SMALL GROUP
MEMBER'S
COMMENTARY

D0910742

Larry Richards is equally at home in the fields of biblical research and group learning theory. The reader gets 2 for the price of 1 in this group commentary which brings together the riches of both – A careful clear understanding of the textual content and a creative group process for enabling groups to be shaped by that Word. Group plans have been made even more versatile by incorporating specific focus for Bible study groups, support groups, recovery groups, singles groups, and mission/outreach groups. Richards has demonstrated again that he is a man of many gifts creating a unique work for multiple occasions.

Julie A. Gorman

Larry has once again developed a valuable resource for Christians who want to grow. His unique combination of biblical insight, life application, and creative learning experiences are evident in *Small Group Member's Commentary*. The fact that small group activities are designed for different types of groups makes this a very versatile tool.

Norm Wakefield

The Small Group Member's Commentary helps resolve a dilemma for Bible teachers. Most commentaries do not help teachers relate the Bible to the problems of life, and most materials for small groups do not take advantage of biblical scholarship. Larry Richards has provided a valuable tool for avoiding the pitfalls of merely pooling ignorance on one hand and merely playing trivial pursuit with Bible facts.

I intend to use the book in teaching my junior boys Sunday School class and in my graduate level classes on curriculum development.

James E. Plueddeman
Chair, Education Ministries
Wheaton College

SMALL GROUP
MEMBER'S
COMMENTARY

LAWRENCE O. RICHARDS

VICTOR BOOKS®

A DIVISION OF SCRIPTURE PRESS PUBLICATIONS INC.
USA CANADA ENGLAND

Copyediting: Pamela T. Campbell
Cover Design: Joe DeLeon
Cover Illustration: Richard McNeel

Recommended Dewey Decimal Classification: 220.7
Suggested Subject Headings: Bible, Commentary
Library of Congress Catalog Card Number: 91-68152
ISBN: 0-89693-055-6

1 2 3 4 5 6 7 8 9 10 Printing/Year 96 95 94 93 92

Contents

Explanation of Symbols

This commentary has special features that are included for those who are using it to lead a small group. The ▶ symbolindicates a word or phrase that is defined to help you better understand the study. The ■ symbol points to the pages in the Victor *Bible Knowledge Commentary* (2 vols.) where you can turn to get a more detailed, verse-by-verse commentary of the passage you are studying. The following symbols indicate activities designed for use with specific *types of groups*: ✍ *Bible Study Group*; ∅ *Missions/Outreach Group*; ✂ *Recovery Group*; ✳ *Singles/Single Again Group*; ♥ *Support Group*.

The Twelve Steps of Alcoholics Anonymous*

1. We admitted we were powerless over alcohol—that our lives had become unmanageable.
2. Came to believe that a Power greater than ourselves could restore us to sanity.
3. Made a decision to turn our will and our lives over to the care of God *as we understood Him.*
4. Made a searching and fearless moral inventory of ourselves.
5. Admitted to God, to ourselves, and to another human being the exact nature of our wrongs.
6. Were entirely ready to have God remove all these defects of character.
7. Humbly asked Him to remove our shortcomings
8. Made a list of all persons we had harmed, and became willing to make amends to them all.
9. Made direct amends to such people wherever possible, except when to do so would injure them or others.
10. Continued to take personal inventory and when we were wrong promptly admitted it.
11. Sought through prayer and meditation to improve our conscious contact with God *as we understood Him,* praying only for knowledge of His will for us and the power to carry that out.
12. Having had a spiritual awakening as the result of these steps, we tried to carry this message to alcoholics, and to practice these principles in all our affairs.

*The Twelve Steps are reprinted with permission of Alcoholics Anonymous World Services, Inc. Permission to reprint and adapt the Twelve Steps does not mean that A.A. has reviewed or approved the contents of this publication, nor that A.A. agrees with the views expressed herein. A.A. is a program of recovery from alcoholism. Use of the Twelve Steps in connection with programs which are patterned after A.A. but which address other problems does not imply otherwise.

Introduction

All over North America we Christians are gathering regularly to study the Bible. We're driven by many different motives. Some of us simply want to know more about God's Word. Some are eager for personal spiritual growth. Some are searching for help to break old, harmful ways of thinking and feeling and acting. Some want more significant relationships and greater support in trying to apply God's Word to their personal life. Some are struggling with singleness, and want to search with other singles for godly ways to deal with loneliness, temptation, single parenting, etc. And some Christians gather in small groups because of a common desire to share the Gospel through missions and personal evangelism.

Why Small Groups?

Whatever it is that drives us, we Christians have found that meeting with others who share our needs and our commitment to Jesus really does help. Small groups, living fellowships of Christians, have vitalized the church from the very beginning. The Bible's very first description of the kind of small group experience we yearn to have today, Acts 2:42, 46, says: "Every day they continued to meet together in the temple courts. They broke bread in their homes and ate together with glad and sincere hearts." In this "they devoted themselves to the apostles' teaching and to the fellowship, to the breaking of bread and to prayer."

In fact, for the first 200 years of the Christian era Christianity itself was a "small group" movement. Christians continued to meet in homes, and so we find many references to "the church that meets in" so and so's house (cf. Acts 5:42; 18:7; Rom. 16:5; 1 Cor. 16:19; Col. 4:15; Phile. 1:2). The few descriptions in the New Testament of church meetings emphasize the active participation, the sharing, and the mutual ministry that best takes place in small groups (cf. 1 Cor. 14:26-33; Col. 3:16; Heb. 10:24-25). This last passage is significant, for it reminds us that we are called as Christians "to spur one another on toward love and good deeds." No wonder the writer exhorts us not to give up meeting together, that we might "encourage one another."

Even a swift glance at these passages makes it clear that the New Testament does not envision meetings of large congregations who gather simply to listen. The New Testament envisions smaller groups of people who meet to share, to learn, to teach each other, and to encourage each other in the Christian life. It's not that there is no place for the larger services today. Not at all. It is simply that meeting in smaller groups is essential too.

The fact is that we Christians have found that meeting in small groups does help us grow. And the fact is that Scripture itself encourages us to meet in this way.

Why a *Small Group Member's Commentary?*

Whatever reason we have for meeting with other Christians in a small group, we share the conviction that the ultimate source of the blessing we seek is God Himself. It is our Lord, working in and through us as we meet in His name, who provides the spiritual power we need for growth and change. It is our Lord, through the gifts given so freely by the Holy Spirit, who enables us to minister to each other. And it is the Scriptures, the Word of God, which are His contemporary voice. It is through the Scriptures that God speaks the Word that brings hope, answers our most pressing questions, and guides us into new and better ways of life. And so, whatever the nature or purpose of our group, if we meet as

Christians, Scripture *must* be given a central place.

But this leads to two concerns. First, we need to accurately interpret and thus rightly understand the Word we study together. And, second, we need to let the Scriptures give shape and direction to our group experience. Any commentary can help us understand the message of a passage we might study. But only this unique *Small Group Member's Commentary* suggests activities that will guide exploring and applying the Scripture as a group—together.

How to Use the *Small Group Member's Commentary*

This commentary is designed to meet both the needs mentioned above. First, you can use it strictly as a commentary, to orient you to any passage in the New Testament that your small group may wish to study. This is not a verse-by-verse commentary, but is designed to give you an *overview of each passage in its context*. Reading this commentary in preparation for a group meeting will help you keep the meaning of the passage clearly in view as you study and apply it with others. Thus, it meets the first need for those in any Bible study group: it helps you accurately interpret, and thus rightly understand, the Word of God.

Second, you can use the commentary *in your group meetings,* or when *planning for a group meeting.* This commentary divides the biblical text into some 103 different units, or "chapters." Each unit which discusses New Testament passages or selected psalms concludes with a *Group Resource Guide.* This is a step-by-step guide to conducting a small group meeting, featuring activities that encourage sharing, fellowship-building, exploration and application of the Scriptures, the meeting of one another's needs through mutual ministry, and worship. Your group *can,* but does *not have to* follow this guide, which is focused on the encouragement of personal spiritual growth and commitment.

In addition, group activity ideas are inserted *within the commentary text.* At times an entire group meeting can be built around just one of these ideas. You'll also note another important aspect of the *Group Activities.* Each specifies a particular *type of group* that the activity is suited for.

    📖 *Bible Study Group* in-text activities feature creative ways to approach the text of Scripture, with a goal of discovering principles that can be applied to the Christian's daily life.

    𝕻 *Missions/Outreach Group* in-text activities focus on discovering and applying biblical principles to enrich the members' understanding of effective evangelism next door and abroad.

    ✂ *Recovery Group* in-text activities apply one of the Twelve Steps, first identified by Alcoholic's Anonymous and currently used by those recovering not only from addiction but also from destructive relationships, attitudes, and habits.

    ✳ *Singles/Single Again Group* in-text activities apply passages to the issues of singleness, ranging from loneliness, dealing with sexual temptation, the need for intimacy, single parenting, etc.

    ♥ *Support Group* in-text activities feature practical ways to explore struggles with such issues as grief/loss, divorce, loss of employment, etc., and to find both comfort and hope in the Scriptures.

To make these resources even more accessible, there's a Group Activity Index of passages especially adaptable for use by each of the five kinds of groups identified above.

Why this *Small Group Member's Commentary*?

For one thing, this is the *only* commentary which is especially designed for members of small Bible study and sharing groups. No other commentary on the market discusses what every New Testament passage means—and shows you how to explore those passages with others in your small group. What's more, no how-to book on group activities provides the sound exposition you expect from a commentary—an exposition so important to make sure your group doesn't wander from the true meaning of the Scripture passages you study with others. You know from experience how wild some folks' ideas are, and how strange some folks' interpretations can become. With the *Small Group Member's Commentary* you have exposition to keep your group firmly grounded in the true meaning of a passage— and you have the *Group Resource Guide* and *Group Activity* suggestions to help your group get the most from your relationship and from God's Word!

Studying the Bible is an enriching experience, whether you study alone or with others. Yet there is something special in exploring God's Word in a group with others who, like you, want to hear God speak and are ready to respond to Him. The author and publisher consider it a privilege to offer you this book, in the sincere hope that God will use it to enrich the time you spend with others studying, sharing, and encouraging one another in the Lord.

MATTHEW'S GOSPEL

Overview

Matthew's Gospel was viewed as the most important by the early church, and is the Gospel most frequently quoted by writers of the first three centuries. Its date is much argued, but all agree it was produced in the first century, a few or several decades after Jesus' death.

The Gospel of Matthew is directed primarily to the Jewish people. At least 130 direct references or allusions to the Old Testament have been identified. The book shows that Jesus truly is the messianic King of Old Testament prophecy. It is designed to help the believing Jew understand what has happened to the kingdom the prophets link with Him.

There are several unique features of Matthew. Of 1,068 verses in this Gospel, 644 contain words of Jesus. Thus more than three fifths of the Gospel is a report of Christ's sayings. Among them are 35 parables. Matthew also emphasizes both Jesus' ethical teachings, and His eschatological teaching (teaching about the future). Matthew's Gospel records 20 of Jesus' miracles, 3 of which are found only in this Gospel (Matt. 9:27-31, 32-33; 17:24-27).

Perhaps the most striking feature of this Gospel, however, is the fact that while it affirms Jesus as Israel's promised King, it also presents Him as a Servant. In Jesus, and in Jesus only, glory and humility, power and gentleness, are perfectly combined.

■ For a discussion of the use of sources, and of outstanding characteristics of this Gospel, see the *Bible Knowledge Commentary*, pages 13-17.

Commentary

When we look at any of the Gospels in our New Testament, we're sure to read of persons, parties, and institutions which were as familiar then as the Kennedys, the Republicans and Democrats, and the postal service are to us today. When we meet these in the Gospels they sound familiar, but most of us may not be sure just what the terms meant in first-century days. So, before we look at a few specific characteristics of Matthew's Gospel, let's look at terms we'll meet in any Gospel that help us to understand the New Testament world.

Parties and Sects

The Gospels tell us about priests and rulers, about Pharisees and Sadducees and Herodians. They mention Galileans and Samaritans. Who were these groups, and what did they stand for in Jesus' world?

Priests The priesthood was an Old Testament institution, established in the time of Moses. Priests were required to be descendants of Aaron, Moses' brother. These priests were the only ones authorized to offer sacrifices, and were to instruct the people in the meaning of the divine Law. While the priesthood was originally a religious office, by the time of Jesus some priests also exerted political influence. The high priest was the president of the Sanhedrin (the Jewish governing body), giving him both religious and political power. The "chief priests" (mentioned 64 times in the New Testament) were temple officers with seats on the Sanhedrin, who also had significant political influence. They should be distinguished from the ordinary priests, like Zechariah (Luke 1:5) who simply carried out their religious function.

The high priest and chief priests, and the aristocratic families from which they came, generally opposed Jesus and later the Apostles.

Rulers. This word, used a number of times in the Gospels, usually indicates members of the Sanhedrin or others with political influence.

Pharisees. While this party arose in the

15

time of Maccabees, its members liked to trace the origin of their teachings to the time of Moses. The name means "separated." It may have been used first in mockery of their resolve to separate themselves from the political parties in their nation. It also surely reflected their determination to separate themselves from sinful practices and to zealously follow God's Law.

The Pharisees were the conservatives of Jesus' day. They held to the authority of the written Law, but also to the authority of the oral traditions that interpreted Mosaic Law and taught how it should be applied. While the Pharisees were truly the orthodox of Judaism in Jesus' day, theirs was a sterile faith. Again and again Jesus had to confront them, showing that their piety was legalistic and hypocritical. In their eagerness to exalt the written Law they missed the love for and mercy toward others the Law was intended to establish.

Tragically, these first-century conservatives would not respond to Jesus. He did not fit their preconceived notions of how the Messiah should behave, and His interpretations of Scripture, which cut through human tradition to original meaning, were not in harmony with their rigid beliefs.

Sadducees. This was the liberal party of Jesus' time. It may have had close links with the priesthood, and was solidly represented in the Sanhedrin.

The Sadducees acknowledged only the Books of Moses as Scripture, denied the existence of angels, and believed in neither resurrection nor the immortality of the soul. They owed their place to their ability to fit in with the pagan power structure, and were not against secularizing their nation and Judaism.

They were in accord with the Pharisees only in their dislike of Jesus, and plotted with them to have Christ killed.

Scribes. The scribes were the scholars of both the Pharisean and Sadducean parties. They were simply authorities on the Law, who were highly respected by the people for their devotion to the study and interpretation of the Old Testament. However, Jesus came in conflict with them as He attacked, not the Law, but accepted scribal interpretations of it.

Herodians. This party was political rather than religious in character. It was linked with the ruling family of Herod, and sup-ported Roman rule. The Herodians were against any political change which might threaten them and their collaboration. They opposed Jesus not so much on religious grounds but because they feared Him as a revolutionary. They saw His claim to be the Messiah as a political threat.

Galileans. This was a political party, as well as a geographical designation. The "Galileans" were what we would call today "freedom fighters," who opposed the Romans and the Hellenization of their land.

Jesus came from Galilee, as did His closest followers. But only Simon the Zealot had been previously associated with the revolutionary "Galilean party."

Samaritans. These inhabitants of the district of Samaria (see map) were descendants of peoples imported after the Assyrians defeated the Northern Kingdom of Israel in 722 B.C. Most of the Jewish people then had been removed, and mixed races had been settled there from many parts of the Assyrian Empire. These people adopted the God of the new land, Yahweh, but continued to worship their old gods as well. Much later, when a small group returned from Babylonian Captivity to resettle Judea, the Samaritans wanted to participate in rebuilding the Jerusalem temple. Their offer was rejected. By the time of Jesus, a deep hostility existed between the Jews and Samaritans. Often people traveling between Judea and Galilee would take a much longer route rather than travel through Samaria.

Palestine. The Palestine of Jesus' time was divided into several districts.

The whole area included in the several districts is only some 140 miles long. In the north it reaches only 23 miles inland from the sea; in the south, about 80. Palestine in Jesus' day was essentially only a tiny mote in the vastness of the Roman Empire.

Galilee. This district was some 60 by 33 miles in area. It held the Sea of Galilee, and many of the places associated with the ministry of Jesus, such as Nazareth, Capernaum, Cana, and Bethsaida.

Samaria. This district lay between Galilee and Judea, and at its greatest extent was 56 miles long and 47 miles wide. Its cities are seldom mentioned in the Gospels, as Jesus' ministry during His lifetime was primarily to the Jewish people, who did not live here.

Judea. Though only 57 miles wide and about 45 miles in length, Judea was the

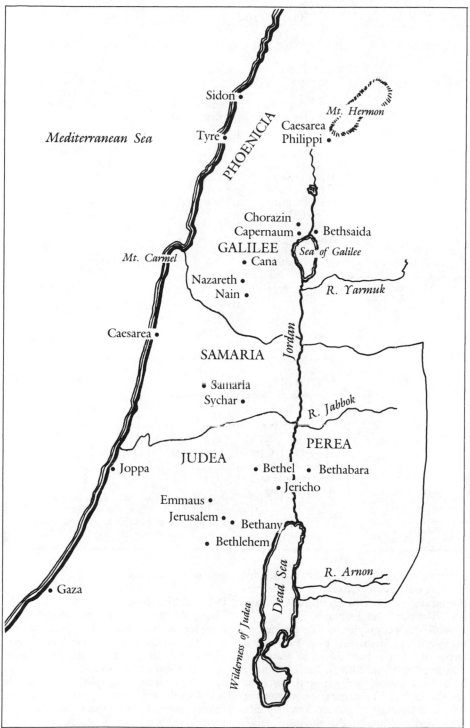

Palestine in the Time of Jesus

The Herodian Family

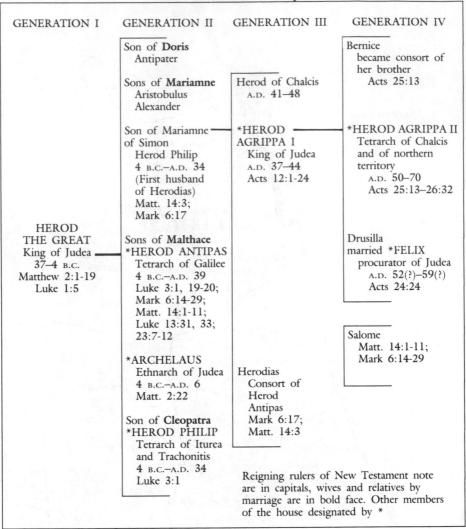

GENERATION I	GENERATION II	GENERATION III	GENERATION IV
	Son of **Doris** Antipater		Bernice became consort of her brother Acts 25:13
	Sons of **Mariamne** Aristobulus Alexander	Herod of Chalcis A.D. 41–48	
	Son of Mariamne of Simon Herod Philip 4 B.C.–A.D. 34 (First husband of Herodias) Matt. 14:3; Mark 6:17	*HEROD AGRIPPA I King of Judea A.D. 37–44 Acts 12:1-24	*HEROD AGRIPPA II Tetrarch of Chalcis and of northern territory A.D. 50–70 Acts 25:13–26:32
HEROD THE GREAT King of Judea 37–4 B.C. Matthew 2:1-19 Luke 1:5	Sons of **Malthace** *HEROD ANTIPAS Tetrarch of Galilee 4 B.C.–A.D. 39 Luke 3:1, 19-20; Mark 6:14-29; Matt. 14:1-11; Luke 13:31, 33; 23:7-12		Drusilla married *FELIX procurator of Judea A.D. 52(?)–59(?) Acts 24:24
	*ARCHELAUS Ethnarch of Judea 4 B.C.–A.D. 6 Matt. 2:22	Herodias Consort of Herod Antipas Mark 6:17; Matt. 14:3	Salome Matt. 14:1-11; Mark 6:14-29
	Son of **Cleopatra** *HEROD PHILIP Tetrarch of Iturea and Trachonitis 4 B.C.–A.D. 34 Luke 3:1		Reigning rulers of New Testament note are in capitals, wives and relatives by marriage are in bold face. Other members of the house designated by *

center of Jewish life. It held Jerusalem, with its beautiful temple. Other Judean localities prominent in the Gospels include Bethlehem, Bethany, and Emmaus.

While the geography of Palestine is varied, with mountains and hills, valleys and fertile plains, it is hard for us to grasp just how small this land truly is. Yet it was here, in a land whose entire population was smaller in New Testament times than the Jewish community in a modern city like New York or Chicago, that the most significant of history's events took place. As in so many things, size here gives no true indication of significance.

Political Situation

The political situation in Palestine was complex, with various overlapping authorities. The Romans held overarching power, represented in Judea by the procurator, Pontius Pilate. Members of the family of Herod the Great, who ruled at the time of Jesus' birth, held various positions of authority over different parts of Palestine. Herod Antipas was Tetrarch of Galilee. Herod Philip, a son of Herod the Great and Cleopatra, was Tetrarch of Iturea.

Herod Agrippa I was king of Judea from A.D. 37–48. The chart traces the Herodian family's role in the life of Palestine during the Gospel and New Testament church era.

In addition, the Jewish Sanhedrin exercised authority over the Jewish population, administering and enforcing Old Testament Law (with its traditions/additions). The Romans taxed the people, and maintained a military force in the Fortress Antonia in Jerusalem. But day-to-day administration of law lay primarily in the hands of the Sanhedrin, who could order any punishment short of execution. Execution had to be ordered by Rome, which is why the Jews brought Jesus to Pilate after condemning Him in their own courts.

Institutions

The Gospels also introduce us to several institutions familiar to the people of Jesus' day.

The Sanhedrin. This governing body of the Jews was both religious and political in character. The Law of the Old Testament was civil as well as religious. The Sanhedrin, headed by the high priest and composed of the "chief priests," scholars of Scripture, and lay members, governed the Jewish population in Palestine, and also had authority over Jews anywhere in the Roman Empire.

The synagogue. When the temple was destroyed in 586 B.C. by Nebuchadnezzar, the Jews were taken captive to Babylon. There they began to meet in small groups on the Sabbath to study the Scriptures and worship God. When the people returned to the land and the temple was rebuilt, these weekly meetings of local communities for study of God's Word continued. Wherever the Jewish people found themselves in the Roman Empire, and many were scattered throughout it, they met together around the Word of God each Sabbath.

Jesus Himself attended synagogue. Luke tells us of one incident in which He was asked to read, and went on to explain a passage from the Old Testament (Luke 4:16-30). Paul and other early missionaries typically went to the synagogue first when they visited any city in the Roman Empire. There they too were often invited to speak, and could share the Gospel with God's ancient people.

The temple. In Jesus' day, the temple that had been rebuilt by the exiles some 500 years earlier had been rebuilt and expanded by Herod the Great. Herod's 40-year building program was intended in part to pacify the Jews. But it was also intended to demonstrate the greatness of this ruler who was known for his cruelty. Many of the events of the Gospels take place at the temple or in its environs. The Jewish people were required to appear at Jerusalem for several of the festivals established in the Old Testament. Jesus often preached on such occasions. And members of the Jerusalem church worshiped in the temple daily, and preached there about Jesus.

This beautiful temple was destroyed in A.D. 70, following another revolt by the Jews against Roman power.

Matthew's Gospel

Author. The writer of this Gospel was the person called Levi in his own Gospel, in Mark, and in Luke.

The story as told in Luke is brief, but powerful.

> After this, Jesus went out and saw a tax collector by the name of Levi sitting at his tax booth. "Follow Me," Jesus said to him, and Levi got up, left everything and followed Him.
>
> Then Levi held a great banquet for Jesus at his house, and a large crowd of tax collectors and others were eating with them. But the Pharisees and the teachers of the Law who belonged to their sect complained to His disciples, "Why do you eat and drink with tax collectors and 'sinners'?"
>
> Jesus answered them, "It is not the healthy who need a doctor, but the sick. I have not come to call the righteous, but sinners to repentance."
>
> Luke 5:27-32

The placement of this incident is significant. Jesus had just healed a paralytic, and announced that He has power to forgive sins (vv. 17-26). Now He called Levi, who was publicly identified as a tax collector and who associated with "sinners." This identification was accurate. Tax gatherers had to bid for their positions, and made their profit by extorting extra from their fellow-countrymen. As collaborators with Rome and as dishonest oppressors, tax gatherers were despised by the general populace.

Now Jesus not only invited one of these men to become His disciple, but even went to a party of "sinners" held in His honor!

Jesus' explanation that He came to call sinners to repentance is magnificently borne out by subsequent events. This "sinner," Levi, became the Matthew whose Gospel launches our New Testament. Jesus, who forgives sins through the power of His forgiveness is able to transform sinners into righteous women and men.

Content

Matthew's Gospel is marked off from the others by several emphases. Each Gospel, of course, tells the story of Jesus. But each Gospel writer lays a particular stress on issues that most concern his intended readers.

Matthew's Gospel, intended for Jewish readers, has these distinctive features.

Multiple Old Testament quotes and allusions. There are some 53 direct Old Testament quotes in Matthew's Gospel. In addition 76 allusions, or general references, have been identified. Several of the direct quotes are linked with Jesus' birth, while many others are associated with His death. Among the latter, intended to show that the death of the Messiah is in harmony with Old Testament revelation, are: Matthew 26:31 (Zech. 13:7); Matthew 27:9-10 (Zech. 11:13; Jer. 32:6-9); Matthew 27:35 (Ps. 22:18); Matthew 27:39 (Ps. 22:7); Matthew 27:43 (Ps. 22:8; 71:11); Matthew 27:40 (Ps. 22:1-2).

In addition there are a number of allusions in these same chapters, notably: Matthew 27:6 (Deut. 23:18); Matthew 27:31 (Isa. 53:7); Matthew 27:60 (Isa. 53:9).

Extended moral teachings. More than any other Gospel writer, Matthew reported the moral teaching of Jesus as Christ challenged His listeners to examine their values, and to set fresh priorities in their relationships with God and their fellowmen. This is particularly set forth in the Sermon on the Mount, found in Matthew 5–7.

Expectations for the future. Jesus also spoke much about the future. He insisted that life's meaning cannot be summed up in our experience in this world. The wise person will lay up treasures in heaven, not on earth. Jesus warned also about hell, speaking more often about it than about heaven! But in addition Jesus did look ahead to events yet to take place on earth. In the extended prophetic discussion found in Matthew 24–26 Jesus shared a vision of the future of this earth held in common by the Old Testament prophets.

In these and all the other themes that are prominent in Matthew, this disciple is concerned with telling the story of Jesus in such a way that His identity with the Messiah of the Old Testament is unmistakable.

Matthew, and only Matthew of the four Gospels, focuses on demonstrating that this Man who lived and died as a servant truly was the Old Testament's promised King.

THE BIRTH OF JESUS

Overview

Matthew was concerned that his readers acknowledge Jesus as the promised Messiah of Israel. Several features of the first two chapters demonstrate his theme. The genealogy we find in Matthew 1 traces Jesus' human ancestry back to Abraham, through David, whose offspring was promised an eternal throne. Matthew referred to acknowledged messianic passages to show that the details of Jesus' birth were in full harmony with the Old Testament. Matthew also emphasized the fear of King Herod, who knew that the promised Deliverer of the Jews was destined to be King. The people of Jesus' time expected the coming Deliverer to be a mighty Ruler and Herod feared the Infant might grow up to threaten his own throne. How little Herod understood of Jesus' kingdom—and of Jesus' purpose on earth. And how clearly we come to understand it as we trace Matthew's revelation of Jesus as truly a King, but a King who came to suffer and to serve.

▶ *Magi.* These Persians were members of a scholarly class that had existed from the time of Daniel. They accurately interpreted the appearance of the star that marked Jesus' birth, and came to honor Him.

▶ *Genealogies.* Hebrew genealogies often skip generations. The record in Matthew 1 includes representative persons who serve to demonstrate Jesus' claim to the Davidic throne.

Commentary
Genealogy of a Man: Matthew 1:1-17

Genealogy is the first emphasis in the Gospel of Matthew. When we think of Jesus, we must realize that we are dealing with a Man. The Person who came from heaven (John 1:1-2) was also fully human, and it is His heritage as a human being that Matthew wants us to first understand.

Sometimes we hesitate here. Somehow being human doesn't seem all that special. We picture humankind as sinful, and recall the vast distortions that sin has swept into our individual and societal experience. We even find ourselves ashamed of our humanity at times. How far this attitude is from Scripture!

At Creation, God made two striking affirmations. One, "Let Us make man in Our image, after Our likeness" (Gen. 1:26, KJV), tells us that our identity is not rooted in this world but in eternity. We bear the image-likeness of God: human nature can only be understood by reference to God, not to some supposed animal predecessor. Only man, of all creation, shares something of the likeness of God as a true Person.

The second affirmation, "Let them have dominion" (Gen. 1:26, KJV), affirms that human beings were created to rule! We were born to be kings.

Even the entry of sin, while it has warped our capacity to rule wisely over creation, and even to rule our own passions, has not changed this destiny. The Psalmist David caught a glimpse of our destiny and expressed his wonder in Psalm 8:

> When I consider Your heavens, the work of Your fingers, the moon and the stars, which You have set in place, what is man that You are mindful of him, the son of man that You care for him? You made him a little lower than the heavenly beings and crowned him with glory and honor. You made him ruler over the works of Your hands; You put everything under his feet.
>
> Psalm 8:3-6

God created human beings—for dominion.

21

Probably the strongest emphasis on this truth in the New Testament is found in Hebrews 2. There the writer quotes Psalm 8, and notes "in putting everything under him [man], God left nothing that is not subject to him. Yet at present we do not see everything subject to him. But we see Jesus, who was made a little lower than the angels, now crowned with glory and honor because He suffered death" (Heb. 2:8-9).

We may not be able to see the glory of that destiny to which God calls us. But we see Jesus glorified—and we realize that the pathway we too must take to dominion is marked by servanthood and suffering.

In Jesus we see our destiny realized. Jesus, the Man of Galilee, fulfilled the destiny of humanity by becoming King, and in doing so was "bringing many sons to glory" (v. 10). Jesus in His death and resurrection was bringing you and me to the place where we could experience our destiny— where we can know the dominion God has always intended human beings to know. Jesus is King of kings. And we are the kings over whom, and with whom, He reigns. Just what the nature of that reign is, of His and of ours, is something we learn about in the Gospel of Matthew.

Old Testament expectations. God's Old Testament people had dimly realized that dominion was their destiny. But they tended to think of dominion in a national sense, as that prophesied time when the nation Israel, under the promised Jewish Messiah, would be exalted over all the nations on earth. Their sense of destiny was accurate. God did make such promises. But their sense of destiny was limited. God intended far more through the ministry of the Messiah than Israel expected.

So it was very important that Matthew, who wrote primarily to the Jews, establish the right of Jesus to the throne promised the Messiah. (This word, Messiah, refers to the Hebrew practice of anointing kings and others to office with oil. Messiah means "anointed one.")

Two genealogical elements were critical if Matthew was to demonstrate Jesus' right to reign. The first was a relationship with Abraham (Matt. 1:1). It was from Abraham that Israel's awareness of her destiny sprang. God called this man from Ur of the Chaldees, and sent him to Palestine. There God gave Abraham great and special prom-ises. These included the promise of posses-sion of the land of Palestine forever, a great people to live in it, a special relationship with God for Abraham's descendants, and ultimately a descendant (seed) through whom all the peoples of the earth would be blessed (see Gen. 12; 15; and 17).

These promises were given in the form of a covenant (a contract, or oath). They would be fulfilled through one Man, who must come from Abraham's line. The gene-alogy in Matthew proves that Jesus comes from the covenant line.

The second significant genealogical ele-ment is the relationship to David. Later in Israel's history God promised to David that the Messiah would come through his family line. The ultimate King would be born from the family of David, Israel's greatest king. In tracing the genealogy of Jesus from Abraham and from David, Matthew was demonstrating Jesus' right to rule. Jesus' genealogy not only established Him as a true Man, but also was the foundation of His claim to the throne of Israel as the promised Seed of David.

In this genealogical record, the focus of Matthew's Gospel becomes even more clear. We are invited to look into this great book, to see Jesus as King. Through Mat-thew's portrait of our Lord, you and I will learn what dominion involves—and how to realize in Jesus the destiny God holds out to humankind.

Ø Group Activity:
Missions/Outreach Group
Jesus is the prototype missionary, who left His own culture (heaven) to enter a total-ly foreign society (man's) with God's good news. Study the genealogy in Matthew 1:1-17. How much planning and prepa-ration does it indicate was involved? What principles of outreach are illustrated: for instance, what attitude toward self, to-ward others, etc.? What does the fact of incarnation itself tell us about the need to truly identify with others to whom we car-ry word of God? When your group has identified at least 12 principles implicit in the genealogy, explore together how you can apply these in personal evangelism now.

The King? Matthew 1:18-25
One problem that Matthew faced in struc-turing his Gospel for the Hebrew reader

was to show that Jesus really was the expected Messiah. Jesus did not seem to be the King the Jews pictured. He did not set out to crush the Roman Empire. He did not act to set up the expected earthly kingdom. He did not behave as the Jews thought their King should behave.

Theologically, then, Matthew had to answer several critical questions which the Jewish skeptic would naturally ask. Such questions as: "Is Jesus really the Messiah? Then why didn't He fulfill the prophecies about the kingdom? What has happened to the promised earthly kingdom of Israel? And, if the kingdom is not for now, what then is God's present purpose?" Each of these questions is answered in Matthew. And Matthew, very much aware of his readers' concerns, immediately tackled the first of these four critical questions.

One of Matthew's approaches to reaching Hebrew readers was to use extensive quotes from the Old Testament. In his 53 direct quotes and many allusions, Matthew draws from no less than 25 of the 39 Old Testament books! Clearly, Matthew was determined to bridge the gap between the Old and the New.

It's very significant to look at the contexts of the quotations used by Matthew in these first two chapters. When we return to them, we see that Matthew insisted his readers view Jesus as the expected King.

Matthew 2:6 quotes from Micah's prophecy that the coming Ruler will be born in Bethlehem (Micah 5:2). In context that Old Testament prophecy speaks of the Messiah, whose origins lie hidden in eternity. He is to rule in Israel in the name of Yahweh, and to be great to the ends of the earth. It is through this Person that Israel is to find peace.

Matthew 2:2 alludes to Jeremiah 23:5. The promised Messiah of the Jews was to be God and man. He is called in this context "The Lord Our Righteousness" (v. 6), and was to be born of David's line. The prophet said that He will reign over a regathered people, who had been scattered over the world. This person is to reign as King, and in His days Judah and Israel will dwell safely.

Matthew 2:23 looks back to Hosea 11:1, and its prophecy that the Messiah will be called a Nazarene. The context emphasized Messiah's descent from David's line. It said

that He will judge and rule with divine wisdom. His rule will bring destruction to the wicked. Gentiles as well as Jews will rally to Him, and in His day the earth will be filled with a knowledge of the Lord. Even the realm of nature is to know unheard of peace.

There are no less than 16 references to the Old Testament in these first two chapters of Matthew. It is clear that Matthew drew from prophecies which affirmed that the Jesus he described was indeed the Messiah Israel had been expecting. Jesus, the Man who lived so quietly, who raised no army, who taught and healed, and who was dragged unprotestingly to an agonizing death, truly is the expected King of glory.

Later the Jewish rabbis would try to explain the jolting contrast between the suffering Saviour and the expected King by postulating two Messiahs: one, Messiah ben David who was yet to come, and who would rule; and two, Messiah ben Joseph, who had perhaps fulfilled the Old Testament prophecies associated with messianic suffering. Yet who would have imagined before Jesus was born and lived His unique life that the pathway to glory led through suffering and self-emptying? Who would have dreamed that the concept of royalty and dominion contains an ingredient of brokenness? Certainly the Jews of Jesus' day, looking for the coming glory, did not see the majesty of suffering. And all too often, you and I miss this dimension as well!

Matthew did not miss it. Matthew made it plain that the Jesus about whom he spoke to us *is* the King of glory. And with this fact firmly established, Matthew went on to describe a King who served; a King whose majesty is enhanced by suffering. A King who shows us how to experience the dominion for which God has destined us — through a servanthood like His own.

✍ **Group Activity: Bible Study Group**
More than Jesus' birth is prophesied in the O.T. Here is a list of prophecies with verses that describe their fulfillment. Compare each set, and then discuss. How clear was the picture of Jesus given in the O.T.? Why might Israel not have recognized Jesus as their Messiah? How can we use prophecy to help others realize who Jesus is, and what his life and death means to them?

Isa. 7:14	*Matt. 1:23*
Ps. 110:1	*Matt. 22:44*
Micah 5:2	*Matt. 2:6*
Zech. 13:7	*Matt. 26:31*
Hosea 11:1	*Matt. 2:15*
Dan. 7:13	*Matt. 26:64*
Isa. 53:4	*Matt. 8:17*
Ps. 69:21	*Matt. 27:34*
Isa. 42:1-4	*Matt. 12:18-21*
Ps. 78:3	*Matt. 13:34*
Zech. 9:9	*Matt. 21:5*
Ps. 22:7	*Matt. 27:39-40*
Ps. 118:22	*Matt. 21:42*
Ps. 22:8	*Matt. 27:43*
Ps. 22:1	*Matt. 27:46*
Isa. 53:9	*Matt. 25:57ff*

Two Models: Matthew 2

It's striking. Matthew no sooner introduced us to Jesus, Son of Abraham, Son of David, Israel's destined King, than he introduced us to another ruler. "After Jesus was born in Bethlehem in Judea, during the time of Herod the King" (2:1). No two men could ever stand in starker contrast.

Herod. Herod the Great was the founder of a dynasty that played a key role in Gospel history. We meet four generations of Herods in the New Testament. It is the founder, who ruled from 47–4 B.C., who was then aged and nearing the end of his life, whom we meet in Matthew 2.

Herod's father had attached himself to Julius Caesar's party, been made a Roman citizen, and appointed procurator (ruler) of Judea. Herod and his brothers were given government roles, but a decade of battling followed before Herod was proclaimed king of Judea by Rome, and was able to enforce his rule. As king, Herod was both brutal and decisive, punishing or executing his enemies, and rewarding his friends. Rivals were murdered. When the decisive battle for the Roman Empire was fought between Anthony and Octavian (later to become "Augustus"), Herod gained the victor's friendship and was given control of additional lands.

While Herod's power was growing, his control over himself and his family was slipping. Herod had married 10 wives and had a number of sons. While these sons schemed to gain the throne, his wives hatched plots and counterplots. Herod became more and more suspicious and paranoid, even torturing his sons' friends to discover any plots against his own life. Herod's own character as a plotter who never hesitated to resort to murder was being reproduced in his family, and this led to the aging tyrant's own sense of terror and fear. Herod finally had the two sons of his favorite wife, Mariamne, executed by strangulation in the very city where he had married their mother 30 years earlier. Antipater, Herod's oldest son and designated heir, tried to poison his father and was put in chains.

When nearly 70 years old, Herod was stricken with an incurable disease.

It was at this time, shortly before his death, that Herod heard of wise men who were seeking to worship the newborn King of the Jews. Herod summoned the wise men and made them promise to report the whereabouts of the child so he could "go and worship Him" (Matt. 2:8). The dying man still struggled to grasp the power that had brought him and his family only suspicion, hatred, and death!

God warned the wise men to return home another way. And God warned Joseph to flee with the Christ Child to Egypt. Herod, realizing that the wise men had returned to the East without reporting to him, had all the male children of Bethlehem two years old and under killed!

It was then only a few days before Herod's own death. Five days before he expired, Herod had his son Antipater executed. Then he called all the leading Jews of his territory to his palace. When they came, he imprisoned them, giving orders that they were all to be killed the moment he died. He wanted to ensure that there would be national mourning at his death, rather than rejoicing!

Herod's dream of power and glory had turned into a nightmare. The desperate king struggled to the last to maintain control over his kingdom, long after he had lost control over himself. And so he died.

Jesus. As the hateful old man was living his last days in the splendor of a marble palace, a Child was born in a stable. There, surrounded by the warmth of the animals which shared His birthplace, Jesus entered our world and became a part of a family so poor that Mary had to offer two doves rather than the prescribed lamb as the sacrifice for her purification.

The Child would grow up in a small

town far from the seat of power. He would become a carpenter, to live and labor in obscurity for 30 years. Finally, as a young Man, the Carpenter from Nazareth would stand on a riverbank to be recognized by John the Baptist as the Lamb of God, destined to take away the sin of the world. For three years Jesus would walk the roads of Palestine, teaching and healing. He would raise no army. He would seek no earthly glory. He would ultimately humble Himself and accept death at the hands of selfish men who saw Him as a threat to their place and their power.

And yet, through it all He would be a King.

A Servant King.

A King in whom you and I find, not only our redemption, but a pathway to the unique dominion over ourselves and our circumstances to which God has destined humankind.

✄ *Group Activity: Recovery Group*
Steps 4 (make a moral inventory) and 5 (admit wrongs to God, myself, and others)
Read Matthew 2 and also the information on Herod provided on page 24. Work together on a moral inventory for King Herod. Focus on shameful events: put yourself in Herod's place and list every area in which you failed to live up to your values, areas in which you feel embarrassed or ashamed. Work together to list at least 20 shameful events.

When you have finished, work individually on two lists of your own. On one list include at least 20 events of which you are ashamed. When you complete this list, make another list of 20 achievements in which you can feel pride.

Now share at least three items from each list with the others in your group. When you have all shared, thank God for His understanding and forgiveness of your weakness, and for the strength He gives to overcome shame.

The Choice
In contrasting Herod and Jesus, Matthew implicitly presented his Jewish readers and us with a distinctive choice. We can see *dominion* in terms of outward power and splendor, as Herod did, or we can look beyond the external to distinguish the inner core of greatness.

There was nothing wrong with the picture the Jews had of the messianic kingdom. Later Matthew reported Jesus' own affirmation that an outward expression of the kingdom was still to come. Even after the Resurrection, the disciples could not shake their longing for the days of the coming glory. "Are You at this time going to restore the kingdom to Israel?" they asked. Gently Jesus responded, "It is not for you to know the times or dates" (Acts 1:6-7). That kingdom will come, in God's own time.

But until then Jesus remains King. And dominion is ours—if we choose it in Him. If we can only shake the Herod dream, and see in Jesus' humility the key to greatness and true glory, you and I can find a distinctive freedom that the world around us, stumbling over the external, can never understand. It is a journey toward just this kind of inner freedom and power that we take as we trace the Messiah's steps with Matthew, the writer of this Gospel.

Jesus *is* King of kings.

In Him, we grasp our title deed to rule.

GROUP RESOURCE GUIDE

Identification: *Share with others*
What have you been told about your birth? Did your parents welcome you, or perhaps resent your coming? How has your impression of their attitude affected your feelings about yourself?

Affirmation: *Express love and concern*
Tell the person on your left one reason why

you are glad he or she is a member of this group.

Exploration: *Probe God's Word*
1. Divide into teams to study the prophecies which Matthew refers to as evidence that Jesus is the Messiah. Passages to look at are: Isaiah 7:14; Jeremiah 23:5-6; 31:15; Micah 5:2, and Hosea 11:1. Based

on these passages, why would the Jewish people have looked forward so eagerly to Jesus' birth? What is there in these prophecies to indicate that Jesus would be special for us as well?

2. Draw on your general knowledge of Jesus as He is described in the New Testament. What did He do that confirmed the impression He was truly a special person? What character traits did Jesus' actions display?

3. Optional. Matthew 2 contrasts Jesus with Herod. Read the passage and discuss: what differences can you see between how Herod and Jesus related to others? Between their motives and values?

Reaction: *respond together to the Word*

1. Share one way in which you believe your character has begun to resemble that of Jesus. Share one area in which you need to resemble Jesus more.

2. Go back to what you said about the attitude of others toward your birth. What do you feel God's attitude toward your birth was? What evidence is there in Jesus' coming that God cared deeply for you even before your birth?

Adoration: *worship and pray*

Meditate quietly for 90 seconds on the love for you God displayed in sending His Son to be your Saviour. In a brief sentence, express your thanks to Jesus for loving you personally.

STUDY GUIDE 3

Matthew 3–4

JESUS' PREPARATION

Overview

Matthew's Gospel skips over Jesus' childhood and adolescence. From the birth story it moves directly to introduce Jesus' ministry. But Matthew gives two chapters to the theme of preparation.

The first preparation theme focuses on the preparation of the Jewish people for Jesus. Matthew 3 reports the preaching of John the Baptist, who announced the approach of the Messiah, and who baptized with water those who wished to publicly repent.

Matthew 4 tells of the personal preparation of Jesus. Our Lord overcame three temptations, demonstrating His sinlessness and His complete commitment to God. With His humanity and His obedience both established, Jesus is seen to be qualified to teach others how to live in intimate union with God.

▶ *Repentance.* Both John and Jesus called on people to "repent, for the kingdom of heaven is near" (Matt. 3:2; 4:17). "Repent" (in Greek, *metanoia*) means to change one's mind and attitude. It is a decision which changes the total direction of one's life.

▶ *Baptism.* The word is an intensive form of the Greek *bapto*, and means "to immerse." In the New Testament it is a technical theological term with different meanings (see Matt. 3:11). This unit looks at "John's baptism." For a discussion of the others see my *Expository Dictionary of Bible Words* (Zondervan).

Commentary

In A.D. 28 one of the Old Testament prophets returned. It had been nearly 400 years, and God had been silent. Malachi, the last of those Old Testament greats, closed his book with a promise — and a warning. "Behold I will send you Elijah the prophet before the coming of the great and dreadful Day of the Lord. And He shall turn the heart of the fathers to the children, and the heart of the children to their fathers, lest I come and smite the earth with a curse" (Mal. 4:5-6, KJV).

Thus, the Jews had been guided to turn their eyes ahead, and look for the day of Messiah's coming. They were promised a forerunner, someone to warn them and turn their hearts back to God's ways. Implicit in Malachi's words was a choice. Unless the hearts of God's people were turned, the Messiah's coming would not bring Israel the expected blessing, but would bring a curse.

Later Jesus would tell crowds that John, then executed by Herod (a son of Herod the great), was the greatest of all the prophets and was, in fact, a messenger sent to prepare Messiah's way. And Jesus added these words: "If you are willing to accept it, he is the Elijah who was to come" (Matt. 11:14). Israel did not accept John's Elijah-ministry. Their hearts would not turn. The golden opportunity slipped by. The Messiah's body came to fit a wooden cross rather than an ivory throne, and Israel was destined to know another 2,000 years of scattering, of ghettos, of pogroms, of unrealized hopes. History would now pivot to focus on the second coming of Messiah. The fulfillment of Malachi's words would await another Elijah.

John: Matthew 3:1-12

John's background. Luke 1 tells us about John's birth. He was born into a priestly family. His father, Zechariah, was one of the many politically unimportant men who served the temple two weeks a year, and lived the rest of the time at his own farm in the countryside. Probably John was trained for the priestly ministry as well. The privilege was passed on from father to son, reserved by Old Testament Law for the descendants of Aaron.

Perhaps John, like Habakkuk, was shaken by the ritualism and emptiness of the religion of his day. We do know that from birth John was filled with the Holy Spirit. Then, as an adult, John left home to live in the wilderness. He ate wild honey and protein-rich locusts, and wore a scratchy shirt made of camel's hair. When the time was right, John began to preach beside the Jordan River.

John's ministry. John's stern and bold preaching echoed the messages of earlier prophets. They too had condemned sin and called God's people back to the way of holiness outlined in Old Testament Law. But there were differences.

The content of John's message was not really new. Luke 3:10-14 gives specific content: to each group or individual who came for guidance, John's prescription was a return to the righteousness and the love expressed in God's Law.

But several things about John's preaching *were* new. There was its sense of urgency. "Hurry," John urged the crowds who came out to hear him, or simply to gaze at the spectacle. "Repent, for the kingdom of heaven is near" (Matt. 3:2). John focused the attention of his listeners not on some distant future, but on the immediate situation.

Another new focus in John's ministry was on the personal responsibility of the individual for his own actions. There had always been a thread of teaching on personal responsibility in the prophets' messages. But now John warned against any hope anchored in relationship to Abraham. "Do not think you can say to yourselves, 'We have Abraham as our father' " (v. 9), he cried, and then urged each individual to repent and to show by his changed life his inner, personal commitment to God.

The third new element was baptism, as a sign and symbol of repentance. Baptism had been known in Judaism before. But John transformed baptism, giving it fresh moral and eschatological significance. One who was baptized by John confessed his sins, identified himself with the renewal of the kingdom under the coming Messiah, and committed himself to live a holy life.

There was a final unique aspect to John's

preaching. John recognized himself as the forerunner, sent to prepare the Messiah's way. Seven times the New Testament records John's announcement that the One to follow him will be greater than he (Matt. 3:11; Mark 1:7; Luke 3:16; John 1:27, 29-30; Acts 13:25). The warning—and the invitation—were both given.

And the crowds came. They listened. Many were baptized. Many, particularly those of the religious elite who were quick to put themselves in the forefront of any popular movement, could see no harm in the rite. But they were withered by John's angry denunciation of them as a "brood of vipers" (Matt. 3:7).

Soon everyone in the tiny land of Palestine had heard of God's firebrand in the desert. They gossiped excitedly about whether he might be the Messiah, and they waited to see what would come next!

✂ Group Activity: Recovery Group
Step 1 (admit powerlessness)
1. John's preaching is described in Matthew 3:1-12 and Luke 3:10-14. He confronted his hearers with things they already knew were right—even though they had made wrong choices.

First list together different ways people might have reacted when they heard John identify their faults and failings. Then discuss: What ideas or feelings about failure might motivate each response? What evidence is there in John's preaching that the people he spoke to were powerless to reform themselves? What makes it so hard for a person to admit powerlessness?

After discussing, privately make a list of evidence from your own behavior that you are powerless to deal with major flaws in your own character. List at least 15 things.

Share at least five of the things on your list with the others in your group.

2. John's preaching was intended to prepare his listeners for the coming of Christ. Discuss: How does admitting our powerlessness prepare us for a new and fulfilling relationship with God?

Jesus' Baptism: Matthew 3:13-17
"Then Jesus came from Galilee to the Jordan to be baptized by John" (v. 13).

Here a fascinating confrontation took place. John objected! It would more appropriate for Jesus to baptize John; John was sure that Jesus did not need his repentance-oriented rite.

It is tempting here to think that John recognized Jesus as the Messiah. But the Bible tells us that the day *after* the baptism John pointed out Jesus as the Messiah to two of his followers, and said, "I would not have known Him, except that the One who sent me to baptize with water told me, 'The Man on whom you see the Spirit come down and remain is He who will baptize with the Holy Spirit" (John 1:33). All the four Gospels agree that John saw the Holy Spirit in dove form descend on Jesus when our Lord came up from the water after baptism. Clearly then, John did not object to Jesus' baptism on the grounds of His messiahship.

The mystery may be resolved when we realize that John and Jesus were probably related. Their mothers were very close (cf. Luke 1:36-45). Probably the two young men, both now about 30, had spent much time together, meeting each year as their families came to the three annual feasts in Jerusalem at which all males over 12 were to appear. And they must have exchanged visits during the rest of the year, as relatives and friends do everywhere. No, John's objection to baptizing Jesus may have been based on a simple fact: John knew that Jesus had no need to repent! John knew that Jesus' life was in fullest harmony with the laws and the ways of God—in fuller harmony even than his own!

Jesus overcame John's objection. It is only right, Christ pointed out, to identify oneself with right things (Matt. 3:15). Entering the water with John, Jesus was baptized, thus identifying Himself fully with John's message as well as with the men and women who flocked to receive that baptism because they *did* need it so badly.

The baptism of Jesus launched His public ministry. But it did even more than that. It demonstrated how fully Christ as a Man identified Himself with humanity. One of the central doctrines of the Christian faith is that of *Incarnation*. Isaiah had foretold it: "A virgin shall conceive, and bear a Son and shall call His name Immanuel" (Isa. 7:14, KJV). The name, giving it the emphasis of its Hebrew form, means *"With us* is God!" God, in the person of the Child of promise, would fully identify Himself as a human being. In every way this promised individual would be God, yet would be God *with us.*

Both Matthew and Luke report the birth of Jesus and explain how Mary, before her marriage to Joseph was consummated, miraculously conceived through the direct intervention of God. The Child was in a totally unique sense the Son of God—God Himself, come to enter the race of man in the only way in which He could become truly human. Jesus is fully identified with us in our humanity. He is God, and He is Man.

Hebrews 2 points out that it was fitting for Jesus to be like us in every way, including His subjection to human weaknesses and His susceptibility to suffering. "Since the children have flesh and blood," the writer explained, "He [Jesus] too shared in their humanity" (Heb. 2:14). Dying, Jesus could then deliver us from our lifelong slavery. God's concern for humanity drove Jesus to "be made like His brothers in every way" (v. 17) and, becoming a faithful High Priest, He offered Himself as the expiation for our sins. The writer to the Hebrews concluded, "Because He Himself suffered when He was tempted, He was able to help those who are being tempted" (v. 18).

The full humanity of Jesus is a basic teaching of our Bible. It was necessary for Jesus to be truly human for Him to become our sacrifice. It was necessary for Jesus to be truly human for Him not only to free us from lifelong bondage, but also to aid us in our own temptations and sufferings.

No wonder John, meeting his relative Jesus on the Jordan riverbank, protested against baptizing Him. John recognized Jesus as a good and righteous Man. Jesus Christ, as a Person, was so completely identified with humanity, that even one most impressed with His spiritual qualities never dreamed He was the Son of God!

There is a lesson here for each of us. What do we look for when we are seeking evidence of God's work in our lives, or in another's? Some startling, miraculous sign? Something that sets the person apart from all other men? Or are we looking for a work of God within: a work of God that produces the love, joy, peace, patience, kindness, goodness, faithfulness, gentleness, and self-control which God values so highly (cf. Gal. 5:22-23). Are we looking for a person who is different, or for a person who demonstrates the very best of what humanity can be? How strikingly our Lord's experience with John points it out. The spiritual person is, in fact, the most humane, and human of us all!

Then, once the voice of God had spoken from heaven, "This is My Son, whom I love; with Him I am well pleased" (Matt. 3:17), John realized the obvious.

Of course Jesus is the Messiah! Of course this most perfect Man had to be the promised Redeemer. The virgin had brought forth a Son, a Son who was the "with us" God. God had identified Himself in every way with humanity. God had come at last, to free us and lift us up to share His throne.

📖 *Group Activity: Bible Study Group*
Which of the following best explains the reason for Jesus' baptism?
(a) Jesus was seeking forgiveness.
(b) Jesus was dedicating Himself to His mission.
(c) Jesus became God's Son when the Spirit anointed Him.
(d) Jesus was identifying Himself with John's message and his movement.
What evidence in the text supports your conclusion?

The Temptation: Matthew 4:1-11
If the baptism of Jesus impresses us with the complete identification of the Saviour with us in our humanity, His temptation stretches our minds to grasp the depths to which Jesus stooped.

In theology, Jesus' self-humbling is called the *kenosis*: the emptying. Paul develops it briefly in Philippians 2, speaking there of Jesus "who, being in very nature God, did not consider equality with God something to be grasped, but made Himself nothing, taking the very nature of a servant, being made in human likeness. And being found in appearance as a man, He humbled Himself and became obedient to death—even death on a cross!" (vv. 6-8) Simply stated, the Bible affirms that when Jesus entered our world He set aside the power and the privileges of Deity. He consciously limited Himself to live here as a man. Even the miracles Jesus would later perform would be attributed by Him to the power of the Spirit (see Mark 3:22-30). The emptying process Paul described is one of progressive

humiliation. Jesus . . .
● emptied Himself
● was born in man's likeness
● was obedient even when it meant death
● accepted even the shameful death of an outcast criminal!

Tempted as a man. When we read about the temptation of Jesus in Matthew 4, we have to read the story against the background of the *kenosis*. When a physically weakened Jesus, after 40 days of fasting in the desert, was tempted by Satan, He did not seek strength from His divine nature to resist! The very first words of Jesus in response to Satan's initial temptation sets the tone.

"If You are the Son of God," Satan challenged, "tell these stones to become bread." Jesus answered with a quote from Deuteronomy: "Man does not live on bread alone, but on every word that comes from the mouth of God" (Matt. 4:2-4). Note the first word.

"*Man* does not live by bread alone!"

Addressed as the Son of God, Jesus affirmed His intention to live on our earth as a human being. Subject, as you and I are, to the hungers and drives and needs which throb within us and seek to pull us into sin, Jesus met every one of Satan's temptations. Rejecting the privilege that was His by virtue of His deity, Jesus cast His lot fully with you and with me.

It is because of this great act of self-emptying that you and I can find hope. Jesus overcame temptation—as a human being! Because Jesus met temptation in His human nature, you and I can find victory too, by meeting our temptations as He met His!

The three temptations. There are three temptations recorded in Matthew, as there are in Luke. But the order differs between the two Gospels. Each writer reported the experience of Jesus with a view to highlighting the culminating test from his own perspective.

Luke, whose focus is on Jesus as a warm and real human being, saw the temptation to throw Himself down from the temple pinnacle (and so prove the Father was with Him) as the culminating test. We all have times when we feel deserted by God; when things have gone wrong and we doubt His continued concern for us. As the Old Testament passages quoted by Jesus stress, the issue in this temptation was that of putting

God to the test, to see "is the Lord among us or not?" (Ex. 17:7)

But Matthew saw this temptation as less significant for Jesus than the vision Satan spread before Christ of all the kingdoms of the world. "All this I will give You," the tempter enticed, "if You will bow down and worship me." The Man born to be King was shown the kingdoms that would be His, and was reminded that they could become His *now*. All the suffering would be avoided—all the anguish, all the rejection, all the pain of a death in which the weight of the world's sins would bear down on the sinless One.

And again Jesus chose. "It is written: 'Worship the Lord your God, and serve Him only' " (Matt. 4:10). Complete commitment to the will of God was Jesus' pathway to the throne. There could be no shortcuts. There could be no other way.

Before Jesus could rule, He had to learn by experience the fullest meaning of submission to the Father's will. The crown lay beyond the Cross.

❋ *Group Activity:*
Singles/Single Again Group
Examine the temptations of Jesus reported in Matthew 4:1-11. On a chalkboard or newsprint draw a three-column chart. Label the first column focus. *Label the second* victory principle. *Label the third* our temptations.

Fill in the columns for each temptation, guided by the commentary. For instance, the challenge to a hungry Jesus to turn stones to bread was directed against His physical nature and needs. The focus *of the temptation thus was "physical nature." Jesus' response, "man shall not live by bread alone," identified an O.T. victory principle. Human beings are not just animals, dominated by the physical nature, but are spiritual, and thus can choose to live by God's will. Go on then to brainstorm and list in column three temptations that singles experience which grow out of our physical nature.*

Follow the same procedure for each of the other two temptations.

When the lists are complete, share one temptation that is very difficult for you to deal with. Let the others in the group respond, sharing not "advice," but telling how they deal with that temptation.

Lessons for Living
Matthew 4 concludes with a brief sketch of Jesus as He launched His public ministry. Jesus took up John's theme and preached that the kingdom was near at hand (Matt. 4:17). He chose disciples (vv. 18-22). He went about Galilee teaching in the synagogues and healing (vv. 23-24). Soon the crowds that had followed John swirled around our Lord.

But Matthew gives us only the briefest sketch of these events. He does not seem concerned here with the public ministry. All the hurry, all the excitement, all the converging of the crowd eager to see miracles and hear the Man who spoke of God with such authority, seem unimportant compared to two initial portraits of the King. First there is the picture of Jesus submitting to John's baptism, identifying Himself fully with humanity. And then comes the picture of an emptied Jesus— suffering, tested, opening Himself to the full force of temptation in His vulnerability as a human being.

What is the meaning of this emphasis for us? We see at least four lessons immediately brought home.

(1) Jesus truly was determined to be a servant. The Incarnation did not mean that Jesus stopped being God, but that He had freely set aside His rights as Deity. The outward exercise of power and glory was not essential to Jesus' majesty. In choosing to empty and to humble Himself, Jesus displayed God's pathway to dominion.

How different from our way. When Cathy and Earl met and fell in love, she determined to become the center of his world. Gradually, she shut out his old friends. After they were engaged she became even more adept in manipulating him to keep him for herself. Cathy took Herod's route in search of power. Manipulating, selfish, she always was trying to control.

Cathy wanted to fill the throne of Earl's life. She wanted to be queen—but a commanding and not a servant queen.

How different with Jesus. Whatever dominion may involve, and whatever it means for us to reign, our destiny is not to be found in selfishness, but in self-emptying.

(2) Jesus' full identification with us in our humanity offers hope. If Jesus had overcome the tempter in His nature *as God*, we could hardly expect to overcome. We

31

are not divine. But Jesus met Satan's tests *as a human*. So we can dare to trust that our dominion destiny includes power to overcome!

Ted, a young man, feels helpless. He sees himself as trapped, overwhelmed by a life that is out of control. Yet seeing Jesus become vulnerable — and victorious! — can change Ted's outlook. "Because He Himself suffered when He was tempted, He is able to help those who are being tempted" (Heb. 2:18). In Jesus the human, you and I realize that we may be vulnerable, but we do have hope.

(3) Jesus' response to the tempter spotlights resources that you and I can draw on to overcome. In each case, Jesus went back to the Word of God and found a principle by which He chose to live.

This is important. It is not simply "the Word" that is our resource. It is the commitment to live by the Word. It is resting the full weight of our confidence on what God says, and choosing in each situation to do that which is in harmony with His revealed will.

This same resource which Jesus used to overcome is our resource too. But we must use Scripture Jesus' way.

(4) Jesus is portrayed in Matthew 3 and 4 as a Person in full control — of Himself! In fact, we might even view this as the central message of these chapters. Jesus demonstrated His right to reign over us by proving that He had authority over the worst of man's enemies — Himself.

Certainly Israel had known in Herod a king who had absolute power over others, but was powerless to control his own hatred and fears. Since then, in our Napoleons and our Hitlers and Stalins, we've seen again and again that enslaving others brings the ruler no freedom within.

Yet it is exactly here that our dominion rule as kings under the King of kings must begin. We must gain power over ourselves: power to humble ourselves, power to submit to God, power to give up our rights, power to obey. Jesus demonstrated just this kind of authority. In His humanity, Jesus was exalted above the greatest men our world has ever known. Jesus alone fully controlled the world within.

No wonder Matthew wants us to grasp this truth. Jesus has overcome! He is worthy to be proclaimed King.

GROUP RESOURCE GUIDE

Identification: *Share with others*
Complete the sentence, "When I think of temptations, I feel . . ." After each person has finished, go around again and tell why you finished the sentence as you did.

Affirmation: *Express love and concern*
Hold hands and repeat in unison Hebrews 4:15 (NIV): "We do not have a high priest who is unable to sympathize with our weaknesses, but we have one [Jesus] who has been tempted in every way, just as we are — yet was without sin."

Still holding hands, turn to the person on your right and say, "I am subject to temptation too, and so I understand your fears and failures.

Exploration: *Probe God's Word*
Examine the temptations of Jesus reported in Matthew 4:1-11. On a chalkboard or newsprint draw a three-column chart. Label the first column *focus*. Label the second *vic-*

tory principle. Label the third *our temptations*.

Fill in the columns for each temptation, guided by the commentary. For instance, the challenge to a hungry Jesus to turn stones to bread was directed against His physical nature and needs. The *focus* of the temptation thus was "physical nature." Jesus' response, "man shall not live by bread alone," identified an O.T. *victory principle*. Human beings are not just animals, dominated by the physical nature, but are spiritual, and thus can choose to live by God's will. Go on then to brainstorm and list in column three the kinds of temptations we experience that grow out of our physical nature.

Follow the same procedure for each of the other two temptations.

Reaction: *Respond together to the Word*
Identify one temptation that you face which is particularly difficult for you to

overcome. Write a paragraph telling how you plan to meet and overcome that temptation during the coming week.

Form groups of three. Share the paragraph you have written with two others. Let each add suggestions or give encouragement from his or her personal experience.

Also jot down a note on the temptations the others in your threesome will work on this week, and promise to pray for them.

It would be good to phone each at least once to report on how you're doing, and to express concern for his or her progress too.

Adoration: *Worship and pray*
Meditate for a moment on Hebrews 4:16, which completes the thought introduced in 4:15 (see "affirmation" above). This verse says: "Let us then approach the throne of grace with confidence, so that we may receive mercy and find grace to help in time of need." We can always come to Jesus with our temptations, whether we have failed and need mercy, or are being challenged and need "grace to help" strengthen us for our time of need.

After meditating for a time, pray spontaneously thanking Jesus for the thoughts in these verses which are most meaningful to you.

THE BEATITUDES

Overview

Matthew 5–7 contains Jesus' famous "Sermon on the Mount." In the context of Matthew's argument that Christ is the expected Messiah-King, this sermon takes on special importance. In giving His moral teaching, Jesus announced as mankind's destined Ruler the lifestyle to be adopted by all who submit to Him.

In this particular study of Matthew 5 we focus on the Beatitudes—a series of "blessed are" or "happy are" statements. The issues explored by Jesus deal with the basic values which human beings adopt and live by. Jesus' point is that the values of this world do not lead to blessing. Instead blessing comes through living by values which the world despises, but which God holds dear.

▶ *Blessed.* Both Old and New Testaments speak of the "blessed." In the Old Testament, and especially the Psalms, the "blessed are" statements describe qualities in a person which bring him or her God's blessing. Here in Matthew the Greek word is *makarios*, which means "happy." Is there a difference? Yes. The Old Testament describes blessings that *will come* to the godly person, and emphasizes material goods. Jesus focused on the *present state* of persons who adopt values and attitudes which permit them to know, now, the inner touch of God in their present lives.

Commentary

Matthew tells us that, after Jesus' baptism, "Jesus began to preach, 'Repent, for the kingdom of heaven is near' " (4:17). Book after book has been written exploring Jesus' "kingdom" emphasis, puzzling over the exact thrust of all His words.

God as King over all. All agree that the Bible pictures God as King over all His cre-

ation. In this sense God is sovereign, marking out the course of cultures and the process of the ages. In a universal sense, everything and all times are to be viewed as God's kingdom: a realm over which He exercises control.

It is also true that the Old Testament brings another focus to God's kingly rule. God in a special way rules over Israel: He is Israel's true King (Deut. 33:5; 1 Sam. 12:12), and Israel is His kingdom (1 Chron. 17:14; 28:5). In a distinctive sense, God involved Himself in the control and direction of Israel's destiny.

When we read in the New Testament that Christ is "Head over everything for the church, which is His body" (Eph. 1:22-23), we have a parallel to the Old Testament emphasis. The rule of God extends over all—but finds special focus in His concern for His own.

God's future reign. A reading of the Old Testament makes it plain that there is more involved in talk of a kingdom than God's overarching rule. God promised through the prophets that a day would come when He will set up an everlasting kingdom on earth, and personally rule from Zion (Isa. 24:23; Micah 4:6; Zech. 14:9-17). Daniel and Isaiah added their descriptions: the King will be God, and yet of David's line. When the Messiah comes, the rule of God will find visible and overwhelming expression as God openly exercises His once-hidden power.

It was this kingdom the Jews expected and yearned for. And it was this kingdom which is described in the prophecies which Matthew relates to Jesus.

So we can hardly doubt what Jesus' listeners pictured in their minds when Jesus announced the good news that the kingdom was at hand. His listeners were sure He meant the eschatological expression of the rule of God. They thought "kingdom of heaven" must mean God's revelation of His power and goodness through Messiah's righteous, endless rule.

Near? It is here that many hesitate. Jesus said that the kingdom of heaven was "near." Yet, 2,000 years have fled since that announcement, and the visible earthly kingdom Jesus' hearers expected has not come. So some have stepped back, and denied the Old Testament vision. They have tried to make the "kingdom of heaven" simply another affirmation that God is in charge, after all.

But why then did Jesus say that the kingdom was finally "near"? Why the urgency? Why, if God has *always* exercised that kind of rule? Clearly some other aspect of the kingdom than God's universal rule must be drawing near.

Particularly significant is the Greek word translated "near." It can mean "at hand," or "has arrived." Was Jesus' announcement of the kingdom an affirmation that in His own coming, God's kingly action was already breaking in uniquely on time and space?

Usually we think of "kingdom" as a place. The "kingdom of Liechtenstein" is geographically defined: a tiny bit of land. Certainly the Old Testament picture of God's ultimate kingdom does involve a place: Palestine is the center from which the Messiah will rule, and the whole earth will be His kingdom's limitless extent. However, in rabbinic literature, kingdom emphasis is not on a *place* but on *action!* "The kingdom of heaven" speaks of that divine action which breaks into our universe and marks out events as God's accomplishment.

No wonder Jesus taught His disciples to pray and say:

Your kingdom come, Your will be done on earth as it is in heaven.
Matthew 6:10

Jesus' disciples, then and now, are to look to God to act on earth just as He acts in heaven itself, to bring His will to pass.

It is most likely, then, that Jesus' announcement of the kingdom had a dual emphasis. On the one hand, Jesus was announcing the nearness of the promised eschatological kingdom in which God will act visibly and dramatically to enforce His will.

That kingdom was near in the person of the promised King!

On the other hand, Jesus also was announcing that the kingdom had arrived! In the personal presence of Jesus on earth, God had acted to take a hand in human affairs. In Jesus, God was already bringing to humankind His final gift of deliverance, and dominion.

Group Activity: Bible Study Group
1. Several phrases in this chapter are critical to its accurate interpretation. Work in teams of four or five to identify the significance of each of the following. Work from the N.T. text only for 15 minutes. Then compare your insights with the information found in the commentary. The key words or phrases:

- *"Blessed are . . ." (5:3, 4, 5, 6, 7, 8, 9, 10, 11).*
- *"You are the light of the world" (5:14).*
- *"I have come to fulfill the law and the prophets" (5:17).*
- *"righteousness [that] surpasses that of the Pharisees and teachers" (5:20).*
- *"you have heard . . . but I tell you" (5:21, 27, 31, 33, 36, 43).*

2. On the basis of your understanding of the nature of this passage, evaluate each of the five ideas about interpreting the Sermon on the Mount found on page 36.

The Sermon on the Mount: Matthew 5:1-11
The impact of the kingdom message does not strike us with the same force that it would have struck the believer of Jesus' day. We have the entire New Testament revelation; we're aware that Jesus acts today in our lives through the Holy Spirit.

But to the men and women who heard Jesus teach, this kingdom concept was new and powerful. They were used to looking ahead to a future when God would act. Jesus' kingdom message made them realize that God was already exercising kingly authority. We can expect God to act *now* to work out His will in you and me!

This kingdom emphasis on an active God underlies what we call the Sermon on the Mount. Only those who throw the full weight of their confidence on God as a King who acts in and for them *now* can ever locate the courage to live the startling lifestyle Jesus laid out for His disciples (Matt. 5:1).

Interpreting the sermon. There have been various approaches to interpreting the Sermon on the Mount. Some are clearly designed to suggest we need not take its teachings seriously.

(1) One view sees the sermon as a salvation message for the world. By "being good" an individual can live in harmony with God and earn His approval.

Only a person who is blind to his own sin and who ignores Jesus' command to repent can see the sermon as portraying a way to find God.

(2) Another view insists that Matthew 5 contains "kingdom truth." The ways of living portrayed there are the ways men will live when Jesus returns to reign. But they are not practical for us until then.

Too often this approach, which has a certain validity, is used to excuse behavior and attitudes that fall far short of the standard Jesus expressed here.

(3) A third view suggests that the sermon is addressed primarily to the church. This too has some validity. But it overlooks the fact that at this stage in Jesus' ministry, Israel, and not the church, was central.

(4) A fourth view synthesizes and provides a better balance. First, the sermon is to be seen as a detailed exposition for Jesus' hearers of what repentance (which literally means a "change of direction" or "about face") involves. Second, it does picture life in the eschatological kingdom. When God is in full charge, at the end of time, everyone *will* live by these guidelines. Third, we have in the Sermon on the Mount the most detailed exposition of God's ethical standards given in the Word. Because these standards reflect God's character and reveal His will, they are relevant to us today as well as in the future kingdom.

(5) To these traditional interpretations we need to add a fifth. *The Sermon on the Mount describes the way in which men are freed to live when they commit themselves to the kingship of Jesus!* When men of any age realize that *in Jesus* the kingdom is "near" to them, they are free to abandon themselves totally to God's will, confident that, as they obey, He will act to shape events.

The Kingdom Now

When Wayne Adams began to dream of making available high-quality art with a subtle yet powerful Christian message, the vision seemed impossible. Wayne had no background or contacts in the art world. And he had no money to finance such a venture.

But Wayne began to pray. Within weeks, believers with all the needed skills were located. Wayne also prayed for funds and left his well-paying job to concentrate on the dream. He sold his car to get enough for a start. When his house was burglarized, insurance payments met other needs. By December 2,000 prints of the first painting, *Born Again*, were completed.

For a number of years Christian bookstores carried Witness Art paintings, and many Christian homes featured these lovely testimonies to some of the great realities of our faith.

Looked at from a "sensible" point of view, everything Wayne did to launch his venture was foolishness. He left his job. He entered a field in which he was less than a novice. He sold his car when the money ran out, and used insurance funds to pay the bills of his project rather than refurnish his home. Everything that Wayne did *was* foolish—unless God's kingdom has broken into our world, and unless God Himself acts in our lives to accomplish His will. Given the reality of God's rule, a person like Wayne, who sets the Lord on the throne of his life, is not foolish but wise.

The Bible makes it clear just how wise Wayne was. According to Colossians, God in Christ "has rescued us from the dominion of darkness and brought us into the kingdom of the Son He loves" (1:13). The Christian has been torn from Satan's grasp and planted firmly in a relationship with God in which Christ is King—a relationship in which Christ acts in our lives.

The Sermon on the Mount is for men who have chosen to be Jesus' disciples and have freely submitted themselves to the King (Matt. 5:1). In it Jesus explains to His disciples of every age what living as a citizen of heaven's kingdom involves. As it meant for Wayne, living in the kingdom means for us, abandoning the ways of the world to adopt a diametrically different set of values and commitments.

New values (Matt. 5:1-12). When first

The Beautitudes: Matthew 5:3-10

Jesus' Values	Countervalues
BLESSED **ARE THOSE WHO ...**	**BLESSED** **ARE THOSE WHO ARE ...**
(v. 3) are poor in spirit	self-confident competent self-reliant
(v. 4) mourn	pleasure-seeking hedonistic "the beautiful people"
(v. 5) are meek	proud powerful important
(v. 6) hunger for righteousness	satisfied "well adjusted" practical
(v. 7) are merciful	self-righteous "able to take care of themselves"
(v. 8) are pure in heart	"adult" sophisticated broad-minded
(v. 9) are peacemakers	competitive aggressive
(v. 10) are persecuted because of righteousness	adaptable popular "don't rock the boat"

heard by disciples, the familiar words of the Beatitudes must have sounded jolting and strange. Familiarity has made them palatable today; their stark challenge to our deepest notions about life is easily passed over. But that first time the challenge must have been almost overwhelming.

What Jesus did in these few verses was to set up a new system of values by which His people are to live. Implicit is a rejection of the values which lie at the core of human civilizations and which shape most individual personalities.

It is difficult to live in our world, to look at men and women who live by the values in the column on the right (chart, p. 541), and be unaffected. We admire this world's "beautiful people." Their sophistication,

looks, pleasures, and importance draw us. We appreciate the values which their lives express. That whole package of values is appealing to us because we tend to associate those values with fulfillment. To be and behave like the people who have status in our society becomes our dream.

Jesus shatters such dreams and rejects such goals in the Beatitudes. He sets up a whole new package of values, proclaiming that in *these* you and I will find fulfillment. Not in pleasure, but in longing. Not in satisfaction, but in hunger. Not in popularity, but in commitment to an unpopular cause. Not in competition and "winning," but in helping others win their way to peace.

The first Beatitude illustrates. "Blessed

are the poor in spirit," Jesus said. Blessed are those who do not approach life with confidence in themselves or reliance on their gifts and talents, sure that they are competent to meet life's challenges. Blessed instead are those who approach life *without* such self-based confidence, "for theirs is the kingdom of heaven." Not, theirs "will be" the kingdom of heaven. But, theirs *is* the kingdom of heaven. In approaching life humbly, and with full reliance on the King, we open up our lives to His direction. We open up our present and future to Jesus' kingly action.

Commitment to kingdom values brings us to the place where we ask the King to reign in our lives. When Wayne Adams surrendered his competencies to God, depending on the Lord to shape events, Wayne responded to the leading of the King and committed himself to the values of the kingdom. In becoming one of the poor in spirit, Wayne discovered the reality of Jesus' promise: "Theirs *is* the kingdom of heaven."

♥ *Group Activity: Support Group*

1. Privately list the three most painful experiences you have had in your life. Then share one of these experiences with the rest of the group, explaining enough so that the others can sense how you felt.

2. Focus on the first two of the Beatitudes. "Poor in spirit," contrasts those who approach life arrogantly with those who come to life's challenges with a humble, reliant attitude. "Those who mourn" contrast those who have experienced grief with those who have dedicated themselves to seeking pleasure without having to have experienced tragedy or reverses.

Talk with one other person about the experience you shared with the group. Tell how the painful experience affected you, positively or negatively. Has pain led to developing either quality commended in one or both of the first two Beatitudes? How?

Remember that Jesus' "blessed are" sayings do not mean painful experiences should be pleasant. It means that if you respond rightly to hurts, you will find God has hidden great benefits within grief.

New behaviors (Matt. 5:13-16). Our values are always expressed in our actions.

What is truly important is the way values find expression in our daily lives.

This is what Jesus alludes to in two brief word pictures. Those who hold kingdom values will witness to those around them the reality of the kingdom. "You are the salt of the earth," Jesus said. In Palestine, flakes of salt form on the rock shores of the Dead Sea at night. In the morning the sun rises. Under its heat the salt loses is saltiness. It blends with the shore and loses its distinctiveness.

"You are the light of world," Jesus went on. Lamps are designed to be put on a lampstand in full view, not to be hidden.

Both these word pictures help us realize that the values which we hold as citizens of Jesus' kingdom are to find expression in our behavior, so that our difference from men of the world will be made plain. Those who come to know us will gradually realize that we are different because of our relationship with our Father "in heaven" (v. 16). The kingdom of heaven is to break into our world, today, through you and me!

Case histories (Matt. 5:17-42). Jesus' kingdom teaching focused first on values and then on the behaviors through which values are expressed. Our Lord went on to give a number of illustrations. This "case history" approach is in full harmony with Old Testament practice. After the Ten Commandments are recorded in Exodus 20, for example, the next few chapters are devoted to illustrating them with examples.

In this sermon Jesus began (Matt. 5:17-20) by explaining that His teaching is not contrary to Old Testament Law. It is intended to "fulfill it." That is, Jesus would explain the Law's true meaning. The kingdom lifestyle that Jesus promoted fulfilled the Law's requirements by producing a righteousness that "surpasses that of the Pharisees and teachers of the Law" (v. 20).

Each of the following case histories demonstrates how the Law is to be "fulfilled" (that is, truly and accurately explained). In each case Jesus shifted the focus of attention from the behavior that the Law dealt with to intents and motives. Here the King works in the hearts of men, changing the values and the behaviors from which behavior springs. In Jesus' kingdom any outward conformity without an inward commitment is unthinkable!

What about murder? Jesus located the root of murder in anger and hatred (vv. 21-26). Rather than nurse anger, which may lead to murder, the kingdom citizen is to value peacemaking. He is to take the initiative to be reconciled to his brother. Later John would write, "Anyone who hates his brother is a murderer" (1 John 3:15).

Adultery? In its true meaning Law does not just speak against the act, for God is concerned with lust itself (Matt. 5:27-30). Jesus sarcastically suggested to men quick to excuse themselves by claims that "I saw her, and couldn't help myself," that they try to rid themselves of their problem by plucking out the offending eye! Impossible? Surely. And so again the issue is focused on the place where the problem lies: "in the heart."

Divorce? Moses permitted it, but Jesus called for lifetime commitment (vv. 31-32).

Promises? Make your word binding by signing a contract—and feel free to break a promise sealed with a handshake? (vv. 33-37) No, be the kind of person whose yes always means yes, and whose no means no.

What about revenge and repaying those who harm you? (vv. 38-48) The Law says you can insist on your rights and on repayment. But in the kingdom, God's blessing rests on the merciful. In relationships with people, the kingdom citizen is called on to be like the Father in heaven and to love even enemies. Does this deny justice? Not at all! It recognizes the fact that in the kingdom, *God* is the One who acts. Paul later put it in these words: "Do not take revenge, my friends, but leave room for God's wrath, for it is written: 'It is Mine to avenge; I will repay,' says the Lord" (Rom. 12:19).

Abandoning the values and the instincts which lie at the root of man's society, the kingdom citizen is to build his life on those peculiar values Jesus taught, values that seem all too shabby to most people. Poverty of spirit? Mourning, meekness, hunger for righteousness? Mercy, purity, peacemaking, willingness to be persecuted on God's account? Yes. On these values Jesus invites His hearers to build new lives.

✂ *Group Activity: Recovery Group*
   Step 10 (continue taking personal inventory)
   On a chalkboard make two columns, one headed *"what others can see"* and the second *"what others cannot see."* Work *through each of the cases Jesus uses for illustration in 5:21-42.*
   For instance:

What others can see	What others cannot see
	5:21-22
Murder Call brother "fool"	Anger Contempt
	5:27-29, etc.

Make a similar chart for your personal use. Review your inner and outer life this past week, and record both "can't see"/"can see" reactions to God, to yourself, and to others. Be honest in undertaking this self-inventory.

Then put a check beside any "can see" items you actually acted out this past week. For instance, you may have become frustrated on the job, and wanted to just walk out. List that, and other possible "can see" actions you might have taken to express your frustration. But put a check mark only next to those "can see" items you actually did act out.

Share charts with one or more other persons in your group. How might you have acted six months before you began your recovery process? How would you like to see the chart you just shared differ after six more months in the group?

Pray together, thanking God for the changes He has made in each of you, and telling God you do depend on Him to keep on making inner changes in your personality.

The Risk

There are two things that are immediately striking about this part of Jesus' Sermon on the Mount. First of all, a person who takes the call seriously and attempts to live as a kingdom citizen takes a great risk. Each of the countervalues of the world seems to have great survival value!

If you aren't competitive and aggressive, how can you get ahead? If you can't take the practical course, and make the expedient choice, you're asking for trouble!

Jesus' sermon calls men to abandon this whole approach to life and to walk out of step with society. We are called to abandon "wisdom" for responsiveness to God's will — whatever the apparent cost. And this involves risk.

The second thing we see in the sermon is the impossibility of the standards Jesus maintains. In shifting attention from behavior to values and motives, Jesus sets righteousness even farther from us than it was before! You and I may have been relatively successful in controlling our behavior. But what about our desires? Our thought lives? Our emotions and feelings toward others? If righteousness in the kingdom means purity in the inner man, each of us is helpless!

But this is just the point of Jesus' an-

nouncement. The kingdom is "at hand"! In Jesus Christ, God has begun to take that action which culminates in our total freedom. In the ultimate expression of the kingdom, Jesus will reign over a renewed earth. But even before Jesus returns, believers of every age have been "brought" by God to the "kingdom of the Son He loves" (Col. 1:13). You and I are in a relationship with God in which He acts for us. When we grasp this, when we open up our lives to Jesus' royal control, He will break into the pattern of our daily lives and into the very heart of our character. Owning Jesus as King, we turn our fears over to Him and seek to rebuild our lives on that which He finds valuable.

Jesus is King. We can take the risk.

GROUP RESOURCE GUIDE

Identification: *Share with others*
Read the Beatitudes silently (5:1-10). Choose one which somewhat describes where you are now in your spiritual journey. That is, are you "poor in spirit," or "meek"? Do you feel a "hunger for righteousness"?

Then share the Beatitude you chose with the group, telling briefly one incident that illustrates that Beatitude's experience in your life, as you understand the Beatitude now.

Affirmation: *Express love and concern*
Consider: have you seen any Beatitude quality displayed in individuals in your group? Briefly give that person or persons feedback on what quality you have noted, and how it has been displayed.

Exploration: *Probe God's Word*
1. Reproduce the chart on page 37 on a chalkboard or sheet of newsprint. Compare each of the values Jesus called blessed with the counter-values held by most persons. Brainstorm each value together: exactly *how* are the values of Jesus better? In what ways might these values find expression in a person's life?
2. One group member should prepare

beforehand to give a report, based on the commentary discussion of Jesus' kingdom found on pages 34-35. Afterward discuss: How does the fact that Jesus rules *today* make a choice to live by the values expressed in the Beatitudes a wise and reasonable one?

Reaction: *Respond together to the Word*
1. Divide into groups of three. Each group should look at the situations Jesus then described, in 5:21-24, 27-30, 31-32, 33-37, 38-42, 43-48. What Beatitude value or values does each case seem to illustrate?

Reassemble to share insights on each situation with the whole group.
2. Think more deeply about the Beatitude you chose as somewhat characteristic of you. List at least five opportunities you expect to have this coming week to put that value into practice.

Then tell the group two of the five things you plan to do to express Jesus' values this coming week.

Adoration: *Worship and pray*
Think how Jesus Himself displayed a Beatitude value in His life here on earth. Take turns praising Jesus for the beauty of His character.

KINGDOM LIFESTYLE

Overview

These chapters continue Jesus' extended teaching called the Sermon on the Mount. In chapter 5 Jesus gave the moral basis for life in His kingdom: Jesus' people are transformed from within, and their godly values are expressed in a holy life that fulfills not just the letter of the Law, but its spirit and intent. In chapters 6–7 Jesus described the lifestyle of those who live in His kingdom.

The major emphases in these chapters indicate that the person who lives, in any age, as a citizen of heaven's kingdom will:

- seek to please God, who sees in secret, rather than men who judge by what is on public view.
- trust God completely to meet material needs, and so concentrate on God's kingdom and righteousness.
- express trust in God in prayer, and by looking to Him to meet every need.
- act on and obey the words of Jesus, which are the only sure foundation for the kingdom lifestyle.

Christians who develop the lifestyle Jesus explains in these two exciting New Testament chapters will experience the presence and the power of our God.

▶ *Kingdom.* A "kingdom" is a realm in which the will and power of a king are expressed. We live in the kingdom Jesus rules when we do His will. Then He will act in our lives and circumstances.

Jesus' listeners were hungry for the kingdom. His message was a jolting one, yet many followed and listened eagerly. They sensed that this Man, who taught with authority, had to know the way to the experience for which they yearned.

That hunger, that longing, is something you and I can understand. We've yearned for a fuller experience of God. We too have been looking for the kingdom where Jesus reigns and acts. All too often we've missed it. All too often we've concluded, wrongly, that the kingdom is wholly future, only to be known when Jesus comes again.

Part of the reason why we tend to look at the kingdom as future only is that we've missed the kingdom when we've looked back into history. Our view of history is distorted, a caricature that has little resemblance to reality. Often the caricature is drawn something like this: "Everything was great as long as the apostles lived. Then it got bad, with the church hardening into a dead and restricting institution paganized by Rome. Then Luther and Calvin brought the Protestant Reformation, and it was alive again for a while. But soon that drifted into deadness as well. Today we're just holding on (sometimes with a feeble grip), waiting till Jesus comes."

This portrait of church history is faulty. It comes in part from the tendency of historians to focus on the institutions, the popes, the cathedrals, and the books written by establishment men to sum up the wisdom of their age. But neither Thomas Aquinas' *Summa* nor John Calvin's *Institutes* expresses the kingdom! The kingdom is expressed in the living witness to Jesus which the Holy Spirit has burned into the lives of those whose hearts turn to the Lord.

For instance, in the twelfth century, the Waldensians, the Poor Men of Lyons, appeared. They gave the Bible to the people in the common language, stressed repentance and conversion, and also emphasized living a Christian life guided by all Scripture—and especially by the Sermon on the Mount.

Long before Luther, John Huss led a great revival in Prague; a revival later forced underground by the persecution which led to Huss' death. For 300 years an underground church existed in Bohemia, with the Gospel passed quietly from father to son, from grandparent to grandchild. Finally these people found refuge in Germany on the estate of Count Nicholas Ludwig von Zinzendorf. Now called Moravians, this group provided impetus for a great missionary movement leading to revivals in Germany, Holland, the Scandinavian countries, France, Switzerland, and America, as well as England. It was Moravian missionaries who met John Wesley while on a ship going to America and introduced him to the possibility of personal faith in Jesus Christ. So, many years before Luther, small prayer and Bible-study groups dotted Germany; when God called Luther to the Reformation leadership, followers had already been prepared.

Today the United States sends out thousands of missionaries across the world. But as late as 1800, there was no missionary movement to reach abroad. Then in 1806, students at Williams College in Massachusetts began to discuss their part in sharing the Gospel with the non-Christian world. A sudden rainstorm sent them dashing into a haystack. Praying there together, God called the first American missionaries. Adoniram Judson, Luther Rice, and Samuel Mills were to lead a host of young men and women, who crossed the oceans to take the Gospel to the world.

These illustrations, which can be multiplied to touch every century and every nation where the Gospel has taken root, bear a striking similarity. A movement of God began in a quiet, hidden way. As far as what has become known as "church history" is concerned, the movements often lie outside the worldly events historians choose to record. Yet the haystack, not the cathedral, is most likely to be characteristic of the kingdom!

True, these movements have often forced their way into the history books. A city set on a hill cannot be hid; a light placed on a candlestick cannot be ignored. But all too often, whether the movement has been Catholic or Protestant, the historical record is one of persecution and antagonism and fear. As in Jesus' day, institutions tend to teach the traditions of men rather than those of God. And such institutions feel threatened by the kingdom.

The kingdom comes into conflict with the world, even as Jesus ultimately was forced into open conflict with the religious men of His day, who demanded, with insistent shouts, "Crucify Him!"

Commentary
Recognizing the Kingdom: Matthew 6:1–7:23

It would be wrong to conclude from what I've just shared that the kingdom of heaven is always in contrast with the established or institutional church. The Wesleyan revival led to the formation of the Methodist Church. The touch of the kingdom was not removed as soon as this church became institutionalized. Today there are Methodist churches which are living expressions of the kingdom—and Methodist churches which know no touch of kingdom life.

The point made by church history is that institutions can never be *identified* with the kingdom. The kingdom can sweep into man's edifices—and sweep out again. To perceive the kingdom, we must look beyond outward appearances to the fleshed-out life of Christ in His body.

This is hard for seekers to grasp. You and I, who are looking for the kingdom of Jesus and are eager for Him to reign in our lives, often become confused. We look to the wrong things for light to guide us. *It is exactly this tendency to miss the inner reality of the kingdom in the outward trappings of religion which Jesus dealt with in the next section of the Sermon on the Mount.*

Jesus gave four warnings—warnings against plausible pathways which will inexorably lead us farther and farther away from the kingdom's presence in our daily lives.

Visible piety (Matt. 6:1-18). "Be careful," Jesus says, "not to do your 'acts of righteousness' before men, to be seen by them" (v. 1).

It's a very natural thing to want to be appreciated as men and women of God, and to be looked up to with respect. It's healthy to want to be a leader. But there are many religious games that people of every age play, which draw them away from the reality of the kingdom.

In Jesus' day, one game was to have a trumpeter announce when someone was going to give alms (charity) to the poor. The poor would come—and so would a host of admiring observers. Everyone would watch as the giver earned a reputation for piety and generosity.

Another common game was played with prayer. When a man wanted to pray, he would go to a busy street corner or a well-filled synagogue and stand, to pray aloud. Often he would pray prolonged and wordy prayers, giving evidence to all that he was pious. Even when men took a vow to go without food, they would be sure to look pained, and would rub dirt into their faces so all could see how much they were suffering for God!

These games were not played for God. They were played for other men, to be seen by them, and to win a reputation with men for piety.

Tragically, many in Jesus' day thought that such people were truly pious! They felt that the way to find the kingdom was by imitating such public acts. Thus an earnest seeker could be drawn into a hypocritical, "play-acting" lifestyle.

In contrast, three times in this passage Jesus instructs, "But when *you* give to the needy, do not let your left hand know what your right hand is doing, so that your giving may be *in secret*. Then your Father, who sees what is done *in secret* will reward you" (vv. 3-4, italics added). And about prayer, "Go into your room . . . and pray to your Father, who is unseen. Then your Father, who sees what is done *in secret* will reward you" (v. 6, italics added). Fasting too is to be seen only by "your Father, who is unseen; and your Father, who sees what is done *in secret*, will reward you" (v. 18, italics added).

It is tremendously important for us to grasp the impact of this repeated emphasis. Kingdom reality cannot be measured by the external things which, done to be seen by men, are singled out in each age as evidence of spirituality.

In one of the churches I attended as a young Christian there were a number of external measurements: attendance at the meetings of the church, praying in King James English at prayer meetings, teaching in the Sunday School, carrying tracts to hand out at the subway station, refraining from smoking and drinking and movies—and from close association with anyone who did indulge in the forbidden three. Most men and women in our little church conformed to these externals. Yet, I know now that beneath the surface of public piety

many suffered the emptiness and pain of alienation, and were unfulfilled. I know also that when I struggled to find reality through conforming, I too wandered away from the reality.

What then is the authentic road? If we are to look away from the ways our culture measures public piety, to what do we look? Jesus' answer is that we are to look to an "in secret" relationship with God as our Father. We are to cultivate awareness that He is present, though unseen, and we are to act to please this One who sees us *in secret*.

How significant is the four-times repeated "in secret"? The world around us does not see the Father. Even our brothers and sisters may see no visible sign of God's presence. In this age, before Jesus comes in power, the kingdom and the Father exist "in secret." But the God who sees us in secret does reward us. The God who sees us *is*, and He does act in the world of here and now.

If we seek the kingdom, we dare not let the traditions of the men of our age draw us away from the God who *is*. It is our secret life with Him which is the key to our experience of the kingdom.

♥ *Group Activity: Support Group*
Many hurt because of an unhealthy relationship with a father as child that continues into adulthood. Such people often find it hard to trust God or to feel worthwhile. In twos or threes, talk about your relationship with and feelings about your father. If possible, place a person with a positive relationship with one or two persons with negative experiences.

Then together underline each reference to God as Father in Matthew 6. Look together at each reference, and complete the following three-column chart:

Characteristic of God	His attitude toward me	How this makes me feel

Note: you can expect some persons with bad fathers to misread the attitude and to feel rejection or condemnation even when the verse is actually positive. Accept these perceptions, but also list the positive attitudes perceived and feelings sensed by those with positive childhood experiences.

When the chart has been completely filled out, discuss: How is our perception of God affected by our experiences with our own fathers? And, how does God the Father differ from the human fathers who have betrayed and disappointed us?

Pray together, telling God you will trust Him as the good Father you never knew. Or ask God to help one of the hurting members of your group trust Him more.

Material success (Matt. 6:19-33). Jesus' second warning focused on possessions. In His day, even the disciples believed that wealth was a sign of God's blessing. Thus, the rich man was viewed as being close to God, while the poor man was somehow thought of as being under His judgment. Jesus put material possessions in a totally different frame of reference in this passage of the sermon.

"Do not store up for yourselves treasures on earth" (v. 19). Instead, treasures are to be laid up in heaven. Once again we are confronted by the fact that the kingdom in our day is in secret. It cannot be measured by material achievement or any of our other standards of "success."

Jesus went beyond warning against such a measurement of His kingdom. He said, "Do not" lay up such treasures. Jesus explained why by pointing out that a concentration on material success would lead to the darkened eye and the divided heart. The eye is the organ of perception through which our whole personality is guided (vv. 22-23). If we focus our vision on what the world calls success, our perception will be distorted and the light of God's revelation of reality will be blocked out. Our whole personality will be darkened.

What's more, our will is affected as well. God and "success" will compete in our personalities, and our values will be shaped by a commitment to one or to the other. "You cannot serve both God and Money" (v. 24).

Then Jesus went beyond, to lay bare the basic issue. Jesus said we are not even to be anxious about necessities! We reject the laying up of earthly treasures, and we reject concern about what we will have to eat and drink! (v. 31) Living in the kingdom means abandoning our very lives to the Father's care so that we can concentrate on seeking "first His kingdom and His righteousness" (v. 33).

How can we find the courage to abandon our lives to God's care? Jesus' illustration answers us. God feeds the birds and clothes the flowers—and you and I are of infinitely more value to our Father! His power orders every detail of the world in which we live; knowing His power and knowing His love for us, His children, we abandon ourselves to His loving care. We know that He will meet our needs.

🖾 *Group Activity: Bible Study Group*
Explore Matthew 6:22-23. Use an illustration like that on page 45 to stimulate thought. Here the pagan sees only material things, and is anxious. But the kingdom citizen sees God's care displayed in nature, and trusts. Develop as many other similar contrasts as you can. For instance, the pagan sees another person as a rival, or sex object. How does the citizen of Jesus' kingdom see others?

✂ *Group Activity: Recovery Group*
Steps 2 (believe in a higher power) and 3 (decide to turn my life over to God's care)
List 15 significant things that painful experience has shown you cannot do for yourself. Then look together at Matthew 6:25-34. How does trying to rely on themselves alone affect the "pagan" in Jesus' story? What emotional impact has trying to rely on myself, and failing, had on me?

Then read Matthew 6:25-34 together. What shows me I can trust myself to God? What shows I must trust myself to God?

If you are ready to make a decision to turn your life over to the will and the care of God, make that commitment in front of other group members.

Authority (Matt. 7:1-14). "Do not judge" are the warning words which mark off the third section of Jesus' guidelines for kingdom seekers. It is directed at those who see in the kingdom the right to exalt themselves above their fellow citizens, who are

What Does our Eye
See and What Does It Mean?

named "brothers" here.

The first warning dealt with seeking approval of men rather than God.

The second warning dealt with having concern for the goods in this world, rather than abandoning such concerns to seek the kingdom and righteousness.

The third warning deals with relationships within the kingdom.

This warning is a vital one; in human society we always go about setting up a "pecking order." We try to settle the question of who has control or influence over another. The whole "chain of command" approach of the military and the business world reflects the concern human beings feel for authority. The right to judge another is a right which the human heart naturally yearns for.

This is true in the church as in any group. Church history is in a real sense a report of the struggle for control over others in the name of religion. This is not true only in the papal distortions of the Middle Ages. It is true in the local Protestant church of today, where a pastor or a board member may struggle to impose his will on his brothers and sisters. Or where a gossip may claim the right to exalt himself or herself over the person whose reputation is smeared. Pushing others down seems such

an easy way to raise ourselves up.

But if we are to find the kingdom, we have to abandon all claims to a right to judge. "Do not judge," Jesus said, and for all time He destroyed the pretentions of anyone who would seek to exalt himself over others in the kingdom (vv. 1-6).

Instead Jesus taught another attitude: that of humility and servanthood. "Ask," Jesus said, commanding us to take the position not of a judge but of a supplicant. We are to approach life in the kingdom with a deep sense of our need for God's good gifts—and with full confidence that our loving Father will supply us with all we need (vv. 7-11). What is more, in bowing down to God we also bow down to our brothers. We commit ourselves not to judge them but to serve them: "In everything, do to others what you would have them do to you" (v. 12).

This truly is a narrow gate. But it leads us to life—the life of the kingdom, now (vv. 13-14).

False leaders (Matt. 7:15-23). Jesus concluded His warnings by focusing on men who will claim Jesus as Lord, but who will seek to use and to savage His flock. How will the false prophet be known? Not by what he says so much as by what he is and does. "By their fruits you will recognize them" is how Jesus put it (v. 20). In context, the bitter fruits are obvious.

Men will come, claiming Jesus as Lord and offering to lead the way into His kingdom. But their lives will be marked by a public rather than a private kind of piety. Their lives will show a concern for, rather than disinterest in, material things. And their lives will be marked by the claim of the right to judge their brothers and sisters.

When these marks are seen, we have Jesus' declaration that, no matter what mighty words they accomplish in His name, "I never knew you" (vv. 22-23). Such men cannot lead us into an experience of the kingdom.

The Kingdom Found: Matthew 7:24-29
Jesus' message concluded with a simple yet powerful illustration, which focuses our attention on the one road to experience the kingdom of Jesus now.

Therefore, everyone who hears these words of Mine and puts them into practice is like a wise man who built his house on the rock. The rain came down, the streams rose, and the winds blew and beat against that house; yet it did not fall, because it had its foundation on the rock. But everyone who hears these words of Mine and does not put them

into practice is like a foolish man who built his house on sand. The rain came down, the streams rose, and the winds blew and beat against that house, and it fell with a great crash.

Matthew 7:24-27

We stand at a fork in a road that leads only two ways—Jesus' way, or another. We too have heard the words of the King. We see the pathway He set out as leading to the kingdom.

In Matthew 5, we heard Jesus focus the issue on our inner lives, and we explored the values by which we are called to live. In Matthew 6 and 7, we see how to distinguish between true and false pathways to the kingdom. What have we learned?

We have learned that to live in Jesus' kingdom, we must abandon concern for the approval of men, and learn to care only for the approval of God. We have learned that we can find release from anxiety over necessities, and so be free to concentrate our attention on righteousness. And we have learned that we are to be humble before God and our brothers: we are not to judge, but to take our place with them as supplicants before God.

Will we find the kingdom if we follow this pathway?

Of course we will. For we will be walking in the footsteps of the King!

GROUP RESOURCE GUIDE

Identification: *Share with others*
Think of a person who you see as a "very fine Christian." Do not mention his or her name, but make a 30-second speech nominating that individual for the title, "Really Fine Christian." After nominations are complete, list together what qualities or traits are most often mentioned.

Affirmation: *Express love and concern*
Write a brief note to a person in your group mentioning one of the listed traits you appreciate in him or her. Give the note to him or her after group session is over.

Exploration: *Probe God's Word*
1. In teams of five focus on Matthew 6:1-6, 16-18. Each team is to identify at least three "games" played by the religious of Jesus' time

(see commentary, pp. 42-43). Try to define the rules by which each game is played, and how a person might "keep score."

Then think of games that contemporary Christians sometimes play. Again, define the rules (tell how the game is played), and what constitutes a score.

Come together and describe the "games modern Christians play" identified by each team.

2. OR study Matthew 6:19-33. Prepare by asking each person to list at least five of his or her "treasures."

Read the passage aloud, having half the group listen and list what the pagan Jesus speaks of seems to treasure, and the other half list what a member of God's kingdom seems to treasure. Record the two lists on a chalkboard or sheet of newsprint—and then brainstorm to add at least 20 items of the same kind to each list. Remember, the items added must be "of the same kind." When the list is complete, discuss what kinds of things are treasures to pagans, and what kinds of things are treasures to Jesus' kingdom people.

Reaction: *Respond together to the Word*
1. Review together Matthew 6:1-18, and underline each repetition of the phrase "in secret." Discuss: How can developing our own "in secret" relationship with God protect us from the temptation to play games with our faith?

For personal self-evaluation after group: If you were handed a note or notes by another group member (see Affirmation, above), evaluate his or her commendation honestly. Have you been playing a game, and fooled the person who gave you the note? Or is what he or she has seen in you evidence that your own "in secret" relationship with God is bearing fruit?

2. OR discuss together the results of having treasures on the "pagan" or "kingdom citizen" lists. Gain your insights from Matthew 6:25-34. Note particularly the contrast between inner anxiety and inner peace, between frantic activity and rest, etc.

After discussing, look privately at the five "treasures" you listed in preparation for the Bible study (above). Do they belong on the "pagan" or the "kingdom citizen" list? How has making these things your treasures affected your emotional life? Your choices? Etc.?

Adoration: *Worship and pray*
In these chapters Jesus emphasizes that God is our Father. Thank God for His Father love, and praise Him for one way in which thinking of Him as Father helps you trust Him more.

THE AUTHORITY OF THE KING

Overview

This extended section of Matthew builds on the Gospel writer's earlier presentation. Matthew showed that Jesus is the One the Old Testament prophets told would come: He fit the prophecies. Matthew showed that Jesus demonstrated in His baptism and temptation dominion over the inner sin which entangles other men: He can lead us to victory. Matthew reported Jesus' Sermon on the Mount: Jesus explained how to live as a citizen of the heavenly kingdom.

Now Matthew moved on to establish clearly the authority of the King. The miracles that Matthew now reported do more than authenticate Him as God's Messenger. They demonstrate the extent of His authority: over sickness, nature, demons, sin, and even over death itself.

Surely this One is to be followed completely, by those who own Him as King. What a privilege to be disciples of our wonderful Lord!

▶ *Authority*. The Greek word expressing the idea of "authority" is *exousia*. It is also translated in English as "power."

The basic meaning of *exousia* is that of "freedom of action." A person with authority has greater freedom to act than a person under authority. The greater the authority, the greater the freedom of action. Jesus in the New Testament is shown to be a Person with *complete* authority. No one or no thing can place restrictions on Jesus' freedom to act—for good—in your life and mine.

Commentary

The live TV audience broke into laughter each time one of the cast asked the "pastor" a question. Why? Well, each time his answer was the same: a decisive "perhaps"!

It is funny. On TV. But not in real life. Kay found that out as she went the rounds of her Christian friends, asking their advice and counsel. Some said one thing. Some said another. No one seemed to be too sure. The uncertain and conflicting ideas confused rather than helped.

No wonder the crowds who listened to Jesus' Sermon on the Mount were stunned. No, not so much by what Jesus said. That hadn't really sunk in yet. The words of the sermon would be remembered and talked about, until finally the new way of life Jesus sketched gradually became more clear. What the crowds who heard Jesus were astonished at was His tone of *authority*. They were "amazed at His teaching, because He taught as One who has authority, not as their teachers of Law" (Matt. 7:28-29). Christ claimed the King's right to govern His people; He spoke with authority. Now all would ask, did He really *have* the authority He claimed?

Authentication: Matthew 8:1–9:34

The next events seem to merge in a fast-paced narrative. The acts of the King are traced as, over and over, they demonstrate the validity of Jesus' claim to authority.

Willing and able (Matt. 8:1-13). Immediately after Jesus' descent from the mount on which He spoke His sermon, a leper met Him. He said, "Lord, if You are willing, You can make me clean" (v. 2). This man sensed Jesus' power, but was uncertain whether Christ would use that power for his sake. Jesus reached out and touched the leper, healing him. The King *is* willing to exercise His authority to help humankind.

Entering the city of Capernaum, a Roman officer met Jesus to ask for the healing of a servant. Christ offered to go with the Roman, who objected. "I do not deserve to have You come under my roof" (v. 8). Instead the Roman asked Jesus merely to speak the word. Jesus spoke; the servant was healed. Jesus is able.

48

Power over all (Matt. 8:14–9:31). The next event shows Jesus' authority over *all* the powers to which you and I are subject.

Sickness	Jesus heals	8:14-17
Nature	Jesus stills a storm	8:23-27
Demons	Jesus casts them out	8:28-32
Sin	Jesus forgives	9:1-8
Death	Jesus makes alive	9:18-26

There is nothing to limit the authority of Jesus, who has demonstrated His power over everything under which you and I are crushed! This Man *is* able to speak "as One having authority" (7:29, KJV) — because He does!

✄ *Group Activity: Recovery Group*
Steps 6 (be ready to have God remove character defects) and 7 (humbly ask God to remove shortcomings)
List and look at the following miracles of Jesus. Tell which you think is greatest, and explain why. The miracles:

Healing	*8:14-17*
Still storm	*8:23-27*
Cast out demons	*8:28-32*
Restores movement	*9:1-7*
Restores the dead	*9:18-26*

Then study together Matthew 9:9-13 with Luke 19:1-10. Matthew became the disciple who wrote this N.T. book. Zaccheus was transformed, made amends, and set out to live a new kind of life. Was the transformation of these two men a greater or lesser miracle than the ones listed above? Why, or why not? How does Jesus' forgiveness and transformation of these two sinners help you trust God, and influence you to turn your life over to Him?

If you are honestly ready to do so, tell God you do believe in Him, and turn yourself over to Him. You can make this decision privately, but during the next week call at least one individual in your group and tell him or her about your decision.

There are three very special riches for us in this extended passage.

(1) *Under authority.* The Roman soldier speaking to Jesus said, "I myself am a man under authority, with soldiers under me. I tell this one, 'Go,' and he goes" (Matt. 8:9). He said this to explain the confidence he had in Jesus which enabled him to ask Jesus to heal from a distance, by the mere speaking of a word. His point was this: As a soldier, his authority over others was *derived*. It was his relationship in the chain of command which gave this military man his power. When he spoke, all the power of Rome's mighty empire, under whose authority he stood, spoke through him.

And what about Jesus? How was Jesus able to speak and have nature, demons, and even death jump to obey? Because here on earth Jesus also operated under authority; the authority of God. When Jesus spoke all the limitless power of God Himself spoke through Him.

It's like this today. We can trust Jesus. The full power of Almighty God is His.

(2) *New wineskins.* A fascinating dialogue here is inserted in Matthew 9:14-17. John the Baptist's disciples had noted that Jesus was unlike their master. They came to ask why. Jesus explained, and added, "Neither do men pour new wine into old wineskins. If they do, the skins will burst, the wine will run out and the wineskins will be ruined. No, they pour new wine into new wineskins" (Matt. 9:17).

You and I cannot stuff Jesus or our experience with Him into our old ways of thinking and living. Life with Jesus is a new and exciting thing. He Himself wants to fill us, to expand our personalities, and to reshape us to fit who He is. When Jesus, the Man with all power, comes into our lives, we are privileged to open ourselves up to newness.

(3) *Dead and blind.* Through these two chapters the acts of Jesus follow a progression. Each portrait shows Christ as having power over a greater enemy than the last: sickness, nature, demons, sin, and then death itself.

Why then does an instance of healing the *blind* follow the raising of the ruler's daughter? For our sakes! You and I can find the faith to believe that Jesus will make us fully alive when He returns. But how often we look at the dead dimensions of our present lives with despair. The blind men were living — but with dead eyes. When they begged for healing, Jesus asked, "Do you believe that I am able to do this?" (Matt. 9:28) They did believe. Jesus touched their eyes. And where the moment before there had been death, now there was sight.

Jesus comes into our lives with hope *for today*. If your personality has died to the capacity to live, or has shriveled in bitterness, or if you have lost the capacity for compassion, Jesus asks, "Do you believe that I am able?" We can answer, "Yes!" Jesus does have the power to revive the deadened areas of our lives.

To really understand the significance of the extended passage we've been considering, we need to note one of its peculiarities. Throughout this sequence of events Jesus referred to Himself as "the Son of man." He did not use the term in the Sermon on the Mount. The first occurrences are here.

The term "Son of man" is found in both the Old Testament and the New. In the New it is used 94 times, and, with 5 exceptions, always by Christ of Himself. Clearly Jesus affirms something important about Himself in His selection and use of this term.

On the one hand, of course, the phrase "Son of man" emphasizes Jesus' full humanity. But even greater significance is found in the fact that, as in Matthew 9:6, "Son of man" signifies Jesus' redemptive work and mission. In the term "Son of man" Jesus presents Himself as the Victor, for He accomplished all that man was intended to do, and becomes all that man was intended to be.

The demons recognized and spoke to Jesus as the "Son of God" (8:29). They were right; they knew Him for who He is. The whole Bible makes it very clear that the One who became Man at Bethlehem truly is the Creator God. John insisted that Jesus is God, coexisting with the Father from the beginning (John 1). Jesus does not hesitate to claim equality with God (John 17). Paul's writings affirm Jesus as God, along with the Father and the Holy Spirit. The Old Testament prophecy identifies Jesus as the "Father of eternity" (a phrase meaning the source or originator of eternity itself!) and speaks of the Child to be born as "a Son . . . given" (Isa. 9:6, KJV). The name Immanuel, as we have seen, means, "With us is God." Jesus had every right to speak of Himself as the Son of God, for that is who He is.

Yet Jesus chose another title for Himself: "Son of man." A Man, with God's prerogative of forgiving sin. A Man, with power to

heal and to give life. A Man, yet Victor over death.

In Jesus the very power of God entered the mainstream of humanity, and in Jesus' authority as the Son of man you and I find an anchor for our hope. Many years ago Johann Burger (1598–1662) caught a vision of the authority of the Son of man, and expressed it in the hymn, "Jesus Lives, and So Shall I."

Jesus lives and reigns supreme;
    And His kingdom still remaining.
I shall also be with Him,
    Ever living, ever reigning.
God has promised: be it must;
Jesus is my hope and trust.

The Man with all power lives today. His kingdom does remain. With Him, we also shall reign. Then—and now.

Shared Authority: Matthew 9:35–10:40
Jesus' authority had been established by His miracles. Then He did an amazing thing. "He called His twelve disciples to Him *and gave them authority*" (10:1, italics added).

Immediately after establishing His own authority, you and I are shown that Jesus intended to share that authority with His followers.

It was human need that moved Jesus to this unexpected decision. Matthew 9:35-38 pictures Jesus continuing His itinerant mission, teaching and healing. Everywhere there were crowds; everywhere Jesus saw men and women who were "harassed and helpless, like sheep without a shepherd" (v. 36). Moved, He turned to His disciples. "Ask the Lord of the harvest, therefore, to send out workers into His harvest field" (v. 38). Jesus determined to multiply His ministry by sending His disciples to every place where He Himself wanted to go.

It must have seemed exciting to His disciples. To be men, themselves harassed and helpless a short time before, and suddenly to have power! "Heal the sick," Jesus told them. "Raise the dead, cleanse those who have leprosy, drive out demons" (10:8). With it all, they were to share the good news that the long-awaited kingdom was at hand. But the thrill and pride must have been dampened as Jesus went on to explain the lifestyle of men who were given the gift of power.

The disciples were not to go in pomp or in luxury. They were to live among their fellowmen as Jesus did—humbly, as servants. And while Jesus' disciples were given authority over sickness, death, and demonic power (v. 8), they were not to coerce men. Some people would receive them; some would hate them. The disciples' role was to use authority to serve.

Lifestyle then. This chapter gives us deep insight into discipleship and helps us see ourselves as kingdom citizens who have power—but who humble ourselves to serve. Note these features of Jesus' instructions:

- Disciples were to be dependent on God, not on their own wealth or possessions, for necessities (vv. 8-11).
- Disciples were to give all men the freedom to accept or reject them and their Lord (vv. 12-15).
- Disciples were to expect and to endure persecution from those who rejected and hated their Lord (vv. 16-25).
- Disciples were to remember their great value to God the Father, and do His will without fear of men (vv. 26-33).
- Disciples were to expect conflict, even in their own homes. In everything, Jesus is to be put first, and pain is to be borne just as Jesus bore the pain of His cross (vv. 34-39).
- Disciples could know they brought great gifts to men, who would be rewarded for their responses to the Father and His children (vv. 40-42).

How very different from the life we expect of a man with power! Instead of wealth, there was self-chosen poverty and dependence. Instead of exercising power over others, disciples extended to all men freedom to choose. Instead of honor and praise, the disciple was often persecuted and maligned. Jesus chose to empty Himself to win us victory as the Son of man. So too disciples are called to wear the humble garb of servants as the badge of their God-given authority.

Ø Group Activity:
Missions/Outreach Group
Matthew 10 tells that Jesus sent His disci-

ples out with authority—but also under His authority, with specific instructions as to how to carry out their mission. Work through Matthew 10:1-42 three times. The first time through, identify and list principles of the missionary/evangelist's relationship with God. The second time, identify and list principles of the missionary/evangelist's relationships with other persons. The third time, identify and list specific instructions given to the missionary/evangelist.

Work with the three lists to develop a "statement of principles" for your own outreach efforts.

Shattered Expectations: Matthew 11

Like chapter 10, Matthew 11 is completely discourse. While Matthew 10 is addressed to the disciples, chapter 11 is addressed to the crowds—crowds who, struggle as they will, cannot see in Jesus their coming King.

The dialogue was initiated by disciples who had come from John the Baptist. The great prophet and forerunner of Jesus was in prison. Soon he would be executed by Herod, his head a prize won by the sensuous dance of a girl with whose mother Herod was living in sin. John had recognized Jesus at His baptism when our Lord was clearly marked out for him by God. But now even John was wondering.

Why? Because John too expected the King and kingdom to burst on Israel with outward power. Not even John had expected the coming of a servant King!

Jesus' answer was to direct John's disciples' attention to the acts of mercy He was performing. "Go back and report to John what you hear and see: The blind receive sight, the lame walk, those who have leprosy are cured, the deaf hear, the dead are raised, and the Good News is preached to the poor" (Matt. 11:4-5). John would grasp the meaning. John, like Jesus, was steeped in the lore of the Old Testament. His thoughts would turn to Isaiah 35 and he would remember that prophet's words about the glory and the majesty of God (v. 2).

Behold, your God will come with vengeance; the recompense of God will come, but He will save you. Then the eyes of the blind will be opened, and the ears of the deaf will be unstopped. Then the lame will leap like a deer, and the

tongue of the dumb will shout for joy.
Isaiah 35:4-6, NASB

John envisioned the glory primarily as recompense; as the day of God's judgment. But the glory of God was also to be seen in the tender care of Messiah for men and women in need. John did not understand then that the servant ministry of Christ had to come first. But the report reassured him. Jesus *was* doing what the Scriptures foretold that Messiah would do.

The crowds were not so easily satisfied. Jesus spoke then of John, and said that if they would accept it, "He is the Elijah who was to come" (Matt. 11:14). Clearly Jesus claimed to be the Messiah whom John announced (vv. 7-15).

But the people of Israel were unable to make up their minds. They were repelled by John's austerity and demand of repentance—he took his religion a little too seriously. Yet they were tempted to dismiss Jesus because, in contrast with John, Jesus lived a normal life and was a friend of tax collectors and "sinners" (v. 19). Like people today, they wanted to have a God who fits *their* expectations. Yet, like changeable children, they could not make up their minds what He should be like. Each time a new candidate appeared, they changed the rules! (vv. 16-19)

Then Jesus uttered His first recorded words of warning and judgment. He spoke of the cities where His miracles had been done, and announced a coming woe. Even pagan Tyre and Sidon, even licentious Sodom, would have repented and believed if a messenger from God had come with such powerful authenticating works as His. But Israel had hesitated—and hesitated still. Israel simply refused to commit herself to her King (vv. 20-24).

The chapter closes with a prayer, and with an invitation. Israel's rejection of the King was also part of the Father's "gracious will." The nation might refuse its King, but all who labor and are heavy laden are called to come to the Saviour.

"Come to Me," Jesus invited, "and I will give you rest. Take My yoke upon you and learn from Me, for I am gentle and humble in heart, and you will find rest for your souls. For My yoke is easy and My burden is light" (vv. 28-30).

The word picture is a beautiful one. The yoke of Jesus' day was a fitted collar-like frame, shaped to rest on the neck and shoulders of two animals. Teamed together, the task was far easier for two oxen than for one. And if one were a young ox, how much easier to have an older, stronger companion to share the burden. To men who called for God's King to reign over them, Jesus offered to be God's Servant, yoked in harness with them.

Today, taking up the yoke that links us to Jesus, we too find rest. We walk beside Jesus. We learn from Him. And because our older, stronger, all-powerful Companion takes His fullest share of all our burdens, when we are linked to Jesus our burdens truly are made light.

GROUP RESOURCE GUIDE

Identification: *Share with others*
Draw three "teeter-totters" on a chalkboard or sheet of newsprint. Each represents a different "balance" between Jesus and His followers. Share briefly which of the three best represents your experience with Jesus this past week.

Exploration: *Probe God's Word*
Two themes are developed in these chapters: the authority of Jesus, and the lifestyle of discipleship. Choose which of these you want to explore. Join a team of two or three others who want to explore the same topic.

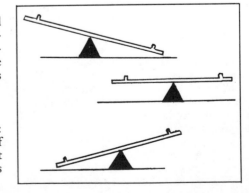

A. Authority study teams: read the descriptions of Jesus' exercise of authority over:

sickness	Matt. 8:14-17
nature	Matt. 8:23-27
demons	Matt. 8:28-31
sin	Matt. 9:1-8
death	Matt. 9:18-26

Discuss: What are we to learn from these miracles? How does seeing Jesus' exercise of this kind of authority affect us?

B. Discipleship study teams: Jesus gave His disciples authority, but with it He gave strict instructions as to how the disciples were to live and relate to others. Study together: 10:8-11, 10:12-15, 10:16-25, 10:26-33, 10:34-39, 10:40-42. Discuss: What are we to learn about discipleship from Jesus' instructions?

Come together and report what each study team learned from its texts.

Reaction: *Respond together to the Word*
Go back to the teeter-totter illustration which shows Christ up and the disciple down. Brainstorm together half a dozen ways in which modern Christians can apply Jesus' instructions to disciples, and so both live under His authority, yet with authority as His agents.

Affirmation: *Express love and concern*
Tell the person on your left one way you see him or her acting as a disciple—or tell him or her one way you wish he or she would grow in discipleship. Remember that even correction offered in love is affirmation. But remember too that even the truth spoken without love can be harmful.

Adoration: *Worship and pray*
Think of one of the miracles reported in this passage, and praise Jesus for what that miracle tells you about Him or the Father.

HARDENING OPPOSITION

Overview

Matthew now comes to his initial explanation of what happened to the promised messianic kingdom.

Matthew's Gospel flows logically from his theme: that Jesus is the Messiah of the Old Testament.

Chapters 1 and 2 reported the birth of Jesus, and demonstrated its harmony with Old Testament messianic prophecy.

Chapters 3 and 4 affirmed Jesus' full identity with humanity—and His victory over every human weakness. Surely this Person can lead us to victory too.

Chapters 5–7, the Sermon on the Mount, contained Jesus' explanation of the lifestyle appropriate for those who choose to live in His kingdom.

Chapters 8–11 proved Jesus' authority over all that binds human beings. And it also shows that in Jesus, authority is expressed through servanthood—in both Master and disciples.

Now, in chapters 12–15, we learn of the response of the nation to Jesus and His message. That response is one of growing opposition, spearheaded by the Pharisees. The Jewish leaders rejected the Lord—and in a series of parables Jesus introduced a modification of the kingdom. If the nation will not welcome the King, individuals who do welcome Him into their lives will live in an unexpected, a mystery form, of Jesus' kingdom.

How wonderful that Jesus is still willing to welcome individuals. How wonderful that His hidden kingdom still exists today!

Commentary

The other night I listened to a late night talk show on which two well-known radio personalities were talking about visits each had made to the South American land of the Aucas. These were the jungle peoples who in the late '50s speared five missionaries—some of whose wives and children later went to live among them and won them to Christ. One of the radio personalities told how impressed he had been with the translated testimony of a converted chief, who had earlier taken 35 human heads, and by the fact that the actual killers of the five missionaries had not only become Christians but were now themselves missionaries to other jungle tribes.

Both men were tremendously impressed by their trips and these jungle peoples. Their interest and curiosity had been challenged—but not their commitment. Faced with the necessity of making a personal choice, neither had responded. And one was clearly hostile.

It must have been something like this in Jesus' day. When Christ first came on the scene, teaching and healing, many were drawn to Him. He was a curiosity, Someone to be impressed with and to talk about. Even the leaders of the people viewed Jesus as God's messenger (John 3:2). But as Jesus' message became more clear, and as He confronted each hearer with the challenge to *choose*, attitudes began to change. Jesus' Sermon on the Mount spoke of the kingdom in unexpected ways. Jesus' own behavior did not fit the popular notion of the coming King. His authenticating miracles could not be denied. But as Jesus continued teaching, He exposed more and more clearly the sinfulness of current attitudes and ways. The leaders particularly became hostile. Jesus was no longer a curiosity. He had become a threat, demanding that they choose between His revelation of God and His ways, and their own dearly held beliefs.

Jesus' authority had clearly been demonstrated in His miracles; He exercised authority over *all* the powers that hold men in bondage. It was clear that no Pharisee or Sadducee had similar authority. Yet their resistance grew. They *would not* believe.

In the men of Jesus' day we see a contemporary issue drawn as well. Rejection of Christ is seldom a choice which hinges on lack of knowledge. Rather, as the issues become more and more clear, our response to truth hinges on our will. We must *choose*. For the non-Christian it becomes a choice to abandon hope in oneself and trust Jesus alone to bring him or her into a family relationship with God. For the Christian there is also a choice. A choice to follow the servant King and to adopt the lifestyle of the kingdom, or to hold onto the attitudes and values and beliefs and behaviors of the world. In tracing growing opposition in these chapters of Matthew, we see some of the issues facing all men—you and me as well. And we are confronted by our own necessity to choose.

⌀ Group Activity:
Missions/Outreach Group

Read aloud the Auca story on page 54. Share: Tell of a time you got a similar reaction when sharing Christ with a friend or acquaintance.

Then look together at Matthew 12, at the open hostility expressed by the Pharisees. How do these persons differ from the individuals you and others just described?

Return to Matthew 12 and explore how Jesus dealt with the Pharisees. What did Jesus say and do? What was His purpose or intent? How did the Pharisees respond?

From your sharing and study, how might you proceed to witness to someone who is interested but indifferent? How if a person is openly hostile and in opposition to the Gospel?

Attack: Matthew 12

The men who seem to have spearheaded the growing opposition to Jesus were the Pharisees. Along with the Sadducees, traditionally their rivals, this band of rigid and committed men were quick to see the great gap between Israel's present lifestyle and Jesus' kingdom truth.

The Pharisees. The name comes from a root meaning "separated." The movement apparently began some two centuries before Christ, and focused on resistance to hellenization of the Jews. The Pharisees were earnestly concerned with the Law and with keeping its minutest detail. But the Pharisees tended to emphasize the "oral law" of the Torah (Pentateuch). This oral law was composed of a vast number of interpretations and explanations of the Old Testament, which over the years continued to grow and grow. Tragically, the oral law increasingly focused on trifling details. For instance, the command not to work on the Sabbath was expanded and illustrated with hundreds of explanations and exceptions. According to the Pharisees' oral law, a person was allowed to spit on rocky ground on the Sabbath. But he could not spit on soft or dusty earth; the spittle might move the dirt and that would constitute plowing, for it might make a furrow! Thus the oral law often robbed the written Law of its real message—a message of godly concern for others. Jesus once rebuked the Pharisees for their practice of "giving" all of their possessions to the temple (to be taken over after their deaths), and then telling poor parents or other relatives that they owned nothing with which to help *them*. God's command to "honor your father and mother" was thus pushed aside in favor of this merely human tradition.

We can see in the New Testament many evidences of the Pharisees' scrupulous concern for the minor details of legalism (Matt. 9:14; 23:16-19, 23; Mark 7:1-13; Luke 11:42). What we often miss is that the movement itself did have healthy roots.

The Pharisees had separated themselves from the rest of Israel because of a deep concern for righteousness. They yearned for the arrival of the kingdom in which God and His ways would be honored in holiness. Until that time, in search of personal holiness, the Pharisees joined communes of others with the same longing. These Pharisees were neither educated nor upper-class men. Instead, they were characteristically middle class, without formal education in the interpretation of the Law. In their closed communities they lived under the direction of a scribe (an expert in the Law), and they sought to separate themselves in order to find righteousness by keeping the whole Law. This high level of commitment won them the admiration of the common people, and gave this group, which in Jesus' day numbered about 6,000, great influence.

Later Paul would write something about the Jews which was characteristic of the Pharisees: "For I can testify about them that they are zealous for God, but their zeal is not based on knowledge. Since they did not know the righteousness that comes from God and sought to establish their own, they did not submit to God's righteousness" (Rom. 10:2-3). In their attempt to find righteousness through legalism, they missed the Old Testament's message of righteousness through faith (cf. Gen. 15:6). The Pharisees became so committed to their own notions of what God's will must be that when the Son of God appeared to reveal the Law's true meaning, they refused to listen. For the Pharisees to respond to Jesus would have meant admitting that the principles on which they had built their lives, and which gave them their distinctive identity, had been wrong. They simply could not and would not abandon themselves, even though it was God who called.

We can sympathize with the Pharisees. Some of us too have had an honest concern for the things of God without real understanding.

But then Jesus confronts us, and calls us to abandon all that we once held dear and true that we might rebuild our lives on Him, and learn His kingdom lifestyle. Too often we too hold back. Dare we surrender all we thought we had and were in order to become something new, just because the King commands and promises?

The Pharisees would not, and could not, make this surrender. They insisted on holding on to their own ideas rather than submitting to the King. Their rebellion against the lordship of Jesus led, not only to their own destruction, but it contributed to the suffering of the nation that they influenced.

Attack (Matt. 12:1-24). We see the Pharisees' mindset in three incidents reported in this chapter. Walking through the grainfields, the disciples plucked and ate wheat kernels. The Pharisees shouted to Jesus, "Hey! They're breaking the Law!"

The "Law" they referred to was the oral law's interpretation of that act as "harvesting." And the disciples were "harvesting" on the Sabbath! But the Old Testament itself never interprets Sabbath Law to demand going hungry.

A little later Jesus entered a synagogue of the Pharisees (v. 9). There He was confronted by a man with a withered hand. This confrontation was apparently arranged by the Pharisees so that they "might accuse" Him (v. 10). So they challenged Jesus. "Is it lawful to heal on the Sabbath?" Jesus responded by pointing out the value of a man to God, and added, "It is lawful to do good on the Sabbath" (v. 12). Jesus then healed the man—and the Pharisees went out and began to plot how to kill Him!

Later Jesus was seen healing, and the crowds wondered aloud if He was the Messiah. Then the Pharisees, hardened in their rejection of Jesus, began a slander campaign against Him. "It is only by Beelzebub, the prince of demons, that this fellow drives out demons" (v. 24).

Jesus' response (Matt. 12:25-50). Much of this chapter is devoted to Jesus' response to the attack of the Pharisees. Responding to the first attack (on the disciples plucking grain to eat as they walked), Jesus pointed out that even God's laws (to say nothing of the oral traditions intended to explain them) are not intended to be rigid, unyielding rules. God is concerned with "mercy and not sacrifice": His Laws are intended to provide a framework for the expression of love. The disciples were guiltless in this situation, for they acted only to meet real need. Their freedom from guilt was pronounced by He who is "Lord of the Sabbath" (v. 8).

The second incident also is revealing. The Pharisees were willing to *use* a man with a withered hand to trap Jesus. They were totally unconcerned about his personal tragedy and his feelings. Jesus' response, affirming God's valuation of individuals, showed up their hardheartedness for what it was. No wonder these men plotted to kill Jesus. In their pursuit of self-righteousness, the Pharisees had lost the deep concern for others that characterizes God. Their religious zeal had, in fact, led them to become *ungodly* (un-Godlike) persons!

With their ungodliness clearly revealed, in contrast to our Lord's own compassion and love, the Pharisees had no choice. They had to either face their sinfulness and abandon the legalistic search for righteousness that had produced it, or to strike out against the One who pierced their pretentions and revealed their lack of love. They chose to strike out.

Several important issues were raised by Jesus in the extended response He made to the Pharisees and their followers.

The unforgivable sin. The Pharisees rejected the evidence of Jesus' miracles and even claimed that Satan's power was behind them. This blasphemy was unique in history; never before had God's Son, standing among men as a Man, by the power of the God's Holy Spirit, performed such obvious authenticating signs. Speaking against the source of Jesus' power was, first of all, a recognition of its supernatural origin, and second, a hardened rejection of Jesus Himself. Completely hardened now, this desperate attack demonstrated the fact that the Pharisees had made their choice. They no longer hesitated. They were committed *against* the Son of God. Their choice, made in the face of all the unique evidence which Jesus Himself had presented to them, was irrevocable: they had chosen to step beyond the possibility of repentance.

Idle words. Matthew 12:36 reports Jesus' warning against "careless words." This is *not*, as some have taken it to be, a reference to chitchat in contrast with "edifying" talk about God. Actually, Jesus is pointing to what is recorded in these very chapters.

The Pharisees, in reacting to the disciples' plucking of the grain and in challenging Jesus concerning the withered hand, had carelessly exposed their hearts! The Pharisees were so careful to appear pious. But in criticizing the disciples and in using the man with the withered hand, they had spoken unthinkingly words which revealed their hearts. No wonder verses 34-35 preface the warning about careless words with this statement:

> Out of the overflow of the heart the mouth speaks. The good man brings good things out of the good stored up in him, and the evil man brings evil things out of the evil stored up in him.
> Matthew 12:34-35

What is in a man's heart will be inadvertently expressed in his words, for "out of the overflow of the heart the mouth speaks" (v. 34).

We can hide our bitterness and lack of compassion. We can disguise hostility under a cloak of religiosity. We can even be rigorously "separated" from all sorts of cultural "sins." But when our reactions and our words reveal a Pharisee-like contempt for men and women whom God loves, our ungodliness is revealed.

The section of dialogue closes with Jesus' refusal to give Israel any more miraculous signs as proof of His identity, and with a renewed warning that judgment must surely come. Nineveh, a pagan land, responded to Jonah's preaching. The pagan Queen of Sheba responded to Solomon's instruction. But Israel had refused to respond to Jesus, though He is greater by far than either Jonah or Solomon.

By turning away from the King, Israel opened herself up to emptiness and a terrifying fate. No longer could physical descent from Abraham be considered a mark of standing with God. Each individual had to see that his relationship was personal, and would hinge on doing the will of the Father in heaven (vv. 46-50).

✂ *Group Activity: Recovery Group*
Steps 8 (list persons I've harmed) and 9 (make amends to people I've harmed)
Positive emotions, such as love, compassion, and concern for others, will be expressed in what we do and say. Negative emotions too, such as bitterness, anger, or cold indifference, will also color our actions and our words. This principle is stated by Jesus in Matthew 12:33-37. Read it, and meditate privately on Jesus' words for 90 seconds.

Then together look at the incident reported in 12:9-11. How did the Pharisees' words display their heart attitude? What attitude did they display toward the man with the withered hand? How might their words have made that man feel? (List suggested feeling words on the chalkboard.)

Individually list the names of (1) members of your household, (2) family members outside your household, (3) people you work closely with, (4) others to whom you are close or spend considerable time with. Under the name of each person list specific things you have said or done that might affect him or her in the way the Pharisees' cruel indifference affected the crippled man.

Choose one person who is especially close to you. Share with the group what you said or did that may have hurt him or her. Tell how you will try to make amends this week.

Follow through and try to make amends

Parables of the Kingdom

The Parable	Expected Form	Unexpected Characteristic
1. Sower 13:3-9, 18-23	Messiah turns *Israel* and all *nations* to Himself	*Individuals* respond differently to the Word's invitation.
2. Wheat/tares 13:24-30, 37-43	The kingdom's righteous citizens *rule over* the world with the King.	The kingdom's citizens are *among* the men of the world, growing together till God's harvesttime.
3. Mustard seed 13:31-32	Kingdom *begins* in *majestic glory*.	Kingdom *begins in insignificance*; its greatness comes as a surprise.
4. Leaven 13:33	Only righteousness enters the kingdom; other "raw material" is excluded.	The kingdom is implanted in a different "raw material" and grows to fill the whole personality with righteousness.
5. Hidden treasure 13:44	Kingdom is *public* and for all.	Kingdom is *hidden* and for individual "purchase."
6. Priceless pearl 13:45-46	Kingdom *brings all valued things* to men.	Kingdom demands *abandonment* of all other values (cf. 6:33).
7. Dragnet 13:47-50	Kingdom begins with initial separation of righteous and unrighteous.	Kingdom ends with final separation of the unrighteous from the righteous.

with this person, and consider how you might make amends with others on your list also.

Remember that although painful, the process of confessing faults and making amends is purifying. Trust God as you do what is right to continue to change you from within, so that in the future your "careless words" will express the new heart He is giving you in Christ.

The Parables: Matthew 13:1-52

The same day that Jesus spoke out, warning His hearers of the tragedy which rejection of the King and kingdom was to bring on them, He sat in a boat to teach the gathering crowds. He "told them many things in parables" (v. 3).

There are a multitude of parables in the Bible. The word itself means to "set alongside," and it is a normal pattern of Scripture to illustrate by setting concrete and familiar illustrations alongside abstract concepts (cf. 2 Sam. 12:1-7; Jud. 9:8-15; and Isa. 5:1-7 for Old Testament examples). Sometimes parables are allegories, such as the story of the Good Samaritan through which Jesus answered the man who wondered aloud, "Who is my neighbor?"

But there is something very different about the parables recorded in Matthew 13. Rather than illuminating what Jesus said, they seem almost to obscure it!

Why then did Jesus speak in parables? There are several hints in the text. Asked this question by the disciples, Jesus said, "Though seeing, they do not see; though hearing they do not hear or understand" (v. 13). The crowds, in rejecting Jesus' clear presentation of Himself as their King, had closed their eyes to truth. Now Jesus would speak less clear words to them, lest they be even more responsible.

It is also possible that Jesus adopted parables here to keep His listeners concentrating on the choice they had to make for or against Him. We need to remember that the Israelites had a clear notion of what the kingdom would be like. They would not be shaken from this single conception to accept new truth, which might modify their expectations. Jesus later explained to His disciples that the parables were spoken to *them* (v. 16). What they dealt with was a dimension of the kingdom which was not the subject of earlier Old Testament revelation. The parables fulfill this prophecy:

I will open My mouth in parables; I will utter things hidden since the Creation of the world.

Matthew 13:35

These parables deal with dimensions of the kingdom which Israel did not suspect existed. They deal, in fact, with those dimensions of the kingdom which you and I experience today and will experience until, at the return of Jesus, the Old Testament's prophesied kingdom rule *is* established.

No wonder the disciples, themselves steeped in the Old Testament's lore, were also puzzled and had to ask Jesus, "Explain to us the Parable of the Weeds in the Field" (v. 36). Only later could they look back and see in Jesus' words the portrait of a time between the Lord's resurrection and the establishment of the earthly kingdom in its expected form. These, then, are parables of *contrast*. By contrast they illuminate key differences between the prophesied kingdom reign and the present servant form of the kingdom over which Jesus now rules.

Jesus concluded His seven parables with a question: "Have you understood all these things?" (v. 51) Afraid to say no, the Twelve nodded yes. Both the old and the new are elements in the kingdom which Christ came to bring. Only later would they begin to understand the deep implications for the church of the unexpected form of the kingdom which Jesus expressed in His parables.

🖎 *Group Activity: Bible Study Group*
Distribute a copy of the chart on page 58 to each group member to use as a guide. Then study each parable, one by one, either as a whole group or in teams of four or five. For each, identify: How does this parable help me better understand what God is doing in our world today? And how does this parable help me see what I can do to live in harmony with God's purposes?

Don't settle for just one or two insights from each parable, but search for at least a half dozen.

If you worked in teams, report and list findings of each team. When this is done, choose at least one purpose that you plan to live in harmony with this week, and tell the others just how you will do so.

Resistance: Matthew 13:53–15:20

The failure to respond to Jesus was becoming open resistance to Him and to His teachings. When Jesus returned to His hometown, He was resented rather than honored (13:57).

John's death at the hands of Herod (14:1-12) added its dampening effect. The early mood of expectancy Jesus' ministry had stimulated was evaporating. The Pharisees had taken sides against Him. Jesus had not acted as the expected King should. The hated Herod had even executed Jesus' cousin John—and Jesus had done nothing. Instead of mounting a vengeful attack on Herod and Rome, Jesus "withdrew . . . to a solitary place" (v. 13).

The crowds followed Jesus. Waiting. Though Jesus would no longer perform miracles as authenticating signs to demonstrate the validity of His claim, He continued to be moved by compassion. Thus Jesus continued to heal—because He cared. And, when the crowds around Him were hungry and there was no source of food nearby, Jesus distributed five loaves and two fish—and fed the thousands who had come.

Late that night Jesus met His disciples on the sea (Matt. 14:22-32). They'd taken a boat; He walked across the waters to them. The rejecting Pharisees and doubting crowd would receive no more such proofs of the King's authority. But the believing disciples would continue to receive miraculous reassurance. So it is even today. The evidence men seek—and then reject when given—is withheld. But the believer who walks with Jesus sees constant evidence that God is ever near.

This section of the story of Jesus closes with the Pharisees returning to Jesus once again. Hating Him as they did, the Pharisees still seemed driven to come and, through confrontation, to find some justification for their stand.

Again the Pharisees attacked at a point developed in the oral law. "Why do Your disciples break the tradition of the elders? They don't wash their hands [ceremonially] before they eat!" (15:2)

Again Jesus bluntly confronted them, seeking to reveal to them the emptiness and hypocrisy of what they had substituted for the heart of God's revealed Law.

"Why do you break the command of

God for the sake of your tradition?" (v. 3) Jesus asked. Their whole approach to life "invalidated the Word of God" (v. 6, NASB) for the sake of their tradition; they were setting aside the intent of God for the sake of a legalistic self-righteousness! Lashing out at these religious men, Jesus cried:

> You hypocrites! Isaiah was right when he prophesied about you: These people honor Me with their lips, but their hearts are far from Me. They worship Me in vain; their teachings are but rules taught by men.
>
> Matthew 15:7-9

Again Jesus focused attention on the heart (vv. 10-20). It is not what a man eats or how he washes that defiles. It is the heart of man that defiles, and it is this with which the King and the kingdom deal. Only Jesus can heal the diseased heart, and His work must be done within.

Coming to the kingdom we must abandon all that we have relied on to perfect ourselves. We must abandon all we are into the hands of the King. We may, like Israel, long for the outward pomp and glory of God's future power. Yet, we must surrender all this for now. If we recognize Jesus as our King, He must be given our individual personality over which to reign.

GROUP RESOURCE GUIDE

Identification: *Share with others*
In the Bible the "heart" stands for "the inner person." Make up a middle name that includes "heart," which tells how you would like to be remembered by others. For instance, someone might say, "I'm Mary Greatheart (i.e., generous) Jones," or "I'm Clark Trueheart (i.e., faithful) Kent." Be creative as well as honest in choosing your new middle name.

Affirmation: *Express love and concern*
Decide together on a new middle name for your group. What would you like to be for each other? What middle name might express the relationship you want to see developed between members?

Exploration: *Probe God's Word*
Matthew 12:34-35 states a vital principle: "Out of the overflow of the heart the mouth speaks. The good man brings good things out of the good stored up in him, and the evil man brings evil things out of the evil stored up in him."

Explore this principle by looking at the two primary figures in Matthew 12–15, Jesus and the Pharisees. From Jesus' words and actions in the following passages, what characterizes a good heart? From the Pharisees' words and actions, what characterizes an evil heart?

Jesus	Pharisees
Matt. 12:6-14	Matt. 12:6-14
Matt. 12:22-28	Matt. 12:22-28
Matt. 14:13-21	Matt. 12:28-45

Reaction: *Respond together to the Word*
Look up and discuss the definition of "careless words" given in the commentary.

Then plan to conduct a "careless words heart check" this week. Choose one person in a relationship that is important to you. Commit to nightly self-evaluation this coming week; a brief period during which you reflect on your interaction with the person you chose. Make a written list of "careless words" that express negative thoughts and feelings, and another list of "careless words" that express positive thoughts and feelings.

As a check, ask the person you chose to make a list of things you may have said or done that hurt/bothered him/her, and of things you may have said or done that encouraged/affirmed him/her.

In preparation for this activity, break into groups of three and share your feelings about the person you just chose to do the "careless words" heart check.

This is intended as a self-check exercise, but if you wish you may share your own list daily with the person you chose. Praise God nightly for those ways in which He is helping you be like Jesus, and commit yourself to His will to change any negatives in your life.

Adoration: *Worship and pray*

Hold hands and thank God for those beautiful qualities you see revealed in Jesus. Ask the Lord to live through you this week in a special way, so His beauty can be revealed in you.

THE TURNING POINT

Overview

These chapters contain the theological turning point in Matthew's story of Jesus and His ministry. The King was rejected by His whole people, not just by the leaders. It was not that they opposed Jesus: they simply refused to commit themselves to Him.

But the rejection was real. From here on Jesus spoke not so much of His kingdom as of His cross. And Jesus began to lay out more clearly the way of life to be adapted by those whom faith bonds to Him.

These chapters also pose several puzzling questions: Why did Jesus speak of a foreign woman as a "dog"? What is the cross Jesus' disciples are called on to bear? What are, or were, the keys to His kingdom? How did Peter line up with Satan against Christ? What is the firm foundation against which even the gates of hell cannot prevail?

These, and other questions, are answered as we explore this critical segment of Matthew's story of the life of Christ.

▶ *Faith.* In these chapters "faith" comes into clear focus. While the term is used in different ways in both Old and New Testaments, faith is essentially a personal, trusting response to God, who speaks words of promise. Faith is our inner response to the Good News that God loves us, and in Jesus has made a way for us to live forever with Him. What a promise! Our God is so trustworthy we need not hesitate to trust ourselves to Him.

Commentary

One afternoon on a flight to Denver I sat next to an orthodox rabinnical student. As we talked, it became clear that I was seated next to a worthy successor of the Pharisees. Like them, he believed that the oral law was given at Sinai; that the complete Jewish faith and lifestyle were communicated then and never have been modified since.

He challenged me about the very incident we looked at in the last study guide: If Jesus were a Rabbi, how could He have justified eating grain on the Sabbath? I explained Jesus' answer: that the oral law is human tradition. As Lord of the Sabbath, Jesus rejected incorporations which actually drained the Law of its intended meaning.

He smiled. Clearly his confidence that he had the entire truth was as unshaken as had been the assurance of the Pharisees of Jesus' day. The way of the Law was the way of life.

Assurance that one knows the whole truth about God's plans and intentions, and that there can be no possible variation which we have not grasped, is always dangerous. If you and I adopt this attitude, we shut ourselves off from new insights from the Word of God and are in danger of ignoring God's Spirit as He seeks to teach us. When we close our minds and hearts and insist that we have all truth, any suggestion of new truth frightens and shakes us.

We can understand, then, that what we are about to see in Matthew 15–17 had great potential to disturb both Jesus' countrymen and His disciples. Jesus went on to further explain the unexpected form of the kingdom which His death and resurrection would install, and which He had already introduced (Matt. 13).

Let's trace through what we've seen in Matthew to date, and note how a shift in Jesus' kingdom-teaching has taken place.

As opposition grew, that particular expression of the kingdom for which the Jews looked receded. Increasingly, Jesus began to speak about an expression of God's kingdom on earth which was unexpected: which had been "hidden from the Creation of the world" (v. 35).

The point of national decision seems to have been reached with an event recorded in 16:13-21. Great crowds had continued to come to hear Jesus and to rejoice in His healings (15:31). In Caesarea Philippi, Jesus asked His disciples, "Who do people say the Son of man is?" (16:13) The disciples reported a variety of ideas. Some thought Jesus was John the Baptist come back; others suggested Elijah or Jeremiah or another of the ancient prophets. This was high praise! Clearly Jesus was regarded as one who was under the blessing and authority of God. But still Israel did not recognize Jesus as the promised Messiah and Son of God. They would not bow down to Him as their King!

Jesus then turned to His disciples and asked, "Who do you say I am?" (v. 15) It is on this foundation—recognition of Jesus Christ as both Messiah and Son of the living God—that any expression of the kingdom must be based. On this foundation, Jesus said, "I will build My church" (v. 18). Then Jesus charged the disciples to tell no one that He was the Christ and, the Bible says, "From that time on Jesus began to explain to His disciples that He must go to Jerusalem and suffer many things . . . and . . . be killed, and on the third day be raised" (v. 21).

From that time the message of the "kingdom at hand" was subordinated to the message of the Cross.

From this point also the Book of Matthew shows a definite shift in emphasis. Jesus increasingly stressed principles on which the present (between Resurrection and return) form of the kingdom would operate.

Focus on Faith—Matthew 15:21–16:12
The section begins with a significant incident. Jesus was met by a Canaanite woman who pleaded with Him to heal her daughter. Jesus refused, saying "I was sent only to the lost sheep of Israel" (15:24). This is a tremendously important saying. What is more, it is not an isolated statement. When Jesus gave authority to the Twelve to preach and heal, He told them, "Do not go among the Gentiles or enter any town of the Samaritans. Go rather to the lost sheep of Israel" (10:5-6).

This, of course, fit the expectations of the Jews. They knew that they were God's chosen people. As the seed of Abraham, they were possessors of God's covenant promises. When the Messiah came, He would

reestablish the Davidic kingdom and rule from Jerusalem, regathering all Israel to share His glory with them. Of course, with the kingdom established, the knowledge of God would fill the earth. Then even the Gentile nations would look to the Messiah (Isa. 11). But the Messiah was *Israel's* King. Just as Israel belongs to God in a special way, (Hosea 11:1-5; Micah 6:3-5), so the Messiah belongs to Israel (Jer. 31; Micah 4:1-5). Until rejected by the people of Israel, Jesus conscientiously made Himself available to them. John put it this way: "He came to that which was His own, but His own did not receive Him" (John 1:11).

Strikingly, the Canaanite woman recognized Jesus for who He is. She addressed Him, "Lord, Son of David," thus giving Him His full messianic title. Rebuked by Jesus, she asked for the crumbs which, overflowing from Israel's future table, would bless the world. Jesus answered, "Woman, you have great faith! Your request is granted" (Matt. 15:28).

The kingdom benefits which Israel as a nation rejected when she refused to recognize her King would be made available to all men—on the basis of faith.

♥ *Group Activity: Support Group*
Share the one greatest need you have just now. Then examine two stories told in Matthew 15:21-28, and Matthew 15:29-39 with 16:13-16. List comparisons and contrasts between the two (see commentary).

What do you learn from the two about how to have your greatest need met? In what ways can the Canaanite woman serve as a model for believers today?

Matthew 15:29–16:12 continues to portray Jesus as offering Himself to Israel. He healed, He fed crowds, He continued to warn against the Pharisees who had been unable to interpret the many signs of the King's presence.

And then Jesus asked the fateful question: "Who do men say that the Son of man is?" And the disciples' report confirmed what had already been made clear. The nation had rejected Jesus. Peter's confession of faith, "You are the Christ, the Son of the living God" (16:16), was a confession which Israel could not and would not make.

Refocused: Matthew 16:13-28

These few verses, coming as they do at the turning point in Matthew's portrait of the life of Christ, have been an object of controversy through much of church history. What is the foundation on which the church will be built? What are the "keys of the kingdom" (v. 19) that Jesus handed to Peter? What are the denial of self and the taking up of one's cross which Jesus said would enable a person to find himself?

The foundation (Matt. 16:17-18). After Peter's affirmation, Jesus called Peter blessed. God had revealed Christ's identity to him. And Jesus went on to say, "On this rock I will build My church" (v. 18).

The ancient church fathers gave various interpretations of this statement. Some said that the rock on which the church was founded was Peter. Others insisted that the name Peter (*petros*, which means "little stone") could hardly be identified as a foundation rock. Other fathers have argued that the church is founded on Peter's *confession*: it is the faith in Christ which Peter professed which is the church's foundation. Still others have seen this as a reference to Christ Himself. Jesus the Christ, the Son of God, is the foundation.

The Epistles seem to support this third conclusion. "No one can lay any foundation other than the one already laid, which is Jesus Christ" (1 Cor. 3:11). Christ Himself, the Messiah and Son of God, is the Foundation of the church and the kingdom.

The keys (Matt. 16:19). What then about the gift of the "keys of the kingdom" and the promise that "whatever you bind on earth will be bound in heaven, and whatever you loose on earth will be loosed in heaven"? What are the keys, and what are the loosing and binding?

Here again there have been disagreements. To some these verses are clear evidence that the church, as made visible in the Roman pontiff, is the "Vicar of Christ on earth." It is held that the power of making binding decisions has been delegated to Peter and his successors. But this notion came late in church history, after the bishop of Rome gained dominance over the other bishoprics.

Other scholars have noted that Peter was chosen by God to open the door of the Gospel to each of the two major groups of mankind recognized in his day. At Pentecost, Peter preached the first Gospel sermon to the Jews. Later still, God chose him to speak to Cornelius, the first Gentile to become a part of the body of Christ (Acts 10–11). Yet, this does not explain binding and loosing.

One thing is clear in the New Testament: Jesus is Head over all things for the church which is His body (Eph. 1:22-23). Jesus was not surrendering His position to any individual or group of men. If we realize our direct link with Jesus as our Head, this will suggest the best solution to the puzzle. How do we on earth speak with such authority? Only because we on earth are, through Jesus' presence within us, an extension of Christ Himself! Our Head, who directs us, acts through His body on earth to loose and bind authoritatively. How fully, then, you and I need to be committed to Christ's lordship, and how fully we need to obey Him. As believers respond to Jesus' direction, the kingdom continues to express its presence on earth.

Jesus' response to the disciples' confession was pointed and striking. He confirmed their awareness that He is the Messiah and Son of God, and announced His intention of building on this reality a "church," literally a "called-out assembly." Moreover, this church is to be the lived-out expression of heaven on earth. In our relationship with Jesus we are to express the kingdom in our generation's "here and now." The destiny of the believer is to *express* the kingdom. We bind and loose; we affirm forgiveness of sin and its retention. We speak God's Word, not on our authority, but on the authority Christ shares with us as He shared it with these disciples He once sent out two by two (cf. Matt. 10).

The portrait given here is an overwhelming one. To *be* the kingdom! To reflect Jesus in our world! To express Him, His grace and His judgments! This is who we are called to be—and become.

This is who we are.

To become (Matt. 16:24-28). Knowing that as kingdom citizens we are to reflect the King may make us feel guilty or unworthy. It is not meant to. Instead, it is meant to help us sense our calling, and respond joyfully to follow our Lord. There *is* a gap between our present experience and our calling. Recognizing the gap, Jesus told His disciples, "If anyone would come after Me" (v. 24). If we want to follow Jesus, we are invited to, and are shown the results.

What results? "Whoever loses his life for Me will find it" (v. 25). This puzzling statement is made more clear when we realize that the word translated "life" here, and "soul" in some translations, reflects a common Hebrew usage. The words (*nephesh*, in Hebrew and *psuche*, in Greek) can mean "soul" or "life." But in Hebrew and in the Greek translation of the Old Testament, the words are often used as a reflexive pronoun. Thus, Jesus warned not of losing one's life, but of losing *oneself*!

"Whoever loses himself for Me," Jesus was saying, "will find himself." And "what good will it be for a man if he gains the whole world and yet forfeits his . . . [self]?" (v. 26) What "self" was Jesus speaking of? Jesus was speaking of who you and I can become if we choose to follow Him!

You and I *can* choose to turn away from all that kingdom citizenship offers. If we do, we will never become what Jesus yearns to make us. Or we can follow Jesus and lose the self we are—the self that feels guilt and shame for so many failures. In following Jesus, you and I can become closer to what we yearn to be.

What does it take? How do we follow Jesus? "He must deny himself and take up his cross and follow Me" (v. 24).

Each of these phrases is significant:

*Self-denial. It would be a mistake to see self-denial as refusing pleasures or joys. The Bible says that God "gives us richly all things to enjoy" (1 Tim. 6:17, KJV). And one of the Pharisees' criticisms of Jesus was that He went to parties! No, self-denial is far more significant than this. It involves a denial of the values, the attitudes, and the emotions of which Jesus spoke in the Beatitudes. For example, bitterness is rooted in the old self and is to be denied. As Christ speaks to us when we are bitter, insisting that we let forgiveness wash away our anger, all that's old in us fights against that choice. Pride, competitiveness, and self-pity all struggle within to direct our reactions. To deny these natural pressures within ourselves involves denying the self we are, in order to follow Jesus. To deny these natural pressures and to choose to forgive helps shape the self that only Jesus can help us become.

*Daily cross. It is significant that Jesus did not ask us to take up *His* cross. Instead Jesus teaches us to be willing to take up *our* crosses. Why the symbol of the cross? No, not because it indicates suffering. The Cross speaks of Jesus' willing choice of that which was God's will for Him. What our crosses symbolize is our willingness to make daily choices of God's will for us—whatever that will may prove to be.

*Follow Me. This is the heart of Jesus' invitation to us. Follow. But not at a distance. Not as someone searching for tracks, to trace a figure long disappeared over the horizon. No, Jesus' "Follow Me" means "*Keep close* to Me." Only when we are close to Jesus can we find the strength for self-denial; only when we are close to Jesus can we sense His daily guidance in our lives.

Denying the old self, choosing daily the Father's will, and keeping close to Jesus, we will—as the first disciples did—find our true selves.

✂ *Group Activity: Recovery Group*
Step 11 (improve relationship with God through prayer and meditation)
Discuss Matthew 16:24-26 to make sure that each member understands the message of these enigmatic verses (see commentary). Individually complete at least 10 and better 15 of the following statement: "Before I decided to turn my life over to God I . . . , while now I. . . ."

Each share at least five completed statements with the group. Then write a prayer expressing praise and thanks for what God has been doing in your life. Memorize the prayer. In the coming week meditate daily on the statements telling what God has done for you, and repeat the memorized prayer whenever you think of God's goodness to you.

Coming Glory: Matthew 17
Jesus' talk of His coming death was deeply disturbing to the disciples (16:22-23). Disturbing too was the choice Jesus then set before His followers. "If *anyone* would come after Me" (v. 24). There was no overpowering "coming" here, to sweep all Israel to a promised glory. Instead, each individual had to face his own private Gethsemane. "Shall I follow the King?" The pathway on which the King walked, a way of self-denial and daily cross, was tremendously

less appealing than the expected Old Testament kingdom.

Yet, Matthew 16 closed with Jesus making another puzzling statement. "Some who are standing here will not taste death before they see the Son of man coming in His kingdom" (v. 28). The next verse says, "After six days Jesus took with Him Peter, James, and John . . . and led them up a high mountain by themselves" (17:1). Some of the disciples, but not all, were about to see the glory all will share when Jesus comes into His promised kingdom.

There on the mountain Jesus was "transfigured before them. His face shone like the sun, and His clothes became as white as the light" (v. 2). There too appeared Moses (who had died) and Elijah (who had been taken up into heaven without passing through death) to talk with Him. The present pathway for Jesus led to the Cross. *But the Cross was the doorway to Glory.*

On the way down the mountain, Jesus warned the three disciples not to share this experience with anyone until He had been raised from the dead. Impressed by the vision and eager for that time of glory to arrive, they seemed disturbed by the fact that Elijah, the forerunner, hadn't accompanied them. They asked, "Why then do the teachers of the Law say that [before the messianic kingdom is established] Elijah must come first?" (v. 10) Jesus answered that Elijah will come first (v. 11). But He also said that if Israel had responded to Jesus, John the Baptist's ministry would have been considered to fulfill the Elijah prophecy.

As the disciples were coming down from the mountain, a crowd led by a man with an epileptic son met Jesus and the three disciples (vv. 14-20). The other disciples had tried to cure the son but had failed. Now the father appealed to Jesus. Jesus responded. A faithless and perverse generation had rejected Jesus as King—and yet constantly sought His help!

Later the disciples asked Jesus why they had been powerless to help. Jesus answered, "Because you have so little faith" (v. 20). The people of Israel, because of faithlessness, were unable to enter the kingdom. And the disciples, who had entered the kingdom through recognition of the King, were unable to experience kingdom power for the same fault: lack of faith.

To enter the kingdom, and to live victoriously in it, faith is required.

The final incident in this sequence (vv. 24-27) sums up in a unique way the message Jesus had begun to communicate to His unresponsive people. The Old Testament established a half-shekel tax to be paid to the temple by each adult male. Met by tax collectors, Peter was asked if Jesus paid the tax, Peter blurted out, "Yes."

At home, Jesus asked Peter, "From whom do the kings of the earth collect duty and taxes—from their own sons or from others?" (v. 25) Peter gave the obvious answer: "From others." "Then," Jesus said, "the sons are exempt."

What was Jesus' point? The Jews had assumed that because they were the physical descendants of Abraham, they had a special relationship with God and a unique claim on Him. But the very fact that God taxed the Jews to maintain the temple demonstrated clearly that they were *not* sons! The physical basis on which the Israelites thought they could claim relationship with God was inadequate, and it had always been so! Men who so confidently claimed Abraham as their father (John 8:33) had failed to realize that Abraham's relationship with God was rooted in faith, not in the Law. They rejected that very quality of the man, whose descendants they claimed to be, which had made Abraham God's man.

Without faith, that generation lost for Israel and for mankind the very kingdom whose living expression you and I are called today to be.

By faith.

GROUP RESOURCE GUIDE

Identification: *Share with others*
Tell briefly about one incident when "my faith almost failed."

Exploration: *Probe God's Word*
Matthew 15:21–17:27 teaches a number of lessons on faith through incidents and instruction. Read each of the following pas-

sages together, one at a time, and "match" each incident with one "lesson on faith" listed below. Discuss how the "lesson" you select is taught in the passage, and how it can be applied to life today.

Passages: 15:21-25; 15:29-39; 16:13-16; 16:21-23; 16:25; 17:14-21.

Lessons on faith:

• God is gracious even to those who do not approach Him in faith.
• We have very little understanding of the power of faith.
• Faith means trusting God enough to risk surrendering our own will to choose His.
• Knowing a lot about Christ is no substitute for faith in Him.
• Faith establishes our only real claim on Christ.
• Faith means we acknowledge Christ's sovereignty and submit to His will.

Reaction: *Respond together to the Word*
Based on insights into faith gained from these passages, share what step or steps of faith you are going to take this coming week.

Affirmation: *Express love and concern*
If the step of faith planned by one of the group members challenges or encourages you, tell him or her so. If the step of faith planned by one of the group seems to call for special courage, tell him or her you will pray for that courage this week—and do so.

Adoration: *Worship and pray*
Meditate on Psalm 27:1 for two minutes:
   "The Lord is my light and my salvation—whom shall I fear?
   The Lord is the stronghold of my life—of whom shall I be afraid?"
Then pray spontaneously praising God that He is a Person in whom we can have total trust.

THE WAY TO GREATNESS

Overview

Each Gospel writer takes the events that he reports and arranges them to develop themes he seeks to emphasize. This characteristic is especially clear in Matthew 18–20, which explores the theme of greatness in Jesus' kingdom.

The sequence begins when the disciples ask Jesus about greatness. It proceeds, through stories Jesus tells about greatness, to incidents that show the emptiness of notions about greatness held by the religious of Jesus' day, to a final demonstration by Jesus Himself of the stunning truth that greatness is found in servanthood.

What an important passage to teach members of your group. We find greatness in a servanthood like Jesus' own.

▶ *Servant and Slave.* Both Old and New Testament terms are often translated by either "servant" or "slave." Yet there are special emphases in each. In Hebrew the root 'abad can indicate voluntary work or forced service. Its derivative, 'ebed means either servant or slave. But sarat indicates significant service, important because one serves an important person in a close personal relationship, doing that which is truly important. In the New Testament douleuo indicates submission of the will, as in slavery. We Christians are slaves of Jesus, for we submit to Him. But diakoneo means serving by giving personal help to another. Christian servanthood means willingly submitting to the will of God, and freely offering help to others.

Commentary

Sometimes we apologize for dreaming great dreams. As a young Christian, I had dreams of becoming another Apostle Paul, just as dedicated to Christ and the Gospel. My dreams were foolish and immature. But I'm sure they were not wrong.

Neither were the disciples wrong when they came to Jesus to ask about greatness. "Who is the greatest in the kingdom of heaven?" (Matt. 18:1) they inquired. Their simple question launched a series of teachings and events which show us in a unique way just how different spiritual greatness is from all that we expect.

It's all right for you and me to want to be great. But we must first grasp what greatness *is*. The vision we often have, looking up to the famous preacher holding large crowds spellbound, or the sensitive counselor whom all respect, or the brilliant teacher all flock to hear, can actually blind us to the fact that a journey toward greatness is a journey *down*, not up!

First Steps: Matthew 18

The disciples' request to know who was greatest in the kingdom stimulated a totally unexpected reply. "He called a little child and had him stand among them. And He said: 'I tell you the truth, unless you change and become like little children, you will never enter the kingdom of heaven' " (vv. 2-3).

Faith (Matt. 18:1-5). The child is the living embodiment of several truths which the disciples of Jesus had missed. The first truth involves faith, a theme developed in Matthew 15–17. Seeking greatness, the disciples must humble themselves, as one of the little ones who "believe in Me."

The people of Israel did not respond when Jesus called them to Him. They stood off at a distance, reserving judgment. When Jesus called the child to Him, the child responded immediately. Without pride, humble and trusting, the child accepted Jesus' invitation at once.

Greatness comes only when we humble ourselves to trustingly respond to our King's every call.

Concern for "little ones" (Matt. 18:6-35).
Jesus then lashed out at those who cause little ones to sin (vv. 6-9). This world is the kind of place in which temptations to sin are bound to come, but "little ones" are to be protected. So Jesus warned, "See that you do not look down on one of these little ones" (v. 10). Who are the "little ones"? All of us who, like children, have responded to Jesus' invitation and put our trust in Him. But, like children, we are to remain little ones in our attitudes toward God—to remain responsive to Jesus' every word.

The three following illustrations show us how to live with each other to preserve the quality of childlike responsiveness to Jesus in ourselves and others.

Matthew 18:10-14. Like sheep, little ones who go astray are to be searched for and restored to the fold. The Palestine shepherd gave each sheep in his flock a name and knew each sheep individually. Rather than driving his flock, the shepherd led. The sheep, knowing his voice, followed him (cf. John 10:3). When a young lamb wandered away, the shepherd left the flock in the sheepfold and braved any weather to find the lost one. Climbing over rocks, searching each crevasse, the shepherd gave himself freely to find the lost one. Finding it, the shepherd gave no thought of punishment, but knew joy that the lost one was restored.

Faith does not make you or me great. But responding to Jesus' call to care about His little ones who stray does. Caring enough to greet them with joy rather than recrimination, with love rather than condemnation.

Matthew 18:15-22. Here Jesus changed the simile. Little ones are sheep—but little ones are also brothers.

"If your brother sins against you, go and show him his fault" (v. 15), Jesus began. Temptations to sin must surely come, as Jesus had already pointed out (v. 7). Even with men of faith, sin will intrude, with all its hurts and pains, to break the fellowship of the family. Such failings are not to destroy family unity. A brotherly desire for reconciliation can keep God's little ones from turning away from Him.

This troubled Peter, who asked, "How many times shall I forgive my brother when he sins against me? Up to seven times?" (v. 21) Christ's answer: "Seventy times seven" [i.e., "always"].

Faith does not lift us above the possibility of sin. But forgiveness can cancel sin's impact on family relationships.

✂ *Group Activity: Recovery Group*
Steps 8 (list persons I've harmed) and 9 (make amends to people I've harmed)
Study Matthew 18:15-22 together. Discuss three key questions: (1) Why is it important to go to persons who have harmed us as well as to make amends to people we have harmed? (2) Why does Jesus say to keep away from people who have harmed us unless they are willing to listen and accept responsibility? (v. 17) (3) Why is praying with others about such a confrontation so important? (vv. 19-20) (4) How does willingness to forgive and keep on forgiving shape our attitude when we do go to a person who has harmed us? (vv. 21-22)

After sharing insights, write down the names of several persons who have harmed you. Tell the group about one of them, without naming names. Then take turns role-playing: act out the way you will go to and talk with him or her. Let others critique your approach and make suggestions.

Remember, the goal of such confrontation is to change a harmful relationship into a positive one. The goal is not to blame, but to show acceptance and forgiveness.

Matthew 18:23-35. Once again the simile shifted. Here we the little ones are seen as servants. Christ, our King, has forgiven us a great debt. In His patience and love, He has treated us gently and lovingly. As servants of such a King, we are now called on to have patience with our fellow believers (v. 29). Failure to have such patience and to extend forgiveness will cut us off from our experience of God's forgiveness. This is not because God is unwilling to forgive. It is because forgiveness is like a coin: it has two sides. We cannot have "heads" (receive forgiveness) without having "tails" (extend forgiveness) too.

Faith does not elevate our status: we are servants, subject to the will of God. And we are to treat our fellow servants as God treats us.

Greatness? The disciples must have been stunned by this discourse. They had asked about greatness, but Jesus spoke only about God's little ones! They had been thinking about great deeds and high position, but Jesus had spoken of sheep and brothers and servants. What did all this have to do with greatness?

Much, for them and for us. To be great in Christ's present kingdom, you and I must first of all take our places as God's little ones — and learn to see our fellow believers in the same way. In our desire to excel, we must never forget that we are sheep, prone to go astray, always in need of our Shepherd's tender care. We must never forget that all other Christians are brothers, and seek to live with them in fullest harmony. We must never forget that we are simply servants living with (not *over*) fellow servants. And we must treat all others with that same patience and forgiveness which Jesus shows us.

One of the most poignant passages in Scripture pictures the Apostle Paul ministering to God's little ones. Paul reminds the Thessalonians:

We were gentle among you, like a mother caring for her little children. We loved you so much we were delighted to share with you not only the Gospel of God but our lives as well, because you had become so dear to us. . . . You know that we dealt with each of you as a father deals with his own children, encouraging, comforting, and urging you to live lives worthy of God, who calls you into His kingdom and glory.
1 Thessalonians 2:7-12

Do you want to be great? Then take your place among God's little ones, and love them into God's kingdom.

Another Way? Matthew 19:1–20:16
Jesus' ideas about greatness are revolutionary. Soon they were contrasted against the ideas of the religious of His day; ideas still popular in our day. And still wrong.
The way of the Law (Matt. 19:3-15). The Pharisees are still the classic example of those zealous for God who expect to find spiritual greatness by rigid adherence to both biblical and human standards of righteousness. These proponents of strict legal-

ism appeared to test Jesus, apparently bringing up a subject which Jesus had spoken on before. "Is it lawful for a man to divorce his wife for any and every reason? (v. 3) Jesus' answer goes back to the Creation account. He pointed out that God intended marriage to unite two persons as one; thus divorce is not His intention.

Immediately the Pharisees struck back. "Why then did Moses command that a man give his wife a certificate of divorce?" (v. 7) The Law permitted divorce. Jesus' answer had to be wrong.

Christ's response reveals the root of legalism's error. "Moses permitted you to divorce your wives because your hearts were hard" (v. 8). Yes, God permits divorce to a sinful humanity which so often falls short of His ideal. But the Law is not a way of some higher or superior righteousness! The permission to divorce shows how willing God is to accommodate His ideal in consideration of human weakness and sin!

The Pharisees' legalism led them to ask the wrong question. They did not ask, "How can we restore the broken relationships which bring such agony into marriage?" No, they asked instead, "When is it all right to permit hurting people to separate?" They did not care about broken hearts, crushed by rejection. The Pharisees took refuge instead in legalism, missing the meaning of the Law by setting up rules as to when it should and should not apply.

The disciples also missed Jesus' point. Jesus had been teaching about greatness, and had shown that true greatness is to restore the straying lamb, to exercise patience, and to continue ever ready to forgive. Others too are God's little ones, and may need years of tender love to help them grow. Failing to relate Christ's teaching on greatness to this legal issue, the disciples blurted out, "In that case, it's better not to marry!" Even they were unwilling to commit themselves totally to another person.

Jesus then spoke to the disciples. The choice not to marry is for some, but "only those to whom it has been given" (v. 11). Within marriage, all who can live by the way of greatness should choose it (v. 12).

Again Jesus drew children around Him. "Let the little children come to Me, and do not hinder them," He said to His disciples (v. 14). The incident is significant. A Jewish person became "a child of the Law"—

that is, responsible to relate to God through the Mosaic Law—at 12. These "little children" were too young to be under Law, yet they could come to Jesus. What God wants is not legalists, but people in intimate personal relationship with Jesus, who will respond willingly to His voice.

❋ *Group Activity:*
Singles/Single Again Group
Divorce is always painful. It is made even more painful by the feeling we have failed God, ourselves, and others. And all too often persons who have experienced divorce are also disapproved of by the very faith community from which they most need support. Matthew 19 is a key N.T. passage on divorce. Here are two interpretations of several key verses in the passage. Which do you believe are most in harmony with God's nature? Which best fits the argument of the passage (see commentary).

● *v. 5. (a) Jesus is stating a new, higher law. (b) Jesus is stating God's ideal.*

● *v. 6. (a) No one is allowed to divorce. (b) No church group has a right to rule on what is essentially a personal issue.*

● *v. 8. (a) O.T. law permitted divorce because God knew His rebellious people would do it anyway. (b) O.T. law permitted divorce because God knew many would cruelly distort what He intended as a healing and nurturing relationship until divorce was better for each person than continuing the marriage.*

● *v. 9. (a) No divorce is possible, and people who divorced for any reason other than adultery must remain single. (b) Divorce involves sin, for it falls short of God's ideal. But like other sins, it can be confessed and forgiven. Jesus spoke bluntly because the Pharisees viewed divorce so lightly, and lacked the sense of failure and responsibility that would help them approach remarriage humbly.*

Share, if divorced, how you felt about your divorce. How did others treat you? What difference would it make to you personally if interpretation A is correct? If interpretation B? If single, share any experience you have had with divorce or divorced people. Has fear of divorce played any part in relationships you have had with others? How?

The way of "goodness" (Matt. 19:16-30).

Immediately after this a young man came up to Jesus and asked, "What good thing must I do to get eternal life?" (v. 16) This young man was a good person, one whose goodness was expressed in his honest observation of the Law. But Jesus challenged him on one point. "Sell your possessions and give to the poor, and . . . come, follow Me" (v. 21).

The young man turned away.

No. This was not a universal command to sell all, given to all the rich. Instead it was a challenge to this individual who measured his goodness by his dealings with other men. Yet, this humanistic benevolence avoids the first commandment: "You shall have no other gods before Me" (Ex. 20:3, NASB). How do we know? Jesus' words were a command from the young man's God. Hearing them, the young man rebelled and put wealth first.

All human goodness fails at this same point. It is good enough to do good to others, but it is not enough. God must be the center and focus of our lives.

As the young man went sadly away, Jesus remarked that wealth makes it difficult to enter the kingdom. The disciples, who, like others in their culture, viewed wealth as evidence of God's favor, asked in astonishment, "Who then can be saved?" The answer? "With man this is impossible, but with God all things are possible" (Matt. 19:25-26).

At this point, Peter blurted out yet another foolish question. The disciples had left all to follow Jesus. What would they gain? Jesus accommodated His answer to their need. They were still concerned about the kind of greatness that involves status and power. Jesus reassured them. "At the renewal of all things, when the Son of man sits on His glorious throne, you who have followed Me will also sit on twelve thrones, judging the twelve tribes of Israel" (v. 28). But, Jesus added, *This is not for now!* For now, "Many who are first will be last and many who are last will be first" (v. 30).

The way of hard work (Matt. 20:1-16). A final parable was added to explain the "last-first" comment. Jesus pictured a landowner who went out early in the morning and hired men to work in his harvest. Later he went out and found more standing idle. He sent them out into his fields as well. Several times during the day this pattern was repeated.

At evening, those who had worked the full day were dismayed to find that others who had worked only two hours received as much pay as they! When they complained, the landowner explained that they were paid what they had agreed on that morning. As for the rest, their reward was a matter not of what they had earned, but what was given by the owner out of generosity. The last had been first.

Like each of the workers in Jesus' parable, we have been invited to serve in His kingdom. What is important is our response to the King when He calls us to our individual tasks. Greatness is not measured by how long or hard we may work trying to gain a reward.

Greg found this out at a Faith/at/Work retreat. For eight years he had directed an evangelistic mission which flooded 70 countries with college students. He labored 16 and 18 hours a day, and his feeling of worth and value was directly related to the length of his day. At the retreat, Greg was confronted by a small group who revealed that they saw him as a man with a "Messiah complex." He was someone who thought he was called to save the world all by himself. Greg broke into tears. For the first time he realized that all his Christian life he had been trying to earn God's favor, caught up in an endless struggle for acceptance. During that week, Greg discovered that he *is* one of God's little ones.

Currently a pastor in Colorado, Greg is now free to respond when God calls, and is finding a rich reward in the conversion and growth of many whom the Lord touches through him.

In the kingdom of Christ's present reign we *are* called to greatness. But we will not find it along the roads that many of the religious have traveled. Christ has another way, marked out for all of us who humbly accept our places as His trusting little ones.

The Servant Leader: Matthew 20:17-28
Again Jesus took the Twelve aside and spoke to them of His death. "We are going up to Jerusalem, and the Son of man will be betrayed to the chief priests and the teachers of the Law. They will condemn Him to death and will turn Him over to the Gentiles to be mocked and flogged and crucified. On the third day He will be raised to life!" (vv. 18-19) In the context of

teaching on greatness, Jesus focused the attention of His disciples on His own choice to give His life.

We see why. Immediately afterward, the mother of James and John, two of the Twelve, came to Jesus to ask for the right- and left-hand seats in the coming kingdom for her sons. These two seats represent power and honor. Momma was politicking for her boys.

It's clear from the context that James and John had asked her to intercede, and were standing close by to hear the Lord's answer. "You don't know what you are asking," was Jesus' weary reply. "Can you," He said, turning to the two listening disciples, "drink the cup I am going to drink?" (v. 22) Authority and power in the kingdom are not what the disciples imagined. The leader will influence others, but he will perform his ministry in the same way that Jesus chose to perform His. Still not understanding, James and John eagerly insisted that they were able to drink Jesus' cup. "You will do that," Jesus replied. But the power and position they yearned for was something Jesus would not promise.

When the other 10 disciples heard, they were indignant at James and John. So Jesus called all 12 around Him, and gave what is probably the most significant instruction recorded in the New Testament about spiritual leadership.

> You know that the rulers of the Gentiles lord it over them, and their high officials exercise authority over them. Not so with you. Instead, whoever wants to become great among you must be your servant, and whoever wants to be first must be your slave—just as the Son of man did not come to be served, but to serve, and to give His life a ransom for many.
>
> Matthew 20:25-28

In this short passage, Jesus once and for all put to rest the pretensions of the spiritual leaders of every age to that kind of "power" which demands the right to command others.

The secular ruler. Jesus set up two models or examples of leaders. The one model was provided by the secular ruler of Jesus' day, the emperor or king or governor who "exercises authority over" others. There are many characteristics of this style of leadership, some made explicit in the text, and others implicit in the example chosen.

For instance, there is a distinctive relationship between the leader and the led: the secular ruler "exercises authority *over*." When I was in the Navy, my commanding officer, Lieutenant Kahle, was about five feet two inches tall, a full foot shorter than I. It was the most peculiar sensation, standing in front of Lieutenant Kahle and still feeling that I was looking up! There is a relational distance between the leader and the led in the secular world.

Another significant characteristic is implied in both the phrases "lord it over them" and "exercise authority." The secular ruler has the ability to enforce his will. He has sanctions to make sure that his orders are obeyed. This was certainly true in my Navy days. If I had not responded to orders, my liberty (time off) could have been canceled. I could have been brought up before the captain's mast (an informal court). I could have been court-martialed. Punishments ranging from restriction to the base, to the forfeiture of my pay, to imprisonment, assured my conformity. Secular leaders have this kind of power.

A third significant characteristic implicit in both the above has to do with *how* leadership is exercised. From his position above, using his power to enforce, the secular ruler *leads by command*. He simply tells others what to do, and they do it.

The servant leader. Jesus chose a servant as the countermodel for His followers. Nothing could be farther from our idea of greatness or leadership. We tend to see, as did the disciples, the pomp of power. The TV cameras focus on the great seal of the United States, a hushed quiet falls, the band in the background plays "Hail to the Chief," and the announcer's voice is heard: "Ladies and gentlemen, the President of the United States." We feel that is greatness. That is what being a leader is all about.

But then Jesus directs our attention to a quiet person standing off camera; a person in overalls with the working tools of his trade. And Jesus says *that* is greatness! That is what being a leader is all about.

This graphic contrast must have jolted the disciples just as it jolts us. Yet Jesus clearly wants us to see each of these people as leaders. Each of them is to be seen as

having authority and the power to move other men. What, then, are the significant contrasts between the two?

While the secular ruler is above those he leads, Jesus said, "Not so with you" (v. 26). Instead of relational distance, there is relational closeness. The Christian leader must seek to be one with those he or she is called to serve.

Instead of "exercising authority" as a ruler who demands and enforces conformity, the Christian leader is to abandon coercion. Jesus said firmly and plainly, "*Not so with you*." Force, manipulation, demand—all are ruled out in the way by which the servant leader exercises Christian authority. Outward force can produce conformity, but it can never produce that inner commitment which moves people to choose to follow Jesus.

How, then, does the servant lead? By serving! The secular ruler speaks the commands, but the spiritual leader demonstrates by his example the kingdom way of life into which he is called to lead others. No wonder Peter picked up this same theme and wrote as an elder to fellow elders, "Be shepherds of God's flock that is under your care . . . not lording it over those entrusted to you, but being examples to the flock" (1 Peter 5:2–3). By serving, the Christian leader demonstrates the greatness of the love of God, and gently motivates others to follow him. "Whoever wants to be first must be your slave—just as the Son of man did not come to be served, but to serve, and to give His life as a ransom for many" (Matt. 20:27-28).

🔊 *Group Activity: Bible Study Group*
Put a T-shaped chart on a chalkboard or large sheet of newsprint. On the left write "secular ruler," and on the right, "servant leader." Take 10 minutes working in pairs to develop contrasts and comparisons between the two kinds of leaders from Jesus' teaching in Matthew 20:25-28. Then together list insights on chart.

Then break into groups to discuss "How can I be a servant leader . . ." based on various relationships. Let each person choose the group he or she wishes to join. Possible groups are: ". . . in my marriage," ". . . of my children," ". . . in my work," ". . . in our church," ". . . in my friendships," etc.

A Last Example: Matthew 20:29-34
The disciples had asked about greatness in Jesus' present kingdom. Jesus had answered them—fully. Greatness involves humbling ourselves and taking our place as one of God's little ones. Greatness involves accepting others as little ones too: seeking to restore when they go astray, having patience, and always being willing to let forgiveness wash away the hurts that sin must bring. Greatness also involves rejecting the attractive but destructive ways in which religious people often seek greatness. Legalism, good deeds, hard work—none of these can produce greatness in Christ's kingdom.

Finally, Jesus has given us His own clear prescription for greatness. Learn how to lead others *as a servant*. Be one of those men or women who choose to drink Jesus' cup and give up their lives for the sake of others.

Then Matthew recorded a deeply moving incident that helps us sense what Jesus' kind of greatness is. As Christ and the disciples were leaving Jericho, a great crowd followed. Two blind men, sitting by the road, heard that Jesus was passing by. They cried out to Him. The crowd callously told them to shut up. But the two only called louder.

And Jesus stopped.

Jesus was on His way to Jerusalem, toward His trial and crucifixion. He was burdened by great crowds who did not care, and by disciples who did not understand. But Jesus set aside His own burdens and need to respond to this call for help. "Jesus had compassion on them and touched their eyes. Immediately they received their sight and followed Him" (v. 34).

Jesus stopped—for the individual in the crowd.

Jesus cared—for the outcasts whom the crowd considered worthless.

This is greatness. To touch in compassion, and to give ourselves for others as their servant, for Jesus' sake.

GROUP RESOURCE GUIDE

Identification: *Share with others*
Tell who has most helped you be responsive to Jesus, and how they have done this.

Exploration: *Probe God's Word*
1. Listen to a previously assigned report on the significance of being one of God's "little children" (Matt. 18:1-11, Commentary p. 69).
2. Break into three groups, each of which is to study a different passage teaching how to preserve "little-oneness" in the Christian community.
- Matthew 18:10-14. How are we human beings like sheep? What attitudes of the shepherd must we adopt in our relationships with others? Test case: A teenager returns after running away. How do his or her parents respond?
- Matthew 18:15-17. How are members of the Christian community like siblings? What typical sibling behaviors can we expect? How are we to respond when hurt by another family member? Test case: You shared a problem with a close friend in strict confidence, and now hear he or she is not only telling others the problem but is also gossiping and faultfinding. How do you respond?
- Matthew 18:21-35. Why is it hard to forgive a person time and time again? Does assurance of forgiveness make repeated violations more or less likely? Why? How has the assurance that God keeps on forgiving you affected your own behavior? Does forgiving a person mean he or she avoids the consequences of his or her choices, or is it a matter of your attitude toward him or her? Your teen skips school, and begs you to write an excuse so he or she can take an important test he or she missed. How do you respond?

After discussing in groups, share your insights into relational principles drawn from each passage.

Reaction: *Respond together to the Word*
Go around the group, telling of one relationship in which you plan to apply one of the "little one's" principles this coming week. Be specific about why you need to apply the principle, and how you will do so.

Adoration: *Worship and pray*
Meditate for two minutes on what it means

to you to be a forgiven person. Then praise God for His forgiving nature and the grace you experience.

Affirmation: *Express love and concern*
If you better understand how the person you identified as one who helped you respond to Jesus did so, write a note of appreciation. Tell him or her how he or she helped.

CONFRONTATION

Overview

Jesus was welcomed by the Jerusalem crowds; hailed as the Messiah on what Christians call "Palm Sunday." Jesus' enemies were aroused by this event, and renewed their attacks. Jesus silenced them — and in turn boldly condemned their wickedness and hypocrisy.

In these chapters we find many of Jesus' most familiar parables. And we find the clearest exposition in the Bible of legalistic pathways which falsely promise spiritual growth. Religious people are all too prone to walk these promising paths, which actually lead to spiritual emptiness and to judgment.

▶ *Praise.* The joyful response of the people to Jesus that first Palm Sunday is a beautiful illustration of praise. Several Hebrew words and concepts enrich our grasp of this richest of words in the vocabulary of worship. *Halal* means "to acclaim," "to glory in," and expresses deep satisfaction in exalting God's wonderful acts and qualities. *Yadah* suggests acknowledging God's works and character, often with thanksgiving. *Zamar* means to "sing praise" or "make music," while *sabah* expresses praise or commendation. What delight we can have in responding to God and His works with growing love and praise.

▶ *Woe.* In both Testaments this is an exclamation of grief or denunciation. How tragic. For those who love and praise Jesus there is joy. But for the rest, as Jesus' words in Matthew 23 reveal, there is only woe.

Commentary

We have a tendency today to see gentleness as weakness.

This tendency probably explains, at least partially, why people of all times tend to draw back from Jesus' picture of leadership as servanthood. "But," they object, "we want leaders who are *strong*. We want leaders with authority!"

The fact of the matter is that only in Christ's kind of servanthood do we find true spiritual strength. Gentleness is *not* weakness. Compassion is becoming to the King.

So it is not Mr. Milquetoast that Jesus sets before us as our example, but Himself. In these next chapters of Matthew, which portray Jesus in direct conflict with His enemies, we see our Lord speak out boldly in His full authority as King. In dealing with little ones the Leader is gentle. In facing foes, He is bold.

The Triumphal Entry: Matthew 21:1-17

It was the Passover week, a few brief days before the Crucifixion. Coming to Jerusalem, Jesus sent two of His disciples to bring a donkey and colt to Him for a long-prophesied entry into Jerusalem. Isaiah and Zechariah had both spoken of it:

> Your King comes to you, gentle and riding on a donkey, on a colt, the foal of a donkey.
>
> Matthew 21:5

Without pomp, humble and on a humble beast of burden, the King would come.

On this day the crowds that soon would turn against Jesus swelled with enthusiasm for Him. "Hosanna to the Son of David!" they shouted. "Blessed is He who comes in the name of the Lord!" (v. 9)

Christ moved purposefully to the temple. There He went into the court, which was to be reserved for prayer, and found merchants.

The Old Testament ruled that only unblemished animals might be offered in sacrifice. The priests set up a very lucrative trade in "approved" lambs and pigeons. Animals brought from the country for sacrifice might easily be disapproved by priestly inspectors, and worshipers forced to buy from the temple merchants. What had been set aside for prayer had become a "den of robbers" (v. 13).

As Jesus stood in the cleansed temple yard, the blind and the lame came to Him and He healed them. With even greater enthusiasm, the crowds proclaimed "Hosanna to the Son of David!" The chief priests and the scribes saw all these wonderful things which Jesus did and "they were indignant" (v. 15). Hardened as ever, the leaders were totally unwilling to acknowledge Jesus as their King.

The Emptiness of Legalism: Matthew 21:18–22:14

When evening fell, Jesus and His companions went across the valley to Bethany for the night. The next morning an incident occurred which gives us the key to understand the events which follow.

On the way back to Jerusalem, Jesus saw a fig tree and went over to it, as if to pluck some fruit for breakfast. Though the foliage was luxuriant, there was no fruit. Jesus uttered a curse, and "immediately the tree withered" (21:19). Impressed, the disciples asked, "How did the fig tree wither so quickly?" (v. 20) Jesus' explanation was simple: "Faith."

The fig tree of Israel which *appeared* luxuriant had produced no fruit. It was to wither away, its fruitlessness to be exposed. Faith was to provide a better way.

Group Activity: Bible Study Group

The cleansing of the temple (Matt. 21:12-17) and the withered fig tree (Matt. 21:18-22) convey the same message using different figures. The temple of God must be cleansed and dedicated. And one who professes to have life must bear fruit. (Note: figs and leaves appeared at the same time; thus, the leafed fig tree made a profession *that was not supported by* product.

Duplicate pages of a concordance that tell N.T. appearances of "temple" and "fruit." Divide into two or more teams to look up references and read their context. From the passages studied ask each team

to develop a report on what it means for Christians today to live as God's temple, and what it means for us to be fruitful.

When reports are in, choose one of the images and determine one specific thing you will do to be a purer temple, or more fruitful Christian.

Immediately on entering the city, Jesus began a series of confrontations and teachings which reveal why the legalism of the Jewish leaders, like the hypocritical fig tree, produced only appearances rather than fruit.

Empty of authority (Matt. 21:23-27). In Deuteronomy, the Jewish people were told to take disputes to their rulers for them to settle. The elders of the people challenged Jesus and asked by what authority He was acting. Christ asked them a question: "John's baptism—where did it come from? Was it from heaven or from men?" The elders were thrown into confusion. If they said "from heaven," Jesus would condemn them for not listening. But if they said "from men," the crowds who held John was a prophet might even attack them! Unwilling and unable to take a stand, or exercise the authority they claimed to have, these men replied, "We don't know" (v. 27).

Untouched by changed lives (Matt. 21:28-32). Jesus then told a parable, which He explained. The leaders were like a son who professes obedience but in practice will not do what the father has asked. Even when the leaders saw sinners respond and change their ways (the disobedient son in the parable later repented and chose to do his father's will), still the leaders did not respond.

They were untouched by the evidence of transformed lives, because they did not, in fact, care about people or about their relationship with God.

The desire for personal power (Matt. 21:33-46). What then *did* the leaders care about? Jesus launched into another parable, about an owner who leased his vineyard to tenants. They were to care for it and then give the owner his share of the profits. When messengers were sent to the tenants, they beat and stoned and killed them. Finally the owner sent his own son. The tenants' reaction? "Come, let's kill him *and take his inheritance!*" (v. 38)

Again the parable was devastatingly clear.

The Old Testament speaks often of Israel as God's vineyard (cf. Isa. 5:1-7). The servants God sent were the prophets, which earlier generations had rejected and often killed. Now, in Jesus, the Son had come. And the reaction of the rulers had been to plot to kill Him!

The Jewish leaders might speak of their pure and holy reverence for God and His Law. But, in fact, their motive was one of lust for personal power. That passion would not permit them to take their place with God's other little ones.

And so Jesus pronounced judgment. "I tell you that the kingdom of God will be taken away from you and given to a people who will produce its fruit" (Matt. 21:43).

Pretentions withered (Matt. 22:1-14). Before this scornful exposé, all the pretentions of the Pharisees withered, just as had the leaves of the fig tree. Looking ahead to the day when Jesus will come into His kingdom, Jesus used the common picture of a marriage feast (cf. Rev. 19:7). Those who were invited have refused to come. They will be replaced by others, both bad and good, who do respond to the King's call. As was the custom, those coming are to be provided with a wedding garment by the Father. Anyone seeking to "crash" this feast will be recognized immediately; his own clothes will not be acceptable. And he will be cast "into the darkness" (Matt. 22:13).

Ø Group Activity:
Missions/Outreach Group
It's important to understand the underlying perspective of those we seek to win to Christ. Matthew 21:23–22:14 records incidents and stories that give us important insights into the ways of those who resist the Gospel. Using the "keys" below, together or in teams examine each passage. What does it tell us about this attitude/response to the Gospel? How might we reach a person who thinks this way today?

Passage	Key
21:23-27	*I'm in charge — but I won't accept responsibility.*
21:28-32	*I know what's right — but I don't do it.*
21:33-44	*I'm serving God — but I insist on doing it my way instead of His.*
22:1-14	*I hear the invitation — but*

I'm too busy.

22:1-14	*I hear the invitation — and I feel hostile at being told I need to respond to the King!*

Finally, does Matthew 22:8-9 indicate that we should ignore those who resist the Gospel and concentrate only on those who seem ready to respond?

Counterattack: Matthew 22:15-46

The religious leaders were desperate now. And they were afraid of the reaction of the people against them if they took direct action against Jesus (21:46). So they determined to try to entangle Jesus in a way that might weaken His popularity.

The Pharisees (Matt. 22:15-22). The strength of the Pharisees was their complete commitment to the Law, and their rejection of all that was Gentile and foreign. The Greek culture which influenced the Sadducee party was totally rejected by the Pharisees, who had a reputation with the people for standing firm for Jewish ways. So a delegation of Pharisees approached Jesus, hoping to trap Him.

"Tell us then," they asked. "Is it right to pay taxes to Caesar or not?" (v. 17)

The Pharisees must have been very pleased at their cleverness. If Jesus directed them *not* to pay taxes, the Roman overseers could be informed and might take action. If Jesus said they *should* pay taxes, the Pharisees were sure He would lose popularity with the people. The insult of paying taxes to Rome through tax collectors, who normally took two or three times what was due, uniquely roused the hostility of the Jews.

Jesus asked His enemies for a coin. When the Pharisees gave a coin to Jesus, He asked them whose inscription and picture it bore. "Caesar's," the Pharisees said. "Give to Caesar what is Caesar's," Jesus responded, "and to God what is God's" (v. 21). Stunned, the Pharisees left Him and went away.

♥ Group Activity: Support Group
Jesus' remark about giving Caesar what is his, and God what He is due (Matt. 22:15-22) has been rightly understood to illustrate a basic biblical principle. We are to fit into the roles assigned us in our society, even when fitting in is difficult. Taxes were heavy in Palestine, and resented. Today we often experience stress

and resentment in our own relationships: in our work, our marriage, our family, our church.

Select one relationship in which you feel stress today, and talk freely about it to the group. How did that relationship begin? What has happened to it? Why are you feeling stress in it now? What is the most painful thing about that relationship? What have you tried to do? How might the "give to Caesar" principle apply?

As group members share, listen not so much to prepare advice, but to sense the pain and understand. See if you have had relationships in which you experienced something similar. In response, share your own similar experience and how you (successfully or unsuccessfully) tried to deal with it. Remember that when people hurt they may need understanding more than advice, so be supportive in all you say and do.

The Sadducees (Matt. 22:23-33). Sadducees have been mentioned earlier in Matthew. But we have not yet focused on them.

For about a hundred years, the Sadducees and the Pharisees were competing parties in Palestine. The word Sadducee seems to come from a root meaning "judge." They were, however, an aristocracy, which controlled the high priesthood and thus gained political power.

Like many an aristocracy, they were exclusive and proud. Theologically they were liberals who rejected the oral law exalted by the Pharisees, and who also rejected such doctrines as that of resurrection and angels. They were the kind of people who were tempted to adjust their views to the "modern" notions of the educated men of their world.

Though in conflict with the Pharisees, the Sadducees had to accommodate themselves to them because of the Pharisees' influence over the masses. But when Jesus appeared, these traditional enemies quickly arrived at a truce. Their mutual hatred and fear of Jesus brought them together.

Now the Sadducees raised one of those hypocritical questions with which they had long taunted those who believed in resurrection. They spoke of a woman who had been successively married to seven brothers. "At the resurrection, whose wife will she be?" (v. 28) the Sadducees asked. Jesus' response was a rebuke, pointing out that

these proud men were strangers both to the Scriptures and to God's power. In the resurrection, people will not marry. And as far as resurrection is concerned, the Scriptures reveal God as One who *is* (not *was!*) the God of Abraham, Isaac, and Jacob. God is God not of the dead, but the living.

The lawyer (Matt. 22:34-45). Once again the Pharisee party attempted to trap Jesus. This time a lawyer (one who was an expert in oral and written Law) asked Jesus to name the first and greatest commandment. Answering, Jesus then asked the Pharisees a question in return.

"What do you think about the Christ [Messiah]? Whose Son is He?" (v. 42) The Pharisees answered correctly: "David's." Then Jesus asked, "How is it then that David, speaking by the Spirit, calls Him 'Lord'?" (v. 43)

The point is, of course, that no human father calls his son Lord, for in the culture of the Middle East the son always owed deference and respect to his father. David's descendant is more than human. He is, in fact, as the Old Testament foretells, the Son of God. Only if David's "son" is his God does David's acknowledgment of Him as Lord make sense.

The Pharisees were unable to utter a single word. They simply went away, and no one dared to challenge Jesus to a debate again.

The Scribes and Pharisees Denounced: Matthew 23

Then, in one of the most scathing indictments imaginable, Jesus cataloged the faults of the Pharisees—faults of which all of us must be wary; particularly those who stand in places of spiritual leadership.

What was wrong with Phariseeism?

- They preached, but did not practice (v. 3).
- They acted only to be seen and admired by others, not to please God (v. 5).
- They were proud, seeking to be prominent and exalted over others (vv. 6-9). Because they rejected servanthood and humility, they were themselves rejected by God (vv. 10-12).
- They were hypocrites who neither responded to God nor let others respond (vv. 13-15).
- They were blind guides who played

with man-made rules and missed the great realities of faith (vv. 16-22).

- They were hypocrites who made a great to-do over strict tithing of the leaves of tiny herbs like mint and dill, but who neglected great matters like justice and mercy (vv. 23-24).
- They were hypocrites who focused on outward appearances, when within they were filled with greed and pride (vv. 25-27).
- They were just like their fathers (e.g., predecessors) who, when they had authority, killed the prophets and wise men God sent to Israel. In this generation's rejection of Jesus, the blood guilt of the ages was coming to rest on them (vv. 28-36).

Yet, against the background of this indictment, we see one last touching portrait of Jesus. As He condemned these hypocrites, His heart broke for them and for the crowds who would soon scream for His death.

In anguish, Jesus cried out:

O Jerusalem, Jerusalem, you who kill the prophets and stone those sent to you, how often have I longed to gather your children together, as a hen gathers her chicks under her wings, but you were not willing. Look, your house is left to you desolate. For I tell you, you will not see Me again until you say, "Blessed is He who comes in the name of the Lord."

Matthew 23:37-39

GROUP RESOURCE GUIDE

Identification: *Share with others*
Using an 8½ x 11 sheet of white poster board and crayons draw a mask that represents a trait or quality you used to have but overcame, or one that you are still struggling with. You might use red, and draw an open, shouting mouth to indicate anger, or green, with narrow, squinting eyes and tight lips, to indicate jealousy.

When done, go around the group, so each person can hold up and explain his or her mask.

Affirmation: *Express love and concern*
Note that "hypocrite" comes from a Greek word that means acting a part in a play. In Greek drama masks were painted to represent characters each actor played. In real life, a "hypocrite" is a person who masks his real self while he plays a part for those around him.

Go around the group again. Tell how you tried to hide the trait represented by the mask you drew. If you can see that God has made a change in a person who is sharing, tell how you have experienced him or her today.

Exploration: *Probe God's Word*
Examine Matthew 23:3-36 to discover and define characteristics of hypocrites. Find at least one characteristic in verse 3, one in

verse 5, one in verses 10-12, in verses 13-15, in verses 16-22, in verses 23-24, in verses 25-27, and in verses 28-36. Discuss each of these characteristics. How might it affect a person's way of life? His priorities? His relationships? His attitude toward himself? His relationship with God?

Before you move on to the next activity, write at least four sentences, each of which is to begin: "Living as a hypocrite is disastrous because . . ."

Reaction: *Respond together to the Word*
Just before launching his attack on the Pharisees, Jesus identified the two greatest commandments in O.T. law: loving God completely, and loving others as yourself (22:34-40). Share one or two of the statements you just wrote about the danger of hypocrisy, and tell how loving God or loving others would—or does—help you avoid that danger.

Adoration: *Worship and pray*
Sing together the familiar chorus, "My Jesus, I Love Thee." After singing several verses, pray, thanking God for ways His love helped you overcome the traits reflected in the masks you created at the beginning of this group meeting.

STUDY GUIDE 11
Matthew 24–25

THE FUTURE OF THE KINGDOM

Overview

Much of the Old Testament speaks about what will happen in the future. And much of that prophecy focuses on a promised kingdom, over which God rules. Jesus also spoke about that coming kingdom, and His words are reported in the Gospels.

Christians do differ on how to interpret the Bible's prophetic portions. But in Matthew 24 and 25 we have several clues. First, Jesus was asked — and answered — several specific questions about what is to come. Second, Jesus referred to events foretold by the Old Testament prophets to explain His answers. In view of this and other features of the passage, it seems best to take Jesus' words in their plain sense. The message will not always be clear, but what Jesus said is not to be taken as symbolic of this Church Age. Here Jesus was answering the one question that Matthew's Jewish readers felt must be addressed.

What *has* happened to the kingdom of which the Old Testament speaks?

▶ *Daniel.* Jesus referred in this passage to the prophecies about the future found in Daniel. Daniel's prophecy is unusual because it predicts the very day that Messiah will triumphantly enter Jerusalem and also predicts an unexpected "cutting off" of Messiah — and a gap between His appearance and establishment of the kingdom.

Commentary

Many people have enjoyed playing games with the Bible, raising all sorts of objections and pointing out all sorts of supposed errors. The foolish raise silly objections that can be easily answered: Where did Cain get his wife? Doesn't the Bible say the earth is flat? How can you believe the Bible since it talks about the sun going around the earth?

This kind of superficial objection is easily explained, particularly as the queries are obviously raised by people who know nothing about the Bible. Any serious student of Scripture can raise far more basic and difficult issues. Without a doubt, one of the most difficult is this: What happened to the prophesied Old Testament kingdom? If God did not keep His word about establishing that kingdom, how can we trust anything in the Word?

The question troubled the disciples. Jesus had told them He was approaching a Cross, not a crown. They could not grasp what was happening. They were sure God's Word is trustworthy, but not at all sure how He would keep His promises if He, the King, were to die.

This concern of the Twelve surfaced as Jesus led them away from the temple after announcing judgment on the Pharisees. Glancing at the towering temple building, Jesus remarked that each stone of the temple would be thrown down, and "not one stone here will be left on another" (Matt. 24:2). This destruction was accomplished four decades later in A.D. 70 by a Roman army under Titus, a general who would later become emperor.

That evening the disciples came to ask Jesus about the future, about that time when Christ would come again and the age would close. In answering them, Jesus gives us our answers as well.

The Future

The Bible speaks a great deal in both Old and New Testaments about the future. Some "prophecy" in both Testaments involves forthtelling: communicating a message from God. But most prophecy involves foretelling which involves telling what will happen *before the historical events occur*.

Foretelling may involve either near events or events that are far distant to the prophet's day. Thus, Jeremiah spoke both of the death of a false prophet, Hananiah (Jer. 28), to take place within one year, and of a New Covenant to be made with the house of Israel which was actually ratified hundreds of years later by Christ at Calvary (Jer. 31).

Prophecy's promise. What is important to note, however, is that in prophecy the *time elements and sequences* are seldom clear. This was Peter's point in 1 Peter 1:10-11, when he noted that the prophets themselves puzzled over "the time and circumstances" the Spirit who inspired their words intended. The prophets had insights into the foretold events, but they could not fit them together.

This is a very important thing to remember when we study prophecy. We do not really know the time when prophesied events will happen, or even the exact sequences. Thus, it is always dangerous to attempt to erect tight prophetic systems in which we confidently sequence the future according to clues provided in the Word. Prophecy is not designed to give us a "future-history book" which can be written before the events. While we do know the broad outlines of the future from Scripture, we can never be too sure about the systems we construct from them.

As a matter of fact, an approach to prophetic studies which majors on constructing systems misses something basic about Bible prophecy. Bible prophecy is meant to have an impact on the present. Prophecy is designed to have a penetrating impact on our lives and values now. Thus, when Peter spoke of the fact that our present universe will one day be dissolved in fervent heat, he did so to challenge values: "Seeing then that all these things shall be dissolved, what manner of persons ought ye to be?" (2 Peter 3:11, KJV) When Paul spoke so beautifully of the Rapture in Thessalonians, it is not so that you and I might argue over whether it comes in the middle or at the beginning of the Tribulation. It is so that we might "encourage each other" (1 Thes. 4:18) with the realization that when Jesus comes, all believers will be together in Him. The dead we mourn will be our eternal companions. When John spoke of Jesus' return it was not to locate it in relation to Daniel's seventieth week, but to help us realize that "when He shall appear, we shall

be like Him; for we shall see Him as He is" (1 John 3:2-3, KJV).

Thus, when we come to a study of the future in any part of the Bible we want to be careful to resist the temptation to speculate on details, and instead seek to discern the major emphasis of the passage. We need to keep the *purpose* of the prophetic passage in clear view.

Relationship between Old Testament and New Testament prophecy. When looking at New Testament prophecy, and particularly at prophetic segments of the Gospels, it is important to be very clear about the relationship between events foretold in the two Testaments.

First, we need to remember that there is full harmony between the Old Testament and the New Testament in prophecy, as in all things. The New Testament does not replace the Old. Thus, we have Christ's own affirmation in Matthew's Gospel that the kingdom, expected on the basis of the Old Testament, *will* come. "I tell you the truth, at the renewal of all things, when the Son of man sits on His throne, you who have followed Me will also sit on twelve thrones, judging the twelve tribes of Israel" (Matt. 19:28). Matthew 24:15 confirms that the future foretold by Daniel and associated with setting up the "everlasting kingdom" will come to pass. There is no doubt that Jesus expected, and promised, a time "when the Son of man comes in His glory, and all the angels with Him, He will sit on His throne in heavenly glory" (25:31).

The glorious kingdom of the Old Testament, expected by Israel and by the disciples themselves, *will surely come.*

Second, since the New Testament does not supercede or replace the Old, we can accept the broad outline of the future developed in the Old Testament as the basic framework within which to understand the teachings of the New. God has not gone back on His Word. Instead, He has demonstrated a greater complexity and variety to His eternal plans and purposes than were earlier revealed.

God's prophetic plan for the "time of the end" as given in the Old Testament involves:

- nations of the earth divided into power blocks.
- the Western power block headed by the Antichrist.

- increasing tension over the Middle East, leading to a treaty in which the Western powers guarantee the integrity of the Jewish state.
- increasing worldwide troubles and disasters, gradually intensifying.
- tremendous tribulation for Israel, involving persecution by the Western powers and finally invasion and desolation by the Northern.
- personal coming and intervention of Christ, the Messiah, who will defeat Israel's enemies and set up a righteous kingdom worldwide.

It is helpful as we read Christ's portrait of the future in Matthew to remember this outline, and to notice that Jesus is clearly speaking within that Old Testament framework.

Third, we want to note that the New Testament provides not a revision of God's plan but rather an addition to it. This, of course, was the point of Jesus' quote of Psalm 78:2 in Matthew 13:35: "I will utter things hidden since the Creation of the world." This is also what Paul was referring to in Colossians where he spoke of himself as a minister charged with making fully known "the mystery that has been hidden for ages and generations, but is now disclosed to the saints" (Col. 1:26).

In short, then, the answer to the question of, "What has happened to the kingdom?" is, "Nothing!" It is still coming.

The Old Testament speaks of both a suffering and a reigning Messiah, but makes no clear time distinctions. The whole intervening age between the Messiah's resurrection and return is not a subject of Old Testament prophecy, but a new dimension of God's eternal plan introduced by Jesus during His lifetime as the "unexpected form of the kingdom." It is the Age of the Church.

With this background, we can go back to look at Matthew 24 and 25. We realize immediately that the questions which stimulated this discourse were asked from an Old Testament frame of reference. Matthew 24 and 25 are, in fact, Jesus' affirmation that the glorious kingdom which Israel expected will surely come. If we understand the content of Old Testament prophecy, we have no doubts about the meaning and impact of Jesus' words here.

✍ *Group Activity: Bible Study Group*
In preparation for reading Matthew 24, read the following O.T. prophecies about the time of the end. Their themes are: (1) world conflict and tribulation, Deut. 4:30-31; Isa. 2:12, 19; 13:6, 9; 24:1, 3, 6, 19-21; 26:20-21; Jer. 30:7; Ezek. 13:5; 30:3; Dan. 9:27; 11:31–12:1; Joel 1:15; 2:1-2, 11, 21; 3:14; Amos 5:18-20; Zeph. 1:14-15, 18; Zech. 14:1. (2) followed by the establishment of an endless kingdom by the Messiah from David's line: Isa. 2:1-4; 4:2-6; 9:6-7; 11:1-13; 24:1-23; 32:1-5; 33:17-24; Dan. 7:1-28; Hosea 3:4-5; Joel 2:28–3:2; Amos 9:9-15; Micah 4:1-5; Zech. 2:1-13; 14:1-21.

With this background, read Matthew 24. What themes of O.T. prophecy can you see in Jesus' teaching? (See the chart on page 84 for comparisons.) Discuss: If a person were totally convinced that what Jesus and the O.T. describe lies in the near future, how would his present choices be affected?

Jesus' Words of Prophecy: Matthew 24:1–25:30

These chapters contain Jesus' answers to three questions posed by His disciples. "Tell us," they asked, "[1] when will this happen, and [2] what will be the sign of Your coming and [3] of the end of the age?" (24:3) The questions were answered, but in reverse order.

Signs of the end of the age (Matt. 24:4-26). The picture given in this section of Matthew 24 is of a time of increasing tension, disaster, and disturbance. Wars and rumors of wars, earthquakes, increasing wickedness, and persecution of Jesus' followers are all involved.

None of these is in itself striking: there have always been wars, and earthquakes often dot the news with tragedy. But there are aspects of this picture which make it the description of a unique time which is the subject of much Old Testament prophecy.

- The common disasters were identified by Jesus as "the beginning of birth pains" (v. 8).
- Events Jesus spoke of are identified in the Old Testament Book of Daniel as taking place in the seven-year period just before the Messiah will establish His earthly kingdom (v. 15).

Matthew's Teaching on the Kingdom

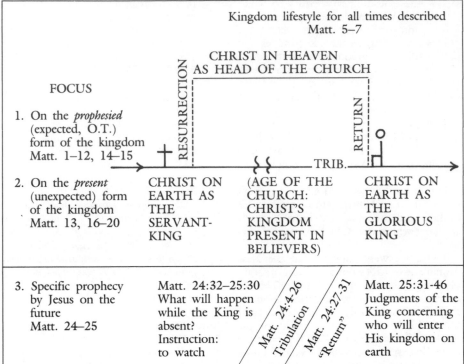

Kingdom lifestyle for all times described
Matt. 5–7

CHRIST IN HEAVEN
AS HEAD OF THE CHURCH

RESURRECTION

RETURN

TRIB.

FOCUS

1. On the *prophesied* (expected, O.T.) form of the kingdom Matt. 1–12, 14–15

2. On the *present* (unexpected) form of the kingdom Matt. 13, 16–20

CHRIST ON EARTH AS THE SERVANT-KING

(AGE OF THE CHURCH: CHRIST'S KINGDOM PRESENT IN BELIEVERS)

CHRIST ON EARTH AS THE GLORIOUS KING

3. Specific prophecy by Jesus on the future Matt. 24–25

Matt. 24:32–25:30
What will happen while the King is absent?
Instruction:
to watch

Matt. 24:4-26
Tribulation

Matt. 24:27-31
"Return"

Matt. 25:31-46
Judgments of the King concerning who will enter His kingdom on earth

• The Tribulation which is said to come then will be a "great distress, unequaled from the beginning of the world until now and never to be equaled again" (v. 21).

In the Old Testament this time of worldwide trouble is given various names: "the time of Jacob's trouble," "that day," "the Day of the Lord," and "the Tribulation." Against this Old Testament background, the disciples would quickly identify the time of which Jesus spoke.

What will be the sign of Your coming? (Matt. 24:27-31) Jesus' answer to this question was far less specific. There is, in fact, no single "sign" identified. Yet, several striking characteristics of Jesus' return are given.

First, Jesus' coming will be visible, seen as clearly as spectacular lightning from horizon to horizon (v. 27). That visible appearance will follow immediately after the Tribulation, and will be accompanied by great and dramatic physical disturbances in the heavens. There will be an unidentified

"sign" in the heavens, with deep mourning as the Son is seen to return in power and great glory (v. 30). Jesus' coming will initiate an angelic regathering of His elect (for this Old Testament context, see Isa. 27:13; Zech. 9:14).

When will this be? (Matt. 24:32–25:30). Jesus answered this third question exhaustively. But only after saying, "No one knows about that day or hour, not even the angels in heaven, nor the Son, but only the Father" (24:36).

Nevertheless, it is this question Jesus chose to explore in greatest depth. It is the answer to this question which has the most significance for the disciples and for us.

This generation will certainly not pass away (Matt. 24:32-35). The Tribulation events previously described are like buds on a tree before the leaves come. The bud is evidence that the time of flowering is near. But one thing Jesus promised: "This generation will certainly not pass away" (v. 34) till all He has spoken of comes to pass.

What "generation" is Jesus speaking of? The term used here does not indicate people alive at that day, but Israel as a race. (Some interpret it to mean the living generation actually undergoing the Tribulation time.) By either interpretation this was Jesus' promise of preservation. The time of trouble will not be the end of the Jewish people or of mankind.

What then did Jesus say about the time of His coming, and the time *until* His coming?

Watch for His coming (Matt. 24:36-44). As in Noah's day, before the Flood swept everything away, the people living in the day just before Jesus returns will be involved in their own affairs, blind to the significance of happenings around them.

Because the day when the Son will come is unexpected, we are to "watch." "So," Jesus said, "you must be ready, because the Son of man will come at an hour when you do not expect Him."

Responsible servants (Matt. 24:45-51). What is to be done by servants who are looking for the Lord's return? They are to remember they have been given responsibility in their Master's household.

The danger Jesus warned against is a real one. He said, "But suppose that servant is wicked and says to himself, 'My master is staying away a long time.' . . . The master . . . will come . . . when he does not expect him" (vv. 48-50). Faithfulness involves taking proper care of God's household, knowing that the Lord will appear at an unexpected time.

The ten maidens (Matt. 25:1-13). This is the well-known story of the 10 maidens who took lamps and went to meet the bridegroom who was coming for his bride. Unprepared for a long wait, 5 ran out of oil when the bridegroom was delayed.

Again, Jesus warned, "Watch, because you do not know the day or the hour" (v. 13).

The talents (Matt. 25:14-30). The Parable of the Talents again emphasizes the same elements. A lord leaves on a journey, making his servants responsible for his possessions. While he is away, the servants are to use the gifts they have been given for the benefit of their master. One day the master will return, and then there will be an accounting.

Each of these stories drives home an im-portant point: What God has promised will come to pass. But our time is not to be spent dreaming of that future day. It is to be spent in the service of our absent Lord who has entrusted His possessions to us. Christ the King has entrusted to us this unexpected and unprophesied form of His kingdom.

Being ready for His coming means being involved as servants in the ongoing ministries committed to us by our Lord.

The Gathering of the Nations: Matthew 25:31-46

Then Jesus turned again to His second coming. "When the Son of man comes in His glory, and all the angels with Him, He will sit on His throne in heavenly glory" (v. 31). Christ went on to discuss the ministry of judgment He will undertake at that day. Again in the Old Testament, roots of the picture He sketched are clear. Christ looked ahead to describe a prophesied time when all the nations on the earth will be gathered before Him.

The peoples of the world will be separated into two groups, one destined to enter the kingdom over which the Messiah will rule. The term "nations" here does not refer to national groups but to the Gentile world in contrast to "brothers of Mine." These Jewish brothers, who will have suffered in the Tribulation, will have been naked, hungry, thirsty, imprisoned, and sick. And some will have reached out to them, while others ignore them.

This passage does not picture the time of final judgment. Instead, as the text indicates, judgment is announced for a generation of men living at Jesus' coming. The prize is not eternal life, but entrance into the kingdom that God has prepared for Gentiles as well as for believing Israel (v. 34).

The Old Testament picture of the future is *not* wrong, for the promised kingdom will come when the King returns. And we can leave the details of that time to God.

There is for us a different focus in life. You and I expect His return, and so we wholeheartedly serve Him. We minister as servants in a household which He has left with us, until He comes to take up His throne.

GROUP RESOURCE GUIDE

Identification: *Share with others*
Describe a time when you could hardly wait for something to happen. After all have shared, discuss: How did eagerly looking forward to the thing you described affect your feelings and your behavior?

Exploration: *Probe God's Word*
In Matthew 24–25 some 37 verses are given to Jesus' prophetic teaching—telling what will happen in the future. But 55 verses are given to exhortation on how to live now, until the future events take place! We should put our emphasis where Jesus does, on what to do until that future comes!

Divide into teams to look at the exhortations Jesus gave. These are found in Matthew 24:36-44; 24:45-51; 25:1-13; 25:14-30. Each team can take one or two of these passages, and look for these common elements:

- the key figure is absent
- the time of return is uncertain
- servants are responsible for the absentee's possessions

- "watch" is a key word
- servants are to be evaluated for what they do while the key figure is gone

Each team should note these themes in their passages, and see what lessons for life today Jesus seems to emphasize.

Reaction: *Respond together to the Word*
Individually, on one side of a sheet of paper list as many phrases as you can that complete this statement: "Because I know Jesus is coming back, I have . . ."

Then on the opposite side of the same sheet list as many phrases as you can that complete this statement: "Because I know Jesus is coming back, from now on I will . . ."

Share at least one statement from the second list with the rest of the group.

Adoration: *Worship and pray*
Divide and, as worship, read responsively Revelation 21:1-6 and 22:1-7. Close with a time of silent prayer.

JESUS' TRIAL AND DEATH

Overview

Each of the Gospel writers speaks in detail of the last few days of Jesus' life. The Cross, with the Resurrection which followed, is clearly the focus of the Gospel story.

Each of the Gospel writers adds details not included by the others. By studying the four accounts, we can know what happened almost hour by hour.

For instance, we know that Jesus had not just one trial, but six! He was taken from court to court, examined (at times in actual violation of Jewish Law), and shunted off to another jurisdiction. Finally He was condemned by Pilate, the Roman governor, who alone had authority to pronounce the death sentence.

Jesus' religious trials

Before Annas	John 18:12-14
Before Caiaphas	Matthew 26:57-68
Before the Sanhedrin	Matthew 27:1-2

Jesus' civil trials

Before Pilate	Luke 27:66–23:7
Before Herod	Luke 23:8-12
Before Pilate	Luke 23:13-25

While the Gospels tell the story of Jesus' death, we need to look to the Old Testament and to the Epistles to explain its meaning. How good to lead our group to sense once again the wonder of what Jesus did on Calvary for you and me. How great the price of our salvation.

Commentary

If Jesus' prophetic picture of the kingdom's future has its roots in the Old Testament, what is about to happen has even deeper roots. All of revelation focuses on the events of the next few days: Millennia and centuries of time strain forward to it, while additional millennia and centuries find meaning by looking back to it.

Matthew puts it in perspective as he gives us Jesus' words: "As you know, the Passover is two days away" (Matt. 26:2).

Passover

The Passover marked the Jewish new year: it was the time of beginnings for Israel. The annual festival recalled a historic event which marked a true spiritual beginning for God's Old Testament people.

Exodus 11 and 12 record the story. Great plagues had ruined the land of Egypt in Moses' day, but they had failed to move Egypt's ruler to let Israel, then a slave race, go. God then determined a final judgment. But He instructed each Hebrew family to select a lamb, to be kept in the home for four days. On the fourth day the lamb was to be killed, and its blood sprinkled on the doorposts and lintel of each Jewish home. The lamb itself was to be roasted and eaten.

The night this happened, God's death angel swept through the land of Egypt. Each home unprotected by the blood of the lamb suffered the loss of its firstborn son. But the homes marked out by the blood of the Passover lamb were safe.

Impelled by the horror of the multiple deaths, Pharaoh released the Jews. Israel had been redeemed by death from slavery, to fulfill its destiny as the people of God.

And God commanded the Jews, each year after this event, to commemorate it by reenactment. Fresh lambs were slain, fresh blood sprinkled, and each generation was taught again the lesson that freedom could come only through the shedding of the blood of the lamb.

This Passover. This Passover, Jesus was about to fulfill the deepest meaning of the Old Testament celebration rite. Passover not only looked back to the Exodus; it looked forward to the Cross. "The Passover is two days away," Jesus said, "and the Son of man will be handed over to be crucified" (Matt. 26:2).

John the Baptist had foreseen it that day back at the River Jordan. "Look," he said, "the Lamb of God, who takes away the sin of the world!" (John 1:29) For three to four years after this Jesus had been among the Jewish people, teaching, healing, caring. But then, when Passover came, like the lambs that represented Him, Jesus had to die. He had to die that through His death those who sprinkle His blood by faith on the doorposts of their hearts might know the ultimate freedom. Through the blood of Christ we are freed from sin and from sin's power—freed even from the fear of death.

The culminating act of service and self-giving had been clearly taught in the Old Testament, even apart from the Passover symbolism. We see it, for instance, in Isaiah 53. The death of Christ and its meaning are so clearly portrayed in this passage that we can hardly believe we are reading words penned over 600 years before Jesus' birth!

He grew up before Him like a tender shoot, and like a root out of dry ground. He had no beauty or majesty to attract us to Him, nothing in His appearance that we should desire Him. He was despised and rejected by men, a Man of sorrows, and familiar with suffering. Like one from whom men hide their faces He was despised, and we esteemed Him not. Surely He took up our infirmities and carried our sorrows, yet we considered Him stricken by God, smitten by Him, and afflicted. But He was pierced for our transgressions, He was crushed for our iniquities; the punishment that brought us peace was upon Him, and by His wounds we are healed. We all, like sheep, have gone astray, each of us has turned to his own way; and the Lord has laid on Him the iniquity of us all. He was oppressed and afflicted, yet He did not open His mouth; He was led like a lamb to the slaughter, and as a sheep before her shearers is silent so He did not open His mouth. By oppression and judgment He was taken away. And who can speak of His descendants? For He was cut off from the land of the living; for the transgression of My people He was stricken. He was assigned a grave with the wicked, and with the rich in His death, though He had done no violence, nor was any deceit in His mouth. Yet it was the Lord's will to crush Him and cause Him to suffer, and though the Lord makes His life a guilt offering, He will see His offspring and prolong His days, and the will of the Lord will prosper in His hand. After the suffering of His soul, He will see the light of life and be satisfied; by His knowledge My righteous Servant will justify many, and He will bear their iniquities. Therefore I will give Him a portion among the great, and He will divide the spoils with the strong, because He poured out His life unto death, and was numbered with the transgressors. For He bore the sin of many, and made intercession for the transgressors.

Isaiah 53:2-12

The Last Days: Matthew 26–27

The culminating events occurred with tragic swiftness. Matthew describes them.

Jesus was anointed with expensive ointment, an act symbolic of preparation for burial (26:6). Judas slipped away to make an arrangement with the chief priests to betray Jesus to them when the crowds were not present. He settled on a price: 30 pieces of silver (vv. 14-16).

When morning came, Jesus sent His disciples to arrange a hall where they would eat the Passover meal together (vv. 17-19). That night, after the meal and before the discourse recorded in John 13–16, Judas left again to finalize plans for Jesus' betrayal (Matt. 26:20-29).

On the way out of Jerusalem, Jesus told the disciples that they would all flee and leave Him to face His fate alone. Peter led a chorus of objectors: no, all would die with Him before they would desert Him! (vv. 30-35)

Arriving at a garden called Gethsemane, Jesus asked His disciples to wait as He went aside to pray. This deeply moving prayer, in which Jesus expressed the agony He felt approaching the Cross, is recorded for us by Matthew (vv. 36-39). But the disciples were too tired to be moved. They drifted off to sleep.

Christ, feeling the utter loneliness of the

condemned, urged them to stay awake to watch with Him. But again they dozed off as Christ returned to prayer (vv. 40-46).

Then the light of flickering torches was seen, and sounds of an armed mob was heard. Led by Judas, the mob hung back until he advanced to identify Jesus with a kiss (vv. 45-50). Immediately the crowd surged forward, and servants of the priests roughly pinned Jesus' arms behind Him!

Bravely, Peter drew a sword and struck out! "Put it away," Jesus told him. If Christ had intended to resist, angel armies could have been summoned. "But how then would the Scriptures be fulfilled that say it must happen in this way?" (v. 54) When Jesus turned to face the mob, the disciples scattered (vv. 51-56).

Then began the long night of trials. Jesus was taken first to the high priest's home, where the council was gathered to try Him at night (an illegal act under Jewish Law). Witnesses were brought forward to accuse Him, but even their lies could not raise an issue meriting death. Finally the high priest asked Jesus directly: "Tell us if You are the Christ, the Son of God" (v. 63). Christ answered: "Yes, it is as you say. But I say to all of you: In the future you will see the Son of man sitting at the right hand of the Mighty One and coming on the clouds of heaven" (v. 64). The high priest rightly recognized this as an affirmation by Jesus of Deity, at which he cried out, "Blasphemy!" And blasphemy is a crime for which the Old Testament prescribes death (vv. 57-65).

The court then passed its judgment. "He is worthy of death" (v. 66). Immediately they began to treat Jesus as a convicted felon, slapping Him and spitting on Him and mocking Him (vv. 66-68).

Meanwhile, Peter was sitting outside the high priest's house. Peter had run. But he still had enough courage to trail the crowd that guarded Jesus. Yet, when Peter was accused by a serving maid and then other bystanders of being a follower of Jesus, Peter denied it with a curse! Then a cock crowed, and Peter remembered that when Jesus told the disciples they would scatter, Christ had also told Peter that he would deny the Lord three times before morning. Sobbing uncontrollably, Peter stumbled away into the dawn (vv. 69-75).

Back inside, the rulers of the Jews had a problem. The Romans ruled Palestine. While the Jews had a large measure of self-government, they did not have the authority to execute. So the leaders packed Jesus off to Pilate, the Roman governor.

Meanwhile, Judas had discovered that Christ was actually condemned to death! Hurrying back to the temple priests, Judas returned the 30 pieces of silver, and wailed, "I have sinned, for I have betrayed innocent blood" (27:4). Unmoved, these men whose office made them mediators between sinners and God, coldly replied, "What is that to us? That's your responsibility" (v. 4). Throwing down the money, Judas rushed out—and hanged himself. And the priests, ever careful to keep the letter of the Law whose spirit and intent they daily distorted, argued over the blood money which it was not "lawful" to put back into the temple treasury! At last they decided to use the money to buy a burial ground for indigents (vv. 3-10).

♥ *Group Activity: Support Group*
Share about an incident or a relationship in which you feel/felt disappointed in yourself. Then compare and contrast the stories of Peter's denial (26:69-75) and Judas' betrayal (27:1-10) of Christ. Each felt sorry afterward. Was there any difference in their sorrow? What was different in how each reacted? What was different about how others responded to them in their need (for Peter, see John 21:15ff, for Judas, Matthew 27:3-4).

Jesus recommissioned Peter, showing us that past failures do not disqualify us from future service.

Freely give support and comfort to any who feel a special need for help to recover from a past failure or mistake.

Jesus then stood before the Roman governor. There He admitted that He was indeed King of the Jews. Beyond this, Jesus refused to defend Himself (vv. 11-14).

Pilate was clearly unhappy with the situation. Even while sitting on his judgment seat, a messenger from Pilate's wife arrived, told Pilate of a dream she had had, and warned Pilate to have nothing to do with "that innocent man" (v. 19). Squirming, Pilate offered the crowd, which had by then gathered, a choice. He would release Jesus or Barabbas, a murderer who was also sentenced to death. And the crowd, urged on by the leaders, shouted out that Barabbas should be freed. As for Jesus, "Crucify Him!" (v. 22)

Pilate tried to reason with the mob. But their only response was to chant, repeating over and over again with bestial rhythm, "Crucify Him!"

Overwhelmed by the passion of the mob, Pilate feared a riot. Historic research suggests that Pilate held his post due to the influence of a man who had recently been executed in Rome. Terrified that the Jews would now accuse him of supporting some other "king" than Caesar, Pilate permitted Jesus' execution. And the Jews accepted the implications of Pilate's symbolic hand-washing: "His blood be on us and on our children" (v. 25).

Then Pilate released Barabbas, and turned Jesus over to the soldiers to be beaten and mocked in preparation for His execution (vv. 26-31).

On the way out of the city to the killing grounds, Jesus stumbled and fell under the weight of His cross. A visitor to the city, Simon, was pulled from the crowd by the soldiers and made to carry it for Him.

At the place of execution, called Golgotha, a sign was nailed to the cross, reading THIS IS JESUS, THE KING OF THE JEWS (v. 37). When all was ready, Jesus refused a drugged drink designed to lessen the pain. Prostrate on the wooden post, spikes were driven through His living flesh. Then, with a tearing jolt, the pole was lifted—hung poised—and dropped into the hole prepared to receive it.

Jesus, King of the Jews, hung outlined against the sky, flanked by two dying criminals.

Jesus, who walked the lanes of Palestine to heal the sick and feed the hungry, to free men and women tormented in the grip of demons, was hanging in suspended agony as passersby paused to watch—and ridicule (vv. 32-44).

Suddenly, about noon, grim darkness blotted out the sun. A hush fell. Near three in the afternoon the figure on the cross convulsed, and cried out: "My God, My God, why have You forsaken Me?" (v. 46) "What's happening?" the watchers whispered to each other. One ran to Him, to again offer Him the drug. Others held back. "Leave Him alone. Let's see if Elijah

comes to save Him." Ghoulishly curious, strangely uninvolved, they watched as the drama unfolded.

Then came another cry from the cross—a cry like a triumphant shout. The figure jerked—then slumped in relaxation against the brutal metal restraints. Finished with His work, Jesus had dismissed His spirit (vv. 45-50).

📖 *Group Activity: Bible Study Group*
Help your group experience the events at Calvary in a totally new way. Give each an 8½ x 11 sheet of paper, containing a sketch of Calvary hill with the three crosses. In pairs read Matthew 27:32-56. Each pair is (1) to identify the individuals and groups who witnessed the Crucifixion, and (2) to locate them on the hill, according to their relative distance from Jesus.

When this is done, each person is to meditate for a time on which of the witnesses he or she feels was most like him or her. Then, each is to speak as if he or she were the person chosen, telling what he or she saw and felt.

Go around the group, letting each person tell the crucifixion story from the viewpoint of the person he or she chose. You will each gain a totally new perspective on the cross and its personal meaning to you.

The very moment Jesus died, the temple curtain, which cut off access to the holy of holies, was torn in two from top to bottom. An earthquake struck, rocks were ripped apart, old tombs opened, and dead men and women stood. Stunned and awe-struck, the Roman officer in charge of the execution detail, blurted out, "Surely He was the Son of God!" (v. 54)

At evening Pilate received a rich man who asked for the privilege of burying Jesus' body. Gently, the servant King's form was laid to rest in a tomb hewn from rock. A great stone was rolled to block the door—and Jesus' sorrowing followers departed (vv. 57-61).

Unmoved by these events just as they had been unmoved by Christ's miracles, the leaders of the Jews hurried to Pilate. They told him of Jesus' talk of rising from the dead, and urged the Roman governor to place a military guard over the tomb to keep the disciples from stealing the body. Soldiers were assigned from troops detailed to the high priest's guard. The boulder was sealed, the guard set.

And the chief priests and Pharisees retired. Triumphant? Afraid? We do not know. But surely Jesus Himself was dead. There was nothing to do but wait.

And so, these men desperately believed, His story had at last come to a fitting end.

Why?

All Christians from the earliest days of the church have looked to Jesus' cross and resurrection as the central facts of the Christian faith, through which the incarnate God reconciled us to Himself. Peter, in his first sermon, said that this Jesus was "handed over to you by God's set purpose and foreknowledge"—and loosed from death because it was impossible for death to keep its hold on Him" (Acts 2:23-24). Only much later would this question be asked: "Why was Jesus' death essential in God's 'definite plan'?"

Atonement theories. One of the first theories advanced saw Jesus' death as a ransom price paid to the devil, in whose kingdom mankind lived enchained. But Christ died not to pay, but to "destroy him who holds the power of death—that is, the devil" (Heb. 2:14). Christ's death was no price paid to Satan but a battleground on which Satan met decisive defeat.

Anselm of Canterbury (A.D. eleventh/ twelfth century) probed more deeply to explore why God's love is expressed through atonement. The *Zondervan Pictorial Encyclopedia of the Bible* (Tenney) summarizes Anselm's answer expressed in *Cur Deus Homo* (Why did God become man?):

His answer was that though prompted by His love to redeem us, God must do so in a manner consistent with His justice. The necessity of the Atonement, then, is an inference from the character of God. Sin is a revolt against God and He must inevitably react against it with wrath. Sin creates an awful liability and the inexorable demands of the divine justice must be met. The truth that God is love does not stand alone in the Bible. The God of the Bible keeps wrath for His enemies (Nahum 1:2); He is "of purer eyes than to behold evil" (Hab.

1:13, KJV). The God of Jesus is to be feared as One "who can destroy both soul and body in hell" (Matt. 10:28). "The wrath of God," Paul wrote, "is being revealed from heaven against all the godlessness and wickedness of men" (Rom. 1:18).

Therefore the death of Christ is the way in which God shows that He is righteous in forgiving sins and justifying him who has faith in Jesus (Rom. 3:24-26). God justly demands satisfaction for one's sins, and since by Christ's death satisfaction is given, the sinner is forgiven and punishment remitted.

Anselm's theory, of vicarious or substitutionary Atonement, has dominated orthodox tradition. Christ's death is seen as *for us*, and *in our place*.

A third theory, which has characterized liberal Protestantism, is the "moral influence" theory. This also has its roots in the eleventh and twelfth centuries. According to this theory, Jesus' death demonstrates God's forgiving love, and stirs up a responding love in men, which leads them to repent of their sins.

Scripture's testimony. Scripture itself speaks with a clear and unmistakable voice about the death of Christ and its meaning. It is so clear that "Atonement theories" hardly seem needed: the Word is explicit.

In fact, the Law requires that nearly everything be cleansed with blood, and without the shedding of blood there is no forgiveness.

Hebrews 9:22

This Priest [Christ] . . . offered for all time one sacrifice for sins. . . . Because by one sacrifice He has made perfect forever those who are being made holy.

Hebrews 10:12, 14

[Jesus said,] "This is My blood of the covenant, which is poured out for many for the forgiveness of sins."

Matthew 26:28

God demonstrates His own love for us in this: While we were still sinners, Christ died for us. Since we have now been justified by His blood, how much more shall we be saved from God's wrath through Him!

Romans 5:8-9

God presented [Jesus] as a sacrifice of atonement, through faith in His blood. He did this to demonstrate His justice, because in His forbearance He had left the sins committed before unpunished— He did it to demonstrate His justice at the present time, so as to be just and the One who justifies the man who has faith in Jesus.

Romans 3:25-26

For God was pleased to have all His full-ness dwell in [Jesus], and through Him to reconcile to Himself all things, whether things on earth or things in heaven, by making peace through His blood, shed on the cross. . . . But now He has reconciled you by Christ's physical body through death to present you holy in His sight, without blemish and free from accusation.

Colossians 1:19-22

But now in Christ Jesus you who once were far away have been brought near through the blood of Christ. For

He Himself is our peace.

Ephesians 2:13-14

He Himself bore our sins in His body on the tree, so that we might die to sins and live for righteousness.

1 Peter 2:24

To Him who loves us and has freed us from our sins by His blood.

Revelation 1:5

He died for all, that those who live should no longer live for themselves but for Him who died for them and was raised again. God . . . reconciled us to Himself through Christ . . . not count-ing men's sins against them.

2 Corinthians 5:15, 18-19

God made Him who had no sin to be sin for us, so that in Him we might be-come the righteousness of God.

2 Corinthians 5:21

Bearing the full weight of our sin, and in our place, Jesus shed His blood. To set us free.

GROUP RESOURCE GUIDE

Identification: *Share with others*
Tell briefly what you thought about Jesus before you became a Christian.

Affirmation: *Express love and concern*
Tell how you feel about the person or per-sons who were instrumental in leading you to Christ. If that person(s) is in the group, speak directly to him or her and tell what he or she means to you.

Exploration: *Probe God's Word*
1. Together develop a simple questionnaire that you might give to a person to find out what he or she thinks about Jesus. Use open ended questions that can be answered in one or two words, such as: "Jesus was. . . ." Be sure to include at least two questions about the crucifixion, such as "Jesus died on the cross because. . . ." or "Jesus' death on Calvary was. . . ."
2. Select Bible passages that explain the

meaning and purpose of Jesus' death for us. Use verses in the commentary section, or select others of your own choice.

Adoration: *Worship and pray*
Thank God for Christ's sacrifice, and for the person(s) who led you to faith in Him. Pray that God might use you to share Christ with others too.

Reaction: *Respond together to the Word*
Duplicate both the questionnaire and the selected Bible verses. Take several question-naires and sheets of Bible verses and go to a mall. Ask strollers to answer the question-naire and read the sheet of Bible verses. Then ask them to complete the questions concerning the crucifixion again, based on the Bible verses they have read. If they do not understand, explain the passages to them. Later return to the group and share your experiences.

Or, take questionnaires and duplicated Bible verses with you to use with neighbors or friends at work. Report what happened when you come together again next week.

ALIVE, FOREVERMORE

Overview

The resurrection of Jesus is one of the best attested events of history. What happened that Resurrection morning, and who saw our risen Lord?

Three women at tomb	Luke 23:55–24:9
Peter, John see empty tomb	John 20:3-10
The women see Jesus	Matt. 28:9-10
Peter sees Jesus same day	Luke 24:34
Two on Emmaus road	Luke 24:13-31
The Apostles, Thomas absent	Luke 24:36-45
The Apostles, Thomas present	John 20:24-29
Seven at Lake Tiberius	John 21:1-23
Five hundred in Galilee	1 Cor. 15:6
James in Jerusalem	1 Cor. 15:7
Many at Ascension	Acts 1:3-12
Paul near Damascus	Acts 9:3-6
Stephen at stoning	Acts 7:55
Paul in the temple	Acts 22:17-19
John on Patmos	Rev. 1:10-19

There were so many witnesses that even though Jesus' enemies started a rumor that Christ's body had been stolen, they could not stop the news of the Resurrection from sweeping the nation, and then the world.

Today we have nearly 2,000 years of church history to demonstrate the validity of our faith. The resurrected Jesus has proved His presence to His people in every age. But do the members of your group grasp just what the reality of Jesus' resurrection means to them, and to other Christians? That is the focus of this study of Matthew 28: the meaning of Resurrection, now.

Commentary

Enemies and friends of Jesus waited. On the third day after His execution, two Marys went to see the tomb. They were shocked to come to a deserted garden.

The guard the Jewish elders had posted was gone. The stone that had sealed the entrance of the tomb was rolled away. Sitting on it was an angel, whose appearance had jolted the guard to insensibility, and who now spoke to the women. "Do not be afraid, for I know that you are looking for Jesus, who was crucified. He is not here; He has risen, just as He said" (Matt. 28:5-6).

The Resurrection

The Resurrection was an unexpected event. Though the Lord had foretold His resurrection, the disciples were unprepared. They even found it hard to believe when the reports began to come in. During the 40 days that Jesus met with the disciples after the Resurrection, many proofs were given. Paul reports:

> For what I received I passed on to you as of first importance: that Christ died for our sins according to the Scriptures, that He was buried, that He was raised on the third day according to the Scriptures, and that He appeared to Peter, and then to the Twelve. After that, He appeared to more than 500 of the brothers at the same time, most of whom are still living, though some have fallen asleep. Then He appeared to James, then to all the Apostles, and last of all He appeared to me also, as to one abnormally born.
>
> 1 Corinthians 15:3-8

The resurrection of Christ is one of the most thoroughly attested facts of history, not only through the written documents of the Scriptures, but also by the transformation of the disciples. From a group of men cowering in a locked room for fear of the Jews (John 20:19), these men were trans-

Resurrection means . . .

"If the Spirit of Him who raised Jesus from the dead is living in you, He who raised Christ from the dead will also give life [now!] to your mortal bodies through His Spirit, who lives in you" (Rom. 8:11).

So . . .

"Forgetting what is behind and straining toward what is ahead, I press on toward the goal to win the prize for which God has called me heavenward in Christ Jesus" (Phil. 3:13-14).

formed into bold and joyful witnesses of the resurrection of their Lord. The historical fact reported in Scripture, accepted by faith by believers, is a cornerstone of our faith.

Resurrection's place in the New Testament. The New Testament gives the resurrection of Jesus a central place. Each of the Gospels climaxes with a description of this great act of God. The earliest preaching of the Gospel takes the Resurrection as its keynote (cf. Acts 2–5; 7; 10). Paul in 1 Corinthians 15, argued that Christianity stands or falls with the Resurrection, the decisive turning point in mankind's history. Dying, Jesus won us forgiveness. Rising, He presents us with all the benefits of a renewed life (cf. Rom. 4:25; 5:9-10; 8:1-2; 1 Cor. 1:30).

✂ *Group Activity: Recovery Group*
Step 10 (continue taking personal inventory)
Divide a single sheet of paper vertically. On the left top draw a backward looking face, on the right top a forward looking face. Begin by looking back over the past week or month, and listing any faults, failures, or sins that have defeated you.

When this is done, draw features on the backward looking face that reflect how those make you feel, and jot down several emotions that recalling failures make you feel.

Share the drawings and the feelings you have written, and also confess at least three of the wrongs you listed.

Then look at Romans 8:11 and Philippians 3:13-14. Because God shares Jesus' resurrection power with you, your failures need not bind you. Draw features on the forward looking face. Thank God that now that you have turned your life over to Him, you can and will increasingly become new.

Resurrection's nature. Christ's resurrection was the resurrection of a real body of flesh. Jesus' followers recognized His face and voice (Matt. 28:9; Luke 24:31; John 20:16, 19-20; 21:12). His body was touched by them (Matt. 28:9; Luke 24:39; John 20:17, 27). He ate with them (Luke 24:30, 42-43; John 21:12-13). He Himself pointed out that "a ghost does not have flesh and bones, as you see I have" (Luke 24:39).

Yet His resurrection body showed a

unique freedom from the limitations placed on us today. He appeared among them in a locked room (John 20:19), and vanished at will (Luke 24:31). He ascended into heaven before the disciples and many witnesses (Acts 1). Though made of flesh and bone, Jesus' resurrection body is called by Paul "spiritual"—not immaterial, but controlled by or responsive to the Spirit (1 Cor. 15:44). In 1 Corinthians 15, Paul described Christ's body as imperishable, glorious, powerful, incorruptible, immortal, and victorious. And we are promised that our resurrection state will be like His.

✍ *Group Activity: Bible Study Group*
What do New Testament passages tell us about the nature of Jesus' resurrection? The fact of resurrection is well established (see commentary overview, p. 94). But what is resurrection like?

Together or in teams study the following passages: Matthew 28:1-10; Luke 24:13-44; John 20:10-31; 1 Corinthians 15:35-58.

Then develop a series of statements about Jesus' resurrection, and ours, that sums up what you have discovered. Title them: This we can believe with confidence.

Finally, share: what differences does the certainty of resurrection make, in our attitude toward life, toward ourselves, toward others.

Matthew's Emphasis: Matthew 28:16-20
Each of the four Gospel writers gives extensive space to the Resurrection, and each has its own particular emphasis. Matthew's emphasis is in fullest harmony with the theme and thrust of his book. Jesus, the glorious King who lived as a servant, did establish a kingdom. Christ's last recorded words in Matthew echo the command of the King to the servants He leaves in charge of His possessions:

All authority in heaven and on earth has been given to Me. Therefore go and make disciples of all nations, baptizing them in the name of the Father and of the Son and of the Holy Spirit, and teaching them to obey everything I have commanded you. And surely I will be with you always, to the very end of the age.
Matthew 28:18-20

All authority. It's important to realize first of all that Jesus' kingdom does exist today. The fact that the Old Testament visible form of the kingdom has not yet been established in no way means that Jesus' power or authority over this earth are limited. The fact is that Jesus reigns now.

His kingdom exists alongside and within human cultures and societies, focused in the men and women in whom Jesus' Spirit dwells. His quiet, unobtrusive rule is nevertheless totally real. Nothing can happen in heaven or on earth except by His will.

Just as Jesus chose during His days on earth to give men freedom to respond to or to reject Him, the pattern of our world today shows a similar freedom. When Christ returns, His righteous ways will be *imposed*. Today, He permits men to choose. How tragic that most men choose the ways of sin. Even so, Jesus continues on the throne. And Jesus does intervene today on our behalf as we choose to live by His will.

Make disciples. Jesus' command to us as servants, left in charge of our Lord's possessions while He is away, is very specific. When Jesus returns and sits on His glorious throne, Christ will impose righteousness on the whole world. Until then, the kingdom continues as a hidden thing, revealed only to the eyes of faith, and experienced only by those who follow in the footsteps of the King.

Christ's words to the disciples in Matthew 16 and 28 give us direction for our lives. "If anyone would come after Me," He told the Twelve, "he must deny himself and take up his cross and follow Me" (16:24). In following Jesus we find not an earthly kingdom but ourselves. We become new men and new women, whose lives are being transformed, and whose personalities are being reshaped to reflect the love, the compassion, and the character of the King.

Making disciples who will be like the Master (Luke 6:40) is the calling which you and I have from our Lord and King.

All nations. The kingdom of God in its present form cuts across all languages and boundaries and societies. Men of every culture are called, not to become like those of some other nation, but to become like Jesus and to reflect Him in their own lands. Baptism, which speaks of identification, is to be into the Father, Son, and Holy Spirit—not into the "Western world" or into America's idea of the church.

Thus, Christ's kingdom is universal, and the Sermon on the Mount is a unique expression of a reality that cuts across all cultures. Unlike the coming kingdom, which will shatter the kingdoms and the cultures of this world, the kingdom today *infuses*. God's kingdom today touches men, shaping within them Christ's unique concern and love for others. Individuals from every land and age respond, and, in becoming followers of the King, demonstrate the transforming power of Christ in fresh and ever-living ways.

Teaching them to observe all that I have commanded you. The disciple expresses allegiance to his King through obedience. Christ's instructions to His disciples about their own lifestyles are to be communicated to each new generation of believers. The Sermon on the Mount, the way of greatness, the challenge to watch and to serve while the Master is away, are all basic to the Gospel today.

In Matthew, we have been shown a way of life, amplified in the rest of the New Testament but unmistakably clear in the Gospel. In Matthew's portrait of Jesus, we have a model of the men and women you and I are to be.

Jesus lived and died as a *servant* King. In the words of this final command, "Obey everything I have commanded you," we hear echoes of Jesus' earlier words.

It is enough for the student to be like his teacher, and the servant like his master.   Matthew 10:25

Whoever wants to become great among you must be your servant, and whoever wants to be first must be your slave — just as the Son of man did not come to be served, but to serve, and to give His life as a ransom for many.
          Matthew 20:26-28

I am with you always. It's important as we face the meaning of Christ's kingdom and His kingship over us, to realize that we are not left alone to do the impossible. Christ has all authority, and Christ promises to be with us. What is impossible for us is fully possible for Him. We are free to follow, for we do not follow alone.

It is this reality that Paul writes of in Romans 8:11: "If the Spirit of Him who raised Jesus from the dead is living in you, He who raised Christ from the dead will also give life to your mortal bodies through His Spirit, who lives in you." Christ was raised from the dead by the power of God. That same resurrection power is available to overcome the deadness in our lives. Because Christ promises to be with us always, we know that His power is always ours.

The King lives.

And reigns.

In us, as in all the world.

⌀ Group Activity: Missions/Outreach Group

Matthew 28:16-20, known as the "Great Commission," is a keystone missions text. Use this group meeting to plan for a series of reports on how this text has shaped and motivated missions worldwide.

First break down the text as in the commentary, focusing on "all authority," "make disciples," "all nations," and "teaching to observe," and "I am with you always." Together list possible questions or research avenues under each heading. Note that some categories focus on informational research: How many "nations" are there, which have been reached, which are unreached, etc.? And, what strategies have been most effective in "teaching to observe," etc.? Other categories focus on personalized research: What experiences of missionaries demonstrate Jesus' authority, or His living presence? Missionary biographies might be the best source for such information.

When you have thoroughly explored how you might go about researching each category, individually or as teams commit yourself to research and report on an area of your choice.

The Breaking: Luke 24:13-35

There is a Resurrection story in Luke which helps us grasp the uniqueness of Matthew's picture of Jesus — and of the kingdom of which you and I are a part.

On that Resurrection Day, two disciples were returning to their Emmaus home, about seven miles from Jerusalem. They were talking about the events of the Passion Week, and the strange reports of the morning.

As they walked they were joined by a

third Person. He questioned them about what had been happening. As they strode along together, the two told the Stranger about Jesus, who they had hoped was to redeem Israel. How amazed they were now at the report that Jesus had been seen alive again!

Then the Stranger interrupted: "How foolish you are, and how slow of heart to believe all that the prophets have spoken! Did not the Christ have to suffer these things and then enter His glory?" (Luke 24:25-26) Then He traced the Old Testament prophecies that foretold the events of that week and of His coming.

When they arrived at the village, the two urged their Companion to stay for a meal and the night. Seated, He took the bread and blessed it—and broke it. And their eyes were opened. They recognized Jesus!

There's something about the breaking of the loaf of bread. The rich odor of its goodness fills the room. The odor awakens hunger—a hunger that demands satisfaction. All this is known in the breaking of the bread.

This is also how Jesus is known. King He is. But at Passover, Jesus identified Himself as "bread." "This is My body, which is broken for you" (1 Cor. 11:24, KJV).

Had Jesus come in glory first, we would have known His power. But God's great love is not known in Jesus' glory, but in His brokenness. Not in the throne, but in the Cross. Not in might, but in servanthood.

As the rich warm odors given off in the breaking of the bread invite men to the feast, it is in the servanthood of Jesus we are shown God's love, that we sense His invitation to draw near.

So it is in our lives.

There will be time enough for glory when Jesus comes. Today the hidden kingdom is revealed in us, as we, following our King, humble ourselves to serve.

Humble and broken, as was our Lord in the service of His fellowmen, we best fulfill His last command.

GROUP RESOURCE GUIDE

Identification: *Share with others*
Divide a single sheet of paper vertically. On the left top draw a backward looking face, on the right top a forward looking face. Begin by looking back over the past week or month, and listing any faults, failures, or sins that have defeated you.

When this is done, draw features on the backward looking face that reflect how these make you feel, and jot down several emotions that recalling failures make you feel.

Share the drawings and the feelings you have written, and also at least two of the wrongs you listed.

Affirmation: *Express love and concern*
Read aloud and meditate briefly on an encouraging word from God's Word: Romans 8:11. God knows our failings and still guarantees our future!

Exploration: *Probe God's Word*
Together discuss each of the following phrases in Romans 8:11. What does each promise for our future?

- The "Spirit of Him who raised up Jesus."
- If (since He) "is living in you."
- Mortal bodies.
- He will give life to your mortal bodies through His Spirit.

Reaction: *Respond together to the Word*
Meditate briefly on Philippians 3:13-14, and then draw in the features of the forward looking face, on the top right of your paper. Let the features show how it feels to know that you can forget what is past, and look foward to an experience of the power God promises us for godly living.

Then list several areas you are going to count on God to enable you to experience His resurrection power this coming week.

Adoration: *Worship and pray*
In groups of three, share at least one of the areas in which you want to experience now Jesus' resurrection power. Then pray for each other, asking the Spirit to enable one another in the specific areas shared.

STUDY GUIDE 14
Introduction

MARK'S GOSPEL

Overview

Papias, about A.D. 140, expressed the view of the early church about this, the shortest of all our Gospels. He wrote: "Mark, being the interpreter of Peter, whatsoever he recorded he wrote with great accuracy, but not however in the order in which it was spoken or done by our Lord."

Like the other Gospel writers, Mark organized his material to achieve a specific purpose. In Mark's case, this purpose was to introduce Jesus through a simple, vivid narrative, to converts from the Roman world. Writing in the blunt, ordinary language of the common people, Mark focused attention on Jesus' acts (rather than His teachings). About half of the book is devoted to the last eight days of Jesus' life.

In this introductory session, you'll guide your group members to look at some of the things that make this short Gospel so special: the fascinating story of its young author, the confrontation of Jesus with demons, the response of observers to Jesus' miracles, and the special insights which the Book of Mark provides into the emotions of Jesus.

■ An excellent discussion of the date of Mark (probably before A.D. 70), the authorship, the sources Mark may have used, evidence that the Book of Mark was probably written in Rome for Gentile Roman Christians, and Mark's theological themes, is found in the Victor *Bible Knowledge Commentary*, pages 95-101.

Commentary

Writings from every center of early Christianity support the belief that this short Gospel was written by John Mark, a young man mentioned no less than 10 times in the New Testament.

Nearly all the material in Mark is found also in Matthew and Luke. Mark seldom quoted the Old Testament. He explained Jewish customs and terms for Gentile readers (cf. Mark 7:2; 12:42), used Latin terms not found in other Gospels (cf. Mark 6:27; 12:15, 42), and used Roman rather than Jewish systems for calculating time (cf. Mark 6:48; 13:35).

Like so many in our own day, the ordinary people in the Roman world were not interested in abstracts. What gripped them was the evidence of accomplishment, not lengthy discourse. Thus Mark adopted a vigorous style, giving in his fast-paced narrative vivid images of Jesus in action. What impresses us as we read Mark today is the vitality and energy of Jesus, the sense of urgency that marked His activity (often heightened by Mark's repeated use of "and immediately"), and the power that Jesus exudes not only in His miracles but in His confrontations with opponents.

The men and women of the early church must have been impressed, as we are today, with Mark's vision of Jesus as a real human being, totally involved in carrying out His mission, always in command as He moved purposefully to His culminating ministry on the cross.

John Mark

John Mark is mentioned 10 times in the New Testament. The references are: Acts 12:12, 25; 13:5, 13; 15:37, 39; Colossians 4:10; 2 Timothy 4:11; Philemon 24; 1 Peter 5:13. From them we can reconstruct the story of his life, and particularly the fascinating incident which led to the splitting up of the Apostle Paul and his earliest companion and Christian friend, Barnabas.

As a young person from a wealthy Jerusalem home, John Mark must have listened often to the preaching of Peter and the other disciples, who met often in his home. He became a believer, and was serious

THE SMALL GROUP MEMBER'S COMMENTARY

enough about his faith to travel from Jerusalem to Antioch to be with the Apostle Paul and his partner, Barnabas. When these two set out on their first missionary journey, Mark traveled with them.

But missionary life seems to have been too difficult for young Mark. We are told that when the team reached Perga, in Pamphylia, Mark returned to Jerusalem. Although we are not given any details, Mark's departure was clearly viewed by Paul as desertion. Mark was one of those whose commitment faltered, and Paul was hardened against him.

We known that Mark's departure was harshly judged by Paul because later, when a second missionary trip was being planned, Paul utterly refused to permit Mark to come along. But Barnabas, ever living up to the meaning of his name as a "son of consolation" (or "encouragement"), wanted to give young John Mark another chance. The dispute between Paul and Barnabas grew so heated that the two parted, and Paul took Silas on the second journey, while Barnabas took Mark and went to Cyprus.

How heated this dispute must have been is understood when we grasp the nature of the relationship between Paul and Barnabas. When Paul had first been converted, only Barnabas had been willing to associate with this man who had been such a bitter enemy of Christianity. Years later it was Barnabas, a leader in the church at Antioch, who had taken a long journey to find Paul and bring him to Antioch to serve with the leadership team there. It was these two who had started out together on the first of several missionary journeys. Paul, who had gained so much personally from the sensitivity and compassion of Barnabas, was bound to Barnabas by a deep love and trust, developed over years of shared ministry.

Yet when it came to taking John Mark on another missionary journey, Paul adamantly refused. And Barnabas, convinced John should be given another chance, would not give in either. John Mark, who had deserted the two earlier, became the occasion for a bitter dispute that separated two Christian brothers who had loved one another deeply and well.

But the story of John Mark does not end here. Some years later Mark was with Peter

in Rome (called "Babylon" in 1 Peter 5:13). And after a few more years, Mark was with Paul in Rome! During Paul's final imprisonment in Rome, he wrote to Timothy, "Get Mark and bring him with you, because he is helpful to me in my ministry" (2 Tim. 4:11). Apparently the division between Paul and Mark had been healed. Barnabas was right. What Mark needed was a second chance. Through a loving, supportive relationship with the mature Barnabas, young Mark became a Christian leader that even Paul learned he could rely on!

What a lesson for you and me. Are we discouraged at times because of our own lack of progress in the faith? Or because of the weakness of the commitment of those we minister to? Let's learn the lesson of Mark, who was given a second chance, and who became a "helpful" Christian: a person whom God used to write the second Gospel, a book which bears his name.

Jesus' Miracles

Mark's Gospel is significantly shorter than the others. Yet while Matthew and Luke each mention 20 of Jesus' miracles, Mark—half their size—speaks of 18 specific miracles and refers 10 additional times to miracles that are not described in any detail. A list of the miracles in Mark shows:

1. Demon-possessed man healed — 1:23-28
2. Peter's mother-in-law healed — 1:29-31
3. Leper healed — 1:40-45
4. Paralytic healed — 2:3-12
5. Withered hand healed — 3:1-5
6. Storm stilled — 4:35-41
7. Demon-possessed man healed — 5:1-20
8. Jairus' daughter raised — 5:22-43
9. Bleeding woman healed — 5:25-34
10. 5,000 fed — 6:35-44
11. Jesus walks on sea — 6:45-52
12. Woman's daughter healed — 7:24-30
13. Deaf and dumb man healed — 7:31-37
14. 4,000 fed — 8:1-9
15. Blind man healed — 8:22-26
16. Epileptic boy healed — 9:14-29
17. Blind men healed — 10:46-52
18. Fig tree cursed — 11:12-14

The 10 general references to other miracles performed by Jesus are: 1:32-34, 39; 3:9-12, 22; 6:2, 5, 7, 13, 14, 53-56. The words used to describe all these miracles are "wonder," "power," "sign," and "miraculous deed."

The nature of miracles. A number of Greek words are associated with miracles in the Gospels. *Dunamis,* often translated as "miracle," is from a root that means "power." This word focuses attention on an event as an explosive demonstration of God's own power. *Semeion* is "sign." This word indicates that the miraculous event links the doer of the act with the divine. The New Testament also uses *ergon,* "work," where miracles are clearly meant.

These words each reflect Old Testament terms. There *mopet,* found only 36 times, means a "wonder" or "miracle." It is used primarily of God's personal intervention through miracles in Egypt to free His people, Israel. *'Ot* means "miraculous sign." Each of the plagues on Egypt is called an *'ot.*

In both Testaments, miracles are unmistakable acts of God—interventions whose nature or whose timing demonstrate God's action in our world of space and time. In each Testament, there was no question in the minds of observers that what they saw was in fact a supernatural act.

In the Old Testament the word indicating this is *pala'.* It is a word describing the impact of miracles on the observers; the sense of awe and amazement at the unmistakable evidence that God has demonstrated His reality in this universe.

No wonder the Old Testament encourages believers to remember what God has done as a source of comfort and confidence. We "remember the wonders He has done, His miracles," and we declare "His marvelous deeds among all peoples" (1 Chron. 16:12, 24).

What is particularly striking in the Gospel accounts of Jesus' miracles is that His fellow countrymen, steeped in Old Testament lore, responded with the same stunned amazement of past generations.

The words Mark uses to describe this reaction emphasizes the stunning impact of Jesus' miracles. *Thaumazo* is usually translated "amazed" and suggests utter astonishment. Yet amazement doesn't automatically produce faith!

Existemi mixes astonishment with anxiety. The miracles of Jesus were so out of the ordinary that they created fear as well as wonder.

Thambeo indicates actual fright. Three times Mark tells us that Jesus' miracles frightened observers (1:27; 10:24, 32).

In fact, the works of Jesus were astonishing and frightening to those who did not believe in Him. As those who believed listened and watched this Man of Galilee, and realized just who He is, His wonders seemed only fitting. He *was* their God; as He had acted in ages past, so He acted now.

There were many differences between the miracles of Jesus and those who claimed to be able to do "magic" in the ancient world. The works of Jesus were performed simply. He used no spells or incantations. He spoke, and His word was enough. His works were performed in public, observed by friend and foe alike. Nicodemus spoke of the ruling Jewish council when he said, "*We* know that You are a Teacher who has come from God. For no one could perform the miraculous signs You are doing if God were not with him" (John 3:2, italics added).

But perhaps most importantly, magic in the ancient world was seen as a mode of controlling or harming others. It was used *against,* rather than *for,* them. But all of Jesus' miracles were exercised on behalf of others, to free them from sickness, pain, and spiritual bondage.

In performing His miracles, Jesus not only demonstrated His power, but also showed the overwhelming love of God for humankind.

What a wonder those miracles were. They documented the reality of God's power to act in man's world, they authenticated Jesus as God's Son, and they revealed in unmistakable ways the love and compassion of God for individual human beings. In the Old Testament God had acted to free the nation Israel. In Jesus He acted to release individuals from the physical and spiritual impact of man's ancient enemy—sin.

Jesus and Demons

Some of Jesus' most notable miracles involved casting out demons, and releasing the demon-possessed from their malignant influence.

What do we know about the demons of which the New Testament speaks?

Most ancient cultures believed in demons who had an evil influence on humans. It is striking in view of the prevalence of this belief that demons are only mentioned twice in the Old Testament (Deut. 32:17; Ps. 106:36-37). Yet the Gospels are full of reports of demons and demonic activity.

Some have suggested that this is because Satan marshaled his forces against Jesus during His life on earth. It does not seem unreasonable that the level of demonic activity then *was* unusual. Perhaps the charge of the Jewish leaders that Jesus was in league with the prince of demons was stimulated by the unusual amount of demonic activity associated with Christ's earthly ministry (cf. John 7:20; 8:48-52).

What we do know is that demons *were* active while Jesus walked the earth. We also know that they demonstrated their hostility toward humankind by harming rather than helping individuals they influenced. Many sicknesses and madness are linked with demon oppression (cf. Mark 1:32; 5:16-18).

We know little about these beings who are called demons or "evil spirits" in the New Testament. The only supernatural beings whose origin and future Scripture speaks of are Satan and the angels who followed him in his rebellion. Regarding these beings, Jesus said, there was "eternal fire prepared for the devil and his angels" (Matt. 25:41). It seems most likely that the demons of the Gospels were actually fallen angels, followers of Satan, and like him, the determined enemy of God and His people.

Several things are significant in the many confrontations that took place between Jesus and demons. First, they invariably knew Him to be the Son of God. Second, they immediately submitted to Him. There was no question that demons could not withstand Jesus: even these evil beings were subject to His authority. Third, Jesus always acted to release human beings who suffered from their evil influence. There is no record that Jesus ever abandoned any person who was demon-possessed or demon-oppressed.

Today many have questions about demons and demon-possession. It is clear from Scripture that demons are real. They can bring misery and cause sickness. But Jesus remains Lord, with authority and power far beyond that of wicked spirits. We can remain confident as we live close to Jesus that He will guard us. As the Apostle John wrote, "The One who is in you is greater than the one who is in the world" (1 John 4:4). It is hard to imagine even Satan himself settling into any relationship with a person indwelt by the Spirit of our Lord.

Jesus and His Emotions

Mark is unusual in that in describing Jesus' acts he often spoke of Christ's emotions. Mark wrote about Jesus as a Person who knew grief, who experienced both anger and compassion. He mentioned Christ's hunger and His exhaustion. We find these mentioned in passages like Mark 3:5; 4:38; 6:6, 31; 7:34; 8:12; 10:14, 21; and 11:12.

Perhaps most striking is the fact that several times Mark refers to Jesus' anger, using at least four Greek words. In Mark 3:5 the word is *orge,* a strong term indicating wrathful indignation. In 9:25, the word translated "rebuked" (*epitimao*) means to angrily reproach. In 10:14 the word rendered "indignant" is *embrimaomai,* which indicates irritation and annoyance.

Jesus was not unmoved by human suffering. But neither was He unmoved by sin in any of its expressions.

These passages raise the question of the anger of God, something spoken of in the Old Testament as well as the New. Both Testaments use similar words to describe God.

But the anger of God is never like a human temper tantrum, nor is it capricious. It is God's righteous response to specific human failures and sins. The *Expository Dictionary of Bible Words* (Richards, Zondervan) says that:

> The Old Testament sees God's anger in a positive rather than negative light. God's anger expresses itself in rebuke and discipline (Pss. 6:1; 38:1; 78:31-38). It is God's righteous reaction to those who persecute His people unjustly (Ex. 15:7; Ps. 7:6). His anger is provoked by wicked deeds (Ps. 106:29). The psalmist says, "Surely Your wrath against men brings You praise, and the survivors of Your wrath are restrained" (Ps. 76:10). God's anger is thus viewed as completely justified, and also as ultimately of benefit to people.

But the Bible does not present anger

as an essential characteristic of God. In fact, God's wrath is set aside when God forgives (Ps. 85:2-3), and even His acts of anger show restraint (Ps. 78:38). Compared to His favor, which lasts a lifetime, God's anger is momentary (Ps. 30:5). God intends only good to humanity, and when it is necessary to act in anger, the intention to do good is never lost.

We can gain special insight into the anger of God by noting in Mark's Gospel just what it is that stimulates the Lord's anger, and the control over this emotion which He exhibits.

Mark's Jesus

There are many attractive things about Jesus as Mark portrays Him. Jesus is a Man of action, yet a Man with deep feelings and emotions. Jesus takes sides: He readily uses His power to help the helpless, and withstand the individuals and forces who would enslave human beings. Jesus in Mark's Gospel remains a servant, dedicated to actively doing His Father's will in the service of humankind.

Yet half of this brief Gospel is given to describe the final eight days of Jesus' life. It is the final act of service that Jesus offered us that is the most significant to John Mark.

Perhaps John Mark's portrait of the strong Jesus is so powerful because Mark himself knew he was weak. Mark, who had failed himself, and had found in Jesus the strength to overcome, reveals to us the Jesus who can act dynamically in our lives.

THE AUTHENTIC SAVIOUR

Overview

Mark's Gospel is the shortest of the four. In powerful prose, Mark tells story after story about Jesus.

Many of the stories bear the mark of eyewitness testimony. The early church believed that Mark, a close companion of Peter, reported what Peter had witnessed, and represents Peter's testimony to the life of his Lord.

Distinctives of Mark are explored in the introduction to this Gospel.

The Gospel can be simply outlined. After a brief introduction (1:2-13), Mark links together stories around simple, clear themes.

Outline

I. Introduction	1:2-13
II. Jesus Authenticated	1:4–5:43
III. Jesus in Conflict	6:1–8:26
IV. Jesus' Instructions	8:27–10:52
V. Journey toward Calvary	11–13
VI. Death and Resurrection	14–16

▶ *Healing.* Mark records a stream of healings in the opening chapters of his Gospel. Christians have often wondered, is there healing for us today? The Bible clearly indicates that God *can* heal. But in New Testament times God did not always heal even His most faithful servants (see 2 Cor. 12:7-10). When one of Paul's dearest friends was ill, the apostle did not "heal" him, but rather prayed and waited for God's answer (cf. Phil. 2:26-28). What Jesus' healings assure us of is that, whatever our need, God cares!

Commentary

The Gospels of Matthew and Luke each carefully describe the miraculous birth of Jesus, and events associated with it. In Mark, Jesus bursts on the scene unexpect-edly, as He must have appeared in His own land. We meet Jesus only as an adult, launching into His ministry in a flurry of vital activity. But Mark makes sure that we do understand who Jesus is.

Authenticated by God: Mark 1:1-13

Mark immediately stated that his Gospel was "about Jesus Christ, the Son of God." Quickly Mark went about marshaling his evidence.

There was a man named John who appeared, baptizing in a desert area in Judea. His message, foretold in the Old Testament, concerned a Person who was to appear. And, "at that time" Jesus came from Nazareth in Galilee and was baptized.

Mark reported that as Jesus was coming up out of the waters after being baptized, John saw heaven "torn open" and the Spirit of God descending on Jesus. And John heard a voice from heaven, saying, "You are My Son, whom I love; with You I am well pleased."

Jesus was first authenticated by God Himself. And John the Baptist was the witness to that authentication. With this beginning, Mark initiates chapters intended to authenticate Jesus as God's Son.

Authenticated by Power: Mark 1:14-39

Witnesses (Mark 1:14-20). Mark first tells us that Jesus selected 12 disciples. This was important to his story, for the disciples would serve as witnesses to the acts which authenticated Jesus as Son of God.

The role of the disciples as witnesses was emphasized. After the resurrection of Jesus the eleven apostles gathered to select a replacement for Judas Iscariot. According to Peter, "it is necessary for us to choose one of the men *who have been with us the whole time* the Lord Jesus went in and out among us, *beginning from John's baptism* to the time when Jesus was taken up from us. For one of these must become a witness with us of His resurrection" (Acts 1:21-22, italics added). The disciples, who accompanied Jesus at all times, would be able to give an eyewitness account of His whole life and ministry, firmly establishing the historical roots of the faith.

There was no room in early Christianity for myth and rumors. The story of Jesus was no hearsay account, based on what someone said that another person heard from a friend. What Jesus said and did was heard by thousands, but in particular there was a group of disciples who saw it *all*— and who in God's time not only traveled the world telling what they had seen and heard, but also saw to it that the story was written down accurately and carefully.

It is no wonder then that Mark notes the calling of the disciples at this point in his story. He wants us to know that witnesses who can authenticate everything he has to tell were actually there.

When we hear of scholars who search for the "historical Jesus," trying to separate strands of the Gospel report into what "really happened" and what was supposedly added later, we need to remember that Mark takes special care to assure us that the Jesus of the Gospels *is* the historical Jesus. What Mark and the other Gospel writers reported is what actually happened, and their accounts are supported by the eyewitness testimony of people who were there.

What was it that the witnesses saw as Jesus launched His ministry that authenticated Him as Son of God?

An evil spirit driven out (Mark 1:21-28). It was Jesus' teaching that first amazed the crowds. Mark, typically, does not tell us *what* Jesus was teaching: simply that He did teach. And those who heard were amazed, because Jesus "taught them as One who had authority, not as the teachers of the Law" (v. 22).

In Jesus' time anyone who wished to be recognized as a rabbi (teacher) went through a recognized process of training. He became a disciple of a rabbi, and from him learned the mass of oral traditions and interpretations which had grown up around the Law. It was common for a rabbi to refer to tradition; to discuss the notion of rabbi this and rabbi that. It was what the long dead had said that the living referred to when teaching. And then Jesus appeared.

And when Jesus taught, He did not hedge His words by references to others. He spoke plainly, powerfully, as One who possessed authority on His own.

The word "amazed" here does not suggest belief. In fact, it suggests skepticism. But, Mark says, "just then" a man possessed with an evil spirit cried out. The spirit identified Jesus as "the Holy One of God!" And Jesus commanded the spirit to come out of him. Shrieking, the spirit obeyed.

News of this act spread. Jesus gave His "new teaching . . . with authority!" And He "even [gave] orders to evil spirits and they obeyed Him."

Even the evil spirits who hated Jesus testified to the fact that He is the Son of God. Jesus' disciples, and the people of Capernaum were witnesses.

Jesus heals (Mark 1:29-34). The first healing Mark reported was of Peter's mother-in-law. But that evening, the ministry of healing was extended to the "whole town," which gathered at the door. This time Jesus' power over the sicknesses that bind humanity authenticated Him as the Son of God. And again the witnesses were, first the disciples, and then the "whole town."

Prayer (Mark 1:35-39). What was the source of Jesus' power? The town did not know. But the disciples did. Mark tells us that "very early in the morning, while it was still dark, Jesus got up . . . and went off to a solitary place, where He prayed." Christ's intimate personal relationship with the Father was the source of His power. This intimacy, witnessed by the disciples, also authenticated Christ as the Son of God.

From there, Mark concludes, Jesus traveled with His disciples to nearby villages, until He had traveled throughout Galilee. Everywhere He went Jesus preached, and His acts of power publicly authenticated Him as the Son of God.

Authenticated by Compassion:
Mark 1:40–3:12

The first set of stories Mark told focused on the emotion of amazement aroused by Jesus' acts of power. Now, in another series, Mark focused on the emotions which moved Jesus, and on the impact of His interventions on the lives of individuals. In this series we realize that Jesus truly was God in the flesh, for He showed God's own concern for individuals who live in bondage.

The healing touch (Mark 1:40-45). Mark had spoken of the crowds. Now he spoke of individuals. The first person Mark mentioned was a leper who came to Jesus, begging Him on his knees.

Leprosy was especially terrible to a Jew. More than what we call leprosy (Hanson's disease) was designated by this name in Bible times. The word was used of any chronic or infectious skin disease. Leprosy was serious in Israel not only because it caused physical pain, but because it made a Jew ceremonially "unclean" (see Lev. 14). Such a Jew could not participate in worship and was to be isolated from others in the Hebrew community.

The leper who approached Jesus had very probably not known the touch of another's hand for years, as all around him were repelled by his disease.

No wonder he was hesitant as he came to Christ and said, "If You are willing, You can make me clean" (Mark 1:40). The leper did not question Jesus' power. But he did question Jesus' willingness to act for him, an outcast.

Mark tells us that Jesus was "filled with compassion." The Greek word used here makes it clear that he was deeply moved. Jesus reached out His hand and actually touched the man! He said, "I am willing," and with a word cured the incurable disease.

With that touch Jesus answered for all time the doubts of those who wonder if God really cares. Jesus not only met the physical need. He understood the loneliness and psychological pain this man must have experienced, and with His touch dealt directly with that inner pain.

✂ *Group Activity: Recovery Group*
Steps 2 (believe in a higher power) and 3 (decide to turn my life over to God's care)
In biblical times leprosy cut a person off from all contact with others and from all participation in the life of the community. Imagine yourself a leper, and write a brief paragraph telling how you feel about yourself. Read paragraphs to one another.
In healing the leper Jesus showed both that He was able to meet the leper's need, and that He cared about this outcast. Di-

vide into teams to look at other miracles of Jesus reported in Mark's Gospel. Each team may take several miracles, depending on the number in your group, and determine what we can learn about Jesus from His works.

1. *Demon-possessed man healed 1:23-28*
2. *Peter's mother-in-law healed 1:29-31*
3. *Paralytic healed* 1:40-45
4. *Withered hand healed* 2:3-12
5. *Storm stilled* 4:35-41
6. *Demonized man healed* 5:1-20
7. *Jairus' daughter raised* 5:22-43
8. *Bleeding woman healed* 5:25-34
9. *5,000 fed* 6:35-44
10. *Jesus walks on sea* 6:45-52
11. *Woman's daughter healed* 7:24-30
12. *Deaf/dumb man healed* 7:31-37
13. *4,000 fed* 8:1-9
14. *Blind man healed* 8:22-26
16. *Epileptic boy healed* 9:14-29
17. *Blind man healed* 10:46-52

Share reports. Then write another paragraph, from the perspective of the leper and from your own. Direct this letter to Jesus, telling Him why you feel you can trust Him and that you are committing your life and will to His loving care.

A paralytic healed and forgiven (Mark 2:1-12). The next story also focused on an individual. The man was a paralytic, brought to Jesus by friends. Confident that Jesus did care and could heal, the friends actually dug through the roof of a home where Jesus was teaching in order to bring the man to Him.

Jesus, in response to this faith, announced not only healing but also the forgiveness of the man's sins! This was too much for some of the "teachers of the Law" who were now listed by Mark as among the observers. These teachers were "thinking to themselves" that Jesus words about forgiveness of sins were blasphemy, because "who can forgive sins but God alone?"

They were right, of course. Only God can forgive sin. But Jesus is God the Son! Jesus answered their unspoken objection in a graphic way. Which is easier: to tell a paralyzed man that he is forgiven, or to heal him? The answer is clear. It is far *easier* to speak of forgiveness. Who could possibly look into a man's heart to see if he was forgiven? It's easy to say, "You're forgiven," because who could really tell? How different to say, "Take up your bed and walk." Everyone can see, then, if the speaker has authority!

Not waiting for an answer, Jesus told the paralyzed man to get up, and walk home. "In full view of them all," the paralyzed man got up and walked away! Jesus' authority as God the Son to forgive sin was authenticated by a healing that took place not just in front of Christ's followers, but in front of His enemies as well!

Levi called (Mark 2:13-17). But is it true that there is no public evidence of Christ's inner work in a human life? Mark focuses our attention on yet another individual. The man was Levi, a tax collector. Tax collectors in New Testament times collaborated with the Romans and often profited by what they extorted from their fellow-countrymen. They were linked by all with other "sinners" from various outcast classes, like prostitutes.

Jesus not only called Levi to become one of His disciples, but even went to his home. There, at a party in His honor, Jesus mixed comfortably with the "sinners" of society.

The Pharisees, witnessing this, were scandalized. In response Jesus simply said, "It is not the healthy who need a doctor, but the sick. I have not come to call the righteous, but sinners" (v. 17).

What is significant about this story is, of course, the fact that the man called "Levi" here is elsewhere called Matthew! He was not only 1 of the 12 disciples, but wrote the Gospel identified by his name!

Jesus' power as Son of God was authenticated not only by healing sickness and disease, but by healing the sin which infects every human being. Jesus came to call sinners. And when His touch is felt on a human life, the sinner responds by becoming a new and righteous man.

Lord of Sabbath (Mark 2:18–3:6). In each of the stories in Mark 2, Pharisees or teachers of the Law have a prominent part. Why?

The people of Israel were truly zealous for God. But their zeal had been misdirected. They thought that God would be pleased if they rigorously kept the details of His Law. In their focus on the details, they missed the real meaning and purpose of God's ancient commands. Our saying, "They couldn't see the forest for the trees," was doubly true of the Pharisees and religious leaders of Jesus' time.

This theme is introduced as Jesus is asked His view on fasting. The disciples of the Pharisees and John the Baptist fasted. What about Jesus' disciples? Did they fast too? Jesus dismissed the question, pointing out that His new wine (His "new teaching") could not be poured into old wineskins. The patterns of thought and religion which characterized Israel were out of harmony with the message Jesus had to share.

Two incidents demonstrate Jesus' focus. Christ's disciples plucked some heads of grain as they followed Him through a grainfield. This was allowed in the Old Testament Law: a hungry person could eat from another's field as he passed by, but could not carry anything away. But this was the Sabbath. And to the Pharisees, who classified the act as "work," the act seemed a violation of the Sabbath Day.

Jesus dismissed their complaint. He did not point out that this interpretation was not found in Scripture but in mere human tradition. Instead, Jesus went back to the Old Testament and noted that even David, when hungry, ate of the shewbread located in God's tabernacle. Though this bread was supposed to be eaten by the priests alone, David was not charged with a sin because he had acted out of real need.

So, Jesus explained, "The Sabbath was made for man, not man for the Sabbath." In other words, God was not angered when real need drove a human being to violate a ceremonial aspect of Old Testament Law. People are more important to God than ritual observances. And this, Jesus said, He now established as One who is "Lord of the Sabbath."

At another time Jesus found a man with a shriveled hand when He entered a synagogue. The Pharisees had apparently planted him there, intending, if Christ should heal him, to accuse Jesus as a Sabbath-breaker. Jesus confronted them. He asked, "Which is lawful on the Sabbath: to do good or to do evil, to save life or to kill?" The Pharisees had no answer—but they were unmoved.

Deeply angered by the stubborn heartlessness of these men, Jesus restored the cripple.

And the Pharisees "went out and began to plot with the Herodians how they might kill Jesus" (3:6).

Mark concluded with another of his typical summary paragraphs. Jesus traveled, taught, healed, and expelled evil spirits who continued to cry out, "You are the Son of God."

What is the significance of this sequence in Mark's story of Jesus? Mark wanted his readers to realize that Jesus is authenticated as the Son of God by His demonstration of God's deep compassion for human beings. He heals our diseases. He forgives our sins. And He shows us that what God desires is not a legalistic relationship with human beings but a relationship marked by loving concern. The love which infused the Law at its giving had been lost sight of as God's people thought of it as rules to follow in order to please God rather than as guidelines showing them how to love Him and one another.

And the Pharisees? They were witnesses of the authenticating marks of Jesus' compassion. And by their reaction they demonstrated to all that their approach to religion was devoid of the love that marks the character of God.

Authenticated by Personal Authority: Mark 3:13–5:43

Mark began this new section with a list of those Jesus appointed as His official apostles (sent ones). He then launched into a series of stories which demonstrate that the Son of God's personal authority is absolutely unlimited. There is only one possible explanation for His acts and His words.

❋ *Group Activity:*
Singles/Single Again Group
On an 8 1/2 x 11 inch sheet of paper draw a series of circles that represent your relationships with others. First draw a circle representing yourself. Then draw circles for any others you choose, identifying each circle with an initial. Show how important a person is to you by the size of his or her circle. Show how close you feel to each by the distance of his or her circle from you. Show relationships persons have with each other by drawing lines between them.

In groups of four or five discuss each other's diagram. What does it suggest about each one's present situation and feelings?

Then read Mark 3:13-19. Some of the 12—James, John, and Peter—were close to each other when called. Others, like Levi, were "loners." Yet in responding to Jesus' call these individuals became "the Twelve," a close-knit, caring group that affected the history of the world!

Discuss: How in following Jesus together can we become a closer-knit, more caring fellowship? What kind of commitment to each other can and should we make? What specific actions do we want to take now?

False explanations (Mark 3:20, 25). The excitement had grown in Galilee, until Jesus was constantly surrounded by crowds. Shouting, shoving people pressed so close that Christ and His disciples could not even find an opportunity to sit down and eat! These people did not try to explain Jesus: they simply mobbed this new celebrity.

When His family heard, they rushed to Him. "He is out of His mind," was their theory. What had happened to this quiet, hard-working carpenter Son and Brother, to make Him run around the country drawing crowds! It seemed so unlike Him!

The "teachers of the Law" who came down from Jerusalem to check out this phenomenon had another theory. "He's demon-possessed!" They tried to explain Jesus' supernatural powers by saying that they were from Satan rather than God.

Jesus exposed the ridiculous theory by pointing out that His powers had been used *against* Satan's minions. What ruler would start warfare between his own subjects? Only if a strong homeowner had been rendered powerless could another carry away his possessions. Jesus' works were done in the power of the Holy Spirit, not of Satan.

Only one conclusion fit the facts. Jesus is the Son of God: His personal authority as God's Son is the only explanation for all He said and did.

Authoritative teaching (Mark 4:1-34). Now Mark gave a sample of Jesus' teaching.

The word Jesus spoke was like seed scattered by a farmer. When the word took root in "good soil" it produced much fruit. Those who hear Jesus are likened to various soils. Some are like stony ground, on which the seed initially sprouts but cannot grow because there is no place for it to take root.

Any trouble or persecution brings rejection of the Word. Others allow concern for the affairs of this life to choke out the spiritual. But on those who are "good soil" (responsive to the Word) it produces a rich crop.

This longer parable is followed by a series of enigmatic statements. Lamps are to be put on stands, not covered with a bowl. The kingdom of God grows gradually, like a planted seed. Taking in the crop awaits harvesttime. The tiniest of seeds can grow into a large garden plant.

Jesus' parables were not explained to the crowds, but "when He was alone with His disciples, He explained everything" (v. 34). The truths hidden in the parables of Jesus were understood by the disciples, and those that relate to the church are woven into the teaching of the Epistles.

Personal authority demonstrated (Mark 4:35–5:43). Now, in his report of a series of miracles, Mark showed us in their ascending significance the full extent of Christ's personal power.

Asleep at sea, Jesus was aroused by His terrified disciples when a "furious squall" struck their fishing boat. He rebuked the storm , , , and suddenly the waters were completely calm! Jesus has power over nature.

In the next story in this sequence Mark told how Jesus cast many demons out of a man, sending them into a herd of pigs. Jesus has power over evil spiritual beings and forces.

📖 *Group Activity: Bible Study Group*
Plan a "pigs or people" party, based on Mark 5:1-20. As each person comes to the group, have him draw a folded slip of paper on which you've written either "pigs" or "people." Read the passage together. Then, depending on the slip drawn, write
down reasons why Jesus valued the demonized man more than the pigs, or the reasons why the Gerasenes placed more value on their pigs and urged Jesus to leave. Write down as many reasons as you can think of.

Collect the written reasons and list them all on a chalkboard or large sheet of newsprint. Then tear off the "pigs" side. And tell how seeing yourself and others in the way reflected by one of the items on the "people" side affects your life.

Finally, celebrate together! Rejoice that Jesus values you more than anything in His universe.

Then Jesus was urged to go to help a dying daughter. On the way He was touched by a woman who had suffered from chronic bleeding for 12 years. She was healed simply by touching Jesus' clothes, and confessed the faith that brought her to Jesus. Even the physical illnesses which bind us and are one of the most obvious results of the Fall submit to Jesus.

When Jesus arrived at the home of Jairus, the man who had begged Him to come to his daughter's aid, she had died. Entering the house with the parents and the disciples, Jesus took her by the hand — and restored her to life! Jesus had power not only over sickness, but over death itself.

Jesus does have personal authority. All that Jesus said and did authenticated Him as the Son of God.

Those who first read Mark's Gospel, as we who read it today, must have been convinced. Jesus is just who Mark claimed Him to be in his first words. What we have read truly is about "Jesus Christ, the Son of God" (Mark 1:1).

GROUP RESOURCE GUIDE

Identification: *Share with others*
Tell briefly one incident you recall from Scripture that sums up your image of Jesus.

Exploration: *Probe God's Word*
Divide into groups to look at the four "authenticating" sections identified in the Commentary. Each group is to study one
or more of the following to report on one incident that sums up who Jesus is for us:

* authenticated as God, 1:1-13
* authenticated by power, 1:14-29
* authenticated by compassion, 1:40–3:12
* authenticated by personal authority, 3:13–5:43

Reaction: *Respond together to the Word*
Go around the group asking each to share one area in which he or she needs now to experience Jesus, as reported by one of the groups. In what area is a touch of Christ's compassion or an experience of His power most needed?

Affirmation: *express love and concern*
Pray at length and specifically for the needs expressed by group members.

Adoration: *Worship and pray*
Conclude with sentence prayers of thanksgiving that Jesus is going to answer the prayers you have just offered for one another.

JESUS' CONFLICTS

Overview

The first few chapters of Mark show us that Jesus is the authentic Son of God. Still, the people to whom Jesus came and showed His powerful proofs did not acknowledge Him! Why?

In two cycles of stories, Mark reveals the reason for Israel's rejection, and demonstrates the response that all must make to Jesus, the Son of God. In these chapters Mark invites us to look at two kinds of hearts. There is the hardened heart of Jesus' followers, who could not seem to grasp the meaning of what they saw. And there are the distant hearts of Jesus' enemies, who refused to even look. Yet Mark also shows us faith, a principle which can open our eyes and our hearts to spiritual reality.

Here, as in the rest of his Gospel, Mark's style is not to preach. Mark simply tells what happened, carefully linking story with story to lead us to discover in Jesus alone a power that can cleanse and renew us.

▶ **Heart.** The theological meaning of "heart" is established in the Old Testament. The "heart" is the conscious self, the inner core of the individual. Jeremiah portrayed the heart as "deceitful above all things and beyond cure" (Jer. 17:9). Every dimension of the human personality has been infected by sin. But only the willfully hardened or distant heart is beyond the power of Christ to change.

Commentary

There has never been any real question about Jesus' authority. The question has always been how human beings will respond to Him. Many throughout history have heard the evidence and hesitated. Others have heard and actively opposed the Gospel. But always one key alone has released the power of the Saviour to operate in the life of the individual.

The Issue Drawn: Mark 6:1-44

Unbelief (Mark 6:1-6). After Jesus' reputation had been well established, He returned to His hometown of Nazareth. When Jesus taught in the synagogue, His words created the familiar "amazement," an amazement linked with doubt rather than faith. As Jesus' fellow-townsmen listened they began to resent Him. How was Jesus better than they? Wasn't He just the village carpenter? Didn't His mother and brothers live next door? Why should Jesus be given such wisdom, and the power to do miracles?

Mark says they "took offense at Him." The word is a strong one. It indicates anger, shock, and even revulsion.

Among these friends and neighbors Jesus did no miracles, except for a few healings. And Mark comments, "He [Jesus] was amazed at their lack of faith."

In this short story Mark established the theme of this section of his Gospel. Mark would examine the response of people to Jesus the Son of God. And he would go about explaining their amazing lack of faith.

The Twelve instructed (Mark 6:7-13). Jesus continued traveling, teaching from village to village. Then He determined to send out the Twelve, giving them authority over evil spirits. Jesus gave them significant instructions. They were to carry nothing for the journey, but depend on those to whom they came. But "if any place will not welcome you or listen to you, shake the dust off your feet when you leave as a testimony against them" (v. 11). The disciples were to preach the Word. Each person was free to welcome or reject the message. But the disciples were to "leave" those who would not respond, and were to "shake the dust off your feet . . . as a testimony against them."

The disciples went out, teaching, healing, and driving out devils. With such abundant evidence of the authority and compassion of Jesus, who would refuse to believe?

Belief is not faith (Mark 6:14-29). Mark interrupted his narrative to tell a story which established a vital principle. Belief, as the realization that certain things are true, must never be confused with "faith."

As more and more stories about Jesus reached King Herod, speculation about Him grew. Some said that Jesus was Elijah; others, another of the ancient prophets. But Herod was convinced that Jesus was John the Baptist, raised from the dead.

Herod had imprisoned John who condemned the king for an illicit relationship he established with his brother's wife. The woman, Herodias, hated John and wanted to kill him. But Mark tells us that Herod "feared John and protected him, knowing him to be a righteous and holy man" (v. 20).

But when Herodias' daughter danced at Herod's birthday party, and he offered her any reward, she asked for the head of John the Baptist.

Herod looked around. All his guests had heard his promise. Their opinion seemed terribly important to him then. Though he didn't want to do it—and though he knew it was wrong—Herod ordered John's execution.

In Greece, hundreds of years before Christ, the philosopher Plato speculated that if only a person knew "the good," he would do it. Herod's act showed how wrong Plato was. It is not enough to know what is good. It is not enough to believe the right things. A person must commit himself to what he knows is right. A person must trust God enough to believe that He exists, and that it is God's opinion that counts; that His will must guide ours.

Herod believed that John was a prophet. He even liked to listen to John's teachings, just as the people of Israel believed that Jesus was a Prophet and crowded around to hear Him speak and to witness His miracles.

But when the time for decision arrived, *mere belief must be transformed into faith.* There must be commitment! A person must not look around, and try to please those who are watching. A person must face the fact that only God's opinion counts, and in the firm conviction that God is and that He is a rewarder of those who

seek Him, that person must commit himself to what is right.

✄ **Group Activity: Recovery Group Step 1 (admit powerlessness)**
The Greek philosopher Plato taught that a person who knows "the good" will choose it. Suppose the Herod featured in the story in Mark 6:14-29 were to join a Recovery Group. Read the passage and from the story, discuss what "good" Herod knew. How did he choose against what he himself believed? What does the text suggest were Herod's reasons for his wrong choice? What do you conclude about Herod's powerlessness, even though he was a king?

Then list at least 10 specific instances in which you knew what you should do, but chose wrongly. Then share: What do you conclude about your own ability to choose the good you know? Illustrate from items on your list.

The first step in recovery is to admit we are powerless to change ourselves. Only then will we be willing to turn our lives over to the One who can free us from sin and failure.

See the Son of God (Mark 6:30-44). Now Mark told another story, one that linked the authenticating marks of Jesus' divine sonship which we noted in the first five chapters.

Crowds followed Jesus out into a wilderness place. Out of compassion He taught them until late in the day. Then, realizing the people must be hungry, Jesus fed some 5,000 men, plus uncounted women and children, from five small loaves and two fish. Jesus' miracle combined the power and the compassion of God, and reminded Mark's readers that this One truly is the Son of God. Surely we cannot only believe in Jesus; in total faith we can commit ourselves fully to Him as God's only begotten Son.

A Matter of the Heart: Mark 6:45–7:37
Hardened hearts (Mark 6:45-56). Jesus sent His disciples ahead by boat so He might have time alone to pray. When the wind came up later that night, Jesus went to join His followers, walking on the water. When the disciples saw His figure amid the waves, they cried out in fear, thinking He was a ghost.

Jesus moved toward them, speaking reassuringly. When He reached them, He climbed over the side into the boat, and the winds died down.

Then Mark gave stunning information: "They were completely amazed, for they had not understood about the loaves; their hearts were hardened" (6:51). Even Jesus' disciples, who had witnessed every miracle and heard every teaching, did not fully realize who Jesus is!

We shouldn't be surprised that the crowds who heard Him and witnessed a few of His miracles hesitated to commit themselves to Jesus. We shouldn't be surprised that the religious leaders were skeptical. Even those closest to Jesus did not fully grasp who this Person they had committed themselves to truly is!

With this story Mark focuses our attention on the heart. As we noted in the overview of this passage, the heart in Hebrew thought is the sum total of the personality, the essence of the individual. It is the testimony of Scripture that the heart of man was tragically warped by the Fall. Sin has darkened human understanding, twisted human motives, crippled human will, distorted human emotions. The grip of sin on each of us is deadly, trapping us in a dark realm of illusion where we can hardly glimpse the truth. Even the disciples of Jesus, who had been so close to Him, were crippled by darkened and hardened hearts.

It is not enough for Jesus to show Himself to be the Son of God. Somehow Jesus must deal with deadened, hardened human hearts.

Distant hearts (Mark 7:1-23). There was no accusation of malice or willful ignorance implied in Jesus' diagnosis of the disciples' hardened hearts. But when the Pharisees and some of the teachers of the Law came to observe Jesus, Christ diagnosed them as victims of an even more terrible spiritual disease.

These men, who took pride in keeping the Law's most minute detail, noted that Jesus' disciples ate with "unclean" hands. Mark explained for his Gentile readers. They were eating with *ceremonially* unwashed hands.

This ceremonial washing was not part of the Mosaic Law. It was instead an interpretation, an application. But the Pharisees held that such oral traditions had the same force as Scripture itself, and so religiously followed the rite. Hands were dipped in water, then raised so that the water ran down the arms and off the elbows. And this was repeated a prescribed number of times. It was unthinkable for the Pharisee to eat until he had completed the required ablutions.

The Pharisees immediately challenged Jesus. As a Rabbi (a Teacher) with His own disciples (students, followers), Jesus was responsible for their behavior. So in asking why His disciples did not wash, the Pharisees were really attacking Jesus. How could Jesus permit them to abandon the traditions of the elders and violate the oral law to which the Pharisees were committed?

Jesus bluntly called them hypocrites and quoted a passage of Isaiah which He said spoke of them:

These people honor Me with their lips, but their hearts are far from Me. They worship Me in vain; their teachings are but rules taught by men.

Mark 7:6-7

The Pharisees had substituted man-made rules for relationships with God. And their rules actually "set aside" the commands of God!

Jesus illustrated. God commanded everyone to honor father and mother. But one interpretation of a regulation about dedicating possessions to God allowed the individual to technically "give" his possessions to God, while using them throughout his lifetime!

However, since what he possessed was technically dedicated to the Lord, he was released from any obligation to help needy parents financially. But this interpretation, this "tradition of the elders" clearly violated both the letter and intent of one of God's Ten Commandments!

How could "religious" people invent such subterfuges? Only if their hearts were far from God; only if they were using religion for their own purposes rather than acting out of real dedication to the Lord.

Jesus went on to explain. In essence, "clean" and "unclean" aren't concerned with externals at all! It isn't what affects the body that makes a person "unclean." No, "what comes out of a man is what makes

113

him 'unclean.' For from within, out of men's hearts, come evil thoughts, sexual immorality, theft, murder, adultery, greed, malice, deceit, lewdness, envy, slander, arrogance, and folly. All these evils come from inside and make a man 'unclean.' "

The Pharisees, with their exaltation of externals and ignorance of the inner meaning of the Law, demonstrated by the very traditions they held so dear that their own hearts were far from God. The tradition of corban (dedication of property to God) revealed that their hearts were full of greed, deceit, and evil thoughts.

And when Jesus held up the mirror of truth to these men whose hearts were so far from God, they hated Him!

Faith, the key (Mark 7:24-37). The disciples' hearts had been willing, but hardened. The Pharisees' hearts had been unclean, tragically far from God. What can be done to heal such sin-infected hearts?

The answer most Jews of Jesus' time would have given was simply to appeal to the covenant. God had made promises to Abraham, and the Jews of Jesus' day were Abraham's descendants. Thus the Jews believed that, because of their physical descent from Abraham, God owed them! They were His people, weren't they? As long as they kept the Law (as best they could) everything would be all right.

And then Mark told of a meeting with a pagan woman, a Greek, born in the Phoenician (coastal) part of Syria. This woman had no basis for any claim on Jesus. She was not a descendant of Abraham. And yet she came to Christ to beg Him to drive a demon from her daughter.

At first Jesus refused. It wasn't right to take what belonged to the family and toss it to their dogs. The Jews *did* have a special claim on God through the covenant promises He had made!

But the woman answered, "Even the dogs under the table eat the children's crumbs." What the children would not eat, but let fall to the ground, could be eaten by others.

Jesus dismissed her, "You may go; the demon has left your daughter."

And the woman went home to find her daughter healed.

What had happened? The disciples, the crowds, and the Pharisees had seen Jesus' miracles and heard His teaching, and still held back. They would not eat this spiritual food spread so generously on their tables. But this woman had believed! Driven by her need, she came to Jesus and acknowledged Him as "Lord." She knew He could heal and expected Him to be gracious even though she had no claim on His grace.

This, and this alone, is the key.

We must recognize Jesus as Lord. We must come to Him, recognizing that we have no claim on His grace, but expecting Him to be gracious. When we do, Jesus Himself will heal our diseased hearts.

Mark concludes this section with yet another story. Jesus was brought a man who was deaf and could hardly talk. His physical senses were as blocked as the spiritual senses of Israel! Jesus took the man aside and said to his senses, "Be opened." And they were! His senses were functioning at last; he was in touch with the world and able to speak.

How wonderful that this same Jesus changes our hearts, and opens our spiritual senses. Those who come to Him with faith, acknowledging Him to be Lord, will be spiritually healed and made truly well.

📖 *Group Activity: Bible Study Group*
In Scripture the "heart" represents the inner person, and often is set in contrast to superficial or external "religious" activities. Duplicate and distribute the article on "heart" from a Bible dictionary or a text like the Expository Dictionary of Bible Words (Zondervan). After reading and discussing, divide into teams to study Mark 7:1-23, and answer the following questions: "What characterizes the 'heart far from' God? How did that heart find expression in behavior? How does one's approach to religion indicate his or her heart is far from God? How does one's relationships or attitudes toward others indicate the same thing?"

Magazines often have self-tests a person can take to check up on the quality of a marriage, job satisfaction, etc. Together develop a 10- or 15-item "heart check up" quiz a person might take, with a brief scoring guide that explains each item.

The Focus of Faith: Mark 8:1-30

Mark again let events speak for themselves, and marshaled his evidence in logical sequence.

He began by showing us the striking reaction of the people in Jesus' hometown. Christ's teaching and the report of His miracles had stimulated active resentment rather than praise and faith! Why? The story of Herod's relationship with John the Baptist illustrated. Herod knew that John was a "righteous and holy man" (6:20). But Herod had acted against this knowledge and ordered John executed. His belief that John had been sent by God had produced no inner commitment to do the will of God. Belief in Herod had not been transformed into faith.

As for Jesus, He continued to perform compassionate miracles. Those who came and who saw what He did had to believe. But would they respond with faith?

In another cycle of stories Mark noted that even Jesus' disciples struggled with hardened hearts that could not fully grasp the impact of what they saw. The natural hardness of sin-infected hearts made faith's full commitment difficult even for those who loved and followed Jesus. We should not be surprised that it was so difficult for those who witnessed what Jesus did to make life's most significant decision and fully commit themselves to Him.

But for some, more than simple hardness of heart was the problem. For the religious leaders the problem lay in the fact that their hearts were "far from" God! Their religion was an external thing; their traditions were masks for their unwillingness to obey God's commands. And their hearts, as revealed in their traditions and acts, were filled with greed, deceit, arrogance, and a host of other evils.

How different they were from the pagan woman who came to Jesus so humbly and begged His aid. She did not trust in her relationship with Abraham; she had none. She did not mention the Law. She simply came to Jesus, acknowledged Him as Lord, and hoped in His grace.

Now, in a final sequence of stories, Mark brought the issue into clear focus, and taught that we must respond to Jesus with faith.

Another miracle (Mark 8:1-13). Mark reported another familiar miracle. Jesus was followed for three days by crowds who now had nothing to eat. Moved by compassion, He shared His concern with the disciples. They were upset since they were in a remote place. Even if they had the money, where would they get enough bread to feed so many?

Again Jesus multiplied a few loaves and a few small fish, and fed thousands—with basketfuls left over. This miracle again expressed both the power and compassion which marked Jesus clearly as the Son of God.

And Mark tells us that "the Pharisees came. . . . To test Him, they asked Him for a sign from heaven" (v. 11). The word "sign" means "miracle." And Jesus' whole ministry had been marked by miracle after miracle, as these men well knew! Mark said that Jesus sighed deeply. These men had all the evidence they needed, yet they would not believe.

The yeast of the Pharisees (Mark 8:14-21). In a boat with His disciples Jesus warned the Twelve against the "yeast of the Pharisees and that of Herod." The disciples, who had forgotten to bring lunch, misunderstood. Exasperated, Jesus reminded them of His miracles multiplying the bread and fish. "Are your hearts hardened? Do you have eyes but fail to see, and ears but fail to hear? . . . Do you still not understand?"

What was Jesus speaking of? The "yeast" of the Pharisees and of Herod are those heart attitudes which distort and permeate the personality. The externalism of the Pharisees, and the concern for the opinion of others that both they and Herod showed, are enemies of faith. For true faith calls on us to make a full commitment to our God, and to make the choices which please Him.

Beginning to see (Mark 8:22-26). Mark told a significant story. A blind man was brought to Jesus. Jesus spat on the man's eyes and touched him. "Do you see anything?" Jesus asked.

The blind man looked around. "I see people; they look like trees walking around."

Once more Jesus put His hands on the man's eyes. His sight was restored, and then he "saw everything clearly."

How like Jesus' relationship with His disciples! These followers of Jesus did see. It was simply that because of hardened hearts, they did not yet see clearly. But the Pharisees, like Herod, whose hearts were far from God, could not see at all!

Who is Jesus? (Mark 8:27-30) Then came

the final incident, which both ended this section of Mark's Gospel and began the next.

Jesus asked His disciples, "Who do people say I am?" The Twelve reported the views of the crowds. Everyone agreed that Jesus was one of the prophets; they disagreed on which one Christ most closely resembled. Then Jesus asked, "But what about you? Who do you say I am?"

Peter answered for them.

"You are the Christ."

And with this response, Peter focused on the central issue of our faith.

Who is Jesus?

When we, with Peter, have faith that Jesus is the Christ, the Son of God, we have established a personal relationship with God. Like the blind man and like the disciples themselves, we may not see clearly at first. But as we continue to trust Jesus and respond to Him, our hearts will melt, and our vision clear. We will know the truth and do it, for Jesus and Jesus alone can transform the human heart.

GROUP RESOURCE GUIDE

Identification: *Share with others*
On a slip of paper mark one of three symbols that indicate how each feels right now. An arrow pointing up means "I feel close to and committed to Jesus"; an arrow going down means "I feel distant from Jesus and even a little hostile." A "0" means "I feel indifferent just now."

Do not tell the symbol you drew or sign the slip, but put all slips of paper together and set them aside for later.

Exploration: *Probe God's Word*
(1) Together or in teams quickly read the following incidents in Mark 5–8. Beside each put one of the three symbols above, to indicate the current attitude of the person(s) in the situation toward Jesus. The passages to mark are:

6:1-6	Jesus in his hometown
6:7-13	Jesus and the Twelve
6:30-42	Jesus and the hungry crowd
6:45-52	Jesus on the stormy sea
7:1-23	Jesus and the Pharisees
7:24-30	Jesus and the Canaanite woman
7:31-37	Jesus and the deaf/dumb man
8:1-13	Jesus and another hungry crowd
8:14-21	Jesus and insensitive disciples
8:22-26	Jesus and the crowd
8:27-30	Jesus and Peter

(2) In pairs or as a group carefully study the passages beside which you placed an "up" arrow. What characterized the persons who were close and committed to Jesus? From your study, how do you believe a person who feels temporarily indifferent or even antagonistic can move toward a closer and more committed relationship with the Lord? List your suggestions.

Reaction: *Respond together to the Word*
Look now at the slips of paper on which symbols were written when you first gathered. Report how many of each symbol there are. If anyone put a "0" or a "down arrow" on his slip of paper, and is willing to share, have him tell why. Share too which, if any, of the discoveries in the Bible study just completed, seem most likely to help.

Affirmation: *Express love and concern*
Gather around any who shared, lay hands on him or her, and ask God to enrich that life by drawing him or her closer to the Lord.

Adoration: *Worship and pray*
Meditate on the eager desire Jesus showed to come close to lost sinners, in His incarnation, and in His acts of compassion while on earth. With eyes closed, visualize Jesus standing at your side, and thank Him for His presence with you.

TEACHING HIS DISCIPLES

Overview

The key to this section of Mark is the repeated note that Jesus "began to teach" and "was teaching" His disciples. Also, five of the six times in Mark that Jesus' disciples call him "Teacher" are found in Mark 9 and 10.

What was happening *before* the events reported in these chapters? Wasn't Jesus teaching then?

Jesus did teach as He traveled from village to village, healing and casting out demons. But it was the crowds that He was teaching. Often that teaching was in parables. Mark does not report this teaching in detail. But what he does tell us suggests that Jesus' teaching was both about Himself and about life in His kingdom.

In this section there is a significant shift. The ones Jesus taught were the disciples. While He began to teach them about His coming death and resurrection, the focus of His teaching is not how to live in Israel's expected kingdom, but on how to live as His disciples now.

The great value for us in these chapters of Mark is to be found in the fact that, as believers, we too are called to be Christ's disciples. How good to learn more of how to live for Him.

▶ *Disciple*. The Greek word means "pupil" or "learner." In its most intense sense discipleship suggests a total commitment to stay close to and to obey the person chosen as one's teacher.

Commentary

In each of the synoptic Gospels (Matthew, Mark, and Luke) one question Jesus asked His disciples marks a turning point. That question is, "Who do people say I am?" (Mark 8:27: see also Matt. 16:13; Luke 9:18)

The disciples reported what the people were saying, people who had seen Jesus' miracles, listened to His teaching, been restored by His healing power, and eaten of the bread and fishes He had multiplied. Everywhere people were convinced that Jesus was among the greatest of the prophets, and might even be one of the ancients restored to life!

And then the synoptic Gospel writers each tell us that Jesus asked His disciples, "But who do *you* say that I am?"

Peter answered for them all.

"You are the Christ."

What is so significant about this incident is that three Gospels tell us that from this point there was a shift in Jesus' ministry. Only then did Jesus begin to teach His disciples about His coming death. In fact, from this point on Jesus focused His ministry more and more on instructing the Twelve.

Why? Because these men acknowledged Jesus for who He is: the Christ, the Son of God. The compliments of the crowds who linked Jesus with the greatest of Old Testament saints fell far short, for they failed to acknowledge Him for who He is. Those compliments in fact constituted a *rejection* of Jesus, a damning with faint praise.

There is no way that people who will not *believe* in Jesus can really profit from His instruction. Without the personal relationship with God which is established by faith, what a person *does* is completely irrelevant. It is only as we believe *and* obey that Jesus can fill our lives with newness. It is only faith *and* obedience that can transform.

And so Jesus now turned to instruct the little core of men who did believe, as you and I believe, how to live as disciples and so to please our God.

Life Through Death: Mark 8:31–9:13

Jesus' coming death (Mark 8:31-33). Matthew, Mark, and Luke agree. As soon as

117

Peter expressed the disciples' conviction that Jesus truly is the Christ, Jesus began to "teach them that the Son of man must suffer many things and be rejected by the elders, chief priests, and teachers of the Law, and that He must be killed and after three days rise again."

This blunt, clear teaching upset the disciples. They didn't want Jesus to die. Peter even took Jesus aside and began to "rebuke" Him!

Christ spoke sharply. "Out of My sight, Satan," Jesus said. And He added, "You do not have in mind the things of God, but the things of men."

This last phrase is especially important. What seems right and reasonable to human beings is often totally out of harmony with God's ways. We must learn to trust the wisdom of God, even when it seems to go against all that seems wise or best to us.

Choosing "death" (Mark 8:34-38). Jesus immediately applied what He had said to discipleship. God had determined Jesus' own death on the cross. Through that death will come new life for Jesus (He will "after three days rise again") and also new life for those who believe in Jesus. But God had also determined that the way for disciples to *experience* that new life was through a self-denial like Jesus' own!

He told the Twelve that if they were to "come after Me," they must also deny self, take up their cross, and follow Jesus.

The disciple's cross is the choice of God's will for the individual, even as Jesus' cross was God's will for Him. Self-denial is a rejection of human wisdom and desires that may conflict with God's will. And "following" Jesus is staying close to Him, living in intimate daily relationship, by adopting His own commitment to please God.

What hinges on this kind of discipleship? Jesus said that the person who rejected discipleship and held on to his (old) life will lose it, while the person who loses his (old) life will save it.

While this may seem complicated, the point is simple and vital. A person who rejects discipleship will never know what he or she might have become if his or her life had been turned over to Jesus. Only if we commit ourselves fully to Him, and make the disciples' daily choice of obedience, can we discover the new life relationship which Jesus makes possible for us!

Glory follows (Mark 9:1-13). Again the sequence of events is important. Jesus had just told the disciples of His coming death and resurrection, and pointed out that the disciples too could be transformed if they would only give up their old lives for Him. Then Jesus told them, "I tell you the truth, some who are standing here will not taste death before they see the kingdom of God coming with power" (v. 1).

While many have puzzled over the meaning of this saying, in each Gospel it is followed by a report of Jesus' visit six days later to the Mount of Transfiguration. There, with Peter and James and John watching (note just *some* who are standing here"), Jesus "was transfigured before them. His clothes became dazzling white, whiter than anyone in the world could bleach them" (vv. 2-3).

The glory that lay ahead for Jesus, a glory to be visible to all when "the kingdom of God come[s] with power," was shown to the three disciples.

The Bible tells us that Elijah and Moses appeared and talked with Jesus, while a voice from heaven said, "This is My Son, whom I love. Listen to Him."

The disciples were given a glimpse of the splendor to come after the Cross. Death truly was the pathway to glory.

The incident was intended not only to reassure the disciples. It is intended to reassure you and me as well. The daily cross of the disciple is hard to bear. Often we will be called on to make choices that seem to us to involve great cost. What we need to remember is that beyond each cross God calls on us to bear, and beyond the little death that obedience may seem to involve, lies the splendor of transformation. Just as Jesus' cross was the pathway to glory, so obedience is the pathway to transformation for you and for me.

The disciples did not yet understand the meaning of what they had seen. They had not even grasped the fact that Jesus would be crucified, and they discussed what "rising from the dead" might mean. But rather than asking Jesus, they moved to safer ground, and raised a theological question: "Why do the teachers of the Law say that Elijah must come first?"

Theological questions and discussion surely are not wrong. But what is most important is in simple faith to take heed to the words that were heard on that mountain. "This is My Son, whom I love. Listen to Him."

If we simply listen to Jesus, and do what He says, our lives will be transformed.

✂ *Group Activity: Recovery Group Steps 6 (be ready to have God remove character defects) and 7 (humbly ask God to remove shortcomings)*
Use crayons to represent, through color and image, a picture of the "ideal person"—someone who is truly beautiful, the person you would like to be. Each color and shape should have meaning to you, though you need not draw an actual person.

Then show and explain your picture to others in your group, and listen as they explain their pictures.

Together read Mark 8:31–9:8. Note that Jesus' death was followed by transformation. Mark 8:34-35 teaches that by "dying" to our old passions and desires, and choosing to follow Jesus, we can be transformed too.

Discuss: What would I be willing to do to become the ideal person I drew? Are there any truly good reasons for not surrendering my will and choosing to follow Jesus? If you have made this decision, share your experience in making that choice and what has happened since, to encourage others.

Pathways to Power: Mark 9:14-50
Jesus then went on to instruct His disciples in the kind of life they would be expected to live. Mark reported just a few of Jesus' teachings, giving us brief and pithy accounts of His sayings. Yet each is distinctively helpful as we try to live our own Christian lives in the twentieth-century world.

Prayer (Mark 9:14-32). When Jesus and the three came down from the Mount of Transfiguration, they found milling, shouting crowds. The disciples and some teachers of the Law were arguing loudly, while people in the crowd shouted out their comments. But when they saw Jesus all ran to greet Him.

Quickly the story came out. The disciples had been asked to cast an evil spirit from a child, but were unable to. When the child was brought to Jesus, the spirit saw Him and "immediately threw the boy into a convulsion."

The father begged, "If You can do anything, take pity on us and help us."

Jesus fastened immediately on the first phrase.

" 'If You can'?"

Hadn't Jesus been teaching and healing literally for years in Galilee? Could there be any doubt?

The answer was, of course there was doubt! People had witnessed what Jesus did but would not commit themselves fully to Him. The man's response to Jesus' statement that "everything is possible for him who believes" was certainly true of the majority in Israel. "I do believe; help me overcome my unbelief."

There was faith, but it was mixed with an unbelief that needed to be overcome.

Jesus rebuked the evil spirit, which shrieked, violently convulsed the child, and left him. Jesus took the near-dead child by the hand and lifted him to his feet.

Perhaps the first lesson for us in this story is that God does not demand perfect faith in people. We *do* believe. But we still need help for our unbelief. Jesus accepts even imperfect faith and generously works His miracles in our lives. As we continue to grow in our relationships with Him, He does indeed "help our unbelief," gradually replacing it with a more perfect trust in Him.

But there is another lesson as well. The disciples who had been unable to help were troubled by their powerlessness. Afterward they asked Jesus privately, "Why couldn't we drive it out?"

Jesus answered, "This kind can come out only by prayer."

For the challenges of our lives as Jesus' disciples we must rely, not on our own strength, but completely on God's. And we express that dependence most perfectly in prayer.

Servanthood (Mark 9:33-37). On the road to Capernaum Jesus' disciples had been arguing about which would be greatest. Christ called the Twelve together and said, "If anyone wants to be first, he must be the very last, and the servant of all."

Greatness is not to be found in self-exaltation, but in self-humbling. Spiritual significance is not won by concern for oneself, but by concern for others. It is only as we give that we receive God's praise.

When Jesus told the disciples to welcome

119

the little children in His name, He illustrated the nature of servanthood. In the Roman world, the "little child" was placed under the authority of slaves. They might be loved, but were of little account until they reached their maturity. But to Jesus, the least important in society were valuable indeed.

In our servanthood, we value the least of men, not just those whom the world considers important.

Nonjudgmentalism (Mark 9:38-41). When the disciples saw a person they did not know driving out demons in Jesus' name, they told him to stop! After all, weren't *they* Jesus' disciples? What right did anyone else have to use His name?

Christ rebuked them, pointing out that no one who does good in Jesus' name one moment can speak against Jesus the next. Even a person who does the simplest good in Jesus' name will be rewarded.

How often through church history Christ's people have forgotten these words to disciples. We are not to condemn others who act in Jesus' name just because they are not part of our group, or our church. Those who act in the name of Jesus are with us, even if they are not of us.

Harmony (Mark 9:42-50). Jesus warned that disciples must do nothing to cause "one of these little ones who believe in Me to sin." In a series of strong statements, Jesus emphasized how terrible sin is. The imagery of cutting off the hand that causes sin, etc., is not meant literally but instead emphasizes the necessity of a decisive rejection of sin.

Disciples are to be "salt," a preservative. If the disciple does not live in harmony with Jesus and with others, but sins or causes others to sin, the disciple will be worthless as salt, and unable to fulfill his or her function.

Sin, in ourselves or in others, is serious. It shatters the harmony that is to exist between us and God, and within the Christian community.

How, then, does Jesus instruct His followers to live as disciples? They, and we, are to live a life of prayer and of servanthood. We are to live with our fellow believers in a nonjudgmental way, a way that promotes harmony by personally rejecting temptations to sin, and being careful not to cause brothers and sisters to sin either.

※ *Group Activity:*
Singles/Single Again Group
Relate some of the things you have done to try to find friends, and tell how they turned out.

Then study Mark 9:33-50 to develop a strategy on how to make rather than find friends. Examine the attitude reflected in each of these passages, and discuss how you can display each in relationships that you currently have.

Mark 9:33-37	*Servanthood*
Mark 9:36-41	*Nonjudgmentalism*
Mark 9:42-50	*Sensitivity*

Threats to Discipleship: Mark 10:1-52

Jesus had shown His followers several keys to living as disciples. Now in a series of incidents that Mark linked together, Christ warned against pathways that have attracted the religious of all the ages. Jesus' disciples, today as then, must be careful not to fall into these spiritual traps.

Legalism (Mark 10:1-16). Again Jesus was met and questioned by some Pharisees. As always, they raised a legal question to "test" Jesus. There is one Greek word that suggests a "test" which is administered from a desire to prove the genuineness of the article tested. That word is *not* used here. The Pharisees did not wish to approve Jesus; they wished to discredit Him.

Each of the Gospel writers reports words of Jesus on marriage. He must have spoken of it often. So when the Pharisees raised the question again to "test" Christ, we can assume that they already knew His position.

Their question: "Is it lawful for a man to divorce his wife?"

This was intended as a trap. If Jesus said no, He would seem to speak against the Law of Moses. If He said yes, He would apparently contradict His own often-expressed commitment to a permanent relationship.

Jesus answered by referring to the Law in which they claimed to trust. "What did Moses command you?"

And they spoke of the "certificate of divorce" that the Mosaic Law permitted.

Jesus' response showed a totally different perspective on the Law than was held by the Pharisees. The Pharisees held that the Law was "the" standard of perfection. They believed God had given that perfect standard to mark out the way of salvation. And they also believed that they, by their zealous effort to keep the Law, would win His approval.

Jesus had a different perspective. He explained, "It was because your hearts were hard that Moses wrote you this law." Look back to Creation, Jesus taught, and you will see God's intention. Marriage is to be a lifelong commitment.

The reference to hard hearts is a reference to sin. It was only because sin warped and distorted this most intimate of relationships that Moses permitted divorce. God was willing to *lower* His standards, to provide imperfect human beings with a way to escape a destructive marriage. Divorce law, then, *proved that Law itself was not the ideal standard the Pharisees thought it to be!* In fact, Law involved a *lowering* of God's standards, permitting men who fell far short of His true ideal to continue in fellowship with Him.

What Law does is to show how far short we fall of the divine ideal, and reveal our need for salvation (cf. Rom. 3:19-20). The Pharisees' assumption that one could be saved by works of the Law, or even win God's approval by legalistic dedication, was completely wrong!

Later the disciples asked about the incident. His answer again focused on the heart, and suggested that the law on divorce was being used simply to change an older mate for a younger one. Anyone who divorces and remarries commits adultery. It is not conformity to the letter of the law, but intent, that God judges.

How careful we must be not to let our living relationships with Jesus be translated into frozen rules that ignore the motives of our hearts and are insensitive to the true desires for our God. And how very careful we must be not to legalistically "test" our brothers as the Pharisees constantly tried to test Jesus, not to approve but to discredit Him.

This sequence ends with another story. People were bringing little children to Jesus. The disciples objected, and tried to send the parents away. But Jesus indignantly commanded them to "let the little children come to Me, and do not hinder them, for the kingdom of God belongs to such as these." He went on to add that "anyone who will not receive the kingdom of God like a little child will never enter it."

What did Jesus mean? In Judaism a "little child" was not considered to be under the Law. Not until one's thirteenth birthday was a person old enough to begin to relate to God through the Law. To receive the kingdom like a "little child" meant to reject Law as a way of entering God's kingdom, and to rely instead as children did on the love and grace of the God who had made great promises to His people.

Humanism (Mark 10:17-34). The "rich young man" who came to Jesus addressed Him as "good Teacher" and asked what he must "do" to inherit eternal life. These provide the key to understanding the next danger to the disciple: humanism.

Jesus immediately challenged the young man's assumptions. Why did he call Jesus "good" and add a merely human title? Didn't he realize that only God is truly "good"?

This is, of course, the key error of humanism. It seeks goodness in human motives and actions, without realizing that only God is good.

To help the young man discover his error for himself, Jesus asked about the commands listed on the second tablet of the Law.

When Moses brought God's Ten Commands down from Mount Sinai, they were written on two stone tablets. The first tablet contained commands that related to loving God. The second tablet contained commands related to loving other human beings. Now Jesus quoted only from the second tablet as He spoke of the commands not to murder, commit adultery, steal, give false testimony, or defraud, and to honor mother and father. This, the young man said, he had done since he was a boy.

This young man was not lying. He *had* been a truly good person. "Jesus looked at him and loved him."

But then Jesus spoke of a great lack. And He told the young man to sell everything, give it to the poor, and then follow Jesus.

The young man's face fell, and he went away sad "because he had great wealth."

What happened here? This young man who represented the best humanism has to offer — a truly "good" (by human standards) person — had related correctly to his fellowmen. But the very first commandment says, "You shall have no other gods before Me" (cf. Ex. 20:3). Jesus' instructions to sell all was a vivid demonstration that this lovely young man, so sensitive in his dealings with others, actually did have another god before God: his money. When the Son of God commanded him to sell his possessions, he made his choice—money.

How hard it was for this rich young man to give God His proper place. Humanistic good—an honest consideration of other people—is not really costly. But putting God first may demand our everything!

The disciples again misunderstood. When Jesus remarked on how hard it is for the rich to enter His kingdom, the disciples were stunned. Surely wealth was a sign of God's approval! If the wealthy found it difficult, who then could be saved?

Jesus answered, "With man this is impossible." No matter how kind and considerate the humanist may be, mere human goodness can never win entrance to God's kingdom. But, "All things are possible with God" (Mark 10:27). In Jesus Himself God has made a way for His lost ones to return.

Still the disciples misunderstood. Fascinated with riches, Peter wondered aloud. "We have left everything to follow You!" Jesus nodded and made Peter, and you and me a promise. In abandoning everything we will without fail receive "a hundred times as much in this present age." In Christ we become the possessors of all things. But many who seem "first" in this life will be last in God's kingdom, and those whom men account "last" will be first.

Authoritarianism (Mark 10:35-45). The third danger to discipleship is the desire for the wrong kind of authority within the believing community. James and John were eager for positions of power in Jesus' coming kingdom. Jesus warned them that one who sought position in His kingdom must be ready to drink from Christ's cup and to be baptized with His baptism. In this He spoke of complete dedication to God's will, and the suffering that this might entail.

Jesus warned them, however, to abandon the notion of "authority" as it was understood in the secular world. There the rulers "lord it over" others and "exercise authority over them." It is not to be this way in Jesus'

kingdom. The person who is great is the one who gives himself to serve others, even as Jesus came to serve and to give His life (vv. 43-44).

There is to be no hierarchy in the church! The greatest is the lowest: the one who dedicates himself not to be served by those to whom he gives orders, but to give service that they might become all that God wants them to be.

⊘ *Group Activity:*
Missions/Outreach Group
Two incidents in Matthew 10 illustrate attitudes that keep a person from responding to Jesus' offer of salvation. The first (Mark 10:1-15) deals with legalism. The second (Mark 10:17-34) deals with humanism.

Analyze each incident as follows:
(1) Define the hindering attitude.
(2) Describe how it shapes an individual's approach to religion/salvation.
(3) Distinguish carefully how Jesus dealt with it.

When each of these steps has been thoroughly carried out, list individually persons you know whose response to Jesus is hindered by legalism, and those hindered by humanism.

Describe each person to the others in your group, and talk about your relationship with him or her. Based on insights gained from the Bible study, the group will brainstorm ways you might approach witnessing to him or her.

The blind see (Mark 10:46-52). Again Mark closed a section with report of a miracle. But what a special miracle. A blind man was given his sight, and was told, "Your faith has healed you."

It is the same with us. Jesus gives us the spiritual sight to see the emptiness in legalism, the futility of mere humanism, and the error of hierarchialism. What is it that truly can heal the disciple and lead him along the pathway of power? Jesus answers us in His words to the blind who now can see. "Go, your faith has healed you." And as with Bartimaeus, "immediately he received his sight and followed Jesus along the road."

GROUP RESOURCE GUIDE

Identification: *Share with others*
Draw your "ideal person," as described in the group activity on page 119. Share the picture with others and explain it.

Affirmation: *Express love and concern*
Whenever you can, give the person sharing his or her picture feedback on ways you see elements of the "ideal" growing in him or her. Be brief and be specific. Describe things he or she has said or done that reflect traits portrayed in the picture.

Exploration: *Probe God's Word*
(1) Have one group member prepared to give a 5-minute overview of the relationship between death and transformation developed in the commentary. He or she should stress the importance of choosing to reject the old self, and following Jesus to become the transformed, "ideal" person we are intended to be in Christ. (2) On a chalkboard or large sheet of newsprint draw a T-shaped chart. Title the left top "Helps" and the right top "Hindrances." Under these titles list:

Helps	Hindrances
Prayer (9:14-29)	Legalism (10:1-16)
Nonjudgmentalism (9:38-41)	Humanism (10:17-34)
Harmony (9:42-50)	Authoritarianism (10:35-45)

Group members divide into teams to explore either helps or hindrances to transformation.

Reaction: *Respond together to the Word*
Teams can report on insights gained from helps or hindrances to transformation. Each team member should share one opportunity he or she has to take a positive step, or one situation he or she faces that contains an obstacle to transformation he or she needs to avoid.

Adoration: *Worship and pray*
Meditate briefly on Mark 10:51-52. Then pray, asking God to open your eyes to both transformation opportunities and obstacles you will face this coming week.

THE LAST WEEK

Overview

As the last week of Jesus' life on earth begins, Mark brings three distinct themes into focus.

In Mark 11 we gain insight into the mission of the Messiah. On Palm Sunday Jesus was hailed as the Promised One. He cleansed the temple, signifying His ministry of purifying religion. He cursed the fruitless fig tree, which symbolized a ritualistic Israel, and explained the power of personal faith.

In Mark 12 we see the futility of Israel's approach to faith explained in great detail. Jesus showed us by contrast how living by faith can please God.

In Mark 13 we have the only prophetic section in this Gospel. Jesus spoke of the end of the age. No one knows just when the events He spoke of will happen. So we are to be on guard, always attending to our assigned task as we expect Christ's imminent return.

There are many familiar stories in these chapters of Mark's Gospel. And there is much to learn from each, as well as from the way Mark linked them to demonstrate his larger themes.

▶ *Pharisees, Sadducees*. You can find background information on these two religious groups of Jesus' time in the introduction to the Gospels, Study Guide 79.

■ See the *Bible Knowledge Commentary* pages 155-173, for a verse-by-verse commentary on each incident.

Commentary

The scene now shifts to Judea. It was the last week of Christ's life, and Jesus now appeared in Jerusalem. This is the traditional center of Old Testament faith. But it is also the center of the corruption of that faith. In a series of incidents and confrontations Jesus demonstrated how the pure religion of the Old Testament had been corrupted, and in those confrontations helps us better understand the relationship that you and I today are to maintain with our God.

The Messiah's Mission: Mark 11:1-26

Triumphal Entry (Mark 11:1-11). Jesus told His disciples where to obtain a colt on which He would enter Jerusalem. Mark did not refer to it, but this fulfilled Zechariah's prophecy that He who is King of Israel will enter in just this way (Zech. 9:9). Jesus now presented Himself in Jerusalem as the promised Messiah.

As Jesus moved slowly toward the city gate, the crowds waved branches and shouted praises. They recognized Him as Messiah: "He who comes in the name of the Lord" (Mark 11:9).

When Jesus entered Jerusalem He went directly to the temple. He did not go to the Fortress Antonia or to Herod's palace. Secular power was not the concern of the Messiah of Israel at this time.

Jesus' choice of the temple established immediately that His first concern was religious. The focus of Jesus' concern was the faith of Israel as a people of God, not the fate of Israel as a nation.

Jesus "looked around at everything." After making this evaluation Jesus left. But He would return the next day.

Cleansing the temple (Mark 11:12-26). On the way back to Jerusalem the next day Jesus saw a luxuriant-looking fig tree. But the tree had only leaves and not fruit. Jesus cursed the tree: "May no one ever eat fruit from you again." He then passed on into the city.

Entering the temple area (its outer courts), Jesus "began driving out those who were buying and selling there." After He had overturned tables and chased out the merchants, Jesus taught, quoting the Old Testament:

My house will be called a house of prayer for all nations.

Mark 11:17

The religious leaders of Judah had made God's house a "den of robbers."

The two incidents are intimately linked. The fig tree represented Israel. Often in the Old Testament the image of a vine or tree is used to represent God's people. In these images God spoke of the fruit which He expected His planting to produce. In Isaiah 5:7 we read that the fruit He desired from the house of Israel, the "garden of His delight," was justice and righteousness.

But like the fig tree, Israel had produced no fruit! Therefore like the fig tree the nation would be cursed, and no one would "ever eat fruit from you again."

But why the link of this incident with the temple which Jesus looked over, and where He returned to drive out merchants? Because in the Judaism of Jesus' day, as in much of Old Testament history, the temple and its ritual were assumed by the Jews to provide special standing with God. The people could do anything they wanted in the temple—even robbing the poor in its very courts by forcing them to buy "approved" animals for sacrifice at inflated prices. They trusted in ritual, unaware that God was unimpressed with great edifices and cared only for hearts tuned to love Him and one another.

The next morning the fig tree had withered away. Its deadness was now exposed, even as Jesus was about to expose the deadness of Israel's religion.

Jesus told the disciples the truth. The true power of religion is not found in buildings or ritual, but in a personal relationship with God which is expressed in faith. The person who trusts God completely can move mountains! We are to pray, believing. We can be sure as we focus our trust in God that we will receive what we ask.

But there is a horizontal aspect to faith as well as a vertical. We are to forgive anyone we have something against when we stand praying. The true religion Jesus the Messiah promotes calls for both love for God and love for our fellowmen.

✂ *Group Activity: Recovery Group*
Steps 4 (make a moral inventory) and

5 (admit wrongs to God, myself, and others)

Mark 11:1-11 is about the Triumphal Entry of Jesus into Jerusalem. It describes how excited and happy the crowds were to welcome Him—perhaps like you when you took steps 2 and 3 and decided to turn your life and will over to the care of God.

But Mark 11:15-17 tells us Jesus went into the temple and began to cleanse it from things that were sinful and wrong! The leaders reacted with fear and furious anger. This is not surprising. When we are asked to take a moral inventory and fearlessly identify where we have done wrong, we too tend to be defensive. We blame others, we deny what we know to be true, we lie, we try to intimidate others, we rationalize our behavior. But Jesus must cleanse our inner selves—our "temple"—if He is to transform us.

So list specific examples of how you have avoided taking responsibility for your behavior. For instance, "Said that I cursed at my sister because she cursed me first." Make a list of at least 10 items.

When done, pray and admit each of these actions to God. Then tell the group at least five of the incidents you reported.

But don't stop now! Take another inventory, and list specific examples of ways you have accepted responsibility for your actions. For instance, "Admitted to my boss that I just overslept."

Share several of the positives as well. Remember that recovery calls for accepting responsibility—and that as God works in your life you will become increasingly honest and real with God, yourself, and others.

Israel's Futile Faith: Mark 11:27–12:44
Mark had established in his first two stories about Jesus' acts in Judea a theme he then developed. How can it be that Israel's faith, rooted in God's Old Testament revelation, had become futile and empty? What was it that had distorted in practice the beauty of the faith God Himself revealed?

Empty of authority (Mark 11:27-33). The "chief priests, the teachers of the Law, and the elders" composed the ruling council of Israel. This group had the power to judge both religious and civil matters in the Jewish community. They even claimed, and exercised, the right to expel people from the synagogue (cf. John 9:22; 12:42).

Since these leaders of the community had never commissioned or recognized Jesus, they liked to think that He spoke without any real religious authority. This, despite the fact that the people were amazed just because Jesus *did* speak as a Man with authority, unlike their official leaders (cf. Mark 1:22).

Now, after Jesus had driven the money changers from the temple, a delegation of leaders challenged Jesus. By what authority was He acting? And who gave Him authority to do what He did?

Jesus asked them one question that exposed how empty of "authority" these so-called spiritual leaders really were. Jesus asked them whether John's baptism was from heaven or from men.

Now, a person who has spiritual authority must derive it ultimately from God. So one who exercises authority must refer to God and God's will in making his decisions. But when these religious leaders discussed Jesus' question, they immediately referred not to God but to the people. "If we say, 'From men.'. . ." The text notes, "They feared the people, for everyone held that John really was a prophet."

Ultimately, they who claimed to be the final court of spiritual appeal, answered Jesus, "We don't know."

No religion which appeals to mere human opinion in making its determinations can have real authority or power. The faith of Israel in Jesus' day was futile because it had exchanged the authority of God and His Word for mere human opinion!

No religion which looks to public opinion to determine its stand can ever be vital and real.

Misuse of authority (Mark 12:1-12). Jesus then told a parable about a person who prepared the land and planted a vineyard. He rented it out to some tenant farmers, and left on a trip. But when he sent servants to collect his share, the servants were beaten and some were even killed. Finally the man sent his only son, saying, "They will respect my son."

Instead the tenants chose to kill the heir, so "the inheritance will be ours."

The leaders realized that Jesus had spoken the parable against them, and were even more determined to arrest Him. They had not used their authority as God's

agents to serve Him at all! They had misused their authority, seeking only their own benefit. Their fathers had been willing to kill God's servants, the prophets, and now this generation was eager to kill His only Son!

Hypocrisy (Mark 12:13-17). The fact that the religion of Israel was now marked by hypocrisy is demonstrated in the next incident.

The Pharisees and Herodians came to try to trap Jesus. The Herodians were a political party that believed in accommodation with the Romans. To them Jesus seemed a dangerous revolutionary. Both these groups, usually opposed to each other, feared Jesus and hated Him passionately.

When they came to Jesus their hypocrisy was made plain in multiple ways. They addressed Jesus as a "man of integrity" who teaches "the way of God in accordance with the truth." They did not believe what they were saying; they said it only to "set Jesus up" for their trap.

They asked Jesus whether or not the Jews should pay taxes to Caesar. The trap was simple. If Jesus told them to pay taxes, He would lose favor with the people who hated Rome. If Jesus told them *not* to pay taxes, He could be accused to the Romans, and would be executed!

Yet this trap was itself a hypocritical one. It was shown to be even more hypocritical when Jesus had to ask *them* for a coin! Here these men were trying to trap Jesus and accuse Him of collaboration with the enemy, and they were the ones who were profiting financially from the Roman occupation, for they were the ones who possessed Roman money!

Jesus avoided their trap by pointing to the portrait and inscription on the coin. These were Caesar's? Then let Caesar have what belonged to him, and give God what belongs to God.

What is it that belongs to the Caesars of this world? Only material things: things that have no lasting value and cannot really reflect the issues of life. And what belongs to God? Our heart, our soul, our love, our obedience, our whole being.

Let Caesar have his *things*, but give God your heart.

The religion of Jesus' day was empty and meaningless because it was all hypocrisy and show. The men who led His people were not moved by a passion for God.

Without understanding of Scripture (Mark 12:18-27). Now the Sadducees — the "liberals" of Jesus' day, who denied the resurrection and life after death, along with angels and miracles — tried to trap Jesus. They raised a hypothetical case. Here's a widow who has been married, in turn, to each of seven brothers. "At the resurrection," they asked (subtly ridiculing this doctrine in which they did not believe), "whose wife will she be?"

Jesus' answer affirmed the authority of Scripture. Their error arose from the fact that "you do not know the Scriptures or the power of God." Jesus explained that there is no marriage in heaven: the saints there, like the angels, will not wed. But as for resurrection, Jesus pinned His teaching on the tense of a verb. God said to Moses, "I *am* the God of Abraham, the God of Isaac, and the God of Jacob." God did not say, "I *was*" their God! Obviously then Abraham, Isaac, and Jacob must be living when God spoke those words, even though they had died physically centuries before.

What a tremendous confidence we can have in Scripture! Even the tenses of words are rooted in reality, and one can trust each phrase to express divine truth.

The Sadducees, like the liberals of every age, were quick to discount the authority of the Word of God. And just because of this fault, they and their religion were "badly mistaken."

Without focus (Mark 12:28-37). There was another fault in the ritual religion practiced by the Jews in Jesus' day. They cluttered up their faith with hundreds of rules derived from traditional interpretations of biblical Laws. But somehow all these laws seemed just as important as all the others. Don't spit on sand on the Sabbath (because you might inadvertently "plow a furrow") was treated with the same importance as "love your neighbor."

When one of the teachers of the Law saw that Jesus was answering well, he raised what to Him was an honest question. "Of all the commandments, which is the most important?"

Jesus answered, " 'Love the Lord your God with all your heart and with all your soul and with all your mind and with all your strength.' The second is this: 'Love your neighbor as yourself.' There is no commandment greater than these."

With this answer Jesus provided the focus for faith which Israel had lost. All of the laws which were so important to the Jews, all the ceremonies and rituals, must be placed in perspective by the realization that man's central duty is to love God and to love neighbors.

The man affirmed what Jesus had said. "To love [God] with all your heart . . . and to love your neighbor as yourself is more important than all burnt offerings and sacrifices" (v. 33).

Jesus said to him, "You are not far from the kingdom of God."

Only when the focus of our faith is squarely on loving God and our neighbor do we even approach the kingdom of our God. Israel's faith was futile because in the preoccupation of the religious with ritual and ceremony and tradition, the true heart of God's revelation of Himself in Law had been totally missed.

The total inability of the religious leaders to understand the Scriptures or its focus is now illustrated by Jesus. The teachers of the Law say that Christ is the Son (descendant) of David. This is clearly true. But how do they explain David speaking of his descendant as "my Lord?"

The crowd was delighted, not because they knew the answer, but because Jesus had shown up the hypocrisy and spiritual fraud of those proud men who claimed to be so much better than common men.

Greed (Mark 10:38-44). The final condemnation drew attention to the true motives of the religious leaders of Israel. These men who loved to be treated with respect because of their superior piety actually "devour widows' houses and for a show make lengthy prayers." They were outwardly religious, but within were moved only by greed.

Jesus and His disciples sat down to watch worshipers contribute money to the temple treasury. Some who were wealthy "threw in" large amounts. The sound of the heavy coins told everyone how much they were giving, and they threw in their offerings with force to make sure all could hear. They were outwardly religious.

But then a widow timidly "put in" two tiny coins, almost worthless. Jesus pointed her out, and said, "This poor widow has put more into the treasury than all the others. They all gave out of their wealth; but she, out of her poverty, put in everything—all she had to live on."

What a difference. The size of the gift the rich could give might impress men. But what they gave was really nothing to them: it cost them not one moment of discomfort. It was no sacrifice at all. But the gift of the widow impressed God. She gave all.

A religion practiced by greedy men who get their wealth by oppressing the poor is a meaningless faith, no matter how much they may "give" to God. What God wants is our love, for out of love we will be willing to give Him not a "tip," but our all.

The End of the Age: Mark 13

This chapter contains Mark's longest report of any connected discourse by Jesus. It closely parallels the report in Matthew 24 and 25.

Jesus warned of terrible tragedies which will be part of human experience while He is away. Finally there will come events foretold in the Book of Daniel and by other Old Testament prophets (Mark 13:14-32). As the end nears there will be "days of distress unequaled from the beginning when God created the world, until now" (v. 19).

That day will close with "the Son of man coming in clouds with great power and glory" (v. 26).

Jesus concluded His predictions about the future with the statement, "This generation will certainly not pass away until all these things have happened" (v. 30). Since that generation is long dead, what could Jesus have meant?

The term translated "generation" here can mean those currently living. But it also can mean a family or national *line*. Jesus had begun His discourse by predicting the destruction of the temple in which the Jews took such pride. Within the lifespan of the generation then living, the temple Herod had spent 40 years beautifying and expanding was destroyed completely. It was destroyed by the Romans in A.D. 70 in response to yet another Jewish rebellion. The generation that had heard Jesus teach and witnessed His miracles—and had rejected the Son of God—lived to see their city razed and their temple destroyed.

What happened to the Jewish people then? For thousands of years they were scattered throughout the world, with no homeland to call their own. And yet they survived. And they maintained their separate identity. That "generation," as represented in the Jewish people (the family and national line) "will certainly not pass away" until *all* the things Jesus spoke of actually take place.

But what about those who believe in Jesus during the interim? Jesus gives His followers this warning: "Be on guard! Be alert!" No one knows when the Lord will come, so each of us must be alert and about his assigned task.

And what, then, must we be alert for? Why, we must be alert that the very things which crept into the religion of Israel and sapped it of its vitality do not slip into the practice of our faith!

How good it is to know that, until Jesus does return, you and I can worship Him, with others, in Spirit and in truth.

GROUP RESOURCE GUIDE

Identification: *Share with others*
Imagine a sharply angled, peaked roof, sort of like an inverted "V." Briefly share whether you see your spiritual journey just now as climbing up or sliding down. After going around the group, discuss: Which is easier, going up or sliding down? Why?

Exploration: *Probe God's Word*
Mark 11 and 12 describe the causes of Israel's failure of faith. Several incidents here pinpoint reasons for a spiritual slide.

Look together at and discuss each of the following, and privately jot down your ideas about how to stop the spiritual slide each passage describes.

The passages to look at are:

11:27-33	Wrongly claiming authority
12:1-12	Misusing authority
12:13-17	Hypocrisy
12:18-27	Misunderstanding Scripture
12:28-37	Lack of priorities
12:38-44	Greed/materialism

Reaction: *Respond together to the Word*
After each passage has been explored, go back and share the suggestions you wrote down as to how to stop the spiritual slide reflected in each passage.

Affirmation: *Express love and caring*
If you indicated your spiritual journey seems downward just now rather than up, share how you are feeling and any insights you may have gained from this study. Let the group members then gather round and pray for you. You join in similar prayers as others also share.

Adoration: *Worship and pray*
Use Mark 13:26-37 as a responsive reading. Thank the Lord for the privilege of being on watch till he comes, and that we can stop every spiritual slide, and keep on growing in Him.

JESUS' DEATH AND RESURRECTION

Overview

Each of the Gospel writers gives us much detail about the last evening Jesus spent with His disciples, and about the trials which led up to His execution. Yet few Christians are aware of the exact sequence of events, or of their locations. In this study, the events reported by Mark and the other Gospel writers are located for you and your group members on a large map which you can duplicate for them to have.

In this *Small Group Member's Commentary* each Gospel's report of Jesus' death and resurrection is given a slightly different treatment, designed to reflect the emphasis of the Gospel.

In the study of Matthew, we explore the meaning of Christ's death as a sacrifice for sins. In that study we answer the theologian's question, "Why did God become man?"

In this study of Mark's Gospel we emphasize the sequence of the events on the day Christ died.

In the study of Luke's Gospel we focus on evidence that, throughout the experience, Jesus remained in control. He *gave* His life; it was not taken.

In the study of John's Gospel we examine Christ's instructions to His disciples at the Last Supper, and the striking confrontation Jesus had with Pilate, the Roman governor.

Through each of these studies we come to appreciate more the suffering of Christ, and sense more of the love He showed to you and me at Calvary.

Commentary

The events associated with Jesus' trials and death took place in and around Jerusalem. While there is debate concerning some of the specific locations, such as the location of Joseph's tomb, we have a great deal of information on the specific places Jesus traveled to on that fateful night.

Jerusalem in the time of Jesus was a typical walled city. The "lower city," built along a steep hillside, was filled with crowded tenement-type structures. The upper city contained the larger city homes of the wealthy, like Caiaphas, the high priest and the beautiful palace of Herod.

It was the temple, however, which dominated the city, and was the focus of the faith of all Jews in every land. Immediately next to the temple was the Fortress Antonia, where a Roman army contingent was stationed and Pontius Pilate held court. Directly across from the temple, separated from it by the deep Kidron Valley, and up on the side of the Mount of Olives lay the Garden of Gethsemane, an olive orchard where Jesus often stopped to rest and pray. On the other side of the city, just outside the city walls, was the public execution grounds, Golgotha—the place of the skull. Many believe that a tomb nearby, hewn into the living rock and matching perfectly the description given in the Gospels, is the very tomb which Joseph of Arimathea surrendered to the Saviour.

This, then, was the setting for those familiar yet terrible events that we know so well as Jesus, near the end of His life on earth, approached the Cross.

Tuesday and Wednesday: Mark 14:1-11

Jesus passed the two days between His confrontation with the Jewish leaders and His final day on earth with friends in Bethany. There He was anointed by a woman who poured expensive perfume on His head. This was a "beautiful thing" done in preparation "for My burial." The woman may not have understood, but she did love the Lord and expressed that love by giving.

Judas, on the other hand, "went to the chief priests to betray Jesus to them" for the promise of money.

Jerusalem at the Time of Jesus

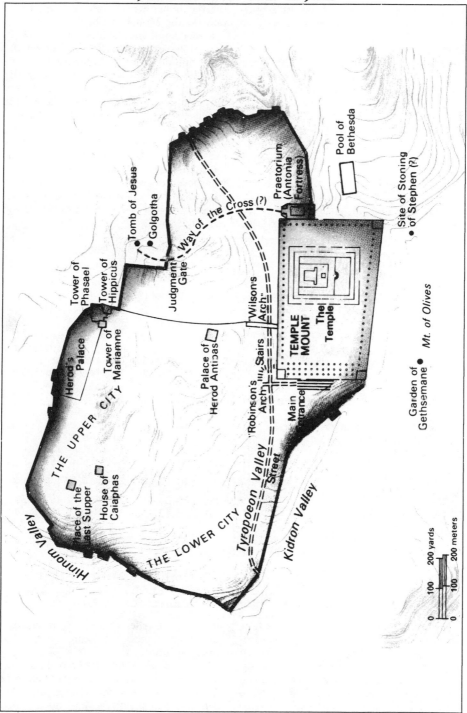

Taken from Zondervan *Pictorial Bible Dictionary*. Edited by Merrill C. Tenney. © 1963, 1964, 1965, Zondervan Publishing House. Used by permission.

What a contrast. The woman gave generously because she loved Jesus: Judas betrayed Jesus because he loved money.

Thursday: Mark 14:12–15:1

The Passover meal (Mark 14:12-26). That Thursday Jesus and His followers met in a room in a house in Jerusalem's upper city.

John's Gospel tells us in great detail what Jesus taught His disciples there. Mark simply tells us that Jesus, seated at the table, told the Twelve that one of them was about to betray Him. Judas then slipped away to go to the chief priests.

Mark tells us that then Jesus broke bread and told the disciples, "This is My body." And He took the cup, saying, "This is My blood of the covenant, which is poured out

for many." After they sang a hymn, they left the house where they had eaten and went to the Mount of Olives.

It was night, and the little party probably went down steps that still lead down the steep hillside near the house of Caiaphas into the valley. Traveling back along the Hinnom Valley into the Kidron, they moved up a path that climbed the Mount of Olives to the Garden of Gethsemane.

Peter's denial predicted (Mark 14:27-31). On the way Jesus remarked that soon all the disciples would desert Him. Peter was incensed. "Even if I have to die with You, I will never disown You." But Jesus told Peter that that very night he would disown Christ three times—three times before the rooster crowed.

	Matthew	Mark	Luke	John
Thursday				
The Passover Meal Held	26:17-29	14:12-25	22:7-22	13:1-38
The Last Supper Teaching				14–16
Jesus' High Priestly Prayer				17
Prayer at Gethsemane	26:36-46	14:32-42	22:39-46	18:1
Jesus Arrested	26:47-56	14:43-52	22:47-53	18:2-12
On Trial before Annas				18:12-14, 19-23
On Trial before Caiaphas	26:57-68	14:53-65	22:54-65	18:24
Peter Denies the Lord	26:69-75	14:66-72	22:54-62	18:15-18, 25-27
On Trial before the Sanhedrin	27:1	15:1	22:66-71	
Friday				
On Trial before Pilate	27:11-14	15:2-5	23:1-5	18:28-38
Taken to Herod			23:6-12	
Returned to Pilate	27:15-26	15:6-15	23:13-25	18:39–19:16
Mocked by Soldiers	27:27-30	15:16-19	22:63-65	
Led to Calvary	27:31-34	15:20-23	23:26-32	19:16-17
Jesus' Crucifixion	27:35-56	15:24-41	23:33-49	19:18-37
Jesus' Body Buried	27:57-60	15:42-46	23:50-54	19:38-42
Saturday				
Women Visit the Tomb	27:61	15:47	23:55-57	
A Guard Set over the Tomb	27:62-66			
Sunday				
The Women Return	28:1-8	16:1-8	24:1-12	20:1-10

Events of Trial, Crucifixion, and Resurrection in Gospels

Gethsemane (Mark 14:32-42). It was now late at night. The tired disciples could hardly stay awake. But Jesus was in anguish, so tormented by His knowledge of what was about to come that He was "overwhelmed with sorrow." Jesus needed their companionship, but the disciples' eyes were so heavy they kept nodding off.

Finally Jesus wakened them. At the base

of the hill, torches could be seen, and the sounds of a mob stumbling up the hill could be heard.

Jesus arrested (Mark 14:43-52). Judas was leading the armed crowd that had been sent by the religious leaders to seize Jesus. He identified Christ with a kiss, and the men roughly grabbed hold of the Lord.

Other Gospels tell us that it was Peter

who then bravely drew a sword and struck out. His blade grazed the head of a servant of the high priest, cutting off his ear. Again, another Gospel tells us that Jesus picked up the severed ear and replaced it. As Jesus rebuked the mob, His terrified disciples all slipped away and fled.

Most believe that the "young man, wearing nothing but a linen garment" who was following Jesus was John Mark himself, the author of this Gospel. When the mob seized Jesus, Mark was so terrified he fled "leaving his garment behind him."

On trial before Annas. Jesus was taken back through the Kidron Valley and up the Hinnom to the steps that led up the hill toward Caiaphas' house. John tells us that He was taken first to Annas, who is also called the high priest. In fact, Annas was high priest emeritus, and was the father-in-law of the current high priest, Caiaphas. He exerted such influence that Luke, in Acts 4, spoke of Annas as high priest.

After a preliminary examination in which Jesus was struck in the face (John 18:22), Christ was sent on to Caiaphas.

On trial before Caiaphas (Mark 14:55-65). The home of the high priest was large, with a handsome courtyard. There the leadership gathered to determine how they might get rid of Jesus. The leaders interviewed those who volunteered to give false testimony against Jesus, but their testimony was not consistent.

Finally the high priest asked Jesus bluntly, "Are You the Christ, the Son of the Blessed One?" Jesus answered, "I am." To the leaders this was blasphemy: Jesus had claimed to be God Himself! And the penalty for blasphemy was death.

Jesus had not yet been officially condemned. The "trial" had been more of a hearing, but a hearing before those who would soon serve as judges. By the time the Sanhedrin met in official session the verdict would be settled.

In the meantime, some began to spit at Jesus, and to strike Him with their fists. In the Jerusalem house that tradition says was that of Caiaphas there is a dark, dungeon-like basement. It may be that the guards who Mark tells us then beat Christ took Him down into that shadowy room.

Peter denies Jesus (Mark 14:66-72). Peter alone of all the disciples had followed the mob that took Jesus all the way back into Jerusalem. There some recognized Peter as one of Jesus' followers. And when Peter spoke, his accent betrayed him as a Galilean. The frightened Peter swore again and again that he did not even know "this Man you're talking about."

It was then the cock crowed . . . and Peter remembered that Jesus had known about his denial. Crushed, Peter "broke down and wept."

On trial before the Sanhedrin (Mark 15:1). Mark 15:1 sums up what Luke 22:66-71 describes. Early in the morning, just before dawn, Jesus was brought back before the Sanhedrin, now officially constituted. Jesus was asked again if He were the Christ, the Son of God. Again Jesus affirmed that He is.

Now the verdict was officially passed. Jesus was guilty of blasphemy for claiming to be God.

There was only one problem, not recognized by the Sanhedrin. Jesus *is* God. The court had met, and had condemned—itself.

Friday: Mark 15:2-46

Jesus before Pilate (Mark 15:2-15). The Jews, like other peoples in the Roman Empire, were granted a great degree of self-government. Of course, local laws were subordinate to Roman law. But only a Roman citizen had access to Roman courts. So most of the civil as well as religious disputes in Judea and Galilee were settled by the Jewish court.

But the Sanhedrin lacked one very important power. It had no authority to execute.

It was for this reason that Jesus was now sent, under guard, to the Fortress Antonia to appear before Pilate. It was very early. But it's possible that even that early in the morning Jesus was taken outside the city, through the narrow valleys, to approach the fortress without being observed. The Jewish leaders would not have wanted to rouse the city that had hailed Christ as the Messiah just a few days earlier.

Luke tells us that after an initial appearance before Pilate, Jesus was taken to Herod Antipas. Herod was technically ruler of Galilee. Sending Jesus to Herod was a courtesy, and Luke tells us that Herod appreciated it. In fact, the gesture healed a rift that had developed between the two.

But Herod, after Jesus disappointed him

by performing no miracle, returned Christ to Pilate. After all, only Pilate had the power of life and death.

Each of the Gospels tells us how hard Pilate tried to avoid condemning Jesus. But Pilate, technically the ruler of this subject people, was unwilling to offend them.

To satisfy the crowd Pilate went against his own conscience, and ordered Jesus' crucifixion!

Mocked by soldiers (Mark 15:16-23). Jesus was then turned over to the military to be prepared for crucifixion. This involved beating, designed to weaken the victim. In this case the soldiers took great delight in mocking Jesus. These Roman soldiers were auxiliaries, probably Franks and Gauls marched across the empire from France to serve in hot, dusty Palestine. They neither understood nor liked the Jews. To ridicule and torment one who called Himself King of the Jews must have stimulated their smoldering hostility and cruelty.

The Crucifixion (Mark 15:24-32). Jesus was taken by a direct route from the Fortress Antonia to the execution ground outside the city. This was located on a major road, where all would profit by seeing what happened to criminals under Roman rule.

Crucifixion was a method of execution that Roman law ordained for the worst of criminals. No Roman citizen could be executed in this way.

The crucified did not die from the wounds in their hands or ankles. The blood in the suspended victims, especially one who had suffered much loss of blood from whippings, was forced into the lower body. The pulse rate increased; after agony which might have lasted for days, the victim died from lack of blood circulating to the brain and heart.

As Jesus suffered crucifixion's excruciating pain, the soldiers on the execution detail gambled for His clothing, while onlookers either mocked or sorrowed. Even the thieves who were crucified too "heaped insults on Him."

Jesus' death (Mark 15:33-41). Jesus hung on the cross from about 9 A.M. to noon. Then, at noon, a terrible darkness blotted out the sun. After three more hours, at about 3 P.M., Jesus cried out, "My God, My God, why have You forsaken Me?"

This cry reflects the real anguish of the cross.

It was not the physical pain that tormented Jesus. It was the fact that, when our sin was laid on Jesus, He was made sin for us (2 Cor. 5:21). At that moment, for the first and only time, the Father turned away from the Son, and Jesus experienced the full meaning of the alienation from God that sin must always cause.

A moment later, the work of redemption done, Jesus "breathed His last." The Saviour was dead.

"The curtain of the temple was torn in two from top to bottom." This curtain cut off the holy of holies, the temple's most inner room, which could only be entered once a year by the high priest, bearing sacrificial blood. This curtain was visible evidence in Old Testament religion that there was no direct access to God for the worshiper. The tearing of the curtain showed that now, through the death of Jesus, the way to God was open to all.

Jesus is buried (Mark 15:42-46). The Jewish Sabbath began at sundown Friday. The death of Jesus moved His followers to act quickly. Joseph of Arimathea, a council member but a believer, hurried to beg Pilate for Jesus' body. Pilate checked to be sure Jesus was actually dead; death usually took much longer. When the death was confirmed by the commander of the execution party, Pilate gave the body to Joseph.

Joseph had to hurry. Rushing back to Golgotha, he wrapped Christ's body in some linen cloth and placed it in his own nearby tomb. The burial must be completed before Sabbath.

It was.

And suddenly the stunning reality must have struck all of those who loved Jesus. He was gone. He was really gone. As the cut stone circle was rolled up to cover the tomb door all their hopes died as well.

Sunday Morning: Mark 16:1-8

Jesus had been put in the garden tomb without normal preparation of the body. So Sunday, when the Sabbath with its restrictions on what one might do had passed, three women brought spices intending to rewrap and anoint Jesus' body.

They were uncertain. A military guard had been set on the tomb, and a seal on the stone. Who would roll the stone away so they could slip into the rock-hewn tomb?

But when they reached the garden the

stone had been rolled away! Inside the tomb there was a "young man" (an angel) waiting for them. "Don't be alarmed," he announced. Jesus is no longer there. "He has risen."

The women, trembling and bewildered, set off to deliver a message to Peter and the disciples. Jesus is alive. "He is going ahead of you into Galilee. There you will see Him, just as He told you."

Jesus had died, yes.

But Jesus lives!

The Cross was not the end, but a new beginning — for us all.

GROUP RESOURCE GUIDE

With this report of Jesus' last days we enter Scripture's "holy of holies." Whatever type group you are a member of, make this session special by entering into Christ's experience in a unique way.

Exploration: *Probe God's Word*
As group members arrive have each draw a slip of paper. If there are not enough group members let volunteers draw two slips. Each slip will have one of the following written on it.

Jesus anointed	14:1-11
The Last Supper	14:12-26
Peter's denial foretold	14:27-31
Gethsemane	14:32-42
Jesus arrested	14:43-52
Before the Sanhedrin	14:53-65
Peter disowns Jesus	14:66-72
Jesus before Pilate	15:1-15
Jesus beaten by soldiers	15:16-20
The Crucifixion	15:21-32
Jesus' death	15:33-41
Jesus is buried	15:42-47
The Resurrection	16:1-8

Each person is to study his or her passage, and then draw a picture of the scene on an 8 1/2 x 11 inch or larger sheet of paper. Using crayons is best. Study the passage from Jesus' point of view, imagining how He experienced the incident you are about to draw. When completed tape pictures to the wall, in sequence.

Reaction: *Respond together to the Word*
Now trace Jesus' steps during the last day and night of His life here on Earth. Each person in turn should tell the story represented in the picture he or she drew. But each should tell the story reverently, and *in the first person,* as if reported by Jesus Himself. Share your insights into what Jesus intended to accomplish at each step, and how Jesus must have felt.

Adoration: *Worship and pray*
Join hands in a circle. Use the rest of your time together to thank and praise God for what He went through for each of you.

STUDY GUIDE 20
Introduction

LUKE'S GOSPEL

Overview

The Gospel of Luke is the longest book in the New Testament. It was written by Luke the physician, a companion of Paul on several missionary journeys (cf. Acts 16:10-17; 20:5–21:18; 27:1–28:16). Luke is the only author of a New or Old Testament book who was probably a Gentile rather than a Jew.

The early church fathers noted the emphases common to both Paul and Luke. Each emphasized the universality of salvation. Even Luke's parables focused on the response of individuals to God's grace, while Matthew's parables concerned the kingdom. Luke, like Paul, spoke often of faith, of repentance, of mercy, and of forgiveness. Thus Irenaeus held that Luke, Paul's companion, "put down in a book the Gospel preached by him," and Origen called Luke "the Gospel commended by Paul." If Mark was the "interpreter" of Peter, Tertullian wrote, Luke was the "illuminator" of the Apostle Paul.

For instance, "grace" is found some 146 times in the New Testament. Of these, all but 21 are in the writings of Paul and Luke. And 190 of the 243 occurrences of "faith" are found in the writings of these two.

It's not surprising, then, that this Gospel, like Paul's ministry, is a Gospel directed to the Gentiles, and particularly for the better educated Hellenists. In some of the most beautiful literary Greek found in any ancient writing, Luke tells the story of Jesus, a true human being who is the Son of God.

Commentary

Tradition tells us that Luke was a physician, who practiced in Antioch. The first Gentile church was established there, and Luke may have been a member during the time Barnabas and Saul (as he was called then) were part of the leadership team. It is clear from the use of "we" in Acts (after 16:10) that Luke often traveled with the missionaries and was a witness of what he wrote.

Perhaps the most fascinating feature of Luke is the beauty of its language. Paul wrote elegant Greek, and displayed a rich vocabulary. About 250 Greek words that Luke used are found *only* in this Gospel in the whole New Testament. And there are another 61 words used only in the Book of Acts, also written by Luke.

In addition, much of the material in Luke's Gospel is found only here, with no parallel in Matthew, Mark, or John. To see its extent, it's helpful to use a highlighter and mark the following passages, identified by W. Graham Scroggie:

Luke 1:1–3:2
Luke 3:10-15, 23-28
Luke 4:1a, 13b, 14a, 15-30
Luke 5:1-11, 17, 29-39
Luke 6:11a, 12b, 17a, 24-26, 33-34, 37b, 38a
Luke 7:3-5, 7a, 10-17, 20-21, 29-30, 36-50
Luke 8:1-3, 12b
Luke 9:9b, 18a, 28b, 29a, 31-33, 43, 44a, 51-56, 61-62
Luke 10:1, 8b, 17-20, 25-26, 28-42
Luke 11:5-8, 12, 27-28, 37-38, 40-41, 44-46a, 53-54
Luke 12:1-2, 13-21, 29b, 32-33a, 35-38, 41, 47-50, 52, 54, 57
Luke 13:1-17, 22-23, 25-27, 31-33
Luke 14:1-25, 28-33
Luke 15:3, 6-32
Luke 16:1-12, 14-15, 19-31
Luke 17:3-5, 7-19, 20-22, 28-30, 32, 37a
Luke 18:1-14, 31b, 34, 43b
Luke 19:1-28, 37, 39-44
Luke 20:16b, 20b, 26a, 35a, 36b, 38b, 39
Luke 21:12a, 18-19, 21b, 22-23b, 24-

136

25b, 26a, 28, 34-38
Luke 22:3a, 15-16, 19b-20, 27-32, 35-
38, 40, 43-45a, 48b, 49, 51, 53b, 61a,
65-68
Luke 23:2, 4-15, 22b, 23, 27-31, 34a,
39-43, 45a, 46, 48, 51a, 53b, 56
Luke 24:4a, 7, 8a, 11-53

We sense the special contribution that
Luke makes to our knowledge of Jesus and
His teaching when we realize that in these
passages above are 15 parables found only
in Luke. Only here do we read about the
Good Samaritan (10:30-37), the Rich Fool
(12:13-21), the Lost Coin (15:8-10), the
Prodigal Son (vv. 11-32), the Rich Man
and Lazarus (16:19-31), and many others.

What else is special in Luke's Gospel?
Over half the verses in this Gospel contain
words of Jesus. Forgiveness and individual
response to the Saviour are emphasized in
this Gospel written for Gentiles. Luke's
concern was not the future of Israel, but
personal salvation.

In a most significant sense Luke is the
Gospel of the Good News for each individual human being born into our world.

While we will explore many of the special
emphases of Luke in the following studies
of his Gospel, there is one important theme
that deserves special study. That theme is
the theme of prayer, for Luke, more than
any other Gospel, emphasizes this dimension of the Christian life.

Scroggie, in his *Guide to the Gospels*
(Revell), notes that prayer-lessons are
taught in this Gospel by exhortation and by
illustration. This introductory session provides a good opportunity to explore prayer,
and at the same time to sense the uniquely
personal aspect of Luke's beautiful telling
of the Gospel story.

Prayer

The Bible has much to say about prayer. To
understand its essence we need to return to
the Old Testament and New Testament
languages, and see how biblical terms are
used to describe this special relationship between man and God.

Hebrew words for prayer. There are a number of different words for prayer in Hebrew. *Palal,* translated "pray," emphasizes
the dependence and humility of the person
praying, and is an appeal for God to act on
the need being presented. *'Atar* emphasizes

the intensity with which a person prays.
Sa'al means to "ask" or "to inquire" and is
often used by those seeking God's guidance. Again, dependence on God is viewed
as very important. *Paga'* suggests intercessory prayer; asking God to help another.
Hanan is a cry to God for mercy, asking
Him to act in grace and meet a need.

Each of these terms in the Old Testament shows us that prayer is an expression
of personal relationship. God is recognized
as Creator and Redeemer, One who is able
to act in this world and One who will act
on behalf of His people. The Old Testament saint who came to God in prayer approached Him humbly, sure that he was
completely dependent on God, just as a little child is dependent on his or her parents.

Prayer in the Old Testament is not really
a matter of ritual religion. God can be approached at anytime, anyplace. Prayer is an
expression of a living, vital relationship between God and His worshiper. Its answer
depends not so much on how the worshiper prays, but on the grace and kindness of a
God who cares.

Greek words for prayer. As in Hebrew, several different Greek words are associated
with prayer. *Proseuchomai* is the general
term for prayer. In the New Testament it
takes on the warmth of conversation, losing
the formal "calling on a deity" characteristic
of classical Greek culture.

Aiteo means "to ask for or request." The
New Testament often emphasizes the fact
that God hears and responds to the requests of His people.

Deomai means "to ask" or "to beseech."
This word places stress on the need which
motivates prayer. The person speaking to
God is hurting, and cries out for help to
Jesus or the Father. The word is also used
of intercessory prayer for others.

While there are other words used commonly of prayer, these are the central ones.

But again it is how the words are used in
the New Testament that gives us our insight into prayer. Here, as in the Old Testament, it is clear that prayer is an expression
of relationship. We who have a personal
relationship through faith with Jesus Christ
have immediate access to God the Father,
and can "approach the throne of grace so
that we may receive mercy and find grace
to help us in our time of need" (Heb.
4:16). In addition, Jesus promised that as

we remain close to Him, we can "ask whatever you wish, and it will be given you" (John 15:7).

It is wrong, then, to assume that prayer is like an obstacle course which believers must successfully negotiate if we are to receive answers from God. What have been called "conditions" for answered prayer are not conditions at all. What are they? They are promises, showing us that as we live in intimate relationship with the Lord we can have confidence that God will hear and answer our prayers. Thus, if we are not living in disobedience (Deut. 1:43-45), unconcern (Isa. 58:7-9), or treating others unjustly (1:15-17), we can rest assured that prayer is no meaningless exercise for us. In the same way the New Testament reassures us. We who seek, knock, and ask are heard (Matt. 7:7-8). When we agree on a matter with others, we can be sure God will act (18:19). When we pray "in Jesus' name," identifying with His character and purposes, we can be sure the prayer is in God's will and will be answered.

How wonderful these assurances are. As we live close to our God, in a warm and dependent relationship, we can share every need and desire with Him and know that God who cares, will answer us.

Exhortations to Pray

Prayer was important to Jesus. Luke tells of nine times when Jesus prayed (Luke 3:21; 5:16; 6:12; 9:18; 9:29; 10:21; 11:1; 22:39-46; 23:34, 46). Seven of these incidents are reported only by Luke.

It's not surprising, since Jesus found prayer so important for Himself, that He often exhorted His followers to pray. Let's see what we can learn about prayer from the exhortations that Luke records.

Prayer for enemies (Luke 6:27-36). Jesus called on His followers to act as sons of the Most High should, modeling their relationships with others on the way God treats human beings. In a familiar passage Jesus encouraged us to actively love our enemies, doing good for those who hate us and praying for those who mistreat us. The call to do good demonstrates the importance of action; the call to prayer demonstrates the importance of heart attitude.

Prayer and ministry (Luke 10:1-3). Jesus urged His disciples to be aware of the need and readiness of people for the Gospel. A plentiful harvest awaited, but there was such a need for workers. Here two things are linked: the call to pray, and the command to go. How striking that those who pray that God will send forth workers become the very workers to whom Jesus says, "Go."

But perhaps it is not such a surprise. It is the person who spends time with God in prayer who is closest to Him, and best able to hear His voice and recognize His call.

Prayer and needs (Luke 11:9-13). Jesus promises, "Ask and it will be given to you; seek and you will find; knock and the door will be opened to you."

The exhortation suggests deep need and uncertainty. And Jesus' comment is intended to assure us that God is eager to listen to our requests and to respond. What human father, Jesus asked, who, if his child needed food, would hand him a snake? How foolish to assume that a human father, who is by nature sinful and bent toward evil, will act more lovingly toward his children than God, the perfect Father, will act toward us.

Again we see the significance in prayer of personal relationship. It is out of confidence that God does love us that we come to Him. And we can come confidently. We can depend on God, who loves us, to give what we need, and to open the door to the future He has in mind for you and me.

Prayer and God's character (Luke 18:1-7). Jesus encouraged prayer by making a comparison (11:9-13). A human father, as imperfect as he may be, gives good gifts to his children. God is a Father too, but a perfectly good Father. How confident then we can be that He will give us what we need when we appeal to Him.

Jesus told a story that reveals something of God's character by contrast (18:1-7). The story of the "unjust judge" underlines the fact that God, unlike him, is a just Judge.

The parable introduces a judge who cares nothing for God or others. It also introduces a widow who had been defrauded, and begged the judge to grant her justice.

The indifferent judge simply ignored the woman's pleas. But the woman would not give up! She kept knocking on the judge's door, and waiting to plead with him on the streets. The judge couldn't go anywhere without the woman showing up and bothering him.

Finally he gave up. He would grant her justice, not because he cared about her, but simply because he didn't want to be bothered anymore!

Jesus asked us to think for a moment about God. How unlike the unjust judge He is! He acts for us because He *does* care, both about us as individuals and about what is right. Remembering these facts should encourage us to keep on praying, and never give up. Let's not be discouraged when God says, "Wait," and our prayers seem unanswered. God will see that His chosen ones get justice. How good to have this assurance as we "cry out to Him day and night."

Prayer Illustrations

In addition to the exhortations, Jesus also told stories which illustrate truths about prayer. Two familiar ones are particularly helpful.

The need for persistence (Luke 11:5-8). Several of Jesus' exhortations to prayer encourage persistence. In this story Jesus used a familiar device: He described a person who was so obviously *unlike* God that a quality of the Lord's which encourages us in prayer seems obvious.

In this story that individual was a "friend." It is important to note that there was no family or intimate relationship implied in "friend." The person might simply be a neighbor, an acquaintance.

At any rate, when the friend was approached at midnight with a need, the friend wasn't very friendly. "Don't bother me," is the shouted response. "The door is already locked, and my children are with me in bed." It's clear that the friendship isn't worth the slight inconvenience involved in opening the door and giving the neighbor needed bread.

But Jesus observed, if you *keep on knocking,* your friend *will* get up and help. He'll not do it for friendship. He'll do it because you are persistent in banging on his door, and he can't get back to sleep.

How unlike God.

God does not sleep. He never locks the door against us. He is always eager and ready to help.

How terrible that we should even inadvertently think of God as like a selfish, heartless person who for any reason would be unwilling to help.

Our attitude in prayer (Luke 18:9-14). In a familiar parable, Jesus told of two men who came to the temple to pray. One was a Pharisee who stood up and prayed "about himself." His prayer was nothing more than a rehearsal of all the things that he did and did not do. He prayed proudly, sure that God must admire such a righteous individual.

The other person was a tax collector. In that day the tax collector was a social outcast. Most were dishonest, and all were counted among Israel's "sinners."

This man could hardly bring himself to approach the temple, and then did not look up. Instead he beat his breast, aware of his need, and cried, "God, have mercy on me, a sinner."

Jesus told His listeners that the tax collector went home justified—not the Pharisee.

The attitude shown here is basic not only for salvation but also in prayer. A person who seeks to be counted innocent by God can hardly come boasting of his actions. We are all sinners. The self-righteous individual will hardly be willing to submit to God's righteousness, which is given on the basis of faith rather than works. For a person to be accepted and acquitted by God, there must be acknowledgment of need and an appeal solely to God's grace as a basis for hope.

It is the same in all prayer. God answers our prayers, not because we deserve His help, but because He is gracious and loving. The root of answers to prayers is sunk deep in the loving and merciful nature of our God; it never grows out of our merely human goodness.

How wonderful then, to know that we can come to God humbly, relying only on His grace. How wonderful that our God *is* gracious, and that He will answer our prayers simply because He cares.

REBIRTH OF HOPE

Overview

Luke's Gospel provides many details about events associated with the birth of Jesus. In these first chapters we find:

- the birth of John the Baptist foretold;
- the birth of Jesus foretold;
- Mary's Magnificat (a hymn of praise);
- the birth of John the Baptist;
- the birth of Jesus;
- the witness of the shepherds;
- Jesus presented as an Infant at the temple;
- Jesus as a Boy visiting the temple;
- the ministry of John the Baptist.

In providing all these details Luke showed us how important it is to establish for his Gentile readers that Christ was no ordinary man. The Gospel itself hinges on the fact that Jesus is the virgin-born Son of God.

▶ *Elijah.* The Old Testament closes with the promise that God will "send you the Prophet Elijah" before "the Lord comes" (Mal. 4:5). Luke reported that an angel told Zechariah, John's father, that the son to be born to him will "go on before the Lord, in the spirit and power of Elijah" (Luke 1:17). John's call and ministry authenticated Jesus as the Christ.

▶ *Virgin Birth.* Isaiah 7:14 established that the Messiah would be virgin born. Mary conceived by the Holy Spirit, so that the Child Jesus was "the Holy One" who must be identified as "the Son of God" (Luke 1:35).

Commentary

Had there been newspapers in the Roman Empire almost 2,000 years ago, some of the headlines that month might have been:

KING ARTAXUS NEAR DEATH
GRAIN SHIPS DOCK, ROME RIOTS END

NINE PIRATE SHIPS SUNK BY SIXTH FLEET
ATHENS STUDENTS CLASH WITH POLICE
OLYMPIC WRESTLER STILL IN COMA
REPORT ANGELS SIGHTED IN JUDEA

Such headlines look very much like the headlines in our newspapers today. For the world of the New Testament was a world very much like ours.

There were wars.

There was sickness.

There was poverty and injustice.

There were people who struggled to keep on living, living by habit long after they had lost any sense of purpose, meaning, or goal.

It was a world like ours, populated with people like ours. *But God had made preparations.* God was about to burst into this world of men. Jesus was about to be born, and after His birth our world, despite all its poverty and injustice, wars and terrorists, has never been the same.

The world that was. God has never desired the kind of world men have made. The Bible tells us that God worked carefully with men. Yet when "He looked for justice, [He] saw bloodshed; for righteousness, [He] heard cries of distress" (Isa. 5:7). Even the people of Israel, who had been given God's laws and had been sent prophets to guide them, twisted life out of shape. The people of Israel were brothers, but in the passion of selfishness they too cheated one another, lied, and tried to use each other. Yet, the more life fell under the control of sin, the emptier life seemed, and the more frustrated people became (cf. Isa. 59).

So God judged the sin of His people. History records a series of defeats and years of foreign captivity. And then, though living in their own land, God's people were crushed under the weight of the Roman Empire. That empire extended over the whole of the Western world. Rome had brought world peace—but with peace came heavy taxes, armies of mercenaries stationed in every land, Roman culture and values, the gladiatorial games, slavery—and misery.

There were still wars.

There was still poverty and injustice.

People still struggled to live, and kept on living by habit long after they had lost all sense of purpose or meaning in life. Not all the power of Rome, nor the progress of our modern technology, have been able to satisfy the basic need all people share to find life's meaning. Neither Rome nor computers have been able to break the bondage of sin that constantly expresses itself in individual life and society.

But something unique was about to happen in an insignificant province in Rome's wide-spread empire. The birth of a Baby would do what no authority or invention of man could. One day that Babe, full grown, would say, "I have come that they may have life, and have it to the full" (John 10:10).

In the birth of Jesus, God acted decisively to bring new life to individuals and transformation to human cultures. In the person of Jesus, God has extended humanity an invitation to new life.

To every person who lives by habit, without direction or meaning or real hope—to you and me—Jesus' birth offers a fresh newness, a life turned around and transformed by the power of God.

This is what the Gospel of Luke is all about: a transformed life. In Luke Jesus is presented as the transformer, with a message of new life for all the world, and with a special message of newness for believers. As we study this exciting book, we and your group members will discover more and more of what it means to *really live*. You will learn and teach the *how* of that full life Jesus promises, and show how that promise can be fulfilled in our daily experiences.

And this is something we all need to learn. Desperately.

Responses to God's Involvement: Luke 1

The Old Testament foretold the coming of a day when God would step into this world of darkness to bring light and hope. A Child would be born, a Son given (Isa. 9:6), and that One would bear the name Immanuel, "With us is God!"

But the announcement that the time was at hand was met with varied reactions.

Zechariah (Luke 1:5-25). Zechariah was a priest who lived in a little hillside town in Judea, except for the two weeks a year when his shift was on duty at the Jerusalem temple. It was during one of these weeks of duty that he was chosen by lot to enter the temple to burn the evening incense. Entering, Zechariah was jolted to see an angel of the Lord standing beside the incense altar! Quieting Zechariah's fears, the angel told him that his prayers had been answered, and his childless wife would have a son to be named John.

Zechariah's response to this announcement was one of hesitation and doubt. "How can I be sure of this? I am an old man and my wife is well along in years." *Zechariah's doubt was based on his understanding of nature!* He had failed to take God into account!

How often we hesitate to believe for the same reason. Answer *my* prayer? "Well, the way things normally work out. . . ." How wonderful that our God is not restricted to the usual, or bound by the merely natural. Our God is a God of the unusual, and the sooner we see God as He is, the more quickly our lives will be transformed.

Certainly Zechariah should have seen the unusual in the angel's appearance. Not only was John's birth announcement supernatural, everything said about the baby marked him off from others.

John's person. John was to be one of God's great men, filled with the Holy Spirit and set apart from birth.

John's ministry. John was to turn many of his countrymen to God. The angel's reference to the "spirit of Elijah" made it perfectly clear to anyone familiar with the Scriptures that this babe was to be the forerunner of the Messiah. John's birth announcement was at the same time an announcement that God was at last ready to act—God was about to intervene in the world of men!

John's significance. There was such a need for John's ministry! To prepare Israel for the Messiah he would be used by God to "turn the hearts of . . . the disobedient to the wisdom of the righteous" (Luke

1:17). How greatly such a ministry was needed is illustrated in John's later preaching (cf. Luke 3:1-20). There were many "disobedient" in John's day, as in ours. Many were uncaring, defrauding others. Many used violence or brutality to extort, and lied for one another in court (cf. vv. 12-14). John was to face this world of sin, and to prepare the hearts of men for the forgiveness and the transformation that Jesus, who came after him, would bring.

Knowing all this from the angel's announcement, Zechariah still hesitated. He still doubted. And because of his hesitation, the Angel Gabriel (1:19-20) announced that he would be unable to speak until the day of John's birth.

After the months of silence, the day came. John was born. Zechariah's tongue was loosed, and he praised God.

Mary (Luke 1:26-56). The Angel Gabriel had another announcement to make. Some months after he had spoken with Zechariah, Gabriel was sent to Nazareth, and there appeared to a young engaged woman named Mary.

Like Zechariah, Mary was startled and upset at the angel's appearance and his greeting. But, reassuring Mary of God's love, the angel told her she would have a Son. This Child would be the "Son of the Most High." He would be of the Davidic line, and would be King over Israel, fulfilling the Old Testament covenant promises. In this one Person, Deity and humanity would be perfectly blended. In this one Person, all the promises of God and all the purposes of God for humankind would be fulfilled.

Like Zechariah, Mary too blurted out a question. "How will this be, since I am a virgin?" (v. 34) The angel's response echoed another Old Testament prophecy: "A virgin shall bear a child, and you will call his name Immanuel" (Isa. 7:14). There was to be no human father. The power of the Holy Spirit was to supernaturally invest an ovum with the germ of life, and the Child to be born would be God the Son (Luke 1:35).

To this explanation Mary had only one response. "I belong to the Lord, body and soul, let it happen as you say" (v. 38, PH).

What a beautiful faith! Zechariah, godly and mature (vv. 5-6), had doubted the possibility of birth because of his age. This young girl, certainly still in her teens, never hesitated or doubted a *supernatural* birth, though she was single!

There is a blessing for those of us who learn to believe in spite of doubt. There is blessing for those of us who respond as Mary did with perfect, childlike trust.

✍ Group Activity: Bible Study Group
Zechariah and Mary represent two different responses of believers to divine guidance. Develop first a list of contrasts and comparisons between the aged priest Zechariah and the teenage Mary. Then compare their responses to Gabriel's message to each. What conclusions can you draw from their stories? How might these apply to your own walk with God?

Mary's faith-response is even more striking when we realize that, according to Old Testament Law, her pregnancy while still single might well be dealt with by stoning! And certainly her fiancé, who would know the child was not his, would hardly go through with the marriage. Yet all these things Mary was willing to trust God to work out!

Instead of worry, joy filled Mary's heart. And her praise song, known as the Magnificat (vv. 46-55), was filled with praise for God and with a vivid awareness of His greatness and love. What was Mary's vision of God?

[He] has done great things (v. 49).
Holy is His name (v. 49).
His mercy extends to those who fear Him (v. 50).
He has performed mighty deeds (v. 51).
[He] has lifted up the humble (v. 52).
He has filled the hungry (v. 53).

Mary knew God as a God of power and a God of concern, the One who cares enough for the humble and the hungry to reach down and to meet human need.

Perhaps this helps to explain Mary's response to the Lord. She had a clear vision of who God is. She knew Him as a God who cares . . . who cares enough to act. May we each know God so well!

✂ Group Activity: Recovery Group
Steps 2 (believe in a higher power) and 3 (decide to turn my life over to God's care)
Using crayons and a sheet of paper, draw

a picture of God as you think of Him. Do not necessarily draw a figure, but use colors and images that best represent how you think or feel about Him. Explain your picture to others in the group.

Then read Mary's Song (Luke 1:46-56), noting together what she says about God and her view of Him. Discuss: What do you suppose Mary's picture of God would look like if she drew Him as you just have?

Mary's images of God are drawn from the Bible and are accurate. Many times a person's images of God are distorted because they are not biblical, but come from experiences with imperfect or even abusive parents. Imagine yourself talking to Mary's God, the true God, and say to Him what Mary said, "I belong to the Lord, body and soul, let it happen as you say" (1:38, Phillips).

After making this commitment, actually draw Mary's image of God as you described it together. Post it prominently to remind yourself of who the God you commit yourself to really is.

The Birth of Hope: Luke 2

Mary's faith was not misplaced. God sent His angel to Joseph too (Matt. 1:19-21), and that good man determined to complete the marriage contract. The two wed, but the marriage was not consummated until the birth of Jesus.

The birth (Luke 2:1-7). As the time of Jesus' birth approached, Caesar Augustus had declared an empire-wide census. So all the people of Palestine went to the towns of their births to be registered. This brought Joseph and Mary, both of whom were of Davidic lineage, to Bethlehem. Though in the late stages of her pregnancy, Mary probably rode a donkey along the dusty roads and waited in weariness as Joseph tried to find accommodations when they reached their destination.

The inns were filled, but Joseph found a sheltered stable, possibly a cave behind an inn. There, in the most common of circumstances, to the simple sounds of animals shifting their weight and munching their straw and contentedly swishing their tails, Jesus was born.

It was a strange unobtrusive birth. No doctors crowded around, no gilt couch held the laboring mother, no fine linens covered the Infant. In simplicity the Baby was born, the quiet was broken by His cries, and His exhausted mother, her labors ceased, wrapped Him in a cloth and lay back to sleep, resting Him beside her where He could sense her warmth and be comforted by it.

We sometimes yearn for great and startling evidences of God's presence. "Oh," we think, "if only I could see miracles now, as in Bible days. If only something *great* would happen to me!" How we long for the sensational.

And how much we have to learn.

For the greatest miracle of all, God's greatest work, was done in quietness and in the simplicity of daily life common to millions of men. A look at the stable, and we may well wonder: Do the great things God wants to do in us and for us bear the same stamp? The stamp and seal of commonness . . . of God's mighty, yet unobtrusive, work in the lives of women and of men?

Shepherds and angels (Luke 2:8-20). While the manger was silent, the hills outside Bethlehem resounded with shouts of joy. Far away, where it would not be observed by the crowds, a heavenly celebration was taking place. Choirs of angels shook the air with joyful shout and song, and as though unable to contain the good news, an angel appeared in a brilliant ball of light to shepherds in those fields, crying, "Good news. . . . Today in the town of David a Saviour has been born to you. . . . Christ the Lord" (vv. 10-11).

But why to shepherds?

Perhaps because shepherds would understand. The Saviour, now lying in the quiet manger, was to be the Lamb of God. And as the Lamb, He was destined to die for the sins of the world, to die for these very shepherds as their Saviour. So perhaps shepherds, who cared for the young lambs, who sat through cold dark nights in the fields to guard and protect their flocks, might understand the shepherd's heart of God the Father—might glimpse what it meant for Him to give His one Lamb for all.

So as the hills throbbed and echoed with the remembered songs of joy, the shepherds left their sheep and hurried off to view God's Lamb.

They found Him. And they told Mary and Joseph about the angelic visitation. Leaving, they told everyone who would lis-

143

ten what the angels had said about this Child.

Dedicated at the temple (Luke 2:21-38). Once more, before the years of silence during which Jesus would grow to adulthood in Nazareth, God gave the parents a special sign.

On the eighth day of Jesus' life on earth, the time for circumcision, Jesus was brought to the temple to be presented to the Lord. Every firstborn son was to be so presented, dedicated to God and to His service. And then the son was to be redeemed (purchased back) with a blood sacrifice. The Law commanded a young bull or a lamb for parents who could afford such an offering. But the poor were allowed to bring two young birds. Joseph and Mary offered only the sacrifice of the poor.

But as they moved toward the altar they were met by Simeon, a man who had eagerly looked forward to the coming of the Saviour, and who had been shown by the Holy Spirit that this Child was the One! Simeon took the Baby Jesus in his arms and praised God.

His praise was echoed by Anna, an 84-year-old woman who had served the Lord in the temple with prayer and praise, and who now told everyone in Jerusalem about Jesus, assuring them that the Saviour had been born.

Jesus' childhood (Luke 2:39-52). Only Luke mentioned Jesus' childhood. He simply said that the child grew and became strong; He was filled with wisdom, and the grace of God.

At age 12 Jesus went up to the temple, where He amazed the teachers of the Law by His understanding. But the most striking note is that afterward, Jesus "went down to Nazareth with [His parents] and was obedient to them" (v. 51). Though the Son of God, and far beyond His parents in understanding even as a Child, Jesus fulfilled the commandment that ordained, "Honor your father and your mother." And so Jesus grew physically and in wisdom, being appreciated by God and by others.

All this Mary stored up in her heart. She must have watched her Son as He grew. She watched as He learned the carpenter's trade from Joseph, His earthly father. She watched as He moved in anonymity around the obscure town where the family was settled. She watched, wondered, and waited.

The Baptist's Ministry: Luke 3:1-22

Then the days of obscurity came to an end.

It began with John, who broke out of the desert like an old-time prophet, boldly announcing God's Word an challenging his hearers to a complete change of heart.

John's words were straightforward, and pierced to the heart of his hearers. He called them a brood of snakes. He warned them not to keep on trusting in their ancestry; their own hearts must be right with God. When they cried out, asking what they should do, John told them plainly, and in telling them John revealed the ways that they hated and hurt one another.

John's message was simple. *There must be a change in your hearts.* God is about to act; judgment is coming. And you must have a new life!

There must be forgiveness first, for there has always been sin. There must be baptism next, as a public sign of a choice to turn from sin (v. 3). And then there must be a whole new lifestyle—a new life that is lived in harmony with God and with holiness, a new life that breaks completely with sin.

And John had one other message.

The Saviour-Messiah was coming. The One who would make all this possible was approaching. He would be here soon (v. 16).

And then Jesus did come. He stood in the waters and, by baptism, identified Himself with the people and with the stand for righteousness that this act symbolized. As He came up, God's voice was heard from heaven: "You are My Son, whom I love; with You I am well pleased."

And, being about 30 years old, Jesus began the work that was to bring the possibility of a truly new life to you and to me.

◯ Group Activity:
Missions/Outreach Group

Look at headlines on the pages of any major newspaper. Discuss: If the coming of Jesus was supposed to make a difference, why is society today still so corrupt?

Together study Luke 3:1-20. How were the sins John identified reflected in our news? What is the remedy John preached? How does his preaching help answer the question posed by corrupt society in the Christian era?

Much impetus for missions today has been drained by the notion that there is "good in all religions" and that somehow any "faith" is acceptable to God. How do the early chapters of Luke, which show that Jesus is unique, and John's preach- ing, that shows "religion" is futile without personal repentance and faith in Jesus as Saviour, define the true focus of Christian missions.

GROUP RESOURCE GUIDE

Identification: *Share with others*
Tell two ways that being a Christian has made a difference in you or in your life.

Exploration: *Probe God's Word*
Three passages in Luke's early chapters convey images of what God intends to do through Jesus in individuals, and ultimately, in society. Divide into teams to look at the following passages. Each team is to list from its passage "What difference does Jesus make?" The passages are:

A. Mary's Song   Luke 1:46-55
B. Zechariah's Song Luke 1:67-79
C. John's preaching Luke 3:1-18

Teams are to report their findings to the whole group.

Reaction: *Respond together to the Word*
The difference Jesus makes in our lives depends on our response to Him. Compare Zechariah (1:11-20) and Mary (1:26-38). Then evaluate these statements, and apply them to your own relationship with Christ.

* The key to Jesus' making a difference is how we respond to His Word.
* Only mature believers can expect to experience the difference Christ makes.
* Maturity is no guarantee a person will be responsive to God.
* I can be like Mary this coming week.

Affirmation: *Express love and concern*
Share one way you would like Jesus to make a bigger difference in your life this coming week.

Adoration: *Worship and pray*
Thank God that Christ does make a difference. And pray specifically for at least one other group member, that he or she will experience that "bigger difference" this week.

OVERCOMING TEMPTATIONS

Overview

Matthew and Luke each paid careful attention to Jesus' temptation by Satan. The Temptation is important to the theme of each Gospel. The King must rule: the perfect Man must possess self-control. Because Jesus has overcome, we can have complete trust in the Son of God. And, because He met temptation in His human nature, He has given us an example which reveals the secret of overcoming to you and me.

This is our focus in this important study: the secret of victory over our temptations.

▶ **Temptation.** The same Greek and Hebrew words are translated as "test," "trial," and "temptation." In the New Testament "temptation" in every instance is *peirazo* or *peirasmos*.

The Expository Dictionary of Bible Words (Richards, Zondervan) says "a temptation is a difficult situation, a pressure that brings a reaction through which the character or commitment of a believer is demonstrated" (p. 593).

James made it clear that temptations are not in themselves evil (James 1:13-15). God permits such situations to prove and' improve our faith. The evil is not in the situations God permits but in responding sinfully to them. Temptations are not designed to trap, but to approve us. God even provides a way with every temptation to overcome it (1 Cor. 10:13).

Commentary

I remember how trapped I felt in high school. It started well. I was running up a flight of stairs and bumped into our football coach. When he got up he said, "I can't wait till you come out for football!" I went out for football. But I was clumsy. I fought it out for a tackle position with my friend, Kayle Craig, and lost. He was a good guy,

and I was glad for him. But it was embarrassing when he'd get his 5'2" frame under by 6'1" frame, and I'd flop like a beached whale.

So I went out for baseball, and discovered that whenever I did happen to hit a pitch, it popped softly 20 feet to the right of second base. Soon, in our practice game, seven guys on the other squad would be standing there by second, waiting for the putout. Fortunately, I got plantar warts on my right heel and was able to withdraw gracefully.

I had similar successes in my social life. For one thing, I have very peculiar hair. It grows out a dozen different directions, and earned me the nickname, Bushman.

I still had my personality, of course. But that didn't help much. I was so shy that I couldn't look a girl from my class in the eye. If I were downtown and saw one coming, I'd cross the street, or look down, or find something interesting in a store window, just so I wouldn't have to greet her.

Things didn't change much in college. I did learn to play Ping-Pong. And once I took a girl on a long walk on a winter night in Yellow Springs, Ohio. We went out to the city dump where we threw snowballs at the jumble of cans to hear the rats jump and scurry.

After two years in college I joined the Navy. A lot of things happened there. After two more years I became a Christian, and joined a little church. I felt better. Before, I'd gone to movies on 42nd Street in Manhattan — two or three triple features a day — and was very lonely. Now I had Christian friends, decided to study for the ministry, became president of our youth group, and just before discharge from the Navy, met a girl on Saturday night, proposed the next Wednesday, and a few months later married.

It was a new beginning all right. But, living in our little house trailer in Saline,

Michigan I discovered it wasn't all that different after all. My boyhood home had been quiet; we didn't get excited. My new wife felt things intensely, and expressed her feelings. When she did, I ran and hid, unable to help her. I felt afraid.

Perhaps all of us feel that way at times. Boxed in. Trapped. Inadequate. Struggling for freedom from our faults and weaknesses; for the freedom to live successfully with loved ones and associates.

When we do have those feelings, it is exciting to realize that Jesus promises us His eternal life, *now*. In fact, even before Jesus began to speak to the people of His day about the new life He offered, Christ gave them a demonstration of the power, and the freedom that He Himself had and that He came to offer to us all.

Christ's Ancestry: Luke 3:23-38

Ancestry was very important to the Jewish people. They traced their lineage back to Abraham. Their whole identity as a people rested on the fact that God had given Abraham promises (Gen. 12; 15; 17) which they, as his descendants, had inherited.

While Jesus' sudden appearance in Judah was not supported at the time by genealogical evidence, both Luke and Matthew felt it was important to show that, on the human side of His nature, our Lord was both in the Abrahamic line of promise and in the Davidic royal line. He was qualified to take the throne that God promised to the Messiah.

We need to note just two things about the genealogy before moving on. First, as is common to biblical genealogies, this one skips. It does not necessarily record each generation; a "son of" someone, in Hebrew usage, might be a grandson or great-grandson. Only the notable in the family need to be mentioned. Thus we cannot estimate times or dates by using Bible genealogies.

The second thing is that this genealogy differs in significant ways from the genealogy in Matthew. Why? Most Bible scholars believe that Luke gives the genealogy of Mary (who was also of the royal Davidic line), while Matthew traces the family of Joseph. Thus by both His mother and His earthly father, Jesus had a right to the throne of Israel.

Jesus' Temptations: Luke 4:1-13

It was important as Jesus launched His public ministry to establish His claim to be the Transformer. Jesus was One who would bring new life to people. But before Jesus offered others new life, *He proved in a personal demonstration that a new life was possible!*

Jesus showed His own freedom from the inadequacies and the sin which trap you and me. In proving that freedom is possible, Jesus gives each of us hope.

The first temptation (Luke 4:1-4). Jesus was led by God after His baptism into the desertlike country where no one lived (vv. 1-2). He was there for 40 days, without food.

Jesus had to prove that new life was a reality in Him.

Those were hard days for the 30-year-old Nazarene. He ate nothing, and the Bible says that afterward He was hungry (v. 2). Physically, Jesus was drained of the natural resources inherent in our bodies.

It was then that the devil came to Him with the first temptation. There are several things to note about it.

"If You are the Son of God. . . ." Satan initiated his attack, not by asking a question, but by making a statement.

There are a number of uses of *if* in every language, but the Greek language usually makes it clear the kind of *if* that is meant. One *if* means doubt: "Well, if you think so, but I can't see it myself."

Another *if* means *since*. Suppose an employer comes home every evening from work and complains about a particular secretary. She's inefficient. She comes to work late. She misfiles things. Finally his wife gets so upset she blurts out, "Well, *if* you're the boss, why don't you fire her?"

This *if* says *since*. Because you are the boss, act like the boss!

This is the kind of *if* that Satan uses here. "Since You are the Son of God, act like God and command these stones be made bread!"

"Man does not live on bread alone." Jesus' response is a thrilling one. He quoted this Scripture, and in selecting the particular verse Jesus identified Himself fully with us. *"Man"* does not live on bread alone. In choosing this verse Jesus told us plainly. *Jesus did not meet the testings of Satan in His deity; Jesus met each test in His human nature as a true man.*

In this we find hope. If Jesus had responded to temptation in His divine nature, there would have been no help here for you and me. Jesus' victory would have proved nothing but that God is greater than Satan. But Jesus was born into our world to live as a human being, and to be hungry and tired, misunderstood and hurt, as we all have been. So Jesus met every temptation *as a man*, and in His victory He showed us the possibility that we will win victory too.

What Jesus did as a man, using the resources available to every believer, *we* can do. The principles on which Jesus' victory was based are principles by which you and I can live too.

"It is written." The next thing to note is that, to find victory, Jesus went to Scripture. And He used God's Word in a particular way.

As a young Christian, I was told that the Bible would give me victory over sin. Yet I was often gripped by a particular temptation. I'd quote a verse that I thought was appropriate -- but as soon as I stopped quoting, I found I surrendered to the temptation!

Why? I was using the Bible as something like a Hindu prayer wheel, saying words over and over by rote as though there were something magical in the words themselves.

Jesus' use of Scripture was very different. He went back to the Old Testament, saying in effect, "Here is a principle to live by . . . and I will live by it." *Jesus chose to act on what God's Word revealed to be God's will.*

So it always must be with the Bible. God's Word is given us to be *lived*. We are to be hearers, but not only hearers. We are to do what it says (James 1:22). It was in doing God's Word that Jesus found His victory, and it is in doing God's Word that we shall find ours.

What then was the principle on which Jesus acted? This particular temptation of Satan was focused on Jesus' physical nature. Christ, after fasting for 40 days, was hungry. In response to the temptation, Jesus recalled, "Man does not live on bread alone." Christ had been led into the wilderness by the Spirit. He had been led to fast. Now He would not let His physical needs or urges dominate: Jesus would choose instead to continue to do the will of God.

The physical is one avenue of temptation for all of us. Some are ruled by gluttony.

Others are firmly in the grip of sexual appetites. One young man and his wife felt led by God to go to a Texas seminary. They arrived, and settled into a small seminary apartment in August, as the temperature hovered over 100 degrees. Within four days they decided God hadn't called them to *this* school, after all. It was simply too hot.

Yes, you and I do have physical needs. And it is all right to satisfy them. But we are more than our bodies. We are more than our sensations. Life for us is far more than the satisfaction of bodily urges and needs. For all of us who feel trapped in a pleasure-seeking society, dominated by our desires, Jesus' victory offers us new hope. The physical *need not dominate in our lives, either!*

With God's help, we can choose to live by the Word of God.

The second temptation (Luke 4:5-8). Then Satan approached Jesus from a different direction. He showed Christ all the kingdoms of the world in a moment of time, and offered them and their glory to the Messiah-King, if He would only bow down to Satan.

Some have felt that this temptation involves worldliness — and have defined worldliness as a desire to possess things, and as the pride of possession. Yet there is more involved in this test than that.

First, we have to realize that authority over all the kingdoms of this world is Jesus' destiny. He is King of kings (1 Tim. 6:15) and to Him one day every knee shall bow and every tongue confess that Jesus Christ is Lord to the glory of God the Father (Phil. 2:10-11).

Certainly what God has planned for Jesus cannot be, in itself, a bad thing — or worldly.

We have to believe also, that it would be a good thing for us if Jesus were to rule. Would there be wars and killings today if Jesus were in charge? Would there be sickness or cancer? Would there be crime, or discrimination, or injustice? Of course not! For the Bible says that "of the increase of His government and peace there will be no end. He will reign on David's throne and over His kingdom, establishing and upholding it with justice and righteousness . . . forever" (Isa. 9:7). The history of the world would have been very different if Jesus had surrendered to Satan's temptation — there would have been peace. There would have been good things.

But this was just the strength of the temptation! It was compelling, because what it seemed to offer seemed so very good!

It's not strange when we think about it. The most powerful temptations are those that involve good things. Not many of us would be tempted if someone said, "Hey, let's go out and commit murder." Or, "Let's have a drunken orgy." Or, "Let's go worship Satan." Oh, no. It is the *good* things that tempt most of us, not the obviously evil.

When Marv was invited to move to Illinois from California, he was troubled by one thing. He had no winter clothes for his three young children, and no money to buy any. Could he move and expose his children to the cold?

Marv's temptation involved a good thing. Shouldn't he have considered the welfare of his children? Oh, yes, it is good desires that make our testings most painful.

How did Jesus respond to His temptation? He again returned to Scripture, and drew from it a principle on which He was willing to stake His life. "Worship the Lord your God and serve Him only" (Luke 4:8). Jesus would not worship Satan. And *Jesus would not serve the good! God's will alone was to determine!*

Choosing God's will was costly. Yet, God intended and still intends to give Jesus the kingdoms of this world. But the pathway to the crown led Jesus by way of the Cross. Suffering preceded glory. Knowing this, Jesus turned His back on the "good," and chose to live by God's will.

You and I know, of course, that the Cross brought a greater good. Jesus might have brought peace to earth as King, but as dying Saviour Jesus brought us peace with God, and eternal life. All the suffering was worth it! God had our greater good in mind as He directed Jesus toward the scourgings and the thorny crown; toward the brutal pain of nails driven into yielding flesh.

It is always this way. God's will brings us the greater good. Marv chose to bring his toddlers to Illinois, even though they had no money, because he felt God wanted the family there. And the warm clothes came — as a gift.

We can never lose by choosing God's will. And we can never gain by selecting what seems "good" if it is not in God's plan and purpose for us.

Are you confronted by a *good thing* that attracts you? Then find freedom in following Jesus' example. Like Jesus, determine to do the *right thing,* determining that in every situation you will worship God, and Him only you will serve.

The third temptation (Luke 4:9-13). The third temptation is particularly subtle and difficult to understand. Perched on the pinnacle of the temple with Jesus, Satan challenged Him to leap off, reminding Jesus that "if You are the Son of God" angels would appear to save Him from even dashing His feet against the stones below.

"If You are the Son of God." The key to understanding this test is found in realizing that the *if* in Satan's challenge of verse 9 is not the *since* of verse 3 — and in remembering that Jesus faced each temptation as a human being. As a human being, the 40 days of hunger, capped by the appearance of Satan to test Him, must have struck Jesus with wonder. And perhaps even with doubt!

Picture a similar situation. Suppose you feel led by God to go to the nearest airport, and buy a ticket to Arizona. You get off in Tucson, and the Lord seems to lead you to a taxi. You get in, and head out of town. Finally you feel led to get out, and you walk down a deserted lane. There, surrounded by scrub and sand and cactus, you sit down. Expectantly. This has been the most unusual experience of your life! How often does God lead a person the way He has just led you? He must have something exciting in mind! And so you wait.

And you wait.

Night comes.

Then another morning. And still you wait. Another night. And another day. Hungry, and alone. And nothing happens!

How long will you wait until you begin to wonder. "Now, did God *really* lead me here, or was it my imagination?" How long before you yearn for some proof that God has been directing you and is still with you?

It was at just such a moment that Satan addressed Jesus. "If [and here we have the *if* of doubt] You [really] are the Son of God, throw Yourself down."

What the passage implies is the question, "Why not settle it?" God won't let His Son come to harm. Prove to Yourself the relationship You claim, once and for all.

"It is written." It's difficult to even suggest this interpretation of the third temptation. One hesitates to believe that, even in His human nature, Jesus might have had doubts. But look at the passage the Saviour then quoted. He turned back again to the Old Testament, to Deuteronomy, and said, "You shall not put the Lord your God to the test" (Deut. 6:16, NASB).

But the Deuteronomy passage also has a reference. It looks back to an even earlier day when God's people, led out of Egypt and given demonstration after demonstration of God's power, ran out of water. At that moment of pressure they forgot all God's goodness, and cried, "Is the Lord among us or not?" (Ex. 17:7) In questioning God's presence and His love, they "put God to the test."

It was this very thing that Satan urged Jesus to do. Make God prove Himself! But Jesus would not. "Do not put the Lord your God to the test" (Luke 4:12). *Relationship with God must always rest on faith, and on confidence in God's trustworthiness.*

Avenue of Testing	Problems in This Area	How Can I Apply Victory Principles?
The Physical physical instincts, desires, needs		
The "Good" letting something besides an appeal to God's will determine our choices		
Doubt failure to trust God when when things are difficult		

Temptations Study Sheet

How subject you and I are to this avenue of temptation. How quickly, when troubles or pressures come, we begin to doubt God and to question His love. How quickly, when we've made a decision and things don't seem to be working out, we cry, "Is God still here? Did I make a mistake?"

When you and I are under pressures like this we need to remember the principle that Jesus Himself applied. We do not need proof. We can trust God. We are not to test Him. In our relationship with God too, faith is demanded.

The temptations of Jesus were now over, for a little while. Yet throughout Christ's life on earth, Satan would attack Him. But our Lord had demonstrated, and would continue to demonstrate, that while He felt the same pressures from testing situations that you and I feel, Jesus never fell under their sway.

The power of a unique life was His. And that same power can be ours as well. For new life is exactly what Jesus offers to all who choose to follow Him.

Rejection: Luke 4:14-44

As Jesus moved out to teach and minister in the power of the Holy Spirit, there was initially great enthusiasm (vv. 14-15). People across the tiny country began to talk about Jesus with great admiration.

Nazareth (Luke 4:14-30). We don't know how long it was before Jesus made a visit to Nazareth, His hometown. But certainly all there had heard about His successes. As a mark of courtesy, the ruler of the synagogue even asked the young Man to read the Scripture.

Jesus unrolled the heavy scroll, and read from a place in Isaiah which His listeners knew described the Messiah.

"The Spirit of the Lord is on Me," Jesus read. "He has anointed Me to preach good news to the poor . . . to proclaim the year of the Lord's favor" (Luke 4:18-19). Then Jesus told them, "Today this Scripture is fulfilled in your hearing." *This was the clearest possible claim that the Carpenter who had been their neighbor was in fact the long-promised Messiah, the Son of God.*

This claim seemed to stun the listeners. They were drawn to Jesus' "gracious words" (v. 22), but over and over they kept saying, "Isn't this Joseph's Son? We've known Him as a Child, a Youth, a young

Man moving among us. Are we now to suddenly see Him as Israel's Deliverer?"

People today are faced with this same dilemma. Many have thought of Jesus as a teacher, as a good man, or a tragic historical figure who was killed because He was too far ahead of His time. But when we meet Jesus in Scripture, and hear His claims, we realize that Jesus calls on us to see Him as the living Son of God.

Jesus' neighbors were confronted with a decision they did not wish to make, and a claim they did not want to hear. The Bible says they "were furious" (v. 28), and that they tried to kill Jesus (v. 29).

In this reaction, this choice, we see a cameo portrait of Jesus' whole ministry. The scene in Nazareth was reenacted over and over during the next three years. In the end the furious anger Jesus aroused expressed itself in implacable hatred, and led to the Cross.

How important that our reaction to Jesus never parallel theirs. When we see Jesus, when we come to recognize Him as Son of God, we must reject either ourselves — or Him.

We may choose ourselves, and surrender to every temptation we feel. But if we do we will never experience the new life Jesus came to bring. Or, we may choose Jesus. And if we do choose Jesus, then we must also choose to respond to our temptations just as Jesus responded to His. We must take our stand on the Word of God, determine to practice that Word, and do it all in the confidence that Jesus, the Son of God, will bring us the victories for which we yearn.

❋ *Group Activity:*
Singles/Single Again Group
Read aloud the story of Jesus' rejection by

His neighbors at Nazareth (Luke 4:14-29). Then jot down words that describe how you think rejection feels.

List the words selected on a chalkboard or large sheet of newsprint. Then go around the group, and tell of a time when you felt rejected by someone who was important to you. After all have shared, discuss: How has rejection affected your feelings about yourself? How has it affected the way you relate to others?

Look again at 4:18-19. Was Jesus rejected because of a flaw in Him, or a flaw in His neighbors? Look at the story again to discern why Jesus was rejected.

Think back over the rejection experience that you described. Realistically, what in you or in the other person caused the rejection?

After sharing, listen to others in the group talk about how they have experienced you and your positive qualities. It is easy when we feel rejection to lose a sense of our worth and value. Let the fact that others see good qualities in you, and that Jesus knew rejection too, encourage you and provide perspective in your daily living.

The promise of power (Luke 4:31-41). Where will you and I find the strength to overcome our temptations, and to validate our choice of Jesus by obedience to His Word? Luke now tells us a series of stories. He shows us Jesus, casting out evil spirits (vv. 31-37). And he shows us Jesus, reaching out to heal and to strengthen the sick.

Surely the One who personally overcame temptation, and who used His power to bring health and wholeness to the sick of His day, will heal our hearts and give us the power to live new, and better lives.

GROUP RESOURCE GUIDE

Identification: *Share with others*
Go around the group and complete this sentence: "The biggest temptation I overcame was. . . . "

Then discuss: Have temptations been more of a positive or negative thing in my experience?

In doing so, talk about this analogy. To

build up muscle tissue a person must exercise strenuously. How can a person build up moral muscle?

Exploration: *Probe God's Word*
Group members previously assigned should briefly explain the three temptations of Jesus (Luke 4:1-12), drawing on material in the

commentary. Discuss each incident until each is clear about the source and nature of the temptations Jesus faced and overcame.

React: *Respond together to the Word*
Individually complete previously prepared charts like that on p. 150, on 8 1/2 x 11 sheets of paper. But add to that chart a third column, titled: "Positive Effects."

First list problems you face in each of the three areas. Take plenty of time and do a thorough, complete job. You may also jot down how you have or might apply victory principles demonstrated by Jesus to overcome your own temptations. Do not write in the third column at this time.

When you are all done, share one or two typical problems from each area. Usually the problems we face will be those others experience as well.

Then share insights as to how to apply Jesus' victory principles to meet your own challenges victoriously.

Adoration: *Worship and pray*
Praise Jesus for meeting temptations in His human nature, and showing us the way to overcome our temptations. Express your personal commitment to respond as He did when you are tempted.

During the next week or two use the third column to record the positive effects of your victories over temptations. Make each victory and advance another occasion for praising God.

Luke 5:1–7:17

THE CHOICE

Overview

These chapters cover what is often called Jesus' early Galilean ministry. Galilee was Jesus' home province. It was not technically Jewish, as was Judea, but contained a large Jewish population. Most of Jesus' ministry was focused near the Sea of Galilee, where Peter and James and John had labored as fishermen.

Strikingly, the Sermon on the Mount, the Transfiguration, and 25 of Jesus' 35 recorded miracles took place in Galilee.

The Jews of Judea, however, looked on Galileans with some contempt. They had a rude accent, and were not considered sophisticated in matters of religion.

This early Galilean ministry took place when Jesus was introducing His teaching and Himself. The later Galilean ministry is associated with hardening opposition.

▶ *Judging.* Luke, Paul, and James each dealt with "judging." They called on us to critically evaluate ourselves, but not others. According to James, passing judgment on others is playing God: "There is only one Lawgiver and Judge, the One who is able to save and destroy. But you—who are you to judge your neighbor?" (James 4:12) Yes, the church is to discipline those who openly and habitually sin. But there is no room in our faith for a critical attitude or judging of others' beliefs, motives, and convictions. We are to give each other the freedom to be responsible to God.

Commentary

Germs

For years the medical world laughed at the germ theory, the notion that infection and diseases are caused by tiny organisms no one can see. They questioned the need for special cleanliness and antiseptics in hospitals, and derided Pasteur and other early proponents of the germ theory.

It was so hard, later, to come to the man they had rejected and to admit, "You were right. We were wrong."

It's always hard to face a person who has been right when we've been wrong, and honestly to admit it—especially if what he has been right about is something really important. Oh, I can admit to one of my children, "You were right; I should have turned two blocks earlier." This doesn't hurt: it doesn't strike at my identity. But how much harder to admit, "Son, you were right. I didn't have any good reason to ground you. I was just feeling angry, and took it out on you. I'm sorry."

This kind of admission is much harder. It hits at something important to me; my desire to be a loving and fair dad, and to be viewed this way by my children.

But it was just this kind—the most difficult of admissions—the admission of being *wrong* about something important to His hearers' identity as Israelites—that Jesus now set out to call from the hearts of His fellow Jews. As Jesus entered the first phase of His public ministry, He presented Himself to Israel as the Lifegiver. To accept Him, people would have to admit that what they had known was not really life. Jesus would in His preaching present a bold picture of life as it is to be lived in God. To accept *this,* people would have to admit that what they were now living was not God's way of life.

These admissions were hard for Israel. They are hard for you and me. But we are faced with the same choice. Will we really follow Jesus, totally, and find in Him the way of life?

Jesus Is Lord: Luke 5:1–6:19

Commitment (Luke 5:1-11). All had been amazed at Jesus' teaching and His power. Yet most still hesitated, waiting for more

153

evidence or for some sign before they committed themselves to Him. But some did not hesitate. They made the choice immediately—and with that choice made the confession commitment must involve.

One day as Jesus was teaching near the shore of Lake Gennesaret (a name for the Sea of Galilee), He was pressured by the crowds that thronged around Him. He got in the boat of a fisherman, and continued His teaching from it. When Jesus was done, He told the owner, Simon (who was later called Peter), to push out into deep water and let down his nets.

By all odds this would be a futile action. The fishermen of Palestine worked at night, when the schools of fish worked in toward shore to feed on the swarms of minnows in the shallower, warmer waters. But Simon did as Jesus told him. And an enormous shoal of fish swarmed into the nets! The nets even began to break with the weight. When a second boat joined them, both were so filled with fish they nearly sank.

This was evidence enough for Peter. He fell on his knees before Jesus, and instead of thanking Christ he begged, "Keep away from me, Lord, for I'm only a sinful man" (v. 8, PH).

Staggered by the haul of fish, Simon had been jolted into recognizing Jesus as Lord. There were no questions left in the mind of this simple fisherman.

It may seem strange that reports of the greater miracles of healing and expelling demons had not moved Simon earlier. Sometimes it is the simplest things that bring a person to realize that Jesus Christ is Lord. But by whatever agency, how vital it is that each of us realizes, as Peter did, just who Jesus is.

Seeing Jesus as Lord raised in Simon's mind a vivid picture of himself. Beside Jesus, Peter was revealed as "only a sinful man." Perhaps if you and I were to compare ourselves with other people, we might have some cause to boast. But when we compare ourselves to Jesus, we see our sin revealed in the light of His perfect purity. Simon, knowing himself, confessed his lack of life and goodness, and his need.

This confession of sin and failure seems so hard to make, until we have made it. Then we discover that, once we have admitted we are sinners, we are freed. For once we see ourselves as sinners we be-

come more ready to hear the healing words of Jesus Christ.

Jesus said, "Don't be afraid; from now on you will catch men" (v. 10).

We who are sinners need not fear God. He forgives us, and transforms us as well. What Jesus told Peter is something He says to each of us who come to Him acknowledging our sin: *from now on, life will be different!*

Peter and his two companions left everything there on the beach—including the great catch of fish—and followed Jesus. All that had been important to them before was now willingly set aside. In the fulfillment found in relationship with Jesus Christ, all of life truly was becoming new.

∅ Group Activity:
Missions/Outreach Group
For use when non-Christians are part of the group. Break down the stories of Peter (5:1-11) and Levi (Matthew) (5:27-32) into "before," "convicted," and "converted" sections. Together or in teams look at each man's experience, and describe him and his activities before meeting Jesus, during his meeting with the Saviour, and after his conversion.

Report and fill data in on a chalkboard or sheet of newsprint. Then ask each person to determine which of the two men he or she is most like, and where he or she is along the journey toward salvation. Share your own conversion with sensitivity, including any fears or doubts you had about making the life-changing decision to trust Jesus. Do not press anyone who is unwilling to share.

Healing the inner man (Luke 5:12-32). Not all who saw Jesus' works and heard His teaching responded as Simon Peter and his friends. So Jesus moved on, to show graphically that His authority extended to the healing of the inner man as well as the outer.

In verses 12-16 we have a touching story that focuses attention on the inner needs of human beings, and shows us Jesus' concern for these needs.

A leper came to Jesus and fell down in front of Him, saying, "Lord, if You are willing, You can make me clean." The leper recognized Jesus' power, but was uncertain of Jesus' love.

We're all so prone to using others. Some give generously . . . to buy a reputation as generous. Some show up for church visitation, to be known as "soul winners." So it was a fair question. Was Jesus *using* the people He healed, just to build a reputation as a healer?

Jesus answered the implied doubt fully. He said, "I am willing." And then as Jesus spoke the healing word, our Lord reached out His hand *and touched the leper* (v. 13).

Lepers in Jesus' day, as in ours, were untouchable. They had to cry out in the streets, to warn others away from them. They lived outside cities, separated from their loved ones and families. They were alone . . . and destined not to know the loving caress or gentle pressure of another's hand. But Jesus reached out and touched the leper!

If you've ever been lonely, ever felt rejected or unloved, you know what that touch must have meant. If you've ever been convinced that no one could possibly care for you, then you understand how that leper must have felt. Jesus' touch was not needed to heal the leprosy, but it was necessary to meet this man's deep, inner need for love.

Later, the leper would follow the Law. He would go, and show his body to the priests, and they would pronounce him cleansed from his disease. Then he would make the thank offerings the Law prescribed.

But what the leper would not show the priests was his heart. They had nothing to do with the heart. But Jesus does. And the touch of love had healed the heart even as the word of power had cleansed the external disease.

If any of your group members have hesitated to trust Jesus, or if they have been convinced of His power but uncertain about God's concern, direct their attention to the leper.

Jesus touched him.

As He yearns to touch all.

In dealing with the inner man, it was not enough for Christ to communicate love. He had to provide forgiveness. So verses 17-26 report an incident that develops this theme.

Many were gathered to hear Jesus teach, including the religious leaders who were to become His implacable enemies. When a paralyzed man was ingeniously brought to Jesus over the dense crowd, Jesus recognized faith. He said to the man, "Friend, your sins are forgiven" (v. 20).

The religious leaders, the scribes, and Pharisees, immediately grasped the implication of this statement. Jesus was acting as if He were God! "Who can forgive sins but God alone?" (v. 21) But Jesus responded to their unspoken thoughts. Jesus asked them bluntly which was harder to say: Your sins are forgiven, or get up and walk? Clearly it is harder to tell a paralyzed man to walk, for then everyone will know immediately if a person speaking has authority to do what he says. But who can tell about authority to forgive sins? Forgiveness doesn't seem to carry the same visible impact.

So, Jesus said to the paralytic, "I tell you, get up, take your mat and go home" (v. 24). And immediately the man did!

What a lesson there is for us here. Jesus was touched by the physical need expressed in the paralysis. But His first concern was for spiritual needs. For the forgiveness of sins. Jesus' acts of healing were truly acts of compassion, but they were performed "that you may know that the Son of man has authority on earth to forgive sins" (v. 24).

There are times when we think that our greatest needs are for healing, for friendship, for more money. Jesus helps us focus on the real issues of life: and our first need is the need for forgiveness and for transformed hearts.

Jesus had asked the Pharisees, "Which is easier to say, 'Your sins are forgiven,' or to say, 'Get up and walk'?" It is clear that there, in that crowded room, it was harder to say, "Your sins are forgiven." A person who says, "You are healed," will be immediately shown to have authority, or shown up as a charlatan. But Luke reminded us that forgiveness too is expressed in a person's behavior!

Levi had been a taxgatherer (vv. 27-32). He was hated, because in those days men paid the government for the right to collect taxes, and then collected far more than was really due. Taxgatherers in Jesus' time were swindlers, money-hungry, and despised as collaboraters with a foreign occupying force. Levi was one of these men, and undoubtedly deserved his reputation as a "sinner."

Then one day Jesus came up to Levi and said, "Follow Me." And Levi followed!

Later Levi gave a party to introduce Jesus to his friends, who were outcasts like himself. When the Pharisees and scribes saw Jesus was associating with such people, they muttered indignantly. No doubt they were secretly delighted to have some apparent cause for criticizing Him.

Jesus answered sharply. Who needs a doctor? The well, or the sick? Jesus wasn't there to sit around with those who thought they were well, but to heal those who realized they were sick!

And what happens when Jesus touches the life of a sinner like Levi? What happens when a sinner accepts forgiveness, and chooses to follow Christ? Scripture gives us an exciting answer. It's found in the first book of the New Testament, a book that bears the name of Matthew, the disciple who was once known as Levi, the tax collector!

If we had known Matthew in his days as Levi, you and I would probably have despised him too. But what a great God we have! We have a God who cares about the despised. A God who can touch the hardest hearts with His forgiveness, and can transform the most warped personality. Through Jesus, the sinner can become a new person.

And this is our destiny too. If we come to Jesus, confess our sin, and receive His forgiveness, Christ will begin a change in us that ends in personal transformation. In Jesus, our life too can become new.

Jesus as Lord (Luke 5:33–6:11). Jesus had demonstrated clearly who He is. How did those around Him respond?

Many hesitated. Jesus recognized the natural hesitation of men to try the new. In the illustration of the new wine (5:33-39), He noted that one who has been drinking an old wine will hesitate to turn to the new. That person will say, "The old is good." But after a time old wine turns sour. When it is time for the new, even the wineskins (which in Jesus' time served as bottles) must be fresh and new.

Jesus had come to bring in the new. Men must choose Him, or would find the old turning sour and worthless.

Others criticized. The leaders particularly tried to find fault with Jesus. When Christ's disciples plucked grain to eat on the Sabbath, these religious men felt it was a violation of Sabbath law. It was not, for their interpretation of Old Testament Law on this point was wrong.

As Lord of the Sabbath Jesus, the Son of God, who had ordained this day of rest, would Himself determine what was right to do on it.

Some hated. On another Sabbath the leaders set a trap. They placed a man with a shriveled hand in the synagogue, and watched to see if Jesus would heal (to them, "work") on the Sabbath. Jesus had the man stand up "in front of everyone" and healed him. The Lord of the Sabbath announced that it was "lawful" to do good, and to save life, on God's special day.

These actions revealed just how sour the old wine of Judaism had become. The religious leaders had no concern for the man they tried to use against Jesus. He was nothing but a pawn to them. In His response Jesus revealed to all the total hypocrisy and emptiness of all their claims to religious superiority. These were nothing but empty men, who loved only their own place and price, and who were untouched by the hurts of those around them. Jesus' words and actions revealed their hearts to others, and they hated Him for it. "They were filled with insane fury and kept discussing with each other what they could do to Jesus" (6:11, PH).

Followers or observers? (Luke 6:12-19) The lines were being drawn. The crowds still hesitated. The leaders were becoming hardened in their hatred and rejection.

Jesus, after a night of prayer, selected 12 men to be His special disciples: men who had chosen to follow Him.

These men had few qualifications. They had little education. No important family connections. Some had dark pasts. They were fishermen; a tax collector; men of quick temper. But Jesus chose them to be with Him. These were men who had believed in Him, and been moved to confess and trust Him. Jesus is the Son of God — and these men believed.

How different the groups we have seen in these chapters. There were the crowds, who gathered around but hesitated to commit themselves to Jesus. There were the leaders, whose pride moved them to hatred. And there were the disciples, who in simple faith stepped out on the pathway toward transformed lives.

How important that we take our place as

sinners at the feet of Jesus, accept His forgiveness, and rise to follow Him.

Discipleship Described: Luke 6:20-38

Jesus was surrounded by crowds who were eager to touch Him. He was a celebrity, and His touch was healing. But when Jesus began to teach what we know as the "Beatitudes," many must have had second thoughts.

The blessed (Luke 6:20-26). The words Jesus uttered seem stark and inexplicable when one first reads them. "Blessed are you who are poor. Blessed are you who hunger now. Blessed are you who weep now. Blessed are you when men hate you." And, "Woe to you who are rich. Woe to you who are well fed now. Woe to you who laugh now. Woe too when all men speak well of you."

The words seem stark, because they seem at first to contradict common sense. Who would willingly choose the "blessed" circumstances of poverty, hunger, weeping, and hatred?

To understand Jesus here, we need to realize that His contrast is not between two sets of circumstances, but between ways people react to life in this world. The contrast is between *Jesus' people* and *other people,* and what gives meaning to each group.

We can state the two principles that Jesus communicates quite simply:

Jesus' people are dissatisfied with what this world has to offer but are happy anyway. Other people are satisfied with what this world has to offer but are miserable.

We know, for example, that there is nothing wrong with riches (1 Tim. 6:17-19). So Jesus was not condemning wealth when He pronounced woe on the rich. It is a love of money which is a root of every evil, not money itself (see v. 10). In desiring wealth, in fixing one's heart on money, a person opens himself up to woes.

Don was 40 when I met him, a middle management executive who, from college days, had determined to work his way to the top of his company and make millions. The week before I spoke in his church, Don had made a discovery that jolted him to the depths of his personality. *He* wasn't going to make it! All that he had worked and planned for, all he'd built his life

around, was destined to elude him. He was not the "successful and rich" businessman he had pictured himself to be—and he never would be!

At first Don hadn't known what to do. His whole image of himself was shaken. And then, as I was sharing from this very passage, Don made a great discovery. The agony he was going through was really God's blessing. God had rescued Don from the misery of becoming the success he had planned to be . . . and, in the process, from seeking to build his life on empty and transient things.

Jesus knows that there is more to life than success; that the meaning of life can't be summed up on a balance sheet or in a bank account. How blessed for Don to weep now, and through his trauma to turn from what this world offers to seek his satisfaction in God. How blessed for Don to be turned, even through pain, toward God's way of living.

It is the same with the other things we set our hearts on. Have you built your life around being accepted by others; on being looked on as one of the "in" people? Are you a person who simply has to have everyone say nice things about you—your looks, your clothes, your personality? Jesus said, "How miserable for you when everybody says nice things about you" (Luke 6:28, PH).

How miserable you must be, to be satisfied with popularity. For you have missed the real meaning of life!

Jesus' Beatitudes pierce to the heart of human values, and force us to ask the basic questions we find so easy to ignore. What is life all about for me? What moves me? What determines my choices? What makes me glad or sad? Am I controlled by my needs, struggling as the pagans do to make sure I have enough? (Matt. 6:25-32) Am I controlled by pleasure, satisfied with the laughter and distraction I can find in amusements? Am I controlled by a desire for wealth, satisfied to see my cash and credit grow? (Luke 6:24) Am I controlled by a need to be liked and admired? (v. 26)

Jesus said, *"How miserable for you!* You might better be hungry, poor, weeping, and hated. For then at least you might turn from these empty things to Me, to find out what life is really all about."

Jesus' words jolted the men of His day,

and they ought to jolt you and me too.

What is your life all about, and the life of your group members? Are they satisfied that they have found life's meaning? Or are they ready to hear what Jesus says about life, and where human beings can find meaning and purpose. For Jesus, the Lifegiver knows the meaning of life. And He tells us plainly.

♥ *Group Activity: Support Group*
Use a balancing scale as a symbol. Then list on the left your personal woes, and on the right, your personal blessings. List woes and blessings experienced in four different periods of your life: childhood, adolescence, adulthood, and "right now."

When the reporting is complete, share in teams of 4 or 5. After you share, let the others share insights. What kinds of things hurt you most? What kinds of things make you happiest? How do you tend to react to difficulties? Give this kind of attention to each person on your team.

Then as a group, study and discuss Luke 6:17-26, guided by the commentary. Apply what you learn from Jesus' teachings to what you have learned about yourself from the charting and feedback. You'll be surprised how woes can be transformed into blessings.

By love (Luke 6:27-38). Jesus went on to tell His listeners, "Love your enemies, do good to those who hate you, bless those who curse you, pray for those who mistreat you" (vv. 27-28). In this Jesus tells us that *the meaning of life for the believer is found in love.* People, not things, are central in the new life that Jesus calls us to live. Giving, not getting, is what life is all about.

In this section's teaching we realize that there is something truly unique about Jesus' kind of love.

Sociologists have labeled one kind of human behavior "reciprocity." They have noted that in every culture this norm, or standard, seems to operate. It's expressed in our saying, "You scratch my back, and I'll scratch yours." This is what reciprocity means: you do something for me, and I'll pay you back. And reciprocity also dictates, you do something bad *to* me, and I'll pay you back for that too.

Most of us are bound by this norm. The Jones family sent you a Christmas card last

year? Somehow you feel you *have* to send one to them this year. The Carlsons invited you over to their house? You know it's your turn to have them for dinner.

This norm of reciprocity operates even in the intimacy of family life. You bought me a present? I'll be warm and loving this evening. Your teenager mowed the lawn without being asked? Well, sure, he can have the car tonight.

The simple notion that we ought to be nice to those who are nice to us, and are under no obligation to be nice to those who aren't, seems to permeate every human relationship.

There is much to be said for the norm of reciprocity. It helps hold society together. If we couldn't depend on people responding in kind, there would be a terrible uncertainty in all our relationships.

It's just that *the Christian's behavior isn't to be governed by the norm of reciprocity!* Another norm, another standard, is to replace it.

The other norm is something we may call *initiating love.* We are to take the lead in initiating love. This is what Jesus meant when He said, "Love your enemies." We are not to love because we expect to be repaid. We are to love, even to lend, without expecting anything back. And we are to love this way because it is the kind of life to which Jesus calls us.

It seems frightening. How can I love, knowing I may be hurt by an enemy who does not respond as he should? How can I do good, uncertain about how others will see and respond to my actions? It *is* frightening. But Jesus lived this way. Even though others did hurt and hate Him.

When we decide to live a life of *initiating love,* we will have two consolations. First, we will be living as Jesus has commanded us; as He Himself lived. And second, we will discover in a love like God's what it means to have a truly abundant life.

We shouldn't get the impression that the life of love Jesus calls for is a totally negative experience, with our enemies taking endless advantage of us. Jesus explains. "The measure you use, it will be measured to you" (v. 38). In rejecting the norm of reciprocity for the norm of initiating love, you and I *set a new standard for those around us!* In becoming a model of Jesus' love, we will find that others do respond to us — and to Him.

✂ *Group Activity: Recovery Group*
Steps 8 (list persons I've harmed) and 9
(make amends to people I've harmed)
Making amends to those who are openly
hostile to us, who view themselves as ene-
mies, is extremely difficult. List everyone
you have harmed who probably considers
you an enemy, or whom you consider an
enemy. List under each name as many
things as you can think of that you have
done that may have harmed them. (Don't
list things they have done to harm you.
You can take responsibility for your own
actions, but not for the actions of others.)

When the lists are complete, read and
discuss together Luke 6:27-38. Talk about
how "the norm of reciprocity" (see com-
mentary) has governed your past relation-
ship with the individuals you listed.

Then list all the benefits to be gained
by obeying Jesus' command to show love to
enemies that you can see from the text or
your experience.

Go back over your list and determine
how you can make amends. Then in
teams of three share what you plan to do
in obedience to Jesus' command.

Power for Our New Lives: Luke 6:39-49

The power of example (Luke 6:39-49). How
does a person learn to live this kind of life?
Jesus points out that we learn to live by
following a person who knows how to live.
And that, "Everyone, after he has been fully
trained, will be like his teacher" (v. 40,
NASB).

This observation strikes at the heart of all
of us who are parents. How will our children learn to live Jesus' way? Will they see
His life in us?

Because Christianity is a way of life that
is learned from Christian models, Christ
calls on us to engage in self-examination (v.
42). We have no right to criticize or instruct another about how to live until we
are sure that our own lives are in harmony
with Christ. If we are blind to God's way of
living, and attempt to lead others, both we
and they will "fall into a pit" (v. 39).

Again in this passage Jesus reminds us
that the issues of life are settled in the heart.
To be a good example, we do not need to
know everything. We do not need to be
perfect. All we need is a heart truly dedicated to Jesus. Out of a sincere heart godly
actions will grow. As Jesus said, "The good

man brings good things out of the good
stored up in his heart" (v. 45).

A final illustration closes this chapter.
How do we grow as Jesus' disciples, and in
our capacity to model His life? Jesus said
that we are to be people who hear Jesus'
words, and do them. Only by full obedience to the teachings and words of our
Lord will we be able to express the love in
our hearts, and come to reflect His likeness
in our world.

Resources for the New Life: Luke 7:1-17

Jesus' picture of the believer's way of life in
Luke 6 portrays a counterculture. All that
Jesus teaches goes against the grain of the
ways men live in our world, and the values
most men hold.

Where do we find the resources to enable
us to move upstream; to be different in a
world that demands conformity?

Jesus was done with His public teaching.
As He entered Capernaum, the next two
recorded events provide the divine answer
to our questions about sources of strength.

A soldier's faith (Luke 7:2-10). The first
incident involved a stranger, a Roman army
officer on occupation duty in Palestine.
While stationed in Palestine this man had
come to know and love the God of Israel
and God's people (vv. 4–6). He had also
heard of Jesus. So when a favorite servant
fell deathly ill, the centurion requested
some of the Jewish elders to appeal to Jesus
to heal his slave.

Jesus listened, and turned to follow His
fellow Jews to the Roman's home. But in
the meantime, the soldier had second
thoughts. He, the conqueror, realized he
was unworthy to have Jesus in his home.
So he sent another message, addressing
Jesus as "Lord." He begged Jesus simply to
say the word. "I myself am a man under
authority," the soldier said. As an officer,
he derived his authority from the Roman
government which had commissioned him.
Because he spoke with Rome's authority,
he could command soldiers and they would
obey. He recognized the fact that Jesus
spoke with the full and complete authority
of divine power! Whatever Jesus commanded would be done.

Jesus "marveled at him" and told the
crowds, "Not even in Israel have I found
such great faith" (v. 9, NASB).

This is our resource too.

159

Faith.

But a particular faith.

Do we realize that the Jesus we know as Saviour *has all power*? Are we aware that He can command, and that His will will be done? We need not fear to live a completely committed Christian life, for we too can have faith in Jesus. His power is unlimited, and He will live out His life in us.

New life (Luke 7:11-17). How great is Jesus' power? Soon after this Jesus met a funeral procession. On the bier was the body of a widow's only son. Jesus saw her tears, and said: "Young man, I say to you, get up."

And the dead awoke.

What a message for us. Have we been dead to Jesus' kind of life? Have we lived the world's way, with thoughts and desires tangled by the cries that distract others? No matter how dead we may have been spiritually, Jesus is capable of awakening us to new life. First comes faith. And then we too hear Jesus' words: Arise!

Arise, and live My new life of love.

GROUP RESOURCE GUIDE

Identification: *Share with others*

Using money—a penny, nickel, dime, quarter, dollar, etc., as an indicator, tell how much faith you feel you have just now. If you wish, tell why you chose that amount, but only if you wish.

Exploration: *Probe God's Word*

(1) Together study Luke 7:1-10. List every indication in the text that this centurian had faith in Jesus. Then come up with a dollar value that seems to you to accurately indicate his faith.

(2) Then in teams of three look at the incidents reported in Luke 5:1–6:49. Be alert for how each incident might build faith, illustrate faith, or call for faith.

Affirmation: *Express love and concern*

The reality of the centurian's faith in Jesus was demonstrated by his words and actions. If you have observed faith in action in one of your group members, tell him or her how you have seen faith expressed.

Reaction: *Respond together to the Word*

Share results of team studies, focusing particularly on "faith building" incidents. Discuss: What is the basis of faith—what we feel about how strong our faith is, or the power of the One we trust?

Adoration: *Worship and pray*

Read aloud Luke 7:11-17. Jesus raised this young man from the dead not in response to faith, but as a spontaneous and sovereign act of compassion. Worship Jesus together. Praise Him that we can trust Him completely, not relying on our "faith" but on His compassion and power.

STUDY GUIDE 24

Luke 7:18–10:24

DECISION TIME

Overview

There are two decisions that are critical in every human life. The first decision is to accept Jesus, the Son of God, as personal Saviour. In the first part of this study we meet some who made that decision.

The second decision has to do with discipleship. Will we follow Jesus completely? In the second part of this study we find the essence of discipleship, and survey the true disciple's life.

Depending on the makeup of your study group, you may want to emphasize the salvation section, or those passages which deepen understanding of discipleship.

What are some of the characteristics of the disciple's lifestyle that your group will find in Luke 9 and 10? Trust. Suffering. Humility. Purpose. Commitment. Involvement. And prayer.

▶ *The Seventy-two.* The other Gospels focus on 12 disciples. But Luke introduces us to a larger corps of close followers. Luke 10 tells us that Jesus appointed 72 that He sent out two-by-two to preach in Israelite towns. We know the names of the Twelve. But the 72 remain anonymous. Yet Jesus knew them and their ministries well. How good that today too we need not be well known by others to be effective disciples of Jesus Christ.

■ For a verse-by-verse exposition of this passage see the *Bible Knowledge Commentary,* pages 222-233.

Commentary

There are some decisions I hate to make.

I particularly dislike deciding what to order from a menu. I'll sit and stare at the listed foods, be the last one to order, and still try frantically to get out of saying to the waitress, "I'll take this."

I had a hard time deciding to buy our last car. I wasn't sure whether it was God's will or my desires that motivated me. And I was very frustrated.

Other decisions — often bigger ones — seem to come easily. It was easy to leave my Wheaton teaching position to move to Arizona, where I had no job or income except through writing. It was clearly the right thing to do.

What can we say about decisions? Some are easy. Some hard. But all of us face decisions that *have* to be made.

This was the situation in Jesus' day as we come to the events described in Luke 7:18–9:20. Jesus had presented Himself as Lifegiver, and had demonstrated His authority. Jesus had openly explained the principles on which the new life He offered is to be built. The counterculture of love had been clearly defined.

And now people had to choose. They had to decide to trust Jesus and commit themselves to Him, or to reject Him.

What were the reactions of people under the pressure of imminent decision? Why did those who hesitated hold back? Looking at them, we can perhaps understand our own reactions to Jesus' claims. And perhaps we too can see why today we *have* to make the choice they tried to avoid.

Why Wait? Luke 7:18–8:3

John the Baptist (Luke 7:18-23). One of those who seemed to hesitate now was John the Baptist! What a shock to see him waver, for the whole focus of his life had been to prepare the way for Jesus. Still, as we look at the circumstances, we can understand.

John was now in prison (Matt. 11:2), about to be executed by King Herod. The personal pressure John faced must have had something to do with the growth of doubt. But even more serious must have been the fact that Jesus' ministry was not taking the direction John had foreseen. John, like the other godly Jews of his day, was entranced with an Old Testament picture: a vision of a messianic King who would throw off the pagan yoke and bring in Israel's promised glory days. But John could see no evidence that Jesus was using His miraculous power to strike a blow for freedom. John did not expect the Messiah simply to go around teaching people to love!

So John sent two of his followers to Jesus to question Him: "Are You the One?" (Luke 7:19, NASB) "At that very time Jesus cured many who had diseases, sicknesses and evil spirits, and gave sight to many who were blind" (v. 21). Turning to John's followers, who had witnessed the healings, Jesus told them to report to John what they had seen.

What had they seen? Miracles? Yes. But *what kind of miracles?* The Old Testament had said the Messiah was to "open blind eyes, to bring out prisoners from the dungeon" (Isa. 42:7, NASB). Messiah would care for those in need. *His ministry would focus on people.* So Jesus sent the followers of John back to him to report. Then He turned to the crowds and He said, "Blessed is the man who does not fall away on account of Me."

John hesitated, because Jesus hadn't done what he expected.

What have you expected of the Christian faith? Have you seen it as a way to become better than others? As a basis from which to criticize sinners? To reject the youth who aches for drugs, or the adult who curses and tries to hide the emptiness of his life behind irreverence or pride.

Jesus told John, *Look at Me! See what I do!* Jesus did not come to judge. He did not come to build religious walls. He came to reach out to people, to heal, to save, to bring hope. To care. And happy are we if we never take our eyes from Him.

If we look at Jesus, we see *love* at the center of the life that He offers and demands. For people who expect something different, something less, no wonder there is hesitancy. But look again at Jesus. And choose.

The crowd (Luke 7:24-35). The crowds around Jesus hesitated for much the same reason John had. While those who knew themselves to be sinners came to John for baptism, the religious leaders held back. And others, aware of their leaders' doubts, held back too.

But Jesus ridiculed these leaders now. John had come, and they all said, "He's too rough. And look at his clothes. What a fanatic." When Jesus came, they said, "He's too smooth! He parties, you know. And goes around with sinners."

Jesus labeled these reactions childish: like sulky children the leaders wanted to play "wedding" when it was time to play "funeral," and when it was time to play "funeral" wanted to play "wedding."

Whoever God sent them, they wanted someone else. And whatever the messenger's message, they wanted another.

We have to watch out for this attitude too. We're too prone to say, "God, I'll let you direct my life—if You give me a wife, a good job, nice children, retirement, etc." We hold back, because we want to retain control over our lives, just as the religious of Jesus' time did. But commitment to Christ involves acknowledging Him as *God!* And to confess this means that we give Him control of our lives.

Christian faith isn't something played by human rules. When we join ourselves to Jesus, we determine to let Him rule.

Rejection (Luke 7:36-50). The final person seen in this section does not hesitate. He simply rejects all that Jesus is because he feels, "I have no need."

The person is a Pharisee, a very religious man. Pharisees were conservatives, not liberals. They believed in God, in angels, in resurrection—in all the tenets of biblical faith.

But the Pharisees were *self-righteous.* They made distinctions between themselves and others, saying in effect, "I'm different." They believed that, even in God's sight, they were good.

As Jesus visited in a Pharisee's home, a prostitute (cf. vv. 37-38) slipped in and began to weep, washing Jesus' feet with her tears. Immediately the self-righteousness of the Pharisee was revealed. He thought, "If this Man were a prophet, He would know who is touching Him and what kind of woman she is—that she is a sinner." And, the implication is clear, a true prophet would pull back from her in horror!

These two propositions express the basic foundation on which the Pharisee's religion was based. *Others* may need cleansing, or punishment. But I'm different. I have no need.

But look at the woman for a moment. The woman, who tradition tells us was Mary Magdalene, knew very well that she was a sinner. She came in tears, and humbly bowed down to kiss Jesus' feet.

How did she have the confidence to come? She surely knew the attitude of the Pharisee; an attitude of contempt, of hatred. But she also must have known the attitude of Jesus. Clearly she had faith that Jesus would not reject her, even in the home of a Pharisee.

Jesus looked into the heart of each of these people. He saw the woman's love and faith. And He saw the Pharisee's criticism and unconcern.

Jesus asked the Pharisee, "Who loves more? One who is forgiven much, or little?" (paraphrase) The answer showed that even the Pharisee supposed that forgiveness and love were linked. The one who is forgiven much loves much.

But the one who will not accept forgiveness will never learn to love!

Of all the figures in the New Testament, the Pharisee is the most tragic. He alone was totally cut off from Jesus' love. He alone *refused* to respond. And why? Because he kept on insisting, "I have no need."

There are things inside each of us that we're ashamed to even think of; that we cringe to imagine another person knowing. Yet Jesus knows. In every detail. And Jesus loves us still. He loves and reaches out to forgive.

Forgiveness unlocked a new life for the woman who recognized her need and came to Jesus. But refusal to admit need, hesitation to take our places before Jesus as sinners, cuts us off from Him as surely as it cut off the Pharisee.

So men hesitated, and found it hard to decide about Jesus for three reasons that Luke unveiled.

- This Jesus isn't what I expected from God.
- Jesus doesn't play by my rules.
- I have no need: I want no forgiveness.

What reasons do we give today? Are they as poor as these three? These were poor, you know, for each fails to reckon with the reality that Jesus Christ is God; that He makes the rules, and that each one of us *does* need the forgiveness that ushers in new life.

❋ *Group Activity:*
Singles/Single Again Group
List the three major things you expect from life; things that you feel you need to make life meaningful.

Share these with each other, then discuss: Has my list changed any in the last ten years? If so, how?

Read and discuss the story of John the Baptist, whose expectations about what Jesus would do were disappointed. How did John react? How did Jesus answer him? (See commentary for explanation.) What evidence is there that John was truly important to God despite his disappointed hopes?

Apply what you have learned from the study of John to yourself. What parallels can you see? What principles found in this story can you apply to your life now? How do these principles relate to the list of expectations you made and shared earlier?

Respond: Luke 8:4-56

Christian decision is essentially response to Jesus Christ and to the Good News about Him. There will always be varied response to Jesus from any group of people. But, whatever the response, there are important things to remember.

The sower (Luke 8:4-15). The Parable of the Sower teaches that the Good News of Jesus falls like seed on men's hearts. The seed falls on different kinds of ground. Some hear, but quickly are distracted and forget. Some hear with delight, but fall away. Some let the cares or delights of this world choke out the good seed.

But why did Jesus speak a parable? He explained: "The knowledge of the secrets of the kingdom of God has been given to you, but to others I speak in parables, so that 'though seeing, they may not see; though hearing, they may not understand' " (v. 10).

Jesus had presented Himself and His message in the plainest of words. The seed had been sown. Those who had responded to Jesus would understand what He said now. Those who refused to respond would soon be unable even to hear.

It seems hard for some to grasp, but it is true. To hear Jesus' message and to hesitate is to reject Him. "Not now" is just as much a "no" as "never"!

And there comes a time when seeds of

truth which have not been allowed to take root are snatched away.

This time had arrived in Jesus' ministry. Men who had seen Him, who had heard His plain words, must now choose. For those who hesitated, and thus implicitly refused to recognize the One they were unwilling to publicly disclaim, it would soon be too late.

Encouraging response (Luke 8:16-21). Jesus had not yet given up on His generation. He gave further exhortations and examples to help men respond with faith.

Jesus Himself had stood out like a lamp, shining clearly where all men could see. He had spoken clearly, so all could hear. Then came the warning. "Consider how you listen. Whoever has will be given more; whoever does not have, even what he thinks he has will be taken from him" (v. 18). The planted seed, the light of truth, both will be removed if not used.

How are we to use the seed and the light? When Jesus' family approached, Christ said, "My mother and brothers are those who hear God's Word and put it into practice" (v. 21). Response brings *relationship,* and our relationship hinges on whether or not we are willing to accept God's message about Jesus Christ. If we hear and believe, we become members of God's family. If we reject, we stay forever outside.

Invitation to trust (Luke 8:22-55). Perhaps the most important thing to remember as we ponder response to Jesus is *who it is* that we are invited to trust and to obey. Jesus' subsequent actions reinforced the awareness of all around Him of who He is.

Jesus stilled the storm (vv. 22-25). Jesus again demonstrated His power over nature, miraculously dispersing a storm and bringing a sudden calm to a raging sea. The creation obeys its Creator; it knows its God.

He freed the possessed (Luke 8:26-39). In Gadara, Jesus met a man possessed by a legion (at least 6,000) demons, whose bondage was revealed in his filthy nakedness and ferocious strength (vv. 26-27). Jesus ordered the demons to leave, and freed the man from their supernatural oppression. Even demons bow before Jesus; Satan knows Him as Lord of all.

He raised the dead (Luke 8:40-56). Shortly afterward Jesus was called urgently to attend a dying 12-year-old. Hurrying to her side, Jesus was touched by a woman in the crowd. The woman had been hemorrhaging for a dozen years; yet at Jesus' touch she was instantly healed. Jesus paused, sought her out, commended her faith, and hurried on.

Arriving at the home of Jairus, the girl's father, Jesus found the women wailing and crying in the traditional Hebrew lament for the dead. Jesus turned them all out of the house, and took the hand of the dead child. Then He commanded her to awake, and presented her alive and well to her joyous parents.

The weeping women had seen her dead. They would now see her alive, and spread the word across Galilee. There was no need for anyone to know just how Jesus had raised the dead in that closed room. It was enough that all would know the girl lived.

Even death gave way before Jesus. He is the Lifegiver, and the Lord of life.

And so, as we think about our response to Jesus, we must remember just who He is. When we see His acts, as witnessed by the men and women of Jesus' day, we know. Jesus is Lord, and our Almighty God.

♥ *Group Activity: Support Group*
List the major problems you face just now. To indicate how "heavy" you feel they are, draw a teeter-totter, with yourself at one end and your problems at the other. Show the "heaviness" by the way the teeter-totter balances, and share any problems that feel really heavy just now.

Together examine the four miracles of Jesus reported in Luke 8:22-56. As you examine each, complete and record on a chalkboard or sheet of newsprint as many appropriate "Jesus is . . ." statements as the group suggests.

Now look at your teeter-totter again, and imagine Jesus seated with you at your end. Does that change the balance? If so, redraw your picture to represent the change.

Pray for others in the group who have shared that they are hurt—both that they might sense Jesus with them lifting their burdens, and that Jesus will act miraculously to meet the need(s) expressed.

Climax: Luke 9:1-22

The climax of the first phase of Jesus' ministry followed immediately. Jesus had presented Himself to men as the Son of God. How would they respond? Would they trust Him? Or, because Jesus wasn't what they expected, would they refuse to admit their need and so reject Him and His forgiveness?

In a flurry of activity, Jesus sent His disciples out again to go from house to house and village to village to proclaim the Gospel and to heal (vv. 1-6). Even Herod, who had beheaded John the Baptist, was perplexed as the reports about Jesus continued to filter in. Could this be John, back from the dead to haunt him? (vv. 7-9)

When the disciples returned from their mission, crowds followed Jesus to a plain outside Bethsaida. He welcomed them, spoke more on the kingdom of God, and cured those who needed healing. Late that afternoon Jesus even met their need for food, performing the familiar miracle of the loaves and fishes (vv. 11-17). These men and women had now heard His words, seen His miracles, and fed on the bread He provided.

It was then that Jesus asked His disciples, "Who do the crowds say I am?"

They answered.

"Some say John."

But they do not say, "Our God."

"Some say Elijah."

But they do not say, "Our God."

"Some say one of the old prophets."

But they do not say, "Our God."

"But what about you?" Jesus asked. "Who do you say I am?" And Peter answered for them all. "The Christ of God."

And this is what it comes down to for all of us. Who do we say Jesus is? A good man? A religious leader? A spokesman for goodness and for truth? Only one answer will do. Only one answer will open the door to forgiveness and new life.

Jesus is the Christ. He is the Son of God.

The Meaning of Discipleship:
Luke 9:23-26

Now the Gospel of Luke shifts its focus. Christ came, and offered new life to a world that, even after conclusive demonstration of who He is, rejected Him. But some believed. This little band of men who said, "You are the Christ, the Son of God," launched out on new life. From now on, while Christ would still speak to the crowds and their leaders, His message was primarily for those who had trusted in Him.

Jesus talked now about discipleship: about how we who are His followers can grow to experience the abundant new life that may be ours in Him.

Life saved or lost (Luke 9:23-25). Many puzzle over Jesus' warning, "Whoever wants to save his life will lose it, but whoever loses his life for Me will save it." We're helped when we remember the focus of Luke. As a Christian, with new life from God, you and I have the potential to be new and different persons. We saw it earlier. Jesus said, "Be like your Heavenly Father." God's intention for believers is that we might bear the family resemblance of His Son. You and I are to develop into persons whose character expresses the very stamp of God's own heredity. *This is our destiny.* We are to be like God throughout eternity, and, in this world, to become more and more like Him all the time.

But the potential self (v. 25) can be lost. We can choose to live the old way, by the values and motives that move men in this world. We can live the *old* life, and let the new remain unnourished, buried deep within us. If we do so choose, what we lose is ourselves, our experience on this earth of the person we could have been.

Earlier we saw a great choice each person must make: Will I accept Jesus' offer of life? Now we see a second choice: Will I become a disciple, put the old behind me, and become new?

This is a question you have to answer. Will you lose your old life, or are you determined to hold tightly to it, to try and save your "self"? Or will you let go, turn away from the old for Jesus' sake, and in so doing become the new, the true, you?

*Let him deny himself (v. 23). Jesus gives a profound three-part prescription to anyone who wants to come after Him (v. 23). The first is: deny yourself.

Self-denial doesn't mean self-rejection. It doesn't mean wallowing in self-loathing, or turning away from everything you enjoy because, "If you like it, it must be bad." God "richly provides us with everything for our enjoyment" (1 Tim. 6:17). We know that, far from being worthless, you and I are of infinite value. Jesus thought enough of you to die for you. If He loved you so, how can you hate or reject yourself?

But denying self is important in discipleship—as long as we understand that it

165

means *deny everything rooted in the old life.* Deny and reject "the lust of the flesh and the lust of the eyes, and the . . . pride of life" (1 John 2:16, NASB).

Carla had been angry. She struck out at her dad with biting words, then ran to her room. After the flood of tears she felt better. But she knew too that for her to follow Jesus would now mean going to apologize. How she fought making that apology! She told herself it had been his fault—and in some ways it was. She told herself she *couldn't* go and say, "I'm sorry." Not when *he* should by rights apologize to her first! Everything in her struggled against the self-humbling that an apology would mean. And for a long time she stayed in her room, as the tension within her grew.

Finally, Carla got up off her bed and, denying the fears and pride of her old nature, went to do what she knew Jesus wanted.

This is self-denial. Growth in the Christian life demands just this: the brutal setting aside of pride and fear and of all the "rights" that the old self demands as its due, to live instead a Jesus kind of life.

*Take up his cross (v. 23). Please note. Jesus did not say, "Take up *My* cross." Instead He says to each of us, "Take up *your* cross."

But what is our cross? Some have thought of the cross as suffering, a reflection of Jesus' agony that fateful Crucifixion day. But that was *Jesus'* cross; that was God's unique will for *Him.* More central than the fact of suffering is the fact that the cross was both God's will for Jesus, and the symbol of Christ's full commitment to do the Father's will.

What is God's unique will for *you?* This is what taking up the cross means: to choose, as Jesus did, to do whatever God wills. This understanding is supported by a little word: "Take up his cross *daily*" (v. 23). Each day, you and I are to decide to do God's will. In this choice we will live as Jesus did, and will be His disciples.

*Follow Me (v. 23). The Living Bible renders this beautifully and well: "Keep close to Me."

How can you and I ever find the strength to reject the old in us, and decide daily to do God's will? By ourselves, we can't. But we have Jesus' invitation, "Keep close to Me."

Jesus does not invite us to a "by-rule" way of life. Jesus invites us to personal relationship. As we do keep close to Christ, He encourages us and enables us. Jesus provides the power we need to live triumphantly, and to grow in that new life which, ultimately, is His.

This, then, is both the way and the necessity of discipleship. To be or not to be disciples is the choice we face: on it hinges the finding or losing of our new selves. We can be disciples as we deny the old in us, choose God's will daily, and follow close to Christ.

And how do we follow Christ? The rest of Luke shows us the way.

✍ **Group Activity: Bible Study Group**
Study the key verses, 9:23-25, making sure each person understands key phrases like "deny himself," "loose his life," "take up his cross," and "follow Me."

Then read the true story of Carla (commentary). Then write anonymously a true or made-up report of a similar event. Collect the stories of all the group members, and read about half a dozen.

Discuss. What is common in our experiences that might help us recognize situations in which we need to deny ourselves?

A Survey of the Discipled Life: Luke 9:37–10:24

We now move on to Luke's description of another flurry of activity. Yet in each incident, we see a little more of what it means to be a disciple. Later in Luke we will see some of these themes developed in great detail. Now we see the critical issues in a quick survey.

Trust (Luke 9:37-43). The very next day an incident occurred which showed the danger of misplaced faith. A man brought his only son to the disciples for healing. And why not? They were associated with Jesus. They had recently been sent by Christ on a healing mission. And yet, when the disciples attempted to cast out the spirit that was the cause of the sickness, they could not.

When Jesus came the man asked Him to look at his son (v. 38). The man had earlier asked the disciples to heal. Now, doubting, he asked Jesus. The failure of the disciples had undermined the confidence of this father in the Master!

Jesus responded almost bitterly. "O unbelieving and perverse generation," Jesus exclaimed. But nevertheless He added, "Bring your son here!"

Do we ask from men what we ought to be asking from God? Is our faith weakened because we have looked too much to Jesus' followers, and not enough to Jesus? A disciple is not a person who acts on his own. A disciple is a person whose trust is fixed in Jesus, and whose response to every need must be to bring that need to Him. Jesus has the mighty power of God. We can trust Jesus.

Suffering (Luke 9:44-45). Immediately after this demonstration of power, Jesus told His disciples that He would be handed over to men for suffering and death. This involved no buffeting by a cruel fate. This was by Jesus' own choice.

Sometimes we suffer too. How good to realize that, as Christ's disciples, we are not being tossed on waves of circumstance. Even as Jesus' suffering was purposive, so is all that we experience in following Him. God will use our experiences for the blessing of others and ultimately for His—and our—glory.

Humility (Luke 9:46-50). The Twelve were eager for the glory that discipleship would bring. They were so eager that each one wanted to be greater than the other! Jesus knew what they were thinking, and that it was rooted in the old self, not the new. He took a child, and told them that, at heart, greatness was to care about the little ones, the seemingly unimportant, the individual.

John quickly changed the subject. He was far more at home struggling with a knotty theological problem. He didn't want to talk about caring for a single child. But Jesus' words stood—and still stand. The great among His disciples are those who, like Him, welcome the least, and humbly stoop to care.

Purpose (Luke 9:51-56). One day on a trip through Samaria, Jesus was refused entrance to one village because He journeyed toward Jerusalem. James and John were incensed. In hot anger they asked the Lord to destroy the town with fire from heaven.

Jesus sharply rebuked them. How far they were from His spirit (v. 55). "The Son of man is not come to destroy men's lives, but to save them" (v. 56, KJV). And so too the disciple who would follow his Lord. We

have a goal in life, a purpose that gives us meaning. Like Jesus, our heart's desire is to heal and to save.

Commitment (Luke 9:57-62). Many in Jesus' day volunteered or were called to discipleship. But many fell short of commitment.

There was the *eager disciple* (v. 57) who volunteered to follow Jesus anywhere—till Jesus warned that discipleship might be uncomfortable. There was the *reluctant disciple* (v. 59) who, when commanded to follow, wanted to wait until his father had died and been buried! Jesus rejected the excuse. "Go and proclaim the kingdom of God." There is no evidence that this reluctant disciple obeyed.

There was also the *someday disciple* (v. 61), who wanted only a little time. Just to say good-bye to the home folks. Then, someday soon, he would follow. This too was unsatisfactory.

You see, what Jesus seeks is the *now* disciple (v. 62). Jesus wants the person who will put his or her hand to the plow and, without looking back, move straight out to do God's will.

The figure of the plowman is succinct. As a teen, I plowed with an old one-horse hand plow, settling the reins around my shoulders, grasping the handles firmly, struggling to hold the blade level and steady, to make an even furrow. As the first furrow was cut into the virgin ground, I picked out a pair of marks at the far end of the field to line up carefully. If I looked back, the plow wandered, and the furrow snaked off across the field. Only by looking ahead, with eyes fixed on my guiding marks, could I do my job.

This is what Jesus asks of us. To fix our eyes ahead, on Him, and not to look back. We are to take the plow, *now,* and commit ourselves to His task.

Involvement (Luke 10:1-20). Then Jesus sent His disciples out again: 72 sent by twos across the land. Discipleship means involvement in the work of Jesus.

And what involvement! We're involved in what Jesus cares about. He is the Lord of the harvest (v. 2). We are involved in Jesus' method of ministering. We go out as sheep among wolves, depending neither on wealth nor status to win a hearing (vv. 3-7). We're involved with Jesus' success: God's power operates through us as we do His will, whether to heal or to bring judgment on those who reject (vv. 9-16). And yes, we're involved in Jesus' joy: we have a sure relationship with God, and we call men to share our fellowship with Him (vv. 17-20).

Prayer (Luke 10:21-24). This last sign of discipleship was one of Jesus' most notable marks. Christ acted in dependence on the Father. Jesus shared His joys with the Father too. In this prayer, Jesus said, "All things have been committed to Me by My Father."

Do you see it?
Do you hear?
Jesus has all power; it is all in His hands. We can come to Jesus, and in full dependence commit ourselves and our needs — in fact our very lives — into His keeping. Then we can step out with confidence, and live!
How good to be a disciple.
How good to learn to really live!

GROUP RESOURCE GUIDE

Identification: *Share with others*
Brainstorm together for specific ideas about what it means to "follow Jesus." Don't stop to evaluate suggestions; just list whatever group members offer on a chalkboard or sheet of newsprint.

Adoration: *Worship and pray*
Before studying the Bible together for a clearer picture of what it means to follow Jesus, take time to praise the Lord for who He is, and that He is worthy of our allegience.

Exploration: *Probe God's Word*
Together or in teams study Luke 9:37–10:24, carefully examining each of the seven characteristics of disciples who follow Jesus, identified in the commentary. As you look at each characteristic in turn, brainstorm how this quality is displayed in life today. The characteristics are:

Trust	9:37-43
Suffering	9:44-45
Humility	9:46-50
Purpose	9:51-56
Commitment	9:57-62
Involvement	10:1-20
Prayer	10:21-24

Reaction: *Respond together to the Word*
Choose one area in which you need to follow Jesus more closely, and share how you are going to do so this week. Be specific: for instance, if you plan to intensify your prayer life, tell when you will set aside time for prayer, what you will pray for, etc.

Affirmation: *Express love and concern*
If any individual in your group has been a model for you of any of the seven characteristics of discipleship you discussed, tell him or her before you break up, or write him or her a note of appreciation and mail it this week.

SPIRITUAL DETOURS

Overview

Luke emphasized the humanity of Jesus. It is only appropriate that many of the teachings of Jesus which Luke recorded show us how to live a human life in union with God.

This portion of Luke contains some of the best-known stories about Jesus' life. Here find the story of the Good Samaritan, the conflict between the sisters Mary and Martha, and the Lord's Prayer. As you show how each of them is linked with Christian spirituality, you will be communicating a vital message to the members of your class or group.

Here your group members can learn to recognize the false trails down which some believers are led, and to recognize spiritual reality from spiritual illusion.

▶ *Spirituality.* In the New Testament the adjective "spiritual" (*pneumatikos*) is contrasted with "soulish" (*psychikos*). The word "spiritual" is used to describe gifts, the law, the resurrection body, understanding, and the believing community, as well as a person. Thus a "spiritual" person or thing belongs to the realm of the Spirit. A spiritual person is, in essence, one who is not only indwelt by the Holy Spirit, but who also lives in obedience to the Spirit's promptings.

Christians have historically been uncertain about the nature of the truly "spiritual" life. Is it a life without sin? A life of prayer, or fasting? A life of withdrawal? In these paragraphs of Luke we begin to understand more of what spirituality is not—and how to live our lives in union with our God.

Commentary

When I was 19, after two years of college, I joined the Navy. At Great Lakes Naval Training Station, I sat in a barber chair and became a "skinhead," was issued my uni-

forms, and was introduced to Navy life.

There I received the traditional misdirection given newcomers in any special group. Left-handed wrenches and lost firing lines, and toothbrushes to scrub cracks in the barracks floor, were just some of the things I was told to fetch. And, because at first I really didn't know what was expected in this strange new life, I was often confused enough to follow false trails. It was all so new. And I wanted to do the right thing.

In many ways it's the same for us as Christians. To become a believer is to launch out toward a unique destiny: to become more and more like God the Father as the new life He has planted in us grows and matures. We are to learn to think and feel and *be* like Him.

This godly way of life we're to learn is distinctly different from the ways we have known. It's far more than mere morality; it's transformation. So it is easy to become confused about the road to personal spiritual renewal. It's easy to wander away from God's pathway, onto sidetracks that look promising but are really only dead ends.

Luke 10 shows how Jesus began to train His followers in discipleship. He began to show them how to live a new life. His words and actions drew contrasts between the way men of the world live and the way His followers are to live. All that is reported in this section of Luke reveals both the straight and narrow path of discipleship, and the dangerous detours and illusions that keep us from our new life's goal.

What are the false trails down which Christians wander? Perhaps members of your group have been disappointed because they have wandered down one or more of them, and missed true spirituality.

Activism: Luke 10:25–11:13

One of the most deeply ingrained human notions is that a person must do something to merit God's favor. We accept gifts from other people. But we seem to want to say of what we receive from God, "I earned it!"

The Good Samaritan (Luke 10:25-37). The activist's approach to life is implicit in a question put to Jesus by an "expert in the Law" (e.g., Scriptures).

But first, it's instructive to note that the man who portrayed the activist attitude put an insincere question to Jesus. He asked, "What must I do to inherit eternal life?" (v. 25) But the man was not really concerned about Jesus' answer. He was not motivated to ask his question by a personal sense of need: he was trying to trap Jesus. If he had been motivated by honest desire, the answer Jesus gave might have been more direct. As it is, the answer came all too clear. It was so clear that the questioner soon realized that *he,* not Jesus, was trapped!

"What must I do to inherit eternal life?" The query contains a contradiction. What does anyone *do* to *inherit?* Why, nothing! An inheritance is something someone else has earned. An inheritance comes as a gift. If your father is a millionaire and makes out a will leaving all to you, what did you do to inherit? Why, you were born into his family. The inheritance is based on relationship, not on performance. You do not *do* something to *inherit.*

Jesus turned the question back on the asker. How did this expert in Scripture "read" the Word? The man answered correctly. The heart of the Old Testament Law, and of all that God seeks to do in the human heart, is expressed in the command to love God fully and to love one's neighbor as oneself (v. 27). All the specific commands in the Law can be summed up by "love," for a person who loves fully and rightly will do what God's Word reveals to be the right thing (see Rom. 13:8-10). This, then, is at once the simplest and most profound demand in the Word of God. Love God completely. And love your neighbor as you love yourself.

Phillips translates Jesus' reply: "Quite right. Do that and you will live" (Luke 10:27).

But this of course is the problem. *Do all that!* Put all self behind; love God purely and perfectly. Love others as you love yourself. *Do all that* and you will live.

These words sounded doom to the questioner. He had been convicted from his own lips. For he, as every person who has ever lived, had fallen short of doing "all that." We have all had selfish thoughts. We have all neglected to put God first. We have all hurt our neighbors. Rather than bring hope, Jesus' demand that a person "do all that" brought dismay.

The expert in the Law now attempted self-justification. This is characteristic of the activist. He wants to earn what he gets. But he wants to use a balance scale to determine value. He wants to weigh his "good" against his "bad," hoping there will be more on the "good" side. Jesus' reply said in effect, "All right. Use your scales. But remember: your 'good' acts are not weighed against your 'bad' actions. Your acts are weighed against the standard of *perfection!* Your acts are to be weighed against *all* that love demands!"

When the expert realized that he had condemned himself, he quickly attempted self-justification. "Who is my neighbor?" (v. 29) How quickly we tend to do this. When we feel condemned, we try to modify the standards, whittling a little off here and shifting something there in a vain attempt to better measure up.

I recently visited a 21-year-old in the hospital. He had shot himself with a rifle. He went to church as a child, but left as a young teen. He said the thing that earned him an invitation to leave the church was a question he asked. "Why, when you're so proud of sending money overseas for missionaries, won't you have anything to do with the poor people across the street?"

Now, I don't blame the church for my young friend's drift to drugs at 13, or for his choice of bad company. But I do wonder. How many of the things we are proud of—our missionary budgets, our separation, our doings and duties—may at heart be expressions of an attempt to whittle God's standard of perfect love down to lists of things we can *do,* and in the attempt feel some pride?

At any rate, the expert in Scripture asked Jesus, "Who is my neighbor?" He didn't want to think he must love everybody!

We all know the story. We know how an injured Israelite lay, beaten and robbed and in pain, along the road between Jerusalem and Jericho. We know how a priest and a Levite (both men who knew and were to teach the Law) hurried on by. And we know that a Samaritan, a foreigner and a hereditary enemy of the Jews, risked stopping to help the injured man. He carried him to an inn and there paid the full cost of his care.

And we know what Jesus said to the expert who had questioned Him. "You go, and do likewise."

The expert in the Law had come in pride, trying to trap Jesus. Now he went away, and we can hope he went away feeling a personal sense of need. For Jesus challenged this activist on his own field of honor: "Go and *do*." You go, and *try. And when you realize that you cannot possibly do all things that are required by the divine law of love, then perhaps you will realize that relationship with God can never be based on human works or accomplishments!*

Go and do. Then, perhaps, this man would recall the message that Jesus so often taught. Life with God begins with confession and forgiveness. Life with God begins when we abandon our works, and throw ourselves on the overflowing mercies of our God.

Ø Group Activity:
Missions/Outreach Group
Sometimes an indirect response is better than a direct answer. Trace the pattern of Jesus' response to an "expert in the law" who, because of his position, was hardly a teachable individual. Work in pairs to answer the following questions about key phrases in Luke 10:25-37.

Phrase	Question
do to inherit	*What does anyone do to inherit?*
love . . . with all heart, etc.	*Who can achieve the standard described here?*
do all that	*Why did Jesus say this?*
Who is my neighbor?	*Why did the expert ask this?*
Go and do.	*What would the expert find if he tried?*

Discuss people to whom you are currently seeking to witness. How might you help them discover their need for Jesus themselves, as Jesus did for this "expert?"

Mary and Martha (Luke 10:38-42). The expert in the Law illustrated an activist attitude distorting the idea of salvation. But is this attitude found only in the unsaved? Tragically, we find it in those who are sincere Christians. The sisters and Lazarus were very close to Jesus. When Jesus and His disciples visited Bethany where the three lived, Martha rushed and bustled about, preparing a special meal for Jesus. Her sister Mary kept slipping away, to sit down and listen to the Lord. Martha, hot and frustrated that Mary wasn't helping, asked Jesus to tell Mary to help! Jesus had to rebuke Martha. Mary, who was staying close to Jesus, had "chosen what [was] better" and that would not be taken away from her. It was not what Martha was *doing for* Jesus that counted: it was that Mary had paused to listen to Him.

The Lord's Prayer (Luke 11:1-4). Activism is an attitude, an approach to life and to relationship with God. The activist wants to put his relationship with God on a "pay-as-you-go" basis. He feels a tremendous need to do something to earn whatever he receives from the Lord.

In unbelievers this attitude is focused on salvation. "Salvation can't be a gift!" they argue. "Let me do something to win God's approval. Let me earn my way to heaven." Like the expert in the Law to whom Jesus spoke, such people have not realized that they truly are lost.

Activism also characterizes the life of many Christians. They too want to live on a pay-as-you-go basis. They feel that they have to work to keep God's favor. But we believers are children of the Heavenly Father! Helpless children, infants, unable in ourselves to love or to do anything well (see John 15:5). Activism, working to earn spiritual growth and gifts—leads only to the frustration that Martha felt as she bustled and hurried—and saw that her sister was closer to Jesus than she!

Then what is God's alternative? If we aren't to grow by self-effort, how *do* we grow? Jesus' answer comes as we see Him help the disciples develop an attitude, not of activism, but of *dependence.*

Consider the implications of the prayer that Jesus taught His disciples, and its relationship to Luke's present theme.

Father in heaven, Holy is Your name. Your kingdom come, Your will be done on earth just as it is being done in heaven. Give us our daily bread. Forgive our

171

sins, as we also live forgiveness with others. And lead us, Father . . . not into temptation, but deliver us from evil.

Luke 11:1-4, author's paraphrase

In this simple prayer, Jesus taught all disciples to come to God as Father, not employer. We are to honor Him, not repay Him. We are to make requests of Him, not to demand earnings. We are to realize our need for constant forgiveness, not to shout in pride, "See how great I'm doing!" We are to request deliverance, not to promise, "I'll try harder."

The activist attitude is based on the idea that we can do something *for* God. The disciples' attitude is based on the awareness that *God can do something* in us!

The prayer applied (Luke 11:5-13). The next few teachings of our Lord recorded by Luke reinforce all that the disciples' prayer implies.

*Persistence (vv. 5-10). The first story teaches by contrast. If you have a friend who is at first unwilling to help you, keep after him. He'll finally come down and help just to be rid of you! And Jesus says in application, "Ask, and it shall be given. . . . Everyone who asks receives (vv. 9-10, NASB). *God is not like an irritable acquaintance!* You can depend on Him, because God cares. Ask Him, and He will give.

*Fatherhood (vv. 11-13). The second illustration explains God's eagerness to meet our every need, and to grant our requests. God is our Father. The key to understanding our relationship with the Lord and His attitude toward us goes back to this fact.

The disciple of Jesus comes to His Heavenly Father. And the Father works in his life, even as the Father worked in the life of Jesus.

This short section in Luke 10 and 11, then, says something basic to each of us. It shows us how we can move on in discipleship and grow to be like our Lord. We cannot grow by attempting to earn. Prayer, not performance, is at the heart of our new life. Spirituality is found in depending, not in doing!

God the Father is eager to see us grow as His sons and daughters. When you and I come to Him, depending on Him to work in our lives and through our actions, asking Him for strength, forgiveness, leading, enablement—*then* God works His sweeping change in our personalities.

Have you grasped the meaning of your relationship with God? To a doer, God is at best a Friend, whose help seems to him to depend on persistent self-effort. To the Christian who has learned to depend, God is a Father, who can be relied on completely. How important then that we be followers of God, "as dearly loved children" (Eph. 5:1).

Do you depend on God? Have you come to Him, listened to His Word, and simply asked, "Father, make this real in me"? The road of the activist is a tragic dead end. The highway to spiritual transformation is the path of total dependence.

Indecision: Luke 11:14-32

The people around saw all that Jesus Himself did in dependence on His Father. But they still hesitated. And they lost the opportunity for new life.

Power over the demonic (Luke 11:14-23). When Jesus cast out demons, people tried to explain it. It could be by the power of God. But might there be some other explanation? Jesus' enemies said His power over demons came from the prince of demons: it was just a trick to fool people into trusting Jesus. Christ's answers (11:17-18, 20) were unable to move them. Finally Jesus confronted them: "He who is not with Me is against Me" (v. 23). The time for indecision was past. People had to choose.

Indecision can spoil the Christian's life too. Coming to Christ as Saviour is only the beginning. One must own Him as Lord and decide for discipleship. But so many of us hold back! And only later discover that we have wandered into an empty way of life.

Vulnerability (Luke 11:24-26). Jesus illustrated the vulnerability of the man who is forgiven, but will not go on to full commitment. Jesus spoke of an unclean spirit cast out of a man. The man was cleansed, freed from the old dominion. But his personality, though put in order, was not occupied! He was like an empty room. What would happen to him? Unless he filled up the emptiness, other spirits even worse than the one cast out would come in.

Even the believer has no defense against evil as long as his or her life is empty. We need the positive, dynamic presence of

Jesus Christ filling our lives. We must invite Him to possess us totally if our lives are going to change. Initial faith not followed by total commitment is another spiritual dead end for Christians.

Filled (Luke 11:27-28). How do we go about filling our lives with Jesus? Christ explained. "Blessed rather are those who hear the Word of God and obey it" (v. 28). *This* "doing" is not to be confused with the activist's self-effort. Instead it is an opening up of our lives to God, a dependence on Christ for enablement which frees us to respond to God's revealed will. This doing is a response, made simply because we want to follow Jesus, and depend on Him to enable us as we keep His Word.

Judgment ahead (Luke 11:29-32). This section closes with a warning of judgment. The people of Jesus' time had heard Him. Except for a small band, they had hesitated far too long. Now the time of invitation was almost past. The next great public evidence of who Jesus is would come in His resurrection (vv. 29-30).

Then Jesus reviewed how great a sin their failure to decide was. When Jonah came to Nineveh, the people of that pagan city responded with faith. Sheba came to Solomon because she had believed the stories of his wisdom. Yet Jesus—far greater than any and all the Old Testament figures—had come to His people. Had they heard? Had they listened? No, they had hesitated, undecided. And they hesitated still, as the last opportunity of the nation to receive Jesus as King slipped away.

What a lesson for us today. Have our group members hesitated too long? Or drawn back from full commitment to Christ as Lord?

How important for us all to remember that Jesus, the One with all power, has said to us, "Follow Me." We cannot afford to hesitate. Hesitation has such a terrible cost. We might lose ourselves, and never know in this world all that it means to be transformed.

How good it is to know that we need not hesitate. Discipleship is not a "try harder" life, that we're afraid to try because we are sure that we'll fail. Discipleship is simply depending on God, our Father, confident in that intimate relationship that God will enable us to do His will, and transform us as He has said.

Illusions: Luke 11:33–12:3

I once spoke at a youth conference on evangelism held at Disneyland Hotel in California.

I had some free time, and visited the Circlevision theater in Tomorrowland. By linking nine cameras, the Disney photographers had provided a 360° vision of historic and scenic America, shown on giant screens that encircled the watcher. I was particularly jolted when the photographers took us inside a car careening down a twisting San Francisco street—and actually *felt* the bodily sensations of tipping and turning. It was as if we were in the car instead of standing on solid, carpeted floor inside the theater. Our eyes literally fooled our bodies; we felt what our eyes saw, what seemed to be happening, and not what was actually happening.

The Bible points to a similar phenomenon: "As [a man] thinketh in his heart, so is he" (Prov. 23:7, KJV). What a person perceives, what he sees as real, affects his whole personality and his behavior.

As Luke moves on in his record of Jesus' training of the disciples, the writer now shows us two particular illusions that can block our spiritual progress. The disciples of Jesus must see life and its meaning as does their Lord. To see as Jesus sees is vital as we seek to *be* as He is.

The lamp and the eye (Luke 11:33-36). Jesus makes this point in Luke with the illustration of the lamp. "[A person] puts it on a stand, so that those who come in may see the light" (v. 33).

Picture the lamp of Jesus' day. It was, in all but the wealthiest of homes, a shallow dish of olive oil in which floated a wick of flax. The wick was lit, and gave off a flickering light. The lamp was never bright. Today, coming into a brightly lit home, we're hardly conscious of the lamps at all. They shed so much light that what we *see* is the room they illuminate. But in Jesus' day men saw the lamp first: they came to the light, and as their eyes became accustomed to the semidarkness, they saw dimly the room that the lamp so imperfectly revealed.

The lamp of Jesus' day, then, was both a focus of attention and an illuminator of all that could be seen, however dimly. The lamp would enable a person to pick out the furnishings of a room, and to pick his way through without stumbling.

Jesus then pointed out to His listeners that the eye performs a similar function for the body. The eye too is a focal point: on it depends our perception of what surrounds us, and so too the choices that we make. We find our way through this life by evaluating what we see. We make our decisions by what appears to us to be the safest and best way. "When your eye is clear," Jesus then noted, "your whole body also is full of light" (v. 34, NASB). But what if the eye is faulty? What if you don't evaluate correctly? Then you are in darkness! Then you will be unable to move without stumbling. And so Jesus warns us, *Watch out that what you mistake as light isn't really darkness! (v. 35)*

With this simple illustration, Jesus had stated a profound truth. If we make a mistake in values, if what we see as important in life is really an illusion, how great is the darkness in which we walk! We will certainly lose our way. We will certainly stumble off the road of the disciple.

What is important? (Luke 11:37-54). After each key teaching, Luke reported events which illustrated his meaning. While Jesus was talking about illusory values, a Pharisee (one of those men whose values were completely distorted) invited Jesus to supper. At that table, Jesus showed a few of the false values against which His disciples must guard.

The conflict in values appeared as they were seated at the Pharisee's table. The Pharisee noted with surprise that Jesus didn't "wash" before the meal.

The washing spoken of here was not for cleansing. It was a religious ritual. Over the centuries the Pharisees had embellished God's Law with many human traditions and interpretations. In Jesus' day, these men were careful about every detail of their lives. In fact, their sense of religious superiority and their claim to spirituality was rooted in this care. So before each meal they would carefully wash, dipping their hands into a bowl of water, raising their arms to let the waters run down their elbows. One who had not gone through this ritual washing would not be considered "clean" enough to eat!

Jesus didn't follow this tradition. And, noting His host's reaction, Jesus launched into a scathing critique of the Pharisee's approach to spirituality, and of the values which lay at its root.

What were some of the externals that seemed important to the Pharisees? Ritual washing. Ceremonial cleansing of every dish from which they ate. Such careful tithing that a Pharisee would count the leaves of household herbs to make sure 1 of every 10 was taken to the temple (v. 42). It was on such compulsive concern for externals that the Pharisees had built their reputation for holiness! And, in their pride, they loved the front seats of the synagogue and to have men bow to them in public recognition of their spiritual superiority (v. 43). And the Pharisees accepted all this deference as their due. They actually thought they were spiritually superior, because they were so careful in keeping the minutiae of what they saw in God's Law.

How easy for us to fall into a pharisaic way of life. We too have our traditions, our own criteria of spiritual superiority. But are such things really measures of spirituality?

Yes, there are lesser duties that we as Christians should perform (v. 42). But we should not be *primarily* concerned with such externals.

As Jesus spoke to the Pharisee He defined the areas of prime concern: justice and the love of God (v. 42).

True spirituality is a matter of the heart. It is a matter of caring about the things that God cares about. And what God cares about is justice and love and doing good to others. Only when our hearts are so tuned will our eyes be cleared of illusion, and we will see reality as Jesus knows it to be.

Jesus was interrupted by an expert in the Law. But later He returned to His theme. "Be on your guard against the yeast of the Pharisees, which is hypocrisy" (see 12:1).

I used to think that hypocrisy was doing something you knew was wrong, to fool others. It can be: one meaning of the original word is "playacting." But there is another emphasis here. Hypocrisy is "outward show." The Pharisees were not pretending. *They actually thought that the outward show, the ritual, the attention to minutiae, was the real thing!* They had mistaken externals for the heart of faith.

Because they mistook outward show for reality, their inner eye was blind. What they thought was light, was darkness! With their values wrong, all that they might do could only lead them deeper into the dark night of the soul.

✂ *Group Activity: Recovery Group Step 1 (admit powerlessness)*
Together read and talk about the Pharisees whose "hypocrisy" (play-acting) Jesus exposes (11:37-41). Then study and discuss the "games" played by the Pharisees, who were so intent on looking good to others that they were not honest about themselves.

Games	Passage
* Put up a good front, and pretend you're OK inside.	11:39-41
* Talk about your strengths, and ignore your weaknesses.	11:42
* Do anything to protect your public image.	11:43
* Take advantage of others by your hiding your faults until your actions actually harm them.	11:44-45
* Demand others live up to impossibly high standards— standards you can't live up to and are unwilling to help them achieve.	11:46
* Criticize others unmercifully and then do the same things you condemn them for—but secretly.	11:47-51
* Don't let anyone suspect you know a remedy for your powerlessness, and refuse to do what you know you must.	11:52

It's all too easy to play the Pharisees' games. In totally honest self-evaluation, on separate sheets of paper list as many specific incidents as you can recall when you played each of these games yourself.

When you are done, discuss together, "Are there any really good reasons why I do not admit powerlessness or that my life is unmanageable?" If you are ready to take this first step in recovery, share at least one sheet recording Pharisee-like games you have played.

If you're not ready for this first step, read aloud what Jesus said about the person who tries to reform himself (11:24-26).

Warning (Luke 12:1-3). It was later that Jesus warned His disciples, and us, against viewing spiritual life as did the religious people of His day. Outward show had become more important to them than the heart; the external had become reality. Yet, there is a day coming when no one will be able to hide behind his illusions! "There is nothing concealed that will not be disclosed, or hidden that will not be made known" (v. 2).

When God reveals reality, how vital that neither you nor I nor our group members be found to have wandered into the cold, dark, empty world of outward show.

GROUP RESOURCE GUIDE

Identification: *Share with others*
Each group member should choose a name tag from one of two piles, green if one is a "do-fer," and blue if one is a "done-fer." A do-fer is a person who tends to take the initiative in doing things for others and around the house. "Here, let me get it," is the do-fer's favorite saying, and he or she is one who jumps up from the table and starts stacking the dishes. But the done-fer is likely to say, "Honey, will you get me the paper?" And after dinner he or she turns on the TV, heads for the sofa, and flops.

Share several incidents that prove you are a do-fer or done-fer. When each has shared, discuss the good and bad things about your type person.

Exploration: *Probe God's Word*
Divide into teams of three or four. Do-fers and done-fers should be in separate groups. Study Jesus' teaching on prayer (11:1-13). Each team is to list specific ways in which Jesus' teaching speaks to its own personality type.

In the process examine each of these paragraphs separately and carefully. Refer to the commentary for additional insights if you wish. Prayer paragraphs: 11:1-4, 5-8, 9-10, 11-13.

Reaction: *Respond together to the Word*
Report team insights to the whole group, listing what each team saw in these verses that speaks directly to the do-fer and to the done-fer. Write down the lists for later meditation, and set aside time to listen to what God wants to say to you about your prayer life.

Adoration: *Worship and pray*
Link hands and pray the Lord's Prayer, slowly and meaningfully. The best way to do this is to pause to meditate for about 30 seconds between each of the following phrases.

Father/Hallowed be Your name/Your kingdom come/Give us/each day/daily bread/Forgive us/our sins/as we forgive/ everyone who sins against us/And lead us/not into temptation.

STUDY GUIDE 26

Luke 12:4–16:31

LIFE'S ILLUSIONS

Overview

Some of the most familiar of Jesus' stories are found in these chapters of Luke. Among them are:

- the Parable of the Rich Fool.
- exhortation not to worry, but to remember the lilies of the field.
- the illustration of the narrow door.
- the Parable of the Great Banquet.
- the Parable of the Lost Sheep.
- the Parable of the Prodigal Son.
- the Parable of the Shrewd Manager.
- the story of the rich man and Lazarus.

Many of the stories involve money, and illustrate the tension that comes as we live in two worlds—the physical and spiritual. Jesus teaches us how to resolve that tension by giving priority to the spiritual, confident that our Heavenly Father will meet our needs.

But the stories also have another theme: they expose the games played by people who want to *appear* spiritual, but who have not really made God's priorities their own.

There is plenty of material in these chapters for several group sessions: many of the parables could each be given an hour or more of time. But there is profit too in seeing how these stories and events fit together, and apply to the issues that we face today while seeking to live as Jesus' disciples in the world of here and now.

■ For a verse-by-verse commentary on these chapters, see the *Bible Knowledge Commentary*, pages 237-247.

Commentary

It is easy for us to fall victim to illusions. Part of the reason is that a disciple does live in two worlds: the material-social world around him, and the invisible, spiritual world operating within and through the visible. Conflicts between these two worlds often occur. A choice that seems wise according to appearances is often not wise at all.

So we seem caught between what we see around us and something that God says is far more real. Standing between the two, the disciple needs to come to the place where he commits himself to one world only. He needs to recognize appearances as mere illusion, and grasp the tremendous fact that what is not apparent to us is far more real.

Carol's mother insisted she work toward a teaching certificate in college, rather than take the training Carol felt she wanted for missions. Carol's mother was moved by a concern for her daughter's security; certainly education was the safest course. So it might appear! But appearances can be misleading.

Between Two Worlds: Luke 12:4-48

Misleading (Luke 12:4-12). Jesus began to teach that appearances are misleading with a simple warning. He told His disciples not to fear (that is, stand in awe of) powers that can kill the physical body. Instead, stand in awe of God, who can give life to or can destroy the living personality (see vv. 4-5).

This instruction might well frighten us were it not for Jesus' next words. Not a sparrow falls, or a hair of our head is lost, but that God knows. So, Jesus said, "Are not five sparrows sold for two pennies? Yet not one of them is forgotten by God. Indeed, the very hairs of your head are all numbered. Don't be afraid; you are worth more than many sparrows." God's power is used *for* us, not against us. We stand in awe of God not because He will destroy us, but because He who has all power cares! We are important to Him!

How important is this realization? Jesus went on to show that when a person acknowledges Christ, that person is acknowledged *by* Christ in the presence of the angels.

What happens on earth is important in heaven! *The two worlds which seem so separated are actually linked . . . and God is in control of both!* How wonderful to realize that God, who does control, values us and will use His power on our behalf.

The rich fool (Luke 12:13-21). It is so easy to think of what is happening here on earth as the important thing. But what a spiritual disaster that is. One man who heard Jesus speak of God's control over the material shouted out, asking Christ to make his brother divide an inheritance. This man had completely misunderstood Jesus' teaching. *This world is not the important one!* So Jesus warned, "Watch out! Be on your guard against all kinds of greed; a man's life does not consist in the abundance of his possessions."

How easily we come to think of this world as the important one, and imagine that life is summed up in what we possess. Jesus told of a "rich fool" who finally felt that he had more than plenty.

He had so much that he tore down his barns to build larger ones. He was comforted to think that he had all he would ever need, and told himself, "You have plenty" (v. 19).

Older versions translate this, "Soul, you have." In the original, the word so translated means the man himself: his living personality. What this man had done was to confuse his life in this world, his bodily needs, with *himself.*

But a human being is more than an animal. He is more than a body and bodily awareness. A human being, formed in the image of God by God's own hand, is a deathless being who will exist in self-conscious awareness throughout eternity—either with God, or separated from Him.

The rich man thought that this world was all; that life consisted of luxury and plenty. How blind! What a tragic mistake! That very night, Jesus said, the man's personality was separated from his body, to leave this world and to answer to God. And all his *things* were left behind.

When we see reality clearly, we come to realize both that the physical universe is under God's control, and that the material is ultimately irrelevant to the real meaning of human life.

Lilies of the field (Luke 12:22-34). Jesus warned the crowds not to assume that abundance and luxury are keys to the meaning of life. Now Jesus spoke to the disciples about their attitudes toward life's *necessities!* The disciple is not to be concerned about food and clothing. His attitude is to be one of trust in God, who knows his needs, and who is in control of all things.

There are two things that Jesus' words bring to our attention.

(1) Disciples need not live in a state of anxiety. We can trust God for our physical needs as for all else. Because we need not worried about such things, when we make decisions we're free to choose God's will, even if it may seem to involve loss of all we possess (v. 33).

(2) Our use of material resources will reflect our commitment to God, and the extent to which our hearts are set on His kingdom and righteousness (v. 31). Jesus said, "Where your treasure is, there your heart will be also" (v. 34). If we treasure things, possessions, or wealth, then our hearts will be drawn away from God. Like the rich fool, we will seek meaning in things. And with our vision clouded, we'll lose our way as disciples.

Group Activity: Bible Study Group
Quickly outline the major categories in your budget, and estimate amounts spent on each. Be as accurate as possible. Then study Luke 12:13-34 together, identifying the major teaching of the story and Jesus' follow-up teaching. Review your spending, and ask yourself: If I felt truly free of all concern for necessities and all desire for luxuries, would my budget be different than it is now?

Watch! (Luke 12:35-48) Jesus closed His discussion of the disciples' attitudes toward the material world with a warning. Be alert!

Christ's coming seems to many to stretch farther and farther into the future. How easy to settle down in this world. How quickly we, as servants of God, can come to enjoy what He has left in our charge while He is away. It is not wrong to enjoy. But we do know the Master's plan. This present world will be dissolved in fire (2 Peter 3:7-13). Thus all that we do here and now should be done in view of the fact of our Lord's appearance. How happy for us if we never let the world around us close our eyes to God. How happy if we resist the constant temptation to build our lives on things rather than on His coming.

♥ *Group Activity: Support Group*
Brainstorm common fears of people, and list on a chalkboard or large sheet of newsprint. Some fears are healthy, some are unhealthy. Privately jot down any fears you have, and identify each as healthy or unhealthy.

Then study together three incidents which have to do with fear: fear of what others might think or do (12:4-12), fear of poverty (12:13-34), and fear of God (12:35-48). Together determine: Is the fear healthy or unhealthy? What is the underlying source of the fear? What are the effects of the fear on behavior? What principles can you see for overcoming unhealthy fears?

Share one of your unhealthy fears and talk about its impact in your life. Together work on principles you might apply to overcome it.

Closing Doors: Luke 12:51–13.9

Christ's ministry was now focused on instruction of His disciples. Yet the door to life while swinging shut, was not yet closed to the crowds. And so Jesus warned them: the time is *now*. You must decide.

Christ asked how people who could judge the weather with a glance toward the sky could fail to interpret the meaning of the times in which they live (12:54-59). The signs had been given: the earth is on its way to court, to appear before the Judge of all. The time to settle is now, out of court, before sentence is passed.

But still Jesus' listeners tried to avoid the issue, and to speak of curiosities. Jesus warned them plainly. Several people killed in a recent disaster were no more guilty than they! "Unless you repent, you too will all perish" (13:5).

The Parable of the Fig Tree (vv. 6-9) is another warning. The tree represented Israel. It had been planted and cared for, but was barren. Now, it was given one last chance. If the tree did not respond, it would be rooted out.

The door is closing.

The Master of the house draws near. Judgment, or joy, awaits.

Are People Pawns? Luke 13:10–14:35

When my oldest son was 12 we got a game called Jarts, which consists of big outdoor darts that one tosses at a circle marked out on the ground. We enjoyed the game until it became clear that my son was taking the competition too seriously, and was frustrated when I scored more points than he did. Finally I got smart, and changed the rules. Instead of seeing who got to 21 first, we began to see how many tosses it would take us to reach that amount adding our scores together. And then we began to enjoy the game.

There's something about any win/lose game that can make for frustration and even humiliation. Eric Berne, in *Games People Play* (Dell), suggests that we all play games with each other; we all try to win. We manipulate other people to make them serve our ends. The desire to "win," to feel ourselves better than others, or to gain a benefit at someone else's expense is all a part of the distortion that sin has stamped on the human personality. It's *natural* to play such interpersonal games, even for the believer. But it is totally contrary to the way of life of the disciple.

Luke illustrated, in the experiences and conversations of Jesus, some of the strategies that people use to gain advantage. And he showed why these are contradictory to the life of discipleship. In probing the inner motives of men, Jesus probes our lives too. He helps us discover hidden patterns in our lives that might hold us back from full experience of the disciple's abundant life.

Formalism (Luke 13:10-21). Teaching in the synagogue on the Sabbath, Jesus saw a woman who had been oppressed for 18 years, bent almost double and unable to straighten up. Jesus called out to her and laid hands on her. Immediately freed, the woman stood upright and praised God. And the president of the synagogue was *annoyed!*

In fact, he was so upset that he announced: "There are six days for work. So come and be healed on those days, not on the Sabbath."

Immediately, Jesus labeled his response hypocrisy: "Outward show." This man was so caught up in the forms and traditions that he lost sight of people! But the same man would think nothing of untying an ox on the Sabbath, and leading it to drink (v. 15).

179

Jesus' illustration pierced through all the pretense to reveal the utter emptiness of formalism. His words "humiliated" the leaders, and then Jesus went on to warn. In the kingdom of God, many birds will come roost on the tree that faith produces. Don't mistake them for fruit! In the kingdom formalism, the notion that outward show and form is the reality, can, like yeast in flour, too quickly permeate the whole.

♥ *Group Activity: Support Group*
Identify the most painful experience you have had as an adult. Then list insensitive things said or done by others in response to your hurt. For instance, a well-meaning person might dismiss the loss of a stillborn child with, "You're young. You can have another."

Read and reread the "case of the crippled woman" (13:10-17). Identify with her in her 18 years of suffering. What are some of the cruel or insensitive things people probably said to her? Together list as many remarks of others as you can think of. Then discuss: How do such remarks make the sufferer feel?

Focus on the acts and words of Jesus in this situation. How did what Jesus said make the woman feel? How did it remove any guilt she might have felt for her situation?

Share the painful experience you identified at the beginning of the group session, and why it has hurt you so much. Respond as each person shares, modeling your supportive words on Jesus' affirming approach to the sufferer.

Name-droppers (Luke 13:22-30). Jesus warned against people who associate with Him without commitment. The day would come, Jesus warned, when such people would find themselves outside! Then they will cry out, "Sir, open the door for us." When the door is not opened they will protest, "We ate and drank with You, and You taught in our streets" (v. 26). Jesus will reject them: "I don't know you or where you come from." *It is origin, not association, that counts!* Spend all the time in church you want. Association with believers won't make you a Christian. You must have the life that comes from God.

Weaknesses (Luke 13:31-35). The Pharisees, who hated Jesus and were plotting to kill Him, now hurried up to warn Christ of impending danger from Herod. The name of this game is, "find the weakness."

The Pharisees would have been delighted if Herod *had* killed Jesus. But even the rumor might help them. Rumors make people worry. A lie here or there might upset a person you don't like. It might produce uncertainty, or even fear. If a weakness shows up in a person's character, you have something to use against him. You have a prop for your own pride; ammunition for belittling remarks. "Did you hear how Jesus just fell apart when He heard that. . . ?"

But Jesus was not afraid. He knew far more than His enemies about His suffering, and He never flinched or drew back. But Jesus took no special pride in His courage. Instead, His heart was touched with compassion for the very men who hated Him and tried to break His spirit. Jesus mourned over the Jerusalem that had rejected, and would soon crucify Him—and in turn would itself be destroyed (vv. 34-35).

Entrapment (Luke 14:1-6). We have a concept in our legal code called *entrapment*. It protects a person from being solicited by law enforcement officers to commit a crime, for which he can then be arrested. Crimes must be committed on the initiation of the criminal, not the police.

But entrapment is one of the games human beings often play with one another. We set up a trap, into which we hope they will fall.

The Pharisees, knowing Jesus had healed on the Sabbath, had Him to the home of one of their most respected members (v. 1). Right across the table from Him they seated a man afflicted with dropsy. And they watched.

Jesus brought the issue into the open. "Is it lawful to heal on the Sabbath or not?" Then, when the Pharisees would not answer, Jesus healed the man and let him go. Again Christ shamed His critics, pointing out that even a cow fallen into a pit would be lifted out on the Sabbath.

This is a bad game to play. Like "find the weakness," it is designed to embarrass another person. It is far worse when we bring in an innocent third party to use against our foe. How had the dropsied man felt? Had the Pharisees cared whether he were helped or not? Hardly! The man was merely a pawn, a way to get at Jesus. It is true. When we see others as pawns, and try to use them for our own advantage, we soon begin to treat others as unfeelingly as did the Pharisees.

Upstage (Luke 14:7-14). Jesus observed behavior at a feast which illustrates another game, one motivated by pride and selfishness. The point in this game is to make sure that everyone sees and admires you. Jesus noted men competing for better seats at a banquet, for seating in those days was ordered, with the most important guests ranked nearest the head of the table.

After pointing out the danger of pushing yourself into a high seat (you might be embarrassed if your host then reseated you lower down!), Jesus noted that anyone constantly trying to gain the spotlight and exalt himself will ultimately be humbled.

How empty when we act from motives of "what will others think?" How meaningless the approval of men, when only God can accurately evaluate, and only His approval counts in the long run.

Jesus suggested to His host that he might better invite the poor and the homeless to his banquet – not friends who would repay in kind. How much better to reach out in love to those who no one knows but God. It is not the spotlight, but the knowledge that God will more than repay acts of love, that should motivate us (v. 14).

📖 *Group Activity: Bible Study Group*
Jesus exposed several games that people play to manipulate others and gain advantage over them. Five of them are identified in the commentary, found in Luke 13:10–14:14. Together or in teams identify each game, and establish the "rules" by which it is played. For instance, the rules of "formalism" might include: (1) Set standards people can't meet. (2) Pretend you meet the standards. (3) Show contempt for others when they fall short. Etc.

Choice (Luke 14:15-33). Then Jesus told a story to those who were too busy with their games and personal concerns to respond to the feast of life God has prepared. In Jesus' story the invitation had been extended (v. 16). Many had been invited, even the game players, whose emptiness Jesus has exposed. Jesus came to save us all,

even the most sinful. Yet in Jesus' story the invited guests began to make excuses. Each was simply too busy with profit and pleasures.

Whatever the excuse, saying no to the divine invitation remains rejection. A person who fails to respond to Jesus' invitation to life has rejected Him. Salvation is a yes or no issue, with no room for maybe.

Tragically, people of every age judge themselves too busy or too involved in their games to respond. But this will not keep God's house from being filled. The Gospel invitation goes out to the whole world, and all who will receive it will be welcomed. For those who will not, the doors will remain closed and they will be excluded from Christ's great welcoming feast.

Jesus then turned to the crowd (vv. 25-33). They too *had* to choose.

Even the closest of human ties that might sway a person against a decisive choice must be set aside. The word "hate" in verse 26 uses an idiom that men of Christ's time would have understood. To "hate" a person in a legal sense was to decisively reject any claim he might have to a portion of an estate given to another heir.

For us, Jesus' words and actions speak clearly. We must reject every little game people play for personal advantage. Formalism? Let us reject empty show, and care about others whom Jesus loves. Let's no longer be concerned with appearance, and value instead our commitment to the Lord.

People, the Prize: Luke 15–16
What ways of living with others does Jesus commend to His disciples? He decisively rejected playing games that treat others as pawns. Instead, Jesus taught that His disciples are to treat people as the prize!

Valuing the sinner (Luke 15:1-10). The Pharisees, whose coldhearted formalism never made them hesitate to use others, began to criticize Jesus for His interpersonal relationships. "This Man welcomes sinners and eats with them" (v. 2). In response, Jesus told a story which establishes the theme of these two chapters in Luke's Gospel, and which clearly reveals the principles that are to guide us as we live with others.

If a man with a hundred sheep loses one (vv. 4-7), he will search for it, and rejoice when he finds it. If a woman loses one coin of her dowry (vv. 8-9), she'll sweep and hunt through the whole house. When she finds it, she will rejoice. It is the same for God, but with people. There is "rejoicing in the presence of angels over one sinner who repents" (v. 10). *To God, people are a prize!* We are important and valued, and the transformation of a single sinner brings joy, not only to God, but also to all who share His heart of love.

Have we grasped what this means? God won't manipulate us or play games with us. We're not pawns, even in God's ages-long battle with Satan. No, each of us is a shepherd's lost lamb, a woman's lost dowry coin. God the Father *loves* us, every one. And all that He does with us will be for our benefit and good.

What a wonderful confidence this is. I am not being used by God to gain some mysterious end of His. I *am* the end, the goal, that in me all His love might be expressed, and that I might thus share His glory.

The Prodigal (Luke 15:11-32). How appropriate that the story of the Prodigal Son follows Jesus' assertion of God's love. Does God really love us? We've rejected Him, wandered in far countries, spent the good gifts He has given us in selfish and often sinful pursuits. What is His attitude toward us now? God, like the father in the Prodigal story, is watching for us. When we turn to God, He comes to greet us. Stilling our confession, He assures us of His changeless love. And He prepares abundant life for us: the fatted calf of transformation.

But there was an older son, who represents the Pharisees, standing by. This son was unmoved by his brother's return. He was angry, and he criticized his father (vv. 25-30). In his anger the elder brother refused the love the father offered *him* — even though the father went out to entreat the angry son to attend the feast.

The story raises a vital question. Whose character do we bear? The father's, whose love overcame and made a way for the dead to live again? Or the elder son's, whose anger at love and at forgiveness so blinded him that he could not even see that *he* needed forgiveness too?

How exciting that when we have experienced the Father's love, we are invited to be like Him, freed forever from the cold self-centeredness that cuts people off from one another and from God.

✂ *Group Activity: Recovery Group*
Step 3 (decide to turn my life over to God's care)
Working together draw on a chalkboard or large sheet of newsprint an imaginative map tracing the journey of the younger son but only up to the point when he became destitute (15:11-16). Talk about his feelings at each stage of his journey before "he came to his senses."

Individually draw a map of your own journey insofar as your experience parallels that of the lost son. Be sure to identify any key choices that set the direction of your life.

Read the rest of the story, and finish the lost son's map. Then discuss: How did the son feel at each step toward his return? What in the character of the father made it possible for him to come home?

The father in the story represents God. Complete your personal map, showing how far you have come toward a personal return to God and home. Share your map and experience with others in the group, to help any who have hesitated to turn their lives and will over to God to do so.

The shrewd manager (Luke 16:1-14). The Pharisees had turned life upside down. They used people to gain things. Now Jesus set the values right, and pointed to the worth of individuals to a loving God. Jesus showed that the servant of God the Father must use things to gain the good of men and women.

This is the point of the story of the shrewd manager, called in some versions the "unjust steward." Jesus commended him because he was wise enough to use things to gain other ends. What he did was not right. But at least it put *things* in perspective as means, not ends.

We too are to determine what is to be used, and what is to be gained. We must then remain faithful in our commitment to the truth that people are of greater value. No man, Jesus taught, can serve two masters. You and I and our group members will either be mastered by our love for others, and give of what we own to meet their needs, or we will be mastered by our love for things, and in the end will use people to gain them (see v. 13).

The Pharisees heard what Jesus said. And they ridiculed Him, because at heart they were lovers of money (v. 14).

The Law and the heart (Luke 16:15-18). Jesus again attacked the Pharisees. "You advertise your goodness before men. But God knows your heart. And all that you hold splendid is utterly detestable to Him" (v. 15, author's paraphrase).

It was then Jesus turned to speak of the Law. Why the Law? Because these proud Pharisees actually rooted their pride in the Law of God! Yet no one can read passages like the first chapters of Deuteronomy, or the Prophet Isaiah, without being impressed by the fact that God is concerned with human beings. His every Word is spoken in love.

The Law, an expression of the way that men might love one another and show love to the Lord, will not pass away. The Law, in which the Pharisees sourced their pride, condemned them, for they had not responded to its central message: Love God. Love your neighbor.

An eternal issue (Luke 16:19-31). This segment of Luke closes with the story of a rich man and Lazarus. It is probably a true story, about real people. Scripture nearly always marks off Jesus' parables and illustrations, and no parable uses an individual's name.

The story draws attention to two men. One was rich, yet love for his fellowman didn't move him to use even a little for the beggar Lazarus.

When death came, the man left his riches behind. With all illusions and false appearances stripped away, he entered the torments of an eternity for which he had not prepared. But Lazarus, who must have sought the meaning of life in God rather than goods, found death a blessing.

Jesus now told of a conversation in the afterworld. The rich man gazed across the gulf fixed between blessedness and woe, and saw Abraham (the father of those who believe) with Lazarus. He called for help. But it was too late.

Then came an unusual request. If only Lazarus could be sent to the earthly home of the man now in torment, to warn his five brothers who were still living. Certainly they would listen if a familiar man returned from the dead to speak with them. Certainly then they would repent and change the direction of their lives.

Abraham's answer must have jolted him. "They have Moses and the Prophets; let them listen to them" (v. 29). They possessed the Word of God, the Word in which even Law breathed love. If they would not listen to God's Word, "They will not be convinced even if someone rises from the dead" (v. 31).

We know how true this is from history. Resurrection did *not* move the Pharisees. The Man who spoke these words was soon to die, and then to be proved victor over death, raised by the Father's power. And still many would not believe.

How important that we open our hearts to the Word of God. Let us listen to His call to discipleship, reject games that use others, and instead view others as God does: as the prize and focus of our new life in Christ.

GROUP RESOURCE GUIDE

Identification: *Share with others*
Tell of one incident where another person has done something which made you feel valuable and worthwhile.

Exploration: *Probe God's Word*
Luke 15 contains three stories Jesus told to express the great value God places on individual human beings. In teams look at each incident, and determine just how the story communicates a sense of value. From each story develop a list of things people can do to send a "you're important" message to others. For instance, one implication of the Lost Sheep story is that the shepherd takes initiative in the relationship and goes out after the sheep.

Develop another list of things that send a "you're *un*important" message. For instance, when the lost sheep was restored the shepherd was joyful. How often after someone has strayed we criticize or condemn!

Reaction: *Respond together to the Word*
Share insights from these stories, and

record both positive and negative lists on a chalkboard or sheet of newsprint.

Identify one personal relationship in which you are currently experiencing some stress. First check the negative list to see how many items on it are characteristic of that relationship. Then check the positive list for ways you can communicate to that person that he or she really is important, to you and to God.

Then, in threes, tell about the person you identified, describe the relationship, and tell what you will do to communicate a sense of worth and value to him or her.

Adoration: *Worship and pray*
Meditate on the three stories and what they tell about God's attitude toward you. Thank God for ways in which the Lord has helped you understand how valuable you are to Him.

ONLY BELIEVE?

Overview

Some object to the Gospel's offer of forgiveness on the grounds that it is too easy. "Only believe?" a Navy buddy once objected. "Why, then you could go out and rob or rape or do anything you wanted to do!"

I tried to explain that a person who trusts Jesus as Saviour doesn't "want to" sin. That faith makes us different inside, and love for God, not fear of Him, motivates holiness. But somehow he just couldn't see it.

We Christians sometimes have just as much trouble seeing that "faith" as belief is *not* enough. Those who truly believe are called on to put faith into practice, and obey the One they have acknowledged as Lord.

In the words and incidents that Luke reports in these crucial chapters of his book, we Christians are helped to see discipleship's link between true faith, and necessary obedience.

▶ *Faith and Works.* Christians have often debated the relationship. But we can agree on certain basic statements. Salvation comes through faith and faith alone, for the death of Jesus purchased our forgiveness and new life. When a person has new life from God, that life will be expressed. Just as a living infant cries and moves, so a person with new life from Christ will express that life—in works. It is not that works bring life, but that those who are alive in Christ will work.

Commentary

We've all seen a child seated in complete concentration, taking apart a new toy. Somehow it seems so important to find out just how something new works.

We may feel the same way about "faith." What does it mean to "believe"? Does it mean sitting back and waiting for God to do something? Or does it mean acting? And how can I tell if my actions are just self-effort, that *activism* which is to have no role in discipleship?

Questions like these plague many Christians, and many who set out to be disciples hesitate at times, uncertain how to proceed.

Jesus' first disciples were uncertain too. Then the Lord taught them the functions of faith. Just as God teaches us the functions of faith through these vital chapters of Luke's Gospel.

Discipleship and Obedience: Luke 17:1-10

One day the question of faith crept unexpectedly into a conversation between Jesus and the Twelve. Christ was speaking a word of woe about those who put temptation to sin in another's way, to cause him to stumble (vv. 1-2). This was not a word for outsiders only: it was a word needed by disciples. Too often our ways of living with others harm rather than help!

Jesus then became very specific. "If your brother sins, rebuke him, and if he repents, forgive him" (v. 3). This is doubly hard. It's much easier to keep still when someone sins against us, and to try to hide the pain. We sometimes even think we're being "spiritual" by trying to ignore the wrong. But failure to be honest, trying to give the "outward show" of nothing wrong when there *is* something wrong, isn't God's way. "[Speak] the truth in love" (Eph. 4:15). Real love speaks out to remove the barrier that even inadvertent sins erect.

The loving thing to do is to rebuke the person who sins against you, for he needs the cleansing that forgiveness can bring as much as you need the barrier of hurt removed. So Jesus said, "Rebuke him."

And if he repents? Forgive! And this is difficult too. For our old self dwells on slights and hurts and takes a perverse pleasure in self-pity and in "righteous indignation."

185

But then Jesus made it even more difficult. "If he sins against you seven times in a day, and seven times comes back to you and says, 'I repent,' forgive him." The disciples were upset at this. "Lord," they cried, "increase our faith!" (Luke 17:5)

I can understand their feelings. When we were first married my wife and I lived in a house trailer 35' by 8'. Our living room was only about 6 feet wide. And I had a problem. Ever since my teen years, I've been driven up the wall by mouth noises—especially gum, chewed with open-mouthed vigor. And my wife was a gum chewer! As I'd sit at the table, way across our 6-foot living room, I'd become aware of a growing, echoing sound: ker-chump, ker-chump, KER-chump, KER-CHUMP!

Finally, in desperation, I'd mention the gum noise, and be given a quick, full-hearted apology. And there'd be silence, as gum and mouth were clamped carefully shut. For a while. But soon, engrossed in reading, she'd forget. And then the sound would reach me again. And grow. Until I just couldn't stand it any longer, and in desperation would speak again. She was always quick to say, "I'm sorry." But after several recurrences, I'd begin to wonder, and to feel upset. "She *couldn't* care! Not and do it *again!*"

No wonder the disciples cried out to Jesus. "Help! If we have to live like *that* with people, then, Lord, increase our faith!"

But how can we understand Jesus' answer? He hardly seemed to sympathize. Instead of promising needed faith, He seems to dismiss their concern. "If you have faith as small as a mustard seed, you can say to this mulberry tree, 'Be uprooted and planted in the sea,' and it will obey you" (v. 6). Now, the important thing to note here is that Jesus was not speaking to Pharisees, who had no faith. He was speaking to the Twelve, who *did* believe in Him, and who *did have faith!*

Jesus' next words explain His reaction. Jesus asked them about a servant—literally, a bond slave. Doesn't his master have him work and do the tasks assigned? Don't both master and slave expect the servant to put his master's needs before his own? (v. 8) And, when the servant has done what he has been commanded, does he deserve any special commendation? Obviously not. *A servant's role is to obey his master: obedience is nothing out of the ordinary for a slave.*

And so Jesus applied the analogy. "So you also, when you have done everything you were told to do, should say, 'We are unworthy servants; we have only done our duty'" (v. 10).

What did Jesus mean? Simply this. Jesus had given His disciples a *command.* When a person sins, he is to be rebuked and forgiven. This is no optional activity, just for persons with exceptional faith! This is the way every disciple is to live with others—this is a matter of obedience to the Lord the disciple has determined to follow! In essence, Jesus said, "Faith is fine for moving mulberry trees, but faith has nothing to do with this!" When it comes to living by Jesus' commands, the issue is not one of faith but of obedience!

How this strikes at our excuses! We're so prone to complain, "Oh, if only I were a better Christian," or, "If I only had more, then, *then* I would do this, or that. Then I'd reach out to love, or pray for my enemy." To such thinking, Jesus has once and for all cried, STOP! You don't need extra faith to obey! What you need to do is to *remember that Jesus is Lord, and we who are Jesus' servants are called to do as He commands!*

This incident revealed the disciple's confusion about the function of faith in the life of a follower of Jesus. It is a confusion that many believers share today. While this incident does not give direct teaching about the nature of faith, Jesus does settle one thing. We can never draw back from doing God's revealed will because we feel we have inadequate faith. Or for *any* other reason. As servants of Jesus Christ, we are to obey when He speaks.

But then Luke showed how Jesus moved on to illustrate and to teach about the role of faith in the disciples' lives.

The Functions of Faith: Luke 17:11–18:17

Faith stimulates obedience (Luke 17:11-19). Jesus heard 10 lepers calling to Him from a hill some distance from the road. They stood away, as society decreed they must. Still, they cried out for mercy (v. 13). In response Jesus told them to "go, show yourselves to the priests." The implication was clear to the lepers. A person who had been healed of an infectious skin disease was told in the Law to show himself to a priest so that he might be certified well. He was then to offer the prescribed offering to God (Lev. 13:2). They hurried away to do just this, and Luke says that *"as they* went, they were cleansed" (Luke 17:14). Because they trusted Jesus, they had not waited for the overt evidence of the disease to disappear. They went, confident that their need had been met, and that healing was theirs.

Faith is like this. It impels us to obey before we see the full evidence of God's work within us. Do you feel inadequate to rebuke, or even to forgive? Then remember who it is that spoke to you. Remember Jesus' power and His love. Let that confidence encourage you to act, and *as you obey* His victory will come.

Only 1 of the 10, when he saw that his healing was a reality, paused. He turned back, praising God in loud shouts, and thanked Jesus. Only 1 found time to return. And he was a foreigner (v. 16).

Do we take time to thank Jesus for our salvation, and our new life? Do we praise God that we have been healed within?

No, our salvation does not depend on gratitude. Jesus said to the leper as He sent him on his way again, "Your faith has made you well" (v. 19). Our salvation does not depend on what we do *after* Christ has spoken forgiveness to us. But how appropriate it is to come back joyfully to Him, with thanks and praise, to offer our whole selves as His willing disciples (cf. Rom. 12:1-2).

🖎 Group Activity: Bible Study Group

Let the story of the healed lepers (17:11-19) challenge you to praise God. Examine the text and note that all ten demonstrated faith: they were cleansed "as they went" in response to Jesus' promise. But only one of the ten returned to thank the Lord.

There is a spiritual danger in taking God's goodness for granted, as the nine did. To avoid it we need to practice praise — and you can make this a "praise practice" session. First, list all the reasons you have to be grateful to God. Then skim the Book of Psalms for verses or phrases that seem to you to capture the spirit of praise.

Develop a combined list of praise verses, and record them for future use. Using the verses you selected as a model, write your own praise psalm expressing your thanks for your personal "reasons to be grateful."

Commit yourself to take two minutes a day: one minute to meditate on one of the praise verses on the list, and another minute to praise the Lord for something He has done in your life recently.

Faith provides certainty (Luke 17:20-37). We live in a world where things are not always as they seem — where, in fact, reality is often hidden by illusion. It is faith that frees us to see through appearances, and know things as they really are.

The Pharisees were men without faith. They insisted on testing reality by sight and senses. What they could see and feel and understand — only that — would they take as real. So they plagued Jesus: "When will the kingdom of God come?" (see v. 20)

They were thinking, of course, of the promised messianic glory, the outward pomp and show. The Lord knew this all too well. "The kingdom of God is not coming with signs to be observed," Jesus responded (v. 20, NASB). Instead, "The kingdom of God is in your midst." Other versions offer various translations. The kingdom of God is "among" you. The old *King James* even says "within" you.

What Jesus meant, of course, was that God's kingdom was *already present in the person of the King!* The kingdom was *there,* then!

The Pharisees just couldn't see it. All they saw was a Carpenter from Galilee; a dusty fanatic who had attacked them and their position. All they saw was a hated enemy whose miracles of healing roused their enmity and fear, instead of their wonder and compassion. *The King was there!* But there were no outward signs of glory then. Only faith's eye could recognize Him, and believe.

Sadly, Jesus turned to His disciples. He spoke of a coming time of trouble, when they too would long to see Christ's visible coming (v. 22). But instead, they would see Jesus suffer, and be irrevocably rejected by their generation. No, there would be no outward signs of His return, even later. Life would go on as it had in Noah's day (v. 26). People would be wrapped up in their own affairs; eating, drinking, marrying, going about the business of living in

187

this world. Men would be unaware that, just beyond the curtain of heaven, Jesus stands poised. He stands, waiting for the day when He is to be revealed to all as King; the day when He steps into history, to judge.

If only the people before the Flood had had faith to see in Noah's warning the reality; to envision the coming waters of destruction. If only the people of Sodom had had faith to heed Lot's warning before fire rained down. And, if only *we* could understand that everything we take as solid reality today is destined to be destroyed when Jesus comes.

It is this, the reality of God and of His purposes, that faith's eye sees, and that unbelief is blind to. Faith provides certainty, for it looks beyond the visible to acknowledge the unseen.

How does faith help us, then? Seeing reality, the man or woman of faith acts. We flee the city of destruction, leaving all behind us (v. 31).

As in every apocalyptic passage, there is in verses 22-37 a concrete description of a real day to come. But of chief importance for us now is not to grasp each detail and try to fit it into the overall prophetic picture. What we need to do is to sense the impact of the whole. We realize that faith, the confidence that God's Word is *true*, enables us to escape entrapment by the appearance of things now. It is the certainty of faith that enables us to commit ourselves to God's values, and it is life by His standards that gives even our present life its meaning and its joy.

Faith motivates perseverance (Luke 18:1-8). Jesus often taught by contrast. He exposed the attitude of others, and against that background His own love and compassion stood out. It could hardly have been otherwise. He is who He is; they were who they were. The vast chasm between the character of human beings and that of God could hardly have remained hidden.

But now Jesus used contrast in a parable about prayer. He told of a judge, cold and unconcerned about God's opinion and uninterested in others' needs (v. 2). A widow appealed to him to right a wrong. The judge had the power and the responsibility, but he would not act.

She kept coming. Everywhere he turned, she seemed to be there. Finally, in exaspera-

tion, the judge decided to settle the widow's case. He still didn't *care*. It was only because she *bothered* him that he finally acted.

Sometimes we pray, and when no quick answer comes we may get the impression that God isn't listening. Perhaps we've prayed for a long time about something important to us with no apparent response. How easy it is then to wonder. Has God heard? Doesn't He care? Why doesn't He act? Discouraged, we may simply stop praying, feeling that He doesn't hear or care. Or we may frantically wonder what we've done to prevent an answer: has sin cut us off from God?

Jesus' illustration forces our attention in prayer away from *us,* to *God.* What is God like, really? Is He like the unjust judge? No, God is a Father, who loves us. Like the judge, God has the power and responsibility of righting wrongs, but unlike him God would never delay for lack of concern.

When faith shows us the person of God, we find quietness and confidence in prayer. We cry to God. He hears. And He *is* acting. We may not see just now what He is doing and what He will do, but we can trust the Lord.

Faith, then, is a central element in prayer. Faith moves us to persevere, not desperately, but with confidence. For faith lets us look beyond our circumstances and fixes our eyes on the Father who cares.

Faith frees us to kneel (Luke 18:9-17). Jesus' next parable speaks of the self-righteous, the person who prays with misplaced confidence. The Pharisee (vv. 11-12) did pray. He came to God. But he only saw himself. His vision was cluttered with the outward show, with the things he did and did not do. Self-satisfied and self-righteous, he saw neither God nor his own heart clearly.

There was also a tax collector there, too ashamed to even raise his eyes to heaven. Humbling himself before God, this man found forgiveness (vv. 13-14). And Jesus said, "Everyone who exalts himself will be humbled, and he who humbles himself will be exalted" (v. 14).

The man who cannot believe that God loves and forgives will always turn to self-righteousness or to despair. Only faith, a faith that lets us see God, frees us to discover our real selves.

Have we been hiding secret sin, even from ourselves? Then let faith's vision of God's love free us, to fall on our knees.

The next incident provides a climax. Jesus said, "Let the little children come" (vv. 15-17). Like children we too must receive God's kingdom. We must each take our place before God and, looking up, see a Father's face of love. And then, in a timeless portrait of what it means to trust, we may reach out, to take the Father's offered hand.

📖 *Group Activity: Bible Study Group*
The commentary identifies several functions of faith illustrated in Luke 17:11–18:17. Faith stimulates obedience (17:11-19), provides certainty (17:20-37), motivates perseverance (18:1-8), and frees us to kneel (18:8-17). List these functions on a chalkboard or sheet of newsprint. Each group member can select one area — obedience, certainty, perseverance, etc. — where he or she feels the greatest need for growth.

Study each passage carefully in teams. Each team should be prepared to summarize the teaching of the passage, and to spell out its practical implications for believers today.

Faith's Object: Luke 18:18–19:10
Faith is a fine thing. But "faith" is not just a subjective phenomenon: it is not something simply inside us, whose reality is measured by how "strongly" we believe. Faith must have an object. And faith is only as solid as that object; only as valid as the thing we put our confidence in.
The rich young ruler (Luke 18:18-34). A wealthy ruler in Israel had listened to Jesus. Convinced that here was a good Man, the ruler posed a question: "What must I do to inherit eternal life?" (v. 18) Jesus probed to reveal the source of the blindness of this ruler, who saw Jesus as good but would not see Him as God, and who wanted to *do* in order to *inherit.*

Jesus listed the commandments that govern relationships between men (v. 20), and heard the ruler claim to have "carefully observed" them from youth. Then, with a single stroke, Jesus revealed the block that kept this man from faith. "Sell all that you possess . . . and come follow Me" (v. 22, NASB).

This was no condemnation of riches, nor was it a general command to all disciples. It was a skilled surgeon's deft stroke revealing a cancer. God spoke to the man: "Sell all; follow Me." And the man went away!

He went away sad, for he was rich.

He chose his wealth over his God!

Here we find echoes of the first and great commandment in the Law: "Love the Lord your God with all your heart" (10:27). Love of wealth had crowded out love for God as the central value in this man's life. And Jesus' command had revealed the flaw.

As the man went sadly away, Jesus remarked to His disciples that it is hard for a man with riches to enter the kingdom (18:24). Why? Because such men tend to misplace their hearts — and their faith.

With God set aside in one's life, a person seeks something else to have confidence in — good works, morality, respectability, even adherence to orthodoxy. Yet so many of our lives are empty today of Jesus' new life because we fail to admit that God is not *first* with us. That our ground of confidence has drifted, and shifted to become something other than Him.

The disciples were amazed (v. 26). They looked on wealth as a sign of God's blessing and approval. Who then could be saved? Only those who look to God for what they themselves can never do. Salvation, impossible with men, is like all things, possible for God (v. 27).

We must fix our faith in God.

He alone can do the impossible.

The disciples didn't understand. Still intrigued by the notion that the rich have difficulties, Peter said excitedly, "We have left all to follow You." Jesus answered them sympathetically. There would be far more in this world than they would otherwise have — and in the world to come, eternal life.

Jesus went on to speak of the great cost to Him of what we so freely receive (vv. 31-34). For God to do the "impossible," and give us new life, Jesus had to die. But "the third day, He will rise again" (v. 33, NASB).

Faith's power (Luke 18:35–19:10). What can faith do? Faith rested in Jesus, and anchored in God's love? The blind beggar whom Jesus passed cried out and was given sight. How can we doubt that faith in this same Jesus can give us sight, to see and

189

grasp reality? (18:35-43)

What can faith do? Faith placed in Jesus and anchored in God's love? Zaccheus was a chief tax collector, who rushed to see Jesus out of curiosity. Jesus pointed to him, and told him, "Come down. . . . I must stay at your house today" (19:5). As the Saviour sat at Zaccheus' home, this tax collector found faith in Jesus. And he changed. Zaccheus showed the reality of the change in his life by repaying fourfold those he had defrauded, and giving half of all he possessed to the poor (vv. 1-8).

What a contrast!

The moral, rich ruler sadly turned away.

The scorned sinner volunteered to give away what had once been the center of his life. And Jesus said, "Today salvation has come to this house." Jesus had found another lost man, and he was saved.

What can faith do?

Faith in Jesus, a full-hearted confidence that frees from every chain and motivates obedience, can transform our lives.

The Cost of Decision: Luke 19:1-40

It's something we need to consider. Salvation is free. But discipleship is costly. Zaccheus (vv. 1-10) not only illustrated the power of faith in Jesus to bring new life, but also introduced the cost of discipleship. What did the disciple decision cost Zaccheus? *Everything!* His life had been built on money. His goals, his purposes, his very identity as a person were built on the importance to him of wealth and material success. But suddenly Jesus came and brought life. And Zaccheus responded; he *chose.* He gave away half of all that he had to the poor, and repaid four times over any he had defrauded. The core of his personality, the values that had given him direction in life, had suddenly shifted. Shockingly, *people* became more important than dollars. *Honesty* became more important than gain. Zaccheus had become a different, new man! Tis is what discipleship will cost you and me.

What are your values? What is your life built on? What is your identity? "Successful businessman?" "Social leader?" "Popular personality?" To the extent that what is important to you is not important to God, to just that extent discipleship will cost you. You will give up what is important to *you* in exchange for what is important to *Him.*

This doesn't mean, by the way, that you will necessarily stop being successful, or pretty, or popular. All it means is that these things will stop being so important. *You* will be different.

Discipleship does cost. This section of Luke raises the question of *how much.* What an important topic to explore with our class or group members as we conclude this exploration of the meaning of our faith.

Zaccheus (Luke 19:1-10). For this man, decision meant rejection of the old values on which his life had been based, and a commitment to the values of Jesus.

Never make the mistake of thinking that we are disciples simply because we agree with what the Bible says. Or go to church. A disciple is a person who has stepped beyond mere agreement to definite action. He has committed himself to *do.*

Actually, our actions always express our true values. Do we *say* that we have a heart for missions? Then how do we spend our money? Our actions express the values to which we are committed. We can lie even to ourselves about what we believe our values to be. But what is truly important to us will always show up in our behavior.

Being a disciple means we choose that which is important to Christ to become important to us too.

The Parable of the Tenants (the 10 minas) (Luke 19:11-28). Immediately after the Zaccheus incident, "as the crowd still listened attentively" (v. 11, PH), Jesus told a parable. The story involves three classes of people: working servants, nonworking servants, and enemies.

Working servants. One group singled out in the story might be called the working servants. They identified themselves as the master's servants, and accepted the responsibility. He gave each a gift, a certain amount of money, and instructed them to *use* this gift until the master returned.

The cost to these servants was simply obedience: they went out and went to work. Yes, discipleship is costly. We are to use our gifts and talents until Jesus comes.

When the master returned, the working servants discovered that this cost was insignificant. The faithfulness of each was commended, and each was given opportunities beyond his dreams. Each received far more than he had ever been able to gain for his master.

Nonworking servant. This person is also identified as a servant of the master. The *relationship* is not in doubt. But this person failed to act as a servant should. He decided not to use the gift he'd been given; not to obey the master's command to work. Being a servant cost him nothing while the master was away, except perhaps the uneasiness of knowing he had disobeyed. But when the master returned, his choice not to obey cost him his reward.

In the end it costs us much more to choose not to live as disciples than any present cost might appear to be.

Enemies. Jesus mentioned some in the parable who have no relationship with the master. They have refused to be identified as servants; they are enemies. And at what a cost to them! When the master returns, they are assigned to destruction and to death (v. 27).

What then is the cost of deciding to be Jesus' disciples? Christ's parable points up the real issue. What will it cost us *not* to decide for discipleship? Only when Jesus returns, and reality is fully revealed, will we know how tragic a price those of us who call Christ Lord, and *do not the things He commands,* will have paid.

Glory ahead (Luke 19:29-40). The final scene shows Jesus entering Jerusalem, riding on a young donkey, fulfilling the promise of prophecy (Zech. 9:9). And the Bible tells us the whole crowd of His disciples shouted joyful praises to God for what they had seen *Him* do.

Certainly this passage has great theological significance. Here, in Jesus Christ, God's promise of Messiah's entrance into Jerusalem came true. But look for a moment at the disciples. See them shouting for joy. See them, thrilled by all they had seen *Him* do.

And with that vision put forever out of your mind the dismal image of discipleship as a drab and dreary existence, or as mere endurance in the desperate hope of something better later on. Realize that discipleship leads to joy. For as we live close to Jesus, He will act in our lives, and we will know the joy that comes from all that we see *Him* do.

Costly?

Not really. Discipleship is gain!

GROUP RESOURCE GUIDE

Identification: *Share with others*
Share an experience you have had with prayer—either involving answered prayer or unanswered prayer. Share also what you learned from the experience or what bothered you about it.

Affirmation: *Express love and concern*
If you have been upheld by the prayers of another person or by the group as a whole, share with the person(s) who prayed what this meant to you.

Exploration: *Probe God's Word*
Luke 18 reports a number of incidents that illustrate prayer principles. Work through them together, or work in-depth in teams on a single passage. Using the following phrases as keys, develop your own list of insights into prayer. Try to find at least five insights in each passage.

Luke 18:1-8	Will not God bring about justice
Luke 18:9-14	Have mercy on me
Luke 18:15-17	Such as these
Luke 18:18-30	What must I do
Luke 18:35-43	Your faith has healed you

Report insights to the whole group and list on chalkboard or newsprint.

Reaction: *Respond together to the Word*
Think back to the prayer experience you talked about at the beginning of the group session, and what you learned from the answered or unanswered prayer. Does anything in Luke 18 provide more perspective on your experience? Share any fresh insights, or ask for the opinions of other group members on questions the study may have raised.

Adoration: *Worship and pray*
Do a creative reading of Luke 18:35-43. Let one person read as narrator, another read Jesus' words, and the whole group

read the blind beggar's words.

Narrator	18:35-37
Group	18:38
Narrator	18:39a
Group	18:39b
Narrator	18:40
Jesus	18:41a
Group	18:41b
Jesus	18:42
Narrator	18:43

Conclude with sentence prayers, expressing your own need, or thanking Jesus that He is willing to stop for us, who like the blind beggar are simply individuals in the great crowd of humanity.

STUDY GUIDE 28
Luke 19:41–24:53

THE PRICE

Overview

Luke has marshaled his evidence and argued his case. He has demonstrated the right of the Man Jesus to our allegiance as Son of God. And he has carefully shown how those who choose to believe must make another choice as well: the choice of commitment to be disciples. Luke has shown us how to be disciples, and the many benefits of discipleship.

Finally, Luke is about to look at price. No, not the cost of discipleship, but at two other terrible costs. First there is the cost of rejecting Jesus. Luke wants us to understand the nature, motive, and the futility of a rejection which will cost human beings everything (Luke 19:42–21:4).

Second, there is the cost *to* Jesus of the new life He came to bring you and me. In the final chapters of his Gospel Luke told the story of the Cross. What Luke emphasized is the fact that Jesus remained in full control as event followed event, leading directly to His death. We need to grasp the fact that while rejecting Jesus will cost *us* everything, our salvation cost *Jesus* everything (Luke 22–23).

But the story does not end with the price. It ends, in Luke's report of the third day, with the prize! (Luke 24) Resurrection. Resurrection for Jesus. And resurrection for you and me!

■ See the verse-by-verse commentary in the *Bible Knowledge Commentary*, pages 253-264, for a detailed exposition of the NIV text.

Commentary

Why do people reject Jesus? Why do believers hold back, and refuse to commit themselves to Him as Lord? As we probe these next chapters of Luke, we begin to better understand the tragedy.

Whatever the motive an individual may have, the decision to reject Jesus is a terrible tragedy. Jesus wept over Jerusalem and the destruction that would inevitably come to the city (Luke 19:41-47). But those tears were no sign of weakness. Immediately Jesus entered the temple, and there expelled again those who defiled God's house. Jesus cared, and pitied the sinner. But Jesus, the Judge of all the earth, is also committed to do right.

The cost of rejection is judgment, and destruction is sure.

Rejection: Luke 19:41–20:44

The nature of rejection (Luke 19:47–20:8). In the temple, day after day, Jesus confronted the chief priests, the scribes (experts in the Law), and the other rulers of His nation (19:47). These were men who claimed divine authority to govern and to rule. So they challenged Jesus' authority. "By what right do *You* act?" (See 20:1-2.)

Jesus responded with a question about John the Baptist. Was he from God, or was his ministry merely human? Those who claimed such authority were silenced. They feared the people, and finally said, "We don't know" (v. 7).

What a picture! Men who pretended to speak with divine authority, forced by fear of the people they led to deny their own claim. With grand contempt, Jesus turned from them. "Then I *will not* answer your question" (see v. 8).

What had happened here? The authority of Jesus (who had clearly demonstrated His power through miracles and had openly claimed to be the Son of God) *was being challenged*. It is this very thing, the questioning of God's authority and the attempt to set up our own authorities (each of which is ultimately forced to make the chief priest's disclaimer) that is at the root of rejection.

When we own Christ as Lord, when we

willingly subject ourselves to His will, we have found the only possible antidote to rejection. We can admit no other authority than God, and must respond to rather than question His Word.

Rejection's motive (Luke 20:9-18). But why should people try to set up their own authorities rather than submit to God? The Parable of the Tenant Farmers explains. They killed the heir to the vineyard, thinking, "Then it will be ours." The motive for rejecting Christ is the desire to play, and be our own, God.

Lucifer became Satan when he rejected the authority of God and determined to raise his own throne above the throne of God (Isa. 14:13). Sin in us constantly throbs out the same message: I, not God, must control.

Yet how empty such usurped authority is. We may claim it by rejecting God's authority over us, but when we try to reach any of our life goals, we will be forced to admit, just as the chief priests were, "I can't." How empty it is to insist on our own way, and then discover that apart from Jesus Christ's enablement we can do nothing!

And how dangerous it is to challenge God's authority. Portraying Himself as the Cornerstone, Jesus warned, "Everyone who falls on that stone will be broken to pieces; but on whomever it falls, it will scatter him like dust" (Luke 20:18, NASB).

Humanity may rush to challenge God. But such men will be broken or utterly crushed. Whatever they may *claim* in their rebellion, Jesus is still Lord and God.

❋ *Group Activity:*
Singles/Single Again Group
Discuss: Why does a person who is rejected often feel guilty?

Share a rejection experience—by parents, date, spouse, or children—and tell how it made you feel about yourself.

Luke 20:9-19 reports a parable Jesus told after He Himself was rejected by the leaders of His people. Surely that rejection hurt Him. But in this story Jesus exposes their motives and fixes blame where it belongs. Read the passage carefully. What does Jesus say about the reason for His rejection? How did the leaders respond when confronted? Why does real guilt seem to make a person more hostile toward the in-
nocent person?

Think back over the rejection experience you shared. Talk with the group about these questions: In all honesty, was your rejection really your fault? How much was it the fault of the other(s)? Has the other's subsequent attitude toward you been like that of the leaders toward Jesus or different? Would it be honest to make excuses for the person(s) who rejected you, or for Jesus to make excuses for chief priests and teachers of the law?

Let others in the group give you feedback about qualities that make you desirable as a friend, child, spouse, or parent.

The futility of rejection (Luke 20:19-44). It's fully human to believe that somehow we are still able to make it on our own, that we really are strong enough even to challenge God's authority.

Men from two groups that opposed Jesus came to challenge Him. Each relied on his group's strengths. And in each case, the strength proved a weakness.

The chief priests and scribes (vv. 19-26) prided themselves on their ability to adapt to changing political and social conditions. They had survived various foreign occupations; now they prospered under Roman occupation as well. Their watchword was compromise. These men had noted Christ's unwillingness to compromise. And so they felt that their strength (their "flexibility") might be used to trap this Man of principle.

Now, the people of Judea were totally antagonistic to Roman rule, and particularly resented the taxes they paid to these Gentile oppressors. If Jesus spoke against taxes, the leaders could report Him to the government and be sure of quick action. If Jesus spoke for taxes, He would surely lose influence with the people. So when these men raised the question of paying taxes they were sure they could not lose!

It did not go as they expected. Jesus asked for a coin (He didn't even have one in His own purse!). He looked at it, asked whose features were stamped on the coin, and told them bluntly, "Then give to Caesar what is Caesar's, and to God what is God's."

Jesus had not compromised.

Instead He had shown His questioners that their supposed strength was really their weakness. In *their* willingness to be "flexible" they had surrendered what was rightfully God's — their total dedication — in exchange for Caesar's gift of their position, and for monetary gain.

The Sadducees tried next. These "liberals" prided themselves on their freedom from dead literalism. So they challenged Jesus, who had shown such respect for the Scriptures, to show up His "unenlightened" position. They asked Him about resurrection — something they themselves did not believe in.

Jesus responded, arguing from the tense of verb (God *is* rather than God *was* the God of Abraham, Isaac, and Jacob) that these men are alive, and not dead.

Then, when Jesus asked *them* a question in return (vv. 41-44), these men hurried away. Jesus could answer His challengers, but they could not answer Him.

How we need to realize that, whatever the strength we rely on spiritually, it will be *our* weakness too. Are we intelligent? Do we rely on our intelligence to guide us through life, rather than seeking God's guidance and direction? This is rejection of God — and our strength when exalted above God will surely be our downfall.

Are we naturally warm and loving? Do we rely on our capacity to love, rather than on asking God to shed His love through our lives? Then we can be sure that our natural emotional responsiveness to people will betray us. We will love unwisely, sentimentally, and make choices that will harm both us and others.

You see, we human beings are not really strong in anything! Only as we submit totally to God's authority; only as we surrender as disciples to His control, can we become the new people we should be.

Rejection, then, is at heart questioning God's authority, motivated by a desire to have what should be His — control of our own lives.

And this rejection, this claim of our right to control, is utterly futile. It is futile, for apart from Christ even our strengths become weaknesses, and life proves over and over again that apart from Him we can do nothing.

Now, Jesus Christ must have control over our lives. We must give Him control or, in that area in which we demand the right to run our own lives, we will not be disciples.

And we will not be transformed.

Results of Unsurrendered Will: Luke 20:45–21:5

If we do not surrender to God's authority, what will become of us? We will become like the scribes that Jesus now described. We will walk around, pretending to be religious and dedicated, while all the time we are simply trying to win the approval of others (20:46-47).

How much better to be like the poor widow Jesus then described, and honored above the wealthy who were throwing thousands of dollars into the temple treasury. She was honored for the few cents she contributed, because what she gave was her *all.*

This is really what God wants from us. Whatever we have. Whatever we are. Surrendered to Him, it will be enough.

The Price Jesus Paid: Luke 22:1–23:56

Several themes are developed in these two chapters. There is the theme of suffering: of Jesus' agony expecting, and then experiencing the cross. And there is the theme of control. The Man dragged before the courts has the situation fully in His own hands! It is those around Jesus who prove to be weak, mere leaves swept by winds of circumstance. And, we see the theme of finality: "It is finished." Jesus' work is done. Salvation is won.

Judas (Luke 22:1-6). The desperate hatred of the Jewish rulers in these last moments of Jesus' life takes form in a plan to kill Him, put into Judas' mind by Satan. The experience of being close to Jesus had not changed Judas' heart. He had held back — now he made his decision to betray. Watch out when we hold back. "Close" doesn't count. The longer a person puts off the decision for Christ, the more likely the choice will be no.

The Last Supper preparations (Luke 22:7-18). As Judas negotiated Jesus' betrayal, Christ made preparation for the Last Supper, the traditional Passover feast. Jerusalem was packed with visitors, yet no room had been reserved. So Jesus sent two disciples to watch for a man carrying a water jug (normally a woman's work). They followed him home, and asked for room there.

Jesus was about to die. But even the

smallest details show that He was still in complete control of every circumstance. And at the dinner, He spoke of His suffering.

The Last Supper (Luke 22:19-22). At the meal Jesus spoke of the purpose of His suffering. "My body *given for you.*" "My blood . . . *poured out for you*" (vv. 19-20, italics added).

Jesus' destiny had been determined. He was committed to follow that destiny to the very end. And He made this choice "for you."

Who is the greatest? (Luke 22:23-30) Jesus' disciples were insensitive. They did not understand what Christ was saying, nor were they aware of His sorrow. Instead they fell to arguing about who would be greatest in the glory days to come.

Jesus remembered how these men had stood by Him through His years on earth. "Yes," He assured them, "you will sit on thrones and rule" (see vv. 29-30). But *now* they were to be servants, as Jesus had been a servant.

Peter's denial predicted (Luke 22:31-34). Then Jesus spoke to Simon. If he only knew how Satan had desired to have him. But Jesus had prayed. *The Lord is still in control.*

Peter was so sure of himself; so proud and confident in his commitment. "Why, Lord, I'll never leave You." Peter was sure nothing could touch his loyalty. He felt self-sufficient and able. But soon he would deny the Lord. Only Jesus was truly confident with a cause.

Prayer (Luke 22:35-46). Jesus continued to warn His followers about the change to expect when He was gone (vv. 35-36). Then He led them out of Jerusalem to a garden, where He prayed. Jesus was in utter agony at the prospect of that next day. It wasn't the physical pain, but the fact that the Son of God would, as He bore the curse of sin, be cut off from the Father. *But He never lost control!* "Your will be done," was Jesus' decision.

And, after prayer, Christ moved steadfastly, ready to meet His destiny—and doom.

Arrest (Luke 22:47-53). Judas arrived with an armed mob and stepped forward to identify the Master with a kiss. Suddenly the disciples recognized the danger: Peter drew a sword and slashed at a servant of the high priest, severing his ear.

Jesus stopped him. With a touch, Christ restored the ear, and then submitted to these picked representatives of satanic power. *Jesus was not forced.* He chose to submit. He was in control.

Peter's denial (Luke 22:54-66). Now the scene momentarily shifted to Peter, who in naive confidence had proclaimed his readiness to follow Jesus even to death. Peter *had* followed. When the others ran, Peter even trailed behind the Lord, and slipped into the courtyard of a house where Jesus was being interrogated.

But Peter's bravery could only carry him so far. Accused of being one of Jesus' people, Peter denied it. Three times. And then as the cock crowed, Jesus, at that moment passing through the courtyard, turned a steady gaze into Peter's face.

With a sickening jolt, Peter realized what he had done. And he went outside, and wept bitterly.

How sickening for us when we realize our inadequacy. How desperately we need to look always to Jesus—for Jesus is always in control.

Trial before chief priests (Luke 22:66-71). Jesus now stood before the rulers of Israel after a night of brutal interrogation. "Tell us," they demanded, "are You the Christ?" Jesus answered, "You are right in saying I am" (v. 70).

Having heard the claim from His own lips, and disbelieving, for them the case was closed. Jesus had to die.

Trials before Pilate and Herod (Luke 23:1-12). Because the Jews, under Roman occupation, had no authority to execute, the leaders took Jesus to the Roman governor.

Pilate, unhappy about the request because he recognized the Jews' motives and found nothing criminal in Jesus' behavior, sent the Lord to Herod, who then ruled an area which included Galilee. How weak Pilate, this man with the power of life and death, was. He lacked the courage to act on his own convictions. He was a prisoner of circumstances; the ruler was ruled. Only Jesus stood tall.

Before Pilate (Luke 23:13-25). Herod's return of Jesus to Pilate is even more revealing. The Roman ruler was actually governed by the threats of his subjects! Against his own sense of justice, Pilate bowed to the mob's cry of "Crucify Him!" Pilate ordered the death of a Man he knew was innocent.

How clearly we see it here. You and I, whoever we are, are not strangers to weakness. We are not stronger than Peter or Pilate. Jesus *had* to die for us. He alone had strength, and strength to spare. Jesus alone was and is in control.

Carrying the cross (Luke 23:26-31). On the way to His crucifixion, staggering under the weight and pain, Jesus was both jeered at and wept for. He turned to the women who cried. "Do not weep for Me; weep for yourselves and for your children" (v. 28).

The city of Jerusalem, which rejected and murdered her Lord, would soon be razed. Within decades, Titus and a Roman army would totally destroy the Holy City, plundering and killing the citizens that disease and starvation would leave alive.

"Weep not for Me."

The burdened Saviour's physical strength seemed to fail, but He remained in control.

Crucifixion (Luke 23:32-43). They came to the hill. The spikes were driven through hands and feet. The pole on which Jesus hung swung skyward, and fell with a sickening, flesh-tearing jolt into its hole. Unable to breathe when His weight hung on His arms, Jesus put His weight on the nail piercing His feet, and endured the searing pain, to lift up His body to gasp a breath again.

Crucifixion.

Life, death, each breath now a blaze of agony. *A blaze of agony which even now, Jesus chose!* He could have called angels to free Him.

Yes, Jesus was still in control.

And He chose to die.

Why?

At first the two thieves hanging beside Jesus both ridiculed, but then one turned, asking Christ to remember him when He came into His kingdom. Jesus' answer was clear: "Today you shall be with Me in paradise" (v. 43, NASB). In these two thieves we see our whole world, and the reason for Jesus' sufferings. For those who take the step of faith, and call on Jesus as did the dying thief, seeing in the crucified Jesus the coming King, there is the promise of paradise. Today.

New life forever.

And new life, now.

Death (Luke 23:44-49). All nature now put on mourning, and as darkness flowed over the scene, the great work of redemption was complete. The veil in the temple that had signified separation from God was torn from top to bottom. Jesus gave a great cry, and *He released His spirit!*

Even in death, Jesus remained in full control.

Burial (Luke 23:50-56). They took His lifeless body and laid it in a rich man's tomb. The body was wrapped in linen; the tomb door was sealed. And on the Sabbath all rested.

For the disciples it seemed the end. Jesus, their hope, had died. Though they planned to minister to the body, packing it in funeral spices, their great dream of God invading history seemed forever gone.

All of life now stretched out ahead, in empty years, meaningless years, years of living by habit, long after the sense of purpose and meaning was gone.

The Prize: Luke 24

Jesus' death must have left His followers with a deep sense of despair and an aching awareness of the emptiness of life. If history's record had closed with the cross and tomb, life for us too would be empty. Life would be nothing but a brief experience of sorrows, swallowed up by endless nothingness and night. But the tomb was not the end. The Resurrection that followed blazes for the power of God, and demonstrates the amazing vitality that transforms death to life—the same vitality that can and will transform our death to new life, even now.

Resurrection (Luke 24:1-11). At dawn on what we now call the Lord's Day, the women started toward the tomb with the burial spices. Their mood was broken when they found the stone that sealed the entrance removed, and two angels standing by the slab where the body had been laid.

Frightened, the women fell, hiding their faces from the angels. But the angels asked, "Why do you look for the living One among the dead?" (v. 5)

It was a good question. Jesus had told them often that He would die and rise again. Christ had been as good as His word. He had risen!

Have we realized yet that it is Jesus' resurrection power that God pours into Christ's followers? Let's not lie among the dead, going through the empty motions that they do, trapped by the same frustrations, the same inadequacies. Let's take Jesus at His word today. He has come to give us abundant life. Let's trust Him, rise up, and live!

When the women reported the angels' words to the 11 disciples (vv. 9-11), they were too disheartened to believe. Sometimes past tragedy or failure so colors our view that we can't even believe eyewitness reports of resurrection. But, whatever our past experiences, *Jesus lives*. And because He lives, we too can live.

Road to Emmaus (Luke 24:13-27). That day, the living Jesus met two discouraged disciples traveling home from Jerusalem to Emmaus. He chose to go unrecognized at first, as they talked of the recent events and the death of all these disciples' hopes (vv. 19-21).

Walking along, Jesus began to show them all that the Scriptures had foretold of the necessity of His suffering and His entry into glory (vv. 26-27).

Today, Jesus offers us a present experience of new life. But everything we experience is rooted in a reality and a truth recorded in God's Word. *New life* is no mere feeling or hope. *New life* is a reality, rooted in the historic resurrection of Jesus and the proof that resurrection provides God's ability and willingness to transform you and me.

Recognition (Luke 24:28-35). The two disciples on the Emmaus Road must have been amazed and deeply touched as that third Man explained the Word. Eagerly they urged Him to enter into their home (v. 29). As He sat at table with them, praying over the breaking of the bread, they recognized Him.

At that moment, everything changed.

It's the same for us today.

We may hear others tell of their new lives. We may read of new life in the Bible. We have been reading of it in Luke's Gospel. *But new life begins when we see Jesus and come to know Him.* Our new life is found only in a personal relationship with Jesus Christ, the Son of God, who died for us, and who rose again.

Appearance and Ascension (Luke 24:36-53). The two disciples rushed to Jerusalem to share their joy. Even as they told the unbelieving disciples of their encounter with the risen Lord, He suddenly stood among them.

Jesus showed His hands and feet: death had truly been defeated by life. And then Jesus opened the Scriptures and helped them to understand.

Finally, Jesus promised His disciples power (v. 49). For the disciples themselves, a new life had just begun.

All the New Testament, all history, bears solid witness to the fact that these men and women were marked by a joy and power that turned their world upside down.

Luke can be closed the same way for you and me, with power . . . Jesus' power . . . available now as we accept Christ and choose to live as His disciples, and with praise — praise to God from each of us who knows by personal experience that Jesus truly does transform.

GROUP RESOURCE GUIDE

This week rather than a regular group meeting hold a special candlelight Communion service, designed to help each person enter into the reality of the death of Jesus for us, and His Resurrection. On an overhead or large sheets of newsprint, duplicate the following, to show with readings previously assigned to various group members. You may wish to choose hymns to go with the service outlined below.

Overhead #1
The Lord Jesus, on the night He was betrayed, took bread, and when He had given thanks, He broke it and said, "This is My body, which is for you; do this in remembrance of Me."

Overhead #2
On the night He was betrayed
First reading: Luke 22:1-6

Overhead #3
He gave thanks
Second reading: Luke 22:39-46
Third reading: Luke 22:47-53

Overhead #4
He broke it
Fourth reading: Luke 22:54-62
Fifth reading: Luke 22:63-65

Overhead #5
Do this
Take a loaf of bread, tear off a piece and hand it to the person on your left, repeating: "This is Jesus' body, broken for you. And I am willing to be broken for you." Repeat until all have a piece of bread, then eat it together.

Overhead #6
He took the cup, saying, "This cup is the new covenant in My blood; do this, whenever you drink it, in rememberance of Me."

Overhead #7
This cup
Sixth reading: Luke 22:66–23:25

Overhead #8
The new covenant in my blood
Seventh reading: Luke 23:26-43
Eighth reading: Luke 23:44-49

Overhead #9
Do this

Pass a large cup filled with grape juice to the person on your right, saying, "This is Christ's blood, shed for you. And I am willing to be poured out for you." Drink from the cup as it is passed to you.

Overhead #10
Whenever you eat this bread and drink this cup, you proclaim the Lord's death until He comes.

Overhead #11
The Lord
Ninth reading: Romans 1:1-4
Tenth reading: Luke 24:1-12

Overhead #12
Proclaim His death
Eleventh reading: Luke 24:36-49

Overhead #13
Till He comes
Twelfth reading: Luke 24:50-53

Conclude the service of worship here, and either break to go home, or share light refreshments and informal talk.

199

JOHN'S GOSPEL

Overview

The Gospel of John is distinctively different from the other three. They tell the story; John interprets through lengthy reports of Jesus' discourses. Only John focuses on distinct theological themes, contrasting throughout his writing such terms as life and death, light and darkness, belief and unbelief, truth and falsehood, love and hate.

While each Gospel presents Jesus as the Son of God, John carefully explains that by this description Jesus was "making Himself equal with God" (John 5:18). A number of times Jesus stated His deity in an unequivocable way (8:58; 9:35-37; 10:36; 14:9; 17:5).

Outline

Commentary

The Gospel of John is a family Gospel. While the others were written to tell the story of Jesus, Matthew to the Jews, and Mark and Luke to the Gentiles, John was written for Christ's church. In this Gospel we have the deepest spiritual and theological teachings of our Lord. Some have noted that the Last Supper discourse (John 14–16) is the "seed bed" of the Epistles. The major emphases of the apostles' instructions to the church developed in the later New Testament all have roots in Christ's final instructions to the disciples.

In this introductory survey we'll see just a few of the things which make the Gospel of John so special, and suggest ways that your group members can sample this Gospel in preparation for a more careful, multiple study exploration of its chapters.

John, the Author

The Gospel does not name its author. But there is no real doubt that this book was written by John, the disciple and later apostle of Jesus.

John is named by the early church writers as the author of the book. Irenaeus, who knew Polycarp and others who were John's contemporaries, wrote that "John, the disciple of the Lord who also leaned upon His breast, did himself write a Gospel during his residence at Ephesus in Asia."

John also is the author of three New Testament epistles, whose use of key terms, such as light and darkness, life and death, link those letters to the Gospel that bears John's name.

We know most of John, of course, from the other Gospels. He was from a family that operated a fishing business in Galilee that employed others beside the sons. John's sentence structure and thought patterns show that he was very familiar with rabbinic methods of biblical interpretation. This suggests that he had gone beyond the basic studies expected of all Jewish men. There is nothing incompatible in Judaism with scholarship and carrying on a trade, so the fact that John was a fisherman in no way suggests ignorance or commonness.

It is clear from reading the Gospels that

John, with Peter and his own brother James, was in the inner circle of disciples. These three alone were invited to witness the Transfiguration. These three went on farther into the Garden at Gethsemane, to provide companionship at Jesus' lowest hour.

But the picture of John found in the Gospels is not always complimentary. He and James had a nickname, "Sons of Thunder," which suggests a wicked temper. That temper was displayed one evening when the two were eager to "call down fire from heaven" on a village of Samaritans who were unwilling to provide lodging because Christ's party was going to Jerusalem, the place where the Jews worshiped (Luke 9:51-55).

John and his brother were also ambitious. It was these two who got their mother to approach Jesus to ask Him for the highest positions in His coming kingdom (Matt. 20:20-28). Jockeying for position, and infighting for advancement, isn't something peculiar to modern corporate life!

Yet it is clear that John, an essentially competitive and achievement-oriented person, was deeply affected by his relationship with Jesus. In his old age he became the apostle of love, and this term, love, dominates his letters and infuses his Gospel with a special warmth. When John wrote this Gospel as an old man, possibly as late as A.D. 90, he had become a truly loving and sensitive person, whose own character reflected the most beautiful qualities of his Lord.

Jesus in John's Gospel

John's Gospel emphasizes Christ's deity to a greater extent than the others. John began not with Jesus' birth, but with a statement of Christ's preexistence as God. John also reported a number of occasions on which Jesus declared Himself to be the "I AM" (John 4:26; 8:28, 58; 13:19; 18:5-6, 8).

This phrase is rooted in events reported in Exodus 3:14. Moses had been told by God to return to Egypt and wrestle God's people from the Egyptians, to lead them to freedom and the Promised Land. Moses hesitated, and among the questions he asked was, "Suppose I go to the Israelites and say to them, 'The God of your fathers has sent me to you,' and they ask me, 'What is His name?' " (Ex. 3:13) It was then that

God announced His name, telling Moses to say, "I AM has sent you," and going on to tell Moses that "this is My name forever, the name by which I am to be remembered from generation to generation" (v. 15).

In fact, the term I AM (a form of the verb "to be") is the root of the Hebrew personal name for God, Yahweh, which is expressed in our English versions as the capitalized LORD. Thus "I AM" is *the* unique name of the God of the Old Testament as He revealed Himself to Moses, and acted in power to redeem Israel from Egyptian slavery! For Jesus to identify Himself as the I AM was to make an unmistakable claim to *be* Yahweh Himself, the one all Israel worshiped as God.

It is no surprise then that the Jewish leaders responded to this claim, as John reported in John 8:59, by picking up stones in an attempt to kill Jesus for blasphemy.

But there is more in John's Gospel than even this powerful claim to full identity with Israel's God. Jesus used seven symbols, linked with the phrase "I am," to show what He is *for humankind*. Jesus is God. But what does the fact of Jesus' deity mean for you and for me? This is what is expressed in the seven symbolic images that Christ used to describe Himself.

The seven are:

1. I am the Bread of Life   6:35
2. I am the Light of the World   8:12
3. I am the Gate for the sheep   10:7
4. I am the Good Shepherd   10:11,14
5. I am the Resurrection and the Life   11:25
6. I am the Way, the Truth, and the Life   14:6
7. I am the True Vine.   15:1

Each of these images, as noted, not only continues to affirm the full deity of Jesus, but tells us what it means for us that Jesus, the Son of God, chose to become man and live among us. Jesus is our bread, who sustains us daily. Jesus is our light, cutting through the shadows and illusions that darken this sin-cursed world. Jesus is the gate, the one door through whom we can go and find safety. Jesus is the Good Shepherd, who cares so much for the sheep that He was willing to give His life for us. Jesus is the resurrection and life; His vivifying power is so great that He is able to bring life even to our mortal bodies, and one day will raise us to total renewal. Jesus is the Way, the Truth, and the Life; no one can approach the Father except through Him. Jesus is the Vine, and as we remain in fellowship with Jesus His life flows into us as branches, enabling us to bear spiritual fruit.

Only because Jesus truly is God can we derive so much from personal relationship with Him.

The Dialogues of Jesus

One of the distinctive features of John's Gospel is its structure. This Gospel alone emphasizes Christ's discourses, while the others emphasize the acts of Jesus.

John's Gospel was written many years after Christ lived. Some believe it was written in the A.D. 90s, some 60 years after Christ spoke the words reported here. Yet we should not be surprised that John reported the words of the Lord so confidently. Undoubtedly John in his teaching had for years told and retold the discourses. We can be confident that his summaries of what were undoubtedly much longer sermons are accurate. Even more important, we can be sure that the Holy Spirit guided John to record just what God intended us to have.

What then are the discourses? Here are key talks that make up the bulk of this powerful Gospel.

1.	On the new birth	3:1-21
2.	On the water of life	4:4-26
3.	On resurrection and life	5:19-47
4.	On the bread of life	6:26-59
5.	On the deity of Jesus	8:12-59
6.	On the shepherd and flock	10:1-21
7.	More on the deity of Jesus	10:22-38
8.	On redemption	12:20-50
9.	On life while Jesus is gone	13:31–14:31
10.	On union with Jesus	15:1–16:33

A number of these discourses display a similar form or pattern. They are launched with a question from a disciple or onlooker.

Jesus made a brief, enigmatic reply. And then Jesus went on to give a wide-ranging explanation.

Chronology

The Gospel of John seems to hold closely to the chronological sequence of events of Christ's life, though some events are not reported. The list on page 203, adapted from Graham Scroggie's *Guide to the Gospels* (Fleming H. Revell), places events in sequence and suggests the traditional dating of each. You may wish to duplicate the list for your group members to have as you study John's Gospel.

Theology in John

John's Gospel is the most theological of the four Gospels. John had a distinctive way of expressing theological concepts. In the Gospel and in his letters, John taught by contrast. He set one concept against its opposite. While this is not done with some theological terms, such as "know," "word," "world," and "glory," most of John's key theological words are explored through contrast.

Among the paired terms that John used often are Life/Death, Light/Darkness, Belief/Unbelief, Truth/Falsehood, and Love/Hate.

If we are to understand John's Gospel we need to have some insight into how he used these terms, not only in his Gospel but also in the letters, 1, 2, and 3 John.

Each of the key terms are defined briefly here. Again, you may wish to duplicate the definitions chart and distribute it to your group members as an aid they can refer to while studying the Gospel or Epistles of John.

For a thorough discussion of each term as it is used by John, see the author's *Expository Dictionary of Bible Words* (Zondervan).

Keeping in mind the way each of these terms is used by John will help you and your group members as you study this rich Gospel.

Events of Jesus' Life

B.C.	
5	Birth of Jesus.
4	Circumcision and Presentation of Jesus. Coming of the Magi.
	Flight into Egypt. Massacre of the Innocents.
	Death of Herod the Great.
	Return of the Family to Nazareth.
A.D.	
8	Jesus' First Passover.
27	The Baptism and the Temptation of Jesus.
	First Passover of Jesus' Ministry (John 2:13, 23)
	Cleansing of the Temple.
28	John the Baptist Imprisoned.
	A Passover, some think, but more probably Purim (5:1).
	Jesus Begins His Ministry in Galilee.
	The Call of Four Disciples at Capernaum.
	Jesus' First Circuit in Galilee.
	The Choice of Twelve Apostles.
	The Sermon on the Mount.
	The Parables of the Kingdom.
29	Commission of the Twelve.
	Death of John the Baptist.
	Feeding of the Multitude. The Discourse on the Bread of Life.
	Peter's Confession that Jesus Is the Christ.
	The Transfiguration.
	Final Departure from Galilee.
	Jesus at the Feast of Tabernacles (7:2).
	Commission of the Seventy.
	Jesus Attends the Feast of Dedication (10:22).
30	Ministry in Perea.
	Lazarus Raised from the Dead.
	Jesus Passes through Jericho on the Way to Jerusalem.
	Public Entry into Jerusalem.
	Second Cleansing of the Temple.
	Jesus' Conflict with the Authorities
	The Prophetic Discourses on Olivet.
	The Supper at Bethany.
	Jesus' Last Passover (11:55; 12:1).
	The Upper Room Discourse.
	Gethsemane.
	The Arrest and Trials.
	The Crucifixion.
	The Resurrection.
	The Appearances.
	The Ascension.

Definitions in Brief
John's use of:

KNOW — "Know" is a relational term. We come to know God by acknowledging Jesus as God's Son and our Saviour. "Know" also speaks of continuing fellowship with God as we live a life of obedience and love. See John 8:19, 31-47; 10:4, 14-15; 1 John 4:15-16.

WORLD — "World" (*kosmos*) as a theological term portrays human society as a system warped by sin and influenced by Satan. The world is energized by the sin nature. See 1 John 3:1, 13; 5:19.

WORD — John affirmed Jesus as the "Word" which existed with and as God from eternity. Jesus is the One through whom God expressed Himself. As the Word, Jesus is the creative power that brought the universe into existence, and the prophetic power that reveals and controls the future. Through faith we can have fellowship with the eternal Word of God. See John 1:1-14; 1 John 1:1-2.

GLORY — "Glory" speaks of God's splendor as seen in His self-revelation. It is an expression in this world of the beauty, power, and greatness of our God. See John 1:14; 17:4-5.

LIFE — "Life" can refer to biological life, but more important it speaks of the vitalizing power of God. We are given God's life when we believe in Jesus. This divine life-force makes it possible for us to live righteously now despite our mortality, and will find expression in our future bodily resurrection. See John 3:15-36; 5:21-26; 1 John 2–3.

DEATH — "Death" too is more than a biological concept. Death speaks of the spiritual state of human beings as separated from God, and morally warped. The spiritually dead lie under God's condemnation and have no way to win His favor. Only the gift of life through Jesus Christ can counteract the death which holds humankind in a firm grip. See John 5:16-26.

LIGHT — "Light" implies holiness, but its primary emphasis is on illumination. Jesus is *the* Light of the world, showing us the way to God. We are to live as His Word shows us how, and so be "children of the light." See John 1:4-9; 3:19-21; 8:12; 1 John 1:5-7.

DARKNESS — Morally, "darkness" describes sinful acts and a sin-filled lifestyle. Theologically spiritual darkness is the dominant evil power which holds the unsaved in bondage. Sinners choose to embrace the dark; only the light provided by Jesus turns us to a God in whom there is "no darkness at all." See John 3:19; 8:12; 1 John 1:5-7.

BELIEF — John often spoke of a superficial kind of belief in Jesus stimulated in observers by His miracles. But the belief John seeks to evoke through his Gospel is an active, continuing trust in Jesus that brings eternal life. The one who truly believes receives Jesus as Saviour, and expresses this faith in obedience and love for others. See John 3; 5; 8:31-32.

UNBELIEF Unbelief is not "doubt," but rather a failure to respond to Christ with belief. Unbelief thus is a moral, not intellectual concept which implies rejection of God. See John 3:16-21.

TRUTH Over half of the New Testament's uses of "truth" (*aletheia*) are found in John. John's focus is on the link of truth and reality. A thing is true because it is in harmony with reality as God knows reality. We can know (experience) reality only by choosing to keep Jesus' words, which show us life as God intends His children to live it. See John 17:17; 1 John 1:6-8.

FALSEHOOD "Falsehood" is not so much a matter of lying in John as it is a matter of deceit and illusion. All the world's notions of reality are at heart illusory. Only God's Word unveils the truth. Only by adopting and living by God's perspective can a person break away from falsehood and know the truth.

LOVE This is one of the most important concepts in the Bible. Scripture reveals God's love for us, and how we can respond to that love. In both Testaments we are taught to show love for God both by obedience and by loving others. John makes it clear that love is not something that flows naturally from the human heart, but must be awakened by God's initiating act of love in Jesus Christ. See John 3:16; 1 John 4:7-21.

HATE As a theological term "hate" speaks of the deep antagonism of the unsaved world to Jesus and His own. See John 3:20; 15:18-25.

STUDY GUIDE 30
John 1:1-18

THE DEITY OF JESUS

Overview

The Gospel of John speaks more clearly than any other of the deity of Christ. There can be no doubt: the Bible *does* teach that Jesus of Nazareth was fully God as well as truly man.

This teaching does not, of course, rest only on what we find in John's Gospel. There are many other passages that affirm Jesus' deity. Among the most powerful are:

Colossians 1:15-20. Jesus who expresses the invisible God was Himself the Creator of all things, and has priority over all.

Hebrews 1:1-13. Jesus is the "exact representation" of God's being, and sustains all things by His own powerful word. He is, as God, above all created beings, including the angels who are so superior to mortal man.

Philippians 2:5-11. Jesus, though "in very nature God" voluntarily surrendered the prerogatives of Deity to become a true human being. Now that He has been resurrected He has been exalted again, and in the future every tongue will confess that Jesus Christ is Lord.

It is this Jesus, God from before the beginning, whom John wants to show us in his Gospel. And from this Gospel John wants to teach us how to respond, from the heart, to Him as Saviour and Lord.

▶ *Grace*. "Grace" reveals both God and man. It shows human beings as helpless, trapped in sin. And it shows God willing and able to meet our deepest needs.

Commentary

The last of the apostles laid down his pen. His fingers brushed away one of the tears that still came so easily when he thought about the death and resurrection of his beloved Jesus. Even after all these years, he could still feel the same sorrow and joy he had felt so intently then.

John had been bewildered when Jesus

died, and amazed by His resurrection. It had taken John and the others so long to understand, so long to really know who Jesus was . . . no, *is*.

John remembered those days just after the Resurrection when Jesus again walked with and taught His disciples. Taking up his pen again, the apostle bent over his manuscript to add: "Jesus did many other miraculous signs in the presence of His disciples, which are not recorded in this book. But these are written that you might believe that Jesus is the Christ, the Son of God, and that by believing you may have life in His name" (John 20:30-31).

John, the last of the apostles to die, gave us in his Gospel one of four portraits of Jesus written in the decades after Christ's death and resurrection. John's Gospel is unique in a number of ways. It was written long after the others, possibly some 40 years after the end of Jesus' life on earth. Unlike the other Gospels, which were written to present Jesus to different cultural groups, John was written as a universal Gospel. It is to all people of all times, and particularly to the church. John's purpose is to unveil the Man, Jesus, and to reveal Him as God.

Of course, the other Gospels present the deity of Jesus, but the central message and focus of John's Gospel is Jesus' deity. John's many years of ministry had taught him the importance of believers coming to know Jesus as God. John wrote his book for this purpose: "that *you* may believe that Jesus is the Christ, the Son of God" (italics added).

But why is this so important? And why is the present tense so important: that Jesus *is* the Christ. Not *was. Is!*

It's important because when we recognize Jesus as the God who lives *now*, we also discover that we "may have life" *now* through His name.

John was making no retreat from the

facts of the Christian faith. John's failure to speak of Christ's birth does not deny the historic events that actually took place in space and time. It does not imply that these are unimportant. It is simply that John's goal was to help you and me see, through the historic Person, the living Christ who is present with us even now. John wanted us to understand not only who Jesus was, but who Jesus *is*. John wanted us to grasp the fact that in our personal relationship with the living Jesus we can experience new life as a present reality.

So, in the Gospel of John, the writer selected and organized historical events in order to unveil the living Jesus of today. As we see His glory, we will find in Him the vital source of a new life of our own.

Why is it so important that Jesus be unveiled? Recently I talked with a girl in her junior year in college, who wondered about her future. Should she continue in her church ministry major? Or take a course in some specialty that will prepare her for a job? How can she look ahead and know what is best for her to do?

Yesterday I spoke with a friend whose wife has asked him to move out. He knows that much of the pain both feel right now has been his fault: they are each struggling with deep hurts and even deeper uncertainties about their futures. Whatever choices they make now will shape the future for their children as well as for themselves.

From your own life, or the lives of members of your class or group, you can add other illustrations. You can point to incident after incident which bring home the fact that we must live in the constant company of uncertainty, and with the possibility of loss. For each of us, the future is hidden behind a veil. We are forced to make our choices blindly, hoping but never sure that what we do will turn out for the best, and hoping as well that the things we fear will never happen.

No wonder it was so important for John to unveil Jesus. We cannot know our personal futures. But we can be free to live with joy when we strip away the veil of history, and see there a Jesus who is the Son of God, and who brings us new life, *now*.

✂ *Group Activity: Recovery Group Steps 6 (be ready to have God remove*

character defects) and 7 (humbly ask God to remove shortcomings)

Work in pairs for three minutes to list "things I can't control." Focus on external things—the weather, the economy, international terrorism, stock market moves, etc. As a group, make a composite list, adding other things as you think of them.

Individually list internal "things I can't control." Here you may think of temper, credit card use, antagonism toward certain persons, etc. Then in pairs again share items on the internal list, and identify those areas that make you most uncomfortable or anxious.

Against this background read John 1:1-18. Together pick out words or phrases that tell who Jesus, the "Word" of this passage is, and discuss what they tell us about who He is, and what this can mean to me. For instance, as "the light of men" He shows us the way to God, right choices, sheds light on our flaws and needs, etc.

Finally, write a letter to Christ, telling Him very specifically the things about yourself that have been impossible for you to control. Turn these things over to Him, and humbly ask Him to remove your shortcomings.

Eternity Unveiled: John 1:1-5

With the first words of the Gospel of John we see that John's task *is* to unveil. The other Gospels begin with the birth of Jesus or with an account of His human ancestry. Matthew and Luke emphasized that a man, a human being, was actually born in the normal way to a young woman named Mary in the ancient land of Judea at the time Herod the Great was living out his last days. John, on the other hand, tells us immediately the Child born then was the eternal God! His origin was not at His physical conception, but, as Micah said, his "origins are from of old, from ancient times" (Micah 5:2). And Isaiah called Him "Mighty God, Everlasting Father" (Isa. 9:6).

John's way of taking us back to eternity was to identify Jesus as "the Word" who was "in the beginning." Moreover, this Word "was with God, and the Word was God." Finally John said plainly that "the Word became flesh and lived for a while among us" (John 1:14).

The Word. The Bible gives many titles or names to Jesus. When He is called "the

Word," we are reminded of His role in the Godhead from the very beginning. Human speech has the capacity to unveil thoughts, feelings, and emotions; to reveal the person behind the words. Jesus is God expressing Himself through Jesus.

When Philip asked Jesus to show the disciples the Father, Christ answered in gentle rebuke. "Anyone who has seen Me has seen the Father" (14:9). Another time Jesus explained to His disciples, "No one knows who the Father is except the Son and those to whom the Son chooses to reveal Him" (Luke 10:22).

This title, "the Word," teaches that Jesus is now, and always has been, the One through whom God expresses Himself. But how did God express Himself in history past, even before the Incarnation? Obviously God was known before Jesus' birth.

In Creation (John 1:3). Paul wrote that "what may be known about God is plain to them, because God has made it plain to them. For since the Creation of the world God's invisible qualities . . . have been clearly seen" (Rom. 1:19-20). The material universe itself speaks of a Maker, loudly shouting His handiwork:

Day after day they pour forth speech; night after night they display knowledge. There is no speech or language where their voice is not heard. Their voice goes out into all the earth, their words to the ends of the world.

Psalm 19:2-4

This Word of Creation is the word of Jesus before the Incarnation. "Through Him all things were made," John said. "Without Him nothing was made that has been made." From the very beginning Jesus has expressed God to humankind.

In life (John 1:4). But it was not just in the creation of inanimate matter that Jesus communicated God. On the spinning sphere hung in the emptiness of space, the Creator placed living creatures. These living creatures are different from dead matter; they moved, ate, responded to stimuli, and reproduced themselves. The creation of life was a voice testifying to God.

Only One who was a living Being Himself could be the source of other life. Dead matter does not generate life now, nor has it ever.

And then, among all the living things, the Creator planted another kind of life that was made "in Our image, in Our likeness" (Gen. 1:26). Not just life, but *self-conscious* life, came into being. This life that came from Jesus the Creator remains deeply rooted in Him. Our very awareness that we are different from all other living creatures is another wordless testimony to the existence of the God whose likeness we bear. Jesus gave us life itself, and by that life He expressed God to us.

In light (John 1:5). This final term introduces one other way in which God has expressed Himself through the preincarnate work of Jesus. In John's writings the terms *light* and *darkness* are often moral terms. Light represents moral purity, holiness, righteousness, good. In contrast, *darkness* as a moral term represents evil, all those warped and twisted ways in which sin had perverted the good in man, and brought pain to individuals and society. "The light shines in the darkness, but the darkness has not understood [or, extinguished] it."

The moral light is one of the most powerful and pervasive evidences of God's existence. Paul described pagans who have never known God's Old Testament revelation of morality, yet they "show that the requirements of the law are written on their hearts, their consciences also bearing witness, and their thoughts now accusing, now even defending them" (Rom. 2:15). There is a moral awareness planted deep in the personality of every person. Different societies may develop different rules to govern, for instance, sexual behavior. These rules may be glaringly different from the pattern set in Scripture. Still, *in every culture, there is the awareness that sexual behavior is a moral issue,* and that no individual can simply have any other person he or she wants, at any time or in any way.

The deep-seated conviction that there is a moral order to things is present in every human society. But society is in darkness; even though some sense of moral order and rightness exists, people in every society choose to do what they themselves believe is wrong. So conscience struggles, and individuals accuse themselves (or perhaps try to excuse as "adult" behavior they know is wrong).

Moral awareness in a world running madly after darkness is another testimony to us that light comes from the preexistent Word. Light, like creation and life itself, shouts out the presence of God behind the world we see.

Then, finally, the Word took unique expression in space and time. "The Word became flesh and lived for a while among us. We have seen His glory, the glory of the one and only Son, who came from the Father, full of grace and truth" (John 1:14).

🔊 *Group Activity: Bible Study Group*
John 1:1-3 makes stunning claims about Jesus. Together list these claims. Are these claims made elsewhere in Scripture? To find out break into groups to examine the following N.T. and O.T. passages: Isaiah 9:6-7; Colossians 1:15-19; Hebrews 1:1-13; Philippians 2:5-11. Report on what each passage adds to our understanding of who Jesus is. Conclude with a time of worship, focusing your thoughts and praise on the Person of Jesus.

Grace and Truth: John 1:6-18
A totally new level of communication begins with the Incarnation. We catch a glimpse of this fact in the ministry of John the Baptist. John, the Bible says, was sent "to testify concerning that light."

What a strange expression. John was sent to *identify* the light! Why? What was there about Jesus as the Light that demanded identification? When we examine the Baptist's message in the other Gospels, we see that John focused his preaching on twin ideas: (1) the promised King of Old Testament prophecy was about to appear, and (2) His coming demanded a moral renewal.

John rebuked sin in ruler and common man alike. His tongue lashed the religious. "You brood of vipers!" he cried scornfully. "Produce fruit in keeping with repentance" (Luke 3:7-8).

The Baptist's prescriptions were clear, simple reflections of Old Testament Law. "The man with two tunics should share with him who has none, and the one who has food should do the same," John told the people. "Don't collect . . . more [taxes] than you are required to," John told the tax collectors. "Don't extort money and don't accuse people falsely—be content with your pay," John told the soldiers (vv. 11-14).

The moral light shed in the Old Testament shone through the Baptist's message. His words pointing to the Person about to appear promised a kingdom in which moral light would not be lost in the darkness, but instead, darkness would be exiled by light. "The true Light," the Gospel writer said, "was coming into the world." And John the Baptist's mission was to make it clear to all that that Man *is* the Light.

But still, why? Why must John announce Jesus? Why did a people who already had the light of the written Law need to have light—an expression of true morality and reality—identified for them? The Gospel writer explained it to us with another term: *grace*. When the Word became flesh, we were given new light—a revelation that the divine morality is "grace and truth."

Law. It is important to understand that all revelations of God before Jesus came were true, but incomplete. Creation spoke of God's existence and power, but not of His essential character. Life testified to God's personhood, but told nothing of His deepest emotions or plans. Light, as awareness of morality, reflected God's holiness, but somehow His heart remained hidden. Even the Law of the Old Testament, which defined holiness and morality more fully and gave a glimpse of God as One who cares about people, still did not communicate God's heart.

There were still some questions left unanswered. What does God truly want with us? How does He react when we fail to meet His standards? "In the past God spoke to our forefathers through the prophets at many times and in various ways, but in these last days He has spoken to us by His Son." It is the Son who is "the radiance of God's glory and the exact representation of His being" (Heb. 1:1-3). In Jesus, the Word is spoken! And what do we hear when the final revelation comes? "Law was given through Moses; grace and truth came through Jesus Christ" (John 1:17). In Jesus we see a morality that goes beyond law and can only be identified as grace.

How is grace portrayed in verses 9-13 of this chapter? The Creator entered the world He had made. He came to His own people, to whom He had given life. But His own people would not receive Him. He was rejected, scorned, and ultimately crucified. In spite of this, He reached out to individuals who would receive Him, and He gave them

209

the right to become the children of God.

The human race did not seek out a family relationship with God. The reaching out was God's, and His alone. In spite of mankind's failure, God drew men and women to Himself and lifted them up, adopting them as His children and heirs. In this act of pure grace, a glorious light bursts into history. In Jesus Christ, the eternal Word, we discover that God's ultimate morality is one of love and of grace.

At first it is hard to realize that the God who spoke in the past is the same God unveiled in Jesus. We had never grasped the full extent of His glory. But John the Baptist was a witness to that light, and testified that He *is* the same. The splendor of God seen in the Son goes so far beyond the glimpses of glory that shine through the Law. Now, we must learn to live in grace's new relationship with the Lord, so that we can share His glory.

And so the theme of Jesus, the Living Word, unveiling God, dominates the Gospel of John. Jesus, full of grace and truth, unveiled now the relationship which God the Father had always yearned to have with humankind. And we, as His sons and daughters, must learn a way of life guided by the splendor of grace rather than by the flickering candle of Law.

For this, we must know Jesus. We must see Jesus as He is, God's ultimate Word of revelation. We must hear His Word, come to understand, and believe in Him. When we trust ourselves to Jesus, forever, and daily, we will learn what it means to "have eternal life in Him."

GROUP RESOURCE GUIDE

Identification: *Share with others*
Complete the following statement: "To me, grace and truth mean. . . . "

Affirmation: *Express love and concern*
Tell one other person in your group how you have observed grace or truth in his or her life.

Exploration: *Probe God's Word*
On 8 1/2 x 11 sheets of paper have written the brief definition of "grace" (p. 206) and of "truth" (p. 205), as well as John 1:17, "The law was given through Moses; grace and truth came through Jesus Christ."

Together read through John 1:1-18, listing on the left side of your papers "evidence of grace" and on the right "truths revealed."

When you have finished, preview John's Gospel in teams of two or three. Let each team take one of the following claims of Jesus; examine the context in which it appears, and determine from that passage just what grace and what truth came to us through Jesus. The claims:

(1) I am the Bread of Life 6:35

(2) I am the Light of the world 8:12
(3) I am the Gate for the sheep 10:7
(4) I am the Good Shepherd 10:11, 14
(5) I am the Resurrection and 11:25
the Life
(6) I am the way, the truth, 14:6
and the life
(7) I am the True Vine 15:1

Report findings to the group as a whole so each can add to his or her list of evidences of the grace and truths revealed through Jesus.

Reaction: *Respond together to the Word*
Repeat the opening activity. Go around the group, with each person sharing "To me grace and truth mean. . . . "

Adoration: *Worship and pray*
John Newton was a slave trader, profane and brutal, until he became a Christian. Later he became a powerful preacher in England, and author of a hymn whose words express a truth he felt deeply: "Amazing Grace."

Rather than sing this familiar hymn, read its words in unison as a prayer of thanks.

STUDY GUIDE 31
John 1:19–4:42

THE NEW HAS COME

Overview

We meet four people in these opening chapters of John's Gospel. They are John the Baptist, Nathanael, Nicodemus, and the unnamed "woman at the well."

John was Jesus' forerunner, sent to prepare Israel for His coming. Nathanael represented the godly Israelite who responded at the very first evidence that Jesus is the Christ, the Son of God. Nicodemus represented the religious leaders who realized from Christ's miracles that Jesus is "a Teacher . . . come from God," but whose spiritual blindness kept them from understanding the true message of the Old Testament, and whose spiritual deadness made them antagonistic to the Son of God. The woman at the well represents the myriad of human beings outside the chosen people who, when they meet Jesus, put their confidence in Israel's Saviour.

The theme of these chapters is salvation—and the way three individuals who typify all humanity respond to the One who alone can bring life to a lost humankind.

▶ **Born Again.** John often used the imagery of being "born of God" (see John 1:13; 1 John 2:29; 3:9; 4:7; 5:1, 4, 18). Spiritual rebirth is supernatural, not natural, and God Himself is the One who acts to give the believer new life (see John 1:12-13). New birth makes us God's children (v. 13), and leads to our moral transformation. One born of God will do what is right (1 John 2:29).

Commentary

Kurt had an uncomfortable feeling about God. As a boy he seldom went to church or Sunday School, but when he did, he was aware that he was with people who had moral standards much higher than his own.

When Kurt learned the Ten Commandments and heard the words of Jesus from the Sermon on the Mount, he was more uncomfortable than ever. The more he learned, the more aware he became of the gap in his own life between what he knew was right, and what he desired and did.

Kurt had all the "light" he wanted! Talk of God only produced flashes of guilt and shame. More light? A brighter light? No thanks! It was much easier to turn away from talk of God and from his own sense of sin.

So John the Baptist's first words about Jesus would surprise people like Kurt if they could understand them. Twice John said that the light of Jesus helps us see that God is "full of grace and truth." What is unveiled in the Son of God is not some higher, more burdensome standard of morality. Instead, Jesus revealed that God wants to relate to us as a Father relates to his children; through *grace,* not *law.*

For everyone who has ever felt like Kurt—that contact with God is painful or condemning—John now had a surprising message.

The Openhearted: John 1:19–2:11

Not everyone is fearful or unable to believe God loves him, as Kurt was. Some have always sensed God's love. It was the same in Jesus' day; some people were very close to God, and immediately responded to Jesus. We are introduced to two of these openhearted men in John 1. We also discover in this chapter a pattern which the writer followed in the rest of his Gospel.

The pattern. Jesus' unveiling of God typically took place *in miracle followed by discourse.*

In the other Gospels, miracles are generally treated as authenticating or teaching signs. For instance, Matthew concentrated reports of miracles in chapters 8 and 9. This section immediately followed the Sermon on the Mount and demonstrated the authority of the King over nature, evil spirits, disease, and even death. But John presented the miracles of Jesus as first steps in each fresh unveiling of the Father and His grace. In general, each reported miracle or group of miracles leads to a teaching discourse. The miracle thus does more than serve as the divine seal of approval on Jesus; it usually illustrates what He is about to teach as well.

So in studying the Gospel of John, we'll find this pattern over and over. New units of thought are introduced by miracles, and concluded with extended explanations by Jesus of some new aspect of God's grace.

John the Baptist (John 1:19-34). John was probably Jesus' cousin, and certainly a childhood friend. John had been sent by God to announce that the promised Saviour of Israel was about to appear. John was called to "testify concerning that Light," a Light much different from Jewish expectations. Even though John had known Jesus from childhood, he never recognized his Cousin as the Son of God. John too was looking for a different revelation than one of grace and goodness.

But when Jesus came to be baptized by John, John, in a private miracle, saw "the Spirit come down from heaven as a dove and remain on Him." John immediately believed.

Nathanael (John 1:35-51). John gave witness to Jesus and pointed Him out as the Son of God. Soon some of John's followers began to trail after Jesus, and Christ began to select men who would join His most intimate circle of followers. One of these, Philip, hurried to Nathanael and told him that they had found the Christ, and that He was Jesus of Nazareth.

Nathanael was skeptical. The prophets said nothing of anyone great coming from the Galilean town, Nazareth. But Nathanael went with Philip to see for himself. And he was stunned by Jesus' greeting: "Here is a true Israelite, in whom there is nothing false."

When Jesus went on to describe the place where Philip had found Nathanael, far out of Jesus' sight, Nathanael was convinced: "Rabbi, You are the Son of God; You are the King of Israel" (v. 49).

What do we learn from these two incidents? First, we note that each of these men had a preconceived idea of what God was like and how He would act. John described the stern judgments the coming Messiah

would execute. Nathanael knew that the Deliverer would come from some place other than Nazareth.

Second, we note that Jesus did not completely fit the preconceived ideas of either. John never dreamed that his gentle, godly Cousin could be the mighty Deliverer that his preaching described (v. 33). Nathanael would find out only later that the Man from Nazareth was actually born in Bethlehem, the place the prophets foretold the coming King would be born. While both John and Nathanael believed deeply in God, both had concepts about His Son that were not fully correct.

Third, each received and responded to a small, personal miracle. Later Jesus would perform many public miracles, and some of these would be absolutely spectacular. It might seem insignificant to us for Jesus to describe the place where Nathanael was when Philip found him (v. 48). But each of these men, John and Nathanael, immediately recognized the hand of God. And *each immediately set aside his preconceived notions, to submit to the authority of Jesus.* Each accepted the fact that Jesus is the Son of God, the Only Begotten of the Father, the revealer of truth as well as of grace (vv. 34, 49).

These insights are important to us at the beginning of our study of John's Gospel. As we explore the written Word, you can expect God to be at work in your own and your group members' lives. God will perform private miracles for you. These probably will not be spectacular, nor will they be public. But, in little ways, God lets us know that He is speaking personally to *us.* And, like John and Nathanael, we each have our own ideas about what God is like and how He will act. But it is vital that you and I, like John and Nathanael, be willing to put aside our incomplete understandings of God and His grace when we discover, in Jesus the Son of God, some fresh unveiling of truth or fresh evidence of grace.

Ø Group Activity:
Missions/Outreach Group
John 1:19-51 displays several approaches to evangelism. One is preaching (1:19-28). Another is personal testimony (1:29-34). The third is networking (1:35-51)."Networking" is using the net of relationships already established by a new convert to further spread the Gospel.

Examine each of these approaches as seen in the text, and together identify characteristics of each approach. When would it be most appropriate to use each?

Then discuss this problem faced by a young friend of mine at Nyack College in New York. He has gone once a week into the city to hold a Bible class for black teenagers. Of the seven or eight who came, all but two have dropped out and joined an agressive black Muslim youth movement in the city that casts whites as "satans." One of the two who come is especially eager to learn. But my friend is deeply concerned about the ones who dropped out, and is frustrated by the fact that he can only come into the city once a week and spend only a few hours with his tiny study group.

What insights would you share about outreach? What would you recommend he do?

The disciples (John 2:1-11). At a wedding in Cana, Jesus sustained the joy of the occasion by turning water into wine when the supply of drink ran out. Few besides the disciples saw the miracle, but, actually, the miracle was for them. In that miracle Jesus began to unveil His glory, and "His disciples put their faith in Him" (v. 11).

Light in the Darkness: John 2:12-25

In the next verses we sense the beginning of Jesus' public, and controversial, action. He and His disciples left Galilee and came up to Jerusalem. There they visited the temple and saw the money changers at work. These were businessmen who exchanged other currencies for coins minted at the temple, because the religious leaders had decreed that only temple money was acceptable to God. Smiling, the money changers inflated the rate of exchange—and probably gave the leading priests their cut. Other temple businessmen sold livestock for the sacrifices. A lamb brought by a worshiper might be rejected because of some blemish when inspected by a priest: it had to be traded then for an animal that was "acceptable." Jesus angrily drove the traders from His Father's house.

Suddenly Jesus was a public figure. He was popular with the crowds, because He challenged the corrupt leaders. In the spotlight more, Jesus began to perform a number of miracles. These signs were so spectacular and compelling that "many . . . believed in His name" (v. 23). But the belief of the people was shallow; so shallow that "Jesus would not entrust [or commit] Himself" to the crowds as He had to the Twelve.

What is a shallow faith? Perhaps it is best to think of it as *a faith that exists only as long as its object fits our expectations.* These people, who "believed" in Jesus superficially, turned away from Him when He did not speak and act as they expected (see 6:60-66). They "believed," but not enough to abandon their own notions and submit themselves fully to Jesus' fresh revelation of God.

May God protect you and me and those we teach from shallow faith as we study John's Gospel. May He help us be willing to abandon our old ideas when He calls us to submit fully to His Son, Jesus, so that we might find life now.

John now turns from a description of the reaction of the crowds to describe in detail the reaction of two individuals. Nicodemus, a ruler of the Jews, and a Samaritan woman, an outcast of the outcasts.

♥ *Group Activity: Support Group*
List on the chalkboard "Needs I have that trouble me deeply." Then read and discuss this observation about "miracles":

"A miracle is nothing more or less than God's intervention on our behalf, whether that intervention is spectacular because of obvious violation of natural law, or is commonplace, because it is performed through what seems to be the most ordinary and natural sequence of cause and effect."

After discussing, look at several "private miracles" reported in John. What conclusions can you draw from John 1:32-34, 1:47-50, and 2:1-11?

Share any "private miracles" you have experienced as a Christian, as God has worked to meet your needs in spectacular or in ordinary ways.

In closing, bring the "troubling need" you identified at the beginning to Jesus, expecting Him to act for you as He has for others.

Nicodemus: John 3:1-21

Nicodemus was identified by John as a "member of the Jewish ruling council" (v. 1). It's important to realize that He was a religious as well as a political leader.

213

In Israel, civil and religious law were the same: the code of the Old Testament, as interpreted by the rabbis over the generations, guided the life of the Jew in the Holy Land, and anywhere a Jewish community existed. Nicodemus was one of the men who interpreted and applied God's instructions to Israelite life. These rulers represented divine authority to the Jews: they "sat in Moses' seat" as interpreters of his Law.

Yet the land of Palestine was under Roman rule as well. Rome was the final authority; only the Roman procurator (governor) could pronounce the death penalty. Still, aside from the taxes Rome collected and the army garrison Rome maintained, day-to-day affairs were administered by the Jewish rulers rather than the Roman overlords. It was much simpler, and some "self-government" did help make subject people less troublesome.

Thus Nicodemus was a significant man: he held a civil power that would be backed by Rome, and he was a recognized interpreter of the Law of God as that Law was expressed in the written Word.

Nicodemus' first words revealed a growing conviction shared among the rulers that Jesus must be "a Teacher . . . come from God. For no one could perform the miraculous signs You are doing if God were not with him" (v. 2). Yet in spite of this belief, the rulers did not make their conclusion public. It's possible that Nicodemus' night visit was made in secret to avoid any impression of public support, and possibly to find out what this new Prophet was going to proclaim.

Jesus immediately jolted Nicodemus with the announcement that to even catch a glimpse of God's kingdom, a person must be *born again*. Nicodemus struggled with this strange idea, and then blurted out: "You can't mean 'reenter the womb and be born'! What do You mean by 'born again'?" (see v. 4) Even Jesus' explanation of the new birth as a work of God the Holy Spirit, and not a physical experience (vv. 5-8) brought the same response: "How can this be?" (v. 9)

Jesus' answer helps us see that His revelation of grace and truth is not foreign to the Old Testament! Grace and truth are imbedded in the very foundations of the Old: they simply had not been recognized. Thus Jesus exclaimed, "You are Israel's teacher, and do you not understand these things?"

To what was Jesus referring? Simply this: God's plan to give men and women a life and a relationship with Him not based on Law is clearly taught in the Old Testament!

For instance, Jeremiah promised a time when "I will make a New Covenant with the house of Israel." This new way of relating to God is specifically said to be unlike the older, Mosaic way. Under the New Covenant, God promised, "I will put My law in their minds and write it on their hearts" (Jer. 31:31, 33). When the new heart is created, new life comes; and one who is "born again" comes to know God in a totally different, deeply personal, family relationship. (See also Ezek. 11:19; 18:31; 36:26).

Through such passages as these, which Nicodemus as a recognized Bible authority should have known and understood, the "new birth" had long been taught. But Nicodemus did not know. And he did not understand. His concept of God was faulty. He knew about the Law, but he missed the promise of grace, which tells us that God loves us in spite of our failures and our sins.

Quietly Jesus went on to explain the grace of God and reveal underlying principles by which grace operates.

God's grace (John 3:16-21).

God loves the world (v. 16). It's easy to see in the Law a dispassionate, impersonal demand for justice and goodness. But God's involvement with us is *not* impersonal. To understand anything about His ways, we must realize that He is consumed with a passionate love for the world. The world may refuse to receive Him (1:12), but God continues to love.

God gave His Son (v. 16). God's love found ultimate expression in His gift of His Son, Jesus, who died in order to redeem the world that hated Him (see vv. 14-15).

God gives eternal life (v. 16). Through the death of His Son, God chose to give eternal life to His enemies. This life is called eternal not only because it will extend into eternity, but also because it is God's own life. He gives us His life; we become His children and have a new heredity (see 1 Peter 1:23).

Apart from this life, all are perishing (vv. 18-21). God had to act on mankind's behalf; apart from Him there was no hope. There is no use going through life thinking that our good and bad deeds are stacked on the weighing pans of some cosmic balance, and then hoping the good will outweigh the bad and earn salvation. There is no use in struggling to keep the Law in hopes that God might accept our righteousness (or at least our efforts). There is no hope for man in goodness, for we are already condemned: "All have sinned and fall short of the glory of God" (Rom. 3:23). To be born again is the only hope for mankind.

Human response to light reveals our lost condition (vv. 19-21). Man's response to moral light, in conscience or in God's Law, has been to choose darkness. This does not mean that every time we are faced with a moral choice each of us always chooses evil. It simply means that *no one* chooses the good every time. Often, even when we do the right thing, we do it from wrong motives or still feel an attraction to evil (v. 19).

How, then, will we respond to Jesus, the true Light who has come into the world? And what response is appropriate to this One who reveals God's ultimate morality of grace? There is only one appropriate response: to believe. To trust the God who offers us life as a free gift. To fully and thankfully commit ourselves to Jesus Christ.

The challenge. Jesus put quite a challenge to this man who had established his identity and his reputation as a religious leader. For all of Nicodemus' knowledge, Jesus told him, he had never even glimpsed the foundation of grace on which God's kingdom is built! How would Nicodemus respond? Would he, like John the Baptist, abandon his preconceived ideas and gladly submit to Jesus, whom he *knew* was "a Teacher who has come from God"?

How Nicodemus responded that night we do not know. Instead, we return to the Baptist (vv. 22-26). When Jesus began to teach, John's importance and popularity began to wane. John's followers became upset. But John told them, "He must become greater; I must become less" (v. 30). Jesus, not a human leader, must be given central place. John stood aside and welcomed Jesus to center stage.

We do know that Nicodemus continued as a ruling Pharisee, and at one point defended Jesus against hearsay accusations (7:50-51). And after Jesus' crucifixion, Nicodemus bought spices and helped to prepare the body of our Lord for burial (19:38-42).

Ø *Group Activity:*
Missions/Outreach Group
Gallup and other polls tell us that a very high percentage of Americans report that they are "born again."

Study Jeremiah 31:31, 33 and Ezekiel 11:19; 18:31; 36:26 along with John 3 to sharpen your own understanding of this common phrase. Then together develop a set of five or six questions that might be used to determine what a person understands by this phrase. Your first question should be: "Over 50% of Americans identify themselves as 'born again.' If interviewed, would you say that you are or are not born again, or that you do not know?"

Use your questionnaire to interview at least ten persons each during the coming week, and report back what you find.

You might wish to either locate a tract that explains being born again to give out after each interview, or develop your own.

The Samaritan Woman: John 4:1-42

No one could have stood in greater contrast to Nicodemus than this woman. She was a Samaritan, a race that the Jews looked down on as having no claim on their God. Apparently the woman was an outcast in her own community as well; she came by herself to draw water from the community well. In biblical lands drawing water and chatting at the well was the social highpoint of a woman's day. In this woman's own village she was ostracized and marked off as immoral; an unmarried woman living openly with the fifth in a series of men.

As Jesus and this Samaritan woman talked, she tried to turn the conversation to theology (vv. 19-26). But Jesus focused on several other issues.

Gift (John 4:7-10). Jesus quickly established the fact, as He had with Nicodemus, that God's dealings with humanity are on the basis of grace. What we do is not the foundation of our relationship with God. Rather we must depend on what God is willing to do for us. Jesus pointed out that her sins made self-reliance foolish. How striking then to discover that the Son of God was willing to "give" what she could not earn.

Eternal life (John 4:11-15). In both conversations the gift Jesus promised was life; eternal life, welling up and supplying every

215

need by its freshening springs.

Belief (John 4:39-42). Again Jesus looked for a specific response of trust, of faith, in Him. In this case that response came both from the woman at the well and from the Samaritan community.

At first many believed because the woman rushed back into her village with word that this Man, the Christ, "Told me everything I ever did." The villagers came out, heard Jesus, and even more responded because they heard Him for themselves.

Differences. In spite of the similarities we've seen in the two confrontations, there are differences in the way Jesus unveiled grace to these two people. To Nicodemus, Jesus stressed the fact that all stand condemned before God. Nicodemus, a religious man, took pride in his keeping of the Law and did not recognize his need for God's grace. But the woman at the well knew she was a sinner. Jesus did not mention man's lost condition to her; she knew! And she learned that Jesus knew too, and still was ready to offer her life as a gift. To this woman Jesus spoke of *worshipers.* He told her the good news that the Father seeks persons to worship Him in spirit and in truth (v. 23).

Why? Because while Nicodemus needed to see himself as a sinner in order to understand grace, the woman who knew she was a sinner needed to see herself as a person of worth and value. God finds us worthy of His concern in spite of our ruin. God values us enough to actively seek us, to welcome us to intimacy, and to rejoice in our worship.

Only a person like the Samaritan prostitute, an outcast from her own, could understand what this means. To be wanted, to be cared for when no one, not even herself, could see anything of value in her! This is grace indeed.

Summary

In these chapters, we've begun to see Jesus unveiling God, and we've begun to learn how to respond to that revelation of God.

John the Baptist and Nathanael were like people to whom faith comes easily. They needed little evidence to believe. They joyfully opened their hearts to learn from Jesus, even when what He showed them was different from what they had thought.

Nicodemus and the Samaritan woman were like those of us to whom faith comes hard. It was hard for Nicodemus, because his piety had earned him a reputation in the community. His image of himself as a good man was deeply ingrained. How hard it is for a person who has honestly tried to be good to realize that all those efforts provide no standing with God, that in spite of everything he stands already condemned and in desperate need of a new life, which can come only as a gift.

For the Samaritan woman, faith came hard because she *knew* she was a great sinner. Her sense of worth was worn away. How hard it was for her to realize that God valued her and wanted her to become a worshiper. How hard to believe that He was offering her eternal life as His love gift.

Yet this is the twin revelation of Light, the ultimate morality of God, which comes to us in John's Gospel. Grace says to each of us, "You count." God knows you as you are, and God still cares. He cares enough to send the Son, that you might have eternal life, become His child, and worship Him.

GROUP RESOURCE GUIDE

Identification: *Share with others*
Tell two or three ideas you had about Jesus before you were converted that changed after you believed.

Exploration: *Probe God's Word*
Use the chart on page 217 to guide your study of John 3–4. Divide into teams to compare and contrast the message of each passage and the ideas each person had to "relearn" about his relationship with God.

Reaction: *Respond together to the Word*
Tell what seems to be the most important truth(s) about Jesus or salvation emphasized in these chapters. Share what at least one of these truths means to you.

Adoration: *Worship and pray*
Praise Jesus for salvation, identifying either

with Nicodemus or the Samaritan woman. Pray in this way: "Lord, like Nicodemus (or the Samaritan woman) I. . . .Therefore I thank and praise You that. . . . "

	Nicodemus	Woman at the Well
THE LESSONS Feelings about self Feelings about God Idea of God's attitude toward him/her Idea of what God wants from people		
THE MESSAGE God's goal God's gift God's attitude toward people Man's response to God What grace is		

THE POWER OF THE NEW

Overview

This segment of John clearly illustrates the structure we've mentioned earlier. John 4:43–5:14 reports two miracles: one the restoration of a child near death, and the other the restoration of a long-term invalid to full health. These lead directly into one of Christ's sermons on the source of life.

John 6 tells first of the miracle of a few loaves and fishes multiplied to feed a great crowd. This miracle too leads directly to another major discourse: Jesus' sermon on the Bread of Life.

Yet the importance of this section isn't found in its structure, but in Jesus' teaching. How important to share with our group members the vision of that new life Jesus brings. And how important to unveil the wonderful truth that what Jesus gives, He Himself sustains.

▶ **Bread.** This was the primary food of people in Bible times. It was made from a variety of grains, often mixed with lentils or beans. The "loaves" were baked flat, about a half inch thick. In the Bible, bread is symbolic as the sustainer of physical life. Thus Jesus' quote: "Man does not live on bread alone" (Matt. 4:4) insists human beings are not mere animals. And the prayer: "Give us today our daily bread," is an expression of dependence on God to meet all our needs for life in this present world.

■ See the verse-by-verse commentary in the *Bible Knowledge Commentary*, pages 288-298.

Commentary

He was never sure when he began to change. At first he had fought against the paralysis. Shame had washed over him when his friends picked up his pallet and carried him to Bethesda pool. His mouth compressed tightly; his forehead was rigid with a frown. One could feel the determination, sense the voice inside him that demanded over and over, "I *will* walk again. I *will!*"

How he had watched that pool! He was so desperate to reach it when the waters were rippled, to win the healing people said would come to the first person to slip in them. He had dug his fingers into the pavement, frantically jerking his body across the stones.

But that was years ago. So many years. The friends were gone now, busy with their own affairs. His world was the tiny space occupied by his pallet on the pavement. He no longer struggled to reach the water. In 38 years he had learned to live with his paralysis; learned to accept his wasted, sticklike legs. All the old dreams were discarded. Now he was satisfied with an extra crust of bread in his begging bowl, or a little warmth when the wind brushed the clouds away from the sun. Thirty-eight years. Life had settled into routine, and he was . . . resigned.

Now, I don't *know* that this is what happened to the man described in John 5. We're told only that he had been ill for 38 years, and that he had no one. But it's easy to imagine what must have happened inside as the reality of his paralysis wore away his spirit. We can imagine his youthful plans; the success or the security he dreamed of, the family he'd have. And then came an illness that stripped him of everything: strength, companions, and finally, hope. No wonder when Jesus saw him, and "learned that he had been in this condition for a long time," His first words were, "Do you want to get well?" (John 5:6)

Do you want to be healed, or would the return of hope now be too painful to bear?

♥ *Group Activity: Support Group*
Read aloud the commentary on this page.

Then ask each person to write down an answer to this question: "If Jesus were to come to you today and ask, 'Do you want to be healed' what would He be talking about?"

Discuss: Which of the following are harder to heal? Why?

bitterness	broken bones
cancer	anger
loneliness	grief

Share the thing(s) you wrote down when asked: "Do you want to be healed?" Talk about how it has affected your life, your relationships, or feelings about yourself.

When all who wish to have shared, close your eyes. Imagine that Jesus is standing beside you, as He stood beside the pool of Bethesda, and that He is asking you. "Do you want to be healed?" If you are willing to be healed, take your problem to Him. Consciously release it, and ask the Lord to make you whole.

If the old feelings come back, you may have to surrender them again. But each time you do, you'll find greater freedom and greater wholeness through Jesus' power.

That question is more wise than it might seem. Lanny and Marie have been married over 20 years. For the past 5 years they've lived together, but apart. For a long time they had struggled, each wanting intimacy and oneness, but over and over again they had failed. The hurts grew deep and bitterness settled in. Finally Marie couldn't stand it any longer. She would stay with him, but not as a wife. And so life for each of them has now settled into polite loneliness. There is caring of a sort and, at times, fun. But always there is an emptiness that somehow hurts less than the pain they had when they were trying so hard.

Lanny and Marie still long for a deeper relationship and a oneness in their marriage. But neither can respond to the offer of a fresh change. The anguish of past failure has made them afraid to risk anymore.

Jesus' offer of new life comes to men and women who have often been in bondage to paralyzing defeat for untold years. For many of us, an invitation to take a fresh start would be heard with doubts and fear. To understand the grace Jesus unveils and see why it is safe to accept His offer, we

need to see more clearly the life that Jesus holds out to us.

The Miracle of New Life: John 4:43–5:18
The incidents in chapters 4–6 take place in different districts: Galilee, then Jerusalem, then Galilee again. But these incidents are linked by the logic of John's pattern of miracle and teaching. And common to each scene is Jesus' offer of eternal life; a life that can release us from our bondage to our past.

The first miracle (John 4:43-54). In Jesus' home district of Galilee, an official begged him to heal a terminally ill son. This was no appeal based on curiosity, or on some perverse insistence that Jesus prove Himself. When Jesus suggested such might be the case, the distraught official could only beg, "Sir, come down before my child dies!" The father was desperate, and he turned to Jesus as his only hope.

Christ sent the man away with the promise that the boy would live. The man believed. As he returned home, he was met by servants who excitedly told him that the boy's recovery had begun the same hour Jesus had said, "Your son will live."

The Word had reached out across the miles and brought life where there had been only the bitter prospect of death.

The second miracle (John 5:1-18). This is the miracle we've already noted. The paralyzed man had lived with death for 38 years. He had suffered the loss of all things and was so empty of hope that he had to be asked, "Do you *want* to get well?"

The man chose healing, and Jesus spoke the life-bringing word: "Get up! Pick up your mat and walk" (v. 9).

These two miracles focused attention on Jesus' claim to be able to bring and to restore life. Strangely, the miracles also created opposition. Jesus had healed the paralytic on the Sabbath, established in Scripture as a day of rest. The man was joyfully carrying his pallet out of the city (as Jesus had told him to do), when he was accused of breaking the Sabbath by "working" on the holy day. When the man explained what had happened, the leaders condemned Jesus because He had dared to heal (another "work") on God's Day. Jesus responded that He and His Father were both still at work (v. 17). This stimulated murderous anger from the Jews, who realized that with these words Jesus was "making Himself equal with God" (v. 18).

Against the background of these two miracles demonstrating Jesus' life-giving power and the fury of Israel's leaders, Jesus began to teach about God's grace.

Sermon on the Source of Life:
John 5:19-47

The Jews persecuted Jesus on the grounds that He was a Sabbath-breaker, and especially because He dared to claim He was equal with God. Jesus unhesitatingly told His angry critics that He and the Father are One. It is just this equality with God that enables Jesus to offer life to us.

One in action (John 5:19-21). The oneness of the Father and Son is seen in that "the Son can do nothing by Himself; He can only do what He sees His Father doing, because whatever the Father does the Son also does." Jesus' actions perfectly reflect the Father's will.

Two acts of Jesus have just expressed God the Father: restoring the official's son and healing the paralytic. Each shows God's desire to bring us life. But Jesus promised even "greater things" that will demonstrate *resurrection power.* God can take the physically and spiritually dead and give them life. In this task of giving life, Father and Son are One.

One in honor (John 5:22-24). Jesus perfectly reflects the Father, for They act as One. Now Christ went on to claim that He has authority to judge.

James warned us about speaking evil of or judging a brother. He pointed out that anyone who does judge steps out of his role as a subject of the Law and, in effect, claims authority over it. "There is only one Lawgiver and Judge, the One who is able to save and destroy" (James 4:12). So when Jesus stated that the Father "has entrusted all judgment to the Son," He was again claiming deity. Only God, who gave the Law, is above it. Jesus must be honored as God, and submitted to in all things. "He who does not honor the Son does not honor the Father who sent Him," is Jesus' inescapable conclusion.

The Jews had just criticized and persecuted Jesus because He healed on the Sabbath. By their definition, Jesus "worked" and so was a lawbreaker. By criticizing Jesus, they placed themselves beside God as judges,

and yet they were outraged when Jesus made "Himself equal with God."

What is the judgment of Jesus to which we are to submit? It is that the one who hears Jesus and believes in God through Him has eternal life. Honor Jesus, and you pass beyond all condemnation, out of the realm of death into life.

The source of life (John 5:25-29). The life that Jesus brings us is resurrection life: life from death. We look forward to a resurrection day in the future; but today, by responding to the voice of Jesus, we can come out of the grave we are living in right now, and experience newness in Him.

Lanny and Marie are afraid to try to rebuild their marriage. Their relationship is wrapped in the graveclothes of the past, buried in the cold ground of old hurts and habits. They can never break out of their bondage to the dead past by themselves. But if they hear Jesus and honor Him, they can experience resurrection power through His gift of eternal life. Then there will be hope for them.

Witness of the Father (John 5:30-36). But how do we know that the Father and Son are One? How can we be sure Jesus is able to provide the eternal life He promises? Jesus pointed His critics to the evidence. It's not just that John the Baptist, a prophet, testified of Him. God the Father added His own unique seal in the life-bringing miracles that Christ's enemies had witnessed! Even the rulers recognized the validity of that testimony, as Nicodemus had admitted, "We know You are a Teacher who has come from God. For no one could do the miraculous signs You are doing if God were not with him" (3:2). The rulers could not deny the evidence. But they still would not commit themselves to Jesus, or honor Him as God.

Witness of Scripture (John 5:37-47). There is yet another witness to Jesus. "You diligently study the Scriptures," Jesus said, "because you think that by them you possess eternal life." They were wrong; studying the Bible or knowing its contents backward and forward does not earn anyone eternal life. What the Scriptures do is point individuals to Jesus.

The Scriptures tell of sin and spiritual death. The message of the Word of God should have led these biblical scholars to do what the father of the dying boy did—recognize that his own efforts were futile, and look for God's grace to appear. These scholars should have recognized that they were no more able to earn God's favor than the paralytic was able to get himself into the pool. They should have been eagerly looking for the prophesied new life, and should have been ready to receive the gift from Jesus' hand.

By refusing to turn to Jesus, who is One with the Father, the men and women Jesus spoke to that day showed how far their hearts were from God. They would not believe; and because they would not believe, Jesus could not give them life.

🔎 *Group Activity: Bible Study Group*
Jesus' teachings in John are complex and difficult. To understand John 5, focus on the concept of "life." Here are key passages in the OT and NT that help us develop a biblical concept of this vital term: Genesis 2:7, 17; 3:6-7; Deuteronomy 19:21; Leviticus 17:11; Deuteronomy 30:19; John 3:15-36; 5:21-26; 6:27-68; 10:10-28; 11:1-44; Romans 5:9-10, 12-21; Romans 6:1-10; Romans 8:1-11; 2 Corinthians 4:1-12; 1 John 2-3; 1 John 5:10-12. Divide in teams to study them and sum up what each teaches about the meaning of "life." (Or, have someone prepared to report on the concept, using a resource like the Expository Dictionary of Bible Words [Zondervan]).

Report on each team's findings, and then with your concept of life expanded work through John 5 together.

Finally, share how you experience this new life that Jesus offers.

New Life Sustained: John 6:1-24
Again John described a miracle and then reported a teaching session growing out of it. This discourse deepens our understanding of the new life Jesus offers us through grace.

The public miracle (John 6:1-24). Great crowds had followed Jesus to see His signs and hear His teachings. They were with Him when mealtime came and passed, and they had had nothing to eat. Jesus took all the food that was available (five small barley loaves and two fish), prayed, and divided it among the people. The 5,000 men, plus women and children, all "had enough to eat," and the disciples collected 12 full baskets of leftovers.

The people recognized that a great miracle had been performed and cried, "Surely this is the Prophet who is to come into the world." Immediately they decided "to come and make Him King by force" (vv. 14-15).

We learn a lot from that phrase; they wanted to take Him by force and *make* Him King! A king is one who rules, not is ruled by others. But the men and women who participated in the miracle of the loaves and the fish were determined to *use* Jesus; they had no desire to obey Him. Jesus, knowing their motives, slipped away. By the next day the crowd had followed Him to the other side of the lake and began to ask Him many questions. He based His teaching on the miracle of the loaves, and presented Himself to the people as the "Bread of Life."

Sermon on the Bread of Life: John 6:25-59
The theme of the message is *life sustained.* Jesus told the crowd about food that "endures to eternal life" (v. 27). He said those who are sustained by it will never go hungry and never be thirsty (v. 35). Jesus promised to sustain a relationship with those who "remain in Me" so that life will be continuously experienced (vv. 56-57). It's not enough simply to have life; life must be sustained and developed. There must be provision for daily growth.

None of this concerned the crowd. They wanted a king who could validate himself by an acceptable sign. And what sign did they want? "Our forefathers ate the manna in the desert." They wanted to be fed, so they would not need to work.

Jesus rebuked them, and exhorted them to focus not on food that perishes but on that which endures to eternal life. They were to look for the true Bread from heaven, and put their trust in Him.

"I am the Bread of Life" (John 6:35-40). Each statement Jesus made stressed the continuing benefits of the life He brings. *You will never be hungry.* God will, in Jesus, keep on supplying that which sustains our new life. *You will never be thirsty.* A human being can go without food for weeks without dying, but he cannot go without water. Jesus promises to satisfy even that most intense of needs; He will see that we lack nothing we need. *I will never drive [him]*

away . . . I shall lose none of all that He has given me. We can be sure Jesus will extend God's grace to us in a daily experience of eternal life as well as in a permanent relationship with God.

"I am the Bread that came down from heaven" (John 6:41-51). The manna God provided for the Israelites during the Exodus is a picture of Jesus as the "living Bread." When God's people traveled through the wilderness, they had to depend on God to provide their food supernaturally. God provided the food in a way that would also teach the people something about their relationship with Him. Every day God gave enough food for that day. No one could gather more than a day's supply. There had to be a continual, constant dependence on God; He was the only source of sustenance.

The Jews murmured against Christ's claim to be "Bread that came down from heaven." They knew this Man and His family; how could He claim a heavenly origin? Jesus answered that it would be God who would draw men to Christ. And Jesus then went on to promise that anyone who believed in Him would have eternal life, and anyone who fed on the living Bread "will live forever."

"Eat the flesh of the Son of man" (John 6:52-59). Many see in those words a reference to the Communion service. "This is My body, given for you," Jesus would say as He instituted the memorial service. This is "My blood which is poured out for you." But to "eat" and "drink" the body and blood of Jesus means far more than to participate in a shared memorial, as the rest of our passage suggests. "Whoever eats My flesh and drinks My blood remains in Me" (v. 56). "He who feeds on this bread will

live forever" (v. 58). "The words I have spoken to you are spirit," Jesus said (v. 63).

Jesus was using *body* and *blood* to represent everything needed to sustain and support life. Our lives will be supported so completely that we never will hunger or thirst. Our spiritual lives will be sustained so completely that they will endure until Jesus raises us up on the last day.

We are to go to Jesus and to Him alone, for all the resources and the strength we need to live our new lives. We can rely only on our Lord.

Rejection: John 6:60-71

The crowds that had been attracted by the prospect of free food now shook their heads. Not only did Jesus fail to produce the expected dinners, but He had begun to speak like some madman! Even a few of those who had been His disciples (in the sense of general adherents, not in the stronger sense of committed followers), "turned back and no longer followed Him" (v. 66).

But when Jesus asked the Twelve if they would leave too, Peter answered for them. "Lord, to whom shall we go? You have the words of eternal life. We believe and know that You are the Holy One of God" (vv. 68-69). Peter and the others understood no better than the crowds. But they were willing to trust Him.

You and I might not grasp the meaning of all of Jesus' words either. We can't yet tell just what "remaining" and "living" in Jesus, or "feeding" on Him, mean. But we do know that if we are to enjoy our new lives, we must keep on looking to Jesus daily to supply our needs, and to sustain us with His grace.

GROUP RESOURCE GUIDE

Note: In preparation for this session, have a variety of colored felt and sufficient burlap for the group to make banners.

Exploration: *Probe God's Word*
Together underline the verbs in John 6:25-59.

Then in research teams of three or four determine which verbs tell (1) what Jesus Jesus has done, is doing, or will do, and (2)

which verbs say what persons are to do as a response to Jesus and/or His acts. There may be differences as to which verbs fit where, but discussion will help clarify the passage and its teachings.

Reaction: *Respond together to the Word*
Still in research teams develop several brief slogans or sayings that sum up one aspect of Jesus' teaching. Choose one saying, then

cut colored felt to form its letters and words. Also cut felt to create symbols appropriate for your slogan. Use them to create a banner on a large panel of burlap.

Identification: *Share with others*
As a team show your completed banner to others. Explain it and tell what its words mean, and why you chose them over other possibilities.

Adoration: *Worship and pray*
When all have shared, have a brief service dedicating the banners to the Lord. You may then give them to a church or Sunday School class, take them home, or put them up in the place where you usually meet.

LIGHT AND DARKNESS

Overview

Jesus said it in a dispute recorded in John 7:24. "Stop judging by mere appearances, and make a right judgment."

In a sense, this is the theme of this important section of John's Gospel, which focuses on "light."

Light and darkness are constant themes in John's New Testament writings. Those who live in darkness are confused, unable to see reality. Lost in a world of illusion they make judgments based on mere appearances, and are simply unable to grasp what is important and true.

Light, on the other hand, cuts through this darkness to unveil the right and the true. And Jesus is the Cornerstone of the kingdom of light; we begin to "see" when we acknowledge Him as the eternal Son of God.

But "light" also has a moral dimension. And it is this moral dimension that Jesus affirmed as He not only presented Himself to Israel as God, but also claimed the right to establish a *grace morality* which is far higher than the *legalistic morality* of the Jews, for it alone truly reflects the morality of God.

▶ *The Jews.* This designation is used often in the Gospel of John. John used it in a technical sense. He did *not* mean Israel, or the Jewish people as a whole. When John said "the Jews" he, unlike other Gospel writers, meant the religious leaders of the people who chose to oppose Jesus, and who represented a distortion of historic Old Testament faith.

Commentary

I hadn't been a Christian very long when I saw a stranger smoking a cigarette in the hall of our little church. I was shocked. I remember the pastor's son's reaction: "We don't smoke in church," Bruce announced in a chilly voice.

I also remember one of the men of that church, a police detective, who cupped his hand around his cigarette, trying to hide it, when he met some of our youth group on the street. I remember my own condemning attitude when one of the girls in our group said she hoped Jesus wouldn't return until she'd had time to enjoy life.

There were so many things that made me and other Christians I knew uncomfortable. There were so many things we considered wrong, in addition to the serious sins the Bible identified. And we felt compelled to judge all the ways in which another person seemed to miss our mark. Of course, if his ways were different enough, we'd have nothing to do with him.

To us, morality was summed up in doing "right" . . . and in cutting ourselves off from any relationship with those who did not do as we did.

We never realized that our attitude might distort true morality. We failed to see the light that Jesus brought into the world.

A World of Misunderstanding: John 7

We saw earlier that *light* and *darkness* are moral terms to John. They represent good and bad, righteousness and evil, as well as truth and falsity. Christ, the eternal Word (John 1) is the One through whom righteousness has always been communicated. Christ planted a moral awareness deep in every person, and revealed the nature of goodness back in the Old Testament. But John tells us that man's understanding and interpretation of light is faulty. Thus Paul can insist that the Law is "holy, righteous, and good," and still be convinced that Law had been an agent of death, stimulating sin rather than quieting it (Rom. 7:7-12).

We can see the distorted perception of the people of Jesus' day by looking at a series of incidents reported in John 7. Jewish thinking about morality was similar to my own in my early days of faith. Against the background of such attitudes, we will be able to see how Jesus displayed the glory of God, as He revealed a new morality, the morality of grace.

Hatred, uncertainty, and fear (John 7:1-13). Jesus' teachings and miracles had become widely known. His uncompromising presentation of Himself as God, and His offer of life to those who believed in Him, stirred up a number of reactions. Each reaction tells us something about the moral climate in Israel.

First, there was hatred (vv. 1, 7). The leaders of the people were charged with teaching God's Word to Israel. But they were so unlike God that they actually hated the Son of God who revealed Him. They in fact responded to Jesus with murderous rage.

Second, there was ridicule (vv. 3-5). Jesus' own brothers (in jealousy?) rejected the evidence of His works, and taunted Him.

Third, there was conflict. People argued with themselves and with each other. This Jesus. Is He a good Man, or a heretic? (vv. 12-13)

Fourth, there was fear. Even those who were convinced that Jesus was a Prophet and a good Man feared to take a stand. They knew they would be attacked, and probably persecuted by their religious leaders (referred to here and in other Johannine passages as "the Jews").

Looking at these reactions, we're forced to ask a question. What kind of results had Israel's interpretation of the divine Law produced? Had God's people become a community of love, caring, and closeness? Not at all! The people of God were angry, antagonistic, bitter, and fearful! There *must* be something wrong with an approach to faith that produces such a lifestyle! There must be a higher and better approach to morality and faith than *this!*

♥ *Group Activity: Support Group*
Read John 7:1-13. Along the continuum lines below, put a check to show how the text characterized relationships in the land divided over Jesus.
Love . . . . Antagonism
Support . . . . Ridicule
Harmony . . . . Conflict

Acceptance . . . . Fear
Discuss: What is it like to live with others when relationships are marked by characteristics on the left? On the right?
Share: Which relationships do you have now that are marked by the left side? The right side?
Relationship with Jesus is intended to create a supportive community characterized by qualities on the left. Do a relationship check on your own support group. On the same continuums, put a check on each line to indicate how you have experienced this group.
Show your charts to each other, and tell specifically what you have experienced that led you to check each line where you have. Be ready to respond to any who have not felt your group's support by expressing acceptance and love now.

God's authority rejected (John 7:14-24). At heart Israel had rejected God's authority. The leaders had made man's ideas supreme, and had missed the real meaning of the Law of Moses, which none kept (v. 19), even as they had rejected the evidence of the miracles that the Father empowered the Son to perform. If any of Jesus' critics had committed himself to do God's will, he would have recognized Jesus' teachings as the Word of God.

This is a critical point for us too. Moral and spiritual blindness are not rooted in our inability to understand. They are rooted in our unwillingness to submit completely to God. If anyone simply determines to do God's will, that person will be enlightened, and will first recognize Jesus as God's Son, and then acknowledge His teachings as God's Word.

Moral cowardice (John 7:25-36). When Jesus appeared at the Jerusalem festival, He taught openly. The rulers had determined to murder Christ, but they were afraid to oppose Him publicly! The crowds knew the leaders' antagonism toward Jesus; why wouldn't they act on their convictions? This led to much speculation. If Jesus were really leading the people astray, it was the responsibility of the leaders to arrest Him. Or "have the authorities really concluded that He is the Christ?" (v. 26) Finally, stung by the criticism, the chief priests and Pharisees gave orders for Jesus to be arrested.

Increasing uncertainty (John 7:37-52).

Jesus continued to offer the crowd words of eternal life, inviting them "to come to Me and drink." The guards sent to arrest Jesus returned to the leaders (who were conveniently absent when the arrest attempt was made!) and reported, "No one ever spoke the way this Man does!"

Furious, the leaders condemned Jesus, and in that act, broke the very code they claimed to uphold, for by Law no man could be judged without a hearing and examination of his behavior.

The authorities' quick condemnation was much like my reaction to the smoker in that church hallway. I felt anger and fear; I had rejected and condemned him without a hearing. I had had no real concern for him as a person.

When our "morality" produces responses that condemn and antagonize other human beings, then the "light" in us is darkness indeed! When we fear others and strike out at them, we are out of touch with the heart of God. And we have not understood the morality of grace that Jesus Himself revealed.

True Morality Revealed: John 8

We have just seen the moral climate of the community in which Jesus ministered; now we see the morality of Jesus Himself.

The woman (John 8:1-11). Unable to arrest Jesus, the Pharisees hoped to destroy His influence by forcing Him into a situation in which He would either directly violate the Law, or would insist on a drastic and unpopular penalty that was seldom enforced. The Pharisees and teachers of the Law brought a woman caught in the act of adultery to Jesus, and they challenged Him. "In the Law Moses commanded us to stone such women. Now what do You say?"

Jesus did not answer. Bending down, He began to write in the dust. Some have suggested Jesus was jotting down the details of sins committed by the accusers. As they continued to insist on a judgment, Jesus looked up. "If any one of you is without sin, let him be the first to throw a stone at her."

One by one the shamed rulers, condemned by their own consciences, slipped away.

Left alone with the woman, Jesus announced, "Neither do I condemn you. Go now and leave your life of sin."

As we analyze this incident, we begin to see the nature of a morality which flows from grace—in contrast to a legalistic morality. That legalistic morality is:

Impersonal. The Pharisees were quick to *use* the woman to strike at Jesus. She had no value in their eyes; they didn't care about her as a person.

But Jesus did care about her, individually. She was guilty, but in spite of her sin Jesus refused to condemn her. Grace salvages, rather than destroys, the individual.

Selective. The Pharisees brought the woman caught in the act of adultery. But where was the man? Their morality excused some while accusing others (see Rom. 2:11).

Jesus, however, raised the issue of universal guilt. "If any one of you is without sin, let him be the first to throw a stone at her," He announced. Every man there was forced to admit that he stood *beside* the woman, before the bar of justice.

The divine morality begins with the affirmation that all have sinned. But the Judge withholds condemnation in order to give life, and to encourage the sinner to "leave your life of sin."

Punishment oriented. The Law was a good and holy expression of righteousness. Adultery is wrong, and we are to care about doing right. But the Pharisees were not concerned with encouraging right action in Israel or with the reform of the woman. Their motives were not righteous, but vengeful.

On the other hand, everything Jesus did was righteous, and was designed to produce righteousness! Jesus affirmed the Law's penalty for sin, but demanded sinlessness from anyone who would execute it! Christ Himself judged the sin wrong, but rather than condemn the sinner, *Jesus withheld the penalty so that she might go and sin no more!*

Immediately after this incident, we are told that Jesus spoke to the people of Israel and said, "I am the Light of the world. Whoever follows Me will never walk in darkness, but will have the light of life" (John 8:12).

What is the light in which we are to walk? What is the moral pattern of grace we see in Jesus, in whose footsteps we are to walk also?

A grace morality cares first and foremost about those involved.

A grace morality humbly affirms solidarity with the sinner, not moral superiority.

A grace morality seeks not to condemn, but to lead others to a righteous life.

In each of these points, the morality of Jesus conflicted with the moral assumptions of the Pharisees, just as it conflicts with my own early self-righteous attitude toward others.

The character of grace morality (John 8:12-59). Now in discourses that follow the incident with the woman, Jesus defended and defined His right to serve as Light to the world. Jesus showed that He is the key, for in Jesus we have a:

Divine standard (vv. 13-20). The Pharisees who challenged Jesus were limited by a human perspective which was itself warped by sin. Thus they judged "by human standards." Jesus does not judge, for He came to bring life rather than condemnation. But were Jesus to judge (as one day He will!), His evaluation would penetrate to a reality that lies beyond human capacity to perceive. Jesus' standards are those of the Father Himself, whom the Pharisees did not even know.

Divine origin (vv. 21-30). The moral roots of Jesus' actions and teachings are from above, reflecting the heart of God. The moral roots of the Pharisees' approach were in this world, and reflect a sinful attitude. Unless the Pharisees abandon their own understanding and come in faith to Jesus, they would "indeed die in [their] sins" (v. 24).

Divine experience (vv. 31-38). True morality is to experience (to put into practice) Jesus' teachings. To know right but to do wrong (as the Pharisees had done) is to live in slavery to sin. But to practice Jesus' teachings is to experience a truth that brings total freedom.

John 8:31-32 combine several of John's key theological words in an illuminating way. To "know" the truth is not to intellectually comprehend, but to experience. To know the "truth" is not to focus on a body of knowledge, but to live in touch with reality as God knows reality. To "hold to" Jesus' teachings is not a reference to doctrinal purity, but to a commitment to put Jesus' teachings into daily practice. To be "free" is not to live selfishly, doing whatever one wants whenever one wants, but to live a disciplined and godly life which re-

leases us from our bondage to sin so that the choices we make lead to what helps us rather than to what hurts. All this can be found if we are only willing to *really* be the disciples of Jesus.

Divine response (vv. 39-47). True morality loves those whom God loves. The Pharisees showed a family resemblance to Satan rather than to God, for they hated Jesus, who came from God. They also had contemptuously dismissed the adulteress, whom God also loved.

Divine claim (vv. 48-59). The Jewish leaders again attacked. This time they insisted that Jesus' teachings and miracles were demonic in origin. The power Jesus displayed was evil rather than good; from Satan rather than God. The dispute concluded with Jesus' affirmation that He existed long before Abraham. In fact, Abraham had believed in Him.

In Jesus' claim, "Before Abraham was born, I am," the Jews rightly recognized that Jesus was identifying Himself with the Yahweh of the Old Testament (see Ex. 3:14; *index* for I AM).

God Himself, in the person of Jesus Christ, has revealed His heart. Jesus has shown us the true nature of morality. And the roots of that morality are sunk deep in grace, and have no reflection of the distorted legalism of New Testament Judaism, or in a legalism of our own.

Group Activity:
Missions/Outreach Group
Evangelism focuses on one issue: Who is Jesus, and what does He mean to us? Many have a general idea of who Jesus is without understanding the unique nature of His deity or the salvation He offers.

John 8:12-58 contains some of the NT's clearest assertions about who Jesus is, as well as a clear teaching on the necessity of belief in Him. Study the passage together to develop a "lesson plan" you might use in an evangelistic Bible study or in one-on-one witnessing. Plan a process that will help others discover for themselves what claims Jesus made, and the great dividing line between "children of God" and "children of the devil."

Group Activity: Recovery Group
Step 12 (carry the 12 Step message to others)

Jot down one thing you have done in the last few days that made you feel ashamed or guilty.

Read John 8:1-11, and together list characteristics of a "morality of law" as represented by the Pharisees (see commentary, p. 226). From the same passage list marks of Jesus' "morality of grace."

Then study John 8:12-59 for evidence that Jesus had the right to operate on, and to establish for us, a morality of grace (see commentary p. 227).

Discuss: How would you feel about admitting the thing you jotted down to a person who holds a "morality of law"? How would you feel about admitting it to others who operate on a morality of grace? If you operate on Jesus' morality of grace, how might your feelings about yourself change when you sin or fail?

One way you carry the message of Jesus' transforming grace morality to others is by modeling it. Can you model self-acceptance by sharing your failure? Can you model grace morality by accepting and supporting others when they share their sins and failures with you? Now is a good time to begin!

The Final Illustration: John 9

Why hadn't the people of Israel responded now that the Light of the world, Jesus, had come and so clearly illumined God's grace? John reported an event that clearly illustrated the reasons, and pointed out a danger that we each face in our own spiritual lives.

Who sinned? (John 9:1-12) The Jewish people knew God was a moral Person. But "morality" was translated into a simple formula: Those who do right will be rewarded; those who do wrong will be punished. It followed, from this formula, that any personal disasters were evidence of sin. Conversely, prosperity was a sign of God's approval.

This formula underlies the disciples' question about a man on the street who had been blind from birth. "Who sinned, this man or his parents?" That is, was the man's blindness a punishment from God for the future sins he would commit, or was his blindness a punishment for ancestral evil?

Jesus' answer was, "Neither." The blind man did not serve as a demonstration of the impact of sin, but rather as a demon-

stration of the power and love of God. His tragedy was a backdrop for blessing!

How often this is true for us. Sue experienced a painful divorce, deserted by her husband when she was three months pregnant and with a two-and-a-half-year-old son. The struggles of the next years were brutal. Yet out of them grew an understanding and sympathy for the needs of the divorced, an active personal ministry, and a book on how Christians individually and as congregations can minister to the suddenly single. The tragedy was a backdrop. It need not be explained by sin, but can be seen as God's avenue to blessing for her and for others.

Jesus healed the blind man. The neighbors were stunned. They brought the man to the Pharisees to see how they would interpret this latest spectacular work of Jesus.

He is a sinner (John 9:13-25). The Pharisees struggled against this new evidence of God's presence with Jesus. The healing had been performed on the Sabbath; here was an excuse to condemn it. Yet some of them hesitated. "How can a sinner do such miraculous signs?" (v. 16) Twice they questioned the man and interrogated his parents. Finally they pronounced their judgment: "Give glory to God. We know this Man is a sinner" (v. 24).

God listens to Him (John 9:26-34). The man who had been blind cut through the hypocrisy. When he was told the Pharisees "did not know where" Jesus came from (e.g., did not know His origins or the source of His powers), the man replied, "Now that is remarkable! . . . [God] listens to the godly man who does His will. Nobody has ever heard of opening the eyes of a man born blind. If this man were not from God, He could do nothing."

Furious, the Pharisees threw the man out on the streets. "You were steeped in sin at birth; how dare you lecture us!"

Your sin remains (John 9:35-41). Jesus found the man whose sight He had restored, and identified Himself as the Son of man (an Old Testament name of the Messiah). The man believed what Jesus said, and worshiped Him.

This blind man's inner vision, as well as his physical vision, had been restored. He recognized Jesus as the Light of the world. The judgment that comes on the world was not a judgment Jesus made, but one the world brought on itself. The blind saw

. . . and those who claimed to see were shown to be blind.

Overhearing this remark, the Pharisees snarled, "What? Are we blind too?"

Jesus answered, "If you were blind, you would not be guilty of sin; but now that you claim you can see, your guilt remains."

The religious leaders of Jesus' day insisted that their moral ideas were right, and so they rejected Jesus and His teachings in spite of all the evidence. If only they would have admitted their moral blindness and turned to Jesus. He would have opened their eyes, even as He restored sight to the man born blind.

The people who cannot see the light are usually the ones who insist their moral concepts are right, and the ones who refuse to submit themselves to God's morality as revealed in Jesus.

In Summary
As the Light of the world, Jesus reveals the morality of God. In Him we see beyond all previous revelations of goodness. In His every action, Jesus gives a clear and unmistakable picture of grace. He shakes our old ideas of morality, and helps us to understand God's righteousness.

Jesus did not in any way condone sin. He even upheld the rightness of sin's ultimate penalty (John 8:7). But Jesus did demonstrate that God reacts to sinners in a far different way than we tend to. Man's legalistic interpretation of morality involves hatred and rejection of the sinner. It leads to judging others, and to the fear of being judged. It also leads to injustice, as some are excused dor their failures while others are never accused. A legalistic morality blinds us to our own condition as sinners, and puts us beside those we have been so quick to condemn.

But God's morality, shown in Jesus, is a morality rooted in grace. It never compromises with sin, but it never rejects the sinner. It accords the sinner love and respect; it says that a person is of worth and value.

The goal of grace's treatment is to rescue the individual from slavery to sin, and to free him to sin no more. The person who lives in the light shed by Jesus is ever aware that he approaches others not as one who is exalted above them to judge, but as one who shares with them a common infirmity that prohibits anyone from casting the first stone.

How can we learn to live this new morality of grace? We are to learn from Jesus, by following Him out of the darkness and into His light (v. 12).

GROUP RESOURCE GUIDE

Identification: *Share with others*
In a sentence or two tell how your attitude toward yourself or toward others has changed since becoming and growing as a Christian.

Affirmation: *Express love and concern*
If you are aware of a significant positive change in another person in your group, express it when he or she shares (above).

Exploration: *Probe God's Word*
1. Read John 9:1-41 aloud. As the passage is read jot down notes about how the different people mentioned (such as the man himself, onlookers, his parents, the Pharisees) respond to the change in the man born blind. For instance, the Pharisees first deny the now-sighted man was born blind, then refuse to believe Jesus did it, etc.

Share your notes and discuss: How have people reacted to the change conversion works in us? Are our changes as obvious? What do we sense or see in ourselves that demonstrates conversion's reality? What should others see? And, what *do* they see?

2. Give a brief report, previously prepared, on how "grace morality" (pp. 226-227) was demonstrated by Jesus and finds expression in the lives of His followers today. This kind of change in attitude and relationships may very well be as stunning as the transition from physical blindness to sightedness.

Reaction: *Respond together to the Word*
In groups of three identify one person to whom you very much want to display Christ through your life. Tell about your relationship with this individual. Talk

together about how you can display Jesus' grace morality in the relationship you have with him or her. Be as specific as possible.

Adoration: *Worship and pray*
Pray in groups of three that Jesus will express Himself clearly through you in the relationship you discussed. Thank the Lord for His own gracious way of relating to you, and commit yourself to represent Him clearly to others.

THE CHOICE

Overview

In these central chapters of John's Gospel we find clear evidence of the decisive rejection of Jesus by His people.

Christ presented Himself as the Good Shepherd who would die for His sheep (John 10:1-21). "The Jews" (John's term for the religious authorities) realized Jesus was claiming to be God, and tried to seize Him (vv. 22-42).

Christ demonstrated His power over death by raising Lazarus, who had been dead for four days (11:1-44). The Jews did not respond to the miracle, but were afraid their people would believe in Jesus and "take away both our place and our nation." They determined that Jesus must die (vv. 45-57).

Christ, acclaimed by the people on Palm Sunday, predicted His death (12:1-36), but the Jews continued in their fixed unbelief (v. 37).

Each of these chapters follows the same pattern. There is a clear presentation by Jesus of His claims, followed by a decisive rejection by the authorities, and a growing determination to kill Jesus to get Him out of the way.

Even so, Jesus did not condemn. But He did warn. "There is a Judge for the one who rejects Me and does not accept My words; that very word which I spoke will condemn him at the last day" (v. 48).

■ For a verse-by-verse commentary on each key phrase in this section see the *Bible Knowledge Commentary*, pages 309-319.

Commentary

Unlike the other Gospels, which trace the development of Jesus' ministry over three years, the Gospel of John focuses on the final months of Christ's life, when the issues had been clearly drawn.

Jesus, the Son of God, revealed over and over again the truth about life and light, and confronted His listeners with the necessity of choice.

John 10 through 12 depicts events that lead up to the Upper Room Discourse. In these chapters we see the final confrontation, and catch a glimpse of the ultimate evidence that will soon be offered to prove Jesus' claims.

The Shepherd and His Sheep: John 10

In the Old Testament, the picture of a shepherd and his sheep was often used to illustrate the relationship between God and His people. "The Lord is my Shepherd," one psalmist said. Another added, "We are the sheep of His pasture."

Shepherd was also a term applied to spiritual leaders in the Old Testament. Jeremiah chose harsh words to describe leaders who perverted their spiritual role: " 'Woe to the shepherds who are destroying and scattering the sheep of My pasture!' declares the Lord" (Jer. 23:1). The prophet declared that God would set His own Shepherd over His sheep when the promised Son of David (Jesus) reigns.

The people would have had these symbolic pictures of divine leadership in mind when Jesus announced, "I am the Good Shepherd" (John 10:11). Jesus then developed a contrast between Himself and the religious authorities of His day. Jesus was concerned for God's people, and exemplified the morality of grace. The Jewish rulers, on the other hand, ignored the welfare of their people. They, therefore, were false shepherds.

By this time, the leaders of Israel were firmly committed not only to rejecting Jesus' claim to divine authority but to destroying Him as well. So in this message Jesus did not speak to the rulers; He appealed directly to the individuals who made up the nation.

True Shepherd recognized (John 10:1-6). In Israel sheep were not herded with dogs or by men who walked behind them. The shepherd of the Middle East *led* his sheep. He knew each one by name, and the sheep recognized his voice. At night several herds of sheep might sleep in the same fold. In the morning, when the one door was unbarred, each shepherd could unerringly pick out his own flock. And each member of that flock would be able to distinguish his shepherd from the others because the sheep would know the shepherd's voice, just as God's people would recognize Jesus as the living Word of God.

The Pharisees who claimed to speak for Moses would be followed, but not by those who belonged to God. The true sheep would hear the voice of the Good Shepherd.

Good Shepherd identified (John 10:7-17). Now Jesus condemned the leaders of Israel, saying, "All who ever came before Me were thieves and robbers." Such men care "nothing for the sheep." Jesus, on the other hand, is the Good Shepherd. The Palestinian shepherd commonly slept in the single opening to the fold through which wild animals might attack. As "the door" Jesus protects His own, by placing His body between the sheep and their enemies. The Good Shepherd guides His sheep to pasture, concerned not only that they have life, but that they "have it to the full." How deep is the commitment of the Good Shepherd to His sheep? "The Good Shepherd lays down His life for the sheep."

How clearly this must have spoken to the men and women of Israel. Their rulers, like religious leaders of many times and many faiths, were quick to demand respect and obedience. They were quick to lord it over others; quick to judge, advise, condemn. But no one in Israel would imagine for a moment that one of the authorities would lay down his life for one of the common people. Those leaders might lay down their lives for truth. More than once the men of Israel had refused to fight on the Sabbath, and had been killed easily by pagans. More than one Israelite had offered his body to Roman swords rather than permit a statue of Caesar, or even the Legion Eagles, to enter Jerusalem. To die for a conviction was not that uncommon. But to die for love of the sheep? Never! Truth was important to the authorities; people were not.

✳ *Group Activity:*
Singles/Single Again Group
It's often hard for a newly single person to do things families take for granted. One recently divorced woman told of some of the sudden challenges that were hard for her to meet including: changing a car windshield wiper blade, stopping a faucet from dripping, making meals for only one person, getting used to sleeping alone.

Together brainstorm things that have been or are hard for you to face as a single.

Then look at John 10:1-15. Individually, pick a single phrase from this passage that sums up the sheep/shepherd image for you. Draw with crayons on a sheet of paper the image this phrase stimulates of your own relationship with Jesus.

Show your pictures, and tell how they express the phrase you chose.

Take the picture home, and the next time you face a difficult task and feel alone, look at it, and remember that though single, you are not alone. Your Shepherd is there.

But to Jesus, the sheep—sinners not worth the contempt of the righteous—were worth dying for!

One with the Father (John 10:18-30). Jesus could die for the sheep because He had the authority from God to lay down His life, and "authority to take it up again. This command," Jesus continued, "I received from My Father" (v. 18).

These words sent the Jews back to the old debate. "He is demon-possessed and raving mad," some said. But others answered, "Can a demon open the eyes of the blind?"

Again the Jews asked the central question: "How long will You keep us in suspense? If You are the Christ, tell us plainly" (v. 24).

Once again Jesus explained that His sheep hear and respond to His voice. To such He gives eternal life. He can bestow this gift because, "I and the Father are One" (v. 30).

Refusal to believe (John 10:31-42). Jesus' renewed claim to be God the Son was recognized by the people: "Again the Jews picked up stones to stone Him."

How strange. "Tell us if You are the Christ." And when Jesus told them, they tried to kill Him because they did not want to hear the truth!

The Jews accused Jesus of blasphemy "because You, a mere Man, claim to be God."

Jesus stunned them with a quote from the Psalms: "Is it not written in your Law, 'I have said you are gods'? If He called them 'gods' to whom the Word of God came—and the Scripture cannot be broken—what about the One whom the Father set apart as His very own and sent into the world?" (vv. 34-36) If those who receive the Word are exalted by the Lord Himself and called "gods," how much more deserving of that name is the One who *is* the Word?

The passage Jesus quoted is Psalm 82:6, "I say, 'You are "gods"; you are all sons of the Most High.' " The life Jesus offers us is eternal life, God's life. When we receive Jesus, we become the sons of God.

As Peter put it, "You are sons of God now; the live, permanent Word of the living God has given you His own indestructible heredity" (1 Peter 1:23, PH). Unable to grasp grace, the Pharisees and other leaders had no concept of what a personal relationship with God meant. They were no more able to understand the gift Jesus offered than they could imagine God could care enough for human beings to become a Man in order to bring us to Himself.

But while the leaders continued to try to arrest Jesus (John 10:39), many others heard in Jesus the voice of God, and began to believe.

The Resurrection, Now: John 11

Jesus now moved to a culminating miracle, a final demonstration of His ultimate authority as God's Son.

During Jesus' public ministry Christ had been very close to Mary and Martha and their brother, Lazarus. When Lazarus became seriously ill, the sisters sent a message to Jesus: "Lord, the one You love is sick." But to the amazement of the disciples, Jesus seemed to make no response. He stayed where He was for two more days before He set out with the Twelve for Bethany. When they arrived, Lazarus was dead and buried, just as Jesus had told His disciples he would be.

Martha rushed out to meet Jesus and, in tears, cried, "Lord, if You had been here, my brother would not have died."

Jesus consoled her. "Your brother will rise again."

Martha thought she understood what Jesus was saying. "I know he will rise again in the resurrection at the last day."

But Christ's words rearranged her thinking. "I am the Resurrection and the Life," Jesus said. "Do you believe this?"

Then Jesus went to Lazarus' grave. When He told the bystanders to roll away the rock that sealed the cave, Martha objected. "But Lord, by this time there is a bad odor, for he has been there for four days."

Jesus demonstrated that His resurrection power was not limited to sometime in the future, but that His power to bring life knows no limits. "Lazarus, come out!" And, at Jesus' word, the man appeared in the cave doorway, still wrapped with the embalming linens. "Take off the graveclothes, and let him go," Jesus commanded.

This miracle stunned nearby Jerusalem. Many came to see Lazarus, and many believed. But the chief priests were still unmoved. They could not deny Jesus' signs. But what they could do was to act immediately on the high priest's pronouncement: "It is better for you that one man die for the people than that the whole nation perish" (v. 50). From that day on, the authorities plotted with renewed determination to execute Jesus.

Then Jesus withdrew and waited. Waited for the Passover, when He would go up to Jerusalem again and, as the Good Shepherd, would die for the sheep. Then Jesus would be restored on the third day, to an endless life.

What is the meaning of the resurrection of Lazarus for us? The same as it was for the disciples and other witnesses in Bethany. *This event is a demonstration of Jesus' ability to make His resurrection power available to His people—now!*

It is one thing to believe that Jesus has the power to raise us up on the last day. He does and He will. But it's something else to realize that Jesus' power is unlimited now; that Jesus can bring new life to the deadened areas of our own personalities; that because of Jesus' power, we can risk taking actions that we might otherwise never have the courage to take. We need never draw back from anything God asks, for the unlimited power of new life is ours in Him.

✄ *Group Activity: Recovery Group*
  Step 11 (improve relationship with God

through prayer and meditation)

Jot down at least five things you've come to believe are too hard for you to accomplish, even though you have made strides in the recovery process.

Then each person in the group needs an 8 1/2 x 11 sheet of paper, near the top of which is a box, over which is written "resurrection power." Up in the right corner draw a tomb with a closed door.

Together study John 11, and on the back of each sheet make notes on Martha's concept of the resurrection power she truly did believe Jesus had. What could that power do? What couldn't it do?

Turn over the sheets of paper and note that the picture of the tomb lies outside the box titled "resurrection power." One problem all of us have is to truly believe in Jesus' power—but to unconsciously assume that some things are beyond the ability of that power to change.

Look up Romans 8:11 and write it on the bottom of your paper. Talk about what this means. Then write down the things that you felt were "too hard to accomplish" either inside the box or outside.

Write them inside if you are going to trust Jesus and rely on His power to enable you, or outside if you are still unable to trust the resurrection power of the Lord.

Pray together that you will know Jesus' will and commit yourself to do that will, enabled by His mighty strength.

The Hour Has Come: John 12

As this chapter opens, it is only six days until the Passover and Jesus' crucifixion. Jesus repeated the truths He had been stressing, and we are given a special insight into how Jesus Himself felt as the tension grew. We will also see in brief vignettes the reactions of those around Jesus.

Prepared for burial (John 12:1-8). At the home of Mary and Martha, Jesus was anointed with an expensive ointment as a sign of life. Mary did not know it, but the ointment (one used in embalming) expressed not only her love but the love of God, soon to be shared as Jesus gave up His life for us.

Triumphal Entry (John 12:9-19). The next day Jesus entered Jerusalem to the cheers of the crowds. His entry fulfilled prophecy and seemed to the elders and priests evidence that "the whole world has gone after Him."

But Jesus' sudden popularity was rooted in the spectacular sign of the raising of Lazarus, not in true faith. A celebrity for a day in our society realizes how quickly such popularity disappears. The Triumphal Entry was an evidence of curiosity and enthusiasm, but not of faith.

Inner anguish (John 12:20-33). The pressure on Jesus in view of His approaching suffering was great. Still He remained firm in His commitment: "What shall I say? 'Father, save Me from this hour'? No, it was for this very reason I came to this hour. Father, glorify Your name."

There are several important spiritual principles in this brief section. It is through death that new life comes; a seed loses its individual identity to become the source from which many grains grow. In the holding onto one's life in this world, we will ultimately lose it. But the person who is willing to follow Jesus' example, turning away from those things that would only be for his own benefit and serving others as Jesus did, will find the true meaning of life. And will find fulfillment. So Jesus warned, "Whoever serves Me must follow Me." The example Jesus set in His death is one we are to follow in our lives.

What then will be the benefits of Jesus' death? He will destroy the power of the ruler of this world (Satan), and will "draw all men to Myself."

In His death Jesus glorified God by bringing you and me into fellowship with Him.

They did not believe (John 12:34-43). Then the crowd that had just cheered Jesus as their King showed the shallowness of their allegiance. They rejected what Jesus said about Himself: "We have heard from the Law [the Old Testament] that the Christ will remain forever, so how can You say, 'The Son of man must be lifted up'?"

The people were still unwilling to submit themselves to Jesus as the Son of God. They insisted that their will, not God's, dominate. The passage says, "Even after Jesus had done all these miraculous signs in their presence, they still would not believe in Him." And those who *did* believe kept their faith secret because they feared the Pharisees and wanted human acceptance (vv. 42-43).

The final choice (John 12:44-50). Jesus said again what He had been teaching among them for months. But this was their last chance. Jesus would not speak to the crowds again.

What did Jesus say?

- I am the revealer of the Father.
- Belief in Me is belief in the Father.
- Whoever believes in Me will no longer live in darkness.
- If you reject Me, you reject the eternal life offered you by the Father.
- If you reject Me, you place yourself under sure judgment.

The living Word has spoken. Now is the time to respond, and to receive life through the Word.

In Summary

The repetition in John's Gospel is there for a purpose. No one must miss the central issues of life and death which Jesus raised. These are issues that you and I face today just as surely as the people of Israel had to face them.

Jesus, the Good Shepherd, revealed the loving heart of the Father. For the first time you and I realize how complete God's concern for us is: He will lay down His life for His sheep.

Jesus, in the incident at Bethany, also showed us the full extent of God's power. The eternal life Christ offers brings us a resurrection power that operates *now*. God is able to bring life even to the dead areas in our personalities today.

But we must respond with faith to the voice of God. Unlike the men and women of Jesus' day who held back, we need to hear in Jesus the voice of the Good Shepherd, and choose to follow Him.

GROUP RESOURCE GUIDE

Identification: *Share with others*
Tell about a time when you prayed earnestly for something really important to you, and no answer came. After each person has shared, talk about how this experience made you feel, and what questions it may have raised about your relationship with the Lord.

Exploration: *Probe God's Word*
1. Read John 11:1-6, 11:17-21, and 11:28-37. How was the experience of Mary and Martha like or unlike the experience you just shared? How must they have felt when Jesus did not respond to their cry for help?
2. Now read John 11:7-16, 23-27, and 38-44. How did the situation, which was one of great suffering and doubt for Mary and Martha, seem from Jesus' perspective? What made His perspective so different from theirs?

Can you talk again about your own experience? How might the situation you shared have seemed different from Christ's point of view?

Reaction: *Respond together to the Word*
Together list the lessons Mary, Martha, and the disciples might have learned from the death and raising of Lazarus. Don't stop at the obvious lessons, but dig deep for every possible implication.

Then look once again at the personal situation with which you have been dealing. Which of these insights might apply and help you accept if not understand the reason for your unanswered prayer?

Adoration: *Worship and pray*
Silently praise God for the mystery of His sovereign workings, and express your confidence that all He does is loving.

JESUS' LAST WORDS

Overview

These chapters contain part of the extended private teaching that Jesus gave His disciples the evening before His crucifixion. It is commonly called the Last Supper Discourse. It is important, for here we find specific teaching on how Jesus' people are to relate to God and others during the Church Age.

Of particular importance is Jesus' emphasis on the Holy Spirit, and the role He is to play when Jesus has returned to the Father.

▶ *Holy Spirit.* The personality of the Spirit is taught in John 15:26. He is linked to both Father and Son, is the subject of a verb (testify) that implies personal action, and is given a name—Counselor. The Spirit's role in this age is so important that Jesus told His followers, "It is for your good that I am going away" for the Counselor could not come until after Christ's death, resurrection, and ascension. The Bible tells of a number of things that the Spirit does for and in believers. He is the Agent in our inner transformation toward Christlikeness (2 Cor. 3:17-18; Gal. 5:22-23). His presence provides the power we need to live a righteous life (Rom. 8:2-11; Gal. 5:5-6). He is the Source of our gifts and abilities to minister to others and enrich them spiritually (1 Cor. 12). How important that we learn to live in harmony with the Spirit, thus letting Him produce in us the fruit of love, joy, peace, and true goodness.

Commentary

Television's "60 Minutes" told the story of a nurse who works with the dying. She counsels the terminally ill patient, helps him or her face death, and plans with the family how to make the patient's last weeks or months most meaningful. Usually, as the end approaches, the patient wants to return home to spend the final days with family and friends.

As we reach these chapters in John's Gospel, we can sense a similar feeling. The mood changes. The sharp tone of conflict is muted. No Pharisee intrudes here. Instead we sense only tenderness and a strange sort of peace. Strange, because Jesus' life is now measured not by months or weeks but by hours. Jesus chose to spend the last hours on earth with His own. To His own—and to you and me—Jesus explains how to practice the presence of, and to know intimate fellowship with, God.

Prelude: John 13:1-30

The introduction to this most intimate scene in any of the Gospels features Judas. When he left the table, only those who loved Jesus remained. Only they would hear Jesus' words of comfort and triumph, spoken in a private room, shut away from doubting crowds and angry enemies.

Judas. Judas represented everyone to whom Jesus offers light and life, and who refuse to respond with faith.

Judas was one of the original Twelve. At the beginning, Jesus chose Judas to be with Him in His public ministry. Like the other disciples, Judas saw Jesus' miracles and heard His teaching. Judas drew close in those private times when Jesus explained His words to the Twelve alone. Judas, along with the other disciples, had often watched Jesus slip away before dawn to commune with the Father.

Yet Judas had failed to respond. Outwardly he looked like one of Jesus' followers. He acted like them. He talked like them. The other 11 did not suspect his inner core of sin and unbelief. But it was there, just as the greed and the uncaring attitude he shared with the Pharisees was always there.

Soon the hidden heart of Judas would be revealed as he opened his personality to Satan's influence, and engaged in history's ultimate crime: he agreed with Jesus' enemies to betray the Lord to them for 30 pieces of silver—the price established in the Old Testament as payment for the death not of a freeman but of a slave!

Judas was later remorseful over the great betrayal. Filled with horror, Judas returned the money to the temple treasury and the priests. "I have betrayed innocent blood," he cried.

Under the Law, priests were charged with comforting and cleansing the sinner, but these priests responded with characteristic indifference. "What is that to us? That's your responsibility" (Matt. 27:4).

Frantic, Judas ran to the edge of one of the cliffs on which Jerusalem stands. With shaking hands he tied a piece of old rope around the limb of a tree . . . around his own neck . . . and threw himself out into space. The rope jerked, stretched . . . and broke. Judas fell to his death on the jagged rocks below (cf. Matt. 27:1-10 with Acts 1:18).

Even when he finally faced his own guilt, Judas still would not turn to Jesus for the forgiveness Christ had spoken of so often during the years they were together.

Judas proved he could wear a mask of piety. He could fit in outwardly even with the most sincere of Jesus' followers. But like the Pharisees, Judas' inner life was evil. He shared their lust for wealth, and he shared their lack of concern for other men and women. Finally, when Judas' betrayal of Jesus exposed his guilt even to himself, Judas still refused to respond to grace. Death seemed preferable to humbly bowing before Jesus, to beg forgiveness at His hands.

How good that Judas need not set the pattern for you and me! We can acknowledge our guilt freely, and trust ourselves to God's grace. We can come to the God each of us has betrayed, and find in Jesus Christ, God's Son, full and free forgiveness. And in Jesus we can find life; a life that fills our personality, remakes our attitudes and desires, and teaches us to reflect to others God's own love.

An example (John 13:1-20). Jesus "loved His own," the passage begins. It then goes on to describe a foot-washing. Clad only in a light robe, Jesus took a basin of water and began to wash His disciples' feet.

Peter was deeply upset. Jesus, his Lord, stooping to serve him like a common household slave! Never!

But Jesus insisted, and later explained. The simple ritual (1) reflected a great theological truth, (2) gave His followers an example, and (3) helped show how we today are to relate to the strangers who slip in among us.

(1) The theological truth. In the ancient world a person might bathe at home or in public baths. After such a thorough cleansing, he would strap on his sandals and walk the dusty streets. When a person entered a friend's house, a servant would wash the film of dust and dirt from his feet. The body was clean, but the feet, having been in contact with the world, needed constant cleansing.

In answer to Peter's objection, and then to his request that Jesus wash "not just my feet but my hands and my head as well," Jesus pointed out that Peter had already been cleansed (bathed). All that was required now was the continued washing away of the dust that might accumulate from traveling in the streets.

Many commentators take this exchange to suggest that in salvation, believers are completely cleansed. But in our daily life we may pick up contaminations that require Jesus' continual washings (forgiveness). "A person who has had a bath needs only to wash his feet; his whole body is clean. And you are clean," Jesus explained (v. 10).

(2) The example. Jesus went on to explain that His actions set an example—an object lesson in humility. If the disciples' Teacher and Lord stooped to wash their feet, they should have no hesitation to stoop and serve one another. "I tell you the truth, no servant is greater than his master, nor is a messenger greater than the one who sent him." Humbling ourselves to serve each other is Jesus' way to greatness.

(3) The challenge. It's striking to realize that Judas was one of those whose feet Jesus washed. The betrayer was served in the same way as the faithful, and through it all, Jesus knew who was going to betray Him.

How is this an example and a challenge to us? You and I know there will be those in a fellowship of believers who have not yet responded to Jesus' message of forgiveness. Will they respond, or will they prove to be like Judas? Should we try to root them out or make distinctions in the way we treat the "true" brothers, and "false"? Never! Within the fellowship of faith we are to serve brother and Judas alike, even as Jesus stooped to wash all of their feet in that Upper Room.

♥ *Group Activity: Support Group*
Silently read John 13:1-17. Hear previously prepared reports on the theological, exemplary, and challenge aspect of Jesus' act in washing the disciples' feet.

Supply a large bowl or dishpan, water, and washcloth. Wash the feet of the person on your right; he or she then washes the person's feet on his or her right. When you have been around the group, talk about the experience. Did you feel most comfortable when your feet were being washed, or when you were washing another's feet? What do we learn from Jesus' washing of the disciples' feet? What did you learn from the actual experience? How can we serve and support one another in our group?

The betrayer departs (John 13:21-30). Jesus identified the one who would betray Him by dipping a piece of bread in broth and handing it to Judas, saying, "What you are about to do, do quickly." The others didn't understand. They thought Jesus was sending Judas out to make a purchase for the festival. Instead, Jesus was releasing Judas to do what he had already determined to do. "As soon as Judas had taken the bread, he went out." The Bible adds, "And it was night."

The New Community: John 13:31–14:31
Within the Upper Room, the vision of a new community was being shaped. In the last few hours of His life on earth, Jesus sketched for His friends a picture of a future that they—and we—are to experience. It's important to realize that this revelation is for us. Here is a picture of your life and mine as Christians, a picture of our experience in Christ. The key to this experience is *relationship:* relationship with each other as members of a new community, and relationship with Jesus, the Enabler of

the new community. Of all the words Jesus could have spoken in that last brief time with His own, these are the words He chose to share. How eagerly we, like the disciples, lean forward to hear each one.

The foundation (John 13:31-35). The foundation of Jesus' new community is a unique relationship. Here is how Christ explained it: "A new command I give you: Love one another. As I have loved you, so you must love one another. All men will know that you are My disciples if you love one another."

These are familiar words, yet strange ones. Love is nothing new; the Old Testament speaks often of love and reminds us to "love your neighbor as yourself."

But on closer examination, there are several things here that *are* new. The Old Testament spoke of loving our neighbors: Jesus focused on loving "one another." We who are Jesus' disciples are still to love our neighbors. But we have been welcomed in Christ into a new, intimate relationship with other believers! In Christ, we have become brothers and sisters, members of a single family (see Eph. 2:19; 3:6). In Christ, our relationship with each other is suddenly more intimate than any human relationship has ever been! In the closeness of our new relationship with God and with each other, love takes on a new savor—and a new necessity.

There is also a new standard by which to measure love. Love of neighbor was to be "as you love yourself." But here we are told to love each other "as I have loved you." Love as Jesus did? Love with a love that *gives* self? Yes, this is new. My brother becomes more important to me than I am!

Finally, there is a new outcome. The Christlike love that permeates the new community of Christian brothers and sisters is a witness to the world that Jesus is real. Only Jesus' living presence can explain such love for others.

This context of a loving community is vital in all that Jesus goes on to explain in these next chapters of John's Gospel. It is in the context of a new community marked off by love that all Jesus outlines can, and will, become a reality.

∅ *Group Activity:*
Missions/Outreach Group
In giving His "new commandment"

(John 13:34-35), Jesus linked effective evangelism with loving one another "as I have loved you." Why?

In teams of three describe a person who has had a strong, positive effect on your personal spiritual growth. Take two or three minutes and try to help the others on your team get to know the person you chose. When all three have shared, individually complete the following, placing a check mark (√) along each continuum line, to show what your relationship with the person you described was most like.

Warm ....*Cold*
Close...*Distant*
Two way* ....*One way*
Knew me**...............................*Not know*
Knew him*** ....*Not know*

* Was your communication one way or two way; did you talk with each other, or did you just listen?
** Did you feel he or she really knew you as a person or not?
*** Did you feel you really knew him or her as a person or not?

When the continuums are completed, compare. Divide the continuum lines into four equal segments. How many checks were in each segment? What do you conclude about the nature of relationships which have a significant spiritual influence on others?

Talk about those whom you are praying for and seeking to win for Christ. What is your relationship with them like? What can you do to make that relationship more like the pattern seen in your combined charts?

Formed while Jesus is away (John 13:36–14:31). The new community is rooted in relationship with Jesus, but not in the same kind of relationship that the disciples had experienced those past three or so years. Instead, Jesus would be away, physically, as the new community took shape.

But how could a community be formed around Jesus when He was not present? That issue nags at us today even as it troubled the early disciples. How are we to experience Jesus and God the Father when our Lord is not *here?*

*Trust (13:36–14:7). Jesus' announcement that He was going and the disciples could not follow shook the 11. Peter promptly swore that he would follow Jesus even to death. Thomas puzzled over where Jesus might hide, and how they would ever find their way to that place. None caught the implications of death and resurrection that we can see so clearly now.

Even so, we can understand the fears that surged up at Jesus' announcement. Sometimes we too feel deserted and alone. When we do, Jesus' words can comfort us even as they comforted the 11. "Do not let your hearts be troubled," Jesus encouraged. He went on to explain two things: while He was absent, Jesus would be with the Father, preparing a place for each disciple and for the community. Then He would return and "take you to be with Me that you also may be where I am." Jesus' absence is temporary and purposive; while He is gone, we are to trust Him.

It's not necessary for us to know the location or to see the star charts that pinpoint the location of our Father's house. Knowing Jesus is enough. He is the Way, the Truth, and the Life.

Here, then, is our first instruction. Remember that knowing and trusting Jesus is enough.

*Prayer (14:8-14). In the Upper Room, Philip still was troubled. "Show us the Father," he begged.

Jesus answered that they had been shown the Father already, in Him! "Anyone who has seen Me has seen the Father." But then Jesus went on to note that even if Philip was unable to *see* God in Jesus' personality, the works God did through Jesus witnessed to the Father's presence. "Believe Me when I say that I am in the Father and the Father is in Me; or at least believe on the evidence of the miracles themselves."

What is important here is to note that while the Father was not present, He expressed Himself in the world through Jesus' actions, words, and character. So God does not need to be physically present to act in our world. Nor will Jesus need to be physically present in order to be a part of and act through the new community. In fact, Jesus promised, "Anyone who has faith in Me will do what I have been doing." Just as the Father acted in Jesus, so Jesus will act in believers.

It is in this context of complete confidence that Jesus tells us to pray. "And I will do whatever you ask in My name, so that the Son may bring glory to the Father. You may ask Me for anything in My name, and I will do it."

This is our second instruction for life in the new community. We are to expect Jesus to continue to act in this world and are invited to bring *everything* to Him in prayer, confident that He will answer.

Following (14:15-31). The third instruction for life in the new community involves responsive obedience. Jesus promised He would send the Holy Spirit as a Counselor "to be with you forever." The Spirit is identified as the "Spirit of Truth," who will give insights to believers which are not available to people who do not belong to Jesus. As the Spirit teaches and brings to our minds the commandments of Christ, and as we obey, we will experience Jesus' presence in our lives. Jesus promised: "If anyone loves Me, he will obey My teaching. My Father will love him, and We will come to him and make Our home with him."

Finally, we are told that through the Spirit's presence we will find peace. This peace is not the kind of peace the world offers; it is a peace that frees us from anxiety and fear, in spite of anything that may happen.

Insights

There are many riches in these chapters that invite deep consideration; more consideration than we can give as we trace the teachings of John's Gospel in an overview. But here are a few for your meditation.

In Jesus' name (John 14:13). Asking "in Jesus' name" means more than simply tacking words on at the end of a prayer. To Old and New Testament people one's name was inextricably tied to his character and mission. Thus prayer is to be "according to His will and instruction, in order that the commission may be fulfilled" (Colin Brown, *New International Dictionary of New Testament Theology*, Zondervan). The "anything" we are invited to ask includes all things that can be identified with the kind of person Jesus is, and the grace He gives.

No wonder the Father will be glorified in answering prayers offered in Jesus' name. In the answers to such prayers the character of God Himself will continue to be revealed.

Jesus' presence (John 14:24). How can we experience Jesus' presence when He cannot be sensed, or seen by others? Where *will* we find Him now that He has gone? Jesus had already promised that He would be with His followers in the person of the Spirit. In this passage Christ explained that we will *know His presence experientially* when love finds expression as obedience.

There's a beautiful and delicate emphasis here. It is not outward conformity to rules that God seeks. God cares rather about a responsive inner attitude, a commitment to act on Jesus' words. We sense that "the" commandments are now "My" commandments, that the Spirit and Scripture's communication are deeply personal whisperings of our loving God. They are directions that lead us to joy and to fellowship.

What can so move us to see the personal nature of God's Word? Love. As we love Jesus, we respond to His commands. As we obey, we draw closer to Him. Step by step, as our love finds growing expression in obedience, we journey toward the Lord. And then, *we find Him*, and realize that He has been with us all the time! What a joy to experience the reality of God manifesting Himself within us.

If there is not love, there will be no inner response leading to obedience. And without the response of obedience, love will die. When love has died, then, like people of the world, we will see Him no more.

Power for the New Life: John 15:1-17

The new community of Jesus asks us to adopt a lifestyle far beyond our capacity. Knowing this, Jesus then explained how a life of fruitfulness is possible for human beings. The fruit Jesus promised here is, of course, the fruit of the Spirit, who will soon settle down into the disciples' lives. The "love, joy, peace, patience, kindness, goodness, faithfulness, gentleness, and self-control" Paul lists (Gal. 5:22-23) are promised in these chapters of John.

Where does the fruit grow? On a living vine, of course. Branches (and this is how we believers are pictured in Jesus' illustration) are unable to bear fruit by themselves. They must be connected to the vine. Roots and trunk support the life of the branch, and only the branch "remaining in" the vine has the potential for fruitfulness.

Several questions are asked about this passage in Scripture. They range from an eager, "What is *remaining in?*" to a fearful,

"What does it mean to be thrown away and wither, especially with the reference to gathering branches and throwing them into the fire?" Let's look at these two typical concerns and then return to the great promise of fruitfulness.

Remain in Me (John 15:4). This often-repeated exhortation is explained here as well as in John 14. If we keep Jesus' commandments, we will remain in His love (15:10). As His words take shape and form in our personalities, as we experience for ourselves the goodness of God's will, we will live in the center of His love. Living close to Jesus is part of remaining in Him.

Thrown away (John 15:6). The simile of the vine and branches focuses on fruitfulness, and does not refer to salvation. This is why the text carefully says, "He is *like a branch* that is thrown away."

In any living vine the function of a branch is to bear fruit. But it cannot fulfill its purpose unless it remains in intimate connection with the vine. Without that intimate "remaining in Me" relationship, it will never accomplish what it was designed for. How empty will the life of a Christian who fails to remain in Jesus be? As empty as that of a branch torn from the vine; it has no potential for fruit bearing. Its only use would be to serve as fuel to provide momentary warmth; then it must disintegrate into ash.

The warning is clear. We cannot become what we are intended to be without having a close relationship with Jesus, with our love for Him expressed in obedience to Him. How tragic if you or I, branches now, fail to experience the joy that comes as we fulfill our potential for bearing fruit.

How tragic if, after life is over, we can point to nothing but ashes.

The promise. But this paragraph is not meant to depress us. It's meant to excite us and to give us joy. *Because we are branches, we can draw life from Jesus the Vine!* What we cannot do by ourselves, Jesus can accomplish in us! The fruit of love, joy, peace, patience, kindness, goodness, faithfulness, gentleness, self-control—all these are possible now. As we live in Him, we will become fruitful. As we remain in Jesus, we will become the kind of people who can make the new community a reality here on earth.

How natural then that Jesus would return to this new-community theme. "This is My command," He repeated. "Love each other." We are Jesus' friends; we are enabled by His Spirit, empowered by His own life flowing through us; and we can fulfill His command to love one another.

Group Activity: Bible Study Group
John 14:15-31 introduces the Holy Spirit as a companion, to be with and in believers while Jesus is absent. Together list everything these verses teach that the Holy Spirit does for us. Then break into teams to explore other key passages that speak of the Holy Spirit's ministry to believers. Each team is to study its passage(s) and prepare a brief report. The passages: Romans 8:2-17; 1 Corinthians 2:6-16; 2 Corinthians 12; 2 Corinthians 3:1-18; Galatians 5:13-25.

After reports, share: How have I experienced one of these ministries of the Spirit? What has this ministry come to mean in my life?

GROUP RESOURCE GUIDE

Identification: *Share with others*
Before the group session begins, read John 15:1-17 and complete the chart (following page). Then share: What positive or negative feelings do you have about the Vine and branches image? What questions does it raise?

Exploration: *Probe God's Word*
"Abiding" is a difficult concept. However,

John 15:10-11 and 14 portray one aspect of our part in abiding. Chapter 14 picks up these same themes, and adds other dimensions to the concept. In teams of three study John 14, and identify additional ways in which we respond to Jesus and ultimately stay close to Him.

Reaction: *Respond together to the Word*
Hear reports on what it means to live as a

branch, united with a life-giving vine. After all teams have shared, identify one step you can take to draw even closer to Jesus.

Affirmation: *Express love and concern*
Return to teams of three and share the "one step closer to Jesus" you can take.

Pray for each other in your team, that you will be able to take that step this week.

Adoration: *Worship and pray*
Worship Jesus as the Vine, the Source who enables you to do what is good and right.

Jesus is like the vine in that . . .	I am like a branch of a vine in that . . .

JESUS' LAST WORDS (CONTINUED)

Overview

These chapters, containing the last words of Jesus to His disciples and a lengthy prayer, are extremely significant, for they focus on the lifestyle of disciples, and on the church. Here we find out more of how we are to live with one another. And here, especially, we begin to see how we are to live as Christ's people in an often hostile world.

These chapters are so significant that literally hundreds of books have been written about them. I have one book of over 400 pages on John 17 alone. It has been suggested that every truth which has been developed by the apostles in the New Testament letters is here, in seed, in Jesus' Last Supper Discourse.

▶ *Be One.* John 17 stresses Christ's desire for believers to "be one as We are One." This has been taken as a prayer for Christian unity, and an argument for denomination unification.

A careful study of the chapter, however, makes it clear that what Jesus prays for is that we might experience our union with Him, even as He had experienced His own union with God the Father throughout His life on earth. Through faith we *are* united with Jesus, linked to Him in an unbreakable bond. But we must experience that union by living in responsive obedience, for the One to whom we are united is God.

■ See the *Bible Knowledge Commentary*, pages 326-334, for verse-by-verse commentary on this passage.

Commentary

Believers across the ages have yearned for the new community Jesus described to His disciples in the Upper Room. We long for the loving fellowship, the humility expressed in foot-washing, the deep experience of Jesus' presence, the sense of remaining in Him.

Some have found this ideal impossible to reach in society, and so they have formed separate communities. The monastery of the Middle Ages and the commune of the twentieth century often have been attempts to withdraw from carnal Christians or from the pollution of pagan culture.

But in these chapters (John 13–17) we do not hear Jesus advocate withdrawal. He calls us to involvement! The Christian does not experience Christ by removing himself from the world; we experience Christ *in* the world, though we are distinctly not *of* the world.

The World

John painted reality boldly, with vividly contrasting concepts. He showed us life versus death, grace versus law, light versus dark. Then he contrasted Jesus' followers (a fellowship of love) with the world (a society of mere men).

The Greek word used here for "world" is *kosmos*. According to the Arndt and Gingrich *Greek/English Lexicon of the New Testament* (Bagsters and Son), *kosmos* has several meanings. It can refer to "the sum total of everything here and now" (the universe as a whole). Or it can refer to "all beings above the level of animals." In this usage it includes both men and angels, or may focus specifically on mankind. In a moral sense, "the world" refers to "that which is at enmity with God," that is, every thought and action, every value and behavior, that is tainted by sin (pp. 202-203).

In this moral sense, the New Testament portrays the world as far more than tainted: it is lost in sin, ruined, and depraved. It is hostile to God and godliness. The principles on which the world operates stand in dark contrast to divine righteousness and a godly life.

To grasp the difference between the two approaches to life, we must be born again. We must be transformed by the renewing of our minds (literally, "perceptions," or "perspective") (Rom. 12:1-3). Because the "whole world is under the control of the evil one" (1 John 5:19), we are to keep ourselves "from being polluted by the world" (James 1:27).

What the world identifies as "adult," we recognize as perversion. What the world praises as "success," we often must label failure. What the world views as the highest of values—material success, popularity, and so on—we recognize as emptiness. There is a deep and abiding antagonism between the society of unredeemed man and the community of Jesus' own.

Because this antagonism always exists, there are two great dangers the Christian continually faces. The first danger is conformity: "Don't let the world around you squeeze you into its own mold" (Rom. 12:2, PH). And John added this warning in his first epistle: "Do not love the world or anything in the world. If anyone loves the world, the love of the Father is not in him. For everything in the world—the cravings of sinful man, the lust of his eyes and the boasting of what he has and does—comes not from the Father but from the world" (1 John 2:15-16). The world's basic approach to life is twisted and perverted. We are to love the people of the world but decisively reject (and fear) the attitudes and values of the world.

The second danger for the Christian is withdrawal. If we do not recognize the world system for what it is, we may unknowingly adopt its lifestyle. When we do recognize the world system for what it is, we may be so repelled that we seek to escape it. This, of course, is the route taken by early monastics; it is the way of the Essenes in Old Testament times, and the way of the Qumran community. It is also the way of a distorted kind of separatism practiced by believers in many churches today. When Christians attempt to protect themselves from the practices of others, they frequently build a wall that rejects people and refuses relationships with those "outside."

The New Testament picture of the world challenges us with important questions. How do we relate to the society in which we live? Should we withdraw? Are there any other options? How do we relate to non-Christians who have only seen worldly values? How can we construct the new community within the ruins of man's society . . . or are we even supposed to try?

Love in the World: John 15:18–16:33

The last paragraph we studied (15:12-17) restated Jesus' command to His disciples: "Love each other." In the context of loving each other, lasting fruit will be produced, intimate relationship with Jesus will be experienced, prayer will be answered. Together we will experience new life. But how will the world respond to this radical new community that is founded on principles so opposed to its own lifestyle and views?

With antagonism (John 15:18-27). Christ immediately warns that as we learn to live out the new community, the world will react with hatred. "Keep in mind that it hated Me first," Jesus reminded the disciples. "If you belonged to the world, it would love you as its own. As it is, you do not belong to the world, but I have chosen you out of the world. That is why the world hates you."

Antagonism develops because light shows up darkness, and grace morality reveals the perversion of sin. Jesus went on to remind His followers that men had seen Him do "what no one else did." They had been forced to recognize their own works as sin and, consequently, "They have hated both Me and My Father."

This witness of Jesus to the Father continues in and through the Christians in the new community (vv. 26-27). God has taken us out of the world. At one time, we were part of that sinful system, and our lifestyles reflected its values. But in Christ we have been "chosen *out of* the world" and have been called to live a new life *in* the world. Our lives and our relationships with others are to be a visible, continuing testimony to God in our godless, hostile world.

Our witness to God will produce hatred and persecution at times. But God the Spirit will shine through our lives, declaring that God is life and love and light.

With persecution (John 16:1-15). At times the world's antagonism has led to persecution, oppression, and death of those who follow Jesus. This would soon be the experience of the 11. Jesus warned, "They will put you out of the synagogue; in fact, a time is coming when anyone who kills you will think he is offering a service to God."

How are we to understand and to respond to persecution—often in small things, but sometimes the ultimate that Christ described, being killed because we love Jesus? Jesus helped us understand by speaking of the advantage to us of His return to the Father. By going away, Jesus made it possible for the Father to send the Holy Spirit to us. When the Spirit came, He would take the witness of the Christian under persecution and use it to prove the world wrong (or, convince, convict) about sin, about righteousness, and about judgment. The world will *see the truth* in Christians, and though the world as a whole will not respond with faith, individuals will believe.

The Holy Spirit will open our hearts and minds to understand the ways and the truth of God. He will make clear to us what Jesus has said in the written Word. He will give us the wisdom we need to apply that Word on a daily basis and to live in responsive obedience to our Lord.

A little earlier I noted two wrong reactions of Christians to the world. We can see more clearly now why they are wrong. If we adopt the values and lifestyle of the world, if we conform to the world system, God is left without a witness to truth and life and grace. But if we withdraw and cut ourselves off from the world's people in order to develop separated communities, God is also left without a witness. *Only by living in the world—by being involved daily with the men and women around us, by being involved in the issues of our own times and society—can we show the contrast between human ways and God's ways.*

The natural response to persecution, to antagonism, to pressure, is to withdraw or to conform. But you and I, like Jesus, are to live under pressure. We are to open ourselves to hurt. We are to resist protecting ourselves and, instead, to expose ourselves, for God yearns to reveal His glory in our lives.

As we learn to love each other, we will have the strength to become involved in the world and to find joy in our suffering, even as Jesus found joy in His. We will begin to love all men, even as Jesus loved us and gave Himself for us.

◊ *Group Activity:*
Missions/Outreach Group
Choose sides, and let four people debate the following: Resolved: To reach people, it is best to set an example by strict separation from them and all worldly practices.

Then study together John 15:16–16:4. What explains the hostility of some people to Christians? What did the believers do to stimulate that hostility? How does this parallel Jesus' way of life among His own people, and responses to Him?

John 16:8-11 assigns responsibility for convicting the unsaved to the Holy Spirit. If it is not our responsibility to accuse and thus convict sinners, how do we cooperate with the Holy Spirit in this ministry?

Prayer is a resource (John 16:16-33). It is all too easy in reading Jesus' warnings to become fearful or depressed and to feel that the Christian life is a burden almost too heavy to bear. Jesus had already pointed to some resources He had given: the Holy Spirit, and Jesus' own continuing guidance. Then Christ spoke of the resource of prayer.

Jesus Himself was soon to leave the 11. At first the events of the Crucifixion would create despair, but soon the disciples would know joy. "I will see you again," Jesus promised, "and you will rejoice, *and no one will take away your joy.*" Life in the world, in spite of hostility and persecution, is a life of secure joy.

How is joy possible? It is possible because *we are not cut off from Jesus!* We are free to bring every need to Him in prayer, and can be confident that He hears us. "My Father will give you whatever you ask in My name," Jesus said. "Until now you have not asked for anything in My name. Ask and you will receive, and your joy will be complete."

Where can we find joy in times of pressure and uncertainty? First, by acknowledging that each of our ministries and everything we possess is God's. Jesus is Lord, and everything I have and do is committed totally into His hands. If Jesus in grace chooses to use it for His glory, I rejoice. And if He chooses not to use it, but to bring all I have planned and worked to achieve to an end, He can use disaster too to glorify Himself—and I rejoice.

To know that Jesus lives, that He hears,

and that He responds as we speak to Him, brings abiding joy whatever the pressures may be.

And so Jesus concluded His words to His disciples. "The Father Himself loves you because you have loved Me and have believed that I came from God." With this assurance, what have we to fear? "I have told you these things so that in Me you may have peace. In this world you will have trouble. But take heart! I have overcome the world."

Jesus *is* Lord.

And God loves us.

No wonder we have peace and joy.

✍ Group Activity: Bible Study Group

Divide into teams of three. All teams are to study John 15:18–16:33, but half the teams are to look specifically for troubles and pressures we may experience as we live the Christian life. The other half of the team is to look in the same passage for resources that help us live joyfully and confidently. This study should take at least 20 minutes.

When finished, ask members of the various teams to share impressions of what it's like to live for Jesus in this world.

It's likely that teams doing each study may have a different feeling about Christian experience. One set of teams may see it as a challenge, or feel it is terribly difficult to live as Christians. The other set of teams may have a much more positive, optimistic outlook. Talk about any differences that emerge. Discuss: How does the viewpoint we adopt concerning trials make them harder or easier to bear?

Talk about any difficulties you face at this time. What perspective on how to meet them do you gain from this passage?

Jesus' Prayer for Us: John 17

The intimate Upper Room experience concludes with Jesus' prayer. This is a prayer for us, His people in the world. "I will remain in the world no longer," Jesus said, "but they are still in the world."

Jesus had described the world's hostility that we will face. Now what will He ask for us? What is His deepest desire?

Glory (John 17:1-5). Jesus first spoke to the Father about Himself, thus giving us a model. "I have brought You glory on earth by completing the work You gave Me to do." This work finished, God would lift Jesus to His presence again and give His Son the glory that "I had with You before the world began."

We live in the world now, but this world is not the end! The end for us, as for Jesus, is glory in the very presence of the Father. The word "glory" speaks literally of brightness, splendor, radiance. Expanded to denote the majesty and sublimity of God, it carries a sense of magnificence and splendor. In the verb form it means more than "to praise or honor"; it means to "clothe in splendor."

With Jesus' work on earth finished, He returned to the Father to be clothed again with the splendor that was His from eternity past. For Jesus, life in this world had a purpose. Christ lived to reveal and to glorify God. But life in this world was only a momentary experience for Christ.

How good to know that for us as well, life in this world is only a momentary experience. Like Jesus, we will be lifted by the Father when our work here is accomplished. Then we too will be clothed in a splendor like Jesus' own. While we are on earth we may never know the glory God intends for us, but one day we will see Jesus, and then, "we shall be like Him, for we shall see Him as He is" (1 John 3:2). Our destiny is to be clothed with our Lord in splendor.

Manifest Your name (John 17:6-10). What is the work God has for us on earth? To be "great"? To be noted evangelists? To be famous teachers? To be known and respected by all? Hardly. God wants a very simple thing, which every believer, no matter how humble, can share in fully. *God wants us to manifest (make known) His name.* We have received Jesus' words (v. 8) and believed in Him. Now we are to live out those words on earth. The quality of our lives is what will make plain to those around us the character of God. Each of us can brighten the world around us by reaching out to others with a grace and love that are like God's own.

Sanctified (John 17:11-19). Christ then prayed that God will guard us while we live in the world's hostile environment. "My prayer is not that You take them out of the world but that You protect them from the evil one." He asked that we be sanctified by God's truth, that is, that we will be set apart to a holy way of life, and then "sent into the world" (v. 18). We are to not only witness to, but are to personally experience Christ's joy as we become more and more like Him. And we have Jesus' added promise that He consecrates Himself to aid our growth in godliness.

Reproductive (John 17:20-26). Jesus then emphasized the fact that He was not praying just for the 11 disciples, but for "those who will believe in Me through their message." You and I, and our local fellowships, along with all believers throughout the centuries are included in this great commitment of Jesus and His Father to all who belong to Them.

The society of those who belong to Jesus is a community that grows in love and then multiplies. Jesus is still reaching out, through you and me, to rescue men and women lost in sin.

There is, of course, one source and one source only for the strength we need to live a God-glorifying life. This is our union with Jesus Christ. Jesus lived in union with the Father, drawing on Him for strength and power. As we are "brought to complete unity" with Jesus and the Father, then the world will know that Christ has sent us and that He loves us still.

GROUP RESOURCE GUIDE

Identification: *Share with others*
Have available lots and lots of "junk" — paper clips, yarn, pencils, construction paper, Tinkertoys, thumbtacks, etc. In groups of five work with the available materials to develop a physical model of the "ideal church." Let your imaginations run wild to represent elements of relationship, etc., which you feel are important.

When the models have been completed, tell the other groups about yours and listen as they tell about theirs.

Exploration: *Probe God's Word*
It's important to have a vision of the ideal church, but it is even more important to know how we can reach that ideal together. Jesus' prayer (John 17) expresses His desire for us as we struggle to live together as His own people.

Work through the passage together, guided by the outline in the commentary:

* Dedicate yourself to glorify God. 17:1-5
* Make God known in word and deed. 17:6-10

* Commit yourself to holy living. 17:11-19
* Share Christ with others. 17:20-26

Record what you learn about each of these Christian life essentials from Jesus' prayer as you explore this great prayer together.

Reaction: *Respond together to the Word*
Go back to your models of the "ideal church," and this time select an item from the "junk pile" that represents *you*. Work it into your model, to show how you personally do or will contribute to achieving Christ's desires for His followers.

Adoration: *Worship and pray*
Have one of the group members conduct a brief closing devotional based on John 17:22-23. Note that being "one" is not being one with others in the church, but being one with Christ, as Jesus was one with God. Verses in John on how Christ lived in union with God, which might be used to develop such a devotional include: 5:9-10; 6:38; 8:28-29; 12:44-45; 14:9-11.

GRACE AND GLORY

Overview

John's themes of grace and life, and his emphasis on light versus darkness, find special expression in the final chapters of his Gospel.

John, like the other Gospel writers, reported in graphic detail the events that are associated with the crucifixion and the resurrection of Jesus. By comparing the treatment of each of the Gospels, we have a more complete picture of this three-day span than of any other period in ancient history!

John's emphasis is on triumph — the triumph of truth, the victory of life over the dark powers of death. How good to be able to share this sense of victory with those we teach. And how good to realize that for us as well, the resurrection of Jesus is the guarantee of life throughout eternity.

▶ *Truth.* Pilate demanded of Jesus, "What is truth?" The passage shows how captive this Roman ruler was to pressures, how controlled by the demands of others. Without a sense of absolutes, and a certainty that there is right and wrong to guide our decisions, we would be just as wavering and tormented. Thank God there *is* truth — that we know reality as unveiled in the Word of God. We need to choose to live by that truth, rather than the uncertainties of expediency.

■ If there are any specific phrases you do not understand, see the *Bible Knowledge Commentary*, pages 334-346 for verse-by-verse comment.

Commentary

The time for words had now passed. Jesus had spoken much about grace and life and light. And also of the darkness that grips those who are of this world. Now, if anyone had questions, those questions were about to be answered decisively.

How deeply is the world entrenched in darkness? How great is God's love for us, and His grace to us? How vital is the life that Jesus offers? How bright is the light by which we are invited to live? The answer to each of these questions is found in the events of the final night and day of Jesus' life on earth . . . and in His resurrection.

A World Entrenched: John 18:1–19:22

Earlier we saw that the context of the last long segment of John's Gospel has a distinctive setting: night. The flickering light of a fire may have lit the Upper Room as Jesus sketched the vision of a new community for His followers. But outside, the forces of darkness were gathering. The hatred of Satan and the antagonism of the world swirled in a dark storm cloud, ready to extinguish the Light of the world.

The context for all the events reported in the next chapters of John's Gospel is darkness. Even Mary's first encounter with the risen Lord takes place "while it was still dark" (20:1). When Jesus appeared to the disciples who were gathered behind locked doors for fear of the Jews, it was evening (v. 19). The mood does not change until John 21:4, when Jesus stood on the shore waiting for His disciples, "early in the morning."

But as Jesus and His friends left the Upper Room for a time of prayer, we see how deep the darkness truly is.

Betrayal (John 18:1-11). Judas, one of Christ's most intimate friends for the past three years, led temple guards and an antagonistic mob to drag Jesus to judgment. At first Peter tried to resist, striking out with a weapon. But Jesus would permit no resistance. Darkness must have its hour.

Desertion (John 18:12-18, 25-27). Peter's act of resistance was a rash yet brave act. But what else can we expect? Hadn't Peter promised to follow Jesus even to the death? Then Jesus was bound and dragged to the high priest (who had already, before the trial, condemned Jesus to death—see v. 14).

Peter followed the crowd, but in the darkness and among Jesus' enemies, His courage faded. When he was accused by servants of being one of Jesus' companions, Peter, shivering in the cold of the dark night, cursed angrily and denied his Lord.

Peter had the courage for an impulsive act, but as the darkness deepened and pressed in around him, that courage drained away.

✂ *Group Activity: Recovery Group*
Step 10 (continue taking personal inventory) .
Write down phrases which complete each of the following "fill in the blank" sentences. If you need to, use a sentence more than one time.
** I intended to*_____
*but I*_____.
* I wanted to _____
*but I*_____.
** I loved*_____
*but I*_____.
* I knew _____
*but I*_____.
ˣ I tried to _____
*but I*_____.

Then together read the story of Peter's denial (cf. John 13:31-38; 18:18-27). Discuss how Peter must have felt: When he expressed his firm intention to stick by Jesus. When he denied Christ. When he realized after the third denial what he had done. For each situation suggest words that describe Peter's probable feelings, such as "strong," "righteous," "hopeless," "ashamed," etc.

Share: As you filled in your sentences and recalled your own actions, which of Peter's feelings did you experience? Discuss: How do you think Christ feels about Peter and us when we intend to do right and fail?

Read and discuss John 21:15-19. What did Jesus' reinstatement mean to Peter? What does it say to us about Christ's attitude toward our failures? In view of what Christ said to Peter, is it easier or harder for us to keep on taking personal inventory and admitting it when

we are wrong? How, and why?

Take this opportunity to add to the list of your completed sentences. Then present all the things you have written to the Lord, admitting them to Him, and thanking Him for His willingness to restore after confession.

Illegal trial (John 18:19-24). Called before an illegally convened court, Jesus was questioned behind closed doors, beaten, and then sent away to the Roman authorities, who alone had the power to condemn a person to death. The other Gospels described this scene in more detail than John did. He seemed to turn from the final revelation of the dark hearts of those religious leaders who were the keepers of the written Word, but now were struggling to suppress its light.

Pilate's weakness (John 18:28-38; 19:1-16). If the religious authority was perverted, what of the secular? Rome had no quarrel with Jesus, who at this time had never confronted or challenged its rule. This is the judgment of Pilate the Roman governor, who announced, "I find no basis for a charge against Him."

Yet, pressured and threatened by the Jews he supposedly governed, Pilate ultimately gave in to expediency and permitted Jesus' crucifixion.

Historic research has suggested some of the possible pressure on Pilate. Tiberius, a sick and violent emperor, ruled Rome. But much of his power had been exercised by Suetonius, the commander of his Praetorian Guard. At last this man was overthrown and killed, and the ever-suspicious Tiberius had many of those who had relied on Suetonius' influence executed. Some have thought that Pilate was aligned with Suetonius' party, and thus was particularly vulnerable. If so, the threat of the Jews to denounce Pilate as "no friend of Caesar" must have been particularly terrifying.

Pilate had no commitment to truth. Though there was no basis in law for the execution of Jesus, Pilate did the expedient thing and chose to compromise his conscience. Jesus would die.

How dark the world is with injustice and fear when there is no commitment to truth.

The crowd's preference (John 18:39-40). It was the habit in those days to release a prisoner (often a political prisoner) at the Passover festival. Looking for a way to save Jesus, Pilate offered the Jews a choice. Which prisoner would they like released: Jesus, or Barabbas, an insurrectionist, murderer, and robber?

The power of darkness was revealed in the swelling cry, "No, not Him! Give us Barabbas!"

The Crucifixion (John 19:17-22). And so the final stage had been set. The degree to which the darkness blinds man's eyes to grace and life and light is about to be revealed.

Because of darkness, a false friend had betrayed the Lord. Because of darkness, a true follower had denied his Master. Because of darkness, men charged with communicating God's truth had turned with murder in their hearts, against the God they claimed to serve. Because of darkness, a man convinced of Jesus' innocence permitted Him to be tormented and crucified. Because of darkness, the crowd that cheered Jesus' entrance into Jerusalem now demanded His death and begged the release of a murderer. In the last events of Jesus' life the nature of sin and the extent to which it had perverted mankind was finally revealed.

In the normal course of events, the depth of the moral darkness in which man lives is disguised with good works, kindness, generosity, caring. But under pressure, under the kind of pressure placed on every actor in Jerusalem that last tense day, the superficial is stripped away. The love that costs us nothing to give is shown to be flimsy cover for selfishness and fear. Only the love of God in Jesus, who remains committed to the ultimate sacrifice, burns steadily and bright.

The Grace of God: John 19:23-42

John's attention was now drawn to Christ Himself. Jesus had suffered the brutal beatings and the mocking that prepared prisoners for crucifixion. His hands and feet had been nailed to the wooden pole. Now Jesus hanged on it, between heaven and earth, His weight resting alternately on the torn flesh of His feet, then on His hands. Around Him indifferent soldiers gambled for His clothing while His enemies smirked in satisfaction at His agony.

Even here, though, we see God's grace revealed, especially as we note incidents reported by the other Gospel writers. Even hanging on the cross, Jesus continued to think of others.

He prayed for His murderers (Luke 23:34). He welcomed the repentant thief with the promise of paradise (v. 43). And John tells of His gentle commending of His mother to the care of the "beloved disciple" (John himself, the writer of this Gospel).

Finally, His suffering complete, Jesus released His spirit and died.

The body was taken down from the cross. A secret disciple, Joseph of Arimathea, and Nicodemus buried the body in a new tomb that had been hewn out of a wall of rock. It was again night.

But the day was at hand.

The Life: John 20

Jesus had often spoken about life and death, light and darkness, grace and Law. He had also claimed to be the ultimate revelation of God.

In His last days, Jesus showed Himself the ultimate revealer of mankind as well. How darkness grips the human heart is evident in the way men responded to Jesus as the Crucifixion drew near. Yet even on the cross Jesus' forgiving, caring concern gives ultimate proof of God's great love for humanity. Only divine love and divine grace can explain Jesus' willingness to sacrifice Himself for those who hate Him. The cross *proves* grace.

But how can life be proven? How can Jesus' claim, "I am the Resurrection and the Life," be demonstrated?

The answer, of course, is the Resurrection! Paul, looking back, saw that Jesus was "declared with power to be the Son of God by His resurrection from the dead" (Rom. 1:4).

The first glimmerings of the ultimate revelation of Jesus as Life came before dawn. Mary slipped into the garden early. She saw that the stone sealing the tomb had been jolted out of its track. In tears she ran to Peter to report that the body of Jesus had been stolen. Peter and John came running to the tomb. John arrived first and, bending over, peered inside. There on a stone shelf were the linen wrappings. John fell back; he must have felt relief as well as disappointment. Jesus' body had not been stolen. He was still there.

But Peter stooped low and entered the

tomb. He saw that though the burial wrappings were still there, the body was gone. It was impossible! But it had happened.

John then entered, and realized that Jesus truly was gone. But, "they still did not understand from Scripture that Jesus had to rise from the dead" (v. 9).

Then the puzzle began to come together. Mary, who was now standing in the garden outside the tomb, met Jesus and realized who He was. That evening, 10 of the disciples were gathered in a room with locked doors because they were afraid of the Jewish rulers. Suddenly Jesus was there, standing among them! Later, Thomas heard their report but refused to believe. "Unless I see the nail marks in His hands and put my finger where the nails were, and put my hands into His side, I will not believe it," Thomas said.

Eight days later Jesus stood before Thomas and invited him to take that test. Convinced at the sight of his Master, Thomas cried out, "My Lord and my God!"

♥ *Group Activity: Support Group*
Thomas' "unless I see the nail marks in His hands" illustrates how difficult faith is. Share some of your own "Unless I . . . " experiences with God. How were they resolved? Did you receive the proof you required? If not, what happened that enabled you to trust?

After discussing, share some of the things you're finding it hard to trust God for right now. What would it take for you to trust, without requiring proof of God's love?

The ultimate power of life was demonstrated in the resurrection of Jesus. Because Jesus is the Life now and forever, the power of death, and the fear of death, associated as they are with sin and darkness, lie shattered and broken at His feet. Because He lives, we too shall live.

The Light: John 21
Even with Jesus' resurrection an established fact, the disciples were uncertain. What were they to do now? Confused, Peter and the others returned for a brief time to their old occupation of fishing, but with little success.

It is here John portrays the return of day.

In the dawn's light, Jesus directed His disciples to cast their net on the right side of the boat. Suddenly the net filled with a shoal of fish, so many that the men were unable to haul them into their boat. When they returned to shore, the disciples found that Jesus had prepared fish and bread for their breakfast.

After the meal, Jesus spoke directly to Peter. Peter had denied his Lord three times. Now Jesus asked Peter three times, "Do you love Me?"

Three times Peter said, "Yes, Lord, You know that I love You."

And three times Jesus charged Peter, "Feed My sheep," and, finally, "Follow Me."

Peter, ever impetuous, now asked what assignment the Lord had for John. Rebuking Peter gently, Jesus let him know that Christ alone will direct His disciples, and that disciples answer only to their Lord.

Think for a moment of what has been revealed in these few brief incidents. Jesus, the Light of the world, has again shown the disciples the path they are to walk, and that they are now to bring light into sin's dark realm

In His resurrection glory, Jesus does continue to serve. He met the occupational needs of His disciples, even when the catch of fish was not necessary for their mission. Jesus stooped to prepare food for them. Jesus restored Peter to fellowship. Jesus helped Peter sense the completeness of his restoration, by telling him that he would be trusted with Jesus' own dearly loved sheep. Peter would now give his life to free, support, and care for other believers.

Jesus also taught that each individual's goal is personal responsiveness to the Lord. Christ will direct each believer into the avenue of service for which he or she has been equipped.

Finally, Jesus showed that in our concern for others we are not to judge them (21:22), but rather are to give each of our brothers and sisters the freedom, and encouragement to be responsive to Jesus as Lord.

For Jesus says, "Follow Me."

How gently Jesus' words echo across the centuries. Jesus, the Light of the world, began a great revelation of God. And Jesus *continues* that unveiling of the grace, the life, and the light in you and me.

GROUP RESOURCE GUIDE

Identification: *Share with others*
Draw a line in the middle of a sheet of paper to represent some difficult decision you face at this time. Above the line draw an arrow pointing downward for each pressure or reason for making a "Yes" (or "Move," etc.) choice. Below the line draw an arrow pointed upward for each pressure or reason for making a "No" (or "Stay here," etc.) choice. Label each arrow with a specific reason or motive pushing you in its direction.

In groups of four or five, show your drawing, tell about the decision, and explain what each arrow represents.

Exploration: *Probe God's Word*
On a chalkboard or large sheet of newsprint draw a dividing line. On one side write "pressures to condemn Jesus," and on the other write "pressures to free Jesus."

Together study the report of Jesus before Pilate (John 18:28–19:16). Draw and label arrows to represent the "condemn" and "free" pressures on this Roman governor. (Be sure to check the commentary for background.) Be as thorough and complete as possible.

Reaction: *Respond together to the Word*
Now evaluate the pressures that Pilate felt morally. Which were "right" or "righteous?" Which were "wrong" or "unrighteous?" Discuss: How important is the moral dimension in making personal decisions?

With this complete, look back over your own "decision" chart. How might you label each of the arrows you drew? Use any categories you wish. For instance, "other's expectations," "selfishness," and "concern for spouse," as well as "it's right" or "it's wrong" might serve as categories.

Affirmation: *Express love and concern*
Return to your group of four or five, and show the labeled chart. Share any insights you received about the decision you must make, and listen to others' comments. Express your concern, praying for anyone facing a really difficult choice.

Adoration: *Worship and pray*
Praise God together that He is sovereign. We can freely do the right thing, confident He will superintend the consequences. And when we are unsure about what God's will is, we can ask for and receive guidance.

STUDY GUIDE 38

Introduction

ACTS AND THE EPISTLES

Overview

The story of Jesus is taken up after the Resurrection by Luke, whose Book of Acts gives a narrative insight into the spread of the Gospel. Acts is, in a real sense, the continuing story of Jesus who, through the Holy Spirit working in men and women of faith, actively continued Christ's own work in our world.

The first chapters of Acts deal with the church in Judea and its initial spilling over into Samaria. But then the focus shifts. Soon Luke's concern is the whole world, for while the Gospel came to the Jew first, it was also for the Gentile.

The shift is reflected particularly in a change of key characters. Peter is the leading figure at first. But soon Paul, the apostle to the Gentiles, takes center stage. We can hardly grasp the import of Acts or the New Testament epistles without paying close attention to this young Pharisee, who was transformed from an enemy of Christians to the most fervent of missionaries for Christ. Not only was Paul the most notable missionary in the history of Christianity, but as the writer of 13 of our 27 New Testament books, he continues to have the greatest impact on the church's faith and life.

In this study guide we'll examine the life of the Apostle Paul and see something of his significance in sacred history. Our time with the Apostle Paul will serve as an introduction both to Acts and to most of our New Testament epistles.

Commentary

The phrase, "New Testament times," is a common one. But its specific meaning is often unclear. It is probably best to think of these "times" as extending from the beginning of Jesus' ministry on earth (about A.D. 30) to the death of the last apostle, John, in the late 90s.

The period of the Gospels focuses, of course, on Jesus Himself. It is His story they tell. Then Acts takes up the tale, and for a decade or so Peter is Christianity's prime mover as the church begins and develops in Palestine. Soon, however, Acts reports the conversion of Samaritans and even Gentiles! The Gospel of Jesus is for everyone. Within a decade the focus of Acts shifts from the Holy Land to the entire Roman Empire. And the central figure becomes a passionate, committed man, the Apostle Paul.

Paul traveled the Roman Empire, proclaiming Christ, founding churches, and writing the letters to young churches which make up the bulk of the epistles in our New Testament.

Tradition tells us that Paul and Peter both were executed in the early 70s. The ministry of evangelism and teaching was taken on by another generation. Only the Apostle John lived on through the first century, to write his Gospel and letters very late in his life.

Yet there is no doubt that the greatest impetus to the spread of the church came in the late 40s and extended into the 70s, as explosive expansion was spearheaded by the Apostle Paul who, with other missionaries, rushed out to share the message of Jesus with the whole world.

If we draw together passages from Acts and from Paul's letters, as well as material from other sources that tell us about life in the first century, we can develop a fascinating portrait of this man whom God used in such a powerful way.

Young Saul

"It's a boy!"

That announcement was always welcome in a Jewish home. Saul, who later became Paul, was born in the port city of Tarsus in Cilicia. It was a cosmopolitan town and important trading center, a strange home for pious Jews. Saul's family may have fled

New Testament Times

A.D.*	Predominant Personality in Acts	Writings
35	Peter	
40		
45		
50	James	James, Galatians
55	Paul	Mark, 1 & 2 Thes.
60		1 & 2 Cor., Rom., Luke
65		Matt., Eph., Col., Phile., Phil., 1 Peter, Acts
70		Jude, 1 & 2 Tim., Titus, 2 Peter, Hebrews
75		
80		
85		
90		
95		John, 1, 2, & 3 John
100		Revelation

*Dates are approximate.

there during the terrible years when Roman armies devastated Palestine. Financially successful, the family had won Roman citizenship. So Saul was born not only a Jew but a Roman, something in which he later took pride, and which was important for his mission (see Acts 22:25-29).

Saul was a product of two worlds. Committed to his Jewishness, he was still at home in the Gentile city. Throughout his life, Saul would seek out such cities, those centers of communication and culture, in his driving desire to communicate the Gospel.

Saul's life, however, centered in the history of his people and his God. As was the custom, by age 5 Saul was learning to read and write and study the Scriptures. By 10 he was taught the traditions which had grown out of generations of interpreting the Law. At 13 Saul entered the community of Israel as a responsible adult, and became a "son of the Law" (*bar mitzvah*). At that age some boys went on to deeper studies in Judaism under well-known teachers. It is a testimony both to Saul's promise and to the family wealth that he traveled to Jerusalem to study under the most famous of first-century rabbis, Gamaliel I. Already Saul had been trained both in the Scriptures and in the trade of tentmaking, for the Jews believed firmly that a scholar should labor, and that a laborer should be a scholar.

Saul talked about these days in the Book of Galatians, where he shared the deep commitment that infused his passionate young heart to the strictest interpretation of Judaistic faith and life, that of the Pharisee. This very passion for God became the motive that drove him to try at first to stamp out a hated heresy, "the Way," as Christianity was then known.

> For you have heard of my previous way of life in Judaism, how intensely I persecuted the church of God and tried to destroy it. I was advancing in Judaism beyond many Jews of my own age and was extremely zealous for the traditions of my fathers.
>
> Galatians 1:13-14

Young Saul was not a terribly attractive figure. Burning with passion, yet cold and untouched by people, this youth who had dedicated himself to the Law of Israel's God would one day, just outside Jerusalem, feel only a fierce joy as waves of hatred from a maddened crowd accompanied each stone that pounded the life from the church's first martyr, Stephen.

Saul's commitment was complete.

Conversion

And then came that day on the road to Damascus when Saul's whole world was jolted. The same Jesus whose followers Saul was planning to imprison confronted him in person! Stunned by the voice and blinded by the light that flashed around him, Saul crumpled to the ground.

At that moment, his world crumpled too. Everything that Saul had believed, and the strict way of life to which he had given his passionate allegiance, were suddenly revealed to be out of focus and off center. Rather than leading him to God, his training and his understanding of the Old Testament had led him to reject God's Son!

It would be a decade before Saul had all the pieces together again. But the next phase of his life would be committed completely to the one solid reality in which he could now believe. Jesus, whom Saul had persecuted, was Lord. Jesus was God's promised Christ, the Messiah. All of the energy of Paul's passionate nature was now focused on serving Him.

The 12 years following Saul's experience on the Damascus Road are hazy. He was probably converted in A.D. 34 when he was about 34 years old. We know that he immediately began to preach Jesus as the Son of God in Damascus (Acts 9:20). We know too that within a few months Saul escaped a Jewish plot to murder him, and returned to Jerusalem. We know that there Barnabas brought him to the apostles, where Saul shared his testimony and where the reality of his conversion was recognized (v. 27). But Saul's story was hardly more dramatic than that of many others in those days. He was certainly not invited to share the leadership of the Jerusalem church.

In Jerusalem Saul's zeal in proclaiming Christ again aroused anger. It is entirely possible that the old, driving, insensitive character of the Pharisee he had been was partly responsible for this reaction, even though the attitude of the Jewish community to Christians had long since hardened. Again Saul was forced to flee for his life, and the brothers took him (perhaps protesting) to the port city of Caesarea and "sent him off to Tarsus" (v. 30).

The next 10 years are obscure. In isolation the man who was God's choice to bridge two worlds, and through whom a clear formulation of the meaning of the Christian faith would be revealed, struggled to reconstruct his own picture of God and his understanding of God's Word. We can imagine Saul, poring over the Old Testament documents, seeking illumination. We can picture him, fasting and praying in the deserts of Arabia, where his final grasp of the Gospel was given him "by a revelation from Jesus Christ" (Gal. 1:12). We can see Saul slipping again into Judea, not this time as the flaming evangelist of his youth, but silently seeking out the apostles to discuss with them his vision of the Gospel. After some 15 days with Peter, and a brief meeting with James, the Lord's brother, Saul went on, visiting many churches incognito as he journeyed toward home. And we can picture Saul at home again in Tarsus — waiting.

How long did he wait? How long did he walk the streets of that great trade city, watching the ships of the Mediterranean world enter the port and slip away again? How long did Saul sit, working thoughtfully at his trade of tentmaking? Why didn't Saul marry during those years of waiting? He must have had the opportunity. But Ananias, the man sent by God to restore the sight he lost on the Damascus Road, had shared with the new convert the Lord's announcement of his destiny: "This man is My chosen instrument to carry My name before the Gentiles and their kings and before the people of Israel" (Acts 9:15). How deeply the sight of the crowded city streets, the swirling groups of men from different lands and backgrounds, must have moved him. As a Pharisee Saul had formerly viewed Gentiles as dogs, deserving only contempt and hatred. Now a Christian, the same man was beginning to see them in a new way—as individuals with worth and value, for whom Christ died.

And so Saul waited.

And then, finally, it was time for God's call.

On Mission

For most of the years of Saul's preparation the church continued to be a movement within Judaism. Then at Antioch came that mass conversion of Gentiles which led to Barnabas' dispatch by the apostles to investigate. It was clear to Barnabas that the spiritual response of the Gentiles was a work of God.

He stayed with the new believers for a time, but soon he recognized the need for help as more and more people were added to the church. "Then Barnabas went to Tarsus to look for Saul" (Acts 11:25).

God had begun that work among the Gentiles for which He had prepared the great apostle.

After a happy year during which Saul shared with Barnabas and others the leadership of the church at Antioch, the two were set aside by God for the first mission to the Gentiles. By the end of a two-year trip, Saul had emerged as the leader, and had taken a new name: Paul. This Romanized name was more appropriate for the Gentile mission than the Hebrew, Saul. The date was early in A.D. 48.

On the missionary journey, all of Paul's studies plus the truths which he had received by direct revelation seemed to come together with exciting clarity. In the crucible of his mission, in the conflict with the Jews who trailed his team and argued against him, in the questions raised by the converts, all that Paul had earlier worked

out for his own peace and understanding was now applied to the church as a whole. The old revelation and the new were not only recognized to be a unified and consistent whole, but the relationship between seemingly conflicting elements was understood. The "Gospel to the Gentiles" and the very nature of New Testament faith had been worked through by this man, the church's greatest theologian and the first apostle to the world.

Again Paul returned to Jerusalem, this time by the Holy Spirit's clear direction, to share privately with the leaders of the Jerusalem church the Gospel which he had been preaching among the Gentiles. It was just 14 years after his conversion.

Paul discovered that the leaders in Jerusalem had nothing to add to his understanding. In fact, they affirmed Paul by recognizing his call as the apostle to the Gentiles, even as Peter was recognized as the apostle to the Jews (Gal. 2:1-10). Paul then returned to Antioch and, assured of the understanding and agreement of the other apostles and the leaders in Jerusalem, Paul began to consider writing a letter to the Galatians (those churches in that area which included the cities visited on the first missionary journey). The urgency of this work was highlighted by a striking incident. Peter came to visit Antioch, freely joining in fellowship with the Gentile converts. Then a party of "Judaizers" arrived. These men were believers, but believers who insisted that all Christians must adopt the Law and the Jewish lifestyle. When these men came, Peter refused to eat with the Gentile believers any longer!

Paul immediately saw that this was a vital issue. It raised the question of the Christian's relationship with Old Testament Law. So Paul "opposed . . . [Peter] to his face" (v. 11).

It is likely that this confrontation and the disturbing teaching of the Pharisee-Christian party led to the Jerusalem Council of A.D. 49, which is reported in Acts 15. Throughout the rest of Paul's life he would accept the burden of contending for the "pure" Gospel. Through his letters you and I too come to understand the uniqueness and joy of our own privilege, of being a part of Christ's church, and of joining with our brothers and sisters in a full experience of the Christian life's great adventure.

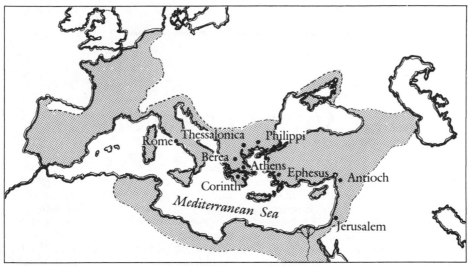

The Roman Empire

Paul, the Man

Eusebius records an interesting second-century description of Paul, perhaps passed on by a grandfather who had known the apostle. He was "a man in a good state of body, with eyebrows meeting and nose somewhat hooked, full of friendliness."

Today it's become popular to think of Paul as a bitter and joyless man, a distant intellectual, a distorter of what Jesus taught, and one who hated women. How far from the picture of Paul the early church drew. And how far from the portrait we have in Scripture! The austere Pharisee had undergone a complete transformation. The man who had cared for God in the abstract now cared for God in a deeply intimate way. And he loved people.

We can't help but realize the depth of this transformation as we look at Paul's words written to the Christians in Thessalonica, recalling his time with them. Paul's remembrance of love and intimate friendships was not written *about* a relationship, but to the very people who had experienced that relationship! What Paul wrote here must be the true portrait; the Thessalonians would have immediately perceived any deceit.

> We were gentle among you, like a mother caring for her little children. We loved you so much that we were delighted to share with you not only the Gospel of God but our lives as well, because you had become so dear to us.
>
> Surely you remember, brothers, our toil and hardship; we worked night and day in order not to be a burden to anyone while we preached the Gospel of God to you.
>
> You are witnesses, and so is God, of how holy, righteous and blameless we were among you who believed. For you know that we dealt with each of you as a father deals with his own children, encouraging, comforting and urging you to live lives worthy of God, who calls you into His kingdom and glory.
>
> 1 Thessalonians 2:7-12

The zealot had learned to love. The rigid Pharisee had become gentle. The man whose vision was the entire world yet found time for "each one of you."

There are many such cameo portraits of the apostle in the New Testament. And, because in teaching the New Yestament you will keep close company with him on his Acts journeys, and live with him in his letters, you'll want to help your group members come to see him as he was.

Seeing him in the intimacy of his sharing, you and your group will also discover the kind of person God uses in spiritual leadership—the kind of person each Christian is called to become.

257

THE ADVENTURE BEGINS

Overview

The "New Testament church" has fascinated Christians through the ages. The excitement, the vitality, the depth of fellowship portrayed in early Acts has attracted us. Many have sought to recapture those days: some by a reemphasis on the Spirit, others by restructuring the church as an institution.

No one can duplicate any moment in history. Yet as we study these first chapters of Acts we do discover principles which will vitalize Christian experience. We probably will not need to abandon our old. But we will need to make a fresh commitment to the God who worked so powerfully in the men and women of the early church. He lives today, and He is fully able to work just as powerfully in us.

▶ *Filled.* The events at Pentecost have been the focus of much theological debate. The text says the Holy Spirit filled the followers of Jesus. Specific signs were associated with that particular filling. There was a rushing, violent wind. Visible tongues of fire rested on each person. And when a crowd gathered each foreigner heard Jesus' followers "speaking in his own native language" (Acts 2:8). To understand the works of the Spirit it is important *not* to identify the Spirit's "filling," or the Spirit's "baptism," with any one of these signs. "Filling" is not itself tongues, or visible fire. For definition we have to go to key passages in the New Testament epistles (see *index*).

Commentary

I remember very clearly walking with five-year-old Paul the day he started kindergarten in Dallas, Texas. Paul was proud and excited—his first day at school! How grown-up he felt, and how grown-up and confident he looked. He was taking an important step into life's great adventure.

Each of us has times like this. For parent and child such moments are a strange mixture of excitement and loss. A whole phase of life is being left behind. We move on, sad, and yet somehow happy to meet the unknown.

It must have been very much like this for both Jesus and the disciples after Christ's resurrection. Their years together were past. The agony of the cross was history, swallowed up in the joy of Resurrection. During the 40 days after Christ rose, as Jesus still met with the disciples, both the Lord and the 11 must have been torn. Both knew the disciples would soon be launched on the greatest adventure the world has ever known, stepping out into the unknown to share Jesus with their whole world. They may have desperately wanted Jesus to remain with them. Yet, deep inside, the disciples must have known that they had been prepared for just this mission. They stood poised, hesitating, and yet eager to move on.

A New Focus

While the faith of Israel served as a foundation for the new faith about to break on a world unaware, what would happen during the months and years ahead was unknown to the disciples. This must have been hard for them. Usually we're most comfortable in familiar surroundings and situations.

We can see this in the disciples. For 40 days Jesus spoke with them about His Father's intention to build His own kingdom in man's world. Jesus also encouraged His disciples: "Wait for the gift My Father promised. . . . In a few days you will be baptized with the Holy Spirit" (1:4-5). Jesus did not push His followers unprepared into an adventure too great for them; He reminded them that He had promised them power. Even so, the disciples still looked longingly at the old patterns of thought and life. "Lord," they asked, "are You at this time going to restore the kingdom to Israel?" (v. 6)

This was a revealing and an important question. The Old Testament had foretold Jesus' coming, but the dominant impression the Jews had received was of His coming to be their King. They had visions of the Messiah rescuing them from Gentile dominion and giving them the exalted political and military position promised by the Old Testament prophets. Jesus' death had been doubly shocking to His followers. Not only had they loved Him, but they had also firmly expected Him to crush Rome's political and military power and to establish Israel as the dominant world power.

The believing Jews in Old Testament times knew that God rules over the whole world of men. Therefore, His sovereignty over history itself was recognized. But the Old Testament saint longed for the day when the hidden authority of Yahweh would be revealed to all, when the Lord's Messiah would rule *visibly* over the world of men. So even the Twelve who were closest to Jesus were disappointed as He continued to teach and preach and heal instead of confronting the Roman Empire.

Jesus had gently taught His followers that the Old Testament also spoke of the Messiah suffering and dying for men's sins. Christ's ministry was leading Him to a cross rather than a crown. But up to the very end, the disciples still had visions of their Camelot: a New Jerusalem, with Jesus (and themselves) ruling the world. The death of Jesus had crushed that hope momentarily. But when Jesus arose, the vision of power and glory again caught and held their imaginations. "Are You *at this time* going to restore the kingdom to Israel?" clearly reflects their longing for the life they had dreamed of so long.

Jesus' answer was gentle (vv. 7-8). First He pointed out that the prophesied kingdom would come, but that its coming was *distant* rather than "at this time." God will keep His promises, and this world will know Jesus' rule. But for now life is to have a different focus for Jesus' followers. That focus, stated in utmost simplicity, is this: "You will be My witnesses."

Jesus Himself is the focus, the center of the believer's life. The meaning of our lives,

the reason that our time on earth can be a great adventure, is summed up in the fact that Jesus is real, and that our every action can be a clear demonstration of the vital impact of the living God on human experience.

This was something that the disciples had not yet grasped, but soon would. Jesus, living within them, would Himself transform their experience. Then everything they were as individuals and as a community would witness to His presence.

These words, "You will be My witnesses," were the last ones Jesus spoke to the 11. As a silent crowd of disciples watched, Jesus rose up, soaring away until the clouds hid Him from sight. Two angelic messengers completed Christ's answer to the earlier question.

"This same Jesus, who has been taken from you into heaven, will come back in the same way you have seen Him go into heaven" (v. 11). This present time, during which the focus of our lives and the heart of our adventure with God is summed up in Jesus, will come to an end. As Old Testament days came to an end in the cross, our age will come to an end when Jesus returns — to establish the kingdom promised in the Old.

Yes, that day will come. But for then the disciples had to turn away from the Mount of Ascension and return to Jerusalem to see what new thing God had in store. There they waited, gathering for prayer. Waiting for a challenge, and a joy, that they could not yet imagine!

The Day: Acts 2:1-21

The days of waiting passed (Acts 1:12-26). The little company of believers, numbering about 120, met daily. On one of these days, they chose Matthias to take the office which Judas had abandoned by his betrayal of Jesus. Judas, overcome with remorse and yet unwilling to turn to Jesus for pardon, had thrown the 30 pieces of silver for which he betrayed the Lord down on the temple floor and, rushing out, had hanged himself.

Now another must take his office as an apostle. Searching among those who had been with Jesus since the beginning of His ministry and who had also been witnesses to the Resurrection, the little company found two candidates. Following an Old

Relationship Between the Old and New Testaments

Unity: in ultimate goal, the "glory of God."
Divergence: in emphasis

Old Testament	New Testament
—*theocratic purpose*	—*soteriological purpose*
1. God will rule the world through the Jewish Messiah's reign.	1. God will save individuals and society through the Jewish Messiah's work.
2. The nation Israel is emphasized.	2. The believing individual and community (the church) are emphasized.

Harmony: in teachings

The theocratic emphasis of the Old does not rule out concern for individuals (see Dan. 4; Ezek. 18; Nahum 1:6-7; Jonah 4).	The revelation of the fullness of God's salvation as it relates to individual transformation does not abrogate the emphasis of the Old (see Acts 1; Rom. 9–11).

Unification: in Christ

Jesus, the promised King of the Old Testament prophets, is also the Redeemer of the New Testament! In His person all of God's purposes will be fulfilled.

Testament practice, they then let God choose between the two by casting lots (much like our drawing of straws).

The company of the Apostles was thus returned to its original number of 12.

Apostles. The word *apostle* means "one sent out." In secular Greek it often referred to a ship or naval force sent on an expedition, seldom to an individual. Yet the word was chosen by Jewish translators of the Old Testament to reflect a Hebrew word that referred to one acting as another's representative.

In the New Testament the word is found 10 times in the Gospels, 28 times in Acts, and 38 times in the epistles, usually referring to men appointed by Christ for a special function in the church. While these men are primarily the Twelve and Paul, others are also called apostles.

No doubt the apostles were given special authority and power. Not only were they witnesses to the events of Jesus' life, but they were also authoritative interpreters of those events. As the body of apostolic teaching grew, it became clear that the church was being "built on the foundation of the apostles and prophets" (Eph. 2:20).

There is no indication in Scripture that the loyal apostles were replaced by others as they died (cf. Acts 12:2). As witnesses and interpreters of the purposes of God in the early days of the church, the apostles stand unique. But as witnesses to the reality of Jesus, the apostles were about to enter into an adventure which they share with all Jesus' followers of every age. And then the day arrived.

Pentecost (Acts 2:1). The Feast of Pentecost was one of the three annual Old Testament celebrations during which the men of Israel came to Jerusalem to worship at the temple. It was a time when Jews from around the world gathered in their ancient homeland and offered sacrifice to the God of Abraham and Isaac and Jacob.

Pentecost was a harvest festival, coming at the time of the grain harvest, just 50 days after Passover. Each year the firstfruits of the harvest were offered with joy and thanksgiving, accompanied by the recitation of Deuteronomy 26:3-10 by the worshiper.

Pentecost was clearly God's choice time for the initiation of Jesus' followers into their great adventure. Just 50 days before, Jesus Himself had been crucified—and raised again. Now, as an indication of the great harvest of everlasting life that Jesus' death had won, the 120 believers were about to be touched by the Spirit of God. They were to be the first of a vast multitude, the first of millions upon millions who would follow them into a unique relationship with God through Jesus Christ.

The choice of Pentecost was also an indication of the meaning of that new relationship for believers. The first words the Old Testament worshiper uttered at the Pentecost service were these:

I declare today to the Lord your God that I have come to the land the Lord swore to our forefathers to give us.
Deuteronomy 26:3

I declare that I have entered in! This is just what Pentecost meant to the first disciples, and what it should mean to us. Through Jesus, we have entered into everything the Promised Land foreshadowed; we are now free to experience the fullness of all the good things the Lord our God has chosen to give men.

And God's first gift was the gift of the Holy Spirit.

The Holy Spirit (Acts 2:2-21). The Bible speaks of the Holy Spirit as a Person, an individual distinct from and yet One with the Father and the Son. As God, the Holy Spirit had various relationships with men in Old Testament times. But the Old Testament also spoke of a coming day when God would enter into a new and special relationship with those who believe. Jesus had spoken often of this. Christ looked forward to a day when He would be back with the Father, and the Spirit "whom those who believed in Him were later to receive," would be given (John 7:39). The promised Spirit was to teach and guide believers (14:16) and, according to Jesus' final promise, to bring power for that new kind of life which bears witness to Jesus' reality (Acts 1:8). In that day, Jesus had said, the Spirit would not simply be "with" the disciples, but "in" them! (John 14:17)

And Pentecost was the promised day!

The Bible tells us that the Spirit's coming into believers was unmistakably marked. A mighty wind seemed to rush through the room where the 120 gathered; flames of fire flickered over each head; and as the Spirit filled them, individuals began to speak in languages they did not know.

This drew a great crowd of the men who had come to Jerusalem for the Pentecost festival. Each person heard the disciples speaking in the language of the land where he was presently living. "How is it," wondered the visitors, "that each of us hears them in his own native language? . . . We hear them declaring the wonders of God in our own tongues!" (Acts 2:8, 11) Perplexed and amazed, they asked each other, "What does this mean?" (v. 12)

All too often that same question is asked today—without listening to Peter's response to those first questioners. All too often the answer given is designed to argue for or against the existence of what has been called "the gift of tongues" in our day. Whatever our opinion might be as to whether God still gives believers this gift, the important point underlined by Pentecost is that now, at last, the Holy Spirit *is* given!

And this was Peter's response to those who demanded an explanation of the disciples: "This is what was spoken by the Prophet Joel:

"In the last days," God says, "I will pour out My Spirit on all people."
Acts 2:16-17

That great gift which God had reserved till the last days was being poured out freely now. All were to know the touch of the Spirit of God; both daughters and sons would be empowered by Him. Most significant of all, in that day on which the Spirit of God would flow out to touch and fill God's own, "everyone who calls on the name of the Lord will be saved" (v. 21).

God was moving out beyond the boundaries of Israel to offer to *all* people that relationship with Himself which is at the heart of eternal life.

The disciples themselves did not understand just then all that the Spirit's coming meant. They didn't see Pentecost as the beginning of the church, as it later came to be understood. They did not realize that the Holy Spirit, living in each believer, would Himself constitute a living link binding each individual to other believers, to form a vital, loving community.

But they did know that God's new day was *now!* They did know that the Holy

Spirit had filled them with Jesus' promised power. And they did begin immediately to explain the striking witness that the rushing wind and the flames and the tongues had given to every observer of the reality of God's presence in these set-apart men.

📖 *Group Activity: Bible Study Group*
The Book of Acts is sometimes called the "Acts of the Holy Spirit" rather than the "Acts of the Apostles." This is because the Spirit plays such a prominent role in the experience of first-century believers and the explosive growth of the early church. Together look up the promises of the Spirit that led to Pentecost (John 7:39; 14:16-17; Acts 1:8; see commentary on Pentecost, Holy Spirit, pp. 260-261). Then use a concordance to locate every reference to the Holy Spirit in Acts.

Divide into teams, each of which is to study about 10 of these references. From them find out: What did the Holy Spirit do? How was His working evidenced? When did the Holy Spirit work (i.e., under what conditions)? What else seems significant about the occasion?

While the Book of Acts is not a book of doctrine, we can learn much about our own relationship with the Holy Spirit by observing His working then. Come together and report both what you discovered and how you see this applying to Christian experience today.

The Message: Acts 2:22–3:26

Jesus' last instructions had been to focus on Himself: "You will be My witnesses" (1:8). Acts 2 and 3 show how clearly the early disciples maintained that focus. The two sermons of Peter recorded here give us a clear picture of the apostolic message and the very heart of the Gospel.

What were the basic elements of the apostolic preaching?

1. *Jesus, the historical Person.* In each sermon Peter began by confronting his hearers with the Person who had lived among them; who was born, lived, performed His wonders, and taught in our space and time, "as you yourselves know" (2:22). This was no mythical person, no invention of disciples parlaying the ignorance of gullible crowds into the beginnings of a new religion. Everyone knew Jesus. He had been a public figure, a chief topic of conversation

for at least three years. Just 50 days before, He had been executed at the insistence of the Jewish leaders, with crowds of the common people shouting for His blood. Peter's words, "As you yourselves know," made it very clear. The Gospel is firmly rooted in historical reality.

And all Peter's hearers knew perfectly well who the historical Jesus was.

2. *Crucified.* A second element of the apostolic preaching involved confronting the hearers with the crucifixion of Jesus, and even confronting them with their own guilt: "You . . . put Him to death by nailing Him to the cross" (v. 23).

3. *Raised.* A third element also involved the statement of historical fact: Jesus was loosed from death's bonds and raised up by God, and "we are all witnesses of the fact" (v. 32).

4. *Correspondence with Old Testament prophecy.* Peter then went on to point out that each of these historical events happened as God had foretold in the Old Testament. Rather than being a threat to the integrity of God's Word, Jesus and the events of His life and death and resurrection are foretold there. What Peter proclaimed was in fullest harmony with God's total revelation.

5. *The promised Messiah.* Peter then went on to interpret the facts he had laid out for his hearers. "Be assured of this: God has made this Jesus, whom you crucified, both Lord and Christ" (v. 36).

The conclusion is so clearly correct that his hearers were "cut to the heart" and begged the apostles, "Brothers, what shall we do?" (v. 37) This question led into the last element of the apostolic preaching.

6. *Repentance and faith.* The word *repent* is a military term meaning make an about-face. The men to whom Peter spoke had refused to accept Jesus as Lord and Messiah. They had hesitated, then passively participated in His execution. Now they were asked to make a clear-cut commitment and symbolize their response of faith by public baptism. And if they did? Then everything that Jesus' death and resurrection promised would become theirs: full forgiveness of sins and the gift of the Holy Spirit. The God they had scorned would welcome even them and, entering their lives, fill them with power to launch out new lives.

So, "Those who accepted his message

were baptized, and about three thousand were added to their number that day" (v. 41).

How vital and contemporary these messages are even today. You and I have been invited by God to enter a living relationship with the historical Jesus. The Son of God lived and died and was raised again, all in accordance with the Scripture, that He might *today* bring forgiveness and power for a new life to all who respond to Him as Lord and Christ. He will be with us, as He was with the first disciples, charging us with the power we need to witness to Him.

Ø Group Activity:
Missions/Outreach Group
Begin by writing a careful description of what was said the last time you witnessed to a non-Christian. Be as thorough as you can in describing the situation and conversation. Then divide into teams of three and read your descriptions.

Come together and compare Peter's two evangelistic sermons reported in these early chapters (Acts 2:14-40; 3:11-26). From these determine the essential elements in this earliest presentation of the Gospel (see commentary, pp. 262-263). Discuss each element so that the importance of each is fully understood by all.

Return to teams of three, and evaluate the witnessing reports you read to each other. What elements of Peter's evangelistic content are present? What elements are absent? How do we effectively communicate the truths Peter stressed to the people of today?

Community: Acts 4
When Frank accepted Christ as his Saviour, his parents saw his conversion as a denial of their family religion. At first they argued and ridiculed. Then, as they sensed the depth of their teen's experience with Jesus, they increased the pressure. They offered Frank that set of expensive drums he'd wanted, if only he'd give up this nonsense! Finally, the Leparises locked their son out of the house. If he would not remain true to the family faith, he would be cut off.

The first exciting days of the church saw many experiences similar to Frank's. There was change and growth. And there was opposition. The contagious enthusiasm of those who believed in Jesus threatened the secure foundations of many people's religious convictions, and uneasy tolerance gave way to hostility. It was then that the little company of believers began to realize that the church was a new community, a community of men and women who could be closer than any family, and who could provide the kind of loving support that believers then — and believers now, like Frank — would always need.

Opposition to the message of a living Christ formed quickly. Peter's sermon, stimulated by the healing of the lame man (Acts 3), was only one instance of the disciples "teaching the people and proclaiming in Jesus the resurrection of the dead" (4:2). Soon some 5,000 men had joined the company of the committed. An annoyed clique of rulers and elders acted. They arrested Peter and John.

The confrontation (Acts 4:5-22). Called before the ruling body of Judaism, the apostles were questioned about the miracle of healing which Peter had performed. Boldly, Peter responded. The miracle had been performed "by the name of Jesus Christ of Nazareth, whom you crucified but whom God raised from the dead" (v. 10). Only in Jesus, Peter went on to affirm, could salvation be found; there is no other name or way.

Such boldness from uneducated and common men stunned the elite group. Setting the apostles outside, the council conferred. There was no way to deny the public healing. Compromising, the rulers called Peter and John back and commanded them to stop all this talk about Jesus. Again speaking boldly, the two believers insisted that they would obey God rather than men. The frustrated rulers, unable to justify to the people any punishment of Peter and John, threatened them and let them go.

The fellowship of prayer (Acts 4:23-31). At this point in time we are introduced to one of the most significant dimensions of the new community's life. Peter and John immediately "went back to their own people and reported" (v. 23). In the brotherhood of the church, Peter and John found others who cared and with whom they could share. Immediately the whole company accepted the burden of the two as their own, and went to God in prayer.

Frank had many burdens to share with us too. There was tremendous pain for him, and often that pain brought tears. But he had Christian friends who cared—friends who would listen, who would encourage, and who joined with him in prayer. Frank discovered as a young Christian what the early church learned in its first adventurous days. *A Christian is never alone!* Not only has the risen Christ sent the Holy Spirit to be with us, but He has also knit us together in a community of fellowship and love.

This is one of the most important things we can learn as we begin our exploration of the New Testament. In the Scriptures we see portrayed a church in which those touched by Christ discover a new capacity to love and to care for one another. The church is more than a group of people who agree in their beliefs. The church is a family of brothers and sisters who experience the reality of Jesus' presence in and through their growing love for one another (cf. John 13:33-34). While some today have not tasted of that reality, this *is* a real and vital dimension of Christian experience. And God invites each one of us to reach out and know this touch of fellowship.

The text of Acts reports that as they prayed together "they were all filled with the Holy Spirit and spoke the Word of God boldly" (Acts 4:31). In the fellowship of prayer, God's power is poured again into our lives.

With one accord (Acts 4:32-37). This is a passage that has captured the imagination of Christians across the ages. "All the believers were one in heart and mind" (v. 32). Growing together, the early church experienced a unique unity. Possessions were sold by the rich, and the proceeds were distributed to the poor. The sense of oneness was so great that no selfish hesitation kept anyone from reaching out to meet another's need. Because concern for the brothers outweighed the value of material possessions, love's expression was both practical and free. "There were no needy persons among them" (v. 34).

This early evidence of the reality of Christian community is not necessarily a standard for the church today. But it is not as unusual as we may think. In our own local church just this kind of expression of love often takes place. Yet, the impact of the passage is not to promote some form of "Christian communism," but rather to highlight the truth of the writer's statement, "All the believers were one in heart and mind."

We are called to oneness in our shared faith. Oneness with our brothers and sisters frees us to share ourselves as well as each other, to support each other in prayer, and to express love in many vital and practical ways.

Homothumadon: One Accord. A unique Greek word, used 10 of its 11 New Testament occurrences in the Book of Acts, helps us understand the uniqueness of Christian community. *Homothumadon* is a compound of two words meaning to "rush along" and "in unison." The image is almost musical; a number of notes are sounded which, while different, harmonize in pitch and tone. As the instruments of a great orchestra blend under the direction of a concertmaster, so the Holy Spirit blends together the lives of members of Christ's church.

The first use of *homothumadon* is found in Acts 1:14. There, in the Upper Room, the 11 disciples and a few women were united in prayer. Earlier strife and jealousies that marred their relationships were gone; the disciples were one, waiting for the Spirit's promised coming. Then in Acts 2:1 we see 120 believers gathered, focusing together on the Lord as they sensed the Spirit's first dynamic touch. The next occurrence is verse 46, as the community (then some 3,000), "continuing daily with one accord [*homothumadon*] in the temple, and breaking bread from house to house, did eat their meat with gladness and singleness of heart" (KJV). Again in 4:24 we see the whole company, moved by Peter and John's report, as they "lifted up their voice to God with one accord" (KJV). As those who are Jesus' own make Him the common focus of their lives and seek to help each other find the Holy Spirit's freedom in their lives, *homothumadon* becomes the mark of Christian community.

Sometimes we look back on these early chapters of Acts as though they picture a church that has been lost—as though unity and love and the experience of Jesus' presence are things that cannot really be ours today. Let's not make this mistake. God's Spirit is still a present reality. *Homothumadon* is still possible in today's shattered and impersonal world. If we look for a reason for emptiness in our own experience, let's look first to our hesitancy to share ourselves with our brothers and sisters. Or look to our failure to let others pick up the burdens of our lives, and bring them in confident prayer to God.

The church, the new community Christ formed, *is* here today. *We are the church.* And God, the Spirit, is able to take our 11s, and our 120s and our 3,000s and, as we joyfully focus our shared life on Jesus, to orchestrate our lives to His wondrous "one accord."

✳ *Group Activity:*
Singles/Single Again Group
Begin by drawing a sociogram that includes everyone in your study group. Draw a circle somewhere on an 8 1/2 x 11 sheet of paper to represent yourself. Then draw circles to represent the others in your group. Indicate nearness or distance from you by space. Indicate links between people by arrows (note that arrows do not need to point both ways: someone may feel close to an individual who does not feel equally close

to him or her. Use initials to label the circles you drew.

Without showing your sociogram, jot down three phrases that you think best describe its climate and atmosphere. Together list these terms on a chalkboard or sheet of newsprint. What strengths of your fellowship do the words reveal? What weaknesses?

Then in teams study three passages: Acts 2:42-47; 4:23-31; 4:32-37. First choose words that describe the climate and atmosphere of these early Christian groups. Then look in the text for what it was that bonded them together so closely.

Come back together and discuss: Why do singles especially need the kinds of relationships described in early Acts? What can we do to draw closer together and develop the bonded, supportive relationship that characterized the earliest church?

GROUP RESOURCE GUIDE

Identification: *Share with others*
Have three concentric circles drawn on a chalkboard or sheet of newsprint. The inner circle represents family, the next circle neighbors, the final circle strangers. Tell briefly about the person who was most influential in leading you to Christ, and put a check mark in the circle where he or she fits.

Affirmation: *Express love and concern*
If persons in your group were God's instruments in bringing you to Christ, tell them directly how much they mean to you.

Exploration: *Probe God's Word*
Acts 1–4 explains both a strategy for evangelism and defines the content of the Gospel we share.

Compare Peter's two evangelistic sermons reported in these early chapters (Acts 2:14-40; 3:11-26). From these determine the essential elements in this earliest

presentation of the Gospel (see commentary, pp. 262-263). Discuss each element so that the importance of each is fully understood by all. Discuss also how each element can best be presented to moderns.

Reaction: *Responding together to the Word*
The *strategy* of evangelism is expressed in Acts 1:8, and is reflected in the Identification activity. We are to reach those in our Jerusalem (family), in Samaria (our neighbors), and in "all the world" (strangers).

Discuss: Which group should have priority in our prayers and efforts? Which group is easiest to reach? Why? Which group is hardest? Why? Talk also about what you are currently doing to share the Gospel with each of the three groups.

Adoration: *Worship and pray*
Praise God for your salvation, and ask Him to help you share His Good News with a specific individual this coming week.

STUDY GUIDE 40
Acts 5:1–11:18

REACHING OUT

Overview

The early church was a dynamic fellowship. It was rooted in faith in Christ, and relationships between Christians were marked by *homothumadon*, that vital principle of "one accord."

But we would be mistaken to idealize the early church. It was a fellowship made up of mere human beings. There were tensions within the church, and pressures from those outside who opposed the Gospel message. All these forces sought to disrupt the oneness of the local body of believers, and to halt its growth. In these next chapters of Acts we look at some of the inner and outer pressures which, unless dealt with correctly, can distort our own churches too.

▶ *Tongues.* For a fuller discussion, see Study Guide 132. However, in these chapters note that "tongues" served a very special function. In Samaria they were an outward sign of union with the Jerusalem church, for they came only when the apostles laid hands on the new converts (Acts 8:14-17). The Spirit came on Gentiles at the house of Cornelius "while Peter was still speaking" the Gospel message. Later Peter argued that this was evidence that Gentiles received "the same gift" as Jewish believers (11:15-17). Thus in Acts speaking in tongues was an outward evidence of the unity of a church just discovering that it was to be composed not only of Jews but of Samaritans and Gentiles as well!

Commentary

"What's happened to us? We were so close before. And then we started growing . . . and. . . . " Carol's words reflect a common experience. A little group of believers comes together, grows close, and forms a local church. There's an exciting sense of closeness and warmth and enthusiasm.

As time passes, growth comes. We become busier and busier. New people come in whom we don't know, and before long the closeness we felt with earlier friends is lost. Soon decisions about buildings and parking lots and programs and staffing and so many other things crowd in on us.

It's easy then to look back at the earlier days and to long for the intimacy of that smaller group. It's also easy, if we've never experienced that kind of fellowship, to doubt whether it is even possible in this day and age.

All such longing is not only useless; it is also foolish. It is in the very nature of life to reproduce. It is in the very nature of Christian faith and life to reach out, to welcome more and more people into the family of God. It may be more difficult to maintain warmth and a sense of oneness in a church when growth comes. But the solution is never to push back to the past. The solution is in finding new ways to affirm and to experience our *homothumadon*.

It was no different in the early church. With growth and expansion came tensions. There were disagreements. There was sin. There were suspicion and misunderstanding. But through it all the early church expected that God the Holy Spirit would enable them to experience the unity that He Himself had fashioned in that bond which knits believers to Jesus and to one another.

Growing Tensions: Acts 5–7

These three chapters of Acts bring us back again to look at the Jerusalem church. There, with growth, came tensions from both within the believing community and from without.

Sin (Acts 5:1-11). The first tension emerged from within. A couple named Ananias and Sapphira wanted a reputation for benevolences like that of other believers who had sold their possessions for the benefit of the whole church. But Ananias and Sapphira didn't want to give all.

There was no demand by God or by the believing community that they should give all. As Peter asked, "After it was sold, wasn't the money at your disposal?" (v. 4) But rather than openly give a part, the two conspired to pretend that they had turned the full purchase price over to the church.

The sin was not in the choice they made for the use of their possessions; the sin was in their hypocrisy and in the lie they attempted to tell, not only to the brotherhood, but to the Holy Spirit.

God's judgment was swift. Both died. And the whole church was gripped with a deep sense of reverence and awe for God (called "fear" in the text).

Here is a remedy for our insensitivity as well. Let's regain awareness of just who this God is who has called us into relationship with Himself. When we are filled with awe because *God* is present with us, the little pretenses and games we play with one another are quickly set aside.

Official persecution (Acts 5:12-42). The aggressive preaching of the apostles, authenticated by "signs and wonders" (healing miracles), led to a revival. "More and more men and women believed in the Lord" (v. 14). This success filled the religious leaders with jealousy; they angrily imprisoned the apostles. But Peter and the others were released by an angel. By daybreak they were again speaking "the full message of this new life" (v. 20) to eager crowds.

The temple guards were ordered to rearrest the apostles. Afraid of the people's reaction, the guards "invited" the apostles to come with them rather than attempting to drag them away. The Jewish leaders were furious at the disciples' continued charge that the Jesus they themselves had killed was now exalted by God to be Saviour and Lord. The leaders now wanted to murder the Twelve as well! Instead, they commanded the apostles not to tell others about Jesus, and they let them go.

The response of the Twelve sets the pattern for our response to similar pressures. "Day after day, in the temple courts and from house to house, they never stopped teaching and proclaiming the good news that Jesus is the Christ" (v. 42).

✂ *Group Activity: Recovery Group*
Step 3 (decide to turn my life over to God's care)

Brainstorm: What are the most frightening things about the prospect of turning my life and will over to God? List suggestions of group members. When the list is complete, talk about each item. Which fears are realistic? Which are not? Why?

Privately write down your answer to this question: "What is the worst thing that can happen to me if I turn my life and will over to God?"

Read and talk about Peter and John, who chose to do God's will and were persecuted for it. What was the worst thing that happened to them? How did they feel about that experience? How would (or do) I feel when I do what God wants, even though it may not turn out the way I'd like?

As a follow-up, read the story of the first martyr Stephen. He did suffer the worst thing — he was killed by a mob! But look closely at 7:54-60. How did he feel about even this fate?

In conclusion, write a brief paragraph telling, if you had to choose between being Stephen and one of his murderers, which would you choose to be, and why.

Suspicion within (Acts 6:1-7). As the number of disciples continued to increase, some of the Greek-speaking Jewish believers felt that their widows were being neglected when the resources of the church were distributed. This group of believers was made up of foreign-born Jews who had gathered for Pentecost from several different lands (see 2:8-10). They first heard the apostles' message in their own languages. Later, not knowing the Aramaic language of Palestine, they could communicate in Greek, the common second language of the Roman world.

Suspicious of the motives of the native-born stewards in charge of the distribution, these Hellenists raised a complaint that might well have hardened into a bitter split if it had not been handled wisely.

What happened was that the apostles called the church together and told them to "choose seven men from among you who are known to be full of the Spirit and wisdom" (6:3). These would be responsible for the distribution. The men they chose had names like Stephen and Philip—names that identify them as Hellenists! The misunderstanding was healed as men who those who had complained would trust

267

were appointed to care for the distribution to all! And "so the Word of God spread. The number of disciples in Jerusalem increased rapidly" (v. 7).

The corporate witness of the church to the reality of Jesus' presence in their community brought its own sure response (see John 13:34).

Hatred (Acts 6:8–7:59). The success of the church, and particularly its constant affirmation of Jesus, now brought a strong reaction. The preaching of the Gospel had polarized Jerusalem. Some responded to the message, while many others became just as hardened against it. These became opponents of the church, even as they had opposed Jesus during His earthly life.

The growing anger now broke out in a vicious mob attack on Stephen. Stephen's defense before the mob (Acts 7) traced the spiritual hardness of Israel from the days of Moses to the present. It was a bold challenge to these men, in which they were charged with faithlessness to the God they claimed to serve. Enraged, the listening crowd dragged Stephen outside the city gates and battered his body with stones until he died.

Thus the church offered up the blood of her first martyr, who prayed for his murderers as he died, "Lord, do not hold this sin against them" (v. 60).

Expansion: Acts 8

Christ in His final charge to His disciples had told them to wait in Jerusalem until the Holy Spirit came to bring them power. Then they were to reach out beyond Jerusalem to share Jesus with the entire world. In 1:8 Jesus gave a pattern for that expansion: "You will be My witnesses in Jerusalem, and in all Judea and Samaria, and to the ends of the earth."

This pattern, in fact, gives us a way to outline the Book of Acts.

There are several ways to outline the Acts' history of the early church. One is to see this record as a report first of Peter's ministry to the Jews (Acts 1–12), and then as a report of Paul's mission to the Gentile world (Acts 13–28). Another is to see it as a history of the development of the Christian movement; its origins (Acts 1–5), its transition days (Acts 6–12), and its expansion to become a world religion (Acts 13–28). However, perhaps the best way to

see Acts is in the framework suggested in 1:8, as the record of an expanding, dynamic life-force, reaching out to bring more and more of mankind into a vital relationship with Jesus Christ.

Judea and Samaria. The death of Stephen launched a great persecution against the church in Jerusalem. The believers, except for the apostles, were driven out and scattered throughout Judea and Jerusalem.

Everywhere the believers went they told others about Christ, and the message was received—even in Samaria.

The response of the Samaritans must have been something of a surprise. While the people of this district were viewed as mongrel Jews until excommunicated by Judaism in about A.D. 300, they were looked down on as a semiheretical and "foolish" sect.

The Progression of the Church

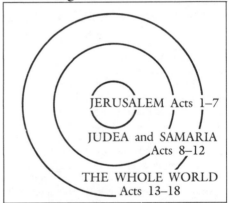

JERUSALEM Acts 1–7

JUDEA and SAMARIA Acts 8–12

THE WHOLE WORLD Acts 13–18

The origin of the Samaritans goes back to the deportation of the people of the Northern Kingdom of Israel in 722 B.C. Those Jews still left in the land mingled with other people imported by Assyria to form a loose culture that retained much of the Old Testament tradition, but developed its own theology and worship system. That the Samaritans had seriously distorted the revealed faith is clear from Jesus' conversation with a Samaritan woman, recorded in John 4, and also from Jesus' clear distinction between Israel and Samaria during His days on earth (cf. Matt. 10:5-7).

Now, however, the Samaritans not only heard the Gospel, but "the people with one accord gave heed" (Acts 8:6, KJV). Hearing reports of the mass conversion, the apostles sent Peter and John to investigate. Discovering that these men and women had truly believed, Peter prayed for them that they might also be given the gift of the Holy Spirit.

This significant incident in the life of the early church receives varying interpretations. What is important to observe here, however, is that the progression of the church outward from Jerusalem (Acts 1:8) proceeded in a series of steps that were given the seal of approval of God's Spirit. Here the Samaritans, later the Gentiles, were shown to be members of the one church of Jesus Christ, led by the apostles of our Lord (10:44-46; 19:1-6).

Since the 700-year-old antagonism between Samaritan and Jew had some of its roots in religious rivalry, it would have been easy for the Samaritans to accept the new faith, but to continue to affirm their identity as a group separate from Christian Jews. By mediating the gift of the Spirit through Peter, God not only affirmed the unity of the church as a single community, but also affirmed the authority of the apostles whom Jesus had chosen to lead it during the early years.

Simon. Acts 8 tells us that Peter's act in Samaria was misunderstood by at least one observer. Simon, a magician who had won a large following among the Samaritans, offered the apostles money if they would only give him such power.

Magicians were well known in the ancient world, and are spoken of in both Testaments. Our word is derived, through the Latin and ancient Greek, from *magi,* a priestly clan in Persia. From the first century A.D. on, the word was used of a variety of magicians, soothsayers, and astrologers. The usual guiding motive behind the life of such a person was acquisition of power to influence people and events through occult knowledge and arcane practice.

The Scripture makes it clear that this stands in direct conflict with God and His ways (see Deut. 18:10-14; Gal. 5:20). There *are* supernatural powers under the control of Satan; seeking knowledge or power through the occult and spirit world is unquestionably anti-God.

Acts 8 records Peter's stern rebuke of Simon. We hear nothing more of this magician in the biblical record. There is, however-

er, early tradition telling of a heretical sect from the same era called the Simoniani. Whether or not this sect sprang from this Simon whom Peter confronted has never been confirmed.

The chapter closes with the report of the conversion of an Ethiopian government official. He was apparently a convert to Judaism, or at least a "God-fearer" who believed in Israel's God but who had not undergone the rites of conversion. The Holy Spirit led Philip away from Samaria and brought him to explain to the Ethiopian eunuch the way of salvation as expressed in the Old Testament passage, Isaiah 53.

Hebrew believers had begun to fan out across the ancient world. The Gospel message was carried with them. This seed would soon bring a rich harvest.

∅ Group Activity:
Missions/Outreach Group

Begin by each ranking the following in order of their spiritual significance: evangelists, missionaries, TV preachers, pastors, ordinary believers. Also list in order of their significance in spreading the Gospel: TV ministries, radio ministries, citywide evangelistic campaigns, church revival meetings, distributing tracts, placing Bibles in hotel rooms, one-on-one witnessing.

Discuss why each of you made the choices he or she did. Then look in Acts 8, paying close attention to the ministry of Philip, particularly: if "numbers" is the criteria you used, why did the Spirit take Philip away from an effective citywide campaign to share with one person, the Ethiopian eunuch?

How might the ranking change if the criterions used were: God's love for each individual; the Holy Spirit's leading; our spiritual gift; or opportunity.

What conclusions can you draw about your own significance in carrying out God's purpose of reaching men and women with the Good News? For a test case, read the Acts' story of Paul's conversion and consequent zeal for Christ. We never know whether the one person we reach for Jesus might have a similar key role to play in God's plan!

Gentile Converts: Acts 10:1–11:18
Chapter 9 of Acts tells of the conversion of

Paul, and events we looked at in Study Guide 117. And then the Acts history sketches one of the least-expected events in the Bible.

Gentile believers were suddenly welcomed into the church, with the same rights and privileges and blessings as the Jewish believers in Christ! And again at this turning point, the central figure is the Apostle Peter.

Peter. Peter and his brother Andrew were both members of the original Twelve. They were fishermen, perhaps in partnership with and certainly friends of James and John.

The Gospels show that Peter was leader of the Twelve. He is listed first in the four New Testament lists of the disciples. He is the most-frequently mentioned disciple. With James and John, Peter was a member of the inner circle of Jesus' intimates. In Acts, Peter clearly had the leading role, from his preaching of the first sermon on Pentecost, to mediating the Spirit to the Samaritans, and then to first proclaiming the Gospel to Gentiles.

While a leader, Peter remained a man of contrasts. He was bold, yet unstable. Quick to recognize Jesus as God's Christ, Peter was just as quick to object when Jesus spoke of the coming cross (Matt. 16). Ready to promise commitment to the death, Peter three times denied the Lord on the night of His trial (Mark 14).

In Acts the inconsistent Peter of the Gospels seems to have emerged as a man of firm and consistent leadership. Yet, later at Antioch, Peter would refuse to eat with Gentile converts for fear of the criticism of other Hebrew-Christians.

Peter stands as a reminder to us to rely on the stabilizing and strengthening power of the Holy Spirit. God can take our strengths and our natural gifts and use them, and He alone can protect us from our weaknesses. Because the Spirit *is* with us, we too can expect to live victoriously.

After these chapters, the focus of Acts shifts to the Apostle Paul. Tradition tells us that Peter continued his ministry among the Jewish people and traveled widely. Two of his last letters are found in the New Testament, the final one being written shortly before his own martyrdom. Early historians seem to agree that Peter died in Rome, executed during the violent persecution of

Christians by the emperor Nero in A.D. 64.

The centurion. In the Gentile center of Caesarea, an officer of the Roman army who had come to believe in God was visited by an angel. The angel told the officer, Cornelius, to summon Peter, who would communicate God's message to him.

The next day, as the Roman's messengers were on the way to Joppa where Peter was staying, Peter had a vision. Three times a sheet filled with animals forbidden by Jewish Law as food (this is the meaning of "unclean" here) was lowered from heaven. Three times a voice commanded Peter to eat. And three times Peter protested against the divine command. Each time the lesson was driven home: "Do not call anything impure that God has made clean" (Acts 10:15).

While Peter was puzzling about the meaning of the vision, Cornelius' messengers knocked at the door.

Gentiles. To understand the need for Peter's preparation and the angry reaction of the Jewish believers when they heard later that Peter had actually entered a Gentile's home, we need to realize the attitude of the Jew toward all foreigners.

For hundreds of years the Jews, full of a sense of their own destiny as God's chosen people, had been politically subject to a series of foreign rulers. Vicious wars, filled with unspeakable atrocities, had been waged by and against the foreigners. Yet the Jews remained in bondage. The fact that this bondage was to men who had no standing or covenant relationship with God made the situation even more galling. Israel was forced to submit to a race they considered unholy and with whom they would never choose to associate. The Gentile was viewed with far greater loathing, and with less respect, than the slave of colonial days. In fact, no pious Jew would ever enter a Gentile's home. He would be contaminated if he did, unable to worship God until he had been ceremonially cleansed.

Thus in the earliest days of the church, the believers were astounded to find God extending His Spirit to the Gentiles! This called for a radical reorientation of their conception of God, and of themselves as the chosen people.

At Cornelius' home. Peter, taught by the vision of the unclean animals lowered from heaven, went with Cornelius' messengers.

He entered the centurion's home and began to speak. "You are well aware that it is against our Law for a Jew to associate with a Gentile or visit him. But God has shown me that I should not call any man impure or unclean" (v. 28). Peter had responded quickly to God; he accepted a concept that, nevertheless, would keep on dividing the church for generations!

Cornelius told of the angel's visit. Now he and his family and friends were eager to hear what God would tell them through Peter.

So Peter began to speak about Jesus. He repeated again the basic apostolic Gospel we've seen in Acts 2 and 3, and again in chapter 4. And as Peter was speaking, the Holy Spirit fell on all who heard.

The Jewish contingent with Peter was amazed. They heard these Gentiles speaking in tongues just as they themselves had at Pentecost. It was clear that God had given these Gentiles the same gift that He had given them. Recognizing that God had re-vealed His will, Peter had the whole Gentile company baptized in the name of Jesus Christ.

Chapter 11 reports the reaction of some in the Jerusalem church. They attacked Peter sharply. Peter went over the events step by step and shared this unanswerable conclusion: "So if God gave them the same gift as He gave us, who believed in the Lord Jesus Christ, who was I to think that I could oppose God!" (v. 17) And the passage reports, "They had no further objections and praised God, saying, 'So then, God has even granted the Gentiles repentance unto life' " (v. 18).

A new and exciting day had come for the early church. Soon the whole world would be invited to believe.

✍ *Group Activity: Bible Study Group*
Examine together the story of Cornelius' conversion reported in Acts 10:1–11:18. Answer the following questions:
* *How were the prejudices of Peter and*

Disruptive Tensions in the Early Church

Acts	Problem Described	Danger	Wrong Responses	Solution	Parallel Problems Today
5:1-11					
5:12-42			Permit sin Ignore sin		
6:1-7		Serious division within the church—destruction of *homothumadon*			
6:8–7:59	Jealousy, anger, and hatred against the church by outsiders				

the Jewish church overcome?
* Why was it necessary to overcome them?
* Why was it easier for the Jewish church to accept a single family of Gentile converts than to later accept overwhelming

mass conversions?
Then together apply your insights. What parallels exist in our society? What would it take for us to overcome prejudices?

GROUP RESOURCE GUIDE

Adoration: *Worship and pray*
Have written on a chalkboard or large sheet of paper "Christ is the Answer." Meditate for 90 seconds on this affirmation, then open with sentence prayers, thanking Jesus for the answer He has provided to a specific problem of your own.

Identification: *Share with others*
Each person should have a chart like that on page 271. Also a large master chart should be reproduced on a chalkboard or sheet of newsprint. Start by working together to complete the first column *(Problem Described)*. When this has been done, discuss how each issue shows up in our churches or relationships. Then select the one area that has most relevance to you

personally, and form a team with others who chose the same area.

Exploration: *Probe God's Word*
In your teamwork study the relevant passage carefully for insights with which to complete the rest of the columns on the chart. Be sure you spend enough time to identify significant parallels in the church and your own experience today.

Reaction: *Respond together to the Word*
Come together and let each team share the results of its study. Complete your own chart with information other teams supply.

Then go around the circle, sharing one thing you have learned that you can apply personally.

THE ERA OF EVANGELISM

Overview

What happens to a local church when the neighborhood changes, and "they" begin to outnumber "us" in a congregation? This is one of the issues dealt with in these chapters of Acts, as well as in significant New Testament letters. In each confrontation, a simple principle is affirmed, one we see developed here in its first form.

"They" don't have to be like "us" to be accepted and acceptable. As Paul wrote to the Ephesians, speaking of Jew and Gentile, whose differences were certainly as great as any that divide people today, "His purpose was to create in Himself [Jesus] one new man out of the two, thus making peace" (Eph. 2:15).

In these chapters of Acts we also read about Paul's first missionary journey, and learn about the evangelistic strategy the apostle developed.

Your group members will be able to gain many insights from these chapters about modern missions — overseas and in your own community.

So teaching this section of Acts can be an exciting adventure for you, and for those to whom you minister! These vital chapters can surely enrich your lives, and strengthen commitment to Christ's truth.

■ A careful discussion of the restrictions placed by the Jerusalem Council on Gentile lifestyle, along with a discussion of each city Paul visited, is found in the *Bible Knowledge Commentary*, pages 382-396.

Commentary

As the number of Gentiles in the early church grew, some congregations developed that were predominantly Gentile. This was an issue the apostles and elders were forced to face, and with which they struggled. How *are* we to relate to those who are significantly "different" from us?

Persecution Increases: Acts 11:19–12:25

Outbreaks of persecution continued in Palestine. The believers were scattered beyond Judea and Samaria. They spread along the Mediterranean coast and crossed the waters to Cyprus. At first these Hebrew Christians shared Jesus only within the Jewish communities. But then some began to speak of Jesus to Gentiles as well. And at Antioch (see map, p. 779), a great number of Gentiles believed and turned to the Lord.

The Jerusalem church again sent an investigating committee, headed by Barnabas, a man we meet first in Acts 4:36-37. Barnabas was delighted by what he found. He encouraged and taught the Gentile converts, and then, led by the Holy Spirit, set out to find a man named Saul, who is known to history as Paul, the apostle to the Gentiles, the writer of the bulk of our New Testament.

Saul was probably then a man in his early 40s. He had been a Pharisee, one of that strict sect of Jews from which had come Christ's most vigorous enemies. A few years before, Saul had been a witness to Stephen's martyrdom. He had been filled with hatred for this heretical sect of "the Way" and had become one of the foremost persecutors in Judea. As the "heresy" spread, Saul had applied to the high priest for a commission to go to the Syrian city of Damascus and bring any followers of Jesus back to Jerusalem in chains.

On the road to Damascus, Paul had been thrown to the ground as a brilliant light flashed from heaven, and Jesus Himself spoke with him. Blinded, Saul stumbled into Damascus and waited in darkness, until the Lord sent a member of the church there to restore his sight.

Converted in this unique confrontation, Saul became an open and vigorous proponent of the faith he had earlier attacked. He'd been so bold that members of the

Jewish community in Damascus had finally determined to kill him. Escaping, Saul had returned to Jerusalem and sought out the brotherhood. But no one would associate with him. They were afraid that his "conversion" was a ruse to break into the Christian "underground."

Finally Barnabas had taken the risk. Convinced of Saul's sincerity, Barnabas had brought him to the apostles.

Saul had begun to boldly and publicly proclaim his new faith in Jerusalem. Again the Jews determined to kill him. Finally Saul was forced to flee from Jerusalem, and was returned by the brothers to Tarsus. Then, for a time, the Judean church knew a relaxation of persecution.

Then Barnabas went to Tarsus to look for Saul. They returned together to Antioch, and the two became part of a leadership team that ministered to the believers there. Later, when the Holy Spirit warned of a famine coming in Judea, Barnabas and Saul were selected to take the funds collected by this Gentile church to their Jewish brethren.

♥ *Group Activity: Support Group*
You are about to welcome a new member to your group: Barnabas. His name means "son of encouragement," and you've heard of him. To make sure each person knows what he is like, divide into teams of five and study N.T. passages describing him: Acts 4:36-37; 9:27; 11:22-30; 12:25; 13:1-50; 14:1-23; 15:2-12, 35-39; 1 Corinthians 9:6; Galatians 2:1, 9, 13; Colossians 4:20.

From these passages determine: (1) What three words best describe Barnabas' personality? (2) What were Barnabas' values? (3) What impact did Barnabas have on the history of the church, and what about him enabled him to have that impact? (4) What qualities of Barnabas would you most like to see in your own life, and why?

Together discuss, what contributions would Barnabas make to our group if he really were here? And, how can we be more like Barnabas in our relationships with each other?

Sometime this week drop a note to the person in your group who you feel is most like Barnabas, and thank him or her for his or her contributions to your life.

In the meantime, persecution had again intensified in Palestine. This time it came from an official source (Acts 12). James, one of the Twelve, was executed by King Herod Agrippa, who ruled as a puppet and vassal of Rome. This so pleased the Jewish community that Herod had Peter arrested as well, intending to execute him at the conclusion of the Passover feast. Peter was miraculously released by an angel and went into hiding. Herod himself now bore the brunt of God's judgment; he was suddenly stricken with an extremely painful disease and died.

Persecution slacked again. Barnabas, with Saul and a young man named John Mark (who later would write the Gospel of Mark), returned to Antioch.

The First Gentile Mission: Acts 13–14

Earlier, witness to the Gentiles had been an unplanned overflow of witness by the Hebrew Christians to other Jews. Now, for the first time, God spoke to the Gentile church of Antioch, commanding that two men be set aside for a specific mission to Gentiles (compare 13:2 and 9:15). As the Holy Spirit directed, Barnabas and Saul (soon to be called Paul in the Acts text) were ordained for the mission.

Acts 13:4-12. At the first stop on the journey Barnabas and Paul began their mission by preaching in the synagogue to the Jews. Soon they were sharing the Gospel not only with the Gentiles but with the Roman proconsul (governor). Here Paul, like Peter, had a confrontation with a magician, an apostate Jew named Bar-Jesus ("son of deliverance"). The evil sorcerer was stricken with blindness; the Roman leader believed.

Acts 13:13-52. Traveling on, the missionary team went to the city of Antioch in the province of Pisidia. Again, as Paul always did, he went first to the Jews and proclaimed Christ Jesus in the synagogue. This pattern in missionary work remained consistent throughout Paul's life. He continued to have a great love for his own people. He was convinced that they, the people through whom the Saviour had been given to the world, must have the first opportunity to hear the Gospel. This approach also had other benefits. In every synagogue there was a reserved place for "God-fearers." These were Gentiles who had been drawn to the high moral precepts and the

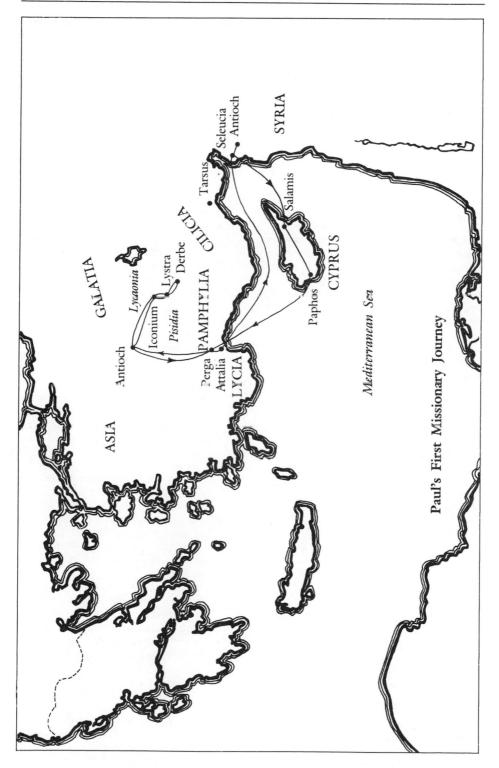

Paul's First Missionary Journey

275

exalted concept of a single, sovereign, Creator God, which then characterized Judaism alone of all the current religions.

In Pisidian Antioch, many Jews and many of the devout Gentiles responded to the Gospel. As the sermon recorded in verses 16-41 shows, Paul's message was the very same apostolic Gospel that had been preached by Peter some 12 or 15 years earlier.

The response was explosive. The next Sabbath "almost the whole city" (v. 44) gathered to hear what the apostles had to say. Many of the Gentiles believed. The Jews stirred up the leaders of the city and drove the missionary team away.

Acts 14:1-7. Traveling to Iconium, the team launched a new mission, and the now-familiar pattern was repeated. Beginning to preach at the synagogue, they soon gathered a crowd of converts from both Jewish and Gentile populations. The unbelieving Jews reacted angrily and stirred up a Jewish and Gentile reaction. The population of the city was divided. Finally the unbelieving majority physically attacked and drove out the missionaries.

EVENTS OF PAUL'S LIFE

A.D. 34	Conversion
A.D. 36	To Tarsus for "the silent years"
A.D. 46	To Antioch
A.D. 47–48	First missionary journey
A.D. 48	Jerusalem Council (Acts 15)
A.D. 49	Writes first epistle (Galatians)
A.D. 50–51	Second missionary journey
A.D. 53	Third missionary journey begins
A.D. 59	Journey to Rome
A.D. 64	Martyrdom

Acts 14:8-28. At Lystra, a city with no significant Jewish population, the mission began in a very different way. The healing of a cripple was observed by crowds, and Paul and Barnabas were mistaken for gods come down to earth. By the time the missionaries grasped what was happening, the local priests were about to offer up an animal sacrifice to them!

Distraught, the missionaries rushed to explain that they were merely men. But they *were* bearers of good news from the God who made all things, and whose many gifts testified to His goodness. The people of the city listened.

At Lystra, another contingent of Jews from Antioch and Iconium arrived. These men had determined to follow the missionaries and try to undo their preaching. And they succeeded in arousing the city against Paul. He was attacked with cobblestones, dragged out of the city, and left for dead.

But the "dead" Paul got up, and returned to the city. The next day the missionary team began to retrace its steps, visiting again those groups of believers which had been formed in every place they had preached.

Several patterns established on this first missionary journey to Gentile lands continued to mark the evangelism of Paul and of other Christians throughout the days of the early church.

- They visited cities and lands where the Gospel had not been preached.
- They began their mission in the synagogues, first contacting the Jewish community and the Gentiles who had been drawn to Israel's God.
- The message was soon shared with the entire city, and the response was more positive from Gentiles than from Jews.
- Initial success led to persecution and opposition.
- After establishing a new group of believers by usually spending weeks or months with them to teach them, the missionary team moved on.
- Later the team returned. Those who had grown spiritually and had been marked off by the Holy Spirit were recognized and ordained as local leaders by the apostles.
- The missionary team, particularly Paul, remained in contact with the new churches. He sent letters of instruction and encouragement, and often sent representatives like Timothy and Titus to guide the new church for a time.
- Each church was, however, to depend on the leading of the Holy Spirit. As the independent congregation matured, that group of believers reached out to the nearby cities and towns to share the message of Jesus in their own local "Jerusalem and Judea" (1:8).

The explosive, multiplying dynamic of the church of Jesus Christ, infused with His Spirit and committed to live life's great adventure by focusing on its Lord, had begun the process by which the Roman world would be reached in a single generation.

∅ *Group Activity:*
Missions/Outreach Group
Study the strategy that the Apostle Paul used in his early evangelistic efforts (p. 276, col. 2). Examine Acts 13 and 14 to see each element of the strategy in action.

You might base a series of meetings on these principles. (1) You might look at the work of class missonaries, like Hudson Taylor and see if— and how—these principles infused their work. (2) You might write to active mission boards today inviting them to compare their strategy with Paul's, or to send speakers to discuss modern missions strategy. (3) You may want to plan and carry out an outreach campaign in your own community, trying to utilize the principles of Paul.

Acts 15

The missionary team returned to Antioch filled with joy, eager to report what God had done among the Gentiles (14:24-28).

But soon another kind of team appeared. These were men from Judea, who had been thinking seriously about the relationship between the Jewish church and the growing number of Gentile congregations. Their solution was to go back to a principle which had operated in Old Testament times. If a person who was not born a Jew wished to become a worshiper of God, he must first convert to Judaism. Identification with the people of the covenant was the only way to enter fully into relationship with the God of the covenant.

And so these Jewish believers traveled to the Gentile churches, teaching that "unless you are circumcised according to the custom [Law] taught by Moses, you cannot be saved" (15:1). To really be a Christian, they thought one had to first become a Jew, or at least surrender one's own culture and identity, and adopt the lifestyle of an Israelite.

This teaching stimulated a serious debate, particularly when it became clear that these teachers had not been sent by the apostles, and did not represent the official position of the Jerusalem congregation.

A delegation was sent from Antioch, led by Paul and Barnabas, to bring this issue to the apostles at Jerusalem. There, in about A.D. 48, the first council of the church was held.

Paul and Barnabas reported on the great moving of God among the Gentiles. Then they heard the demand made by some believers who were also Pharisees (the most strict of Judaism's sects when it came to stressing man's obligation to keep both the written Law of Moses and the oral traditions): "The Gentiles must be circumcised and required to obey the Law of Moses" (v. 5).

The Law. In studies of Romans and Galatians we'll discuss the Law in depth. For now, it's important to realize that the term "Law" is used in a number of ways, both in and out of Scripture.

At times "law" (*nomos* in Greek) is rendered "custom." At other times our word "principle" is more fitting. But even when *the Law of Moses* is specified, there may be different things on the writer's mind. At times *the Law* may be a way of referring to revelation itself, meaning God's total revelation of Himself and His will in Scripture. Finally, *the Law* spoke of the lifestyle of Israel, regulated as it was by biblical commands and traditions, which patterned the way the Jew spoke and thought and acted. The Pharisees surely believed that *the Law* indicated that distinctive way of life which set the Jews apart from all foreigners, and had for centuries marked them off as God's peculiar people.

In Acts it seems clear that the challengers were asking for more than moral and ethical purity from the Gentile converts. "It is necessary," they insisted, "to circumcise them, and to charge them to keep the Law of Moses." Circumcision was the sign of entry into covenant relationship with God; the visible mark of being a Jew. The Pharisees were demanding that Gentile converts reject their own culture and heritage, and adopt both the name and lifestyle of the Jew to be accepted as true Christians!

Acts 15 reports the struggle of the leaders with this issue, and the exciting outcome. The Law, Peter declared, was a burden no one had ever been able to bear successfully (v. 10). Since salvation is by the grace of God for Jew and Gentile alike,

277

why burden the Gentile believers with the Jewish Law?

After further discussion, James summed up the council's conclusions. God clearly had acted to save the Gentiles, *as Gentiles!* In fact, the Old Testament prophets foretold a time when such a thing would happen, and even Gentiles would be called by God's name (v. 17). The Hebrew church then had to let the Gentiles keep on being Gentiles. They had to accept these Gentile brothers and sisters *as they were!*

There were, however, four specific warnings which related to aspects of the Gentile lifestyle which James felt should be brought to their attention. These warnings seem rooted in prohibitions which were stated by God before Law was given (see Gen. 9). The Christian converts were to have nothing to do with the idol worship which characterized their culture. They were to keep away from illicit sex (again, a common feature of the Gentile lifestyle). They were to give up unbutchered meat (something tremendously offensive to the Jew, which could have made it very hard for a Jew to have fellowship with a Gentile brother) (cf. Lev. 17:10-14; Deut. 12:16, 23-25), and they were to abstain from shedding blood (this probably means cruelty, murder, and even possibly service in the army). Later

many Christians did take it this way: many in the early church refused to do military service, and were executed. Others did serve in the Roman army, but were persecuted for their refusal to enter into the official religious practices expected of soldiers.

The delegation returned joyfully to Antioch. The Jerusalem church had officially welcomed the Gentiles into the fellowship of the church. It had affirmed the fact that every culture has equal standing before God. From Jew and Gentile, God was about to form one new man. In Christ, the differences could be accepted and forgotten. Jesus, not our differences from one another, is to always be the focus of our shared life.

The problem would, of course, surface again and again. Paul, the leader of the Antioch delegation, would himself be the one to spell out in letters to the Galatians and the Romans just what the Law does mean to a Christian. But those days were still ahead.

For now, another great stride had been made. And the church knew a special sense of joy and peace.

■ For a discussion of Paul's split with Barnabas, see the *Bible Knowledge Commentary,* pages 396-398.

GROUP RESOURCE GUIDE

Identification: *Share with others*
"Sharing" isn't always a warm fuzzy kind of thing. Sometimes it involves conflict, when what we share is a deeply held conviction that clashes with the convictions of others. To experience this, draw one of four previously printed roles, which you play for the first 20 to 30 minutes of your group meeting. Have previously prepared two "leader" roles, 60% "Jewish" roles, 20% "Gentile" roles, and 20% "neutral" roles. You will then meet together to decide what the Gentile Christians will have to do to be accepted as equals by the Jewish Christian majority.

Leader Role
You are responsible for helping the group discern God's will. You know that God

wants a unified church, not one made up of "first-class" and "second-class" members.

Jewish Role
God has chosen your people and given Israel special promises. He has also given Israel a Law through Moses that defines righteous living. It is obvious to you that if any Gentile is to have a relationship with God, the same standards apply to him as to you. You accept the fact that Jesus died to save Gentiles as well as Jews. But you cannot accept the heretical notion that believing Gentiles can just go on in their old ways without adopting the way of life which God Himself gave your people. Clearly, unity in the church is possible only if Gentiles live like messianic Jews.

Gentiles
You have been saved through faith in Christ, and are members of a vital Gentile congregation. You have turned your back on paganism and immorality and are excited about your new life in Christ of prayer, commitment, and evangelism. You have nothing against Jews, but their customs and notions are strange to you. You do not intend to abandon your own culture to become a Jew, and all your experience as a Christian makes you sure God does not intend that you should. You're troubled by the Jewish insistence that you change, but at the same time you resent it.

Neutrals
You're a happy Christian, enjoying your life in Christ. You don't see why all the fuss over whether or not Gentile Christians must keep the Law of Moses. Why doesn't everyone just worship the Lord, and let other folks alone?

When roles are assigned, let the leader(s) call the conference together, ask each side to present its case, and then lead a discus-

sion of the differences.

After 20 to 30 minutes, stop the process and talk about what has happened. How did members of each faction feel? Were they trying to find God's will or to "win"? How did this kind of sharing make them view the other side?

Exploration: *Probe God's Word*
Together read Acts 15, which describes the Council at which the early church dealt with this very issue. What were the keys that led to the full acceptance of Gentiles as Gentiles?

Reaction: *Respond together to the Word*
Discuss: What have we learned about how to share with others when that sharing involves serious differences in conviction? How can we apply what we have learned to our group, as well as to other relationships?

Adoration: *Worship and pray*
Praise God for a unity in Christ which permits us to love and accept each other despite differences.

THE GENTILE CHURCH

Overview

This portion of Acts contains the report of Paul's second missionary journey (see map), and a portion of the report of his third. During these years of journeying we find Paul moving from the provinces into the very cultural and trade centers of the Roman Empire.

A congregation founded in a central location, like Thessalonica, could become the hub from which the Gospel was spread throughout its area of influence. And this is, of course, exactly what happened. As Paul wrote in a later letter to the Thessalonicans, "The Lord's message rang out from you not only in Macedonia and Achaia—your faith in Christ has become known everywhere" (1 Thes. 1:8).

This was the true secret of the early spread of the Gospel: it did not rest on the shoulders of key men like Paul alone. Enthusiastic evangelism was a ministry shared by all.

But what made the first-century world so receptive to the Gospel message? In this study guide we look not only at the events reported in Acts 16 through 19, but also sketch the religious and moral climate of the first century. That world, like our own in so many ways, was ready to hear the Gospel message when it was appropriately shared. And it was ready to respond.

■ The Victor *Bible Knowledge Commentary,* pages 398-412, gives helpful information on the cities and people mentioned in these chapters.

Commentary

The world into which the church now advanced was very different from the provincial land of Palestine. Centuries earlier the conqueror, Alexander the Great, had begun a process which spread Greek culture and language across the Middle East. Asia Mi-

nor, Egypt, the Greek Isles, and the ancient Empire of Persia all fell to the conqueror and, after his early death, to the four generals who divided Alexander's spoils.

The spread of the Greek language and culture unified and linked the world of the New Testament. The vision of "one world" and of a "united nations" is no modern invention. It was Alexander's dream, hundreds of years before Christ. By the days of the early church, this dream had been realized to the extent that missionaries like Barnabas and Paul did not have the language barrier that missionaries face today. They could communicate everywhere they went in Greek, the second language of elite and commoner alike.

Greece conquered the world culturally. But it had taken the expansionist and brutal power of Rome to weld the world together politically. Under the first emperor, Augustus, the *Pax Romana* (Roman peace) had been imposed by force of arms. The empire which Rome held included not only Egypt and the Middle East, but extended even to the British Isles, encompassing France, Spain, and what is now West Germany (see Map of Roman Empire, p. 760). Roman government and Roman law brought an unprecedented stability to the world through which the missionaries traveled. There was no trouble with passports, no detours to avoid wars between bickering states. During the first years of Christianity's expansion, the new religion was considered a sect of Judaism by the government. As such the Christian faith was a "licit religion," with its freedom of practice guaranteed by the Romans!

The Roman world was far less unified religiously. The official religion of the empire was the cult of emperor worship. The classic religion of the period of the Roman republic (with its worship of a pantheon of interchangeable Greek and Roman gods and goddesses headed by Zeus [Jupiter]) now received only perfunctory attention. But existing alongside the official and the classic religions were a number of secret cults, generally referred to as "mystery religions." These originated in the East and became more and more popular, as the aberrations of succeeding emperors eroded confidence in the official faith. The austere and distant gods of Greece and Rome offered no personal relationship, and provided no personal religious experience. To fill this need, cults like the Eleusinian, the Dionyisian, the cult of the Great Mother (Cybele), and that of the Egyptian Isis and Osiris, spread through the empire.

These mystery religions featured initiation rituals, rites, and myths. The cults had little or no ethical content. Most stressed fertility in a female deity and had both sexual and social appeal. In the sense of belonging that came through initiation into the cult, and in the promise of a special relationship with a mythical deity, many looked for a meaning that life in the Roman Empire, for all its stability, did not provide.

The world, empty of promise or hope, was ready for the coming of the Saviour. And this world over which Rome ruled was uniquely shaped to permit the explosive spread of the one faith which actually does meet the deepest needs of man. A faith which rests not on myth, but on the historical fact of God's entrance into the world in the person of His own Son, Jesus Christ.

The Core
It is clear from our reading of Acts 16–19 that the Apostle Paul was sensitive to first-century culture. But it should also be clear that Paul was careful never to compromise the core issues of the Christian faith.

The distinction is often lost. It's so easy to take a practice sanctified by tradition and mistake it for a core issue.

For instance, for many years in the United States, Sunday evening was dedicated to evangelistic church services. Non-Christians could be brought to church, and an evangelistic message, with an invitation, became the expected thing. As American society changed and new recreational and entertainment patterns developed, Sunday evening no longer was a time when the unchurched slipped into the pew. Even the

annual "revival meetings" were now attended primarily by believers. Yet, the approach to evangelism continued to be the Sunday evening or special revival service. A "Gospel message" was expected, even though the Gospel might be familiar to everyone present.

How different this picture is from Acts. There, Paul took the Gospel to people where they were, and he adapted the form of presentation to his listeners. We see Paul searching out a riverside place of worship, and sitting down to talk the Gospel over with Lydia and her friends. We see Paul moving into the synagogue and there debating in the classic way from the Old Testament Scriptures. When Paul stood before the philosophers in Athens, his presentation took the form of philosophic argument, using even pagan religious poetry and an Athenian altar to "An Unknown God" as points of contact. His presentation there never once referred to Scripture! And, in Ephesus we see Paul in the lecture hall of Tyrannus, holding "discussions daily" (Acts 19:9) like other itinerant teachers of his day.

As Paul moved to different settings and different cultures, he *adapted*. He easily shifted the location, and even the form of the Gospel presentation, to fit patterns his listeners were most likely to recognize and to understand.

Perhaps we too need to develop the cultural sensitivity of the early missionaries. Perhaps if we were more sensitive to our culture, and less rigid in our terminology, we too might be more effective in our modern evangelism.

Form and Content
It's important to realize that, while Paul clearly adapted the form of his Gospel presentation to fit the listener and the culture, Paul did *not* compromise the core itself. D.R. Jackson, in the *Zondervan Pictorial Encyclopedia* (5:725), noted that Paul spoke "in the way most appropriate to his hearers' circumstances and cultural background," but that certain basic themes are consistently present. The themes that Jackson suggests are: "(1) Christ's death, (2) Christ's resurrection, (3) witness testimony, (4) Scripture testimony, (5) power, and (6) forgiveness." Wherever the Gospel message was preached, to Jews or others who had the

background of the Old Testament, these elements were emphasized. But in the Acts 17 report of Paul's speech to the philosophers of Athens, the proclamation went further.

Paul began in Athens by affirming the existence of a "God who made the world and everything in it" (v. 24). This God is Himself the sole source of the material universe and animate life. The God who made the world has design and purpose woven into His Creation. History's ages are moving toward a divinely determined end; an end in which God "will judge the world with justice" (v. 31). The proof of God's reality and His concern for mankind lies in the fact that God Himself entered space and time in form, undergoing death and then experiencing a bodily Resurrection from the dead (see v. 31).

Here we have a true confrontation with the first-century world. Paul might have adapted the cultural forms for those to whom he spoke, but there was no compromise of the Gospel message. And that message went against the grain of the most basic beliefs and values of Paul's listeners, just as biblical Christianity contradicts the beliefs and values of modern man today!

A weary world view. Acts 17 mentions the two prevalent schools of philosophy in the time of the early church: Epicureanism and Stoicism. While differing from each other, both philosophies had the same practical purpose: each sought peace of mind. Stoics saw man as a rational being, felt that the world had a moral order, and emphasized a kind of universal law that pantheistically pervaded the universe. Epicureans saw man as a feeling being, emphasized the supremacy of the individual, and affirmed that the universe was but a random combination of atoms, mechanistically determined. They maintained that seeking pleasurable experience was the best way of life.

Neither philosophy had any place for a divine Creation. One viewed matter as eternal, while the other regarded matter as pervaded by, and essentially equivalent to, the Divine. Without a personal, supreme God who created for His own purposes, the universe had no known origin, and history had no direction or goal. An individual's relationship to either the universe or God (such a god as there was) had no meaning beyond its own existence; no purpose for

life could be found outside the brief span of years allotted to an individual.

To someone seeking the meaning of human existence these ancient philosophies could only say, "Exist!" (Eat, drink, and be merry) or "Endure."

It is true that very few first-century men and women were philosophers, just as relatively few people of our own day consciously struggle with basic questions. But the emptiness of the then-current philosophies was reflected in the attitudes and ideas of the general population.

Even the old faith had no adequate explanations. The pantheons of ancient gods and goddesses were simply immortal men and women, freed to indulge in the sins and pettiness their worshipers yearned for themselves. These gods and goddesses had no real concern for humans. Oh, they might choose to favor a special hero, such as Achilles or Hercules, for a time. But they would capriciously turn away from him on a whim at any moment, or they might make him a pawn in a battle with some rival. What's more, the gods themselves were not all-powerful! Like men they were helpless before an impersonal fate. The average individual in the first century saw himself as caught under the crushing weight of chance, helpless to affect the course of his own life, and without any hope of establishing a relationship with a trustworthy supernatural power. Such people had only superstitious ritual or magic practices with which to ward off evil.

Even those mystery religions, which attracted many in the first century, offered at best some revival of life in the underworld, or the prospect of an escape from punishment, or escape from continued imprisonment in a succession of bodies (reincarnation). The concept of a conscious, bodily resurrection was unthinkable.

The view of reality in the ancient world was characterized then by these elements:

- an impersonal universe,
- an impersonal fate,
- an essential purposelessness,
- no hope for relationship with a faithful deity.

Within the framework of this common belief, man lived out his life. The lifestyle of the age had gradually lost the optimism of early Greek culture (ca. 400 B.C.) and was now burdened down with:

- pluralism (with many competing philosophies of life advanced),
- relativism (with each individual choosing his or her own thing, accepting the notion that what might be "right for me" may not be "right for you"),
- superstition (with a variety of straws grasped at in the hope of finding something to satisfy),
- syncretism (with religious and philosophical notions from many sources combined and recombined in an effort to find meaning).

Captured in a world they did not understand, men and women lived lives of quiet desperation or hopelessness. In the words of Paul, they existed "separate from Christ, excluded from citizenship in Israel and foreigners to the covenants of the promise, without hope and without God in the world" (Eph. 2:12). In the fullest meaning of the word, the first-century world was *lost,* wandering in meaningless illusion, never penetrating to the reality underlying the universe, and never knowing that a God exists who offers humanity a relationship through which we can recover both meaning and hope.

𝒫 **Group Activity:**
Missions/Outreach Group
According to the commentary, the Gospel met some of the deepest human needs unmet by the culture and values of the first century Roman Empire. With your group, take a four-step approach to analyzing how to best present the Gospel to our society.
   Step 1: Examine this list of features of contemporary Western culture, and determine what values are reflected in our society.
* *Massachusetts passes liberal abortion law.*
* *Laws require employers in health-care professions not to test employees for AIDS even though patients would be at risk.*
* *Persons are concerned about guilt feelings but not about guilt.*
* *A large denomination permits ordination of practicing homosexuals.*
* *Schools distribute contraceptives to teens; sex ed classes give detailed instructions in positions for intercourse.*
* *Suicide becomes third largest cause of death of teenagers.*

* *Homosexuals demand the government give live-in lovers the same benefits provided for married couples.*
* *The teaching of evolution as a scientific fact, with human beings merely an advanced animal, is mandated in many states.*
* *Capital punishment is decried as murder.*
* *Abortion is supported as a "woman's right to choose."*
* *Nudity and profanity increasingly characterize daytime and primetime network TV.*
* *Research shows "loneliness" is the most common complaint in U.S. society.*
* *Some 40% of U.S. children are brought up in homes in which one parent has been divorced or remarried.*

   Step 2: After determining values expressed in these traits of our society, develop a set of contrasting Christian values.

   Step 3: Evaluate the impact of each set of values on persons. Which set of values makes for a happier, more meaningful life? Which produces strength of character and valuing of self and others?

   Step 4: Discuss: How could we best present the Gospel so that it presents a clear, positive alternative to the unconverted in our own society?

No wonder it was a weary world that the early missionaries invaded! And no wonder that, when we look beyond the surface — past the material peace and prosperity and the often unbridled sensuality — we discover a world of men and women desperately ready for the Gospel's Good News.

And today? How like the first century our day is! With all its material prosperity, our age is marked with a sense of weariness and hopelessness. Disillusioned by the unfulfilled vision of scientific conquests, as well as by the patriot's dream, more and more people turn to ancient avenues in search of hope. For most today the universe is as impersonal as it seemed in the first century. With sophistication we explain origins by an evolution that supposedly took place by random chance, bringing life from lifeless matter. From this empty, impersonal origin we seem to move toward a meaningless

283

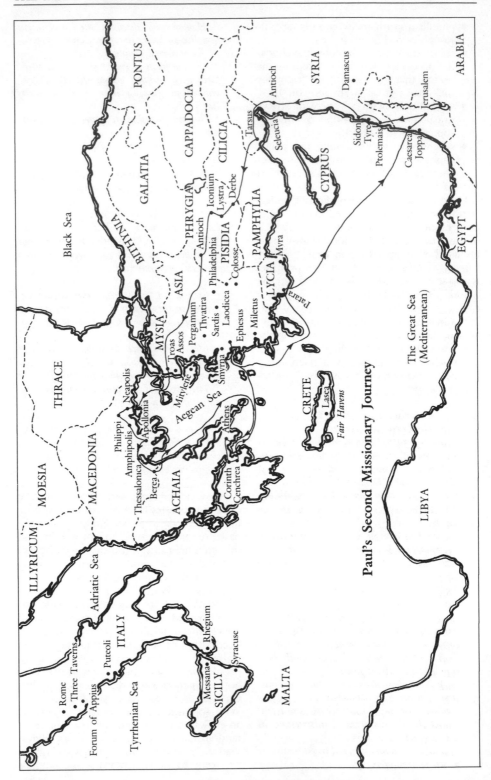

Paul's Second Missionary Journey

end. If that end doesn't come soon through a destructive atomic war, mindless depletion of earth's natural resources, overpopulation, or pollution of the environment, then the end will still come in some distant age when the universe itself runs down, the stars wink out, and an endless dark descends.

No wonder that within such an impersonal universe men and women increasingly turn to drugs, to hedonistic sensualism, to astrology or the occult, or to modern mystery faiths from the East, in a desperate search for meaning and for hope.

For perhaps the first time in centuries, the world view of modern man closely resembles the world view of New Testament times! The revolutionary truths so familiar to the Christian are truly revolutionary again. Returning again to the Gospel core, you and I are invited by a living Word to experience again the exciting days of the first century, when the church was vital, and the faith was young.

∅ *Group Activity:*
Missions/Outreach Group
It is important to contextualize the content *of the Gospel so it speaks directly to the real and sensed needs of people in a society. But it is also important to select* presentation strategies *that are effective. Evaluate the following methods of outreach for their "fit" to today's world:*
1. Pass out tracts on the street.
2. Hold revival meetings at church.
3. Put evangelistic sermons on TV.
4. Use TV spots to present Christ.
5. Hold a debate on a college campus.
6. Start a one hour radio call-in show.
7. Sponsor a Divorce Recovery Workshop in the community.
8. Hold Bible studies in homes.
9. Canvass your community, house-to-house.
10. Do a telephone poll on loneliness, offering a free book to those who answer your questions.
11. Plaster your car with "Jesus Saves" stickers.
12. Organize a mayor's prayer breakfast.
13. Sit in the local bar and try to strike up conversations with regulars.
14. Mail an evangelistic newsletter to everyone in your community.
Discuss each of these ideas, deciding
why they do or do not have promise in our society. Select the three best ideas—and see if you can come up with five to ten more strategies like them.
Select your very best idea(s) and plan to put them in operation!

Comments on the Text: Acts 16–19

Timothy (Acts 16:1-5). Immediately we are introduced to Timothy, a youth who typifies the first-century world. The son of a Jewish mother and a Greek father, Timothy reflected his century's melting-pot quality. Races and cultures united, retaining something of their heritage but also forming something democratic and new.

Conversion in Philippi (Acts 16:11-15). Luke, the author of Acts, who had joined the missionary company, identified Philippi as a "Roman colony and the leading city of that district of Macedonia" (v. 12). Originally Roman colonies were garrison settlements of Roman citizens in captured territories, often populated by army veterans and their families. They had such rights as autonomous government, freedom from taxation, and the legal privileges of those living in Italy. A crossroads for both sea and land trade routes, Philippi was an important center of business, government, communications, and culture. It was typical of the metropolitan centers that the missionaries chose for church-planting.

Lydia and the women with her were most likely Gentile proselytes (converts) to Judaism. While there was a state religion and mystery religions which featured myths and ritual, neither had any particular moral or ethical content. It was not surprising, in this complex religious climate, to find a group of women drawn to Judaism and gathering outside the city for worship. Nor was it surprising to see Paul sit down and informally share the Christian message.

Occultism (Acts 16:16-21). Inside the city we see another aspect of the religious climate of the Roman world. Paul and the others were followed by a slave girl who "had a spirit by which she predicted the future" (v. 16). As a fortune-teller, she earned a great deal of money for her owners—until Paul, in the name of Jesus, cast out the spirit.

Occultism was a feature of the first-century world just as it is a growing element in our own. Exorcism was well known (19:13-16); witchcraft and sorcery were practiced (vv. 17-20). Despite the many religions and philosophies, the average man sensed his hopelessness and knew uncertainty and fear. As Merrill Tenny pointed out, "The pagan world took for granted that men were under the influence of invisible forces of evil which continually sought their destruction. Only by obtaining ascendancy over these powers through magical arts could they retain their freedom" (*New Testament Times,* Eerdmans).

Roman citizens (Acts 16:35-40). Jailed in Philippi because of mob violence stimulated by the slave girl's owners, the missionaries were miraculously released. When the magistrates discovered that they had "publicly without a trial" (v. 37) beaten men who were Roman citizens, they quickly came to appease the missionary party. Such official misconduct might have cost them their positions, or even led to severe punishment! Roman justice, including the protection of the rights of the individual, was swift and fair. As today, federal justice superseded state and local systems.

Thessalonica (Acts 17:1-4) Moving on to Thessalonica, Paul went first to the Jewish synagogue there. In the first-century world there were probably some 4 million Jews, and less than 20 percent lived in Palestine. Most major cities had colonies of Jewish citizens engaged in trade, banking, or manufacturing. In these Jewish centers the Old Testament faith had been maintained, and some of the Gentile population was attracted to Judaism. These Gentiles often became "God-fearers," adherents to the moral and theological teachings of Judaism but not full converts to its restrictive lifestyle.

Such Jewish centers were normally the place where Paul began his mission.

Athens (Acts 17:16-21). In Athens, Paul was confronted with a city full of idols and with philosophers constantly speculating on the nature and meaning of life. Luke noted, "All the Athenians and the foreigners who lived there spent their time doing nothing but talking about and listening to the latest ideas" (v. 21). This rather graphic description may remind us of today's intelligentsia.

Paul gave the residents of Athens a unique exposition of the Gospel, starting from the assumptions and ideas of his listeners and then leading them to a confrontation with revealed truth. His sermon here, so different from Peter's sermons recorded earlier in Acts, "recognizes the philosophical cast of mind of his audience and presents his message under-

standably to them in terms of the three great questions of philosophy: 'Whence,' 'What,' and 'Whither'; or otherwise stated, 'the origin,' 'the nature,' and 'the end of all things' " (Carter and Earle, *The Acts of the Apostles,* Zondervan). In his exposition Paul quoted, not from Scripture but from Greek religious poetry!

Corinth (Acts 18:1-5). Moving on from Athens, Paul came to Corinth, a city that typifies another dimension of the first-century world. *Corinth* was a byword for licentiousness and moral corruption, so much so that "to Corinthianize" was a common phrase meaning "to carry on immorally."

Here Paul lived for some time, teaching in the synagogue until he was expelled, and then teaching in the home of a believer next door to the synagogue.

Priscilla, Aquila, and Apollos (Acts 18:18-28). Two of Paul's well-known converts were Priscilla and Aquila, a couple who are also mentioned in Romans 16:3; 1 Corinthians 16:19; and 2 Timothy 4:19. Aquila and Priscilla went with Paul to Ephesus where they met Apollos who spoke powerfully of the coming Messiah. Apollos had known only about the ministry of John the Baptist, and had not yet heard the full Gospel. Rather than speaking up publicly, the quiet Priscilla and Aquila invited him home, and explained the Gospel "more adequately." This sensitive and loving instruction quickly won the open Apollos, who went on to become a powerful witness and evangelist.

How important that we do not correct others in a way that embarrasses or alienates them! How much we need the spirit of Priscilla and Aquila in the modern church.

Ephesus (Acts 19). Moving on to Ephesus, Paul found himself in one of the world's great religious centers. This city's life was dominated by the temple and cult worship of Diana (or Artemis). Here Paul again taught, first in the Jewish synagogue, then, when expelled, in the lecture hall of Tyrannus, who apparently was one of the many teachers of rhetoric or philosophy found in first-century cities. Paul rented his facilities for use when the owner was not teaching.

Within two years, the Gospel message had such an impact on the city that the business of the silversmiths and other craftsmen, which was based on selling religious items to tourists and pilgrims, had fallen off significantly. The leader of the tradesmen warned his fellow craftsmen not only of a loss of trade but "also that the temple of the great goddess Artemis will be discredited, and the goddess herself, who is worshiped throughout the province of Asia and the world, will be robbed of her divine majesty" (v. 27).

Again a riot ensued, but this time it was squelched by the city officials, who insisted that the swelling Christian movement "neither robbed temples nor blasphemed our goddess" (v. 37). Christianity did confront the culture and faith of the first century, but the confrontation was on the deepest levels of human experience, and not marked by disrespectful actions or language.

The church in mission is neither rebellious nor destructively radical. The Christian revolution takes place within the hearts of men. Confrontations that invariably follow the Gospel message are the outgrowth of personal transformation. With the Gospel comes a rediscovery of reality, and a recovery of hope. And *these* are the key to building the kingdom of God.

GROUP RESOURCE GUIDE

Identification: *Share with others*
Think of a woman, not a parent or spouse, who has made an important contribution to your growth as a Christian. Jot down her name, and briefly describe in writing the contribution she made. Set this description aside for use later in the session.

Exploration: *Probe God's Word*
Two Christian women are prominent in these chapters. Divide into teams of three to study the following passages, and sense specifically what their contributions were. Look behind the text, and sense what is implied as well as what is stated specifically. What was this woman like? What strengths and gifts did she have? How did she use them in service to the Gospel? The women and verses are:
Lydia: Acts 16:11-15,
Priscilla: Acts 18:1-4; 18:18-28; Romans 16:3; 1 Corinthians 16:19; 2 Timothy 4:19

Reaction: *Respond together to the Word*
Share the insights developed by each study team. Discuss: How can we affirm the importance of women within the body of Christ? Ask the women in your group: Do you feel valued and affirmed? If not, what do we need to do to help you be a Lydia or a Priscilla among us?

Affirmation: *Express love and concern*
If the person you identified and whose ministry you described (as the group session began) is in the group, tell her that you named her and explain the impact she has had in your life.

Adoration: *Worship and pray*
Praise God for His grace in giving every person in the body of Christ a ministry to others, and for making each one important. Ask Him for a greater sensitivity to the contribution of the women He has placed among you, and thank Him for His ministry through the women in your group.

PAUL'S IMPRISONMENT

Overview

These last chapters of Acts tell a tale of high adventure. Paul concluded a third missionary journey, undertaken to encourage churches already founded (20:2). The journey ended in Jerusalem.

There Paul was attacked by an angry Jewish mob. He was rescued and then held in prison by a Roman governor, till Paul exercised his right as a Roman citizen to be judged in the Emperor's court! After a stormy journey Paul arrived in Rome, where he awaited trial for two years in his own rented residence.

The Book of Acts ends here. But tradition suggests that Paul was acquitted. He traveled to Spain on another missionary venture, but was arrested again. During his second imprisonment Paul wrote his second Letter to Timothy. This time his imprisonment was ended by execution, and the great apostle joined the Lord whom he had loved and served so well.

While these Acts chapters are filled with adventure, they also suggest many lessons that we Christians need to learn. This study guide focuses on lessons that will be especially relevant to you and your group.

■ The chart analyzing reports in Acts of speaking in tongues (p. 794) is taken from the *Bible Knowledge Commentary*, page 408. This chart is typical of the helpful data contained in this excellent verse-by-verse resource, which should be referred to for answers to questions on details not dealt with in this *Small Group Member's Commentary* survey.

Commentary

There is only a brief report of Paul's third missionary journey in Acts (19:1–21:16). It's clear that this trip of encouragement was also a farewell journey: Paul felt the Spirit's compulsion leading him to Jerusa-

lem, to terrible danger, and to a new phase of his ministry. Yet there is much we can learn from the brief report of that journey, and from the adventures of the apostle in the Holy Land and on his way to Rome.

The Power of the Gospel:
Acts 19:1–21:15

These chapters highlight elements in Paul's ministry which we have seen earlier in Acts, but which raise questions that deserve our attention.

Is there a modern role for miracles in evangelism? (Acts 19:1-22) Luke's report of Paul's arrival in Ephesus makes several references to the supernatural.

First (vv. 1-7) he tells of Paul's meeting with "some disciples" whom Paul asked about receiving the Holy Spirit. These men had not even heard of the Holy Spirit. As Paul probed further, he discovered that they knew only of John's ministry announcing the Messiah was at hand. It was "John's baptism" (as a sign of repentance) rather than Christian baptism (as a sign of faith in and union with Christ) that they had received. Paul shared the Gospel message, and the men immediately responded. The Holy Spirit "came on them, and they spoke in tongues and prophesied."

If we analyze this and other incidents reported in Acts we note that not every reference to filling by the Spirit and not every reference to conversion tells of speaking in tongues. In the three cases which do speak of it, this experience seems to have served as a special sign to Jews (see chart).

This does not prove or disprove any modern view about speaking in tongues. But it does suggest that while that experience was real, it had a special purpose in New Testament times and was not always associated with evangelistic ministry.

But Luke went on immediately to tell of "extraordinary miracles" that God did

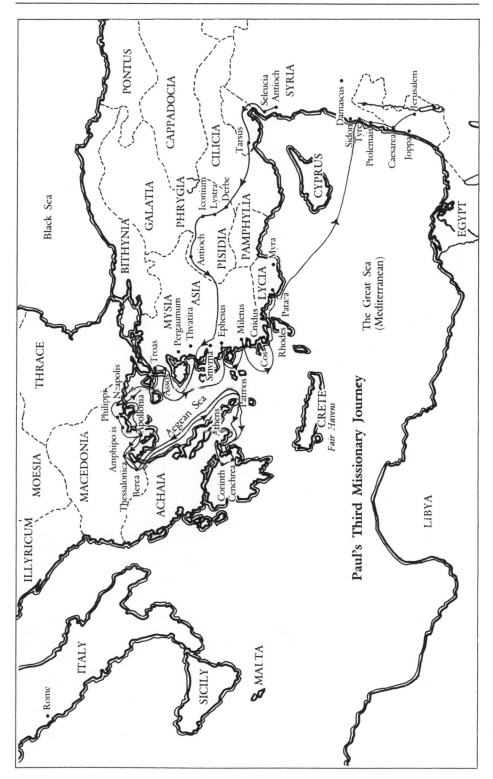

Paul's Third Missionary Journey

Speaking in Tongues in Acts

PASSAGE	TONGUES-SPEAKERS	AUDIENCE	RELATED TO SALVATION	PURPOSE
2:1-4	The 12 Apostles and others	Unsaved Jews	After salvation	To validate (for Jews) the fulfillment of Joel 2
10:44-47	Gentiles (Cornelius and his household)	Saved Jews (Peter and others) who doubted God's plan	The same time as salvation	To validate (for Jews) God's acceptance of Gentiles
19:1-7	About 12 Old Testament believers	Jews who needed confirmation of the message	The same time as salvation	To validate (for Jews) Paul's message

through Paul in Ephesus (vv. 8-22). Clearly in Ephesus miracles were associated with missions. But just as clearly this was "extraordinary" (v. 11) rather than the normal course of events. Acts mentions miracles in other missions settings (13:9-11; 14:3, 8-10; 16:18). Yet in other cities where the apostle spent varying amounts of time, such as Pisidian Antioch, Thessalonica, Berea, Athens, and Corinth, there is no mention of miracles. What conclusions are we to draw?

There are helpful hints here in Acts 19. The passage tells of seven sons of a Jewish priest who were apparently exorcists who tried to cast out an evil spirit using Jesus' name in a magical way. The demon-possessed man beat and stripped all seven! The demonic activity this suggests was very likely stimulated by the devotion of many in Ephesus to occult practices. Many who were now Christians had been involved in such evil, and those who had practiced sorcery publicly burned books of magic worth in our day some $2.5 million! *In a city where Satan had gained a foothold and the supernatural was a dominating theme, God's Spirit performed miracles that demonstrated Jesus' power over supernatural powers!* In cities like Athens, where the orientation was to the philosophical, there are no miracles reported, but Paul's presentation of the Gospel was tailored to the speculative bent of his listeners. This may provide us with our principle. The Gospel confronts human beings where they are. Where there is

demonism and sorcery, the Holy Spirit may act to demonstrate the lordship of Jesus. Where there is moral and mental darkness, the Spirit may act through the holy lives of God's people and the simple message of the Gospel to demonstrate that in Jesus there is a better way.

How are Christians to confront evils in society? (Acts 19:23-41) The temple of Artemis in Ephesus was one of the ancient world's wonders. It was the very center of the city's life, for the temple served not only as a worship center but as a bank, to which not only individuals but nations came for loans. The idol representing the goddess had been shaped from a meteorite (v. 35), and silver medals and miniatures sold there were critical to the area's economy.

When Paul brought the Gospel to this city and its surrounding area he did not attack Artemis directly. The city clerk testified that the Christians "neither robbed temples nor blasphemed our goddess" (v. 37).

What the missionaries did do was to confront the assumptions that lay at the root of idolatry. Paul presented no man-made god, but the God who made men. He told not of a lifeless lump of metal, but a living Person who came from heaven and who, resurrected after His death for our sins, returned there. The message and the power of the living Saviour themselves revealed the emptiness of idolatry. The result of the positive presentation of Christian truth was to discredit the false!

What an exciting concept. We *do* need to confront evils. But not by railing against them so much as by positive affirmation of Christian truth.

Was Paul right to go to Jerusalem? (Acts 20:13–21:15) Some have argued that Paul ignored divine warnings and went to Jerusalem against the Lord's will. It's clear that Paul was deeply aware of the danger he faced. Paul told the Ephesians he did not know what would happen, but that "in every city the Holy Spirit warns me that prison and hardships are facing me" (20:23).

These two chapters tell of several warnings Paul received. But the theory that Paul's insistence on going to Jerusalem in spite of them was disobedience cannot be sustained. Paul said his journey was "compelled by the Spirit" (v. 22). The warnings simply prepared Paul for what would happen, and strengthened his resolve. As Paul affirmed, "I am ready not only to be bound, but also to die in Jerusalem for the name of the Lord Jesus" (21:13).

The evidence of God's leading in our lives is *not* that everything we do turns out well. At times God leads us into hardship, just as He led Paul. What we need is Paul's resolve to do God's will, whatever that will involves, and the faith to believe with Paul that God's will is ultimately good.

♥ *Group Activity: Support Group*
Tell about a time when you had a very difficult decision to make. Who did you ask for advice? Who volunteered advice without being asked? What role did the advice of others play in making that decision? Did the advice prove helpful, or did it make your decision more difficult?

Study Acts 20:1–21:16. Did Paul receive advice about his decision to go to Jerusalem? Why was Paul so adamant about making this trip? How would you evaluate the advice and reaction of others — helpful? positive? stressful?

Discuss this statement and its implications for any difficult decisions you must make, and any advice you are asked to offer: "We are to help others seek God's will for hard decisions, and always preserve their freedom to be personally responsible to God."

Paul, the Jew: Acts 21:17–23:22
It would be wrong for us to idealize the

Apostle Paul. He was a great man. And in most things he is a fine model for Christians. But Paul was human and had his faults. His unyielding nature was a strength when he confronted Peter in Antioch over Peter's refusal to eat with Christian Gentiles (see Gal. 2:11-16). Yet that unyielding nature was a weakness when he broke with Barnabas over his old friend and partner's desire to take John Mark on a second missionary journey (see Acts 15:36-41).

We can't sustain the charge of some that Paul went to Jerusalem against the expressed will of God (20:13–21:16). But a more significant question has been raised about Paul's conduct when he reached Jerusalem.

The charge. The charge some raise against Paul goes something like this. "Paul, you've always insisted that Christian faith has replaced Judaism. Yet when you came back to Jerusalem, you pretended to be a traditionalist. You took an Old Testament vow, and offered sacrifices at the temple, as though the old purification rites were still valid."

When Paul was later taken before the Sanhedrin (the Jewish religious and civil court), he claimed to be a Pharisee on trial because of his hope in the resurrection. While this might be partly true, it wasn't *really* truth, and Paul just said it to get the Pharisee and Sadducee parties in the Sanhedrin arguing.

It's true that Paul did speak out boldly about Jesus. But that was only when he had been accused of desecrating the temple. The problem is that Paul clearly compromised his convictions. He *knew* the Jewish ceremonies had no more meaning, but he went through them. He knew that his Christian faith was the real issue, but he tried to mislead the Sanhedrin. In Jerusalem at least, Paul was a *poor* example for Christians today, a man who compromised his convictions for convenience and safety.

𝄞 *Group Activity:*
Missions/Outreach Group
Study Acts 21:17-26. Paul has often been criticized for "compromise." The theory is that by allowing himself to be purified at the temple he went back on his commitment to demonstrate by every act that salvation and sanctification are by faith,

apart from works of the law. How might Paul respond to this charge?

How far are we to go in seeking to win a hearing with non-Christians? What acts that some view as "compromise" may not be compromise at all? What acts really would compromise the Gospel itself?

The defense. Those who speak in Paul's defense note that the apostle had learned how to fit into different cultures to best present the Gospel in ways that were most likely to win a hearing. Earlier, in a letter to the Corinthians, Paul wrote, "To the Jews I became like a Jew, to win the Jews. To those under the Law I became like one under the Law (though I myself am not under the Law), so as to win those under the Law. To those not having the Law I became like one not having the Law (though I am not free from God's Law but am under Christ's law), so as to win those not having the Law" (1 Cor. 9:20-21).

Because Judaism's practices *were* irrelevant to relationship with Jesus, Paul felt free to adopt them if this would help him relate to the Jews he yearned to win to Jesus! In the same way, because Gentile lifestyle was irrelevant to relationship with Jesus, Paul was free to adopt it if that would help him relate to the Gentiles he yearned to win to Jesus!

A major theme in apostolic preaching was always the resurrection of Jesus. Paul wisely raised this issue, not to mislead, but to gain an opportunity to appeal to those Pharisees in the group who might be moved to defend—and thus be open to hearing—his resurrection message.

In fact Paul is an excellent example for modern Christians. He shows us how to adapt to the people we seek to minister to. He teaches us not to confuse irrelevant cultural issues with the core of the Gospel. And, as these chapters also demonstrate, Paul did not hesitate to proclaim the Gospel boldly when the opportunity came (cf. Acts 21:37–22:22).

Paul, the Roman Citizen: Acts 23:23–26:32

The Roman Empire was a conglomerate of many peoples, bound together by the military power of Rome and a common second language, Greek. The Romans did not try to impose their own patterns of laws and cus-toms on subject peoples. Instead each national group continued to govern itself to a large extent, using its historic institutions and laws. Thus a Jew in Rome was governed by Jewish law.

In fact, Roman law was superior to and superseded the laws of subject peoples. But a noncitizen could not bring a suit in a Roman court: he had to go to his national court for justice. Yet a Roman citizen could bring suit in a Roman court against a native of another nation. In such a case, it's obvious who would be favored!

Roman citizens also had special privileges. A noncitizen could be tortured in a judicial examination: a Roman citizen could not even be beaten before being condemned. And a citizen could never be put to death in some of the more brutal modes adopted in the empire.

Paul had used his citizenship in earlier situations. He had been beaten (illegally) and imprisoned (illegally) in Philippi (Acts 16). When the local officials learned that Paul was a Roman citizen, they were forced to come in person to apologize and to respectfully usher the missionary party out of their city.

In Jerusalem Paul was about to be "flogged and questioned" after the riot his preaching stimulated (22:1-25). When Paul revealed his citizenship, the "commander himself was alarmed when he realized that he had put Paul, a Roman citizen, in chains" (v. 29).

This position not only led the Roman military commander in Jerusalem to protect Paul, but also gave him an excuse to send him (protected by a detachment of nearly 500 soldiers!) to the provincial seat of government, Caesarea (a port city built by Herod the Great and a center of Greek and Roman culture).

Paul was kept there for two years, and had many opportunities to witness to the Roman governor and other royal personages (Acts 24:24-27).

When a new governor, Festus, was appointed, the Jewish leaders pressured him, as a favor, to return Paul to Jerusalem. Paul knew that in Jerusalem the Jewish leaders would find a way to take his life. And so he said, "I appeal to Caesar."

This was a legal expression, and the right of a Roman citizen. A citizen who appealed to Caesar was released from the jurisdiction of lower courts, and could take his case to

Rome itself, and to the Emperor's court.

Within days King Agrippa, a grandson of Herod the Great and ruler of northeast Palestine, came to pay his respects to the Roman governor. Festus, confused over the issues raised by the Jews and by Paul's talk of resurrection, told the king about Paul and arranged for Agrippa's contingent to hear the apostle. Paul spoke respectfully to him, for the king was a practicing Jew who believed the prophets and was well-acquainted with Jewish faith. Agrippa advised Festus that Paul could simply have been released: there was no substance to the charges against him. But since Paul had appealed to Caesar, he must be sent to Rome!

Through the whole ordeal Paul never hesitated to use his citizenship to advantage. It is not wrong for a believer, who is a citizen of both this world and heaven, to use the tools this world provides.

📖 *Group Activity: Bible Study Group*
Take private "yes/no" votes on the following questions.

1. I would not sue a person who defrauded me.
2. I would not run for political office.
3. I don't believe a Christian should hire a lawyer to make out a will or other document.
4. I refuse to pay taxes.
5. I would not call the fire department if my house was burning.
6. I would not apply for welfare or food stamps even if destitute.
7. I would not sign a petition to rid my neighborhood store of pornographic material.
8. I would not vote.
9. I would not write my congressman to lobby on a social issue.
10. I would not take part in a neighborhood watch against crime.
11. I would not call the police if robbed.
12. I would not defend myself if sued.
13. I would not attend a school board meeting to express my opinion on a sex education or science curriculum.
14. I would not let my children go to public school.
15. I would not pledge allegiance to the flag.
16. I would not join a military service.

When all have voted on each issue, poll the group. Discuss items on which you differed. Then together try to determine a "Christian policy" governing the believer's relationship with secular government.

After the policy has been agreed on, look at Paul's references to his Roman citizenship, in Acts 16:16-40; 18:28-41; 22:22-29; 25:1-12. From these passages, do you believe Paul acted in accord with your policy statement or not? If not, what modifications would you have to make for Paul to agree to it with you?

To Rome and Beyond: Acts 27–28

Paul traveled to Rome by ship. In New Testament times many took passage on ships to travel the Mediterranean. These ships were not passenger vessels, but were coastal freighters who took on passengers in addition to their normal load. Wrecks of ships like the one Paul probably sailed on have been located and studied by underwater archeologists.

The sailing vessels of that era were not particularly maneuverable, and generally ran before the winds. Against Paul's advice the Roman army officer escorting him to Rome set out to sea too late in the season. The boat was caught in a "wind of hurricane force" and tossed so violently for two weeks that, even with the cargo and ship's tackle heaved overboard, no one could eat and all were sure they would be lost.

The story of an angel's appearance to Paul promising him the lives of all aboard, and the subsequent shipwreck, has proven a favorite story for boys and girls as well as adults. How good to know that no matter how dark the future seems, God is able to deliver us.

In Rome Paul waited for his case to appear on the docket. He spent two years waiting, living in a rented house. But those days were not wasted. Paul met with Christian brothers, and spoke to the Jewish community's elders, some of whom believed, but many of whom rejected the Gospel message. Acts concludes with these words: "Boldly and without hindrance he preached the kingdom of God and taught about the Lord Jesus Christ." What an epitaph for the great apostle. Or for any one of Jesus' followers of any age.

Epilogue. Paul won release from this first imprisonment. During those two years he wrote four New Testament letters known as the "Prison Epistles," Ephesians, Philippians, Colossians, Philemon.

After his release Paul probably traveled to Spain to continue his ministry of church-planting. Later he was arrested again, and this time the verdict of the court was death. But during that second imprisonment Paul wrote what are known as the pastoral epis-tles, which include 1 and 2 Timothy and Titus.

The churches Paul founded did flourish, and the Gospel message continued to ring out. And, through the ages his letters have guided Christians and churches of every time and place.

GROUP RESOURCE GUIDE

Identification: *Share with others*
If you had to describe the Apostle Paul in one word, what word would that be? Jot your word down, then list it with other words suggested by group members.

Exploration: *probe God's Word*
Divide into teams to check your impression of the Apostle Paul. Each team should take one set of chapters: 19–20; 21–22; 23–24; 25–26; 27–28.

Reading carefully, how does the Acts' description of the great apostle fit or call into question the words you listed at the beginning of the group session?

Reaction: *Respond together to the Word*
Come back and discuss your findings. If any impressions of Paul have changed, tell how and why. If any have been supported, tell how.

Affirmation: *Express love and concern*
Think of a single word that describes your first impression of a person in your group—an impression that has changed since you've gotten to know him or her. Go around the group, with each telling the person you thought of how the impression of him or her has changed.

Adoration: *Worship and pray*
Focus on the Lord. Praise Him for traits of His that you have come to understand and appreciate as you have grown to know Him better.

ROMANS

Overview

Romans, perhaps more than any other New Testament letter, is a theological treatise. The letter explains carefully the nature of the righteousness that God demands from—and gives to—human beings.

The "by faith" kind of righteousness that Paul explains in Romans is distinctly different from the righteousness the Jews thought they would find in keeping the Law of Moses. In fact, Paul argued that one must not confuse righteousness and Law. The Christian is "not under Law, but under grace" (Rom. 6:14). Yet the Christian under grace is not free from righteousness: he or she is freed for the first time to truly *be* righteous!

The teachings of this New Testament letter are foundational to our understanding of our Christian faith. And truths revealed here are foundational to our experience of a victorious Christian life.

In this study guide we gain an overview of the Book of Romans, sum up the teachings of its major sections, and examine two concepts which must be understood to grasp Paul's teaching: the concept of righteousness, and the concept of Law.

It is well to remember that the conversion of Martin Luther, the great Lutheran reformer, and of John Wesley, who brought revival to Great Britain, came through study of passages in this great book. God still touches hearts and changes lives as He makes these truths real to men and women today.

Commentary

"But that means you can do anything you want to and still go to heaven!"

I heard that objection often from my Navy buddies. Faith alone the way to salvation? No careful keeping of the divine Law as an additional requirement? Then, what is to keep a person from going out and sin-

ning as much as he pleases? Doesn't God care about righteousness anymore?

This is how my witness to Christ as a young Christian affected some of my friends, and how Paul's teaching affected many in New Testament times. How could faith be enough? There must be Law too. Or else God doesn't care anymore about righteousness. To most people now as then, Law and righteousness seem inseparably linked.

Some years into his ministry the great apostle wrote a letter to the church at Rome. In his letter Paul answered the objections of the people of his day, and he answers the doubting of our time. Paul's answer is found in Romans' careful explanation of how the Gospel is related to righteousness—both to God's righteousness and to our own.

Rome

As early as the second century B.C., a Jewish colony existed in Rome. After 63 B.C., when Judea became a part of the Roman Empire, this colony grew. By 59 B.C. Cicero wrote of it as powerful and influential.

At times the Jews suffered expulsion from Rome, and as in an A.D. 19 financial scandal. Yet, within a few years the Jews would drift back again to this center of finance, trade, and political power. In A.D. 49 Claudius expelled the Jews from Rome in an act mentioned in Acts 18:2. Strikingly, the historian Suetonius said that the cause of Claudius' action was the "constant indulgence of the Jews in riots at the instigation of one Chrestus." Apparently the message of Christ divided the Jewish community at Rome and, as it did in the cities to which Paul journeyed on his missions, provoked bitter and violent controversy! Priscilla and Aquila, whom we meet later in this letter and who are mentioned in Acts 18, were apparently converted at this time.

They were already believers when Paul met them.

Claudius' expulsion edict, like the earlier ones, had no lasting effect. A few years later the Jewish colony again flourished and, as before, included Jewish believers in Christ. By the time Paul wrote this letter to the Romans, a large number of Gentile and Jewish Christians comprised a typical church.

Paul had longed to go to Rome, both to minister to the believers there and to be encouraged by them. But he was not able to go just then. So instead Paul sent a lengthy letter. In his letter we have our most careful, thorough, and detailed explanation of that Gospel which God called Paul to preach. In Galatians we catch glimpses of themes that Paul now fully develops. As we study Romans, we see that in Christ, God has truly taken a new and dynamic approach to the question of righteousness. The cage of the Law was designed to restrain *unrighteousness*. The freedom of the Gospel is *designed to produce in man the righteousness of God*. "In the Gospel a righteousness from God is revealed, a righteousness that is by faith from first to last" (Rom. 1:17).

This is God's gift to us too.

To live a truly righteous life. Not by the Law, but by faith.

Outline
Romans 1:17 is the verse that states the theme of Romans. Any adequate outline of the book must reflect the theme of righteousness.

As we trace through this outline, we discover that God has called us to lives of:

● Deliverance
● Victory
● Community

Romans in Brief
What will you and your group members find as you study Romans together? We can sum up the contribution of each major section of this towering New Testament book.

Deliverance (Rom. 1–5). Paul began by showing in his first three chapters that both Jew and Gentile desperately need righteousness, because each group stands guilty before God. The Jew had not lived by the Law God revealed, and the Gentile had not

Romans
Revealing Righteousness from God
I. Introduction (1:1-17)
  A. Salutation (1:7)
  B. Personal items (1:8-13)
  C. Theme (1:14-17)
II. Deliverance: Righteous Standing a Gift (1:18–5:21)
  A. Universal need of righteousness (1:18–3:21)
    1. Guilt of the Gentiles (1:18-32)
    2. Guilt of the Jews (2:1–3:8)
    3. Proof of universal guilt (3:9-20)
  B. Provision of righteousness (3:21-26)
  C. Harmonization: Justification and the Law (3:27-31)
  D. Illustration: Justification in the Old Testament (4:1-25)
    1. Abraham, David, and justification (4:1-8)
    2. Circumcision and justification (4:9-12)
    3. Inheritance and justification (4:13-17)
    4. Faith and justification (4:18-25)
  E. Exaltation: The certainty of justification (5:1-11)
  F. Summation: The universality of justification (5:12-21)
III. Victory: Righteous Living a Possibility (6–8)
  A. The basis for victory: Union with Christ (6:1-14)
  B. The principle: Enslaved to righteousness (6:15-23)
  C. The relationship: Freed from the Law (7:1-25)
    1. Law and the believer (7:1-6)
    2. Law and sin (7:7-12)
    3. Indwelling sin and the believer (7:13-25)
  D. The power: The Spirit within (8:1-17)
  E. The end: Glorification (8:18-39)
IV. History: Righteous Dealings a Certainty (9–11)
  A. Israel's present rejection is just (9:1-33)
  B. Israel's present rejection explained (10:1-21)
  C. Rejection not complete (11:1-36)
    1. It is not total (11:1-10)
    2. It is not final (11:11-36)
V. Community: A Righteous Reality (12–16)
  A. Christ's impact (12–13)
    1. In the community (12:1-21)
    2. In society (13:1-14)
  B. Christ's attitude incarnated (14:1–15:13)
    1. Uncondemning (14:1-13)
    2. Self-sacrificing (14:13–15:4)
    3. Purposive (15:5-13)
  C. Paul's farewells (15:14–16:27)

lived by the moral sense, experienced as conscience, which God has implanted in all human beings.

But God had acted in Christ to provide righteous standing before God to those who believe in Jesus. The death of Christ was a sacrifice of propitiation, on the basis of which God freely forgives sins past and future. That death is a demonstration not of our righteousness but of God's. The holy God must punish sin: the loving God was willing to take that punishment on Himself.

While the Jews object that this makes Law meaningless, Paul argued that the Gospel actually restores Law to its intended place. Law from the beginning was intended to serve as a mirror, to reveal sin. The Law was not a standard we must struggle to achieve, but a measure against which we might discover how far short we each fall.

As for faith, the Old Testament itself introduced the principle of a justification that comes by faith. Abraham and David are examples of men who were called righteous by God not on the basis of their good deeds, but because they trusted in His Word.

Paul can only conclude that we who have come to God by faith have sure and certain peace with God. We have been saved by the death of Jesus for sinners: our safety is guaranteed by His resurrection.

Yes, sin came into the world by one man's sin—Adam's. Because of that original sin death cast its pall over the whole human race. But now God has acted in one Man—Jesus Christ. And Jesus has brought humanity the promise of righteousness and life.

Victory (Rom. 6–8). The first chapters of Romans deal with the question of righteous standing before God. How can God pronounce sinners "not guilty"? Only because those sinners have trusted in Jesus, who died as their substitute, taking their punishment on Himself.

But when God pronounced such people righteous in His sight, His decree was no legal fiction. Christians are, by faith, actually united to Jesus Christ. That union is real: we were in union with Jesus when He died, so our death was real and not simply imputed. We were in union with Jesus when He was raised. Thus, the power of God's Spirit, which raised Jesus from the dead, is also available to us in our mortality. The One who raised Jesus from the dead gives

new life to us as well. Because of this new life, and because the Spirit's power energizes us, we can actually begin to live righteous lives here and now!

But *how* are we to live righteous lives? As a new Christian Paul tried to do right by struggling to obey the Law of God. He found that despite his struggles, he kept on falling short. At last Paul abandoned his efforts, and instead appealed directly to God the Spirit for power and leading.

This was the key. It is the Spirit within, and not the Law without, that the Christian looks to and depends on. One who lives in this way experiences his union with Jesus, and discovers that the Spirit is creating within a righteousness that the Law required but was never able to produce.

As we will see in our study of Romans 7 and 8, learning to relate *directly* to God the Spirit rather than seeking to relate to God indirectly through Law is a vital key to victorious Christian living.

History reviewed (Rom. 9–11). One of the questions Paul's exposition raises is, "Has God been fair? Was God Himself 'righteous' in His treatment of Israel?" Paul argued that God is the only judge of what is fair, and showed that Israel's present rejection is both justified and temporary. God has not abandoned His covenant people, nor has He gone back on His Old Testament commitments.

Community (Rom. 12–16). In his first two major sections Paul showed that God has given individuals who believe in Jesus a righteous standing, and has also acted to bring their state into harmony with righteousness. In this final section Paul looked at the righteous community, at the church which has been formed of those who believe. It is not only the individual Christian who is to live a victorious, righteous life. We Christians are a family, called to live together in a righteous, loving community.

Paul first explores acceptance, which makes it possible for those whose convictions differ to continue to live in community. He then shows us how the uncondemning, self-sacrificing attitude that marked Jesus' own personal relationships helps us create a loving, holy community of those who have faith.

What an exciting book you and your group members are about to study! What wonderful truths. Study of the Book of Romans can bring us assurance of salvation, can show us how to live a righteous, Spirit-filled life, and can help us be contributing members of a local congregation. What a privilege to study and to teach this great New Testament book.

Key Concepts

In our brief review of the Book of Romans, we've already touched on two concepts that must be understood to grasp the nature of our New Testament faith. Let's look at each of them more closely, as background for our study of this Book.

Righteousness. The Old Testament introduces the theme of righteousness, teaching that God's acts are "always righteous" (Jer. 12:1), for all God does is in harmony with His character. God, as the Creator and the moral Judge of the universe, is Himself the one valid standard of what is right.

God's righteousness is expressed in the Old Testament in the "righteous decrees and body of laws" God set out for Israel through Moses (see Deut. 4:8). In terms of God's own actions, two things display His commitment to righteousness. God will "judge the world in righteousness" (Ps. 9:8) and He will also "deliver [the sinner] in [His] righteousness" (31:1). Both God's acts of judgment and of salvation display His righteousness.

The Gospels, however, portray Jesus' teaching that those who seek relationship with God must find a righteousness that goes beyond the Law-based righteousness that engaged the attention of the scribes and Pharisees of His day (Matt. 5:20). Their view of righteousness was summed up in "lawful" behavior: Jesus called for a righteousness in which the very heart of the individual mirrors the heart of God (see vv. 21-48).

This emphasis of Jesus called for a dramatic shift of focus. Righteousness is not to be measured by what a person does or does not do. Righteousness is to be measured simply by whether or not a person truly is, in his heart, like God!

In Romans Paul demonstrated that this kind of righteousness simply is not possible for human beings. Our hearts are corrupted by sin. We reflect, not God's character, but the twisted motives and desires of Adam after his fall.

It is Romans that most clearly expresses God's solution. God fulfilled His commitment to judge sin by taking our sins on Himself as Christ died on Calvary in our place. And then through union with Jesus and by the gift of the Spirit, God set about the process of remaking us from within. His concern is not just that we act righteously, but that we truly *be* righteous. And to be righteous is to literally be like Him in our innermost character.

Thus Paul wrote that we will surely be "conformed to the likeness of [God's] Son" (Rom. 8:29).

To understand righteousness as a biblical concept, we must see that righteousness is at heart nothing more or less than God's essential moral character. God expresses His righteousness in judging sin, and in saving the believing sinner. The Law is at best a definition of how a human being who *is* righteous will behave, and in fact is God's revelation to humanity of how far we each fall short of being like God.

We must also see that the righteousness to which we are called cannot be defined by Law, which measures only behavior. If we are to be truly righteous, our character must be fully in harmony with God's own. And this is exactly why Jesus died and rose again. In Christ, and through faith in Him, we are declared righteous by God, and through His Spirit made righteous by an inner transformation toward Christlikeness.

While we will be perfectly righteous only when we too are raised from the dead, we are even now growing toward Christlikeness, and through Christ we can live a righteous life now. As Paul wrote in 2 Corinthians 5:21, "God made [Jesus] who had no sin to be sin for us, so that in Him we might become the righteousness of God."

Law. The theme of Law is one of the most significant in the Scriptures. It is also one which must be understood if the freedom we have in Christ, and the pathway God has marked out for us to live by are to be found.

The Hebrew word *torah* (translated "law" in the Old Testament) has complex meaning. Its basic meaning is "teaching" or "instruction." Depending on context, *torah* may have this general meaning, or may refer to the specific instructions given to Israel by Moses. In this later sense it may refer strictly to the Ten Commandments, to the whole set of ordinances established in the

Mosaic writings, to the five books of Moses as a whole, or even to the whole Old Testament. The content of the *torah,* God's instructions to His people, thus includes not just moral but also ceremonial and civil matters.

This Law of Moses was, however, given to a special people for a special purpose. God had made covenant promises to the children of Abraham, Isaac, and Jacob. These people, known as Israel, were given the Law to teach them how to live in fellowship with God so that they might receive the benefits promised by the covenant.

While the moral aspect of the Law is universal in that it is an expression of the character of God and thus a divine definition of right and wrong for all, the Law itself was *not* given to Gentiles (see Deut. 4:32-40).

The true believer in Old Testament times loved the Law of God in all its aspects, for it was one of the primary means of God's self-revelation. The believer yearned to know God, and to be like Him, and thus found the Law (as God's revelation) precious (see Pss. 19:7-11; 119:12-16).

Jesus shared the appreciation of the Jew for the Law of God. He affirmed the whole of the Old Testament as God's sure Word (Matt. 5:18-48). But in the same context Jesus announced that He had the right to explain the Law's true meaning. In a series of "you have heard . . . but I say" teachings, Christ showed that the Law's external demands had always witnessed to the fact that God cares about the heart-attitude of human beings. Christ's statement that the whole Law can be summed up in the command to love God and to love one's neighbor underlines this fact. One who truly loves God and others will not do any of those things that Law marks out as a "thou shalt not" (see Matt. 7:12; 22:36-40).

While the Law, as an expression of God's character and of righteousness, was not done away with, its function as a guide to the believer has been done away with. Thus Jesus taught that "the Law and the Prophets were proclaimed until John. Since that time the Good News of the kingdom of God is being preached" (Luke 16:16).

The New Testament "law" is *nomos.* This Greek term functions in the New Testament with several different shades of meaning. On one hand, it captures and expresses the Old Testament's view summed up in *torah.* In other contexts Paul uses such phrases as "law of sin and death," meaning the "principle of sin and death" at work in every human being's life.

Paul, however, had one very special usage which helps us understand what to many seem contradictory viewpoints. In that use Paul viewed "Law" as an operating system, composed of the revealed moral code and human nature. If we take the moral law objectively, without considering any interaction when it is related to fallen man, then law is "holy, righteous and good" (Rom. 7:12). In pure beauty the moral law reveals the character of the God who gave it, and we are moved to worship and to praise.

But what happens when we bring law into contact with fallen men and women? Then Paul noted, "The very commandment that was intended to bring life actually brought death" (v. 10). Sinful human beings are not stimulated by the Law to do good, but are provoked to do wrong! Paul concluded that the problem with the moral Law was that it is "powerless" for it is "weakened by the sinful nature" (8:3).

We might use this simile. The sun that our planet circles is bright, beautiful, and beneficial. Without its heat and light our world would be dead, cold, and lifeless. But neither you nor I can look directly into the midday sun without going blind. The sun's rays will burn out our eyes.

Is this the fault of the sun? Does it change its character as a bright and beneficial thing? Not at all. The problem lies in the very structure of our eyes, which makes it impossible for us to look into the sun's fierce beauty without suffering our sight's destruction.

It is just this way with God's Law. It is beautiful and beneficial. But if human beings seek to relate to it the wrong way—if we link our moral efforts to Law and figuratively fix our gaze on it—we find only destruction. The fault is not in the Law nor in the sun. The fault is in the weakness of our physical and moral nature.

Whenever Paul spoke of God's Law in a negative way, it is this that he had in mind—not the Law in itself, but the way human beings and Law interact. Paul was urgently concerned that Christians did not make the mistake made by Israel, and seek righteousness by staring intently at God's Law.

It is not the task of Law to make men righteous. It is the task of the Law to show men how desperately they need a righteousness which comes from God rather than a righteousness based on their own futile, frustrated efforts.

The key to our understanding of both righteousness and the Law, as well as our understanding the secret of victorious Christian living, will be found as we examine further this great New Testament book.

THE QUEST FOR RIGHTEOUSNESS

Overview

The first three chapters of Romans carefully argue that all men are guilty before God. No one who relies on his observance of the Law will be declared righteous in the divine court. The Law, as a moral revelation of righteousness, offers no hope; it testifies against us so that "every mouth may be silenced and the whole world held accountable to God" (3:20).

Yet the devastating critique of our human condition ends on a note of hope. God has found a way to give us a righteousness that is apart from Law.

Romans' argument is interspersed with theological terms that we need to understand.

▶ *Circumcision.* The Old Testament rite was a physical sign and symbol of a person's participation in the covenant God made with Israel. Paul argued, however, that true circumcision is of the heart: a person *in* the covenant must live by the covenant's regulations. The true Jew is one inwardly, not just in the flesh.

▶ *Conscience.* Evidence that Gentiles have an implanted moral law is found in conscience. Every culture has standards of right and wrong, and every person fails to live up to what he himself believes is right. Conscience offers no hope, but is as condemning as the Law.

■ See the *Bible Knowledge Commentary,* pages 435-452, for verse-by-verse discussion of these chapters.

Commentary

I remember how guilty I felt.

As a young teenager, I had traced pictures of female underwear models from the Sears catalog, and hidden the "pinups" under my mattress. When Mom changed the sheets, she found them. And left them, exposed on the top of my bed.

Burning with shame, I'd tried to brazen it out. With attempted enthusiasm I hurried out to the back garden to offer Dad, who was trimming a peach tree, my help.

There were other times I felt guilty too. Like the time John Weimer and I picked the only plum on the new tree just before it ripened. Mom had been heartbroken; she'd looked forward so much to tasting that one plum. John and I hadn't even eaten it! We'd opened it and thrown the still-hard flesh of the fruit on our garage floor.

Guilt.

Sometimes it comes because of a willful choice of what is known to be wrong. Sometimes it overwhelms us for unwitting failures. Either way, to feel guilt is pure agony; a recognition of our failure and inadequacy.

Feelings of guilt are common in our society. Sometimes the feelings are rooted in specific acts. A spouse is unfaithful. A mother neglects a young child who is later injured. A teenager lies to his parents about where he is going. A businessman cheats on a government contract.

Sometimes our feelings of guilt are rooted in the growing awareness that we are unable to cope with life. We fall short over and over again. Somehow we must be to blame. The sense of guilt grows. Plagued by the awareness of our inadequacy, we may try any of several approaches to break free.

● One approach to handling guilt is to deny it. Our feelings of guilt, we say, come from hang-ups that society imposes on us. So we insist that everyone has the right to do his own thing, that there are no absolute moral standards that are binding on us.

● Another approach to handling guilt is to explain it away. We look back into our childhood and find reasons why we couldn't help ourselves; we made some of those bad choices because we had to. Often criminal behavior is explained away as being due to societal conditions rather than the individual's choice. Denying personal responsibility is a popular way to attempt to rid ourselves of guilt.

• A third approach to handling guilt is to punish ourselves. We feel "bad," and so we drink, or fail at our work or marriages to make ourselves suffer. Somehow we hope that if we suffer enough we won't feel guilty, even though failing actually will deepen our general sense of guilt and worthlessness.

• A fourth approach to handling guilt is to construct a system of do's and don'ts which we *can* live up to. Then we reassure ourselves of our goodness by meticulously keeping the rules we construct. If we still feel guilty, we compare ourselves with others who don't live up to our high standards, and remind ourselves how much better we are than others. This has historically been a favorite approach of the religious.

• Of course, there's a fifth approach. Just enjoy sin! The first pangs of conscience will recede if we throw ourselves into the pursuit of sinful pleasures. Perhaps we can sear our consciences enough so that we will no longer be troubled by guilt—except late at night when we wake up feeling empty and fearful and alone.

Guilt is such a big thing with us, and is felt so intensely by so many, that it is hard to grasp the fact that the Bible does not really speak about guilt feelings. Instead, Scripture speaks only of real guilt, of responsibility for acts of sin. Even here, guilt is hardly a dominant biblical theme. *Young's Analytical Concordance* lists only 6 New Testament references to guilt or guiltiness, and of the 17 Old Testament references, 8 are found in Leviticus 4–6 and refer to the sin offerings through which guilt was to be covered.

God seems far more interested in speaking to us of forgiveness than of guilt!

The most frequently used Old and New Testament words which speak of forgiveness have the same root meaning: to send away. In each case, what is sent away is not those feelings of guiltiness aroused by our sins or our inadequacy, but the sin itself. It is the *sin* that is forgiven and sent away.

The act of God in forgiving us through Jesus is the source of a new freedom for us. The New Testament quotes an Old Testament promise: "I will forgive their wickedness and will remember their sins no more" (Heb. 8:12). In another place this is repeated: "Their sins and lawless acts I will remember no more" (10:17). Because of Jesus, our sins have been dealt with fully and completely. As far as God is concerned, the issue is settled. Forgiveness is so complete that sins are no longer even remembered.

Then what of guilt?

Because our sins are dealt with and sent away, we are no longer guilty! We stand uncondemned before God! Justified by faith, we now "have peace with God through our Lord Jesus Christ" (Rom. 5:1). And in Jesus we can find inner peace as well.

Sometimes guilt feelings linger on after we have accepted Jesus and His forgiveness. This is one of the things we learn to overcome as we grow in our faith. A child frightened by a dog may grow up terrified of even the tiniest poodle. The fear remains, long after the reason for fear is gone. Often Christians feel guilt long after Christ has taken away their sins, and the real guilt is gone. How good to grow to the place where we can acknowledge the nature of sin, can accept Jesus' forgiveness, and can go on in our Christian lives freed from bondage to guilt feelings after the guilt is gone.

Yet before we can discover this freedom we must face the grim facts that Paul presents in the first three chapters of Romans. We must realize that we are guilty before God and utterly without hope in ourselves. Only when we face that fact are we likely to abandon our futile attempts to deal with guilt on our own, and come to Jesus for release.

The Power of God: Romans 1:1-17

In his introduction Paul affirmed first that God has good news for humankind in Jesus Christ, His Son, who "was declared with power to be the Son of God by His resurrection from the dead" (v. 4). The Gospel, the Good News from God, is infused with this same life-giving vitality, for "it is the power of God for the salvation of everyone who believes: first for the Jew, then for the Gentile" (v. 16). And what does the Gospel message reveal? That there is a righteousness from God, which is available to human beings, and that it is "by faith from first to last."

Thus Paul's opening paragraphs are filled with promise. God has a message for us in Christ, a good word about a salvation which does not depend on what we do to earn it, but comes as a gift which can be received only by faith.

Later in Romans Paul examined each theme introduced here. He explained carefully the astounding nature of "salvation," and how it is that both life and righteousness are involved. Later too Paul helps us understand the nature of "faith." But first of all, Paul wanted to make sure that we fully understand why we need this salvation.

The reason is grim. Without salvation, we have no spiritual life. Without it, we have no righteousness. Without it, we stand guilty and condemned before the holy God. There is no hope for any person aside from the by-faith salvation that God offers us in Jesus!

No wonder Paul saw himself as "obligated both to Greeks and non-Greeks, both to the wise and the foolish" (v. 14). Paul had the Gospel, the message that can bring life to the lost. As a fellow human being like you and I, Paul was obligated to share the Good News of salvation with all.

Ø Group Activity:
Missions/Outreach Group
In Romans 1:1-6 Paul shares his convictions about Jesus and what his calling as a servant of Christ means to him. Use Paul's words as a pattern, and write your own confession of faith and servanthood statement. Share what each of you have written.

Then discuss three key phrases in 1:1-17: "I am obligated" (1:14); "I am so eager" (1:15); "I am not ashamed" (1:16). How do each of these find expression in your daily life? In your group outreach efforts?

The State of the Lost: Romans 1:18–3:20
As Paul penned these first chapters of Romans, one reality dominated his thoughts. That thought is stated in a critical verse in Romans 5: "By the trespass of the one man [Adam], death reigned" (v. 17). Our understanding of salvation must grow from

our awareness of man's utter lostness.

All too often human beings begin their thinking about relationship with God with different assumptions. To some, a human being seems a person born with spiritual life who forfeits that life only when he personally chooses sin. Others believe that a person is born neutral. To them, the issue remains in doubt until the final judgment, when our acts will be weighed in a set of divine balances. If, at that time, there is more good than bad (so the thinking goes), eternal life will be the reward.

Paul had no such image of man. He took seriously the Old Testament picture of the Fall, and was convinced that all human beings are born spiritually dead and alienated from God. Both by nature and by choice, human beings willingly choose sin, even when they know the good. So the basic question is, "How do human beings receive spiritual life?"

This is a question that Paul himself never asked or even thought of in his early years. As a young Pharisee, the 30-year-old Saul assumed that life was his, and that he could please God by a rigorous keeping of the Law. Only later, jolted by the appearance of Jesus on the road to Damascus, did Saul go back to probe the untested assumptions on which his whole life had been based.

Now, writing to the Romans, Paul realized that there would be many others like himself who would not have traced the implications of the Gospel back to the basics. So in the first three chapters of this book Paul sought to demonstrate the deadness of humanity. He sought to prove our guilt, and utter lack of righteousness. Paul argued that we do not die spiritually because of sin; our sins demonstrate that we are spiritually dead.

Human beings never needed Law to show them how to live. Mankind's need has always been for life itself—something that is not communicated through God's Law.

Spiritual deadness (Rom. 1:18-32). Paul was familiar with the sinful lifestyle of the pagans, a lifestyle adopted and expressed in the stories of their gods and goddesses. The Gentiles had not come to this depraved state because they had no opportunity to know God. Paul pointed out that ever since Creation, God's invisible qualities have "been clearly seen" (v. 20). That which can be known about God through nature "is plain to them" (v. 19).

The question is, "How have human beings responded to God's revelation of Himself in Creation?" What has happened is that, when confronted by God, "they neither glorified Him as God nor gave thanks to Him" (v. 21). Instead they reacted *against* Him, exchanging "the glory of the immortal God" for dead images and idols.

An analogy helps. We've all seen two lovers walking side by side. We've seen their hands brush, then seen them grip. The love that exists between the two attracts: a touch stimulates a handclasp, and soon an embrace. We've also seen what happens when a hand brushes a hot iron or stove. There's a sudden jerk; the hand is pulled away. Instead of attraction there is repulsion.

This, Paul said, is what has happened between God and man. When God brushes against human beings, unveiling just a bit of Himself in creation, humanity jerks away! Humans desperately repress the truth, not thinking "it worthwhile to retain the knowledge of God" (v. 28).

To Paul and to us this reaction is evidence of the spiritual deadness of humanity. To contact God—the Bible's God of love and righteousness—and to be repelled! And then to choose all sorts of corruption and wickedness rather than Him! How plain it was to Paul as he went on to list the spiritual and moral wickedness that human societies have so clearly displayed. Such people must be both guilty and spiritually dead! If there were any life at all, they would respond as a lover to the God who loves each of us so.

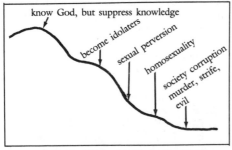

Romans 1:18-20 21-24 24-25 26-28 29-30

✄ *Group Activity: Recovery Group Steps 6 (be ready to have God remove character defects) and 7 (humbly ask God to remove shortcomings)*

Romans 1:18-30 traces the downward

slide of a humanity which suppressed truth about God and blocked Him out of their lives. Use a chalkboard or sheet of newsprint, and together trace the downward pattern (see illustration), labeling attitudes or actions which show growing character defects. Then talk about the pattern, and what it means for people today.

Individually draw a chart showing the downward pattern of your past life. Label attitudes and/or actions along the way that show your own character defects. Then circle those defects which God has already removed from your life.

Share one or two shortcomings God has removed, and tell the others how this has affected your lifestyle.

Then share at least one defect you are ready now to have God remove. When all have shared, ask God to do this for you, and pray for the others who have shared as well.

God's judgment (Rom. 2:1-16). Paul then made it clear that God will surely judge the sins of humankind. No human being can lightly condemn others, for we too have sinned, and deserve judgment. What is called for is repentance. The Jew might be proud because he knew more of God than the Gentile. He had received God's Law. But what God is concerned with is not *knowing* good. It is *doing* good that counts (vv. 7-11).

Verses 14-15 are an interesting aside which have often been misunderstood. These verses read:

Indeed, when Gentiles, who do not have the Law, do by nature things required by the Law, they are a law for themselves, even though they do not have the Law, since they show that the requirements of the Law are written on their hearts, their consciences also bearing witness, and their thoughts now accusing, now even defending them.

Paul here was pointing out that the Jews, recipients of the revealed Law, were not the only ones with moral standards! The Gentiles too had a moral nature, and a conscience that identified moral issues and led them to set up standards of right and wrong by which to judge themselves and each other. "By nature" they do what the concept of Law requires: they weigh, measure, and evaluate human behavior by moral criteria. They realize that moral failure calls for judgment, and they try to excuse and defend their failures. When God's Judgment Day comes, both Jew and Gentile will be shown to have fallen short of whatever standards each approves!

This is helpful for those who are honestly concerned about God's "unfairness" in failing to reveal His standards to everyone. God will not judge pagans by Scripture's standards of right and wrong. He will judge all men by their own standards.

But it makes no difference. For all fall short. The failure of individuals and of societies to live up to standards they themselves establish is additional evidence that men are both lost and dead. There is no help for us in ourselves.

⌀ **Group Activity:**
Missions/Outreach Group
List all the reasons you can think of why people might ask, "Are people who have never heard of Jesus lost?" Then study Romans 1–3 to put this issue in perspective. Key points to explore are: God has revealed Himself to all human beings (1:19-20; cf. Ps. 19:1-4). All have moral standards, and God will judge each person's acts on the basis of standards a person has (2:12-14, 25-27). The sinful condition of mankind is demonstrated by the failure of persons to respond to God's self-revelation, and by their failure to live by the moral standards they hold. Universal human experience testifies to the truth stated in Scripture (3:9-20).

Then study together Romans 3:21-26. What specific answers does it give to those who question whether people who have never heard of Jesus are lost, and to the reasons they ask this question?

You may wish to take the role of a person who raises this question for one of the reasons you suggested, and see if another person in the group can give you a helpful answer from these Scriptures.

Jews and the Law (Rom. 2:17–3:8). Paul then spoke directly to the Jew, who relied on the Law and "brags about your relationship to God." Simply knowing the Law does not make a person superior: one must *observe* the Law.

In essence, Paul was accusing Judaism of having become a religion of externals. It took pride in having the Law, but Jews "dishonor God by breaking the Law." Judaism took pride in physical circumcision, but ignored the inner circumcision of the heart accomplished only by God's Spirit. The Jews had many spiritual advantages (3:1-2). But their unfaithfulness (v. 3) had not shaken God from His commitments. God will still judge those who sin.

Righteousness (Rom. 3:9-20). Up to this point Paul had sought to demonstrate that all humanity is spiritually dead, and thus under God's judgment. Human beings are repelled by contact with God. They choose wicked acts, and even though Jew and Gentile alike have moral standards, they do not live up to them.

Then Paul moved from demonstration to proof! And for proof, he went back to the Old Testament, quoting various Psalms which tell us "there is no one righteous, not even one" (v. 10). This collage of Old Testament verses goes beyond argument. The evidence of history and personal experience Paul drew on is impressive. The statements of God in His Word are conclusive.

It is at this point that Paul returned to the Law. Whatever the Law has to say, it speaks to those who are under the Law (e.g., the Jewish people). And what it says is that all are guilty! Crushed by requirements that no one has ever perfectly met, the mouth of every human being under the Law is silenced, and "the whole world [is] held accountable to God" (v. 19). Since it is the function of the Law to condemn the sinner and demonstrate guilt, "no one will be declared righteous in [God's] sight by observing the Law." Instead "through the Law we become conscious of sin" (v. 20).

So humanity *is* lost. We are spiritually dead, and the very Law to which the Jews looked with such hope is actually an instrument of condemnation.

What Is the Gospel? Romans 3:21-31
Paul launched Romans by referring to the Gospel—Good News from God. What is that Good News? How is it possible for God to provide us with a "righteousness from God, apart from Law"?

Paul then said that "this righteousness from God comes through faith in Jesus

305

Christ to all who believe" (v. 22), for there is no difference between Gentile and Jew, since all have sinned.

The basis on which God makes this offer is the blood of Christ, poured out as a "sacrifice of atonement" (v. 25). Our salvation rests on the work of God in Christ; there is no human contribution. God's grace, His free choice to *give* what we do not have and cannot earn, is at the root of salvation. All God asks from us is faith.

Paul also noted here that the Cross demonstrates not only grace but also God's justice. In the past too God offered believers forgiveness. But how could the holy God let sin go unpunished? The Cross shows the God who does not relax His standards. The penalty which justice demands — death for the sinner — was paid by God Himself. Ours is not cut-rate salvation. Ours is no cheap forgiveness. But it is God who paid the price in the blood of His Son.

The Gospel, then, is simply the message that God forgives guilty sinners, and does so righteously, on the basis of Christ's sacrificial death.

Law and faith (Rom. 3:27-31). To all who object that this robs the Law of honor, Paul responded, "Not at all!"

The principle of faith does exclude human boasting. And it makes salvation accessible to all. But this principle of faith actually *upholds* Law.

What Paul meant is, the Gospel finally puts Law in clear perspective, establishing in every eye the role that God has given the Law — not the role human beings mistakenly assigned to it. The Law's place as the revealer of our lostness is established. The Law's role is even exalted, for now we know. Law itself is a compelling call to look to Christ for a righteousness which can come only as God's gift, and only through faith.

GROUP RESOURCE GUIDE

Identification: *Share with others*
Choose one word that tells what "guilt" feels like. List your word with those suggested by others, and talk together how the experience of guilt affects different individuals.

Exploration: *Probe God's Word*
On the basis of Romans 1:17–3:20 examine the following definition of "guilt." Together work to change the definition if necessary, to reflect the teaching of this passage more accurately. The statement:

Guilt is rooted in man's personal, conscious, and responsible choice to do something which that person knows to be wrong and for which he or she merits punishment. All are guilty, for all have knowingly done what he or she believes to be wrong.

Reaction: *Respond together to the Word*
Discuss: How did you react when you first became aware of personal sin? How did you try to deal with your sense of guilt? How did that affect your life?

Do you still have feelings of guilt sometimes, even as a Christian? How do you deal with them now?

Adoration: *Worship and pray*
God chose to deal with our guilt by taking on Himself the punishment due our sins — and then freely forgiving us in Jesus. Because of Christ, our sins are gone, and we are declared "not guilty!"

Meditate for five minutes on Romans 3:21-26. Then express your praise to God, by leading in a chorus, praying aloud, or sharing a personal testimony.

It would be especially appropriate to conclude this group session with a brief Communion service.

BY FAITH

Overview

Paul had shown that all humanity lies, spiritually dead and without hope, under the judgment of God. The Law in which Israel had hoped was no aid to salvation, but rather a mirror set up to display the sinfulness of human beings.

Yet Paul did not abandon hope. Jesus Christ by His atoning sacrifice has made salvation possible. His blood released the flow of life and righteousness which comes to us as a gift.

But how is this gift received? In Romans 4 Paul reviewed sacred history, and highlighted a principle which has operated from the beginning, but which Israel had overlooked: faith. This towering chapter is one of the Bible's clearest and most powerful explanations of the nature of faith, and particularly of saving faith.

In Romans 5 Paul invited us to experience the peace that faith in Christ brings. We have been reconciled to God through Christ's death; we will be saved through His life.

Romans 5 then examines the theme of life. Adam's sin brought death into the world. This dark heritage has been the burden of every human being born of Adam's line. But Jesus, a new Adam, brings life and the gift of righteousness as well.

And then, in a pivotal section of this book, Paul taught that the key to our new lives is the union that faith forges with our resurrected Lord. Because we are now in Him, life and true goodness can and will be ours.

Commentary

Like other chapters in Romans these chapters are theological in character, and introduce theological terms. It is helpful to preview them, so that when we meet them in the text each passage's teaching will be clearer.

Justification. The Greek word translated "justify" or "justification" means "to acquit," "to vindicate," or "to pronounce righteous." These are important judicial terms, and the theological meaning is borrowed from the courtroom. In justification God clears those who have been charged with sins or failures. The Bible makes it clear that God will clear no one of the charge of sin on the basis of his or her efforts to keep the Law. One can be justified—declared righteous—only on the basis of faith.

The exciting revelation of Scripture is that with the *declaration* of righteousness God has also made possible the *experience* of righteousness. Thus in many contexts "justification" includes both God's "not guilty" verdict pronounced over the forgiven sinner, and the moral transformation of the sinner, which also is by faith.

Grace. God's gift of righteousness is received by faith, but is rooted in His grace. Grace is a dominant theme in the New Testament, but has Old Testament roots. Those roots are sunk deep in the compassionate and caring nature of God, who can be appealed to for mercy "according to Your unfailing love; according to Your great compassion" (Ps. 51:1).

In the New Testament "grace" (*charis*) has become a pivotal theological term. There grace affirms a radical view of relationship with God. It affirms God's attitude of love and acceptance. It affirms each person's helplessness. Grace is action of a caring God who stoops to lift us up, not because of any merit in ourselves, but simply because of His great self-sacrificial love.

Reconciled. This term is not a common one. But it is important. The word implies a restoration of relationship, a return of the harmony that once existed between God and human beings. The point is that conversion brings both a change of position, and a psychological and spiritual change, so our inner attitudes are brought into harmony with the divine reality. We who were once enemies of God now "rejoice in God through our Lord Jesus Christ" (Rom. 5:11).

Baptized. This term appears in Romans 6, which speaks of believers as those who are "baptized into Christ Jesus."

As do words in every language, "baptism" refers to different things. One reference is water baptism, which is a symbol of the spiritual reality spoken of in Romans 6. Another is the baptism by the Spirit spoken of in 1 Corinthians 12:13, which that passage defines as an act of the Spirit which unites us to Jesus and to other members of His body. In Romans 6, "baptism" is our union with Jesus itself: a bonding to Christ that is so real that we are considered both to have died with Jesus and to have been raised with Him. So "baptism" in Romans 6 does not speak of water baptism (the symbol) but of our union with Jesus (the reality that water baptism symbolizes).

For an in-depth discussion of each of these key terms, see the author's *Expository Dictionary of Bible Words* (Zondervan).

Faith: Romans 4

What is this "faith" that Paul proposed as the key to experiencing that salvation Christ has won for us?

Faith and justification (Rom. 4:1-8). "Faith" is what justified Abraham and David, representative Old Testament saints. "Abraham believed God, and it was credited to him as righteousness" (cf. Gen. 15:6).

It's not a question of what Abraham and David did or did not do to please God. The question is to whom does God *credit righteousness?*

In this argument Paul again asked us to be clear on the character of those involved in the transaction. Abraham and David, like you and me, were sinners. But God is the God "who justifies the wicked" (Rom. 4:5).

The term justification is central here, and its meaning is summed up well by Article 21 of the Augsburg Confession: it is "as when my friend pays the debt for a friend, the debtor is freed by the merit of another, as though it were his own. Thus the merits of Christ are bestowed upon us."

Paul's return to the Old Testament to demonstrate justification by faith is important. God is One, and Scripture is in full harmony with Scripture. The whole Word of God testifies to God's willingness to justify the ungodly, and in every context that justification is by faith.

Justification for all (Rom. 4:9-12). The Jewish reader was likely to object that this justification was for God's covenant people alone. Paul pointed out, however, that Abraham was counted righteous before he was circumcised! Thus he is the "father" of all those who believe, circumcised and uncircumcised alike. Faith is a universal principle that applies to all humanity's relationship with God.

Abraham's offspring (Rom. 4:13-17). The term "father" here is used as "founder of a line or family." That which makes a person one of Abraham's offspring is not physical descent, but rather faith in God. Those who are physically Abraham's descendants and those who are not must alike become members of his spiritual family. This is possible only by believing in the God in whom Abraham believed.

Resurrection (Rom. 4:18-24). Abraham's faith, portrayed so powerfully in the Old Testament, has a distinct New Testament flavor. When God told Abraham that he and Sarah would have a son, it was a promise that life would spring from the bodies of those who were "dead" as far as childbearing was concerned. Abraham faced this fact—"that his body was as good as dead—since he was about a hundred years old—and that Sarah's womb was also dead." But Abraham did not "waver through unbelief." He believed the promise God had given. And this faith was "credited to him" as that righteousness his actions showed he did not possess.

We too believe the message of life springing from death—the message of a resurrected Lord, who died for our sins and was raised for our justification. And for all of us who, like Abraham, commit ourselves to the God we are "fully persuaded . . . had power to do what He had promised" (v. 21), there is a righteousness we do not possess credited to our account.

✍ *Group Activity: Bible Study Group*
Explore the nature of "faith" in Romans 4, a key passage on this basic biblical theme.

First try this "true/false" quiz.
1. *Faith is believing in God.*
2. *Faith is believing God.*
3. *Saving faith is different than daily faith.*
4. *Faith is a New Testament doctrine.*
5. *Faith is an Old Testament doctrine.*
6. *Faith is better than good works.*
7. *Faith makes us righteous.*
8. *Faith wins us forgiveness.*
9. *Faith is a matter of grace, not law.*
10. *Faith is confidence in God's Word.*

Discuss the reasons each person answered the quiz questions as he or she did. In some cases either T or F may be correct depending on the reasoning involved.

Then in teams study what Paul says about Abraham's faith relationship with the Lord. What was the nature of Abraham's faith? What specifically did Abraham believe? How was his faith expressed? What were the results of his faith? What specifically are we to believe? In what ways is the model of Abraham's faith to be applied by us today?

New Life: Romans 5:1–6.14

A life of peace (Rom. 5:1-11). The result of our justification through faith is "peace with God through our Lord Jesus Christ."

This peace with God is objective and subjective. Objectively we have "gained access" to God, for the ground on which we stand is one of grace and not of works (v. 2). Subjectively, our new "at peace" relationship with God has multiple expressions. We "rejoice in the hope of the glory of God." "Hope" here and in the rest of the New Testament is a special term. It is *not* a word suggesting uncertainty (as, "Well, I *hope* I can make it.") It is instead a word of *confident expectation.* Christian hope is a sense of certainty that brings us joy, even if present circumstances are painful.

Paul specifies the basis of this joy producing hope. First, we know that present suffering is intended by God to produce the inner transformation of our character that God has always intended (vv. 3-4). Second, the Holy Spirit who has been given us pours out God's love in our hearts. There is the inner witness of the Spirit that God does love us as His own (v. 5). Third, there is the object evidence of God's love for us seen in the Cross. Christ died for us when we were still numbered among the ungodly. Surely the One who died for us when we were sinners and saved us from God's wrath will, now that we have been reconciled to God, save us "through His life" (vv. 6-11). The ever-living Jesus will keep us, and bring us through this life to the glory for which we hope (v. 2).

✂ *Group Activity: Recovery Group*
Steps 2 (believe in a higher Power) and 3 (decide to turn my life over to God's care)
Brainstorm images that people have of God, such as the policeman, the nagging mother, the hanging judge, etc. After all you can think of are listed on a chalkboard or large sheet of newsprint, pick one image that has affected your life in the past. Tell the others what that image is, and explain how thinking of God in this way affected your life and your relationship with Him.

In teams study Romans 5:1-11. Your job is to first come up with several alternate images of God suggested by these verses. Then list "God is . . . " sentences drawn from these verses that sum up what these verses tell you about God.

Together again, share one image and one sentence that makes it easier for you to decide to turn your life over to God daily. You may wish to actually draw that image on an 8 1/2 x 11 inch sheet of paper, to take home and display as a reminder.

A life of righteousness (Rom. 5:12-21). We come now to one of the key passages in the Scripture—one which theologians pore over. Despite the questions the passage raises (for instance, as to the nature of imputed sin), the primary message of the passage is exciting—and clear.

Sin entered the world through Adam, and all descending from him have been sinners. Spiritual death, as God had clearly warned (Gen. 2:16-17), struck humankind. While no one was charged with "sin" (in the technical sense of a violation of divine law) until the Law was given, all *were* spiritually dead. Thus death reigned, bringing all humankind under necessary condemnation.

But then Jesus Christ came into the world, bringing a grace-gift to us. What flows from Jesus is not death, but life. What relationship with Adam meant was death; what relationship with Jesus means is eternal life—and righteousness.

For *just as sin is associated with and expresses spiritual death, so righteousness is associated with and expresses spiritual life!* Through Jesus, we come to life again and our new life will be marked by the reign of righteousness!

Union with Christ (Rom. 6:1-14). Paul here described a great reversal. We who were dead through Adam lived in sin. Now we who are alive through Jesus are dead to sin.

All this flows from the fact that our union with Jesus is in fact a *real* (not merely symbolic) union. We were bonded to Jesus so that His death was ours, and His resurrection ours as well. In this union our "old self" died to sin. A new self was created that is "alive to God in Christ Jesus." This new self is intended to live a righteous life.

Paul calls on us Christians to acknowledge by faith the reality of our death and new life, and to "not let" sin reign. As those who have been brought from death to life, we are to offer ourselves to God "as instruments of righteousness." We who relate to God through grace rather than Law will not be mastered by sin.

These few verses in Romans 6 are pivotal in the Book of Romans and in our lives. In Romans they serve to shift our gaze from what Jesus' death means for us in our standing with God, to consider what Jesus' death means for us in our present experience. And as pivotal verses, they deserve a closer look.

Romans 6 Revisited: Romans 6:1-14

In Romans 1–5 the Apostle Paul proclaimed the Good News of peace with God. Christ's redemption, received by faith, offers the forgiveness of sins.

Now, writing in the distinctive form of the diatribe, in which the writer inserts periodic objections which an imaginary opponent may make, and then answers them, Paul raised an important question. What shall we conclude from this promise of a salvation by faith, and an imputed righteousness? "Shall we go on sinning so that grace may increase?" (v. 1) That is, is the assurance of forgiveness a license to sin? Some might even go further. Since our sin seems to give God the chance to display His grace, shall we go on sinning so that even greater displays of grace might take place?

Paul responded to this idea with an exclamation: "By no means!" We might paraphrase it as an explosive, "Never!" And Paul says, "We died to sin; how can we live in it any longer?"

What happened to the sin nature? Paul's exclamation, and the verses which immediately follow, are the key to understanding the victory over sin which Christ has won for us.

Historically, there have been many different approaches to the "victorious Christian life." Each of them is related to a particular idea of what has happened to the Christian's sin nature.

*Eradication. According to this theory, when a person becomes a Christian the sin nature itself dies. This means that the very capacity to sin is removed; whatever a Christian desires or chooses must flow from the new in him and not the old. Our common experience as well as the Bible's promise of *continued* forgiveness makes it plain that this theory does not fit the facts.

*Suppression. According to this theory, when a person becomes a Christian he or she is given the power to control the sin nature. The capacity and the desire for sin are still present, but the Christian is responsible to hold down that desire.

In this approach a great deal of emphasis is placed on the Law as a tool for suppression. Guided by the Law's demands, and always aware of his own personal responsibility, the individual fights for mastery over his old self.

This grim struggle is something that Paul described in Romans 7. The apostle himself apparently once took this route—and failed.

*Self-crucifixion. Noting that we were crucified with Christ (see 6:6; Gal. 2:20), this approach to the Christian life visualizes our sin nature as something that struggles to get off the cross again. It is the believer's responsibility, then, to live the "crucified life." Each temptation calls for renewed surrender to God.

At times this approach to Christian living has led individuals to see every human desire and pleasure as an indication of sin. When this happens, they have been led into a joyless life of denying themselves those

Romans 6:1-14

What Identification Means	How We Respond to Find Victory
I. Union with Christ in His death. *Sin* in our bodies is rendered inoperative, robbed of its lordship.	I. Understand what union with Jesus means. We were crucified with Christ that the dominance over the body of our sin nature might be rendered inoperative.
II. Union with Christ in His resurrection. We are made alive with Christ, free to serve God.	II. Believe (count what God says as true: "reckon"). Stop turning yourself over to sin. Trust God's promise that you no longer must sin.
	III. Act on what you believe. Present yourselves to God rather than to sin and do His will.

very things which God gives us "richly . . . to enjoy" (1 Tim. 6:17, KJV).

Penalism. This approach views all temptations as attacks of Satan. The problem is never located within us; it's always the fault of Satan. The right response to Satan's attack is rejection. We are to resist Satan on the authority of Jesus, who at the cross won final victory over His enemy and ours, the devil.

But what Paul taught in Romans 6 is different from each of these four ideas. Paul's argument rested on a unique understanding of what did happen at the cross. And Paul taught us a unique way to respond when we sense sin's inner pull; a way that promises a freedom such as we have never known!

This way of release is based on the realization that through Christ's work on the cross our sin nature was *rendered powerless.* Oh, it still exists. And it still pulls us toward evil. But we do not *have* to respond. We are no longer slaves to sin!

Union (Rom. 6:1-4). Paul began here with the concept of identification, of our union with Christ. Paul's point was that this union with Jesus is not merely "legal" but is real. Because we who believe are now "in" Christ, His death was our death, and His resurrection was our resurrection.

Being "in Christ" is the very root and essence of the new life of the Christian. We have passed from death to life (the powers of death have no hold on us anymore). We are not "in the flesh," or "in sin" anymore. It is as if we were citizens of a new country—in Christ.

This being the case, we have a share in Christ's triumph over the forces of death and hell. As they could not hold Him in their power, they no longer hold us in their power. The Cross, irradiated with the light of Easter morning, is the fundamental fact which will determine not only the history of the cosmos but our own personal history as well.

"Old self" (Rom. 6:5-10). This crucifixion of the "old self" (a term for the sin nature) did not eradicate the old desires or motives. They continue to betray our "place of origin," as a tell-tale accent marks our speech. The crucifixion of the "old self" did not remove the pull of temptation. Instead, what happened was that the "body of sin" (that whole package of old and warped responses) was rendered powerless or inoperative (v. 6). We will still feel the temptations, *but are not in their power.* Our days of slavery are ended. We are now free to choose the good.

Like Jesus, you and I are now alive to God, and we can choose to live for Him.

Response to sin (Rom. 6:11-14). How is the believer who feels a temptation to sin to respond? Paul's answer is, with faith. For salvation is a matter of "faith from first to last" (1:17).

We are to consider ourselves to be dead to sin (6:11). In other words, consider what God says about the "death" of your sin nature in respect to its power over you to be true. Realize you do not *have* to surrender to your temptations. Then, with full trust in the life that Jesus has given us, actively yield yourself to God, surrendering all to Him for acts of righteousness. In essence, we are to step out and *do* what is right, confident that as we obey the Lord, He will strengthen and enable us.

Donald Grey Barnhouse used to give this analogy to explain. He told of a crew whose captain went mad and was replaced in mid-voyage by the first mate. Now the old captain had no authority; the new captain was the one to be obeyed. Yet Barnhouse suggested that the crew might very well find itself jumping to obey when the old captain shouted out his orders.

What the crew had to do was to constantly remember that the old captain need no longer be obeyed, and learn to respond to the voice of the new.

It's like this with us, Barnhouse suggested. Our old natures will keep on shouting out orders. But they have been stripped of all authority over us. We *can* obey them, but we *do not have to.* What we must do is to listen for the voice of our new Captain, Jesus, and choose to obey Him. He and He alone is to be obeyed, for the sin nature no longer can rule our lives.

The truths that Paul presented here in these early verses of Romans 6 do promise us a victory and freedom of which many have only dreamed. And the practical implications of this teaching are astonishing.

The past is now powerless. One of our greatest bondages has been to our past. In a very real way, our pasts determine our futures. The habits we've developed and the tastes we've cultivated have "programmed" our personalities. Each time we surrender to a temptation, we make it harder to resist the next time. Each sin in which we have indulged has paved the way for the next.

But that whole cluster of programmed responses was dealt with on the cross! We still feel the pull. But our future choices are no longer determined by those bad decisions we made in the past. "I can't help myself" is no longer true!

We have so many ways to talk about the bondage we experienced in the past. "I can't stop myself" is a cry that expresses hopelessness. So is, "The temptation is more than I can bear." No matter how true such statements may have been once, they are no longer true. Now, at last, there is release and hope.

On the solid basis of God's own Word I am assured that the power of the past over my present has been broken by Jesus. And I choose, by faith, to act upon that good word.

The next time inner conflict comes, I will present myself to God and let His righteousness find expression in me.

GROUP RESOURCE GUIDE

Identification: *Share with others*
Complete the sentence "When I feel a temptation to sin, I usually. . . . " When each person has had a chance to complete the sentence, discuss briefly what the phrase "a victorious Christian life" means to you.

Exploration: *Probe God's Word*
Listen to a previously prepared report on various theories about what happens to the sin nature when a person becomes a Christian (commentary, p. 310). Then in teams of three study Romans 6:1-14.

Work with a copy of the chart on page 311. First find a phrase or phrases in the text that corresponds with each point listed on the chart. Then find and underline the active verbs in this Romans passage that defines our part in actually experiencing the victory Christ has won for us.

Reaction: *Respond together to the Word*
Review the way you and others completed your "When I feel a temptation to sin, I usually . . . " statements. Write down how you would change your response on the basis of what Romans 6:1-14 teaches. Then go around the group, sharing what each of you wrote, and explain why.

Adoration: *Worship and pray*
Focus your thoughts on Jesus as King. Dedicate yourself to let Him—not sin—rule in everything you do. Consciously and verbally, "offer the parts of your body to Him as instruments of righteousness."

POWER

Overview

Romans 6:1-14 was a pivotal passage in Paul's argument. On the one hand it was the culmination of Paul's presentation that those who are spiritually dead can have life — through union with Jesus! It was also the launching pad for another presentation: an affirmation of freedom to live a righteous life. Here, in brief, is the line of thought we trace.

Not Under Law,
But Under Grace (Rom. 6:14)

(Digression: are we then free to sin? [6:15-23])

How can we legally be freed from the Law? (7:1-3)

Why must we be freed from the Law? (7:4-6)

(Digression: if the Law is so closely linked to sin, is Law evil? [7:7-12])

What happens to a believer who tries to relate to God through Law? (7:13-25)

What happens to a believer who relates to God through the Holy Spirit? (8:1-8)

What is the source of our victory experience? (8:9-17)

Keeping this simple line of thought in mind can help us grasp the powerful teaching of this vital New Testament passage.

Commentary

We often picture Romans as a doctrinal book, full of deep and difficult truth. In fact, the Book of Romans is totally practical. In seeking to understand the human condition Paul did not turn to abstract theory. He simply looked around him, and saw in society and in each individual's experience a daily demonstration of the reality of sin.

In seeking to explain faith, Paul again resisted the philosophical approach. He simply went back to look at a flesh and blood man in a historical situation. He noted that, for Abraham, faith meant unwavering trust in God's promise. And in turn his unwavering trust led Abraham to respond to God's word.

Then, like the practical person he was, Paul turned his attention to how faith works in us to produce a righteous life. In particular, he explored how we find the freedom to be righteous. Oh, it is good to know that sin in his life had been "rendered inoperative." But we do still feel its pull! At times when we honestly want to respond to God, we may find ourselves actually choosing the opposite way. What does it take for us to live victoriously? How do we experience the flow of the divine power?

Paul's answer was simple, but surprising. "Sin shall not be your master, because you are not under Law, but under grace" (Rom. 6:14). Somehow release from the Law, to live a Christian life under grace is vital to our experience of freedom.

Chapters 7 and 8 in Romans hinge on this affirmation. In them Paul answered the questions his statement had raised, as outlined in this study guide's *overview*.

But before we look more at these chapters, we need further backgrounding.

Earlier in our study of Romans we noted that the concept of spiritual death lurked in the background of Paul's teaching in Romans 1–3. Another concept casts a shadow across the teaching in Romans 6–8. This is the concept that the believer has "two natures."

The Bible speaks very bluntly about human "sin nature." This is an inbred tenden-

The Believer

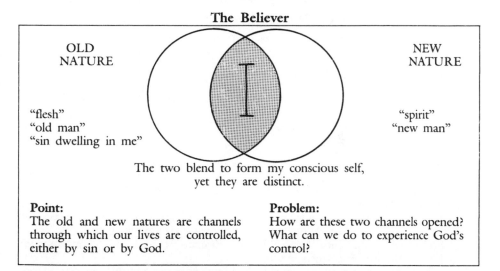

OLD NATURE		NEW NATURE

"flesh"
"old man"
"sin dwelling in me"

"spirit"
"new man"

The two blend to form my conscious self,
yet they are distinct.

Point:
The old and new natures are channels through which our lives are controlled, either by sin or by God.

Problem:
How are these two channels opened? What can we do to experience God's control?

cy to sin which warps and distorts the human personality. Human nature, which in the original Creation reflected the character of God Himself (Gen. 1:26-27), was twisted out of shape by the Fall. That fallen nature, warped and twisted, with its capacity and passion for every way but God's, remains with us. What God in Christ has done is to add a "new nature," or "new creation." Those who believe are "made alive" in Christ, with a new capacity for goodness which we did not possess before. Now at last we have both the desire and capacity to respond to God.

But these two natures, the old and the new, are at war within us. Christians are to "put to death" what belongs to the earthly nature, for the "old self with its practices" are to be put off and a "new self, which is being renewed in knowledge in the image of its Creator" put on (see Col. 3:5-11).

So now in one person there are two capacities. The one oriented to good and the other to evil. In each believer reactions, motives, desires, values, and behavior become channels through which God will express Himself in righteousness, or evil will express itself in sin.

The challenge of the Christian life is to learn to live as the new people we have become, and to increasingly reject the old we once were.

This distinctive understanding of the believer and our difference from other men and women is basic to Paul's prescription for victory. Understanding this back-

ground, we can move on to examine, in order, the answers to the questions raised by Paul, and answered in Romans 7 and 8.

Human Nature and the Law: Romans 7
How can we legally be free from the Law? (Rom. 7:1-3) Paul turned to marriage for an illustration. A married couple is bound to each other under the Law until one of them dies. The death of a partner frees *both*, so that the living partner is free to remarry. Our union with Jesus is a real union too, so when He died we were legally released from any obligation to the Law. God considers us to have "died to the Law through the body of Christ" (v. 4), and so to be free from any past obligation to live "under" it (6:14).

Why must we be freed from the Law? (Rom. 7:4-6) This is an extremely significant question. It is, in fact, central to the Bible's whole teaching on the Law and the believer. What Paul said here is that the old nature (our "sinful passions") is aroused (literally "stimulated," or "energized") by the Law! And the result of this stimulation is that we produce sin's deadly fruit.

But since we are "not under Law," we can relate to God in a new way. This new way is by the Spirit, who speaks to us directly from within. And, while Law energized the old nature, the Spirit energizes the new nature! The result of the Spirit's ministry is that we produce the fruit of righteousness.

We see the energizing principle at work

315

Two Ways of Relating to God

Through the Law	Through the Spirit
The Law energizes the old nature which produces fruit to death	The Spirit energizes the new nature which produces fruit of righteousness

everywhere. The child who is told, "Don't touch the cookies, they're for company," finds his hunger for a cookie increased! The forbidden seems far more desirable.

When we approach life as interpreted through the Law, all marked off by "do's" and "don'ts," our old sinful nature is charged with energy. But when we approach life in God's new way, seeing each challenge as an opportunity to let God express Himself through us, we are on the way to victory.

What is the experience of the believer who places himself under the Law? (Rom. 7:13-25) Paul again showed his practical bent. He looked back to his own experience after his conversion when he tried to live the Christian life under the Law. And Paul shared the discouragement he felt then. No matter how hard Paul tried, sin kept on expressing itself in him.

You and I and our group members have had the same experience. We have wanted to do good. We've tried to keep what we saw as good laws or rules, and we've known the shame and agony of failure. Paul's deeply felt anguish, expressed in this rough paraphrase, reflects feelings that we have known only too well.

I don't understand my own actions. I don't do what I want—I do the very thing I hate. Because I don't want to do the things I do, it's clear that I agree that what the Law says is good and right. I'm that much in harmony with God, anyway. But somehow I'm not in control of my own actions! Some sinful force within me takes over and acts through my body. I know that nothing good exists in the old me. The sin nature is so warped that even when I desire good I somehow can't do it. Sin, dwelling in me, is to blame for this situation. It all seems hopeless! The fact is

that when I want to do right, evil lies close at hand. In my inmost self I delight in God's law. But another principle wars with the desire to obey, and brings me as a captive to my knees before the principle of indwelling sin.
Romans 7:15-23 (author's paraphrase)

Paul's effort to keep the Law, with which he agreed, had failed. The sin nature had retained enough control over him to make it plain that no matter how he tried to keep the Law, he fell far short of the holiness and goodness it reveals.

Victory: Romans 8

Romans 7 ended with a cry: "What a wretched man that I am! Who will rescue me from this body of death?" (v. 24)

Romans 8:1-2 answered. "There is now no condemnation . . .because through Christ Jesus the law [principle] of the Spirit of life set me free from the law [principle] of sin and death." Sin within is overcome by a new and powerful principle, that of "the Spirit of life." Put simply, Paul found his answer in realizing that even as a believer he could not keep the Law . . . and was no longer trying! Paul no longer felt any *obligation* to try! Paul had finally accepted himself as really a sinner, with no hope of pleasing God. So Paul turned his gaze back to the Cross, and found joy in the thought of "no condemnation."

But then Paul made the great discovery! When he stopped *trying*, and instead relied on God to express His own divine life through Paul's personality, then "the righteous requirements of the Law" were "fully met" in him (v. 4). Sin lived in Paul. But Christ lived in Paul too. If Paul concentrated on keeping the Law rather than on trusting Jesus, his old nature was stimulated and he sinned. When Paul concentrated on trusting Jesus, the Spirit energized his new nature and he found himself living a righteous life.

Our obligation, then, is not to the Law, but to respond to the leading of the Holy Spirit (vv. 12, 14). The Law has been replaced by an intimate, personal relationship with God.

Baseball provides an analogy. We want to get to first base. But to do so the batter does *not* look at first base. He watches the ball. He focuses all his energy in concentrating on hitting the ball as it is pitched.

In a sense the "righteous requirements" of the Law are first base to us. We yearn to get there. But too many believers focus their attention on first base — and constantly strike out! What Paul said was keep your eye on the ball — on Jesus Himself — and you will discover that you arrive on first base (a righteous life) without even trying.

How can relationship be the key to moral victory? How does relationship produce righteousness? Paul showed us that as we deepen our relationship with the Lord, the Spirit of God gains more and more control over our lives. Then the Spirit will "give life to your mortal bodies" (v. 11). Yes, in our mortality we are in the grip of sin. It has always taken resurrection, life from the dead, for God to express Himself in human beings. And resurrection is exactly what God provides for those who "live in accordance with the Spirit" and "have their minds set on what the Spirit desires" (v. 15).

Likeness of Jesus (Rom. 8:18-30). In Romans 5 Paul concluded his explanation of the Gospel by stating an underlying principle: all men are spiritually dead; they desperately need righteousness, and can only receive it as a gift.

Then, in Romans 8, as Paul concluded his explanation of how the Gospel produces righteousness in a believer, he again stated a principle which supported his argument. God had chosen to shape redeemed men in the likeness of His Son, Jesus Christ (v. 28). It is our destiny to be like Jesus. God is committed to produce in us all the love, all the joy, all the patience, all the long-

Comparison: Romans 7 and 8

Chapter 7	Chapter 8
I struggle to keep the Law.	I yield myself to Jesus.
Battlefield: self-effort	*Battlefield:* enablement
Combatants: law of sin in the flesh vs. law of the mind	*Combatants:* law of sin in the flesh vs. Spirit of life in Christ Jesus
Outcome: I serve sin.	*Outcome:* The requirements of the Law are fulfilled in us.
Summary: Romans 7:4-6	*Summary:* Romans 8:8-11
NOTE Relating to God through an impersonal code: "law"—20 times "I"—22 times "I do"—14 times	NOTE Relating to God personally through faith: "law"—4 times "Holy Spirit"—20 times

suffering, all the goodness, and all the gentleness of Jesus.

This divine commitment means ultimately the renewal and transformation of the whole creation. It means that one day sin will be eradicated and that we will be "brought into the glorious freedom of the children of God" (v. 21). It also means that we *now* have hope. In another passage, Paul spoke of a progressive transformation, of a *growth* in Christlikeness which we can expect to take place. "We . . . are being transformed into His likeness," Paul wrote the Corinthians, "with ever-increasing glory, which comes from the Lord, who is the Spirit" (2 Cor. 3:18). As the Spirit of God shapes the likeness of Jesus within us, we need never concern ourselves with Law. The life of Jesus will overflow in spontaneous righteousness.

What the Law never was able to produce, the Spirit of God within us *is* producing, even now.

The New Testament on the Law

At this point, then, we need to review and summarize the New Testament teaching on Law.

The Law itself is, objectively, "holy, and the commandment is holy, righteous and good" (Rom. 7:12). As such, the Law has several important characteristics.

• Law establishes standards by which people can measure and evaluate their behavior.

• It provides a partial explanation of righteousness, illustrating righteous behavior and specifying what is unrighteous.

The Law (defined in this context as the moral and social commands given to Israel) is definitely *revelational;* it is designed to help us know more about both God and about what is good. The Law's revelation of the holy has several functions. These, strikingly, relate to the "old man" or the "sin nature."

• The Law is designed to bring the knowledge of sin (3:19-20). When a person looks at the Law's demands and then reflects on his own deeds, he becomes aware that he is a sinner.

• The Law is designed to stir up sin within us. This overlooked function is one often mentioned in the Bible. "The Law was added so that the trespass might increase" (5:20). It is because man *is* a rebel

that God's commands stimulate his rebelliousness. Yet even this function has gracious intent: unless we recognize the sin within us we are unlikely to seek God's forgiveness in Christ.

• The Law is designed to demonstrate human need of redemption. Only a person who has given up, and ceased to rely on his own efforts to gain favor with God, is likely to turn to faith. It is our natural tendency to "try harder." If we look honestly at our lives, in the clear reflection provided by the Law, we see how futile our self-effort really is.

The Law and the believer. In theology it is common to distinguish "three functions" of the Law: (1) to reveal God, (2) to convict of sin, and (3) to guide the believer in his or her life with God. This third function is one over which there has been conflict. Some say that during the Old Testament era believers were guided by the Law to respond to God, but that the New Testament introduced a new way. Others believe that the Christian should be expected to keep the Law today, and that Law is still the means God uses to guide Christians to please Him. But neither of these notions seem to fit the New Testament facts.

The point made in Romans 7 is that Law *always* relates to the old nature (the capacity for sin in man). What's more, the Law always *energizes* that sin nature. This is true whether a person is spiritually dead (and possesses only one nature) or is spiritually alive (and possesses the two natures—the sin capacity and the new life capacity). The Law has *never* been the way that believers related to God (see 1 Tim. 1:8). Always the true believer, in Old and New Testament eras, responded to God directly and personally. Even when listening to Scripture's words, the true believer heard through the Law the loving voice of God, and was freed by faith to respond to Him.

The Old Testament principle of life by faith (presented by Paul in Rom. 4) was missed by historic Israel. They distorted the Law into something it had never been intended to be. They tried to make it a way of salvation. They tried to make it a ladder on which to climb, rung by rung, to claim a place beside God as good. In so doing, they lost sight of God Himself, ignored a personal relationship with Him, and thus fell from grace.

And so may we.

We too can read about righteousness in the Scriptures, and take the Bible's teachings as rules and laws to live by. We can make the mistake of seeing God as a rule maker, and the Bible as a rule book for the game of life. We can throw our energies into vigorous attempts to fulfill the "oughts" and "shoulds." But in so doing we will take our eyes off the Lord and our personal relationship with Him. For what we are called to in Christ is a growing closeness, a deepening love. What we are called to is the warm, loving guidance given by the Spirit, and the eager, "Yes, Lord," which moves us to respond.

If we try to live by Law, we miss the joy, and our inward battle wears away our hope.

How wonderful to know that God accepts us as we are: imperfect, falling short of goodness, and yet, because Christ *is* in us, we are growing toward His likeness. For our present sins and failures we have forgiveness. And for the rest of our lives we have the promise of progress toward God's goal—likeness to Jesus.

In another passage, Galatians 2:20, Paul summed it up this way, "The life I live in the body, I live by faith in the Son of God." As Jesus' life surges up within me, all the righteousness which the Law ever envisioned, and even more, will find its expression in me.

In Jesus we have peace.

And power.

GROUP RESOURCE GUIDE

Identification: *Share with others*
Duplicate the paraphrase of Romans 7:15-23 found on p. 316 and distribute a copy to each person. Remember one situation in which you felt the way Paul seems to, and describe it briefly to the others.

Exploration: *Probe God's Word*
This is a difficult but critical section of Romans. To help teams of three work through the passage duplicate the following material.
Key Questions:
1. How can we legally be freed from Law? (7:1-3)
2. Why must we be freed from Law? (7:4-6)
3. Is the Law evil? (7:7-12)
4. What happens when a believer tries to relate to God through Law? (7:13-25)
5. What happens to a believer who relates to God through the Holy Spirit? (8:1-8)
6. What is the source of our victory? (8:9-17)

Also, provide copies of the charts on p. 315 and p. 316 (labeled Rom. 7:4-6), and p. 317.

Take plenty of time to work through the passage in triads, referring to the commentary for help when necessary.

Reaction: *Respond together to the Word*
Picture "Law" as an employer, who says, "You have to," and threatens severe punishment if you fail. And picture "Grace" as a dearly loved parent who says, "Come on, honey, I'll help you."

Discuss: How might you feel and react differently to the very same task set for you by each of these persons?

Adoration: *Worship and pray*
Read aloud and meditate on the last four paragraphs of the commentary, beginning with "If we try to live by law. . . ."

Then write a brief poem celebrating God's grace, the Holy Spirit's presence, or your freedom from the Law.

Read these aloud as expressions of praise and thanksgiving.

RIGHTEOUS IN HISTORY?

Overview

These middle chapters of Romans have not been as popular as the rest. They shift from the meaning of Jesus' death and endless life for us to other issues. And they introduce concepts over which Christians still debate.

Many of Paul's readers in New Testament times were Jewish, and a Jew might well wonder if *God* was being righteous in justifying all by faith. After all, God had given Israel great covenant promises. And this Gospel of salvation by faith totally ignores the covenants. How could Paul dare to speak of as *righteous* the God who broke and ignored His ancient word?

Romans 9–11 contains Paul's answer to this major objection to the validity of the Gospel of salvation by faith. Part of that argument rests on two difficult theological concepts.

▶ *Sovereignty.* The word is not found in Scripture. But the concept—that God is free to act as He chooses, without any limits set by the actions of another—is deeply rooted in the biblical concept of God.

▶ *Election.* The New Testament often uses the term "the elect" or "God's elect" to identify believers (cf. 2 Tim. 2:10; Titus 1:1; 1 Peter 1:1). The Greek words indicate a "choice or selection." Some Christians believe that election implies God's choice of who *will* believe, while others say it implies His choice of those who *do* believe. See Ephesians 1:4, 11.

Commentary

"But I want to draw like Paul *now!*" Every so often my youngest, Tim, was filled with an awful sense of urgency. He felt such a terrible need at 13 to be able to do everything his 19-year-old brother did. And to do it just as well.

I heard it on the basketball court when Tim missed. *Now* was such a burden for Tim. He knew so many things he would be able to do only in the future.

I could understand my youngest son's feelings. You can too. Often you and I feel the same kind of urgency to see more evidence of Christ's presence in our lives. We want to be like Jesus *now.* The dimensions in which we still need to grow bother us deeply. We feel like the Apostle Paul when he placed himself under the Law and struggled to live up to the righteousness he saw expressed there. He tried. And when he failed, he felt condemned.

But then God taught him those truths which he shares with us in Romans.

God has taken us out from under the Law. Law did its work in making us aware of our sin and failure. The Law did its work in making us feel condemned. The Law did its work in forcing us to look away from ourselves to God—to find some other way.

And God had that other way prepared. Righteousness is imputed to men by faith. The death of Christ provided a basis on which forgiveness could be extended, freely, to all. What's more, the faith through which forgiveness comes also is the secret to actually becoming righteous. Through faith, in a deepening personal relationship with God, the new in us grows, and the Spirit's power is released to shape Christ Himself in our personalities.

The Law shouted out demands, telling us what we should be but are not. Grace invites us to accept ourselves as forgiven sinners—and to trust God to help us become new.

But *becoming* takes time. And becoming sometimes disturbs us. We fail to see that God seeks progress rather than perfection. When we step out from under the Law and realize that we have been given time enough to grow, the pressure is removed.

What joy! We can be ourselves—as immature and unskilled in God's ways as Tim was in his games—and yet we can rejoice in the fact that we still please God. We are growing, and it is growth He seeks.

God does not condemn.

Nothing can separate us from the love of Christ.

Paul's words of praise in Romans 8:18-39 culminate in a joyful shout. And we shout for joy along with the great apostle.

It's hard for us to grasp at first, but those words brought outraged objection from many Jews. Their thinking went something like this. "If God is so steadfast in His love, why has He abandoned Israel? Why have the promises to God's Old Testament people been so summarily set aside, to the benefit of Gentiles? Can Paul's God of righteousness justify His behavior toward the Jews?"

On the surface, the Israelites had a strong case. We cannot read the Old Testament without being struck by the fact that God outlined there a glorious future for the Jews. They, the descendants of Abraham, are promised the land of Palestine as a perpetual possession. They, the descendants of Abraham, are promised a special relationship with God in which He claims them as His own. They, the people of David, are promised that one day a Descendant of David will mount His throne and rule not only over Israel but over the entire earth.

When this promised King, the Messiah, comes, then Israel is to enter her days of glory. Israel's God will be recognized by all. The Gentiles will come to the Jews to learn about God, and will recognize the Lord as Lord of all. In those days of glory, peace will cover the whole earth, and the Messiah-King will enforce righteousness. Thus, the blessing of all humanity depends on the Jews. The proud, despising Gentile will recognize that Israel has been God's own all along.

This, the Jews firmly believed, was Israel's heritage. This was Israel's hope. And it was all rooted in what the Old Testament prophets proclaimed.

But when Jesus came, everything seemed to change! This Person, whom Christians proclaimed as Messiah and Lord, rejected the throne and chose a cross instead. And now Paul was preaching Jesus and faith to the Gentiles—and the Gentiles were believing in Him! Becoming like Jesus, not ruling with the King, was the focal point of the great missionary's concern. And those promises of a kingdom for Israel seemed to be set aside while Paul went on and on about "righteousness."

With all Israel's dreams of glory seemingly shattered, how could Paul speak of God as "righteous"? Hadn't God's Word and promises been broken? How dare Paul write with such confidence of God's enduring love?

These are challenging questions. Yet Paul in Romans 9–11, went about answering them. He began with history. And ended with a look ahead, into the future.

This same approach, looking back and looking ahead, is important for you and me in our own spiritual lives. When we—like Tim—sense the gap between what we are and what we yearn to be, we need to look back and see what God has done in our lives. And we need to look ahead, to see what God will do as He shapes Christ in us. We are *in the process* of moving toward that goal; we cannot truly know ourselves or God's grace until we see our lives from the perspective of the whole of God's great plan for us.

It's this way too in God's dealings with Israel. The Jewish objectors failed to see God's actions as righteous. They lacked perspective. They failed to understand history—and they failed to look far enough ahead.

Paul, looking back and looking ahead, shows us that God is righteous—and sovereign too.

Israel's Rejection: Romans 9:1-33

The true Israel (Rom. 9:1-6). Paul was proud of his Hebrew heritage, and was anguished over those of his race who had not responded with faith to Jesus, their Messiah. He fully acknowledged his Jewish critics' claim of a special relationship between Israel and God: "Theirs is the adoption as sons; theirs the divine glory, the covenants, the receiving of the Law, the temple worship and the promises" (v. 4).

Yet present events did not mean that God had gone back on His word (e.g., that "God's word had failed"). The failure was not God's but Israel's! The keystone of this first argument was Paul's statement, "For not all who are descended from Israel are Israel."

Descendancy (Rom. 9:7-13). Paul went back into sacred history and showed that, first of all, the promises *never* included *all* physical descendants of Abraham. Ishmael, though a child of Abraham, was not included in the covenant promises; only Isaac was (Gen. 21:12). Later Jacob and Esau were born as twin sons of Isaac and Rebekah. But God's purpose included one, and excluded the other! Before the boys were even born (and thus before they could have done either good or bad, so that their actions were no basis for God's choice), God announced that one was chosen and the other rejected as a participant in the covenant line.

Note here that "hated" (Rom. 9:13) is used in a legal rather than emotional sense. It reflects an ancient inheritance formula. God chose Jacob to be heir to the promise, and decisively rejected any claims of his brother, Esau.

So far, then, Paul had established from history that the idea of "Israel" has *never* meant simply the physical descendants of Abraham, Isaac, and Jacob.

✂ Group Activity: Recovery Group Step 1 (admit powerlessness)

Romans 9 looks at people who argued that they were OK. Paul admits that they did have many advantages (9:1-5). But it doesn't follow that they are personally in control of their lives or right with God because they come from a godly family line (9:6-9). Even if both parents are believers, the children born into the family can have different destinies (9:10-13). Even trying hard to make it on our own is no help because everyone falls short and needs God's mercy (9:14-16).

Follow this pattern in analyzing your own situation. (1) List the advantages you have had through your upbringing or associations. (2) List the things you have relied on to give you control over your life. (3) List things you have done in an effort to give you control.

Share the advantages, the things you have relied on, and the things you have done in trying to take control of your life. Then talk about three things: what feelings make you realize you can't make it on your own? What experiences make you realize you can't make it on your own? What specific failures make you realize you can't make it on your own?

In closing, repeat this verse together until you have it firmly committed to memory: "It does not depend on man's desire or effort, but on God's mercy" (9:16).

Sovereignty of God (Rom. 9:14-23). At this point Paul's readers might make another objection. Paul had said that God *chose* Isaac and Jacob. Was it fair for God to choose some and reject others?

Here Paul took a definite stand. The God revealed in the Old Testament is a Sovereign God. He acted freely, without His actions being limited by what mere humans might do. And among His freedoms is the freedom to:

> Have mercy on whom I have mercy . . . and I will have compassion on whom I have compassion.
>
> Romans 9:15

Historically Pharaoh was given authority in Egypt by God—so that God might "display My power in you and that My name might be proclaimed in all the earth." So, Paul argued, God has mercy on those He chooses to, and He hardens those whom He wants to harden.

Paul reemphasized his position. A potter forms the clay into vessels that suit his own purpose. Who are men, mere lumps of clay, to argue with the God who shaped humanity?

This strong view of sovereignty has repelled some. Yet two things need to be considered. First, Paul in emphasizing sovereignty is *not* dealing with free will. If we go back into the Old Testament we find the Bible speaks both of God hardening Pharaoh's heart, and of Pharaoh hardening his own heart. God did not, in exercising His choice, violate the freedom of choice of His creatures. God did not *force* Pharaoh to do anything he would not have freely chosen to do.

Second, *all* humanity lies lost in sin, willingly and willfully alienated from God. The divine choice was made in eternity past that some be saved, even though all deserve condemnation. God was not and is not obligated to see to it that all are saved, even though the death of Christ is sufficient payment for all. While some see Paul's reference to two groups—"us," the "objects of His mercy," and the "objects of His wrath—as evidence that God acted to choose each individual among "us," others see it only as evidence that God decided there would be two groups. In this second view, which group a person belongs to is strictly a matter of his or her own free choice.

Yet however we interpret its implication, it is clear that Paul argued from his conviction that God *is* sovereign. God is free to act, and has acted in history as He chose to act. And God as God has that right!

Gentile salvation (Rom. 9:24-33). Returning to his theme, that never in history has "Israel" included all the physical descendants of Abraham, Isaac, and Jacob, Paul quoted the Old Testament to make two points. First, the Old Testament has *always* taught that Gentiles would be saved (vv. 24-26). And second, the Old Testament has *always* taught that only a remnant (a part and not the whole nation) of Israel will be saved (vv. 27-29). So Paul's Gospel of salvation by faith is actually in complete harmony with the Old Testament, and does not suggest that God is unfaithful! It is just that "faith" has become the key to bringing in the Gentiles, and to separating the spiritual remnant from the merely physical descendants of Abraham.

Israel's Rejection Explained: Romans 10

Paul's desire (Rom. 10:1-4). Paul had dealt theologically with the issue the Jews had raised. Then he moved to an emotional level to express his deep passion for his own people.

Paul again shared his deep desire that the Jewish people come to know Jesus Christ. And he pinpointed Israel's problem: they have disregarded the "righteousness that comes from God and sought to establish their own," refusing to "submit to God's righteousness" (v. 3). It is this spiritual orientation, not God's unfaithfulness, which had led to the current rejection by the nation.

Hope (Rom. 10:5-13). Yet there is hope for the individual Jew, just as there is now hope for the individual Gentile. Christ has come down from heaven, died, and risen again. All that is left for a person to do is to believe. It is not a matter of "doing" the Law, but of confessing that Jesus is Lord, and believing in Him in one's heart. Everyone, each individual, who calls on the name

of the Lord *will* be saved. Thus God *is* faithful still, and this Gospel message (as Paul's Old Testament quotes in this section prove) is in full harmony with the Word God spoke in the Old Testament to the Jews.

History (Rom. 10:14-21). One issue remained. Faith is stimulated by a hearing of the Good News, the Word of God. Had Israel had that opportunity? Of course! History demonstrates, in the prophets who cried out to Israel over the centuries as well as by the written Word Israel received, that God *had* spoken the Word to Israel that was to be received by faith. But those same prophets testified that Israel, though hearing, had not as a nation ever understood! In the words of Isaiah:

All day long I have held out My hands to a disobedient and obstinate people.
Romans 10:21

We can sum up Paul's argument to this point quite simply. History indicated that "Israel" had *never* meant every physical descendant of Abraham, Isaac, and Jacob. It has meant *some.*

On the one hand the fact that only some are involved reflects a clear choice by a Sovereign God. On the other hand, the fact that only some are involved reflects a clear choice by individuals. For Israel *had* heard the Word. Yet historically the nation had not heard or understood, but remained obstinate. It has always been *some* who have responded with faith to the message of God, but not all.

Thus, the charge of the Jews that the God of the Gospel is unrighteous (for the principle of faith would mean that God had abandoned His Old Testament people), is shown to be totally wrong. There has *always* been a Gospel, a message from God that must be received by faith. And in history past as today, only some believe and are saved.

∅ *Group Activity:*
Missions/Outreach Group
Use Romans 10 as a tool to evaluate your group's strengths and weaknesses. The passage focuses on four elements of outreach:
1. Caring (Rom. 10:1-5). How deeply do we care for the lost?
2. Confessing (Rom. 10:6-14). How clearly do we present the central issue of

trust in Christ, that others might believe in and confess Him?

3. Calling (Rom. 10:15-17). How aware are we of being sent with the Gospel?

4. Confronting (Rom. 10:18-21). How persistent are we in the face of resistance or rejection?

Break into four teams to explore each of these issues. First carefully study the passage itself for principles and underlying concepts. Then use these to evaluate everything your group is doing in missions and outreach. Be realistic about both strengths and weaknesses. When you find a weakness, suggest ways to shore up that area.

Reassemble to hear reports and recommendations.

Israel's Rejection Incomplete: Romans 11

A remnant (Rom. 11:1-10). Paul then picked up the Old Testament concept of the remnant, and showed that Israel's present situation could hardly be described as "rejection by God." After all, Paul himself was a Jew, and he was a believer. For its first decade the church was a Hebrew church. Thousands of Jewish men and women in Paul's day were Christians—and thousands of Jewish men and women *today* are Christians as well! "So too," Paul argued, "at the present time there is a remnant chosen by grace" (v. 5). And even this has historical precedent: in Elijah's time God told His prophet that in all Israel there were some 7,000 God "reserved for Myself who have not bowed the knee to Baal."

Gentiles (Rom. 11:11-24). Here Paul introduced an aside to his Gentile readers, who might have been feeling superior to the Jews. The company of believers is like an olive tree, Paul suggested. Its roots are Jewish, sunk deeply in Old Testament history and God's ancient commitment to His chosen people. Gentiles are like branches that have been grafted into this tree. Recognizing this, the Gentile has no cause for pride. Rather we should consider how easy it will be for God to graft *back* the "natural branches" when the time for regathering comes at last.

All Israel saved (Rom. 11:25-36). With this said, Paul looked far into the future. He did not want his Gentile brothers and

sisters to be conceited, or think that they had won Israel's promised place. The hardening of Israel is temporary, to last only until "the full number" of Gentiles has come into the church (v. 25). When the time comes, "all Israel will be saved" just as the Old Testament prophets promised (v. 26).

This was a new theme!

Paul had explained that God's present actions were in full harmony with the way God had acted in sacred history, so that the Jewish accusations of, "Unfair!" were groundless. But then Paul said that one day all the Old Testament promises to Israel will in fact be kept!

Today it is "everyone" who calls on the name of the Lord. In the future it will be "all Israel" (the nation) that experiences God's grace.

Why is this? It is because God *has* made Israel covenant promises and, Paul said, "God's gifts and His call are irrevocable" (v. 29).

In the future, history will demonstrate it. God's plans and purposes are far more complex and involved that we have supposed. Israel's vision of the future was not wrong, just incomplete. Our own vision of a heaven to be won and a hell avoided is also incomplete. God's glory will yet be displayed on earth as well as in eternity, as Jesus returns to take the throne as Israel's promised King. No wonder Paul concluded with a powerful doxology of praise:

> Oh, the depth of the riches of the wisdom and knowledge of God! How unsearchable His judgments, and His paths beyond tracing out! Who has known the mind of the Lord? Or who has been His counselor? Who has ever given to God, that God should repay him? For from Him and through Him and to Him are all things. To Him be the glory forever. Amen.

Conclusions

The Jews who accused God of unfaithfulness to His Word erred in underestimating the Lord. They had only a superficial grasp of God's plan and purposes. And, rather than submit to God, and seek out the whole, these men dared to condemn the Lord!

Tragically, you and I are sometimes found doing the same thing. We come to teachings that we do not understand, and rather than acknowledge our own limitations, we begin to lay charges against God.

For instance, we bridle at Paul's blunt statements about God's sovereignty and wonder that God should choose some to receive mercy (Rom. 9). We can't understand how this fits in with the revelation in Jesus of a God of love who is unwilling that *any* should perish (2 Peter 3:9). Instead of trusting in God's wisdom, righteousness, and love, we, like the unbelieving Jews of Paul's day, cry out, "Unfair!"

So what if we cannot understand? Is God accountable to us? Or can we, like Paul, see such things that are beyond our comprehension as fresh evidence of the depth of the wisdom and knowledge of God? We cannot fathom the wisdom and knowledge, but we *can* surrender in trust.

There are other things too. We complain and grumble about the slowness of our growth. Why the ups and downs? Why do some of our problems persist so long? "Am I really profiting from these years of bouts with depression? Why has God put off healing the hurts which divide my home?"

Yet Scripture demands that we see everything happening in our lives as an aspect of God's good plan for our growth and glorification. "In all things God works for the good of those who love Him," Paul affirmed (Rom. 8:28). We have been called "according to His purpose" (v. 28), and our lives are designed so that His purpose, of forming Christ within might proceed at God's carefully planned pace.

Looking at the pattern of my life, I must be willing to surrender my perspective to Him. He is Lord. I am not His adviser. His wisdom is beyond my own, and I surrender, praising, to that wisdom.

How tragic when we underestimate God. How tragic when we, like the ancient Jews, fail to read the lesson of history past and of history yet to come. God's wisdom *is* far beyond anything we can understand or grasp. *But what God says is true!* With complete confidence in the wisdom of God, I can bow before Him and surrender my wisdom to His.

From this day forward, I can live.

By faith.

And, in Jesus, I will experience the greatest adventure of all.

For from Him and through Him and to Him are all things. To Him be the glory forever! Amen.

Romans 11:36

GROUP RESOURCE GUIDE

Identification: *Share with others*
Respond to one of three words, sharing what it makes you think of, and how it makes you feel. The three words are: sovereignty, predestination, and election.

Then sort the positive and negative feelings suggested by group members, listing positive words used on one side of a chalkboard and the negative words used on the other side of a chalkboard.

Exploration: *Probe God's Word*
Divide into teams, with one set of teams formed of those who were mainly positive about the three terms, and one set of teams formed of those who were mainly negative. Each team is to read through Romans 9–11 quickly, identifying verses that support its members' feelings about sovereignty, predestination, and/or election. For instance, the "positive" teams might note that God is one who "has compassion" (9:15), while the "negative" teams note the phrase "He hardens whom He wants to harden" (9:18).

When each team has identified its supportive verses, come together and share findings. Then work through the three chapters, guided by the commentary, to see if you can put both kinds of verses in perspective.

Because of the difficult nature of the material in these chapters, most of your group time will be spent in this direct Bible study.

Reaction: *Respond together to the Word*
Very briefly tell one thing you have learned about yourself, about God, or about the Bible from this session.

Adoration: *Worship and pray*
Read in unison the doxology ("words of praise") with which Paul concludes this section of Romans (11:33-36).

A RIGHTEOUS, LOVING CHURCH

Overview

Paul had described God's gift of righteousness to humankind. He had shown that God's righteousness is both legal (providing a basis on which sinners can be acquitted before the divine court) and dynamic (providing an inner power which leads to the transformation of the believer from within).

Now Paul went on to make yet another vital point. Those individuals who have received the gift of God are to band together in community. In the community of those who believe, fresh aspects of God's goodness and His beauty will be expressed.

However, not every local church has experienced the joy of community. Why not? In these vital chapters of Romans, Paul described the attitudes and the actions which bond believers together in love, and which create a relational climate in which maximum personal spiritual growth can take place. How wonderful these chapters of Romans are! And how we need to take them to heart, making them our guidelines as we learn how to live together as God's holy, loving family of faith.

▶ *Accept.* This key term appears in Romans 14 and is used to describe our attitude toward all who are fellow-believers, even though they may differ from us in significant ways. The Greek word, *proslambano,* means literally "welcome," to actively draw another into one's society or circle of friends.

Commentary

I don't know why we picture righteous people as dull. But we do.

And we picture them as rather grim. As standing to one side, with a disapproving look on their faces while others frolic. Somehow the righteous person shows up dressed in black, while everyone else wears bright and colorful clothes. In the old movies we watch on TV, the scoundrel is the warm, engaging person who quickly makes friends.

How tragic when we let the world force our thinking into Satan's mold. Righteousness isn't like that at all! The righteousness that God gives us, and the righteousness that His Spirit is at work to shape in us, is a warm personal kind of thing. Rather than isolate us from others, for the first time we find it is possible to draw truly near. We find that the first fruit of the Spirit, love, warms and deepens our relationships with others who have become our brothers and sisters, one with us in the forever family of God. The second product, joy, makes the fellowship we share bright and colorful (see Gal. 5:22-23).

So let's exchange our old, mistaken picture of righteousness for the reality. Let's take off our imaginary suits of black. Let's put on our brightest party clothes. Let's reach out to others . . . stretch out our hands . . . touch . . . smile! Let's call for the music to play, the celebration to begin! Let's move out into the sunlight, feel its warmth, shout together, share our joy!

The righteousness of God finds its fullest expression in Christ's new, loving, and joyful community.

Homothumadon. In our study of Acts we introduced this Greek term which means, "with one accord." It was a word that God chose to describe the fellowship that existed within the earliest church. That word portrays the unique harmony and love that so impressed early observers. "See how they love one another," was the remark. These early Christians, so varied in background (there were both rich and poor, Judean and foreign Jew), found a unity and love that observers could hardly believe.

Jesus had spoken of this dimension of Christian community before His crucifixion. He told His followers, "Love one another as I have loved you. All men will know that you are My disciples, if you love one another" (John 13:34-35). God's plan for believers includes the demonstration of His righteousness in and through a loving community. Christ's church is to demonstrate to all the world that righteousness, correctly understood, means love and joy!

The church is also to be the context in which growth and transformation take place in believers. We are to be nourished in our growth toward Christ's likeness by one another. In the acceptance and love of our brothers and sisters, we're to sense God's own acceptance and love, and to grow in that freedom from Law which Paul explained so carefully. "Grow up into . . . Christ," Paul called it in Ephesians 4:15. Growing up, together, into Christ.

It is tragic that just as the Law has sometimes been distorted and misused by Christians, the church has too. Sometimes, rather than the joyful community of God's plan, the church has become a joyless assembly. Rather than loving and accepting one another as brothers on a common pilgrimage, some churches have become legalist assemblies where conformity and pretense are the price of admission. The vital dimension of growth in Christ as a way of life has been set aside, and agreement on our doctrines, or our convictions and customs has been imposed. No longer are imperfect people welcomed, loved, and accepted as they are, in the calm assurance that growth in Christ is all they need. Instead, the believer in such a church is forced to try to hide his imperfections, and struggle to live up to a new legalism, imposed not by God but by men.

No wonder then that Paul, all too familiar with this same tendency in his own day, turned in the closing chapters of Romans to outline for us the way to the righteous, loving community that God seeks to shape. Paul here gave us clear, simple guidance for shared experience of God's joy.

Christ's Impact: Romans 12

Romans 12 begins with familiar and famous words. "I urge you . . . in view of God's mercy, to offer your bodies as living sacrifices, holy and pleasing to God—which is your spiritual worship." We can never have a truly Christian relationship with others until we are fully committed to God. Only when we are surrendered to Him will the world be powerless to squeeze us into its mold, and will we be transformed and able to live out God's good will.

This is important here, launching a section on interpersonal relationships. We can never substitute quality relationships with other Christians for quality relationship with the Lord. The real source of quality relationships with others is full commitment to the Lord. With this principle established, however, Paul does call us to look closely at the relationship we have with the brothers and sisters whom God has given us.

Mutual ministry (Rom. 12:3-8). The world's way is all too often to measure people *against* each other. How well we compete, and how much better we are than others, are ways we are measured.

This competitive dimension of society shows up in everything. School grades are a way of measuring people against others. Sports are designed to select winners, and to separate them from losers. Our economy and businesses are again expressions of a competitive approach to life. The way we view others and our opinion of them are all directly related to how they compare, in terms of skills, education, looks, talents, character, etc. In tremendously significant ways, measured against others, each individual stands or falls alone.

But when we come to the church, this perspective changes. God views us as members of a body. In the body relationship we do not compete; we cooperate. "In Christ we who are many form one body, and each member belongs to all the others" (v. 5). Each of us has a different function, but our differences do not make anyone better or worse than another. The reason is that, whatever our gift (function), each of us contributes. Each of us is necessary!

How then are we to evaluate ourselves? We are each to focus on using our own gift to serve others. *We find fulfillment not in comparing ourselves with others, but in being ourselves and using whatever talent God has given in ministry!*

How exciting this is. No longer am I any more important than my brother, or he more important than I. We are each important, in and of ourselves.

It is impossible to overestimate the impact of this perspective on ourselves and on interpersonal relationships. When I develop the divine viewpoint:

- I am released from jealousy.
- I can find fulfillment in being who I am, rather than wanting to be like someone else.
- My friendships are not distorted by status—I am awed by none, and look down on none.
- I appreciate others for themselves, without feeling they must be different or must be like me.

Learning to take God's view of others as members with me in a body where cooperation, not competition, has value initiates a whole new way of relating to others that is unlike anything the world knows.

This is the first key to building a righteous, loving community. To see ourselves and others as God does, as valuable contributing persons in a family of faith.

Love's priority (Rom. 12:9-21). The key to life in the Christian community is love. Paul makes this very clear. "Love must be sincere. . . . Be devoted to one another in brotherly love. . . . Live in harmony with one another. . . . Overcome evil with good" (vv. 9-10, 16, 21).

The kind of love that Paul described is not a passive thing. Instead it involves an aggressive reaching out to care for others. "Share with God's people who are in need" (v. 13) is one practical expression of love. "Practice hospitality" (v. 13) is another. "Be willing to associate with people of low position [in society]" (v. 16) is yet another.

A climate of love is absolutely basic to the church of Jesus Christ. Without such caring, and reaching out to touch one another's lives, the church will fall tragically short of God's intended experience of His "good, pleasing and perfect will" (v. 2).

♥ *Group Activity: Support Group*
Share briefly how you have experienced support from members of your group. Then look together at Romans 12 which identifies and describes three commitments: commitment to God (12:1-2); commitment to minister (12:3-8); and commitment to love (12:9-21). The first is foundational, the other two are expressions of our dedication to the Lord.

In teams of three or four look at each phrase found in 12:3-8 and 9-21. By each

phrase that describes what is already happening in your support group, put a plus. By each phrase which describes something that any one of you feels is not currently happening, put a minus.

Come together again and share both pluses and minuses. Be sensitive, for anyone who senses a minus may be expressing a personal need others have been unaware of. Use such expressions as clues to help you see how to better support and care for other group members.

Church and State: Romans 13

In one sense this is a digression. In another it is not. The church is a body, uniquely different from the secular society of which it is also a part. How are Christians to relate, not to each other, but to the state and to its secular citizens?

Human government (Rom. 13:1-7). Paul taught that God had instituted human government as a restraining power, an agent of justice to bring punishment to wrongdoers. This is no blanket endorsement of every and any form of human government. It is, however, an astute observation. Any state, for its own self-interest, must be concerned with morality and moral order! If citizens lied and stole and murdered one another, the state would fall to enemies from outside or to corruption from within. Thus human government, for its own sake and not out of respect for God, serves as God's agent in enforcing basic morality.

Christians are to recognize that the state (human government) has been ordained by God, and are to respect it as a divinely intended institution. Out of respect for God we are to pay taxes, show respect for those who govern, and in other ways be good citizens of the countries in which we live.

✍ *Group Activity: Bible Study Group*
Many significant church/state questions have been raised in the U.S. in the past decade. Romans 13 defines certain basic concepts about the nature and function of the state. Study the passage, to identify guiding principles. For instance, the state exists to protect the freedoms of those who do right.

After listing as many principles as you can agree are implied in the passage, see which can be applied to contemporary issues such as: Should tax credits be given to those who want to educate their children in Christian schools? Should Christian teens be allowed to have Bible Study clubs that meet on school property? Should the government pass laws that relate to moral issues, such as pornography and abortion? Should Christians use civil disobedience to protest laws they believe contradict biblical principles?

Personal corruption (Rom. 13:8-14). The citizen is to fulfill all his public obligations. Yet there is one debt which can never be paid: the debt we owe to all our fellowmen to love them (v. 8). Everything the commandments speak out against *harms* others (vv. 9-10). If we truly love them, we will do nothing to bring them harm, and thus love will lead us to fulfill divine law as well as keep us from violations of human law.

We who are Christ's need to concentrate on love, rejecting all those sins that attract the lost. Love calls us to "clothe [ourselves] with the Lord Jesus Christ, and . . . not think about how to gratify the desires of the sinful nature" (v. 14).

Maintaining Harmony.
Romans 14:1–15:13
Paul's primary concern in this section of Romans is not how the Christian is to conduct himself in society, but how we express our new life within the believing community.

This is not because society is unimportant. *It is because the Christian community as well as the individual is to witness to the reality of Jesus.* On the one hand, the Christian community is the context in which individual believers can grow to their full stature as Christ's people. On the other, the love which marks Christian relationships is itself a powerful testimony to Christ's presence. For each of these purposes to be achieved, the church must truly be the righteous, loving community which Scripture describes with *homothumadon.*

It's no wonder, then, that Paul described attitudes toward others which build community. Strikingly, each of the attitudes reflects Jesus' own attitude toward us.

Accepting (Rom. 14:1-13). Paul dealt with an issue which often creates conflict in churches: convictions. These are *not* matters which Scripture identifies as "sin." They are, however, issues which seem "wrong" to some believers, and "right" to others.

Actually, all of us differ from others in significant ways. We Christians have different opinions about what a believer should and shouldn't do. Some think women should be ordained; others violently disagree. Some, in Paul's day, thought it was "Christian" to be vegetarian, while others liked a good steak. Some then felt Christians should observe special "holy" days, and others felt all days are alike.

These differences tended then as now to divide believers into subgroups of "them" and "us." And all such antagonistic divisions are harmful to community! All distort the unity and ministry of Jesus' church.

How does Romans teach we are to deal with such differences?

Positively. Paul suggested several positive steps and attitudes we are to develop. First, we are to actively welcome even those with a weak faith (v. 1). Second, we are to recognize Jesus as Lord (vv. 6-12). Christ arose (and thus is alive) so that *He* might be Lord for His people. Each of us is responsible to Jesus as Lord; we are *not* responsible to each other. Third, we are to each explore the issues over which believers have convictions and "be fully convinced in his own mind" (v. 5).

Negatively. What we are *not* to do in our relationships with other Christians is clearly identified. We are *not* to condemn others whose convictions differ from ours (v. 3). We are *not* to look down on them for being "less spiritual" than we (v. 3). Bluntly put, *we are not to judge them at all* (v. 1). Jesus is Lord, and they are responsible to Him. If they have sinned, Jesus will judge them. We have no business intruding into this relationship of responsibility of a fellow believer to the Lord (v. 13).

We should look to Christ as our model. "Accept one another, then, just as Christ accepted you, in order to bring praise to God" (15:7). God does not condemn the brother we judge, but has accepted him (14:3). As far as his future is concerned, Jesus is able to make our brother or sister stand (v. 4).

How important then, that like Jesus, we love and accept each other, and try to build each other up rather than tear one another down because of the ways in which we differ.

329

❋ *Group Activity:*
Singles/Single Again Group
Discuss: Are other people more or less likely to tell singles or single-again persons what they ought to do than they are to give such "advice" to marrieds? List some specific "you ought to" or "you have to" opinions others have expressed that have hurt or outraged you. Explore too how the well-meant but demanding advice of others has made you feel: more competent or less? More confident or less? Etc.

Then study Romans 14:1-13. Sum up its teaching in brief, pithy statements, such as: "stop judging," "extend freedom," "let Jesus be Lord," and "let me be responsible."

In conclusion talk about two things: How does this passage's teaching empower me as a single person? And, how can I stand up for the freedom and the responsibility God has given me as a single person to make my own decisions?

Self-sacrifice (Rom. 14:13–15:13). Often the differences that do exist between us will trouble an entire fellowship. Some, who have the freedom to do what others question, may in the exercise of that freedom, cause the brother harm.

Paul is very clear here. Nothing (that is not identified in Scripture as sin) is unclean or wrong in itself. But neither is it more important than our brother or sister. So we Christians walk a fine line.

We affirm our freedom and responsibility to live by our own convictions. Yet we are careful not to flaunt them, so that others may follow our example despite personal doubts, or may condemn us for what we ourselves believe to be good and right.

In this area, Paul gives several practical suggestions:

"Whatever you believe about these things keep between yourself and God" (14:22).

"Make every effort to do what leads to peace and mutual edification" (v. 19).

"We who are strong ought to bear with the failings of the weak and not to please ourselves" (15:1).

The goal toward which we are to work, giving it priority rather than convictions, is "that with one heart and mouth you may [together] glorify the God and Father of our Lord Jesus Christ" (v. 6).

Farewells: Romans 15:14–16:27

Paul's farewells are also revealing. He expressed confidence in the Spirit who was within the Romans. They did not need him, for they had been fully equipped by God for a life of faith (15:14-16).

While Paul had long wished to visit Rome, God had not yet let him. Eagerly he looked forward to such a time, perhaps as a side visit on the way to Spain. What an adventure there: Spain! A land where the Gospel had not been heard.

Romans 16 is filled with personal greetings. If ever we wondered about the apostle and his relationships with others, these greetings are revealing. Paul had never visited Rome. He must have met these people elsewhere on his journeys. Yet, he had kept such close track of them that he knew the details of many of their lives.

What a warm and loving fellowship Paul must have experienced with his beloved brothers and sisters in the Lord. How real the community of which he wrote in these chapters must have been to him. Saul, the lonely Pharisee at 30, isolated from everyone in that distorted righteousness of works, had become Paul the apostle, a man of warmth and love, wrapped in the comforting cloak of Christian friends.

God's kind of righteousness has broken through the isolation of the lonely heart and, in the fellowship of those who love one Lord, brought celebration and joy.

With Paul		At Rome	
Men			*Women*
Timothy	Aquila	Rufus	Priscilla
Lucius	Epenetus	Asyncritus	Mary
Jason	Adronicus	Phlegon	Tryphena
Sosipater	Ampliatus	Hermes	Tryphosa
Tertius	Urbanus	Patrobas	Persis
Gaius	Stachys	Hermas	Julia
Erastus	Herodion	Nereus	
Quartus	Olympas	Junias	
Phoebe	Apelles	Philologus	

In Christ, community is ours. Yet our names are known individually.

What a lesson. Our individuality is not surrendered, yet in the bonds of love in Christ's church each one can at last, severally and together, become all we were ever meant to be.

✍ *Group Activity: Bible Study Group*
Put the list of men and women mentioned by Paul in Romans 16 on a chalkboard or sheet of newsprint. First brainstorm: what conclusions can you draw from the list itself, without looking further into the text?

Then look into the text, and list the kinds of things Paul says about these people (e.g., "fellow workers," etc.). About whom does he say these things?

Now examine what is said about the women on the list. Are they described in the same ways men are or in different ways? What roles did women apparently have in the churches Paul founded?

If this were the only passage in the N.T. that mentioned women in the church, what conclusions would you have to draw about them and their role in congregational life?

GROUP RESOURCE GUIDE

Identification: *Share with others*
Tell one thing you do or do not do in order to avoid criticism from other Christians rather than because of personal conviction. When all have shared discuss: How comfortable are you in conforming to expectations? How do you feel about those who impose their standards on you? How does conforming make you feel about yourself?

Exploration: *Probe God's Word*
Together read Romans 14:1-17 and list on a chalkboard or sheet of newsprint statements that summarize its teaching.

Reaction: *Respond together to the Word*
Write down how Romans 14 (1) will affect your attitude and behavior toward others, and (2) will affect your personal decision-making.

Then discuss the two case histories below identifying with one of the persons in each. Talk about how you would likely have reacted without Romans 14 teaching, and how you would respond now that you understand Romans 14.
The case histories are:

Case 1: Linda's children are in school now, and she wants to go back to work. Her husband Jim is opposed. His coworkers are convinced men should be the providers, and women should stay at home. If Linda goes to work, the others in their Bible-Belt town will look down on him. Besides, he has the feeling the Bible is against women working. Why does Linda want to work anyway?

Case 2: Bob isn't ready to buy the opinion expressed by the church's pastor that drinking alcohol is always wrong. Didn't people drink wine in NT times? Of course, drunkenness is wrong. But what's wrong with a single cold beer to help a guy mellow out after work? Charlie, a recovered alcoholic, has come to believe this is a vital moral issue, and that any drinking at all is absolutely wrong. How is the church to deal with these divergent views, and how are Bob and Charlie to relate to each other?

Affirmation: *Express love and concern*
If you have experienced unconditional acceptance from anyone in the group, tell him or her how much you appreciate that quality in him or her.

Adoration: *Worship and pray*
Focus on a sheet of paper on which has been written, "Christ is Lord." Together praise Jesus as Lord in your life, and Lord in the lives of each of the others in your group. Pledge yourselves to let Jesus be Lord, and not to take any of His perogatives by judging, condemning, or looking down on Christians whose convictions differ from your own.

A UNITED CHURCH FAMILY

Overview

First Corinthians is the New Testament's "problem epistle." In it Paul deals with a series of problems that existed in that young church, introducing each new issue with the phrase, *peri dei,* translated in our versions as "Now concerning," or simply, "Now. . . ."

The problems sound like a catalog of problems experienced by local churches today:

- Division in the church (1–4).
- Discipline (5–6).
- Marriage and divorce (7).
- Doctrinal disputes (8–10).
- Misunderstanding of spiritual (charismatic) gifts (12–14).

In addition, the letter touches on the role of women, the importance of the Lord's Supper, and on the centrality of the Resurrection in Christian teaching.

Within each section, Paul gives us a carefully reasoned discussion of the problem, and how to deal with it, making this letter one of the most practical and important for Christians today.

▶ *Wise/wisdom.* In 1 Corinthians 1–4 "wisdom" (Greek, *sophia*) is the perspective from which a person deals with the issues of life. Humans are "foolish" when they fail to realize that their notions must be subjected to divine evaluation. Only when a person abandons what seems wise by human standards to accept without hesitation the divine viewpoint as revealed in Scripture can he or she be truly wise.

Commentary

Near the end of his third missionary journey, Paul wrote a letter to a church in trouble. Some seven years before, he and his companions had founded the church in Corinth. Even though the members of the

believing community were richly gifted, the process of transformation toward Christ-likeness seemed constantly blocked.

Paul kept in touch with the Corinthian fellowship, as he did with all the churches. Finally, after a verbal report from the family of Chloe, and after a delegation arrived from Corinth asking for Paul's judgment on specific questions, this first letter to the Corinthians was written.

This is an important letter for us to read and to master. It is important because it helps us realize our own struggle for a real and vital faith may be a long one. And it is important because this letter presents principles that you and I and our group members can apply to help resolve problems that continue to plague modern Christian fellowships.

Corinth was an important city and had been from ancient days. It was situated on the isthmus bearing its name, and controlled land and sea trade routes. In New Testament times, it was not only an important commercial city but also the administrative center of the Province of Achaia.

Roberth H. Gundry's description of the city (*A Survey of the New Testament,* Zondervan) gives us an idea of the cosmopolitan character of Corinth.

The athletic games at Corinth were second only to the Olympics. The outdoor theater accommodated twenty thousand people, the roofed theater three thousand. Temples, shrines, and altars dotted the city. A thousand sacred prostitutes made themselves available at the temple of the Greek goddess Aphrodite. The south side of the marketplace was lined with taverns equipped with underground cisterns for cooling the drinks.

Noted for its lax morals and scandalous lifestyle, Corinth was a completely pagan society—a society that created many difficulties for the believers who lived there.

Even though the Corinthian church was struggling, and is the only congregation that Paul called unspiritual in one of his letters, Paul began his letter with words of commendation and confidence. He was writing to people who had been "sanctified in Christ Jesus and called to be holy, together with all those everywhere who call on the name of our Lord Jesus Christ." Paul assured his readers that Christ "will keep you strong to the end, so that you will be blameless on the day of our Lord Jesus Christ. God, who has called you into fellowship with His Son Jesus Christ our Lord, is faithful" (1 Cor. 1:2, 8-9).

What a wonderful thing to remember always. No matter how much our own Christian experience may seem to involve struggle, how slow our growth, it is God who has called us into fellowship with Himself. And God is faithful. God *will* work in our lives, and will keep us strong.

But once Paul expressed his confidence, he plunged immediately into an analysis of the Corinthians' problems. And these problems were serious indeed.

A Method of Study
The Bible contains many different literary forms. There is narrative storytelling, as in Genesis and the Gospels. There is poetry, as in Job and the Psalms. There is the preaching of the prophets—and the carefully reasoned argument of many of the New Testament epistles. Each of the different literary forms are, in Scripture, a mode of the divine revelation. Yet each is to be studied in ways that are appropriate to its special character.

When we come to tightly reasoned passages of Scripture, the most appropriate Bible study method is to trace the writer's line of argument. That is, we must study carefully to follow his train of thought. This approach will guard us from taking a verse out of context, and interpreting it as if it stood alone. But most important, this method will enable us to truly understand what God is teaching us in a particular book or passage.

First Corinthians is one of the most closely reasoned of Paul's letters. In it Paul dealt with problems—and in it he carefully explained the principles, the very "thoughts of God," which we are to apply to resolve the problems.

It would be appropriate, then, to apply a particular type of Bible study *designed to trace an argument* to your group's study of 1 Corinthians. If you do, you will not only help your group members discover the deeper truths this great book teaches, but will also train them in an approach to Bible study which will enrich their own personal reading of God's Word.

In each of the 1 Corinthian study guides we'll apply this particular method, which you may choose to use in teaching. But we'll also discuss the key truths taught in each section, and provide alternative methods so you will not *have* to use this study approach if you feel it is not appropriate for your particular group.

How then do we trace the argument (the line of thought) of a closely reasoned passage of Scripture?

1. Read and reread a section to determine its subject.
2. Make a one-sentence summary of each paragraph within the section.
3. Rework sentences into a brief paraphrase of the section.
4. Go back and examine each paragraph in the text in more detail.
5. Determine and apply major teachings (principles).

If we apply this method to the first four chapters of 1 Corinthians, here's what may be discovered.

The Subject: 1 Corinthians 1–4
When we read through these chapters quickly, several things are apparent. First, Paul talked here a great deal about *wisdom*. This word, and *wise,* appear no fewer than 27 times in this four-chapter section!

At the same time, it is clear that Paul is not concerned with an intellectual debate about the relationship between faith and philosophy. Paul immediately expressed his central concern: "I appeal to you . . . that there may be no divisions among you and that you may be perfectly united in mind and thought." The Corinthians had formed parties, or cliques, based on the supposed superiority of various Christian leaders. There was a "Paul party" and a "Peter party"; an "Apollos party" and a very spiritual type, "Jesus-only party." These divisions had shattered the unity of the local congregation, and created dissension. This whole section is basically about divisions, and how to maintain unity.

So we might give the section a title like this:

Maintaining Unity in the Church Family

As noted, wisdom is somehow critical here. But before we know just how, we need to trace the progression of Paul's thought, paragraph by paragraph. When we do, we will see that something called God's wisdom provides the solution to this very common, very human problem.

A Sentence Summary: 1 Corinthians 1-4

The goal here is to capture in a single sentence the main thrust of each paragraph.

For instance:

I appeal to you, brothers, in the name of our Lord Jesus Christ, that all of you agree with one another so that there may be no divisions among you and that you may be perfectly united in mind and thought. My brothers, some from Chloe's household have informed me that there are quarrels among you. What I mean is this: One of you says, "I follow Paul"; another, "I follow Apollos"; another, "I follow Cephas"; still another, "I follow Christ."

1 Corinthians 1:10-12

Now, what is the subject of this paragraph? What is its focus? If we emphasize the problem, we might summarize this way: *The division in your church fellowship is wrong.*

If, however, we emphasize the goal, we'll pick up from Paul's first sentence: *I urge you to resolve your differences and restore unity in your church fellowship.*

Very often in translations of Paul's writings we'll find that the first sentence of a paragraph is a key to his subject. So let's choose the second summary (above) as the summary of this paragraph, though the first is not wrong. In developing summary sentences, there is always room for different ways of stating the same things.

If we work through the entire four-chapter passage, we may come up with summary sentences like those on the chart.

Paraphrasing: 1 Corinthians 1-4

When we have the summary sentences complete, we then read them over and see if the thought of each is closely linked to what precedes it and what follows. Can they be read aloud together, and so follow the apostle's thinking? Does the whole make sense?

In a paraphrase we do just this: we link the summary sentences and, if necessary, go back to any paragraph whose links to what goes before and comes after are unclear to us.

Paraphrasing in this way protects us against a common flaw in Bible study. We all tend to lose sight of the whole. As a result, we may misinterpret single verses or short paragraphs. A good paraphrase will bring the whole passage into clear view—and keep it in view—thus guarding us against "proof texting" or taking a thought out of context and misinterpreting it.

What might a paraphrase of 1 Corinthians 1-4 look like, and what will it tell us about Paul's line of thought? Here are the sentence summaries, reworked into a paragraph.

Unity in the Church Family
1 Corinthians 1-4

I urge you to resolve your differences and restore unity in the church family. Remember, Christ is the center of our lives and in Him we *are* one.

This may not sound like a very "wise" argument, but then the message of Christ and His cross has always been at odds with human wisdom.

And Christ, not some super "wisdom," brought you your righteousness, holiness, and redemption. That's why I kept my message simple when I was with you, that you might rely only on the crucified Lord.

Of course there is a divine wisdom, but it comes by revelation and not human discovery. This wisdom involves learning to think God's thoughts, something that requires both hearing the revealed words and being enlightened by the Holy Spirit.

But you! Why, your jealousy and quarreling make it very clear that you think and act like mere men. Who do you think is important: we servants, or God who works through us? I'm thank-

Paragraph	Verses	Summary Sentence
1	1:10-12	I urge you to resolve your differences and restore unity in your church fellowship.
2	1:13-17	The central fact is Christ, and that in Him we are one.
3	1:18-25	God's wisdom as shown in Christ is really at odds with man's "wise" approach to things.
4	1:26-31	In fact, it is Christ and not some superior wisdom who has brought you righteousness, holiness, and redemption!
5	2:1-5	I purposely kept my message simple when with you in order that your full reliance might be on the crucified Jesus.
6	2:6-10	Of course, there is a divine wisdom—but this comes through revelation, and its source is not in man's discoveries.
7	2:11-16	This wisdom involves a person coming to grasp God's thoughts, something that demands both hearing the revealed words and being enlightened by the Holy Spirit.
8	3:1-4	But you! Your jealousy and quarreling make it clear that you think and act on a merely human level.
9	3:5-9	Who do you think is important—we servants, or the God who works through us?
10	3:10-15	I'm thankful for the privilege of serving, but my foundation is Jesus, and what I build will be evaluated one day.
11	3:16-17	But don't you realize that the true construction is going on in your lives, that *you* are God's sacred temple, and that we all must build (not tear down!) the growing structure?
12	3:18-23	So don't fool yourselves with all those childish arguments about which leader is better; abandon that kind of thing, and focus on all that God has given you in Christ.
13	4:1-7	Grasp this principle: God Himself is the source of all that a man possesses, so how can anyone boast about having "superior" gifts or skills?
14	4:8-13	Rather than trying to build our own little empires, we apostles have abandoned all, having chosen humiliation, weakness, hunger, and persecution as our lot.
15	4:14-16	As your father, I warn you to imitate me in this and get your priorities back into harmony with reality.
16	4:18-21	And I warn you: unity in the family is so vital that in God's power I will discipline you when I come unless you abandon your worldly arrogance!

ful I can serve, but my foundation is Jesus, and one day what I build will be evaluated. (Don't you even grasp the fact that the true construction is going on *in your lives* and that *you* are God's sacred temple? Building up people, not tearing them down, is doing God's work!)

So don't deceive yourselves with all those childish arguments over leaders. Abandon that foolish game and focus again on all that is yours in Jesus, you who are not on trial before any human jury! Can't you grasp the basic principle? God Himself is the source of all. How then can we boast about anyone's superior gifts or skills?

Why, rather than trying to build our own little kingdoms, we apostles have abandoned all that, and have chosen humiliation, weakness, hunger, and even persecution as our lot. So I warn you. Imitate me in this, and get your priorities back in order. And this *is* a warning. Unity in the family is so vital that, in God's own power, I will discipline you when I come unless you abandon your worldly arrogance!

What a powerful passage! And what a vital message for divided Christians today.

Reviewing the Text: 1 Corinthians 1–4
At this point, with the overview of the argument in mind, we can go back and look into each paragraph more closely. It is *now* that a verse-by-verse approach to Bible study can be helpful, for now our understanding of the thoughts and phrases will be guided by an overview of their context.

Often at this point we will make exciting discoveries, and see fresh meaning in verses that have become so familiar that we read over them, without thought. Often too we'll make a discovery that will lead us back to our paraphrase to make a change that brings the whole into clearer focus. In short, *a study of the details of the text is always more fruitful when we have first grasped the argument of the larger unit.*

This very point is one that Paul made in 1 Corinthians 1 and 2. He pointed out that man's ways of thinking (human "wisdom") and God's ways of thinking (His "foolishness") truly do *not* correspond. The Cross is given as an example. What human mind would have imagined that God would give us righteousness, holiness, and redemption by means of the execution of His Son as a criminal!

To the Greek mind the whole notion was idiotic: salvation, if there were such a thing, would have to come through some appeal to man's capacity to achieve. Furthermore, the Greek mind viewed God as immutable and unchangable. The Gospel presentation of Incarnation, the Cross, and Resurrection were simply ruled out; the Gospel contradicted one of the axioms of classical Greek philosophy.

To the Hebrew, the whole thing was foreign as well. Deliverance would come in another Exodus, with God breaking into history to perform miracles and punish Israel's enemies. A suffering Saviour? Never! Israel would settle for nothing less than a conquering king.

While the Greek and the Jew each clung to his own notion of how God must act, God had His own ideas. The Cross meant that each must surrender his own way of thinking, and submit to *a divine wisdom that operates on principles which are basically different from those that appeal to human thought!*

Man is impressed by human accomplishment: God chose to use things man despises.

Man is impressed by strength: God chose to use weakness.

Even in the church, the human tendency is to seek to build little kingdoms around differences—different leaders, different doctrines, different ways of baptizing, different likes and dislikes in music. It is *God's* way to reject that kind of thinking, and to build *unity* around the one thing that Christians have in common: Jesus!

Paul's whole argument is a warning to the church at Corinth—and to us—that we must learn to look at issues from the divine viewpoint. We must realize God doesn't think the same way we do. We must be willing to surrender our own way of thinking and earnestly search out His.

How? God has revealed His thoughts "in words taught by the Spirit" (1 Cor. 2:13). And God has given believers the Holy Spirit to interpret the written Word (vv. 9-15). In the Word and in the Spirit we have been given an astounding gift: "We have the mind of Christ" (v. 16). Searching the Word, guided by the Spirit, we are to learn

God's way of thinking (His wisdom), and gradually learn to evaluate all things from His unique perspective.

This is why a tracing-the-argument approach to Bible study is so important. We're prone to grasp a single verse or teaching, and try to make it fit our way of thinking. We're apt to use the Bible to try to prove our point of view, or to disprove another's. But Paul here teaches us to study the Scripture so we can learn to *abandon* our own points of view, and submit ourselves instead to God's. By disciplining ourselves to trace the argument of a section of Scripture, we guard against our natural tendency to misuse, and we set ourselves to grasp the very thoughts of God.

Application: 1 Corinthians 1–4

When we have understood the flow of thought of a passage, and have gone back to understand details in the light of the whole, *then* we can discern principles and apply them. It is fascinating to see how all that Paul has said in these first chapters underlines two basic principles which are to guide you and me and our groups as well as they were to guide the Corinthians.

First, *Christ is One.* Unity in the church is vital, because unity alone can model this reality. A church that is splintered by disputes so that its members are at odds, dividing and competing, ignores Christ's call that we be "perfectly united in mind and thought."

Second, *Christ is the Source and focus of our faith.* The Corinthians had exalted mere human leaders to that position. "I'm a Paulite." "I'm a Peterite." In modern terms we might say, "I'm Methodist," or, "I'm Baptist," or even say, "I'm a Calvinist" or, "I'm a charismatic." Use of any such term to identify us makes that particular association or belief the defining difference — the focus of our identity. Paul argued that Jesus, and Jesus alone, is the basis for Christian self-identification.

To exalt leaders, or denominations, or doctrines, or experiences, to the level where they make us "different" from our brothers and sisters in Christ is to operate on that mere human wisdom which is nothing but foolishness in God's sight. As for leaders, they are merely servants of God. There is no place in the church for pride *in* a human leader, or *by* a human leader. If God blesses us through one of His servants, we are to address our praise to the Lord, and are to be loyal to God, not the leader.

There is one foundation and one only (3:11), and that foundation is Christ Jesus. Any person or group that tries to rest its faith, all or in part, on any other is foolish indeed.

How wonderful that Jesus *is* our foundation. And how wonderful that we can live by God's wisdom, refusing to let any of our "distinctives" separate us from heartfelt fellowship with brothers and sisters who, whatever our differences, still own Jesus as Saviour and Lord.

GROUP RESOURCE GUIDE

Identification: *Share with others*

If you have ever met other Christians with whom you have felt slightly uncomfortable, describe. What was it that made you feel uncomfortable? How did you react in that situation?

Exploration: *Probe God's Word*

The believers in Corinth were divided into different groups based on church leaders they claimed to follow and honor more than other church leaders. Brainstorm to list beliefs, practices, or traditions that divide Christians today.

Then study these chapters for basic principles teaching us how to relate to others with whom we differ so as to maintain the unity the NT says is essential (cf. 1:13-17). Key passages to study are:

1:18-31. What is God's perspective on our differences?

2:1-16 How do we maintain God's perspective on essential issues?

3:1-22 What is the spiritual nature of divisiveness?

3:1-21 How are we to evaluate the differences that divide us?

Reaction: *Respond together to the Word*
Choose four persons to debate the following proposition: "Resolved, to maintain spiritual unity we must all have the same beliefs, practices, and honor the same traditions."

Affirmation: *Express love and concern*
Speak directly to someone whom you know differs significantly from you in some belief, practice, or tradition. Identify the difference, and then say, " . . . ,but I am committed to you and love you despite our difference(s)."

Adoration: *Worship and pray*
Praise God that Christ's church is one, united around the crucified Savior, united despite other differences we may have from one another.

CHURCH FAMILY DISCIPLINE

Overview

"Church discipline" is an important, but often misunderstood and ignored, aspect of Christian congregational life. Dealing with a specific situation in Corinth, the Apostle Paul laid down principles which can help us deal with a variety of contemporary church situations—and can guard us from interfering in situations which are *not* subject to church discipline.

In brief, your group members will discover in this two-chapter passage that:

- professing Christians who practice immorality are to be expelled from fellowship;
- disputes between Christians should be settled within the church rather than by law;
- sexual immorality is *never* right, for we are to honor God with our bodies.

▶ *Sexual Immorality.* "Sexual immorality" encompasses all sexual intercourse outside of marriage. The serious nature of adultery and fornication (intercourse between *un*married persons) is seen in this powerful Corinthians passage as well as throughout the Scripture. There are two basic reasons: first, sex is sacramental, intended to bond two people together in the most intimate of human relationships. Second, marriage is a covenant, a commitment of mutual loyalty which is to reflect the commitment of God to His people. Within the context of covenant and sacrament, sex is beautiful and right. In any other, it is destructive and wrong.

Commentary

I recently talked with the pastor of a church I serve as an elder. One of the women in the local congregation, who for a time was growing rapidly in the faith, recently went through a painful divorce. At one point she had an affair with a neighbor, a situation about which we had confronted her, and had been assured it was over.

Just two days before the phone call, we discovered that she was living with her paramour. And as members of the family of God, we realized we were responsible to discipline her.

It wasn't an easy prospect.

We naturally drew back from this kind of confrontation. In the family of God, our deepest desire is to support and love, so discipline seems harsh and unloving. Can we really *care*—and at the same time deal decisively with sin in the fellowship, even passing judgment on sin and sinner as Paul did in 1 Corinthians 5? How, after Paul had spoken out in 1 Corinthians 4:1-5 against judging him and other leaders, can we judge a fellow Christian? Why, Paul had just written that he is not even competent to judge himself (v. 4).

Yet, in a society like first-century Corinth, there was a sure need for discipline. Immorality was an accepted part of the Corinthian lifestyle. The old passions and desires, the old way of looking at sexuality, were sure to crop up again and again in the church.

We have many parallels today, when the Playboy philosophy reflects the attitude of so many. Today in our individualism and relativism, many stress "freedom," and demand that each person be allowed to do his own thing without criticism. Today too many insist that what may not be right for you is not necessarily wrong for them. The modern label of the pornographic as "adult" and "mature" duplicates the mindset of the Corinthians and their culture. The sophisticated of Corinth were as adept as the sophisticates of today in pretending that evil is good and good evil.

In a world like ours and theirs, in which the "rights" of the individual are stressed, while old distinctions between right and wrong are blurred, there are sure to be times when immorality and other kinds of sin infect the church. The old ways of thought die hard. Transformation, while real, is gradual and progressive. On the journey to Christian maturity, both individuals and local congregations can falter.

That's what happened in my own congregation. And that's what happened in the Corinthian church. Facing the issue head-on, Paul helped the Corinthians — and us — to think through a number of difficult questions. In the process, Paul helped us learn more about God's mind and heart. And more about what it means to truly love one another.

Paraphrase

If your group members are studying this passage inductively, using the 5-step approach explained in Study Guide 129, let your group members compare their sentence summaries and paraphrases with each other. The paraphrase may look something like this one, which highlights central issues.

Discipline Is Essential
1 Corinthians 5–6

Deal decisively with that case of sexual immorality you've been tolerating — put the man out of your fellowship! How can you have been proud of your toleration? Don't you realize such old taints can spoil the new person you are in Christ? Earlier, I told you not to associate with the sexually immoral, and I meant specifically those who call themselves brothers. I don't judge non-Christians; it's those within who are to be judged — and in this case expelled.

Even such things as lawsuits and disputes are to be settled within the family. Why, the continued existence of such things is a tragic spiritual defeat. People practicing sin have no place in God's kingdom; you *were* like that, some of you, but after being washed and sanctified and justified in Jesus, all that is to be put behind. Don't misuse the, "Everything is permissible" principle. This is subordinate to the fact that Jesus is Lord. You can never take that body of yours, a member of Christ, and unite it with some prostitute! Utterly reject sexual immorality, for, as the temple of God's Holy Spirit, you belong to Him now.

At first glance, this summary does not seem to help much in answering the difficult questions about church discipline, and the necessary dimension of judgment. Yet as we examine this passage in our Bibles, we do find answers — and we learn what the right questions are!

Answers to Our Discipline Questions: 1 Corinthians 5

Let's deal with this passage first by looking at its answer to the five questions raised above about church discipline.

How dare we judge others? This is an important question, especially in view of Paul's statements in 1 Corinthians 4 about being judged by a human court (vv. 1-6). If we go outside this letter, we find more warnings. Jesus said, "Do not judge, or you too will be judged" (Matt. 7:1). And James asked, "Who are you to judge your neighbor?" after pointing out that God alone is "Lawgiver and Judge" (James 4:11-12).

Yet when we look at 1 Corinthians 5 we find that Paul had "already passed judgment" on one member of the Corinthian fellowship (v. 3). He commanded the church to assemble and "hand this man over to Satan" (v. 5). He told them "not to associate" with sexually immoral persons, which necessarily calls for an evaluation of who is and who is not immoral!

While on the surface this may seem contradictory, it is not when we make a simple distinction. *There are some things which we Christians have no right to judge. But there are other things which we must judge!*

This is really quite an obvious principle. I'm not a nuclear physicist, so I wouldn't be called in to judge the safety or danger of a new atomic power plant. I have no criteria or skill for making such an evaluation. On the other hand, I am a Christian educator. As such I'm often invited to churches or schools to evaluate their curriculums and programs. So in areas where I am not competent to judge, I refrain. In areas where I am competent, I should speak up.

We are not competent to judge another's motives or service (1 Cor. 4). Both Christ and James were speaking of critical evaluation of others who, while perhaps different from us, are not subject to us but to Jesus as Lord (see also Rom. 14–15). In 1 Corinthians 5, Paul was talking about *sin*.

And this, as we shall see, is one area in which we must accept our responsibility, and judge!

What kinds of things are valid causes for discipline? As we look at the Corinthian passage, it becomes even more clear. *God has made us responsible to judge those things that He Himself has declared to be sin!* We have not taken the judge's robes and declared "immorality is sin." Not at all. God has already spoken. When we act to discipline a brother who is practicing sin, all we are doing is agreeing with God in the judgment He has already pronounced!

It is understandable that the other things Paul mentioned in this chapter are things which Scripture also clearly identifies as sin: idolatry, adultery, homosexuality, thievery, drunkenness. God has announced His judgment on all of them. In these areas, the church must speak with God's voice. Our judgment must agree with His.

But note two things. First, the text speaks of "idolaters" rather than idolatry. It says "homosexual offenders" rather than homosexuality. This wording is important, not because it indicates a *person* rather than a sin, but because it indicates *a person who is habitually practicing the sin!* Paul is not saying that an individual is to be disciplined by the fellowship for a single act or failure. After all, transformation is not instantaneous; we need to give each other room to grow. But when a person habitually practices sexual immorality or thievery or homosexuality, *then* the family is to accept its responsibility and is to discipline.

Second, our judgment is limited to those who are professing Christians. Paul makes it very clear that his instruction not to associate with the immoral was given, "not at all meaning the people of this world who are immoral," for it is no business of the Christian to "judge those outside the church" (1 Cor. 5:10, 12). But those *inside* "must" be judged, and the "wicked man" must be expelled from the fellowship.

What church discipline involves, then, is judgment (1) of a practice which God's Word has unequivocally condemned as sin; (2) when that sin is habitually practiced; (3) by one who claims to be a member of the family of God.

Why must we discipline within the family?

One answer is given in this passage. The family of God is to reflect the Lord's own purity. Permitting sin in Christ's body will taint the whole and will spread (vv. 6-8).

This point is particularly significant when we remember that the church is God's chosen agency for transformation. Within the fellowship of the family we find our examples, our support, our encouragement, our instruction, our admonition—all those influences God uses to help us enter into the great realities we are called to experience in Christ. A church family torn by disputes or soiled by the presence of those committed to habitual sins loses its power to transform. For the church to fulfill its purpose, holiness and discipline are necessities.

There's one other point, not made here but in 2 Corinthians. Discipline is also the *loving* way to deal with the sinner. The goal is not to cut him off, but to work for his restoration by helping him sense the seriousness of sin, and respond to God's call to holiness. When the Corinthian church obeyed Paul's demand, the result was restoration of the sexually immoral brother to fellowship with God and with the congregation (see 2 Cor. 2:5-11).

How do we discipline? In the case of habitual sin and continuing immorality, we know that Paul had earlier given them instruction in a now-lost letter (see 1 Cor. 5:9-11). We can assume that Paul's instruction included an explanation of the process which Jesus outlined in Matthew 18:15-17.

In that pattern, Jesus called for loving admonition from a Christian friend. If this failed, the leaders of the local congregation were to meet with the sinning believer. If he or she still refused to repent and give up the sin, then that person was to be cut off from fellowship. In Jesus' words, "Treat him as you would a pagan or a tax collector." In Paul's restatement, which captures the meaning of those words exactly, he said, "With such a man do not even eat" (1 Cor. 5:11).

What about Paul's reference to delivering the sinner up to Satan? The thought is that the sinner who has not responded to the church must now suffer affliction and perhaps even physical death (cf. 10:10; 11:30, 32 with 1 Tim. 1:20 and 1 John 5:16).

Doesn't discipline violate others' rights? This question reflects an individualism characteristic both of Hellenistic times and of our own. Then, as now, people claimed personal freedom and privilege, insisting "everything is permissible" (1 Cor. 6:12). In our day this arrogant attitude has been expressed in law suits brought against churches which have expelled members for immorality.

But the argument from personal rights is an empty one. We Christians no longer belong to ourselves; our "rights" are no longer paramount. For we belong to the Lord. "You are not your own: you were bought at a price" (1 Cor. 6:19-20). Our bodies are now the temple of the Holy Spirit, who is in us (v. 19). Our bodies, as well as our hearts and minds, are God's. It is *His* right to be Lord, not our right to do as we please.

While we are free from external bondage, we are to exercise our Christian freedom within the limits imposed by God's purpose in our lives. When it comes to discipline in the church of Christ, we are not to hesitate to act because we feel we might violate a brother's rights. Instead we *must* act because God has charged us to uphold *His* rights.

And, of course, we discipline because we love the sinning brother or sister. He will only discover the meaning of his life, and we of ours, as we remain in full fellowship with our Lord. Because we love we discipline, and through discipline we invite our straying brother or sister to return.

Other Teachings: 1 Corinthians 6
Judging disputes (1 Cor. 6:1-8). Paul looked at one other case in which Christians are to judge. The word "judge" comes from a Greek root that means simply "to discern." In the case of church discipline, the word carries a legal connotation, and suggests passing judgment as on a criminal. In the "trivial cases" in 1 Corinthians 6, it should be understood to emphasize evaluation with a view to settling a matter in dispute as in a civil case.

The matters in dispute in the Corinthian church were the kind of things that today we might bring to small claims courts, or even make an issue in a civil suit. Christians who felt that another believer had cheated or defrauded them in some way angrily went to the civil courts to accuse one another.

Paul considered it shameful for believers to take a family dispute before secular courts, whose judges were not believers. He reminded them that one day God's saints will have a role in judging the world and angels; surely such comparatively trivial matters as those in dispute could be settled by a committee of Christians appointed to work out a fair resolution.

How much better to trust our differences to those we know love us and our opponent, rather than to an impersonal court of secular law.

Sexual purity (1 Cor. 6:12-20). Paul began by putting the principle: "Everything is permissible for me," into perspective. This principle is one that Paul himself taught, as seen in Romans 14:14. No doubt those who were sinning in Corinth remembered what Paul had taught them, and were using this Pauline principle to justify their behavior. This "permissible" principle is circumscribed by other principles. For instance, "Not everything is beneficial." A Christian *can* do things that do not particularly benefit him or others, but a wise believer will choose what is beneficial. Again, "I will not be mastered by anything." Some things a Christian *can* do may develop into habits that master him. For instance, some become slaves to their appetite for rich food. Yes, a Christian *can* overeat—but a wise believer will not develop such a habit.

But sexual immorality does not fall into either of these two limiting categories. The "all is permissible" principle does not apply at all, for "the body is not meant for sexual immorality, but for the Lord" (v. 13).

Sexual immorality is one of the worst of sins, for it violates the intimate relationship which a person has with Jesus Himself and the indwelling Holy Spirit. Jesus, who is Lord of the body, requires that we honor God in our bodies rather than sin against Him.

❊ *Group Activity:*
Singles/Single Again Group
Sexual temptation is amplified in our society. Together list as many pressures as you can on Singles or Singles Again to engage in sex outside of marriage. The pressures may be social ("dates expect it") or internal ("I'm lonely").

Then list as many reasons to refrain from sex outside of marriage as you think of together.

Note that pressures too are often intense and offer immediate gratification. In contrast, reasons not to are often intellectual, and painful consequences lie in the (distant) future. What we need is a source of immediate feedback we can rely on in a pressure situation.

Together study 1 Corinthians 6:12-20, and identify the strongest motive(s) a Christian can have for refraining from sex outside of marriage, and link them with specific words of the text.

Afterward determine one or two things you might do to reward yourself when you honor the Lord and overcome sexual temptation. Pick something relatively small but meaningful. A trip to the Bahamas is probably out, but a new pair of earrings or a chocolate sundae needn't be. When next in a temptation situation, remember the words you chose from this text. As soon as you are out of that situation, reward yourself, as a symbol of the larger reward you will receive in glory for honoring and pleasing the Lord.

GROUP RESOURCE GUIDE

Identification: *Share with others*
React to this situation, by telling what you would do if you were a church leader.
One of the women in our congregation had been growing rapidly as a Christian. But then in anger at her husband she had an affair with a neighbor. When confronted by the leaders she assured us it was an isolated incident, and it was over. Two days ago you learned that she has now moved out of her apartment and is living with her paramour. What will you do?

Exploration: *Probe God's Word*
Put Paul's advice to the Corinthians who faced a similar situation on a chalkboard or sheet of newsprint: "Put [him] out of your fellowship."
Then study 1 Corinthians 5:1-13 together or in teams to answer the following questions:
1. How dare the church judge believers?
2. What things are we to discipline others for?
3. Why is church discipline important?
4. How is discipline to be exercised?
5. Does discipline violate the rights of others?

Reaction: *Respond together to the Word*
Make up a true/false quiz that could be administered to see if Christians understand the NT teaching on church discipline. You might include such statements as:
* Everyone is responsible for church discipline.
* We are to discipline those who hold false doctrine.
* As soon as a person sins he or she is to be expelled from fellow-ship.
* Only a person who habitually practices and refuses to give up what the Bible clearly identifies as sin is subject to church discipline.

Affirmation: *Express love and concern*
Share: Have you ever been involved in a church discipline situation? Was it handled biblically? How might the situation have been handled differently if it was not? Was it easy or difficult to exercise discipline? What was the final outcome?

Adoration: *Worship and pray*
If you are aware of any situation that may call for church discipline, ask the group to pray with you for the person or persons involved (without naming them!). Commit yourself to bring the issue to the leaders of your church, and ask God to prepare the hearts of the leaders and the person who needs to return to fellowship with the Lord.

CHURCH FAMILY DISPUTES

Overview

NOTE: 1 Corinthians 7 is discussed with 1 Corinthians 11, in Study Guide 54.

The Corinthian church was troubled by many problems. There were cliques and divisions, and there was immorality. Now we discover that the believers in Corinth were also divided over a doctrinal issue!

In 1 Corinthains 5 we saw that to maintain the unity and purity of the local congregation, God calls on us to discipline brothers and sisters who habitually sin. But what do we do to maintain unity when doctrinal differences emerge?

This passage gives us a surprising answer. We are to admit the fact that one side or the other will be more "right" in their belief. But who is "right" is not the most important issue! No matter who is "right" we are to maintain harmony by affirming love, and by refusing to let our disagreements force us into opposing camps. The "right" and the "wrong" are to continue to live together as members of a caring family!

How is this possible? The answer is found in these important Corinthian passages you are called to teach.

▶ *Doctrine.* The Greek word simply means "teaching." It is found 21 times in the New Testament, 15 in the Pastoral Epistles. Typically it means divinely communicated content, binding on the Christian community as God's truth.

Commentary

It seems peculiar. In a faith that claims to possess truth, Paul insisted on protecting the right of brothers and sisters to be wrong!

This is actually what we discover in this powerful section of 1 Corinthians. Among the issues raised by the folks at Corinth, and carried to Paul by Stephanus, Fortunatus,

and Achaicus (1 Cor. 16:17) was a doctrinal dispute. The church appealed to Paul to settle the dispute, by telling them which side was right.

Paul settled it. But by explaining how such disputes are to be dealt with! Paul was careful not to give either side a club with which to bludgeon the other. Something else, Paul taught, was involved in the doctrinal conflict; something that takes priority because it is more important than being "right." When we grasp what Paul is teaching here, you and I and our group members will have a very necessary guide for us in modern times.

We need to remember that the New Testament church broke into the Hellenistic world with a Gospel of revolutionary truth *and* with a revolutionary relationship: love. The impact of the church was related to both truth and love, and to the fulfilled promise of personal transformation. It is to be the same in our century: the message of God is to be communicated, and the power of the Gospel is to be demonstrated in a loving community, peopled by transformed individuals.

Truth, love, and transformation are all essential.

But what happens then when there is a disagreement in Christ's body over truth? What happens when we are forced by our convictions to disagree, not over favorite leaders (as in 1 Cor. 1–4), but to disagree over truth itself? Is there any way to preserve love in such a dispute?

At most times in church history the answer has been, "Contend for the truth. Break with those who are not doctrinally 'pure.'" A few times the answer has been, "Emphasize love. Surrender truth for the sake of harmony." But each of these solutions is wrong! Each short-circuits the dynamic of the body of Christ. In New Testament times and in our own it is the *harmonious* testimony of truth, love, and transformation that has provided compelling evidence of the reality of Christ, and has overwhelmed the defenses of pagan cultures.

Our solution to the problem of doctrinal differences *must* affirm truth. But it must also maintain love, and facilitate personal transformation. And it is the pattern for just such a solution that Paul offered in 1 Corinthians 8–10.

Cultural Background

Before summarizing the thrust of this passage in a paraphrase, it's helpful to point out that the confusion in Corinth was compounded by the fact that there were *two* problems linked with this dispute over "food sacrificed to idols" (8:1).

Leon Morris, in *The First Epistle of Paul to the Corinthians* (Eerdmans), helps us understand why this issue was so important to the believers in the first century.

First, it was an accepted social practice to have meals in a temple or in some place associated with an idol. "It was all part and parcel of the formal etiquette in society" (Moffatt). The kind of occasion, public or private, when people were likely to come together socially was the kind of occasion when a sacrifice was appropriate. To have nothing to do with such gatherings was to cut oneself off from most social intercourse with one's fellows. . . . Secondly, most of the meat sold in the shops had first been offered in sacrifice. Part of the victim was always offered on an altar to the god, part went to the priests, and usually part to the worshipers. The priests customarily sold what they could not use. It would be very difficult to know for sure whether meat in a given shop had been part of a sacrifice or not. Notice that there are two separate questions: taking part in idol feasts, and the eating of meat bought in shops, but previously part of a sacrifice.

What should the Corinthian Christians do? Not go to dinner at friends' homes because the food served there would have been offered previously to pagan gods or goddesses? (Actually, Paul had taught in 1 Cor. 5:9-12 that believers were *not* to cut themselves off from pagan contact—even with idolators.) As for the Christian's own homes, the temple meat markets were the normal places to shop. Should a Christian become a vegetarian?

In struggling with this issue, the Corinthians rightly went back to basic truths. They searched the truths revealed by God (Christian teaching, or doctrine) for guidelines. But different people came up with different answers! This truly became a doctrinal issue—not just a matter of personal conviction. It divided many in the church, and the dispute became so sharp that the parties appealed to Paul, asking him to tell them who was right.

Many commentators feel that Paul, in writing his answer, actually quoted from their own arguments. Here are phrases which seem to most to represent the doctrinal views that led one party to the conclusion that both the social practice and shopping at a temple meat market were acceptable.

- Doctrinal argument one:"An idol is nothing at all in the world" (8:4).
- Doctrinal argument two: "Food does not bring us near to God; we are no worse if we do not eat, and no better if we do" (v. 8).

In fact, these arguments are strong, and they reflect something of the spiritual growth of those who made them! God is *One!* All the gods and goddesses that the Corinthians had once feared and tried to appease, or had worshiped in the unlikely expectation of some kind of aid, did not even exist! These believers were freed from the emptiness of that whole system! They now laughed at the lumps of stone and metal that had once held them in bondage. When they attended social events, and idols were honored, the Corinthians felt only joy that they knew the true and living God, and dismissed the idolatry as empty and meaningless. Those who objected to their participation seemed to these men and women, so thrilled by the truth they now knew, to still be in bondage to false beliefs about pagan gods and goddesses that a Christian should discard.

As for food, this party also realized that all the rituals by which they once tried to please the gods were meaningless. Their relationship with Christ was a living reality, a vital, personal transaction. What a person eats or doesn't eat fails to delight God. It is what is in our hearts, not in our stomachs, that is Jesus' concern (see Matt. 15:17-20).

So this party in Corinth, basing their practices on what seemed to be sound doctrinal reasoning, participated in social idolatry without a qualm of conscience. They were right in their doctrine. And Paul gently agreed with their insights. But then Paul went on to show them how it is possible to be "right" and still be wrong!

Tracing the Argument
It is difficult to summarize paragraphs so packed with ideas as some are in this section of 1 Corinthians. But your group members' paraphrases may read something like this:

The Right to Be Wrong
1 Corinthians 8–10

Let's begin thinking about this idol question in terms of *love* rather than *knowledge.* Beginning from knowledge, we do conclude that idols are nothing. But this isn't the customary view. Someone might be led by your example at an idol feast to eat against his conscience. If you thus damage a brother for whom Christ died, *that* is a sin against the Lord Himself.

Look, you know I'm an apostle. As such, I too might claim certain rights, such as the right to be supported by you. But I gave up this right, and I work to earn my living. I freely surrender my rights and choose to live as a slave to everyone in order to reach them.

✒ *Group Activity:*
Missions/Outreach Group
A missionary in the Philippines noticed a group of men sitting and whittling on a wharf each Sunday morning. He invited them to church, but they never came. Then one Sunday morning he got a knife, and sat down on the wharf with them.

Evaluate this true story. Did the missionary do the right thing or not? Why?

After discussion, study what Paul says in 1 Corinthians 9:19-23. How might this apply to the situation above? How might our own efforts to reach others be affected if we followed Paul's example? Be specific and apply to actual relationships

you now have with persons you hope to reach with the Gospel.

It's like an athlete. He gives up many things while in training in order to win the prize. Well, my prize is people.

Now, as to your "knowledge," don't be ignorant of the fact that Israel's experience speaks to us Christians. Idolatry led Israel into all sorts of immorality, and brought on God's judgment. Are you to feel secure in your knowledge of the emptiness of idolatry? Watch out that you don't fall into the common temptations associated with it!

Really, flee idolatry. Our communion is with Christ, and our identity is with those who are one in Him. While idols are nothing, pagan sacrifices are offered to very real demons who are behind the pagan systems. So *don't* participate in idol feasts. Don't insist on your rights and your freedom. Choose what is beneficial to you and others.

But don't make a big issue of meat purchased at temple meat markets. If someone else makes an issue of it—like saying, "This is temple meat!"—then don't eat it, for his sake. God *doesn't* care what's in your stomach, but even eating and drinking can be done to God's glory. In this case, that means considering the impact of your actions on others—Jews, Greeks, and your brothers—and being guided in what you do by concern for their good rather than for the rightness of your position. This is what I do as I follow Jesus, so you follow my example.

What an exciting answer! But to understand it, we need to be sure we grasp several critical points.

Keys to Understanding Paul's Argument: 1 Corinthians 8–10
Limitations on knowledge (1 Cor. 8:1-3). In these chapters Paul was responding to the stance taken by the Corinthians. In the dispute there each side was concerned with only one issue: "Who is right?"

Each party based its conviction that *it* was right on an appeal to revealed truth, and on the belief that it had a better grasp of truth than the other party.

So Paul began with a warning. Approaching *any* issue from the viewpoint of superior knowledge alone is inadequate, and is dangerous. Why? Because each side in the argument will have at least *some* grasp of God's truth ("we all possess knowledge" [v. 1]). But if we put our emphasis only on knowledge of the truth, we are sure to develop a spiritual pride—pride that we know more and better than others ("knowledge puffs up" [v. 1]). But in fact any human being's grasp of truth is incomplete ("the man who thinks he knows something does not yet know as he ought to know" [v. 2]). Thus the attitude that we know the truth and that we are "right" is not only dangerous, but it is wrong.

In these opening verses Paul established an important fact. *The Corinthians had gone about dealing with the disputed issue in the wrong way!* In their focus on knowledge of God's truth they forgot love! They ignored the imperfection of human understanding, and, in effect, cut themselves off from growth in knowledge, for their pride about what they thought they knew cut them off from learning more!

Well, if the Corinthians' approach was wrong, how *do* we deal with doctrinal disagreements? *Be sure to begin by affirming love.* First, because love is the key to transformation. In the loving family of God, the Holy Spirit works to transform attitudes, values, behavior, understanding—our total personality. *Where there is love in the body, there will be openness to God.* As we open our lives to God, the Spirit guides us into "the knowledge of the truth" (Heb. 10:26).

We can visualize Paul's key concept here this way:

Dispute Handled through Knowledge

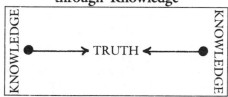

In the confrontational approach, each side claims to have a better grasp of the truth than the other. This leads to pride, and encourages a closed mind to aspects of truth not yet grasped. It does not help either side to open up to the Spirit of God for further teaching, and it causes divisions in the body of Christ.

In what we can call the commitment approach, each side affirms its love for and acceptance of the other. Side by side, without false pride, each humbly admits the limitations on human knowledge and concentrates on helping the other love God better. This leads to both sides remaining open to God, and to the teaching ministry of the Holy Spirit.

Dispute Handled through Love

When differences are approached in love, there is no retreat from our community to truth. Instead, there is a deep desire to know truth and to grasp it more fully—together.

Paul's rights (1 Cor. 9). At first it is a temptation to think that chapter 9 is unrelated to chapter 8. How did Paul move from talking about meat offered to idols, to the subject of apostolic rights?

The connection is this. Paul was high lighting something that the Corinthians had overlooked, an issue that was vitally important even though their dispute was essentially doctrinal. This issue is the *attitude* of those who knew an idol had no real existence, and who thus concluded: "I've got the truth, and according to truth I have a *right* to attend idol feasts and eat sacrificed meat." The attitude suggests that these people believed doctrinal correctness *in itself* justified their behavior.

Paul, however, confronted these believers with a factor they had not considered. Even if they were right about idols, and even if they were able to eat meat at idol feasts with a clear conscience, was their *insistence on exercising their rights* a truly Christian attitude? Which should have priority—our rights, or our brother's well-being? What do we care about most—a good steak dinner, or members of God's family who may not have our "mature" viewpoint?

In 1 Corinthians 8 Paul concluded that the Corinthians, rather than taking pride in their knowledge of the truth, really should have been ashamed of their lack of concern for others. First Corinthians 9 is a personal illustration: Paul was not just "preaching at" the Corinthians. Paul had himself chosen to give up *his* rights and privileges as an apostle, for their sake!

More truth (1 Cor. 10). Chapter 10 grows out of Paul's initial warning that our knowledge of truth is incomplete. He did commend the Corinthians for recognizing that an idol was "nothing at all in the world" (8:4). But now Paul pointed out the dangers of idolatry.

As far as participation in idol feasts was concerned, such things had always been associated with immorality. Did a person identified with Jesus think it was right, by participating, to link himself with all that the culture associates with idol feasts? In idolatry there are temptations common to all men: Christians are not exempt (10:13).

What's more, while the idols themselves are "nothing at all in the world," idolatry has always been used by demonic powers, which *are* real. Can a Christian, who shares in Communion and drinks "the cup of the Lord," go to an idolatrous feast and "drink . . . the cup of demons too?" (v. 21)

Clearly Paul had ruled that the "go to idol feasts" party was *wrong!* Their claim of a grasp of Christian doctrine was foolish, for they justified their actions on only part of the truth.

Finally Paul shifted focus to deal with the second issue: eating meat that may have been purchased at a temple meat market. Paul pointed out that this was not the same as participating in a festive and idolatrous party which had been dedicated to some pagan god or goddess. If the host at a private dinner party made an issue of the meat having been offered first to an idol, then, for the sake of *his* conscience, the Christian should not eat. But otherwise, Christians shouldn't make an issue of it. Just remember, Paul advised, that while the food in itself is morally neutral, in eating and in drinking, and in whatever we do, we are to seek God's glory, and to be sensitive to what will lead to the salvation of the lost, and to the benefit of our brothers and sisters.

♥ *Group Activity: Support Group*
*Begin by expanding your concept of "temptation." For instance, when you ex-*perience a great loss, you may be tempted to withdraw, to sink into self-pity, to blame and try to punish yourself, etc. So first share one thing you are struggling with at the present, even though it may not be what we traditionally think of as a "temptation."

Then help each other look at how you are trying to deal with the thing you shared. Describe your feelings, your behavior, etc. For instance, do you find yourself sleeping more to avoid facing a feeling of emptiness? Or do you watch TV till exhausted enough so you can sleep? Sharing in this way will help you sense the nature of the "temptations" involved in your present struggle.

Then look together at three emphases in 1 Corinthians 10:13. (1) Your experience is "common to man." You're not alone in your suffering or your struggle. (2) "God is faithful." Pain doesn't mean God has deserted you. It's when you hurt that He draws closest to you. And (3) He makes a "way out so you can stand up under it." The "way out" is not a way out of the struggle, but a way out of the unhealthy ways we are tempted to respond to suffering, grief, loss, or pain.

Try to understand God's "way out" of temptation in your struggle. Let others who have experienced something like you have share what helped them. And ask God to show you His way to help you endure and grow.

Analysis

There are several vital lessons for us in Paul's handling of this early doctrinal dispute.

Begin with a commitment to love. Even if a brother or sister is wrong doctrinally, we are not released from the obligation to love.

Maintain a concern for truth. Paul kept a balance. He continued to love those on both sides of this issue, but he did not hesitate to make the truth clear, even when it revealed one position to be wrong.

Be sensitive to the relational implications of truth. One side in Corinth was so sure it was right—and sure that orthodoxy gave them the right to participate in idol feasts—that they disregarded *other* truths about relationships in the family. No single truth has priority, but must be held in balance with other truths. Our adherence to one doctrine does not justify ignoring other teachings in God's Word.

Don't treat one truth as the whole truth. We need to look beyond a doctrine that is being disputed, in order to see related truths in Scripture. By building their whole argument on the single truth that idols are nothing, the one faction in Corinth overlooked the reality of demons and the immoral cultural associations of idolatrous celebrations. By overlooking these other relevant truths the "I can eat" party in Corinth was "right," but reached a wrong conclusion.

Keeping these principles in mind can help us today when we have honest doctrinal differences within our congregations.

Paul's pattern. The way in which Paul dealt with error in Corinth was beautiful for its sensitivity and love. Paul even commended those who were wrong, for grasping those truths they had apprehended! Paul also commended them for their "strong" conscience. How wonderful that these men and women were able to cast off the attitude of a lifetime and, on the basis of God's Word as they understood it, find freedom from idolatrous bondage and fear. Anyone who is aware of the difficulties pagan peoples have with release from such bondage would commend these people too!

So, rather than beginning by saying to the "We can eat" party, "You're wrong," Paul began by commending and affirming them.

In the rest of the discussion Paul kept the focus on the relational, and encouraged all the Corinthians to act for the benefit of their brothers and sisters. Paul let them know he expected as much; that he really believed they cared. Paul did point out that because of two factors (two truths) the one party had overlooked, they were wrong. But at the same time Paul kept his appeal focused on *both* truth and love.

Paul's premise. How did Paul find the freedom to deal with error so gently? How was he able to commend those who were wrong, and to actually affirm their right to be wrong?

The answer comes when we realize that Paul operated with a basic premise — a premise that needs to be ours as we live with other Christians. You see, *Paul expected the Corinthians to grow.* He did not insist that everyone be doctrinally correct *now.* Paul knew that in the context of a loving family, in which even the erring brother is worthy of affirmation and concern, spiritual and personal growth *will* take place. As life is opened up to the Spirit of God, He will lead the people of God into all truth.

This premise helps you and me to relate to those who differ doctrinally today. our brothers — and we too! — are young. We have a long way to grow, and much more to learn. At best, our grasp of truth is incomplete. But if we keep on loving one another, God will bring us by His transforming power to a place where we both have a more complete knowledge of God's wonderful truth.

GROUP RESOURCE GUIDE

Identification: *Share with others*
Think of a conflict you have recently had with another person — in your family, your church, at work, etc. Write down a line or two about each of these topics: (1) the problem, (2) what the other person(s) said and did, (3) what I said and did, and (4) the outcome. Hold these descriptions for use later in the group session.

Exploration: *Probe God's Word*
Have one group member previously prepare and now give a lecture on Paul's principles for handling disputes. Use the illus-

trations and commentary on pages 346-348 in developing the lecture.

The person prepared might want to use an interactive lecture approach. This simply means that after summarizing a point, he or she gives the group members time to read the verses summed up, and to ask questions about them. However, no more than 20 minutes should be given to this foundational part of the group session.

Reaction: *Respond together to the Word*
In groups of four or five look at two or three of the conflict reports you prepared at

the beginning of this session. Evaluate each of the four elements of each report in view of Paul's principles:

The problem: What is the "truth" element?

What is the "love" element?

Others: Did the other(s) approach the dispute as a conflict with you (a win/lose approach), or as a dispute you needed to resolve together (a "love," or win/win approach)?

You: Did you deal in a win/lose or loving, win/win way with the other person?

Outcome: What was the result? How was the conflict resolved (short-term outcome)? What happened to your relationship with the other(s) (long-term outcome)?

When an analysis is complete, let the person who wrote the report suggest what he or she might have felt or done differently to obtain a better short-term and long-term outcome. After the person involved has reevaluated the experience, others on the team may wish to add their insights as well.

Work through as many of the conflict reports as you have time to do.

Adoration: *Worship and pray*
Praise God as a God of love, who enables us to love even in difficult circumstances.

Affirmation: *Express love and concern*
If anyone in your team was particularly helpful to you, or provided a particularly good example of how to resolve conflicts in a godly way, drop him or her a note expressing your appreciation.

1 Corinthians 12–14

CHURCH FAMILY GIFTS

Overview

One of the problems in Corinth focused on spiritual gifts, and their relationship to spirituality. Today too similar questions surface, and similar confusion exists. Yet in this three-chapter section of 1 Corinthians Paul provided clear teaching. For instance, our study of 1 Corinthians 12–14 will tell us which of the following are true and which are false—and explain why!

- T or F? The more important the spiritual gift, the more mature and spiritual the person.
- T or F? The major evidence of the Holy Spirit in a person's life is his or her ability to speak in tongues.
- T or F? We must ask God for the spiritual gift we want.
- T or F? A person "under the influence" of the Spirit can't help shouting out.
- T or F? Some Christians have little to contribute to others.
- T or F? In church meetings, only the pastor should teach, because he's usually the only one with seminary training.
- T or F? There is no real test for "spirituality."
- T or F? Some people are more important than others in the church as in every other situation.

If your group members have ever had questions like these, or are uncertain about spiritual gifts and their relationship to Christian spirituality, this study is especially for them!

Commentary

It should be very clear by now in our study of 1 Corinthians. The New Testament church was not utopia!

Sometimes we imagine that it was. When we're plagued by problems in our local congregations, or unhappy about our personal spiritual progress, we long for those early days. We feel that somehow the church has lost its power; we wonder how to recapture those supposed days of constant victory.

Well, the New Testament church *was* dynamic. The truth, the love, the transformation that marked the Christian fellowship was distinctive in a world that was void of each. But that same trio is meant to characterize the family of God in every age, and in each we must struggle to maintain their balance. The way to victory now as in New Testament times was marked by struggle, setbacks, slow growth, and time. Maturity then as now comes only gradually, and often seems choked out by problems.

Actually, we need not be discouraged if at times our churches are marred by differences, problems, and disputes. Let's remember that Paul wrote 1 Corinthians when the church was young and vital and alive—and that even a vitally alive congregation will have problems. It is not the absence of problems, but *how we deal with them,* that determines our continued growth toward the full experience of blessing.

In Paul's letter, he guides us as well as the Corinthians to this understanding. Paul wanted us to know *how* to deal with issues that are likely to trouble any local church—including problems that may arise from confusion over tongues.

Background

Once again, some insight into the first-century world is helpful as we approach what seems to be a very contemporary issue.

Tongues. In the New Testament we first meet tongues in Acts 2, when on the Day of Pentecost the Holy Spirit welded the disciples into a new body, the church. Not only were there miraculous signs of fire and wind but, filled with the Holy Spirit, the disciples began to "speak in other tongues as the Spirit enabled them" (Acts 2:4).

"How is it," the observers asked in amazement, "that each of us hears them in his own native language?" (v. 8)

Later, when we meet tongues in Acts, they again seem to be foreign languages (see 10:44-46; 11:17).

Coming to 1 Corinthians, we learn that the tongues-speaker himself did not understand what he was saying unless a person with the gift of interpretation explained. Here interpretation of tongues is identified as a separate gift—a gift often possessed by a fellow believer in the congregation. Tongues, then, was not used evangelistically in the early church to reach outsiders, but was exercised within the family, and then only when an interpreter was present to make the message intelligible to others (1 Cor. 14:28).

Nothing in this passage ruled out tongues as a valid expression of the Holy Spirit's ministry through one of God's children. Instead, Paul was concerned in these chapters with putting this rather spectacular gift in perspective.

Cultural context. Perspective was especially important in a place like Corinth. It was universally accepted in the Hellenistic world that some were especially close to the gods. Usually this closeness was supposed to be manifested by trances, ecstatic speech, and other unusual or bizarre forms of behavior. All this was taken as evidence of special spiritual endowment. A person with epilepsy, for instance, was said to have the "divine disease." The oracles at religious centers were often given drugs to provoke their utterances. The oracle at Delphi, so prominent in the early days of Greece, breathed volcanic fumes from a cleft in the rock of the temple floor, and her unconscious mutterings were then interpreted by the priests.

It is not surprising, given this cultural perspective, that the Christians in Corinth were attracted to the gift of tongues. Nor is it surprising that they thought of such people as especially spiritual.

But their assumptions led to real problems in the Corinthian church. And Paul launched these chapters by challenging the assumptions carried over from paganism. Paul's very first words were: "Now about spiritual [gifts], brothers, I do not want you to be ignorant" (12:1).

The word "gifts" really should be placed, as I have, in brackets. It is not necessarily implied by the Greek word *pneumatikon.* As the alternate reading in the *Revised Standard Version* suggests, it might as well be rendered "spiritual *persons.*" This probably better reflects the issue that troubled the Corinthians. It was the issue of *spirituality itself,* and how spirituality is expressed in Christian experience.

We need to remember that the Corinthians were pagans just a short time ago, "somehow or other . . . influenced and led astray to dumb idols" (v. 2). It was dangerous for them to carry over into the Christian faith old notions about spirituality! But apparently they had been so influenced by the old assumptions that when someone in an ecstatic trance had pronounced an *anathema* ("be accursed") against Jesus Himself, a few of the Corinthians had actually been swayed! They had taken the state of the person making the utterance as evidence of divine inspiration!

Paul said firmly that no one could say, "Jesus be cursed," by the Spirit of God. Neither would anyone caught up in such an experience (as were the oracles of pagan faiths) ever announce, "Jesus is Lord," unless indwelt by the Holy Spirit. The state of the speaker was not to be taken as evidence of inspiration or of spirituality!

Paul dealt with this issue because there was then, as now, a great danger that in their ignorance some Christians would be led away from true spirituality by an unwarranted emphasis on this more spectacular manifestation of the Spirit. In his argument Paul did *not* attack the gift of tongues, or reject it. Rather he gave a lengthy explanation of how the Spirit does work in our lives, and in our churches.

Tracing the Argument:
1 Corinthians 12–14

Our insight into backgrounds helps us entitle this important section of 1 Corinthians, and also helps us trace the apostle's train of thought. A paraphrase condenses the argument, and makes it more clear.

True Spirituality
1 Corinthians 12–14

Brothers, don't view spirituality from your old pagan perspective. God is at work in all of us, but the Spirit's work is manifest in different ways. Yet, it *is* the Spirit who shows Himself behind each gift, and these expressions of His presence are dedicated to our common good. (Just how He works in each individual is *His* choice.)

Actually, we Christians are the body of Christ, many parts united in one. Like parts of the human body, we each have our own functions, as a "hand" or "foot" or "eye" or "ear." And we're each necessary; no one contribution should be singled out and exalted. So you're each in the body, and *this* is what's important. But if we were to rank gifts by their importance, tongues would hardly be at the top of the list.

Really, there's a better way to measure true spirituality: love. No gift profits a person exercising it unless he loves. You want to measure spirituality? Then look to kindness, patience, and those other practical expressions of real love. For it is love that lifts us out of childhood; love is the mark of spiritual maturity.

Focus on love, and realize that the gifts used for communicating God's Word should have priority when you meet. You see, intelligible speech builds up our brother, and it is such building up gifts that we should value. So, in church don't burst out in a tongue unless an interpretation can be given. And don't misunderstand! I speak in tongues more than you all; I'm not rejecting this gift. But I'd rather speak 5 words that will help someone than 10,000 words in a tongue no one can understand.

So get over your childish preoccupation with tongues. Tongues are certainly *not* meant to be a sign of special spirituality within the body; as that kind of sign, their only appeal might be to pagans, as an indication of God's presence.

In church meetings let each one participate — but no more disorderly clamor! Take turns. God's work is marked by order, and you *can* control yourselves. As for the women who've been disrupting your meetings, they especially need to learn submissiveness. Tell them to be quiet in church and to discuss their questions with their husbands at home.

And if anyone there still wants to claim a "special spirituality," let him recognize the fact that I speak with God's own authority. So, brothers, don't forbid tongues, but do concentrate on communicating God's Word in your meetings.

Observations on the Text:
1 Corinthians 12–14

Several points within this extended passage have been disputed and discussed by Christians who differ doctrinally. Some are very important in tracing the apostle's thought and, in fact, interpretation of this passage may hinge on the grasp of the entire argument when more than one option is open to understanding individual verses. Here are observations that may be helpful.

To each one (1 Cor. 12:7) Each Christian has a spiritual gift, or "manifestation of the Spirit." The gifts differ, but have these common elements. (1) Each is a manifestation of the Holy Spirit's presence. (2) Each is "for the common good," that is, each is intended to build up the body of Christ. (3) Each is given "as He [the Spirit] determines." There is no true Christian in whom the Holy Spirit has not worked, providing a divine capacity enabling him or her to make a significant contribution to other believers.

Prophecy (1 Cor. 12:10). The emphasis on the ministry of prophets in Old and New Testaments is not on prediction, but on setting forth clearly what God has said. In the New Testament church *prophecy* can be (1) a gift, and/or (2) an office associated with authoritative expression of God's message.

It is best to always link prophecy with Scripture, either as an exposition of the Word, or as a message subject to the Word for authentication.

Desire the best gifts (1 Cor. 12:31). This is *not* an exhortation to individuals to ask the Spirit for any particular spiritual enablement. Instead it is an exhortation to the Corinthian congregation, needed because their attention had been drawn to "tongues" and they had actually ignored the more important ministries of the Holy Spirit.

The most excellent way (1 Cor. 12:31). The Corinthians had made two mistakes. First, they had taken a spectacular but less significant spiritual gift and given it priority in their meetings (see 1 Cor. 14). Second, they had carried over the pagan notion that such ecstatic utterances were a mark of spirituality—of special closeness to God. First Corinthians 13 dealt with this second issue. Here Paul answered the question, "How *do* we recognize special closeness to God in ourselves or in others?" All too often we yearn for a closer walk with the Lord. If we do not understand the closer walk, we're likely to grasp at an unusual experience such as tongues as the key. We're likely to listen to the person with the unusual experience, and take his gift or experience as the mark of divine favor.

Paul wanted the believers in Corinth to recognize the priority of the more important gifts in the ministry of the church, but he also wanted them to see that true spirituality is *completely unrelated* to the gifts a person may have from the Spirit. After all, Paul identified the Corinthian church as "still worldly" (3:3). Yet there was an exercise of *all* spiritual gifts in that body! (1:7)

The "most excellent way" Paul now introduced is the way to a deeper walk with God. *Love* is the key to our growth toward maturity, and love is the indication (a practical indication, according to 13:4-7) of true spirituality in others.

❋ *Group Activity:*
Singles/Single Again Group
Love is something we all need to both give and receive. But in our society the word "love" often conveys a distorted image. Use 1 Corinthians 13:4-7 to purify your concept of love, of its giving and of its receiving.

On an 8 1/2 x 11 sheet of paper draw horizontal lines to provide 14 equal sections. Label each section with one of the qualities described in 13:4-7. Then draw two vertical lines, labeling the sections "past receive" and "present receive" and "present give."

Then work individually to fill in the "past receive" column with specific things you have experienced as a child or adult that demonstrated the appropriate aspect (the 14 qualities Paul lists) of love.

When you finish this column, share in teams of four or five. Have you experienced real love in the past? When? Who has loved you in this way? What did the experience of love mean to you then, and what does it mean to you now?

Come together again and talk about how understanding "love" can be important to you. For instance, many are caught up in a "Hollywood" view of dating and marriage and find themselves attracted to persons who would make totally disastrous mates! How can an understanding of love from 1 Corinthians 13 be translated into a profile of a person we would consider dating or "falling in love" with?

Perhaps more important, consider whether the love we all need may be supplied in nonsexual relationships. See if you can fill in the other two columns with present experiences of receiving and giving the kind of love Paul describes. Reaching out to love in a godly way can satisfy a need for intimacy far better than that need which is met in many marriages.

The church assembled (1 Cor. 14:1-19). With the principles explained in chapters 12 and 13, Paul moved on to apply them to church gatherings. Apparently these assemblies had become a bedlam. Brothers and sisters were shouting out in tongues at the same time; prophecy was discounted, and the prophet often interrupted; and apparently a group of women had become very aggressive about their gift of tongues. Paul told the church to correct these abuses. The principles he laid down are fascinating.

First, all believers could contribute—and tongues were not to be forbidden. After all, all are gifted, and these gifts are given "for the common good" (12:7). If participation is restricted, many will not contribute and their gifts will be lost, and the whole group suffer. (This is an interesting observation in terms of the contemporary church which tends to allow only one person to minister when the congregation gathers—the pastor.) Second, order must be maintained. There were rules to follow. Anyone claiming to have been "swept away" by the Spirit so he or she couldn't help interrupting was *not* acting by the Spirit. ("The spirits of the prophets are subject to the control of the prophets," 14:32). As for the women who had become so aggressive and dominating, they needed to learn to be quiet at church and to discuss things with their husbands at home. Submission was a principle these women needed to apply for their own personal spiritual growth—and for the sake of the congregation.

How like Paul! The most significant of Christian truths have the most practical application.

A sign to unbelievers? (1 Cor. 14:20-25) This is one of the most discussed passages in Scripture, and there are several explanations of why Paul seemed to say first that tongues are for, and then say they are not for, outsiders. One explanation is this.

In Greek culture, ecstatic utterances were taken as signs of the divine presence. Paul noted that unbelievers may view tongues as signs, even though believers were *not* to take them as a sign of spirituality (v. 22).

But such signs have limited impact on the unconverted. If an unbeliever should attend a Christian meeting and see everyone shouting out in tongues, his impression is likely to be, "What a madhouse!" (See v. 23.) But if he comes to a Christian meeting and hears the Word of God in plain talk, he'll be convicted by the Spirit and converted (vv. 24-25).

The point is, then, that while outsiders may *come* to a Christian meeting because they have heard about a miraculous sign, seeing the sign in action in the church will not lead to their conversion. That requires a presentation of the Gospel in words the visitor can understand.

Summary. Paul gave vital and clear teaching about an issue that divides believers today just as it troubled the early church. In this passage we find no license to reject the gift of tongues as a valid manifestation of the Holy Spirit. At the same time, we find a corrective to an overemphasis on this gift, which would attempt to make it *the* evidence of God's Spirit's presence, and *the* test of spirituality.

Once again Paul gently and delicately guided the Corinthians, and us, to affirm brothers who differ from us, and lifted up the vital role of love.

The Body: 1 Corinthians 12

In discussing spirituality and spiritual gifts, Paul introduced a powerful image of the church of Jesus Christ.

Two major images are given in the Bible: the church is a family, and the church is a body.

The concept of family is used often, and communicates the warmth of love and intimacy that is to mark the fellowship of believers. We are sons and daughters of God now through Jesus; as children of God we are also brothers and sisters. Learning to look at each other as brothers and sisters, and to think of ourselves as family, helps us realize why love truly is the mark of Christian fellowship.

Here, however, Paul asked us to see the faith community as a living body, and to visualize each believer as a functioning part of the body. While "family" speaks to us of relationships, "body" speaks to us of ministry.

♥ *Group Activity: Support Group*
Celebrate the "body" nature of Christian interpersonal relationships. Read and discuss 1 Corinthians 12. Then look at a rough drawing of a human body sketched on a chalkboard or sheet of newsprint. Look around your group and, thinking of how individuals have ministered to you, pick a part of the body that best represents each.

Focus on each group member. Members of the group will tell each in turn, "Susan, I'm glad that you are a (part of the body) because as a (that part of the body) you have. . . ."

This simple procedure can help you and the other group members better sense your spiritual gift, and better experience the reality of the body image. We do need each other. And in our differences we do contribute to one another's spiritual growth.

These two images of Christ's church are never held up in contrast. Instead, they are two perspectives on a single reality. The *family relationship* is *context for ministry*. And *ministry* is the contribution that love leads each of us to make to our fellow family members.

The picture of a body also helps us see how Jesus continues to perform His work in our world. In Ephesians Paul tells us that Jesus is the "Head of the body" (Eph. 2:20-22). Jesus as living Head directs us— we who are His hands and feet and eyes and ears and mouth—to continue His own mission in our world. The compassion Jesus showed to the sick and weary and the sin-tormented, He still shows—through His body. When we as individuals and local groups of believers mature and become sensitive to the Lord's guidance, Christ ministers to us and through us.

Fellow members. Paul developed the analogy of the body in this passage to teach us about our relationship with each other. We are *dependent* on each other. No one person is fully equipped with all the spiritual gifts. Instead, each is given his own distinctive gift or gifts; each then makes his own unique contribution to "the common good" (1 Cor. 12:7).

It is through cooperation and coordination that each of us makes his or her contribution and, in turn, is helped and aided to grow. Individualism, with its emphasis on competition to discover the "best" and "greatest," is totally foreign to the body of Christ.

Yet the whole spirit of the Corinthian church was individualistic; they exalted favorite leaders, they competed doctrinally, they even competed to be given special individual "honor" because of the gift possessed. They were unable to see that each person needed the other and they were *interdependent,* not *independent.*

How much we need to rediscover the reality of the body of Christ today! For our age too is ruggedly individualistic. We too exalt competitiveness and individual achievement. We too find it hard to work with others in a team relationship. But we *are* a body. And it is as a body—honoring each part, ministering and being ministered to—that we must learn to live in God's family.

The more excellent way to experience life in Christ's body, and to find fulfillment in ministry, is to live the life of love that binds us together in harmonious unity.

GROUP RESOURCE GUIDE

Identification: *Share with others*
Jot down the name of the "most spiritual person I have known." Then describe him or her briefly to the group, and listen carefully to their descriptions of their "most spiritual" persons.

From the descriptions given, brainstorm "qualities of the spiritual man or woman" and list these on a chalkboard.

Exploration: *Probe God's Word*
Do a "reverse paraphrase" of 1 Corinthians 12–14. Have copies of the author's paraphrase of these chapters (commentary, pp. 352-353). In teams of three compare the paraphrase with the text of the Bible itself, and trace how the author arrived at each summary statement.

This team activity will provide a general grasp of the passage needed to apply its truths to life.

Reaction: *Respond together to the Word*
Work through the T/F questions found at the beginning of the commentary portion (p. 351). Then individually write at least seven additional true/false questions that deal with main points made by Paul in these important chapters. At least two of the questions should focus on some way in which the passage can be applied by members of your group.

When done, read your questions for the group to answer, and answer the questions of others.

Affirmation: *Express love and concern*
Go back to the description of the "spiritual" person developed by your group at the beginning of this session. Would you change it now, and if so, how? If someone in your group seems to you to provide a good example of spirituality and Christian maturity, feel free to express appreciation to him or her during or after the group session.

Adoration: *Worship and pray*
Read 1 Corinthians 13:4-7 aloud. Then praise God in sentence prayers for the way He exemplifies one of the 14 qualities of love found here. That is, "love is patient," so thank God for His patience with you in some specific situation. Etc.

WOMEN IN THE CHURCH FAMILY

Overview

One of the problems faced by the early church was understanding the new role of women. It may be hard to grasp, but Paul's teaching stimulated one of the first "Women's Lib" movements! In Christ, possessing spiritual gifts, each woman could view herself as an individual of great personal worth and value.

The impact of this discovery, and the struggle to understand the implications of lifting women up to stand beside men, rather than crouching in their shadow, is reflected in questions posed for Paul to answer.

One of the questions had to do with divorce. In 1 Corinthians 7 Paul dealt with this issue, raised primarily by women who were seeking emancipation by questioning their traditional role as wives. In 1 Corinthians 11, Paul spoke to first-century Christian women who campaigned for the right to attend public worship with uncovered heads, to symbolize their equality with men. Some of these even disrupted the meetings by noisily challenging those who taught.

It is striking how many of the contemporary cries of women in our society are reflected in these passages.

In Paul's handling of these issues here, we are helped to see God's unique answer; an answer which affirms the full personhood and full participation of women in the body of Christ, and yet gently guides us away from drawing false conclusions about what full personhood means.

Commentary

It is important first to notice that the Bible takes a consistent stand in its basic attitude toward women. Genesis 1 affirmed the full personhood of Eve, and her full participation in God's image as that image is stamped on humankind. Eve also shared fully in the "dominion" which God intended mankind to exercise over creation.

So God created man in His own image, in the image of God created He him; male and female He created them. God . . . said to them, "Be fruitful . . . and subdue."

Genesis 1:27-28

With sin, a new necessity was imposed on the race. Woman was forced into a subordinate place, just as later the destructive nature of man's sinful impulses forced the imposition of government on society (cf. Gen. 3:16; 9:6 with Rom. 13:1-4). This subordination implies no demeaning of women. It made a wife no less important than her husband as a person—just as today a mayor, governor, or even President is no more important than a person who is an ordinary citizen. Romans 13 insists that the ruler's role is in fact to serve the citizen; and service rather than power is implied in Genesis 3's reference to a husband's authority.

But sin has a way of warping all things. Just as governments tend to become tyrannical, so "submission" became a denial of worth, and "authority" became the right to use and discard. The divine order, rather than upholding the worth of women, has actually been accused of denying it!

In Old Testament times, most cultures viewed women as chattels; they were denied rights commonly granted to men, and could be treated any way their husbands or owners pleased. It is probably difficult to grasp now, but the Old Testament's laws relating to women were significantly more liberal and supportive of women's rights than those in the rest of the world. Not that the Old Testament laws reflect the full restoration of women. Many Old Testament laws do *not* reflect God's ideal. They are accommodations to man's "hardness of heart," as Jesus pointed out in Matthew 19:8. Law itself does not present the standard of perfection, but represents an accommodation to the capacity of men to respond.

Yet, even in the Old Testament, there were indications that God would one day act to reaffirm woman's position *beside,* and not beneath, men.

With Christ, those promised days came! One of the most dramatic transformations was in men's attitude toward women, and in women's understanding of themselves. We see it so often throughout the Word.

> There is neither Jew nor Greek, slave nor free, male nor female, for you are all one in Christ Jesus.
>
> Galatians 3:28

The old ways of valuing and classifying people are no longer valid! In Christ, we are members of one body.

> I will pour out My Spirit on all people. Your sons and your daughters will prophesy.
>
> Acts 2:17

Since the Spirit's coming at Pentecost, *every* member of the body has been given a gift, and called to minister. Even the gift of prophecy, which Paul identified as very important (see 1 Cor. 12:27-30), is shared by women!

> I commend to you our sister Phoebe, a servant of the church at Cenchrea. . . . She has been a great help to many people, including me.
>
> Romans 16:1

Paul not only valued women, but he recognized them as eligible to hold office in the church. In the same context he called Priscilla and Aquila "my fellow workers in Christ" (v. 3).

It is difficult to see how some accuse Paul of a narrow, Pharisaic attitude toward women, or insist that the New Testament documents maintain a degrading, culture-bound view of the place of women in marriage and in the church. *It was exactly because the early church rejected society's view of women that the Corinthian problem arose!* Paul's guidelines here are not designed to put women "back in their place," but rather to help newly liberated women find their identity as persons of worth and value. . . and to help men, stunned by this sudden recognition of women as God's ministers in the body of Christ, to explore the implications of the new relationship.

Marriage Problems: 1 Corinthians 7

In every age there are twin tendencies to distort the search for a depth relationship with the divine. One of these is asceticism, the notion that by rigorous denial of bodily drives and desires one attains special holiness. The other is licentiousness, often rooted in the belief that the physical does not matter and that, therefore, full expression of any passion is acceptable.

Paul had devastated this second view while in Corinth, and he repeated his condemnation of immorality in this letter (1 Cor. 5). It's clear that some Corinthian Christians had carried over the playboy philosophy of Corinth into the church, and continued to regard women as men's playthings.

But others had taken the ascetic route. The affirmation of women as sisters in Christ, with full rights in the body of believers, tended to encourage this thinking. If women are to be regarded fully as persons now (and not just as *female*), doesn't it follow that marriage and the physical side of sexuality is ruled out? This notion gave rise to some of the questions the Corinthians raised, particularly as reflected in something Paul had taught: "It is good for a man not to marry" (7:1).

Looking over this passage, and outlining it, we can see the different kinds of marriage-related questions that troubled the Corinthian church.

7:1-9	Does women's full equality rule out marriage?
7:10-11	What about divorce?
7:12-16	What about unbelieving spouses?
7:17-24	A basic principle stated.
7:25-38	What about our virgin daughters and engaged couples?
7:39-40	Any word for the widows?

Let's look at each of these segments in order.

Does women's full equality rule out marriage? (1 Cor. 7:1-9) As was his practice, Paul began by commending. It *is* "good for a man [person] not to marry." But immediately he corrected the misapplication of this saying, which he himself probably taught while with them (see v. 7). "Good" here does *not* imply "morally required," nor even imply "better." In fact, Paul went on to say that marriage is the normal state! And marriage means *marriage*—with its full sexual expression. The "holy marriage" of the celibate, which some in Corinth promoted, is not marriage at all.

Paul stated very clearly that life in this world means life in the body, and that human beings have bodily needs. One of the purposes of marriage is to help us satisfy those needs in a holy way; Christian couples are not allowed to deprive one another sexually (v. 5). Then Paul made a striking statement. In Christian marriage, it is not only the man who has marital rights, needs, and desires. The woman has them as well. She actually "owns" her husband's body just as much as she "owns" hers!

What a devastating break with the culture! Full sexual equality and partnership is an early Christian teaching which must have jolted Paul's readers thinking, as it does the thinking of some today.

What about divorce? (1 Cor. 7:10-11) To those Christians who for any reason were initiating divorce action, Paul passed on this blunt command: "No." Should this teaching, stated by Jesus, be rejected, the divorced person was to remain unmarried, or to be reconciled to his or her spouse.

The fact that Paul was thinking primarily of wives here suggests that some of the newly liberated women in Corinth felt that to "find themselves" they had to step out of the "bondage" of their marriages. Sometimes a sudden rediscovery of a woman's personhood does bring an individual to want to lead her own life, and build her own identity outside of the old relationships and "restrictions" of marriage. Paul made it clear that this is not the way to affirm individuality. But he also realized that some women in Corinth would divorce, despite his injunction. In that case, Paul insisted that such a woman either remain unmarried, or be reconciled to her husband.

Almost as an afterthought Paul added, "By the way, you men aren't to divorce your wives either." Clearly the divorce question was stimulated by actions taken by women, rather than men, and this leads us to suspect that the "women's lib" movement in the church was the cause.

What about unbelieving spouses? (1 Cor. 7:12-16) Even if a believer's spouse is not a Christian, the believer is not to initiate a divorce. Christ's presence in the believer reaches out to touch the unbelieving family members; spouse and children are "sanctified" (v. 14) in this way, in the sense of being privileged to experience the influence of Jesus through the believer.

At the same time, if the *unbeliever* initiates a divorce, the Christian partner need not feel guilty about it. In fact, when this happens, the believer is not "bound" (under obligation). The marriage is dissolved.

A basic principle (1 Cor. 7:17-24). Paul now spoke to a basic issue underlying these inquiries. In each case, the believers seem to be trying to "find themselves" or develop a new identity *by changing the conditions under which they lived.* A wife wanted to get a divorce so she could have a separate identity. A man wanted to make his marriage "spiritual" by eliminating sex. To these people, and to us, Paul replied, "Each one should retain the place in life that the Lord assigned to him and to which God has called him" (v. 17). What was Paul saying?

First, that God is sovereign.

God Himself has *assigned us* our roles in life. And God has *called us* to live in that role.

The newly liberated women in Corinth would not find themselves by seeking emancipation, or by trying to be like men. Instead, identity and fulfillment would be found in living out their calling as women, and as servants of the Lord. A slave's self-identity did not hinge on his being free. Possessing freedom doesn't make the free man any less Christ's slave. A Jew should not deny his cultural heritage, and a Gentile need not deny his (vv. 18-19). Instead, each believer is to make every effort to live for Christ *in the state in which he or she is called.*

It is by serving and loving God *as we are* that we discover our true selves, and find our fulfillment.

What about virgin daughters and engaged couples? (1 Cor. 7:25-38) Paul's advice to parents concerning arranging marriages for their unmarried daughters (which was the practice then), and to betrothed couples, was to put off marriage "because of the present crisis" (v. 26). In that particular crisis situation—about which we know little today—concern for a husband or a wife might threaten the believer's commitment to God. For instance, it is easier for most to face martyrdom and torture than to permit the torment of family members.

Still, Paul let the believer know that God will guide differently in some individual cases. Such persons will not sin if they marry. After Paul's defense of marriage in the opening paragraph of this chapter, it is clear that the apostle does *not* hold an ascetic or puritanical view!

A word to widows (1 Cor. 7:39-40). As for widows, of course they were free to remarry—but only to other Christians. And Paul said they might well be happier if they did not marry just now (contrast 1 Tim. 5:14).

And so Paul moved on, in 1 Corinthians 8–10, to another subject. But he returned to another problem that arose out of the restoration of women to full personhood in chapter 11. When he did return, his argument rested on the principle in 7:17.

We find fulfillment in being who and what we are.

God is sovereign.

God has assigned us our roles in life, and calls us to live in that place. It is by affirming the worth and the value of who we are, not in struggling to be something we are not, that we find fulfillment.

✍ *Group Activity: Bible Study Group*
Use the following letters to advice columnist "Dear Paul" to stimulate exploration and application of truths taught in 1 Corinthians 7. When uncertain, check with the commentary.

#1
Dear Paul,
I yearn to be spiritual. So I've told my wife the physical side of our marriage is over, so I can devote myself to prayer and Bible study, undistracted. She objects. But Paul, isn't it wrong for a woman like her to want sex? I mean, doesn't sex sort of belong to the darker side of our nature? Should I get a divorce, or just pray for her?
[1 Cor. 7:1-9]

#2
Dear Paul,
What do you really think about mar-
riage? I'm engaged, but I'm kind of uncertain. What are the pros and cons of getting married in the first place? Will I be sorry later?
[1 Cor. 7:1-2, 7-9, 25-35]

#3
Dear Paul,
Now that I'm a Christian I realize I'm really "me," not just a wife and not just a mom. I've got to explore who I am as a person in my own right, so I'm divorcing my husband and starting out on my own! It's scary, but I sure appreciate the sense your teaching has provided that I'm a person of worth and value too. So I just wanted to write and say "Thanks," and see if you have any advice for me as I start my new life.
[1 Cor. 7:17-24]

Women in the Church: 1 Corinthians 11
The subjects taken up in this chapter of 1 Corinthians all have to do with public worship. The first subject focuses on several practices of the Christian women's liberation party. The second topic is the practice of the Lord's Supper. It is the first subject we want to concentrate on.

Paul began by praising the believers—including the women—for holding to his previous teachings (v. 2). Paul then went on to answer some who had challenged his teaching.

Again we need to understand the cultural background before looking at the passage itself. What really is at issue is the Corinthian women's desire to dispense with the veil (to go "uncovered") in public worship.

The veil covering. Sir William Anderson gives us some insight into the cultural implications of the veil:

In Oriental lands the veil is the power and the honor and the dignity of the woman. With the veil on her head she can go anywhere in security and profound respect. She is not seen; it is a mark of thoroughly bad manners to observe a veiled woman on the streets. She is alone. The rest of the people around her are nonexistent to her, and she is to them. She is supreme in the crowd. . . . But without the veil the woman is a thing of nought, whom any man may insult. . . . A woman's authority and dignity vanish along with the all-covering veil that she discards (cited by Robertson and Plummer in *Corinthians One,* International Critical Commentary, p. 311).

Anderson's point is simple. The veil served *to affirm the woman's dignity as a woman.*

Why did the Corinthian ladies want to remove their veils in church meetings? Because they felt a need to symbolize their new status as full participants in the body of Christ. If they were equals of men, they wanted to be like men and to worship unveiled!

Paul's response is not a put-down. Instead, it is a reaffirmation of the fact that a woman can be valuable and worthwhile *as a woman.* No woman needs to seek liberation by struggling to become like man!

An inappropriate symbol. It is significant here that Paul does not argue, as he might have, from the cultural implications of going unveiled. In that society, the discreet matron would demonstrate her propriety in the way she dressed, while the *heterai* "available for hire") would advertise herself by her dress. Surely Paul could have taken the approach of shaming the Corinthian women for acting like harlots.

But Paul did not. Instead, he affirmed these women. He argued that there *are* differences between men and women, and that it is no disgrace to recognize the differences. Acting in ways appropriate for a woman to act in no way denies the Christian woman's worth and value, and it in no way threatens her participation in the body of Christ.

An unnecessary demand. In verses 2-16 Paul explained that there *are* differences between men and women that are to be acknowledged. But the differences are designed to make men and women *interdependent*, not to make one sex of lesser importance.

Paul's argument here is a theological one, finding its roots in the order of Creation. The man does have a certain priority; he was created first, and woman was shaped from his flesh. Eve was created to meet Adam's need for companionship rather than vice versa. This order in Creation is reflected in the relationship between a man and his wife. He is the "head" of the woman,

even as Christ is the Head of man.

Usually it is at this point that the modern person rebels. "Head" to most of us means "power," and in our day that connotes suppression and oppression. But note that this is not the way Paul viewed it here. Man is the "image and glory" of God (v. 7). *Rather than indicating oppression by God, the Lord's headship over man implies an exaltation of man!*

So too with the woman. Man's headship over the woman does not imply subservience, but instead the lifting up of the woman. Headship does not proclaim the rights of men to enslave. Just the opposite. It insists that men should recognize the high value God places on woman not only as fully a person, but as man's "glory"! Thus, in wearing a veil (that "sign of authority"), the Corinthian women would be displaying for men and angels as well, the stunning fact that *in Christ it is no shame to be female!* Each time women participated *as women* in the ministry of the church, they would show again the value, worth, and glory of womankind.

In verses 11-16 Paul did make a cultural appeal. At that time long hair *was* womanly, and men would be ashamed to let their hair grow long. Would a woman ever think of shaving her head and appearing in public without her hair? Of course not! Why? She'd be ashamed. Somehow, without long hair, she would be denying her femininity.

So, Paul said, it really isn't proper to appear in church and pray unveiled either. For this too is a denial of feminity. A woman would be denying herself—not finding herself—by attempting to become like a man.

Echoes

It is here that we find echoes of the principle Paul stated in 1 Corinthians 7. We find fulfillment in being who and what we are.

God is sovereign.

He has assigned each of us our place. He has called us to live in that place. This is the message that echoes from those first-century days to our own. In tones of love, the great apostle reminded women who were breaking out of old, distorted images and shaking off feelings of worthlessness and unimportance that it was not necessary to deny their womanhood to find their new identities. Rather, they would find fulfillment in accepting themselves as women, and glorying in that fact. For a woman *is* important, not in spite of being a woman, but *as* one.

There are other passages in the New Testament relating to women in the church. Some of them are more difficult to understand than these two in Corinthians. But if we keep in mind the cultural background, and the argument developed by Paul in this particular chapter, we can understand better the point Paul makes.

In 14:33-36, on disorder in the congregational meeting, Paul is not telling women to "stifle yourselves." He is warning some of the more aggressive of the women's libbers to stop shouting and interrupting with their argumentative questions. They should instead talk things over with their husbands at home, and in the process learn a submission that is appropriate for them as wives.

First Timothy 2:11-15 does not teach that women cannot exercise their spiritual gifts when the body meets. We know that women can, and are to (Acts 2:17; 1 Cor. 12:7; 14:26). Instead the passage has a more narrow focus, on the role of a ruling elder. To "teach" (1 Tim. 2:12), as defined "with authority" is an elder's function. This particular function in the body of Christ—and only this function!—is reserved for men.

How important that today, we like Paul affirm believing women, and lift them up to become full participants as partners in our homes, and as ministering persons in Christ's church.

GROUP RESOURCE GUIDE

Identification: *Share with others*
Divide into two groups, men in one and women in the other. The men are to discuss, "How Christian men really see women." The women are to discuss, "What attitudes do Christian men display toward women in the church, home, and workplace?" Take at least 15 minutes to explore these questions.

Have each group summarize for the other, and together identify areas of tension.

Exploration: *Probe God's Word*
Have two or three women previously prepared to summarize the teaching of critical passages in these two chapters that speak to the special concerns of Christian women in the church, home, and workplace.

Reaction: *Respond together to the Word*
One of the most important things we can do is to really listen to others' concerns. Let the men serve as a listening team as the women in your group tell them "what we really want from men."

After the women have had a chance to share, each man is to jot down "three things I heard you say you want from us." Each man in the group will then read his "three things." If one or more does not reflect what the women were really saying, the women should restate their concerns so they do reflect what they have been saying accurately.

Adoration: *Worship and pray*
Let the men in the group pray, thanking God for all of the women and stating specifically what they are thankful for.

RESURRECTION: THIS FAMILY IS FOREVER

Overview

The belief in a personal, bodily resurrection is basic to biblical faith. While one of the Jewish theological traditions (the Sadducees) rejected the concept, it *is* taught in the Old Testament (see Job 19:25; Pss. 17:15; 49:7-12; 73:23-26; Isa. 26:19; Dan. 12:2).

Jesus affirmed the resurrection in His teaching (see Matt. 22:29-32), and demonstrated His personal power over death by raising Lazarus (see John 11). Yet the raising of Lazarus and others by Jesus (see also Matt. 9:18-26) was merely a restoration of earthly life. It was not the total transformation exhibited in Jesus' own resurrection—and promised believers when Christ returns. What we do know is that when Christ returns the believing "dead will be raised imperishable, and we [who live then] will be changed" (1 Cor. 15:52.)

Then, the limitations of our present nature will be lifted, and we who are now perishable will be imperishable; we who are weak will be filled with power; we who are mortal will be immortal. Forever and ever, Amen.

▶ *Resurrection.* Because the idea of resurrection was foreign to Greek thought, there existed no technical words in Greek to describe it. The Bible uses two common words, one meaning "to raise, to arouse" and the other "to awaken."

■ See discussion of difficult verses in 1 Corinthians 15 in the Victor *Bible Knowledge Commentary*, pages 542-547.

Commentary

Christ promised the believer an inner transformation. And there *was* transformation.

Believers found striking changes were taking place—within themselves, and in one another. The attitudes and ideas and ways of paganism died hard. Yet, there was clear evidence of God's work within the Corinthian body.

In spite of differences and divisions, and in spite of lax discipline, people were being delivered from superstition and fear. The bondage of idolatry was shattered; an exciting new freedom was experienced. God's presence in Corinth was abundantly demonstrated; all the spiritual gifts were operating in the body, and the church was excited about each new experience of the Spirit. The Corinthian's attitudes and values were changing too. They took very seriously Paul's teaching on marriage--and even went beyond what he intended in some cases.

The believers appealed to Scripture and to God's Word for guidance (through the apostolic teachings), and were praised for holding to the practices which Paul taught them. Women were breaking out of their servitude, rejoicing in their liberation, and asserting themselves in bold (if sometimes misdirected) ways. In general, the Corinthians seemed very responsive to truth; Paul always expected that they would respond obediently to his instruction.

Each of these facts give witness that transformation had begun. These believers *were* changing and growing, becoming new and different persons.

At the same time, their growth was retarded, apparently because of a lack of that vital quality Paul spoke of so often in his letters to the Thessalonians. To the church at Thessalonica Paul could say, "About brotherly love we do not need to write to you, for you yourselves have been taught by God to love each other" (1 Thes. 4:9). But to the Corinthians, Paul had to say, "knowledge puffs up, but love builds up" (1 Cor. 8:1), and then go on to show them how to handle their differences lovingly. It was to the Corinthians that the great exposition of love in chapter 13 was addressed, and one of Paul's last reminders to them was, "Do everything in love" (16:14).

A process. All this helps us realize again that growing toward Christian maturity is a process. God does work His transformation in our personalities, but that work takes place over time, and sometimes over more time than we desire!

Sometimes growth seems slow as we face problems like those that plagued the church at Corinth. We need to keep three things in mind here. First, as newness comes, there will be tension between the old and the new. Transition times are sure to bring problems.

Second, building the climate of love in the body will ease tensions. Love, like truth, is essential. By affirming our love for each other in spite of differences and strains, and by affirming together our commitment to truth, we *will* grow. We are being freed from the world's mold—that old way of thinking, of valuing, and of perceiving ourselves and others. We are being transformed in a process to which God has committed Himself. Words Paul would later pen to encourage the Philippians hold as well a promise for the Corinthians—and for us! "He who began a good work in you will carry it on to completion until the day of Christ Jesus" (Phil. 1:6).

And this brings us to the third thing. A day of completion is coming! In the day that Christ Jesus returns, our transformation will be complete.

Resurrection: 1 Corinthians 15

The culminating experience in our personal transformation is to be resurrection. Yet, some in Corinth denied this completion. They carried over into their new faith the typical Greek attitude toward life after death; they could not accept the idea of a bodily resurrection. Christian faith might have meaning for the here and now. It might even offer some astral form for their personalities after death. But, a *literal* resurrection? No.

Paul vigorously corrected them. If our hope is limited to this life, then we Christians are "of all men most miserable" (v. 19, KJV). Transformation begins in the present, but completion will come in the day of Jesus Christ. Then we will actually "bear the likeness of the man from heaven" (v. 49). What God does in our earthly lives not only excites us, it holds the glittering prospect of perfection to come. The trans-

formation process finds its ultimate meaning in attaining this goal.

It *is* our destiny to *be like* Jesus. What is more, the Good News of Jesus rests on the fact of our Lord's own resurrection. Christ was raised bodily from the dead. His resurrection both demonstrates the power of God, and is the ultimate proof of His ability to provide forgiveness. Jesus' resurrection and our own are so intimately intertwined that to doubt either constitutes a denial of the Gospel message itself!

Eager to explain this vital truth, Paul, in 1 Corinthians 15, gives the classic and definitive New Testament explanation of resurrection.

Christ's resurrection (1 Cor. 15:1-11). Paul began by reminding the Corinthians of the content of the "Gospel I preached to you." In that original presentation, the Resurrection was given a central role.

> For what I received I passed on to you as of first importance: that Christ died for our sins according to the Scriptures, that He was buried, that He was raised on the third day according to the Scriptures, and that He appeared to Peter, and then to the Twelve.
>
> After that, He appeared to more than 500 of the brothers at the same time, most of whom are still living, though some have fallen asleep. Then He appeared to James, then to all the apostles, and last of all He appeared to me also.
>
> 1 Corinthians 15:3-7

In this summary we note two things: the events the Gospel affirms actually happened in the real world, and were neither mystical nor mythic in character. And the events took place "according to the Scriptures"; as predicted and in full harmony with earlier revelation. The fact is that both these elements—the historical nature and scriptural roots—were *always* emphasized in apostolic preaching of the Gospel (see Acts 2:14-41; 3:11–4:12; 10:34-43).

The Gospel is simply not the Gospel if the element of Resurrection is removed. So Paul reminded his readers, "This is what we preach, and this is what you believed."

Believer's resurrection (1 Cor. 15:12-19). Paul then linked the resurrection of the believer to the resurrection of Jesus. If Jesus was raised, how can some say, "There is no

Theme of 1 Corinthians

Passage	Theme	Principles
1 Cor. 1–4	Overcoming Barriers to Divisions	Reject pagan approaches, seeking to understand God's patterns of thought. Regard human leaders as servants; reserve glory for God.
1 Cor. 5–6	Discipline	Deal firmly with sin in the family. Act to resolve disputes equitably.
1 Cor. 8–10	Doctrinal Disputes	Love and truth are both required for resolution. Being "right" does not remove love's obligation to build up our brothers.
1 Cor. 12–14	True Spirituality	Possession of certain gifts is not evidence of spiritual achievement. Love is the key indicator of spiritual maturity. As a body, family members are interdependent; each gift is important, and each person's ministry is needed.
1 Cor. 7;11	Women's Identity	Affirm the worth and value of women. Equality as persons does not mean "sameness." Each person finds fulfillment in the role God has sovereignly chosen for him or her— and is *called* to that place. Because women are affirmed as equally valued persons in the body of Christ, no woman needs to deny her womanhood.
1 Cor. 15	Resurrection	Ultimate transformation is assured.

resurrection of the dead"? If there is no resurrection, then Christ could not have been raised, and in that case "your faith is futile; you are still in your sins."

In the bluntest possible way Paul said that the doctrine of resurrection—the resurrection of Jesus and of the believer—is essential to Christian faith. Robbed of the resurrection, Christian faith would be an empty and futile thing indeed.

Resurrection: past and future (1 Cor. 15:20-28). But Christianity is *not* like one of the empty religions or mystery faiths that the first-century world practiced. "Christ has indeed been raised from the dead."

The resurrection is the key to our understanding of the past, and the doorway of hope for the future. Death came into the world through Adam's sin; life comes to humanity through Jesus' resurrection. The future will now unfold according to the plan of God: Christ is raised first; when Jesus comes, those who belong to Him will be raised, and then at the end—Jesus takes His kingdom and ultimately hands it over to God the Father. The ultimate enemy, death, will be put away forever as part of the "everything" Scripture promises will be put under the Messiah's feet (e.g., totally defeated and destroyed) (see Ps. 8:6).

Baptism for the dead (1 Cor. 15:29-34). In this aside, Paul noted the practice of some in Corinth of being "baptized for the dead." Between 30 and 40 explanations have been given for this phrase. The simple meaning of the words seems to suggest that some at Corinth were undergoing baptism on behalf of friends who died without that sacrament. In referring to the practice, Paul did not endorse it. In fact, he disassociated himself from it by referring to "those" people, and saying "they" rather than "we."

It's clear that in the cases mentioned in this paragraph, Paul was reasoning from experience rather than from revelation. Why bother, he said, to undergo such a baptism if your friends are simply dead and gone, and there is no resurrection? Why should the missionary team with Paul keep on endangering their lives if death is really the end? If this life is all, why not live by that contemporary maxim, "Eat and drink, for tomorrow we die"? (v. 32)

No, it is the prospect of the final transformation that leads the Corinthians to this peculiar practice, and to Paul's own commitment to his mission.

Paul's point was simply this: wandering from the truth about resurrection will certainly have an impact on daily life. What the Corinthians and Paul have been doing makes sense only if there *is* a resurrection coming. Once this conviction is abandoned, both practices and commitments which reflect the belief are sure to change.

The paragraph raises an important question for you and me. What do we do because we too believe in resurrection? How would our lives be different if we were to abandon this hope?

Resurrection body (1 Cor. 15:35-49). It was only natural that in the debate over resurrection some should inquire, "Well, what will this resurrection body be like, anyway?" Others challenged, "How can men rise when their bodies have decayed?" Paul replied that the objection is foolish. A dead-looking seed is planted in the ground, and a vital, living plant appears. Just as God gives the planted seed a form appropriate for its new life, so the resurrected saint will have a glorious body appropriate to full transformation.

No, the resurrection body will not be the same body we have now; natural life will be replaced by spiritual. The likeness we bear then will not be Adam's but, instead, we shall "bear the likeness of the Man from heaven" (v. 49).

This last phrase may be the key to our best approach to visualizing the resurrection state. The *Expository Dictionary of Bible Words* (Richards, Zondervan) notes:

Many have found it fascinating to observe the capabilities of the resurrected Jesus and speculate on what being "like Him" might mean. For instance, the resurrected Jesus had "flesh and bones" (Luke 24:39). Why not flesh and blood? Is it because "the life of a creature is in the blood" (Lev. 17:11) and a resurrected person is infused with a different kind of life? Others have noted Jesus' sudden appearance among His disciples in a locked room (John 20:26). Is this teleportation? Or can a resurrected person move between the atoms of the physical universe?

While such speculation has a fascination, we do best to let the issue rest with

God, as John and Paul did. We do not yet know what we will be, but we will be like Him. The limitations of our physical nature will be gone, and, whereas we are now perishable, we will then be imperishable. Power will replace weakness; immortality will end mortality.

Conclusion (1 Cor. 15:50-58). Paul was now caught up in the glory of what lies ahead. Paul saw the dead being raised, the living caught up—all transformed! He saw the bright splendor shine as the perishable fades, and mortality is clothed with immortality. And then—then comes the triumphant shout: "Death has been swallowed up in victory" (v. 54).

Paul's conclusion is important: in view of the coming resurrection we are to stand firm, and let nothing move us. Since we see beyond this world, and beyond death, to realities others cannot see, we can follow Paul's admonition to "always give yourselves fully to the work of the Lord, be-cause you know that your labor in the Lord is not in vain."

Concluding Remarks: 1 Corinthians 16

This letter concludes with a note about a collection for needy brothers, a topic that is amplified in 2 Corinthians.

Paul shared a number of requests, added notes to friends, and also shared an exhortation:

Be on your guard; stand firm in the faith; be men of courage; be strong. Do everything in love.
1 Corinthians 16:13

What a good word for the Corinthians and for us. We too may have problems, and we may not be growing as quickly as we would like. But as we remain committed to Jesus and to each other, we will experience more of the Spirit's transforming touch, as we move on with our brothers and sisters to God's glorious resurrection day.

GROUP RESOURCE GUIDE

Identification: *Share with others*
Jot down ideas, and then describe in detail what you expect to be doing in 20 years. Include where you will live, activities you'll engage in, what you'll look like, the car you'll drive, etc.

After sharing this with the group, jot down ideas and describe in detail what you expect to be doing in 100 years. Include everything you know or speculate about eternity. Take plenty of time to share your ideas.

Exploration: *Probe God's Word*
Divide into at least three teams. One is to study 1 Corinthians 15 to determine "Is Jesus' Resurrection real?" Another is to study 1 Corinthians 15 to determine "What differ-ence does Jesus' resurrection make?" The third is to study 1 Corinthians 15 and John 20–21, and determine "What can we know about our resurrection?"

After 20 minutes or so each team can share its findings with the rest.

Reaction: *Respond together to the Word*
Reverently and slowly, read aloud Revelation 20:11–22:6.

Adoration: *Worship and pray*
Meditate on 1 John 3:2: "Dear friends, now we are children of God, and what we will be has not yet been made known. But we know that when He appears, we shall be like Him, for we shall see Him as He is."

2 Corinthians 1–3

THE INADEQUATE MAN

Overview

Second Corinthians is an intensely personal letter. In it the Apostle Paul shares his inner feelings in an attempt to help his readers understand principles on which ministry must be based. For you and me and those we teach, this is an important letter. Seeing the heart of one of the most effective ministers of all time helps us establish a firm foundation for our personal ministries.

Outline

▶ *New Covenant.* The "New Covenant" is a key New Testament term, with roots in the Old Testament. The "Old" Covenant with which it is contrasted is the Mosaic, or Law Covenant. The Law defined righteous *behavior,* and God's people were promised blessing if they lived by its regulations. But the Old Testament promised a New Covenant would be given, "not like" the older one (Jer. 31:33-34). Under the New Covenant, initiated by the death of Christ, God makes believers righteous by inner transformation. This letter helps us understand how to live under God's New Covenant, and to truly *be* righteous through and through.

Overview

Paul's earlier letter to the Corinthians had a mixed reception. For instance, the brother living immorally was turned around. Yet others bridled at Paul's teaching. It is clear from 2 Corinthians that some challenged Paul's authority and apostleship. They charged him with unwarranted pride and overconfidence, and with saying one thing one time and something else another. The recriminations of this segment of the Corinthian church were furious and bitter—so serious that Paul had to respond, to express his deep love for and continuing confidence in the immature congregation.

While Paul intended to deal with several specific questions (such as giving), the main thrust of his letter was to reassure the Corinthians. In spite of what Paul's enemies were saying, he did trust them completely. And he did care for them. Paul's motives and feelings, as well as his teachings, had been twisted by his critics. For the Corinthians' own benefit, Paul now opened his heart in complete self-revelation.

Earlier Paul had written to the Thessalonians and referred to his motives. "You know how we lived among you for your sake," he said (1 Thes. 1:5; see also 2:5). Paul's whole approach to ministry was to live among the members of a new body as a completely transparent man. He freely and openly expressed his motives, his feelings, his values—everything. Paul so loved his converts that he was ready to share with them not only the Gospel but his own self as well.

Certainly Paul had been this kind of man among the Corinthians. There could be no reasonable basis for doubting him, or for questioning his motives. Yet a group in Corinth did question. Their backbiting and innuendos were troubling the whole body of believers. Perhaps these were people converted after Paul left Corinth, people who never knew him. Or perhaps they were simply proud and bitter people whose pretensions of superiority—whether based on a claim of superior "knowledge" or on the supposed superiority of the gift of tongues—had been gently destroyed in Paul's earlier letter. At any rate, these people did attack Paul—bitterly. They could not refute his teaching, so they attacked him personally, seeking to undermine Paul's influence by making him appear to be a weak, plastic, venial man.

It should not have been necessary for Paul to defend himself against this kind of attack. Many in Corinth had been converted under Paul's ministry. But apparently even their confidence in Paul had been shaken. The weakness and failures which Paul identified in that first letter must have devastated the faithful; even they began to doubt that Paul could love and continue to respect them.

And so Paul wrote 2 Corinthians—which should have been an unnecessary letter. Yet in this letter Paul ministers to us in unique ways. We find answers to some of the most basic questions about spiritual leadership that face the church today. And we find, in the self-revelation of the apostle, a picture of the kind of person God is calling each of us to become.

Special Contributions of 2 Corinthians

What are some of the specific values your group will receive as you teach this great New Testament book?

Gain insight into transformation. Several times in the Corinthian letters Paul urged young believers to "follow my example, as I follow the example of Christ" (1 Cor. 11:1). "Transformation" sounds like such an abstract thing. Even when we say that transformation involves growth in Christlikeness, it is hard for us to grasp the meaning. But in the person of Paul (a living, breathing, real human being whom the body could watch and observe and listen to), Christlikeness took on fresh reality. In the close, personal relationship that Paul developed with his converts, they could learn the lifestyle of one who had traveled further than they down transformation's road.

The invitation of Paul to believers to "imitate me" or to "let me be your example in this" was not rooted in pride. It was rooted in the apostle's awareness that a living example is essential in the communication of Christian truth. As we see in other New Testament passages, the bridge between knowing God's truth intellectually, and building it into one's life, is often the modeling of truth in another's life.

This is one reason why 2 Corinthians is so important to us today. We don't know Paul as a person. We don't live in his first-century world. But in this letter, we not only meet Paul face-to-face, we meet him heart-to-heart. In this most intimate biblical portrayal of Paul as a person, we discover in him the kind of person God is calling us to become.

Learn how to motivate. In a nationwide survey of 5,000 pastors I conducted through Renewal Research Associates, a Phoenix foundation, *every respondent,* when asked to identify the greatest need he saw for strengthening the life and ministry of his church, gave "getting my lay people more involved as ministering people" a first- or second-priority ranking. The problem these pastors faced was one of motivation. How could they move others to follow Jesus? What is the *motivational key* to making disciples?

All too often we hear a presentation of the Scriptures that is encased in an "ought" framework. We're made to feel guilt or shame for what we haven't done; we're urged to try harder. Such guilt-producing approaches, however, create a sense of hopelessness, and actually retard transformation. At best, they force us into a flurry of activity which we call "ministry."

God has a far better way; a far more freeing way! In 2 Corinthians, we'll come to know Paul the motivator, and will discover a different avenue to making disciples.

Discover how to exercise spiritual authority. A final focus in our exploration of this intimate letter will be authority. This too is a question troubling the church today. What is the nature of spiritual authority? How is it expressed and exercised? How can we have authority that isn't oppressive, impersonal, restrictive—even degrading?

In observing Paul gently exercise his authority with the Corinthian church, we gain new insights into how Christian authority operates. In the process, we'll find guidance for our own lives, in our homes, and in the church of God.

This New Testament letter truly is a rich and exciting one. Once again God's Word will speak to each of us. In listening, and taking what Scripture teaches to heart, we will find new and open doors leading to faster personal spiritual growth.

Biographical Study

Because this letter is such a personal one, one effective way to study it is by using the biographical method. As noted in an earlier study, the basic method for exploring the New Testament Epistles is what is called the *synthetic* method. That is, we try to trace the thought of the writer over extended passages, and then put it all together, often by using paraphrase. In this study I'll continue to trace the flow of the apostle's thought so your group members will be able to master content. But you may also wish to help your group members come to know Paul, the man better. For his words, "Let me be your example," are written not only for the Corinthians but for Christians throughout the ages. In exploring Paul's motives, values, and attitudes; in sensing his feelings and emotions, and discovering the basic convictions that shaped him, we will learn much about what it means for us to be truly Christian men and women.

There is another reason for use of the biographical method of Bible study. It helps us understand truth in ways we might not if we remained strictly "logical" in our approach. Truth in Scripture is *not* divorced from life. When seen in and through life, we often discover dimensions of truth we might not otherwise glimpse.

Truth in life. Yet, it's important to remember that what we see in Scripture through the filter of life is rooted in revealed truth. The living example of men like Paul does not have validity in itself; instead, the lifestyle is valid only when it expresses truth.

For instance, in this letter we'll meet Paul as vulnerable and inadequate. We'll see that Paul, under attack from the Corinthians, did not respond from a position of strength. Instead, he responded by revealing his weakness! At the very beginning of this letter Paul wrote, "We do not want you to be uninformed, brothers, about the hardships we suffered in the province of Asia. We were under great pressure, far beyond our ability to endure, so that we despaired even of life. Indeed, in our hearts we felt the sentence of death" (2 Cor. 1:8-9). How striking! Paul immediately exposed himself to his enemies.

How they might have used that against him! Can't you hear Paul's critics now? "Paul's not so great. Look, he gets de-pressed just like some new believer! Why, what does he know of victorious Christian living? He even admits feeling despair."

Or, "How can you ever respect a weak person like that! Paul needs help!"

Why did Paul give his enemies this kind of edge? Why didn't he simply exercise his great power as an apostle and strike out against his critics? Why didn't he at least begin by recounting his strengths, rather than by revealing his weaknesses?

Paul's underlying motive for this approach was his desire to minister to the Corinthians. Paul knew that, to minister effectively, he would have to identify with them in their humanity before he could show them a way to rise beyond themselves. Paul also grasped a basic truth — and realized its full implications. In order to truly minister to others, you must be completely honest and real with them.

❋ *Group Activity:*
Singles/Single Again Group
Suggest one word which sums up your present impression of the Apostle Paul as a man. List your word with those of the others on a chalkboard or sheet of paper.

Then in teams of three read 2 Corinthians 1:1–2:4 carefully, to draw as clear as possible a picture of the apostle's personality. How did he view himself? Others? Is he sensitive or insensitive? What are his motives and goals? Etc. Be as thorough and careful as possible. Then together sum up what your team feels Paul was really like, and share your insights with the others.

Discuss: Are most "first impression" reactions to others accurate or not? How do you tend to err — idealizing a person you've just met, or dismissing him [or her] on superficial grounds? How do we gather the kind of information needed to build an accurate picture of others? What kinds of situations do we need to see them in? Why is a date not an adequate setting? What qualities are important to you, and how can you find out if another person has those qualities?

God's Comfort: 1 Corinthians 1:1–2:4

Paul was concerned first of all in laying a basis for continuing ministry to the Corinthians — and especially to his critics. He knew that a basis for ministry to others calls for sharing, not preaching. That is, we are most effective in helping others when those others see us as like them. If we are truly like others, then there is hope, for those who are overwhelmed by a sense of weakness cannot learn from people they view as strong—and therefore not like them.

Paul *could* have begun his letter with an appeal to his unique authority as an apostle. However, Paul wanted all the brothers and sisters in Corinth to identify with him as a mere human being, so that they would see the divine power which was expressed in his life as something they could draw on too.

This is the significance of Paul's statement that God "comforts us in all our troubles, so that we can comfort those in any trouble with the comfort we ourselves have received from God." It is because I have known troubles, and experienced God's enablement, that I can understand and come alongside those who have troubles like mine. If a brother or sister realizes that I am speaking about God from personal experiences that are like their own, they will be able to receive God's comfort from me.

Because of this conviction Paul was willing to share his weakness, even revealing his times of despair, to build a foundation for a solid continuing ministry to that church.

✂ *Group Activity: Recovery Group*
Step 10 (continue taking personal inventory)
Discuss reasons why it is hard to admit we are wrong or to reveal a weakness. Start by talking about these reasons, and add more of your own:
  * *People will lose respect for me.*
  * *It can be carried too far.*
  * *I feel too ashamed or embarrassed.*
  * *I won't be able to correct my kids or others if they know I make mistakes.*
  * *I get angry when I think of admitting faults.*
  * *I feel worthless when I do wrong, and hate the feeling.*

  * *I feel. . . .*
Read Paul's "confession" in 1:8-11. Did it fit an apostle's "image" to feel despair? Why didn't Paul hide this weakness to preserve his image? What in Paul's example suggests positive outcomes of admitting to ourselves, to God, and to others when we are wrong?

Individually make a personal inventory of your own wrong or weak acts this last week. List the acts you recall. Then write a "confession." Be aware not only of your responsibility for your actions, but of God's grace in preserving you even when making errors or doing wrong.

Share your confessions with others in the group, and share also any ways in which you see God graciously involved. For instance, you became angry and said something wrong and harmful, but stopped before going as far as you used to.

Continuing inventory has a strongly positive impact: we keep aware of our need for God's help, and at the same time see progress even while making mistakes.

♥ *Group Activity: Sharing Group*
Page 372 contains a diagram showing the sharing process by which we can best minister to others, adapted from the author's book, Youth Ministry (Zondervan, p. 144). Duplicate, and provide a copy for each group member.

Then together study 2 Corinthians 1:3-11, relating Paul's teaching and personal sharing to the process shown on the chart. Be sure you understand the process and its rationale.

Then work in pairs, alternating the roles of Person A and Person B. Select real rather than imaginary issues to talk about, and seek to truly help each other rather than simply practice a skill.

Take the chart home and review it. You can use this process within the family as well as to share meaningfully with friends or coworkers.

11. Person A
returns with new
solutions

Person A	10 decide together to put solutions into effect	Person B
1 shares problem		2 listens carefully

9
Person B
shares solutions
he used in
solving present
conflict of
Person A

4 responds, goes into more detail		3 humbles self, shares similar problem
6 reveals past fully: "really wasn't going to tell"	8 Person B shares solutions and Scriptures he used for past	5 humbles self, selects certain conflicts and tells them

7
response and
acceptance . . .
disclosure of
"real self"

The Case for Openness: 2 Corinthians 2:12–3:18

The context makes it clear that Paul was speaking about something he called a "New Covenant" ministry. As a result of that ministry, the Corinthians themselves were a letter of recommendation, for Christ through Paul had engraved His own person on their hearts. They were living letters, "written not with ink but with the Spirit of the living God, not on tablets of stone but on tablets of human hearts" (v. 3). It is this unique ministry of inner transformation that Paul spoke of when he said that God has "made us competent as ministers of the New Covenant" (v. 6).

Ø *Group Activity:*
Missions/Outreach Group
Sharing Christ has a pattern something like an upside-down Υ. Our role is to com- *municate the message. But that communication brings one of two responses: rejection, or acceptance of the Gospel message. Use an upside-down Υ chart to explore implications of 2 Corinthians 2:14–3:3.*

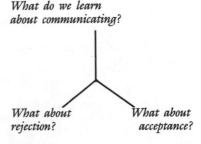

What do we learn about communicating?

What about rejection?   *What about acceptance?*

Focus together on the acceptance branch of the Υ. Are we effective in following up and nurturing new converts? How do we go about the process of aiding the Spirit to "write" Christ's presence on the hearts of new believers?

Paul contrasted his ministry with the ministry of Moses. That Old Covenant ministry had a certain fading glory, but is not to be compared with the splendor of the present ministry of the New Covenant. Paul brings the issue into focus:

Therefore, since we have such a hope [that is, the hope of inner transformation], we are very bold. We are not like Moses, who would put a veil over his face to keep the Israelites from gazing at it while the radiance was fading away.
2 Corinthians 3:12-13

What Paul was referring to was the Old Testament description of Moses, entering the tabernacle of God and returning to speak with the Israelites, transfused with a radiance and splendor.

Remember that Moses was leading a group of people much like some of the Corinthians. The Israelites were constantly challenging Moses' leadership. They murmured, complained, plotted against him, and at times were on the verge of stoning Moses to death! But when Moses came away from the Presence of God, with that visible splendor shining on his face, the people must have been stunned into temporary silence. We can even imagine Moses taking daily walks through the camp, pleased by the quiet that fell.

But then Moses noticed that the splendor faded. The glow went away! And "Moses . . . put a veil over his face to keep the Israelites from gazing at it while the radiance was fading away" (v. 13). *A process of deterioration was taking place, and Moses could not bear to have others see it.*

But ah, the contrast! Paul said, "We are not like Moses"; instead, "We are very bold." And Paul explained:

Where the Spirit of the Lord is, there is freedom. And we, who with unveiled faces all reflect the Lord's glory, are being transformed into His likeness with ever-increasing glory, which comes from the Lord, who is the Spirit.
2 Corinthians 3:17-18

What did Paul mean? Simply this: I unveil and reveal myself in order that you might see Jesus in me. Jesus is not revealed in some supposed human "perfection," but rather in our progressive transformation. It is not, "See how good I am," that witnesses to the reality of Jesus, but, "See what God is doing in such a sinner."

So Paul revealed his weaknesses. And in doing so, he also revealed the reality and the power of Jesus. Paul *was* weak, but the Spirit of God was constantly at work in him, working His transformation, overcoming his weaknesses, and infusing him with new strength. By taking off the veil that hid the real Paul from others, Paul knew that his critics would discover a weak and needy person. But Paul also knew that these people *would also see Jesus!*

Core truths. How stunningly clear. In Paul's explanation of his openness and vulnerability, we see reflections of basic truths testified to by the Word of God.

- We are sinners, warped and twisted out of shape, far from being the persons we want to be, or that God intends us to be.
- Jesus Himself enters the life of the believer; once born again, we receive "His own indestructible heredity" (1 Peter 1:23, PH).
- God is *in the process* of working His transformation in us believers; we "are being transformed into His likeness with ever-increasing glory" (2 Cor. 3:18).

To Paul, the implications of these truths were compelling. As a leader, called to be an example, Paul *had* to take the veil off his life and personality, and let others see him as he really was. Of course, Paul realized that the Corinthians would discover he had weaknesses; his transformation, like our own, was incomplete. But Paul also knew that since Jesus was in his life, his brothers and sisters would also be beholding the Lord's glory (2 Cor. 3:18). As others saw Jesus at work in Paul, they would find the confidence to hope for their own transformations.

It costs to be this kind of Christian. Some will misunderstand and try to use our weaknesses against us. Others will tend to look down on us. But once again, Paul has opened for us God's way of thinking—a way so very different from man's. Not pride or self-protection, but humility and self-revelation. Paul's understanding of this truth led to his commitment: "We have renounced secret and shameful ways; we do not use deception, nor do we distort the Word of God. On the contrary, by setting forth the truth plainly, we commend ourselves to every man's conscience in the sight of God" (2 Cor. 4:2).

May the Lord use Paul's example to free us and our group members to live, and to minister, in this same open, powerful way.

GROUP RESOURCE GUIDE

Identification: *Share with others*
Jot down on paper one evidence you're aware of concerning Christ's transforming impact on your own life. Do not share these, but save what you have written.

Affirmation: *Express love and concern*
Tell each person in the group, in turn, of any growth and/or positive changes you have noticed in him or her during the time you have known him or her. Be sure each person in the group receives some of this feedback.

Exploration: *Probe God's Word*
Together study 2 Corinthians 3:12-18, using the illustration below to focus its message.

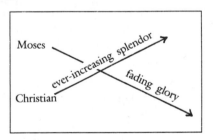

Moses veiled his face when he left God's presence because a process of deterioration

was taking place—the radiance was fading. The Christian is "bold" and removes veils because God is present within and the Holy Spirit is actively transforming us. The radiance of that transformation shines "with ever increasing glory." Only when our veils are removed—and people see our flaws—will they sense Jesus' presence through the transformation they note over time (see commentary).

Reaction: *Respond together to the Word*
Look at the item you wrote down at the beginning of this group meeting. Did people mention it as evidence they have seen of God's transformation in your life? Discuss: What does it mean about my own openness if no one mentioned the item I wrote down? What does it mean about my openness if several mentioned it?

Discuss: Why is it hard to be open and honest with others about our struggles and flaws? Why is it important? How can we foster openness in our group meetings?

Adoration: *Worship and prayer*
Meditate on Jesus' words: "Without Me you can do nothing" (John 15:4, KJV). We don't need to pretend that we've arrived: Our failures simply demonstrate the fact that Jesus is essential to us and to all.

THE MINISTRY OF RECONCILIATION

Overview

Paul's vision of his New Covenant ministry was rich in the promise of a progressive transformation for believers. "We . . . are being transformed into His [Jesus'] likeness with ever-increasing glory, which comes from the Lord, who is the Spirit" (2 Cor. 3:18).

Yet the Corinthians displayed less evidence of transformation than did other congregations! We know from Paul's first letter to them that their fellowship was marked by divisions, by doctrinal disputes, by confusion over spiritual gifts, even by immorality that was winked at by the local body.

How could Paul maintain his confidence in this unspiritual church, despite all the evidence that existed to the contrary? The answer is given in 2 Corinthians 4–5; an answer that gives us hope as parents, as members or leaders of modern congregations which, like that in Corinth, fall short of God's ideal.

▶ *Reconciliation.* This theological term means "to bring into harmony." In this passage Paul argued that the death of Jesus brought humanity to a place of harmony with God; where forgiveness can flow. But there is also an experiential dimension to reconciliation. We are to *live* in harmony with God, reflecting in ourselves the righteousness of God. It is to this end that Paul ministered—and in this passage he shows us the key to a ministry of reconciliation of our own.

Commentary

Paul was not only a great evangelist and teacher. He was a master motivator. In 2 Corinthians we see Paul at his best, and discover how first of all the apostle maintained his own optimism, as well as the way he motivated others to full commitment to Jesus Christ.

Actually, we are given hints in the first three chapters. These hints are found in phrases like:

- "Our hope for you is firm" (1:7).
- "You help us by your prayers" (v. 11).
- "We will boast of you in the day of the Lord Jesus" (v. 14).
- "I was confident of this" (v. 15).
- "I had confidence in all of you" (2:3).
- "Reaffirm your love for him" (v. 8).

The same encouraging optimism is expressed in a phrase from chapter 4: "Life is at work in you" (v. 12).

How are these phrases related to Paul's own optimism, and to spiritual motivation of others?

The football coach who chews out his players is doing it to motivate them. The parent who demands, "Sit down and do your homework *before* you go out," is seeking to motivate. The pastor who preaches a fiery sermon on coming judgment is seeking to use fear to motivate his congregation to action.

We have so many ways of attempting to move people. We set goals for them, and urge them to achieve. We make rules, and insist that others keep them. We shame, urge, condemn, and plan competitions in the hope that *something* will move others to respond. The unhappy wife nags her husband, the disappointed parent belittles his child, and even the proud parent withholds praise in an effort to stimulate still higher achievement. And all of them, at times, wonder, "Why?"

"Why doesn't my husband improve?"

"Why doesn't my child *try?*"

"Why don't members of our congregation get involved?"

The answer to all these questions is the same. It's because we're trying to use man's approach to move others. And as Paul taught in 1 Corinthians 1 and 2, human wisdom is not God's kind of wisdom. God has His own unique and vital way of doing His work in our lives.

The Role of the Leader

One of the basic elements in God's approach to moving believers to follow Jesus is a theme repeated over and over in the Corinthian epistles. It is the theme of the leader's *example*. Paul could, and often did, say to his readers "Imitate me in this," or, "Follow me as I follow Jesus."

In these chapters we see revealed two factors in Paul's own attitude which are critical if we as parents or leaders are to create a climate which will free others to respond and to grow.

Unconditional love. This is the first characteristic of the effective parent or leader. How often we see it stressed in this book.

Apparently Paul's first letter was taken by some in Corinth as rejection; an indication that Paul no longer loved them. They took his gentle explanation as "cold and unfeeling" reasoning. So over and over in this letter Paul reassured them. "We are not withholding our affection from you" (2 Cor. 6:12).

Sometimes we hear psychologists suggest that to withdraw love is an effective way for parents to discipline children. Far from it! In fact, it is the awareness of unconditional love—that sense of certainty that we are supported by a love that will never let us go—that creates the context for growth. Where there is uncertainty about love, there is also uncertainty about our personal worth and value. There is also fear of failure, and an unwillingness to take a risk. It seems safer not to try; safer never to fail, safer never to risk the possible withdrawal of love.

Whatever we can say about human approaches to motivating others—about nagging, shaming, expressing anger, chewing out, or demanding achievement, one thing is sure. These do *not* communicate unconditional love.

Expectant confidence. This was the second key to Paul's approach to motivation. Paul let the Corinthians know that he was confident they would grow. "I have great confidence in you," Paul said. "I take great pride in you. I am greatly encouraged; in all our troubles my joy knows no bounds" (7:4).

Here, remember, Paul was not writing to the Thessalonians, whose work of faith and labor of love and endurance inspired by hope were so abundantly plain. No, Paul was writing to the Corinthians, the church marked by division and marred by troublesome disputes.

It is easy to see how Paul might have expressed confidence in believers like those in Thessalonica. But the Corinthians? Yet, over and over, Paul assured the recipients of this letter that he had confidence in them. And his confidence was not because of the Corinthians' achievements, but in spite of their lack of achievement!

While the Corinthians had begun to lose confidence in themselves, Paul strongly affirmed that his confidence had not been shaken. Paul would believe in these men and women—until they were finally able to believe in themselves.

This is the key. For growth, there must be the assurance of love, and the prospect of hope. For a person to be motivated, there must be a confident expectation of success. That expectation cannot be based on performance alone. For no matter how we may try, our efforts are bound to fall short at times.

As parents or as leaders, we need to not only extend others our unconditional love, but we need a basis on which we can honestly and confidently express our own confidence that even the most hopeless will succeed.

A Basis for Confidence: 2 Corinthians 4–5

Paul's confident reassurance of the Corinthians was not an attempt to manipulate them. It was not just a motivational technique. Instead, what Paul was doing was sharing with these uncertain and ashamed believers what he really felt about them.

Expressions of confidence, if honest, do motivate. But such expressions cannot initially be based on others' past performance. If our hope for ourselves and for others is based on performance, there is bound to be a growing sense of discouragement and ultimately, the loss of hope.

This is a trap that parents often fall into with their children. Time after time they instruct or encourage or request. And time after time the child fails to respond, or "forgets," or simply ignores. He doesn't do his homework. She forgets to make her bed. He neglects his chores. She keeps on resisting correction. He won't confess misdeeds, no matter how gently or firmly you deal with him. She won't clean up her room.

Before long, a parent's confidence is worn away. Before long, the parent *expects* the child to disappoint. And the child, sensing the parent's attitude, begins to expect himself or herself to fail.

The child learns to live by the expectations of failure that we have communicated.

It is so important for us to learn Paul's secret. The secret of maintaining one's own confidence, and thus being able to build confidence and hope—and motivation to change—into others' lives. What is that secret? Paul explained.

"We do not lose heart" (2 Cor. 4). Paul was deeply aware that he had been entrusted with his ministry by God. As to the Gospel message, God is able to make its light shine in dark hearts. Ultimately, God is the source of all change in human hearts (vv. 1-6).

As for Paul himself, he was deeply aware that he was a mere "jar of clay." Despite the terrible pressures under which he must have lived (vv. 7-12), Paul spoke out with faith and confidence. He knew that "the One who raised the Lord Jesus from the dead will also raise us with Jesus and present us with you in His presence" (v. 14). The message of Christ glows with a vitalizing power: the very power that raised Jesus from the dead, at work in human beings.

"Therefore," Paul said, "we do not lose heart" (v. 16). The foundation for Paul's confidence in the Corinthians was his bedrock belief in Jesus, and the Resurrection power that the message of Jesus unleashes.

At this point Paul laid down an important principle which was at the core of his confidence. Outwardly Paul admitted deterioration: we are "wasting away." But inwardly Paul experienced a daily renewal. As a result Paul said, "We fix our eyes not on what is seen, but on what is unseen. For what is seen is temporary, but what is unseen is eternal" (v. 18).

This concept deserves exploration. What Paul said is that *anything* that exists in this world of time and space is subject to change. Children grow up. Job descriptions change. Buildings decay. Civilizations fall. Even cliffs are eroded by wind and rain. Anything that we can see is by its very nature subject to change!

This is true of those children of ours who can't remember to make their beds—and of the Corinthians, who could not seem to get beyond disputes and arguments. If what troubles us is a behavior that we can see, then we need to remember that it is temporary. It will change, by the very nature of things in this world of change! How foolish then to become discouraged and give up, even if behavior that bothers us persists for months or years. We need to remember, with Paul, that what we see can change. And it will change.

But Paul did more than remind us that things in this world are temporary. He affirmed realities which are *not* subject to change. "We fix our eyes . . . on what is unseen. For what is . . . unseen is eternal."

There are realities which God knows, and has revealed, that are utterly stable and on which we can count. In our ministry with others, we must not only remember that some things are temporary. We must fix our hope on unseen things which are eternal.

Heaven ahead (2 Cor. 5:1-10). In a brief aside Paul looked at some of those unseen things which are utterly real. There is an "eternal house in the heaven" that will replace our mortal body. Aware of this reality, we look beyond our earthly life and yearn to be present with the Lord. Because we believe completely in this unseen reality, we "make it our goal to please Him," aware that our deeds on earth will be evaluated, and we will "receive what is due" based on how we live our present lives.

It is important here to note that the "Judgment Seat of Christ" (a *bema*) has nothing to do with salvation. The believer's acts are judged, with a view to rewarding him or her (see 1 Cor. 3:15; 4:5).

A ministry of reconciliation (2 Cor. 5:11-12). To understand this passage, we must realize first that Paul was not talking about evangelism when he spoke of his "ministry of reconciliation" (v. 18). "Reconciliation" literally means to "bring into harmony." When we set our watch by the electric clock in the kitchen, we are "reconciling" our watch to the clock. We change the one so that it keeps time set by the standard of the other. This is what Paul wanted for the Corinthians; to bring their lives into harmony with the pattern set by God.

Paul pointed out that it's only appropriate that we live by the heartbeat of God's life rather than by the old heartbeat of humankind. Since Jesus loved and died for believers, they should "no longer live for themselves but for Him who died for them and was raised again" (v. 15). As they do this, they will "become the righteousness of God" in Him (v. 21).

It is this goal of leading believers to life in full harmony with God's righteousness that Paul had in mind when he said, "We implore you on Christ's behalf: Be reconciled to God" (v. 20).

With this understood, we can go back and look at Paul's explanation of how he could express such amazing confidence even in the Corinthians.

Paul began the paragraph assuring the Corinthians that his expressions of confidence were no insincere attempt at flattery (vv. 11-12). Yet how could Paul be totally honest and, while criticizing the Corinthians' behavior still speak of his joy and confidence in their future progress? Paul explained that this is because his approach was so different from "those who take pride in what is seen rather than what is in the heart" (v. 12).

This statement takes us back to the core concept expressed earlier. Some base their pride on what can be seen and measured. "Aren't the folks in my congregation spiritual! Fifty percent of them show up on prayer-meeting night." And, "My Johnny is an ideal Christian boy. Why, he reads his Bible every day."

This is *not* to say we shouldn't be pleased by evidence of spiritual progress or commitment. But pride in the 50 percent who come means shame on the 50 percent who don't! And, neither coming nor not coming provides a basis for judgment of individual spiritual progress. Indeed, because anything that can be seen is temporary and subject to change, those who boast in externals set themselves up for a fall when the percentage drops off, or Johnny forsakes his Bible reading.

What then *are* we to take pride in? Paul said, "What is in the heart." We can't *see* what is in the heart, of course. We can't measure it. But the Christian knows that Jesus Himself is resident in the heart of believers. And Jesus is eternal. He will not change no matter what.

Paul told the Corinthians his view wasn't madness (v. 13). It was utter sanity. Because, Paul said, "Christ's love compels us" (v. 14).

Paul's point was this. There is only one thing that will really bring about change in a believer's life, and move him or her toward Christlikeness. That is the love that Christ Himself pours into the heart in which He dwells. Mere human forms of motivation—the attempts to coerce, to shame, to move by guilt—may bring conformity of action. *But they will never change the heart, and it is the heart—the unseen world within—with which Christian ministry is concerned.*

Paul now stated a powerful theological argument. Christ died for all. He died for us in order that we who live should stop living for ourselves, and begin to live for Him. *That is, God's purpose in the Cross was to change us, and change the focus of our lives.* Paul was confident that Jesus, who now lives in the hearts of believers, will bring about the change that He died to gain! It is inconceivable to Paul that the purpose of Jesus' death on the cross could be thwarted. God *would* change the Corinthians. Paul had hope and confidence, not because of what he saw in the Corinthian's actions, but because he looked beyond appearances and saw Jesus living in these believers' hearts.

The next paragraph is important, because it shows us how to live with others to encourage this change Jesus has come into their lives to make. Paul said that from now on "we regard no one from a worldly point of view" (v. 16). That is, we simply do not judge them by what we see. If we looked at Jesus in this way, we would see only an idealistic Carpenter, murdered by wicked and selfish men. But we look at Jesus through the eyes of faith! In the Cross we do not see defeat, but victory! Though we do not see Jesus with our physical eyes, we recognize Him as the living God, our Saviour and our Lord.

In the same way, we must learn to look at our brothers and sisters with the eyes of faith. We must affirm, with Paul, that "in Christ" they are "new creations." The old *has* gone, the new has come within. And because the new has come, in time, behavior too will change and our loved ones or friends *will* learn to love the One who died for them.

How do we help them come to this commitment? Paul said that Jesus' ministry of reconciliation was accomplished by "not counting men's sins against them." God doesn't count our sins. He doesn't say, "You've failed 32 times. Oh, my, there's 33." And He doesn't hold our sins against us. He keeps on loving, keeps on holding out hope.

This is just how we are to treat others—our children, our spouses, our brothers and sisters in the Lord. We don't say, "That's the thirty-second day you forgot to make your bed, and tomorrow will be 33." And we don't hold failures against them.

Instead we remember that, in Christ, there is a newness rooted deep within. We keep on expressing love. And we keep on expressing confidence and hope. And through it all we make God's appeal. Bring your life into harmony with who God is, that "in Him [you] might become the righteousness of God."

A Life of Love: 2 Corinthians 6–7
Paul had revealed the convictions which enabled him to maintain confidence in the Corinthians. Now he shared more of what love means.

Love means urging (2 Cor. 6:1-2). Unconditional love does not rule out exhorting. Paul called on his readers not to receive God's grace in vain.

Love means self-sacrifice (2 Cor. 6:3-13). Paul reviewed the hardships he had suffered in ministry. He had endured everything as a servant of God, out of love. Paul had been completely open and caring—it was time for the Corinthians to open wide their hearts to Him as well.

Love means separation (2 Cor. 6:14–7:1). The Christian will refuse to be linked with evil. Commitment to Christ calls for purification "from everything that contaminates body and spirit."

❋ *Group Activity:*
Singles/Single Again Group
What relationships are OK for a Christian Single to have? What relationships are out?
Together brainstorm to develop complete

lists in three categories: Definitely Out, Debatable, Definitely OK.
When you have finished study 2 Corinthians 2:14-18 and 1 Corinthians 5:9-13. Based on these two passages develop a set of "Guiding Principles for Singles."
Now go back to your lists. See if applying the principles developed from these passages leads you to shift items from one list to another.

Love means joy even in pain (2 Cor. 7:2-16). Paul's relationship with the Corinthians had brought both of them great pain. Paul felt great anxiety over the Corinthians, as well as deep hurt. And Paul's letter caused the Corinthians sorrow. Yet that sorrow was beneficial—the godly repented and changed. And the change in them was complete (v. 11). As a result the sorrow each experienced was one of those temporary things Paul had been speaking of in these chapters.

And the pain even produced joy. Paul felt joy when Titus came and told the apostle "about your longing for me, your deep sorrow, your ardent concern for me so that my joy was greater than ever" (v. 7). Titus too felt joy as he learned the sincerity of the Corinthians' faith, and saw their responsiveness to instruction.

And so a great danger was avoided in Corinth, and the church there was set back on the path to righteousness. And through it all, Paul in total honesty was able to encourage his friends, and to say with a full heart, "I have great confidence in you; I take great pride in you. I am greatly encouraged; in all our troubles my joy knows no bounds."

How wonderful when we have learned Paul's secrets of motivation, and have taken them to heart, so that we say to others who are struggling, "I am glad I can have complete confidence in you" (v. 16).

Because we believe in Jesus, and hold the unseen far more real than what is visible to the eye, we can reach out with unconditional love and confident hope, and by our example help others to grow.

GROUP RESOURCE GUIDE

Identification: *Share with others*
How did your parents try to motivate you? What was the result of their approach? Did it develop your confidence? Did it make you feel good about yourself? Did you feel affirmed and accepted?

Discuss your experiences for 10 or 15 minutes. Then consider this question: Did your parents feel confident that you would turn out all right, or not? How did this affect their approach to parenting?

Exploration: *Probe God's Word*
1 Corinthians 4–5 are basic but difficult chapters. They explain the basis on which Paul—and parents today—can have confidence in ministry even when those ministered to seem unresponsive.

Because it is so vital to trace the flow of thought in this passage, use one of these two unusual approaches to be sure its teaching is understood. (1) Distribute copies of the commentary on these chapters, pp. 375–379. Read and underline, comparing the commentary to the text. Then in groups of three discuss key points and questions. (2) Have someone previously prepared give a minilecture, carefully covering each point. Be ready to answer questions, and make sure each person thoroughly understands the teaching of these chapters.

Reaction: *Respond together to the Word*
Reevaluate how you were brought up. Did your parents "not count" your failures "against you"? Or did they count them, and remind you of them?

Then look at your relationships with others—your spouse, your children, your employees or coworkers. Do you exhibit an attitude that promotes reconciliation? What can you do to become more effective as a reconciler?

Affirmation: *Express love and concern*
Affirmation sometimes is experienced as constructive feedback, even when this may not seem pleasant. Find out how others in the group experience you. Do you seem accepting, positive, encouraging—a reconciler who does not count trespasses against others? Or do you seem negative, counting and remembering others' faults, holding flaws against them, etc?

Adoration: *Worship and pray*
Focus on the cross, and its message of reconciliation. In the Gospel God comes to us with the good news that He loves us as we are, and that through forgiveness (not counting our sins against us) He introduces a dynamic that will ultimately make us "the righteousness of God in (Christ)." Praise Him for His attitude toward you, and the freedom Christ brings you to grow and change.

STUDY GUIDE 58

2 Corinthians 8–9

NEW TESTAMENT PRINCIPLES OF GIVING

Overview

John wrote in the introduction to his Gospel, "the Law was given by Moses; grace and truth came through Jesus Christ" (John 1:17). In a sense, the rest of the New Testament is an exposition of the grace and the truth which came through Jesus.

Here, in 2 Corinthians 8 and 9, the Apostle Paul outlined the grace principles governing a New Testament pattern of giving which supplants the Old Testament principle of the tithe.

The way Paul developed this topic also illustrates his approach to New Covenant ministry. In the preceding chapters Paul had expressed a confidence in Christians based on the reality of Christ in their hearts. Now, rather than command or coerce, Paul simply taught and encouraged his readers to give as a free and personal response to Christ.

These chapters also are an illustration of Paul's use of spiritual authority, which we explore in the next study guide. Rather than demand, the apostle carefully guarded the freedom of individuals to be personally responsible to God, and reminded us all that response to God must not be made "reluctantly or under compulsion, for God loves a cheerful giver" (2 Cor. 9:7).

What a privilege to be able to affirm the grace of God as we teach, and to encourage in our group members a free, spontaneous and loving response to Jesus which the Lord Himself loves to see in you and me.

Commentary

It's said most Sundays in most of our churches. As the collection plate is passed, the congregation is encouraged to give God "tithes and offerings."

There's nothing particularly wrong with this familiar phrase. Unless we make the mistake of reading into it a theology of giving that has its roots in Old Testament Law

rather than in the vital new principles of grace-giving that the New Testament establishes for God's people. It is significant that the Epistles mention no tithes, and the offering which God seeks is that of the person himself as a "living sacrifice . . . which is your spiritual worship" (Rom. 12:1).

Background

The tithe in the Old Testament. The Law established a concept of tithing which, at first glance, seems simple. Leviticus 27:30-33 says that a "tithe of everything from the land" was to be set aside for use as God might command. Other passages expand this initial instruction. According to Numbers 18:21-32, tithes were to be used for the support of those dedicated to serve God. According to Deuteronomy 12:5-14 and 14:22-26, the 10 percent was to be brought to a central sanctuary, later established by David at Jerusalem, for distribution.

However, 14:27-29 and 26:12-15 introduce *another* tithe, this one to be collected every third year and distributed locally to the needy! Some students of Scripture believe that as many as three separate tithes can be identified. But surely there are two: the yearly 10 percent taken to support those who led Israel in worship, and a triannual 10 percent used to support widows and orphans.

In Old Testament times this giving posed no threat to the believer, and Scripture does not see it as a burden. God is able to make the land produce abundantly, so His people will have all they need and more. Giving is a way of worship; a way to express confidence in God (see Mal. 3:10).

In addition to the tithes which the Israelite *owed* to God, the Law established a principle of voluntary contributions. These contributions, called "freewill offerings," were given spontaneously, out of love. They were not a duty, and they were not considered "bribes" to buy divine favor.

Thus in the Old as well as the New love flowed: beyond duty there was the privilege of expressing devotion through one's giving to God, and of expressing concern for God's people by lending to the needy.

As we move into the New Testament era, however, we note several important contrasts. The Epistles never call for a tithe. There is no single worship center and no priesthood to be supported by the old, annual temple tithe. While giving to support individuals who minister full time is mentioned in the New Testament, no letter suggests this be done through a local tithe. The New Testament emphasizes a deep concern for the poor and needy, especially within the family of faith. Paul and others did organize offerings to be taken up for those in hunger-ridden foreign lands. But the guidelines for giving that Paul laid down nowhere mention or imply that the tithe is to be used to measure a Christian's obligation.

So we need to look carefully in our study of 2 Corinthians 8–9 to see if new principles of measure are introduced.

The New Testament view of possessions. The principles of giving which we find in 2 Corinthians reflect an attitude toward possessions which is consistent throughout the New Testament.

Jesus taught that the believer is not to trust in possessions, nor consider material things treasures (Matt. 6:19-33). The manager in one of Jesus' parables was considered shrewd because he *used* worldly wealth to prepare for his future (Luke 16:9). Jesus went on to show that no one can serve two masters: we will either love God and reject money as the focus of our lives, or we will love money and God will take second place. "You cannot serve both God and money" (v. 13). The believer, then, will give God first place and use money in God's service.

The New Testament Epistles reflect this teaching. The love of God will be reflected in sharing what we have. "If anyone has material possessions and sees his brother in need but has no pity on him, how can the love of God be in him? Dear children, let us not love with words or tongue but with actions and in truth" (1 John 3:17-18).

Paul told Timothy to "command those who are rich in this present world not to be arrogant nor to put their hope in wealth, which is so uncertain, but to put their hope in God, who richly provides us with everything for our enjoyment. Command them to do good, to be rich in good deeds, and to be generous and willing to share. In this way they will lay up treasure for themselves as a firm foundation for the coming age" (1 Tim. 6:17-19).

While it is not wrong to be wealthy, and while material riches can be used to help others, the love of money *is* a problem, a "root of all kinds of evil" (v. 10).

The composite we draw suggests that worldly riches are not in themselves evil. The issue is one of how they affect our values and choices. If we put God first, and respond lovingly to the needs of others, we can use our possessions to prepare for eternity. But if we put money first, we will fall short of full commitment to God and fall short in our obligation to love others.

Our use of our resources then becomes one means of measuring our dedication to God and our commitment to eternal values.

Grace Giving: 2 Corinthians 8–9

Several things help us put this passage's teaching on giving in perspective. In the early New Testament church there were no buildings to finance, no curriculums or programs to support. Yet there were needs within the body. Funds were given to the apostles and to others who traveled as missionaries. Often local elders would be supported to free them for a full-time ministry. Paul wrote to Timothy about needy widows who were also supported by the congregation. However the first obligation for their support fell on children and grandchildren. The great collections of which the New Testament speaks here and in other passages (cf. Acts 11:27-30; etc.) were, however, intended for the support of Christian brothers and sisters in lands struck by famine or some other natural disaster. Essentially then "giving" in the New Testament was focused on meeting "people needs." Its goal was to enable others to simply survive, or to carry on ministries recognized as important by the church.

It is not surprising then to discover that the term used for "giving" in this New Testament context is not the typical Greek word for making a gift. Instead the New Testament adopts the Greek word *koinonia,* which means "sharing." As Christians shared life in Christ, their family relationship was expressed by a sharing of financial and material resources.

In these chapters of 2 Corinthians then Paul wrote to encourage members of this congregation to share their material possessions with needy brothers. His whole approach and argument was a demonstration of the revolutionary approach to motivation explored in our last study guide. Paul held no rallies and called for no pledges. He sent no letters filled with underlined appeals. Paul set up no "buy a brick" campaigns; he put no red ribbon threaded through a giant thermometer to creep upward toward Paul's campaign goal. There was not even an every-member canvass. In fact, Paul seems to have found an entirely different way.

If we keep in mind these two factors, that "giving" is really sharing to meet needs in the body of Christ, and that New Testament giving focuses on people needs, we will be able to better understand what Paul teaches us here.

Two examples (1 Cor. 8:1-9). Paul began by telling about the way the churches of Macedonia had shared generously despite extreme poverty. Their act of service was viewed as a privilege, and their example provided a standard against which the Corinthians could measure their own earnestness.

But the Macedonians were not the prime example of the grace of giving: Jesus is. Jesus demonstrated this grace in that though He was rich, He gave all ("became poor") that through His poverty we might become rich.

There is no appeal here to the tithe as a standard against which to measure our giving. Instead Paul pointed to other believers and to Jesus, whose love moved them to give, first themselves and then money.

Willingness (2 Cor. 8:10-12). Paul was pleased that the Corinthians had earlier expressed a strong desire to help. But the Corinthians needed to carry their intentions through to completion, "according to your means." This is an important factor in grace giving. Paul said it again. "If the willingness is there, the gift is acceptable according to what one has, not according to what he does not have."

On the one hand, one need not be a millionaire for his or her contribution to be significant. Even the gifts of those who have little and can give little are acceptable. What God is concerned with is the willingness: the love that motivates the believer to share (cf. Luke 21:1-4).

The principle of "equality" (2 Cor. 8:13-15). Here Paul laid down an important principle. The goal in grace giving is "that there might be equality." This is *not* Christian communism, in any sense. Paul's vision is of a worldwide church, an international body. In the first-century world, as in our own, there were at times famines or other natural disasters, which left whole populations on the verge of starvation. The collections which Paul spoke of here were for the relief of Christians in such areas. What Paul pointed out is that, at present, the plenty enjoyed by the Corinthians could supply others' needs. In their turn those others might one day supply the Corinthians when they had needs.

The body image is appropriate here. Just as the food we take in is digested and distributed to all parts of the body, in order that every bodily part can function, so the funds God supplies to believers are to be shared with those in need so they can live and function as God intends.

♥ *Group Activity: Support Group*
Study the principle laid down in 2 Corinthians 8:13-15. Then discuss whether, and how, it would apply in the following situations.

(1) Carla, a young divorced mother of two, is about to lose her house because the payments are just too large for her to make on her earnings. The trouble is that rent payments will be about the same, and she doesn't know what to do.

(2) Joy suffered brain damage at birth and is in a Christian residential care facility. Her parents have been told the facility must raise its prices again. They are already stretched to the limit, and don't know how they can manage another $100 a month.

(3) Herb has just been laid off from his job—and just after buying a new car for his wife too. She doesn't want to go back to work, and Herb knows he'll be without work for at least three months.

(4) Carrie quit school before graduating. Now the only job she can get is at Mc-Donald's—and the pay isn't enough

to live on. She's smart enough, but was kind of wild in her teens, and now at 23 is paying the price.

Move from the hypothetical to the real situation. What financial difficulties do group members have? How have they been resolved? What could (or should?) the church or other Christians do? How do we support each other when our problems are primarily financial?

Action encouraged (2 Cor. 8:16–9:5). Paul told the Corinthians that Titus and another brother were coming to take and distribute their liberal gift, and urged them to "show these men the proof of your love and the reason for our pride in you" by having it ready.

Giving as sowing (2 Cor. 9:6-11). Paul turned to another image that had its roots in the Old Testament. Sharing with others is like sowing seed: the more generously one sows the more he or she will reap.

This is *not* a promise that one who sends in $7 will get $77 in return. Instead it is an affirmation of God's ability to outgive His people. "God is able to make all grace abound to you, so that in all things at all times, having all that you need, you will abound in every good work." *The conviction that God is able to supply our needs is intended to free us to give generously, without fear that we will deprive ourselves or our family by responding to meet the needs of others.*

In this context Paul said that "each man should give what he has decided in his heart to give, not reluctantly or under compulsion, for God loves a cheerful giver." Again, Paul was careful not to place believers under any obligation to give, and not to specify any percentage as appropriate. Each is to give "what he has decided in his heart," and that decision is not to be made reluctantly or under compulsion.

The outcome of grace giving (2 Cor. 9:12-15). Paul now summed up the results of generous giving. It supplies the needs of God's people. It overflows in expressions of thanks to God, and stimulates praise. It demonstrates the obedience (commitment) that is appropriate to our profession of faith. It generates prayers for the giver by the one who receives.

And, as Paul had shown earlier, it permits us to experience the faithfulness of God who is able, and does supply our needs as we use our material possessions to help our brothers and sisters.

Implications

In an earlier study we saw that the Apostle Paul abandoned typical approaches to motivating others. He did not demand. He did not try to produce guilt. He did not manipulate. Rather Paul put great trust in the fact that Christ does live in the believer, and he based both his confidence and his appeal to others on this reality.

What kind of pattern might we see in our local churches if we were to build our stewardship programs on the gracious principles Paul presents in 2 Corinthians 8 and 9?

It seems that such a program would feature these elements:

We would present needs. Paul did not hesitate to share with the churches the needs of those for whom he planned to take up a collection. The needs emphasized were human needs. It is not *wrong* to give today to support the local church as an institution, or to support denominational programs. But the strongest and best motivation for giving is to respond to brothers or sisters whose needs are real and basic.

We would encourage our people to evaluate our own needs in view of the resources and against the needs of their brothers. Wealth is comparative. In some situations a person with a thousand dollars is rich; in others a person with that amount is poor. In some societies all our needs can be met with the expenditure of a few thousand dollars a year. In other situations our most basic needs may require the expenditure of many thousands of dollars. God does not set a fixed amount that Christians are to give, but He does call on us to evaluate what we have (and need) and to look honestly at what others have (and need).

We are then to give what we can and what we wish to, but not what we cannot spare or are unwilling to share.

We would reject manipulation. Like Paul we would protect the freedom of our brothers and sisters to respond to God as they themselves choose, and do nothing to force or manipulate giving.

We would teach freeing truths. While Paul did not manipulate, he did not hesitate to teach truths which release Christians from fear and from bondage to the material. Like

Paul we might remind others of God's great gift in Christ. We might emphasize God's commitment to us, and affirm that we cannot outgive a God who is able to make all grace abound to us. We might also teach that the person who gives sparingly will reap sparingly, and that giving generates many spiritual benefits.

These are principles we need to implement in our churches. But before we apply them to stewardship in the church, we can apply them in our own lives. As we take to heart the truths Paul taught here, we experience both freedom and release. We are freed from compulsion in our Christian lives. And, through growing trust in God, we are released from our bondage to possessions and enabled to respond freely, and generously, to meet others' needs.

GROUP RESOURCE GUIDE

Identification: *Share with others*
Give your opinion and one reason for it: "Our church ought to establish a fund to help people who are in real financial need."

Exploration: *Probe God's Word*
Assume that your church actually did establish such a fund, and that you have been assigned to develop policies governing its administration. In teams explore 2 Corinthians 8–9. Assign different teams policy development in the following areas.

1. How will the program be presented and funds be collected?
2. What needs will qualify for assistance, and what needs will not?
3. What will we ask those who receive help to do?
4. What will the relationship of this fund be to regular church giving to support the ministry and pay for buildings?

After teams have researched the passage and come up with recommendations, report to the group as a whole, explaining the basis for each recommendation.

Reaction: *Respond together to the Word*
Keep on exploring in one of two ways. (1) Continue the hypothetical approach, and apply your guidelines to see how they would work in the cases described on the group activity, page 383. Or (2) Get personal. What kind of financial obligation do we have individually — not through a church program — to other Christians? What does this passage suggest about how much to give, and where to direct giving? How close is our practice to the biblical ideal?

Adoration: *Worship and pray*
Choose one verse in this passage that speaks to you of God's giving. Go around the group, each reading the verse chosen, and expressing your appreciation to God for His giving nature.

SPIRITUAL AUTHORITY

Overview

In 2 Corinthians Paul shared principles of his New Covenant ministry. That ministry leads to the inner transformation of believers, as promised in Jeremiah's ancient prophecy (31:33-34).

The New Covenant ministry is one of openness and transparency, for God the Spirit is at work within and we see Christ in each others' lives as the process of transformation is revealed (2 Cor. 1–3). New Covenant ministry relies on the reality of Christ in the heart to motivate change, and is not discouraged by apparent lack of progress. The New Covenant minister expresses confidence in others, "not counting their trespasses," sure that Christ will move believers to live a righteous life (2 Cor. 4–7). New Covenant ministry, as illustrated by grace giving, guards the freedom of each individual to respond personally to God, while teaching truths that release us to respond generously (2 Cor. 8–9). Now, in the last chapters of this most personal of Paul's books, we see how the apostle exercises spiritual authority in such a way that it builds others up rather than tears them down.

▶ *Authority*. The Greek word is *exousia,* and its basic meaning indicates "freedom of choice." A person with great authority has maximum freedom of choice; one under authority has his or her freedom limited. The secret of spiritual authority is that it creates rather than limits others' freedom of choice.

Commentary

"Authority" is such a difficult word. We use it in so many ways.

- An encyclopedia is cited when someone asks, "What's your authority for that statement?"
- Professor so-and-so is introduced as an "authority on cybernetics."
- "Where's your search warrant?" is a demand for evidence of authority.
- "By the authority vested in me, I now pronounce you man and wife."

Yet, in our society, the idea of authority has had many negative connotations. To many it tends to imply control, restriction, coercion, and impersonal command. "Authority" and "authoritarian" can seem almost synonymous, and it's hard for most of us to imagine how we might exercise authority without somehow asserting a right to control or command.

It's no wonder that spiritual leadership and authority are misunderstood. And it's no wonder that a parent's authority over a child can be distorted. No wonder those called to lead the church of God, and given His authority for that task, are often troubled and uncertain. No wonder we often resort to a worldly approach to the exercise of authority—and stimulate rebellion rather than response.

Paul's Approach to Authority: 2 Corinthians 10–13

We may not be aware of it as we read 2 Corinthians, but it is true that in this letter the apostle was exercising spiritual authority.

We're not likely to realize it, because Paul did not even mention authority until chapter 10. His second and final mention of authority came near the end of this letter, in chapter 13. In each of these two contexts Paul gave a definition of the purpose of authority in the body of Christ. Authority was given to Paul by the Lord "for building you up rather than pulling you down" (10:8; see also 12:10). How much Paul hoped, as he closed this letter, that when he visited he would not be forced to be "harsh in my use of authority" (13:10).

We tend to think of authority as something essentially harsh. But in the body of

Christ, the use of authority is marked by a distinct gentleness. Even the Corinthians missed the authority in the apostle's approach. Deceived again by their reliance on their old ways of understanding, they could not understand why the apostle did not simply insist and command and demand. "Why," they must have wondered, "doesn't this leader *lead*?" They mistook Paul's wisdom for weakness. We know that, from Paul's "defense" in the opening of chapter 10.

> By the meekness and gentleness of Christ, I appeal to you—I, Paul, who am "timid" when face to face with you, but "bold" when away! I beg you that when I come I may not have to be as bold as I expect to be toward some people who think that we live by the standards of this world. For though we live in the world, we do not wage war as the world does. The weapons we fight with are not the weapons of the world. On the contrary, they have divine power to tear down strongholds. We demolish arguments and every pretension that sets itself up against the knowledge of God, and we take captive every thought to make it obedient to Christ.
>
> 2 Corinthians 10:1-5

God's approach to authority operates on divine power. Through God's methods, Paul would be successful in taking "captive every thought" and making it "obedient to Christ."

What are some of those methods? Listen, as Paul's letter itself unveils them:

- "Not that we lord it over your faith, but we work with you for your joy" (1:24).
- "I urge you, therefore to reaffirm your love for Him" (2:8).
- "Dear friends, let us purify ourselves from everything that contaminates body and spirit, perfecting holiness out of reverence for God" (7:1).
- "I am not commanding you, but I want to test the sincerity of your love" (8:8).
- "Here is my advice about what is best for you" (v. 10).
- "Was it a sin for me to lower myself in order to elevate you?" (11:7)

And the freedom that Paul found to exer-cise his authority in such gentle ways was rooted both in his knowledge that this *is* God's way to use spiritual authority, and in the knowledge that it is *God* who exercised authority through him.

In 2 Corinthians 13 Paul gave a warning: he would not "spare" those who failed to respond to his letters. Yet even here Paul himself would not act. What Paul would do was expect *God* to act, because Christ truly was speaking through him. The Lord would enforce the spiritual authority of His servant—Paul would not rely on worldly ways to punish those who did not respond.

> On my return I will not spare those who sinned earlier or any of the others, since you are demanding proof that Christ is speaking through me. He is not weak in dealing with you, but is powerful among you.
>
> 2 Corinthians 13:2-3

♥ *Group Activity: Support Group*
One of the most painful things we have to deal with is people we care about who misunderstand our motives or actions. Read 1 Corinthians 10–13 together, to make a list of ways in which Paul was misunderstood by some in Corinth.

Then share: Does anything on this list remind you of a personal experience? Tell about it.

Return to the text, but in teams. Examine each misunderstanding you located, and see how Paul handled his hurt and disappointment. What did he do to try to straighten the relationship out?

Report insights, and then see if they can be applied to the personal experiences you shared. What did you do, or can you do, to deal with misunderstandings?

Authority Principles

The issue of spiritual authority is complex and important enough to warrant an entire book, not just part of a chapter in this *Teacher's Commentary*. But we can sketch basic characteristics of spiritual authority as demonstrated by Paul, which will give us perspective and help to sensitize us to what is behind the last, most intimate chapters in this very personal epistle.

Source. Spiritual authority, unlike secular authority, is not rooted in position. An officer in the army or the president of a corporation has authority by virtue of his or her office. Spiritual authority, however (even though it may be associated with an office in the church, or one's position as a parent), is actually rooted in one's *gift*. Paul relied on "the authority the Lord gave me" (13:10) in his dealings with the Corinthians.

This is important to grasp. If our authority is truly given us by the Lord, then He will be responsible for authenticating it! This is why Paul could say to those who demanded proof that Christ was speaking through him, "*He* [Christ] is not weak in dealing with you" (v. 3, italics added). Jesus will vindicate the authority He has given.

Goal. Paul made it very clear that the purpose or goal of spiritual authority is to "build up." His authority was exercised purposefully and wisely: he used the spiritual weapons in God's arsenal to "take captive every thought to make it obedient to Christ" (10:5).

A very important concept is expressed here. It is *Jesus* who is the Head of the church. And He is the Head of every man. The spiritual leader does not use authority to bring believers to obey the leader. Instead, spiritual authority is always exercised to lead the local body and individual believer to obey Christ. The spiritual leader is not to attempt to exercise control over others; instead, he seeks to free them to be responsive to Jesus.

There are a number of reasons why this concept is vital. Authority that seeks to *control* focuses on externals. A person can "exercise authority" to manipulate or control another's behavior through all the secular motivation methods looked at in the last study guide. One reason why these methods are so often adopted by Christian leaders is that they are successful! But this is true only if we measure success by conformity. It is true that many leadership methods are adapted to produce different kinds of achievement. Using them, we can raise money, build bigger buildings, increase attendance in Sunday Schools. But the one thing that such methods cannot do is to produce *commitment*. Commitment is a change within the human personality, an aspect of transformation. Commitment comes when a person freely chooses to respond to God.

All this underlies Paul's statement that authority has been given him to "build up." Rather than gain control over others' behavior, *Paul's exercise of authority was designed to free them to choose God's way willingly*. This thought also finds expression in Paul's confident assertion that "Christ's love compels us" (5:14). It was the reality of Christ within, not external pressures, that Paul relied on to motivate believers to respond to the Lord.

Relationships. Paul had also, in relinquishing any claim to a supposed right of authority to control, helped us to see more clearly the relationships appropriate to spiritual leadership. Paul did more than hint when he spoke of meekness and gentleness and insisted to the Corinthians that he would not "lord it over your faith" (1:24) but rather would "lower myself in order to elevate you" (11:7).

Rather than be relationally *over* others, the person with spiritual authority takes his or her place alongside the other and thus lifts them up. We can illustrate the distorted and appropriate concepts of authority with simple diagrams like those on page 389.

The "chain of command" diagram represents the leader as *between* God and the person under his or her authority. This is the kind of structure used to chart military or business (and too often church) organizations. It indicates lines of control and responsibility. But this concept significantly distorts the biblical concept of authority.

An approach charting authority actually requires two diagrams. The first represents the *fact* of authority. While the leader *is* "above," and the led "under," *the leader is not between the individual and God.* Instead, both the leader and the follower recognize Christ's lordship over each of them, and over both of them together.

The fact of authority does admit the right of the leader to lead, but it denies the right of the leader to control. Instead, the leader's *influence flows from his or her gift* (the fact that Christ *is* speaking through this person), and it flows from the example the leader gives as a person who has experienced significant growth and transformation.

But even this chart is inadequate to represent how the leader *exercises* spiritual authority. We need another diagram for this; one that shows the leader choosing to humble himself, even to "lower myself in order to elevate you." How did Paul lower himself?

Paul requested rather than ordered. He gave advice rather than commands. Paul shared his weaknesses, and thus took a stand beside men and women who knew themselves to be weak. Paul refused to "lord it over your faith," even when the Corinthians' worldliness made them critical of Paul's shameful lack of "boldness"!

The characteristics which the Corinthians associated with leadership were as foreign to true spiritual leadership as are the traits that we associate with it today!

What Paul had done was to take to heart, and to put into practice a servant leadership demonstrated by Jesus, and commanded by Jesus for those who would minister in His church.

> You know that the rulers of the Gentiles lord it over them, and their high officials exercise authority over them. Not so with you. Instead, whoever wants to become great among you must be your servant, and whoever wants to be first must be your slave—just as the Son of man did not come to be served, but to serve, and to give His life as a ransom for many.
>
> Matthew 20:25-27

Attitude. What is the appropriate attitude of the leader? A servant attitude. A servant who sees others, not himself or herself, as important. A servant who humbles himself, concerned only with doing his master's will. A servant who willingly sets aside every outward symbol of power and relies completely on the power of God within the men and women he or she leads to stimulate response.

It almost seems embarrassing to read the words Paul writes in these last chapters of this letter. We're almost ashamed for him as he speaks out of the intensity of his love and pain. He seems almost, well . . . weak.

And yet Paul was strong. Strong in God's way. "For Christ's sake, I delight in weaknesses, in insults, in hardships, in persecutions, in difficulties. For when I am weak, then I am strong" (2 Cor. 12:10). This was Paul's perspective. And it should become ours.

God's ways are not our ways, and His thoughts are not our thoughts. And so our greatest need is to learn His ways.

♥ *Group Activity: Support Group*
Describe a time when you were deeply conscious of personal weakness or helplessness. Include what you did, and how you felt about your situation.

Look together at Paul's personal confession and testimony in 2 Corinthians 12:1-10. Label points on the "Paul's Time-Line" chart to trace his emotional ups and downs. Then complete the chart by extending the line to reflect where you feel Paul was emotionally when he adopted the perspective reflected in verses 9-10.

Authority Concepts

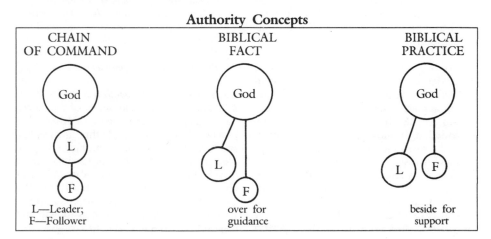

CHAIN OF COMMAND	BIBLICAL FACT	BIBLICAL PRACTICE
L—Leader; F—Follower	over for guidance	beside for support

Paul's Time Line

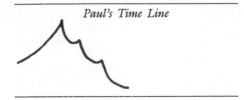

Go back down and draw a similar time line for your own experience, showing your ups and downs, but particularly, where you ended up emotionally. Many of us have never fully recovered from a terrible grief, loss, or other "down" experience, but continue to suffer from it. So don't feel you have to conclude with an "upper."

Share your charts, and then discuss. How can (or have) we apply Paul's insight to our own situations?

Comments on the Text

The marks of leaders (2 Cor. 11). The Corinthians, still superficial and still evaluating by worldly criteria, were attracted to "strong" leaders. These were persons who as "trained speakers" (v. 6) seemed very impressive. They claimed the right of support, and like most of us the Corinthians seemed more impressed by that for which they paid than that which came at little cost (v. 7). But they presented a distorted Gospel (v. 4), and Paul called them "false apostles" who were masquerading as Christian leaders.

What are the marks that we see in Paul of one who is a true Christian leader? Paul first of all cared deeply about the Corinthians' spiritual welfare (vv. 1-3). He refused to burden anyone financially in order to demonstrate that he was no spiritual profiteer (vv. 7-11). Paul's commitment has led to deep suffering—floggings, hunger, thirst, danger after danger (vv. 16-27). Paul felt deeply with the weakness of the weak; was in anguish when he heard of a believer's sin (vv. 28-30). In short, Paul not only identified with those to whom he ministered, he cared enough for them to accept personal hardship in order to benefit them.

What an example the apostle left for you and me. Ministry to others is *not* just a matter of sharing our knowledge of the Word. It is a matter of sharing ourselves: of being the caring, self-sacrificing kind of person

whose spiritual authority is matched by his or her commitment to others out of full commitment to Christ.

Overcoming weakness (2 Cor. 12:1-10). Bible students agree that Paul suffered from some unidentified disease. How did it happen that Paul, whom Acts tells us did miracles of healing (see Acts 14:8), was not himself healed? Despite Paul's prayer God chose this physical disability as the apostle's lot. Finally God revealed to Paul, "My grace is sufficient for you, for My power is made perfect in weakness" (2 Cor. 12:9). God's grace worked through Paul despite his weaknesses: the Gospel's power did not rely on human strengths or abilities.

What a wonderful lesson to us, not only in our times of sickness, but also as we contemplate spiritual leadership. God does not rely on the strengths that our society exalts. God's power can and will flow through even those who are "weak" in the qualities secular leaders count on to make them effective.

❋ *Group Activity:*
Singles/Single Again Group
In these very personal chapters (2 Cor. 10–13) the Apostle Paul expresses in revealing terms the kind of relationship he yearned for—and that many in Corinth coldly rejected. In teams, examine these chapters to develop a description of the intimate relationship Paul was looking for.

Share insights and discuss: Which aspect of the relationship Paul wanted is most important to you? Which seems most difficult to establish? In what ways have your experiences been like those of the apostle?

Look back through the text together. What is Paul doing to try to build the desired relationship, despite the Corinthians' reluctance? How can we employ Paul's principles in our own relationships?

Christ is speaking though me (1 Cor. 13:1-10). This is the ultimate secret of the Christian leader's authority, and of his or her power. Christ does speak through leaders, and Christ is "powerful among" His people. Christian leaders do not need to rely on merely human means to motivate or to discipline. God Himself authenticates the Christian leader, moving believers to respond, and acting in those who will not respond to discipline and to change.

GROUP RESOURCE GUIDE

Identification: *Share with others*
Complete the following sentence: "To have authority means a person is. . . . " List the phrases group members suggest on a chalkboard or large sheet of newsprint.

Based on the phrases suggested, do most of us seem to feel it's comfortable or uncomfortable to "have authority"? To "be under authority"?

Exploration: *Probe God's Word*
This is another of those times when it is best to have someone previously prepared to give a careful lecture on the nature of authority in Christian interpersonal relationships, based on the text of 1 Corinthians 10–13 and the commentary.

Reaction: *Respond together to the Word*
One setting in which we all experience or have experienced authority relationships is in the family, as children, parents, and spouses. Have group members pair off. They are to use three circles, representing God, husband, and wife, to create two diagrams showing the "authority relationship" existing between the three. The first diagram is to be "traditional." The second is to reflect the teachings of Christ (Matt. 20:25-27) and Paul (2 Cor. 10–13) on spiritual authority (see Authority Concepts chart, below, for possibilities).

Compare and discuss the diagrams, and see if together you can develop one or more that seem to sum up the NT's teaching.

Finally, if your group is composed of married couples, pair off and have couples discuss: Does our relationship express the biblical ideal? If so, how? If not, how can we change?

Affirmation: *Express love and concern*
If anyone in your group is a good example of a servant leader, tell him or her so, and express your appreciation.

Adoration: *Worship and pray*
Consider Christ as suffering servant, who although He was God in heaven, possessing all sovereign Authority, chose to die for our sakes.

Praise Him, and ask Him to fill you with His own attitude toward others.

THE GOSPEL

Overview

Paul's brief letter to the Galatians is one of the New Testament's earliest, probably written around A.D. 49. Like Romans, it explores the relationship of the Mosaic Law to the Gospel of Jesus Christ and, like Romans, concludes that Law was temporary. It has now been replaced by a better, more effective way of relating to God through the Spirit.

Also like Romans, Galatians is concerned with the experience of holiness, and how God's people can live a righteous life. Paul shows us here that, though it may initially seem frightening to remove the strictures of Law, God's better way produces a righteousness which the Mosaic Code could never produce. Christ has set us free for freedom—not freedom *from* righteousness, but freedom to be truly good (Gal. 5:1). This little book has proven exciting to generation after generation of Christians, who through it have realized that they are saved by faith—and that the Christian life is *lived* by faith as well!

▶ *Gospel*. The "Gospel" is mentioned a number of times in the first chapter of this letter. The Greek word simply means "good news." But Paul intended us to understand a specific content: there is an unmixed "Gospel of grace" which Paul preached, and an "other gospel" which is a mixture of faith and works, grace and law. In this little book we and our students are helped to understand the real Gospel, the Gospel of grace.

Commentary

It was early when the apostle rolled over on his pallet and saw the shafts of morning sunlight sifting through the shutters.

The confrontation over Peter's sudden unwillingness to eat with Gentile converts (Gal. 2:12) had heightened Paul's awareness

of the dangers facing the young church. Then messengers had come, reporting that delegations of Christian Pharisees had visited the cities where churches had been planted. They taught that the Gentile Christians must place themselves under the Law of Israel, and many were obeying them.

Deeply burdened, Paul had called a number of the brothers together and prayed with them through most of the night.

Now, fully awake, Paul decided to act. Filled with a deep sense of urgency, he found a pen and papyrus sheets and attacked the task he had set himself. His pen raced; passionate phrases appeared. All the churches in southern Galatia must receive a copy of this, his first letter of instruction and his first attempt to set down a theology for the new Christian movement.

"Paul, an apostle—sent not from men nor by man, but by Jesus Christ" (1:1). These Judaizers claimed to be authorized by the Jerusalem church. As if man's authorization counted!

"I am astonished that you are so quickly deserting the One who called you by the grace of Christ and are turning to a different gospel" (v. 6). Yes, God knows it *is* a different gospel! The Gospel rests solely on the grace of God. These Judaizers would make it a gospel of works-plus-faith. But works-plus-faith is not the Gospel; it is a distortion that robs the Good News of its grace. It is a different, perverted gospel!

"Am I now trying to win the approval of men, or of God? Or am I trying to please men? (v. 10) The gall of those Judaizers! "Paul just tried to make it easy for you," they had suggested. "He was trying to please you, afraid of your response if he didn't make the Gospel easy. But," they had continued, "there's no such thing as 'easy believism' to the Gospel. God insists that your faith cost you something!"

Paul's pen raced on. *"The Gospel I preached is not something that man made up. . . . I received it by revelation from Jesus Christ"* (vv. 11-12). On and on, the words filled sheet after sheet. How exciting now to put down on paper all the deep understanding and struggles that the one-time Pharisee had spent years working through in his own life. How exciting to share with the brothers—the little children he himself had midwifed into God's kingdom—the full glory of what the Gospel is, and the glorious fulfillment that is offered to all who believe in Christ!

The scene just sketched is imaginary. But it must have been much like this. It's easy to visualize Paul pouring out his love and concern in those passionate words to the Galatians which we read in our New Testament.

And even today, Paul's words are needed. Today too questions arise and Christians feel concern about the true nature of the Christian Gospel. Isn't it a little too easy to just "accept Christ"? Can we really say that salvation is through faith and by grace, plus *nothing*? Shouldn't a Christian at least be expected to live a certain holy life after he has come to know Jesus? Shouldn't God have a right to reject a person who believes in Jesus, but shows no respect for God by continuing to sin?

In a later letter to the Romans (which we'll study with the last chapters of this book) Paul goes on to define the relationship of the Gospel to righteousness. He shows just how the Gospel produces a holy life. But in Galatians the focal point of Paul's instruction is different. The relationship between Law and God's grace is at issue. The question is, "What lies at the heart of the pure Gospel?"

Paul's Defense of His Gospel: Galatians 1:1–2:10

After Paul and Barnabas returned to Antioch from their first missionary journey, they found men who had come from Judea and were teaching that "unless you are circumcised, according to the custom taught by Moses, you cannot be saved" (Acts 15:1). This teaching implied far more than simply accepting circumcision.

In the Old Testament, circumcision was a key element in the covenant God had made with Abraham. A Hebrew boy, on the eighth day of his life, was to have the fold of skin covering the end of his penis cut off. God said to Abraham, "Any uncircumcised male, who has not been circumcised in the flesh, will be cut off from his people; he has broken My covenant" (Gen. 17:14). To the Judaizers this act symbolized, as it does in Scripture, becoming a true Jew. In other words, this teaching implied that to be a Christian, one must first become a Jew. And the Bible makes it clear that the Judaizers intended exactly this: "the Gentiles must be circumcised and required to obey the Law of Moses," just as every Jew was required to do! (Acts 15:5)

The Judaizers were apparently aggressive, visiting not only Antioch but also going to other Gentile churches. And these men, who apparently did believe in Jesus, claimed a special authority for their teaching: "We are from *Jerusalem*! We're members of the first (and thus the true?) church!"

Paul and Barnabas vigorously opposed the men who taught this in Antioch (v. 2). So Paul and Barnabas, along with some others, were appointed to go to Jerusalem and see what the apostles and elders there had to say about this question.

The Judaizers had *not* been commissioned by the Jerusalem church. Nonetheless, once this issue was raised, this first council of the church held "much discussion" (v. 7) on the matter. The result was that the church recognized the fact that God showed He had accepted the Gentiles "by giving the Holy Spirit to them, just as He did to us. He made no distinction between us and them for He purified their hearts by faith." It would thus be wrong for the Judaizers to "try to test God by putting on the necks of the disciples a yoke [the Law] that neither we nor our fathers were able to bear." The Judaizers insistence on circumcision and Law was rejected, for "we believe it is through the grace of our Lord Jesus that we are saved" (vv. 8-11).

All this seems to have happened after Paul wrote his letter to the Galatians, though this is debated. Surely Paul made no mention of the determination of the Jerusalem Council, which it seems likely he would have if its determination had been made before he wrote.

All in all, we can credit both Paul and Barnabas with recognizing the threat to the

Gospel posed by those who would mix it with Law. Even Peter, as we'll see later, did not "act in line with the truth of the Gospel" in this matter (Gal. 2:14).

In his letter to the Galatian churches, then, Paul could not defend his position by referring to the determination of the gathered leaders of the Christian church. Instead, Paul had to develop a different line of defense.

Another Gospel (Gal. 1:6-10). The Greek language makes a clear distinction between "others." There is another of the same kind (*allos*), and another of a different kind (*heteros*). Paul, after a few words of greeting, launched immediately into a confrontation with the Judaizers. What the latecomers preached was *not* the Gospel Paul had shared: it was a "different gospel" which because of the difference was "no gospel at all."

With no equivocation, Paul condemned that perverted gospel, and also those who preached it: let such a person "be eternally condemned" (v. 9).

The Judaizers had accused Paul of weakening the Gospel to "please men" and to "win the approval of men." That is, they claimed that Paul shaded the truth because he didn't want conflict, and instead wanted an "easy" message. Paul's confrontation with those who preach the "different gospel" would now show just how willing the apostle was to fight for the truth of the Gospel he had been charged by God with delivering (v. 10).

Received by direct revelation (Gal. 1:11-17). Paul had been a persecutor of the church when he was converted. He "went immediately" into Arabia, and there struggled to understand the Old Testament in light of his experience with Jesus. Paul stressed, "I did not consult any man, nor did I go up to Jerusalem to see those who were apostles before I was."

This was important to Paul. The Judaizers claimed an authority they said was derived from Jerusalem. Paul claimed an apostleship equal to that of the Twelve, and a revelation which came to him directly by God.

Confirmed by the other apostles (Gal. 1:18–2:5). Paul spoke of twice going to Jerusalem to "get acquainted with" the leaders there.

His second trip was directed by God, to "set before them the Gospel that I preach among the Gentiles" (2:2). The leaders confirmed Paul's Gospel, and affirmed that he had been right in confronting the "false brothers" who sought to introduce legalism. On that trip the Jerusalem leaders had accepted Titus, a Greek, as a brother and had not even suggested he should be circumcised.

Paul's experience with the other apostles, then, suggests that there was no conflict with the Gospel he preached and the Gospel as it was understood by leaders in Jerusalem.

Paul's commission affirmed (Gal. 2:6-10). The leaders in Jerusalem "added nothing to my message." Instead they recognized Paul's calling, to take the Gospel to the Gentiles, even as Peter's calling was to bring the Gospel to the Jews in the Holy Land and throughout the world.

The only concern the leaders in Jerusalem expressed was that the Gentile churches should "continue to remember the poor," which Paul was eager to do.

Paul thus has buttressed the claim which he made when he began this argument:

> The Gospel I preached is not something that man made up. I did not receive it from any man, nor was I taught it; rather, I received it by revelation from Jesus Christ.
>
> Galatians 1:11-12

Paul stood for the Gospel because he was convinced that the Good News he presented is true, and that he held a commission from God Himself to proclaim it in Gentile lands (see vv. 15-16).

Confrontation: Galatians 2:11-21

It's clear from both Galatians and Acts that the confrontation that occurred between Peter and Paul in Antioch dealt with a basic issue. And at that point, only Paul realized what this issue was.

Peter had come to visit the church in Antioch, and at first had gladly participated fully in the body's life. But when some of the Judaizer party arrived as well, Peter drew back from the Gentile believers. And other Jewish believers in Antioch followed Peter's example!

This action, which divided the church into two camps, was not "acting in line with the truth of the Gospel."

There's no doubt that Peter's action and that of the Jewish minority must have hurt the Antioch believers personally. It implied that Gentile believers were second-class citizens in God's kingdom.

But Paul saw more than the momentary hurt, and more than the hypocrisy. Paul saw the deadly intrusion of Law into the Gospel message. Paul reacted. He confronted Peter publicly, and charged him with hypocrisy.

We who are Jews by birth and not "Gentile sinners" know that a man is not justified by observing the Law, but by faith in Jesus Christ.

Galatians 2:15-16

Those who put their faith in Christ ought not to mix Gospel and Law, but affirm a justification that comes from faith alone. "A man is not justified by observing the Law, but by faith in Jesus Christ. . . . Because by observing the Law no one will be justified" (v. 16). God's verdict, declaring a person forgiven and free from the guilt and penalty his sins deserve—and God's power, breaking the bondage of sin to free an individual to become truly good, have nothing to do with the Law. Justification is a gift of grace, freely extended to all who put their faith in Jesus Christ.

"I do not set aside the grace of God," Paul insisted, "for if righteousness could be gained through the Law, Christ died for nothing" (v. 21).

♥ **Group Activity: Support Group**
Discuss: What makes it hard to confront a friend or loved one when we feel something he or she is doing is wrong?

Then study Galatians 2:1-21. What do we learn about confrontation from the background to and story of Paul's rebuke of Peter? As you explore, consider:
a. Peter's/Paul's previous relationship
b. Specific behavior in the situation
c. The issue involved
d. The reason for a public confrontation
e. The outcome: cf. 2 Peter 3:14-16.
After studying discuss: Am I willing to be confronted and rebuked by others in our support group? Who am I close enough to to feel comfortable confronting?

How important is it for us to be confronted by each other, anyway?

Life and Law. It is still a little difficult to grasp what Paul was saying. That is, until we see the key place of Galatians 2:20:

I have been crucified with Christ and I no longer live, but Christ lives in me. The life I live in the body, I live by faith in the Son of God, who loved me and gave Himself for me.

Galatians 2:20-21

Jesus' mission on earth was not to utter some new call for redoubled effort to keep the Law. Jesus' mission, and the heart of the Gospel—was to issue an invitation to life. It is tremendously dangerous to let our own focus shift from *life* to the *Law*.

Righteousness can never come through the Law. Only new life can bring us that justification from God which means both (1) entrance into a new relationship with God and (2) the dynamic of God's power within to make possible the love, goodness, and holiness which all religions hold out as an ideal, but only the Christian faith is able to produce.

This issue is clarified in Paul's climactic statement to Peter. And with this said in the letter, Paul moved on immediately to an explosive statement that analyzes the differences between the two approaches to the Gospel. Is the believer to work out his relationship with God through the Law, or is he to do it by recognizing the nature and dynamic of life?

As we move on in this letter, we will discover *why* the legalistic approach to Christian experience is doomed to fail. And we will catch the New Testament's first glimpse of the life principle which brings us freedom.

For any who have ever felt burdened in his or her Christian life, or felt weighed down by "oughts" and "shoulds," these next chapters contain the charter deed to personal freedom and to joy.

In the Victor *Bible Knowledge Commentary* Dr. Donald K. Campbell has this helpful explanation of Galatians 2:20:

In Galatians 2:20 Paul enlarged on the meaning of verse 19. He "died to the Law" because "he [Paul] was crucified with Christ"; he was able to "live for God" because Christ lived in him. Basic to an understanding of this verse is the meaning of union with Christ. This doctrine is based on such passages as Romans 6:1-6 and 1 Corinthians 12:13, which explain that believers have been baptized by the Holy Spirit into Christ and into the church, the body of all true believers. Having been thus united to Christ, believers share in His death, burial, and resurrection. Paul could therefore write, "I have been crucified with Christ" (lit., "I have been and am now crucified with Christ"). This brought death to the Law. It also brought a change in regard to one's self: "And I no longer live." The self-righteous, self-centered Saul died. Further, death with Christ ended Paul's enthronement of self; he yielded the throne of his life to Another, to Christ. But it was not in his own strength that Paul was able to live the Christian life; the living Christ Himself took up His abode in Paul's heart: Christ "lives in me." Yet Christ does not operate automatically in a believer's life; it is a matter of living the new life "by faith in the Son of God." It is then faith and not works or legal obedience that releases divine power to live a Christian life.

What a wonderful affirmation we have here of the core of the Gospel. It is by faith from first to last, for faith releases the power of God to be at work within our personalities, to express Jesus through our lives.

GROUP RESOURCE GUIDE

Identification: *Share with others*
Read Galatians 2:21. Let each person make some comment on it, either raising a question, making an explanatory statement, or expressing a feeling.

Exploration: *Probe God's Word*
Read Galatians 1–2 and put a check mark beside each verse that expresses Paul's concern about mixing the Gospel and Law.

The commentary on pp. 318-319 summarizes the N.T.'s teaching on Law. In addition the following N.T. passages make significant statements about the Law and its relationship to human beings. Study these verses and refer to the commentary as background to explain Paul's obvious upset and concern. Key verses and passages are: Romans 4:13-16; Romans 6:14; Romans 7:4-6; 1 Corinthians 15:56; Romans 7:21-25; Romans 8:3; Galatians 3:10-14; Galatians 3:21-22; Galatians 5:1-6.

After study sum up your findings by together completing the following with as many significant endings as you can: "The Gospel and Law cannot be confused because. . . ."

Reaction: *Respond together to the Word*
The Christian's alternative to a life lived as a response to Law is summed up in Galatians 2:19-20. Memorize this verse together. By depending only on Christ, His resurrection life expresses itself in and through us. Faith, not law, is the victory.

Adoration: *Worship and pray*
Preselect several hymns that express this "open secret of the Christian life." For instance, "Faith is the Victory," "Christ Liveth in Me," etc.

Sing the selected hymns together, including spontaneous prayers as group members wish.

GOOD NEWS OF FAITH

Overview

In Galatians we have Paul's first powerful defense of the Gospel. Some from the Pharisee party in Judea who had trusted Christ apparently retained their zeal for the Mosaic Law. They traveled to the churches Paul had founded, and taught that the Gentile Christians they must be circumcised and must keep the Law of Moses to be saved. In essence, they said that to be a true Christian a Gentile must become Jewish in lifestyle, and live by the Old Testament's code.

Paul confronted this view, insisting that what these men taught was different gospel from the Gospel of God's grace in Jesus Christ. Paul insisted that there can be no mixture of Law and grace in the Gospel of Christ without robbing the Gospel of its power.

Now, in the extended and carefully argued bulk of Galatians, Paul explained *why* the Law is not for Christians now. Paul's argument emphasized three points: The Law is opposed to life (3:1-18). The role given Law in Scripture is a limited one (3:19–4:7). And, the Law is an inferior path which leads to spiritual disasters (4:8–5:12).

For further background on the New Testament's view of Law as it relates to the Christian life, see Study Guide 126.

■ It will be helpful as you prepare to teach this important passage to read through a good verse-by-verse commentary like the *Bible Knowledge Commentary*, pages 596-606.

Commentary

In Paul's initial defense of his Gospel he reported a conflict which he had with Peter in Antioch. When even Peter was influenced by members of the Pharisee party, and separated himself from Gentile Christians, Paul confronted him.

"We who are Jews by birth," Paul said, "know that a man is not justified by observing the Law, but by faith in Jesus Christ" (Gal. 2:15-16). Paul then pointed out that all the Law was able to do was to demonstrate that the one under it was a lawbreaker. There was no power in the Law to create holiness.

But the Christian is not under Law, because "through the Law I died to the Law so that I might live for God" (v. 19). That is, because of the Christian's union with Christ the believer is legally released from the Law. How? By dying with the Saviour. For a person who is "dead" is not responsible to keep the Old Testament code, but is released from its hold.

Thus the Christian, as the old man who was crucified with Christ, no longer lives. But our union with Jesus was not just union in His death (Rom. 6:1-6). It was also union with Jesus in His resurrection. Now "Christ lives in me." In fact, the daily life of the believer is the Christ life, lived "by faith in the Son of God, who loved me and gave Himself for me" (Gal. 2:20).

This is the key to understanding the Gospel. What the Gospel offers is not just forgiveness, but new life! And that new life is lived by faith, *not* by a return to the Law. And so, Paul concluded, "I do not set aside the grace of God, for if righteousness could be gained through the Law, Christ died for nothing" (v. 21).

This powerful and wonderful affirmation of life in Christ, and of faith as the key to our experience of that life, is the background against which Paul now analyzed Law. The Law, while an expression of the holiness of God and good in itself, could never produce life, and indeed has nothing to do with life. If we think of the Gospel of God's grace in terms of the new life it provides, and then understand the faith principle which enables us to experience the new

Life Versus Law

GALATIANS 3–5

Why isn't the Law for us now?
I. The Law is opposed to life (3:1-18). This is demonstrated by:
   A. Experience: How did you first receive and live your spiritual life? (3:1-5)
   B. Example: How did Old Testament saints receive spiritual life? (3:6-9)
   C. Exposition: What does the Scripture teach about how life is to be received? (3:10-18).
II. The Law's role (3:19–4:7) is shown in Scripture to be severely limited:
   A. In extent: It is temporary (3:19-20).
   B. In ability: It cannot make alive (3:21-22).
   C. In function: It was a custodian (3:23-24).
   D. In force: It is nullified today (3:25–4:8).
      1. Because we are "in Christ"
      2. Because we are now sons
III. The Law is an inferior way that now leads to tragic results for the believer (4:8–5:12). Law leads to:
   A. Dissatisfaction: It robs us of joy (4:8-19).
   B. Bondage: It robs us of freedom (4:20–5:1).
   C. Powerlessness: It turns us from expectant faith to hopeless effort (5:2-12).

life, we will see why legalism is futile.

In Galatians 3:1–5:12 we look at the first part of this spiritual equation: the futility of trying to link Law with life. Then, in Galatians 5:13–6:16, we see the second part: the secret of how to live our new life in Christ by faith.

Paul in Galatians rejected the "different gospel" of the Judaizers who would bring Law back into the believer's relationship with God. The contrast that Paul drew between life and Law is the key that helps us trace his argument and outline this great book.

Why Not Law? Galatians 3:1–5:12

The major portion of Galatians, as reflected in the outline, is a devastating critique of looking to the Law for help in living the Christian life. Before we trace through each passage, let's take a look at some of the particularly significant points Paul made.

Importance of faith (Gal. 3:10). Paul spoke in this passage to "all who *rely* on observing the Law." He did not suggest that the Law itself is somehow bad or wrong. What he did insist was that the Law had never had anything to do with faith, and therefore that reliance on the Law, either as a way of salvation, or as a way to work out one's salvation, was inappropriate.

Paul made an interesting point in verses 15-18. If the Law was so important, how did people ever get along without it? The Law wasn't even introduced until some 430 years after Abraham's day. Certainly Abraham and the other patriarchs had meaningful relationships with God!

Most important, however, is the fact that the principle of faith in God's promise (v. 16) which was introduced in Abraham was never set aside by the subsequent introduction of Law. Faith has *always* been the way to God; God's promise has never depended on keeping that latecomer, the Law.

Law for restraint (Gal. 3:19-29). The Law was introduced because of sin, and thus it relates to sin, not holiness. The Law was to be a *temporary* expedient, to function only until Christ came.

Picture, if you will, a raging tiger trapped behind bars. The bars were introduced because the tiger's wild impulses make him dangerous to all. Would anyone expect the *bars* to tame the tiger? Of course not! That is not the purpose of bars; they are to *restrain*. What happens, then, if someone does succeed in taming the tiger, using a different principle than putting him in a cage? The bars can be removed! There is no longer any use for them.

This, essentially, is Paul's argument. Now that faith has come and believers have been "clothed . . . with Christ" (v. 27), we have been truly tamed! How foolish, then, to insist that the tamed beast continue to live behind bars! Especially when all along God had affirmed His intention of removing the bars as soon as the new and living Way came (see Jer. 31:31-34).

Law as teacher (Gal. 4:1-7). Paul used another illustration to make the same point. It was common in the Greek culture of his day to place a young child under the supervision of a family slave, called a *pedagogue* (a word sometimes translated in Gal. 4:2 as "guardian," "trustee," "manager," etc.). The pedagogue made sure that the child obeyed the parent, whether the child wanted to obey, or not. Until the children would "receive the full rights of sons" (v. 5) they were, in fact, no more than the slaves of a slave! They had to obey a slave who obeyed their father.

But then the great day came when a child was accepted as an adult. Now the father spoke directly to him. Now the son responded directly to his father. The pedagogue had no more place in their relationship.

The Law, Paul said, was a pedagogue. Jesus' redemption act is that great event in history marking the transition from childhood to sonship. The Law, which up until Jesus had a pedagogue's purpose, now had nothing to do with our relationship with God! "So you are no longer a slave, but a son; and since you are a son, God has made you also an heir" (v. 7).

It is striking to see what happens when people, still fearing the tiger in them and unable to grasp the fact that Christ really does tame, seek to hide behind the bars of legalism. Such legalism seems at first to promise a certain kind of security. Its bars not only keep us in; they keep others out.

But Christ's people are not made to cower in barred caves and cages! We have been shaped by God to live on the plains and in the mountains and, yes, in the jungles of the whole wide world. Jesus Himself set us the example. He stepped boldly from the security of heaven and was caught up in the rush and swirl, the joys and agonies of human experience. He entered the homes of publicans and sinners, enjoyed the wedding parties, reached out to touch and heal the hurting, and confronted the hardened Pharisees. Jesus was totally involved—yet uncontaminated. He rubbed shoulders with sinners—and remained pure. He lived with and like other men—and revealed God. His whole life was an adventure.

It is to just this kind of adventurous life that you and I are called today. Jesus did not come to bring a new set of bars for our cages. He came to tame the tiger in us and to release us, to live as He Himself lived in the world of men.

The meaning of our lives, the adventure of it, isn't to be found in the cages that Christians make for themselves and decorate so attractively. No, meaning and joy

Law, the Pedagogue—*Until* Christ

"No longer a slave, but a son" (Gal. 4:7)

for us are to be found in stepping outside the old cages, dismissing the no-longer-needed pedagogues, and setting out into the future to live as *sons*.

All too often, Christians draw back.

We fear.

We don't realize that as God's sons we now have His life. Like the Judaizers of Paul's day, we hurriedly try to shape new bars as fast as God tears them down. In deepest agony Paul cried out to the cage-builders of his day, "How is it that you are turning back to those weak and miserable principles? Do you wish to be enslaved by them all over again?" (v. 9)

You will lose your joy there (v. 15).

You will lose your freedom (5:1).

You will lose your power (v. 3). You will lose all that Jesus died to make available to you as you live your new life in Him.

Falling away (Gal. 5:4). This verse has troubled many. It reads, "You who are trying to be justified by Law have been alienated from Christ; you have fallen away from grace." What was Paul saying?

It's important to realize that here Paul was focusing on present-tense salvation, not on past-tense. What Paul meant when he warned against falling away from grace must be grasped from the context of the passage.

Paul had shown that the Law was a pedagogue. Once, Law was the avenue through which a believer experienced his relationship with God. But now that relationship is direct and personal, as with a child who at last receives the "full rights" of sonship (4:5). What, then, if a son keeps going back to his old pedagogue for directions? Clearly, he has alienated himself from the personal relationship. Such a fall from grace back into old practices and ways means simply that the individual *is no better off than he was before*! All the freedom, all the joy, all the adventure of the life a child of God is to live by faith, has been drained away—traded for something that is worse than nothing. "Christ will be of no value to you at all" means simply that being a Christian will not make the *difference* in daily life He intends it to. A person will be no better off than he was before being a Christian, as far as living the Christian life is concerned.

This seems a hard thing to say. No better off? Why, heaven has been won, at least.

Yes, but the Christian faith is not solely concerned with eternity. The Christian faith includes God's affirmation that life *now* is important too—important to God, important to others, and important to you.

The wonderful life that God offers you and me in Christ is one which provides a solid hope for meaning, joy, and fulfillment today. And that life is appropriated by faith, not by trying to keep the Law.

✄ *Group Activity: Recovery Group*
Step 11 (improve relationship with God through prayer and meditation)
Discuss: Which of the following two messages is most likely to help a person grow and improve: "You're bad, and you must do better," or "You're good now, and I'll help you do better"?

Galatians 3:1–4:7 examines both approaches. "Law" says, "You're bad, and you must do better," and leads us to struggle unsuccessfully to do right. "Promises" says, "You're My children now. Trust Me, and I'll help you do better." So divide into two sets of teams. One set will study this passage to determine why the "law" approach does not work. The other set of teams will study the same passage to learn about the "promise" approach that does work. (Note: Each set of teams can be given the boxed outline found on page 399.)

Each set of teams is to prepare to report on why the "law" or "promise" approach works as it does, and also, to illustrate how we take that approach in our own daily lives.

After the reports, meditate for a time on 4:6-7. Close your eyes and for five minutes picture yourself as one of God's sons, equipped with the Holy Spirit, an heir to His great power. Then share with the others the images that came to mind, and share with God in prayer what it means to you to be a son of the King.

Observations on the Text: Galatians 3:1–5:12

The Law is opposed to life (Gal. 3:1-18). Paul launched his argument against the "different gospel" of the Judaizers by expressing amazement. Their own experience with God was rooted in faith, not Law (vv. 1-5). "Did you receive the Spirit by observing the Law, or by believing what you heard?" It was not Law that brought them life; the key in their conversion was faith. "Are you so foolish?" Paul asked, that "after beginning with the Spirit, are you now trying to attain your goal by human effort?" (v. 3) The Spirit actually had operated among these churches and worked miracles not through observing Law, but "because you believe what you heard."

It is clear, then, from the experience of modern Christians that life in Christ is a matter of faith from first to last. If life is received and lived by faith, why then turn to the Law as an aid to spiritual attainment?

Not only has faith proven to be the key to modern Christian experience, but it was also the key to the experience of Old Testament saints (vv. 6-9). Abraham "believed God" and it was his faith that was credited to him as righteousness.

But *why* hadn't the Law functioned in the spiritual experience of Abraham and all those generations after him whose relationship with God was rooted in faith? Because the Law and faith are contrary principles. Law condemns, bringing under its curse all who do not "do everything" written in it (v. 10). Christ died to release us from the "curse of the Law" so that we might relate to God through faith.

The Law, according to the Scriptures, is severely limited (Gal. 3:19–4:7). First, Law was not only added long after faith was introduced as the principle by which we relate to God (3:17-18), but was always intended to be *temporary,* in effect only until Christ (the Seed) came (vv. 19-20).

Second, Law never had the function of bringing life; that was the role given to faith (vv. 21-22).

Third, Law was merely a pedagogue, a family slave intended to watch over young children until "faith should be revealed." Its goal was to "lead us to Christ that we might be justified by faith" (vv. 23-24).

Finally, the Law is no longer in force as far as we are concerned (we are "no longer under the supervision of the Law"). In Christ we are now "sons" and as such not subject to a pedagogue. We all—male and female, slave and free—have received the "full rights of sons."

The phrase, "full rights of sons," reflects Roman law rather than Jewish traditions. In Roman law the father had authority over every member of his family. He was also

considered to own his children's property, and had the right to control their behavior, including the right to discipline. But the father was also committed to help his child, and as an heir, what the father possessed was considered to belong to the child as well. All the resources of God become ours as heirs of God, and we are able to draw directly on them to live our new lives.

This relationship is an immediate and personal one, and is not mediated through some go-between who, like Law, has no more standing than a family slave.

Attempts to live by the Law lead only to spiritual disaster (Gal. 4:8–5:12). What happens within when a believer tries to live as if under the Law rather than as a son with a direct, immediate relationship with God?

The person who tries to relate to God by rigorous legalism will, as the Galatians, lose his or her joy (see 4:15).

That individual will find himself or herself in bondage, living as a slave rather than a freeman (4:21–5:1). Paul considered a historical event a figurative expression of a basic principle (see. Gen. 21:8-21). Sarah, childless, had urged Abraham to follow contemporary custom and father a child with her slave, Hagar. The child of this "surrogate mother" would legally be Abraham's and Sarah's. Abraham had finally given in, and Hagar bore a son, Ishmael. But rather than joy, the child brought Sarah only pain. Hagar looked down on her mistress, for it was now clear that her childlessness was not due to Abraham's inability to father a child. Ishmael thus became a constant reminder to Sarah of her own failure as a wife.

Later, when Sarah did have the child God promised Abraham, Isaac, Sarah's resentment increased. By custom Ishmael would receive a major share in Abraham's estate. Sarah wanted it all for her son, Isaac. She demanded that Abraham send Ishmael away.

At first Abraham refused. He not only cared for Ishmael, but in those days to reject Ishmael would be a crime against the boy.

But God intervened.

God told Abraham to expel Ishmael and Hagar, and God promised that He would Himself take care of Ishmael and bless him. Reassured but reluctant, Abraham did as his wife urged, but only at God's command.

Looking back, Paul realized why God told Abraham to do something so foreign to his character. Sarah had been right, but not for her selfish reason when she said, "Get rid of the slave woman and her son, for the slave woman's son will never share in the inheritance with the free woman's son" (Gen. 21:10; Gal. 4:30). The principle of promise and of Law simply do not and cannot mix. Only the one who is a son on the basis of God's promise can inherit God's blessing. There is no hope for one who seeks relationship on the basis of Law.

Paul concluded his argument with a powerful statement. Anyone who lets himself be circumcised (that is, places himself under Law) finds that "Christ will be of no value to you at all" (5:2). What did Paul mean?

It's as if you stood at a fork in the road, with one path leading to the north and the other to the south. You must choose one path or the other. You cannot choose both, for they lead in opposite directions.

The Galatian Christians, like you and I, stand always at just such a fork. We must either take the path of relating to God through Law, or of relating to God through the faith. *We cannot have it both ways.* If we are trying to relate to God through the Law, we are not living by faith. And if we are living by faith, we turn our backs on all that Law implied. Being a Christian will make no practical difference in our lives ("Christ will be of no value to you"). We who are called to live in the sphere of God's grace will fall from that grace. Our hope for transformation now will be replaced by futile self-effort, for "the only thing that counts is faith expressing itself through love" (v. 6).

❋ *Group Activity:*
Singles/Single Again Group
Focus on Galatians 5:6 for this session: "The only thing that counts is faith expressing itself through love."

In context Paul's point is that relationship with God does not find expression in trying harder to keep the law, but in the practical expressions of love for Him and for others that faith in Christ generates.

So make this session a "celebration of faith." Begin by writing notes to other group members thanking them for specific ways in which they have expressed love to you. Hold on to the notes when finished.

Then together create a visible symbol of what God has been doing in your relationship. Use a mural format on which is drawn a wall-sized tree with many branches, or a potted tree, or actual tree branches. Based on the notes you have just finished, and without mentioning names, tell what specific expressions of love you have experienced. As each loving act is reported, tape or tie a construction paper cutout of a fruit on the mural or actual tree. When all have contributed, consider the fruit-filled branches that are evidences of God's work through and for you for each other.

Join hands, and celebrate love's expression of faith by praising God. And, before you leave, make sure the "thank-you" notes you wrote are distributed.

As we go on in Galatians we will discover more about what it means to live by faith. But for now, we know one thing for sure. Focusing our attention on trying to keep God's Law is not the answer, either for salvation or for the abundant Christian life.

There is something, something linked with faith, that provides a far better way.

GROUP RESOURCE GUIDE

Reaction: *Respond together to the Word*
Give teams of three a cutout picture of a tiger. Have available all sorts of "junk" material—blocks, paper clips, string, etc. Explain that the tiger is vicious and dangerous, and that each team is to use these materials to creatively "tame its tiger."

When the teams are done, let each show its solution for taming the tiger.

Exploration: *Probe God's Word*
Read aloud the author's illustration of transforming rather than caging the tiger (p. 399, *Law for restraint*).

In teams or as a group work through Galatians 3:1–5:12, guided by the boxed outline (p. 399). Determine why tying to the law (the cage) is not God's answer, while claiming our sonship in Christ and responding to the Holy Spirit's promptings is.

Identification: *Share with others*
Share two things that have been particularly helpful in helping you grow as a Christian. List what each person shares on a chalkboard or sheet of newsprint.

When all have shared, look over the items on the list. How many are "law" or "restrictive" type items? Discuss: What does their presence or absence suggest to you?

Adoration: *Worship and pray*
Consider God's grace in making us sons and heirs and giving us His Spirit. Praise Him for His grace, which frees us to love Him and others.

GOOD NEWS OF FREEDOM

Overview

In Galatians Paul was deeply concerned with contrasting his Gospel with a counterfeit taught by Judaizers—men who insisted that to be a Christian one must keep the Mosaic Law.

Paul first characterized his Gospel. It is a Gospel of life; life that is ours through faith in Christ. The Law could never produce life, nor enrich it. Law was a temporary expedient, a household slave charged with directing the immature till Christ appeared. Now that Jesus has come and reaffirmed the ancient place of faith, Law is no longer relevant. Now there is an exciting freedom: freedom found in a new, direct relationship with God; freedom to live a truly good life.

Now, in the final section of the Book of Galatians Paul explained how the dynamic of faith operates in the believer to produce a righteousness that Law was never able to generate. As we read it, we need to be aware of several key terms, and how each of these terms is used in Paul's argument. The key words are:

- freedom
- sinful nature
- the Spirit
- new creation
- fruit

There are also key phrases. Among them are "live by the Spirit" (5:16), "led by the Spirit" (v. 18), and "keep in step with the Spirit" (v. 25).

As we study this passage we will realize in a fresh way the wonder of the Good News of Jesus, and its promise for each life.

Commentary

For the first time in his life, Jim found himself wildly cursing. The vicious words poured out, fed by a rage that both frightened and exhilarated him. His face twisted with anger, Jim shouted out words that he had been too ashamed even to think.

"Good! Good!" encouraged the young professor when Jim's rage finally collapsed in sudden exhaustion. "Jim, you're really learning to express your feelings. The real you is finally surfacing."

The scene is imaginary, but it has been repeated many times. The young professor represents one particular school of psychological therapy. "We're only allowed to talk about the here and now. And we're going to learn to express what we really feel. So whatever you feel—about yourself, about anyone else here—I want you to express it openly and honestly."

Such instructions are designed to break through the barriers of convention that cause people to repress their feelings, and to help them find a kind of release. The notion seems to be that by bringing negative feelings out into the open, the person will rid himself of them. Somehow this process is supposed to give a new freedom to individuals to find themselves, and to grow.

This is *not* a picture of Christian freedom. Such excesses can turn us away from the whole idea of freedom. Some of us are frightened to discover that God has now taken away the bars of the Law and has left us uncaged. No wonder that we, like the Galatians, rush to build new cages! We not only seek safety from a hostile world, but we just as desperately try to place restraints on our hostile selves. We know only too well the hidden thoughts and motives, the secret desires, that we struggle to keep buried. If the bars of the Law are taken away, won't something terrible in us be released?

Freedom

The Bible insists, "It is for freedom that Christ has set us free" (Gal. 5:1). Scripture is not speaking of the kind of freedom the young professor was encouraging. For the Bible says, "Do not use your freedom to indulge the sinful nature; rather, serve one another in love" (v. 13). Christian freedom is designed to help us grow in goodness.

Let's be sure of one thing. In affirming freedom, the Christian is not expressing a desire to release sinful passions. In affirming freedom, the Christian responds to God's own call to shake off old bonds and to find Christ's pathway to goodness. The Law, throughout its long history, never succeeded in producing righteousness. We are to look beyond Law now—to a better way.

The group therapy offered Jim a counterfeit freedom. Encouragement to express anger and other negative feelings (in order to "get rid of" them or to "get in touch" with oneself) has been shown to produce just the opposite of the desired effect. The more a person expresses hostility, the more deeply he seems to feel it. And the more quickly he interprets others' actions as a cause for anger. For a person without Christ in a society of people who do not respond to God, the Law's restraints are both wise and necessary. Unchecked, the tiger within man does quickly take control.

But there is a basic difference between the believer who has established a personal relationship with God through faith and the unbeliever who has not. The Christian is no longer under the Law because, unlike other men, he can now "live by the Spirit" (v. 16). An entirely new principle of life governs and guides the believer and provides a basis for Christian freedom.

Made alive. One of the most exciting themes in Scripture is that of life. In Genesis we see God giving life to all His Creation. We see Him breathing a special life into Adam and Eve: physical life, and more! They were spiritually alive, aware of God, capable of fellowship with Him.

When Adam and Eve chose sin, they died spiritually (Gen. 2:17). This spiritual death was passed on to their children and became the one great devastating flaw in humankind. Dimly aware of God and goodness, man's spiritual deadness leads him to respond to the self-centered drives of his sin-warped nature rather than to God. "As for you, you were dead in your transgressions and sins," Paul wrote later in Ephesians 2:1. "All of us also lived among them at one time, gratifying the cravings of our sinful nature and following its desires and thoughts. Like the rest, we were by nature objects of wrath" (v. 3).

Man needs both human law and divine Law. Without restraint, with each individual given license to express his cravings, society would fall and individuals would prey on those weaker than they and, in turn, be a prey to the stronger.

If we think this picture is exaggerated, we are ignorant of history. The wars, the rapes, the murders, the systematic crimes of economic oppression, the private brutalities—all fill in the details of man's Fall. The very fear which so many feel when one speaks of freedom from the Law's restraint is adequate testimony that, deep down, each of us is already aware of man's depravity—by each being aware of our own.

But the Bible story does not stop at death. The Bible goes on to share the Good News of *life*. God "made us alive with Christ even when we were dead in transgressions" (v. 5). When we come by faith into a relationship with Jesus Christ, God plants His own new life within our personalities. All the New Testament writers speak of it. Peter, the other apostle on whom the Book of Acts focuses, put it this way: "For you are sons of God now; the live, permanent Word of the living God has given you His own indestructible heredity" (1 Peter 1:23, PH). There is a new kind of life swelling up within the Christian. It is God's kind of life, and our possession of God's life changes everything.

We wisely are afraid to remove the restraints from our old selves. But who feels a need to restrain God?

The Spirit. Now we will begin to penetrate to the root of our freedom. Six times in the next few verses of Galatians (5:16-25) Paul spoke of the Holy Spirit.

"Live by the Spirit" (v. 16).

"The Spirit . . . is contrary to the sinful nature" (v. 17).

"Led by the Spirit . . . not under law" (v. 18).

"The fruit of the Spirit" (v. 22).

"We live by the Spirit" (v. 25).

"Keep in step with the Spirit" (v. 25).

The dynamic of Christian freedom is found not only in the possession of new life but also in the person of the Holy Spirit. God Himself has entered us with His gift of power.

In affirming freedom, Paul was not telling us to let the old nature go on an orgy of selfish self-expression. Instead Paul was asking us to trust ourselves to God the Holy Spirit, and to look to Him alone to express through us that quality of life which is both new, and His own.

Only if the tiger in me is truly tamed do I dare take the bars away. With new life and through the Holy Spirit's power, I can at last find the courage to be free.

Observations on the Text: Galatians 5:13–6:18

This vital and exciting passage contains Paul's explanation of what he meant when he wrote in Galatians 2:20, "I no longer live, but Christ lives in me. The life I live in the body, I live by faith in the Son of God, who loved me and gave Himself for me." Paul found freedom not to be "himself," but to be his *new* self. And Paul realized that new life as God's own.

Christian freedom (Gal. 5:13-15). We are never to mistake Christian freedom for the kind of liberty the therapy group tried to force on Jim. Christian freedom is always in harmony with the Law, though it does not rely on the Law.

Christian freedom is not freedom "to indulge the sinful nature" but rather freedom to "serve one another in love." Here Paul argued, as he did in Romans 13:8-10, that the entire Law can be "summed up in this one rule: 'Love your neighbor as yourself.' " Thus the person who expresses the new life within him or her by loving others will find his actions actually fulfill the Law of God (see 8:3-4).

The problem with the Law has always been that while it warns us if we misuse freedom, it can never produce love. But now, with a new life from God and with the Holy Spirit granted to us, love *can* be produced in our hearts, and expressed in loving acts.

New nature and Holy Spirit (Gal. 5:16-18). The Holy Spirit is not motivated by the cravings of a sinful nature, for He does not possess one. We do possess a sin nature, which Law has never been able to change. So the real issue in the Christian life is whether we will live according to the old nature, or the new that has been given us in Jesus.

Paul argued that Law is linked with the old nature, for it speaks out against its sins. On the other hand, the Holy Spirit is associated with the new nature. If we surrender ourselves to the Spirit, to let Him guide or control us, then the Spirit will see to it that we do not "gratify the desires of [our] sinful nature" (v. 16).

The who issue of Christian life and freedom *has nothing to do* with the Law.

Acts of the sinful nature (Gal. 5:19-21). All those things which the Law speaks out against and is designed to protect society from are listed here. And they flow from the old, sinful human nature. As long as our sinful nature is in control, and its desires expressed in our actions, Paul's list of evils will appear in our lives.

Fruit of the Spirit (Gal. 5:22-26). As the sin nature produces its fruit in an individual's life, so the Holy Spirit also produces fruit. That fruit, love, joy, peace—all those things we yearn for—stand in stark contrast to the fruit produced by man's sinful nature. And that fruit appears as we walk by, and keep in step with, the Spirit of God.

And against this fruit no law has ever been passed.

Christian freedom must be understood in the context of man's two natures. Freedom is a release from the domination of the old and warped within us, and a release which gives the Spirit full reign to produce good fruit. Christian freedom is the capacity, and the strength, to act in love, to know and share joy, to experience and promote peace, and all those other blessings that come only through the Spirit of our God.

✂ Group Activity: Recovery Group Step 10 (continue taking personal inventory)

Taking personal inventory can be an exciting, positive experience when we take the longer view. Think back to when you were at your lowest point. Use Galatians 5:19-21 to stimulate your memory, and list specific things you did that led you to recognize your powerlessness. Then use the list in Galatians 5:22-23 to stimulate your thinking, and list specific things you do now that show God is at work in your life.

When the two lists are complete, draw a teeter-totter to show where you feel you are today on your personal spiritual journey. Perhaps you're just beginning to make progress, and so the tilt is slight, weighted in one direction or another. Perhaps you've not begun at all, or have come

Freedom to Live

GALATIANS 5

"sinful nature" (death)	"Spirit" (new life)
Characteristics	
* not responsive to God	* responsive to God
* in conflict with the Spirit	* in conflict with the
* ruled by its cravings	sinful nature
	* ruled by God
Products	
immorality	love
impurity	joy
debauchery	peace
idolatry and witchcraft	patience
hatred	kindness
discord	goodness
jealousy	faithfulness
fits of rage	gentleness
selfish ambition	self-control
dissensions	
factions	
envy	
drunkenness	
orgies	
Relationship to the Law	
The Law is "against such things" (5:23) and was added "because of transgressions" (3:19).	NONE "Against such there is no law" (5:22).

a long way, and so the tilt is extreme in one direction or the other.

Show the teeter-totter you drew to the others in your group, and talk about why you drew it as you did.

Ask others for prayers in areas where you are still weak, and praise God together for the growth you have each experienced.

Greetings and injunctions (Gal. 6:1-18). The last chapter of this early New Testament letter contains several injunctions and personal greetings. The brothers are encouraged not to deal harshly with those who are learning to walk the new life (vv. 1-2). One who falls should be restored gently. Each brother should seek to help others along the way and fulfill Christ's new commandment to love (John 13:33-34). Recognizing the divine source of the new life, each man can rejoice in his own gifts and actions without the kind of pride that comes from feeling better than someone else (Gal. 6:3-5).

♥ *Group Activity: Support Group*
Galatians 6:2 and 6:5 mention two kinds of "burdens." The Greek word in 6:5 is the normal pack carried by a soldier when marching. The Greek word used in 6:2 means an unusually heavy or crushing weight. On a sheet of paper list on the left burdens you have to carry that are normal for people in your situation. Then on the right list any burdens that you experience as unusually heavy, as crushing.

Share lists, and talk about the ways you and others cope with the normal loads people carry.

Then share and talk about the burdens you experience as crushing weights. What might others do that would help you carry them? (6:2) As individuals and as a group, find ways to help "and so fulfill the law of Christ."

In all of life's adventures, we can live in total honesty with ourselves and with God. We will never deceive ourselves into believing that Christian freedom is a license to sin (vv.7-10). We can always commit ourselves

407

to doing good, sure that "at the proper time we will reap a harvest" (v. 9) of joy.

Summing up (vv. 12-18), Paul again pointed us to the cross of Jesus Christ, where He (and each believer too!) was crucified. Jesus died—but He rose again. In Him, you and I have risen as well to a new life in a new world. It is a world not ruled by the old Law but one filled with the vital presence of God Himself. In this new world "neither circumcision or uncircumcision means anything" (v. 15). Jew and Gentile meet at the cross, and at the cross each abandons his old lifestyle and culture, to find, as Christ's new creation, a new and better way.

GROUP RESOURCE GUIDE

Identification: *Share with others*
Complete the following sentence: "Freedom is not. . . . " After each has contributed, talk about your own feelings. Do you feel free, or restricted? When are you most likely to feel one or the other?

Exploration: *Probe God's Word*
Each person should have a copy of the "Freedom to Live" chart on page 408. In groups of three work through Galatians 5:13-26, guided by the chart.

Reaction: *Respond together to the Word*
Individually and privately put a check mark beside any item or any "product" on either of the two lists on your chart that characterize an action you can recall taking this past week. Be sure that you have a specific incident in mind before you check any item.

Then discuss: What does it mean if I have many checks on the "sinful nature" side? What if I have many checks on the "new life" side? What if checks are evenly distributed?

Adoration: *Worship and pray*
Write a brief poem on freedom, in which you express your feelings to God. Your poem should express confession, yearning, confidence, or praise.

When done, conduct a brief worship service featuring the reading of your poems as modern-day "psalms." Read them in the following sequence:

Yearning for freedom
Confessions of failure
Confidence in God's provision
Praise for freedom found

STUDY GUIDE 63

Ephesians 1–2

ONE PEOPLE

Overview

Ephesians was written by Paul to a congregation established on one of Paul's later missionary journeys (Acts 19). It was written from Rome, probably in A.D. 62 or 63.

The theme of Ephesians is the church as a living organism, the actual body of the living Christ. It is a key book for understanding our personal relationship with Jesus, and how to live with our fellow Christians in a nurturing, ministering relationship.

Ephesus was "the" religious center of the province of Asia. The great temple of Artemis there drew tourists and worshipers, and served as a giant bank from which cities and nations as well as individuals applied for loans. This highly successful institutionalized religion is the backdrop against which Paul gives us a vision of the church of Jesus Christ. This church is no institution: it is a body, a family, a holy but living temple. It reveals a glory in the living personalities of its members which far outshines the glory of the stone temple of Ephesus, even though that temple was four times the size of the Parthenon of Athens.

This book is an important one for Christians to study today. It helps us not to think of our own churches in institutional terms — as buildings and programs and activities alone. It helps us to see ourselves, and one another, as living expressions of a Christ who still expresses His glory in human lives.

Commentary

When we skim the first two chapters of Ephesians, one brief paragraph stands out. In it, Paul expressed a prayer for the assembled believers in Ephesus. When we read that prayer today, we see again the theme of knowing Christ personally, and the desire for a daily experience of the divine power. We become aware that Paul included *us* in his sweeping request that all God's people might experience Him as present, filling "everything in every way" (Eph. 1:23). Look at that prayer now, and visualize Paul praying for you and those you teach.

I keep asking that the God of our Lord Jesus Christ, the glorious Father, may give you the Spirit of wisdom and revelation, so that you may know Him better. I pray also that the eyes of your heart may be enlightened in order that you may know the hope to which He has called you, the riches of His glorious inheritance in the saints, and His incomparably great power for us who believe. That power is like the working of His mighty strength, which He exerted in Christ, when He raised Him from the dead and seated Him at His right hand in the heavenly realms, far above all rule and authority, power and dominion, and every title that can be given, not only in the present age but also in the one to come. And God placed all things under His feet and appointed Him to be Head over everything for the church, which is His body, the fullness of Him who fills everything in every way.

Ephesians 1:17-23

Ø *Group Activity:*
Missions/Outreach Group
Conversion is an act; salvation is a process. When a person comes to Christ, the process of transforming him or her has just begun — and the one used to reach the new convert takes on an important responsibility: nurture.

Two prayers in Ephesians (1:17-23 and 3:14-21) alert us to what Paul saw as his own converts' greatest needs. Study these prayers and (1) develop a "prayers for new converts" list showing how to pray for them, and (2) outline a "follow-up" pro-

gram for new converts. The follow-up program should indicate what truths, and what experiences, new converts might need to be grounded in their new faith.

Your group can use — and share — the prayer list when praying for the work of missionaries you support. If your group members are reaching others with the gospel, see how you might implement your follow up ideas.

Grasping the Hope

Helen hung up the telephone. "O Lord," she whispered, "give me strength."

Lucille, an older friend from her Thursday evening Bible study, had asked for Helen's help. "You're the only person I know who cares," Lucille had said. "I can talk to you."

Last week their study group had met at Lucille's home, and Helen had stayed after the others left. She'd listened as Lucille, a divorced woman with two grown sons, told of her husband's unfaithfulness and desertion. She shared how her sons blamed her; she described her loneliness and her struggle to get in touch with God. In tears, Lucille said how grateful she was for Helen. Helen really seemed to care.

But caring wasn't easy. Helen had grown up believing she was inadequate and unable to love. Her sense of inadequacy had led to a series of choices that turned her away from others. Now, at 37, it was almost impossible for Helen to reach out.

It had been easier that night after the Bible study. She was already at Lucille's house. No choices had to be made. There was no time to think about a coming confrontation; no time to worry about what she'd say or do. No time to feel the tension grow and the perspiration come cold and clammy. But to choose to visit Lucille, to get into the car and drive the dozen miles across town to where she lived, that would take time. As the days passed, as fear gripped her each time she thought of Lucille, the strength never seemed to come.

How different Helen's hesitation is from Paul's prayer. Helen asked for strength. Paul asked that you and I might *grasp the power that is ours.* Helen was asking for something she already possessed! Having failed to grasp the hope of Christ's calling, she was living in unnecessary defeat.

Paul's vision of the present power of Jesus is one of the most striking emphases of this Christological epistle. Even the word "hope" takes on special meaning in the New Testament. We say, "I hope," and mean "I would like, but am uncertain about." New Testament hope has no note of uncertainty. It is a term of *expectancy.* "Hope in God" (Ps. 42:11) is a call to an active faith which *expects God to act.* Paul's prayer is that you and I might grasp all that we confidently expect, as God's new people. For we are a people in whom God's own incomparably great power is even now at work!

If the "working of His mighty strength" is available to us now, how inappropriate are the desperate, hopeless prayers we so often utter. How tragic Helen's cry, begging for a power to act that has been her heritage ever since she was "included in Christ."

And how important these first chapters of Ephesians, for they help Helen — and us — realize just who we are as a people of God through Jesus Christ.

An Overview: Ephesians 1–2

There is nothing more influential in shaping our actions than our self-image. That is, how we see ourselves, how we feel about ourselves. A person who sees himself as capable will act confidently. A person who sees himself as weak, and unable, is all too likely to refuse to try.

In our spiritual experience too our image of who we are plays a significant role. And it is to just this issue that the first two chapters of Ephesians are addressed. They help us to develop a vital, correct sense of our identity in Christ. They help us understand who we really are as Jesus' people, and thus help free us from our bondage to old frustrations and inabilities.

The Godhead (Eph. 1:3-14). In these powerful verses Paul drew past, present, and future together. He looked at the work of each of the Persons of the Godhead as it relates to you and me. God the Father, in eternity past, chose us in Christ to be holy and blameless. He predestined us to be adopted as sons, pouring out His grace on us in Christ. God the Son, in history past, redeemed us through His blood, bringing us forgiveness and lavishing on us gifts of wisdom and understanding. Even now we are "included in Christ," and looking forward to the complete fulfillment of God's plan and the glory that fulfillment holds for us. Now too we have been sealed by God's gift of the Holy Spirit, the living guarantee of our inheritance to come.

What stunning truths! Somehow you and I, with all God's people, have been the focus of His concern from before the Creation of the universe! Each person of the Godhead— Father, Son, and Holy Spiirt—has been involved in bringing us the grace in which we now stand. In view of all this, there is *no way* that a Christian can see himself or herself as insignificant, unimportant, or ineffectual. The focused energies of God have been spent on our redemption because in Christ we are significant to Him. We are important. And, with God's Spirit present in us, we have the power to live "to the praise of His glory" (v. 14).

Prayer (Eph. 1:15-23). Paul desired, then, that we might enjoy a full experience of our position in Christ. We have a new identity now—we are "saints" and we experience "His incomparably great power for us who believe." And it is *His* power: the power of a Jesus who is now raised from the dead, seated at the Father's "right hand" (the ancient place of authority), far above every competing natural or supernatural authority. Perhaps most significantly, Jesus is Head "over everything for the church, which is His body." This theme, that we are members of a living organism over which Christ is the living Head, is a theme Paul picked up in later chapters of this powerful little book.

Alive in Christ (Eph. 2:1-10). God is fully aware of who we *were*. We were "dead in . . . transgressions and sins" and we used to follow "the ways of this world." We were dedicated to "gratifying the cravings of our sinful nature." So in affirming our new identity in Christ, there is no question of misunderstanding. God knew full well what we were.

But it is *were*. We are no longer what we were! Now we have been "made . . . alive" in Christ. His grace has been poured out on us and we were "raised . . . up with Christ," recipients not of a reward but of a gift. Who are we now? "We are God's workmanship, created in Christ Jesus to do good works, which God prepared in advance for us to do."

God knows who we were: it is up to you and me to take Him at His word about who we now are! We can no longer think of ourselves in the old way, or burden ourselves down with past guilts. In Jesus we are renewed: we are His own fresh creations, shaped by the divine hand for the good works He calls us to do.

One in Christ (Eph. 2:11-18). Another aspect of our new identity has a direct impact on our relationship with other Christians. We once defined our relationships with others on the basis of the things that made us different, even as Jew and Gentile were aware of the cultural and religious gap that not only separated them, but also made them enemies. But now in Christ the gap has been closed, and Jesus has made peace. From even such hostile elements God has made "one body." By being reconciled to God, we are at the same time reconciled to one another.

Family of believers (Eph. 2:19-22). The "one body" theme is important, for the new identity we are urged to grasp is not found in isolation. We are to see ourselves as "fellow citizens with God's people" (v. 19). As members of God's household, we are "being built *together* [italics mine] to become a dwelling in which God lives."

This last theme is one that Paul developed carefully in both Ephesians and Colossians. We have been given new life, and have been given power to live it. But we do not live isolated lives. We grow to full stature in Christ as members of a household. It is in the fellowship of other believers that individuals are formed into a living, growing organism that "rises to become a holy temple in the Lord" (v. 21).

This focus on the community of faith gives us a new perspective on personal growth and identity. It also gives us a new perspective on Christ. In Ephesians we no longer see Jesus primarily in relationship to the believing individual. We see Jesus as Head of a living body. We see God's intention to:

- "bring all things in heaven and on earth together under one Head, even Christ" (1:10);
- place "all things under His feet" and appoint "Him to be Head over everything for the church, which is His body" (vv. 22-23); and
- set Christ Jesus Himself as the chief Cornerstone. "In Him the whole

My New Identity

Portrayed in Ephesians 1 and 2

What God has done

1:5 _____
1:8 _____
1:13 _____
1:13 _____
2:5 _____
2:6 _____
2:8 _____
2:13 _____
2:19 _____
2:22 _____

What we now have

1:6 _____
1:7 _____
1:7 _____
1:9 _____
1:13 _____
1:18 _____
1:19 _____
1:23 _____
1:23 _____
2:4 _____
2:5 _____
2:13, 18 _____
2:14 _____
2:16 _____
2:19 _____
2:20 _____
2:22 _____

Record above your own discoveries of your identity in Christ. After your research, write below which of your findings seems most significant to you and why:

_____

_____

_____

building is joined together" (2:21).

As we read on in Ephesians we will see Christ pictured more and more as Head of the body. In the first two chapters, however, Paul focused on *our* identity. What does it mean for us to be "in Christ"? What does it mean to have been snatched from death and given life? Just why was Paul so sure that our daily lives will be transformed if we grasp the hope of our calling, if we know what we can expect as members of Christ's body?

♥ *Group Activity: Support Group*
"I feel uncomfortable with people who . . ."

Together brainstorm ways people might finish this statement. List as many likely (or even unlikely) responses as you can think of.

When the list is complete, put checks beside items which people feel intensely. You can use up to five check marks to show intensity.

Then evaluate. What's the reason for the discomfort with items that receive at least two or three check marks? Record the reason or reasons given.

Now study together Ephesians 2:11-22, which teaches that differences based on culture are not valid grounds for drawing back from true unity with other believers. After you feel you have mastered the passage, go back to your list and re-evaluate the more heavily checked items. Which "uncomfortable" feelings are valid reasons for separation from others? Which must we deny in order to truly welcome Christian brothers and sisters? How can we develop real closeness to people from whom we differ?

Focus then on your own group. Have

any differences between you and other members made you uncomfortable? Have they changed as you've come to know the other(s) involved? What do you need to do to promote real unity with others in your support group?

One way to help our group members build a picture of our new identity is to read and reread these first chapters of Ephesians, noting what Paul says we have in Christ, and what God has done for us. How rich to realize that, now, what we do have in Christ includes redemption. Power. Life. Peace. Membership in the family. Christ Himself to guide us.

And how wonderful to realize what God has done for us in Christ. That He has chosen us to praise Him. That He has adopted us as sons, and reshaped us. That our personalities now bear the mark of His workmanship.

As we explore these chapters, the wonder grows. In Christ we truly are a new people! We have a new identity now, individually and together. With the newness that being in Christ brings, we shrug off forever the bondage of past hopelessness.

✂ *Group Activity: Recovery Group*
Steps 2 (believe in a higher power) and 3 (decide to turn my life over to God's care)
Share briefly why you believe in God. Then use the New Identity chart on page 412, and together look up each verse. First work through the "What God has done" items, then the "What we now have" items.

Write a brief paragraph in response to this study that states why, in view of who God is and what He does for us, you feel secure in turning your life and will over to Him.

Share your paragraph and listen to the paragraphs written by the others. Then openly express your commitment. Either tell how you have turned your life over to the Lord and what this has meant to you, or state that you now turn your life over to the Lord and will commit to do His will, or tell that you are not yet ready to turn your life over to the Lord, and share why.

God, who has done so much for us, welcomes all who come to Him, and waits pa-

tiently for those who are considering this decision.

In the Spirit of Worship
We would miss the tone of these early chapters if we failed to note that Paul's great affirmation of our hope is framed in liturgy. Many commentators see major blocks of these two chapters as early church hymns; credal confessions used regularly in the worship of the first century.

These liturgical elements are found in chapter 1:3-12, 20-23 and in chapter 2:4-10, 14-18. Each lifts our hearts to the person of Christ, to appreciate all God has done for us and for His own glory.

Worship was important in the life of the early church, and it is important now. Not only is worship vital because God merits our praise; it is important to the worshiper. Only when we shift our gaze from ourselves and our inadequacies to God and His power of endless life can we believe that we too have been "raised up with Christ and seated . . . in the heavenly realms" (v. 6). Worship is not selfish; we do not worship God because of the benefits we receive. Yet in losing ourselves in praise and adoration, we discover more of who God is. And an adequate view of God will free us from the bondage of our own inadequacies.

This emphasis on worship helps us remember something else. In the early church, gatherings of the church body were not just to hear a sermon.

The life of the church was focused on reaffirming community by a liturgy of Communion and the Word. Justin Martyr, writing his *First Apology* about A.D. 150, gave two accounts of worship in the early church.

On finishing the prayer, we greet each other with a kiss. Then bread and a cup of water mixed with wine are brought to the president of the brethren, and he, taking them, sends up praise and glory to the Father of the universe. . . . When the president has given thanks and the whole congregation has assented, those whom we call deacons give to each of those present a portion of the consecrated bread and wine and water. And on the day called Sunday there is a reading of the Apostles, or the writings of the Prophets are read as long as time permits. When the reader has finished, the president in a discourse urges and invites us to the imitation of these noble things. Then we all stand up together and offer prayers. And, as said before, when we have finished the prayer, bread is brought and wine and water, and the president similarly sends up prayers and thanksgivings to the best of his ability, and the congregation assents, saying the "Amen"; the distribution and reception of the consecrated elements by each one takes place and they are sent to the absent by the deacons. Those who prosper, and who so wish, contribute, each one as he chooses to. What is collected is deposited with the president, and he takes care of orphans and widows, and those who are in want on account of sickness or any other cause, and those who are in bonds, and the strangers who are sojourners among us, and briefly, he is the protector of all those in need.

Robert Webber, a professor at Wheaton College and author of a number of books on worship, notes that early church worship services had this general form:

Liturgy of the Word
Lessons from Old and New Testaments
Sermon
Prayers
Hymns

Liturgy of the Eucharist
Kiss of peace
Offering of bread, wine, water
Prayers over elements
Remembrance of Christ's death
Amen, said by all
Communion
Sharing of material possessions

In this structure, worship—focused on Christ through Word and Communion—marked the gathering of the local congregation. In the reading, the prayers, the responses, and the sharing with one another, the body of Christ came together to focus shared praise on her Lord. Paul reflects this same kind of service briefly in Colossians 3:16.

As we read Ephesians, we again sense that worship was the heartbeat of the early church. We find hope by grasping who we are in Christ. But hope becomes a reality when we confess Christ with other believers.

The better we come to know God through worship, the more clearly our astounding new identity becomes real to us. For Christ is the source of our reality. Apart from Him, we are nothing. In Him, we experience the fullness of the one Person able to fill us in every way.

GROUP RESOURCE GUIDE

NOTE: Before the group meets have a team of several members prepare a worship service on the theme of what God has done for us, following the pattern that was used in the early church, as reported by Robert Webber above. Plan for up to 2/3 of group time for this unique worship experience.

Exploration: *Probe God's Word*
Give each person a "My New Identity" study sheet (p. 412). Work through the first two chapters of Ephesians together, and fill in the blanks. When done, give three minutes for each person to fill in personal reactions about his or her identity in Christ.

Adoration: *Worship and pray*
Briefly explain the Early Church's pattern of worship. Then be led in worship by the team that has previously prepared.

ONE BODY, ONE FAMILY

Overview

Ephesians gives us three images which help us think about the church. Two of these images are brought into focus in the mid-section of Ephesians.

The three images that are intended to give us a vision of who we are as Christ's church are those of a *body,* a *family,* and a *holy temple.*

The three images share a common emphasis. Each reminds us again and again that we are one with our brothers and sisters, even as we are one with Christ. But each of the images also has its own distinctive emphasis.

The biblical picture of the church as a body reminds us that we are called to a life of good works. Even as our own bodies act to carry out the intentions of our minds, so the body of Christ acts on earth to carry out the intentions of Jesus, our living Head.

The biblical picture of the church as a family reminds us that we are called to a life of love. As the human family is the context for growth and intimacy, so the family of God is a context in which God's love is expressed to welcome each other and to help each other grow.

The biblical picture of the church as a temple reminds us that we are called to a life of holiness. As a temple reminds us of the worship of God, our calling as a holy temple is to bring God praise and honor and glory.

■ See the *Bible Knowledge Commentary,* pages 628-637 for a verse-by-verse discussion of these chapters.

Commentary

The New Testament gives us three vivid pictures of what the church is. Each is found in Ephesians. Each differs from other biblical illustrations that describe the church. These show us not what the church

is *like,* but what the church *is.*

Of course, we know that the church is people. Not organizations or buildings or programs, but people. The Greek word *ecclesia* means "congregation," and more specifically a "called-out congregation." Those who have responded to God's invitation in Christ are called out from humanity to fulfill all of mankind's ancient dreams in a vital, new community. Each of us responds to that invitation individually, but once we respond, we are part of a great company. We are suddenly members of a new community, linked intimately to other men and women who have joined their lives to Jesus. It is important for us to realize that now our identity is to be found not in isolation but in and through the community of Christ's church. We grow in our capacity to live as God's persons within this fellowship.

So it is vital to learn what the church is. Discovering the nature of the church and learning to live as its members is critical to our personal growth and fulfillment.

The body of Christ. All believers are "members together of one body, and sharers together in the promise of Christ Jesus" (3:6). Stress here is laid on the church's unity. Each of us is linked to Christ and one another. This oneness is a truth we must accept.

Also implicit in this portrait is the notion that the church lives only as she responds to her Head. Christ alone is Head of the church. We look to Him for direction and guidance. What is His goal? Scripture tells us that Christ continues His work in our world. He is absent in one sense, seated at the right hand of God (1:20). Yet in another, He is physically here, alive and active in our century. Christ is in heaven, but His body lives and moves on earth. We who have been "created in Christ Jesus to do good works" (2:10) carry out God's hidden plans. You and I, together with all believers, are called to be a contemporary incarnation of the living God. Christ reveals Himself in human flesh, the human flesh of His living church.

The family. This second portrait of the church in Ephesians is that we are all "members of God's household" (v. 19). The "whole family of believers . . . derives its name" (3:14) from God the Father. That name is "family," and from God's name as Father we learn that we are children together. We are brothers and sisters now in the loving, intimate context of a home.

It was in our parents' home that we first learned to love. Now, in God's family, we learn of His love, and to love one another.

A holy temple. The third picture of the church is found in 2:20-21. Here we see a building being raised. We see the Foundation and Cornerstone clearly—Jesus Christ. And we see the process—stone is joined to stone by the Master Builder. As the building grows, we discover that it is a temple. A holy temple, Scripture says, "in the Lord" (v. 21).

This too is the church. Fallen humanity, re-created by God, and now in Christ, a fitting expression of the holiness of God.

Each of these three pictures highlights aspects of who and what we Christians are. Each helps us to understand ourselves as individuals, and to understand the importance of developing an appropriate lifestyle together as God's new community.

✳ *Group Activity:*
Singles/Single Again Group
In a couples-culture Singles often feel left out, as if they don't fit in. Ephesians reminds us that the church is—and is to function as—a living body (1:20-22; 3:6); as a family (3:14-19); and as a holy temple (2:20-21). Each image helps us understand who we are, and the nature of the satisfying relationships we can develop with each other.

Distribute copies of the Word Pictures of the Church chart (below). Select one image of the church, and in a team of others interested in the same image, read quickly through Ephesians 1–5 to pick up ways the church (as a community of Christians) is similar to a body, a family, or a temple. Then identify implications of this image for your own life and relationships. Note: Don't major on the failings of your local church and its people. Focus first on your singles' group as an expression of the church. Then focus on what you can do to further develop body, family, and holy temple relationships with others.

Comments on the Text: Ephesians 3:1–4:6

The argument (flow of thought) in this section emerges from Ephesians 2. Verses 11-18 teaches that Christ's great act of reconciliation brought sinners to God, and welded them together in a new creation. "One new man" (v. 15) was formed from individuals of different cultures and backgrounds. Differences, even those which had caused hostility, were made irrelevant, as interpersonal peace came with a shared access to our common Father.

Word Pictures of the Church

	Ephesians 1:15 through 2:22	
	Similarities	Implications
Body		
Family		
Building (Temple)		

In what ways is the church a body, a family, and a temple? What are the implications of these realities for us as members of Christ's church?

Paul concluded (vv. 19-22) that both household and temple rest on a single foundation, Jesus Christ. And oneness is characteristic of both.

A mystery revealed (Eph. 3:1-6). Paul now called the church a "mystery." The word (*mysterion*) is used in the New Testament primarily by Paul (20 of 27 occurrences) and is always associated with a verb of revelation. What is a "mystery"? It is an insight made available to Christians which was not made clear in the Old Testament.

The "mystery" here is the fact that the Gentiles would be "heirs together with Israel, members together of one body, and sharers together in the promise of Christ Jesus" (v. 6). While Isaiah and others had foretold that Gentiles would one day be saved, all thought theirs would be a subordinate position. No wonder Paul repeats and repeats in Ephesians the doctrine that the church is *one*.

God's wisdom revealed (Eph. 3:7-13). Paul, as the Apostle to the Gentiles, had been called by God to reveal this unexpected aspect of God's eternal plan. Paul reminded us that that plan expressed the "manifold" (that is, complex or multifaceted) plan of God. God is at work in the church, doing far more than we may imagine. What is important for us however is to realize that "in Him [Christ] and through faith in Him we may approach God with freedom and confidence" (v. 12).

Another prayer (Eph. 3:14-21). In this prayer Paul again expressed his desire for believers. To understand it we must note the context: it comes in a section in which Paul had been affirming the unity of a church made up of many differing individuals. Here Paul prayed that "being rooted and established in love" we believers might experience the love of God and be filled with His fullness. What "love" are we to be established in? In context it is not the love *of* God, or even love *for* God. It is *love for one another as members of the family of God!* It is in the context of loving relationships within the church that we experience, through one another, the depths of God's love. It is in this context that we grow to the fullness of Christ.

All this is possible only because God is "able to do immeasurably more than all we ask or imagine, according to His power that is at work within us."

✂ *Group Activity: Recovery Group*
Step 11 (improve relationship with God through prayer and meditation)
Talk about the following events reported in Scripture. What does each tell us about the power of God?

(1) God created the material universe.
(2) God unleashed miraculous plagues on Egypt that forced them to let their Israelite slaves go free.
(3) God's power through Jesus gave sight to a man born blind and healed others who were crippled from birth.
(4) God raised Jesus from the dead.
(5) God changed the Pharisee, Saul, who persecuted Christians, into the Apostle Paul, the greatest Christian missionary.

After talking about God's power and the ways it is expressed, stop and list the specific areas in your life in which you need to experience God's power now. When done, share your list with the group. If the group is large, share with three or four others in a smaller team.
Together memorize Ephesians 3:20-21. You may do it by writing the verse on a chalkboard and reading it, and erasing one word or phrase at a time while repeating the verse together. By the time all words have been erased, you should have the verse memorized.
In your teams, look together again at the "need power" lists you've shared. What do the verses you memorized say to you? What promise can you claim? What reality can you hold on to when you fear or sense your own weakness?
Hold hands, and repeat Ephesians 3:20-21 together as an affirmation of confidence, and as a prayer.

Living in love and unity (Eph. 4:1-6). Paul's exhortation and prayer for an experience of unity closes with an exhortation. Live in love. Maintain unity. We, Christ's church, *are* one. We know—as no mere association of men can—"one body and one Spirit . . . one hope when you were called—one Lord, one faith, one baptism; one God and Father of all, who is over all and through all and in all" (vv. 4-6).

Implications of Oneness
Paul's stress on oneness troubles many.

There have always been differences within the church. Presbyterians have their distinctives, Baptists theirs. Calvinists disagree with Arminians. Some appreciate formal worship; some ask only for a small room where a few can sit in silence and listen to the voice within. Today some hesitate to links hands with anyone who fails to speak in tongues, while others draw back from any who do. More recently, some have insisted that we view the doctrine of inerrancy—that the Bible as originally written contained no errors—as the criteria to divide the "true evangelical" from the false. And yet we hear Paul say, the church is one. And we wonder. If we are one, why does division mark us instead of unity?

A number of answers have been suggested. Here are a few.

• *Unity is only spiritual.* "The invisible church is one, but the visible church, made up of human beings, will always fall short of unity."

• *Organism vs. organization.* "A true bond exists (and can be affirmed, among believers) but this bond need not be expressed in any kind of organizational union."

• *Local unity.* "The only true expression of the church on earth is found in local congregations. Thus the oneness of the local body is all that was ever intended."

• *True church.* "All others outside our group who claim to be Christians are deceived. Since we define all who are unlike us as out of the body, it's easy to claim that unity exists—right here among us."

Each of these, and other formulations, are honest attempts to deal with a difficult question. Yet each falls short of Scripture's affirmation of our oneness as body, family, and temple of God. Looking at Ephesians carefully, we can see errors in each view.

In Ephesians 2:11-18, Paul dealt with deeply rooted cultural and social differences. Jew and Gentile had lifestyles and world views which were incompatible. These led to hostility. When the Gospel message was first shared in Judea, only Hebrews responded. Then, as the word of the Good News spread, Gentiles began to believe too!

One faction in the early church insisted that, to come to Christ, Gentiles must give up their heritage and become Jews. A council was called in Jerusalem to decide that issue. Relationship with Jesus, not culture, made a Christian. The right of Gentile and Jew to their own cultural heritage was affirmed.

Not everyone could stand the tensions such differences caused. Some in the early church still insisted that unity could come only from sameness. But again Paul affirmed the right to be different. God made one new man from *two.* He did not bring harmony by removing differences, but by destroying barriers. He attacked "the dividing wall of hostility" (v. 14), and made its foundation, the Law, irrelevant. In Christ *life* is the only issue. Have we been made alive in Christ? Then we *are* one body, one family, one temple being constructed by the Lord.

In the early church, the Jewish believer continued to live the Hebrew way. The Gentile continued in his way. Each turned from sin, but cultural distinctions were retained. And yet, they still affirmed their identity as one. In Gentile lands Paul took up collections for poor believers in Jerusalem. The family reached out to help. When the Greek-speaking minority in the earliest church in Jerusalem, felt their widows were being treated unfairly in the daily distribution, they complained. Seven deacons were selected to supervise the funds. And every one of the seven bore a Greek name! (Acts 6) Not only in daily fellowship but also in organization, the early church affirmed God's Word. There were differences, but the church was one.

We need to be very careful here. Do I as a dispensationalist draw back from the covenant theologian? As a noncharismatic do I reject the brother who praises God in tongues? Do I let differences cut me off from fellowship with my brothers, or from organizational expressions of our unity? In Christ my brother and I *are* one. My life with him must affirm, not deny, a unity that God says *is.*

In Ephesians 4:1-6, Paul spoke of several aspects of our oneness: one hope, one Lord, one faith. I can accept and ignore many differences. But what about differences in doctrine? What about the person who claims to have the divine life, but whose beliefs differ from mine?

There were doctrinal differences in the early church. Neither Scripture nor early church history suggest that oneness is possible with those outside the body. But here again, life is the issue. One who has Christ's life is to be acknowledged and affirmed no matter how he may differ from us in ideas about Scripture, gifts, separation, predestination, or whatever. Paul's expression of one faith, one baptism, and one Lord is not meant to be exclusive, as a test of purity. Rather it is inclusive, demonstrating the broad-based reality believers know and affirm.

This same approach was taken in the early church. Irenaeus, writing about A.D. 190, offered evidence that the substance of Christian faith received from the apostles was confessed by the church everywhere. This can be our confession too: the confession of a company of men and women who share a common life and know a common Lord. In this confession, we affirm our unity with the church visible and invisible, the church past, future, and present everywhere today. Listen to the ring of the ancient words:

Now the church, although scattered over the whole civilized world to the ends of the earth, received from the apostles and their disciples its faith in one God, the Father Almighty, who made the heaven, and the earth, and the seas, and all that is in them, and in one Christ Jesus, the Son of God, who was made flesh for our salvation, and in the Holy Spirit, who through the prophets proclaimed the dispensations of God— the comings, the birth of a virgin, the suffering, the Resurrection from the dead, and the bodily reception into the heavens of the beloved, Christ Jesus our Lord, and His coming from the heavens in the glory of the Father to restore all things, and to raise up all flesh, that is, the whole human race, so that every knee may bow, of things in heaven and on earth and under the earth, to Christ Jesus our Lord and God and Saviour and King, according to the pleasure of the invisible Father, and every tongue may confess Him, and that He may execute righteous judgment on all. The spiritual powers of wickedness, and the angels who transgressed and fell into apostasy, and the godless and wicked and lawless and blasphemers among men He will send into the eternal fire.

But to the righteous and holy, and those who have kept His commandments and have remained in His love, some from the beginning of life and some since their repentance, He will by His grace give life incorrupt, and will clothe them with eternal glory.

Having received this preaching and this faith, as I have said, the church, although scattered in the whole world, carefully preserves it, as if living in one house. She believes these things everywhere alike, as if she had but one heart and one soul, and preaches them harmoniously, teaches them, and hands them down as if she had but one mouth. For the languages of the world are different, but the meaning of the tradition is one and the same.

Living a life worthy of this calling—a humble, patient, loving life—we will maintain the unity of that body which *is* one in Christ.

Comments on the Text: Ephesians 4:7–5:2

Paul now developed implications of the church's life as the body of Christ. The risen Christ is pictured as giving gifted persons to the church "to prepare God's people for works of service, so that the body of Christ may be built up" (4:12). Several aspects of this statement may seem strange to us.

Gifted persons (Eph. 4:11). Other passages on gifts focus on various talents or abilities. We recall gifts such as teaching, faith, and showing mercy, and we tend to define gifts as heightened capacities to serve God and others. Usually when we speak of spiritual gifts, we wonder, "What can I do to contribute? What special ability has God given me?"

This is no error. While each of us has faith and exercises that faith in prayer, some have a heightened capacity to believe. While each of us has a capacity to communicate, to teach, some of us have that ability in a special degree. *This* is the gift of teaching. While each of us can reach out in love to care for those in need, some are gifted to a special degree with the capacity to show mercy. And each believer has one or more of such supernatural endowments.

But in this passage, Paul was not talking

419

THE SMALL GROUP MEMBER'S COMMENTARY

about spiritual gifts! Some people have *become* gifts! Some are given to the body for special purposes. Who are these gift-persons? Apostles. Prophets. Evangelists. Pastor-teachers. And what is their calling?

Leadership's task. Gift-people are "to prepare God's people for works of service" (v. 12). Leaders are not to *do* the work of the ministry; leaders are to prepare the laity to minister.

It is here that we have often missed the implications of the body portrait, and developed congregational patterns that deny rather than express what the church *is*. All too often leaders are hired by a congregation to do the "work of the ministry." The pastor is expected to teach. To evangelize. To counsel. To visit the sick. To pray with the discouraged. If the church grows in size and new members are added, it is taken as an indication that their local congregation is healthy and the minister is doing his job. If the church fails to grow or the budget is not met, the one to blame is the minister. After all, he was hired by the church to minister.

How different is this view from the Bible's portrait of a living body! In a living organism, *every cell contributes*. The body's health depends on each member fulfilling its special function. No one person can carry out the functions of the living organism the Scripture describes. No one person or team of paid professionals was ever intended to. The role of leaders within the church has always been to help the members of the body grow in capacity to minister; to help each individual find and use his or her spiritual gifts. The role of leaders has always been to lead all believers into a fulfilling life of service.

When we miss this, and put the ministry of the church onto the professional, we have lost sight of who we are. The local congregation becomes weak, unable to respond as a healthy body to the directions of its Head.

Becoming mature (Eph. 4:12-16). Paul here set an initial goal for our works of service. We are to build up the body, "until we all reach unity in the faith . . . and become mature" (v. 13). *The first ministry of believers is to other believers.*

It is vital that we "grow up into Him" if we are to be a valid expression of Jesus in this world. The whole body "grows and builds itself up in love, as each part does its work" (v. 16).

This is sometimes hard to accept. We look at the world and are burdened by the need for evangelism. We look at the poor and are burdened by the need to establish justice. We look at the suffering and are impelled to comfort and to care. So sometimes we slip into the trap of organizing the local church to undertake one or more of these tasks. We program evangelistic efforts and buy more buses. We commit ourselves to an active social welfare involvement. All too often we lose sight of the fact that the first function of the body is to build *itself*.

When my oldest son was about five, he wanted to mow our lawn. We had a push mower then. The kind in which the blades moved only when the wheels moved, and the wheels were moved by people power. Well, Paul pushed and strained—and finally found an answer. He leaned on the handle, lifted the wheels off the ground, and easily moved the mower on just the back roller! How busy he looked, chugging up and down across our lawn. And how little grass he cut!

After a while, I would explain. "Soon, Paul, you'll grow, and then you'll be able to make those blades turn. Then you can help a lot."

How often in the church we concentrate on organizing spiritual five-year-olds to push better lawn mowers, and wonder why so little of God's grass gets cut! The church is called to "grow up into Him who is the Head, that is, Christ" (v. 15). Maturing within the body, growing more and more like Jesus, is the believer's first calling. To equip the church for service, believers must minister to one another and to the world.

Don't misunderstand: this focus on building one another up is not "selfish." It is essential. Only as we grow toward maturity together can we respond fully to Jesus as He directs us to serve in the world. Only a strong and healthy body can carry out the tasks assigned to it. Our effectiveness in communicating the Gospel and the love of God to the world around us depends on our growth toward maturity. This kind of growth takes place as we—members together of one body—build each other up in love, each part doing its own ministering work (v. 16).

420

✍ *Group Activity: Bible Study Group*
Analyze Ephesians 4:11-16. This critical passage is vital to our understanding of how believers grow and mature. Approach your study by looking three separate times at each of the following phrases in the text. The first time, list "questions this raises." The second time, list "principles this suggests." The third time through list "actions we need to take."

The phrases to highlight and examine in this threefold way are:
* *He gave [leaders]*
* *To prepare God's people*
* *For works of service*
* *That the body of Christ may be built up*
* *All reach unity*
* *Become mature*
* *Attain . . . the fullness of Christ*
* *No longer infants*
* *Speaking the truth in love*
* *From Him the whole body*
* *Grows and builds itself up in love*
* *As each part does its work*

Sharing (Eph. 4:17–5:2). At times we make living in and as a body more difficult than it is. We think of ministering relationships, and we wonder, "How do we develop them?" "What are we to *do*?" And, uncertain, its all too easy to draw back. We forget that living in Christ's church is like living in a family.

The apostle brings us back to the concept of simple sharing by pointing out in 4:16 that the body builds itself up *in love*. Paul then exhorted us to "live a life of love, just as Christ loved us and gave Himself up for us" (5:2). Over and over Paul brought into focus the personal relationships that are to be developed by members of the body. In the context of these natural relationships, our giftedness grows.

As members of the body, we must no longer live as the Gentiles do (4:17-19), but become a loving family in which growth can take place. How do the Gentiles live? Without sensitivity, indulging themselves in sensuality. This is a picture of men and women who see others as something to use. Love never degrades others or places things above human values. "I tell you this, and insist on it in the Lord, that you must no longer live as the Gentiles" (v. 17).

The Church Is a Body

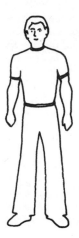

Visualizing the church as a body, do the following:

1. What part of the body are leaders (remembering that Christ alone is the Head)?

2. What part of the body would you most like to be?

3. What spiritual gifts (see Rom. 12 and 1 Cor. 12 for typical gifts) seem most closely associated with the part you selected?

⚔ *Group Activity: Recovery Group*
Step 10 (continue taking personal inventory)
Ephesians 4:20-32 contrasts the "old man" we were without Jesus with the "new man" that God forms as we grow through faith in Him.

First discuss denial. How do people go about trying to hide "old man" flaws in their way of life? For instance: Blame others for their failures ("he made me mad"); dismiss them ("it only happened twice"); compensate ("but look at the good things I've done!"); etc. Together list as many ways we try to hide "old man" flaws — making sure your favorite ways are up there with the rest!

The problem is that growth takes place only as we are honest with ourselves, with

421

God, and with others—and let God deal with our failures. So make a list of the "old man" acts found in Ephesians 4:25-31. Then focus on each in turn, honestly reexamining your own behavior this past week or month. Each time a phrase in Ephesians stimulates you to remember something you have done, write that action down. When you have worked through the list, first confess your wrongs to God. Then share several with others in the group, and tell what you plan to do to make amends if this is appropriate.

Conclude the session with an affirmation of faith. In Christ you are being "made new in the attitudes of your minds." Commit yourself to "put on the new self, created to be like God in true righteousness and holiness."

How are we taught to live together in Christ? Putting off the former way of life (vv. 20-32), we are to live with a totally new attitude: a new self that is like God in true righteousness and holiness. How does righteousness find expression in human relationships?

• *By putting off falsehood and speaking truthfully.* This involves more than not lying. It involves an open sharing of ourselves with one another, rejecting deceit.

• *By rejecting the sinful actions anger drives us toward.* Anger is not given a place. Before evening comes, we are to move toward reconciliation.

• *By rejecting gossip and unwholesome talk.* In our conversation we seek to build others up, not tear them down.

• *By ridding ourselves of bitterness, rage, slander, and every form of malice.* In their place, we are to express kindness and compassion, forgiving each other as God has forgiven us.

"Be imitators of God, therefore, as dearly loved children and live a life of love" (vv. 1-2). In every New Testament passage that teaches that the church is a body, we also find an emphasis on the loving relationships that are to develop between believers. It is through living with one another in love that ministry opportunities are created, and ministry takes place.

This is the simplicity we sometimes miss. The love that grows between family members and draws us closer to each other, moves us to care. As we care, we reach out to bear one another's burdens, to encourage and support—we minister. It is in loving that our spiritual gifts come into play.

Local churches. The Ephesians' description of a life of love helps us define the characteristics of a healthy local church today. We have already seen that a local congregation must have a biblical understanding of ministry. The church that has a biblical understanding:

• Sees leaders as equippers.
• Sees each member as a minister.
• Pays close attention to maturing and building believers up in Christ.
• Seeks to help individuals and groups within the church serve as Christ leads.

Through such ministry, the maturing congregation has the greatest impact on the world around.

Now we see another critical aspect of local church life. Relationships within the church are to be marked by love. Jesus spoke of that at His Last Supper. "Love each other," He told His disciples, "as I have loved you" (John 15:12). This new commandment also contained a promise. "All men will know that you are My disciples if you love one another" (13:35). Christ placed His highest priority on love within the body, for He knew we could only become one through ever-deepening personal relationships. Only through love can we build each other to maturity. Only through love can the church bear compelling witness to Jesus as Lord. When others see Jesus' love lived out in the brotherhood of faith, there is no explanation but one: God is real.

If our local congregation wants to be the church, we need to:

• *Come to know each other well.* We cannot love a person we do not know.
• *Learn to share our lives with each other.* Love involves bearing each other's burdens. We need to trust others enough to reveal our burdens to them.
• *Reach out in caring to meet others' needs.* As burdens are shared, we want to respond.

These are very practical guidelines. They let us look at a congregation's lifestyle and see ways to encourage growth. Do people know each other well? If not, we need to plan time to be together. Do we share? If not, we need to grow used to opening our lives to one another. Do we reach out? If not, we need to concentrate on ways to minister to people. In short, we need to see what the New Testament reveals: that the heart of ministry is not to run a program or fill an organizational slot, but to focus on people and their needs.

"Live a life of love," Scripture says (Eph. 5:2). *Be* the church—the family of God—that you *are*.

GROUP RESOURCE GUIDE

Identification: *Share with others*
Ephesians 5:2 says "live a life of love." React to this verse, sharing what these words make you think of or how they make you feel.

Exploration: *Probe God's Word*
Together or in teams define from the Ephesians text what it means for Christians/for the church to "live a life of love." Build your study on the three images of the church given us in Ephesians:

Living love as a family (3:1-21)
Living love as a body (4:1-16)
Living love as a holy temple (4:17–5:2)

When you team has fully defined what a life of love entails, report and hear the reports of others.

Affirmation: *Express love and concern*
If you have experienced another person living the life of love your teams have described from the text, now is a good time to tell him or her so.

Reaction: *Respond together to the Word*
Discuss: if your group members were to make just one commitment that would bring you all closer to living that life of love Ephesians calls for, what would it be?

Adoration: *Worship and pray*
Focus on God's ability to work in you individually and as a group. Meditate on Ephesians 2:20-21, and make God's "immeasurable" power the focus of your prayer and praise.

ONE IN LOVE

Overview

Ephesians affirms the oneness of Christians, bonded together in Christ. We've looked at that oneness as expressed in the images of a body and of a family.

Each of these is an image not of what the church is *like*, but of what the church *is*. Each is an image of what we are called to experience, together, as God's people.

In this study we look at the third image, that of the holy temple. We also examine a basic attitude which is vital to adopt if we are to truly *be* Christ's church: the attitude of submission. Finally, we look at those schemes of the devil which are focused on distorting our life together—and at the armor God has provided for us to enable us to withstand.

How good to look into this, one of the deepest and most important of Paul's letters, and learn with our students how to build oneness through a truly practical love.

▶ *Submission.* The New Testament emphasizes a voluntary (James 4:7) rather than a forced (Luke 10:17) submission. Submission is appropriate in social roles (as citizen or slave, see Rom. 13:1; Titus 2:9). It is also appropriate in Christian interpersonal relationships. Here the image is one of responsiveness and willingness to yield to one another out of love.

Commentary

Each section of Ephesians adds to our understanding of our identity together as the church. Each shows how we can help each other know Christ better. Looking back over these sections, we can sense the wonder of it all—and see practical guidelines for a vital new lifestyle.

Ephesians 1–2. Here we see Jesus, raised from the dead to the Father's side as Head of the church. And we see our new identity in Him. We, who were cut off from God by

sin, are forgiven and provided with spiritual life. The power that raised Jesus from the dead fills us, lifting us out of our inadequacy and empowering us for something new. We now live in hope, because we are in constant touch with a God who has committed Himself to us.

All this is ours because of Jesus Christ. Seeing Him as the Source of our life moves Paul to expression after expression of praise.

Ephesians 2–3. In these chapters we learn that power for the new life God has given us is channeled through the community of the church. We are not to live isolated lives; we are to live in intimate relationship with other believers. To illustrate this, Paul portrayed the church as a body, a family, and a holy temple. Each of these images stressed the fact that the church is one. We are to seek, and maintain unity in order to experience together the divine power.

Living together as a body, we build one another up and grow toward maturity. As family, we find our attitudes and values changed as love becomes the touchstone of our lives. As God's temple we find our lives taking on a holiness which exposes evil for what it is. *Learning to live together as the church is the key to individual growth, love, and holiness. As we live in true fellowship with others we discover the living presence of God.* The relationship between Christ and the individual is experienced in the fellowship of the saints.

Ephesians 4–5. The practical meaning of living together as a body, family, and temple is amplified in these chapters. Living in the body means each person ministers to other members, using the spiritual gifts supplied by God and developed by gifted leaders. Living as members of the family means coming to know and care for one another deeply, expressing that care in openness, compassion, forgiveness, and a deep involvement in each

Ephesian Emphases

Chapters	Doctrine	Emphasis
1–2	Christ is exalted as Head over all.	We have life and power in Him.
2–3	The church is one body, one family, and one holy temple.	Unity is to be maintained.
4–5	The church is to learn to live as body, family, and holy temple.	We love and minister to each other and live together righteously.

others' lives. And, as we'll see, living together as a holy temple means rejecting dark things and building our commitment to goodness, righteousness, and truth. All of these are learned within the context of the new community, created and led by Christ.

Again we see it clearly. To know the living presence of Jesus, we are called to experience the fellowship of the church. In the church, the new creation of God, we each will find renewal.

Renewal as a Holy Temple: Ephesians 5:3-20

The church is a holy temple. Therefore, we are to live as God's holy people.

Here the contrast is that of night and day, darkness and light. It's as though we've passed through a pitch-black tunnel—stumbling, mired in dirt and filth—and then suddenly broken into the light. At first we're blinded by the brilliance. Then, as our eyes adjust to the shimmering glow, we realize where we are. We're in a new and different world, a world without impurity or greed or idolatry. A world of goodness, righteousness, truth, and purity. And this is how we are to live—with eyes opened to holiness, making the most of every opportunity to do God's will. What is it like, this holy life? This too is found in relationships—in the way we live with others inside and outside the church. What are the marks of holiness in contrast to the ways of darkness?

As we live in love, caring for others rather than using them, we reveal the righteousness of God and we expose evil for what it is.

How does the church expose evil? By mounting a crusade, or picketing? Hardly. *Evil is exposed by providing an example of righteousness.*

Paul put it this way: "Everything exposed by the light becomes visible, for it is light that makes everything visible" (5:13-14). As children of light, we reveal darkness for what it is. In the light shed by the holiness of God's people, evil is revealed as evil.

And so we again see the church: a body, a family, a holy temple. A *people* of God, not just individual Christians.

Individualism

In reviewing what Ephesians teaches, we see a major difference between the church and our culture. *Competitiveness* is valued by our society. We are a nation of individualists; we approach life's issues *alone*.

In school we work individually for grades, and compare with others to see whose score is highest. In sports we sometimes compete by teams, but always we keep individual statistics. In business the company that grows makes the best product, or promotes it most effectively. Each salesman works to make his quota, to be in the top for the month or year. We measure ourselves against others by our educations, our incomes, our cars, our vacations, and even by our roles in church organizations. Our society appreciates rugged individualism. The exaltation of one person above others is reflected in our ways of living together, and in our idea of what leadership

Darkness	Light
sexual immorality	goodness
impurity	righteousness
greed	truth
obscenity	thanksgiving
coarse joking	
idolatry	
drunkenness	

involves. To win, compete, excel—all these things a person does *against* the crowd.

And then we come to the church of Christ, and enter another world. Here we see a living body that "grows and builds itself up . . . as each part does its work" (4:16). Every person ministering to others is the sign of a healthy body. Not competition but cooperation is the heart of the Christian lifestyle. Even leaders are not exalted as "the" ministers, but are subordinated to the members, whom they are to serve by equipping them for *their* ministering work!

Like a family, the church is more concerned with brothers' and sisters' needs than their accomplishments. It is more committed to love than victory. Love is what Jesus showed when He gave Himself for us. "As dearly loved children," we are to "live a life of love" (5:1-2) that is just like Christ's! We are invited to surrender personal ambitions and subordinate our needs to the needs of others, being willing to give ourselves up for those who have become so dear.

Here too we see a holy temple, in which the struggle to lift ourselves above the others—to use them for our gain—is rejected in favor of goodness, righteousness, and truth.

The lifestyle of the church decisively rejects the individualism of society, and values cooperation over competition. This lifestyle does not exalt the leader over the led, but sees serving others as the highest calling. Unity leads us to abandon pride of place or position and accept each other as fully equal in the community we share. Paul portrays this new attitude in the Book of Philippians:

If you have any encouragement from being united with Christ, if any comfort from His love, if any fellowship with the Spirit, if any tenderness and compassion, then make my joy complete by being like-minded, having the same love, being one in spirit and purpose. Do nothing out of selfish ambition or vain conceit, but in humility consider others better than yourselves. Each of you should look not only to your own interests, but also to the interests of others.

Your attitude should be the same as that of Christ Jesus: Who, being in the very nature of God, did not consider equality with God something to be grasped, but made Himself nothing, taking the very nature of a servant, being made in human likeness.

And being found in appearance as a man, He humbled Himself and became obedient to death—even death on a cross!

Philippians 2:1-8

This is the new world of relationships, so dramatically different from the world of individualism we have known.

But this new world raises many questions. What about the differences in station and position that exist in society? What about the great distinctions between slaves and free, parent and child, husband and wife? How do we live our new lives in our roles in society? Do we reject social order, to affirm the unity Christ has formed within the church? Paul turns to these questions in Ephesians 5.

Submission: Ephesians 5:21

It seems strange to find Paul speaking of

submission in view of his emphasis on unity. Accept a subordinate position? We who are lifted up in Christ, made so completely equal that Paul himself insisted, "There is neither Jew nor Greek, slave nor free, male nor female, for you are all one in Christ Jesus" (Gal. 3:28).

This idea of superior/subordinate positions—of submitting within the framework of societal roles and relationships—must have troubled the early church as it does us today. In three of the New Testament letters this same issue is explored. We hear the same message from each: "Wives, submit to your husbands" (Eph. 5:22; Col. 3:18; see 1 Peter 3:1). "Children, obey your parents" (see Eph. 6:1; Col. 3:20). "Slaves, obey your earthly masters with respect and fear" (Eph. 6:5; see Col. 3:22; 1 Peter 2:18). And for all, "Submit yourselves for the Lord's sake to every authority instituted among men" (v. 13). It is in the framework of the real world of human differences and inequalities that the church's oneness is to be expressed.

How can this be? How can we experience oneness while recognizing and respecting the rights of those placed "over" us?

Mutual submission. Whenever we move into this area of authority, we tend to emphasize the "rights" of the superior to control or influence the person below. Paul immediately showed that control is not the frame of reference from which to begin. His discussion began with the command, "Submit to one another out of reverence for Christ" (Eph. 5:21). We are to maintain a humbleness that considers others—whatever their place in life—as "better than yourselves. Each of you should look not only to your own interests, but also to the interests of others" (Phil. 2:3-4). Maintaining an attitude of loving concern for one another strips authority of its "rights" and also strips submission of its humiliation. Whatever role we have been given provides an opportunity to serve our brothers and sisters in the Lord.

Mutual responsibilities. Reading through the passages in Ephesians, Colossians, and 1 Peter that deal with human relationships and societal roles, we find that *the scales are not weighted in either direction!* The child obeys parents in the Lord, but parents are not to exasperate or embitter their children. Discipline is to be distinctively Christian.

The slave is to serve wholeheartedly. But masters are to treat the slave with consideration and concern, doing what is right and fair.

Within the context of whatever role, the Christian's deep concern for others as persons is to guide and control.

Occasion to serve. The underlying thought is that authority and submission are not to be viewed as humiliation, but as *providing different opportunities to serve.* If I am a master, I serve my slaves by treating them with fairness and respect. If I am a slave, I serve my master with wholehearted loyalty.

The Christian attitude toward authority and submission is drastically opposed to the perceptions of the world, which see the one in authority as exalted, and the other as debased. There, each person's value is determined by the position he holds. But in Christ's church that whole pattern is rejected. Each persons' value exists *apart from his role.* The slave is just as important to God as the master, the child as the parent, the woman as the man. It is simply that one who is a slave has a different kind of opportunity to serve than does the master. The Christian view of authority and submission shifts the focus completely from power, to service.

🖎 Group Activity: Bible Study Group

Select one of the following statements and tell why you agree or disagree.

* *Authority is power over others.*

* *Submission is weakness.*

* *Submission is an admission of inferiority.*

* *The Christian ideal is mutual submission.*

After sharing, study the parallel passages on submission (see chart, page 428). What are the implications of (1) each person having responsibilities to the other? (2) Paul's command to "submit to one another out of reverence for Christ"?

Summarize the author's observations on submission (pp. 426-429: Submission: Ephesians 5:21 and Husband/Wife Relationships: Ephesians 5:22-33), or read the commentary section aloud.

Then describe and evaluate the way you function in your own authority/submission roles.

427

Parallel Passages on Submission

Relationship	Eph.	Col.	1 Peter*
Husband/wife	5:22-23	3:18-19	3:1-7
Parent/child	6:1-4	3:20-21	
Master/slave	6:5-9	3:22–4:1	2:18-21

*Note that Peter speaks of relationships with persons who are *not* within the church. Ephesians and Colossians speak of relationships within it.

Questions to explore
● How does each "superior" relationship provide an opportunity to serve?
● How does each "subordinate" relationship provide this opportunity?
● How might each person's attitude toward authority affect the relationship between them?

Husband/Wife Relationships: Ephesians 5:22-33

Nowhere is this concept seen more clearly than in marriage.

The pagan view. In Paul's time, pagans saw women as inferior beings, playthings for the dominant male. To be "head of the house" was to accept the common notion that authority was the male's rightful providence. Children and wives were only responsible to obey. The wife was not equal to her husband as a person, or in any other way. His needs and concerns dominated the household, and the wife existed to fulfill those needs and to serve him.

Contemporary interpretations of Ephesians 5 that describe the wife as finding total fulfillment in her relationship with her husband and household reflect the pagan, not the Christian view. So does the notion that the wife is so "under" the authority umbrella of her husband that she is not to speak or act except at his direction.

The Christian view. The Christian view is quite different. Women are seen as persons of equal worth and value. In the structure of society, men are given the role of head of the house, a role affirmed by God in this passage. But their headship is modeled on the way Christ loved the church, not on human systems of authority. This headship focuses attention on the way a "superior" is called to serve the "subordinate"! Specifically, Ephesians 5:27 portrays Christ as giving Himself up for the church "to present her to Himself as a radiant church, without

stain or wrinkle or any other blemish, but holy and blameless." In pursuit of this ministry, Christ nourishes and cares for the church. In the same way, husbands are to nurture their wives, seeking always to help the wife grow as a person and as a Christian.

What a contrast with the pagan view! Suddenly things are reversed. The wife is transformed from an unimportant adjunct, who exists only to meet her husband's needs, to a person of intrinsic worth and value, becoming the focus of her husband's concern. Instead of demanding that she live for him, he begins to live for her! Rather than keeping her under, he seeks to lift her up. Christian headship lifts the wife up as the rightful object of a husband's loving concern.

In this context, the husband serves by being a Christlike head; the wife serves in responsive submission to one who lifts her up and holds her beside him.

📖 *Group Activity: Bible Study Group*

Each person in the group should write a letter to his or her spouse, stating how he or she feels about the way authority/ submission works out in their home. The letter is to be folded and slipped into an unsealed envelope.

Hear a previously prepared lecture on Ephesians 5:22-33 contrasting the "pagan" and "Christian" views of headship in marriage.

Then discuss the following case history,

examining how the couple might deal with the situation if they held the pagan view, and then how they might deal with it if they held the view Paul explains in the Ephesians passage.

Case History

Sandra wants to go back to school for pre-med training. Her goal is to become a doctor, so she can help others, and so she can support herself and her three-year-old daughter if anything happens to Dan.

This really upsets Dan. In his family, the husband is supposed to take care of his wife. Besides, a three-year-old needs her mother. Every time Sandra mentions school, Dan gets really upset.

Sandra doesn't like housework, and feels her God-given talents are being wasted. Besides, Sandra is worried. Dan's been out of work twice in the last six years—once for nearly eight months! Deep down Sandra isn't convinced that Dan will always be able to take care of them. And she isn't about to see their daughter on welfare! Not if she can help it.

After thoroughly discussing the case history, sum up by looking at Ephesians 5:22-33 again, and restating what Paul has said about husband/wife relationships.

Then take out the letter you wrote to your spouse, and add to it. Has anything that you've studied in Ephesians suggested a change in what you've said? Deepened your convictions? Made you more uneasy about your relationship, or even more comfortable? And, if there is anything you want your spouse to consider to build more of an Ephesians 5 relationship, spell it out.

After the group meeting exchange letters, and then talk about what each of you has written.

In summary. What both Paul and Peter do in their letters is to help us realize that our place in society is irrelevant to the oneness that is to exist in the church. For the Christian, who lives to serve others, the role in which that service is offered is unimportant. Slave and master are one in Christ, lifted up and seated with Him. How foolish then to define a brother first of all as "master," and feel the alienation that "au-

thority" often creates. How foolish to think of ourselves as unimportant if our role is that of "slave." How useless to bridle against being a woman, as though it were better to be a man! How foolish, when we are all members of one body, one family, living stones in that holy temple constructed by the Lord. How freeing it is to realize that my worth and value as a person rests on who I am in Christ, and that my position in the world simply defines my opportunities to serve.

The Devils' Schemes: Ephesians 6:10-20

Paul concludes this letter with a warning. Satan is actively struggling against God. All his energies are focused on shattering the unity of the church. The enemy will attempt to cripple the body, to introduce dissension into the family, and to corrupt the holy temple. Against the enemy's attacks God has equipped us with His own armor: "The full armor of God so that you can take your stand against the devil's schemes" (v. 11).

Many different interpretations of the armor have been given, and its equivalents in the panoply of the Roman soldier of Paul's day have been discussed. But what is most important has often been overlooked: Paul here describes *the armor which enables us to stand against attacks on our life together as Christ's new community.* Viewed from this perspective, what are the divine resources we have been given?

The belt of truth. Put off falsehood and speak truthfully to your neighbor, Paul has warned, for we are all members of one body (4:25). Openness and honesty gird us together; misunderstanding and hidden motives divide.

The breastplate of righteousness. "There must not be even a hint of sexual immorality, or of any kind of impurity, or of greed" (5:3) among God's holy people. Righteous living is essential, guarding the very heart of our shared lives.

Feet fitted with the Gospel of peace. More than once in this letter Paul has stressed how the Gospel brings peace, reconciling us to God and making us one. In Ephesians, peace is the bond that holds the unity created by the Spirit. When unity is maintained, Christ's church is enabled to move in full responsiveness to its Head.

The shield of faith. We maintain a confi-

429

dent hope in the reality and power of God. This trust extinguishes doubt. We are inadequate in ourselves, yes. But our trust is in God, who "is able to do immeasurably more than all we ask or imagine, according to His power that is at work in us" (3:20).

The helmet of salvation. Salvation has brought us a new life and identity. By keeping our identity as Christ's living church constantly before us, our perception of life is transformed. Satan's dreams of distorted relationships cannot cloud the mind of a person who grasps the full meaning of the salvation we enjoy in Christ.

The Spirit's sword. Why does Paul explain here that the sword is "the Word of God"? (6:17) It is because, in all of Ephesians, Paul has not discussed Scripture as he has the other elements of our armor. This vital tool is needed for us to wage our spiritual warfare.

And, in it all, on all occasions, we need prayer.

GROUP RESOURCE GUIDE

Identification: *Share with others*
Complete the following sentence: "I feel closest to others in our group when. . . . " After all have shared, discuss: What builds and maintains the unity that is so important to God and to us?

Exploration: *Probe God's Word*
The "devil's schemes" are designed to destroy the unity Jesus' people need to function as a body, a family, and a holy temple. In Ephesians 6:10-20 Paul uses the figure of a heavily armored soldier to sum up what he has been teaching in this NT book.

Divide into teams, each of which is to take one of the following:
* the belt of truth
* the breastplate of righteousness
* feet fitted with the Gospel of peace
* the shield of faith
* the helmet of salvation

Each team is to read through Ephesians to find references or allusions to topics such as "truth," "righteousness," etc. (Note: if not clear on the topic involved, see Commentary.)

After locating allusions, each team is to study the context and determine how this theme is related to maintaining Christian unity, and be ready to report to the group.

Reaction: *Respond together to the Word*
Do an evaluation of your own group. Is God's armor fully on? Are some parts slipping? How can you strengthen your relationships and better be body, family, and holy temple in Christ?

Adoration: *Worship and pray*
Praise God as your protector against Satan and his schemes.

CALLED TO JOY

Overview

This brief, warm letter was written to Philippi from Rome in early A.D. 63. Paul was especially close to the church in this, the leading city in Macedonia. His letter, rather than a reasoned exposition or corrective of a local error, is simply an expression of friendship and of shared joy in a common faith.

Three things seem particularly special about this short letter. First, its key word is "joy." "Joy" and "rejoice" occur again and again, and suggest a helpful strategy for the book's study.

Second, Philippians contains one of the most powerful New Testament affirmations of Christ's deity and lordship. Jesus who was God from eternity emptied Himself to become a man and, after suffering death, was raised again to His original glory and given a name above every name: Lord.

Third, Paul shared his own personal goal in life—his yearning for a present experience of that transformation which will be his at the resurrection.

How great an opportunity we have, to teach this short, but warm and powerful review of what we Christians have in Christ.

▶ **Joy.** Old Testament terms cast joy in terms of the worshiping community's response to God. Relationship with Him is the key to joy. The key New Testament term (*chairo*) indicates both a state of joy, and that which brings us joy.

Commentary

The New Testament makes it abundantly plain. It is relationship with Jesus that is a vital source of our joy. Jesus Himself spoke of two ways that we might find joy in Him. He said, "If you obey My commands, you will remain in My love, just as I have obeyed My Father's commands and remain in His love. I have told you this so that My joy may

be in you and that your joy may be complete" (John 15:10-11). And, "Until now you have not asked for anything in My name. Ask and you will receive, and your joy will be complete" (16:24).

As we go on we make other discoveries about joy. We see that it is produced in us by the Holy Spirit, and is a fruit of His presence (see Luke 10:21; Gal. 5:22; 1 Thes. 1:6). It is not linked with material possessions but rather is an overflow of salvation (Acts 8:8; 16:34).

Even persecution could not dampen the joy that glowed in early Christians, for their joy was not dependent on external circumstances (see Acts 13:52; 2 Cor. 7:4; James 1:2). Peter even said that "in this [salvation] you greatly rejoice, though now for a little while you may have had to suffer grief in all kinds of trials. These have come so that your faith—of greater worth than gold, which perishes even though refined by fire—may be proved genuine and may result in praise, glory, and honor when Jesus Christ is revealed" (1 Peter 1:6-7).

It is true that even pagans can know joy, as they find it in the good things that God has given to all human beings so liberally. But the Christian knows a heightened joy; a joy that is rooted in the bond that exists between the believer and the Lord, and the bond that exists with other believers whom we have come to love (see Rom. 16:19; Phil. 1:4, 25-26; 2:2, 29; 4:1; Heb. 13:17; 1 John 1:4). The deeper our relationship with Jesus and with His people, the greater the joy that awaits us, and the less that joy is dependent on external circumstances.

Who is Jesus? Philippians 2:1-13

To understand why Jesus is the key to joy, we must grasp who Jesus is. Paul, in a great and powerful affirmation of faith, made Christ's true identity perfectly clear. Many believe that the words in Philippians 2:5-11 are from an early Christian liturgy, used as a confession of faith in the churches which Paul founded.

Jesus is our example (Phil. 2:1-5). Paul looked with awe at Jesus' willing surrender of the prerogatives of Deity to become a human being, and to die for us on a cross. But the self-sacrifice of Jesus is also a powerful call to the believer. Those of us who look to Jesus as our Saviour are also to look to Him as our example! In fact, our "attitude should be the same as that of Christ Jesus."

When we adopt His attitude, there will be a dramatic impact on our relationships with others. We will be "like-minded." What Paul envisions here is a *community* of believers who model their personal relationships with each other on Jesus. Such a community will be united, having "the same love," and being one in spirit and purpose (v. 2). Our unity will not be based on having the same convictions (see Rom. 14–15), or even on holding exactly the same doctrines (see 1 Corinthians 8–10). Ours will be a unity that grows out of love; out of a Christlike attitude.

Paul then looked at how that attitude is expressed in individuals. It is expressed by doing "nothing out of selfish ambition or vain conceit, but in humility consider others better than yourselves. Each of you should look not only to your own interests, but also to the interests of others" (Phil. 2:3-4). It is this total unselfishness that we see exhibited so powerfully by Jesus. He did not "grasp at" His equality with God. He "made Himself nothing" to come to earth as a human being— a Servant. Here He even humbled Himself to the extent that He willingly died a criminal's death. And all for us.

If you and I have this attitude toward our brothers and sisters in Jesus, there *will* be Christian unity. And we will truly be one, in spirit and purpose. We, like Jesus, will live to serve. And in serving we, like Jesus, will find the way of exaltation.

♥ Group Activity: Support Group

Write down the names of others in your support group. By each name write one way in which that person surpasses you, and one need or concern he or she has.

Together study Philippians 2:6-11, and sum up: What does this tells us about Jesus' attitude toward Himself and others? Check your results against 2:1-5, in which Paul shows how Christ's attitude is to infuse our relationships.

Now go around the group, focusing on one person at a time. Each person is to tell the individual under consideration what superiorities he or she sees, and the concern he or she listed. Afterward the individual under consideration can respond, especially sharing any burdens the others may not be aware of. This process when completed will give you a good check on the depth of relationships in your group—and go a long way toward strengthening them.

Finally read and consider Philippians 2:12-13. We can work out our own problems together, guided by God, as long as we are bonded together by the love and attitude displayed by Jesus.

This, of course, was part of Paul's total vision. Because Jesus humbled Himself, God the Father exalted Him—"to the highest place" (v. 9). For us as well as for Jesus, the way *up* is down. For us, as for Jesus, God exalts us when we humble ourselves in service of others.

Jesus is God (Phil. 2:6-11). This is the foundational truth in Christianity. In this confession the early church affirmed the pre-existence of Jesus as God, affirmed His incarnation as a true human being, affirmed His death on the cross, His resurrection and His coming again to be revealed as Lord of all.

We should note that the phrase stating Jesus was "found in appearance as a man" does *not* imply that Christ only *seemed* to be a human being. The Greek word here is *schema*, which lays stress on what was visible to the beholder. The Son of God was seen by men to be a man, and He truly was what He appeared to be: one of us.

What a passage for meditation today as we remember our Lord, and focus our thoughts on who He is—and how much He has done for us. For this is One:

Who, being in very nature God, did not consider equality with God something to be grasped, but made Himself nothing, taking the very nature of a servant, being made in human likeness. And being found in appearance as a man, He humbled Himself and became obedient to death—even death on a cross! Therefore God exalted Him to the highest place and gave Him a name that is above every name, that at the name of Jesus every knee should bow, in heaven and on earth and under the earth, and every tongue confess that Jesus Christ is Lord, to the glory of God the Father.

Jesus is the source of our salvation (Phil. 2:12-13). Paul concluded with an exhortation to the Philippians to continue obeying his instructions, as they had. In this way they were to "work out your salvation with fear and trembling, for it is God who works in you to will and to act according to His good purpose."

This call to "work out your ['own,' as some versions have it] salvation" has troubled some. They have seen it as a demand to perform, or perhaps salvation will be lost. But this is not what Paul is suggesting here.

The word commonly translated "salvation" does look at personal salvation, in the Christian sense of salvation from sin. But that salvation has several aspects. There is the initial forgiveness won through faith in Jesus. There is present deliverance from the dominating power of sin in our lives. And there is ultimate salvation; deliverance from even the presence of sin when resurrection day arrives.

Here the word "therefore" links Paul's words with what had been said before. And Paul had been speaking to the Philippians about a unity to be found by adopting the attitude of Jesus—a unity which 4:2-3 tells us was at least strained in the local body.

What Paul was saying, then, is that the church is to work out (to express) in their lives together the deliverance which Jesus has won for them, and is to do this with a proper sense of awe, realizing that God Himself was at work within them, present to will and act according to His good purpose.

As the Christians at Philippi modeled on Christ, and adopted His attitude, they would find deliverance from the things that divided them and would in fact give visible expression, together, to the salvation that was theirs in Jesus Christ.

Yes, the Jesus we worship truly is God. And, as the God-Man, Jesus set us an example, showing us the attitude which is the key to Christian unity, and is also the key to expressing in our fellowships the salvation which is ours in Him.

Paul's Personal Goal: Philippians 3

If there was ever a man who was deeply aware of his need to experience the present-tense salvation referred to in 2:12-13, it was the Apostle Paul.

Paul's later ministry, expressed in this book and in Colossians and Ephesians, increasingly focused on the present impact of Jesus on His church. Toward the end of Paul's life, arrests grew more frequent. He spent an increasing amount of time in prison. With less and less personal contact with the congregations he founded, Paul kept in touch through correspondence, friends, and disciples such as Timothy and Titus. Paul watched as the early flush of excitement and expectancy was tempered by the sober necessity of living in a hostile world. Challenges to the faith were raised. Some wanted to blend the philosophies of paganism or the ritualism of Judaism with the new Way. Clearly the church needed a better understanding of its uniqueness. The Good News of God's action in the past and His promise for the future must not obscure the fact that God *is,* and that "the present time is of the utmost importance" (Rom. 13:11, PH).

So Paul's prison letters turned the attention of believers to Christ Himself and to an exploration of what it means to live as members of Christ's body.

In Philippians Paul shared a very personal testimony. Centering his own attention on Jesus, Paul spoke of his own present experience—and his daily goal in life. He is one of those who:

Glory in Christ Jesus, and who put no confidence in the flesh—though I myself have reasons for such confidence.

If anyone else thinks he has reasons to put confidence in the flesh, I have more: circumcised on the eighth day, of the people of Israel, of the tribe of Benjamin, a Hebrew of Hebrews; in regard to the Law, a Pharisee; as for zeal, persecuting the church; as for legalistic righteousness, faultless.

But whatever was to my profit, I now consider loss for the sake of Christ.

What is more, I consider everything a loss compared to the surpassing greatness of knowing Christ Jesus my Lord, for whose sake I have lost all things. I consider them rubbish, that I may gain Christ and be found in Him, not having a righteousness of my own that comes from the Law; but that which is through faith in Christ—the righteousness that comes from God and is by faith. I want to know Christ and the power of His resurrection and the fellowship of sharing in His sufferings, becoming like Him in His death, and so, somehow, to attain to the resurrection from the dead.

Philippians 3:3-11

Paul's deeply personal desire, expressed here, is not a yearning for some distant future. Paul concentrates instead on his *ongoing daily experience with God,* an experience that can lift the endless repetition of emptiness, and give life vitality and meaning. To understand, we need to note several of Paul's themes here.

Knowing Christ (Phil. 3:8). Paul focused here on relationship; on a personal experience of Jesus Christ that deepens as the days pass. This is Paul's first goal.

Having righteousness (Phil. 3:9). Again Paul was not looking ahead. Paul was concerned about moral transformation *now.* We Christians are to experience a holiness, rooted not in the do's and don'ts approach of Law, but in a dynamic goodness that only divine power can bring.

Resurrection power (Phil. 3:10). It is easy to misread these words. Paul was not referring to the future resurrection promised to believers. Paul spoke later of that time (vv. 20-21). Here Paul expressed his deep yearning to experience God's resurrection power.

Paul had expressed this earlier, in Romans. "He who raised Christ from the dead will also give life to your mortal bodies through His Spirit, who lives in you" (Rom. 8:11). But Paul had not yet arrived at a full experience of that power (Phil. 3:12). The daily goal that Paul set for himself was a fuller experience of Christ's resurrection life, bringing vitality and power to his present.

Reading Paul's words, we become aware that life does have meaning. In Christ we too are called heavenward (v. 14). We are invited to know the touch of a God who is always present. We are invited to a deepening personal relationship with Jesus; to a growing and dynamic righteousness; and to an experience of power that can transform us and our lives. What a goal for you and me—and our group members—to adopt. What examples we have, first in Jesus, and now in Paul.

✂ *Group Activity: Recovery Group Step 1 (admit powerlessness)*
It's common to rely on props that hide the fact of our inadequacy. In the first century men called Judaisers followed Paul around and tried to convince his converts they needed to keep the O.T. law in order to be good Christians—and that only by doing so could they please God. In other words, these men taught we have to rely on our own efforts. But Paul knew that all these things were props that merely papered over man's helplessness, and made it easier to fool ourselves about our powerlessness.

Study Philippians 3:2-6 and make a list of the props that Paul himself once used. When this is done, privately make a list of the props that you have used to hide your powerlessness from yourself and others. Share your personal list with the others, and together make a master list of modern props people use to help them pretend their lives are not unmanageable.

Then discuss: Why don't the props work? How do we know, despite the props, that we really can't make it on our own? And, What does it take to make us admit we are powerless and that our lives are out of control?

Conclude by reading and talking about Philippians 3:7-11. Paul exchanged his useless props, which he now calls "rubbish," for a righteousness and resurrection power that come from God. Why not admit helplessness, and exchange your props for God's gifts right now?

The Search for Joy: Philippians
As noted at the beginning of this commentary, the theme of "joy" is woven throughout this small New Testament book. This theme probably should guide us in our teaching, as we help our group members examine what it is that can bring believer's inner joy.

Sources of joy in Philippians 1. Paul was in prison, his chains restricting him to a small rented house in Rome. The apostle, whose life had been dedicated to establishing churches by traveling to the key cities in the Roman Empire, had been set aside.

Yet as Paul wrote to the Philippians we sense the warmth of his love, and we also sense a confidence and joy. Paul reached the most distant lands by prayer, and was reassured about his converts by his conviction that "He who began a good work in you will carry it on to completion until the day of Christ Jesus" (v. 6). But there were other sources of confidence as well. Though in chains, Paul had the opportunity of witnessing to the Praetorian guards assigned to watch him. And Paul heard that others, stimulated by his imprisonment, had become more zealous in preaching the Gospel.

In verses 4-5 Paul speaks of praying "with joy" for the Philippians "because of your partnership in the Gospel from the first day until now." This was not a sharing in salvation, but rather partnership in spreading the Gospel. Paul and the Philippians had a common concern for communicating the Gospel to the lost.

In fact, this theme is expressed again and again in the first chapter. Even Paul's imprisonment should have been gladly accepted by his friends because "what has happened to me has really served to advance the Gospel" (v. 12).

Paul's chains stimulated some to speak out more courageously. But others, who saw Paul as a rival, had increased their own missionary effort out of "selfish ambition." Paul was glad, for from whatever motives "Christ is preached" (v. 8), and "because of this I rejoice."

In this first chapter, then, Paul presented sharing the Gospel as a basic source of Christian joy. As we reach out to others with the Good News of Jesus we too will discover, with Paul and the Philippians, an overflow of Spirit-produced inner joy.

Ø Group Activity:
Missions/Outreach Group
In Philippians 1:12-29 Paul puts his imprisonment in unique perspective. What might seem a tragedy, setting him on the shelf, has actually turned out to have advanced the promotion of the Gospel! Study the passage carefully to determine how this "setback" has had unexpected consequences.

God often uses setbacks, and personal troubles to advance the Gospel. Take time out to review your own lives, the history of your mission, or your group's outreach efforts. What setbacks or troubles have you experienced? How has God used them in promoting the Gospel?

Let this review of your individual and group experience reassure you, even as Paul reassured the Philippians. God is sovereignly at work in our every experience, constantly shaping our lives as instruments for sharing Christ's good news.

Sources of joy in Philippians 2. Paul now looked to other believers and viewed them as a source of joy. Paul's joy would be complete when the Philippians adopted Christ's attitude and were "like-minded, having the same love, being one in spirit" (v. 2).

Paul next used an Old Testament image. He saw himself and his own likely execution as a "drink offering" poured out on a sacrifice. This drink offering was voluntary, and intended to add its own rich savor to the basic sacrifice. Paul viewed his coming death not as loss, but as a joyful service he willingly offered on behalf of all who had come to Christ through him. And Paul urged the Philippians not to be upset, but rather to rejoice with him that he has been privileged to give himself for their sake.

Finally, Paul spoke of being "glad" (rejoicing) in the recovery of a messenger from Philippi, who had been extremely ill.

Throughout this chapter, the focus is not so much on the Gospel itself as on those who have responded to the Gospel. And the joy Paul spoke of wells up from being able to serve others, and from seeing God at work in others' lives.

Sources of joy in Philippians 4. Finally Paul spoke of a joy that is ours in the Lord Himself. He told us to "rejoice in the Lord always. I will say it again: Rejoice!"

And Paul went on to tell us how we can experience joy in knowing Jesus. We are to remember that the Lord is near, and rather than being anxious are to present every need to Him with thanksgiving. As we do, God's own peace will fill us. And, to keep our hearts and minds fixed on the Lord we are to focus on whatever is true and noble,

435

putting our faith in Jesus into practice, and thus experience God with us.

❋ *Group Activity:*
Singles/Single Again Group
It's good to share personal struggles with others who understand. It's good to gain insights from other Singles' experiences.
But there are also some universal, basic principles that Singles can apply in any situation.
List three significant problems you've had to face as a single this past year. Then without sharing them, look together at Philippians 4:4-9. Create a two-column chart, on the left listing every active verb, which tells us what to do. Against these on the right list the results of doing what Paul exhorts.
Be thorough and analyze the passage carefully.
Then in groups of three, share the "significant problems" you listed. Talk about how you dealt with them. Then together look at the chart of Philippians 4:4-9 you've created. How would (or did!) applying any of the advice Paul gives relate to each situation? How would (or did) it help you come through the situation more successfully?
When each has had a chance to share and relate this passage to his or her personal life, come back together. Discuss: Which advice is most important to you as a single? And why?

GROUP RESOURCE GUIDE

Identification: *Share with others*
Brainstorm things that most people think will make them happy. Then briefly share: How have you personally experienced either the possession or lack of these things?

Exploration: *Probe God's Word*
Together go through Philippians and underline or circle each occurrence of "joy" or "rejoice" in the book. Then divide into teams. Each team will explore either chapter 1, chapter 2, or chapter 4 to isolate the sources of the joy that Paul speaks of so frequently.

Reaction: *Respond together to the Word*
Have copies of the "Happiness vs. Joy"

chart for each person (page 436). As each team reports fill in the "joy" column with the sources of joy which Paul tapped. Feel free to ask questions of the reporting team(s) so you fully understand what is in their chapter.
Then together complete the "What we can do" column by suggesting ways that you, individually or as a group, can experience joy from these same sources.

Adoration: *Worship and pray*
Offer personal testimony of your experiences of joy through these, or other, spiritual sources. Close with a time of praise, that God is a God who fills us with a joy that is vital and real despite our circumstances.

Happiness vs. Joy

Happy	Joy	What We Can *Do*
Money Security Nice home Success	chap. 1 sharing in Gospel Christ preached	
Health Love Friends Leisure Travel	chap. 2 other believers sacrifice self for others	
Family etc.	chap. 4 Lord Himself	

A NEW HUMANITY

Overview

This brief but significant letter reflects a challenge raised by false philosophical systems that attempted to infiltrate and distort Christianity in its early centuries. This system, known as Gnosticism, is known in its developed form from second-century writings. Its basic tenets are confronted here by the Apostle Paul.

The Gnostics claimed a special, hidden knowledge not available to ordinary Christians. But their beliefs in fact contradicted basic Bible truths!

In responding to the challenge Paul powerfully affirmed basic tenets of the biblical faith. He made it clear just what God is like, who Jesus is, how we come to know God, and how we can experience a vital spiritual life through relationship with the Lord. The book can be outlined quite simply.

Paul wrote this letter while in Rome in prison, and sent it in A.D. 62 or 63.

Outline

■ For a discussion of background and a verse-by-verse commentary on key concepts developed in Colossians, see the Victor *Bible Knowledge Commentary*, pages 667-686.

Commentary

Two of the most powerful words in advertising, I've been told, are *new* and *free*.

When the Gospel message echoed across the first-century world, both these elements were emphasized. "It is by grace you have been saved, through faith—and this not from yourselves, it is the gift of God—not by works" (Eph. 2:8-9). The Gospel is free! And, God created one "new man out of the two" [Jew and Gentile], thus making peace" (v. 15). The Gospel brings that which is refreshingly new!

Suddenly all the old categories men used to define themselves, and the old ways they attempted to understand the world and their relationship to the divine, were shattered. The new had come. Commenting on Colossians 3:11, Ralph Martin (in *Colossians: The Church's Lord and the Christian's Liberty* [Zondervan]) observes:

> In the society of Christians a new type of humanity is being formed. Christ's life flows out to His people and is reproduced in their midst. One proof of this new life was seen in the canceling of restrictions and inhibitions which made the ancient world so socially stratified and class-conscious. Paul had shown how in the church barriers of race, social distinction, and sex were being broken down as Christians acted on their baptismal profession of initiation into the body.

But many in the ancient world struggled against the idea of "new." They were attracted to the church but tried to adjust Christ to fit their old categories. They tried to define Christianity in terms of their human philosophies rather than letting Christ define them as a new humanity.

We have the same problem. We have seen that the church is a living organism. Yet today we still persist in diagramming its structure as a business rather than a body. The leadership is called to equip members of the body. Yet all too many Christians view the pastoral staff as men hired to do the teaching and evangelism that is the body's ministry.

We see in the New Testament that a dynamic holiness is to mark the character of believers, and the believing community. And yet we persist in trying to define our righteousness by lists of things we do and things we don't. Constantly the temptation is to push and squeeze the totally new into the old and familiar ways. In Christ, the *new* has come, and in the church—God's new humanity—we find a life that calls us to a fulfillment that can be found only in Christ's completely different way!

Understanding this, it is not too surprising to discover that in the once-important center of Colossae, the church was being drained of power by a group of men who claimed advanced knowledge (*gnosis*) but were attempting to fit Christianity into an old and empty philosophic system: the Gnostic way.

Not until the middle of the second century did the church fathers combat a developed form of Gnosticism. Yet most scholars see the terms Paul uses in Colossians and the concerns he deals with as indicating the presence of this heresy in Colossae. These Gnostics were concerned about issues explored by people of all ages:

- What is God like and what is His relationship to the world?
- How does a human being gain access to God's true presence?
- How does the human being find fullness of spiritual life?

Gnosticism not only posed these questions, but claimed to answer them. When a local congregation formed at Colossae, early Gnostics hurried in to redefine Christ and the Gospel in their own terms.

What is God like? The Gnostics were dualists. They saw all things in terms of two contrasting principles. On the one side was good, which was associated with the spiritual and the immaterial. On the other side was evil, which was associated with the material universe. God Himself was perfectly good, spiritual, and totally disassociated from the material. He would not pollute Himself by any such contact! The material universe was an accident or, at worst, the error of the last of a long series of supernatural beings—intermediaries—ranked between God and matter. To God, the pure Spirit, the world was alien and despicable.

To the Gnostics how jolting was the idea of an Incarnation! God become man? God take on human flesh? Never! Christ must be a lower intermediary or an "appearance"—a shadow of God cast on a screen. But God in human flesh? Unthinkable!

It was also unthinkable that God might wish to enter believers' lives. Instead the Gnostics saw the human being as trapped; a spark of the divine held captive in a fleshly prison. Salvation meant release from bondage to all that was material, including our own bodies! Resurrection? God's life, lived out in a corporate body shaped of loving men and women, in whom Christ now walks this world? Ugly! Horrible!

How does a human being gain access to God? The Gnostic saw God as remote and inaccessible. God might be approached through the long chain of intermediaries that stretched between Him and matter. Jesus Christ might even be one of these intermediaries. But since Jesus had contact with this world, Christ's rank within the chain must be low. Here is a partial explanation of Paul's reference to the worship of angels (Col. 2:18): people were striving to gain the attention and support of beings who form a chain leading to God. These powerful spirits should be placated, the Gnostics taught, for human destiny lay in their hands, not in God's.

How does a human being find fullness of life? The Gnostics said, by practicing the way of life they propounded. That way of life stressed asceticism and rigid regulations, abstinence and self-punishment. For liberation from the evil, fleshly body must be good. The angelic intermediaries were honored by ritual and self-discipline. In this way, the fullness might be found.

So some at Colossae were imposing this approach to spirituality on the church there. And Paul wrote this letter to refute the false teaching that warped both faith and Christian experience.

God's Way: Colossians 1–2

The Gospel of Christ simply did not fit the Gnostic's categories, which were drawn from well-known philosophies of that time. Only a drastic reordering of these old categories enables the believer to grasp the fantastic new hope held out to man. The body of Christ—the new and living organism of which you and I are a part—is at the heart of that newness. Christ living in His body forms the new humanity, and transforms us

Gnostic Way Versus God's Way

Gnostic Way dualistic	God's Way in Colossians
"good" "evil" spiritual material divine nondivine to know to do There is no contact between these two systems. *Christ*—a lower intermediary or an appearance. *Man*—a divine spark imprisoned in an evil, material body. *Salvation*—freedom from the evil, material prison. *Way of salvation*—found through special knowledge, asceticism, and honoring angelic intermediaries. *Individual morality*—ascetic self-denial of needs, drives, desires, and appetites. *True religion*—subjective, speculative. Escape to a realm in which the material plays no part. *Angels*—powers between God and men who must be honored and used as access to the fullness.	

as well as all our old ideas about life. So the Book of Colossians not only challenged the people to whom it was addressed; it challenges us now. Am I able to set aside my old ways of thinking about spirituality and to enter joyfully into the new?

Commendation (Col. 1:1-8). As always, Paul began with a commendation. The Colossians' lives were marked by love for all the saints. God's Gospel had taken root among them, and was growing and producing fruit.

Concern (Col. 1:9-14). At the same time, Paul had a deep concern for this church, a concern he expressed in his prayer. Paul was eager that God would fill the Colossians "with the knowledge of His will through all spiritual wisdom and understanding" (v. 9), that through knowing God's will their lives might be worthy of Him.

Paul was eager that growth, good works, and empowerment might be theirs. He was eager that they experience fully what it meant to live *now* in the kingdom of God's Son.

✂ *Group Activity: Recovery Group*
Step 11 (improve relationship with God through prayer and meditation)
At times celebration needs to take precedence over self-examination in recovery groups. Key this celebration to Colossians 1:13: "He has rescued us from the dominion of darkness and brought us into the kingdom of the Son He loves."

Share the "then" and "now" contrast that Christ has made in your life since you've turned yourself over to Him. After all have shared, bring out snacks and treats and have a party! Congratulate each other when this is appropriate, and conclude with a time of praise to God for the light you enjoy in the kingdom of His Son.

Who Jesus is (Col. 1:15-23). The kingdom is Christ's. Clearly then, we must grasp who Jesus is. In this passage, which was possibly adapted from early liturgy, Paul contradicts every Gnostic category!

- Jesus is the express "image of the invisible God" (v. 15). He is not some distant, inferior reflection.
- Jesus is the direct Creator of all things in the material and spiritual universe—even of the angelic hosts. By Him and for Him everything was made (vv. 16-17). Clearly God and the material universe are not at odds!
- Jesus is Head of the body, and He is supreme in everything (v. 18). The fullness of God resides in Him alone (v. 19).
- In a real Incarnation—in Christ's physical body through death—God *has* reconciled us, bringing us into His very presence. In Christ we are "holy in His sight, without blemish and free from accusation" (vv. 20-22). In fact *spiritual effects are accomplished in the physical body.* Again, our life in this world and our life with God are not at odds, but harmonize.

Paul concluded that the Colossians should continue in their faith, "established and firm, not moved from the hope held out in the Gospel" (v. 23). In this way they would experience the reality of being new men and women in Christ. Christ is the sole focus, the center, and to understand newness, we must keep our lives centered in Him.

Mystery (Col. 1:24-29). Paul now showed that his ministry was to help the saints grasp this great mystery. No knowledge is hidden, as the Gnostics claim. All has been revealed, even the great secret that "Christ is *in you,* bringing with Him the hope of all the glorious things to come" (v. 27, PH).

In Christ (Col. 2:1-15). Here Paul appealed to the Colossians to realize that Christianity calls us to live our present life "in Christ." This involves not only reliance on the Head, but also participation in the body (vv. 6-7). In being joined to Christ by the Spirit's baptizing work (v. 12, see also 1 Cor. 12:13), we were so completely united to Him that we experienced not only His death but also His resurrection. Having thus been made alive with Christ (Col. 2:13), we are freed to live a resurrection kind of life *now.* Christ's death canceled and made irrelevant all the old things that once cluttered life and opposed us (v. 15). Life is now the issue; our sole goal is to live Jesus' life in this world.

God's new humanity (Col. 2:16-23). How empty the rigorous life the Gnostics proposed! Keep regulations. Worship higher powers. Eat this. Don't eat that. Strictly observe rituals and taboos. In Paul's judgment, "Such regulations indeed have an appearance of wisdom, with their self-imposed worship, their false humility and their harsh treatment of the body, but they lack any value in restraining sensual indulgence" (vv. 22-23).

Paul's point is that while such self-discipline may limit expression of certain kinds of sins, the sin nature will still find occasion to express itself—as in spiritual pride.

The person groping for a touch of God loses connection with Christ when he or she focuses on the shadows of human effort. That taste of true spirituality, for which we all yearn, is found in relationship with Jesus Christ as Head of a living body. It is from the Head that "the whole body, supported and held together by its ligaments and sinews, grows as God causes it to grow" (v. 19).

And so both Colossians and Ephesians emphasize that the church as Christ's living body is the key to understanding—and becoming—God's new humanity.

What is God like, and what is His relationship to the world? God *is* Jesus, Creator and Sustainer of all things visible and invisible. And God walks the world today in that body of which Christ is living Head.

How does a human being gain access to God's true presence? By the reconciliation won through Christ's blood and death and by intimate relationship with others who have life through Jesus.

How does a human being find fullness of life? That question will be answered as we finish our study of Colossians by examining chapter 3.

The Threat

Gnosticism in the early church was no harmless alternative to faith. It challenged the very core of living faith by attempting to set Jesus aside, and make Him something less than the center of our lives. Gnosticism also attempted to set the body of Christ aside, by raising many objections to oneness. Love and caring became less important than fulfilling rituals. Unity was displaced in favor of hierarchy, not only in the spirit world but also in the church. Those with "special hidden knowledge"—the Gnostics—were at the top. Next were those whose rigid adherence to rituals and other religious duties made them "more spiritual" than the herd. The attitude that calls us to "consider others better than ourselves" (Phil. 2:3) gave way to rank and pride. Living with other believers in harmony and peace was set aside as unimportant.

Gnosticism also rejected the concept that the Christian's calling *is* to live in this world. The kingdom was viewed as far-off, and spiritual. Good works were ridiculed. After all, the world is the corrupt dwelling place of sin. Only by withdrawing could one find a touch of the divine. The kind of commitment Jesus knew—to walk and talk and love a band of sweaty men as the perspiration poured down His own back—was unknown to the Gnostics. The idea that Jesus, through His body on earth, might desire to touch the filthy among sin-warped humanity was foreign to their thought. (Sometimes it is foreign to us as well!)

Yet a study of the Gnostics against whom Paul wrote is helpful to us. It raises questions that each of us need to face.

Where do we center our faith? In Jesus, or in the practice of religion?

Where do we place our priorities? On knowing and loving each other as members of one body? Or have other things intruded and led us to build our own hierarchies and establish our own little rules: rules that enable us to keep our brothers at arm's length and to feel better than they?

And, where do we see our calling? Are we simply to worship, in some cloister set apart from the world? Or are we to *be* God's kingdom now, and reach out to touch the poor and the lost?

"He has rescued us," Paul wrote to the Colossians (1:13). Rescued, we are the new humanity. Old categories no longer fit, and we cannot define ourselves by them. To discover who we are, we must submit all thoughts to Christ.

GROUP RESOURCE GUIDE

Exploration: *Probe God's Word*
Each person needs a copy of the Gnostic Way versus God's Way chart (p. 439). One person should have previously prepared to explain each note on Gnosticism (see Commentary). When each has a general understanding of Gnostic tenets, divide into teams of four or five. Each team will study Colossians 1 and 2 to find the biblical view on each theme.

When teams have finished, regather and go over discoveries. In cases of uncertainty, see the Commentary for discussion of significant verses.

Identification: *Share with others*
Paul's point is that the spiritual always finds expression in our everyday life in this present world. This happened with Christ in Creation and Incarnation (1:15-18) and in the salvation Jesus won on the cross (1:19-23). And it is to happen with us (2:13-23). We do not win spiritual points by religious acts: the new spiritual life God has given us expresses itself in a righteous life that flows from the change within.

Go around the group sharing how your own spiritual experience has affected your choices, your interests and activities, and your actions.

Adoration: *Worship and pray*
Consider the Cross, through which Jesus reconciled us to God and made the differences in your life which you have just spoken of. Worship the Christ of Calvary, and praise Him for the sacrifice which brings us new life.

441

Colossians 3–4

A NEW LIFE TO LIVE

Overview

In the first two chapters of this Bible book, Paul set out truths which contradict the notions of those later known as Gnostics. This heresy taught that the material was evil, and the immaterial good. God, good and spiritual, was isolated from the universe in which we live by His own moral character and nature. Jesus, in this system, was either an unreal shadow or a lower-order of angelic being.

Paul directly confronted this view. Jesus is God in the flesh. And it was in His real human body through death in that body that Jesus accomplished the greatest of all spiritual tasks: our redemption. What is more, Jesus Himself is the Creator of both material and immaterial worlds, and holds authority over each. We Christians find our fulfillment in Jesus and in relationship with Him. There is no "higher knowledge" than knowing Jesus, and no spiritual secrets that are not unveiled in Him.

Now, in Colossians 3, Paul applied these basic truths to our Christian lives. Spirituality is not withdrawal from this world, but is living Jesus' life *in* the world. What a privilege to help our group members discover the characteristics of true spirituality, and to help each see how he or she can live in intimate union with Jesus.

▶ *Holiness.* New Testament holiness involves joyful commitment to God and to good, expressed in all we say and do.

Commentary

A famous preacher of an earlier day wrote a book about his early search for a full life in Christ. He told of his struggle for holiness — hours of prayer for purification from selfishness and wrong desires. He told how he guarded his every word and action, struggling to bring them into conformity with God's will.

Finally exhausted by the pursuit, he contracted TB and spent a year in a sanitarium. There he met a young woman of his denomination who was recuperating from the same disease. She seemed so tranquil and pure. He watched her for weeks and became convinced that she had found the secret that eluded him. One night as he struggled in prayer, he felt he could wait no longer. He rose to find her, determined to ask for the way to peace.

Before he could leave, there was a knock on his door. There she stood, her face contorted as her body shook with sobs. "Brother Harry," she gasped. "I've watched you all these weeks. If anyone has found the secret of holiness, it's you. I've *got to know!*"

Spiritual Reality

This true story illustrates the deep frustration many have felt in their search for an answer to the Gnostics' third question: How does a human being find fullness of life? How do we experience the reality of Christ and know the meaning of a Spirit-filled life?

Many suggestions have been made. Many different descriptions of true spirituality and how to find it have been given. Often the prescription promises a shortcut: immediate attainment of a higher kind of life. Among these ways are:

The special experience. As the result of one dramatic moment, the Holy Spirit's power will flow unimpeded for the rest of your life, eradicating sin and lifting you to fullness.

This is an attractive view. The change is sudden. It is clearly supernatural; God's work alone. And it promises freedom from the nagging tensions that have been our lot. No more struggle! Just surrender and be lifted to a higher plane.

We must be careful not to dismiss special experiences altogether. God sometimes brings us to crisis confrontations with Himself, and these result in valid spiritual breakthroughs. But we deceive ourselves if we expect any such experience to confer instant sainthood.

Special knowledge. This also seems attractive, appealing to our feeling that there must be something more to the simple message of Christ than meets the eye. Sometimes we expect special knowledge from learning to read the Hebrew and Greek of the original biblical documents. Sometimes it is a special key to interpreting the Bible, a key not given to the ignorant masses who take Scripture in its plain sense. Sometimes it is theosophy or some modern cult that imposes a system so like Gnosticism on Scripture that they are almost indistinguishable.

And how attractive it is to believe that once I know the hidden thing, I will have fullness. How attractive to feel that knowledge sets me above others and brings me closer to God.

Ritual observance. Here fullness is attained by careful keeping of prescribed rituals and taboos. We refrain from eating meat, keep Sunday or the Sabbath, guard our behavior, and keep everything within prescribed rules. Soon we have developed lists and traditions defining every situation and telling us what pleases God.

This is probably the least satisfactory approach. Our attention to details leads us further and further from relationships with others. Even fellowship with Christ is set aside in our commitment to rules. But the feeling that life is empty will always intrude.

Self-denial. This approach will always tempt those who are ascetically inclined. Pushing down desires, controlling the body by severe fasting or punishment, and being suspicious of anything associated with the material world has a strange appeal. It seems so spiritual! Escape from life to an ethereal plane!

The Gnostics chose to do so. Spirituality had to be found beyond the world of things and persons. And so the body and desires associated with this world had to be denied.

It is true that Paul told the Colossians to "put to death, therefore, what belongs to your earthly nature" (3:5). The Christian life has always been a walk of discipline. But it is not discipline for discipline's sake; we deny ourselves certain things because Christ has called us to something better.

Licentiousness. This obviously is not a way to find spiritual fullness — but some have reasoned that since our bodies are part of the evil material universe, it doesn't matter what they do. They can indulge every fleshly desire, for whatever is done cannot contaminate the spiritual element within. Spiritual reality is found through special knowledge, subjective experience, or the ritual observations totally divorced from daily life.

We have something of this same notion today — the idea that what we do on weekdays, in business, or other relationships has nothing to do with Sunday faith. Spirituality is pressed into a single compartment and never integrated into our total experience.

Our Hidden Life

In contrast to these shortcuts, Paul encouraged us to think in terms of gradual renewal and growth.

"All over the world this Gospel is producing fruit and growing" (1:6). Paul's prayer for the Colossians was that they might also be "bearing fruit in every good work, growing in the knowledge of God" (v. 10). Live in Christ "rooted and built up in Him" (2:6).

The Colossian prayer provides important background for our understanding of Paul's pathway to spiritual fullness. That prayer reveals something that I have called in another book, the "Colossians cycle" (p. 445).

The prayer that explains the cycle is found in Colossians 1:9-11. Here Paul asks God to:

> Fill you with the knowledge of His will through all spiritual wisdom and understanding. And we pray this in order that you may live a life worthy of the Lord and may please Him in every way; bearing fruit in every good work, growing in the knowledge of God.

The first element, a "knowledge of God's will," is literally a knowledge of "what God has willed." That is, the apostle has not looked to personal experiences of leading, but to revelation. God has made Himself and His will known to us in the Word. Personal experience of God begins with this revelation of Himself through the Prophets and Apostles.

The Colossian Cycle*

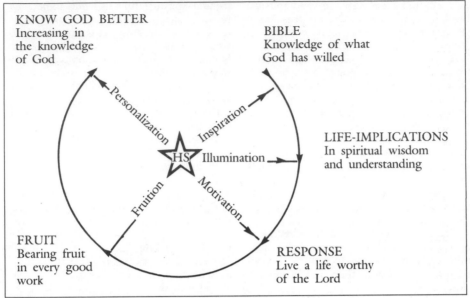

*from *Creative Bible Teaching*, Richards, Moody Press

But we are to hold this knowledge with "all spiritual wisdom and understanding." Each of the terms here focuses our attention not on intellectual knowledge or information. Each speaks of practical knowledge: of ability to apply what is known to daily life, and see its implications for our choices and actions.

As we apply what God has willed to our everyday lives, wisely letting God's Word guide our choices, we will live lives that are truly worthy of the Lord.

In this process God Himself will be actively at work within and through us, producing the Holy Spirit's fruit in our personalities even as we are active in every good work.

Finally, we will be "growing in the knowledge of God." This culminating thought is not of growth in knowledge *about* God, but growth in knowing Him personally. We will experience God in our lives, and find personal spiritual fulfillment, only in this way.

What a corrective to many of our own practices and assumptions. Knowing the Bible is not the key—applying what God has revealed in our daily lives is what counts. Knowing what we should do is not enough—it is putting what we know into practice to live a life worthy of God.

As we, encouraged by the Holy Spirit, fulfill these responsibilities God Himself produces His good fruit in our lives, and makes Himself real to us.

It is against this background that Paul in Colossians 3 now shows us how to grow in a spiritual—and holy—life here on earth.

It is only natural for Paul to emphasize this. He thinks of Christianity in terms of *life*. And all living things grow. Growth is a natural, gradual process. There is direction to growth, but the change is often imperceptible day to day.

Paul's call is to "continue to live in Him [Christ], rooted and built up in Him" (2:6). This exhortation helps us resist those tempting promises of instant spiritual maturity. We are to be satisfied with Christ, to accept the growing processes of life in Him, and to resist the glamorous promises of hidden knowledge or special experiences that offer us shortcuts to glory. No wonder Paul spoke of a "new self, which is being renewed in knowledge in the image of its Creator" (3:10). Renewal is a process; growth is a way of life. Keeping our hearts fixed on Christ, we are to be satisfied with progress—not to demand perfection now.

Paul also focused on the hiddenness of spiritual life. Experiencing fullness may not be the exciting, obvious, or supernatural thing we dream of! Paul pointed out, "Your life is now hidden with Christ in God. When Christ, who is your life, appears, then you also will appear with Him in glory" (vv. 3-4). The glory will be seen when Christ appears. Don't look for it until then!

Our perception of fullness in Christ is much of our problem. What do we expect fullness to be like? Some aesthetic experience? No wonder some look for it in a sudden endowment. Some visible mark of piety? No wonder some look to ritual and observances.

In fact, we should not expect spiritual fullness to be marked off by its striking difference from ordinary living! Remember Jesus' incarnation? What set Him apart during the early years? He was a Man among men. He laughed. He enjoyed companionship. He ate and drank like other men. He was so much a man that His own people did not recognize Him. His claim to be the Son of God was heard with amazed disbelief, for He did not fit their image of the Divine. And yet, God walked the earth in the Man Jesus. In His life, we see God unveiled. We discover holiness in the love and compassion of One whose company was sought out by prostitute and sinner. His glory? That we will see when He returns in power.

Godliness in human flesh lives a Jesus-kind of life. And this is exactly what the apostle wanted us to realize. Holiness is not being "different." Holiness is not being "strange." It is being the same kind of loving person Jesus was. True holiness is hidden in daily life, expressed in the ordinary, and revealed in our living relationships with other people.

With this background, we can understand how jolting the teaching of Colossians 3 and 4 really was. Holy living, the fullness of living our relationship in Christ, is to be sought in the context of our ordinary lives in this world.

✍ **Group Activity: Bible Study Group**
Each person needs a copy of the Colossians Cycle chart (p. 444) duplicated at the top of an 8 1/2 x 11 sheet of paper. Work through the cycle, guided by the discussion in the commentary (pp. 443-445, Our Hidden Life).

Then individually trace the experience of this cycle in your own life, by selecting at least three truths of Scripture you have come to understand, see the implications of, and put into practice.

When all are done, share with the whole group or in teams of five. When all have shared, discuss: How has knowing, understanding, and acting on God's Word affected our character and our personal relationship with the Lord?

Comments on the Text: Colossians 3–4
Raised with Christ (Col. 3:1-4). Paul began by stressing the fact that we have been raised with Christ. Earthly regulations and concepts of spirituality are to be set aside. Our attention is to be fixed on things above, on Jesus, for it is only in Him that our real life can be found.

Two ways of life (Col. 3:5-11). Paul compared two ways of life. One way flows from what is called the "earthly" nature. This is not the *material nature* (e.g., the physical body) but the sin nature shared by all of humanity. The evil things that flow from the human heart are to be rejected by God's people. There is no place in the spiritual life for "sexual immorality, impurity, lust, evil desires and greed." The believer is to be rid of such things as "anger, rage, malice, slander, and filthy language." It is these things which pollute us and block our experience of Christ, not the fact that we exist as material beings in a material universe.

Evidences of holiness (Col. 3:12-17). But the truly spiritual life is not an empty life. That is, it is not so much characterized by what is absent from it as by what is present. So Paul tells us that as God's chosen people we are to cultivate such virtues as "compassion, kindness, humility, gentleness and patience." In our relationships with others we are to "bear with [put up with] each other and forgive whatever grievances you may have against one another." Love, which motivates all these expressions of our new life, is to characterize all our personal relationships.

All this may fall short of our dreams and images about spirituality. But these common things are the material from which spirituality is forged. These are the evidences of true holiness.

Opportunities to serve (Col. 3:18-4:1). Different stations in life become irrelevant when holiness and spirituality are in view. In every relationship—as children, spouses, citizen, and/or slave—we have full opportunity to live a holy and truly spiritual life.

Prayer (Col. 4:2-6). The way of life that Paul sketched is supernatural. Thus Paul emphasized the role of prayer. We are to depend on the Lord ourselves, and encourage others to focus their lives on God.

Greetings (Col. 4:7-18). Paul concluded with greetings to his Colossian friends, and by claiming a runaway slave, Onesimus, as his "faithful and dear brother" (v. 9). For the touching story of this young slave, see the Book of Philemon.

Summary

The Gnostics, whose influence was shaking the Colossian believers, had a notion of spirituality that drastically distorted the Christian way. It was rooted in a doctrine that robbed Jesus of His central place. Rather than seeing Jesus as the focus of all God's acts, the Gnostic pushed Him aside as one of a series of intermediaries. Thus Jesus would no longer be the touchstone by which the believer measured his life, or the source of power and daily guidance we all so desperately need.

Jesus would also no longer be the pattern for the truly spiritual life. The "compassion, kindness, humility, gentleness and patience" (3:12) that marked Jesus' days on earth were far too ordinary to be viewed by the Gnostics as "spirituality"! Though Jesus lived the truly spiritual life, His incarnation was not seen as the model of the Christian's calling. Instead, an individual under the Gnostic influence wandered off in a futile search for some experience or hidden knowledge that would transform the mundane.

How important that Jesus truly be the center of your life and mine—and the center of the life of those we teach. He and He alone is the hope of glorious things to come in this life as well as in eternity (1:27). And it is Jesus who calls us to live the same life on earth that He lived; a life of holiness, as holiness is expressed in the ordinary events of each succeeding day.

GROUP RESOURCE GUIDE

Identification: *Share with others*
React. "When I think of 'holiness' the image I see is. . . . "

Exploration: *Probe God's Word*
Study Colossians 3–4 together or in teams to develop a biblical profile of holiness.

But before you begin, together brainstorm a series of "Questions we have about holiness." Be sure to include questions about its source, its nature, its practical expression, etc.

If you do study in teams, be sure to re-

port so the whole group has a common understanding of this vital biblical theme.

Affirmation: *Express love and concern*
On the basis of your study, tell members of your group how you see holiness expressed in their lives.

Adoration: *Worship and pray*
Look in these same two chapters for many things God has done for you for which your group can praise Him—and do so.

1 Thessalonians

THE WORD: HEARD AND LIVED

Overview

Many believe that the Thessalonian letters are the earliest written by Paul. Though the apostle and his team had little time in Thessalonica (cf. Acts 17:2), the church he founded there grew rapidly, and reached out to promote the Gospel in the surrounding province. Paul's letter is one of warm encouragement, a restatement of many truths which he had already taught them.

The book can be outlined simply, using the theme of the Word of God and response to it.

Outline

Two characteristics of this letter suggest a special study approach. First, it is rich in a variety of *repeated themes*. This suggests that a thematic study, rather than a verse-by-verse or paragraph-by-paragraph exploration can be helpful. Second, the book is personal, expressing beautifully how the Apostle Paul himself went about sharing God's Word with his converts. This suggests a special exploration of relationships in ministry.

Each of these approaches is taken in our present study of this small, but exciting, New Testament letter. And each will prove especially enriching to those you teach, seeking as Paul to help them live lives worthy of our Lord.

Commentary

We know from Acts that Paul did not stay long in Thessalonica. The disturbance described in Acts 17 forced the missionaries out of the city; later attempts by Paul to return were blocked (see 1 Thes. 2:17-18). Yet, looking at this early missionary letter,

we see how quickly Paul communicated core truth to new converts, and the impact the truth had. "You became imitators of us and of the Lord," Paul reminded his Thessalonian readers. "The Lord's message rang out from you . . . your faith in God has become known everywhere. . . . How you turned to God from idols to serve the living and true God, and to wait for His Son from heaven, whom He raised from the dead—Jesus, who rescues us from the coming wrath" (1 Thes. 1:6-10).

Paul here pointed out the complete reorientation that came when people of the first century grasped the meaning of the Gospel's core.

- A personal God lives.
- The God of the universe calls us to know and serve Him.
- This God invaded history in the person of His Son, and through His Son's death and resurrection God rescues us from coming judgment.
- Jesus' return testifies to the promise that the universe has an end as well as a beginning.

Within the framework of the Gospel's glowing revelation of reality, individuals could once again find meaning, purpose, and joy. The underlying reality is God Himself. The life-transforming fact is that this God calls us into personal relationship with Himself!

We get a clearer impression of Paul's exposition of core truth through Charles Horne's discussion (in the *Zondervan Pictorial Encyclopedia*) of the doctrines referred to in the two Thessalonian letters:

First, as respects the doctrine of God, Paul indicates that there is one true God (1 Thes. 1:9). From this one true and living God the Gospel is derived (1 Thes. 2:2). To Him they submit themselves for approval of their labor (1 Thes. 2:4, 10).

He providentially directs their lives (1 Thes. 3:11), and He is the one who will perfect the Thessalonians at the coming of Christ (1 Thes. 5:23). He has both chosen them (1 Thes. 2:4) and is even now calling them unto His own kingdom and glory (1 Thes. 2:12). And this God is faithful; He will accomplish the work which He has begun (1 Thes. 5:24).

Second, as respects the doctrine of Christ, the apostle so unites the Son with the Father that their essential unity is indicated (1 Thes. 1:1). He is described as "the Lord," the common term for God among the Jews of this time.

Third, as respects the doctrine of the Holy Spirit, the apostle teaches that it is the Spirit who makes the message effective in the hearts of the hearers (1 Thes. 1:5). The Spirit gives joy in affliction (1 Thes. 1:6); the Spirit calls believers to a holiness like His own (1 Thes. 1:7). . . .

Fourth, as respects the doctrine of eschatology, the apostle has considerable to set forth. From the futuristic perspective the "obtaining of salvation" is principally conceived in the Thessalonian epistles (1 Thes. 5:9; 2 Thes. 2:14). The basic emphasis theologically in the Thessalonian epistles is eschatological. The definite announcement of the Second Coming rounds off each step in the apostolic argument.

The new converts had been firmly grounded in core truth. A new view of reality, penetrating beyond the mists of illusion and empty human reasoning to the Person who made the universe for His own good and loving purposes, literally revolutionized the lives of first-century people.

The Power of Love

It would be a mistake to believe that the New Testament church captured the first-century world on the power of a "better idea" alone.

Paul did not preach a new philosophy. The response of new converts was, at heart, a response to a personal God who, in Jesus, offers forgiveness and an endless relationship with Himself. This is the Gospel's real power.

The revelation of God as a Person who loves came as a jolting surprise in the first century. W.W. Tarn, in *Hellenistic Civilization* (London, Edward Arnold), notes that two vital elements in the new religion, quite apart from the figure of the Founder, had no counterpart in Hellenistic thought. The first was the revelation of personal immortality and resurrection. The second was the fact that:

> Of all the Hellenistic creeds, none was based on love of humanity; none had any message for the poor and the wretched, the publican and the sinner. Those who labored and were heavy laden were to welcome a different hope from any which Hellenism could offer.

The mystery cults offered initiates a mystical association. Help was given in case of illness and with burial costs. But cult members were not family. Their god or goddess did not love them, nor were the initiate's fellows brothers and sisters bound together in a mutual commitment of love.

And then the Gospel message came.

God loved them. Christ died for them, according to the Scriptures. God invited them to receive forgiveness of sins and to become a member of His family, *forever*. The message of the Gospel was then, as now, the stunning word that *God seeks to establish a permanent personal relationship with you!*

It was the personal dimension of the Gospel message, even more than its core truth, that captured hearts. When Paul addressed the Thessalonians and wrote, "Brothers loved by God, we know that He has chosen you," he was striking a totally new chord (1 Thes. 1:4)

Essentially Paul's mission was to communicate not only the truth about God, but also the love of God.

So, how did He communicate the love of God? And how does the New Testament indicate that we are to communicate today the wonder of personal relationship?

Paul's time in Thessalonica. Paul and his companions had gone to Thessalonica early in his second missionary journey (about A.D. 49). Acts 17 tells us that he first approached the Jewish community and for three Sabbaths presented the Gospel. It's likely that he stayed in this Greek city for up to six months, until finally the Jews marshaled opposition and expelled him. Thus the Christian church there was largely composed of Gentiles (1 Thes. 1:9; 2:14; Acts 17:4).

Thessalonica, as was typical of the cities in which Paul chose to found new churches, was located on the main highway from east to west, had a good harbor, and was a trade center. It was also the largest and most important city in Macedonia, and its capital.

The church founded there was a vigorous one; it grew rapidly, both in size and commitment.

"You became a model to all the believers in Macedonia and Achaia. The Lord's message rang out from you not only in Macedonia and Achaia—your faith in God has become known everywhere" (1 Thes. 1:7-8). Since this letter was written in A.D. 50 or 51, it is clear that the Gospel not only took root quickly but also that within a very short time this new church moved out aggressively to plant more churches throughout the province of Macedonia.

Paul had not only succeeded in communicating God's love and the reality of a personal relationship with Jesus. He had somehow equipped the new believers to communicate that same relationship to others. Perhaps this is what Paul meant in chapter 1 when he wrote, "You became imitators of us and of the Lord" (v. 6). Turning from their empty idols, they joyfully committed themselves to know and to serve the "living and true God" and were willing to "wait for His Son from heaven" (vv. 9-10). These new believers embraced both the relationship and the content of the Gospel.

✂ *Group Activity: Recovery Group*
Step 10 (continue taking personal inventory)
Turning our lives over to God in Christ does make a difference. Look at the impact of God's Word in Thessalonica—how the Gospel came (1:4-5), how it was welcomed (1:6-7), and how it was subsequently spread (1:8-10).

Taking inventory involves more than being sensitive to the flaws we must continue to work on. As in the case of the Thessalonians, taking inventory means being aware of what God has already done in our lives.

After exploring the impact of the Word in that ancient Greek city, list parallels of the Gospel's impact on your own life. How did it come to you? How did you respond? What changes that have taken place in your life show you have "turned to God from [your former] idols"?

Share the lists you have made, and celebrate the process of recovery, which is also the progress of God's transforming grace.

Reality. Looking at 1 Thessalonians 2, we begin to sense how Paul and others in the first century communicated the reality of this Gospel relationship. The means is so simple and so obvious that we might tend to overlook it when we read this epistle. Yet, it rests on a profound and basic principle.

The Scriptures claim to reveal the truth about life and its meaning. We're told in its core truths about a God who created the universe in which we live. We're told that He created man in His own image, and that even though man sinned, God determined to redeem him. We're told that one day Jesus, who was born into the real world, who lived and died here and was resurrected bodily and ascended into heaven, where He now is with the Father, will one day return in triumph. The great questions about the origin, the meaning, and the goal of the universe are given a distinctive and positive answer. We're told that this is an accurate description of reality; that one day we will be present when God's Son returns from heaven. Then we will *know,* because we will participate in that great final denouement.

But we must take all these affirmations on faith. We cannot test these realities personally. We cannot experience them directly now. The core truths of the Gospel *are* true. We believe them. But we cannot test them experientially.

However, the Gospel also presents relational truth! The Bible affirms that God loves us and that, to Him, each person is a precious and valuable individual, worth even the ultimate sacrifice. The Bible claims that when you and I respond to Jesus, God draws us into His family; we become His sons and daughters, and we become brothers and sisters in a new and loving community.

This Gospel truth is also presented as reality. And this reality we can experience now! We *can* test it experientially! *We can know the love of God as He loves us through His family.*

This theme occurs so often in Scripture that it is hard to see how we sometimes miss it. "Christ's love compels us" (2 Cor. 5:14). "You are a letter from Christ," he explained, "written not with ink but with the Spirit of the living God, not on tablets of stone but on tablets of human hearts" (3:3). The living personality of the Christian becomes the message as God writes His own character and personality on us.

No wonder Jesus gave us the new commandment to "love one another as I have loved you" (John 13:34). *The reality of the love of God is communicated in our love,* both for one another, and for the lost for whom Christ died.

The Gospel claims about relationship are testable. And the test of that reality is love.

The pattern. 1 Thessalonians 2, particularly verses 7-12, gives us a picture of the intimate relationships which characterized Paul's own ministry in this new church. The picture is all the more striking when we realize how short a time Paul had with them. It is a picture of a person who validates his message of love by loving.

> We were gentle among you, like a mother caring for her little children. We loved you so much that we were delighted to share with you not only the Gospel of God but our lives as well because you had become so dear to us.
>
> Surely you remember, brothers, our toil and hardship; we worked night and day in order not to be a burden to anyone while we preached the Gospel of God to you.
>
> You are witness, and so is God, of how holy, righteous and blameless we were among you who believed. For you know that we dealt with each of you as a father deals with his own children, encouraging, comforting, and urging you to live lives worthy of God, who calls you into His kingdom and glory.
>
> 1 Thessalonians 2:7-12

A stranger might come to town and propound new doctrines in order to gain a following. In the New Testament world, it was expected that such an itinerant teacher *would* come, and that he would make a living on the fees he charged his disciples before he moved on. But no passing philosopher or proselytizer would ever arrive, undergo hardships to support himself, and actually *love* those he taught! No one had ever before shared *himself* as well as his philosophy. No one had ever spoken of a father-child relationship with a loving God, and then gone on to actually treat his disciples with that same tender family love he insisted that God offers.

Paul's communication of the Gospel characteristically involved building a personal relationship with new believers, in which the reality of God's love would be experienced, now.

Ø Group Activity:
Missions/Outreach Group
First Thessalonians 1 focuses on the "word," the conceptual content of the Gospel. First Thessalonians 2:1-12 focuses on the relational content of the Gospel. Both are important in effective missions and evangelism.

First, in teams of three, describe at least two persons you are currently seeking to reach for Christ. Tell what each is like, how much Gospel truth you have been able to share, and what your relationship with that person is like.

Then study 1 Thessalonians 2:1-12. Consider together: If you were a new believer in Thessalonica, how would you know that Paul loved you? Be exhaustive in developing your answer from the text — look carefully at every word and phrase.

Back in your groups of three, talk more about the two persons you described earlier. What can you do to make your relationship with each more like that described here by Paul.

Together again, share briefly about the person(s) who won you to Christ, and tell what your relationship with him/her was — and still may be — like.

The dynamic church of the New Testament — as well as the dynamic church of every age — is a church in which the twin thrusts of truth and love are understood and kept in balance. Just as there is a place in evangelism for the presentation of core truths, so there must be a place in evangelism for communicating the love of God, through building personal, loving relationships with others.

Transformation

Hellenistic religions and philosophies did have moral content. Some were highly ethical and proposed strict standards, while others seemed actually to foster immorality. But none gave the adherent any real hope.

Then the message of Jesus broke out on the world with the promise that not only would believers have a new relationship with God, but they would also become new and different people as well! Christianity promised the power to *become* righteous. True to this promise, believers in Thessalonica began to experience a progressive transformation that touched every aspect of their personalities. "Your faith is growing more and more, and the love every one of you has for each other is increasing," Paul wrote in his second letter (2 Thes. 1:3). The capacity to trust and the freedom to love were increasingly characteristic of these young believers. God was working an inner transformation.

Looking yet again through the Thessalonian epistles, we gain a clear impression of the extent of the transformation that Christianity provides.

Anxiety and fear marred many lives, then as now. Increasingly the Thessalonians were able to act in faith, trusting not only God but one another (see 1 Thes. 1:3, 10; also 2 Thes. 1:3-4). Even when suffering affliction, these men and women were able to retain their confidence (1 Thes. 3:4).

Isolation was as much a fact of first-century life as of our own. Individualism created the lonely crowd then as now. But when Christ entered a person's life, this changed. Increasingly the new believers developed the capacity to care. As a result, they reached out in love to others, and others drew close to them as well. Barriers between people of differing cultures were breached as Christ's transforming power brought a new freedom to love (1 Thes. 1:3; 2:7-11; 3:6-10, 12; 4:9-10; 5:13). Love for God and man became a reality.

Moral compromise was replaced by steadfastness and commitment. The courage to live by inner convictions, unswayed by circumstance, developed naturally with growth in the new faith (1:3; 2:14; 3:4, 8).

Motivations also underwent an increasingly dramatic change. The self-interest, materialism, natural drives, and passions that once controlled thoughts and actions were replaced by new values and desires (1:6; 2:4-6, 14; 3:3; 4:3-6, 11-12; 5:8, 12). The very core of the personality underwent a gradual transformation as believers experienced more and more of the power of Jesus Christ.

Personal failures, an inability to be what they wanted to be, must have nagged first-century men and women even as it does us today. But disappointment and shame were gradually replaced too as believers discovered a new power for holiness. God's transformation worked within to make these growing believers more and more like the Lord (3:12; 4:1, 3, 7; 5:23).

Lack of goals and meaning plagued many lives. With Christ, even this changed. The letters to Thessalonica show us that a new sense of purpose and meaning, which could be expressed practically in daily life, now gripped the believers. A commitment to good deeds, to honest work, and to right behavior took on fresh and deeper meaning as Christians recognized that every action could reflect credit on their Lord (4:1, 11-12; 5:14-15). Daily duties as well as the privilege of serving others began to bring new satisfaction.

The newness of this life did not come from improved circumstances or from sudden prosperity. The newness of these Christians' lives was deeply rooted within the believers' own personalities. The fulfilled promise of transformation is part of the secret of the early church's power. "Do not conform any longer to the pattern of this world, but be transformed" (Rom. 12:2) lost all tinge of mockery, and brought a living hope.

This transformation is not automatic. It wasn't in New Testament times, and it's not today. But transformation is uniquely provided in the Holy Spirit's working, through distinctive resources closely associated with God's Word.

We saw in 1 Thessalonians 2 that God communicates His love through human beings. His truth about relationships is validated by love within the body of Christ.

It is important to remember that *church* in the New Testament has an uncluttered meaning. Today we commonly associate the term with a building, Sunday morning

451

services, or an organization with membership, officers, programs, and planned activities. None of these ideas was characteristic of the church of New Testament times. At that time, *church* meant something basic and clear, namely, *community*. The church was an assembly of people, called out of the world into the closest of all possible relationships. The church was and is the family of God.

Thus *church* in the Scripture is a *relational* term. Always in view are the people, who share a common relationship with one Father and with one another as brothers and sisters. In the intimate context of family relationships, God chooses to work His transformation in human lives.

It shouldn't be too surprising, then, to find that when a person is born again as a child of God, the Lord chooses to put him in this family. Here growth toward Christian maturity takes place. "Therefore, encourage one another and build each other up, just as in fact you are doing," Paul urged the Thessalonians. "Live in peace with each other. . . . Warn those who are idle, encourage the timid, help the weak, be patient with everyone" (1 Thes. 5:11, 13-14).

The Thessalonian letter helps us see the quality of relationships appropriate to the family of God. As believers strive together to be responsive to the Word, they provide continual examples for each other (1:7; 2:14). Within the family is an intense love, a love that reaches out and seeks to draw others close. "You yourselves have been taught by God to love each other. And in fact, you do love all the brothers," Paul praised the Thessalonians (4:9-10). In the closeness of the family, we verbally exhort and instruct each other (2:11; 4:1). In our concern for each other, we comfort and encourage (4:18; 5:14). The love is so real, the belonging so sure, that we don't hesitate even to admonish or to discipline (v. 14).

♥ *Group Activity: Support Group*
Focus on the comfort found in hope-filled grief.

Let any who still feel intense grief at the loss of a loved one share. (Remember that intense grief isn't limited to recent loss, but may continue for years.) Encourage each person who shares to talk about the things that bring his or her loss to mind, and what is hardest for him or her to bear. Others in the group should listen with empathy, not offering advice, but seeking simply to understand.

When all who wish to do so have shared, talk together about v. 11. Christians do grieve — but in a different way from "the rest of men, who have no hope." Discuss: How is a Christian's grief different from that of "the rest of men"? Also share: How does our faith, which affirms reunion with our loved ones, and affirms Christ's presence now and His power in our lives, help us in our grief?

Read through 1 Thessalonians 4:11-18 and do as verse 18 says. Select specific words from this passage, and "encourage" one another by speaking words of comfort and hope to those who have shared their grief.

How wonderful to view the world in a fresh, new way shaped by the core truths communicated in the Word of God. How wonderful to experience even now the reality of God's love. And how wonderful to experience personal transformation, aided and encouraged by others in the loving family of our God.

GROUP RESOURCE GUIDE

Identification: *Share with others*
Briefly share two significant ways in which conversion has affected your life.

Exploration: *Probe God's Word*
The Book of Thessalonians focuses on a number of areas in which acceptance of and growth in Christ make a difference in our lives. Based on the things you shared, select one of the following areas to explore:
  * Differences in perspective
  * Differences in relationships
  * Differences in lifestyle
  * Differences in motivation
Each team will either read through this brief book together and list differences they

discover, or scan the book and select a single chapter to study in depth.

Reaction: *Respond together to the Word*
After the teams report on their findings, repeat the opening activity. Share at least two ways in which conversion and spiritual growth has affected your own personality and/or life.

Adoration: *Worship and pray*
Praise God for being constantly active through His Word. What He did in the Thessalonians in the first century, He is doing in His people today.

THE DAY OF THE LORD

Overview

This brief note is closely linked to Paul's first Epistle to the Thessalonians. It was written within three or four months of the other, and intended to clear up confusion about the future.

Growing persecution had led some in the city to believe that the "Day of the Lord" of which Paul had taught had arrived. Paul wrote to explain, and to teach them how to live under persecution.

The letter can be outlined simply.

Outline

As we approach this study of a book that emphasizes prophecy, it is important to remember that in Scripture prophetic teaching is *practical*. That is, the Christian vision of the future is intended to have application to the believer's present experience. Prophetic teaching is not focused on constructing prophetic systems, which link future events in any particular sequence. We are able to fit prophesied events together, to some extent. But the major emphasis of the Bible itself is on seeing the relevance of yet-future things to our lives today.

■ For a verse-by-verse commentary, see the *Bible Knowledge Commentary,* pages 713-725.

Commentary

Paul's first letter was full of references to the future. In fact, the new faith the Thessalonians had adopted so enthusiastically had captured their own imaginations, and created a vital new hope. The Thessalonians were eagerly waiting "for His Son from heaven, whom He raised from the dead—Jesus, who rescues us from the coming wrath" (1 Thes. 1:10). They had caught something of Paul's own attitude, for the apostle had fixed his hope, and joy, and gloried in the crown which would be his "in the presence of our Lord Jesus when He comes" (2:19). How motivated these new believers were to "be blameless and holy in the presence of our God and Father when our Lord Jesus comes with all His holy ones [angels]" (3:13).

While the Thessalonians looked forward with Paul to Christ's coming, there were still confusions and uncertainties. Paul had only had a few brief months in their city. It's not surprising that some had misunderstood his teachings.

Some there were very upset about believers who had died. They apparently viewed the return of Christ as imminent, and assumed that the Second Coming would take place in their own lifetimes. They were uncertain about what would happen to those who died before this event took place.

Paul did not correct their assumption that Christ's coming was imminent. Like them, Paul believed the Lord could return at any time. But Paul did not know *when* that "anytime" would be. So in his first letter the apostle described the Rapture, in which believers are caught up in the air to be with the Lord. He did not fit this event into any prophetic scheme. He simply wanted the believers to realize that death had not cut their loved ones off from the hope of glory to come. Both those who live at Christ's return, and those who have died, will be caught up together!

> Brothers, we do not want you to be ignorant about those who fall asleep, or to grieve like the rest of men, who have no

hope. We believe that Jesus died and rose again and so we believe that God will bring with Jesus those who have fallen asleep in Him. According to the Lord's own word, we tell you that we who are still alive, who are left till the coming of the Lord, will certainly not precede those who have fallen asleep. For the Lord Himself will come down from heaven, with a loud command, with the voice of the archangel and with the trumpet call of God, and the dead in Christ will rise first. After that, we who are still alive and are left will be caught up with them in the clouds to meet the Lord in the air. And so we will be with the Lord forever. Therefore encourage each other with these words.

1 Thessalonians 4:13-18

Paul emphasized that "about times and dates we do not need to write you" for "the Day of the Lord will come like a thief." But in view of its certainty, the believers are told to "encourage one another and build each other up, just as in fact you are doing" (5:1-2, 11).

In view of all these references in Paul's first letter, it is clear that eschatology—teaching about the future—had a significant place in the instruction of those congregations the great apostle and missionary founded throughout the Roman Empire.

While eschatology had a central place in early Christian teaching, as we have noted, misunderstandings did arise. And this was particularly true in Thessalonica, where Paul had so little time to ground the new believers before he was forced to travel on. Paul's first letter emphasized the Christian's hope, and answered one question they had about those who had died. But more questions arose. And so a second letter was sent. This letter centered on the future—and on the impact our vision of the future is to have on Christian life.

When Paul wrote his second Letter to the Thessalonians, it dealt with three specific issues that had surfaced in Thessalonica. Each was directly related to prophecy.

Persecution: 2 Thessalonians 1
Paul had been driven from Thessalonica by persecution organized by jealous Jews (Acts 17:5). A mob attacked several of the brothers, and a riot ensued. Paul was forced to leave that very night. Despite the fact that a number of Greeks and a few prominent women were members of the new congregation, the mob actions had apparently stirred up considerable opposition. In this second letter Paul wrote movingly about "all the persecutions and trials you are enduring" (v. 4). There were a number of enemies who actively "troubled" them. The Greek word, *thlipsis,* is a strong one, and suggests great emotional and spiritual stress caused by external or internal pressures.

Here the context suggests both kinds of pressure. The external pressures are suggested by the riots and physical mistreatment described in Acts, and undoubtedly continued after Paul left the city. The internal pressures came as the Thessalonians wondered: how could this God who loved them permit them to experience such suffering? How does this relate to Jesus' deliverance of believers "from the coming wrath"? (1 Thes. 1:10) Aren't troubles here an evidence of divine judgment?

To answer, Paul turned to Scripture's vision of the future. He commended them for their perseverance and faith despite the persecutions they endured. And then explained just what will take place when Jesus returns.

God is just: He will pay back trouble to those who trouble you and give relief to you who are troubled, and to us as well. This will happen when the Lord Jesus is revealed from heaven in blazing fire with His powerful angels. He will punish those who do not know God and do not obey the Gospel of our Lord Jesus. They will be punished with everlasting destruction and shut out from the presence of the Lord and from the majesty of His power, on the day He comes to be glorified in His holy people and to be marveled at among all those who have believed.

2 Thessalonians 1:6-10

The justice of God might well be questioned if only what happens in this life is considered. But when we realize that God has set a future time to fulfill His role as Judge, then our inner pressures are relieved. The stress that is natural under external persecution is quieted when we look ahead, and realize that God has created a truly moral universe. God will both "pay back trouble to those who trouble you and give relief to those who are troubled." When Jesus returns all will be set right.

Paul said that it was "with this in mind" that he shaped his prayers for the Thessalonians. He did not pray that they might have relief *now* from their troubles. Instead Paul prayed that God would continue to work among them, "so that the name of our Lord Jesus may be glorified in you, and you in Him, according to the grace of our God and the Lord Jesus Christ" (vv. 11-12).

 Group Activity: Support Group
Express agreement or disagreement with the following series of statements, and then discuss the attitudes each displays.

*Christians should be immune from suffering.
*God's love is shown by delivering His people from trouble.
*Christians who suffer are likely to doubt God's love.
*We should always pray that suffering believers will be delivered from their troubles.
*If God was both good and all-powerful, He would not let His people suffer. Therefore He must either not be good or not be all-powerful.

After discussing, study 2 Thessalonians 1. Then reevaluate the statements above in view of what Paul says about suffering, justice, and punishment of the wicked when Jesus returns.
Finally, rewrite the sentences to reflect what this chapter teaches. And make your rewrites personal: that is, instead of saying "Christians," make "I" the subject of each rewritten saying.

∅ **Group Activity: Missions/Outreach Group**
The Thessalonians contain two powerful images of the return of Christ and its meaning for human beings. Compare and contrast the two by studying 1 Thessalonians 4:13-18 and 2 Thessalonians 1:3-10.
What are the implications of each passage for missions and evangelism? How do we best communicate the significance of

eternal destiny to people—both Christians and non-Christians—who are often so focused on this present life that they lack perspective?

Anxiety: 2 Thessalonians 2:1–3:5
The troubles experienced by the Thessalonians led to another, very specific worry. Paul had taught them that Jesus would return, to catch the believers up into the clouds. The dead would be raised and the living taken with Him.

Paul had also taught them about "the Day of the Lord." This is a technical theological phrase in both the Old and New Testaments. It always identifies a span of time during which God directly or indirectly, but personally, intervenes in history to accomplish some specific aspect of His plan. In most cases the phrase draws our eyes toward the culmination of history, when great acts of terrible judgment will shake our earth. The prophets describe this coming day in graphic, powerful language.

Woe to you who long for the Day of the Lord! Why do you long for the Day of the Lord? That day will be darkness, not light.

Amos 5:18

The great Day of the Lord is near—near and coming quickly. Listen! The cry on the Day of the Lord will be bitter, the shouting of the warrior there. That day will be a day of wrath, a day of distress and anguish, a day of trouble and ruin, a day of darkness and gloom, a day of clouds and blackness.

Zephaniah 1:14-15

The believers in the Thessalonian congregation, who were first recruited from "God fearers" who were Gentile adherents of Judaism (Acts 17:4), were familiar with this apocalyptic vision. They had understood Paul's own teaching about the coming Day of the Lord. But now, under intensifying persecution, the rumor had spread that they were already *in* that "day"!

This disturbed them intensely, because they expected "the coming of our Lord Jesus Christ and our being gathered to Him" to take place *before* the great time of troubles (2 Thes. 2:1). Had they missed the Rapture? What was happening?

Paul answered by a reference to other familiar Old Testament prophecy: prophecy he must himself have touched on when he taught the young church. They were to disregard rumors that "the Day of the Lord has already come" (v. 2). This will not happen "until the rebellion occurs and the man of lawlessness is revealed" (v. 3).

This individual, identified in Daniel's prophecy, and also spoken of by Jesus, is the person we know as the Antichrist. (For background, see Study Guides 67 and 90.)

Note that Paul was *not* saying the rebellion must precede Christ's appearing. He simply said the "Day of the Lord" will be ushered in by the Antichrist's rebellion.

How then do we explain present persecution? Paul said the "secret power of lawlessness is already at work." The forces of evil are presently active in our world. But they are currently restrained (most believe by the Holy Spirit) (v. 7).

Paul made it clear that the appearance of this Satan-empowered person will be unmistakable. He will come "in all kinds of counterfeit miracles, signs and wonders." And he will delude the mass of humanity.

Again, Paul's concern in this teaching on prophecy was practical. Paul wrote to reassure the Thessalonians that the trouble they experienced, while inspired by active evil at work in the world, were *not* the troubles Scripture speaks of when describing the end times.

Paul concluded his instruction. He exhorted the Thessalonians to stand firm, and hold to the teachings he had given them. Understanding how painful their persecution was, Paul asked that the Lord "who loved us and by His grace gave us eternal encouragement and good hope, [would] encourage your hearts and strengthen you in every good deed and word" (vv. 16-17).

And finally Paul asked for prayer for him, that the message of Christ might spread rapidly and be honored, and that he might be delivered from evil men so he could continue his ministry. As for the Thessalonians themselves, "We have confidence in the Lord that you are doing and will continue to do the things we command. May the Lord direct your hearts into God's love and Christ's perseverance" (3:4-5).

Idleness: 2 Thessalonians 3:6-18

So far we've seen that two of the concerns of the Thessalonians were resolved by a reference to prophetic truth. The doubts caused by present persecution were resolved as Paul made it clear that God's judgment on the persecutors is reserved until the time of Jesus' return. For now, believers are to persevere in spite of troubles, sure that God will make all things right in His own time.

Confusion about the "Day of the Lord" was also rooted in present persecution. The Thessalonians' troubles seemed so intense that some thought the time of the end had come. But if this were so, why hadn't the Lord come to deliver them? Paul simply pointed out that the time of ultimate trouble indicated by "the Day of the Lord' will not come until the Antichrist – the "lawless one" – appears. And as his appearance will be marked by apparent miracles and wonders, that appearance will be well marked.

The last issue Paul raised in chapter 3 also is linked with his teaching on the Second Coming. But this is a very practical rather than theological kind of concern. It seems that some in Thessalonica reasoned that, since the Lord might come at any moment, it made little sense to plan ahead. Why even work, if Jesus might come before evening? Why plan, or prepare for the future, if Jesus' arrival might make any preparations moot?

So those who reasoned this way simply sat back, idle, and refused to work! They let other Christians feed them, and sat around gossiping their lives away.

This was a total misunderstanding of the meaning of imminence. The fact that Jesus *may* come at any moment does not mean that He *will* come during our lifetimes! God calls us, not to sit and wait, but to be actively and responsibly involved in the affairs of this life. Paul wrote very bluntly:

You yourselves know how you ought to follow our example. We were not idle when we were with you, nor did we eat anyone's food without paying for it. On the contrary, we worked night and day, laboring and toiling so that we would not be a burden to any of you. We did this, not because we do not have the right to such help, but in order to make ourselves a model for you to follow.

For even when we were with you, we gave you this rule: "If a man will not work, he shall not eat."

We hear that some among you are idle. They are not busy; they are busybodies. Such people we command and urge in the Lord Jesus Christ to settle down and earn the bread they eat. And as for you, brothers, never tire of doing what is right.

2 Thessalonians 3:7-13

It is true that all God's plans focus on a grand, future culmination linked with the second coming of Jesus. But what we know about those plans is intended to motivate us to godly living now. And they are intended to resolve doubts and uncertainty caused by painful experiences in this present life. When we realize that the universe is moving toward God's intended end, and that in history's great culmination all of His good purposes will be fully realized, we are strengthened to live for Jesus now—to live with perseverance, to stand firm, and to actively do the will of God.

❊ *Group Activity:*
Singles/Single Again Group
List things that Singles have to be personally responsible for that children may leave to parents or marrieds may leave to a spouse. After listing, select those that apply specifically to you, and discuss: How do these responsibilities make you feel? Do you meet them successfully? What have you gained or lost by being left with these responsibilities?

The theme of 2 Thessalonians 3 is responsibility. Study the chapter to develop a "theology of personal responsibility." Note that woven into the chapter is another theme, that of purposefulness. Believers who have a sense of goal and purpose—of the meaningfulness of life—approach responsibilities differently than others. Compare also 1:11-12; 2:13-16; 3:1-5.

Go back to the list you made together, and to your earlier discussion. What positive things might God intend to do in your life and character? What special opportunities for personal growth does singleness provide?

GROUP RESOURCE GUIDE

Identification: *Share with others*
How has the Bible's teaching on prophecy affected your life—or not affected it? After sharing, discuss: What beliefs about the future do you personally hold, and do group members hold in common?

Exploration: *Probe God's Word*
Divide into teams to read key passages describing the future. Each team can take one passage, or several. Each is to sum up its chapter's major images of the future, which are unmistakably clear, and be ready to report on them. The chapters to read are:

2 Thessalonians 1   2 Peter 3
2 Thessalonians 2   Jude
1 Thessalonians 4   Matthew 24

When this study is complete, hear reports and list the major prophetic images/teachings on a chalkboard or large sheet of newsprint.

Reaction: *Respond together to the Word*
Compare the list of prophetic images discovered in these passages to the beliefs the group members held in common before the study. How do these passages deepen your understanding of what lies ahead? More importantly, how does the Bible's portrait of the future affect our present lives? What attitudes do we need to reexamine? What goals and values might we need to change?

Adoration: *Worship and pray*
Meditate for five minutes on God as Lord of the future. Envision Him weaving all the strands of history together, guiding and directing history to the end as revealed in prophecy. Then envision yourself, and our times, in the perspective of history's flow from eternity past to eternity future.

With the sense of God and yourself that this provides, express your feelings in worship and in prayer.

Introduction to
1, 2 Timothy; Titus

THE PASTORAL LETTERS

Overview

Paul wrote three brief letters to two young men he had trained for ministry. These letters, 1 and 2 Timothy, and Titus, are called the "Pastoral Epistles." Each was written between A.D. 64–67, near the end of Paul's life. Second Timothy dates during Paul's second imprisonment in Rome, just months before his execution.

Neither Timothy nor Titus were what we today would call "pastors." Each was, however, a young leader who traveled to churches in various cities of provinces when problems emerged, or special guidance was needed. We can sense a number of the problems they had to deal with by reading Paul's instructions to them: problems ranging from selection of local leaders, to order in the churches, to confronting heresy, to maintaining a stress on godliness and good works.

Each of the three letters has a somewhat different focus. Yet the content of the three overlaps significantly. For this reason, it's helpful when teaching the pastorals to look at major themes occurring in each, and draw together the teaching in these books to gain a comprehensive picture. In our studies in the pastorals we will do just this, looking at what these epistles contribute to our understanding of Christian teaching, of the qualifications of leaders, and of the way leaders are to function in the church.

■ For a verse-by-verse study of each individual book, see the *Bible Knowledge Commentary*, pages 727-767.

Commentary

I like to read the last words of famous men, even when I suspect someone else may have put those words in the celebrity's mouth. Examples of questionable but famous last words, include those of the Emperor Julian, vigorous opponent of Christianity in the A.D. 360s, who supposedly said, "Thou has conquered, O pale Galilean." And there was the millionaire whose last word to his gathered sons was reported to be "Remember — buy low and sell high."

But last words do give us insight into the values, concerns, and focus of a life. If I could record not just a saying, but a solid core of guidance for future generations, what would I say?

Pretentious. It would be pretentious for you or me to presume to look ahead and give words of wisdom to guide future generations of our families. We are so limited in our understanding that we cannot see what next year holds, much less the coming decades. But as we come to Paul's final letters in the New Testament, and to other late writings, we realize that we are reading "last words" which *do* apply to us today. These letters contain guidelines for living as God's family in a world that is all too often an enemy of Christian values.

These letters of Paul are more than words of wisdom from a gifted leader; they are words written under the inspiration of the Holy Spirit.

The first 30 years of the New Testament era had passed now. Jesus had entered history. The church had grown and developed after His death and resurrection. The power of the Gospel had brought hope and new life to millions of first-century pagans. The church had met opposition and attack, and had affirmed Jesus Christ as the center of its life. The church had come to understand itself as Jesus' body, and God's family and holy temple. The men and women who were the driving force in these early years — Paul, Peter, Barnabas, John, Apollos, Priscilla, and the others — were now old.

There had been other changes. Christianity was no longer a novelty. The church knew second-and-third-generation believers. Once each Christian was a convert from paganism or Judaism, but now young men and women had grown up knowing the truths of the faith from childhood. Soon the Roman government would take an official position against Christianity. Within the faith, false teachers intruded, infiltrating twisted doctrine and warped lifestyles.

A clear form of organization with definite offices and roles had developed within the church. How that organization was to function, without taking on the unhealthy characteristics of bureaucracy, was another challenge the church had to face.

During the decades of the 60s through the 90s, Paul and the others looked ahead to foresee these emerging problems and needs. They knew that they must commit their ministry to others who would faithfully carry on the work of God. Thus they were led to leave us, in books like 1 and 2 Timothy, Titus, 2 Peter, Jude, and the three letters of John, their last words. These letters speak to us today with a living authority and a wisdom that is part of our heritage from the Apostolic Age.

Paul, Timothy, and Titus

Paul. The Book of Acts closes with Paul imprisoned in Rome. Most commentators feel that he arrived there (Acts 28) about A.D. 59. Paul was kept under very lenient restraint. He had his own rented home, and welcomed many visitors. It was during this time that he wrote the Prison Epistles — Colossians, Ephesians, Philippians, and Philemon. The apostle eventually gained his opportunity to appeal to the emperor, and won his release.

Paul then very probably made his intended visit to Spain. An early church father, Clement of Rome, reports that Paul went "to the extreme limit of the west" before he suffered martyrdom. We can gather that he also had time to visit Ephesus in Macedonia (1 Tim. 1:3) as well as Crete (Titus 1:5). Paul planned to spend the winter in Nicopolis on the west coast of Epirus (3:12). Certainly the apostle was again free, totally immersed in his ministries as a missionary and church supervisor.

But when Paul wrote 2 Timothy, he was imprisoned a second time, and this time under no gentle restraint: he was in chains (2 Tim. 1:16). He lacked warm clothing and books (4:13). The prospect was so grim that Paul wrote, "I am already being poured out like a drink offering, and the time has come for my departure" (v. 6).

What had happened?

Paul's release from his first imprisonment probably took place around A.D. 60 or 61. His journey to Spain may have taken two years, say till 63. On his return Paul revisited many churches and wrote supportive letters to young Timothy and Titus (early 64). Then came a series of events that unleashed opposition to Christianity throughout the empire!

Nero Claudius Caesar was Emperor of Rome from A.D. 54 to 67. Though a vicious and unbalanced man, his first five years were marked by sound administration, because he was content to let two supporters, Seneca and Burrus, run the empire. By 62, however, the young emperor grasped the full power of his position, having put to death those who had previously restrained him (including his mother). The situation rapidly deteriorated. In July of 64 a fire broke out in a slum and destroyed half of Rome, and the rumor circulated that Nero had put his capital to the torch in order to have more space for one of his grandiose building schemes.

The increasingly unpopular emperor looked for a scapegoat upon whom he could turn the wrath of the people. Christians, already hated by the Roman mob, were chosen. During the next five years suppression of Christianity became the official policy of the Roman state, and persecution was intensified.

Paul was rearrested, tumbled into a maximum security prison in Rome, and, within months after writing his second letter to Timothy, was executed. Deserted and alone during his last days (see v. 16), the aged apostle's final thoughts were for the harassed church, and the youthful leaders who must now accept the burden of guiding its course.

Timothy. Our impressions of Timothy come from Acts and from the letters he received from Paul. Timothy was a youth of good reputation, probably a resident of Lystra (Acts 16:2). His father was a Greek and his mother a devout Jewess who, with his grandmother Lois, instructed Timothy in the Old Testament Scriptures (Acts 16:1; 2 Tim. 1:5, 14). Timothy was probably a teen when he first joined Paul; fifteen years later Paul could write, "Don't let anyone look down on you because you are young" (1 Tim. 4:12).

It's uncertain how heavily Timothy was involved in missionary work during the intervening years; however, his name keeps appearing in association with Paul and Silas. Certainly Paul had known this young man intimately. And Paul now committed to Timothy much of his own ministry, and gave him his last words of advice. Certainly, Paul was aware not only of the difficulties facing the church but of Timothy's own weaknesses. Bastien Van Elderen, New Testament scholar and archeologist, sums up the impression of Timothy conveyed in Paul's writings in the *Zondervan Pictorial Encyclopedia*:

He was a fairly young man who was somewhat retiring, perhaps even a bit shy. He appears to be sincere and devoted, but at times perhaps frightened by his opponents and their teachings. This perhaps is also reflected in his apparent inability to cope with the problems in the Corinthian church.

How encouraging it is to see the mission of the church being committed to ordinary people. Retiring. Perhaps a bit shy. Sincere, but uncomfortable with opposition, and all too often unable to cope. Just ordinary people, like you and me. Yet Christ's church has endured and, from generation to generation, communicated the life that is our Saviour's enduring gift to those who choose to make Him their own. How important then Paul's last words to Timothy would be. They comfort us ordinary people, and give us guidelines for maintaining the church of Jesus Christ as His living, growing family.

Titus. We know even less of Titus than of Timothy, yet the infrequent reference in the epistles to this young leader is consistently favorable. He shows genuine devotion and concern (2 Cor. 8:16-17); he is committed to those he serves (12:18). And Titus was apparently effective even in areas in which Timothy proved indecisive. Van Elderen reflects on the impact of Titus' visit to Corinth as Paul's emissary during a time of antagonism against the apostle.

When Paul arrived in Troas, he did not find Titus (2 Cor. 2:13). Although there were promising opportunities for mission work in Troas, Paul's concern about Corinth and Titus led him to proceed to Macedonia. . . . In Macedonia Titus brings to Paul a comforting report about the Corinthians, which gives him much joy and peace of mind (2 Cor. 7:6-14). Titus seems to have established a good rapport with the Corinthians and Paul exuberantly expresses his gratitude for the happy turn of events.

Aside from this portrait of an effective and promising young leader, we know only that Titus was a Gentile who remained uncircumcised. He, like Timothy, accompanied Paul and later Barnabas on missionary journeys. Now, like Timothy, Titus must provide leadership in place of the apostle, and like Timothy, would profit from Paul's final advice.

Issues and Answers

The emphasis in each of these three letters is different. We might suggest that in 1 Timothy Paul's focus is the life to which the church is called. In 2 Timothy Paul's focus is on the work to which leaders are committed. The letter to Titus, on the other hand, emphasizes the way in which the church is to accomplish God's purposes in this world.

Yet despite different emphases, there is constant overlap of content, and there are recurring themes which find parallel expression in each book. The chart shows the areas of overlap, and helps us to see how certain critical issues grasped the apostle's attention during his final days. We can best understand the teaching of these last letters, not by studying each separately, but by examining them together, looking for Paul's answers to the common and recurring problems he dealt with.

What a heritage these letters are. Christ's church was designed to endure. Though at times our grasp of spiritual realities has seemed weak, and our life flame dimmed, the church *has* endured.

Yet, enduring is not God's sole goal for His family on earth. God yearns for us to live fully. The gift of His life is ours in Christ: the great desire of God's heart for us is that we might experience that life to the full.

Our problem of how to experience real,

Common Content in the Pastoral Epistles

The Life of the Church 1 Timothy		The Work of Leaders 2 Timothy		The Way of the Body Titus	
1:3-7	Goal of ministry: love from pure heart	1:3-12	Called to holy life, fervent love	1:1-4	Concern for "knowledge of the truth that leads to godliness"
1:8-11	Lifestyle *contrary* to *sound doctrine* described	1:13-14	Must guard *sound doctrine*		
1:12-17	Paul an example of a saved sinner; "eternal" life	1:15-18	Onesiphorus an example		
1:18-20	Timothy's goal to be a minister of the faith	2:1-7	Timothy to entrust truth to faithful men who will minister		
2:1-7	Pray and live to bring salvation to others	2:8-13	Paul's endurance for the salvation of elect		
2:8-10	Examples of godly life	2:14-19	Leaders must live godly lives		
2:11-15	Special limits placed on women's role	2:20-21	Limits placed by individual's response		
3:1-15	Leader's qualifications	2:22-26	How a leader lives, teaches, and corrects	1:5-9	Leader's example
				1:10-16	Leader's duties
4:1-5	False lifestyle	3:1-9	False leaders		
4:6-10	Danger of distraction from godliness				
4:11-16	Need to set example in faith, speech, life, etc.	3:10-17	Need to continue in godly life and teaching		
5:1-8	Respect toward others in the family: "put religion into practice"	4:1-5	Need to preach and live true doctrine	2:1-15	Godly life and doctrine applied
5:9-16	Widows' role				
5:17-20	Elders' responsibility				
5:21-25	Various injunctions				
6:1-2	Slaves' attitudes				
6:3-10	False doctrine; wrong motives				
6:11-21	Charge to pursue godliness, truth, love, etc., keep faith in Christ central	4:6-18	Paul an example of persevering workman, athlete	3:1-11	Practical results of our common salvation

vital life in an enduring institution—the ongoing, structured church—has been answered in the providence and purpose of God. The answer is one we will come to understand to an even fuller degree as we meet ourselves in the issues raised by these final letters of the Apostle Paul.

CALLED TO TEACH

Overview

The church of Jesus Christ is called to endure. But it is also called to experience fully the life that God shares with us in Christ.

One of the most challenging tasks faced by Christians in any age is to maintain the vitality of Christ's life in what is at the same time a family—and an institution. And too often our approach to teaching and learning is institutionalized, as we model on the public school rather than on what is unique in the nature of our faith.

Teaching and learning is one of the major themes of these "last word" letters of Paul. New generations must have faith's life communicated to them. New converts too must be taught. And so 1 and 2 Timothy and Titus each contain instructions from the apostle on the communication not just of Bible truths, but of life in Christ.

What a thrill to learn from the apostle how you and I can better teach God's Word. And how we can have an even greater impact on the spiritual lives of those God has called us to instruct.

▶ *Teach.* There are a number of Hebrew and Greek words that can be translated as "teach," and a number translated as "learn." Yet both agree that *what* we teach is the Word of God that comes from outside the realm of human experience. Our challenge is to communicate this Word from "outside" in such a way that it is woven into each believer's life.

Commentary

Over and over again in Paul's last words to Timothy and Titus he returned to the theme of teaching. His concern seems obvious. Certainly the continuation of the church across the ages demanded transmission of Bible truths. Probably one of the most quoted verses from the Pastoral Epistles is 2 Timothy 2:2: "And the things you have heard me say in the presence of many witnesses entrust to reliable men who will also be qualified to teach others."

This verse appears on the seal of the seminary I attended. It's a common theme at seminary commencements. Much of our education in Sunday School as well as in special training and discipleship classes hopes to do just this: entrust the task of teaching so that truth may be passed on to the next generation.

But we are so confident we know what "teaching" means that we may fail to ask what it meant to Paul when he wrote to Timothy and Titus.

Education

The *Random House Dictionary* defines *education* as "the act or process of imparting or acquiring general knowledge, developing the powers of reasoning and judgment, and generally of preparing oneself or others intellectually for mature life." In our society *education* implies *school,* and to us the key phrases in this dictionary definition are "imparting or acquiring knowledge" and "preparing oneself intellectually." To teach or to learn, education focuses on knowledge and on the intellect.

This is, of course, an accurate definition for our society. School systems teach reading and writing, history and science, business and law, so learners will be "prepared intellectually for the mature life."

In our society teaching is imparting knowledge and processing information; learning is acquiring knowledge and using information. It's hard for us to realize that teaching did not have the same meaning for Paul or Timothy or the other early readers of these letters.

William Barclay, in *Educational Ideals in the Ancient World* (Baker), suggests that Jewish education was very different from our notions of teaching and learning.

The very basis of Judaism is to be found in the conception of holiness. "You shall be holy for I the Lord your God am holy." "And ye shall be holy unto Me: for I the Lord am holy, and have severed you from other people that ye might be Mine." That is to say, *it was the destiny of the Jewish people to be different.* Holiness means difference. And their whole educational system was directed to that end. It has been precisely that educational system which has kept the Jewish race in existence. The Jew is no longer a racial type; he is a person who follows a certain way of life, and who belongs to a certain faith. If Jewish religion had faltered, or altered, the Jews would have ceased to exist. First and foremost, the Jewish ideal of education is the ideal of holiness, of difference, of separation from all other peoples in order to belong to God. Their educational system was nothing less than the instrument by which their existence as a nation, and their fulfillment of their destiny, was ensured.

See what Barclay is saying? The Hebrew concept of education was *not* "to impart knowledge" or to "prepare oneself intellectually." It was to produce holiness and to impart a distinctive lifestyle. When Paul wrote to Timothy and Titus about the importance of teaching in the church, his concept of education was Hebrew, not twentieth century.

What does this mean for us? First, it illustrates why we must guard against reading a twentieth-century meaning into Bible words. Secondly, it encourages us to explore Scripture in order to determine from the Bible itself the meaning of such terms as *teach* and *instruct*.

We need to carefully examine these letters to find out what kind of teaching and learning Paul was so concerned about. Do we have this kind of teaching in our churches today? Are there better ways to communicate our faith to coming generations than we have found? How do we pass on our living relationship with Jesus Christ to others?

✂ *Group Activity: Recovery Group*
  Step 12 (carry the 12 Step message to others)

Paul reviews his own recovery process. He realized his own life was unmanageable, admitted his sin, and turned to Christ (1:12-15). He discovered a new purpose and goal in life (1:16). He praises God in a beautiful doxology (1:17). And he urges his friend Timothy to imitate him, and keep "a good conscience" — by making right choices, and when wrong choices are made by admitting the wrong and making it right.

Draw a vertical line on an 8 1/2 x 11 sheet of paper. On the left, list the topics Paul chose to review his own recovery:
● *Face unmanageable life*
● *Admit wrong (sin) to self, God, others*
● *Find new purpose in life*
● *Experience and praise God*
● *Maintain faith and a good conscience*
Together talk over what you may know about Paul's life, and fill in information under these categories.

Then use the same categories to fill in your own personal recovery history on the right side of the sheet. When done, share your story in groups of three.

Goals of Education

In each of his three last letters Paul seems to plunge immediately into statements about the goal of Christian teaching. In 1 Timothy he warned against false doctrine and urged commitment to the truth. Paul stated succinctly his goal in teaching the truth: that goal is "love, which comes from a pure heart and a good conscience and a sincere faith" (1 Tim. 1:5). In 2 Timothy, Paul brought up the same issue. "What you have heard from me, keep as the pattern of sound teaching, with faith and love in Christ Jesus" (2 Tim. 1:13). And in the opening of Titus, Paul spoke immediately of "the knowledge of the truth that leads to godliness" (Titus 1:1). The goals that Paul had in mind for teaching in the church aren't limited to gaining intellectual knowledge. In fact, Bible knowledge is never an end in itself! It is to produce love, faith, and godliness in our lives.

Measuring learning. Paul was not so much concerned that believers *knew* the truth as he was that the truth produced a distinctive way of life in them. The measure of effective teaching is not how much a person knows, but how well he or she lives.

Schools evaluate learning by testing and

measuring knowledge. How many books has the student read? What was his final grade? Were the answers on the exam correct? Even in the church there's a tendency to think that the "educated" Christian is the one who has gone to Bible school, a Christian college, or seminary. The individual who has memorized the most Bible verses, who always has the right answer to a doctrinal quiz, or who can authoritatively chart a premillennial picture of the future, may be viewed as the model of a well-taught Christian.

But if we take our stance with the Apostle Paul, we realize that evidence of Christian learning is not found in what is known. It is instead found in the love, faith, and godliness that are to mark the believer's life. Paul urged Timothy and Titus to be engaged in the kind of teaching that links truth with life; the kind of teaching that has as its product loving, trusting, and godly men and women. Paul would say that character is a better indicator of a well-taught Christian than knowledge.

Truth . . . and Life

One of my old friends, a coprofessor at a school where I taught, is a dichotomous thinker. That is, he tends to think in opposites, in either/or fashion. At one time the faculty senate began to talk of redesigning our curriculum, to better equip young people for the practical demands of the ministry. My friend was visibly upset. If our curriculum were to be "practical," we would have to sacrifice "academic respectability." Education must be either "academic" (concentrating on truth) or "practical" (concentrating on methodology), and *he* was going to stand firmly on the side of truth! He could never see education involving *both* the academic *and* the practical. For him it had to be either one or the other.

Yet nothing could be further from the Apostle Paul's thought in these letters. To him, teaching's goal is knowledge expressed in love, faith, and godliness. Truth and life — the "academic" and the "practical" must be intimately linked.

- Paul said sinful acts are "contrary to sound doctrine" and do not conform to the "glorious Gospel of the blessed God" (1 Tim. 1:9-11).
- Paul expressed concern about "how

people ought to conduct themselves in God's household, which is the church of the living God, the pillar and foundation of the truth" (3:15).
- Paul's goal was "knowledge of the truth that leads to godliness" (Titus 1:1).
- Paul taught that temperance, self-control, faith, love, endurance, and reverence are "in accord with sound doctrine" (2:1-3).
- Paul encouraged Titus to stress basic doctrinal truths "so that those who have trusted in God may be careful to devote themselves to doing what is good" (3:8).

Looking over these statements, we can see several things. (1) Knowing the truth, being committed to sound doctrine, must lead to godliness, love, self-control, reverence, etc. (2) Not only is truth expected to have an impact on life, but life is to be in harmony with truth. Our good works will reflect our beliefs. (3) Truth produces the godly lifestyle, not vice versa. Being a "good person" does not bring one to the truth. But truth, accepted and applied, does produce godliness in us.

The kind of teaching that Paul urged links truth and life and communicates both content and lifestyle. Teaching that attempts to communicate the faith simply as a good way of life is woefully inadequate; but teaching that attempts to communicate the faith merely as a system of beliefs is just as wrong.

Our twentieth-century emphasis on teaching as the transmission of information is *not* an adequate model for teaching God's Word.

What then *is* the teaching that Paul so urgently demands?

♥ *Group Activity: Support Group*
In a single sentence sum up what people who were important to you when you were growing up thought of your abilities.

Then discuss: What impact does the way people viewed you as you were growing up still affect you?

First Timothy 4 is advice the Apostle Paul gives to Timothy, a gifted but hesitant and uncertain leader who still suffers from what we would call a "low self-image." Study the chapter, and then write a

Titus 2

You must teach what is in accord with sound doctrine. ²Teach the older men to be temperate, worthy of respect, self-controlled, and sound in faith, in love and in endurance.

³Likewise, teach the older women to be reverent in the way they live, not to be slanderers or addicted to much wine, but to teach what is good. ⁴Then they can train the younger women to love their husbands and children, ⁵to be self-controlled and pure, to be busy at home, to be kind, and to be subject to their husbands, so that no one will malign the Word of God.

⁶Similarly, encourage the young men to be self-controlled. ⁷In everything set them an example by doing what is good. In your teaching show integrity, seriousness ⁸and soundness of speech that cannot be condemned, so that those who oppose you may be ashamed because they have nothing bad to say about us.

⁹Teach slaves to be subject to their masters in everything, to try to please them, not to talk back to them, ¹⁰and not to steal from them, but to show that they can be fully trusted, so that in every way they will make the teaching about God our Saviour attractive.

¹¹For the grace of God that brings salvation has appeared to all men. ¹²It teaches us to say "no" to ungodliness and worldly passions, and to live self-controlled, upright and godly lives in this present age, ¹³while we wait for the blessed hope—the glorious appearing of our great God and Saviour, Jesus Christ, ¹⁴who gave Himself for us to redeem us from all wickedness and to purify for Himself a people that are His very own, eager to do what is good.

¹⁵These, then, are the things you should teach. Encourage and rebuke with all authority. Do not let anyone despise you.

letter to yourself, or to the member of your group who seems to you to be "most like" Timothy. The letter should paraphrase Paul's advice by putting it in contemporary terms.

When your letter is finished, share key phrases and thoughts, and together develop a master summary of Paul's advice.

Finally, again in a single or in a few sentences, tell one area in which you can put Paul's advice to Timothy into practice.

Teaching

In Paul's First Letter to Timothy, he gave him quite a list of subjects to teach, including: exposure of false doctrines, myths and genealogies; law; sound doctrine; the glorious Gospel; mercy; truth; dedication; prayer; harmony; women's dress and appearance; marriage and dietary practices; qualifications for leaders; conduct; sayings, truths of the faith; the practice of religion; relationships with fellow Christians; treatment of widows; ways to select elders; contentment; righteousness; faith; love; endurance; hope in God; and doing good.

In looking over even this incomplete list, someone may argue, "But this isn't about *teaching!*" That argument, of course, presupposes the narrow view that teaching involves only the verbal communication of beliefs and concepts.

But this is the whole point. Paul was concerned with communicating doctrine,

mercy, commitment, conduct—truths *plus* a whole new way of life. *Christian communication is to touch the entire person;* to shape beliefs, attitudes, values, and behavior.

To teach the whole person, instruction must go beyond processing information. Even true information. As we look at 1 Timothy we realize that biblical teaching *does* involve verbal instruction. But it also involves urging, pointing out, commanding, setting an example, giving instructions. Christian teaching calls for a personal involvement that touches every aspect of the learner's life.

If we study the Pastoral Epistles carefully, we see that Paul's stress on instruction typically focused more on shaping lifestyle than passing on truth! These second-generation Christians knew and accepted the basic doctrines of our faith. What they needed most was to learn how to live lives that were in harmony with the truths they knew! We might summarize Paul's view of teaching by using his own words: teaching is helping the people of God learn how to "conduct themselves in God's household" (1 Tim. 3:15).

A key chapter. Titus 2 can help us understand what is involved in this kind of teaching.

Let's look at each of the boxed words and see what they mean. "Teach" sound doctrine is *laleo*, "to speak, assert, proclaim." What is to be the subject of this vocal instruction? Not "sound doctrine" itself, but a lifestyle that is in harmony with the revealed truths that shape our understanding of God, and of the meaning of life in this world.

"Teach" (v. 2) is not in the original. The Greek, however, does have a common grammatical construction that implies an imperative, urgent communication. What is to be given such urgent attention? Why, a way of life which is "temperate, worthy of respect, self-controlled, and sound in faith, in love, and in endurance."

"Teach what is good" is *kalodidaskalous*, used only here in the New Testament. The older women are responsible themselves to be admirable persons, and then to instruct the younger women.

"Train" here is *sophrontizo*. It means "to encourage, advise, urge." In New Testament times the word focused on teaching morality and good judgment. In essence the older women were to show concern for the moral development and improvement of the younger women.

"Encourage" is *parakaleo*, which means to "encourage or exhort." It suggests a close relationship; a closeness allowing the individual to correct a younger man.

"Example" is *typon*. This word means more than a "visible impression." It suggests "a pattern or example to follow." We teach others God's ways by *showing them by our way of life what those ways are.*

"Teaching" in verse 7 is *didaskalia*, "the act of [typically verbal] instruction."

"Teaches" (v. 12) is *paideuousa*. The word suggests giving parentlike guidance and daily correction, as to a child.

"Teach" is again *laleo*, "to speak."

"Encourage" is again *parakaleo*. Finally, "reprove" in verse 15 is *elencho*, which means "to bring to light, expose." In context it means to convince, to reprove if necessary in order to convict.

When we integrate all these terms and concepts into our notion of teaching, what do we discover? First, the teaching ministry is one of shaping lives, not simply one of passing on even true information. Second, Christian teaching deals with every aspect of our lives. The tensions of daily life, relationships with others — all these are the concerns on which Christian teaching is focused. Third, we would conclude that "teaching" is a very broad term. It simply means bringing the insights of Scripture to

bear on the daily lives of learners by modeling, instructing, encouraging, advising, urging, exhorting, guiding, exposing, and convicting.

✳ *Group Activity:*
Singles/Single Again Group
What should Singles Again look for to provide meaning in life now? Look together at this chapter, and discuss its implications for younger singles. For older singles. For local churches.

✍ *Group Activity: Bible Study Group*
Work together as couples, or if single, work individually to develop an estimated budget. Be sure to include: income, taxes, medical, housing, food, clothing, recreation, giving, savings, and any other major expense categories.

Then brainstorm: What would you do if your income were suddenly to jump by $20,000 a year? What would you do if your income were to suddenly drop by $2,000 a year?

After working on your actual budget, and revising it for increased and decreased income, study together 1 Timothy 6:3-19. Agree on and list the major points that the apostle makes.

Then discuss: If each of us were to live totally by Paul's principles, how would it affect our budgeting?

On Guard

Paul's balanced approach to teaching was intended to help the early church, and you and me today, avoid tragic errors. On the one hand, Christians cannot neglect doctrine if we are to know reality. On the other hand, if believers think that only orthodox doctrine is important, we can end up with debates, antagonisms, and finally sterility of life. We can take pride in being right — but cut ourselves off from others who may differ from us. And with all our knowledge we can fail to experience the warmth and vitality of a growing relationship with God, and with our brothers and sisters in Christ.

The kind of teaching that stresses *only* knowledge is all too likely to produce sterile Christian experience. When we teach our children by stressing mastery of stories, of information, of doctrines, we may produce youth who have the right answers but who do not know the loving touch of

Jesus. Paul urged us to guard against this pitfall by communicating the full Gospel: the Good News that "faith" involves both adherence to truth, and commitment to a truly Christian lifestyle.

GROUP RESOURCE GUIDE

Identification: *Share with others*
Talk together about your own Christian education experiences. What kind of teaching have you had? What have you learned? Who were your primary teachers? What were the strengths and weaknesses of your experiences?

Exploration: *Probe God's Word*
Each person needs a copy of Titus 2, with key words and phrases boxed (see p. 467). Talk through these words and phrases, guided by the commentary. Then together determine what is to be taught, and how it is best taught.

Reaction: *Respond together to the Word*
In teams of five compare and contrast the Christian education Titus 2 describes with the following traits of "education" as it is generally practiced in our country, where "schooling" involves:
 * a focus on content/information
 * a classroom setting
 * a defined, logical curriculum
 * a teacher with a defined role
 * students with defined roles
 * a tendency to rely on lecture
 * a gaining of knowledge as a goal
Come together again to compare insights.

Affirmation: *Express love and concern*
Share how your group experience and members of your group have contributed to your growth in a Titus 2 rather than "schooling" way.

1, 2 Timothy; Titus

CHRISTIAN LEADERSHIP

Overview

The process and content of teaching are both important in Christianity. But so is the *person* of the teacher or leader. Paul, about to die, now emphasized to his young successors the importance of selecting reliable local church leaders.

First Timothy 3 and Titus 1 are the key New Testament passages which describe the qualifications for spiritual leaders. There are many other passages in the New Testament that help us understand Christian spirituality. First Corinthians 13 looks at it from the perspective of love. Galatians 5 looks within, and describes the fruit that the Spirit produces in the person who walks in step with the Lord. Other passages describe the quality relationships that mark the church as God's family (as Eph. 4 and Col. 3). But the pastoral passages are unique. *They describe the spiritual person in terms of observable behavior!*

You and I cannot look into the heart of another person and measure his peace and joy. But we can observe an individual's way of life, and see by what he or she does the extent of that person's progress toward Christian maturity.

Strikingly, it is spiritual maturity that is to be considered when we choose leaders. It is not how much a person knows, not how many degrees a person may hold, not a person's status in society. What Christians are to consider in choosing leaders is the extent to which a person's life demonstrates the transforming touch of Jesus Christ.

Commentary

Not long ago the headlines carried news of two 747s that collided on the ground in a fog, killing hundreds. The verdict of the investigators? "Human error." The safety system was foolproof, but one of the pilots had not followed procedures.

Today there's a great debate about the use of nuclear power to supplement power generated by coal, oil, and water. "Unsafe!" the environmentalists cry. "Foolproof," the electric companies reply. Yet there is the nagging fear that no matter how foolproof the system, there may be room for human error.

Our systems may be perfect, but people are not. We must always consider the human element.

A communication system. In our last study we noted Paul's deep concern with effective communication of the faith to succeeding generations. Sound doctrine and the distinctive Christian way of life must be taught. The Pastoral Epistles even describe a system of teaching that is divinely designed to transmit both truth and life.

Dr. Merrill Tenney pointed out that the topics touched on in Titus alone constitute a fair digest of New Testament theology, and goes on to list the following:

- The personality of God (2:11; 3:6)
- The qualities of His love and grace (2:11; 3:4)
- His title as Saviour (2:10; 3:4)
- The saviourhood of Christ (2:13; 3:6)
- The Holy Spirit (3:5)
- The implication of the Triune Being of God (3:5-6)
- The essential deity of Christ (2:13)
- The vicarious atonement of Christ (2:14)
- The universality of salvation (2:11)
- Salvation by grace, not works (3:5)
- The incoming of the Holy Spirit (3:5)
- Justification by faith (3:7)
- Sanctification (purification) of His own people (2:14)
- Separation from evil (2:12)
- Inheritance of eternal life (3:7)
- The return of Christ (2:13)

These truths are to be affirmed and maintained. But if we read Titus again, we find that this brief book also gives a fair summary of Christian lifestyle! Here we read about:

- Godliness (1:1)
- Faith (1:2; 2:2)
- Qualities of leaders (1:5-9)
- Ministry of leaders (1:8-9)
- Temperance (2:2)
- Love (2:2, 4)
- Self-control (2:2, 5-6)
- Endurance (2:2)
- Dedication to doing good (2:7; 3:1, 8, 14)
- Personal integrity (2:7, 10)
- Seriousness (2:7)
- Subjection to authority (2:9; 3:1)
- Trustworthiness (2:10)
- Rejection of sin (2:12)
- Humility (3:2)
- Considerateness (3:2)
- Peaceableness (3:2)
- Harmony (3:10)

It is both doctrine and a way of life that Paul yearned to pass on to the next generation through the system of teaching and communication that the pastorals describe.

Yet the apostle was deeply aware that no system is foolproof; we must pay the closest attention to the human element. So over and over Paul focused attention on the "reliable men" (2 Tim. 2:2) to whom the transmission of the faith is to be entrusted. Men who will be "qualified to teach others."

◯ Group Activity:
Missions/Outreach Group
In this passage Paul focuses on Timothy's childhood heritage (1:5), which provided the foundation on which he himself was later able to build (1:13-14).

Poll the group, or as an experiment call and ask these questions of 10 percent of the members of your church, selected at random: Were you brought up in a Christian home? How influential was a parent in your conversion and spiritual growth?

On the basis of the passage and the data gathered in your polling, list issues that leaders in a local church should discuss when thinking of outreach. After listing issues, and based on implications of 2 Timothy 1, see if you can come up with guiding principles for a local church's outreach and evangelistic efforts.

Selection of Leaders: 1 Timothy 3, Titus 1
In both 1 Timothy and Titus, Paul described the qualifications and responsibilities of church leaders.

They are to manage (take care of) the church (1 Tim. 3:5).

They are to be entrusted with God's work (Titus 1:7).

They are to both encourage sound doctrine and to refute those opposing it (v. 9).

In essence, leaders are responsible for both the beliefs and the lifestyle of the local Christian community. Whether our leaders are called pastors or elders or deacons, they are responsible for the communication of the faith.

What sounds foreign to us about Paul's guidelines for selecting these leaders is that he did not stress academic or intellectual equipment. True, leaders must "keep hold of the deep truths of the faith with a clear conscience" (1 Tim. 3:9), and "hold firmly to the trustworthy message as it has been taught" (Titus 1:9). But apart from this commitment to sound doctrine, and a grasp of truth that enables the leader to encourage, rebuke, and explain (2 Tim 4:2), little is said about knowledge. What the apostle did stress was character, or quality of life. The person recognized as a leader and given responsibility for teaching in the church is to be above reproach, married to but one wife, temperate, self-controlled, respectable and upright, hospitable, not an alcoholic, not violent but gentle, not quarrelsome or quick-tempered, not a money lover, a good manager of his family, not a recent convert (who might be susceptible to conceit), well respected by non-Christians, not overbearing, a lover of good, holy and disciplined. Qualities such as these, rather than verbal skills or success in business, or the capacity to preach a good sermon, are to be given first consideration in selecting local church leaders.

A chart found in my *Theology of Church Leadership* (Zondervan) lists 28 such characteristics, and gives a brief explanation of each.

We should ask, "Why?" Why not give first consideration to a seminary transcript, or capacity to preach, or previous success, talent, or spiritual giftedness? Yet on such qualities Paul was silent when giving directions on the choice of leaders!

"Paul, what spiritual gifts should a leader

Qualifications for Leadership

Scripture	Qualification	Explanation
Titus 1:5-9	1. Above reproach	Not open to censure; having unimpeachable integrity.
	2. Husband of one wife	A one-wife kind of man, not a philanderer (doesn't necessarily rule out widowers or divorced men).
	3. Having believing children	Children are Christians, not incorrigible or unruly.
	4. Not self-willed	Not arrogantly self-satisfied.
	5. Not quick-tempered	Not prone to anger or irascible.
	6. Not addicted to wine	Not fond of wine, or drunk.
	7. Not pugnacious	Not contentious or quarrelsome.
	8. Not a money-lover	Not greedy for money.
	9. Hospitable	A stranger-lover, generous to guests.
	10. Lover of good	Loving goodness.
	11. Sensible	Self-controlled, sane, temperate.
	12. Just	Righteous, upright, aligned with right.
	13. Devout	Responsible in fulfilling moral obligations to God and man.
	14. Self-controlled	Restrained, under control
	15. Holding fast the Word	Committed to God's Word as authoritative.
	16. Able to teach sound doctrine	Calling others to wholeness through teaching God's Word.
	17. Able to refute objections	Convincing those who speak against the truth.
Additional from 1 Timothy 3:1-7	18. Temperate	Calm and collected in spirit; sober.
	19. Gentle	Fair, equitable, not insisting on his own rights.
	20. Able to manage household	A good leader in his own family.
	21. Not a new convert	Not a new Christian.
	22. Well thought of	Good representative of Christ.
Additional from 1 Peter 5:1-4	23. Willingly, not under compulsion	Not serving against his will.
	24. According to God (in some Greek texts)	By God's appointment.
	25. Not for shameful gain	Not money-motivated.
	26. Not lording it over the flock	Not dominating in his area of ministry (a shepherd is to lead, not *drive* the flock).
	27. As an example	A pleasure to follow because of his Christian example.
	28. As accountable to the Chief Shepherd	Motivated by the crown to be gained—authority to reign with Christ.

have?" No answer.

"Paul, what kind of training should a leader have?" No answer.

"Paul, should we select a successful businessperson or a community leader?" Only silence.

"But Paul, isn't it important for a leader to be able to preach an interesting sermon?" Again, except for his remark that a leader should be adept at teaching, there is no response. Instead, Paul points us away from such considerations and says over and over again to look first to the *quality* of the life.

But *why*?

It is because Christian leaders must *live* God's truth.

If teaching in the church involved only *knowing*, then those whose knowledge was superior should be leaders. But for Christians, truth and life are both vital. Using biblical knowledge to form sound doctrine means knowing by experience; it leads invariably to the distinctive lifestyle Paul highlighted in these letters. The goal of teaching sound doctrine is to produce love (1 Tim. 1:5) and godliness (Titus 1:1).

Isn't it obvious, then, that we should choose as leaders those who are approaching this goal, rather than those who may simply be starting on the way? Isn't it clear that the conceptual, schooled knowledge of the Bible, while it may be a step toward truly understanding Christian truth, does *not* indicate achieving that goal? Anyone who is short of the goal, who relies on his or her intellectual knowledge alone, should never be considered for spiritual leadership.

This is the underlying reason that Paul repeated his list of qualifications for leaders in the church. A person recognized as a teacher in the community of faith must himself or herself have *learned*. And we recognize such a person by character, not transcript.

✍ *Group Activity: Bible Study Group*
List aspects of our society which deeply disturb or frighten you. For instance, the high percentage of teens with STDs (sexually transmitted diseases), the increase of date rape on college campuses, the increase of violence, etc. List also trends in some church bodies which may disturb you as well.

Then compare what Paul says about trends in society. What should we expect any human society to become? More importantly, what are Christians to do when societal corruption multiplies?

How Leaders Teach

So far we've seen that teaching, in the biblical sense, is not "teaching" as we know it in secular education. For the distinctive task of transmitting both true doctrine and a godly lifestyle, we are to choose leaders whose qualifications are a demonstrated Christian life—evidence that they themselves have *learned*. Those who are spiritually mature will be able to guide and teach the church. The immature, no matter how much they know, will not be able to maintain or build God's family.

These final letters of Paul are full of insights into *how* leaders can build and main-

Christian Lifestyle and Leaders

Christian lifestyle includes	*Christian leaders are*
● godliness	● above reproach
● faith	● temperate
● temperance	● self-controlled
● love	● respectable and upright
● self-control	● hospitable
● endurance	● not alcoholics
● dedication to good	● not violent but gentle
● integrity	● not quarrelsome or quick-tempered
● seriousness	● not money-lovers
● subjection to authority	● well-respected by nonbelievers
● trustworthiness	● lovers of good
● humility	
● considerateness	
● peaceableness	

tain the church family.

How Paul taught Timothy. "Pursue righteousness, faith, love and peace," Paul urged (2 Tim. 2:22). "Continue in what you have learned and have become convinced of " (3:14). Timothy is not only to command and teach truth; he is to "set an example for the believers in speech, in life, in love, in faith and in purity" (1 Tim. 4:12). He is to give himself wholly to his ministry and to "watch your life and doctrine closely" (v. 16), "so that everyone may see your progress" (v. 12). The process of communication does involve instruction, but it also requires that the teacher be willing to *live out* his teaching. The person whose life is an illustration of the faith is essential in God's plan for Christian teaching and leadership.

What is striking is to note that the Christian lifestyle which Paul urges, and qualifications for Christian leaders, show striking correlations.

Looking at the two side by side makes it clear. It takes a person like the one described on the right to teach the way of life described on the left!

Think how foolish it would be to expect a violent or competitive person to help others become peaceable and humble. How foolish it would be to ask a money-hungry or morally loose person to teach others godliness. How impossible to ask an intemperate or impulsive person to guide others into a life of self-control and integrity!

Ability to communicate may not depend on character. A individual may express information brilliantly. But only a person who *lives* the Christian life can lead others into the lifestyle that truth produces.

The Bible's approach to teaching by word and example has several implications. The first is that the classroom or lecture hall, in which individuals gather infrequently for impersonal contact with an instructor, is inadequate for the kind of total communication the Bible portrays. Somehow the learner needs to see the teacher in real life if lifestyle is to be caught.

A second implication grows immediately from the first. It's important that a personal relationship between the Christian leader and the learner be developed. How can we learn faith, patience, temperance, love, and self-control from a stranger? We need a Paul/Timothy closeness, which enables us to say too, "You . . . know all about my teaching, my way of life, my purpose, faith, patience, love, endurance, persecutions, sufferings" (2 Tim. 3:10-11). We can know these things only if leader and learner are close, sharing friends.

Each of these considerations implies a kind of fellowship and closeness that is uniquely a part of the body of Christ. As we come to know and love one another, we have opportunity to learn from each other and especially from leaders to whom God has entrusted the health of the church and the communication of the faith.

Leaders Alone?

Scripture teaches that leaders bear the responsibility for the community: they are entrusted with the task of building and maintaining both soundness of doctrine and depth of Christian experience. In this context they are portrayed as the overseers and managers of the local congregation. Peter exhorts those recognized as leaders (elders)

Principles of Communication

Principle	Passage from Deuteronomy
The Word is lived out by the model, who is its teacher.	These commandments that I give you today are to be upon your hearts.
A close, "among" (= family) relationship exists between the teacher and the learner.	Impress them on your children.
The context of teaching is a daily life shared by teacher and learner alike.	Talk about them when you sit at home and when you walk along the road, when you lie down and when you get up (Deut. 6:6-7).

to "be shepherds of God's flock that is under your care, serving as overseers . . . not lording it over those entrusted to you, but being examples to the flock" (1 Peter 5:2-3).

But is this kind of communication the sole preserve of leaders? Or is it open to all of us? The Bible says that *each of us is to communicate our faith in exactly the same way — by Word and by life.*

In the Old Testament, Scripture commands parents to communicate the reality of God. "These commandments that I give you today are to be upon your hearts. Impress them on your children. Talk about them when you sit at home and when you walk along the road, when you lie down and when you get up" (Deut. 6:6-7). The teacher is qualified by having the "Word in the heart," having an intimate relationship, and being a daily example — observable and available for sharing. We who are parents communicate our faith by instruction as example, as God helps us reach our heart's desire, bringing up our children in the Lord.

It's the same in communicating our faith to unbelievers. Peter encouraged us to "always be prepared to give an answer to anyone who asks you to give the reason for the hope you have," speaking "with gentleness and respect"(1 Peter 3:15). In the context it is clear that Peter expected the Christian's unusual way of life to be observed and to raise questions. Example leads to explanation, and together the spoken Word and demonstrated life portray to those outside the faith the reality of Jesus Christ.

It's clear, then, that the system of communicating Christian faith described by Paul is *not* limited to leaders alone. And that the character of any person who seeks to teach is of utmost importance. All who want to share Jesus' love have the powerful and inseparable resources of the Word and their life example to enable them to reach others with the good news that new life is ours through Christ.

GROUP RESOURCE GUIDE

Identification: *Share with others*
Jot down the name of one or two persons whose integrity you trust, and whose example or advice you are willing to follow.

Share the names, and discuss: How well do you know the person(s) named? What is your relationship with him/her?

Exploration: *Probe God's Word*
Duplicate for each person the chart summarizing qualifications for leadership found on page 472. Also duplicate the chart on page 474 that compares aspects of Christian lifestyle vs. qualities to be possessed by leaders.

Have someone briefly explain the concept of "teaching by example" (pp. 474-475). Then work through each chart as a group, discussing what each quality listed teaches the Christian community, and why it is essential in a leader.

Affirmation: *Express love and concern*
A person need not be an elected church leader to be a true spiritual leader. Express your confidence to anyone in your group who you see as a spiritual leader, whose integrity you trust and whose example has already had an impact on your Christian life.

Reaction: *Respond together to the Word*
Each Christian is a leader — at least in his or her own home. Your influence is also felt through ordinary interpersonal relationships.

Focus on the person(s) you most wish to influence for Christ. Then based on the charts, your discussion, and your own experience with others whom you view as spiritual leaders in your life, write for several minutes on what you can do to be a better spiritual leader and influence in your chosen relationship.

Adoration: *Worship and pray*
Thank God for those whom He has used in your life to lead you into a closer walk with Him.

CHURCH LEADERSHIP

Overview

The Pastoral Epistles are Paul's last words to leaders of the young church. These brief letters to Timothy and to Titus have their own unique value. They show us how we are to communicate our faith (Study Guide 72). They teach us how to recognize and select spiritual leaders (Study Guide 73). And they give us insight into different categories of leaders, and how our local church leaders are to function.

In these brief letters we meet apostles, overseers (bishops), elders, and deacons. What do we know about the role of each, and how each functioned?

In addition, the pastorals raise a question linked with a sensitive modern issue. Paul told Timothy to commit what he had been taught to "reliable men." And he said that he did "not permit a woman to teach or to have authority over a man" (1 Tim. 2:12). Does this mean that women cannot function as leaders in the church? And, if so, what specific leadership roles are they not to take?

The structure of modern churches is not the same as that of the first-century church, even though we use some of the same identifying terms. Even so, there is much we need to learn about leadership from the pastorals and to apply today if we too are to maintain healthy, vital congregations.

For a complete discussion of this subject see the author's *Theology of Church Leadership* (Zondervan).

Commentary

When Paul and the other early missionaries established a new church, they characteristically stayed for a time, teaching and instructing. They would make another visit to the young church at a later time to complete what was unfinished "and appoint elders in every town" (Titus 1:5). From this practice, referred to in the Book of Acts and several New Testament Epistles, we draw both principles and some questions.

- Paul (with Timothy and Titus) did not function as local church leaders. What were they?
- Elders (plural) were to be established in every town. Nothing is said about ordaining a "pastor" of a local church. What was the task of elders? What about pastors?
- Elders were appointed on the missionaries' *return* visit. Why not on the first?
- New Testament letters dealing with leadership seem to assume (or to explicitly teach) male leadership. What about women in the local church? Can they be leaders?

Exploring questions like these does not necessarily lead us to challenge our own forms of church government. But it does help us think more clearly about spiritual leadership and its function in the local church.

Leadership Terms

Several different words identify church leaders in the New Testament.

Apostle. This word, which in the New Testament can mean "ambassador," "delegate," or "messenger" (e.g., "missionary") is used predominantly of the original 12 disciples and of Paul. These, whom we might call "the Apostles" had unique authority in all the churches. But there were also others called "apostles," such as Barnabas (Acts 14:14), and even the little-known Andronicus and Junias (Rom. 16:7). These apostles were itinerants, who traveled widely founding and then guiding a number of local congregations, much as do modern missionaries.

Whether or not there are modern apostles is often debated. But if so, they surely fall into the category of "apostle" and not "Apostle."

And if there are apostolic ministries, they will surely, as in New Testament times, extend beyond ministry in a single local church.

Bishops. The Greek word we translate "bishop" in some versions means "overseer," or "one who takes care of." Jesus is called "Bishop of your souls' (1 Peter 2:25, KJV). The word suggests a special responsibility to superintend, or to watch out for.

The parallel descriptions of qualifications for the bishop (or *overseer*) in 1 Timothy 3 and for the *elder* in Titus 1 suggest that these two terms, along with "shepherd," "presbyter," and "pastor," are synonyms. Titus especially seems to use "bishop" and "elder" interchangeably. And Paul's letter to the Philippian church is addressed to three groups in the congregation: "all the saints . . . with the overseers and deacons" (Phil. 1:1).

Though we do not know the specific duties of the overseer, it's clear that the overseer worked within a functioning, local congregation.

Elder. This Greek word, like our own, refers first to age: "older one." The Romans had a similar term in Latin: *sonatus,* or "senator." The Jews used "elder" as a title for members of local councils and for the inner group of the Sanhedrin.

In early Christianity, teams of elders were responsible for overseeing local congregations (see Acts 14:23). The *Expository Dictionary of Bible Words* (Zondervan) discusses the appointment and tasks of elders.

The appointment of elders is mentioned in both Acts and Titus. The term "appoint" need not imply apostolic selection of elders; but it does indicate official apostolic recognition and installation. Apparently elders were appointed only on subsequent visits of the missionaries to congregations they had established (Acts 14:21-23; Titus 1:5). It was necessary for a congregation to exist for some time before those whose growth toward maturity and whose gifts would be recognized by the local community could be appointed as elders. The religious con man might temporarily deceive with smooth words. But within a community that shared life intimately, time would reveal true character and motivations.

Scripture gives no well-defined job description for elders. We do know that elders functioned within local congregations and assembled with other elders to consider matters that affected Christians. The word "elder" probably suggests age, and certainly indicates spiritual maturity.

The role of elder requires distinctive spiritual gifts, as well as developed Christian character. After all, every one of God's people is called to spiritual maturity. But not every mature believer is called to serve as an elder.

One critical ministry of elders is mentioned in 1 Timothy 5:17: "The elders who direct the affairs of the church." A hint about the directing role is found in the concept of overseer (*episkopos*). By the way it was used in the secular society, this word, often translated "bishop," suggests both administrative and judicial functions. The same meaning seems applicable to the church, particularly when the concept is linked by Peter with the image of shepherding (1 Peter 2:25).

Although we have no detailed description of the tasks of an elder, the hints found in the New Testament are suggestive. The church is a body, with its own unique organic kind of life. Gifts of overseeing are needed to understand and guard those processes and relationships which permit the local community to function in an organized way. Thus, being an elder calls for insight into the nature of the church and an understanding of how the body functions and the way the gift of administration operates.

Deacons. The Greek word means "to serve" or "to wait on." A deacon literally is the servant of someone. A deacon in the New Testament church was a helper, or agent, of the governing authorities.

In Acts 6 the apostles appointed deacons to supervise food distribution to needy Christian widows. There were high spiritual qualifications for this service; yet it was recognized as a subordinate ministry established to free the apostles for teaching and prayer.

What is important to note is that on both the local and "national" levels there were those who accepted responsibility for maintaining sound doctrine and the holy lifestyle in the church.

Multiple Local Leadership

Some see the Pastoral Epistles and other New Testament books as challenging our contemporary practice of hiring a single pastor. It is clear from 1 Timothy 5:17-18 that some local church leaders in Paul's day gave their full time to ministry and were supported by the congregation, "especially those whose work is preaching and teaching" (v. 17). So the problem does not seem to be whether or not local leaders should include paid professionals.

Where we are more seriously challenged by the New Testament is in our typical local church structure which sets a lone pastor as the "man at the top." We often see this structure as a pyramid with the pastor (or "senior pastor") at the peak, and all others (associate pastors, board members, committee members and ordinary laymen) as under.

But Paul speaks explicitly of "the elders who direct the affairs of the church" (v. 17; Titus 1:5). From these references it's clear that the New Testament concept of local church leadership is that of a *team*, rather than of individual "superstar" leadership.

Why multiple leadership? There may be several reasons. (1) No individual can expect to have *all* the spiritual gifts needed to adequately oversee the life of a congregation. We need a blend of gifts. (2) Leaders need to be close to individuals in the congregation and to be aware of doctrinal and practical needs. No one individual can develop close enough relationships with all members of a typical congregation. (3) We are all human and fallible. Team leadership permits discipline, correction, and instruction of leaders by other leaders. (4) Leaders give leadership by *example*. While an individual may provide a good example of individual qualities, no individual can model a functioning body. A leadership team can be an example of the loving, caring community the whole church is to become.

What can we learn about how local church leaders are selected? I noted earlier that elders were "appointed" by the apostles or men like Titus when they made *return* visits to churches. Why? Because elder qualifications focus on personal growth and spiritual maturity, evidenced both by life and by grasp of sound doctrine. Men needed time to mature before their qualifications could be distinguished.

But who then selected them? In the New Testament, the apostles or their representatives seem to have made the official appointment. The word "appoint" is *epitithame*, which has the meaning of "ordain" or "give official recognition to" rather than that of "select." The process seems to involve growing congregational trust in certain members and acknowledgment of their maturity. It was only then, when leadership qualities had developed and been recognized in the local congregation, that leaders were given official recognition by apostolic "appointment."

📖 *Group Activity: Bible Study Group*
Have someone previously prepared summarize the leadership roles and patterns found in the pastoral epistles (see commentary). Then obtain a copy of a church constitution (your own church, if your group is composed of members of one congregation). Compare the N.T. pattern with that reflected in the church constitution.

The two patterns may very well differ, as reflections of different times and cultures. The things you should look for, however, are: Does the church constitution conflict with N.T. principles at any point? And, Does the N.T. pattern incorporate principles which are neglected or left out of the constitution? If either of these two situations are found, how might you change the constitution to more closely follow N.T. principles?

Reliable Men?

Of all the questions raised about church leadership, one is particularly important and deeply felt these days: "Must leaders always be *men*? May women be elders? May women be pastors? And if not, why not?" The discussion is often blurred by a semantic problem: what we in the twentieth century have defined as the elder role is usually not what Paul was talking about. Hence, is it even relevant to apply his qualifications to a job that sometimes more resembles a business manager than a spiritual leader?

Nevertheless, each of us, in whatever ecclesiastical arrangement we find ourselves, must face the general question of women's role in church leadership.

To respond to this issue, we need first of all to review how the New Testament affirms the equality of women with men in the body of Christ. In a day and culture that typically counted only men, the emphasis on women is surprising. Women were with the original disciples after Jesus' ascension; and "they all joined together constantly in prayer" (Acts 1:14). The conversions of individual women are noted (Lydia in 16:14-15; Damaris in 17:34). In other cases, Scripture records that "not a few prominent women" and "a number of prominent Greek women" believed (vv. 4, 12). Paul ended his letter to the Romans with a list of notes to special people in the church there; a third of these are women!

There are women whom Paul called his "fellow workers" who "have contended at my side in the cause of the Gospel" (Phil. 4:3). Paul used the word *fellow worker* to describe Timothy (Rom. 16:21), Titus (2 Cor. 8:23), Demas and Luke (Phile. 24), Priscilla (Rom. 16:3), and Euodia and Syntyche (Phil. 4:3), the last three being women.

Phoebe was a deaconess (Rom. 16:2), and many commentators feel that 1 Timothy 3:11 refers not to deacons' wives but to deaconesses. In the practical, ongoing work of the church for which the deacons were responsible, there would be certain tasks clearly more suited to women (such as assisting another woman at baptism, counseling women on relating to husbands and children, etc.).

In this Age of the Spirit, even the gift of prophecy (which many feel includes proclamation or preaching) is for daughters as well as for sons (Acts 2:18; 1 Cor. 11:5). In the church, each person is a priest, and each has spiritual gifts through which he or she can contribute to the health and ministry of the whole. It is completely out of harmony with the Bible to make artificial distinctions between men and women in the church, relegating women to a second-class position. Each woman and each man in the church is free to find fulfillment as a ministering person. "There is neither Jew nor Greek, slave nor free, male nor female, for you are all one in Christ Jesus" (Gal. 3:28).

Women leaders? Why then in the pastorals does the same writer, Paul, "not permit a woman to teach or have authority over a man"? (1 Tim. 2:12) Why are they to "learn in quietness and full submission"? (v. 11) Why are bishops and deacons referred to as "husbands" and "men" (1 Tim. 3:2, 8, 12; Titus 1:6) without exception?

In the whole context of Scripture (where women *do* prophesy!) it is clear that Paul is not suggesting a woman may not open her mouth when men are present. Church leadership is the topic of the pastorals, and since leaders oversee the purity of the Christian community's doctrine and lifestyle, it is clear that the particular "teaching" Paul refers to is the "teaching with authority" that Paul urges on Timothy and Titus as their ministry. It was Timothy's role to "command and teach" (1 Tim. 4:11) the things of God as an apostolic representative. Apparently Paul did not permit a woman to be ordained to such an office of responsibility.

As to the "quietness and full submission," the *Bible Knowledge Commentary* (Victor) notes (p. 735),

> The word *hesychia,* translated "quietness" in 1 Timothy 2:11 and "silent" in verse 12, does not mean complete silence or no talking. It is clearly used elsewhere (Acts 22:2; 2 Thes. 3:12) to mean "settled down, undisturbed, not unruly."

Today? What about today? Well, there are many who would disagree with this instruction of Paul's.

- Some suppose that Paul was simply a male chauvinist. He spoke from the context of his own time, and thus shared a common prejudice against women. "For our enlightened day," they suggest, "such a limit does not apply."
- Some, less eager to discount Scripture, still suggest that the restriction was peculiar to first-century culture. In that society, a woman leader would not have had the same respect as a man. In today's world, the situation has changed, so we are free to suppose the restriction no longer applies.
- Others suggest that it is all right for women to serve on the church board "at the invitation of" (and thus under the authority of) the men of the congregation.

Among those who take Paul's restriction at face value are the following:

- Some say that his ruling is based not on culture but on creation. God ordained male headship as long ago as

Genesis 2, not because of any superior intelligence or strength, but simply because headship had to be tested somewhere to prevent anarchy. In everyday society, we may rearrange roles and responsibilities to our hearts' content, but in the home and the church—divinely ordained institutions—we are bound to follow the order demonstrated in Scripture.

- Some extremists make this teaching the foundation of an attack on women as persons, declaring that the disqualification for church leadership demonstrates female inferiority.
- Still others simply say that, whatever the reasons behind this teaching, it is better to follow it than to debate it.

What strikes me as being of most concern here is not so much whether women are or are not to be affirmed as pastors or as elders. On this issue each of us is responsible to examine the Word for guidance, and to follow what we believe to be God's will. I feel free to hold my own convictions, and to permit others to hold theirs.

What most concerns me is that the debate about women *leaders* may cause us to lose sight of the fact that women *are* full and equal members of the body: gifted, valued, ministering members.

Another concern is that women may be tempted to make the issue of ordination a symbol of their acceptance as persons.

Either of these is tragic. On the one hand, the whole church in our day needs desperately to affirm women as people and open itself in every way to the ministry God intends to offer the whole body through them. On the other hand, women and men both need to learn to live comfortably and affirmatively within whatever limitations God has placed on them. Each of us needs to develop a healthy self-esteem based not on position but on recognition of who we are in Christ. We each have God-given gifts with which to serve others.

If a women *should* be disqualified from an office in the church, such a disqualification would in no way make her less significant as a sister, a person, or a unique and utterly vital member of the body of Christ.

The Well-being of the Body

God's church is to glorify Him. It is meant to praise and worship its Lord and Head, Jesus Christ. It is also meant to build up and to encourage its individual members. God desires that we be whole persons, and one of the reasons He has given us the church is to help our individual growth.

Not every member of a congregation will hold an office, but every member ought to be ministering to others and exercising the gifts he or she has been given.

On what basis do we choose leadership in the church? First, we look at the qualifications for leaders that Scripture sets out. We look for those who are mature, and who are ministering now in ways that leaders are to serve the people of God. We rid ourselves of the notion that church leadership is some sort of reward system or status symbol. Instead, we seek to affirm those whose gifts and calling demonstrate that they are God's choice for building up the church of God. And the more we mature, the more clearly we realize that we need one another and the contribution each of us makes to all.

Roles of Men & Women

Men father children serve as elders, deacons	*Men & Women* • in image of God • given spiritual gifts • ministering people ("fellow workers") • "prophesy"	*Women* bear children, mother serve as deaconesss

GROUP RESOURCE GUIDE

Exploration: *Probe God's Word*
Two bodies of content are necessary for the group to deal meaningfully with the issues raised. These might be covered by two persons who have previously prepared brief lectures.

One person should review the principles of church leadership developed in Study Guide 74. A second person should summarize the leadership terms used in these letters, and the way in which multiple elders guided the life of the local Christian community (see commentary, pp. 477-478).

Reaction: *Respond together to the Word*
Discuss: Based solely on the principles governing how spiritual leaders are to lead, is there any reason why women cannot function as leaders? Do men in our group tend to dismiss the qualities and abilities of women in our group just because they are women?

After discussing, divide into two teams, one of men only and one of women only. The women are to discuss whether or not they feel their gifts and contributions are affirmed within the group. The men are to discuss how they feel about the contribution of women, and to list specific ways that individual women in the group have ministered to them personally, or what individual women contribute to the group as a whole.

When the teams come together again, each team is to share what members said with the other.

Exploration: *Probe God's Word*
This session, an unusual second trip into Scripture, is important. Read aloud 1 Timothy 2:8-15, and discuss the interpretation the author suggests in the commentary (pp. 478-481), using the chart on p. 480.

Divide again into teams, to discuss: Is this interpretation helpful to Christian men? Is this interpretation helpful to Christian women?

Adoration and Affirmation: *Express love and concern through worship and prayer*
Pray aloud together. Men, praise God for specific godly women in your group who have ministered to you. Women, thank God for specific men who you feel accept and value you for your contribution.

NOTE TO A FELLOW WORKER

Overview

This short letter, just 335 words in Greek, was written by Paul while he was in prison in Rome, about A.D. 62 or 63. It is a personal note, written to a well-to-do Christian named Philemon about a runaway slave, Onesimus.

The slave had apparently stolen funds from his master and planned to lose himself among the masses in Rome. There he met Paul, was converted, and under the apostle's gentle teaching, determined to return to his master.

The letter is important in two respects. First, it shows the "moral suasion" approach to spiritual leadership that Paul adopted. This approach is explained in 2 Corinthians, in which the apostle explained the basic principles which guided his relationships with his converts.

Second, the letter gives us insight into how early Christianity dealt with an evil institution. Slavery then as at any time in history was repugnant—a denial of the dignity and worth of human beings. Yet Christians launched no crusade against slavery. Rather, as Paul shows us here, Christ introduced love into the heart of master and slave. As a slave Onesimus sought to be profitable to his master (v. 11); as master Philemon would learn to see Onesimus also "as a man and as a brother in the Lord" (v. 16). It is Christ's power to transform relationships that has, in history, motivated movements which have led to emancipation.

Commentary

Slavery was an important institution in the Roman Empire. Most slaves were laborers, the machines of their day. Yet a number of slaves were educators, physicians, skilled artists, and administrators. Materially, slaves were often better off than the poor freedmen, who had to work for a daily wage. Their food and clothing were compa-rable, and slaves were often better housed.

Yet slaves were not people in a legal sense, though the law did provide a minimum of protection for them. A slave with marketable skills might also earn enough money on his own time to one day purchase his freedom, a thing alluded to in 1 Corinthians 7:21.

Yet, as the *Expository Dictionary of Bible Words* (Zondervan) notes, slavery was still slavery:

> However, much the bondage of slavery might be mitigated by the comparatively good conditions in which a slave lived, the central fact of slavery remained. A slave was not his own person. He was required to do his master's will, not his own. He was bound to serve, not his own interests, but the interests of his master. This reality underlies many sayings in the Gospels. The Roman soldier said to Jesus, "I say to my servant [*doulos*, "slave"], 'Do this,' and he does it" (Matt. 8:9). Jesus spoke (Luke 17:7-10) of the *doulos* who worked in the fields and then prepared his master's supper: only afterward did he sit down to eat. "Would he thank the servant because he did what he was told to do?" Jesus asked (v. 9). The answer, of course, is no. In obeying, the *doulos* only did his duty.

There were three sources of slaves in the first century. First was capture in war. Second was being born of a slave mother. Third was through sale. A parent might sell a child, or an adult might sell himself to pay debts. Release from slavery might also come through different avenues. It was not uncommon for a slave to be freed by his master. Or a slave might purchase his own freedom with funds he earned and saved. And, of course, a slave might die. Yet, while a person lived as a slave, he or she was morally and legally perceived as one who owed loyalty to his or her master.

Despite the wrong deeply imbedded in this institution, and its violation of the most basic of human rights, slavery was one of the foundations of first-century economy and society. Giving wholesale freedom to slaves would have meant starvation to great segments of the population. In that age there simply were no available alternatives which might have provided the slave population with employment and housing. It is against this background that the New Testament instructs both slaves and masters (Eph. 6:5-9; Col. 3:22; 1 Tim. 6:1-2; Titus 2:9-10; 1 Peter 2:18). Slaves are to serve their masters faithfully, while masters are to be considerate of their slaves and treat them with respect. A believer need not be free to live a truly Christian life; a believer need not even free his slaves to treat them in a Christian way.

Yet, while Christianity posed no immediate threat to this accepted institution, Christ brought a new perception of human beings and a new relationship between master and slave which ultimately led to emancipation. Only, as in the early years of this country, by somehow defining a slave as less than human could the institution persist.

Philemon

This brief letter contains several clearly defined sections.

Greetings (Phile. 1-3). Paul expressed his appreciation and love for Philemon, a "dear friend and fellow worker." It seems possible that Philemon lived in Colosse. Paul, in that letter, noted that the letter carrier, Tychicus, "is coming with Onesimus, our faithful and dear brother, who is one of you" (Col. 4:9). Paul very probably included this brief personal note to Philemon with the letter sent to the Colossian congregation.

Thanksgiving and prayer (Phile. 4-7). The form here is typical of first-century letters. Secular letters from the first century also express thanks to the gods and assure of prayers. But Paul filled this form greeting with unique content: he thanked God for Philemon's faith and love, and prayed that Philemon might continue to be active in sharing his faith. Paul also expressed personal appreciation: "Your love has given me great joy and encouragement, because you, brother, have refreshed the hearts of the saints."

Paul's plea (Phile. 8-22). It is in this, the major section of the letter, that we see Paul's "moral suasion" approach. The apostle did not use his authority to command Philemon to accept Onesimus back (and, implicitly, not to charge or punish him for his earlier theft). But Paul did not hesitate to state his case strongly.

On the one hand this is an "appeal," and Paul wanted Philemon's response to be "spontaneous and not forced." Philemon could refuse to respond.

On the other hand, Paul pressed his appeal. He reminded Philemon of their mutual love. He expressed his own love for Onesimus. He spoke of Onesimus' conversion. He pointed out that the runaway slave was now a brother, and will be "useful" to him once again. He reminded Philemon of all that individual owed Paul, and asked that Onesimus' debt be charged to his own account. In view of all this, Paul made his request with confidence that Onesimus would obey.

Final greetings (Phile. 23-25). Again using a pattern common to first-century letters, Paul closed by sending greetings from mutual acquaintances and friends.

GROUP RESOURCE GUIDE

Identification: *Share with others*
Think of a favor that someone recently asked you to do for them that you didn't want to do. Tell why you either did or did not do the favor asked.

Exploration: *Probe God's Word*
Someone previously prepared should give a brief summary of slavery in Roman times, and outline the NT's teaching (see commentary).

Then listen together to a tape recording of Philemon, read as it was, a letter from Paul asking a friend for a favor.

Discuss: Would this favor be easy for Philemon to grant? What reminders does Paul include that might motivate Philemon to grant the favor? (In case details slip your mind, rather than reading Philemon, listen to the tape recording again, and as often as necessary.)

Reaction: *Respond together to the Word*
What kind of relationship frees us to ask others for favors? What kind of relationship motivates us to grant any favors we can when we are asked?

Affirmation: *Express love and concern*
If you are fully ready to do so, make the following commitment aloud to the other members of your group: "Because you are so dear to me, I will do anything in my power to help you when you ask—and I encourage you to ask."

Adoration: *Worship and pray*
Praise God for the gift of others who do care about and support us because we are dear to them and for Jesus' sake.

HEBREWS

Overview

This letter was written to Hebrew Christians who apparently were disturbed by legalistic Jews who traveled to young churches, arguing that an Old Testament lifestyle must be maintained by believers in Jesus. The letter shows that Christ is the reality which Old Testament institutions only foreshadowed. Believers need not go back, but must go forward to experience a new life in Christ which does not depend on the old ways.

Outline

■ For a technical introduction to the Book of Hebrews and a verse-by-verse commentary see the *Bible Knowledge Commentary,* pages 777-813.

Commentary

The authorship, date, and addressees of Hebrews are uncertain. One early tradition identifies Paul as author. Another mentions Barnabas. But the letter itself does not say, and the literary style is quite unlike that of the great apostle.

It seems likely that the book was written in A.D. 68 or 69, primarily because the writer speaks of the Old Testament sacrifices as if they were still being offered. These sacrifices were made only at the temple in Jerusalem, and that temple was destroyed with the city itself in A.D. 70 by the Romans.

While the letter seemed to have been written to a particular congregation (see Heb. 13:23) — perhaps in Palestine — its destination is not specified. But it is clear that the intended readers were Christians of Jewish background. The writer not only spoke constantly of Old Testament events and institutions, he also contrasted Jesus, and His position and His ministry to them. Clearly the Book of Hebrews is intended to demonstrate the superiority of Christ and the way of life built on faith in Him to the way of life expressed in Old Testament Law and custom.

As we read Hebrews we can sense something of the desperation that its readers may have felt. They seem, like many Christians today, to have been people who yearned desperately for a satisfying spiritual life — and felt uncertain of achieving it. So members of this Hebrew-Christian congregation were wondering about what they had given up — and what they had gained. They were looking back longingly at the old ways of Judaism, at the traditional pattern of life that had seemed so stable and secure. They were wondering if the way of life they had left wasn't perhaps better than the new one they had adopted.

We can sympathize with their uncertainty and their unhappiness. The Old Testament faith bore the stamp of divine revelation. God had spoken through the prophets, through angels, through history itself, and through acts that were clearly miraculous. He had spoken by means of the seven annual festivals of worship that marked the Hebrew year, and in the sacrifices that dealt with sin and gave the worshiper a way to express praise. God had spoken in the closely regulated way of life of the committed Jew, and in the divine Law, which expressed the highest moral tone. A man who was born a Jew and whose heart was warm toward God found in the total pattern of life under the Old Testament a great sense of fulfillment and identity.

But then Jesus came—the Messiah the prophets had foretold—promising a salvation that included, but went beyond, the glimpses given in the Old Testament. These Hebrew men and women had believed in Jesus. They turned from what they had known all their lives, and ventured out to discover a new way of life, and a new identity. And then, somehow, the venture threatened to turn sour. They had tried, but had somehow missed the promised maturity. They had missed the wholeness.

The Book of Hebrews points out that in Christ there *is* far more than an Old Testament faith offered. There is a maturity, an experience with God, a full and complete salvation that through history had awaited Jesus' coming. And it is this *full* salvation that the Book of Hebrews explains.

In this introductory session you can sample some of the exciting truths in Hebrews—and raise questions that will be answered in a study of each section of this vital book.

What might you sample? The superiority of Jesus as revealer of God (Heb. 1:1-3). A key concepts chart that pinpoints life-changing truths in each chapter. And a preliminary study of three warnings that are given in the course of this book's argument.

The Superiority of Jesus: Hebrews 1:1-3

The Book of Hebrews begins with Jesus. Total confidence in Him must be the basis of our new life, and of our identity as Christians.

It was particularly important to begin with Jesus in writing to these Hebrew Christians. The Hebrew Scriptures had given glimpses of the truth that the "God of Abraham, Isaac, and Jacob," as the Jews often identified Him, was really one God in three Persons. However, the doctrine of the Trinity was never explicitly taught in the Old Testament. It could be glimpsed in the plurals of Genesis 1, as God said "Let *Us* make man in *Our* image" (1:26, italics added). It could be detected in the very term by which the unity of God was affirmed each Sabbath in the synagogue: "Hear, O Israel! The Lord is our God, the Lord is One" (Deut. 6:4, NASB). That "One" in the original permits a compound unity, such as that of a single bunch of grapes which is composed of numerous units. Glimpses of the Trinity could also be seen in the many Old Testament references to the Spirit of God as distinct from God Himself.

Yet, only when Jesus came and taught, "I and the Father are One" (John 10:30) was truth about God as three Persons fully disclosed. When it was disclosed, and Jesus began to explain that "no one comes to the Father except through Me" (14:6), it became vitally important that believers learn to rest their full confidence in Him.

It also became important to realize that *all there is* of salvation for us is to be found in Jesus. There is nothing higher or greater than knowing Jesus. There is nothing beyond knowing Jesus that is key to a supposedly "higher" spiritual experience. The Bible says of the Holy Spirit, "He will bring glory to Me [Jesus]" (16:14). In everything in our Christian lives, God has determined that the focus should be on Jesus. We can come to know Jesus better . . . but we can never find anything better than knowing Jesus.

So it is important for us to begin with an accurate impression of Jesus—just as it was vital that the Hebrews to whom this letter was written grasp just who He is. Our vision must leave no doubts that Jesus is God.

How powerfully these first verses of Hebrews portray His glory:

In the past God spoke to our forefathers through the prophets at many times and in various ways, but in these last days He has spoken to us by His Son, whom He appointed Heir of all things, and through whom He made the universe. The Son is the radiance of God's glory and the exact representation of His being, sustaining all things by His powerful word. After He had provided purification for sins, He sat down at the right hand of the Majesty in heaven.

Hebrews 1:1-3

Sonship belongs to Jesus (Heb. 1:2). This term has been used by some to question the full deity of Jesus. But the term "son" is designed to emphasize relationships between the Persons of the Godhead, not to suggest that Jesus is a created being. Even the term *firstborn* (v. 6), according to Arndt and Gingrich's *Greek Lexicon,* "is admirably suited to describe Jesus as the One coming forth from God to found the new community of saints" (p. 734). He is "Firstborn" in that He is the Founder, the Model, the One with the Father's full authority to act (see Rom. 8:29; Rev. 1:5).

The clearest evidence of Jesus' position as a full Member of the Godhead is given in these early verses, as we see who Jesus is, all He accomplished, and all that will be His.

The coming kingdom belongs to Jesus (Heb. 1:2). Jesus has been appointed "Heir of all things." He will inherit and purify this world at His coming, and then create a new heaven and a new earth. He is Heir to all, and this constitutes a promise that one day all will be fully God's.

Creative power belongs to Jesus (Heb. 1:2). Jesus is the One who spoke, and in speaking caused our whole vast universe to appear. Jesus is the One who billions of years ago acted to shape stars so distant that astronomers can only guess at their existence.

The original glory of God belongs to Jesus (Heb. 1:3). The phrases "radiance of God's glory" and "the exact representation of His being" are both strong assertions. *Radiance,* the light shining forth from a luminary, is all that the human eye can see. Similarly, all that we can see of God shines through Jesus! *Exact representation* assures us that there is a total and complete correspondence between the eternal God and the Man, Jesus. If you and I look at Jesus, we see exactly what God is like, for Jesus is God, and reveals Him exactly.

Sustaining power belongs to Jesus (Heb. 1:3). Even today the entire universe would flicker out of existence if it were not for the power of Jesus, energizing the so-called "natural laws" that govern our physical universe.

Redemptive work belongs to Jesus (Heb. 1:3). As a Man, Jesus walked our earth and knew our nature and weaknesses. But now, once

again, He has returned to "the right hand of the Majesty in heaven." His work has been fully accomplished. He rests now, knowing that He has provided a salvation able to make us whole. Now, seeing Jesus, the focus of our praise and worship, restored to glory, we need to learn to rest in the fact that Jesus *is* God.

Key Concepts in Hebrews

The writer of the Book of Hebrews constantly returned to the basics of our faith. His first words direct our attention to Jesus, for He is the foundation and the core. In nearly every chapter the writer continued his perceptive, direct approach, and continued to highlight truth which, when appropriated, will bring us to wholeness in our Christian experience.

The key concepts chart (p. 989) summarizes the truths your group will discover in Hebrews — and the meaning of those truths for every life.

Warnings in Hebrews

There are three extensive warning sections in the Book of Hebrews. They are understood by some to be warnings against the loss of salvation. As we examine them in context, however, we can see that actually they are warnings to Christians against missing out on the full experience of that salvation Jesus provides. They are warnings to a people who are almost ready to abandon the only process that can produce maturity.

You may want to use some of this introductory session to look quickly at these warnings.

Hebrews 3–4. The first of these warning passages is found in Hebrews 3 and 4. Looking back we can see several significant features of the warning that sets a pattern repeated in the other warning sections as well.

In the warning, two directions or courses of action are examined. One is for believers to obey when they hear the voice of God. The other possible response is to disobey; to hear what God is saying, but to harden our hearts against Him and doubt that His direction is best. When this happens we will rebel.

Each of these two courses of action has an outcome. If we disobey, we will never experience God's rest. Entry into a Sab-

Key Concepts Chart

Hebrews	Theme	Concept	Key Verses	Key Words	Meaning
Chap. 1	Jesus' identity	Jesus is God	Heb. 1:1-2	whole, complete	Jesus is enough . . . there is nothing more I need.
2	Our identity	We are Jesus' brothers	Heb. 2:11	mastery, dominion	I need to see myself raised to mastery of life in Jesus.
3 & 4	Life-principle	Experience our position	Heb. 4:10	rest, faith, response	When I trust and obey God I enter His rest.
5	High Priest	Jesus links us with God	Heb. 4:16	weakness, link	When weak, I can come confidently to Jesus for forgiveness and aid.
6	Maturity	Security stimulates growth	Heb. 6:18	insecure, foundation	I can forget myself and launch out in reckless trust that the Atonement is complete.
7	Priesthood	Relationship is assured	Heb. 7:25	guaranteed relationship	I can have assurance of salvation: Jesus is my Guarantee!
8 & 9	Law	Righteousness is necessary	Heb. 8:10	commandment law, inner law	I can trust Jesus to make me progressively more righteous as I trust and obey Him.
9 & 10	Sacrifice	Holiness is ours	Heb. 10:14	guilt, cleansed	I can see myself in Jesus as a holy, not a guilty person.
10	Warning	Maturing takes time	Heb. 10:35-36	process, persevere	I can know that daily commitment to God's will will produce maturity.
11	Faith	Faith enables	Heb. 11:6	enablement, obedience	I can meet any challenge enabled by faith in God.
12	Discipline	Faith becomes commitments	Heb. 12:10	patience, holiness	I can discipline myself to full commitment to faith's life.
13	Love	Faith produces love	Heb. 13:20-21	externals, grace	I can find life's real meaning in others and in Christ.

Left margin labels: "Foundation Truths . . ." (chaps. 1–6); "Deeper Truths . . . Identity" (chaps. 7–10); "Deeper Truths . . . Lifestyle" (chaps. 10–13) bath-rest (a peace despite troubles) which Christ has made available to us simply cannot be experienced by those who refuse to trust and obey. But if our daily life *is* marked by obedience, then we will experience His rest. As the Scripture says, "Today, if you hear His voice, do not harden your hearts" (3:15).

Thus the first danger that can rob us of the full experience of salvation is presented. We are warned against *unbelief* and *disobedience*. We are reminded that for progress in the life of faith we need to keep a firm trust in Jesus and respond in obedience to whatever He says to us.

This is hardly an exhilarating or startling insight. It doesn't appeal to our eagerness for instant maturity. Instead it sets before us a disciplined pattern of daily life. It describes a process that is to be lifelong, yet a process which both satisfies our hearts with present rest and promises constant progress toward beginning to reach maturity.

Hebrews 6. This chapter contains the second great warning. Note that the pattern set in the earlier warning is repeated here, and that the issue is basically the same.

The warning is addressed to believers. It examines two courses which the believer can take. One course is that which leads to maturity. The other is to "become lazy" (v. 12), and lay faith-foundations over and over.

Each of these courses also has an outcome. We're told that if we fail to go on, our lives will be marked by unfruitfulness (vv. 7-8), and that we will fail to possess all that being in Christ provides. We're also encouraged. If our approach to life in Christ is one of building on the foundation already laid, we will fully grasp the hope within. How exciting that phrase is! Our hope is that Jesus, who is eternity-now for you and me, will reshape us into His likeness.

This too is a significant warning for people who were becoming discouraged with their Christian lives. They looked back and wondered if they were "really" saved. Over and over again they tried to lay a foundation that Jesus had laid once for all in His death. They were so preoccupied with these foundational matters, which were actually settled already, that they had grown slack about daily obedience and daily growth.

This is common too. One of Satan's attacks on God's children is focused in just this area. You're discouraged about sin cropping up in your life? You're unhappy about your lack of progress in the faith? Satan is sure to suggest, "Well, maybe you're not saved. Maybe you need to run to Jesus again. Maybe you need to keep going back until it 'takes' and your sin problem is settled, and perfection comes in a flash."

Don't let Satan deceive! The sin question has been settled. In Jesus' death for you, you stand holy and forgiven in God's sight. But perfection does not come in a flash. Perfection and maturity are things you grow toward, with the benefits of Jesus' death being progressively applied as you trust and obey God. Through that process you *grow toward* what will ultimately be the full experience of that costly, blood-won salvation which is yours in Him.

Hebrews 10:26-39. When we come to the third great warning passage in chapter 10, we find the same themes repeated. God is again warning a people eager to hurry up the process and to find instant maturity. God is saying, "When the growing gets rough, My way for you is not to turn back, but to tough it through."

This warning also follows the pattern set in the others. First, it is addressed to believers: "We" are the subjects" (v. 26ff).

Also, two courses are contrasted. The one involves throwing away our confidence in the completeness of Jesus' work (v. 35), and shrinking back (v. 39). The other course of action is, as in early days, to stand fast (v. 32) and "to persevere so that when you have done the will of God, you will receive what He has promised" (v. 36). Again a commitment to disciplined doing of the will of God stands contrasted with giving up on Jesus, and striking out to find some other way to live.

The critical issue here then is clear. If, understanding what Jesus has done, the Hebrews now shrink back and turn away from Him, they can *never* find the fulfillment for which they yearn. There is only one way to experience salvation fully. The product of maturity never comes apart from the process.

In one sense, these warnings are frightening. They are given in all seriousness, and should be listened to seriously as well. Yet the fright that Christians have felt has often been misplaced: we have feared the wrong thing!

Warnings in Hebrews

Question	Heb. 3–4	Heb. 6	Heb. 10:26-39
Who is being warned?			
What are they told to do?			
What are they told *not* to do?			
What consequences follow the wrong response?			
What benefits grow from the right response?			
What is the danger against which we are being warned?			

This will be clear as we go on to teach Hebrews 3–4 and Hebrews 6 in future sessions. But the reason for the fears, and the reasons why many are unfounded, both become clear as we continue to look at Hebrews 10.

If we deliberately keep on sinning after we have received the knowledge of the truth, no sacrifice for sins is left, but only a fearful expectation of judgment and of raging fire that will consume the enemies of God. Anyone who rejected the Law of Moses died without mercy on the testimony of two or three witnesses. How much more severely do you think a man deserves to be punished who has trampled the Son of God underfoot, who has treated as an unholy thing the blood of the covenant that sanctified him, and who has insulted the Spirit of grace? For we know Him who said, "It is Mine to avenge; I will repay," and again, "The Lord will judge His people." It is a dreadful thing to fall into the hands of the living God.

Hebrews 10:26-31

To understand these verses, we must remember where they come in this book. They come *after* the writer has explained the full meaning of Jesus' death. They follow his clear presentation of the fact that Jesus' sacrifice "has made perfect forever those who are being made holy" (v. 14).

At this point in the book the readers *know* that perfection is promised, and that they can draw closer to it daily as they "spur one another on toward love and good deeds" (v. 24). But what happens if they refuse to count on these things as true? What happens if they still turn back—to Judaism or to any of the other routes that are seen as possible shortcuts to maturity? According to Scripture, this would be to "deliberately keep on sinning after we have received the knowledge of the truth" (v. 26). According to this same verse, if we make this choice and turn away, "no sacrifice for sins is left, but only a fearful expectation of judgment."

This terrible portrait immediately conjures up visions of the loss of our salvation. Yet it seems that from chapter 6 on the writer of Hebrews has tried to show us that salvation *can't* be lost! Jesus' death is the perfect sacrifice that makes us holy.

What then is meant? Simply this. The phrase "no sacrifice (or "offering") for sins is left" lets us know that God cannot apply the benefits of salvation until we deal with our own sin by confession. It's not that Jesus' blood is inadequate to cleanse from willful sin after conversion. It is simply that even God's perfect provision cannot benefit us in our present experience if we persist in rejecting God's truth about how to go on to maturity.

And not only this. The temptation to seek shortcuts also opens us up to judgment and punishment. People who rejected the Old Testament Law given by Moses were punished severely—even by death (10:28). How much more worthy of punishment is a person who looks at Jesus' blood and its meaning and then turns away to look for fulfillment in Judaism—or in tongues, or in "groups," or in witnessing, or in pet doctrines? God says that it is the "blood of the covenant" that sanctifies (v. 29). It is the power of the blood of Jesus that makes us holy, and it is our constant reliance on Jesus, expressed in daily trust and obedience, that applies that blood to our experience and makes us grow.

Trampling the Son of God underfoot (v. 29) by seeing Him as *insufficient* is one of the grossest rejections of God's grace. Believers who do so will taste the discipline of the God who accepts responsibility to judge His own people as well as men of this world (v. 30).

And so the writer urged, "Do not throw away your confidence" (v. 35). Persevere. Do the will of God, and you *will* receive what He has promised.

JESUS, THE LIVING WORD

Overview

In Ephesians, Paul described the armor that equips believers to live in one body. Only one piece of this armor is explained—the sword of the Spirit, which is "the Word of God." In Hebrews, God's Word is again a sword (Heb. 4:12-13). It is "living and active. Sharper than any double-edged sword, it penetrates even to dividing soul and spirit, joints and marrow; it judges the thoughts and attitudes of the heart."

Yet there are questions about the Word. When we want guidance and help, how do we experience it as "living and active"? When we are uncertain, how do we tap its "penetrating" power?

And, does God speak to us only through His written Word? Or may Christ speak to us with another voice? Often when we want to know God's will we become confused.

In Old Testament times it seemed so simple. God had given laws and rules through Moses that regulated every aspect of life. When special guidance was needed God sent a prophet, authenticated by miracles. Now, however, as the Hebrew Christians apparently felt, though we too have a written Word, the voice of God is less certainly heard.

The writer of Hebrews understood. And he moved immediately to make one thing clear to his readers. In Christ we have an even greater revelation than that from Moses. And, through relationship with Jesus, we have access to the very voice of the living God.

Commentary

In Israel's past God communicated to His people in many ways. The writer identifies some in the first verses of this book—and then goes on to say that *now* God "has spoken to us by His Son" (1:12). A person who wishes to hear God's voice must now look to the Son, who is the "exact represen-

tation" of God's very being.

The writer then went on to show the superiority of Jesus *as One who reveals God* to first angels, and then to Moses.

Jesus' Superiority as a Revealer of God: Hebrews 1:4–3:6

Jesus' superiority to angels (Heb. 1:4-14). The writer now began an extended argument to prove that Jesus is superior to angels. Why is this important? The answer is seen in 2:2. There the writer referred to "the message spoken by angels," which was binding on Israel. The Jews believed that their Old Testament had been mediated through angelic messengers. The Word of God was deeply respected in part because of this supernatural mediation. But now, the writer said, *the Spokesman is greater than the angels!* The Messenger is God Himself, exalted above the ancient messengers, for He is the very Father of eternity.

The Hebrew Christians, aware of the Bible's teaching about angels and aware that angels had been intermediaries in the past, found it difficult to fully accept the fact that, in Jesus, God had established direct communication. There was the temptation in the early church to think of Jesus as a "high" angel. To counter this, the writer of Hebrews made it clear at the outset that Jesus is superior to all angels.

*Superior relationship (1:5). Jesus stands *beside* God the Father as His Son, not *below* Him as a creature.

*Superior as Deity (1:6-9). None of the angels is called God, and no angel is worshiped by his fellows. Yet Jesus is given the name of God, and the angelic hosts worship Him.

*Superior as Creator (1:10-12). Like the angels (who are immortal, not knowing birth or death as we do) Jesus will outlast the universe. Unlike angels, however, He was there "in the beginning" when He laid

the foundations of Creation. Angels change and grow in knowledge as the centuries unfold God's plan, but Jesus remains the same; as God He knows all.

Superior in destiny (1:13). No angel was ever invited to share the rule of the universe as God's equal. But for God to picture Jesus "at My right hand" indicates that Jesus shares God's rule even now.

In every way Jesus is superior—and thus it must be that the revelation He brings, and the salvation He offers is superior to the fragments offered in the Old Testament. There is no need to look elsewhere.

In Jesus we have the whole truth—and in Jesus the best possibility of being made whole.

An application (Heb. 2:1-4). It was this writer's habit to apply what he said as he moved along. In Colossians and Ephesians Paul spent several chapters developing doctrine. Then, toward the end of the books, he focused on the practical meaning of his earlier teaching. Not so in Hebrews. This writer was always ready to interrupt the flow of his thoughts to make application, which in turn stimulates more teaching.

What is the application of this initial presentation of Jesus as the ultimate spokesman? "We must pay more careful attention, therefore, to what we have heard" (v. 1). We dare not ignore the message of a great salvation, which has been announced by the Lord Himself and confirmed by Spirit-given signs.

The great salvation (Heb. 2:5-18). What is the "great salvation" that the writer described? Hebrews views salvation as nothing less than the exaltation of humanity (vv. 5-13), and as an escape to freedom (vv. 14-18). And what the writer said will sound strange to us if we persist in identifying human beings primarily as "sinners."

Of course, we have all sinned. All humankind, apart from Jesus, lies dead and deadened underneath the curse. But still, beauty lies within the sleeping corpse.

Before the poisoned fruit, beauty lived. Then beauty died but somehow remained within, awaiting the kiss of life. Christ, stooping to claim His bride, quickens us to life and restores the beauty.

Quoting the Old Testament, the writer recaptures the wonder of the psalmist who has discovered man's lost identity:

What is man that You are mindful of him, or the Son of man that you care for him? You made him a little lower than the angels; You crowned him with glory and honor and put everything under his feet.

Hebrews 2:6-8, quoting Psalm 8:4-6

God made man in original glory, "in His own image" (Gen. 1:27) and God gave him "dominion" (v. 28, KJV). That dominion was lost in the Fall, shattering God's glorious intention. But the Fall did not shake God's love. Man was still God's concern, still cared for. And so Jesus stepped down to become Man, suffering death that He might bring "many sons to glory" (Heb. 2:10). *This is the exaltation of humankind!* In Christ, we have been lifted up to share the Son's glory, becoming in Him so fully "of the same family" that we are called by Jesus Himself, "My brothers" (vv. 1-12).

This exaltation, vaulting us far above the angels to be Christ's brothers in God's family, is also our deed to freedom. Satan, who held the power of death, was destroyed by Christ's self-sacrifice. Now we are freed. There will still be temptations to fall back into the way of death. But now Christ lives as our faithful High Priest to help us when we are tempted. We who have been dead are now alive and now we can hear and respond to the voice of God calling us back to beauty.

❋ *Group Activity:*
Singles/Single Again Group
Briefly list persons to whom you are important. Share your list. Then discuss: What makes a person feel he or she is important to someone else?

God wants us to feel valued and important and to know the comfort and confidence that this brings. Work in pairs for 10–15 minutes on Hebrews 1–2 to find answers for the following:

* What does this passage teach about Jesus?

* What does it teach about angels?

* What does it teach about the relationship of Jesus to angels? Our relationship to angels?

* How is our relationship with God different from His relationship with angels?

When finished, regather to share findings.

Also, look together at the chart on

p. 494 which sums up the impact of these chapters' teachings on angels.

Conclude by writing yourself a "letter from God" about your importance to Him. If you have time, share several of these letters, as reminders that in our most important relationship of all—with God through Jesus Christ—we are totally valued and loved.

Hebrews 1 and 2 describe our relationship with angels and Jesus. He "was made a little lower than the angels" for a time (2:9), that He might bring *us* to glory. We can chart it like this:

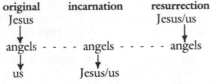

original	incarnation	resurrection
Jesus		Jesus/us
angels - - - -	angels - - - - -	angels
us	Jesus/us	

Jesus is not only exalted above the angels, He has lifted us up to share this destiny with Him! To experience the full meaning of salvation we must never drift from the amazing truth that, in Christ, we *now* have the capacity for mastery and dominion.

Jesus' superiority to Moses (Heb. 3:1-6). Moses stands as an example of faithfulness to God in the Old Testament and in history. Not only was the written Word of the Pentateuch given through Moses, but God commended this faithful man. Yet Jesus surpasses Moses, for Jesus is the Builder of the house in which Moses was a servant! We, who are the "house" that Jesus is now building, are to fix our eyes on Jesus, not on Moses, and to give Jesus honor.

Hearing God's Voice: Hebrews 3:7–4:13

It is important to keep in mind when we read the Old and New Testaments that the relationship between them is that of fragments to the whole. Visualize a picture puzzle, half completed on the table, with many parts spread, unconnected, beside it. That is like the Old Testament. The outline, the basic themes and colors, may be clear. But still the whole is not seen. Come back later, when the puzzle is complete, and suddenly it all fits. Things you saw in part are now clear. The real shape and form of that bit of green is different than you imagined; it's far more beautiful and complex than you'd dreamed. Yet, when you see it together, it is clear that even the fragment suggests the whole.

Throughout the Book of Hebrews the writer referred back to the fragments of truth given in the Old Testament, and reinterpreted them in light of the whole. He spoke of them as "shadows," which dimly outline the reality and yet are not reality. Through it all, the writer showed that the reality which has now been fully revealed in Christ truly was there all along.

When we begin to think then about the Christian's new "way of life," we are not suggesting that it *contradicts* the Old Testament way of life under Law. Instead, we're saying that shadowy truth about spiritual truth which was contained in the Law has been brought into fresh focus. *Now, at last, the basic, heart issue of the believer's lifestyle has been isolated and revealed.* From the complicated details of Old Testament regulatory laws, the Book of Hebrews isolates the critical principle. This principle now is to guide us, in Christ, into a life of rest.

The example drawn (Heb. 3:7-11). Quoting Psalm 95:7-11, the writer focused our attention on an *attitude* that characterized the relationship to God of a particular Old Testament generation. It is the generation of those freed by God's power from slavery in Egypt, and led by Moses toward the Promised Land. These men and women heard God's voice at Kadesh Barnea telling them to enter the land, but they hardened their hearts and refused to respond. As a result, God was forced to declare, "They shall never enter My rest" (Heb. 3:11). In this context, *rest* clearly refers to the land of Canaan, promised to Israel by God, toward which God had led His people after releasing them from slavery (see Ex. 3–11).

An application made (Heb. 3:12-15). The writer immediately made his point. We have been raised to take a position in Christ. Our share in Him makes us the new men and women we are, and opens up the possibility of a victorious life. But our share in Christ will be of no practical value to us if we permit the same attitude to develop in us as was displayed by Israel of old. This attitude, characterized here as sinful and untrusting (v. 12), can harden us and keep us from responding to God's voice when He speaks to us.

The focus in our life with Jesus today is not to be on lists of do's or don'ts, or even on the Bible's revelation of right and wrong behavior. The primary issue and the focus of our concern as believers is to be this: Is my heart open to God? Am I eager to learn what God wants me to do, and am I willing to do it?

✂ Group Activity: Recovery Group
Step 3 (decide to turn my life over to God's care)
List five times in your life when you consciously chose to do something you knew was wrong. Recall what happened in each case. Then share with the others to see if their experiences parallel yours.

Together study another case history found in the O.T. Read Numbers 14 aloud, and discuss. How did the Israelites know the right thing to do? What did they do? What were the consequences of their disobedience?

Hebrews 3 looks back on that experience, warning us when we hear God's voice in our day, we must obey to avoid personal disaster. We can only experience God's rest (his best, blessing, and inner peace) if we respond with obedience.

Read silently and think about Hebrews 3:1-15. After rereading and considering the passage, list three things you know that God wants you to do. Make specific plans to respond and do God's will.

In teams of five, tell the three things you listed, and talk about what you intend to do. If you feel you need encouragement or strength, ask for others' support and prayers. Then close in teams with prayer for one another.

A tragic end (Heb. 3:16-19). The writer now returned to that Old Testament generation, to identify them clearly, and to mark off sharply the tragic results of hardening hearts and lives to the Lord. Who were the rebels? They were actually men and women who had experienced the mighty acts of God by which He freed them from slavery in Egypt! With whom was God angry? These very people who sinned—and whose bodies ultimately fell in the wilderness, never to know the rest of entering the Promised Land. And who does God declare can never experience His rest? No one who disobeys God can ever enter His rest!

A "rest" remains (Heb. 4:1-11). This section of Hebrews is complicated by a multiple use of the word "rest" and by a complex argument. We can best follow the thought if we sort out some of the elements, rather than attempt to analyze the passage verse by verse.

*The promise stands. This is the thought with which the chapter begins (v. 1). Even though a later, obedient generation did enter the Promised Land, that entry did not completely fulfill the promise of a "rest" for God's people. In fact, much later, in the time of David, the promise and the warning were repeated: "Today, if you hear His voice" (v. 7). If God's full blessing for His people had been granted when Joshua led Israel into Palestine, then the promise of a rest would not have been repeated much later to the people of David's day, or by the writer of Hebrews to Christians then and now.

*The nature of rest. The word "rest" is used in Hebrews 3 and 4 in three distinct senses. First is the usage we've seen. Entry into the Promised Land, so large a feature of Old Testament history, is a portrait—a tangible example—of the idea of rest.

It was an appropriate picture. God had promised the land to Abraham and his descendants. During the years of Israel's slavery in Egypt, pagan peoples had populated and improved the land. They had built houses, planted vineyards and orchards, and tamed the wilderness. Yet their lifestyle more and more evidenced the grossest of sins. The time of their judgment by God corresponded with Israel's release from slavery. In coming into Canaan, Israel would be God's instrument of judgment on sin—and would inherit riches for which she had not labored. The people would sit under trees they had not planted and drink wine made from grapes of vines they had not cultivated. They would come into a land where the work had been done—and they would rest.

Like Israel of old, you and I in Jesus have been delivered from slavery. Sin's power in our lives has been broken, and we are called by God to enter a "Promised Land" experience, in which we will rest. We are to enjoy the benefits of the work Jesus has done for us. The Christian life is not one of struggle to carve out a bare living in the wilderness. The Christian life is one of appropriating all the benefits of the spiritual abundance that Jesus so richly provides.

495

A second connotation of "rest" is seen in the application of the term to God's own rest on completion of Creation. The Jewish teachers had noted a fascinating feature of the Genesis account. For each of the first six days, the text speaks of "evening and morning." The beginning and the end were clearly marked off. But the seventh day has no such demarcation. The rabbis took this to mean that God's rest has no end. With the creative work complete, God is not *inactive*, but He no longer creates, for that work is done.

Strikingly, it is *His* rest (4:5) that believers are invited to enter! We are to come to the place where we appropriate fully what God has done, and while never becoming inactive, we do stop *laboring*. The load of a Christian life that some experience as a struggle is lifted. The pressure of trying harder is gone.

Entering rest. The analysis of the early generation that failed is a specific application to the believer's experience. "There remains, then, a Sabbath-rest for the people of God" (v. 9). The Bible tells us that we are to rest from our own work, just as God did from His (v. 10). The lifestyle of the person who is raised to mastery of life in Christ is not to be the ceaseless struggle some know. There is to be an experience of rest.

In chapter 3's analysis of the early generation that failed to experience the promised rest, we saw that the critical problem involved their attitude toward God. This people heard what God said. But they hardened their hearts, and would not respond. Unwilling to trust God, they were unable to obey.

Modern psychology thinks of an "attitude" as a disposition or tendency to respond. Attitudes are always linked to behavior. To say that a person has a critical attitude implies that in many situations he will tend to criticize (rather than appreciate) others.

The rebellious attitude exhibited by the men and women Moses led out of slavery also had clear consequences. When God spoke to them, their tendency was, first of all, to fail to trust Him. And, second, to disobey.

In the Bible these two characteristics, trust and obedience, are always linked. Trust in God (believing what He says to us is prompted by love, and actually does mark

out the very best pathway for us) is critical to the kind of obedience God desires. A person who does not trust, but rather fears, might produce an *outward conformity* to the orders of a tyrant. But only trust and love enable us to make a willing, inner commitment to follow the instructions of our Heavenly Father. When we trust God, we are freed to obey from the heart.

What then contrasts with the rebellious attitude of the disobedient generation? A *responsive* attitude. When we hear God's voice today, what is important to God and to us is simply that we trust ourselves to Him and obey.

Faith in God, expressed in obedient response to His voice, is the critical principle which sums up the lifestyle expected of God's children. What you and I are to concentrate on in our Christian lives is entering God's rest by making faith's response whenever we hear His voice.

How can we sum it up? Let's realize the implications of God's own rest. Since Creation itself, there has been no contingency for which God has not planned; no problem for which He hasn't a solution. God has been active while at rest, for all has been cared for. For us to enter God's rest means simply to learn to be responsive to God's written and contemporary voice, and let His living Word guide us to the solutions He has already prepared for our every difficulty. Like God, we remain active. But amid all our work, we are at rest. We are not troubled, burdened, or loaded down. We know that God will lead us through His living Word, and that we will find His prepared and Promised Land by listening to Him.

Some have interpreted the next words in Hebrews 4 as a threat:

The Word of God is living and active. Sharper than any double-edged sword, it penetrates even to dividing soul and spirit, joints and marrow; it judges the thoughts and attitudes of the heart. Nothing in all creation is hidden from God's sight. Everything is uncovered and laid bare before the eyes of Him to whom we must give account.

Hebrews 4:12-13

To those who fail to see themselves as Jesus' brothers, and to understand the thought of Hebrews 3 and 4, it may seem frightening. Such people might cringe as they imagine these verses describe God examining *them,* to highlight each hidden fault. But this is not the point at all! The writer has just explained rest. That rest goes beyond the promise of Palestine to Israel. God's rest is a rest of soul and spirit, a rest of thought and attitude. The inner person is to be at rest as well. And we can rest, for nothing is hidden from God's gaze. He knows our deepest, most secret needs, and with His Word lays bare that need — and guides us into rest.

God's Living Voice

Today too Jesus is the voice of freedom for you and me. As the ever-living Word, He calls us today to enter His Promised Land of rest.

But we still wonder. How do we hear Christ's "today" voice? In a verse torn from context? In circumstances? In a friend's advice? As far as Scripture is concerned, it is clear that God's voice is heard *in the flow of the Bible message.* But that flow is not itself God's voice. God's voice speaks to us through the understanding we gain from grasping what the Scriptures teach.

What I mean is this. Note how carefully the writer of Hebrews develops his argument. Step by step he has helped his readers see the superiority of Christ, and realize their own release through Him. Such careful development tells us that God does not depend on shedding light in snatches! God works carefully to help us understand a whole new way of thought. *It is in the understanding — in the context of the message — that the living voice is heard.* Yet God's voice is itself subjective and personal. The Holy Spirit speaks through the Word to you with His answer for your problem — for your most pressing present need. And He speaks through the same word with His answer for my problem, though my needs may be different. The Holy Spirit within us actively applies God's truth to our individual situations, and He Himself is the voice of our living Lord.

It is true that the Spirit may speak to us through circumstances. And God may use a Christian friend. But always, the voice is heard within the flow of the message given us in Scripture's written Word, as God the Holy Spirit looks deep within our souls and spirits and applies His truth to you and to me.

And when we hear this living voice, telling us God's way, then we hurry to obey in joyful trust and faith. By obeying, we enter the land of rest and freedom that Jesus has proclaimed.

GROUP RESOURCE GUIDE

Identification: *Share with others*
Try reading Hebrews 4:12-13 aloud. Several of you can read in a threatening tone, and several as if these words were an exciting, positive promise. Then share your reaction: How do these verses make you feel, and why?

Exploration: *Probe God's Word*
Scan Hebrews 3:7–4:13, and underline the following key words: Today, Voice, Hardened hearts, Rest, Unbelief, Disobedience. Then in teams of three work from the text to define each term, and to describe how each is related to the others. When done, reassemble and compare. If there is disagreement, check with the commentary.

Reaction: *Respond together to the Word*
Write down brief descriptions of two situa-

tions in which you have been uncertain about what you will do. Then answer each of the following questions:

* Is your uncertainty because you don't know the right decision to make?

* If so, have you listened to God for His direction?

* Is your uncertainty because you don't like what you think you should do?

* If so, is your idea about what you "should do" based on your best reasoning, or on a conviction about God's will?

* Are you ready to do what God wants — whatever that is — when you do hear God's voice giving you "today" guidance?

Share, not necessarily the situations, but your answers to the questions above.

Adoration: *Worship and pray*

Read aloud the author's explanation of Hebrews 4:12-13. Because God's Word searches and knows our innermost being, He understands thoroughly our deepest needs and is able to guide us into those paths which provide the rest we need.

Hebrews 4:12-13 is not a threat, but a wonderful promise.

Meditate on these words as promises. And then praise God for the wisdom and love with which He speaks words of guidance to us today.

JESUS, OUR HIGH PRIEST

Overview

In the Old Testament the high priest was the man appointed to represent the people before God. He was the man who dealt with sins and weaknesses by offering the necessary sacrifices for sins (Heb. 5:3). But as a link between God and man, the Old Testament priest was never enough. He was a shadow representing the coming perfect intermediary.

Hebrews 4:14 affirms that in Jesus "we have a great High Priest." As a human being He is able to sympathize with us in our weaknesses. Yet He is also God: the Son has "gone into heaven" to take His stand in the very presence of the Father.

Because Jesus is both God and Man, He is an adequate link between us and the Father. So the Scripture says, "Let us then approach the throne of grace with confidence, so that we may receive mercy and find grace to help us in our time of need" (v. 16). When we fail and are ashamed, or when we are overwhelmed and need help desperately, we need never draw back. Jesus, human like us, will understand. And Jesus, God as is the Father, is able to aid.

It is important, when we have heard the voice of God calling us to act, and still feel inadequate, that we turn to Jesus as High Priest and realize all that He is able to do for us.

In this important study, then, you will guide your group members to see Jesus as their High Priest, and rely on Him.

Commentary

For the Hebrew Christians to whom this letter was written, the ministry and qualifications of a priest were well known. For the modern reader, without any intimate experience of the Old Testament priestly concept, these may seem strange. Yet what these chapters teach is important, for they speak not only of the shadow pictures of the old economy but of realities vital to Christian experience.

The Priestly Ministry: Hebrews 5:1-10

This passage begins by making three statements about the priesthood . . . and then by commenting on two.

Its function and qualifications (Heb. 5:1-3). The priest represented other men "in matters related to God" and offered "gifts and sacrifices for sins." Jesus of course offered Himself, and by that one sacrifice, opened the door to permanent relationship with God. Anyone who desires to come to God can come through Jesus. Thus Jesus fulfills everything that the Old Testament hinted at concerning relationship with God.

The high priest of the Old Testament had to be "selected among men" and be "able to deal gently with those who are ignorant and are going astray, since he himself is subject to weakness." Jesus was surely chosen from among men, for He became a Man. But what about "subject to weakness"?

Hebrews 4:15 says that Jesus is able "to sympathize with our weaknesses" because as a Man He was "tempted in every way just as we are—yet without sin."

This verse is often misunderstood, in part because of misunderstanding of weakness. Weakness does not refer to our human tendency to give in to temptation, but to our capacity to feel it! Our weakness is human frailty itself: the hungers, the desires, the pains to which we are subject and which push and pull against our wills. Jesus, in taking on human nature, took on our *weaknesses* as well. At every point in every way, Jesus was tested as we are. In fact, He was tempted *beyond the point at which we give in!*

Imagine two prisoners of war being tortured to make them do a propaganda radio broadcast. One, after two months, can stand it no longer and yields. The other resists beyond the two months for years, even though the pressures increase. Both learned something of their weakness as the pressures grew. But only the one who continued to resist *really* knew how weak he was, as he daily had to cope with and overcome his human frailty. Only the one who continued to resist understood the full weight of pain that being a human being involves.

And this is what the Bible says about Jesus. He knows more about human frailty than we do. He really understands how terrible it is to be *weak*. And because He understands, He is able to sympathize with us when we find ourselves tempted.

In Hebrews 5 the writer says more about Jesus' humanity and its relationship to His present high priestly ministry. First, in Gethsemane Jesus knew a desperate extremity which drove Him to pray "with loud cries and tears" (v. 7). Note that Jesus prayed to One who could "save Him from *death*," not "save Him from *dying*." And God did, taking Jesus from the very grip of death in Resurrection. Yet Jesus' suffering extended through the ultimate – dying itself. Jesus surely *does* understand human weakness: He experienced all that it means.

This full and total identification with us enables Jesus to "deal gently" with us when we go astray. The Greek word, *metriopatheia*, suggests a balanced involvement. We've seen mothers so upset at a child's accident that they are unable to help. *Metriopatheia* suggests both feeling with the injured, yet being detached enough to react and to act for the other's good.

Second, the writer says that Jesus met His dying with "reverent submission." Thus He was able to "learn obedience" from the things He suffered (vv. 7-8). We never benefit from our trials or sufferings when we react rebelliously or in panic. God seeks to strengthen us through every experience of life. Meeting life with reverent submission frees us from being overwhelmed, and helps us grow in our own ability to feel with those who are hurt or needed without becoming so "sympathetic" that we are unable to help.

Finally the writer notes that these experiences and His suffering "made [Jesus] perfect" (v. 9). The phrase does *not* suggest that Jesus fell short, as God or as a human being. The Greek word, *teleios*, speaks of *a perfection that is related to the purpose or function for which a thing or person is designed.* If

Jesus were to be fitted for the task of High Priest. He "learned," in the sense of personally experiencing, the pain of being human and the cost of obedience when suffering is involved.

And thus, as a truly qualified Person, Jesus was appointed by God, who alone has the right to determine who will be High Priest to His people (vv. 4-6), to His priestly ministry.

♥ *Group Activity: Support Group*
Jot down the name of the person in your support group who you feel best understands you. Without sharing the name, discuss: What factors led you to name the person you did rather than some other person in your group?

Hebrews 4:14–5:10 encourages us to come to God's throne of grace "with confidence," and assures us that Jesus is able to "deal gently" with us in our weaknesses. Explore this passage in pairs, identifying what it is that makes Jesus so sympathetic and understanding. Also jot down any questions you may have.

Share findings, and if necessary refer to the commentary to answer questions the passage may raise.

Then meditate in silence on Jesus as a Friend – one who understands and is sympathetic because He has shared our struggles and pain, and knows how difficult life can be.

On to Maturity: Hebrews 5:11–6:8

The writer was discouraged. If only these Jewish believers could grasp the import of Christ's High Priesthood! If only they would grasp these basic truths, apply them, and by "constant use [application]" go on to maturity! But these Christians are immature, and "slow to learn," not having grasped even the elementary truths of the Gospel.

Deep controversy has raged over what the writer is about to say in Hebrews 6. There are few passages that have stimulated more debate. Over the years, four main interpretations of Hebrews 6 have been suggested:

(1) These verses speak of Jews who had *professed* Christ but stopped short of true faith.

(2) These verses refer to believers who have fallen into sin, and will lose their reward.

(3) These verses refer to believers who have slipped back into unbelief, and have lost their salvation.

(4) These verses give a hypothetical case, used to demonstrate the foolishness of a panic which insists "hold on" when Christians should instead "go on."

Before we select one of these, let's look carefully at what verses 1-4 call elementary teaching, or if you will, foundation truths.

Foundation truths. It is important to see these truths for what they are—truly foundational. Remember that a foundation is a solid and secure base on which one can build. Once the foundation has been laid, we can trust ourselves to it and get on with the business of construction. What the writer identified for these panicky Jewish believers who look back to the Old Testament faith and lifestyle are foundational truths that should provide security. Grasping them, feeling secure, these believers should have gone on to maturity.

What are the foundation truths on which we can rely?

- Repentance from dead works. Coming to Christ we realize that our works had nothing to do with salvation or the life Jesus offers. We turn away from a "works righteousness" in the Christian life as well.
- Faith in God. Trust in God is the key to salvation. That transaction of saving faith is complete.
- Instruction about baptisms. In the early church, careful instruction preceded baptism. It is likely this refers to the basic doctrines taught and accepted before baptism took place.
- Laying on of hands. This may refer to church discipline (leaders were appointed with the laying on of hands) or perhaps to teaching about the Holy Spirit (whose entry into the believer was so symbolized).
- Resurrection of the dead and eternal judgment. These doctrines summarize the believer's hope.

The writer, then, is asking us to believe so fully that when Christ came into our lives *all these things were settled* that we no longer worry about our relationship with the Lord. We *know* that He loves us. We *know* that we are saved.

The emphasis on an already laid foundation, and the Hebrews' tendency to look away, leads us to conclude that the fourth suggestion best explains the teaching of verses 4-10. The writer is posing a hypothetical case to demonstrate just how foolish the Hebrews' panic and uncertainty are. The writer says, "Let's not go back again as if there were no foundation to rest on." The fact is that *the basic issues of death, faith, and resurrection have been settled by the finished work of Christ.* So the writer asks:

What would you want to do? View your failure as a falling away of God, so access is now lost? How then would you ever be restored—you who have been enlightened, tasted the heavenly gift, shared in the Holy Spirit, and known the flow of resurrection power? Do you want to crucify Jesus all over again, and through a new sacrifice be brought back to repentance? How impossible! What a disgrace, this hint that Jesus' work for you was not enough.

Hebrews 6:4-6, author's paraphrase

The point here is simple. God wants us to know that Jesus' death is enough. There is no more need for sacrifices for sin. By His one sacrifice Jesus made "perfect forever those who are being made holy" (10·14). *You and I, like the Hebrews, are free to get on with the business of living for Jesus because He has resolved forever the question of our relationship with God.*

Two brief paragraphs that follow reinforce this understanding. From 6:7-8 we learn that the issue is one of fruitfulness. God is (and we are to be) concerned with the products of maturity.

Verses 9-12 are words of encouragement. Calling the readers, "dear friends," the writer looks at the fruit they have already produced. Their work, their love for God, and love for God's people, show that they have taken first steps, and are making progress. But how we each need, not hesitant progress, but a full commitment to that obedience which brings us maturity.

✍ *Group Activity: Bible Study Group*
The interpretation of Hebrews 6:1-12 has been much debated in church history. Yet it clearly follows the pattern established by the three other "warning" passages in this book.

Begin by distributing to each person or

drawing on a chalkboard or sheet of newsprint the "Warnings" chart on page 491. Together look at the other three passages on the chart, and fill in each cell on the chart.

Individually, try a rough paraphrase of the Hebrews 6 passage, remembering that the pattern of the passage follows that of the other warning segments. Then together try to fill in the chart cells for this passage too, and work toward a common paraphrase. If you have questions, refer to the commentary.

Finally, read 6:13-20 aloud, and thank God for the certainty we have when we put our trust in our promise-keeping God.

Our anchor. Just to make sure that his readers had not misunderstood, the writer spoke of the confidence we can have in the full access won for us by Jesus. Our access is guaranteed by God's oath, so that "we who have fled to take hold of the hope offered to us may be greatly encouraged. We have this hope as an anchor for the soul, firm and secure. It enters the inner sanctuary behind the curtain, where Jesus, who went before us, has entered on our behalf" (vv. 18-20).

✂ *Group Activity: Recovery Group Steps 2 (believe in a higher power) and 3 (decide to turn my life over to God's care)*
Jot down the names of two people: the least trustworthy person you have known, and the most trustworthy person. Together, thinking of these individuals, develop a cluster of characteristics of the person you would be willing to trust, and the person you would not be willing to trust.

Hebrews 6:13-15 notes that God made promises to Abraham and kept them. In teams, read one of the following stories about Abraham. How does it make God's commitment to keep His promise more impressive?

A. Genesis 12:10-20
B. Genesis 16
C. Genesis 20

After each team has reported, read on through Hebrews 6:16-20. Then discuss: What do I personally see in Genesis and in this passage that makes me willing to turn my life and will over to God?

More on Priesthood: Hebrews 7:1-8:13
The writer's previous references to Melchizedek are now explained. This mysterious figure, who was king of Jeruslaem in Abraham's day, was offered tithes (the tenth part of one's goods, set apart by the Old Testament Law for the priesthood) by the patriarch himself! To the writer, this demonstrated the superiority of the Melchizedekian priesthood, for the unborn Levi, head of the tribe from which Old Testament priests were drawn, might be said to have paid tithes to Melchizedek through his great-grandfather, Abraham (7:1-10).

The writer now contrasted Christ's priesthood with that of the Old Testament order (vv. 11-28).

- The new Priest's ministry does not rest on family line but on "the power of an indestructible life" (v. 16).
- The former priesthood was set aside because it was unable to provide perfect access. In Jesus, we have "a better hope . . . by which we draw near to God" (v. 19).
- The former priests died. Jesus continues forever as a permanent Priest. "Therefore He is able to save completely those who come to God through Him, because He always lives to intercede for them" (v. 25).

This, the writer exults, is the High Priest we need. You and I, living in a culture in which the priesthood principle is relatively unknown, may dismiss these arguments as irrelevant. But our High Priest is a present reality, a reality we need to grasp and know. Because Jesus lives as our High Priest, we too have guaranteed access to God. In failure, we can claim the promised mercy. Under the daily pressures of our lives, we can claim the help of a Man who knows our every need, and who knows as well the path of victory.

The writer now made an important observation. The change in priesthood indicated a change in other elements of the Old Testament system. And one of those changes was a change in covenant—that is, a change in the nature of the promises God has made to us that define how He relates to us as His people.

The Old Testament itself promised that one day the Old Covenant of Mosaic Law would be replaced, because it was inadequate. Thus the Hebrews' yearning for the old ways was doubly unwise. But where does the superiority of the new lie? Why is it so much better for us? In part because, in Jesus, we have a better High Priest. But also because of *the impact of the New Covenant on our very personalities.* God had said that when the new comes:

> I will put My laws in their minds and write them on their hearts. I will be their God, and they will be My people. No longer will a man teach his neighbor, or a man his brother, saying, "Know the Lord," because they will all know Me, from the least of them to the greatest. For I will forgive their wickedness and will remember their sins no more."
>
> Hebrews 8:10-12

God's change in the system is a simple one. He takes the laws which express righteousness and puts them, not in external commandments, but on inner tablets of mind and heart. Notice that two things are necessary. We must know *what* God's righteous standards are and *how* to translate them into personal experience. The Law can tell us what the standards are. But only a changed heart will enable us to live by those standards.

This is what is so exciting here. God now puts His laws in our minds and writes them in our hearts.

It is through the Bible that we come to understand the will of God. And it is here we find the principles that show us how to live a righteous life. But it is only the transformed heart, which spontaneously responds to God and His Word, that will move us to righteousness.

We can summarize then what Hebrews here reveals. Mosaic Law does deal with righteousness. The shadow it cast across the Old Testament showed that God, its Giver, is righteous. The shadow shows us something of what righteous behavior is. The shadow shows us that God really cares about seeing righteousness in us. But commandment law was only a shadow; it could not *produce* righteousness. It dealt with externals, but did not touch the heart.

Then Jesus came. In Jesus' human personality, the full righteousness of Commandment Law was expressed as living truth. Then Jesus died. And in His death and resurrection, Jesus snatched us up and, calling us "brothers," brought us into the divine family. In making us sons, God planted deep within us something of Jesus' own personality. "Christ in you," Paul says, is "the hope of glory" (Col. 1:27). When Jesus entered our lives He brought righteousness with Him. That which had been expressed in external commands now is expressed in our hearts and minds. That very element of the old system which broke down (the human element) has now been changed.

The outer Commandment Law of the old has become an inner law through the new.

And all this is enhanced as we see Jesus as our High Priest. When we see Jesus as High Priest, we realize that the shame of failures that once drove us from God no longer matters. Jesus understands, He sympathizes, and He can help us overcome our weaknesses. Because of Jesus we run *to* God, not from Him.

And Jesus as High Priest promises not only access but also renewal. He is constantly at work within us, writing His law and very personality in our inner selves. This too is ours through Jesus, our High Priest.

Because of Jesus, the door to God is always open, and so we always have hope. The old doorkeepers, the Aaronic priests, are gone. Their struggle to keep open the crack that the Old Testament opened in relationship to God is ended. Jesus has come, and He has not only thrown open the door, but He stands in it to welcome us personally when we turn to Him.

GROUP RESOURCE GUIDE

Identification: *Share with others*
In a single sentence sum up how you feel about yourself when you sin or fall short of your own ideal. Then list key words from these sentences on a chalkboard or sheet of newsprint.

Exploration: *Probe God's Word*
Divide into teams of three. Each is to read one of the following passages and determine from it how God feels about us when we sin or fall short. Also, what does He do, and what are we to do?

Passages to read are: Hebrews 4:14-5:10; 7:1-26; and 8:1-13. After 20 or 25 minutes, come together and report what each passage teaches and/or suggests.

Reaction: *Respond together to the Word*
These chapters cast their answer to these questions in the context of Jesus' priesthood. Together list key features of Christ's priestly ministry, and identify how each applies to our present experience. (If in doubt, see commentary.)

Adoration: *Worship and pray*
Give each person a string of three linked paper clips, using a colored clip for the middle link. The middle link symbolizes Jesus, who as High Priest holds us in living relationship with God. Praise Him for this ministry, reminding us again that our security does not depend on the strength of our grip on faith, but on God's grip on us through His promise and grace. And keep the string of three clips as a reminder of the strength of your present relationship with the Lord.

Jesus grips US

THE FATHER

CHRIST is the link that holds us in living relationship with God

Our High Priest

His high priestly ministry

Us, His adopted sons

As our High Priest, Jesus is the link between us and God. As High Priest, He holds us. Our safety does not depend on *our* grip, but on His.

JESUS, THE PERFECT SACRIFICE

Overview

The sacrificial system was a vital element in Old Testament faith. The Mosaic Law code established standards which, while shaping the lifestyle of Israel, no individual could live up to. And anyone who fell short, in even one point (James 2:10-11), was guilty of sin.

Yet God made provision for sinners. With the Law, God gave Moses the pattern for building a tabernacle, and established a sacrificial system. A sinner could bring a required blood sacrifice, have his sins covered, and so approach God. The one way into the tabernacle—the only door to the courtyard of the place of meeting with God—opened onto the altar of sacrifice. There was no other way for a sinner to approach God. Only blood on the altar could cover human sin.

The writer of the Book of Hebrews argued that the Old Testament sacrifices spoke of Jesus, the perfect Sacrifice, who has done what animal sacrifices could never accomplish. Jesus has actually *perfected* the sinner washed in His blood, and made the sinner holy in God's sight! There is no need for repeated sacrifices, for by His one sacrifice on Calvary Jesus has fully met our need, freeing us completely from sin, guilt, and shame.

Why is this teaching so important to believers today? Because, when we understand just what Jesus has done for us, we find our conscience cleansed and experience release from our bondage to past failures. And we have hope that we will live a new and holy life.

Commentary

There's something almost soft (too soft?) in the tone of the previous four chapters of Hebrews. It's almost as if, in emphasizing the compassion of Jesus our High Priest, the writer is saying, "Don't let sin bother you. It's all right with God."

After all, the promise of sympathy, the guarantee of access, the assurance of mercy—all these seem to indicate indifference to something we are sure the holy God must care about deeply. How can God deal so gently with those of His family who resist His voice and rebel against Him?

In fact, God is *not* being soft. Or indifferent. But to see what He is saying, and to grasp its impact, we need to understand the difference between shame and guilt.

Shame and Guilt

Let's suppose a person cheats on his income tax returns by misrepresenting income and expenses. Let's further suppose the fraud is discovered, and we're listening in on an interview between the individual and an Internal Revenue agent:

"OK, I guess you've got me."

"Yes, Mr. Anderson. I'm afraid it's all pretty clear."

"Well, you can't blame me for trying. I suppose everybody gives themselves the benefit of the doubt."

"I think you've gone beyond that. This is a pretty clear case of fraud, and we're thinking of prosecuting you."

"Now wait a minute! I'll pay the tax you say I owe, and the penalty too. But you can't prove I didn't just make an honest mistake."

"I think we can prove fraud, Mr. Anderson. And it's very possible that we'll try."

"Please. I won't try to talk you out of it. But—well, will my children have to know?"

Notice the three different evaluations of the same act. And the three possible responses.

- *Guilt.* Mr. Anderson committed fraud. He was guilty of breaking the law. No matter how he felt about himself or his actions, the objective guilt remained.

- *Guilt feelings.* This is the personal sense of guilt Mr. Anderson might well feel, but apparently did not. Instead, he justified his actions: "Everybody gives themselves the benefit of the doubt."
- *Shame.* No matter how Mr. Anderson may justify his action, the question, "Will my children have to know?" shows more was involved than guilt and guilt feelings. There was also shame, that agonizing worry about what other people would think.

We need to distinguish between each of these. Guilt speaks of the objective blame that has accrued through a specific act, and that merits punishment. Guilt feelings focus on how a person feels about himself. Shame springs from fear of others' disgust, disappointment, or ridicule once they know.

In our society we concentrate almost entirely on guilt feelings. Strikingly, the Bible seldom speaks of them. The focus in Scripture is on guilt as an objective reality. But today much Gospel preaching promises release from *felt* guilt through faith in Christ.

Sometimes missionaries, moving into another culture, begin by proclaiming freedom from guilt feelings and are stunned that no one seems concerned. As they learn more about the culture, they discover that the deep-felt need there relates to shame. To be exposed in the eyes of others—there is the terror.

In shame cultures the Gospel presentation may well shift from the emphasis given in guilt cultures. And if it does, we find that Scripture presents Jesus as the answer for shame as well as guilt.

See, I lay a stone in Zion, a chosen and precious Cornerstone, and the one who trusts in Him will never be put to shame.

Isaiah 28:16, author's paraphrase

The Hebrew culture was distinct in that both guilt and shame were understood. And in Jesus, God promises to these believing Hebrews the one remedy that speaks to *all* our needs. In Jesus, God provides release from guilt, guilt feelings, and from shame as well!

This is the answer to the uncomfortable feeling that perhaps our compassionate High Priest, revealed in Hebrews 5–8,

shows too little concern for holiness. The picture of Jesus holding open the door, and inviting us to come to God relates specifically to shame. Our failure to respond to God's voice drives us to hide ourselves from Him. We cannot face God, knowing that He knows. But in the High Priest, we discover that God does not condemn or ridicule. In His eyes, we remain precious and respected. Jesus knows the weakness of our flesh: He understands, and His response is one of sympathy.

This is how God deals with our shame. But how does He deal with our guilt and with our guilt feelings? The answer to this question is found in Hebrews 9 and 10.

Observations on the Text: Hebrews 9–10
The earthly tabernacle (Heb. 9:1-10). The writer immediately launched his readers into the argument. The Old Testament system included a sanctuary carefully designed by God. The inner sanctuary, representing the very presence of God, was entered only by the high priest. Even then, he entered only once a year and always carried the blood of a sacrifice he had offered "for himself and for the sins the people had committed" (v. 7). The veil, which covered the inner sanctuary at all times and was pulled aside only briefly for the animal sacrifice, was God's visual aid, a reminder that the door to God was not yet thrown open. In the same way, it was clear that the repeated sacrifices, which never succeeded in removing the veil, "were not able to clear the conscience of the worshiper" (v. 9). Sins were merely "covered." This is the meaning of the Hebrew word *kaphar*—"atonement." But sin had not been removed, and so the guilt remained.

I read in the newspaper about a woman who lost both kidneys to disease. For eight months she had lived on a dialysis machine. Pumped through the machine, her blood was kept clean of impurities. The machine took the place of kidneys temporarily. The article went on to tell how she had been disappointed three times as donor kidneys were thought available for transplants, then refused. The transplant was her real hope. She only used the machine until real kidneys became available.

It was like this with the Old Testament saints. The sacrifices, like the dialysis machine, kept them going. But the real hope

Jesus Deals with Sin

An act of sin . . .	generates	Jesus deals with sin as	providing
	Shame	High Priest (compassionate)	Access (Heb. 5–8)
	Guilt	High Priest and blood sacrifice	Forgiveness (Heb. 9–10)
	Guilt feelings	High Priest and blood sacrifice	Cleansing (Heb. 9–10)

for life was that someday a *cure* could be found. Someday transplanted life might deal with the sickness from within. And until then, the repeated sacrifices only reminded Israel of how sick with sin they really were.

Then Jesus came to effect the cure. He came to deal with the poison of sin from within, not to cover it but to cleanse from it. Jesus, the true Sacrifice to which all the animal sacrifices had pointed, in one unique act, *perfected forever* those of us set apart to God by His death.

An interesting phrase in Hebrews 10 helps us get a better glimpse of what God is trying to communicate to us, "In practice, however, the sacrifices amounted to an annual reminder of sins" (10:3, PH). Rather than removing the sense of being sinners and guilty in God's sight, the Old Testament sacrifices reminded men of their helpless and guilty state. How? In the same way that every time that kidney patient came to a dialysis machine to take another treatment she was reminded that she was *ill*. The machine that saved her life was a constant reminder of how near death was!

Jesus has come. The cure has been effected! And you and I are to be overwhelmed with a joyous sense of being *well!*

Christ's blood (Heb. 9:11-15). Then the writer contrasted the old system with Christ. As High Priest, Jesus:

- Entered   not the   but heaven.
             earthly
             sanctuary
- Offered   not the   but His
             blood of   own blood.
             animals
- Obtained   not   but eternal

temporary   redemption
covering   for us.

As a result, Jesus has succeeded in cleansing our consciences from those acts that led to death "so that we may serve the living God" (v. 14). Jesus' death was to set us free from sin and guilt—totally free!

✂ *Group Activity: Recovery Group*
Step 11 (improve relationship with God through prayer and meditation)
Read Hebrews 9:14. Briefly tell your reaction to what this verse says, and listen to the reaction of others.

Look at a copy of the chart on the top of this page, "Jesus Deals with Sin." Discuss: How have I been affected by shame? Guilt? Guilt feelings? How important to us is it that Jesus died to set us free from each?

List the sins and failings that continue to trouble you, even though you have turned your back on them since beginning your recovery process. List also sins and failings that you have admitted since beginning the recovery process, but which still nag at your conscience.

If you are willing today to take God's promise to welcome you, to forgive your sins, and to cleanse you from every residue of your old life, take your list to a place where you can read it aloud, and then burn it. Let the symbolic burning remind you that you are forgiven, you are welcomed, and that through Christ you will be continually cleansed and renewed.

One sacrifice (Heb. 9:16-28). Now the writer turned to one of those typically Jewish arguments understood by the Hebrew

Christians. Why death? Because inheritance (see v. 15) comes only after the death of a benefactor. So our inheritance in Christ came after—and through—His death. But more than that, death has always been associated with cleansing. The Old Testament in fact "requires that nearly everything be cleansed with blood, and without the shedding of blood there is no forgiveness" (v. 22). It was sufficient that the earthly sanctuary, which copied heavenly realities, be cleansed with animal sacrifices. But heaven itself demanded a higher sacrifice. And so the writer concluded that "now He [Christ] has appeared once for all at the end of the ages to do away with sin by the sacrifice of Himself" (v. 26).

By a single, sufficient sacrifice, Jesus has done what all the old repeated sacrifices could never accomplish. Sacrificed once, He took away the sins of His people.

Once for all (Heb. 10:1-10). This is a theme the writer wished to stress. Endlessly repeated sacrifices could never take away sins. In fact, their repetition was a reminder of guilt! If guilt were truly gone, there would have been no need for an annual sacrifice. But now Jesus has offered a single sacrifice, and "we have been made holy through the sacrifice of the body of Jesus Christ once for all" (v. 10).

Completeness (Heb. 10:11-18). In summing up, the writer made perfectly clear how completely Jesus has dealt with sin and guilt. By that one sacrifice "He has made perfect forever those who are being made holy" (v. 14). Sins are remembered no more. With forgiveness extended, "there is no longer any sacrifice for sin" (v. 18). *We have been cleansed.*

Hope of forgiveness (Heb. 10:19-25). Now comes another of those familiar digressions. Let us draw near to God, realizing that shame and guilt have been taken away by our great High Priest. Cleansed from a guilty conscience, we hold on to the hope forgiveness brings. Indeed, we now concentrate on "how we may spur one another on toward love and good deeds" (v. 24). With this cleansing, we are free to concentrate on living together for God.

God's dealings with His people (Heb. 10:26-39). A reaction almost always follows such a definite proclamation of forgiveness. Will the promise of forgiveness stimulate a believer to live carelessly? After all—if we're forgiven anyway. . . .

This reaction misunderstands many dynamics of the Christian life. Fear will not motivate us to respond to God. It is love and an awareness of who we are in Christ that frees us to hope. And it is God's power within our new lives that enables us to respond. But there are always some who misunderstand. Even some believers. And so the writer pens a warning. If there is deliberate, continuous sin, we do not benefit from Christ's sacrifice. Instead of freedom we find judgment—and that judgment is severe. The blood of Christ is not to be trampled underfoot, as though it were associated with unholiness. God "will judge His people" (v. 30), and under that judgment, we will know the terror roused by an angry Father.

But note—God is still dealing with His people. He acts, because the proclamation of full forgiveness is not meant as a license for sin. The message of forgiveness is intended to lead us into a life of holiness!

We are to keep on living God's way and find the same kind of holiness Paul described in Ephesians and Colossians. "You stood side by side" with those who were persecuted. "You sympathized with those in prison and joyfully accepted the confiscation of your property" (vv. 33-34). Confidence in God must not be thrown away because of difficulties in our lives. Holding fast to God and doing His will, "you will receive what He has promised" (v. 36). The holiness the writer speaks of is ours in Christ, something each of us will experience in our own daily lives.

Holiness Now?

Looking back over these two chapters, we find some amazing statements.

- Jesus "obtained eternal redemption" for us (9:12).
- Jesus cleansed "our consciences from acts that lead to death, so that we may serve the living God" (v. 14).
- God has made us "holy through the sacrifice of the body of Jesus Christ once for all" (10:10).
- Jesus by His one sacrifice "has made perfect forever those who are being made holy" (v. 14).
- "Their sins and lawless acts I will remember no more" (v. 12).

All of this, argues the writer, cleanses us

from a guilty conscience (v. 22) and frees us to draw near to God and live in hope.

There is no equivocation in these statements. No "ifs." No carrot-and-stick approach to life, holding out promises for performance of God's will and threatening condemnation should we fail to heed His voice. Instead there is a promise and the firm conviction that with our consciences cleansed we *will* "serve the living God."

What are the "acts that lead to death," and how do they affect our consciences so that we cannot serve God?

Guilt and forgiveness. In our day the meaning of the word "guilt" has shifted in the minds of most people from a biblical to a nonbiblical sense. We tend to use the word in the sense of "guilt feelings." The sense of being guilty or unclean is generally what we mean when "guilt" is used in print or conversation. But this sense of guilt feelings is *never found* in the Bible. There the word "guilt" means actual guilt incurred by acts of sin.

Actually, the word "guilt" appears seldom in the Scripture. There are only 6 occurrences in the New Testament and 16 in the Old. Instead the emphasis in Scripture is on forgiveness: 60 times the New Testament speaks of forgiveness, and the Old Testament many times more.

Forgiveness in the Bible is never seen as "passing over" guilt. The root meaning of both Hebrew and Greek words for forgiveness is "send away." God deals with guilt by *sending off* sin, not by overlooking it. With forgiveness, the source and cause of "guilt feelings" is removed, for the sin and guilt are gone.

Holiness. When we realize that our sins are truly gone, and will not be remembered against us, God's Spirit works in our consciences to cleanse and free us.

Conscience is that faculty which not only evaluates acts morally, but which *looks backward* and evaluates *past* actions. The Greeks saw conscience in a very negative light, as the accuser of mankind. In reminding of past failures it tormented men and women. The memory of the acts stored there lead to death in that they are chains: they bind us to an awareness of our inadequacies and weaknesses. They remind us of patterns of failure that have become part of our personalities. In this way, by shaping our sense of who we are, conscience robs us of our freedom to risk obeying God, by robbing us of our faith in His ability to change us.

And then Christ's good word comes to us, affirming forgiveness. The acts stored up in our consciences, the past failures and sins that bind us, are sent away. God remembers them no more—and we too are to forget our past! Instead of looking *backward* we are to look *ahead*! Rather than heeding conscience's message that we are sinners, we are to heed Jesus' message that we are now holy! And, convinced that Jesus truly has changed us, we have faith enough to step out and to obey, acting as a holy people would act.

It is this that the writer of Hebrews teaches. As long as our consciences were archives of failure, its reminder of our sin programmed us for death. Cleansed, our minds and hearts filled with a sense of holiness, we are now filled by God with that confidence and faith which lead us to actively serve Him.

God wants us to respond to Him, stepping out in joyful obedience. But He knows that a sense of guilt and shame will block responsiveness, not encourage it! Feelings of guilt and shame focus our attention on ourselves and not on God, from whom our strength must come. Feelings of guilt and shame make us hesitate; we dare not risk the burden of still more. A sense of guilt and shame blocks the flow of love which is the key motivation in the Christian's life. God does not seek to *make* us respond to Him. Instead He sets us free and invites us to shake off our past failures, and step out to experience liberty.

As a basis for this freedom—to assure us of our acceptance even if we should fail—God clearly announces the great realities. Jesus has once and for all dealt with sin. With sin forgiven, both guilt and shame loose their grip.

● God is not ashamed of you.

● God does not condemn you as guilty.

Because of what Jesus has done as our High Priest, God views you and me as perfect forever. In God's eyes, we are holy. And in proclaiming freedom God undertakes to make our experience of holiness coincide with who we are in Jesus, His Son.

GROUP RESOURCE GUIDE

Identification: *Share with others*
Listen to a previously taped recording of the dialog found on p. 505. What in a single word sums up what you think the "taxpayer" is feeling?

Exploration: *Probe God's Word*
In pairs read through Hebrews 9, and then answer the following questions based on Hebrews 10:
 (a) 10:1-4 shows the OT system for dealing with guilt was inadequate and frustrating. How?
 (b) 10:5-10 explains the purpose Jesus came and what He had to accomplish. What was it?
 (c) 10:11-18 explains the implication of repeating the OT sacrifices. What was it? What is the meaning of Jesus' one sacrifice?
 (d) 10:19-22 tells how we are to see ourselves in view of Jesus' one sacrifice. How is that?

 (e) 10:23-25 tells us how we are to relate to one another. How is that?
 Share your discoveries, and relate them to the chart found at the top of page 507.

Reaction: *Respond together to the Word*
God offers us complete acceptance and complete forgiveness in Christ. In addition, He promises to progressively cleanse and transform us. Share: Which of these is more important to you? How does knowing what God has done for us affect your feelings about God? About your past? About your future?

Adoration: *Worship and pray*
Select one verse from Hebrews 10 which sums up the chapter's most important contribution to you personally, and use it as a basis to construct a brief, written prayer.

JESUS, OUR SANCTIFICATION

Overview

The author of Hebrews demonstrated the superiority of Jesus over the Old Testament system, which foreshadowed His ministry. Jesus is superior as a revealer of God. Jesus' priesthood is far superior to the priesthood of the Old Testament, just as the covenant He makes is superior to the old Law Covenant which came through Moses. And Jesus has offered a superior sacrifice — Himself — which purifies the worshiper and deals once for all with sin.

On the basis of what Jesus has done for us, we are now made holy — and are enabled to live a holy life! Thus Jesus produces a righteousness which the old system was never able to do.

In the last chapters of Hebrews the writer went into just *how* we appropriate the sanctification that Christ provides. In chapter 11, we see the role of faith, not only for our own lives but in the lives of believers of every age. In chapter 12 we see the importance of making every effort to move toward the goal of holiness — and learn how to respond to the loving discipline of the God who is committed to bring His children to a godly maturity. Finally, in chapter 13, we are given a final warning and shown how the practical holiness is demonstrated in Christian behavior.

In these, as in other chapters of Hebrews, we and our students are invited to a fresh, exciting vision of how great our privileges are as God's own.

Commentary

The last thought of Hebrews 10 launches into a new major section of this book. We are not people who cower back and are ruined, but who fasten on faith, and so preserve and enrich ourselves.

With this thought the writer launches us on an adventurous exploration of how the believer, secure in his new identity as one of God's holy ones, is to live. With the "deeper truths" about who we are in Christ explained, the writer moves on to explore indepth truth about our new way of life.

Fasten on Faith: Hebrews 11

Often when we think of "faith" our image is one of subjective experience. But the validity of Christian faith does not rest on either our sincerity or our fervency. Christian faith stands or falls on the *truth* that the Word of God reveals. Thus the writer began Hebrews 11 by helping us realize that it is confidence in the reality of things we cannot see that lies at the root of faith. It is only "by faith we understand that the universe was formed at God's command, so that what is seen was not made out of what was visible" (v. 3).

Much of what the writer has told us about our new selves is invisible too. We can't see Jesus, standing as the link between us and heaven. We can't see ourselves as God does, holy and cleansed by the one great sacrifice of Christ. But when our minds accept these as fact, and we become certain of them even though we cannot yet see their full reality revealed, *then* we are ready to begin to live by faith.

But faith is more than conviction of the reality of the facts that God has unveiled. Faith also exists as response to those facts. The Scripture makes it clear: "Without faith it is impossible to please God, because anyone who comes to Him must believe that He exists and that He rewards those who earnestly seek Him" (v. 6). Faith is focused confidence in a person who not only exists, but who seeks a personal relationship with us. God loves us. He is *not* uninvolved. Instead, He is a rewarder of those who diligently seek Him.

When we are willing to accept as fact what God's Word says, and in response reach out to seek and to experience relationship with

Him, then we have begun to live by faith. And then we will be rewarded.

This living by faith—accepting as fact the truths that we cannot touch or feel or see, and then acting on them—seems such a simple prescription for life. Lest we make the mistake of equating simplicity with ineffectiveness, the chapter moves on to detail the accomplishments of faith.

Enablement (Heb. 11:4-31). In this extended passage the writer invites us to look into the lives of a host of heroes of the faith, and to see how faith expressed itself in their experiences. We see as the writer analyzes each life that, essentially, faith *enables.*

Faith enabled Abel (11:4). Aware that God required blood sacrifice (see Gen. 3:21; 4:7), Abel offered a sheep rather than fruit and vegetables. Faith found for Abel the way of acceptance, and "by faith he was commended as a righteous man."

Faith's first enabling step for us is the same. Pleading Jesus' one unique sacrifice, we receive the same testimony of imputed righteousness.

Faith enabled Enoch (11:5-6). The four verses devoted to Enoch in the Old Testament say twice that he "walked with God" (Gen. 5:21-24). One verse affirms that he walked with God for 300 years. His relationship was consistent.

For each of us too faith promises the possibility of a daily, consistent walk with the Lord, for faith enables us to please Him.

Faith enabled Noah (11:7). Noah lived in a time when all had turned their backs on God. He alone remained faithful. When warned of a coming flood, Noah devoted 120 years to the building of a great boat miles from any sea. Faith enabled Noah to cut through the contrary views of his contemporaries and to accept the warning of impending disaster as fact. And faith enables us to withstand social pressures and respond with reverence, obeying the command to build.

Faith can enable us to be different as well. We can build our lives on a revelation of the future that men who do not know God count foolish.

Faith enabled Abraham (11:8-10). The life of faith is a life of risk, of stepping out into the unknown with nothing more solid before us than God's command. Faith en-

abled Abraham to take an uncertain journey, not knowing where he was going, but only that God had summoned him.

Faith can enable you and me to take risks as well. We can even stand long periods of uncertainty (v. 9), for faith assures us that God's summons rests on His eternal purposes. What a solid foundation for our lives!

Faith enabled Sarah (11:11-12). Here is a most encouraging example. When Sarah first heard the promise, she doubted and laughed (Gen. 18:12-15). But first doubts were overcome. Faith swept in to enable her dead womb to gain the vitality needed for childbearing.

Often we're overcome by first doubts. Parts of our personalities seem deadened and withered. But faith can be restored. Even such "second-chance" faith can enable us to experience vitality in areas of our lives we saw as being dead.

Faith enabled all (11:13-16). Sometimes we have a difficult time identifying with great men of faith like Abraham. How good then to know that countless *unnamed* men and women looked ahead, lived, and died, assured that the promises would yet be theirs. These may remain unknown to us—but not to God.

It isn't our greatness in the eyes of others or even in our own eyes that's important. Faith enables unknown people as well. Faith enables each of us to count on God's promises—and because of faith "God is not ashamed to be called their God" (v. 16).

Faith enabled Abraham (11:17-19). Faith was of constant importance in Abraham's life, as it is in ours. The first steps of faith led to further steps, until finally the ultimate test came. Abraham was commanded by God to sacrifice his only son on an altar. Faith enabled Abraham to take even this jolting command in stride, and never lose confidence in God. He was even ready to believe that God could raise his son up, even if he were dead, for God had promised that Isaac was the key to his descendants (v. 19).

We too can trust God even this much. When we view Him as totally trustworthy, even the most difficult steps of obedience are made possible.

Faith enabled the patriarchs (11:20-22). Each father mentioned here looked ahead to a future that was unknown, but yet was guaranteed by God. Counting God's picture of tomorrow as sure, each ordered the life of his children as if that future were present.

Sometimes it's easier to let God have control of our lives than to guide our families into full commitment to Him. The sacrifice we'd willingly make ourselves we hesitate to impose on our boys and girls, wishing instead for their "happiness." Faith gives us a clearer view. We look across the generations and commit ourselves and our loved ones to the realities He says will be.

Faith enabled Moses (11:23-29). The many ways faith changed the life of Moses are stamped vividly on the pages of the Old Testament. Here we're reminded that at every critical stage in his life, faith shaped him for his ultimate ministry. His parents' initial faith saved his life (v. 23). Growing up, faith led him to throw in his lot with the slave people of Israel rather than his adoptive royal family (vv. 24-26). Faith enabled him to defy rather than give into Pharaoh, remaining obedient to the heavenly King (vv. 26-27). Faith led Moses to command the people to keep the first Passover, and to walk boldly into the Red Sea (vv. 28-29).

Almost every difficulty, every challenging experience, every danger, every decision in Moses' life was faced on the basis of faith's obedient response. Faith enabled each obedient act, and the pattern of faithful obedience that emerged made Moses the man he finally became.

It's the same with us. In everything in life we need to be guided and enabled by faith. As we live by faith, we will progressively become the persons God wants us to be.

Faith enabled Rahab (11:30-31). Faith took the godly Moses and made him even more a man of God. But Rahab was a prostitute! Did faith enable her?

Yes. This inhabitant of Jericho, a city marked for destruction, believed God. She acted in faith to save the Jewish scouts, and instead of sharing the fate of the disobedient, she became a member of the people of God.

Whatever your past, and whatever your old associations, faith can produce a great transformation. Through faith you can lose your old identity as sinner—and become a child of the living God.

Faith enables you and me. This is, of course, the point the writer of Hebrews

made. As example after example is given, we are shown that *faith works!* Faith does enable.

A promise of success? (Heb. 11:32-40) The pathway of faith that Hebrews commended is the answer to our search for meaning and progress in the Christian life. But it is no guarantee of good times.

Here the writer gave examples of victories won by faith's obedience (vv. 33-34), but he also presented the record of those whose lives of faith led to suffering (vv. 35-38). He told of those tortured to death, of others mocked and flogged and bound in prison, and still others killed by stoning or murdered by the sword. Some lost everything and fled naked into the desert, to live like animals in caves or holes.

No, taking the path of faith and committing ourselves to obey God no matter what, in no way promises that the circumstances of our lives will be pleasant.

Yet how comforting. Hebrews speaks to us in our difficult situations and in our failures, and it reassures us. Faith doesn't guarantee good times. Faith guarantees our realization of the hope we have for transformation *within.* Through faith, we are enabled to catch from day to day a growing hint of what we will be at Jesus' return, when the complete experience of perfection will be fully known.

🖊 Group Activity: Bible Study Group

Scan Hebrews 11 quickly, and identify the particular hero of faith listed there whom you are most like, or wish to be like. Meditate for several minutes on what the text says about the role of faith in his or her life.

Then take the role of that person. Go around the group, and each share "How faith enabled me," speaking as the chosen biblical character.

After sharing, dig into Hebrews 11 and together discuss what it says about these three issues: what faith is (Hebrews 11:1-6); what faith enables (11:7-31); and, what faith does not guarantee (11:32-40).

Discipline's Way: Hebrews 12

In Hebrews 11, the writer concluded that God has provided us with something the ancients waited for. His "something better" (v. 40) is to be made perfect in a maturity marked by the present experience of God's holiness. But how will God accomplish this promise now that the foundation for holiness has been laid by Christ?

Follow God's way (Heb. 12:1-4). The writer just listed a great group of men and women who witness to the value of a life of faith. In addition, the reader can fix his eyes on Jesus and see him walk God's pathway—and receive the crown! Yes, Jesus' path led to a cross. But His suffering was not the end. Holding fast to God's will by faith, Jesus chose to endure far more than such a choice could ever entail for these Hebrew Christians. Jesus' obedience cost Him life itself. The Hebrews, like you and me, had not yet resisted sin to the point of bloodshed.

The testimony given by people of faith and by Jesus Himself urges us to set aside everything that hinders and follow God's way.

Encouragement (Heb. 12:5-13). Now comes a word of encouragement. God will help! God commits Himself as a good Father to discipline and even to punish those He loves.

Several important characteristics of God's discipline are given:

*Discipline is a family thing. If suffering (one aspect of discipline) comes, some may fear God is angry or rejecting them. Not so. Even hardship is part of God's guidance for His sons (v. 7).

*Discipline's purpose is our good. Whatever motive human parents may have in discipline, God's sole concern is our good. He is motivated only by love (vv. 6, 10).

*Discipline has a clear goal in view. Through discipline, God helps us to share His holiness (v. 10).

*Discipline's product is assured. Though an extended time may be involved, and our experience during this time may be painful, we can rest assured. God's discipline does produce "a harvest of righteousness and peace for those who have been trained by it" (v. 11).

When we understand God's attitude and purpose for disciplining care, strength replaces feebleness. Discouragement gives way to hope.

Toward holiness (Heb. 12:14-28). Again, the writer turned to application and exhortation. Progress toward the goal of holiness is vital. We are to concentrate on working out holiness in our relationships with everyone (v. 14).

One danger is that we might miss God's grace in the discomfort of discipline. If we do, bitterness may grow up. Another is immorality—that focus on the sensual that led Esau to exchange God's promise for a cup of soup.

What is to protect us from such misunderstandings? Our vision of God. In the Old Testament, this vision brought terror. He was revealed in a mountain of burning fire, associated with darkness, gloom, and storm. Even Moses was terrified and reacted, "I am trembling with fear" (vv. 18-21). But what is *our* vision of God? In Christ, He has been revealed with "thousands upon thousands of angels in joyful assembly" (v. 22). Looking beyond shadow to see the reality, we greet the God who speaks as a Judge—yet His judgment has been executed in Jesus, and He now counts us "righteous men made perfect" (v. 23).

Yet, we can never forget that it is *God* who speaks (vv. 25-29). We reach out to touch the hand of a God who "is a consuming fire" (v. 29). But we are warmed, not burned! Yet still the fire consumes! The universe itself is shaken at His word; created things flee away. Only that which cannot be shaken will remain. What is that? The kingdom we are called to share. "We are receiving a kingdom that cannot be shaken," the writer concluded. "Let us be thankful [note, not fearful!], and so worship God acceptably with reverence and awe" (v. 28).

And so the writer promises us that God *will* guide us into an experience of His holiness. At times our way may seem difficult. But so was Jesus' way. Through it all, we are assured of the Father's changeless love. The fire that sears the universe merely warms God's sons and daughters. With this confidence, we can endure hardships and move on to holiness.

♥ *Group Activity: Support Group*
Write a brief description of a childhood incident which you associate with discipline. Then share your experience, and tell how it made you feel.

After sharing, consider: How have your experiences of discipline as a child affected the way you react to pain or suffering as an adult? Do you have the same feelings just described when you experience a loss, a disappointment, or grief? If not, how do your feelings differ?

Then together explore Hebrews 12:5-13, which speaks of God's discipline. Try to answer the following questions:

* What do I learn about God?

* What do I learn about myself as God's child?

* What do I learn about my painful experiences?

Finally, review the feelings that your painful experiences engender. How might keeping the perspective of Hebrews 12 in mind affect the way you deal with difficult times?

The Holy Life: Hebrews 13

In the closing exhortation, Hebrews almost sounds familiar. Here are many echoes of Ephesians and Colossians. And why not? Living holiness is the same for the believing Hebrew as for the Gentile Christian. The common element is, "Keep on loving each other as brothers" (v. 1). Love is holiness lived out in the body of Christ.

Caring (Heb. 13:1-3). Caring for others is described briefly. A concern for those in prison or the mistreated is a common theme.

Ø *Group Activity:*
Missions/Outreach Group
Hebrews 13:1-3 calls for involvement with the outcasts of society. Bringing strangers in, and going out to visit those in prison (cf. James 1:27) are two expressions of concern for all people.

If you have a prison or jail nearby, check with the prison officials or chaplain to see what Christian groups minister to prisoners. If there is no community ministry, evaluate the need and see what your group might do to establish one. (If you need help in getting started, contact Charles Colson's Prison Fellowship.) If a community ministry already exists, some of you may want to become involved.

Value people (Heb. 13:4-6). Placing value on people rather than on things, and being willing to use things but not people, is also a reflection of Old Testament and New Testament teaching.

We will never find contentment in pos-

sessing things. Our contentment will be found in God, and in the good news that He has promised never to leave us. We are His.

Authorities (Heb. 13:7-8, 17-18). The theme of respecting authorities is also a common one. This time the emphasis is on relationships with leaders in the church. We are to remain responsive to them, and to imitate their faith.

Jesus is superior (Heb. 13:9-14). The ritualistic approach—in Jewish rather than Gnostic systems—is set aside. Our hearts are strengthened by grace; the altar we serve is supplied with the living Bread.

What is the reference to going "outside the camp"? (v. 13) In the Old Testament system, the offerings for sin were made on an altar, but the animal carcasses were eventually burned outside the camp, away from populated areas. Similarly, the writer notes, Christ died on Golgotha, outside the city walls.

Nothing in Hebrews suggests that the old way was wrong. As a system instituted by God, it was good. But the old was temporary. It foreshadowed only. When the new that it mirrored came, reality replaced shadows. The old priesthood faded away as a single High Priest took His stand in the heavens. A single sacrifice replaced the endless repetition. And the promise of perfection became a present possibility.

This is the call Hebrews makes to these believing Jews. Recognize the superiority of Jesus. Make Him the center of your life. Leave the walls of the old city—the old system—and going outside it find everything you need in Jesus Christ.

Benediction (Heb. 13:20-21). The book closes with a great benediction.

May the God of peace, who through the blood of the eternal covenant brought back from the dead our Lord Jesus, that great Shepherd of the sheep, equip you with everything good for doing His will, and may He work in us what is pleasing to Him, through Jesus Christ, to whom be glory forever and ever. Amen.

Hebrews 13:20-21

GROUP RESOURCE GUIDE

Identification: *Share with others*
Share one time when you felt God had deserted you or was far away. After all have shared, discuss: What do your experiences have in common?

Exploration: *Probe God's Word*
Divide into teams to examine what Hebrews 12:1-13 says about our painful experiences. Half the teams should read the passage from God's point of view, to identify His purposes and His attitudes in bringing such experiences into our lives as discipline.

Half the teams should read the passage from the sufferer's point of view, with close attention to how we are to respond, and the benefits to us of appropriate response.

After 15 minutes or so come together to share findings.

Reaction: *Respond together to the Word*
Go back to the incident you described at first. In teams of three, review it. Then describe how you responded to it, any good that God may have worked in you through the experience, and evaluate how you responded during it. If you had kept Hebrews 12 clearly in mind, would your feelings have changed in any way? Would you have done anything differently?

Adoration: *Worship and pray*
Consider Jesus as "Author and Perfector of our faith." By enduring the cross He showed us that the deepest anguish we experience can be transmuted into good by our loving God. Praise Father and Son for teaching us that suffering truly can be a gift and expression of love.

FAITH'S LIFESTYLE

Overview

James is thought to be the earliest of the New Testament's letters. It was written when there was a company of Jewish believers, probably between A.D. 45–48. The author is James "the Lord's brother," not James the Apostle (see Acts 12:17; 15:13; 21:18; 1 Cor. 15:7; Gal. 1:19; 2:9). James the Apostle, the brother of John, was martyred about A.D. 44 (Acts 12:1-3).

Like the other brothers of Jesus, James did not believe in Him at first (John 7:2-5). But after the Resurrection this brother was not only converted but became a key leader in Jerusalem and at the Jerusalem Council (Acts 15). One tradition nicknames James "camel knees," because of the calluses he was supposed to have developed from long hours spent in prayer.

James' theme is "faith." But here faith is not saving faith, or justifying faith. James' theme is practical: he looked at the *lifestyle which is to be produced by faith in Jesus.* James knew, with Paul, that true faith generates obedience, and so he gently encouraged the early Jewish church to live a life that was worthy of their profession of Jesus as the Christ.

In structure, James is much like Proverbs. He gave a series of short, pithy exhortations, touching on a variety of subjects important in the Christian life. What a wonderful book to teach if we, like James, want to help our people learn to live for the Lord.

Commentary

The church we see portrayed in the early chapters of Acts was both typical of what the church is to be, and yet different. At first the Jewish people viewed Christianity as a sect, as much an expression of Judaism as Sadduceeism, Phariseeism, or the withdrawn Essenes. Recognized and named 'the Way," the Christian community took part in the life and culture of Judea, worshiped at the temple as did the others, and maintained the lifelong patterns of obedience to the Law.

It is in this context that the first of our New Testament letters was penned. Later sharp distinctions would occur between Christians and Jewish doctrine and practice. Later would come the exploration of the meaning of a faith that reaches out to encompass the Gentile as well as the Jews. But none of this is found in the Book of James. Instead of emphasizing salvation by faith, James presupposed the apostolic teaching we see in Acts 2 and 3. What James emphasized is the life of faith, which followers of "the Way" are encouraged to live.

By Faith

One of the striking features of the Book of James is its frequent references to faith. In spite of this, though, James had not always been well received. Martin Luther, that great advocate of faith from the time of the Protestant Reformation, looked on James with suspicion and called it an "epistle of straw," certainly not a letter with the weight or importance of his favorites, Galatians and Romans.

Why did Luther hold such a dim view of the Book of James? The reason is not hard to find once we set Luther's position against the backdrop of his cultural context and personal religious odyssey.

In Luther's day, the church was enduring one of its periodic cycles of corruption where the pattern of biblical truth was perverted. A playboy pope, Leo X of the house of Medici, had succeeded to the papal chair and was selling the offices of the church to whomever could pay well for the privilege. The archbishop of Mainz, the primate of Germany, having borrowed the money to buy his office, was allowed to issue indulgences to recoup his expenses. These indulgences promised the complete and perfect remission of all sins to those (or their dead relatives or friends) who subscribed to the building of Saint Peter's Cathedral in Rome (though only one half the money went for this purpose, the rest repaying the archbishop's loan). A popular jingle of the time phrased the promise well:

As soon as the coin in the coffer rings,
The soul from purgatory springs.

Luther had recently discovered for himself the tremendous truth that salvation, a person's entrance into a personal relationship with God, is a free gift received through faith in Jesus Christ. He realized that the Gospel then consists of what God, in Christ, has done for human beings. No one could ever buy salvation!

Thus Luther and the other Reformers were drawn to those books of the Bible which stress the meaning of Christ's cross for all who trust Him. James, with its ethical and practical emphasis on man's response to God's initiative, found little favor. In their situation, James even seemed at times to support the other side!

Interpreting Scripture

Luther's suspicion and others' misunderstanding of the Book of James point out an important feature of good biblical interpretation. *We must be careful to read Scripture in the context of its own time — not of our time.*

Viewed from the perspective of the Protestant Reformation, James even seemed to contradict what is taught in the Books of Galatians and Romans. All of James' talk of being "justified by works" seemed to deny Paul's affirmation that justification is by faith alone. With "salvation" viewed as the *entrance into* relationship with God, James' approach (in which salvation is viewed as the continual outworking of the meaning of Christ's presence in the believer's life) is easy to misunderstand.

Today too if we approach the New Testament with neat definitions of Bible terms fixed in our minds, remaining unaware of possible other meanings, we are liable to misunderstand some of the interplay of great Bible truths.

One of the best ways to avoid misunderstanding the Bible then is to take a look at the circumstances in which a book was written. Then we go on to define the author's purpose. An important corollary is to look at the range of possible meanings of each significant Bible term and then decide which, in the context of the author's purpose and time, is intended.

We will want to keep the following two principles of interpretation in mind as we read the Book of James: (1) understand the settings, and (2) look at all the possible meaning of terms. These two principles will help us discover not only the message of James, but the message of many other passages in God's Word.

The setting. What then was the setting in which James wrote? What was his purpose? And how do these differ from the setting of a book such as Galatians?

James wrote to the earliest church. He wrote in the days when the church was Hebrew-Christian, made up of men and women who had known the God of the Old Testament and who, under the dynamic preaching of the Apostles, now recognized Jesus of Nazareth as their resurrected Lord and Saviour. The Book of James is *not* an evangelistic book written to people in a culture where faith is foreign. The Book of James is a book of guidelines for living, which was written to the family who had a full knowledge of who Jesus is, and who had chosen to make Him the center of their lives.

Essentially then James was concerned with how the new faith in Jesus is to find expression in the lives of members of that early community. James and Paul were, in fact, exploring different aspects of a common salvation. Paul, the obstetrician, was explaining what happens at birth. James, the practical nurse, was changing diapers and holding the hands of toddlers as they learned to walk. Because the setting and the purpose of the two writers differed, a difference in emphasis naturally followed. As John Calvin pointed out in Luther's day, "It is not required that all handle the same arguments."

It is helpful to note several contrasts between the setting of James and the setting and purpose of Paul's letters.

JAMES	PAUL
stresses the *work*	*stresses the work*

of the believer in
relation to faith
is concerned that
the *outcome of faith*
be fruit (2:14), so
that no one be able
to confuse creeds
with Christianity

of Christ in
relation to faith
is concerned that
the *object of faith*
be Christ, unmixed
with self-reliance
or self-righteous-
ness

writes shortly after
the Resurrection,
when the church is
Jewish and the Old
Testament well
known

writes later, when
the conversion of
Gentiles raised
questions never
asked or thought
of earlier

These are important contrasts which help us see that we must study James in James' own terms, not in view of later developments in the early church or in church history.

Key terms. We've already noted that "faith" is a key term in the Book of James. And we have suggested that faith has more than one kind of impact in a believer's life. It is by faith we enter into relationship with God. But it is also by faith that we continue to live the Christian life (see Rom. 1:17; Gal. 2:20). What we must avoid when we read the Bible then is reading *either* the "saving" or the "lifestyle" meaning of faith into a particular verse until we have considered which meaning is intended by the author. Studying God's Word demands that we read to discover the writer's meaning, not to read our own impressions and theological biases into the text.

Another word that is often *read into* rather than read, occurs not only in James but also throughout the New Testament. It is "saved." To many people, whenever this word is found, it is automatically read as though the passage deals with entrance into a personal relationship with God. With some passages this creates no problem: "Everyone who calls on the name of the Lord will be saved" (Rom. 10:13), or, "There is no other name under heaven given to men by which we must be saved" (Acts 4:12). Clearly these verses are dealing with that invitation to enter into eternal life through faith in Jesus.

But some other passages trouble those who have only a narrow view of the meaning of "saved." James asks in chapter 2, "Can such faith save?" (v. 14) He seems to answer

that human works are somehow necessary. Is he denying Paul's teaching of salvation by grace through faith, apart from works? (Eph. 2:8-9)

Paul himself wrote in Philippians 2:12, "Continue to work out your salvation with fear and trembling." Was Paul contradicting here what he had written elsewhere? Is the Bible inconsistent? Is its teaching about salvation unclear?

The answer comes when we go back into the Old Testament and note that the root meaning of "salvation" is *deliverance.* In most cases the deliverance the Old Testament speaks of is from present dangers and enemies. Only infrequently does "salvation" in the Old Testament context look beyond this life to focus on an individual's eternal destiny. The underlying theme is that God is a real Person who does intervene in human affairs on behalf of those who trust Him.

In the New Testament it is more clearly defined just how God intervenes. Strikingly, God's intervention is pictured as something with past, present, and future implications. In the past, God acted in Jesus Christ to provide us with forgiveness of sins and a new life. By a simple act of faith, we enter into all that Christ has done for us in history, and at that point we "are saved."

But God's intervention for us is not finished yet! In the person of the Holy Spirit, Jesus Himself has come into our lives. He has linked us to Himself with an unbreakable commitment; and because He is present in us, we are also "being saved." This is clearly what Paul spoke of in Philippians: "Work out your salvation with fear and trembling," he wrote, "for it is God who works in you to will and to act according to His good purpose" (Phil. 2:12-13). We approach life seriously, but with confidence. Christ's *present-tense deliverance* is being worked out in our lives even as we continue to trust and rely on Him, and as we demonstrate that trust by meeting life boldly, head-on.

There is a future dimension of salvation as well. The Bible tells us that Jesus will return, and then we will be *fully* saved. We will be fully delivered from all that sin has done to twist our personalities and to warp us away from God (see Rom. 8:18-24).

It is important then when we come on the word "saved" in the Bible not to impose a single or narrow meaning on it. What "salvation" is in view here? Past tense? Present tense? Future? If we make this simple distinction and realize that each aspect of salvation affirms God as One who acts in the lives of those who trust Him, we are freed both from misinterpreting our Bible and from many an agonizing doubt about our personal standing with God.

James

Let's return then to the Book of James, and view it as God's guidance concerning *present-tense* salvation. Let us see it as guidelines for living our faith; for a lifestyle that emerges from a vital, intimate relationship with the Living God.

Outline

Faith's Personal Impact: James 1:2-18

After a very brief introduction, James immediately confronted his readers with a number of practical, personal implications of a living faith. Each of these looks within, and asks the individual to probe his own reactions, values, and perceptions.

Our attitude toward trials (James 1:2-4). James called on us to actually welcome trials and difficulties. These are to produce unmixed joy, not because the trials themselves are pleasurable, but because we look beyond the immediate experience to foresee the result. God permits such experiences as a test (intended to show the validity, not weakness) of our faith. Such trials call for perseverance, which in turn produces maturity and spiritual wholeness. If we are able to look beyond the present and see the product God intends to produce through our suffering, we will experience joy.

This perspective is impossible for most men. But those who have confidence in God value character above pleasure, and eternity above the present moment.

Our expectation of God's aid (James 1:5-8). Trials are likely to panic us. When a person doesn't know which way to turn, he or she may fear to make decisions or may constantly change his or her mind. James reminded us that ours is a giving God, and one of His gifts is wisdom.

This "wisdom" is practical: it is the capacity to apply spiritual truth to daily decisions.

James promised that God will show the person who asks the way to go. "Belief" here suggests a willingness to respond and act on God's guidance. The wavering individual, who hesitates to respond obediently, will be unable to receive what the Lord is eager to give.

Our awareness of our identity (James 1:9-11). Human beings tend to evaluate themselves by various standards. One of the most common has to do with status and income. James called on those who are poor and once angry about their poverty, to throw off the old attitude and realize that, in this new relationship with God, they have been raised to riches. And the wealthy, once confident in their pride, are to remember their spiritual poverty. The old symbols of status, like this present life itself, are as perishable as grass.

Our acceptance of responsibility (James 1:12-15). Faith brings the believer a new sense of personal responsibility. It's common for human beings to excuse sins by blaming God or Satan ("The devil made me do it" is for some more than a saying). James knew that many different circumstances may stimulate our desire to turn from God's way.

But James analyzed the situation carefully. It is not the external thing itself that tempts us; it is our reaction to it. An alcoholic may be tempted overwhelmingly by the smells wafting from a brewery, while a teetotaler is repelled. The odor is the same in each case. What differs is the reaction the odor causes. Candy is a terrible temptation to a fat person on a diet, but another who dislikes sweets won't even notice it.

James showed us that God brings no experience into our lives in order to drag us down. His gifts are always and only good. If we feel temptation, the problem is in our own inner desires. Unless we deal with our temptations on this basis, our initial desire will grow into sinful acts, and this to a sinful lifestyle.

If we recognize temptations as flowing from our own nature, we can deal with them by rejecting sin and responding as the new in us directs.

Our expectation from God (James 1:16-18). James reminds us that we are to expect only good gifts from God. And there is a good gift which counters the tendency to sin that makes us susceptible to temptations.

God has chosen to "give us birth through the word of truth." The old nature which responds wrongly is balanced now by a new nature, which responds to God, for it has been created as a "kind of firstfruits" of all He created. The promise of complete righteousness in the resurrection is guaranteed as we see God creating righteousness within our hearts now.

Faith's lifestyle then calls for us to adopt various personal perspectives on life. We are to see the long-term purpose in trials, and rejoice in that purpose. We are to expect to receive wisdom from God, and to ask for and act on His guidance. We are to see our identity as rooted in relationship with God, to accept responsibility for our temptations, and to expect God's good gift of a new nature to enable us to overcome.

✄ *Group Activity: Recovery Group*
Step 10 (continue taking personal inventory)
List all the excuses that you and others have used to deny responsibility for your actions—from "the devil made me do it" to "she made me angry."

Then make a list of situations in which you personally are most likely to lose it, and do wrong.

Together study James 1:13-15, which analyzes the nature of temptation. What the passage teaches is that "temptation to do wrong" is not in the situation, but in us and in our response to it. See if you can define the steps by which initial emotions or desires become acts of sin.

In teams of three select one of the situations on your list and describe the inner process you go through that has in the past led to doing wrong.

Together again look at James 1:16-18. James' point is that God has given us a gift—a new birth—which enables us to counter the inner pressures that transmute initial thoughts and desires into acts of sin.

Finally, go back to your list of situations, and describe one incident when you felt temptation, but with God's help were able to choose not to do wrong.

Thank God for the gift of personal responsibility, and the new birth which enables us to choose what is right.

Faith's Interpersonal Impact: James 1:19–2:13

James then moved on to explore another aspect of faith's life. Men and women in relationship with Jesus find that that faith also transforms their relationships with others.

Our responses to others (James 1:19-21). Human nature is charged with selfishness and pride. These show up not only in immorality (the use, rather than the valuing of others), but also in anger and antagonism. James told us that the quick, hostile reactions of men to one another are changed by faith. Patience and meekness replace anger and pride.

Our standards of behavior (James 1:22-25). At the heart of the believer's new way of living with others is the realization that God's Word is to be acted on, not just heard. The doer of God's Word is "blessed" in his doing (v. 25).

Our view of religion (James 1:26-27). Christian faith gives us new perspective on religion. It no longer is a ritual kind of thing, but now is seen to be a response to others that mirrors the concern of the God who is Father to humankind. Pure religion is now understood to "look after orphans and widows in their distress and to keep oneself from being polluted by the world."

Our welcome to others (James 2:1-7). The unity found in Christ has its source in the fact that in His church, all are family. Rich and poor stand side by side in Him. Thus, in the church, believers are to reject all artificial distinctions and to affirm unity in every way. Rich and poor are to be treated with equal respect and appreciation as persons; anything else is to blaspheme the name by which we are called.

Our calling of love (James 2:8-13). As persons of faith, responsive to the royal law (the command to love one another was uttered by King Jesus [John 13:33-34]), we are to love our neighbors without partiality. Making distinctions between rich and poor and thus showing favoritism, is as much a violation of the divine intent as the more obvious sins identified in the Law.

It's important to understand James' point when he said "whoever keeps the whole Law and yet stumbles at just one point is guilty of breaking it all." The Law of the Old Testament is a unity. As a whole balloon is broken by just one pin prick, so a person becomes a "lawbreaker" by violating just one requirement of the Mosaic Law.

♥ *Group Activity: Support Group*
James 2:1-13 describes a common temptation that has the potential to corrupt Christians in any culture: a "favoritism" which views others in terms of status ascribed by society rather than in terms of the family relationship rooted in our common relationship with God through Jesus Christ.

Study the passage together. First read it aloud, then work through it verse by verse, listing observations made by group members on a chalkboard or large sheet of newsprint.

Then write your own paraphrase of James 2:1-4, but write it concerning a difference between people which you believe lead Christians to show favoritism in our own day, and in your own community.

Read several paraphrases, and then list the differences you each think might lead today to the kind of "favoritism" James is against. Discuss. How is this seen in our own group? How is it seen in our church, or our personal lives? And, what are we to do to correct it?

James, as a leader of the Jerusalem congregation, was showing a pastor's heart in this brief letter. He knew that faith in Jesus can and will change our lives. And he encouraged his congregation by showing them the new attitudes and relationships which faith will produce.

GROUP RESOURCE GUIDE

Identification: *Share with others*
Tell one difference that your faith in Christ has made in the way you live.

Affirmation: *Express love and concern*
Tell one other person in your group a way in which you see his faith has positively affected his life.

Exploration: *Probe God's Word*
A person previously prepared should briefly orient the group to the "lifestyle" emphasis of James 1–2 (see commentary).

Divide into teams of three to work through these chapters. Each team is to (1) title the following paragraphs, (2) identify the attitude or actions that faith inspires, according to that paragraph, and (3) contrast it with the attitude that might be dis-

played in those without faith. The paragraphs to study are: 1:2-4, 5-8, 9-11, 12-15, 16-18, 19-21, 22-25, 26-27; 2:1-7, 8-13.

Reaction: *Respond together to the Word*
After the paragraphs have been titled and attitudes identified, choose the topic which is of greatest interest to you personally. Then meet in a smaller team with any others in the group who chose the same paragraph to discuss its implications for your daily lives.

Adoration: *Worship and pray*
Thank God for the new attitudes and outlook that faith produces in every Christian's life.

FAITH'S CHALLENGES

Overview

The Book of James is about faith. But it is *not* about "saving faith." It is about the role faith plays in the life of a person who is already a believer.

In our last study we saw James' insights into personal and interpersonal aspects of the life of faith. A believer's character (1:2-4), attitudes (vv. 5-8), emotional responses (vv. 19-21), behavior (vv. 22-27) and priorities (2:1-13) are all reshaped by faith. Thus participation in the community of those who take Jesus as the focus of their lives brings a total reorientation of the individual, and of all that he or she is. Christian faith is not merely assent to a set of propositions about Jesus: it is a living trust in the Lord which leads to a whole new way of life.

In this study you will help your group grasp a basic principle that underlies this faith-lifestyle (vv. 14-25), and examine problems to be faced by the man or woman of faith (chaps. 3–4). Finally you will look together at the prospects for the person of faith—redress of wrongs when Jesus returns, and until then all the resources we need to overcome.

▶ *Justify.* The Greek word means "to vindicate" as well as "to pronounce righteous." Depending on the context, *justify* can mean "found innocent" or "vindicated in a particular course of action." It is important to keep each meaning in view as we study James 2.

Commentary

James was a man deeply concerned that those who have faith in Jesus express that faith in an appropriate lifestyle. Knowing God means a total reorientation for human beings who were before blinded and lost. It is against this background of concern that those who claim Jesus live a life of faith

that James, in chapter 2, penned a paragraph which greatly troubled Martin Luther and others who thought that James suggested a salvation that is won through human effort rather than by the work of Christ on Calvary.

Principles of Faith: James 2:14-26

Here is what the troublesome passage says:

What good is it, my brothers, if a man claims to have faith but has no deeds? Can such faith save him? Suppose a brother or sister is without clothes and daily food. If one of you says to him, "Go, I wish you well; keep warm and well fed," but does nothing about his physical needs, what good is it? In the same way, faith by itself, if it is not accompanied by action, is dead.

But someone will say, "You have faith; I have deeds."

Show me your faith without deeds, and I will show you my faith by what I do. You believe that there is one God. Good! Even the demons believe that— and shudder.

You foolish man, do you want evidence that faith without deeds is useless? Was not our ancestor Abraham considered righteous for what he did when he offered his son Isaac on the altar? You see that his faith and his actions were working together, and his faith was made complete by what he did. And the Scripture was fulfilled that says, "Abraham believed God, and it was credited to him as righteousness," and he was called God's friend. You see that a person is justified by what he does and not by faith alone.

In the same way, was not even Rahab the prostitute considered righteous for what she did when she gave lodging to the spies and sent them off in a different direction? As the body without the spirit is dead, so faith without deeds is dead.

We can avoid misunderstanding if we only look at the thesis James stated so clearly. He was speaking of an individual who claims to have "faith," but whose "faith" has not produced any change of life. He asked, "Can *such faith* save him?" (v. 14, italics added)

James thus was looking at a particular *kind* of "faith," that actually stands in contrast with what Paul and other New Testament writers call "faith." While the kind of "faith" James examines does exist as intellectual acknowledgment of God (e.g., "God exists"), it does *not* exist as a trust in God that generates response. In this it is like that of demons, who know full well that God exists, but who rather than trust and love Him "shudder" (v. 19).

This kind of faith is seen in human beings who, despite their claims to "believe" in God are unresponsive to the needs of their brothers and sisters. *It is not linked with response* — either to God or to God's children.

James then contrasts dead faith with a real and vital faith in God. As seen in both Abraham and Rahab, true faith produces fruit. Abraham's "faith and his actions were working together, and his faith was made complete by what he did. And the Scripture was fulfilled that says 'Abraham believed God, and it was credited to him as righteousness'" (vv. 22-23). That is, God's recorded statement that "Abraham believed God" was demonstrated to be true by Abraham's subsequent obedience to the Lord! Where there is true faith in God, that faith will never exist apart from works, but will find expression in the believer's way of life.

But what about the statement that "a person is justified by what he does and not by faith alone"? (v. 24) Doesn't this conflict with the teaching that salvation is by faith, apart from works?

Here we turn to the second meaning of *justify* as "vindicate." The *Expository Dictionary of Bible Words* (Zondervan) says:

It is not beyond our efforts to resolve the apparent conflict between Romans and James. Consider the following: James does not teach that Abraham was pronounced righteous on the basis of his actions. James teaches that Scripture's announcement that Abraham *was* righteous is vindicated on the basis of Abraham's subsequent obedience. He did right because God's action actually worked within him to make him righteous! James is speaking of two kinds of faith, only one of which is saving faith. He teaches that saving faith will be vindicated by the actions that flow from it and in this sense complete it.

What is particularly significant to us here is that James joins Paul in suggesting that justification is something more than a judicial declaration. True, in response to faith, God does declare sinners acquitted and righteous before Him; but He does more than that. God acts within the believer to make righteousness a reality. Thus the Gospel offer of salvation by faith includes more than a pardon: it also includes a transformation. God will declare the sinner righteous, and then God will act to *make* the sinner what God has declared him to be.

The kind of faith which saves also transforms, and that transformation will show up in the lifestyle of the true believer.

And so James calls us today to look at our Christian faith not only as *what* we believe, but also as *how* we believe. Has our response to God been a dry, intellectual kind of thing? Have we simply accepted as true the historical facts about Jesus' life and death and resurrection? Or have we gone beyond recognition to a wholehearted trust in Jesus? A trust that involves not only the confidence that He has forgiven us, but also involves the commitment of our whole person into His loving hands. A commitment of all that we are and have to Jesus now. When we make this commitment, "This kind of faith" not only will save us but will also transform our lives.

Group Activity: Bible Study Group

Do an individual paraphrase of James 1:14-26. Then together work toward a group paraphrase of this "troublesome" passage. Discuss each phrase until you are all satisfied that your rendering expresses its meaning as well as possible.

The process should lead you to discover and debate key issues raised in the pas-

sage. When in doubt, refer to the commentary, or check other Bible commentaries.

After your group paraphrase is complete, discuss: What is the main truth James intends to convey? How do we take that truth and apply it to our own lives?

Problems for Faith: James 3–4

After his sweeping assertion of the principle that faith must find expression in our lifestyle as well as in our beliefs, James focused on problems that each of us must deal with. These are, in essence, challenges to the way of life that faith promotes.

What is so surprising is that these are such common, ordinary problems. There is no demand here that our faith move mountains, produce miracles, or at the very least lead us to venture overseas without support, to carry the Gospel to distant tribes. Rather than the extraordinary feats we sometimes associate with great faith, James directs our attention to the unspectacular business of the common man's ordinary daily life.

Taming the tongue (James 3:1-12). The tongue is the first challenge for faith. It's so easy for us to slip and to criticize or say something cutting about our brother. It's so tempting to gossip. The person who has his or her tongue under control has definitely matured in the life of faith.

❊ *Group Activity:*
Singles/Single Again Group
The following phrase is written on the chalkboard: "I'd share more in our group, but I'm afraid someone would gossip if I were to share about really personal things." Decide whether you agree, disagree, or are uncertain, and share your opinion with the rest.

James 3:1-12 focuses on the difficulty we have in "taming the tongue." Read the passage aloud, and talk about your own personal experience with speaking too quickly, or saying too much. What have you learned from these experiences?

Go back to the statement on the chalkboard. Lovingly confront anyone in the group who has betrayed a confidence by talking about something you've shared. Tell how this made you feel, and how it affects your participation in the group now. If someone confronts you, accept

your responsibility and apologize.

Assurance of confidentiality is vital if a group is to deal with the deeper needs of its members in a healing, loving, and Christian way.

Subduing the self (James 3:13–4:10). Each of us has natural desires and passions that constitute another challenge to faith. We can recognize the influence of the old passions when we see "bitter envy and selfish ambition" in our hearts.

On the other hand we can recognize the divine wisdom by its traits. It is "pure . . . peace loving, considerate, submissive, full of mercy and good fruit, impartial and sincere" (3:17).

What is so serious about our desires? If we act out of the old passions our relationships with others will be marked by conflict. There will be "quarreling and fighting" (4:1-2). What is more, the *things we desire* will be wrong. We will not obtain them, first because we have not associated them to our lives with God (v. 2), and second because when we *do* ask God, we "ask with wrong motives" (v. 3)

James went on to further emphasize the seriousness of the materialistic and selfish viewpoint that is linked with our old lives. "Friendship with the world is hatred toward God" (v. 4). Here "world" is used in its theological sense as the world system: the whole set of values, attitudes, desires, and passions that characterize sinful human society.

The challenge for faith, then, is to submit oneself totally to God. We are to adopt His viewpoint and His values, even at the cost of personal pain and humbling ourselves before Him (vv. 8-10). The reorientation of life which comes when we make full commitment to God will transform our desires, and by making us those who love rather than those who desire, will change our relationships with others as well.

Judging the judge (James 4:11-12). Another common problem faced by all of us is our tendency to judge and evaluate each other in a negative, condemning way. James pointed out that God alone, who makes the law, is competent to judge. Faith struggles against this tendency to judge and criticize a neighbor.

Humbling the haughty (James 4:13-17). Finally, faith comes into direct conflict with pride and the human tendency to rely on one's own self. Arrogance, boasting, and approaching life as though our lives were under our control rather than in God's hands is likely to grow with success and accomplishments. Faith maintains the awareness that we are each dependent on God, and faith frees us to relax in the assurance of His loving guidance for our lives.

Prospects and Promises: James 5:1-20

The men and women to whom James wrote lived, as we do, in a time when injustice was common and suffering the all-too-often lot of believer and unbeliever alike. What does a life of faith promise to Jesus' followers? What are the rewards of joining with others on faith's great adventure?

The prospect (James 5:1-6). James wanted to recognize immediately that there is no promise in Christianity of utopia now. Instead James spoke out for the oppressed, warning the wealthy who defraud the poor laborer while they live "in luxury and self-indulgence" (v. 5). Earthly treasures will rust away, and the very rust will be evidence against the oppressors in the coming judgment.

The impact of this message is not to call the poor believer to vindictive joy at the prospect. Instead, James sought to call rich and poor alike to realize that a day *is* coming when God will show His justice as well as His love. To the rich this is a call to repent. To the poor it is a message of hope. This world is not the sum and substance of reality. When Jesus comes, the world as well as individuals will be renewed.

Present promises (James 5:7-20). What about now, as we wait patiently for Jesus to return? James tells us that the person of faith has many resources.

There is patience (vv. 7-12). Job waited, trusting God's timing. And the end of Job's life demonstrated the compassion and the mercy of God (Job 42). Like Job, the suffering believer today can commit himself and his suffering to the Lord.

There is prayer (James 5:13-18). We have the privilege of joining with our brothers to bring both illness and sin to God for healing. James insisted that we not underestimate the importance of prayer. "The prayer of a righteous man is powerful and effective" (v. 16).

Note that many see the promise of healing here as linked with confession, and the sickness as a divine judgment. In any case, we are to bring all our needs to Jesus, confident that He does hear and answer prayer.

There is caring (vv. 19-20). This last resource is seen in the final words of James, "My brothers, if one of you should wander from the truth" (v. 19). The response of the believing community is not to condemn but to seek to restore. The family is a community of life. Whatever life may hold, within the family there is the certainty of caring and concern.

♥ *Group Activity: Support Group*
James 5:7-11 calls for patience in times of suffering. Write the word "patience" on the board. Then respond to it: When is patience most needed? When is it most difficult? What helps us be patient when things are tough?

Then together do a time line of Job's experience, referring to the Book of Job for details if necessary. Along the time line show his years of blessing, the disasters that struck him, etc., on to his final restoration. Then discuss: What does God intend for us to learn from Job's experience? How is his story to impact our lives?

Then do a time line of your own life, showing the major griefs or losses you have experienced up to the present. When done, share the time lines in teams of five and talk about how you have (or are) dealing with the pain they cause(d) you.

Finally, look ahead and complete your time line to reflect what seems to you an "ideal" expression of God's "compassion and mercy." What are you looking forward to? When do you expect this to happen?

God is a God of compassion and mercy. He may not show it in the way we expect, or just when we expect it, but blessing does lie ahead.

GROUP RESOURCE GUIDE

Identification: *Share with others*
Tell one way you want your faith in Christ to change your life or outlook in the next five years.

Exploration: *Probe God's Word*
James 3–5 identifies several specific areas in which faith is supposed to change our lives or outlooks. Together read through the chapters and identify these areas. Then divide into teams of three to five, each of which is to study one of the topics you have identified, and prepare a report on the nature of the problem, and the change that a real faith is expected to make in believers.

After about 20 minutes let each team report briefly on its findings.

Reaction: *Respond together to the Word*
How many of the things shared by group members when the session began are the same things that James deals with? On the basis of this James study, what changes might each of you make in your expectations for the future?

Repeat the opening process, telling one way you want your faith in Christ to change your life or outlook in the next five years.

Adoration: *Worship and pray*
Consider God as a transforming God, who has entered your life to change it and you for the better. Praise Him not for what He has done, but for what He is surely going to do for and in you.

THE CALL TO SUBMISSION

Overview

Peter's first letter was written in a time when the church was beginning to feel the flames of persecution. Written to the "scattered" by Peter, this letter was probably directed to clusters of believers in various cities of the empire.

Peter's letter is a call to holiness in troubled times, and a recognition that even suffering can be a gift from God. No fewer than seven different Greek words for suffering in this letter suggest the intensity of the persecution.

Perhaps the most striking feature of the letter is Peter's emphasis on submission as the Christian's response under pressure. Despite suffering, discrimination, and ridicule, the path of holiness involves acceptance of our pain and an awareness that even suffering can be a gift from God.

In this first session on this striking New Testament book, you will help your group members explore this path that we find so difficult to travel.

▶ *Submission.* The Greek terms are *hypotasso* or *hypotage*. The words indicate a subjection or subordination. While this may be forced (as the demons who submit to God, Luke 10:17), Christian submission is voluntary. We submit to secular authority (Rom. 13:1), to one another (Eph. 5:21), and Christian slaves even choose submission to harsh masters (1 Peter 2:18). Here Peter called on us to submit when persecuted, and keep on trusting God.

Commentary

The first-century church was divided by two cultural traditions—Jewish and Gentile—from which people were drawn to become one in Christ.

At first, the church was Jewish. The community of faith grew immediately after Jesus' resurrection as a sect of Judaism. These first believers were surprised that God would accept pagan outsiders just as He accepted the chosen people—by faith in Christ. Still, for its first two decades, the new community was primarily Jewish.

Then came the explosive days of missionary expansion. Spearheaded by Paul and others, the Gospel was carried throughout the Roman world. And thousands responded. The makeup of the church changed: Gentiles predominated. Teachers began to explore the new faith's relationship to Hellenistic philosophies and ways.

Looking back at Ephesians and Colossians, it is clear that Paul wrote to men and women of Hellenistic orientation. It is equally clear that the Book of Hebrews was written to Jewish believers, for it deals with Christian faith in the traditional categories of Old Testament theology. Despite their differing audiences, all three books consider the very same issues. They help readers grasp the superiority of Christ. They each affirm Jesus as the center of our faith, the heartbeat of our new lives.

Christ is superior to the cosmology of the pagans and to the revealed shadow-truths of the Jews. New life in Jesus cannot be found through the ascetic self-denial of Gnosticism or the ritual observances of Judaism. Identity is found in our resurrection life, portrayed in Ephesians and affirmed in the Hebrews' pronouncement that we have been lifted to glory as the sons of God. Theme after theme in these books compares, though each is adapted to the history and to the Gentile or Jew to whom it is addressed.

One implication of this is clear. As the church continued to mature, its identification with either tradition was gradually being lost! Believers shook off the tendency to identify themselves as Gentile-Christians or Jewish-Christians, and found a new, common identity in Christ alone. Shaking off old identities to understand who they were in Christ became a vital issue for a worldwide church, composed of such diverse elements.

And, as Christians began to view themselves as a separate and distinct people in themselves, so the world around began to realize that Christianity was not just a sect of Judaism. It was a religion in its own right—and it was not a "licit," or governmentally approved religion either!

There is much controversy over 1 Peter. Most theologians agree that it was written near the end of Peter's life. Probably he wrote from Rome, just before his martyrdom under Nero around A.D. 64.

The debate focuses on whom Peter wrote to. He addressed his letter to the "scattered," to *diaspora* (1:1). This word identified Jews who lived in major Gentile cities throughout the world. Along with Peter's identification as an "apostle to the Jews" (see Gal. 2:7), this seems to prove that the letter was meant for Christian Hebrews.

On the other hand, the book speaks of "the empty way of life handed down to you from your forefathers" (1 Peter 1:18) and gives a catalog of distinctly Gentile vices (4:3-4). These references and others make it hard to limit Peter's readers to Hebrew Christians. It is possible that Peter addressed this letter to mixed communities, composed of both Hebrew and Gentile Christians. But it is certain that Peter, like Paul and the writer of Hebrews, addressed common issues, and emphasized those themes which soon made the Christian church distinct.

Foundation Truths: 1 Peter 1:1–2:12

Looking at the introductory section of Peter's letter, we are struck by the familiarity of the truths he developed. These are the very same truths portrayed throughout this study as the foundation for a life of holiness.

For instance, Peter began with praise to God, who has in His great mercy "given us new birth into a living hope" (1:3). How familiar this is! Paul emphasized that the dead have been raised to a resurrection kind of life in Ephesians 2. And again in Colossians, he said, "God made you alive with Christ" (2:13). This belief was shared by the writer to the Hebrews. In Christ, we have been lifted up, freed from our fear of death, and made members of God's family (Heb. 12:7-10) and called to *keep* on loving one another as brothers (13:1). Our hope of holiness rests on this foundation.

✂ *Group Activity: Recovery Group*
Step 11 (improve relationship with God through prayer and meditation)
First Peter 1:1–2:12 lays a foundation for God's call to us to live holy lives. Use the chart (below) to guide the study of this passage, and summarize what Peter says about the new identity we have in Christ.

What is Peter's concern for this church we belong to, and which in Christ has a unique identity? Reading through the book quickly, we note a number of repeated themes, including a constant emphasis on suffering.

Common Foundation Themes
A basis for holiness

	Summary	Parallels		
1 Peter		Eph.	Col.	Heb.
1:3, 23	New, resurrection birth			
1:4	Inheritance			
1:9-12	Present experience of salvation benefits			
1:14				
1:15-16				
1:17				
1:19-20				
1:22				
2:5, 9				
2:10				
2:11				
2:12				

Peter warned that life in this world may involve suffering grief in all sorts of trials (1:6). Suffering as Jesus suffered is not unexpected (2:18-23).

In fact, we may even suffer for doing what is right! (3:14) Christ suffered, we are reminded. So we should arm ourselves with His attitude (4:1) and not be surprised at painful trials (v. 12).

Another repeated theme is submission. Peter seemed to place great emphasis on living appropriately under human government (2:13), within the framework of society's other institutions (v. 18; 3:1), and within the church (5:5).

While these themes are often repeated, neither seems to sum up Peter's major concern. Instead, Peter seemed most concerned with holiness. We have been called in Christ, Peter said, to be holy (1:14-15). After all, we "are being built into a spiritual house to be a holy priesthood" (2:5). We are, he insisted, a "chosen people, a royal priesthood, a holy nation, a people belonging to God, that you may declare the praises of Him who called you out of darkness into His wonderful light" (v. 9).

Peter called Christ's people to "live such good lives among the pagans that, though they accuse you of doing wrong, they may see your good deeds and glorify God on the day He visits us" (v. 12).

Peter, writing to the church of God — not the Jewish church or the Gentile church but the church that finds life in Jesus alone — called us to *a life of practical holiness*. While that life involves, as we expect, a commitment to "abstain from sinful desires" and to "live such good lives" that our "good deeds" are evident, one of its major features is submissiveness! A holy life is a life of Christian submission.

Submission's Path: 1 Peter 2:13–3:9

In the Bible holiness is associated both with an active love for others and a decisive rejection of every kind of evil. These themes are found in Peter too. "Now that you have purified yourselves by obeying the truth so that you have sincere love for your brothers, love one another deeply, from the heart" (1:22). And, "Rid yourselves of all malice and all deceit, hypocrisy, envy, and slander of every kind" (2:1). A life of practical holiness will always be marked by these two qualities.

But Peter went on to develop in great detail an aspect of a holy life that Paul only mentioned: living in willing submission within the framework of authorities that exist in society. At first, it seems peculiar to relate this to holiness. But, as we trace Peter's argument, we understand why the relationship does exist in God's eyes.

Man's authority (1 Peter 2:13-17). We Christians submit to authorities "instituted among men" (v. 13) for the Lord's sake. Doing good is always within the framework of our society. Our freedom in Christ is not an excuse to flaunt human laws or to withhold respect.

Unjust authorities (1 Peter 2:18-25). What if people in authority treat us unjustly?

Selecting the critical area of potential mistreatment in his own society, Peter looked at the relationship between slave and master. The slave is to submit, Peter wrote, and to maintain due respect "not only to those who are good and considerate, but also to those who are harsh" (v. 18). This is not an endorsement of slavery. Nor is it suggesting that a person should not seek relief, if society makes it possible. Peter simply focused on an extreme case to provide a clear illustration of the principle of submission. In Peter's world, a slave had no right to demand considerate treatment. It was perfectly legal, though morally wrong, for a master to treat his slave harshly.

Did harsh treatment release the Christian slave from his obligation to submit with respect? No, Peter said firmly. The Christian's call to a life of submission is *not conditional.* Another person's failure to live God's way does not release us from our responsibility to so submit.

To show us that God does not ask of us any more than He was Himself willing to do, Peter invites us to look at Jesus. Christ suffered, for doing only good! Even though He might have, Jesus did not retaliate. In His submission Jesus gives us an example of how we are to live. After all, if the body is incarnate Christ in the world today, we would expect Jesus to want us to live the way He did.

♥ *Group Activity: Support Group*
Complete "I've got a right to. . . ."
open-ended statements. Do not complete
them as you yourself would, but as the

"average person" might. The statements are:

* My boss doesn't pay me enough, so I've got a right to. . . .

* My spouse cheats on me, so I've got a right to. . . .

* The government raised taxes unfairly, so I've got a right to. . . .

* My church doesn't treat women like real persons, so I've got a right to. . . .

* Members of my support group don't listen to me, so I've got a right to. . . .

Share how you completed each and compare it with the responses of the others in your group. Discuss: How are we supposed to respond when some situation in our lives is unfair?

Then study 1 Peter 2:18-25. How are we to respond to unfair situations? Why are we to respond this way? What motivates us to respond in this way?

After thorough discussion, go back to the open-ended statements. How do you suppose the Apostle Paul might have completed each? Work together to develop the best response possible in each of these situations.

Finally, identify one situation which is unfair to you just now. Describe it, and listen as the group members suggest how you might apply this passage in dealing with it.

Husbands and wives (1 Peter 3:1-7). In the husband/wife relationship, submission is again enjoined. Here Peter was addressing a problem that exists today, when Christan wives are married to men who "do not believe the Word" (v. 1). Peter did not suggest aggressive evangelism. Instead, the wife is to adopt a course of *aggressive submission.* Quietly demonstrating the inner beauty Jesus brings, wives are to communicate the Lord through the holy way of submission.

Of course, believing husbands are to be considerate (v. 7). But, as the slave is not released from the holy way if he has a harsh master, neither is the wife with an inconsiderate spouse.

Attitude toward suffering for good (1 Peter 3:8-12). In it all, our goal is to "live in harmony with one another" (v. 8). And how? "Be sympathetic, love as brothers, be compassionate and humble. Do not repay evil with evil or insult with insult, but with blessing, because to this you were called"

(vv. 8-9).

It is so natural to strike back when we are treated unjustly, to focus our energy on anger and rebellion, and to rage against injustice and find ways to overthrow the person or system under which we live. But Peter called us to a different kind of life. Rather than exploding, we focus our energy on love.

Every human society has its share of evil. Each of us who are hurt or mistreated by the system might easily be drawn into endless crusades. It is not that we are to compromise with evil or fail to work for social change. However, *we are never to be drawn away from the first calling of holiness: to live God's love.* So Peter's concern is that unjust treatment never tempt us to return evil for evil, and forsake our commitment to good.

Compromise: 1 Peter 3:10–4:6

It is hard to grasp what Peter's teaching implies. Was he compromising with evil? Should we simply *adjust* to sin? Are we to be unmoved by injustice? To ignore society's festering sores?

To some who have read the prophets' ringing calls for justice — because God is committed to justice — Peter's stress on submission seems to contradict the Lord.

Romans 13. Yet Paul deals with the issue of submission, and in the same way. "Everyone must submit himself to the governing authorities" (v. 1), Paul said. Because human government is instituted by God for a good purpose, one who rebels against this authority is rebelling against what God has created.

Note that only rebellion is at issue here. Paul did not speak of changing governments or obtaining redress within existing law. Both he and Peter instructed believers not to *rebel,* even when they receive unfair treatment. The issue is not abstract. It is how we respond when someone in authority treats us unjustly.

Sovereignty. Peter's exhortation was grounded in theology. He went far beyond Jesus' example here. Peter's approach was rooted in the concept of a sovereign God — a God who permits injustice in our world and works His good purpose despite them. The conviction that God is sovereign underlies both of Peter's references to Jesus as our example of living with injustice. Now, tracing his argument, we are led to a totally new understanding of submission and suffering.

Christ, the Suffering Servant (1 Peter 2:18-25). In thinking of harsh treatment given a servant, Peter naturally thought of Jesus. Christ often spoke of Himself as a Servant (see Matt. 20). Like the harshly treated slaves of Peter's example, Jesus was persecuted by those He served—and for doing good. In this experience, Jesus never retaliated or threatened. He bore the insults and pain, even to Calvary. How did Jesus find the grace to respond righteously? The Bible says, "He entrusted Himself to Him who judges justly" (1 Peter 2:23). Jesus looked beyond the immediate circumstances and saw the sure, steady hand of God!

Christ acknowledged as Lord (1 Peter 3:10–4:6). In a carefully developed argument, Peter helped us understand his earlier reference to Jesus' committing Himself to God.

Peter began by explaining how a Christian is enabled to react with love rather than in anger. A quote from the Old Testament explains that "the eyes of the Lord are on the righteous, and His ears are attentive to their prayer" (3:12). God is carefully superintending the lives of His children.

This is especially important to remember in the unlikely circumstance that one suffers for doing what is good (vv. 13-14). Peter explained carefully how we are to respond in such a circumstance.

- First, don't be frightened.
- Second, remember and acknowledge in your heart that Christ is Lord.
- Third, be ready to explain why you are able to maintain a hopeful attitude despite the injustice.
- Fourth, maintain gentleness and respect in your response, keeping a clear conscience.
- Fifth, your behavior will shame those who have spoken evil of you.

Peter then comforted us. How much better it is to suffer for doing right than for doing wrong! This kind of suffering is truly Christlike. Jesus too suffered for sins that were not His (v. 10). In fact, Christ's death was the ultimate injustice: He was executed, instead of His persecutors who deserved to die. But God used this miscarriage of justice in a wonderful way! Through His death Jesus brought us to God. From tragedy and injustice, God brought good.

And this is the point! *When we do right and suffer for it, we can be sure that God intends to use our experience for good.* Whatever happens to members of God's family, we can be sure that our loving Father is at work for good.

The next passage, which seems obscure, should be understood as an analogy. Peter showed us the far-reaching extent of Jesus' work by going back to the great Genesis Flood, when an ark carried eight people through the waters of raging judgment. Jesus is our ark. In our union with Him—for this is the impact of "baptism"; (see 1 Cor. 12:13; Col. 2:12)—we have been lifted *beyond* fact, we have been delivered to a new life! *And we are to live this new life now.* Freed by Jesus from bondage to "evil human desires," we are to live our new lives by "the will of God" (1 Peter 4:2).

The analogy is a powerful one. Noah and his family were snatched from an old world that was destined for destruction. Carried safely through judgment's storms, their ark landed in a new world. Here great changes were made. The waters once suspended in the atmosphere had fallen to earth. Ecology had changed. Now, human government was instituted and man given meat to eat (see Gen. 9). Noah's family had to develop an entirely new way of life.

This is exactly the case with you and me. We have been snatched from an evil world dominated by Satan. As members of Christ's kingdom who now walk in light (1 Peter 2:9), we must learn to live in His new creation. Old things are to be put aside. Now our lives are to be according to the will of our God (4:6).

Submission? As Peter explained it, submission is not compromise. It is an expression of the Christian's confidence that Jesus is Lord. It is also an expression of our commitment to live by God's will rather than by the drives and passions of a lost humanity. God's will may lead us into experiences of injustice. It did for Jesus. Yet, in Jesus' submission we find not only an example but also hope. Jesus' death and resurrection—accomplishing our salvation—made it plain that God worked His good through His Son's suffering. And He can work good through the suffering of His other children as well.

By committing ourselves to God when we suffer injustice, we let Him work in and through our lives.

And so submission *is* an aspect of holiness. Yes, holiness is love, and holiness is goodness. But holiness is also submission to the will of God when that will leads to the suffering of injustice. Love, goodness, and submission each demonstrate the fact that we are separated to God, and to Him alone.

GROUP RESOURCE GUIDE

Identification: *Share with others*
Tell of one time you tried to do right, and things worked out badly or disasterously.

After all have shared, talk about these experiences. What is disturbing about them? How have you tried to explain them?

Exploration: *Probe God's Word*
Work through 1 Peter 3:8–4:11, discussing each phrase and thought, guided by the commentary.

Reaction: *Respond together to the Word*
In teams of three review the experience you shared earlier. How did you respond when you tried to do right, but things went wrong? Which of the "steps" Peter gives in 3:12-17 did you follow? Which didn't you?

How did your reaction to the situation affect you, and/or others?

Then share: Is there any situation now in which you are trying to do right, but things aren't working out? How can you apply Peter's instruction in these chapters to that situation?

Affirmation: *Express love and concern*
In the entire group again, commit to pray with anyone who is facing a 1 Peter 3-4 situation now. And do so together.

Adoration: *Worship and pray*
Thank God for His ability to transform injustice in good. Praise Him for His wisdom and His unmatched grace.

THE CALL TO SUFFER

Overview

Peter's first letter focused on the themes of submission and suffering. Yet the book is vibrant with optimism. We sense this tone in the opening chapter. Peter praised God

- for new birth
- for a living hope
- for an inheritance that can never perish
- for shielding by God's power.

In view of these great blessings we have joy, even though "now for a little while you may have had to suffer grief in all kinds of trials" (1:6).

Such trials are precious, for they are intended not to trip us up, but to demonstrate the genuineness of our faith, that when Jesus Christ comes He—and we—might receive praise, glory, and honor for our faithfulness.

So salvation does *not* promise an easy life here. Instead we can expect difficulties and trials. After all, Jesus Himself was not immune to suffering. And we are called to walk in His steps.

The subject of suffering is not a popular one. But it is an important one. For none of us is immune to the pain associated with our human frailties. How important to help those we teach come to see suffering in God's perspective, and so strengthen both their faith, and their hope.

■ For a verse-by-verse commentary on each reference to suffering in this Bible book, see the *Bible Knowledge Commentary,* pages 837-857.

Commentary

Throughout the later letters of our New Testament, hope predominates. We Christians have hope because of our participation in Christ. Even suffering changes when viewed as the continuation of Jesus' life on earth, and as the life He continues to live through members of the body.

And so Peter called us to "rejoice that you participate in the sufferings of Christ" (4:13). A Christian's suffering is no cause for shame. It is to be seen as God's hand at work in our lives, shaping and equipping us in wise discipline.

In thinking about our own suffering, it is instructive to remember what we read about Jesus in Hebrews. "Although He was a Son, He learned obedience from what He suffered and, once made perfect, He became the source of eternal salvation for all" (Heb. 5:8). Suffering was necessary to perfect Jesus for His role as sympathetic High Priest. Of course, Jesus was already perfect as God. But to become our High Priest, Christ had to experience human weakness.

We often misunderstand the nature of weakness. All too often we think of it as sin or as giving in to temptation. Not so. Our *weakness* is feeling the pressures life places on us. Our *flaw* is choosing to surrender to sin. Jesus did not choose sin. He was without flaw. But Jesus did know hunger and exhaustion. He knew the pain of rejection, and the hurt of ridicule. Jesus knew feelings of abandonment and felt the anger of those whose hearts fed on hate. In all this, Jesus suffered. And in all of it, He experienced what it means to be human. Having learned, He became our salvation.

It's very possible that suffering is necessary to perfect us in the same way. Jesus is the High Priest, but you and I are a royal and holy priesthood (1 Peter 2:5, 9). We not only participate in Christ's experiences, we participate in His ministry. And for us to sympathize, we need to know what it means to hurt.

This is an important thought. Our calling does not pull us *away* from the world. Instead, it leads us *to live Jesus' life in the world*! Jesus' ministry was to seek and to save. He never forgot the lost; instead He lifted them up to become sons.

Perhaps one good that God brings through our suffering is to remind us of our fellowmen—of the pains they know and the suffering they experience, without any source of joy. If we remember who we are, we may be moved to reach out as Jesus reached out. Instead of drawing away from those who sin, we reach out with a firm and loving grip and draw them to Jesus, who holds the door open wide.

Pain and Suffering in Scripture

The ancient Stoic philosophers saw suffering as man's fate in an impersonal universe. Even the wisest have, throughout history, been forced to shrug off the question as unanswerable. And those who are antagonistic to God have argued that the very existence of suffering in a universe supposedly created by a good God proves that "God" either does not exist, or that He is not good.

Yet the Bible affirms God, and teaches both His power and goodness. And, in the context of a personal universe, the Bible speaks directly about human pain and suffering.

Pain and suffering in the Old Testament. The Hebrew language has many different words that communicate the ideas of pain and suffering. Here are some of the more frequently used:

Ka'ab emphasizes pain. While physical pain is involved, words derived from *ka'ab* are most concerned with the mental anguish associated with hurt.

'Asab and its derivatives. These words are translated as grief, sorrow, and wound. Here too both physical and mental pain are in view.

Use of hil. This is a graphic word that is very strong: it suggests writhing in agony, and is used of terror at disaster and extreme mental anguish.

A study of the use of these words in the Old Testament draws attention not to painful events themselves, but to how human beings are affected by life's tragedies. If it were only the bout with illness, or the loss of a job, or an unjust lawsuit, in itself, but the real suffering is in how such events affect us within—the doubts, the uncertainties, the fears, as the future we looked forward to seems dashed and all ahead black,

The Book of Job reminds us that while the Old Testament is sensitive to human suffering, it offers no easy answer. God permitted Satan to assault Job, a truly good man. Despite the most intense suffering Job maintained his trust in God—until three friends tried to explain *why*. Then Job too was catapulted into an attempt to explain his experience.

Job and his friends had an image of God as righteous Judge. So the friends concluded that Job's suffering must be a punishment from God. Job had not knowingly sinned, and so would not admit fault. Yet Job himself had no other explanation. Overwhelmed by what seemed betrayal by the God he trusted, Job began to challenge the beliefs of his friends about how the Lord works in human affairs.

Job's inability to explain his suffering, and the accusations of his "friends," brought the sufferer close to despair. How clearly we see in Job, stripped of hope and fearful in a universe he suddenly did not understand at all, reflections of our own feelings during times of intense personal suffering.

At the end of the Book of Job God did intervene. He restored Job, and corrected his friends. *But God did not explain.* Job was left without answers, to simply trust a God whose motives and purposes no human being can fully know.

There are, however, fascinating insights in the Old Testament. First, as Job illustrated, the reasons for the suffering of the good man are often hidden. We must simply trust God to bring good in the end, even as He restored and blessed Job.

Second, Job's friends were right in that *sometimes* suffering is associated with sin. God "does not leave the guilty unpunished" (Num. 14:18). Yet suffering can also be instruction: It can be a means of grace by which God shows the sinner his need for repentance. It was suffering which often led people to call on the Lord for relief (Isa. 14:3).

Third, several of the words for suffering in the Old Testament are associated with childbirth. The *Expository Dictionary of Bible Words* suggests that in Hebrew terms, "Pain's essence is summed up in the writhing body and straining muscles of the woman in the pain of childbirth. The image is theologically significant. It offers hope, in that the outcome of the pain is the emergence of fresh life into the world." God intends that our suffering will in some mysterious way give birth to good!

One other theme in the Old Testament is important. Isaiah looked ahead to the appearance of a "Suffering Servant." This Individual would come to do God's will, even though that will brought Him intense pain. If ever good was given birth in suffering, it was so in the death of Jesus. As Isaiah said:

Surely He took up our infirmities and carried our sorrows, yet we considered Him stricken by God, smitten by Him, and afflicted. But He was pierced for our transgressions, He was crushed for our iniquities; the punishment that brought us peace was upon Him, and by His wounds we are healed. We all, like sheep, have gone astray, each of us has turned to his own way; and the Lord has laid on Him the iniquity of us all.
Isaiah 53:4-6

Pain and suffering in the New Testament. There are many Greek words for pain and suffering in the New Testament, most with broad meanings that parallel those of the Old Testament.

But most New Testament references to suffering use the Greek word *pascho* and its derivatives. Strikingly, these words constantly are linked with the events associated with Jesus' crucifixion. He is the primary example of suffering, and in a study of Jesus' suffering we learn much about its nature.

Many of the special insights come from our Book of 1 Peter.

Suffering and sin. The Bible definitely links suffering and sin. In the Fall Adam and Eve, and all the human race, became subject to suffering. At times suffering is *directly* related to our own sin, in that suffering comes as a consequence or punishment of our own acts. A person who is imprisoned for a crime obviously is suffering both as a consequence of and as a punishment for his or her sins.

On the other hand, suffering is often *indirectly* related to sin. A person shot or injured by a criminal suffers not because he did something wrong, but because of the sin of another.

In our sin-cursed world we are subject to much suffering that is "unjust" in the sense that we suffer because of others' actions rather than our own. But, whomever's the fault, it is sin in our universe which is the cause.

Peter gives us the ultimate example of unjust suffering. He points out that Jesus suffered "the righteous for [*hyper*, lit. "on account of"] the unrighteous" (1 Peter 3:18). The sins for which Jesus suffered on the cross were not His own. In the immediate situation, it was the sins of Jesus' enemies among the Jews that brought about His pain. In the grand context of eternity, however, Jesus suffered because of your sins and mine. It was the sin of all humanity which brought Christ to the Cross.

So the Bible never suggests that our experience of pain and suffering will be "fair." Like Jesus, we will often suffer not for what we do but for what others have done, or simply because sin has warped society itself out of God's intended shape.

Suffering and God. While the Bible associates suffering with sin and sees sin as the basic cause, Scripture affirms that our Sovereign God is also involved.

We Christians are told, when overtaken by unexpected and unjust suffering, to "set apart Christ as Lord" (v. 15). We are to remember that God is Sovereign, and nothing is permitted to happen except by His will.

In looking again at Jesus we realize that His own suffering was "by God's set purpose and foreknowledge" (Acts 2:23).

Suffering and purpose. Again, the suffering of Jesus demonstrates that though an injustice, Jesus' suffering had a purpose. Through it God intended to bring us to Him through the death of Christ (1 Peter 3:18).

So the suffering of Jesus teaches us important truths. Sin can be the indirect as well as direct cause of suffering. And when we suffer unjustly, God not only is sovereignly involved but also is at work through the experience, to bring about some good purpose of His own.

Suffering and the Christian. The New Testament does speak directly to the issue of the suffering saint.

First Peter 1:3-9 points out that the suffering we experience now demonstrates the genuineness of our faith and will bring glory when Jesus comes. Romans 5:3-4 adds that "suffering produces perseverance; perseverance, character; and character, hope."

So suffering is intended to make a contribution to the inner transformation of the Christian.

First Peter 2:13-25 encourages us to bear up under unjust suffering, and commit ourselves to live good lives, "conscious of God" (v. 19). We are to remain aware that by living godly lives under pressure we follow Jesus' example and walk in His steps.

Paul even spoke of such suffering as fellowship (lit., "participation") in Christ. Christian suffering is associated with God's plan to complete the mission of Jesus in our world (see Phil. 3:10).

A Theology of Suffering?

Human suffering is and will remain largely a mystery. Yet from 1 Peter, which draws together so many themes seen in both Old and New Testaments, it is possible to develop a practical theology of suffering, which links God's view, purposes, and role in human suffering in a positive, redemptive view. The chart below identifies key verses in 1 Peter, from which a study group can work.

♥ *Group Activity: Support Group*
Discuss: What kinds of suffering are worse: Physical? Emotional? Loss? Uncertainty?

Then work together to complete the "Practical Theology of Suffering" chart on this page, looking into the many passages in 1 Peter that deal with this topic.

When you have explored each thoroughly, develop together what you feel is a Christian view of suffering.

Together: 1 Peter 4:7–5:11

Use of gifts (1 Peter 4:7-11). Peter reminded us that we can see in the very sins of our society which causes human sufferings the end of all things. God will judge. Until then, we believers must be deeply committed to each other, to help and encourage each other to keep on serving God.

Suffering (1 Peter 4:12-19). How much we need encouragement. Especially when we suffer as Christians, experiencing pain unjustly. Then the encouragement we receive, will help us commit ourselves to our "faithful Creator and continue to do good."

A Practical Theology of Suffering

1 Peter passage	Teaching
1:3-6	
1:7-9	
2:18-20	
2:21-25	
3:10-18	
4:1-2	
4:12-19	
5:6-7	
5:10-11	
A Christian view of suffering	
1.	
2.	
3.	
4.	
5.	
6.	
7.	
8.	
9.	
10.	

Authority in church (1 Peter 5:1-4). We have seen many exhortations in Peter about living under authority. Peter now advised those in authority in the church. Leaders are to provide an example to the flock. Autocracy, selfish motives—none of these are appropriate for those who walk in Jesus' way.

Submission and humility (1 Peter 5:5-6). Submission within the church and humility in all relationships is fitting for Christians. We live under authority in every aspect of our lives.

God's care (1 Peter 5:7). Is submission surrender? Not at all. As we have seen, submission is an expression of trust in a sovereign God. Knowing that God is *God,* we can cast all our anxieties on Him, because He does care for us.

The devil (1 Peter 5:8-9). Satan will attack the church's ways of life. But we are equipped to resist.

Finally, Peter gave his benediction. It's a reminder of the glory and power that suffuses and transforms all the suffering we might know.

The God of all grace, who called you to His eternal glory in Christ, after you have suffered a little while, will Himself restore you and make you strong, firm and steadfast. To Him be the power forever and ever. Amen.

1 Peter 5:10-11

GROUP RESOURCE GUIDE

Identification: *Share with others*
Jot down at least three phrases with which you might complete the sentence, "Suffering is. . . . "

Exploration: *Probe God's Word*
Take notes as a person previously prepared reviews on O.T. and N.T. words for suffering and what can be learned from them (see commentary).

Then work in teams of five to study and summarize the 1 Peter passages listed on the chart on page 537. When complete, compare your summaries with those of other teams.

Reaction: *Respond together to the Word*
Complete the chart on page 537 together by developing statements that sum up a Christian perspective on suffering.

When done, repeat the opening activity, by individually finishing the sentence, "Suffering is. . . . "

Adoration: *Worship and pray*
Praise God for the comfort He gives us in suffering, by assuring us of His continuing love and sovereign control.

2 Peter; Jude

DANGER!

Overview

The later letters from the New Testament era show a growing awareness of dangers facing the young church. In 2 Timothy, the last letter Paul wrote before his death, we find grim warnings about false teachers and a growing pollution of the church. Now, in two other late letters, one written by Peter and one by Jude, we discover the same strong note of warning.

Because 2 Peter and Jude are so closely linked, not only in theme but also in specific content, it is helpful to teach and study them together.

Most believe 2 Peter was written just before the apostle's death, in A.D. 67 or 68. Jude may have been written as many as 10 or 15 years later.

While 1 Peter deals with dangers from outsiders hostile to the Christian community, 2 Peter and Jude examine dangers that emerge from within. Each book warns us about the same two problems: the emergence of false teachers, and of false teaching.

For anyone concerned today with heresy, or with recognizing false teachers and cults, these two books are extremely valuable. They are also helpful to the average Christian, for they call us back to the simplicity of a godly life, and teach us to commit ourselves to loving God and doing good.

■ For a verse-by-verse commentary on each of these short New Testament books, see the *Bible Knowledge Commentary,* pages 859-879 and 917-924.

Commentary

One of my family's favorite TV series used to be "Lost in Space." The Robinsons, two passengers, and a friendly robot moved through the galaxy facing new threats each week. When the robot sensed some dark, mysterious force approaching, he would shout out, "Danger! Danger! Danger!"

In the last half the first century, a threat far more sinister than those dreamed up by TV scriptwriters assailed the churches. The two short books of 2 Peter and Jude were written to sound an urgent alarm. As we move on in time (rather than in space), we too need to be alerted to spiritual dangers and be prepared to meet them.

Peter and Jude

Who were these two men, and what was the historical context in which they wrote?

Peter. The writer is, of course, the most prominent of the Twelve in the Gospels and the dominant figure in the early chapters of Acts. This is the second of two letters Peter wrote to the early church. It too is a "last days" letter, written at the end of the apostle's career.

According to the early church historian, Eusebius, Peter was martyred during Nero's persecutions (about A.D. 67–68). The letter was most likely written one of these years.

Heresy was clearly threatening the church, a heresy that challenged both doctrine and lifestyle. The books of 2 Peter, Jude, and 2 Timothy all contain clear teaching that combats this danger.

Jude. The writer's identification of himself in verse 1 and in early church tradition have led to the conviction that Jude was a younger brother of the James who led the Jerusalem church, and thus was a younger half-brother of Jesus. It is very difficult to establish a date for Jude's short letter; suggested dates range from the late 60s to the 80s. The similarity with 2 Peter does not indicate that one copies the other. Instead it suggests how widespread the threat within the church had become, and that there was a common body of teaching to help congregations deal with such dangers.

Paul's Concern

Actually, early words of warning come from

Paul in 2 Timothy, as well as from Jude and Peter. Paul warned Timothy of the teachers who have "wandered away from the truth" (2:18). He spoke of "terrible times" when "people will be lovers of themselves, lovers of money, boastful, proud, abusive, disobedient to their parents, ungrateful, unholy, without love, unforgiving, slanderous, without self-control, brutal, not lovers of the good, treacherous, rash, conceited, lovers of pleasure rather than lovers of God." Worst of all, these people will retain "a form of godliness but denying its power" (3:1-5). While Timothy was to teach, correct, rebuke, and encourage with "great patience and careful instruction," he was also to realize that "the time will come when men will not put up with sound doctrine." They will instead shape doctrine to "suit their own desires" (4:2-3).

Times of stress are coming. Christians must recognize the signs of danger and be prepared to protect the purity of the church.

Persecution. When Paul, Peter, and Jude were writing these letters, danger signs were all around. Gentile nations had recognized Christianity as a faith distinct from Judaism, and the Jews had also become hateful and envious.

Other sources of opposition existed. In 2 Timothy Paul mentioned Alexander the metalworker, who did him "a great deal of harm" (4:14). He was probably one of those whose living came from selling images of the gods. His livelihood was threatened by the growing Christian movement. Later even the butchers who sold meat for pagan sacrifices lost income because the people were forsaking the temples. The Emperor Nero would soon formally accuse Christians of "hatred of mankind" and put many of them to horrible deaths.

The Roman world was used to multiple faiths, all tolerated and existing side by side. Just as in the modern East a person may be both a Buddhist and Shintoist, the Roman world saw no problem with one person worshiping many gods or having several religions. Christianity challenged this ethos. The Christians refused to worship the emperor, which left them open to the charge of treason. They disturbed families with their insistence on total allegiance to one God. Many refused to serve in the military and to worship the legion eagles. All in all, Christians were becoming a disruptive force in society. Often in the next decades local magistrates would initiate persecutions against these strange and unpopular people.

By the time of Trajan (about A.D. 100), problems caused for the empire by the spread of Christianity were serious. Pliny the Younger, governor of Bithynia around A.D. 112, executed a number of Christians. Then he wrote to the emperor asking for advice and instruction. Trajan instructed Pliny that those who admitted they were Christians and refused to give up their belief were to be executed. But the governor should not hunt Christians down or accept anonymous accusations. And, of course, any Christian willing to give up his or her faith and offer sacrifice to the emperor was to be released.

Within 30 years after Jude's and Peter's letters, Christians would face a world in which their faith was itself adequate cause for execution! Yet, as we read these "last letters" of the Bible, we note a strange thing. *The danger that most concerned the apostles is not the danger from without!* They were confident that, when believers were called before judges, God would stand beside them and give them the words for their defense (see Matt. 5:11, 44; 10:17-20; Luke 21:12-19; John 15:20-21; Acts 4:1-31). Throughout history, persecution has tended to strengthen rather than weaken the church. We see in fact that the great danger to Christians does not live in the antagonism of outsiders at all!

📖 **Group Activity: Bible Study Group**
Examine 2 Peter 3:3-13, which reports that society will scoff at the biblical view of the Creation and judgment by a God who is able to intervene in the material universe. How does rejection of a biblical worldview affect personal and public morality?

Peter warns in 2 Peter 3:3 that "in the last days scoffers will come, scoffing and following their own evil desires." Look through copies of several days' newspapers. What evidence do you find in them that moderns like the ancients "scoff at" (belittle, flaunt, mock, scorn) biblical values and teachings?

Then together answer the question posed by Peter in 3:11.

Perversion. The great danger to the early

church, as to us today, is that what is central in the life of the corporate body might be perverted. Outsiders can never prevail against the body of Christ. But if the church is to remain strong and vital, it must be strong *within*. And inner strength depends on sustaining sound doctrine *and* a godly lifestyle.

Paul warned Timothy that opposition will come from "men of depraved minds" (2 Tim. 3:8).

"There will be false teachers among you," Peter then warned. These "will secretly introduce destructive heresies. . . . Many will follow their shameful ways and bring the way of truth into disrepute" (2 Peter 2:1-2).

Jude appealed to the church to contend for the faith, "For certain men . . . have secretly slipped in among you. They are godless men, who change the grace of our God into a license for immorality and deny Jesus Christ our only Sovereign and Lord" (v. 4).

Each of these letters warns against the twin threats of false teaching and ungodly living *within* the church.

Twin Threats

It helps us, in reading 2 Peter and Jude, to have an overview of the nature of the dangers with which they are concerned. Let's look at each threat separately.

False teaching. There was a body of teaching or doctrine, entrusted by God to the prophets and apostles and recorded in the Scriptures (2 Peter 3:2). A number of false teachings are mentioned in these letters and in 2 Timothy. Paul pointed out the mistaken belief that the resurrection of believers had already occurred. Peter warned against those who question Jesus' second coming and the certainty of the final judgment (2 Peter 3:6-10). However, both Peter and Jude made it clear that the critical heresy that threatened the church had to do with who Jesus is. The godless men who secretly slipped into the fellowship change God's grace and "deny Jesus Christ our only Sovereign and Lord" (Jude 4). Peter insisted, "We did not follow cleverly invented stories when we told you about the power and coming of our Lord Jesus Christ" (2 Peter 1:16). The false teachers who secretly introduced destructive heresies were actually "denying the Sovereign Lord who bought them" (2:1).

The crucial doctrinal danger is to deny Jesus as Sovereign Lord.

We can understand why. The New Testament teaches that Jesus is the center of our faith, our life, and hope. Continuing in a personal relationship with Jesus is the only means we have to break the hold of sin or to give us freedom from tension, fear, or guilt. Christians have no power in themselves to produce a life of wholeness.

Any teaching or doctrine that denies Jesus Christ His primacy or reduces Him to less than God robs Him of His glory, and us of our hope. Such a system of belief is what Paul calls a counterfeit faith.

An ungodly life. While the necessity for sound doctrine is much in the minds of Peter and Jude in these warning letters, it's clear that they warn against moral decline even more. Just as Paul insisted that leaders be chosen for their spiritual maturity, so Jude and Peter warned against leaders whose lifestyles mark them off as perverters.

A number of terms and concepts here need explanation, lest we think an ungodly way of life is simply a life of gross and open sin. For instance, what is the "depraved mind" Paul speaks of? (2 Tim. 3:8) And what are the "passions" or "evil desires" that find such frequent mention in these letters?

The Greek word translated "mind" here is *nous,* and is much more than intelligence, or the organ of thought. Greek scholars point out that this term refers to the sum total of the mental and moral outlook or state of being. We might call the biblical "mind" an attitude, a perspective, a way of thinking about and approaching life.

Is there a distinctively Christian life perspective? Of course there is. We are to find worth and importance in people rather than things. We are to love, not to use or abuse others. The Christian perspective measures material against eternal values, and finds the unseen more real than the visible. The Christian outlook on life enjoys holiness and finds sin uncomfortable; it rejects instinctual responses in favor of self-control. By loving God and others, a Christian finds fulfillment that no other focus for life could possibly provide.

Anything that draws us from this distinctive Christian perspective on life is a dangerous threat to the church. Only by building our lives on God's values can we find the holiness that gives the Christian fellowship its vitality and its power.

What may draw us into the world of illusion that is secular society's "mind"? Jude and Peter spoke often of passions and instinctual desires. It would be a mistake to understand these as merely sexual terms. The word translated "passions" or "desires" is a Greek word *epithumia*. In classical Greek the term is morally neutral; it simply means "desire." It could mean having a longing for something worthwhile, or it could imply desiring a forbidden object.

When a person enters into a friendship with Jesus, he gets a new life in which the old desires, thoughts, and choices are to be transformed. The "desires" (*epithumia*) that concerned Paul, Peter, and Jude are leftover drives and stirring passions of our old way of life. Peter identifies them as "the evil desires you had when you lived in ignorance" (1 Peter 1:14). We are not to conform to them or be "enslaved" by all kinds of passions and pleasures (Titus 3:3).

It's not wrong for a Christian to have feelings and wants. After all, God Himself promises that He will give us "the desires of our heart" (Ps. 37:4). We are free to move toward that which we want deeply; and as we live with God, He Himself will cause us to desire His best (see 103:5).

One difficult lesson for an astronaut to learn is that his old physical reactions, adapted to earth's gravity pull, are inappropriate in weightlessness. He takes a normal step, and bounds off the floor, He needs to learn to shuffle his feet to keep contact between magnetic shoes and the metal spacecraft. He grasps a wrench to turn a bolt, and finds himself, not the bolt, turned by the force he exerts. In his new environment the astronaut's old instinctive reactions are wrong!

The Christian too lives in a new environment: a kingdom ruled over by God's dear Son. The desires that shaped our perspective before we knew Christ produce the wrong responses now. Thus Peter and Jude warned us against men who claim to be spiritual leaders but whose lifestyles indicate that they "follow the corrupt desire of the sinful natures" (2 Peter 2:10) and react "like brute beasts, creatures of instinct" (v. 12), their personalities shaped by the *epithumia* of fallen humanity.

The real threat to the church is not persecution from without but corruption from within. How can we recognize this danger? Corruption from within involves a desertion of sound doctrine. When we "reinterpret" or reject the apostolic teaching recorded in Scripture, and especially when we deny the central teaching of Scripture about the person and work of Jesus, we wander from the truth and place our generation in jeopardy.

But corruption from within also involves a retreat from a holy life. When we begin to respond to life situations as instinct tells us, motivated by the old *epithumia* that gripped us before we knew Jesus, our whole perspective becomes warped. The Bible says it: "Do not conform any longer to the pattern of this world, but be transformed by the renewing of your mind [*nous*]" (Rom. 12:2). We must understand that a commitment to both sound doctrine and a godly life is essential, not only for church leaders, but for all believers. Any retreat from either, and we hear, through Peter and Jude, God's own danger alarm.

A Positive Christian Life

In our next study we will look carefully at these books' descriptions of false teachers and false teaching. For now it is important to note that we have protection against the influence of evil within. *In a sense, there are certain commitments of the Christian which immunize him or her from the threats of false teaching!*

Productive lives (2 Peter 1:1-11). God has given Jesus' people great promises and gifts. These provide "everything we need for life and godliness through our knowledge of Him" (v. 3). Through God's provision we partake of the divine nature and thus "escape the corruption in the world caused by evil desires" (v. 4).

Our first protection against corrupting influences from within is a commitment to that godliness which God's work in Christ has made possible for us. Peter calls on us to "make every effort" to develop qualities that reflect God's nature. These qualities are (vv. 5-7):

- faith   as full commitment to Christian teaching.
- goodness   literally, "virtue," or moral excellence.
- knowledge   as understanding drawn

- **self-control** from God's revelation. as the ability to "hold yourself in."
- **perseverance** as steadfastness in the face of opposition.
- **godliness** as conduct that shows we are aware of God's presence.
- **brotherly kindness** as a real affection for our fellow Christians.
- **love** as a real commitment to do good to others.

Such qualities will "keep you from being ineffective and unproductive in your knowledge of our Lord Jesus Christ" (v. 8).

The person who is fully committed to living for Jesus is unlikely to be drawn away to follow false teachers or false teaching. It is rather the lukewarm and indifferent Christian who is susceptible.

God's sure Word (2 Peter 1:12-21). A parallel line of defense is full confidence in "the truth you now have" (v. 12). Peter reminded us how great a confidence we can have in the Scriptures, whose prophetic words about Jesus have proven true, thus demonstrating that the Spirit truly "carried along"

Scripture's writers so that the Word has its origin in the will of God.

A vision of reality (2 Peter 3:1-13). Unlike those who scoff, we know that this present world will be destroyed. Looking forward to that great cataclysm we fix our hope not on anything in this material universe but on the new heaven and earth God will create. Our vision of the future, and values shaped by the expectation of Christ's return, motivate us to live "holy and godly lives."

Persevering in the faith (Jude 20-22). Jude closed his letter with a description of the life to which we are to commit ourselves. As we focus on these things, we will be immune to the appeal of false teachers and false teaching.

What are we to concentrate on? Praying. Keeping ourselves in God's love (which 1 John 5:1-4 defines as loving one another and obeying the Lord). Looking expectantly toward Jesus' coming. Being merciful to those who waver, and seeking to snatch them from judgment even while keeping clear of all that corrupts them.

If we lead lives like this, we and the church itself will be safe from all influences that would corrupt.

GROUP RESOURCE GUIDE

Identification: *Share with others*
If you have ever been led astray by a religious teacher, or have accepted teaching you now believe is false, tell about the experience. What attracted you to the person or teaching? What led you to rethink your allegiance?

Exploration: *Probe God's Word*
Read quickly through 2 Peter and Jude, putting a check mark beside any verses that deal with false teachings or false teachers.

Together make a master list of relevant verses. Develop symbols to mark each verse as to its emphasis: on characteristics of false teachers, on the appeal of false teachings, on false doctrines taught in the first centu-

ry, and on the appropriate response to false teaching.

Reaction: *Respond together to the Word*
Discuss how prevelant you feel false teaching and false teachers are today. How sensitive are we to the danger they represent?

Adoration: *Worship and pray*
In preparation for worship talk about the godly persons who have influenced you, taught you, and helped shape your faith. How many influential persons can you list? What has each contributed to you?

Then thank God for His goodness in providing the godly leaders who do hold to and communicate His truth.

HERESY

Overview

Throughout church history, many who have been labeled heretics have been tortured and put to death, or driven from their homes. Even Luther called on the princes to repress a peasants' movement for equality in his day. And Calvin did not hesitate to affirm the death penalty for an early unitarian in Geneva.

But often those called heretics by the majority were the true believers! The followers of Huss were brutally repressed by the church, and the Huguenots (French Protestants) were mercilessly massacred. Wars on the continent and even in England were often motivated, or at least justified, by religion.

This raises a question. What is heresy, and who is the heretic? How is the church to guard against heresy? And how is the heretic to be treated?

These may seem irrelevant questions in our society. We value tolerance so much that taking a stand for truth, or for righteousness, is foreign to us. Yet the early church did take a stand, in a society much like our own. The early Christians insisted that Jesus is the only way to God.

Certainly we do not execute heretics today, and we do not persecute those who differ from us. We don't want to. But we should be able to recognize heresy. And we should know how to respond to false teachers, like those against whom Jude and Peter warned, who creep into the church today, to introduce their still "destructive heresies" (2 Peter 2:1).

Commentary

The *Random House Unabridged Dictionary* defines *heresy* as an "opinion or doctrine at variance with the orthodox or accepted doctrine." In Roman Catholic tradition, the reference continues, a heretic is "a baptized Roman Catholic who willfully and persistently rejects any article of faith." Both these definitions focus attention on doctrine, but in Scripture the word has a wider application.

The Greek word from which *heretic* derives is *hairesis,* and means "sect, party, or school" (as of a school of philosophy). It was used of the "party of the Pharisees" in Acts 15:5, which Paul called "the strictest sect of our religion" (26:5). In the Christian movement heresy came to refer to a dissenting faction or group holding some opinion or dogma that marked them off from the rest of the body (1 Cor. 11:18-19; Gal. 5:20). In essence, heretics seem to be individuals within the church who hold to some way of thinking or living that sets them off from scriptural doctrine, lifestyle, and fellowship.

As we saw in our last study, factions may develop over various teachings such as the Resurrection or the Second Coming, but the truly critical element in "destructive heresies" has to do with the person of Christ. No doctrine that fails to give Jesus preeminence as God and Sovereign Lord can be considered "Christian."

But heresy also involves variation in lifestyle. God's people are called to holiness. When we desert Christian attitudes and values, turning to a licentious following of old impulses and desires, we have also fallen into heresy. We have become a faction, dividing the body.

An Overview of Jude: Jude 1-2

Even a cursory reading of Jude helps us sense how serious heresy is.

Godless men (Jude 3-4). Jude intended to write an encouraging letter, but felt compelled to urge his readers to resist "godless men" who had "slipped in among you" and who both denied Jesus and twisted grace into a license for immorality.

Judgment (Jude 5-7). Jude reviewed God's

acts of judgment, and warned against modern outbreaks of immorality.

False teachers (Jude 8-10). Jude portrayed the false teachers as ignorant of spiritual realities, reacting as "unreasoning animals" in that they were driven by instincts rather than higher faculties. This failing was reflected in their contempt for authority. The reference to a dispute about the "body of Moses" in verse 9 is to a book called the *Assumption of Moses*. Jude did *not* suggest this book is Scripture: his point was that even in devotional literature a powerful angel like Michael does not show contempt for an angel of higher rank, Satan, but waits for the Lord to rebuke him.

History of rebellion (Jude 11-13). Like Cain, these leaders harmed their brothers. Like Balaam they were moved by a passion for money. Like Korah they wanted to be leaders though God did not call them for leadership. Each of these suffered judgment—and so were the false teachers who troubled the church.

Enoch's prophecy (Jude 14-16). Jude again referred to well-known devotional literature. Even here God is known as One who will judge the ungodly

Perseverance (Jude 17-23). The writer closed with a call to the true believers to persevere, faithful to and contending for the truth of the Gospel.

Analysis of Heresy: 2 Peter; Jude

When we study the details of the Book of Jude, and compare them with 2 Peter, we gain a clear picture of false teachers and false teaching.

Characteristics of false teachers. Paul instructed Timothy and Titus to officially recognize those in the churches who had matured in the faith and who demonstrated their reliability by adhering to sound doctrine, and by living exemplary Christian lives. Now Peter and Jude identified false teachers by the opposite characteristics.

False teachers claim a special knowledge or interpretation that differs from the common core of belief in the Christian community. They charge that the doctrine recorded in Scripture is "cleverly invented stories" (2 Peter 1:16). They also reject the authority of Scripture, and of the present leaders of the Christian community (2:10; Jude 8, 10). False teachers can be recognized by their insistence that they alone have the truth. Sooner or later in their denial of apostolic teaching they attack the person of Jesus, and seek to rob Him of His centrality.

False teachers also claim freedom to live a life moved by the old passions. They are competitive. Rather than serve, they use and exploit others. They rationalize their immorality and "are grumblers and faultfinders; they follow their own evil desires; they boast about themselves and flatter others for their own advantage" (v. 16). At every point their characters lack the qualities Paul said are to be found in spiritual leaders.

Jude warned that some "have secretly slipped in among you" (v. 4), which implied that neither the false teaching nor the sinful lifestyle may be evident initially. No wonder Paul warned that those considered for leadership "must first be tested" and then serve an apprenticeship as deacons "if there is nothing against them" (1 Tim. 3:10). He pointed out that while "the sins of some men are obvious," the "sins of others trail behind them" (5:24). Because flaws of character are not always readily apparent, selecting church leaders should never be a hasty or careless process.

Appeal of false teachers. How does it happen that those who introduce heresies all too often find followers within the church?

First, it's clear that their appeal is to the immature: those who are not deeply grounded in sound doctrine or the fellowship of the church. No wonder Peter began his letter with the exhortation to "make every effort to add to your faith goodness; and to goodness, knowledge; and to knowledge, self-control; and to self-control, perseverance; and to perseverance, godliness; and to godliness, brotherly kindness; and to brotherly kindness, love. For if you possess these qualities in increasing measure, they will keep you from being ineffective and unproductive in your knowledge of our Lord Jesus Christ" (2 Peter 1:5-8) Growth in the disciplines of the Christian life must follow our initial step of faith if we are to resist the lure of false teachers.

But what *is* their appeal? In part it is an appeal to pride in a superior and special knowledge that sets some apart from others. "They may believe that, but *we* know better!" Yet the main thrust of heresy's appeal seems to lie in its promise of freedom

545

to indulge our instinctual desires. "They mouth empty, boastful words," Peter said, "and, by appealing to the lustful desires of sinful human nature, they entice people who are just escaping from those who live in error. They promise them freedom, while they themselves are slaves of depravity—for a man is a slave to whatever has mastered him" (2 Peter 2:18-19). Certainly it is inviting to "follow mere natural instincts" (Jude 19). It's hard to surrender our desires to God for reshaping and to deny ourselves the sensations our old way of life has led us to crave. The false teacher justifies any and all behavior by corrupting God's grace into a "license for immorality" (v. 4).

Some time ago on a talk show, a young challenger insisted to Billy Graham that sexual intercourse was the same as a ham sandwich. Sex and hunger are both "natural" desires, he argued: when you feel a desire, you satisfy it. After all, if God has made an experience pleasurable, then it must be good.

The false teacher seeks to encourage within the church a passion for pleasure that draws people away from the life of holiness and self-control to which the Christian is called. Some will become "lovers of pleasure rather than lovers of God," Paul warned (2 Tim. 3:4).

Yet the Christian life is not a miserable withdrawal or a dreary denial of every pleasant thing. But we are to find our pleasure in what God calls holy, not in distorted passions and desires. Scripture promises, "At Thy right hand there are pleasures forevermore" (Ps. 16:11, KJV).

Any invitation to share a special revelation that the rest of the church does not possess, or any promise of freedom to indulge our every "natural" desire with God's blessing, should be a warning to us. We may have met a false teacher who seeks to shatter the oneness of the body in which God has placed us.

Our Response to False Teachers

Jude tells us that we are to "contend" for the faith. To some in history, contending for the faith has meant to attack those who deviate from sound doctrine. Such an approach led to men and women burned at the stake, to wars, and inquisitions fashioned in order to enforce conformity. Yet there is no hint in the Bible of a crusade to exclude the deviate. How then do we "contend"? Here are several principles from these letters to help us.

Stand on unshakable foundations. Paul reminded Timothy that in spite of doctrinal challenges from Hymenaeus and Philetus, who have wandered away from the truth. . . . God's solid foundation stands firm, sealed with this inscription: "The Lord knows those who are His," and, "Everyone who confesses the name of the Lord must turn away from wickedness" (2 Tim. 2:17-19).

We may proceed with the firm conviction that, while we may be uncertain who belongs to the Lord, He does know. But at the same time, one who confesses the name of the Lord "must turn away from wickedness." *Open sin* calls for judgment and discipline in the Christian community.

Give gentle instruction. Rather than trying to silence the false teacher with shouting, Paul instructed, "Don't have anything to do with foolish and stupid arguments" (v. 23). Debate may be exciting, but it is not productive. Instead, the leaders of the Christian community are to "gently instruct" those who oppose (v. 25). We prayerfully communicate sound doctrine "in the hope that God will grant them repentance leading them to a knowledge of the truth, and that they will come to their senses and escape from the trap of the devil, who has taken them captive to do his will" (vv. 25-26).

The fleshly approach of the false teacher is to attack, challenge authority, ridicule, strike out, and abuse. The Christian must respond with love, recognizing that he is not battling against an enemy but *for* a fellow human being. In this spiritual confrontation, the warfare is between God and Satan. As for us, we are to simply "be merciful to those who doubt, snatch others from the fire and save them; to others show mercy mixed with fear—hating even the clothing stained by corrupted flesh" (Jude 22-23).

Depend on divine judgment. Our response to heretical challenges to the Christian community should not be confused with compromise. There can be no retreat from truth, *or* withdrawal of love. God "knows how to rescue godly men from trials and to hold the unrighteous for the day of judgment" (2 Peter 2:9). Both in this life and the life to come, the Lord involves Himself directly in the judgment of those who persistently rebel against Him. We can trust the false teacher to God and be free to concentrate on building ourselves up in the faith.

These letters then not only warn of dangers from within the church but also describe safeguards. If we as individuals and fellowships are firmly committed to these principles, we can be confident that we will be immune to any heresy which might appear. So let's:

- Be aware of the characteristic of false teachers and false teaching, so we can recognize and reject each.
- Follow only leaders who meet the qualifications given by Paul in his letters to Timothy and Titus.
- Study to understand the apostolic doctrine preserved for us in Scripture.
- And commit ourselves to the holy way of life and the unique values to which God calls us in His Word.

2 Peter

To see even more fully God's plan of protection for His own, we'll trace the thought of 2 Peter.

Peter began by reminding us that God "has given us everything we need for life and godliness through our knowledge of Him who called us by His own glory and goodness" (1:3). Jesus is sufficient; we don't need to look for something beyond a relationship with Him. Chapter 2 is devoted to a description of false teachers and their end. Chapters 1 and 3 encourage and exhort believers, showing us how to avoid the growing dangers from within.

Growth vital (2 Peter 1:5-11). The faith that brings us into relationship with God marks only the beginning of our life with Him. We are to concentrate on maturing in character so that we are no longer attracted by the false teacher's alluring promise of liberty. If you do these things," Peter said, "you will never fall" (v. 10).

Apostolic teaching trustworthy (2 Peter 1:12-21). Peter reminded the readers that the sound doctrine of the church is rooted in reality. The apostles did not relate "cleverly invented stories" but communicated historical facts to which they were eyewitnesses. All they reported is in harmony with the prophetic Word of the Old Testament. The two

Testaments stand as one, giving sure witness to the foundational truths of the church.

In this passage one phrase of verse 20 has been puzzling. The *New International Version* translates it "no prophecy of Scripture came about by the prophet's own interpretation," while the *King James Version* renders it "no prophecy of the Scripture is of any private interpretation." The original Greek supports either of these renderings, and both have suggestive implications. In the first case, we are reminded that it is God who spoke through His prophets and apostles. The Word is trustworthy because it is His own. In the second we are reminded that a false teacher may quote Scripture but give his own interpretation, which will differ from what the whole Bible teaches and from what the church has historically taught. When a sect, such as Jehovah's Witnesses, presents its own distinctive interpretation of Bible passages to deny the deity of Christ, we can look to the Word itself to refute the heresy. We can also look to the church as a whole, past and present, to see the voice of faith universally affirm that these verses teach that Jesus *is* God, fully human, and yet one with the Father from all eternity.

While there have been, and are, differences in interpretation of minor details of doctrine, the core of apostolic faith, as represented in the Apostle's Creed, has been the joyful affirmation of the church universal.

Judgment coming (2 Peter 3). This chapter is a striking affirmation of the trustworthiness of God's Word. Looking across the coming generations, Peter warned scoffers who will doubt Christ's return and question the certainty of judgment. They will insist that "since our fathers died, everything goes on as it has since the beginning of Creation" (v. 4). Yet God *did* intervene in the past to destroy the world in judgment, and this same God will intervene again, to destroy the works of human society (vv. 10-13).

We are not to let scoffers shake us from our certainty that Jesus will keep His promises. Because this universe will pass out of existence, we are to concentrate on that which is eternal. "So then, dear friends," Peter urged, "since you are looking forward to this, make every effort to be found spotless, blameless, and at peace with Him" (v. 14).

As we concentrate every effort on pleasing Him who has delivered us into the kingdom of Jesus Christ, we will be untouched by the lure of false teachers. They offer only the fleeting pleasures of a world that will someday flare up, and then burn out.

GROUP RESOURCE GUIDE

Exploration: *Probe God's Word*
Divide into three interest groups, each of which will explore one of these themes as it is developed in both 2 Peter and Jude.
Characteristics of False Teachers
Appeal of False Teachers
Response to False Teachers
If you have previously completed study #85, build in the verses keyed at that time. If you have not completed that study, begin with the identification activity suggested on page 543.

Reaction: *Respond together to the Word*
It is important not to identify everyone with whom we may disagree as a "false teacher."

Together discuss the following three questions:
What must we know about a person before we identify him or her as a false teacher?
What teachings can we list that should undoubtedly be considered "false teachings"?
What teachings can we list that should not be considered "false teachings"?

Adoration: *Worship and pray*
Tell one Bible truth you have come to know, trust, and experience, and share how it has changed your life. After all have shared, praise God for His revelation of transforming truth, so different from the sterile heresies that have deceived so many over the centuries.

WALKING WITH GOD

Overview

John's letters are probably the last written of our New Testament. Despite the persecution of the last part of the first century, John's warm, pastoral letters call Christians to live a life of simple love and obedience. It is the inner life of the man and woman of God that concerned John, for the deepest issues of life lie within.

John's letters are not closely reasoned or marked by step-by-step arguments. Instead, John stated and then returned again and again to the themes that concerned him—themes like light, love, and truth. In simple, powerful prose John reminded us of the basic truths that shape our lives and relationship with the Lord.

Outline

Commentary

It's quite easy to sense the personalities of Peter and Paul from material in the New Testament. In the Gospels bombastic Peter blurted out his first thoughts; in Acts a matured and Spirit-filled Peter dominated early-church history. And Paul spoke so openly of his feelings and motives that sometimes we're embarrassed by his totally honest revelations.

But it's hard for us to visualize John, so humble that in his Gospel he cannot bear to name himself. With quiet joy he refers obliquely to "the disciple whom Jesus loved" (John 21:7). We know that John was one of the inner circle along with his brother James, and with Peter. We know that at the Last Supper John found a place as close to Jesus as possible. But what else do we know about this quiet apostle? And what do we know about his writings?

John and His Writings

The man. When John and his brother James, the sons of Zebedee, began to follow Jesus, they were apparently quite young and passionate. Once the disciples were passing through Samaria on the way to Jerusalem. James and John went on ahead to find lodging in a village. When the Samaritans, who hated the Jews as much as they were hated, learned the party was traveling to Jerusalem, they refused them shelter. Furious, James and John confronted Jesus. "Lord," they asked, "do You want us to call fire down from heaven to destroy them?" (Luke 9:54) Their nickname was appropriate: "Thunderers."

Another time the disciples saw a man driving out demons in Jesus' name, but the man was not one of their company. "We told him to stop," John reported, "because he was not one of us" (Mark 9:38). John was again corrected by Jesus because his zeal had missed the spirit of his Master.

A final Gospel incident (Matt. 20:20-28) completes John's portrait. He and his brother whisper privately to their mother. Shortly she approaches Jesus. Could the places of authority at Jesus' right and left hand be reserved for her sons when the Lord takes power in His kingdom? Jesus explained to the mother and to the two sons that He did not have the authority to grant such a request. Later the other disciples heard of the pair's attempt to gain advantage, and reacted with understandable anger. Then Jesus explained to the Twelve that greatness in His kingdom is not found in authority but in servanthood: a servanthood far removed from the self-concerned attitude of James and John.

We can understand John; we've all known (and possibly been) such firebrands. We understand his quickness to take offense and the anger that urged him to strike back. We understand the pride that held others at arm's length. We understand the drive to succeed, the hunger to be somebody and gain a high place even at the expense of friends. We understand all this because these are the motivating passions (*epithumia*) in our world. These are the desires that the New Testament encourages us to replace with a set of values summed up in the concept of holiness. Yes, we understand young John only too well. He is so much like us!

But when we come to John's writings, we meet a different man. We meet a man whose favorite word was *love,* a man who was gentle, so selfless that he hardly mentioned himself or his feelings, except as they related to the needs of the men and women to whom he ministered. We meet a man who *was* transformed, who demonstrated in his own personality the Bible promise that we can be changed by beholding Jesus (2 Cor. 3:12).

John emphasized the love Jesus had for him even in the days before he matured; thus he calls himself, "The disciple whom Jesus loved." What a message for you and me. Jesus loves and accepts us, no matter what our stage of growth. Jesus' new life *will* grow within us and, as John, we will become more and more like our Lord.

John's writings. John's epistles were probably written from Ephesus and circulated in the churches in Asia. They were immediately accepted by the whole church: we even have evidence of an exegesis (study and explanation) of John's Gospel from as early as A.D. 150.

Like Peter and Jude, John counseled the church about dangers from within. He warned against antichrists who were trying to lead believers astray. Like the others,

John identified the spirit of antichrist with the denial that "Jesus Christ has come in the flesh" (1 John 4:2). The person of Jesus is the central doctrinal truth, and a relationship with Him, who *is* God, is the irreplaceable essence of our Christian experience. He also reminds us that sin by any name is the devil's work: we are not to be moved by appeals to our passions.

Invitation to Joy: 1 John 1:1-4

The heresy emerging in the days of Peter and Jude was an even greater danger during John's last years. As competing teachers introduced conflicting doctrines, many Christians became confused about who was the false teacher, and who was the true. Confusion also arose as the drive for holiness brought an unexpected reaction: those who slipped into sin began to wonder if they still had a personal relationship with God.

John focused on the doubts, fears, and uncertainties that well up in believers of every era who try to follow Jesus, yet who often find themselves stumbling and unsure.

John immediately shared with us his deep personal concern. He wrote in order "that you also may have fellowship with us. And our fellowship is with the Father and with His Son, Jesus Christ" (v. 3). "Fellowship" is the Greek word *koinonia.* It's a word of intimacy and means "communion; close relationship; participation; sharing." John's desire for us is what we ourselves yearn for: a warm, comfortable relationship with God in which we are aware of being close to Him in heart and mind.

John has seen in the historical Jesus (vv. 1-2) the reality of *life.* In Jesus eternal life entered time, and through Jesus John personally experienced that fellowship he desired for all of us. We can almost picture the old man deeply aware of how close he now stands beside his Lord, beckoning you and me to come closer and share with him that intimate relationship with the Father and Son that makes joy complete.

♥ *Group Activity: Support Group*
Focus on 1 John 1:3: the disciple's commitment to share "what we have seen and heard": i.e., his personal experience with Jesus. Recall one of your most difficult times, and how God ministered to you in it. Tell the others in your group about it

and how Christ ministered to you. Through your celebration of God's living presence, others will be strengthened and enabled to experience joy.

Walking in the Light: 1 John 1:5–2:2

How can we have fellowship with God? In this familiar yet vital New Testament passage, John unlocked truths that can transform us—and our attitude toward ourselves as well as toward God.

Light (1 John 1:5-7). John's first answer to the question of how believers can have fellowship with God was simple. God is Light. If we walk in the light, we will have fellowship.

Often when John spoke of light (and he used the term 30 times in his writings), he was quoting Jesus: "I am the Light of the world. Whoever follows Me will never walk in darkness, but will have the light of life" (John 8:12; see 9:5; 12:46). The essential nature of God as light sets God apart from man. Man's sinful condition has made the world lie in darkness. Even worse, "Men loved darkness instead of light because their deeds were evil" (3:19). Confronted with the nature of God, men twist and struggle to turn away from such holiness. "Light" and "darkness" are *moral* terms in John's writings. The character of God is expressed as light; the character of sinful man is expressed as darkness.

So in this first letter, John confronted us with a disconcerting reality. If we are to be comfortable with God and live in intimate fellowship with Him, we must "walk in the light, as He is in the light" (1 John 1:7). Our values, our behavior, our attitudes, our commitments must be in harmony with God's character rather than with the natural passions of fallen humanity.

But this seems to raise a terrible barrier. If we must walk in light to have fellowship, how can we, who feel sin's pull and all too often give in to temptations, ever be comfortable with God? Isn't each sin a retreat to darkness? If sinlessness is the avenue to fellowship, who then can stand in the presence of God?

But John was *not* talking of sinlessness. "If we walk in the light," he said, "the blood of Jesus, His Son, purifies us from all sin" (v. 7). Even those walking in the light need forgiveness, and cleansing from sins they commit. While it is possible for us in

Christ not to sin, we can never claim that it is impossible to sin.

John's primary target here seems to be those who "claim to have fellowship with Him yet walk in the darkness" (v. 6). These men and women speak glowingly of their closeness to God and the fellowship they enjoy—and yet make a practice of sin! Their lifestyle is not godly; it is patterned after the ways of the false teachers described by Jude and Peter. No one who makes a practice of sin can claim fellowship with God. God's nature is light, not darkness. Those who walk in light as He is in the light may fall, but they will quickly turn away from that old lifestyle to find forgiveness in Jesus.

We might sum up John's teaching this way; if the direction of your life is toward the Source of light, you will find forgiveness for your failures and inadequacies. But if the direction of your life is toward the darkness, then you may be sure you have nothing in common with God.

Confession (1 John 1:8-10). John's readers were confused by two false teachings. The first was the claim that those who choose sin's lifestyle can maintain fellowship with God. This John labeled as a lie (v. 6). The second claim was by those who said they were without sin (v. 8). They based their claim to fellowship with God on the belief that they matched God in His moral perfection! John called this claim self-deceit: "We deceive ourselves and the truth is not in us" (v. 8).

Truth and falsehood are not related so much to the trustworthiness of the teller as they are to correspondence with reality. The problem with the claim of sinlessness is not that the motives of the claimant are unpure. His or her report may be made with honest conviction. But the report of sinlessness is mistaken: it does not correspond to reality. "We deceive ourselves and the truth is not in us."

What is the reality of sin for the Christian? The simple fact is that while in His death Jesus dealt fully with sin, the sin nature within us is not eradicated. The ingrained responses still tug. We still experience pride, lust, anger, hatred, and fear. The capacity to sin remains ours and will be an ever-present burden until we find our full release in resurrection.

But the capacity to sin, and even the

temptation to sin, are not really the issue in the Christian life. What is at issue are our *choices*. While we can feel the old passions stirring, we also have a new appreciation for godliness. We *want* to be like Jesus! Now two sets of desires war within us, and we have been given the freedom to choose. We can walk in the light and live in the radiance shed by the Living Word. Or we can turn our backs and chase off into the darkness after the illusive pleasures of sin. The choices we make, not the temptations we experience, are what move us into darkness or into light.

But again John is sensitive. Men and women who turn toward the light, and begin that hesitant journey toward holiness, find that their sinful "deeds will be exposed" (John 2:20). In the radiance of the light of Jesus, we become aware of pools of darkness in ourselves. Things we did that before seemed natural and proper become tawdry and shameful. Motives we suppressed come to light. The action we justified we see to be a petty release of antagonism. Our drive to succeed is recognized as a materialism that has pushed aside the needs of family and replaced the value of persons with the love of money.

The more we live in the light Jesus sheds, the more aware we become of how unlike God we are. Rather than feeling comfortable in His presence, we pull back in shame and hopelessness, deciding we are forever separated from Him. Or, unable to face the reality, we deceive ourselves and deny the blemishes that surface. "My sin is gone," we insist. And since pettiness and antagonism are wrong, we rechristen our reactions "righteous indignation." We dare not acknowledge our materialism and distorted values, so we justify our drive to succeed by the money we can give to missions. Closing our eyes to reality, we wander through life, insisting on our sinlessness and yet wondering why we have only an aching void inside rather than fellowship's joy.

But what's the alternative? How can a sinful and sinning human being maintain a joyful and comfortable relationship with a holy God? John says, "If we confess our sins, He is faithful and just and will forgive us our sins and purify us from all unrighteousness" (1 John 1:9). *The basis of our fellowship with God is not our sinlessness, but His forgiveness.*

✂ *Group Activity: Recovery Group*
Step 10 (continue taking personal inventory)
Each, in turn, either enter a totally dark room or submit to blindfolding. The room each will walk through should have a clear zig-zag pathway created through it, but the area off the pathway can be sprinkled with Rice Krispies. The challenge is to walk through the room in the dark or blindfolded without crunching a Krispie.

After each has tried it in the dark or blindfolded, each can go through the room with the light on or blindfold off.

Then read 1 John 1:5-10. Here "walking in the light" is being totally honest with ourselves and with God, admitting our sins when we do wrong so that we can be forgiven. Walking in darkness is "claiming to be without sin" when we do wrong, living in pretense and so denying both the truth and God.

Talk about your darkroom or blindfold experience. How did you feel trying to find your way in the dark? Also, how did it feel before you began your recovery process and denied your faults and failures? We are always tempted to pretend with ourselves and others, but that pathway leads us only into darkness and uncertainty.

Take time now for personal self-examination, and list every wrong or failure you are conscious of. Confess them to God and claim His promise that He is "faithful and just [to] forgive us."

Then share at least one of the things for which you have just been forgiven. Or: Tell how this will change you in the future.

Let's remember the development of John's explanation before going on. You and I are invited to live our lives in intimate relationship with the Lord, in comfortable closeness and joy. The key to experiencing this kind of fellowship is to walk in light, not darkness. Some may claim fellowship while obviously choosing sin. They lie. Others may claim fellowship on the basis of a supposed sinlessness. They deceive themselves. The reality is that we are imperfect— and yet can have fellowship!

To have fellowship involves choosing a basic direction *toward* godliness; walking *into* the light, we can see God and reality.

But we also become aware of our sins and failures. We will become aware of all that God still has to do within us to make us truly godly.

We cannot live in fellowship with God if we live a lie: to walk in the light means we must face and deal with the reality of our sin.

How do we deal with sin? We confess (lit., "acknowledge") sins. Instead of pretending or hiding our sins, we acknowledge them to God. And God "will forgive us our sins and purify us from all unrighteousness." God's forgiving grace will remove every barrier between the believer and God, even that of remembered guilt, so that we can be comfortable in the very presence of our Lord.

One last important promise is given us by John. God will not only forgive us as we acknowledge the sins we discover, but He will also purify us. God will touch our motives and desires, and He will gradually reshape us. Like John himself, as we walk into the light of Jesus, we will gradually lose the old anger and drive for prestige, and will become men and women who love.

A dangerous promise? (1 John 2:1-2) Some, reading John's letter, were sure to object to his teaching. "If we know we can be forgiven," they say "then why not sin? If that's all there is to fellowship, why make the effort to follow Jesus?" The objectors of course misunderstand. Only the person who *wants* to live in darkness will pervert the promise of forgiveness into a license for sin.

John was writing to help us avoid sin. "But if anybody does sin, we have One who speaks to the Father in our defense— Jesus Christ, the Righteous One. He is the atoning Sacrifice for our sins, and not only for ours but also for the sins of the whole world" (vv. 1-2).

How completely sufficient is the blood of Jesus Christ! Enough for the whole world, it surely is enough for you and me. Let us then go on boldly, with full confidence in Him, and walk in the light. We are moving toward holiness. But on the journey, we do not need to hide our sins. We need to acknowledge them, and receive not only forgiveness but the purifying power of our God.

GROUP RESOURCE GUIDE

Identification: *Share with others*
Share one sin, personal flaw, or failure you were able to admit to yourself only with great difficulty.

Discuss: Why is it so hard to be honest with ourselves, much less with God and others?

Exploration: *Probe God's Word*
Together work through 1 John 1:5–2:2 verse by verse, guided by the commentary. Make sure that each person understands the implication of each phrase. Or have one person previously prepared summarize the teaching and answer questions.

Reaction: *Respond together to the Word*
Choose one of the following three persons whom you see yourself "most like."
* Myra: You always feel like a failure. Never did well in school. Boys stayed away from you in droves. You have the feeling no one likes you very well. You thought

that becoming a Christian was the answer. But you've failed so many times to be a "good" Christian that you're close to despair.
* Jana: You never fail. You always got top grades. Popular. You graduated third in your law school class and are moving up in your firm. As a new Christian, you expect not to fail in your faith. After all, if you put out the necessary effort you can always make good. In fact, you won't even consider the possibility of failure in any effort.
* Sally: You're an average person. Win a few, lose a few. Of course, now you've got a really important goal: to live close to God. That's what's bothering you, in fact. You're so, well—average. How can you be special enough to get really close to Him?

Divide into teams based on the person each felt "most like." In teams, share why each of you chose this individual as someone you were like. Then explore: What does John 1:5–2:2 have to say to a person like me? What special needs does my type person have that this passage meets?

Affirmation: *Express love and concern*
In teams, thank anyone whose sharing or insights has helped you better understand yourself and this passage's meaning.

Adoration: *Worship and pray*
Together list the qualities of God emphasized in this passage. Then express thanks to God for who He is, by offering sentence prayers of praise.

WALK IN LOVE

Overview

When John called us to fellowship, he called us to "know" Jesus. Paul uttered the same call: "I want to know Christ and the power of His resurrection and the fellowship of sharing in His sufferings, becoming like Him in His death, and so, somehow, to attain to the resurrection from the dead" (Phil. 3:10). Knowing Jesus opens the door to a present experience of resurrection power.

But how can we tell if we "know" Him?

Part of our problem is that we can be confused by different meanings of the word "know." For instance:

- "I know *that*" means I have information.
- "I know all about bass" may be a claim that I can catch them.
- "I know Henry" may express friendship, acquaintance, or simply ability to identify a person in a crowd.
- "I know Plato" probably is a claim to understand his philosophy.
- "I know what you mean," can even be an expression of sympathy.

What then does it mean to "know" Jesus? *The Dictionary of New Testament Theology* (Zondervan) points out that the Greek word used here, *ginosko,* means basically "grasping the full reality and nature of an object under consideration. It is thus distinguished from mere opinion, which may grasp the object half-correctly, inadequately, or even falsely."

How important then, John's promise, 'We know that we . . . know Him" (1 John 2:3).

Commentary

Inner Evidence of Relationship: 1 John 2:3-17

John wrote to people who knew about Jesus, but who were not sure that they knew *Him.* We know about Jesus, but our grasp of truth may be incomplete, or we may have been misled by a false system of doctrine. How can we be sure that in spite of gaps in our understanding, we have a close personal relationship with the Lord?

John launched into an explanation of how we can be sure, not theoretically but experientially, that we know Jesus. He wants us to be free from nagging doubts and fears.

We respond to His commands (1 John 2:3-6). Jesus said, "My sheep listen to My voice; I know them, and they follow Me" (John 10:27). Those who belong to Jesus are responsive to His voice.

It's important not to misunderstand here. John does not suggest that relationship with God is *established* by obedience; rather, that relationship is *demonstrated* by obedience.

Sometimes people claim to know God but are unresponsive to His Word and His way of life. Such a person may possess accurate information about God and may be able to debate finer points of theology. Such a person may have memorized much of the Bible and regularly be in church. But unresponsiveness to God's voice shows the claim, "I know Him," to be false. Relationship is demonstrated by walking "as Jesus did" (1 John 2:6).

The central command (1 John 2:7-11). This idea of responsiveness can be distorted into a legalism in which the list of do's and don'ts grows longer. We try to measure our relationship with God as we do the temperature—by degrees.

To avoid this error, John quickly noted a central command from which all else flows. That command has been known and revealed through both the Testaments, but has been given fresh meaning in Jesus' coming. Jesus calls us to "love one another. As I have loved you, so you must love one another" (John 13:34). John said that the one who hates his brother cannot be walking in the light (1 John 2:11).

If you or I wonder if we're really responsive to Jesus' voice, we don't have to measure ourselves against a list of things we do or don't do to please Him. All we have to do is look within to see if we are reaching out, to care for our fellow Christians.

The listeners (1 John 2:12-14). John seemed to have more confidence in the people he wrote to than they did themselves. He didn't question their relationship with Jesus. He was sure that they did know Him and that they could live in fellowship with God.

John had reasons for his confidence:

● These little children had made an initial commitment to Jesus, and their sins had been forgiven.

● These fathers had lived in relationship with a God who had demonstrated Himself to be stable and trustworthy from the beginning of the universe.

● These young men had been challenged in their faith by the evil one, and God's strength and His Word in them had enabled them to overcome the threat.

These people could take the test John suggested. They could examine themselves and discover that they were responsive to Jesus' voice; they had begun to love. These inner drawings toward Jesus help us to be sure that we do know Him.

Divided hearts (1 John 2:15-17). John helps us look within to discover evidence of the reality of our relationship with Jesus. Now John warned that in order to love and respond to God, we must stop acting from the motives that reflect the world's value system.

Again John gave a common word a distinctive moral slant. *Kosmos* ("world") in Greek can mean the universe itself, the planet on which we live, or mankind. In a moral sense, however, "world" refers to the created universe and to mankind *as fallen*. This world, John says later (5:19) "is under the control of the evil one." The values and the attitudes that characterize the world— "cravings of sinful man, the lust of his eyes and the boasting of what he has" (2:16) do not come from God.

A Christian cannot live with a divided heart, responding one moment out of love for God and at the next turning to the world for pleasure. If we want to demonstrate (to ourselves, as well as to God) that we know Him, we need to make a clear-cut commitment to do the will of God rather than respond to the world's passions.

Warning Against Antichrist: 1 John 2:18-27

John helps us see inner, subjective evidence that we know Jesus. You and you alone know if you are responsive to God's voice. A new Christian might be responsive, but as yet show little change in lifestyle. And you and you alone know if you are beginning to love. If you find the stirrings of obedience and love within yourself, then you can have confidence that you know Jesus.

But what are the objective criteria? How about those who claim to be Christians, and even to be teachers, but who are instead antichrists? How can we recognize false teachers and false prophets?

John gave several principles to guide us. First, they "went out from us" (v. 19). The false teacher comes into a local fellowship, begins to teach his lies and, when he cannot influence the whole group to follow him, takes the little band he has deceived and starts his own sect or movement. Watch out for those who would divide and separate Christ's people. They go out because "they did not really belong to us" (v. 19).

Second, they deny Jesus is the Christ. Rejecting the Son, they reject the Father also. Jude and Peter as well have stressed that the false teacher sooner or later distorts the Bible's teaching on who Jesus is.

Finally, there is a subjective element in discerning false teachers. God the Holy Spirit has taken up residence in every true Christian. Our resident Teacher is a sound interpreter of the written Word and of the teachings of men. "You do not need anyone to teach you," John boldly declared (v. 27); the Holy Spirit will "guide you into all truth" (John 16:13).

This whole passage is a great corrective for our own day. Are we afraid to fellowship with those who have differences from us, yet are brothers and sisters in Christ? Are we worried when small groups of believers get together in homes to pray and study the Bible, afraid that they may go astray without the pastor there to answer every question and correct every misunderstanding? If so, we have fallen far short of a biblical confidence in the Holy Spirit's ability to teach and guard His own.

So, there *are* objective criteria by which to test relationships with Christ. There is also the prompting and loving guidance given by that Person who has taken up permanent residence in our lives.

The Sin Question: 1 John 2:28–3:10

The emphasis on looking within to find a subjective basis for confidence that we know Jesus does raise a serious question. Paul insisted that leaders be chosen whose lives demonstrated holiness. Jude identified false teachers by their actions. Why then did John seem to retreat from a clear-cut call for active holiness? Why did he first assure us of forgiveness when we fall, and then go on to reassure us that we can be sure we know Jesus by looking within to sense responsiveness and love? Doesn't what we *do* matter anymore?

John was writing to ordinary people like you and me who became Christians, looked forward to a new kind of life, then perhaps were crushed to discover that everything wasn't different after all. The promised freedom from old habits and sins didn't come.

Experiences like these are common, because the Christian life involves growth. We are born again into a new world through faith in Christ.

Yet the old *kosmos* that we knew so well has patterned our personalities. The gift of new life does *not* include spiritual amnesia, or wipe away old thought patterns, emotions, and responses. All these are still there; still deeply ingrained. The old *will be* replaced, but gradually—through growth and grace.

It is the "gradually" that so troubles us. We want to be rid of the old immediately. We want to be all new, *now*. When we stumble and fall and then fall again, it's only natural to wonder if we've made a mistake about our relationship with God. Perhaps we are *not* born again. Perhaps our failures and stumbling into sin indicate that we only *thought* we believed!

John wrote to release us from this torment. If you want to be sure you know Jesus, first look within. If you are responsive, even in a stumbling way—if you find love in your heart—you can be confident.

But what about our failures and sins?

"Dear children," John wrote, "*continue* in Him" (2:28).

How comforting! Take your place as a child. Don't expect to be mature yet. But do continue in Him. Do keep on growing. And as you mature, you *will* come to the place of victory over sins.

John said several important things about sin in this short passage:

- Through faith we are now God's children. When Jesus appears we will be completely like Him. As we keep His promise of transformation in view, and fix our desire on the goal of perfection, we will grow in purity here and now (3:1-3).
- There is no compromise with the sinfulness of sin. Violating God's standard of righteousness is sin. There is no sin in God. No one living in Him keeps on sinning (vv. 4-6).
- Objectively we can say that one whose life is committed to habitual sin is "of the devil" rather than of God. No one "born of God will continue in sin" (vv. 7-10).

Reading these verses we become aware that John was talking about the pattern of a person's life. He was not talking about isolated acts of sin, but about the direction of one's journey. The question is not, "Does he sin?" but, "Does he make sin a habit?" When God's life takes root in the human personality, that "seed remains in him" (v. 9), the life of God within struggles against sin, and the Spirit nudges us in a new direction.

So, over time, there *is* objective evidence of a righteous life to match the inner witness of love and responsiveness to God. Over time. Not necessarily immediately. But the objective evidence *will* come.

John promised, "No one who is born of God will continue to sin" (v. 9). It is not possible for sin to keep us in bondage, because the life of God within us will overcome the evil.

Love's Way: 1 John 3:11-24

From the beginning God's message to man has been "love one another" (v. 11). Yet somehow the attitude of Cain has intruded. The Old Testament commanded, You shall "love your neighbor as yourself" (Lev. 19:18). *The Dictionary of New Testament Theology*, (Zondervan) comments, "Love in this context means devotion toward one's neighbor for his sake, accepting him as a brother and letting him come into his own."

Yet among the passions that move us, a spontaneous love for others is missing. We can respond affectionately and even unselfishly to those with whom we have a special tie. But even family relationships may degenerate into the anger of Cain. Hurts, frustrations, real and imagined slights, all build up. The exploding divorce rate and the deep canyons of alienation that mar so many families today are vivid evidence that the way of Cain is still with us.

The contrast is especially glaring when we see how John used the word "love" (*agape*). Love is a central reality of God's nature. "God is love," John reminded us (1 John 4:8). God expresses love in the gift of Jesus; we receive that gift by a response of love. Knowing that we are loved and loving in return drives out the fear that destroys trust (v. 18). One who is God's and who walks in His light will necessarily live in love. Such love will not only change the character of an individual's relationship with God but also the nature of his relationship with other people. If we truly live in God, then we will live in love, for God is love.

God promises us who know Jesus that the reactions and responses of Cain will be replaced by the reactions and responses of Christ. John immediately confronts us with this contrast: "Do not be like Cain, who belonged to the evil one and and murdered his brother" (3:12). Did the murder drive Cain into Satan's hands? Not at all. In fact, the murder demonstrated how deep Cain already was in the evil one's grip.

Why did Cain murder Abel? Was it due to slights or parental unfairness? No, it was "because his own actions were evil and his brother's were righteous" (v. 12). Abel's good revealed Cain's sinfulness. Rather than acknowledging his sins, Cain tried to hide them from himself. He turned his shame into anger at Abel; antagonism welled up in his heart; he murdered in hatred. The entire process makes it plain that Cain did not know God.

And so we return to the theme of John's letter. How can we be confident that we know God? As we love our brothers, we can be reassured that we walk not in Cain's darkness but in Christ's light.

Contrast (1 John 3:11-15). John held up Cain and Christ for us to compare. Cain reacted with hatred to a brother who was good. Christ responds with love to sinners who reject God. Each expresses his feelings in action. Cain took another's life. Christ gave His own life for others. Cain's actions revealed him to be evil. Christ shows Himself to be good, a God of love.

Earlier John contrasted light and darkness to help us understand the Christian life. Now he contrasted love and hatred. No one who hates lives in God. But one who lives in God will love.

Love's expression (1 John 3:16-20). John is quick to note that love is not a feeling or an intention. Love is a choice that binds us to a distinctive course of action. "We ought to lay down our lives for our brothers," John said. "If anyone has material possessions and sees his brother in need but has no pity on him, how can the love of God be in him?" (vv. 16-17) Love is not a matter of words but of acts.

♥ *Group Activity: Support Group*
"Love" is communicated to different people in different ways. To some a hug says "I love you." To some it is help with the dishes. Take a few moments and jot down how you experience love, by completing 10 "Love is . . . " statements.

Read 1 John 3:11-18 together. Then sum up what this passage tells us about the nature of love.

Share your "love is" statements, and then tell how you have experienced love from the different members of your group.

Use the insights you gain from this way of looking at love expressed "with actions and in truth" to better show your affection and concern for one another in the future.

Then John added, "This then is how we know we belong to the truth, and how we set our hearts at rest in His presence whenever our hearts condemn us" (vv. 19-20). John noted earlier that we may become discouraged when we find ourselves slipping, unwillingly, into sins. He encouraged us to look within and see love awakening in our responsive hearts. When you and I sense responsiveness within, we can be sure we know Him.

Dealing with Uncertainty about Relationship with God

UNCERTAIN	CONFIDENT	UNCERTAIN
Because we see ourselves slip into acts of sin.	Because our hearts are responsive and we feel loving.	Because we feel ourselves drawn to sin and antagonistic to our brothers.
Then . . . examine heart, and sense the desire to be responsive.	*Then* . . . we choose to be obedient and practice love.	*Then* . . . examine actions and see obedience and love practiced.
This is evidence we know Him.	This is evidence we know Him.	This is evidence we know Him.

But *what if our hearts condemn us?* What if, looking within, we become aware of feelings of antagonism toward a brother? What if bitterness blocks us off from giving or receiving forgiveness? If our hearts condemn rather than justify us, then it would seem logical that we do *not* know Him.

All too often you and I are aware of failure within us that others may not see. Depression may come, and with depression everything looks black. We feel guilty and helpless. John, with his deep sensitivity to our human experience, understands and answers. When it is your heart that causes you uncertainty about your relationship with God, then look for another evidence of relationship. What evidence? Love. Not as a feeling or emotion, but love expressed "with actions and in truth" (v. 18). When we choose love's way in spite of our feelings, we have evidence that we know Him.

God's desire is for each of us to find rest. But if we find ourselves troubled by a nagging uncertainty because of either our actions or our hearts, God wants us to continue to trust. As we live in Him, His Spirit *will* purify and transform us.

✂ *Group Activity: Recovery Group*
Step 11 (improve relationship with God through prayer and meditation)
Which do you usually feel most like:
    * Uncertain, because you see yourself slip into acts of sin?
    * Uncertain, because you feel yourself drawn to sin and antagonistic to your brothers?
    * Confident, because you feel love for your fellow Christians and you consistently obey God?
    Join a team with others who feel as you do. Together, referring to the chart at the

top of this page, read through 1 John 2:3–4:21, and put a check mark beside each verse that seems to speak directly to you. Go back then and discuss each verse, finally choosing two or three that are most helpful to persons who feel as you do.

Come together again and share the verses you chose and the reasons.

Then choose one verse that you feel is especially directed to you personally. Meditate on it for three to five minutes. Then write a prayer that is a response to what God has said to you through "your" verse.

False Teachers: 1 John 4:1-6
John returned briefly to the theme of many late New Testament letters. How can we test for counterfeits and false prophets? First, doctrinally. Jesus, God's Son, has come in the flesh. This confession will never be made by false teachers. And second, by lifestyle. The world, with its "cravings of sinful man, the lust of his eyes and the boasting of what he has" (2:16), is put away by the mature believer. When a teacher speaks from the viewpoint of the world, we know he is not from God.

The true believer will also recognize John's writings as God's truth. The Holy Spirit will confirm it. When teaching is out of harmony with the written Word, the Spirit Himself will bring disquiet within the believer.

Dimensions of Love: 1 John 4:7-21
In these next verses John helps us see the way of love in the Christian community. He wanted us to experience close fellowship with Jesus and the Father, and live in intimate community with fellow-believers. John was not exhorting us to pump up the

emotion we call "love." He was explaining why love is valuable to the church, and how we can *choose* to live love.

In these verses there is no threat to make us feel guilty if we have fallen short of love. John did not lay a burden of obligation to make us struggle harder to do something we cannot do. Instead he simply pointed out that God is love, and to live in fellowship with Him is to live in love. If in our association with other Christians we fall into the world's way of antagonism and selfishness, then we are not experiencing God's presence.

These words of John bring hope. If we have failed to love, we acknowledge our sin to God and experience His forgiveness and cleansing. Only if we deny the importance of love in our relationships within the church, and let barriers arise between people have we lost our way. What do believers need to understand about love in order to experience fellowship with God? Let's trace the thought of the passage.

Love is central (1 John 4:7-8). Because God *is* love, the person who shares God's love *will* love. This is simply a fact; a reflection of the reality that where there is no will to love, God is absent.

Love initiates (1 John 4:9-12). John made abstract love personal when he explained that God loved us and "sent His Son as an atoning sacrifice for our sins" (v. 10). God's action is especially striking since *we did not love God* when He gave Himself. Loving meant initiating action without immediate return (and, in the case of many whom God loves, without *any* return). Here is a model for love in the Christian community. Since God loved us in this same way, we ought to love one another in the same manner.

Relationships in society are usually governed by reciprocity. I am nice to those who are nice to me. Jim invites me to lunch; I invite him in return. I borrow tools from Stan; he borrows tools from me. Even sinners, Jesus once commented, love those who love them (Matt. 5:46). But love in the Christian community is not to depend on repayment. We are to take the initiative in loving, even when the ones we reach out to do not respond.

At first this seems like a strange instruction. Won't such lovers be taken advantage of? Won't the unresponsive drain the people who do care? John's answer is twofold. First, the capacity to love in this way exists in every person who is born of God. Thus, it is not a few loving the rest, but *it is all of us loving one another*! Each of us has the opportunity to reach out and initiate actions that meet the deepest needs of our brothers and sisters.

Second, as we take up the joyful burden of loving others, God, who no one has seen, becomes strangely *visible* in the church. We see God Himself as He "lives in us and His love is made complete in us" (v. 12). As God becomes more real among us, even those who have not responded will be touched by His love.

God does live in us (1 John 4:13-16). Is such love possible? Of course! We don't rely on any capacity of our own to love our brothers. In the person of the Holy Spirit God lives in us and will love through us. We learn to share God's love for us.

Love frees us from fear (1 John 4:17-18). John has an exciting prospect for the fearful and doubting. As we see God's love taking visible shape in the community of faith, we become more confident and more like God. "In this world," John said of the believing community, "we are like Him" (v. 17). Love transforms us. We realize that God is not angry or eager to punish; love has driven out fear.

The way love drives out fear is beautiful. When Stan became a Christian, he was antagonistic, bitter, and quick to take offense at others whom he thought slighted him. Burdened by a poor self-image, Stan could not believe that God accepted him with all of his faults. Every time something went wrong, Stan was sure God was punishing him and he cringed. Even when everything seemed to go smoothly, there was always an aching fear that kept Stan from feeling peace or satisfaction.

Then Stan became a member of a truly loving church whose members accepted him as he was. They understood his behavior, overlooked his insults, and returned only love. They invited this unpleasant young man into their homes.

Gradually Stan began to realize that these people loved him in spite of himself. He could be real with them, and they still cared. For a time Stan became worse, testing their acceptance to see if it were real. Finally he was convinced. *He was loved!*

With this discovery came a great release. Through the love of his brothers and sisters in Christ, Stan experienced the reality of God's love. The message of Calvary he had accepted intellectually now released the knots of guilt and fear deep within. When Stan found a community of people who were like God in this world, he was freed to grow into a loving person himself.

Love is our proper response to God (1 John 4:19-21). Stan was freed to love only by being loved. John pointed out that it is the same with all of us. We did not love God; God loved us. God reached out first. But in being loved by God, we are freed to love in return. Then we can reach out to others.

Who do we love when God's love frees us? Yes, we do love God. But we also love our brothers. In fact, love of God and love of His family are so inseparably linked that John flatly stated, "If anyone says, 'I love God,' yet hates his brother, he is a liar" (v. 20). Love wears no blinders that cut off some while focusing on others. When love touches us, our whole personality is affected. We see God and sensing His love, are drawn to Him. We see people for the first time. We reach out to touch and to care. Love has transformed us.

In Christ, and in His community of faith, we *will* learn to walk in love.

GROUP RESOURCE GUIDE

Identification: *Share with others*
In a single sentence express what it means to you to "know" God.

Exploration: *Probe God's Word*
Check several dictionary definitions of "know" to get a sense of the broad meanings of this term. Then together read 1 John 2:3-17 and determine: What kind of "knowing" seems important to John? How can that kind of knowing be measured?

Then divide into teams, each of which is to explore one of the following passages to find answers to the question: How can I come to know God better? Refer to the commentary for help with any difficult passages or phrases.

* 1 John 2:15-29   * 1 John 4:1-21
* 1 John 3:1-24
After 20 minutes regather and share findings.

Reaction: *Respond together to the Word*
Write a brief paragraph stating what you intend to do as your personal response to the teaching of 1 John 2–4. Then read aloud what you have written.

Adoration: *Worship and Pray*
Read aloud what God chose to do to show His love for us, specifically 4:7-16. Thank God for what He has done, and commit yourself to love one another as He has loved you.

STUDY GUIDE 89
1 John 5; 2, 3 John

WALK BY FAITH

Overview

"Life" and "death" are key words in John's Gospel as well as in his epistles. They are not, however, just words about our future. They are terms describing the present experience of human beings.

A person who has a personal relationship with Jesus Christ has experienced a new birth, and *has* eternal life now. A person without that very personal relationship which is established by faith is spiritually and eternally dead, even while physical life persists.

In this last chapter of John's pastoral first letter, he wrote about life, eager that believers should *know* that they have life now.

The very brief letters of 2 and 3 John reflect themes seen in all John's writings. There are love, obedience, truth, warnings, and notes of joy.

How clearly the pastoral concerns of John shine through—giving you and me an example as we too share God's living Word.

■ First John 5 contains three passages over which theologians debate. This study guide discusses each, but you may wish to check further in a verse-by-verse commentary like the *Bible Knowledge Commentary,* pages 900-904. The three disputed passages are:
  - 1 John 5:6-7: Jesus came "by water and by blood."
  - 1 John 5:14: We are to pray and ask "according to His will."
  - 1 John 5:16-17: There is a sin that "leads to death."

Commentary

"I can hardly wait to die so I can live."

This rather strange statement actually reflects the attitude of some misinformed Christians, who suppose that eternal life is something we inherit only after death. Such

people, who look at their present lives with despair, and think that only eternity holds hope, need to hear John's concluding thoughts. "God *has given* us eternal life, and this life is in His Son. He who has the Son *has* life" (5:11-12, italics mine). Eternal life is ours, and we are to enjoy it *now*.

Faith: 1 John 5:1-12

The core meaning of "faith" (*pistis* in Greek) is a personal relationship established by trust and trustworthiness. For a Christian to say, "I believe in Jesus," is not so much a statement affirming certain beliefs *about* Jesus as it is an affirmation of trust. It is a confession that the Person, Jesus Christ, about whom I learn in the Bible, has become more than a historical figure to me. I have recognized Him as a real and living Person, and I have not drawn back in fear. Instead, I have confidently placed all I am and all I hope to be in His hands. Faith is abandoning ourselves and our efforts and resting in Jesus' promise of forgiveness and transformation.

John's special emphasis within this core of meaning is this: Jesus' claim to be true and trustworthy has been authenticated by God.

Only faith will receive the testimony about Jesus. John wants us to know that faith brings life. As we respond in faith to Jesus, we become one of a great company who *have* eternal life, now.

Faith's focus (1 John 5:1-5). John makes it clear that new birth, through which we receive life from God, comes through faith in Jesus Christ alone. This first verse says literally, "Everyone believing 'Jesus is the Christ' is born of God." John went on to point out that believing is a trust response and that there can be no relationship with God except through Jesus.

Faith's initial act of trust ushers us into a new world in which we love God and dem-

562

onstrate that love by obedience. The presence of eternal life now means that we will be able to overcome problems that trouble us. We will be strengthened by the eternal life that has taken root within our personalities. The things that are impossible for us today will become possible tomorrow.

Faith's testimony (1 John 5:6-12). The meaning of verse 6 is obscure, and is the subject of much debate. The verse identifies Jesus as "the One who came by water and blood" — not by water only. Did John mean "came into the world"? Or "came into our lives"? Or perhaps he simply meant "presented Himself to us." Does the water speak of the bag of waters in the mother, that breaks just before the child is born? If so, John referred here to the Incarnation, and affirmed the fact that Jesus, God's Son, entered the world as a Human Being to live in space and time and history. His presence was verified by men, and recorded for all generations to come.

Or does the water refer to Jesus' baptism by John in the Jordan River, the initiation of His public ministry?

Does the blood refer to the sacrificial death through which Jesus freed us? Certainly this is the central New Testament usage of the term.

Or did John use both terms in a very specific way, to echo what he wrote in his Gospel — that on Golgotha "one of the soldiers pierced Jesus' side with a spear, bringing a sudden flow of blood and water"? (John 19:34)

Whatever John may have in mind for the first two sources of testimony, he added a third that is very clear. God the Holy Spirit gives a testimony to each believer that is in harmony with the other two. History tells us of Jesus' birth as a Man. Scripture records His death and resurrection and explains the meaning of those events. As we hear the Gospel story, God's own Holy Spirit confirms its truth within us. These three witnesses provide a unified testimony to Jesus that we can accept, for God's testimony is sure. When we hear and believe, we *know*; God the Spirit confirms the truth within our hearts (1 John 5:10).

What of those who hear the Gospel promise of life and prefer to seek God in someone or something other than Jesus? John's answer was clear and unequivocal. Such a person has made God out "to be a liar, because he has not believed the testimony God has given about His Son" (v. 10). Since eternal life is only in the Son, "He who has the Son has life; he who does not have the Son of God does not have life" (v. 12).

The claim that Jesus is the only way to God angered the people of the first century. They wanted to search for God in their own ways. They wanted their philosophies, their gods and goddesses who embodied human passions and reflected the image of man. Today too people demand the right to do their own thing in morals and religion. They reject the idea of an absolute.

But John was not concerned with what people *want* to believe about God. John was concerned with *reality*. The fact is that God has spoken. *He* has said that only in Jesus can life be found. You or I may reject what He says, but our rejection will not change reality.

It's important for us to grasp the implications of the unchangeable nature of God's Word. Conferences and councils may meet and announce changes in doctrine and practice. Those who claim to represent the church may announce that homosexuality is now acceptable, but that will not change the fact that God condemns that lifestyle. Some who claim to represent the church can announce that as we evangelize, we must respect the good in other religions, and never suggest that their traditional faith might not lead to God. But God says that life can be found only in Jesus.

Today, as in John's day, we need to communicate to a hopeless world not the acceptable illusion people desire, but the reality they need. Jesus, God's Son, is the promise of victory — and the only way to God.

⊘ Group Activity:
Missions/Outreach Group
Focus on 1 John 5:12: "He who has the Son has life; he who does not have the Son of God does not have life." Together brainstorm at least 10 questions that this verse answers decisively.

In teams of three develop a creative greeting card by which you might communicate this truth to folks today.

Concluding Remarks: 1 John 5:13-21
John's concluding remarks summarize and

apply his teaching. John helps us to realize how great a gift we have received in Jesus, and in each other.

Prayer (1 John 5:13-15). Our whole attitude toward prayer is changed when we know we possess eternal life now. We are not probationers, waiting uncertainly just outside the door until death ushers into life. No, John wrote so that we who believe "may know that you have eternal life" (v. 13). How does such knowledge affect our prayers? John explained that it gives us "assurance . . . in approaching God" (v. 14).

Will God accept us? Have our failures made Him angry? Will God turn His back on us because of some inner attitudes that lurk, still unchanged, in our personalities? Or will He ignore us because of some habits we are not yet able to break? Such fears keep us from praying with confidence.

But John's letter has quieted these fears. There have been failures, but the blood of Christ cleanses. Sin, confessed, forgiven, and forgotten is no barrier to fellowship with God. Is an inner attitude still warped? Are aspects of my lifestyle still unchanged? John told us we *have* eternal life through faith in Jesus. We will see His life in us overcome our shortcomings.

With such concerns laid to rest, what should be our major prayer concern? Only that what we ask—what we desire—be what God wants too. Whatever we ask that fits His will, we can be sure we will *have*.

The word for God's will here is *thelema.* It does not usually refer to God's decree or unalterable plan, but what God desires to happen. We might say that praying in God's will means harmonizing our wishes and desires with God's.

How is such a harmony possible? First, God reveals His values, attitudes, plans, purposes, and intentions to us. We know, for instance, that the pride of possessions that motivates people of the world is rejected by God. He values persons, not things. It follows then that a request to God expressing a prideful desire for possessions is not according to His will. We can expect such a request to be refused. But we can expect a request that *is* in harmony with God's own deep concern for persons to be heard and granted. So understanding and adopting God's values helps us pray in His will.

It is also possible for us to pray according to God's will because the Holy Spirit lives within us. His voice is heard by believers. He can lead us to desire and pray for those things God wants for us.

It's important to realize that John is *not* stating a "condition" we must meet before we can expect God to answer prayer. Just the opposite! With our relationship to God established in Christ, we can approach God with confidence. As God the Spirit works within us, our prayers will more and more harmonize with God's will. We can look forward to answered prayer as a daily experience in our Christian lives.

Sin in the fellowship (1 John 5:16-17). When we acknowledge our sins to God, He forgives and cleanses us. But what if we see a fellow Christian slip? John encouraged us to pray for the brother or sister. God will answer our prayers, and bring our brother back.

John does note, however, that there "is a sin that leads to death" (v. 16). Was John teaching that those who have eternal life can lose it?

In the Bible, "death" has several meanings. Biological death comes to all the living. Spiritual death, the legacy of sin, grips each of us until its hold is broken by Christ. And there is the realm of death, which is that experience of alienation from God, of captivity to the world's ways, from which the believer is rescued.

John tended to overlook biological death. To him, the glorious present possession of eternal life was so vital and real that the moment of transfer from this world to the world beyond was hardly of concern.

Yet even for the believer, sin can lead us back to experience death. What sin? Sin denied or unconfessed. Sin justified by excuse and argument. Sin not brought under the covering of Jesus' blood because we choose to turn from the light to wander in darkness. What John seemed to be saying here is that there is sin that opens directly into this realm of death. Not every sin catapults us into the world of illusion from which we have been delivered, but some do.

If we see a brother or sister whose angry spirit leads him to strike out at others, or whose desires are still captivated at times by greed, we are to pray for him. Such wrongdoing is sin, but it does not necessarily blind our brother to the light.

But some sins are so dark that choosing them returns a person to the deepest darkness of this world. What are these sins? John didn't say.

What he did say is that the one born of God *will not continue to sin.* The life of God within will struggle against sin and bring the believer again to the light. The whole world may be under the control of the evil one, but the one who has new life from God is kept safe: "the evil one does not touch him" (v. 18).

While John did not define the sin that leads directly to the realms of death, it is possible to speculate. All the later New Testament letters are concerned with heresy, with false teaching about doctrine, and lifestyle. John himself said that false teachers wormed their way into the fellowship of the church, but later "went out from us, but they did not really belong to us" (2:19). It seems likely that the sin of which John was speaking is that of apostasy: of turning away from both Christian truth and Christian lifestyle.

Wait, John was saying. If you see a brother turn away from Christ, pray. And if the person has been born of God, he will not continue in his sin. God will protect him from Satan's grasp, and bring him back. But if he continues, departure indicates he is a false brother, cease your prayers. Let him settle down in the world of death and darkness, which is his home and his destiny.

How delicately John put it all. For you and me, there is no question about our personal relationship with Christ. We each know our own hearts; we receive God's testimony and his assurance of eternal life. But we do not judge another who claims to be a brother. We pray when we see one brother troubled by sin's remaining taint. And, if another turns dramatically away from Christ, we wait. If he is one of God's own, he will be kept safe, and will return.

About others—we withhold judgment.

About ourselves—ah, about ourselves we can be sure!

2, 3 John

These two brief letters to individuals show how completely the themes seen in John's first letter dominate his later thinking. Joy is found by walking in the truth. We are called and commanded to "walk in love" (2 John 6). As we continue in the teaching of Christ, we are protected from deceivers, who snap and tear at Christ's body on earth.

While each of the letters might be studied in its own right, the letters can also be looked at as a summation of John's thoughts. It is this way that you can best use these two pastoral notes to sum up the major teachings of the apostle of love.

GROUP RESOURCE GUIDE

Identification: *Share with others*
Mention one "condition" you have been told you must meet before God will answer your prayer.

List all the "conditions" suggested by the group on a chalkboard or sheet of newsprint. Discuss: How do you feel about praying when you remember one or more of these conditions?

Exploration: *Probe God's Word*
Read 1 John 5:13-15 and discuss. Is John trying to create assurance and confidence in prayer, or doubt about it? Is the "if we ask according to His will" a "condition," or something else? If this is a condition, how could we possibly meet it?

Then discuss the author's explanation in the commentary (p. 564, Prayer). In teams read either 2 John or 3 John. What key words describe the kind of relationship in which confidence in knowing God and His will takes place? Remember that the key to our prayer life is fellowship with God; that comfortable assurance that we love Him and are living as He wants us to live.

Reaction: *Respond together to the Word*
Look back at the earlier "conditions" you listed. How can each be explained as something other than a condition? What might God be saying to us in Bible verses that suggest each?

Then have fun brainstorming "prayer

isn't" statements. For instance, "Prayer isn't jumping over hurdles," "Prayer isn't walking a sidewalk without stepping on any cracks," etc.

Adoration: *Worship and pray*
Meditate for a time on the fact that God is your loving Father. Visualize yourself as a little child, running to Him with arms outstretched. See Him stoop down to pick you up in strong arms, bending near to listen to everything you have to say.

Then praise Him aloud for the beauty and simplicity of prayer, which grows out of our personal relationship with the Lord, and expresses the confidence we have in His Father love.

REVELATION

Overview

The Book of Revelation was written by John the apostle, apparently in exile on the Isle of Patmos. Even though it is an unveiling, or "revelation," it is without doubt the most difficult book to understand. At the same time, its basic outline is clear.

Outline

While we can outline the content of this great book, saying just what each event portrayed means is something else again. And yet study of this book contains a unique promise of divine blessing: "Blessed is the one who reads the words of this prophecy, and blessed are those who hear it and take to heart what is written in it, because the time is near" (Rev. 1:3).

Commentary

There are a number of reasons why it's so hard to be "sure" about our interpretation of Revelation. We can illustrate two of the most significant.

Symbolic words. Look at this paragraph from Revelation 1, in which John describes Jesus as He appeared in John's vision:

> Among the lampstands was Someone "like a Son of man," dressed in a robe reaching down to His feet and with a golden sash around His chest. His head and hair were white like wool, as white as snow, and His eyes were like blazing fire. His feet were like bronze glowing in a furnace, and His voice was like the sound of rushing waters. In His right hand He held seven stars, and out of His mouth came a sharp double-edged sword. His face was like the sun shining in all its brilliance.
>
> Revelation 1:13-16

It is clear from the repetition of "like" that this vision of Jesus has special significance. Each element has some meaning beyond its mere appearance. Each has *symbolic* meaning, affirming a reality beyond itself.

If we look through the rest of Scripture we gain impressions of what various elements suggest. John Walvoord, writing in the Victor *Bible Knowledge Commentary,* suggests several possible references:

● *White hair*	Purity and eternity of Jesus as God (cf. Dan. 7:13).
● *Fiery eyes*	Judgment of sin (cf. Rev. 2:18).
● *Bronze feet*	Material of altar of Old Testament sacrifice, suggests judgment (see also v. 18).
● *Seven stars*	Held in right hand,

• *Sword*   A type of sword *(rhom-phaia)* used to kill, refers also to judgment.

they symbolize Jesus' sovereign power of the churches.

Note that several kinds of clues are used in an attempt to understand the symbolism. First, there is a search of other biblical material to find similar references (as the white hair), or specific use of the material (as the bronze). There is also a search of context (the seven stars) and a general reference to culture (the significance of holding them in the right hand, and the particular use put to the type of sword mentioned in the text).

But we also need to note that several of the elements of this vision simply cannot be explained by looking to any of these sources. And we must also remember that there is no guarantee that our explanations are correct.

Strikingly, Scripture often does explain the significance of symbols and acts. For instance, the New Testament explains the veil that hung in the Old Testament temple between the holy of holies and the outer room as signifying that the way to God was not yet open. When Jesus died, that veil was miraculously torn from top to bottom (see Matt. 27:51; Heb. 9:8).

Likewise, the miracles God did in bringing Israel out of Egypt were explained. They were performed as a judgment on the gods of Egypt, and to let both Israel and the Egyptians know that the Lord truly is God.

So we have a long biblical tradition of explanation of symbols, as well as the appearance of some symbols which are not explained. When the text of Scripture does not itself explain symbols, it is not wise to be dogmatic about their meaning.

This is one thing which makes the Book of Revelation hard for us to understand. It often uses symbolic language which is not explained in the text. For this reason, there are some things reported about which we must remain unsure.

Apocalyptic vision. There is another thing that makes it unwise for us to be too dogmatic about Revelation. John described what he saw in his vision of the end times. In giving us this description, he *was limited to the language and images of his own time.*

For instance, imagine that one of our great great grandfathers, who lived 150 years ago, was suddenly transported to our time. He witnesses a traffic jam, sees a TV football game (replete with replays), is taken in a 747, and goes to an air-conditioned movie. Then he is returned to his own age, and given the task of explaining it all to his contemporaries.

He lacks all the terms and images we use to describe what are to us commonplace events. He has experienced something that no one else in his day can even imagine. How terribly difficult it must be for him to struggle for words to communicate what he has seen.

Well, this was exactly John's situation. What he saw are real events. And John reported what he witnessed. But he had to struggle with an inadequate vocabulary, and use imagery that may communicate something of his vision to the people of his day—even though his imagery did not exactly describe what he saw.

Look, for instance, at this passage. What, really, was John describing? The events are real, surely. And they will happen. But just *what* is he talking about?

The first angel sounded his trumpet, and there came hail and fire mixed with blood, and it was hurled down upon the earth. A third of the earth was burned up, a third of the trees were burned up, and all the green grass was burned up.

The second angel sounded his trumpet, and something like a huge mountain, all ablaze, was thrown into the sea. A third of the sea turned into blood. A third of the living creatures in the sea died, and a third of the ships were destroyed.

The third angel sounded his trumpet, and a great star, blazing like a torch, fell from the sky on a third of the rivers and on the springs of water—the name of the star is Wormwood. A third of the waters turned bitter, and many people died from the waters that had become bitter.

Revelation 8:7-11

It is clear from this description that John described terrible cataclysms that will strike our earth. Some imagine that what he saw and tried to describe was a terrible atomic war, or perhaps a space war. But the fact is, we can't *tell* just what it was John saw.

We know that it was terrible, and associated with worldwide divine judgment. We can also be sure that when it does happen, we'll recognize the events. But till then there is much uncertainty.

These are two of the reasons why it is not easy to understand the prophetic visions relayed to us in the Book of Revelation. We sense the power and terror of the last days that John described. But we dare not be dogmatic in our interpretation of them.

The History of Interpretation

Across the centuries of church history there have been various interpretations of Revelation and of prophecy in general.

My *Word Bible Handbook* (Word) sums up the history succinctly:

> *The Early Church.* The *Didache* was probably written about A.D. 100. It gives this picture of the future as understood in the post-apostolic church: "Watch for your life's sake. Let not your lamps be quenched, nor your loins unloosed; but be ye ready, for ye know not the hour in which our Lord cometh. When lawlessness increaseth, they shall hate and betray and persecute one another, and then shall appear the 'world-deceiver' as Son of God, and shall do signs and wonders, and the earth will be delivered into his hands, and he shall do iniquitous things which have never yet come to pass since the beginning. Then shall the creation of men come into the fire of trial, and many shall be made to stumble and shall perish, but they that endure in their faith shall be saved from under the curse itself. And then shall appear the sign of an opening in heaven, the outspreading of the heaven; (b) then the sign of the sound of the trumpet; and the (c) third, the resurrection of the dead, yet not of all, but as it is said: The Lord shall come and all His saints with Him. Then shall the world see the Lord coming upon the clouds of heaven" (Ante-Nicene Fathers, Vol. VII, 382).
>
> In A.D. 140–160 Justin Martyr wrote, "I, and as many as are orthodox Chris-

tians, do acknowledge that there shall be a resurrection of the body, and a residence of a thousand years in Jerusalem, adorned and enlarged, as the Prophets Ezekiel, Isaiah, and others do unanimously attest" (Fathers, Vol. 1:239).

Irenaeus, a great missionary and church father, who died in A.D. 202, summed up the picture of the future taught in his day. "When the Antichrist shall have devastated all things in this world, he will reign for three years and six months, and sit in the temple at Jerusalem; and then shall the Lord come from heaven in clouds, in the glory of the Father, sending this man, and those who follow him, into the lake of fire; but bringing for the righteous the times of the kingdom, that is, the rest, the hallowed seventh day; and restoring to Abraham the promised inheritance, in which the kingdom of the Lord declared that 'many coming from the east and from the west should sit down with Abraham, and Isaac, and Jacob' " (Fathers, Vol. 1:560).

It is clear from these early fathers, as well as from the writings of Tertullian, Cyprian, Lactantius and others, that for some 300 years the church did integrate Old Testament and New Testament prophetic pictures and took them in their literal sense. They expected Christ's return to precede a time of blessing, promised in the Old Testament, before the world would end.

To the Reformation. A review of commentaries on the Book of Revelation shows a shift in understanding prophecy occurred after the early centuries. A leader of the African church, Tyconius, wrote a commentary around A.D. 390 in which the events Revelation describes were spiritualized. His allegorical approach was adopted, and later used to justify the development of the papacy as a political power. The allegorical method of interpreting Revelation was followed by Pirimasius (ca. A.D. 550), Alcuin (A.D. 735–804), Maurus (A.D. 775–836), and Strabo (A.D. 807–859).

Joachim of Fiore (ca. A.D. 1130-1202) challenged the dominant allegorical interpretation by introducing a chronological division. He divided all of history into three ages: the Age of the

Father (Creation to Christ), the Age of the Son (Christ to his own day), and the Age of the Spirit (his time, until final judgment). When the Reformation came, this chronological approach was fastened on by Luther, Calvin, and others. The Antichrist-beast of Revelation 13 and the harlot of Revelation 17–18 were interpreted as the papacy, and as Rome. Events in the history of western Europe were linked to the various seals and trumpets of the book.

The Catholics responded with a commentary on Revelation in which Francisco Ribera (A.D. 1537–1591) argued that the Antichrist was an individual who would come in some future time, not the pope. Other Catholic writers argued that Revelation applied only to events before the fall of Rome, in A.D. 476.

The medieval scholars, the Reformers, or the later Catholic theologians attempted to relate Revelation to the prophetic picture found in the Old Testament and build a unified picture of the future.

In modern times three different views of the future have been expressed in prophetic systems. Each system tends to take a different view of Revelation.

Premillennialism is the view of the early church, revived in the nineteenth century by the Plymouth Brethren.

The premillennialist believes that there is a literal Antichrist who will appear. He will bond Europe into a single power, make a treaty with Israel as foretold by Daniel, and then break that treaty and try to set himself up as god. The Old Testament prophecies of invasion of the Holy Land and destruction of a Northern (Russian) army by God will then be fulfilled. After seven years of intense Tribulation, Jesus will return and crush the Antichrist's forces, and chain Satan. He will establish a redeemed Israel as this world's premier nation, and rule from Jerusalem for a thousand years. Afterward Satan will be released and lead a final rebellion. This universe will then be destroyed, final judgment be pronounced, and God will create a new heaven and earth.

This vision of history ahead, all agree, is one that fits the *literal sense* of the words of both Old and New Testament prophecy.

But not all agree that the literal sense is the intended sense in prophecy.

Postmillennial. This view, which had gained in popularity before the First World War, sees a gradual conversion of humanity through the spread of the Gospel. When the world has been converted, an era of peace will be known, and society purified by the Christian majority. This era of peace is what is foretold in the Old Testament

Modern Prophetic Systems

Interpretations of Revelation

Chapter	Futurist	Modern historist
4	Suggests the Rapture of the church.	Suggests awe-filled worship by church of all ages.
5	Relates scroll to Daniel 7:13-14 as deed to the Old Testament's promised Davidic Kingdom.	Scroll speaks of redemption and believer's rule in Christ today.
6	Initiates events that Jesus described in Matthew 24:5-8, leading into the Great Tribulation.	Shows impact of the Gospel on the earth, as Christ conquers through the message of His cross.
7	Sees the 144,000 as Jewish missionaries active in Tribulation.	Sees 144,000 as symbolic "perfect number" of the saved.
8	Initial judgments of Tribulation.	Natural disasters are a warning to the unsaved.
9	Demonic enemies are released to torment man.	An invasion of anti-Christian forces operating in the spiritual realm.
10	An interlude.	A message that God will not abandon believers.
11	The two witnesses are Moses and Elijah (Matt. 17:10-11), who preach for 3½ years in Jerusalem and are killed near end of first half of the Tribulation.	The period of 3½ years is symbolic. Witnesses are the true church speaking against false faith.
12	The Jewish people are preserved by God from Satan during Antichrist's rule.	War in heaven is a picture of Jesus' victory on Calvary preserving the church from persecution.
13	The Antichrist and false prophet appear and form European state.	Symbolic expression of Satan's attack on church by anti-Christian governments and false religion.
14	An overview of the final judgment of God on human society, represented by "Babylon."	An image of final judgment.
15–16	Literal descriptions of events on earth at the end of the Tribulation.	Symbolic descriptions of final judgment.
17	"Mystery Babylon" represents false religion of Antichrist.	The woman is pseudo-religious influences in the world today.
18	Civil, secular, and military power of the Antichrist.	Represents all past, present, and future materialistic centers.
19	Jesus returns as foretold by Old Testament prophets to battle enemies.	Symbolizes the complete victory of Jesus over all enemies.
20	Jesus sets up 1,000-year kingdom, then destroys Satan in last great battle.	Satan was "bound" at birth of Jesus. 1,000 years is symbolic of believer's present exaltation of Christ.
21	The vision is of eternity.	The vision is of the triumphant church, not of a literal city or new earth.
22	Jesus is coming again, soon!	

and suggested in the image of the thousand years ("the Millennium"). Some post-millennials do expect an outburst of evil before Jesus returns.

Amillennial. This group rejects the idea of a time of blessing on this earth. The Old Testament prophecies like the images of Revelation are thought to be symbolic, and to symbolize the spiritual blessings Christians experience through relationship with God. Thus this school does not believe prophecy should be taken in its literal sense.

Within these traditions there are currently two major approaches to the interpretation of Revelation. The *futurist* has a premillennial orientation, and tries to understand the events John describes by reference to Old Testament and New Testament prophecy. The modern *historist* sees Revelation as a panorama of history itself, but does not try to link it to specific events in the history of Rome or of western Europe. The modern historist generally believes that the seven major visions of Revelation simply look from different perspectives, at all of history between First and Second Comings.

The chart sums up the interpretations of these two schools of Revelation's major segments.

Summary

The Book of Revelation will continue to cause debate. However, whatever our approach to interpretation we cannot help but be stunned as we read John's sweeping descriptions of judgment. God *is* in control. Judgment day *will* come. And nothing human beings can do can thwart or change the sure purposes of our God.

Revelation 1–3

LETTERS TO SEVEN CHURCHES

Overview

Many believe that Revelation 1:19 is the key to understanding the book. That verse records words spoken by Jesus to John telling him to write "what you have seen, what is now and what will take place later."

According to this division the vision of Jesus recorded in Revelation 1 is "what you have seen."

"What is now" is reflected in the message to seven existing churches found in Revelation 2–3.

"What will take place later" is in the bulk of the book, chapters 4–21.

In this study we look at both "what you have seen," John's vision of Jesus, and at "what is now," his letters to seven churches.

Many commentators see these churches as representative of churches in every age. Their strengths and weaknesses are typical, and we are to gain insight into our own congregations by studying them. Others see the churches as representative of the ages of church history, with the first, Ephesus, representing the apostolic church and the last, Laodicea, representing the church of our own day. Whatever one's view, there are many insights we can gain as we learn how Jesus Himself evaluates His people — and there are many warnings we can heed.

What a privilege for you and me to lead others in a study of this book which uniquely unveils Jesus, not in His humanity, but in the glory we shall see when He returns.

Commentary

There's no more puzzling book in the Bible. The vivid images and the sketches of terror on earth and cataclysmic disaster in the universe beyond are hard to grasp. And even harder to interpret.

Are these outlines of future history . . . of events that will actually happen in space and time? Are they pictures of past history, using vivid imagery to describe persecutions under pagan emperors? Or are these symbolic presentations of experiences believers may undergo now and that will finally be seen to be elements in God's final judgment?

It is easy to become involved in debate about interpretation as we explore this final book of the New Testament. It is easy to become caught up in constructing systems, debating how a detail fits into our prophetic program, or arguing against another person's system. The problem is that we can develop a prophetic system with some confidence, and still miss the point of this great book! For this final, culminating book of the Bible begins with a statement and a promise to which we need to pay the closest attention. The statement is:

> The revelation of Jesus Christ, which God gave Him to show His servants what must soon take place.
> Revelation 1:1

And the promise is:

> Blessed is the one who reads the words of this prophecy, and blessed are those who hear it and take to heart what is written in it, because the time is near.
> Revelation 1:3

Concerning the statement, Dr. John Walvoord says, "It is a revelation of truth *and* Christ Himself, a disclosure of future events, that is, His second coming when Christ will be revealed" (in *The Revelation of Jesus Christ,* Moody). Walvoord's point is simple. *The central focus of this book is Jesus!* Everything we read must be interpreted and understood in relation to what the events disclose about Him.

For instance, Revelation 6 describes four horsemen who bring war, anarchy, famine, plague, and death to earth. If we focus on a prophetic system we will ask, "Is this a literal event to come? Does it describe the first or second part of the Tribulation? What are corollaries with Old Testament prophecy? How can we fit this in the time sequence of past, or future history?

Yet if we focus on such questions and debate these issues, we miss the dominant and jolting impact of John's picture. It is the Lamb of God (v. 1) — the gentle Jesus who allowed Himself to be led away and crucified — who has opened the seals in order to loose these awesome judgments on the earth! God's love has been firmly established; now we see a new quality expressed. The judgment so long and patiently withheld begins, and we are introduced to the wrath of the Lamb.

The "things that must soon take place" are related to this new and final unveiling of God. As we read Revelation we will gain a new awareness of who God is and how His character as righteous Judge will find expression at history's end.

And the promise? "Blessed is the one who reads . . . and takes to heart what is written." As we experience this book, we want to catch a clearer vision of Jesus — and take what we discover of Him to heart and into our lives.

Revelation: Revelation 1

The word "revelation" comes from the Greek *apokolupsis*. It means to reveal, bring to light, or disclose. It is often used of God's communication to us of supernatural secrets — of information we could never discover if God did not tell us. The secrets are about His plans, intentions, motives, or interpretations of events, and we could only guess about these without a divine word.

But "revelation" is also God's *self-disclosure*. He wants us to know *Him,* and as He presents information, God also communicates Himself.

To John this revelation of the person of God is always a central concern. In his Gospel, John showed that Jesus came in the flesh to show us the Father (John 14:9-11). The Incarnation, through which God entered history to share our humanity, was an unveiling that is recognized by faith. Now, in the Bible's last book, John describes another coming — one still future — in which Jesus' unveiling of God will be recognized by all humanity. Then "every eye will see Him" (Rev. 1:7). All those who have rejected Jesus as the One "who loves us and has freed us from our sins by His blood" (v. 5) will see His glory, and "all the peoples of the earth will mourn because of Him" (v. 7).

Comparisons (Rev. 1:4-11). We can see a number of comparisons between the way John unveiled God's person in his Gospel and what he revealed of God in the Book of Revelation. This is summed up in the chart. As we look at it, we begin to realize that in this New Testament book we will meet our Lord not in His role as Servant, but as the One who is high and lifted up, the Sovereign God.

To know Jesus now as "Him who loves

The Revelation of Jesus

Features	John's Gospel	Revelation
Who is unveiled	Jesus	Jesus
What is unveiled	Life, Light Grace, Truth	Wrath of the Lamb (Rev. 6:16)
For whom is the unveiling	Those who believe believe (John 20:21)	Every eye will see Him (Rev. 1:7)
Quality of God emphasized	Love (John 3:16)	Holiness (Rev. 4:8)
Expression of that quality	Washed us from our sins in His blood (John 3:16; Rev. 1:5)	Wrath (Rev. 6:16-17)
Man's response	Believe in Him (John 6:69; 10:41) Praise (Rev. 1:6)	Fear, anger (Rev. 9:20-21)

us and has freed us from our sins by His blood, and has made us to be a kingdom and priests to serve His God and Father" (vv. 5-6) brings believers joy and leads to praise. To be confronted by the Jesus we meet in Revelation will bring terror to unbelievers and stimulate them to intensified rebellion (9:20-21).

Yet God wants *us* to see Jesus as the wrathful Lamb as well. You and I are to look at history's end and through John's vision realize more fully who He is who loves us. We need to see the ultimate impact He will have on the created universe and on all the world's people.

As we see the Lamb finally releasing His wrath, you and I will be better equipped to make daily choices and evaluate our present view of eternity. And we will gain a far greater sense of what it means to live with a Jesus who is the *holy* God.

✍ Group Activity: Bible Study Group

Jot down two words that convey your dominant impression of Jesus. Then list words of all group members on a chalkboard or newsprint.

Read aloud Revelation 1:9-20. Look at the symbolism in the description of Jesus (commentary p. 574, First glimpse). Brainstorm words that express the impression of Jesus conveyed in John's vision. Then compare the two lists. How do they differ? Why do they differ? What do they suggest about the Jesus we are to meet in the Book of Revelation? What do they suggest about the completeness of our own understanding of who Jesus is?

First glimpse (Rev. 1:12-20). Now John plunges us into his own unsettling experience.

John the apostle was now a very old man, in his eighties or nineties. The year was A.D. 95 or 96, over 60 years after the death and resurrection of Jesus. Under a wave of persecution stimulated by the Emperor Domitian, John had been exiled to the little island of Patmos, a forbidding and craggy spot in the Aegean Sea. While he was cut off from fellowship with the church he loved, and deeply concerned about the persecutions his "little children" were undergoing, John was given a great vision. He was taught that Jesus is the center of history to come, and a mighty voice commanded him to "write what you see." And so the Book of Revelation is, in essence, a report by an eyewitness.

The first sight John saw was Jesus Himself, in a startling and unexpected form:

> Someone "like a Son of man," dressed in a robe reaching down to His feet and with a golden sash around His chest. His head and hair were white like wool, as white as snow, and His eyes were like blazing fire. His feet were like bronze glowing in a furnace, and His voice was like the sound of rushing waters. In His right hand He held seven stars, and out of His mouth came a sharp double-edged sword. His face was like the sun shining in all its brilliance.
>
> Revelation 1:13-16

John's reaction to this vision was to fall in terror at the figure's feet. But then the man reached out a hand and touched John, saying, "Do not be afraid."

What is most striking about this brief vignette is that it is *John* who falls stunned and terrified before Jesus! Remember, John is the "disciple whom Jesus loved." John is the one who was always closest to Jesus, reaching out to touch Him, straining to hear every word, catching and focusing for all of us the glorious love of God communicated in the Son. John, the apostle of love these 60 years, meets again the object of his love . . . and his first reaction is fear!

We, like John, will meet in the Book of Revelation an aspect of God's character that, while we have always known it is there, might not seem to fit the personality of the One we've come to love. But Jesus' words calm us as they did John. Whatever terrible visions may unfold in this revelation of Jesus, we will not fear. Jesus places His hand on us, and says, "Do not be afraid." Then we remember that we are His.

But what about this strange description of Jesus? What is the significance of the white hair and feet like molten bronze? And why seven stars?

Symbolism. The Book of Revelation is filled with symbols and symbolism. There has been much debate about the reason for, as well as the meaning of, particular symbols. Yet throughout Scripture, and especially in prophetic literature, similar imagery can be found. It is particularly helpful in trying to understand Revelation to look in the book itself for an explanation, or to look for Old Testament corollaries.

For instance, the "seven golden lampstands" (v. 12) are identified almost immediately (in v. 20) as representing seven churches to whom John is told to write. Because when the number seven is used in the Bible it often suggests wholeness or completion, many conclude that the seven churches represent all churches. Our own congregation may well be reflected in one of these pictures.

The white hair and brazen feet are not explained in the text. But the hair reminds us of Daniel 7:9, where God is described as "the Ancient of Days. . . . His clothing was as white as snow; the hair of His head was white like wool."

The feet of burning brass might suggest the altar of sacrifice and the life that had to be offered for sin (see Ex. 38:2). The altar and the other articles used in the sacrifice were always of bronze.

But, however we understand the elements of this description, the overall impact of this revelation of Jesus is clear. There is glory. There is holiness. There is awesome majesty. And there is terror.

John even felt terror at the vision, until Jesus' touch removed fear. That touch reminds us that the overpowering Person we are about to see in action is also the God we love—and who loves us.

Letters to the Churches: Revelation 2–3

The majestic figure now instructed John to write what he had seen, and then dictated to John letters to seven churches.

These are historic churches that existed in John's day., Each was marked by the characteristics the letter describes. Yet in these churches we see pictures of our congregations of today. Some commentators have also felt they found a portrait of church history—with each of the seven churches representing a different development in the Christian era, from New Testament times to the present.

What is more important for our understanding of these two chapters is to keep in mind again that the Book of Revelation *is primarily a revelation of Jesus Christ*. The most important question we can ask is, "What does this passage tell of Him and

my relationship with Him?"

If we ask this question we're struck by the fact that John's vision of Christ as Judge places Him among the lampstands, and the lampstands are the seven churches. Jesus may not be *visible* in our congregations in all His glory. But *He is among us!* We sense Jesus' presence in these letters, and we also see something of the way we are to respond in view of His presence. If we can catch a glimpse of Jesus *among us* in all His glory, we will respond to the pressures of wealth, poverty, or persecution in the way these early churches were exhorted to respond.

As we see through faith what John saw, our confidence in the power of God and our freedom to live committed lives will grow.

The church in Smyrna. Let's look at one of the seven churches in more detail and see how we can receive help or guidance from these letters.

The city of Smyrna lies about 35 miles north of Ephesus. In New Testament times it was a port city, and very wealthy, one of the finest in Asia. Under the Emperor Diocletian pagan and Jew alike focused intense persecution on the believers in Smyrna. This oppression led to extreme poverty among the Christians—not simply "being poor" but being destitute, possibly because they had been robbed of all their goods by their persecutors.

Tragically, the persecution Jesus speaks of was to increase. Yet Christ said that as the intensity of persecution grew, the Smyrnan believers were to "not be afraid of what you are about to suffer" (2:10). They were to remain faithful, even though faithfulness might bring them death.

It would be easy to be overwhelmed by such a message. We are to remember that Jesus, in all His power and glory, is *among us*. And we are to remember Him as "the First and the Last, who died and came to life again" (v. 8). Jesus too has undergone suffering and death . . . and Jesus has been raised to new life. He understands, for He has experienced what they are experiencing. He is fully aware of their afflictions and poverty (v. 9).

How then was the church in Smyrna guided by this letter, and what can we learn about our own experiences of suffering?

First, Jesus *is* there, aware of His people's

Church	Characteristic	Description of Jesus	Desired Response
Ephesus, the steadfast church (2:1-7)			
Smyrna, the persecuted church (2:8-11)	undergoing suffering, poverty, persecution	the One who died but is alive again	remain faithful
Pergamum, the morally compromising church (2:12-17)			
Thyatira, the doctrinally compromising church (2:18-29)			
Sardis, the counterfeit church (3:1-6)			
Philadelphia, the obedient church (3:7-13)			
Laodicea the materialistic church (3:14-22)			

The Seven Churches

needs. He Himself has experienced suffering like theirs. Yet now He is alive; the end of His suffering came, and glory followed.

Second, aware of His glorious power, the believers are to fear none of the things they will suffer. There will be persecution. Some will even die. Yet the persecution will result in Jesus' gift to them of a crown of life. They will have eternal life, and will be untouched by the *second death* . . . the ultimate judgment of God on those who do not know Jesus, or respond to Him.

Jesus understands our suffering because of what He has suffered. Knowing we will share in His ultimate victory over sin and death gives us courage to live fearlessly in times of pressure.

You and I and our congregation may not be a Smyrna church just now. But we do experience our own pressures, suffering, and afflictions. And whenever we do, the vision of Jesus standing among us in all His glory, and the words of promise He speaks, will sustain and guide us.

GROUP RESOURCE GUIDE

Identification: *Share with others*
Imagine Jesus were to send a personal message to the churches in your town today. Tell one thing you think He might probably say to you.

Exploration: *Probe God's Word*
Jesus did send a personal message to seven churches of John's day, found in Revelation 2–3. On an enlarged copy of the chart on this page, work with three others to list

the characteristics of the church, the description of Jesus, and the desired response in the message to each of the seven. If you wish, each team of four can work on one or two churches, and then report findings so each person can fill in his or her chart.

Reaction: *Respond together to the Word*
Choose the one of the seven churches of Revelation which seems to you to be most like churches in the U.S. today. With oth-

ers who have selected the same church, discuss the similarities you saw.

In view of the similarities, what do Christians today need to do in response to Jesus' words? What does your group's members need to do? What do you need to do?

Adoration: *Worship and pray*
Focus your attention on Jesus as He is described in Revelation 1:9-18. Hear His words as they are spoken by the resurrected Christ, glorious, exalted, of awesome power. Worship Him, and respond to His commands appropriately.

PRELIMINARY JUDGMENTS

Overview

With chapter 4 of Revelation, the scene shifts. Here is how John describes it:

After this I looked, and there before me was a door standing open in heaven. And the voice I had first heard speaking to me like a trumpet said, "Come up here, and I will show you what must take place after this." At once I was in the Spirit, and there before me was a throne in heaven with Someone sitting on it.

Revelation 4:1-2

In these two verses we have moved from earth to heaven, and from the then present to what is to come. We have moved from Christ standing among the candlesticks (churches), to the Father on His eternal throne.

From this point on in the Book of Revelation, we are thrown ahead in time.

The question most Bible students ask is, "How *far* ahead?" Do we see in Revelation an unfolding of church history, as some have argued. Or are we seeing events associated with history's end?

Whichever position we take, the powerful images and terrible descriptions continue to remind us that our God is a flaming fire; a God whose righteousness and whose justice will surely strike terror in the hearts of those who reject Him.

Commentary

I have suggested that our most fruitful approach to the study of Revelation is to avoid majoring on the details of this or that interpretive system. Even so, we need to review how believers have approached this book before looking into its major section.

We can distinguish four major systems of interpretation taken by those who have a high view of Scripture as God's Word to man.

Allegorical. This approach, with its roots in early church history (Clement of Alexandria and Origin) regards Revelation as a writing of encouragement. It was intended to assure the first-century reader of the ultimate triumph of Christianity, not to predict the future. As the Book of Revelation shows us vision after vision, we are convinced of God's "sure triumph, glorious over and amid them all" (R.C.H. Lenski, *Interpretation of St. John's Revelation,* Luthern Book Concern).

Preterist. This approach views Revelation as a record of conflicts between the early church and paganism/Judaism. The final chapters are thought to portray a contemporary triumph of the church. In this view, the focus of Revelation is the first century itself. The book's value is in revealing principles of God's action, not in delineating specific time periods or events.

Historical. This approach has traditionally suggested that Revelation is a symbolic overview of church history, culminating in Jesus' second coming. During Reformation times this was the most popular interpretation, with the beasts of Revelation 13 identified as the pope and the papacy. The major problem with this approach is its great flexibility; over 50 different interpretations of history have emerged, and each has identified the events and characters of Revelation to fit a particular historical point of view.

Modern historists tend to see the book not as images of specific events but rather as seven parallel pictures of how God is at work within history.

Futurist. This approach looks at Revelation as prophetic, and suggests that with the beginning of chapter 4 the book describes events that are still to come, not only for John but for us as well. This system of interpretation suggests the events describe a time period just preceding the return of Christ, the Tribulation time mentioned in Matthew and in the Old Testament.

The Old Testament prophetic passages are expected to be fulfilled literally, and Jesus is to rule on earth as glorious King. Thus Revelation is correlated with pictures of the future given by Daniel, Isaiah, Ezekiel, and other Old Testament prophets.

Which one? It's clear from a quick glance at these different systems that the approach we take to Revelation will affect our understanding of it, and may even distract us from its chief value! If we take a historical view, we may try to correlate events with councils, persecutions, and movements in church history. If we take the allegorical, we may look for meaning, but deny that the events described could ever happen. If we take the futurist view, we might easily become involved in speculation about how a specific future event correlates with others described in this book or in the Old Testament.

To me, the futurist view seems most in harmony with the whole of Scripture. But I do not want to argue for the futurist position. Nor do I think we should try to build a detailed picture of history to come from the teachings of this majestic book. What I want, for myself and those I teach, is a fresh vision of Jesus, standing as an awesome figure at history's end.

When we do study Revelation to meet Jesus, and our vision is drawn beyond time to an eternity in which He is Lord, our lives and our faith will be enriched.

The Framework: Revelation 4–5

The general framework for a futurist interpretation is provided in Revelation 1:19. There John is told to write "what you have seen, what is now" (chaps. 2–3) and "what will take place later" (chaps. 4–21).

But beyond noting that we will treat the rest of Revelation as describing events at history's end, we need spend no more time on systems. We can instead take John's viewpoint, and see these events from the perspective of heaven. We will stand beside the Lord in heaven and keep our eyes fixed on God.

Lord God Almighty. Seated on a throne, in a blinding riot of color, is a figure. Lightning plays around Him, flashing on four angelic beings who praise Him day and night, saying:

> Holy, holy, holy
> is the Lord God Almighty, who was, and is, and is to come.
> Revelation 4:8

Just beyond this inner circle are 24 elders, who also worship. They joyfully lay their crowns before the throne and say:

> You are worthy, our Lord and God, to receive glory and honor and power, for You created all things, and by Your will they were created and have their being.
> Revelation 4:11

This first vision of God immediately focuses our attention on His holiness. He, the Eternal, the Creator, the Source of all being, is holy, holy, holy. *What we are about to see in the events of history to come is a revelation of the holiness of God.*

That revelation of holiness does not repel those who know Him. Instead, it stimulates those who live in His presence to worship Him and give Him "glory, and honor and thanks" (v. 9). A revelation of God's holiness will always lead those who know Him to praise and to purity. But soon we will see an entirely different reaction from those who stand in rebellion against Him.

The Lamb. The figure on the throne is holding a book, a scroll that is sealed (locked) and cannot be opened. With John, we are heartbroken that no one can be found to open the book. Somehow we sense that the scroll *must* be opened and read.

Then one of the elders announces that there is One who "has triumphed" and can open the scroll and its seals. "Then," John records, "I saw a Lamb, looking as if it had been slain, standing in the center of the throne, encircled by the four living creatures and the elders" (5:6). The elders and four living creatures give the Lamb the same worship they offered to the Father (a clear identification of Jesus as God). They break into a song of praise:

> You are worthy to take the scroll and to open its seals, because You were slain, and with Your blood You purchased men for God from every tribe and language and people and nation. You have made them to be a kingdom and priests

to serve our God, and they will reign on the earth.

Revelation 5:9-10

The singers are now joined by millions of angels who praise the Lamb, saying:

Worthy is the Lamb, who was slain, to receive power and wealth and wisdom and strength and honor and glory and praise!

Revelation 5:12

Finally, in antiphonal response, "Every creature in heaven and on earth and under the earth and on the sea" joins the choir:

To Him who sits on the throne and to the Lamb be praise and honor and glory and power, forever and ever!

Revelation 5:13

And those around the throne echo: "Amen."

God who is God. These two chapters of worship and praise are a necessary introduction to John's description of things to come. They are as necessary for us as they were for him.

Perhaps we have been so filled with wonder at a God who loves us and gave Himself for us that we tend to miss an important reality. Though God in Jesus gave Himself for us, *He remains the center of the universe.* It is God, not man, for whom all things were and are created. It is His glory, not our glorification, that is important. As the Westminster Catechism states, "The chief end of man is to glorify God and enjoy Him forever." We must never neglect this reality or come to feel that somehow the chief end of God is to glorify man! We must never measure what happens or what is described in the Book of Revelation from a human viewpoint. All that occurs must be measured against who God is.

Judgment Begins: Revelation 6–9

We must realize God is the ultimate measure of every event before we come (in chapter 6) to the breaking of seals on the scroll God holds. For as each seal is opened, new terrors are unleashed on earth. If we see only the impact of those judgments on mankind, we are likely to criticize God's holy actions. But it is only after cen-

tury upon century of grace that God unleashes the punishment required for sin.

Looking at man's unwillingness to respond to God's grace, Paul asked, "Do you think you will escape God's judgment? Or do you show contempt for the riches of His kindness, tolerance and patience, not realizing that God's kindness leads you toward repentance?" (Rom. 2:3-4)

Now, after humanity has rejected God's kindness for millennia, and only now, the dam of God's patience breaks, and judgment floods the earth. Paul's warning is fulfilled: "Because of your stubbornness and your unrepentant heart, you are storing up wrath against yourself for the day of God's wrath, when His righteous judgment will be revealed" (v. 5). The wrath that comes only underlines the grace of God, for now we see what human sin and unwillingness to repent has always deserved.

The seals (Rev. 6). As the seals are opened, war and famine and disease invade the earth, and millions are killed. A fourth of earth's population dies under this first wave of judgment. Then comes a second wave, with cataclysmic earthquakes and jolting changes even in the stellar universe. These events are so obviously supernatural that even unbelievers are convinced of God's intervention in the world. "They called to the mountains and the rocks, 'Fall on us and hide us from the face of Him who sits on the throne and from the wrath of the Lamb! For the great day of Their wrath has come, and who can stand?' " (vv. 16-17)

As this terrified howl issues from earth, we hear other voices as well. Those who were hated by the world and have been martyred because they responded to God's call: "How long, Sovereign Lord, holy and true, until You judge the inhabitants of the earth and avenge our blood?" (v. 10)

God's judgments on mankind are not unjustified. They are in fact required by man's own injustice to man, and by humanity's hatred of those who have responded to God's love.

The multitude (Rev. 7). In chapter 7, we see a group of men and women "that no one could count, from every nation, tribe, people and language" (v. 9), who stand before God redeemed. We are told who they are. "These are they who have come out of the Great Tribulation; they have washed their robes and made them white in the blood of the Lamb" (v. 14). Seeing them, we realize that even in the time of wrath God has remembered mercy!

The chapter opens with the calling of 144,000 people, 12,000 from each of the 12 tribes of Israel. At the beginning of the time of wrath these are set aside to serve God. (Many Bible students believe they are evangelists who will go throughout the world calling people to faith in God during the Great Tribulation.) Whoever they may be; one thing is clear from the chapter: *God's love will operate to call men to Himself even in the time of wrath!* God's tender love has reached down amid the terrors with continuing promise of personal relationship and caring:

> Never again will they hunger; never again will they thirst. The sun will not beat upon them, nor any scorching heat. For the Lamb at the center of the throne will be their Shepherd; He will lead them to springs of living water. And God will wipe away every tear from their eyes.
>
> Revelation 7:16-17

Even in the days of wrath, only a person's hardness of heart can keep God's love out.

The seventh seal (Rev. 8). The book now continues with descriptions of more judgment on earth. Again these pictures are cataclysmic, so immense they seem unreal.

> The second angel sounded his trumpet, and something like a huge mountain, all ablaze, was thrown into the sea. A third of the sea turned into blood, a third of the living creatures in the sea died, and a third of the ships were destroyed.
>
> Revelation 8:8-9

John is clearly struggling to find words. It's helpful as we read these chapters to remember that what we have here is a *description* of events beyond imagination, events impossible to portray in words. It is as though someone from colonial days were suddenly dropped into our century and asked to explain to one of his contemporaries such sights as spaceships and jet planes, television and skyscrapers. He would have had no words to adequately convey such a vision out of the future.

So we should not find it hard to see why John has to struggle for words. "Something like a huge mountain, all ablaze" is the closest he can come to describing the sight he sees. Many reading these words see visions of atomic warfare. That may be. Whatever it is John describes, it is destruction beyond our wildest dreams, beyond our greatest fears.

Demonic invasion (Rev. 9). In this new plague (apparently demonic) beings from the Abyss torment, but do not at first kill, the people remaining on the earth. After five months, more supernatural beings are released, and they destroy a third of the human beings who have survived the earlier judgments.

Yet, in spite of all these supernatural judgments:

> The rest of mankind that were not killed by these plagues still did not repent of the work of their hands; they did not stop worshiping demons, and idols of gold, silver, bronze, stone, and wood — idols that cannot see or hear or walk. Nor did they repent of their murders, their magic arts, their sexual immorality or their thefts.
>
> Revelation 9:20-21

They had rejected the love of God. Now not even the wrath of God could persuade their hard hearts to repent.

Interlude: Revelation 10

As we move on into Revelation 10, it is apparent that all that has gone before is preliminary! Now John hears an angel announce, "There will be no more delay! But in the days when the seventh angel is about to sound his trumpet, the mystery of God will be accomplished, just as He announced to His servants the prophets" (vv. 6-7).

John is told to take a scroll from an angel and then to speak out "about many peoples, nations, languages and kings" (v. 11). In these next chapters, we will meet the individuals, the forces, and the institutions that emerge to struggle in deadly conflict with each other and with God Himself, as history draws to a close.

Two Witnesses: Revelation 11

In this chapter a specific period of time is

mentioned. During these 42 months, Gentiles will "trample on the Holy City." Daniel 12 mentions this same period of time, as well as many of the individuals and forces we meet in Revelation.

Now John introduces us to two individuals identified as "witnesses." In spite of the victory of Gentile powers over the Holy City, these witnesses are given supernatural powers that protect them and enable them to strike back against God's enemies. Finally, after 42 months of testifying, the two are killed by a supernatural being who comes from the Abyss. Their bodies lie in the open, and the whole world rejoices at the death of the two prophets who used truth to torment those who lived on earth.

But after three and a half days, we see the witnesses restored to life! Their enemies watch in anger and terror as the two ascend to heaven in a cloud. At that very hour an earthquake strikes the city, destroying a tenth of it.

Many have debated the identity of the two witnesses. Often they are said to be Elijah and Moses. Whatever their identity, their ministry during the time leading up to the end is clear. They will testify to the power of God. After they ascend into heaven, we hear again the praise of those before the throne:

> We give thanks to You, Lord God Almighty, who is and who was, because You have taken Your great power and have begun to reign. The nations were angry; and Your wrath has come. The time has come for judging the dead, and for rewarding Your servants the prophets and Your saints and those who reverence Your name, both small and great — and for destroying those who destroy the earth.
>
> Revelation 11:17-19

Those Who Destroy: Revelation 12–14

The first figure John describes is a pregnant woman who is under attack by a great red dragon. The dragon is identified as Satan (12:9). We are told that he is the leader of a group of angels who rebelled against God.

While some see this as a description of Satan being cast from heaven originally, the passage clearly relates these events to the 42 months of Tribulation on earth. The woman, probably representing Israel, is taken to a place of safety in the desert while the war in heaven is fought.

When the enemy loses the battle in heaven and is cast down to earth, he pursues the woman. When he is unable to reach the woman, he goes off "to make war against the rest of her offspring — those who obey God's commandments and hold to the testimony of Jesus" (v. 17).

Now the dragon is joined by a beast who rises out of the sea. Satan (the dragon) gives "the beast his power and his throne and great authority" (13:2). The symbolism here parallels again the prophetic picture in Daniel 7. Given supernatural powers, this world ruler exercises "authority over every tribe, people, language and nation" (Rev. 13:7). He receives worship from all who do not belong to God (v. 8). Satan, who has always yearned for the worship and the place belonging to God alone, now seems to achieve that goal through the counterfeit Christ who rules in his name.

Finally, to these two is added "another beast, coming out of the earth" (v. 11). The unholy trinity is now complete. The second beast acts as spokesman for the first, using miraculous powers to force men to worship Satan and the Antichrist. He kills all who refuse to worship and forces "everyone, small and great . . . to receive a mark on his right hand or on his forehead, so that no one could buy or sell unless he had the mark, which is the name of the beast or the number of his name" (vv. 16-17).

These are the destroyers. Satan's heart is revealed at last. God acts in love, giving people freedom to choose to follow Him; but Satan acts in hatred, *forcing* people to surrender their freedom to Him.

But we are encouraged as the voice from heaven says that Satan "is filled with fury, because he knows that his time is short" (12:12).

He knows his time is short, because the Lamb stands beside the throne of heaven. There is anguish and antagonism on earth, but the glorious figure who dominates Revelation is about to do battle with His enemies.

> He will act on behalf of His saints
>   To finally,
>   utterly,
>   completely,

ultimately,
destroy the destroyers.

And so chapter 14 returns us to the side of the Lamb. We watch as an angel proclaims the message of the "eternal Gospel . . . to every nation, tribe, language and people" (v. 6). Believers who are being persecuted are encouraged to have "patient endurance" and "obey God's commandments and remain faithful to Jesus" (v. 12).

But as for anyone who worships the beast and his image, another angel delivers a message of judgment. "He, too, will drink of the wine of God's fury, which has been poured full strength into the cup of His wrath. . . . There is no rest day or night for those who worship the beast and his image, or for anyone who receives the mark of his name" (vv. 10-11).

Further Judgments on Earth: Revelation 15–18

Now more judgments are released on earth, and "with them God's wrath is completed" (15:1).

Before these judgments begin, those who belong to God and were victorious over the beast praise God in song. Against the background of human sin and Satan's rebellion, the righteous judgments of God call forth our praise.

Great and marvelous are Your deeds, Lord God Almighty. Just and true are Your ways, King of the ages. Who will not fear You, O Lord, and bring glory to Your name? For You alone are holy. All nations will come and worship before You, for Your righteous acts have been revealed.

Revelation 15:3-4

It is important to remember that the judgments are righteous as we read of ugly and painful sores, of scorching heat, and of waters turning to blood. We must remember the figure of Christ as we read of people who gnaw their tongues in agony and curse God because of their pains. We must keep the perspective of the angel who declared:

You are just in these judgments, You who are and who were, the Holy One, because You have so judged; for they have shed the blood of Your saints and

your prophets, and You have given them blood to drink as they deserve.

Revelation 16:4

The persecutors of God's people, in all their pain, "refused to repent and glorify Him" (v. 9); in all their agony "they refused to repent of what they had done" (v. 11). Even in the final judgment, with earthquake and lightning and volcanic holocaust, "they cursed God on account of the plague of hail, because the plague was so terrible" (v. 21).

Another woman (Rev. 17). From Reformation times, commentators have identified the woman of chapter 17, portrayed as the "great prostitute," and named "Babylon the Great," with apostate religion. The Reformers saw her as papal Rome. We can broaden their interpretation by seeing that when Scripture speaks of Babylon as a religious system, it points to a counterfeit faith—sometimes pseudo-Christian, often pagan in nature.

During the end times apostate religion apparently will form a relationship with the secular power that is Satan's emissary. Raised to world power, false religion will join eagerly in this persecution of those who remain faithful to Jesus.

Finally, the secular power, consolidated from at least 10 national entities into a single state, acts to destroy even the apostate church and permit only the worship of Satan and his beast (see vv. 12, 16-17).

There is much detail and much symbolism in Revelation 17. Here again we are reminded of Daniel's prophecy of the development of the final world rule of the Antichrist (Dan. 12). Certainly the detail is significant, and to examine the passage would provide a clearer picture of the future; but what is important to us is to see God revealed against the final patterns of history.

By this criteria, what is important here is to see that *religion may be the enemy of God.* It is not belief that is important; *what is important is the one in whom we believe.* A counterfeit faith, no matter how much it may seem in harmony with our culture, is an enemy of God. One day Satan will no longer need to hide behind these attractive counterfeits, and he will sweep away the facade and demand that all people worship him.

The city of Babylon (Rev. 18). From the

beginning of Scripture, "Babylon" has been significant. Genesis 11 describes people building a tower at Babel to reestablish a political basis for unity. In the Old Testament, "Babylon" was a symbol of godless political and economic power. God's people have always been warned to flee from Babylon (see Jer. 50:8-9; 51:6, 44-45).

Revelation 18 makes it plain that Babylon here represents not only political power but also material wealth and luxury. As God's judgment consumes the city of Babylon, her merchants and kings and sea captains and sailors will weep and mourn for their lost riches:

Because no one buys their cargoes anymore—cargoes of gold, silver, precious stones and pearls; fine linen, purple, silk and scarlet cloth; every sort of citron wood . . . and bodies and souls of men.
Revelation 18:11-13

But earth's weeping and mourning over Babylon's destruction is matched by heaven's joy!

Rejoice over her, O heaven! Rejoice, saints and apostles and prophets! God has judged her for the way she treated you.
Revelation 18:20

When the state and its leaders trample the individual; when *things* have more value than *persons*; when all is bent to the warped pattern set by Satan . . . then the fall of Babylon will bring joy to the godly.

Characters in the Drama

In Revelation 10–18 we see personalities against whom Jesus, the Lamb, stands in sharp contrast. As we look at each element in the drama, we can see why God's wrath is just. We can also better understand His character as we see what He hates.

The witnesses. These men reveal unregenerate mankind's deep-seated antagonism to God's spokesmen. These prophets draw vicious anger from the world, in spite of divine protection and authenticating miracles. Just as Jesus was slain by men who angrily rejected Him, so the witnesses are constantly under attack. Finally, the world gladly takes sides with the devil himself and rejoices at the apparent destruction of these

men of God.

Only when this concentrated hatred for God and His people fully manifests itself does Jesus take up His great power and begin to reign.

The evil trinity. This trio is made up of Satan, the first beast (the Antichrist), and the second beast (a false prophet), and is a counterfeit of God the Father, Jesus, and the Holy Spirit. Satan is the key figure here. He empowers the other two (who are apparently human beings) to deceive and coerce the world into a willing worship of Satan. This is a trinity dedicated to destruction, not redemption. They do not serve men, but instead demand that men serve them. They do not die for humanity, but rather take lives when people will not obey their unholy commands.

At every point Revelation's portrait shows us a stark contrast between the motives, values, and character of Satan and those of God. In the final confrontation, Satan knows his time is short. He is eager to bring all those he can snare with him, to destruction. Most of humanity eagerly joins this rush toward disaster, angrily rejecting repentance even under the most severe of warning judgments.

Counterfeit religion. Humanity has always been religious. No culture is without some faith, some ritual practice of religion. But religion, while on the surface a good thing, has never been a friend of God. At the time of the end a "world church" joins the beast (secular power) in a systematic assault on believers, seeking their deaths.

It's all too easy in our pluralistic society to be tolerant of false religions or even to attempt to compromise Scripture's teaching in order to make room for their adherents in the family of faith. In Revelation we see the unveiling of reality. These faiths at heart are enemies of God and His people. Against them, totally committed to care for His own, stands the Lamb in all the glory of His power.

We are not to attack adherents of false faiths now. But we are to recognize the essential anti-God character of religion. We are to hold even more firmly, not to religion but to our relationship with the One who is Lord of lords and King of kings.

Political Babylon. Here we see the final culmination of world government. It leads to unparalleled prosperity but also to unparalleled regimentation. The mark of the beast is needed before a person can buy or sell anything; there is total control over the individual. The luxuries, the power, the seeming security convince people that they have no need to depend on God. Pride and self-reliance mark the rise of the world state; mourning and anguish over lost wealth mark her destruction.

In Revelation 18 we see this Babylon being destroyed. The treasures people lay up for themselves are subject to rust and theft, and to the destroying fire. No political system can unify the world or bring the blessings God alone can provide for His people. The Babylon system has to be destroyed, for it is a political system that feeds on in-justice and pride and that encourages rejection of God. It is a political system that leads persons and nations astray (v. 23). It has no room for either saint or prophet, and kills those willing to witness of the reality of God (v. 24).

And what do we see of God through political Babylon? Against the transitory glimmer of human achievement, we see the glow of God's changeless glory. Against the background of the wealth destroyed in Babylon's fall, we see the treasures stored up for us in the presence of Christ Himself. Our destiny is to worship Him, not wealth or power. Man's Babylon will fall. But the city of God will stand forever and ever.

GROUP RESOURCE GUIDE

NOTE: Revelation can be studied image by image, and the meaning of each event described and debated in depth. But Revelation is better read through, letting each image build on the preceding, creating its intended impression of judgment and of a Sovereign God whose will will ultimately be imposed on rebellious humanity. Make this group meeting an experience rather than a study.

Exploration: *Probe God's Word*
Have a pad of paper on which to draw doodles or jot down words and impressions. Listen actively as one person reads Revelation 4–18 straight through. (Or listen to a professionally done tape of this extended passage.) As you listen, doodle, draw pictures, or jot down your major impressions.

Reaction: *Respond together to the Word*
When the reading is complete, sit in silence for three to five minutes, and try to feel the impact of Revelation's terrible vision of history's end.

Adoration: *Worship and pray*
Praise God, expressing aloud what He has said to you through this dramatic and powerful portion of His Word.

ENTRANCE TO ETERNITY

Overview

These final chapters of the Bible give us Scripture's clearest portraits of eternity. In them we see the destiny of saved and unsaved alike.

One stereotype of Christianity that is found in literature and the media is the "hellfire evangelist." He is usually portrayed as an Elmer Gantry: someone so twisted by his own sins that he finds release only by laying a burden of guilt on his listeners. He frightens them with visions of a God who seeks any excuse to drag people away to endless torment.

Often Christians, captivated by the vision of God's love in Jesus, turn away from the picture of a lake of fire and the idea of eternal damnation. A few theologians have also looked for other ways to describe the destiny of those who resist God's grace to the end. Some have suggested annihilation—the idea that for the lost, death is simply the end. The evil people of this world slip into death as into some endless and dreamless sleep; they simply cease to exist. Others have supposed a final reconciliation of all with God. Colossians 1:20 is taken to mean that the Hitlers of this world will find a place in glory with those they massacred.

But the Bible affirms the existence of a real heaven—and a real hell. And the Bible also answers the question, "How could a loving God condemn anyone to a lake of eternal fire?"

Yet we do not need to fear hell. In Jesus, our destiny is heaven.

Commentary

As background to understanding these last chapters of Revelation, where we are confronted with a lake of burning sulfur as well as a renewed and holy earth, we need to think about the nature of human beings. To see who humanity is, we must go back before the Fall (Gen. 3) to the story of Adam and Eve, told in Genesis 1–2.

"Let Us make man in Our image, in Our likeness. . . . So God created man in His own image, in the image of God He created Him" (1:26-27).

There are many other statements in Scripture that speak of man's identity and destiny. "You made him [man] a little lower than the heavenly beings," the psalmist exults (Ps. 8:5). Short-lived though we are (144:4), yet only we in all creation have a share in the image and likeness of God. Only we have been chosen to be lifted to glory (Heb. 2:10) and to be called "brethren" by the God who stooped to take on human nature (v. 17). God has always intended an unimaginable exaltation for His people.

The fact that sin broke into human experience and tainted the race has not changed God's commitment to us. In fact, our sin became the occasion for the fullest expression of God's love: He came as a Man to bear sin's punishment so that we might become righteousness in Him (2 Cor. 5:21).

At the same time, God's act of rescue, and Scripture itself, tells us that human beings are not mere sparks that glow in the dark and then are gone. God's gift of life to man, investing in us His own likeness and image, made us more than the animals. We are persons in the same way God is a Person. *Because we share this with Him, we are too significant to disappear as though we had never been. The very nature of human beings as bearers of the divine likeness demands that even after the body has returned to dust, the personality, the "living being" of Genesis 2:7, must remain.* Unlike God in that we have a beginning, we are like God in that once we are born we have no end!

To suppose that even the lost can suffer annihilation is to deny a significance to the individual that the Bible and the death of

Jesus for us constantly affirms.

Who Is God?

To see each human being as a person of eternal significance tells us something about God as well. He is a Person who loves *eternally*. You and I know what it means to suffer the loss of a loved one. Even a child suffers when a pet dies. But what a difference between the two. We know that our loved one still lives, while the pet is gone. The human being has eternal significance; the pet lives for a brief moment and then exists only as a memory. But God could not create a race to be the focus of His love whose members would lose their being and live only in His memory. He gave us something of His own nature in Creation so that He might love us and know our love forever.

When we ask the question, "Who is God?" we can only reply that He is a Person who, in love and perfect holiness, chose to create beings with whom He would share Himself, whatever the cost. And the cost was one *He*, not we, had to pay!

- It was the price of anguish, as over and over His loved ones rejected His love.
- It was the price of crucifixion-death, as His loved ones nailed Him to the cross.
- It was the price of seeing many of His loved ones reject forgiveness, selecting instead an endless death.

If we were to be truly like Him, truly free beings with choice and personal responsibility, then God could not demand that we accept His love against our will. He could not program us so that we did not have the possibility of real choice. He chose to suffer His own deep pain over each one who refuses to turn to Him. He allowed people the freedom to be endlessly separated from Him.

All this may sound speculative or philosophical. But several things are clear. He does not want "anyone to perish, but everyone to come to repentance" (2 Peter 3:9). Certainly God's choosing to suffer in order to rescue beings who turned against Him demonstrates once and for all that God takes no delight in our punishment. God is not the kind of person who would enjoy condemning anyone to a lake of fire.

It is because there is no other way to deal with the results of sin in beings whose nature grants them endless existence that the lake of fire of Revelation will exist. But for man to be truly human, and for God to share Himself with man, some such way to deal with sin had to be. It is not desirable. But it is necessary.

Hallelujah: Revelation 19

In spite of the pain, there is joy in heaven as history's end comes. As the glorified figure of the Lamb prepares to battle His enemies on earth, we hear the multitude shouting:

> Hallelujah! For our Lord God Almighty reigns. Let us rejoice and be glad and give Him glory!
>
> Revelation 19:6-7

Heaven open (Rev. 19:11-21). Immediately Christ Himself enters the battle. "He is dressed in a robe dipped in blood," and "He treads the winepress of the fury of the wrath of God Almighty" (vv. 13, 15).

The armies of the beast are gathered on earth to make war against Christ. . . . But their efforts are futile. The two human members of the evil triumvirate are "thrown alive into the fiery lake of burning sulfur" (v. 20). As for the rest of their army, all are killed in the battle, and "all the birds gorged themselves on their flesh" (v. 21).

The irresistible power of the Lamb who is also King of kings and Lord of lords ends the battle almost before it begins!

Interlude: Revelation 20:1-10

The thousand years. Now we find, somewhat surprisingly, that the battle described in Revelation 19 is followed by a period of a thousand years (20:3-4, 6-7).

During this period several things happen. First, Satan is "locked and sealed" in the Abyss, to "keep him from deceiving the nations anymore" until the thousand years end (v. 3).

Second, there is a "first resurrection" at which believers killed during the time of terror and the Antichrist's rule are given new life. "They will be priests of God and of Christ and will reign with Him for a thousand years" (v. 6). The text specifically says that the rest of the dead will not come to life until this thousand-year period is over.

Then, after the thousand years of Christ's

rule on earth, Satan is released from his prison, and the final battle is fought (vv. 7-10).

Why a thousand-year interlude? Many suggestions have been made. Certainly the Old Testament prophecies of a glorious kingdom on earth can be fulfilled during this time span. But even more may be involved.

One suggestion is that during this time sin's true nature will again be demonstrated. Sin has found expression throughout the ages in the characters of both individuals and societies. Often today society itself is blamed for individual failure: the environment, some argue, programs people into actions which, in a just and moral society, they would never voluntarily choose. The rule of Jesus and the resurrected saints will provide a truly just, moral society, and thus an ideal environment. Individuals will be released from those social pressures that now stimulate them toward wrong choices. Will human beings be "good" under ideal conditions?

Revelation suggests that once Satan is freed (v. 8), he will succeed in deceiving the nations. Millions will choose, *against their environmental setting,* to follow Satan and rebel against God.

As we look at Revelation's terrible picture of final judgment, we can never forget that those who have taken sides against God have done so by their own free choice. The character of sin is again revealed in the final rebellion, and the judgment of God is shown to be just. Fire flares from heaven to destroy the rebellious host. The devil is "thrown into the lake of burning sulfur, where the beast and the false prophet had been thrown." And Scripture adds, "They will be tormented day and night forever and ever" (v. 10).

The Great White Throne: Revelation 20:11-15

Now suddenly earth and the heavens are gone. We're shown an empty universe . . . empty except for the throne of God and for humanity, gathered before Him. *Of all that God has created, only human beings, whose personalities are indestructible, remain.* All the dead not raised in the first resurrection are here, and each person is judged according to what he has done. All whose names are not written in the Book of Life are judged by their works. Since this judgment is based on the criteria of their own actions rather than on their faith in Christ, all fall short (Rom. 6:23). Then the Scripture states clearly and simply, all are "thrown into the lake of fire."

Two resurrections. This is one of the concepts taught in Revelation that is only hinted at in the Old Testament. Daniel spoke of a resurrection in which those who "sleep in the dust of the earth shall awake: some to everlasting life, others to shame and everlasting contempt" (Dan. 12:2). But dividing the resurrection into two widely separated events is a distinctive contribution of the Book of Revelation.

Forever and ever. The second resurrection, a prelude to official condemnation, is a resurrection to death rather than to life. When the believer is resurrected, he is transformed, changed to the image of Christ (Rom. 8:29; 1 John 3:2). In the resurrection of the unsaved, the individual is *unchanged.* He is conscious, aware, but his character and his attitude toward God retains sin's twist. The man consumed with anger is an angry man still. The jealous person is still jealous. The lustful still lust. In the lake of fire, the old desires burn, but are forever unsatisfied. This is one reason why the lake of fire is called the second death (Rev. 20:14). It is an endless captivity to what one is when he dies. There is no hope for change, no hope for growth, no hope for transformation. Fixed forever, unchangeable, the personality of the lost burns as much from inner torment as from the cauldron John can only liken to burning sulfur.

In this picture you and I can find no pleasure. And neither can God. But because the human personality does have endless conscious existence, and because people were made free to choose so that they might freely choose to love God, those who will not respond to God condemn themselves.

Now we can understand a little more of God. Against His own desires that all might be saved, God

- *did* create man like Himself, and so give the gift of endless life to all.
- *did* create man like Himself, and so give each of us the freedom to choose.
- *did* come in Incarnation to take on Himself the suffering that brings us forgiveness.
- *did* offer that forgiveness as a grace/

gift to all who will receive it by faith, and

- *did* withhold the punishment sin deserves, extending the day of grace and postponing judgment. But ultimately
- God *will* bring all mankind before Him to face the final judgment that holiness demands.

God's desire is to bring all to everlasting life. But Scripture says that "the cowardly, the unbelieving, the vile, the murderers, the sexually immoral, those who practice magic arts, the idolaters and all liars—their place will be in the fiery lake of burning sulfur. This is the second death" (21:8).

Another View: Revelation 21:1–22:6
The description of the final judgment has been somber and sparse. There are no psalms of praise here, no sounds of joy and gladness. There is only a grim description of what must come.

But in the last two chapters of Revelation there is an obvious change of tone. We are given another view of eternity. With the task of judgment past, now the family gathers to share the joy of God's presence and the rich gifts He has prepared for those who love Him.

In these chapters we have a hint of what we call "heaven." It is a different picture from the stereotype of the dead becoming "angels," and then relaxing on the clouds with harps.

Instead we see a scene in which we each keep our individual identity—yet a world where everything is truly new.

The New Jerusalem. The first vision is of a sky city, coming down from heaven over a newly created earth. This is the Holy City, the New Jerusalem, and is identified as the dwelling place of God. From now on He will be "with men, and He will live with them" (21:3). God's presence will bring perfect peace and joy; "He will wipe away every tear from their eyes. There will be no more death or mourning or crying or pain, for the old order of things has passed away" (v. 4).

This magnificent city is described as a cube some 1,500 miles long and wide and high. Its walls are of pure gold; its foundations are of precious stones; its streets are transparent. Most importantly, the city has no temple. Nor does the city need sun or moon; God's presence within it gives light:

"The nations will walk by its light, and the kings of the earth will bring their splendor into it" (v. 24).

John then goes on to picture the river of the water of life. Its clear water flows from the throne of God right through the middle of the city. The trees by its banks yield fruit; its leaves are for the "healing of the nations." In this new universe there is no curse; there is personal access to God; there is no night. God's presence provides light, and the people "will reign forever and ever" (22:5).

New cosmology. Other passages of Scripture tell us that the present heavens will "disappear with a roar; the elements will be destroyed by fire, and the earth and everything in it will be laid bare" (2 Peter 3:10). So, Peter continued, the Christian is one who looks forward to a "new heaven and a new earth, the home of righteousness" (v. 13). Peter echoed Isaiah, who prophesied:

Behold, I will create new heavens and a new earth. The former things will not be remembered, nor will they come to mind.
Isaiah 5:17

New humanity. Little is said here about the future of mankind, aside from the implication that kings and nations still exist. Men are still men, not angels. And none who enjoy this new and endless existence are tainted by sin.

To see more of what the future holds for us, we need to look at other New Testament passages. We find that when we stand in God's presence, we will be transformed into Jesus' likeness. "We shall be like Him, for we shall see Him as He is" (1 John 3:2). And Paul said that God has predestined us "to be conformed to the likeness of His Son" (Rom. 8:29). All that mankind potentially is . . . all that Jesus was as a Man . . . we will be.

Paul told the Corinthians that the believer's resurrection body will be imperishable in contrast to our present perishable body. It will be marked by power rather than weakness. It will be controlled by the spiritual, rather than subject to the physical. Yes, the dead "will be raised imperishable, and we shall be changed" (1 Cor. 15:52, see vv. 35-54). When the mortal becomes immortal, then death itself will be swallowed up in our great victory.

In these words of Scripture we see a glorious promise. But the scene is so far removed from our present situation that it is hard to get any clear picture. We can perhaps see more in the Gospel's description of Christ after His resurrection. He was able to eat with His disciples; He had flesh and bones (Luke 24; John 21). Yet He also could "appear" among them in a locked room (20:19). He was recognizable: the same individual, yet different.

Jesus' new capacities will undoubtedly be ours as well in resurrection. The greatest wonder of all is that we shall be like Him, freed from every stain of sin. To be perfected and yet retain our individual self—this is our glorious destiny. "He who overcomes," God promises, "will inherit all this, and I will be his God and he will be My son" (Rev. 21:7).

New dreams? Many have asked, "What will we *do* then?" God has given every believer gifts for ministry; each one of us participates in the great work God is doing in our world. One of His first gifts was the gift of work to Adam and Eve, so they could share in the Creation act (Gen. 2:15). He made people able to have dominion and capable of taking an active role in the supervision of God's universe. Would our creative and active God shape eternity for a *passive* existence?

Against this background, some have made fascinating suggestions about our ministry in eternity. One great Bible teacher, Dr. Donald Grey Barnhouse, used to tell of his expectation that one day God would say to him, "Donald, go create a world, people it, and govern it for Me." The endless universe itself seemed to Dr. Barnhouse a stage for the fulfillment of God's plan for man. We, who have been made in His image and likeness, and given a destiny of dominion, must (it seemed to Barnhouse) fulfill that destiny in some universal way.

But all such ideas are speculation. We are not told in Scripture just what our role or ministry in eternity will be. Yet we do know that God shaped us uniquely for Himself and for His glory. We can be sure that eternity will be full, and fulfilling, to each one of us.

Coming Soon: Revelation 22:7-21

Three times in these closing paragraphs the promise is made, "Behold, I am coming soon." Eternity may seem far off. Yet for each of us the return of Jesus and the events foretold in Revelation have an immediacy. "Soon" may be tomorrow! *There is nothing that must happen before the events we have read of in Revelation may begin.*

These paragraphs also make it clear that we are to learn to live with this sense of immediacy. Thus John reports, "Blessed is he who keeps the words of the prophecy of this book" (v. 7).

But how can we keep the words of the prophecy? We have been shown what God Himself will do at history's end. What is there for *us* to keep? The next verses explain.

The vision of a glorified Christ, stepping into history to judge, will have an impact on every reader. It is *not* an evangelistic impact: no one can be frightened into heaven. The good news that brings salvation is the story of the love and forgiveness God offers human beings in Jesus.

And so the voice of John warns, "Let him who does wrong continue to do wrong; let him who is vile continue to be vile; let him who does right continue to do right; and let him who is holy continue to be holy" (v. 11). *The words of this book will move each reader in the life direction he or she has chosen to go!*

If we have taken to heart God's call to holiness, seeing the future in Revelation will stimulate us to a holy life. If we have taken to heart God's call to do right, then seeing Jesus at history's end will deepen our desire to do right.

Illusion is always the enemy of holiness. We delude ourselves into thinking that what we do now is unimportant, that we need not make choices, that we need not act responsibly. We may feel that we only need settle down and wait for Christ to come, and all our problems will be over. But we are ministers, members of the body of Christ! As such, we are His voice and arms and legs and hands and feet in this time of grace. And the present time *is* of utmost importance. The present time is the Age of Grace, the time of God's kindness and tolerance and patience, meant to lead all persons to repentance (Rom. 2:4). In this age of God's extended kindness, you and I, as agents of His reconciliation, are called to grow more like Him and to com-

591

municate by our own love His love for others.

The unveiling of the righteous Judge in Revelation is not meant to overpower us with guilt because of what we may not have done in the past. It is rather to help us look ahead and motivate us to live for Christ and for others. He *is* coming soon; the judgment will then begin. While we yearn for that coming for our sakes, we also yearn to share the love of God with others *now* . . . for their sakes.

Revelation, then, is a book for believers. The Spirit and the Bride say, "Come." And because we are convinced that He will come soon, we dedicate ourselves to do right and to be holy. But for the others, the message of judgment will not melt the heart like the message of God's love. For them the Good News of Jesus' life and death, unveiled in John's Gospel as the coming of grace and love, is the message we have to share.

GROUP RESOURCE GUIDE

HELL
Identification: *Share with others*
In a single word, sum up your impression of "hell."

Exploration: *Probe God's Word*
Look up and read aloud the following passages that have to do with final judgment and the state of the lost. As each passage is read, work together to make a master list of major teachings.
> Daniel 12:1-2
> Luke 16:19-31
> Matthew 25:41-43
> 2 Thessalonians 1:5-10
> Revelation 19:11–20:15

Reaction: *Respond together to the Word*
Discuss: What purposes might God have in providing such clear pictures of eternal judgment? How are they supposed to affect our outlook? Our view of others? Our motivations and actions?

What, specifically, will be different in your life if you keep the Bible's vision of hell clearly in mind?

Adoration: *Worship and pray*
Consider the Father's grace and Christ's love. At great personal cost God has acted to save us from the fate our sins deserve. He deserves our thanks and our praise.

HEAVEN
Identification: *Share with others*
In a single word, sum up your impression of "heaven."

Exploration: *Probe God's Word*
Look up and read aloud the following passages that have to do with the blessing God intends to provide for his own at history's end. As each passage is read, work together to make a master list of major teachings.
> Daniel 12:1-3
> John 14:1-4
> Isaiah 65:17-25
> 1 Thessalonians 4:13-18
> Revelation 21:1–22:7

Reaction: *Respond together to the Word*
Discuss: What purposes might God have in providing such clear pictures of eternal blessing? How are they supposed to affect our outlook? Our view of others? Our motivations and actions?

What, specifically, will be different in your life if you keep the Bible's vision of heaven clearly in mind?

Adoration: *Worship and pray*
Consider the Father's grace and Christ's love. At great personal cost God has acted to take us into His family, and guarantees an eternity of blessing that we do not merit. He deserves our thanks and our praise.

PSALMS

Overview

The Psalms have a wonderful capacity to capture the reality of our human experience. Dr. Samuel Schultz notes in *The Old Testament Speaks* (Harper and Row) that "they express the common experience of the human race. Composed by numerous authors, the various psalms express the emotions, the personal feelings, attitudes, gratitude, and interests of the average individual. Universally, people have identified their lot in life with that of the psalmists."

In every experience of our own, no matter how deep the pain or how great the frustration, or how exhilarating the joy, we can find psalms which echo our innermost being; psalms which God uses to bring comfort or to confirm release.

The psalms were written over an extended period of time, most probably coming between 1000 and 400 B.C. They were written by several different authors, and at several times new groups of psalms were added to the collection. Seventy-three of the psalms were written by David. Forty-nine are anonymous.

The psalms were used in public worship in Israel, as well as for private devotions. They show us how intimate and free our relationship with God can be as we share every thought and feeling with Him.

Understanding the Psalms

The era of David, about 1,000 years before Christ, brought not only political change but also literary revival. Many of the psalms recorded in the Scriptures come from David's own pen, and many others were written during his reign.

The 150 psalms are organized into five books, which represent four later collections added to the first worship book. Book I (Pss. 1–41) is Davidic, compiled prior to his death. Book II (Pss. 42–72) was most likely added in the era of Solomon. Books III and IV (Pss. 73–89, 90–106) were probably collected during the Exile, and Book V (Pss. 107–150) in the time of Ezra. This last book is the most liturgical.

The various books of Psalms, then, are not organized by content but by the time they were added to the official worship collection. It is likely that many if not most of the psalms were used before the official compilations were made.

The structure of the books is just one of several things we need to know to understand this wonderful Bible book and its contents. We also need to have a grasp of the principles of Hebrew poetry, and some sense of the themes of the psalms.

Hebrew poetry. Unlike English poetry, which emphasizes rhyme and meter, Hebrew poetry relies on other characteristics for its impact. These are parallelism, rhythm, and figures of speech.

Parallelism. English verse manipulates sound, and emphasizes rhyme and meter. Hebrew poetry repeats and rearranges thoughts rather than sounds. There are several types of parallel arrangement of thoughts, with three being basic.

* *Synonymous parallelism* is the repetition of the same thought, repeating it in different words. For instance,

> But God in heaven merely laughs! He is amused by all their puny plans.
> Psalm 2:4 (TLB)

* *Antithetical parallelism* emphasizes a thought by following it with a contrasting statement. For instance,

> The lions may grow weak and hungry, but those who seek the Lord lack no good thing.
> Psalm 34:10

* *Synthetic parallelism* involves a more

complex pattern, in which thought is added to thought to develop an original expression. For example,

> He is like a tree planted by streams of water, which yields its fruit in season and whose leaf does not wither.
> Psalm 1:3

When reading the Psalms or any other Hebrew poetry, it is important to be aware of parallelism. Our understanding of the text, and our interpretation of it, hinges on sensing these thought patterns.

Rhythm. In the original text there are accent marks, which indicate stress to be placed on words and phrases. But this rhythm is not metrical; it cannot be distinguished in English translations.

Figures of speech. Hebrew poetry, like the Hebrew language itself, uses vivid images, similes, and metaphors to communicate thoughts and feelings. These, like parallelism, are easily translated into other languages, even though at times idiomatic uses may be obscure.

In reading Hebrew poetry, then, and especially in reading the Psalms, we need to be sensitive to these literary distinctives. We need to be aware of the role of repetition and imagery in the Psalms, and discover their meaning within the framework provided by these linguistic characteristics.

Themes of the psalms. While the books of Psalms are not organized by topics but by the era they were added to the official collection, the Psalms do show a number of repeated themes. So we can classify some psalms by their content. What types of psalms have been identified? Here are the major ones:

* *Praise psalms.* These focus on the person of God and praise Him by describing His nature or His qualities. This type of psalm is well illustrated by Psalms 33, 103, and 139, and by such expressions as:

> Praise the Lord, O my soul; all my inmost being, praise His holy name. Praise the Lord, O my soul, and forget not all His benefits—who forgives all your sins and heals all your diseases, who redeems your life from the pit and crowns you with love and compassion.
> Psalm 103:1-4

* *Historical psalms.* These review God's dealings with His people. Illustrations are Psalms 68, 78, 105, and 106, and such expressions as:

> In spite of all this, they kept on sinning; in spite of His wonders, they did not believe. So He ended their days in futility and their years in terror.
> Psalm 78:32-33

* *Relational psalms.* These psalms express the personal relationship which exists between the believer and God. They are illustrated by Psalms 8, 16, 20, 23, and 55, and such expressions as:

> Keep me safe, O God, for in You I take refuge. I said to the Lord, "You are my Lord; apart from You I have no good thing."
> Psalm 16:1-2

* *Imprecatory psalms.* These are psalms in which the worshiper calls on God to overthrow the wicked. Among them are Psalms 35, 69, 109, and 137. They contain such expressions:

> May those who seek my life be disgraced and put to shame; may those who plot my ruin be turned back in dismay. May they be like chaff before the wind, with the angel of the Lord driving them away.
> Psalm 35:4-5

* *Penitential psalms.* In these the psalmist expresses sorrow over his failures and confesses his sins to God. Examples are Psalms 6, 32, 51, 102, 130, and 143. They contain expressions like:

> O Lord, do not rebuke me in Your anger or discipline me in Your wrath. Be merciful to me, Lord, for I am faint; O Lord, heal me, for my bones are in agony. My soul is in anguish. How long, O Lord, how long?
> Psalm 6:1-3

* *Messianic psalms.* These psalms refer in some way to Christ, who is to come from David's family line. Many such psalms are indicated by references in the New Testament. Psalms which the New Testament in-

dicates refer to Christ are Psalms 2, 6, 16, 22, 40, 45, 69, 72, 89, 102, 109–110, and 132. Others may also have messianic elements or make prophetic reference.

* *Liturgical psalms.* These are psalms which were used in Israel's worship at special times of the year or on special occasions. While most of the psalms were used in public worship, these are linked with such events as coming up to Jerusalem for one of the annual festivals. Liturgical psalms may be illustrated by Psalm 30 (used in the dedication of the temple), 92 (a psalm for the Sabbath), and Psalms 120–134.

Personal Messages from the Psalms

The Book of Psalms has long been recognized as a guidebook for prayer. As we read the psalms, there are a number of very personal messages about prayer that come through with clarity and beauty.

It's all right to be human. The Bible tells us that in Creation God viewed man, the culmination of His creative work, and affirmed that work as "very good" (Gen. 1:31). Man, the Bible says, was made in God's image, and we are taught to value our humanity. As people we do bear a certain likeness to the Lord.

Sometimes, aware that sin has entered the race and warped mankind out of the intended pattern, Christians have come to view their humanity with shame and guilt rather than pride. A person who tends to locate the identity of mankind in our character as sinners, rather than in our nature as those who bear God's image, is likely to repress human feelings and emotions. Struggling for "control," such people may be uncomfortable with strong emotions and may attempt to hold them down or to deny them.

The Bible really does teach us to affirm our value and worth as human beings. Psalm 8 speaks in wonder that God should have created man "a little lower than the heavenly beings" and "crowned him with glory and honor." Hebrews 2:10 echoes the thought that we are never to let slip the awareness that God's intention in Christ is to bring "many sons to glory." Christ calls Himself our brother; He was "made like His brethren in all things" (2:17, NASB). Far from being ashamed of his humanity, the Christian is free to rejoice in who he is,

knowing that in Creation and in redemption God has affirmed our worth.

Such teaching passages might help us grasp this affirmation about man intellectually. But we are gripped by it when we read the Psalms! For here we see our own inner experiences openly shared without shame or hesitation, and we discover that God values man's inner life enough to record this dynamic record of it in His own Word.

When we read the Psalms and see in them our own emotions and struggles, we find a great release. It *is* all right to be human. It *is* all right to be ourselves. We need not fear what is within us or repress the feeling side of life.

There's a way out. One reason why emotions frighten us is that many people do not know how to express or release them. In our culture, the recognition and expression of feelings is not encouraged—especially of negative feelings. Feelings are feared. To feel anger well up within and to sense that we're on the verge of losing control is a frightening thing.

For Christians there is the added pressure of the notion that it's wrong to feel anger or sense tension. "If only I were a good Christian," we're liable to tell ourselves. "If only I were really trusting the Lord." So we feel guilt over the emotions that well up, and then, all too often, we try to deny this very important aspect of personhood.

Reading the Psalms carefully, however, we note that they often trace a process in which the writer begins with strong and almost uncontrollable feelings. We see how he struggles with them, and we see how he brings his feelings to God or relates them to what he knows of the Lord and His ways. In reading Psalms, you and I can learn how to handle our emotions creatively, and how to relate feelings to faith.

Psalm 73 is a good example of this "working through" process. It begins with the writer confessing that he has become envious of the wicked—certainly not an unusual experience when we face difficulties and then see everything going well for the person who cares nothing about God!

The psalmist shares:

For I envied the arrogant when I saw the prosperity of the wicked. They have no struggles; their bodies are healthy and strong. They are free from the burdens common to man; they are not plagued by human ills. Therefore pride is their necklace; they clothe themselves with violence . . . . They say, "How can God know? Does the Most High have knowledge?" This is what the wicked are like—always carefree, they increase in wealth. Surely in vain have I kept my heart pure; in vain have I washed my hands in innocence. All day long I have been plagued; I have been punished every morning.

Psalm 73:3-6, 11-14

How hard it seemed! What good was it to be good? Frustration, envy, self-pity—all had gripped Asaph, the Levite who wrote this psalm, and who now faced rather than repressed his inner state.

The passage goes on to explain how the writer handled these feelings. First of all, he tried to think the problem through, but "it was oppressive to me" (v. 16). He went to God with his problem, to pray at His sanctuary. There God gave him an answer. Asaph's thoughts were directed to the end toward which the sinner's life leads.

Surely You place them on slippery ground; You cast them down to ruin. How suddenly are they destroyed, completely swept away by terrors! As a dream when one awakes, so when You arise, O Lord, You will despise them as fantasies.

Psalm 73:18-20

The easy life of the scoffers had led them to forget God, and their success had not permitted them to sense their need of Him. The very wealth and ease which Asaph had envied were "slippery" places that Asaph's trials helped him to avoid!

This new perspective changed Asaph's feelings. His past feelings were "senseless and ignorant; I was a brute beast before You" (v. 22). His emotional reactions in this case had not corresponded with reality. Yet, when God showed Asaph reality, his emotions changed.

Yet I am always with You; You hold me by my right hand. You guide me with Your counsel, and afterward You will take me into glory. Whom have I in heaven but You? And earth has nothing I desire besides You. My flesh and my heart may fail, but God is the strength of my heart and my portion forever.

Psalm 73:23-26

Real life always holds such struggles for us. There is nothing wrong with them. The emotions we feel then are not bad; they are part of being a human being. The glory of the believer's privilege is that, because he knows God, his emotions can be brought into fullest harmony with reality. You and I can face all of our feelings—and find freedom to be ourselves with the Lord. What a privilege to be ourselves with God, and to experience His gentle transformation!

We can be honest with God. This is a third great message of Psalms. Just as we need not repress our feelings, we need not try to hide our feelings from God. He loves us and accepts us as we are—yet always so creatively that we are free to grow toward all that we want to become.

How freeing to realize that God's love is unconditional. He is concerned about every aspect of our lives, inviting us to share all that we are with Him, that in return He might share Himself with us and bring us to health and wholeness.

Psalms, then, speaks directly to our inner lives. The patterns of relationship we find there guide you and me in our prayer lives.

Like the poetry of other peoples, Hebrew poetry is not designed so much to communicate information as to share the inner life and feelings of its writers.

This characteristic of the Psalms is very important to us, and is a dynamic aspect of divine revelation. Through the Psalms we are able to see the men and women of Scripture as real people, gripped by the feelings that move us. We are also able to sense a relationship with God that is deeply personal and real. Every dimension of the human personality is touched when faith establishes that personal relationship. God meets us as whole persons—He touches our feelings, our emotions, our joys and sorrows, our despair and depression. Faith in God is not just an intellectual kind of thing; it is a relationship which engages everything that we are. Thus, in the Psalms we have a picture of the relationship to which God is calling us today—a relationship in which we have freedom to be ourselves, and to share ourselves freely with the Lord and with other believers.

Nine Special Psalms

This *Small Group Member's Commentary* concludes with an invitation to explore the personal meaning of nine very special psalms, which touch on several vital aspects of our relationship with the Lord.

Psalm 1 encourages us to consider the outcome of our choice of life's two possible paths: that of the wicked and that of the righteous. Each path has a distinct pattern, but the ends are dramatically different.

Psalm 23 is undoubtedly Scripture's most familiar image of a relationship with God, portrayed here as a Shepherd who guards and guides His own. Possibly no passage of Scripture has offered more believers more comfort than this brief, simple expression of trust in a loving God.

Psalm 32 calls us to look within and find the source of the emptiness and anguish that sin brings. This psalm shows us the healing pathway of confession, followed by a response to God's counsel which leads us out of the pit of despair to a fresh new life.

Psalm 35 is a unique invitation to express to God our frustrations and anger against those who persecute us. Many are troubled by the strong "negative" feelings expressed in this and other imprecatory psalms. And yet it is not right when we or others are victimized. This psalm shows us how to channel our emotions both wisely and righteously by committing our cause to the Lord.

Psalm 37 is a rich feast of insight into the nature of trust offered us by King David, who experienced multiple disappointments and setbacks, and yet he found inner peace in his relationship with the Lord.

Psalm 51 is perhaps Scripture's prime example of confession, and one of its clearest expositions of the freedom that we find in forgiveness. This public confession by David of this sin with Bathsheba reminds us that God can "create a pure heart" within us, whatever our past transgressions. And that only His new creation can cleanse and release us from our bondage to the sinful acts of our past.

Psalm 69 finds David in despair. His moving expressions of despondency remind us that our faith does not make us immune from tragedy, or from the anguish that is a part of every human life. Yet even this psalm, which lingers so long on David's pain, ends in praise and expressions of confidence in God. In the end, our despair too must give way to the realization that we are objects of God's unshakable love.

Psalm 73 touches on another common painful human experience: jealousy or envy caused by comparing our troubles with the life of ease apparently enjoyed by the wicked. The frustrated psalmist asks for us: What's the use of trying to please God if our life is filled with trouble and disappointment? The psalmist does find the answer. And in sharing it, gives each of us a new perspective on what is of value in life.

Finally, Psalm 89 captures the exalted spirit of praise that finds its purest expression in many of these great worship poems. As we enter into the worship experience of the psalmist, we are lifted up and given a unique taste of the glory that is found in loving, praising, and glorifying our God.

The psalms we explore in this *Small Group Member's Commentary* are an introduction only, not just to the wonders of this great Old Testament book, but also to the richness of sharing it with others. For it is together, as a people of God, that Old Testament saints celebrated their relationship with the Lord. And it is together, as God's new community in Jesus Christ, that we too celebrate and explore the wonders of our own relationship with the Lord.

LIFE'S CROSSROAD

Overview

The psalms reflect major themes of Old Testament life and thought. Perhaps no theme is more central to the Old Testament's concept of morality than the stark contrast that exists between the "wicked" and the "righteous."

These terms appear again and again throughout the older Testament. They remind us that while shades of gray may make some decisions difficult for us, the central issues of life are boldly drawn in vividly clear black and white. There is such a thing as the way of the righteous, and there is such a thing as the way of the wicked. These two pathways are dramatically different, not only in the goals toward which each leads, but also in the characteristics of the choices one makes along the way.

Today we may tend to drift through life, making decisions without a clear grasp either of their implications for the future or even of the fact that moral issues are involved. But the godly of Old Testament times never lost sight of the fact that every choice must be weighed by the righteous. For if we ignore the moral dimension of even ordinary choices, we may find ourselves wandering unaware along the path trodden by the wicked. And drawing nearer and nearer to their certain—and dreadful—end.

Commentary

Psalm 1, like God Himself, is concerned with blessing. That's why the very first phrase announces the happy fate of the person "who does not walk in the counsel of the wicked" (1:1). The Hebrew word, *ashrey,* can be translated "How happy." The very best in life, the deepest satisfaction, the richest joy, hinges on the moral decisions we make in response to God's revelation of his "righteous," or "right," way.

It's important when considering this to remember that God's moral standards are not impersonally *imposed* by a Deity who insists that His creatures behave as He wishes, simply because He is God. In fact, God's moral standards are an expression of God's character, and His earnest desire that the human beings He shaped in His image might experience a richly rewarding life here and hereafter. God's standards are intended not as chains to bind us, but as a key that unlocks our bondage to moral uncertainty and opens the doorway to blessing. So it is no wonder that the psalmist begins his exposition on life's most significant choice with the exclamation, "How happy!"

If we walk in the way God's Word illuminates we *will* be happy. If we walk in the way God's Word illuminates, we will find blessing. And, if we walk in the way God's Word illuminates, we will find a source of inexhaustible strength. Even in life's driest moments we will not wither away, but drawing stamina from the Lord we will survive and triumph.

The Old Testament illuminates the choice implied in this psalm in its frequent exploration of the words that characterize each option. We can choose the way of the wicked. Or we can choose the way of the righteous.

The way of the wicked vs. the way of the righteous. The Hebrew term most frequently translated "wickedness" in the Old Testament is *rasa*. This masculine noun occurs more than 250 times in the Old Testament, and is part of that Testament's vocabulary used to portray sin. The root on which this noun is constructed is *ra*, which means "evil" or "bad." When used of a person, it focuses on those particular moral flaws which move a person to injure other human beings. Sinful attitudes lie at the root of wickedness. But wickedness itself in the

Old Testament is acting in such a way that God's standards for the treatment of other people are violated. Thus "wickedness" does not look at an act in relationship to God, as do terms like "iniquity." Wickedness views acts in terms of their impact on others. In essence, wicked acts are criminal in character. They violate the rights of individuals, and threaten the whole fabric of justice that is to hold a community together. As we glance through the Bible's descriptions of wickedness, we see that the wicked are proud and vicious, and delight in dishonesty, in violence, in oppression, in extortion, fraud, and other sins that damage other human beings.

✄ *Group Activity: Recovery Group*
Steps 8 (list persons I've harmed) and 9 (make amends to people I've harmed) Job 31 contains the OT's clearest exposition of the way of the wicked. Remembering that "wickedness" is that which we do which harms others, work through Job 31:1-34 and develop a list of "wicked" acts. When complete, discuss how each act might hurt or harm others.

Individually go through the list. Whenever an item reminds you of specific harm you have done to another person, jot down his or her name and notes about the circumstances. Take time to do a thorough and honest appraisal.

Then circle the names of those to whom you can attempt to make amends.

Then in groups of five share at least one action for which you think you can make direct amends. Admit honestly what you did, how it harmed the other person(s), and what you plan to do to make amends. Let the others in your team of five give you feedback on your plan to make amends and make suggestions. Then you can help them consider how to make amends for any of the wicked acts they are willing to share.

Righteousness (*sedaq* or *sedaqah*) is a broader term, whose basic meaning in the Old Testament is abiding by God's standards as these are revealed to human beings in His Law. Yet when righteousness is contrasted with wickedness we can take it to imply the mirror image of those active, destructive, interpersonal acts.

In looking at Job 31, quite probably the Old Testament's clearest description of the contrasting ways of the wicked and the righteous, we note several important things.

First, the "heart" mentioned again and again (cf. Job 31:7, 9, 27) is critical. It is our inner orientation that controls our actions. The righteous keeps his or her heart pure, while the wicked are drawn away from righteousness by impure motives and desires.

Second, the tendency of the heart is revealed in our acts. It is futile to complain, "I wanted to do the right thing." The fact is that our actions reveal what we truly want. When our acts are sinful, they show that we wanted to turn away from God to creature comforts—and did so.

Third, wickedness can be displayed in a failure to act as well as in the actions we do take. Thus Job speaks of keeping his bread to himself and refusing to share it with the fatherless, or failing to provide the needy man with the warm clothing he needs to survive (31:17, 19). Righteousness not only requires us to do no harm, but to actively do good.

Thus the morality called for in Psalm 1 is not a passive thing. It is not simply refraining from doing what damages other persons. It is a commitment to help and to heal persons who are in need. The choice Psalm 1 calls for us to make is a strikingly active one. We are to travel the path of the righteous, not sit, uninvolved, alongside life's highway. It is the person who cares for others, and reaches out to aid them, who discovers the reality of that "How happy!" blessing promised in Psalm 1.

What kinds of blessing can the righteous expect? *The Expository Dictionary of Bible Words* (Zondervan, p. 534) sums up: "Righteousness brings many blessings. The person who serves God and chooses to live by his standards will be blessed (Ps. 5:12) and upheld (Ps. 37:17), will flourish (Ps. 92:12) and be remembered (Ps. 112:6). The righteous may have troubles, but the Lord will help them (Ps. 34:19), and they will neither be forsaken nor fall (Ps. 55:22). Proverbs adds that their home will be blessed (3:33), they will not go hungry (10:3), and their desires will be granted (10:24). Their prospect is joy (10:28), and they will never be uprooted (10:30). They will thrive (11:28) as they are rescued from trouble (11:8), and they will even have a refuge in death (14:32).

♥ *Group Activity: Support Group*
Recall a difficult decision that you are proud of having made. Describe it to your group, explaining what made the decision hard and why you are proud of having made it.

In teams of three take a page from a concordance that contains the phrase "the righteous," and look up each O.T. occurrence. List the things that these verses tell about the righteous—their character or actions, and the benefits they receive from doing what is right.

Then discuss: How many of the decisions you were proud of had moral dimensions? How many were made because of the conviction that what you did was the right thing? Also, why are you glad you made it? Were there immediate benefits, or simply the satisfaction of doing the right thing?

The Past—Two Pathways: Psalm 1:1-2
When we remember the nature of Hebrew poetry, we realize Psalm 1:1 capitalizes on *synthetic parallelism* to make its point. That is, the poet uses a series of roughly parallel thoughts that build a clear picture of what he intends to convey. At the same time, each of the phrases in this verse is progressive, and also captures the process by which a person is enmeshed in wickedness.

The process starts with "walking in the counsel of the wicked." Here the picture is one of chance association. We stroll along life's path, and come across those who are wicked. Thrown together, we walk together for a time. But soon the conversation of the wicked betrays his or her orientation to life. "Counsel" here has the meaning of "plan" or "purpose." It doesn't take long for us to sense the values and commitments—or lack of them—of the people we meet in life. What this phrase suggests is that the person who today finds himself enmeshed in wickedness once had an opportunity to make a better choice. We don't have to continue in our association with the wicked. We can walk with them. Or we can walk away from them and their influence.

The next phrase is "stand in the way of sinners." The word "way" (*derek*) is consistently used in a symbolic sense to indicate

conduct. Unless we break away from the wicked, we find our freedom to choose gradually draining away. We "stand," someone unwilling to act even though it is increasingly clear that the wicked, who never hesitate to harm others, are "sinners" who are in rebellion against God. Somehow association with the wicked dulls our conscience, and we begin to think and feel as they do.

The final stage of decline is expressed as sitting "in the seat of mockers." The mocker (cf. Prov. 15:12; 21:24) makes light of God's laws, dismissing them as meaningless and insignificant. The "seat of mockers" conveys the image of the elders of a local community in Old Testament times. There the wise men of the city sit, serving as judges as cases in dispute are brought to them, and instructing the young in the principles on which life in the community is conducted. The person who fails to break away from the wicked, and begins to conduct himself as a sinner, will in the end be so confirmed in wickedness that he himself will actively promote it!

The point the psalmist makes in this simple verse is profound. We can have *nothing* to do with wickedness. We must reject it, and reject those who follow its ways. Our life must take a different path.

Psalm 1:2 is strikingly different from 1:1. The first verse portrays a process. The second a commitment. That commitment is to the Law of the Lord, which the believer finds a "delight." The word translated "delight" here is *hapes,* which emphasizes a person's strong emotions about the object of his delight. This delight is expressed by constant meditation, or consideration, of God's Law "day and night." What God says to this person is gratifying, enriching, and pleasant. There's no sense of need to look elsewhere for something satisfying. Scripture "sticks to the ribs," meeting every need, unveiling what is beautiful and good. When our commitment is to the Word of God, and when we focus our attention on understanding and doing it, we will not be enticed by the wicked.

There is another fascinating contrast here. In 1:1 it is the wicked themselves—other persons—who lead the foolish down their pathway to sin and scoffing. Here what the believer relies on is not the purposes and plans of mere men, but the revealed purposes and plans of God. Commitment to God's Word protects us from being confused and led astray by other human beings, however persuasive they may be.

And so these first two verses confront us with a choice. Will we commit ourselves to God, take counsel from His Word, and reject those who follow the way of the wicked? Or will we hesitate, keep company for a time with the wicked, and thus be drawn into their way of life?

✳ *Group Activity:*
Singles/Single Again Group
On a chalkboard or sheet of newsprint draw a chart featuring three categories: "innocent but wrong," "consciously wrong," and "definitely evil."

Together brainstorm moral choices that singles have to make, and record each in one of these three categories. Try to be as exhaustive as possible, and include all of the kinds of moral choices you have faced as a single.

When the chart is complete, look at Psalm 1:1 and discuss the progression it implies. Look back at the chart, and discuss: What links exist between the actions in the first and second column? Between the second and third?

Finally, focus on 1:2. What guidance does Scripture give about each of the issues you have listed? If there isn't clear moral guidance available, how will you best handle each of the "innocent but wrong" situations you have described in column 1?

The Present—Consequences:
Psalm 1:3-4

The psalmist has looked at the choices his readers must make or have made. There is a fork in every man's road where a moral imperative is felt. It comes like a weight, bearing down on us, making us conscious that right and wrong are at issue. It isn't always a dramatic choice. A person can find himself almost unawares "walking in the council of the wicked." But even then there is always a point at which the consciousness of a need to choose arises. And that choice affects the whole of the rest of our lives.

Now the psalmist turns to imagery to convey the import of that choice on our present life. The person who commits himself to God's Law, and takes delight in it, is like a tree. But he is like a very special tree: one "planted by streams of water."

Much of the holy land is dry and desolate. In the hills rainfall is carried away down well-defined runs, which most of the year are filled only with dust and stones. The rains fall; the waters rush down the stream beds, and flood away, leaving them desolate. Yet in some parts of the land streams contain water all year round. Even in the dry season, alongside these streams a strip of verdant green can be seen; a ribbon of life stretched across a dead landscape. How fortunate the tree that does not depend on the vagaries of a fickle nature, which all too often in that land withholds rainfall. How fortunate to be a tree whose roots stretch out and down, to tap a constant supply of moisture. There, close to a stream of water, a tree produces fruit, and remains green whatever the weather may be.

This, says the psalmist, is the blessing we can expect as we delight in the Law of God. For God is the source of water; His Word the stream that holds the life-giving fluid. As we remain planted by that stream, we—and whatever we do—will prosper indeed.

But the wicked? Again the psalmist uses a familiar image. They are like chaff that the wind blows away.

One of the most familiar sights in Palestine during the grain harvest was the farmer, his figure outlined against the sky on some hilltop. After the stalks of grain had been cut they were carried to some usually bare and windy spot on a hilltop. There the stalks were trampled and crushed, often by oxen pulling heavy wooden sleds over the cut grain. The crushed stalks were then tossed into the air by the farmer. The wind plucked at them as they fell, allowing the heavy kernel of grain to fall in a heap, blowing the lighter straw a few feet away, and whipping the lightest bits of chaff away to disappear. The wicked are like this, the psalmist says. Bits of chaff, insubstantial, flimsy, so frail and fragile that they disperse in the slightest breeze. Their life is meaningless. Their time on earth is short. They are here today, but tomorrow they will be gone, and no remnant of them will be found.

What a powerful contrast. A tree, vital and green. Or chaff, lifeless and transitory. Will we choose righteousness and life, or

601

will we walk in the way of the wicked, and by that choice extinguish every hope for a meaningful life?

The Future—Judgment: Psalm 1:5-6

The Old Testament saint was deeply aware that judgment has present as well as future aspects. God as Moral Judge of His universe is involved in the events of every life, weaving the experiences that make up the fabric of our existence. The saint is not immune to suffering and loss. And yet the saint lives in the sure confidence that God is at work in his life, shaping events to bring us a better tomorrow and a glorious forever.

It's likely that these last two verses of this first psalm do focus on the present experience of sinner and saint. The wicked will not stand the judgments God will bring upon them during this life, much less in eternity. Without spiritual substance, the slightest breeze will blow them away. When tragedy strikes, and trials overwhelm, the wicked are without an anchor and without hope. The sinner who when first tempted did not separate himself from the "counsel of the ungodly" will himself be separated from "the assembly of the righteous."

There is, however, even more reassurance here for the believer. The Lord "watches over the way of the righteous." God is intently interested in all that happens to his own. If you will, the psalmist pictures the Lord, bending over so He can see, absorbed in the events of our lives. Even more, "watches" implies active involvement. God sovereignly shapes the "way of the righteous." He sees not only our todays, but also our tomorrows, and He so directs the flow of our personal history that what happens to us today contributes to the blessing He intends to bring into our lives in the future.

There is one more reassuring word as well. David says "the way of the wicked will perish." The wicked himself, as insubstantial as chaff, is blown away. But more, his "way" will itself come to an end! In the day of God's judgment wickedness itself will be done away with. No more will human beings harm one another by cruel or criminal acts, for earth will be populated by a redeemed humanity, and God will reign over all.

GROUP RESOURCE GUIDE

Identification: *Share with others*
Jot down the names of any persons with whom you presently associate, or have associated with in the past, in which the relationship troubles you morally.

Then share briefly what it is about the person or the relationship that gives you trouble.

Exploration: *Probe God's Word*
Together study the progressive decline implied in 1:1, checking answers to any questions in the commentary. Be sure you understand the implications of each phrase.

Reaction: *Respond together to the Word*
In teams of five, go back to the relationship you identified as troubling. Where do you feel you are in the relationship: walking, standing, or sitting?

Talk about that relationship and why you are still in it if it troubles you. What would it take to break it? Why have you hesitated so far? How is the relationship affecting you?

Affirmation: *Express love and concern*
Have sketched on the chalkboard a tree, filled with leaves and fruit, and also chaff blown in the wind. Share what you felt about yourself as you described the relationship you chose: Do you feel more like a tree when you consider the relationship, or like chaff? When others share do not give advice, but do make clear your concern for any who are troubled or hurting.

Adoration: *Worship and pray*
Read the whole psalm aloud, either in unison, or by taking one phrase in turn. Then meditate in silence on 1:6, praying silently for wisdom and strength to act in your troubling relationships in a way that pleases God and is in harmony with His Word.

STUDY GUIDE 96
Psalm 23

THE SHEPHERD PSALM

Overview

Certainly no psalm is as familiar. It is one of the first Scriptures memorized by the young, and perhaps the greatest comfort to the aged. In times of stress, in moments of danger, this simple poem penned by David three millenniums ago is the one literary work people of every tongue and nation are most likely to turn to.

The images of sheep and shepherd, so familiar a part of life in Old Testament or New Testament times, retains the power to convey a sense of security and love even in our own time. No matter how familiar this psalm may seem, it is a mine full of rich insights, worthy to be reexplored by any Christian study group.

Commentary

The shepherd psalm does not appear in a vacuum. Indeed, images of the sheep and shepherd are found frequently in both Testaments. Looking at the verses which deal with sheep and shepherds both literally and figuratively provides a background which helps us better sense the connotations of each verse of David's poem.

Sheep in Old Testament times. There are several different words for "sheep" in the Hebrew language. One, *keseb,* or *kebes,* is usually translated "lamb" and is found in passages that speak of animals offered up in sacrifice. While Jesus, the "Lamb of God," served as our sacrifice, there is no hint of God's surrendering up His people as burnt offerings. Another word which is used figuratively but only a few times is *seh.*

The most common Hebrew word for sheep is *so'n,* which means "small cattle," and is used only of domesticated flocks. This word often stands as a symbol for the people of God, as in Psalm 100:3 and Isaiah 53:6. It is this word that reminds us how significant sheep, and the persons who cared for them, were in ancient times. In the early times flocks and herds of domesticated animals were often the basis of a person's wealth. It was exactly so with Abraham and with Job.

Sheep and goats provided the wool that was woven into everyday clothing. Their milk sustained the family, and their meat was used in the highly spiced dishes served on special, happy occasions. Even the skin of the goat was scraped, cleansed, and sewed together to create a vessel that could contain water or wine, or be used in the transformation of milk into a type of yogurt. Hides were also tanned and then sown together to make tents. In short, sheep were more than valuable. They were vital to the well-being of the people who kept them, and the shepherds who were charged with their care guarded them lovingly.

One of the first impressions we receive, then, as we look at the role of sheep in ancient Israel, is that sheep were an integral and vital part of the life of a pastoral people. Even when Israel conquered the land of Canaan and the economy shifted to an agricultural base, many families in the upper highlands remained dependent on the flocks and herds they maintained. Sheep truly were important to and valued by the people of God.

How appropriate then that the psalmist says in Psalm 100:3, "Know that the Lord is God. It is He who has made us, and we are His; we are His people, the sheep of His pasture." We belong to God. And we truly are important to Him.

Characteristics of sheep. While biblical images of herds of sheep consistently emphasize their value, sheep themselves are described in less flattering terms. The Old Testament portrays sheep realistically as helpless, dependent, and none-too-wise creatures. Building on well known characteristics of these familiar animals, Isaiah remarks that "We all like sheep, have gone astray, each of us has turned to his own way" (Isa. 53:6). This tendency of sheep to wander off is also reflected in one of Jesus' most familiar stories—that of the 99 sheep and the one who goes astray:

What do you think? If a man owns a hundred sheep, and one of them wanders away, will he not leave the ninety-nine on the hills and go to look for the one that wandered off? And if he finds it, I tell you the truth, he is happier about that one sheep than about the ninety-nine that did not wander off. In the same way your Father in heaven is not willing that any of these little ones should be lost (Matt. 18:12-14).

This story is also well known, for it reveals God's attitude toward us despite our propensity for sin. We wander, but God searches for us. We sin, but God forgives. And when He finds us He takes us up in His arms. When He finds us and brings us to Himself He is not angry, but filled with joy over the lost one who has been rescued at last.

This inability of sheep to find their own way emphasizes our need for our Heavenly Shepherd. While God may delegate to human beings a role as undershepherd, and such ministry is required (cf. Num. 27:17), the Old Testament saint recognized the great truth affirmed by David in Psalm 23: "The Lord is my Shepherd."

The portraits of sheep and shepherds found in the Bible, then, emphasize the dependence of sheep and their weakness for going astray. Only by belonging to a shepherd, and following close to him, could a sheep be secure. Only when we can say with David, "the Lord is MY Shepherd," can we be safe from ourselves as well as from the dangers of life in this world.

David as a shepherd. David's psalm grew out of long personal experience with his father's flocks. It was typical in Old Testament times for younger sons, as they approached adolescence, to be given the task of watching the family flocks. David, as the youngest of eight sons in the family of Jesse of Bethlehem, was away "tending the sheep" when Samuel arrived at the family holdings to anoint him as the successor of the rejected King Saul. Many of David's na-ture psalms, as well as Psalm 23, undoubtedly grew out of this period of David's life.

Later, when David pled with Saul for the opportunity to face the Philistine giant Goliath, he explained his lack of fear:

Your servant has been keeping his father's sheep. When a lion or a bear came and carried off a sheep from the flock, I went after it, struck it, and rescued the sheep from its mouth. When it turned on me, I seized it by its hair, struck it, and killed it. Your servant has killed both the lion and the bear; this uncircumcised Philistine will be like one of them, because he had defied the armies of the living God. The Lord who delivered me from the paw of the lion and the paw of the bear will deliver me from the hand of this Philistine (1 Sam. 17:34-37).

The sheep were to be defended, even at the risk of one's life. And God, who cares for His people as a shepherd cares for his sheep, will defend the one who puts his trust in the Lord.

David's own years as a shepherd, as well as his identification of himself as one of God's sheep, provided the insights reflected in Psalm 23. David knew what it was to protect, and what it was to need protection. He understood God's heart, and he understood his own need. As we read his simple yet profound poem we too sense God's love and commitment to us, despite our own waywardness. And our vision of God the Shepherd protects us from despair.

Christ, the Good Shepherd. Of all the passages in Scripture that take up the image of sheep and shepherds, none is more significant than John 10. Here Jesus presents Himself as Shepherd, and shows us how great indeed the shepherd's commitment is to his sheep.

As shepherd, Jesus is the "gate for the sheep" (John 10:7). At night sheep were assembled in a corral of stones or thorny plants. The shepherd slept in the gate, interposing His body between the sheep and any predators. Jesus is Himself the "gate" for us; His body and blood is our protection from the evil one.

As shepherd, Jesus comes "that they may have life, and have it to the full" (John 10:10)." The shepherd's concern is not only to protect his sheep, but to see that they have all they need for maximum well-being. Jesus is concerned with our salvation, but also with providing an abundant life for us here and now.

As good shepherd, Jesus "lays down His life for the sheep" (John 10:11). David risked his life to protect his sheep from the lion and the bear. Jesus gave His life on Calvary to save us, His sheep, from the consequences of our sins. Despite the terrible cost to Himself, Jesus did not abandon us in our desperate need.

As good shepherd, Jesus knows us and is known by us (John 10:14-18). In Old Testament times shepherds did not drive their sheep from behind, but went ahead of them. The voice of the shepherd was familiar to the sheep, and because they recognized his voice they followed him. Yet perhaps even more significant is Jesus' claim to "know" His sheep. In biblical times it was not unusual for the herds of several shepherds to spend the night in the same enclosure. In the morning, as they filed out the doorway, each shepherd recognized the individual sheep that belonged in his flock. What's more, the individuality of each sheep was affirmed in the fact that it was not only recognized, but had been given a name.

What an encouragement for us. God does not view us as merely part of a herd. We are individuals to Him. He recognizes us, He names us, and makes sure when He calls His flock that each one of us recognizes His voice and trails close behind.

All this is background for David's comforting Shepherd's psalm. And with this background, we can see its rich promises even more clearly than before.

Psalm 23

The Lord is *my* shepherd (Ps. 23:1). Each word in this first phrase of David's psalm is significant.

"The." There is no uncertainty here, no fumbling among many gods for one that might be of help. Instead there is a quick focus on a single Deity: "the" Lord, who is a shepherd to me. In a time when many pagan deities vied for the allegiance of God's people, it was vital to focus on "the" Lord—the only one among the many who had the power to help. The only one who was real.

We may think that uncertainty was characteristic only of ancient times. It is not. Even now people hesitate between competing voices that cry out for their allegiance. Is money to be the thing I rest my hopes on? Is popularity? Love? Success? Health or happiness? Not at all. There is still only One who can serve as a secure foundation for our life, and that One is "the" Lord.

"Lord." The Hebrew is *Jahweh*, the personal name of God. As Lord, God has revealed Himself to us as Creator. As Lord, God acted at the time of the Exodus to show Himself able to intervene to help His own. As Lord, God comes to us as One who is always present. He is here, beside us now, powerful, ready and able to save.

"Is." This simple verb affirms both the reality and the presence of our God. God our Shepherd *is*. He is no invention of man's imagination. He is no creation of primitives who appealed to the supernatural because they failed to understand the "scientific" explanation for natural phenomena. Our God *is,* and because He is real, He can and will act for us. Our God *is,* and because He is real we can face an uncertain future with confidence and hope.

"My." The indifferent and distant God of the philosopher is unknown to Scripture. The God of the Bible is a Person, and as a Person He seeks a personal relationship with the human beings He created. The "my" of this phrase reminds us that it is in the context of a personal relationship with God, established and maintained by faith, that we experience His Shepherd care. When we can affirm that God is "my" Shepherd, all the benefits David recounts in this psalm immediately become ours!

"Shepherd." All that the culture, all that David's personal experience, and all that Jesus shows us about God's commitment to us, invests this image with its meaning. Here love, caring, intimacy, and self-sacrifice are woven together in a way that reassures us. Because God is our Shepherd, we are safe.

I shall not be in want (23:1). What a difference between "I shall not want" and "I shall not be *in* want." Like sheep who tend to "go astray," how quickly our attention wanders from God and His path as one of the world's delights presents itself before our eyes. We're so like children, trailing mommy through the store, fascinated by every bright object and crying out again and again, "I want that!"

God is not a "fairy godmother," present to wave a wand and magically produce whatever we desire. God is a Shepherd, whose wisdom is vastly greater than that of the sheep. He gives us not what we want, but what we need so we will not be in want.

He makes me lie down in green pastures, He leads me beside quiet waters (23:2). The structure here displays that parallelism which marks Hebrew poetry. The first phrase and the second are synonymous, each image deepening the sense of well-being David intends to convey. The wants of the person who has God for a Shepherd are guaranteed, and so in that relationship we find rest.

The images of rest are themselves fascinating. Lying down in green pastures is not only an image of plenty, but of satisfaction. Sheep stand to graze, bending their heads down to nip off the blades of grass. Only when they have had enough do they lie down, their hunger sated, comfortable and fully at ease.

Even the image of green is significant. Shepherds in Palestine ranged over the hills to find food for their sheep. Those hills are more often brown than green, and the sheep search among rocks for blades of grass that too often are dry and tasteless. What is more, sheep "overgraze." Unlike cattle, sheep bite the grass off so close to the ground that the roots are destroyed, and any range can quickly be stripped of its ground cover. But God leads us, His sheep, to green pastures. We cannot overgraze in God's fields, for where He is there is an ever-abundant supply of all we need to sustain our life and satisfy our appetite.

There is a similar message in the "quiet waters." Most streams in Palestine rush quickly over rocky stream beds, filling them during the rainy season, but draining away during the hot summer months. Quiet waters are found only where the land is relatively flat, and where a pool or lake, or living spring, fills a hollow and maintains it throughout the year. God brings us too to quiet waters, and wherever the steps we take in following His lead may take us, we find ourselves beside an inexhaustible supply of what we need to quench our inner thirst.

He restores my soul. He guides me in paths of righteousness for His name's sake (23:3). In Hebrew the soul, or *nepes*, is not an immaterial part of man that survives after death, but rather a term better translated as "person," "self," or "being." It is the very essence of the individual person that is intended by "soul."

The Hebrew word translated "restore" here is *sub*, one of the most common of Hebrew verbs. Its basic meaning is one of movement, spatially or spiritually. Man is a wanderer, prone to stray away from moral and spiritual moorings. Yet God the Shepherd restores us, working in our hearts to move us away from that which harms us, back to Him and His ways.

David describes God's restorative work as guiding us "in paths of righteousness." The basic idea here is one of straightness, of happy conformity to the pattern of life God has laid down for us in the Law. And why does God so guide us? "For His name's sake."

The "name" in Hebrew culture was understood to capture the essential nature of the person or thing named, and so to represent him or it. We would put it this way: God restores us spiritually and guides us into righteousness *because it is His nature to do so.* God is a righteous and loving person, totally committed to good. How natural then that He would commit Himself to restore His straying sheep, and guide those who are His own into righteous ways.

Even though I walk through the valley of the shadow of death, I will fear no evil (23:4a). Sheep even though beloved by a shepherd remain sheep. And human beings, though loved by God, remain creatures. This means that we share with sheep a terrible vulnerability. We are subject to the laws of the physical universe and so must one day walk into the shadows toward an inevitable biological death.

What relationship with God does for us in our vulnerability is to free us from the fear of "evil." The Hebrew root translated evil, *ra'*, is extremely complex. On the one hand "evil" is applied to moral acts which violate God's standards and His intent for humankind. On the other hand "evil" is used to describe the consequences of sin. Adam's violent rejection of God and His ways in Eden, and the heritage of sin which corrupts every human being, makes each of us vulnerable to the tragedy, the distress, the calamity and harm that necessarily follow the doing of wrong. The weak are victimized, the strong take but are denied satisfaction, and each man faces the certainty of biological death, made fearsome by the threat of judgment to come.

Yet David cries out, "I will fear no evil." In becoming one of God's sheep, in experiencing the restoration God brings, and in faithfully responding as God's Word guides us into righteous paths, death loses its fearfulness. There is "no evil" which can befall us that is serious enough to break the bond trust has established between us and God. He is our Shepherd now. He will be our Shepherd as death approaches. And even after our body feels death's cold grasp God will be our Shepherd, and snatch the essential "me" away to be with Him.

For You are with me; Your rod and Your staff, they comfort me (23:4b). The sting of threat of evil is drawn in looking up, and realizing that even as death's shadow falls across our frame, "You are with me." It is the presence of God the Shepherd that comforts us.

But why the "rod and staff"? As a shepherd David had carried rod and staff. This was a heavy instrument, an aid to walking along the way, but used primarily in defense of the sheep. The sturdy rod is a reminder to David of God's protective power. The God who walks with us is not unarmed. Whatever danger may threaten He is equipped, as is the human shepherd with a rod and staff, to protect His sheep.

How comforting to remember just who it is that is with us. We never walk alone. Nearby, just ahead and leading our way, is the God whose imagination shaped the universe and whose spoken word called it to reality. No power in heaven or earth can compete with His power. We are utterly, totally safe.

No, we are not immune from trouble. We are not spared death. But the one thing we need not fear is "evil." In every experience our Shepherd commits Himself to supply us with what we need, and to translate what we fear into the good we were not wise enough to desire.

You prepare a table before me in the presence of my enemies. You anoint my head with oil; my cup overflows (23:5). Now David leaves the image of the Shepherd with his

sheep to call up another familiar scene.

In Old Testament times hospitality was both a virtue and an obligation. Even the stranger who came to the door was to be welcomed, fed, and housed. How much more the friend would be welcomed and entertained.

But hospitality meant even more than offering a passerby a meal. When a person came into your home and shared food, you accepted the obligation of protecting him. In various cultures the specific obligation varied. Perhaps it was for three days, perhaps five. And perhaps one was only obligated to protect a table-guest until he had traveled a certain distance from your home. But throughout the ancient world a host accepted certain obligations to his guest, and those obligations were some of the most binding of society.

Struggling to explain the security David felt because of the presence of God, the psalmist envisioned himself a table-guest of the Lord. God Himself had prepared a table, and as host invited David to partake. David was "in the presence of my enemies." But suddenly their enmity was meaningless to him. He sat at God's table. He was under God's own protection! What could his enemies do to harm him? Nothing at all!

There is even more. David is a guest whose head God Himself has anointed. The immediate allusion is to God's choice of David as King, confirmed when Samuel anointed his head with sacred oil. But even in the context of guests in the home, anointing has significance. It was a mark of special favor for the host to provide a guest with sweet-smelling oil with which to anoint his head and beard. It was an even greater mark of favor if the host himself performed the act, rather than leaving it to a servant. David reminds us that the relationship we have with God is one marked by deep love and full commitment. His love for us cannot be plumbed, for we are of infinite value to our Lord. He has chosen to shepherd us. He has invited us to His table. In each role He has committed himself fully to protect us from whatever might do us harm, and affirmed for all time that He truly cares.

Surely goodness and love will follow me all the days of my life, and I will dwell in the house of the Lord forever (23:6). What can we look forward to, as sheep of the Divine

Shepherd, and table-guests in His universe? We can confidently expect goodness and love to be our companions throughout this life. And after this life is over, we can expect to dwell in God's presence. Forever.

It is true that the parallelism of Hebrew poetry makes it likely that the same basic thought was in David's mind as he penned these words. And yet, under the inspiration of the Spirit, they surely convey more.

How long are the days of our life? They are hardly limited to the few fleeting moments we spend on this earth. The days of our life, because our life is bound up in that of God Himself, extend beyond time and flow on, unchecked, throughout eternity to come. The goodness and love we experience here are but the foretaste of a future that will be glorious beyond our capacity to imagine.

GROUP RESOURCE GUIDE

Identification: *Share with others*
Take a consecutive number between one and five as you go around the group. Match your number with one of the words below, taken from the first verse of Psalm 23.

1	2	3	4	5
The	Lord	Is	My	Shepherd

Think about the implications of the word that matches your number, and share what that word suggests to you in context.

Affirmation: *Express love and concern*
Tell any person in your group who reminds you of a shepherd what it is about him or her that conveys that impression.

Exploration: *Probe God's Word*
Listen as someone previously prepared gives a brief summary of the meaning of the biblical image of sheep and shepherd (see commentary).

Then divide into six teams. Each is to look at one of these verses: 1, 2, 3, 4, 5, or 6. Each team is to seek to draw as much meaning as possible from its verse, and take notes for a report to the rest. *Only when you have drawn as much from your verse as possible* should you look at the commentary for further information.

When you have found as much in the verse as possible, discuss how its images might be applied by Christians today.

Reaction: *Respond together to the Word*
Have one person in your team sum up your findings about the verse. Then briefly relate an experience in which you personally have found one of the truths suggested in your verse meaningful to you.

Adoration: *Worship and pray*
Meditate on God as your Shepherd. Then as a prayer recite Psalm 23 together.

THE PSYCHOLOGY OF SIN

Overview

"Sin" is a familiar term for Christians. It is part of our vocabulary, even though the idea may be scoffed at by the people of the world. But perhaps even our perspective is slightly distorted, with so much emphasis on the acts which are wrong, and on the punishment sin merits, that we overlook the devastating inner impact that sin has on the human personality.

This is not something that the psalmist overlooks. In fact, David devotes one of his most significant psalms to sharing the psychological impact on his own life of sinful acts. As we trace David's thoughts, and listen for echoes of his emotions in our own experience, we better understand both the psychological impact of our sins—and the wholeness which comes when we release ourselves to God and accept His forgiveness.

Commentary

One of the greatest dangers to the maturing of our faith is our tendency to be satisfied with pat answers and with superficial understanding. One reason why the personal evangelist may have such a difficult time in reaching others is that he or she approaches this issue of "sin" on just such a level.

You've done wrong.

You deserve to be punished.

Jesus took your punishment.

If you don't accept Him, you'll go to hell. Each of these propositions is, of course, absolutely true. But somehow the argument doesn't seem compelling to most non-Christians. "You've done wrong" is often met with agreement, but then dismissed with "But so has everyone else," or "I'm a lot better than George," or "But on balance, I'm more good than bad."

"You deserve to be punished" is often rejected out of hand. "My sins are little ones. Criminals deserve to be punished, but I don't." In fact, many people believe God owes them, and if things don't work out they wonder why God should punish *them!*

Without a sense of the sinfulness of sin, and without dread of the punishment that lies ahead, the good news that Christ took our punishment seems bland and meaningless to the secular man. Hell seems far away, and besides, unconvinced of the seriousness of their sins, most folks expect to muddle through to heaven on balance, their merits outweighing their demerits, even if the scales barely tilt in their favor.

And so the Christian experiences great frustration in trying to share with the unconverted. Our special vocabulary uses words that have such meaning to us, but seem unintelligible to the lost. We speak of sin, they think of crime. Sin and its consequences remain unreal, and the lost man or woman sees no need for Christian salvation.

Even the saints of the Old Testament were sometimes confused on the issue of sin and its consequences. Job struggled to understand the devastating tragedies that struck him and failed, primarily because he saw sin and punishment in materialistic terms. If a person sinned, something bad should happen to him. But because Job had not sinned, Job felt God was acting unfairly in permitting him to suffer. Habakkuk saw the sin that permeated his society despite a superficial religious revival, and asked how God could permit this to happen. When told that God was not overlooking Judah's sin, but was about to send the Babylonians against His people to punish them, Habakkuk was even more concerned. He could understand the coming exile as just punishment. But how could God let the Babylonians, surely a more evil people than the Jews, succeed in their sinfulness?

It is in the Book of Habakkuk that we are shown most clearly the principles underlying the reality David shares with us in Psalm 32. And it is this reality that deepens our understanding of sin and its consequences—and provides a significant, new approach to effective evangelism.

Habakkuk has posed his challenge to God: "How can you let evil people [the Babylonians] get away with sin?" (Hab. 1:12-17) As Habakkuk listens, God explains that he is not letting the Babylonians "get away with" anything! Even in their moments of greatest apparent success, the wicked are *being* punished!

But the present punishment God imposes on the wicked is not one of disaster or tragedy. No building collapses to kill them, no dread disease robs them of health until they repent. No financial disaster wipes out their wealth. To all outward appearances, the wicked may continue to prosper. No, the present punishment God imposes on the wicked is *inner* punishment; a punishment that has a devastating *psychological* impact, either directly within the individual's psyche, or indirectly, by setting up currents in personal relationships which draw the wicked inexorably to certain doom.

What are these hidden, inner punishments that God imposes on the wicked? First, there is *dissatisfaction* (2:4-5). However much the wicked gain, they remain greedy and unsatisfied. Success does not bring fulfillment, but only makes the fires of ambition burn brighter. What a terrible punishment this is. Even when one gains everything he or she thought she wanted, it is never enough. Down deep there is always an ache, always a yearning, never a sense of having arrived or of being at rest.

But Habakkuk continues. The wicked so distort social relationships that they arouse hostility, and so guarantee future repayment of the wrongs they have done others (Hab. 2:6-8).

Deep down the wicked are aware of their vulnerability. They desperately pile up wealth and power, intent on making themselves secure. But every effort is futile, and the very stones of the strongholds they construct cry out against them (Hab. 2:9-11). Isaiah 57:20-21 puts it this way: "But the wicked are like the tossing sea, which cannot rest, whose waves cast up mire and mud. 'There is no peace,' says my God, 'to the wicked.' "

What is more, material possessions are all the wicked have, and *material things decay* (Hab. 2:12-14). The spiritual realm is true and lasting reality, this world a passing illusion. Everything which the wicked grasp at, even when they hold it in their desperate clutch, withers in their grip.

In the end, even in this world, the wicked receive *repayment in kind* (2:15-17). The financial empire built on fraud collapses, leaving the man who defrauded others bankrupt as well. The dictator who pursued and killed his enemies is himself pursued by armed rebels. The heartless lover who violates the trust of women and leaves them weeping alone comes to his life's end, with no one to hold his hand and no one to weep beside his grave.

Most of these are hidden, subtle punishments. Some are never witnessed by others, for they are buried deep within the individual heart. Yet even if the "rich and famous" never speak of inner pain, an awful emptiness and anguish do exist. Sin's terrible psychological consequences are utterly, terribly real—and every human being experiences them.

The difficulty is that they are felt—but not connected to man's alienation from God and commitment to wrong ways. The secular man goes not to the priest, but to the therapist, there to be told his feelings are a heritage of old, outworn ideas about right and wrong. He is given absolution by being told to do what he wants, and given pills to dull pain. But the ache remains. For there is no healing for sinners other than the blood of Christ, no remedy but forgiveness, no hope but in grace.

Ø Group Activity:
Missions/Outreach Group
Brainstorm for those emotions and inner evidences that a person is out of harmony with God. For instance, the lack of peace mentioned in Isaiah 57, the dissatisfaction and sense of vulnerability identified by Habakkuk, etc.

Then divide into teams, each of which is to further explore one psychological phenomenon you have identified. How does this show up in a person's life? How does it affect his or her relationships? Sense of self? How could we present it in such a way that most people who experience this would identify themselves as victims?

During the week meet together as a team and explore the theme in Scripture. What does the Bible say about peace and how to find it? What does the Bible say about security? and satisfaction? When you have studied your topic thoroughly, take a shot at writing a tract or a 90 second radio spot. Then try them out — and see if this approach will better convince the sinner of his or her need of the Savior.

Psalm 32

This psalm, sometimes called the "testimony of a forgiven sinner," is developed in five distinct sections. Verses 1 and 2 express the joyful relief experienced when a sinner is reconciled to God. Verses 3-5 describe the effects of undealt with sin, using physical terms to express the psalmist's inner, psychological sufferings. Verses 6-7 are evangelistic, pointing the reader to God as One who protects the penitent from every danger. Verses 8-9 express God's promise, and a warning. The Lord will surely guide His own, but with guidance *from* God comes a responsibility to be responsive *to* God. Verses 10-11 sum up. There are but two pathways open to man. The way of the wicked not only leads to eternal punishment but is paved with "many woes." But the righteous, who trust God, are surrounded by the Lord's unfailing love, and so go on their way rejoicing.

The relief of reconciliation (Ps. 32:1-2). It's not surprising that the psalmist begins by expressing relief, and ends this psalm with an utterance of joy (v. 11). When you or I feel a sense of despair, everything seems dark, and all we can think or talk about is distorted by our pain. But when the darkness lifts, and the anguish is behind us, it's as if a great weight were lifted. Then, basking in the sunshine, we feel buoyed up, cheerful and bright. In fact, it is release from pain that often gives us our happiest moments, and we rediscover blessings we had begun to take for granted. The sun shines brighter. The song of the birds seems more cheerful. And we notice the delicate hue of flowers, and wonder why we'd glanced at them so casually before.

This is the tone that pervades the first two verses of this psalm, and David celebrates his release from an inner turmoil that had darkened his days, and filled his sleep-less nights with gloom. For here, as is usual in the Psalms, "Blessed is" (*'asere*) means "How happy" or "Happy is the one." David is very clear about what it is that has made him happy. Three different Hebrew nouns are used to indicate "sin," and three different verbs indicate how God has dealt with sin.

The nature of sin. The three nouns used here indicate "rebellion," "failure," and "deviation from the right path." Whenever we think of sin, it's important to keep all three in mind.

Sometimes we are aware of sinning willfully. We are aware that what we are considering is wrong. We tell ourselves we won't do it. Yet somehow we let ourselves get into a situation where we have the opportunity to sin — and in that moment our resolve dissolves, and we consciously choose to do what we told ourselves we would never do. These are sins of rebellion.

Sometimes we honestly try to do what is right and good. We understand God's ways, we approve of them, and we try to keep them. But an unexpected word of gossip slips out. Or we realize too late we've failed to help a friend. In a moment of selfishness we've turned our back on another person in need, or told a "little lie" when the truth was too painful to reveal. These are sins of failure, or falling short.

Sometimes without being consciously aware the whole pattern of our lives shifts and changes. The moment comes when we realize that we've lost contact with our Christian friends, and have no time for fellowship. Or that in an attempt to fit in we've neglected to witness for our Lord. TV has squeezed into the time we once spent with God, and prayer has become a casual, infrequent exercise. The pattern of our life has shifted away from the path of godliness. These are sins of "deviation."

And we are vulnerable to them all.

Soon the psalmist will remind us what happens when we let these sins retain their grip on our lives. But now he celebrates. He had sinned. He had rebelled. He had failed. He had wandered from God's path. But God, in grace, provided a remedy!

The nature of forgiveness. The three different verbs David uses help us understand the nature of forgiveness. These verbs suggest "lifting up" or "carrying away," "blotting out," and cancellation of a debt.

The Hebrew verb *nasa'*, "to lift up" or "carry away," is found over 650 times in the Old Testament. It is linked with sin in three different contexts. When human beings act in evil ways they "take up" sin, and it becomes a burden they carry. But the guilt or punishment of sin can be "taken up" and "carried" by a substitute, as the Old Testament sacrificial system illustrated (Lev. 10:17; Isa. 53:4). And, God Himself can "take up" our sins, by His action taking them away. This is the foundation of the forgiveness we are offered by God. Through His gracious action in Christ, God has taken away the very acts of sin that make us guilty, and by punishing our sins in Christ has released us from the threat of judgment. Even our sins of open rebellion, the psalmist reminds us here, "are forgiven" (v. 1) – taken away by God, and no longer borne by you and me.

The Hebrew verb *kapar* means "to cover," and is associated in the Old Testament with sacrifices of atonement. It is found some 150 times in the Old Testament, and there suggests removal of both ritual defilement and personal sin. Here David praises God for his failures, those sins represented by falling short of his own as well as God's intended goal, are atoned for by the Lord and so removed.

A verbal phrase is used to give the final image of the forgiveness David has experienced. Those sins of deviation from God's path are not "counted against" David. The language is in effect a bookkeeping term: the debt David owed has been canceled. God in forgiving forgets, and so completely wipes out the debt we owe that there is not even any record left of our wrongs.

It's no wonder then that David celebrates! He has sinned against God. Like the rest of us he has rebelled, failed, and deviated from the path of godliness. But relief floods David's soul as he realizes anew that God has acted to deal with his sins. God has lifted the burden from David's back. He has covered over David's failures. And he canceled every penny of David's debt.

God, in Christ, has done the same thing for you and me. No wonder we Christians rejoice! We are a forgiven people. We are free of our past, free to face the future with our hand comfortably resting in God's own.

✂ *Group Activity: Recovery Group*
Step 3 (decide to turn my life over to God's care)
List the three kinds of "sin" described by the nouns in Psalm 32:1-2 on the chalkboard. Discuss, till everyone has some idea of the kind of thing described. Then privately list acts of your own which fit each category. Be thorough, and honestly list as many acts of rebellion, as many failures, and as many deviations from God's path as you can recall.

Without telling specific sins you listed, tell how looking back on them makes you feel. Pessimistic? Optimistic? Ashamed? Etc. Make a list of the words group members suggest.

Now match the three verbs of these verses to the nouns, and discuss until each person understands the nature of the forgiveness God provides. Discuss too how assurance that the sins of our past are gone might affect our feelings about ourselves and our future – those words just listed by the group.

Take the opportunity now to confess each sin you have listed to God, asking Him to keep His promise and take away, cover, and wipe out every sin. When you have done this, tear the list into tiny pieces, and mixing them with the pieces of lists torn up by others in your group, burn them.

In confessing sins and accepting forgiveness we accept God into our lives. How gladly we can now turn our lives over to Him!

The effect of unconfessed sin (32:3-5). The Old Testament more than once uses medical terms in a figurative way to describe spiritual condition. Isaiah says of the nation of his day, "From the sole of your foot to the top of your head there is no soundness – only wounds and welts and open sores, not cleansed or bandaged or soothed with oil" (Isa. 1:6). It is not surprising then that David adopts the same figures of speech to describe the psychological impact of sin on his own life.

"When I kept silent" reflects a choice. David had decided to deny his sins, and to pretend to himself and others he had done nothing wrong. In that state of denial he refused to bring his sins to God for forgiveness and healing. And so David suffered the pains experienced by any person whose spiritual life is unbalanced; who is out of fellowship with God, and alienated from the Lord.

The state of denial and the inner unease that grows out of undealt with sin is something known by Christians as well as by unbelievers. The rift is far greater in the latter case, for the unsaved have as yet no contact with God and no hope of relief. But any rift in our own relationship with God brings inner pain. Only when we are in a state of fellowship with God will we experience His peace.

David's description is powerful, and awakens memories in us all. All might have seemed well to observers. But deep within

> my bones wasted away
> through my groaning all day long.
> For day and night
> Your hand was heavy upon me;
> my strength was sapped
> as in the heat of summer.

Somehow none of us are able to go it alone. When sin breaks the bond that holds us close to God, and we are abandoned to our own puny resources, we soon do find ourselves in the grip of unease and inner pain.

As long as we keep silent, as long as we deny to ourselves and others that we have done wrong, we remain spiritually sick and debilitated. Only in turning to God is there hope that we can be made whole and well.

At last the anguish was so great that David was forced to be honest with himself and honest with God. And so he says, "I acknowledged my sin to You." When David did this, honestly facing his failures and exposing himself to God, "You forgave the guilt of my sin."

Earlier David used a phrase that is vital for us to understand. He expressed joy in forgiveness, announcing the blessing experienced by the person whom God forgives, "and in whose spirit is no deceit." This phrase is vital, for it helps us understand the essential nature of confession. You see, it is easy for us to make excuses for our sins. It's so easy to blame our anger on someone else, saying that they "made" us angry. It's so easy to pretend that what we feel is "righteous indignation," and that our vindictiveness is motivated only by a "desire for justice." Yet however we relabel sinful acts to hide their true nature, sin re-

mains sin. And the only person we deceive is ourself!

But if we are deceived, how can we confess our sins? If we pretend to do no wrong, how can we bring the wrongs we do to God and claim the forgiveness He promises us? And—if we continue to deceive ourselves—what will we do when our lives too are marked by moaning, when our strength is sapped, and when fears and dissatisfaction testify that we no longer have our hand in the hand of God?

So the blessings of forgiveness truly are reserved for the one "in whose spirit is no deceit." We need to look honestly and fearlessly at ourselves. We need to examine our acts. And whereever, or whenever we discover sin, we need to bring that sin to God, that we might immediately be forgiven and blessed.

An appeal to the godly (32:6-7). The godly are now encouraged to "pray to You," eagerly seeking God "while You may be found." The point is not that God will move to some new and hidden abode. The point is that if we keep moving away from God, we won't know where to seek Him!

And if we remain close to God? Then even when disaster strikes the land, we will not fear. When our inner life is right with God, external circumstances cannot shake us. Our confidence in the Lord remains firm, and we know that He will protect us from trouble and surround us with songs of deliverance (32:7).

God's promise, and warning (32:8-9). Sometimes sin is rebellion. Sometimes failure. Sometimes deviation from a known path. But few if any of our sins are rooted in true ignorance. One of the things God has done is to "instruct you and teach you in the way you should go." (ref.???)

This promise has both general and personal dimensions. Its general application is to all humankind, for God instructs man in morality both by giving every person an inner moral sense, and by giving humanity itself a specific, special revelation of His will in Scripture. The unbeliever may scoff at biblical concepts of right and wrong. But in most societies there is some knowledge of what God's standards are. Christians especially, who study the revelation of God's will given to us in Scripture, are instructed and taught in the way we should go.

Yet another aspect of this promise is personal. God knows each of us intimately. He knows the choices we must make, many without clear guidelines provided in Scripture. And so God says, "I will counsel you." When we do not know which way to turn, if we are living in fellowship with the Lord we can always turn to Him. He is watching over us, and He will show us the choice we are to make.

But with this promise comes a warning. We are not to be "like the horse or the mule." The beast does not and cannot sense the will of God, but must be controlled with bit and bridle. God does not control us this way. He does not force. He does not demand. He counsels and guides. And only when we are looking to Him, sensitive and willing to do His will, can we know the direction He wants us to take.

David's summary. The psalm began with a happy cry, an exclamation uttered by David who had reclaimed his position as a forgiven man by confessing his sins to God, and rediscovering the joy of fellowship with Him. The psalm ends in the same way, as David turns his back on the woes known by the wicked, and rejoices in the Lord whom he now follows once again.

Once again David is aware that he is surrounded by the Lord's unfailing love. He has rejected deceit, and faced his sins. He has acknowledged his sins to God, accepted forgiveness, and David has been healed.

May we find inner healing too, and the grace we need to abandon the self-deceit that steals our peace and isolates us from the joy others experience in the Lord.

GROUP RESOURCE GUIDE

Identification: *Share with others*
Look at a copy of Psalm 32, in which a wider space separates each of these verses: 1-2 from 3-4 from 5 from 6-7 from 8-9 from 10-11. Decide which of these sets of verses best describes where you are in your inner life right now.

Share briefly which verses you chose, and why. Then join a team of others who chose the same verse(s) you did, to discuss more thoroughly where you are spiritually just now, and what it is like.

Exploration: *Probe God's Word*
Hear reports from three persons who have prepared previously. One report should be on the nature of sin and forgiveness. One report should be on the inner consequences of unconfessed sin. One report should be on the dangers of self-deceit and the importance of honesty in our relationship with God. Each person who prepares a report should base it as much as possible on Psalm

32, but can draw on other passages. For suggestions, see commentary.

Reaction: *Respond together to the Word*
After the reports are heard, return to your team and discuss. Which report is most relevant to the experiences you've shared in your team? How might the truths explained be put into practice? What difference might acting on them make?

If you wish, you might invite the person who gave a report of special interest to you to join the group, and then further question him or her.

Adoration: *Worship and pray*
Choose one word from this psalm, and meditate on it for three minutes. Then share briefly what that word tells you about God and your personal relationship with Him.

When all have shared, let those who wish to pray in closing do so.

Psalm 35

WHEN LIFE ISN'T FAIR

Overview

To say that "life isn't fair" is true—and a truism. Everyone experiences circumstances that crush dreams. Everyone has at some time been mistreated by others, perhaps even severely oppressed or persecuted. At times like these it's not surprising that we feel frustrated. It's not surprising that we feel anger at our oppressors or even at God.

Christians have often been upset having such "negative" feelings. Shouldn't the believer, whose trust is in God, simply bless his or her enemy and keep on smiling? Shouldn't the sting of injustice be drawn by our knowledge that God is Sovereign and in control, and so lead us to praise Him even in our pain?

Perhaps. But such a response isn't easy. And, as the psalms suggest, there is often a process that we must work through before we find peace. Anger at injustice, even when we are the victim, may well be justified! The question is, what can we do with our anger?

Psalm 35, which has been dismissed by some as "somewhat monotonous and repetitive," is a poem which grows out of an experience of life's unfairness. The psalmist rides the same emotional roller coaster we do in such circumstances. He alternates between sorrow, anger, cursing, and thanksgiving. In it all, he struggles, as we do, to relate life's unfair experiences to the Lord.

Commentary

"I've got a right to be angry" is something more than one person has exclaimed. In three major sections, David explains his frustration and the anger that have moved him to appeal with such agitation to the Lord. Verses 1-10 contain an appeal to God for protection. His enemies are unjustly trying to bring him down. Verses 11-18 are a complaint. Men who were once David's friends have turned against him, and are now his enemies. Verses 19-28 contain another urgent appeal, for David's opponents are accusing him falsely, and only God knows the truth. We can identify with David in each of these experiences. We've been surprised when others to whom we've done no harm treat us as an enemy. We've been hurt when friends have turned on us, telling lies or spreading untrue gossip. And we've felt the loneliness that overwhelms when everyone seems ready to believe the lies, and no one will listen to the truth. In times like these hurt, anger, self-pity, hostility, and a host of other "negative" emotions may well compete for dominance.

The psalm never suggests that God is angry with us for our reaction to injustice. But it does suggest that we can grow beyond the negative feelings to reach a deeper level of trust in our relationship with the Lord.

♥ *Group Activity: Support Group*
Look at each of the three sections of this psalm (vv. 1-10, 11-18, 19-28). Together identify and underline the "feeling words" in each section. Then choose one of the three sections as "most like" experiences and emotions you have had.

Form teams based on the section each person chooses. Share one experience or emotion you have had which led you to choose this psalm section. When those who chose the same section have shared, look for answers to the following questions:

A. What specific emotions does David share?

B. What reasons does he have for feeling as he does?

C. What does David do to deal with his emotions?

D. What brings David a sense of release and peace even though the situation has not yet changed?

Still in your teams, talk about the expe-

riences you shared before. How was your response like, and how unlike, that of David? What have you learned from this psalm that you can apply now, or in the future?

An Appeal for Protection (35:1-10)

The first verse sets the tone of this section of Psalm 35. "Contend" is *rib*, a Hebrew word that is most often used in describing a court case or legal dispute. When the psalmist begs God to "contend with those who contend with me," he is asking God to enter the case, and act as his advocate. The same word is sometimes used in a military context of fighting between two persons. While this sense would fit the second phrase, "fight against those who fight against me," David clearly intends the legal context in verse 23. The point is, of course, that whether in court or on a battlefield, David feels himself to be under attack. What's more, he feels helpless before his enemies. For some reason he cannot defend himself effectively, and so is thrown back completely on the Lord. Only if the Lord actively enters the case, only if God straps on His armor and enters the battle, will David be victorious (35:2).

David feels helpless. But David also feels angry and upset. Those who contend with him have no reason to hate David. They have no reason to attack him. And because David is innocent, they are guilty. It may be well and good for Christ to ask the Father to forgive those who unjustly crucified Him, and for the martyr Stephen to beg forgiveness for those who hurled the stones that broke his bones. But David just isn't at the place where he can forgive and forget.

Perhaps this is because, in the case of Christ and of Stephen, the battle was over and the enemy apparently victorious. It may be easier, as life ends, to look kindly on those who victimize us, realizing that we are about to enter the land of the blessed. What wonderful perspective death gives on things that loomed so large while we were enmeshed in the cares of this life. Perhaps David, still struggling to win or maintain his crown, lacks perspective.

But there is another issue to consider. And, when we do, it sheds a totally different light on David's expressions of anger and his "worst wishes" for his opponents. That issue is simply that God is a God of justice. Yes, He will settle every account in full at history's end. But even here and now He does act to punish the sinner, and when He does, justice has been done. In asking that those who seek David's life "be disgraced and put to shame" (35:4), David simply asks for justice, now. David is angry and upset. Yet when David asks that the path of his enemies be dark and slippery (35:6), or that those who dig a pit for him fall into their own trap (35:7-8), he only asks for what is fair.

The idea of most folks about justice is rooted in something called the "norm of reciprocity." If someone invites us to their house for dinner, we feel an obligation to invite them to ours in return. If someone does us a favor, we know we owe them a favor in return. On the other hand, if someone trips us so that we fall, most would say it's fair to trip them back. If someone injures us, we have a right to injure him. Now, this is a human notion. And David does not adopt it. He does not say, "I'm ready to take this into my own hands, Lord. Just help me get 'em." Instead David says, "Lord, You take charge, and You see that they get what they deserve."

In essence, David is committing his case into the hands of God, fully aware that as a God of justice, God *will* act. And it is most likely that God will act in history, and turn the plans of the wicked against them.

So even in his imprecations, and his "worst wishes" for the wicked who attack him, David is acting with restraint and with faith. And this is not the first time!

Remember how David, when pursued by Saul, had the opportunity to kill the wicked king? (cf. 1 Sam. 24) His men urged him to act, seeing Saul's vulnerability as evidence that God had delivered this enemy into David's hand. But David held back. David explained, "I will not lift my hand against my master, because he is the Lord's anointed." Then David went on to say, "May the Lord judge between you and me. And may the Lord avenge the wrongs you have done to me, *but my hand will not touch you*" (24:10-12).

It was not wrong for David to want or even expect Saul to pay for the wrongs he had done. But it would have been wrong for David to take the matter into his own hands, and to try to pay Saul back himself. Recognizing this, David simply turned everything over to God, and trusted God to do what was right.

Actually for us to say, as David does, "May the Lord avenge the wrongs done me," is not unspiritual at all! It is in a very real sense an affirmation of faith. It is an expression of our trust that justice exists in our universe, and that God will see to it that justice is done.

What's more, calling on God to avenge us is God's way of helping us deal with the anger and hurt we feel when we are treated unjustly. We face our feelings, we acknowledge that they exist, and then we discharge those negative emotions by turning the whole situation over to God. Later, with our feelings discharged, once again sensing the supportive love that God offers us, we may very well achieve the perspective of Christ and Stephen, and pray as well, "Lord, forgive them, for they know not what they do."

❋ Group Activity:
Singles/Single Again Group
Think about a person or persons who have hurt you deeply and wronged you. Briefly tell about him or her, and the wrong done to you. Share too how you have felt about yourself and about that person. Then focus on Psalm 35:4-8, and the "worst wishes" David expressed for his enemies.

Make a list of your own "worst wishes" for the person or persons you have described. Make them fit the situation as much as possible, and be sure they express your feelings as well. For instance:

* May the young bimbo he left me for gain three hundred pounds in six months.

* May the guy who spread rumors about me to get that job have to take work home every night.

Write at least a half dozen "worst wishes." Then read your list of worst wishes to the rest of the group. When all have read their lists, vote for three "classics."

Then use your "worst wishes" list as a basis for closing prayers, and in expressing them turn the entire issue over to the Lord.

David concludes this first major section of Psalm 35 by expressing confidence that God will act (35:9). When He does, David will finally feel complete relief. Yet the very act of turning the whole issue over to the Lord has restored David's sense of joy and

his peace. Rather than focus on his situation, and stew in his feelings of frustration and anger, David has shifted his gaze to God, and committed the whole thing to Him. As a result David is now filled, not with anger, but with wonder and with joy.

My whole being will exclaim,
"Who is like You, O Lord?
You rescue the poor from those too
    strong for them,
the poor and needy from those who
    rob them."

Remembering these truths about the Lord, and bringing our anger and our hurt to Him, we too can find release, peace, and even joy.

A Heartfelt Complaint (35:11-18)
It hurts when those who we counted our friends turn on us. It is this experience that underlies David's complaints in this section of his psalm.

Ruthless witnesses (35:11). In the Old Testament legal system a witness (*'ed*) was a person with firsthand knowledge of some act, who could report what he or she had seen or heard. It was the obligation of any person who knew of a criminal act to bring it to the community's judges. Thus the witness was often an accuser as well as one who gave testimony during a formal trial.

Because of the power this gave an unscrupulous person, provisions in Old Testament law guarded against its misuse. To sustain a charge, the law required at least two witnesses. In addition, if the accuser lied, he or she was to be punished with the penalty required by law for the crime of which he accused the other (Deut. 19:15-21).

Here David complains because there are ruthless witnesses (plural!] who accuse him—but they accuse him of "things I know nothing about." David did not do what he is accused of doing. The witnesses are false witnesses. But because there are several to conspire to lie about him, David has no legal redress. He is frustrated, for he is condemned unjustly.

They repay me evil for good (35:12-16). David is not only frustrated because he is innocent, but because the accusers' action constitutes a betrayal. David has done good to them, and they have repaid him with evil. He gives a specific example. When his accusers were ill, he was truly concerned.

617

He mourned for them. He was as upset as if they were members of his immediate family.

But when *David* experienced troubles, "they gathered in glee." They took David's troubles as an opportunity to slander him. In our parlance, they gleefully joined in to "kick him when he was down."

We're not told of the historical situation out of which this psalm grew. We do know that David knew many ups and downs. But surely one such experience is described in 2 Samuel 15-16. These chapters tell of the rebellion led by David's son, Absalom. Gradually the young man had "stolen the heart" not only of the ten northern tribes of Israel, but had also won the allegiance of men who had been David's friends and supporters for decades. Among them was Ahithophel, David's wisest counselor, and others who had been members of his inner circle.

How it must have hurt David. He had given his life to build a secure kingdom for his people, and now they were ready to kill him. He had offered friendship to Ahithophel and the others, and yet they threw their support to a usurper. It is one thing when enemies attack us. But it is something else again when those we have loved and been good to turn on us.

Perhaps no one feels this quite so much as a parent, whose child scorns him or her and goes his own way, or a spouse, who after years of faithful commitment to a marriage is abandoned by the one he or she has loved. None of us is totally innocent of wrongdoing. David too had flaws, and many faults. Yet what troubles David so much is that he is innocent of the things he is being accused of, and that he surely does not deserve such treatment from those who have been his friends.

When an adult child says, "You never cared about me," or scornfully blames us for his or her own faults, it both confuses us and hurts us. When a spouse abandons, saying "You never *really* loved me," or says our selfishness drove him away, and we know we have and still do love, and have sacrificed for his career, we are both confused and deeply hurt.

This is what David is talking about. And this is what drags a cry of utter despair from David, a cry that begins as an almost hopeless prayer.

O Lord, how long (35:17-18). This is such a familiar cry. How well we understand it. It isn't just the hurt. It's the fact that the pain continues, on and on. We try to put it behind us. But everything we do seems to remind us of our loss. Even though we believe, with David, that healing will come someday, and we will again be able to give God thanks, the *now* pains us. And so we do cry out, "how long?"

There is no answer to the how long. Grief is something that only time and grace can heal. Healing will come. And we need to hold on to that reality. But until it does, it is all right to cry out to God, and exclaim, "O Lord, how long?"

He understands.

And He cares.

❋ *Group Activity:*
Singles/Single Again Group
Abandonment by a spouse is one of the most painful of human experiences. It is bad enough to lose a loved one by death. But the tearing apart of an intimate relationship, the isolation, is often even more traumatic when the cause is divorce.

It is important in working through the grief involved to have others who can listen and care. So why not give at least one group session to the Singles Again among you who have lost a spouse to divorce.

Pattern the sharing on Psalm 35:11-18. Encourage the re-singled to talk about phrases that bring to mind the unfairness of his or her experience. If a long time has passed, and healing has begun to come, talk about the process of recovery and the setbacks along the way. It's likely that those who have shared this experience can be of more help to each other than others can, although anyone can help by listening compassionately.

A Plea for Vindication (35:19-28)
The last section of this psalm contains David's plea for public vindication. All of us are sensitive to what others think of us, and want the majority to think well. It may be right, but it is also unrealistic, to expect us to be satisfied with "I know I didn't do it, and God knows I didn't do it." Even when we have this assurance, it hurts when we think others are looking at us accusingly. And he especially does not want his enemies to slander him with impunity.

And so David voices an appeal for *public* vindication. "Let not those gloat over me who are my enemies without cause" (35:19). And, "do not let them think, 'Aha, just what we wanted'!" In essence David is saying, don't let my enemies assume that they've won.

This is another reason why public vindication is important. It is not just something we need for peace of mind. It is something the whole community needs, for in exposing those who do wrong, bystanders are warned against similar wrong acts.

And so David is right to ask, "May all who exalt themselves over me be clothed with shame and disgrace" (35:26). These terms, "shame" and "disgrace," are synonyms. While in some cases they may indicate an inner state, in most cases these words indicate an objective situation which exposes the person shamed by the failure of some endeavor to which he was publicly committed. Thus David's enemies, by their attacks, publicly committed themselves to bring him down. If their charges are proven false, or *if they fail* in what they are trying to do, their true character is exposed, and thus, they are publicly shamed.

It's important to remember that in uttering this prayer David isn't concerned with how his enemies feel. He isn't asking God to make them as miserable as they have made him. "Payback" is not really involved. What David is asking for is vindication: the public exposure of his enemy's lies, and the failure of their attempts to bring David down.

Ultimately, of course, every sin will be exposed and believers will be vindicated before the whole universe of men and angels.

While the Old Testament tends to look for vindication in this world, the New Testament shifts our focus beyond time to eternity. This is, in fact, a significant difference between the orientation of the two Testaments. And so Paul reminds those suffering unjustly in first-century Thessalonica,

> God is just: He will pay back trouble to those who trouble you and give relief to you who are troubled, and to us as well. This will happen when the Lord Jesus is revealed from heaven in blazing fire with His powerful angels. He will punish those who do not know God and do not obey the Gospel of our Lord Jesus (2 Thes. 1:6-8).

So you and I may need to be satisfied with the certainty that public vindication will come. And yet we may, as David did, find that God will so shape the circumstances that we are vindicated now—as a grace gift to us, as discipline for those who have treated us unjustly, and as a lesson for the whole community of faith.

And so David prays that while those who oppress may be put to shame, those who "delight in my vindication" may find joy and comfort. Seeing what God does in David's life, they will be encouraged, and with renewed trust exclaim, "The Lord be exalted." For God is the kind of person who "delights in the well-being" of His servants (Ps. 35:27).

No wonder, looking confidently now for the vindication to come, David's hurt and anger are drained, and he is able to say, "My tongue will speak of Your righteousness and of Your praises all day long."

GROUP RESOURCE GUIDE

Identification: *Share with others*
Choose one of these two statements, with which you either agree or disagree. Tell what statement you chose, and explain your reaction to it.

Either
Time heals all wounds.
Or
Time wounds all heels.
After sharing, read quickly through Psalm 35. Jot down individually, and then list

together, what David seems to feel, what causes his feelings, and how he deals with them.

Exploration: *Probe God's Word*
Choose one of the psalm's three sections to explore in depth with others. Select the section which you feel is most likely to speak to your personal feelings or situation. The three are:

35:1-10 An appeal for protection.
35:11-18 A heartfelt complaint.
35:19-28 A plea for vindication.

Share one experience or emotion you have had which led you to choose this psalm section. When those who chose the same section have shared, look for answers to the following questions:

* What specific emotions does David share?

* What reasons does he have for feeling as he does?

* What does David do to deal with his emotions?

* What brings David a sense of release and peace even though the situation has not yet changed?

Still in your teams, talk about the experiences you shared before. How was your response like, and how unlike, that of David?

Reaction: *Respond together to the Word*
Listen as someone previously prepared sums up the lessons of each section of this psalm, as presented in the commentary.

Then go around the group so each of you can share what you have learned from this psalm that you can apply now or in the future.

Adoration: *Worship and pray*
Consider David's concept of God as revealed in this psalm. Who is the Lord? How does He relate to us when we are victims of injustice? What can we expect from Him, and how much can we trust Him?

After meditating on these questions for a time, close in prayer, praising God for that aspect of His character which has become more clear and precious to you.

WORDS FROM THE WISE

Overview

Psalm 37 is an acrostic; each of its verses begins with a different, consecutive letter of the Hebrew alphabet. It is also a collection of proverbs—of wise sayings—intended to distill the insights of men and women of faith, and make these insights available to us. Because David, who offers these insights, has experienced troubles and injustice and during his long life has successfully put them in perspective, this psalm has been cherished by believers throughout the ages. Because here David uses proverbs rather than argument or description of a single personal experience, this psalm is particularly difficult to outline. In fact it is best to read it with a series of "rests." That is, to read a verse or two as a thought unit, and then to rest a moment and think about what we have read.

What is special about this psalm, and has made it a favorite of generations, is that there is a special word here for each of us, for at least one thing here is bound to speak to every heart.

Commentary

As we read through Psalm 37, we're struck by the number of times David uses the phrase, "the Lord."

Trust in the Lord and do good (v. 3).

Commit your way to the Lord;
    trust in Him, and He will do this (v. 5).

Be still before the Lord and wait
    patiently for Him (v. 7).

Wait for the Lord and keep His way.
    He will exalt you to possess the land
    (v. 34).

The salvation of the righteous comes
    from the Lord; He is their strong-

hold in time of trouble (v. 39).

In essence, David is not simply giving us advice in this psalm. He is inviting us to constantly relate our experiences to God.

When we look behind the meaning of the phrase, "the Lord," we see he is inviting us to see God in a very special way. For the roots of this name for God go back to the beginning, and its unique meaning was first revealed to Moses at a critical moment in that great leader's life.

Moses had been a man of ability and ambition. Considered the "son of Pharaoh's daughter," the Jewish child found by the Egyptian princess floating in a bullrush basket (Ex. 2) had been adopted by the royal family. He was given the benefits of an education in all the wisdom of that great ancient civilization. As the right to Egypt's throne frequently passed through a daughter rather than a son, Moses may even have been in line to become Pharaoh!

But Moses had a dream. Despite his many advantages, he had identified himself with the Hebrew people, who were slaves in Egypt. And Moses firmly intended to see to it that his people were freed.

But the story is tragic as well as familiar. Moses, seeing one of the Hebrew slaves being mistreated, kills the Egyptian overseer. When Moses later learns to his horror that others know of the killing, he is forced to abandon his dreams and flee Egypt. After forty years at the center of that time's mightiest and most sophisticated empire, Moses is forced to settle in the arid lands of the Sinai peninsula, where he joins a nomadic tribe and spends his days in the hills, watching sheep. For forty more years, until he is eighty years old, Moses vegetates in one of history's dreary backwaters. His dreams die. And with them his youthful vision of himself and his gifts dies too. The young crusader is turned into a weary, disappointed, and oh so hesitant old man.

And then one day God appeared to Moses and spoke to him from a burning bush. God told Moses to return to Egypt. The dream was to become reality! Moses was commissioned to become Israel's deliverer.

Even though Moses now objected, God continued to insist. "I have indeed seen the misery of My people in Egypt. I have heard them crying out because of their slave drivers, and I am concerned about their suffering. So I have come down to rescue them . . . and to bring them up out of that land into a good and spacious land, a land flowing with milk and honey" (Ex. 3:7-8). What good words these are! And how often we need to hear them. God hears our crying as well. God is concerned about our suffering. And God is eager to rescue us, to bring us up into His good land.

But Moses hesitated.

As we often do.

"Suppose I go to the Israelites," Moses objected, "and say to them, 'The God of your fathers sent me to you,' and they ask me, 'What is His name?' Then what shall I tell them?"

God's answer established forever the way you and I are to view this one whom David presents to us in Psalm 37 as "the Lord."

"I AM WHO I AM," God replied. "This is what you are to say to the Israelites: 'I AM has sent me to you' " (Ex. 3:13-14).

What is significant here is that I AM, this simple affirmation of the verb "to be," is the basis of the Old Testament's personal name for our God: *Yahweh*. The Old Testament has many different terms *describing* God: "the Almighty," "Sovereign Lord," "God of Hosts," etc. But Yahweh is God's personal name. And in giving Moses this personal name, God unveiled something unique about who He is as He stands in relationship with believing human beings.

The name YAHWEH is constructed from the Hebrew verb meaning "to be." Thus Moses was told to report that "I AM" had sent him. In essence, Moses is told that if God's people want to know Him, want to know His essential identity, they must realize that He is the I AM.

What a stunning message!

In Moses' time Israel had not experienced God as I AM. They had heard of Him as the great I WAS who spoke to their forefather Abraham some 400 years before. They even trusted Him as the great I WILL

BE, who in some future time might act to deliver them from Egypt and return them to the Promised Land. But in Moses' time the Hebrews were slaves. They were the lowest of the low in Egypt. They had no educational or other advantages. They had no hope. All they were experiencing, all of what seemed real to them, was the burden of their oppression.

And then Moses came with the wonderful announcement that God is really I AM — and to prove it, God burst into history with a series of mighty acts that brought mighty Egypt to its knees. In a devastating series of miracles God showed His people that He truly is I AM — a God who is present with them, able to act, willing to deliver. All this is expressed in the name, the Lord.

And God said to Moses, "This is My name *forever, the name by which I am to be remembered from generation to generation*" (Ex. 3:15).

And this is what puts Psalm 37 in perspective, and what gives us perspective in our troubles. God is I AM for us too. God is "One who is always present." So when David calls on us to "trust in the Lord," he is really saying "trust the One who is with you now." Rely on God as a present reality in your life, and you will have hope. Even though you have waited as long as Moses, your dreams need not die. For God is present with you, and all things are possible with Him.

And so David's advice, given in this wonderful psalm, can best be understood if we read its key verses with a clear understanding of the meaning of the phrase, "the Lord."

Trust in God, who is with you at this moment, and do good (v. 3).

Commit your way to the One who is with you even now; trust in Him, and He will act (v. 5).

Be still before Him who is ever with you, and wait patiently for Him (v. 7).

Wait for the One who is with you, and keep His way (v. 34).

The salvation of the righteous comes from the God who is at their side each moment; He is their stronghold in time of trouble (v. 39).

God is. He is present with us now. And this is what gives Psalm 37 its wondrous power.

Psalm 37

Do not fret (37:1-2). This is the first advice offered by David. The word translated "fret" suggests a mixture of anxiety and anger. This is the impact of "evil men" who "do wrong" on both individuals and on society. The social order is violated, and we become anxious and wonder if perhaps we're next. Hostility toward evildoers grows, deepening our fears as the system seems powerless to punish them or to protect us! Yet David encourages us to take a longer view. Evil men are as fragile as the grasses that wither away. Surely we who love God and do right will outlast them.

Trust and do good (37:3-4). Trust in the Lord (v. 3) and delighting in the Lord (v. 4) are closely linked. Through trust we establish a personal relationship with Him. As we grow to know Him in that relationship, we become more and more favorably disposed toward Him, and experience great pleasure and joy.

It is significant that "and do good" is interposed between trust and delight. The only way to deepen a personal relationship with God is by committing ourselves to His ways. As we do good, we remain close to Him, and grow to know Him better. As intimacy grows, God Himself becomes a vital source of our joy. And our closeness to Him makes it possible for God to give us "the desires of [our] heart."

Note the subtlety of this verse. The closer we are to God, the more our relationship with Him will shape what we desire! Thus God first gives us desires for that which is good. And then He is satisfies them. Only if we desire what is good can God in good conscience give us what we desire.

Commit your way (37:5-6). The Hebrew verb here is *galal*, which is translated "commit" only three times in most English versions. The verb means "to roll" or "to roll away." What the psalmist is saying is that we can roll every burden, every concern for the future, on the Lord. He is willing to accept responsibility for us and for our future.

But what is the relationship between rolling our concerns onto the Lord and the associated promise, "He will make your righteousness shine"? Simply this. The person who keeps on trying to carry the burden of his future will be tempted to make moral decisions on the basis of how he expects those decisions will affect his or her future. But if we roll the burden of our future off onto the Lord, so that He becomes responsible to supervise the consequences that flow from our choices, we are free to make every choice on the basis of conformity to God's will! In committing our way to God, we determine to do what is right, and "let the chips fall where they may"—sustained by the knowledge that a God who is ever present with us supervises each chip's fall.

Be still and wait patiently (37:7). It's so hard to remain still and patient when things aren't going well. We fret, we become anxious, we pace up and down, and then when we can't stand it any longer, we act.

David's advice goes contrary to our nature. He says, "sit and wait." But the reason behind his advice lies in two things. The first thing is David's encouragement to be still "before the Lord." In Old Testament times those who wanted to petition God or to worship Him oriented themselves toward the temple in Jerusalem. Ideally they came to that city and worshiped there before the temple. But even when they were far away, they turned toward the holy city. That physical position was a symbolic act, indicating that the full attention of the petitioner was centered on the Lord.

This is the first thing David urges us to do when we can hardly bear to wait. Focus your full attention on the Lord. Don't be caught up in the circumstances of the moment, but consciously bring God into your calculations, and make Him the most important factor.

The second thing David tells us is "wait patiently." Here David's reasoning lies within the word he uses for "wait." The Hebrew *yahal* is most often translated "hope." It reminds us to look ahead with confidence even though our present experience may painful. The fact is that God Himself will act in the future, and that when He acts He will save the person whose hope is in Him. Thus, it is appropriate for us to wait, patiently, until God does.

Certainly David, who as a young man waited for years for God to make him king, understood how difficult it is to remain patient. Even when persecuted and deeply discouraged, David knew that timing was a vital element in God's will. And David was so sure of God's love and commitment that he was willing to wait.

So, even when the wicked carry out their schemes successfully, we too need to keep our eyes on the Lord, and to wait confidently for His time.

Refrain from anger (37:8-11). The wrongs done to us do fester. The more we think about them, the more we relive past experiences, the more anger is likely to build.

David reminds us feeding on anger has disastrous consequences. "It leads only to evil." That *only* is a powerful word of warning. Feed on anger, fan the flames of hostility, and the actions you take will hardly express the love, the grace, the forgiveness that characterize the truly good. Anger leads us not to correct the evil but to become like them!

What's the alternative? It is to remember two things. Evil men will be cut off. God is the moral judge of His universe, and there is no way that the evil will prosper in the end. So the first thing to remember is that we leave any vengeance up to God.

The second thing to remember is that our reverses, like the evil man's prosperity, is a transitory, quickly passing thing. What is our destiny? With others who hope in the Lord, our destiny is to "inherit the land."

We are heirs to all the good things God has in store for His people. Why then let anger dominate, and lead us into the pathway taken by the evil who are destined to be cut off in just a "little while"?

The Lord laughs (37:12-13). People have a tendency to take themselves and others much too seriously. The wicked seldom have much sense of humor, and almost never laugh at themselves. The trouble is the godly seldom laugh at the wicked. We get upset. We get agitated and angry. We wonder why they don't get what they deserve. In David's terms, we "fret" (37:1, 8).

Not God. God laughs contemptuously at their posturing and shortsightedness, for He knows that "their day is coming."

The same thought in found in Psalm 2, a vision of the future when God's Messiah returns to establish righteousness. The kings of the earth, taking themselves oh so seriously, take their stand together against the Lord. And

The One enthroned in heaven laughs;
  the Lord scoffs at them.
Then He rebukes them in His anger
  and terrifies them in His wrath.

Ultimately the wicked pose no more serious a threat to God than some sullen adolescent gang, trying hard to look dangerous, standing on a street corner and glaring at passersby would pose to the forces of Desert Shield or Desert Storm. When God rebukes them they will scatter, terrified, and disappear.

This does not mean that the evil the wicked do is not something to take seriously. What David means is that we are not to take the wicked themselves at face value, as though they were a serious threat to the stability of the moral universe. They are not. They are clowns, posturing on the stage of history, thinking all the while they are dramatic actors who hold the lead role. Looking at them, and recognizing them for what they are, we can join in God's derisive laughter. Like God, we know their day is coming. Soon.

Their swords will pierce their own hearts (37:14-15). David continues to explore the problem of the wicked. Their intent is evil and serious: they draw the sword and bend the bow to "bring down the poor and needy." But again the imagery ridicules the wicked. The swords they draw "pierce their own hearts."

Picture if you will a remake of *The Three Musketeers.* The brave swordsmen are surrounded by the guards of the evil Richelieu. It's a dramatic and terrifying moment, for our heroes are unarmed and helpless. The malevolent guardsmen, eager to kill their defenseless enemies, draw their swords. And suddenly they are revealed to be buffoons. One slips on a banana, and his blade pinks the foot of another, who hops away off camera. Another, distracted by the accident, turns and inadvertently clips the belt of a third, who loses his trousers and tumbles facedown in a puddle.

The wicked *are* bumbling. In the end their ridiculous posturing will be exposed. And the swords they draw will be deadly indeed—to themselves.

Better the little (37:16-26). Now comes a series of observations on the wicked and the righteous.

It is better to be righteous and have little than to be wealthy and wicked (37:16-17). God guarantees the inheritance of the righteous and provides for them in desperate times. But the wicked are destined to perish (35:18-20). The way of the wicked is profitless, and they will be reduced to borrowing, while the way of the righteous leads to prosperity (35:21-22). The person in whom God delights may stumble. But the Lord is there to lift him up (35:23-24). And then David adds his personal testimony. David has grown old, and watched generation succeed generation. But never has he seen the descendants of the righteous reduced to begging. To trust and love God, and to do good, is not only the way to find blessing for oneself. It is the way to bless our children as well (35:25-26).

For the Lord *loves the just (35:27-40).* Having drawn his contrast between the experience of the wicked and the just, David concludes with a series of proverbs which refocus our attention on the Lord. The just are blessed, because God will never forsake the one who trusts in Him (35:27-29). Trust in God gives us a sensitivity to His Word, and a love for His Law. And the Law provides the insight into life the righteous need to make wise choices (35:30-31). God will not abandon the righteous into the hands of the wicked (35:32-33). And so we can "wait for the Lord," all the while keeping His way, confident in the future God has for us (35:34).

It is clear that David's vision of God has made him more future oriented than time bound. Yes, the wicked do flourish at times. But if we wait and watch we will observe that the ruthless man soon passes away. And, if we wait and watch, we will also see that "there is a future for the man of peace" (35:35-38).

Why? Simply because the Lord is a God of salvation. The righteous know this. The righteous experience it, as their deliverer "comes from the Lord" in their times of trouble. As long as we hold on to this reality, that God is ours, and that God delivers those who take refuge in Him, we will have peace.

GROUP RESOURCE GUIDE

Identification: *Share with others*
Share briefly one time when you found it hard to trust God.

Exploration: *Probe God's Word*
Work together to complete a chart summarizing the themes found in Psalm 37.

Reaction: *Respond together to the Word*
In a team with four others, review the experience you shared at the beginning. What about the experience made it hard to trust God? What were your thoughts and feelings? What did you do?

Particularly, what did you find in this psalm that might give you perspective for future, similar situations? What will you do if such a situation should arise?

Adoration: *Worship and pray*
Have someone previously prepared sum up the implications of the name, the Lord, which is repeated so often here by David. Praise Him together for what you have learned through this psalm that His presence means to believers.

A CALL TO CONFESSION

Overview

"Confession of sins" is often misunderstood. Some confuse it with saying "I'm sorry," and assume that that's all it takes to heal broken relationships. Some confuse it with penance: the idea that when we do something wrong, we have to offer God some service which will make it all up to Him.

Biblically, however, "confession" is best understood as openly acknowledging our sins to God. When we stand in judgment on ourselves, and agree with His determination that the act in question is sin, God is able not only to forgive us but to initiate a cleansing process intended to make us more and more like our Lord.

But confessing sins isn't easy. Something inside us fights against admissions of wrong. We've all experienced this. And certainly it was experienced by the Old Testament saints who wrote the great worship book of Psalms. From them, and especially from David, we need to learn how to confess. And how confession brings us freedom and renewal.

Commentary

Most psalms grow out of personal experience. Many of the psalms of David can be traced back to specific incidents reported in the historical books that give us his life history. Certainly Psalm 51 has its roots in just such an incident: an incident which not only reveals the human side of David, but which reminds us that every human being is vulnerable to the dark power of sin that crouches within his or her personality.

In David's case it all began innocently. David was restless. His initial goals as a united Israel's ruler had been achieved. David had unified the kingdom, established Jerusalem as both political and religious center of his kingdom, and expanded Hebrew-controlled territory several times over.

Like many of us when we reach the goals we set for ourselves, David seems to have felt uncertain, with no new challenges to meet. So one year when his armies marched out for their spring campaign, David did not lead them but stayed at home.

The story of David's downfall is told in 2 Samuel 11, and begins with the phrase, "One evening David got up from his bed and walked around on the roof of the palace" (11:2). Many of us have nights when we can't sleep. But in David's case this seems to have been a symptom of his general restlessness. His enormous energy seems to have been dissipated, and he was distracted and ill at ease.

As the restless David wandered on the roof of his palace, perched high on one of Jerusalem's steep hills, he chanced to look down on the homes on the slope below. And there he saw Bathsheba, bathing in the moonlight in the privacy of her inner courtyard.

Often believers have tried to polish David's image by suggesting Bathsheba was a shameless seductress, who purposely set out to corrupt Israel's godly king. In fact, the biblical text does just the opposite: it goes to considerable lengths to protect Bathsheba! It points out that David should have been away, at the head of his troops, where kings of that time were expected to be. It points out that even if at home, David had gone to bed, and might well be expected to be there instead of wandering on the rooftop. Homes of the well-to-do were built around an inner court. There Bathsheba could surely expect privacy for her bath. Perhaps she waited till night to bathe just because then only from the top of the palace roof could anyone have possibly witnessed her washings.

But that night David was on the roof. And when he glanced down, and saw the beautiful Bathsheba bathing in the moonlight, he didn't look away. Instead he watched, and watched lustfully.

The text continues the story. David sent someone to find out about her (11:3). When David learned she was married, and to an officer in the army that even then was out fighting his wars, the king did not hesitate. Driven by desire, he "sent messengers to get her" (11:4). Powerless to resist Israel's absolute monarch, Bathsheba accompanied the king's guard. And there, in the royal palace, David "slept with her" (11:4).

We have no idea how Bathsheba felt about all this. And the reason is simple. How Bathsheba felt about it didn't matter. David was king. And David had his way with her. Stripped to its essential nature, this act was nothing more or less than rape. No knife may have been held at Bathsheba's throat. But the power of the king implied exactly the same kind of threat.

And when David had had her, he sent her back to her house. Bathsheba was used. And discarded.

This part of the familiar story is terrible enough. The king, whose dedication to God was public knowledge, whose commission was to do justice and care for God's people, had himself violated one of God's most significant decrees, and in so doing done violence to one of the sheep he was to shepherd. And worse was soon to follow!

David's rape made Bathsheba pregnant. When she sent a messenger and informed the king, he was frantic to cover up his act. Undoubtedly after it happened David had been ashamed. Usually the aftermath of passion brings a perspective easily lost in its heat. But David was not ashamed *enough* to acknowledge his culpability! So David sent for Uriah, the husband of Bathsheba, expecting Uriah to sleep with his wife and so be deceived into believing that the child was Uriah's own.

But Uriah was an unusual man. Deeply aware of the hardships faced by his men on the battlefield, Uriah slept on the floor in the king's palace. Uriah felt he could hardly lead men when he accepted privileges they did not share. And so the dedication of Uriah not only revealed him to be an unusual and admirable man, but also frustrated David's plans.

David now was driven now by the fear of exposure. The consequences of his initial sin, and his refusal to acknowledge it, compelled him to commit another, surely more depraved act. Consciously, calculatingly, David masked his intent with pretended friendship, and sent Uriah back to the army with sealed orders. And those orders were, "Put Uriah in the front line where the fighting is fiercest. Then withdraw from him so he will be struck down and die" (11:15).

Then, when Uriah was killed, David took Bathsheba into his house as one of his several wives.

This, its superscription tells us, is the experience which, in time, gave rise to Psalm 51 and to a public confession by David of his terrible, very private acts.

Lessons from David's experience. There are many insights we can find in and draw from this story, and from the psalm which marks a spiritual turning point.

In the first place, we learn that even the godly truly are vulnerable to the grossest of sins. David did love God and sought to honor Him. But David also possessed the sin nature to which all humanity is heir. Let's not make excuses for David. David fell—and so can you or I. We have to be constantly on our guard against the deceptiveness of sin; constantly intent on seeking and serving God.

In the second place, we're reminded that one step down the path of sin can quickly lead to more. Unless we deal with failings quickly and decisively, unless we acknowledge our sins and put them behind us, each is sure to lead to more. Covering up, as President Nixon found, is frequently more damaging to us and others than open admission of error.

In the third place, the story and the psalm demonstrate the stunning power of God who works through confession and forgiveness to redeem the most sordid of experiences. For the story does not end with the rape, or with the death of Uriah, or with David's marriage to Bathsheba.

In a way, the story is not fully told until David lies on his deathbed. We join that scene in 1 Kings 1. David is old now, and one of his sons, Adonijah, decides to take the succession in his own hands and declare himself king in David's place. The old prophet Nathan enlists the help of Bathsheba to block Adonijah's power play. He sends Bathsheba in to see the king first.

Bathsheba too is old, and the bloom of her erotic beauty long faded. Yet as she kneels beside the king we can sense a bond of deep, true love between the two. Kneeling there Bathsheba reminds David that he had promised to make her son, Solomon, king after him. And she shares her fears. If David fails to confirm Solomon as his successor, "as soon as my lord the king is laid to rest with his fathers, I and my son Solomon will be treated as criminals" (1 Kings 21). Then Nathan appears, and confirms the immediacy of the danger. And the old king stirs himself. Calling Bathsheba back, he confirms his promise to her. Struggling against the weakness of his great age, David calls in priest and prophet and orders them to "blow the trumpet" and to proclaim Solomon king."

What has happened here? How has a relationship which began in lust, was consumated by rape, and led to murder, been transformed into a loving marriage which produced not only Solomon, Israel's king-to-be, but also according to 1 Chronicles 3:5, three other sons as well? The answer lies in the act of confession that David reports in our psalm.

Not that it was easy to bring David to the point of confession. In fact, the king grimly hardened his heart against God and refused to face his sin for many months. It was only when Bathsheba was about to deliver that the Prophet Nathan was finally sent to confront David and force him to acknowledge his guilt. The story is told in 2 Samuel 12. Nathan tells the king the story of a poor man whose one lamb was taken from him by a wealthy neighbor who possessed many lambs of his own. David explodes in righteous indignation and condemns the offender—only to be told by the prophet, "You are the man!"

Stunned, David falls back, and as Nathan publicly recounts the sins David committed in secret, the enormity of his act is driven home. Finally David admits the truth that he has struggled to hide not only from others but from himself: "I have sinned against the Lord" (12:13). At last the dam of deceit has been broken, the corruption flows out, and the healing process can begin.

Oh, there were consequences. The child conceived in sin died, not as a judgment on him but as a grace gift. Death freed that child from the burden of growing up with parents whose attitude toward him must necessarily have been colored by the fact that his very existence was a reminder of their sin. We can be forgiven. But we cannot expect to avoid every consequence of our sinful acts.

And yet God redeemed the situation, and transformed the relationship of David and Bathsheba. David had violated her; he had abused her in the most terrible ways possible. And yet in doing so David had acted *out of* rather than *in* character. His confession of sin constituted acknowledgment of his responsibility for their situation, as well as reaffirmed his commitment to God. By acknowledging responsibility David laid a foundation for hope that he would change, and the passage of years enabled Bathsheba to develop ever-growing trust. In the end they did put their past behind them, and developed a lasting love, witnessed not only in the children they produced together but in David's final act of love, in protecting Bathsheba's future by confirming Solomon as king in his stead.

There is a vital point here. It is impossible to be right with God without a willingness to confess our sins. And it is impossible to restore shattered relationships without a willingness to acknowledge full responsibility for our acts. The abusive husband who blames his wife for making him angry will never change. That relationship will continue to be destructive, and the wife will continue to be a victim as long as she remains with him. Only when a person accepts responsibility for the wrong he or she does to another is there any hope at all for healing in a relationship.

David, in confessing his sin, not only accepted the forgiveness God offers every sinner and the cleansing which follows, but also laid the foundation for a healthy, holy marriage with Bathsheba. Confession had its redemptive effect on the king, and on the bond he now was able to forge with his wife. For even Bathsheba found in the humbled David a man she could respect and learn to love.

✂ *Group Activity: Recovery Group*
Steps 4 (make a moral inventory) and 5 (admit wrongs to God, myself, and others)
Listen to the story of David's sin, confession, and its long-term outcome.

Discuss: What does the serious nature of David's sins tell us? Why did David find it so hard to confess doing wrong? What in David's experience parallels experiences of our own? What in David's story helps us face our own sins and failures honestly?

Suppose that Nathan the prophet were to confront you. With what sins would he be most likely to charge you? Make a list, including everything you think Nathan might charge you with.

When the list is complete, first think about and face the nature of your own acts. Then acknowledge them before God by confessing them to Him in prayer.

Finally, determine which acts you need to admit to others as evidence that you are taking responsibility for your actions and are counting on God to help you change. In teams of three, describe the sins and tell who you feel you must admit them to to begin the healing process.

Psalm 51

The structure of the psalm is clear and logical. David pleads for forgiveness, based on the merciful character of God rather than on any merit of his own (51:1-2). His confession is genuine; he has examined his acts, and at last grasps the true nature of his sin (51:3-5). The next verses reveal his yearning for an inner renewal (51:6-12), and a clear understanding of the obligations that forgiveness will lay upon him for a future reformation (51:13-17). What is more, David senses the implications of being forgiven as an individual for the believing community. For only as a forgiven people can God's covenant community live and worship together (51:18-19).

Merciful God (51:1-2). The key words in these two verses delineate the character of God as David knows Him. God is marked by mercy, characterized by unfailing love, and filled with compassion.

God's "mercy" is *hanan,* a word that draws attention to the way a person able to help responds to another who is in need.

God's "unfailing love" is *hesed,* a unique word associated with God's covenant commitment to His people. It is in essence a bond of loyalty that knows no bounds; an unshakable choice to care deeply for another.

And God's "great compassion" is *raham,* a word which means "to love deeply" and thus "to be compassionate."

In essence, David knows God as one who loves him, who is committed to him, and who surely will reach down to help in view of David's present helplessness. Ultimately only God can deal not only with the consequences and guilt of sin, but with the terrible urge toward evil that lies, perhaps dormant but truly present, in the heart of every man.

Understanding who God is and His attitude toward us is the source of the courage we need to acknowledge our sin—to ourselves, much less to others. Without God we have no hope of absolution or of change, and so dare not look our sins in the face. We can only turn our backs on them, deny their existence, and like the little child aware of unreal monsters under his bed, pull the covers over our heads. With God, the God of Scripture, everything changes. We can look at our sins and acknowledge them, for God offers us hope of both forgiveness and of change.

I know my sins (51:3-5). David's awareness of who God is and what He is like gave him courage to face his sins. The key words in these verses indicate that David not only faced them, but that he also examined his actions carefully. Like an oncologist, intent on knowing the full extent of the cancer that has found a foothold in his patient's body, David searches out every trace of the sin that burst out in his shocking acts of rape and murder.

The psalmist uses three distinctive words for sin in these verses, which show us how carefully he examined himself in light of his actions. The Old Testament's principal word for sin is *hata',* which means to miss a mark. Most of its 580 occurrences in the Old Testament indicate a failure to reach some standard that God has set for humankind. *Pesa'* is frequently translated "rebellion" or "transgression," and this indicates a revolt against the divine standard. The third term, *'awon,* usually rendered "iniquity" or "guilt," suggests deviation from the standard set by God, or a twisting of that standard.

Each of the principle words for sin, then, depends on the conviction that God has revealed, in human nature itself and especially in His Law, standards which are binding on humanity. When David cries out "Against You, You only, have I sinned," he is not discounting the harm his act did to Bathsheba. Rather, he acknowledges the fact that the standards he has violated are God's standards, and that thus all sin is essentially "against" God.

Moderns try to find comfort in the notion that "sin" is against one's conscience, or against the standards of the community. Right and wrong, good and evil, are not absolutes, but are flexible expressions of mere human values which one can bend or break, with the only real cost a twinge of guilt feelings. David knows better. Sins are committed against God, and are measured against standards that He has set. The penalty for falling short, for rebelling, and for deviating from the standards is to incur *real* guilt. And real guilt brings with it the immediate penalty of alienation from God, of corruption of personal relationships, and of punishment not often here, but certainly in the future.

All this David knows as he reexamines what he has done, and finds that he is totally guilty of violating God's standards in every sense. *The Expository Dictionary of Bible Words* (Zondervan, p. 566) quotes these verses, with the Hebrew terms included. Here is how the passage reads:

Have mercy on me, O God, according to your unfailing love; according to your great compassion blot out my transgressions [*pasa'*]. Wash away all my iniquity [*'awon*] and cleanse me from my sin [*hatta't*]. For I know my transgressions [*pasa'*], and my sin [*hatta't*] is always before me. Against you, you only, have I sinned [*hata'*], and done what is evil [*ra'*] in your sight, so that you are proved right when you speak and justified when you judge. Surely I was sinful [*'awon*] at birth, sinful [*hete'*] from the time my mother conceived me.

This last phrase contains a vital insight. In performing his shameful acts David has discovered that his very nature is twisted [*'awon*], and that he falls short [*hata'*] of being what human beings were originally created to be. It is not just that David's acts have been sinful. *David* is a sinful person. He is flawed in his essential nature, and thus, is truly in desperate need of God.

This is a discovery each of us must make as well. We can't go through life dismissing our sins as an aberration, or explaining away our unkind acts as some sort of just retribution. David might well have followed the path all too many take, and blamed Bathsheba. She was too beautiful, so it was her fault. She shouldn't have taken her bath in the courtyard at night instead of inside some room. Uriah shouldn't have been so dedicated. If he'd just acted like a normal man, David wouldn't have been forced to plot his death. If . . .

And so it is that many desperately splash whitewash on their acts, in hopes of covering up what deep down each of us knows full well. The seed of sin is planted deep within us, in our very nature. "Surely I was sinful at birth, sinful from the time my mother conceived me." Unless we come to this painful self-knowledge, and examine the acts through which our sin nature expresses itself, there is no hope for us. And this itself will be impossible until we see God as He is, and He has unmistakably revealed Himself in Christ to be. Overflowing with mercy. Filled with unfailing love. An unending source of great compassion.

Personal renewal (51:6-12). But David knows even more about the God of Scripture than His motivation. David knows what God is able to do in the heart of a believer. And it is this that David now appeals for, using three powerful verbs.

"Cleanse me" (51:7-9). The mention of hyssop is significant. This plant was used in services of sacrifice. Its roots were dipped in the blood of the sacrificial animal, and that blood sprinkled on the object or person to be purified from uncleanness (Ex. 12:22). David believes that God can cleanse him. But he recognizes that this can only be accomplished through the death of a substitute. In this, as in the whole sacrificial system of Israel, the Old Testament looks forward to the death of Christ and the purifying power of His blood. David did not understand the mystery which sacrifice implied. But he did know that God could and would cleanse the sinner who approached Him through a sacrifice that God had ordained.

And what does cleansing accomplish? Objectively, it blots out all our iniquity. Subjectively, it releases us from our past, so we can again "hear joy and gladness."

"Create in me a pure heart" (51:10-11). David realizes that apart from an act of God recreating him as a new person, and apart from the sustaining presence of God's Spirit, he will fall again. Cleansing without renewal is useless. Yet when God forgives us He does create in us the new heart David yearned for, and He gives us His presence generously.

"Restore to me the joy of your salvation" (51:12). Again the objective and subjective elements are both emphasized. Forgiveness brings release. And release wells up as joy.

I will (51:13-17). As David concludes this great psalm, used in public worship, he acknowledges another great truth. The person who has been granted forgiveness, who has been transformed within, and who is sustained by God's Spirit, is now obligated to the Lord who saved him. The obligation is not one marked by the demand, "you must." Instead it is marked by the spontaneous, joyful, "I will." Because God has loved us, we love Him.

What will a restored and renewed David do? "I will teach transgressors Your ways" (v. 13). "My tongue will sing of Your righteousness" (v. 14). "My mouth will declare Your praise" (v. 15). In fact, whatever God delights in David will gladly bring to the Lord, beginning with "a broken and contrite heart" (v. 17).

Isn't it fascinating that only when our heart is broken can it be repaired?

Only when we see and acknowledge our sins, only when our pride is shattered by the discovery of the terrible flaw we share with the rest of humankind, will we submit ourselves to God and, with no illusions left, beg Him for mercy. And when that mercy flows, and we rise up cleansed and renewed, how gladly we commit ourselves to serve and to praise our wonderful Lord.

Zion prospers (51:18-19). David's prayer has been intensely personal. It is his sin he has confessed. It is his heart that has been purified and restored. But in his confession and renewal David has unveiled the secret that will bring prosperity not just to himself, but the whole believing community. Only in confession and renewal can the people of God find unity *with* the Lord, and unity *in* the Lord. When we all learn and apply this lesson that David learned at such terrible cost, Christ's church will prosper, and righteous sacrifices will be offered up by the people of God.

GROUP RESOURCE GUIDE

Identification: *Share with others*
Sit on jury with others while four members of your group put on a mock trial. The four are a judge, a prosecutor, a defense attorney, and the defendant. The situation is simple: the defendant is accused of attacking a neighbor's wife, and then contracting for the murder of her husband. The actors can make up details as they go along.

When the "trial" has established the facts and heard the defendant's defense, the "jury" will vote on a verdict.

After the vote, however, each jury member is to identify (privately) one charge that might be brought against him of which he or she is personally guilty.

Exploration: *Probe God's Word*
The mock trial dealt with the question of establishing guilt. Psalm 51, which of course has a parallel situation, raises a far more important question. Once we pronounce ourselves guilty of some sin, how do we deal with it?

Break into teams, each of which is to look carefully at Psalm 51:1-12, and identify in the following passages three things which a person must do to deal with the sins of which he or she is guilty. The three are:

Psalm 51:1-2
Psalm 51:3-5
Psalm 51:7-12

If team members are uncertain, they can check for insights in the commentary.

Take plenty of time in teams, to identify and explore the implications of each of the principles illustrated. Then come together and report.

Reaction: *Respond together to the Word*
Listen as someone previously prepared tells the story of David and Bathsheba, as interpreted in the commentary. Then meditate

on the fact that God can and will redeem even the situations created by the personal sins each of you identified after the mock trial.

Adoration: *Worship and pray*
Consider either who God is (51:1-2) or what God is willing to do for you (51:7-12). Then in prayer of confession or of praise, honor Him for His goodness to those who appeal to Him for cleansing and renewal.

Psalm 73

A CURE FOR ENVY

Overview

We're all familiar with the proverbial "green-eyed monster." Call it envy. Call it jealousy. Whatever we name it, it's at root a deep dissatisfaction with our lot when compared to the lot of someone else.

In believers it is often a spiritual malady, mixed with more than a little disgruntlement. After all, we've committed ourselves to God. We do our best. We try to please Him. And when others who we know are far less righteous than we seem to prosper, well, why not be upset! It's not only that our desires are being frustrated. It's also the fact that God just isn't being *fair*.

If you've ever felt that green-eyed monster stirring in your heart, you know how the writer of this psalm felt. And you surely need to know the antidote he discovered when he was about to give in to feelings he knew deep down were wrong.

Commentary

Psalm 73 tells a story. It describes the experience of a godly man in the grip of envy. Despite his personal commitment, the writer can't help feeling betrayed when he compares the well-being of those he knows to be wicked to his own distress (73:1-12). Deep within he feels that his dedication to God has been in vain. Yet, because he is a spiritual leader he keeps his thoughts to himself, and finds that he bears a double burden (73:13-16). And then, unexpectedly, the writer experiences a sudden illumination. The easy life of the wicked is itself God's judgment, for their very prosperity keeps them from facing their need of God. Their first inkling of spiritual reality will come when judgment suddenly descends, and sweeps away all their illusions (73:17-20). Given this perspective the psalmist sees how foolish he was, "senseless and ignorant; I was a brute beast before you." What the psalmist has is God, holding his hand,

guiding him, ultimately to take him into glory. His faith restored, the psalmist cries out, "earth has nothing I desire besides You" (73:21-26). At peace at last, his heart freed of envy and totally satisfied with his state, the psalmist is at peace. "It is good," he says, "to be near God" (73:27-28).

Envy of the arrogant (73:1-3). Both "envy" and "arrogant" are vivid, powerful words in Scripture. Envy portrays a strong emotion, and the Hebrew word, *qana'*, is used in both positive and negative senses. Positively, "envy" suggests a high level of commitment. When used of God's deep concern for His own people it is often rendered "jealous" in our English versions. But when used negatively it is a strong desire for something that is not properly one's own, and more of a bitterness that poisons our life when envy gains a grip in our personality. When the psalmist became "jealous of the wicked" what he experiences is a strong desire for the pleasures they seemed to enjoy or the material goods they possessed.

"Arrogant" is the translation of words constructed on the Hebrew word *zid.* They convey the impression of self-importance, of a pride so great that it leads to acts of rebellion and to willful disobedience. The arrogant man is a person who sins with impunity, scornful of God and equally scornful of the opinion of society. It is fascinating that arrogance often brings material prosperity. The person who does not care what others think, and laughs at the laws society holds dear, is free to violate the rules with impunity. He acts for his own profit, in his own interest, and let the buyer beware! It is even more fascinating that once the arrogant amass their fortune, the rest of the community seems to envy them! Maybe they're not nice. But they are rich!

And this is what has happened to Asaph, a Levite who in the time of David served with his sons as the chief minister of music at the temple in Jerusalem (1 Chron. 6:39; 15:17, 19). He knew very well the nature of the arrogant. But he could not help noticing their prosperity. And he could not help the feelings of envy that welled up within him.

Perhaps there were many who envied Asaph. He did hold an important religious position. He was close to the king. He surely was not poor. But each of us knows others better off than himself. And each of us knows the private disappointments that have intruded to disrupt our lives. No one is immune from envy. Whatever we may have, in health, in family, in possessions, in position or social status, there are always others whom we perceive as better off than we.

Looking back Asaph says in his psalm, "my feet had almost slipped; I had nearly lost my foothold." There is great spiritual danger in envy. Envy introduces bitterness and dissatisfaction into our lives. If envy grows, it will block our awareness of the Lord, and may lead us down the very path taken by the arrogant!

They have no struggles (73:4-12). If we look only on the surface of things, the wicked often have much to be envied. Asaph provides us with a list.

They have no struggles.
Their bodies are healthy and strong.
They are free from burdens.
They are immune to human ills.
And, "always carefree, they increase in wealth."

Asaph's list is drawn from years of observation. Life seems good for the arrogant. But Asaph is always aware that the arrogant have paid a price for their "blessings." That price was paid in psychological currency, each bill paid by another step toward:

Violence.
Callousness.
Iniquity.
Malice.
Scoffing.
Tyranny.

Impiety, as they learn to view God as an impotent and irrelevant notion with no impact on life in this world.

What the wicked gain in the material realm they lose in the moral and spiritual.

Rich in possessions, that become poverty-stricken in character. And yet, as Asaph observes them, as he sees their carefree life, he can't help envying the wicked, even though he sees the price they have paid. What the wicked have has become more important to Asaph than what the wicked are.

In vain I have kept my heart pure (73:13-15). What bothers Asaph most is that if one considers what a person is, Asaph stands head and shoulders above the wicked. He has kept his heart pure. Morally and spiritually Asaph is a man of real stature. But if a person considers what Asaph has, he seems poverty-stricken beside the wicked.

It isn't just a matter of money. Asaph complains that he has been "plagued" and "punished." A number of Hebrew words convey these ideas, and all suggest a variety of personal calamities or troubles. Life hasn't turned out for Asaph as he expected. Perhaps he is bothered by ill health. Perhaps it's the loss of a wife or other loved one that has left him lonely. Perhaps he experiences his responsibilities as a burden rather than a privilege. Even among religious leaders there is often competition and some even stoop to slander. Perhaps Asaph is a victim of this kind of disparagement from the temple hierarchy. Whatever it is, life has left a bitter taste in Asaph's mouth. He deserves better! The wicked are carefree, while Asaph feels himself burdened down.

The problem here is rooted deeply in the Old Testament saint's conviction that God was obligated to bless the righteous, and to punish the wicked. The covenant God gave Israel through Moses seemed even to provide a guarantee. Moses said,

If you pay attention to these laws and are careful to follow them, then the Lord your God will keep His covenant of love with you, as He swore to your forefathers. He will love you and bless you and increase your numbers. He will bless the fruit of your womb, the crops of your land—your grain, new wine and oil—the calves of your herds and the lambs of your flocks in the land that He swore to your forefathers to give you. You will be blessed more than any other people (Deut. 7:12-14).

Although this promise was made to the

nation, it was applied in popular theology to individuals as well. Do good, and God will bless. Do wrong, and He will punish. The formula was simple, but in most cases it did work out. Every life knew some discomfort, but in general the godly enjoyed the blessing of God.

And so his troubles were a double burden for Asaph. He tried so hard. He worked at keeping his heart pure. But God didn't play fair. The plagues and the punishments that should have fallen on the wicked fell on him instead. And so the bitterness grew, and the discontent. And Asaph found himself becoming envious of the wicked.

Asaph knew his envy was wrong. He knew he could not express his feelings and still be faithful to his calling. And yet, knowing his envy was wrong, he felt it. He held it in. But it dominated his thinking, and it robbed him of peace.

I tried to understand (73:16-22). There are times when understanding just doesn't help. Asaph knew all the arguments. He knew the pat theological answers that might have been offered by a counselor of his day. But knowing was no help at all. And then Asaph experienced a flash of illumination; a moment when God spoke not to his mind but to his heart.

This happened when Asaph "entered the sanctuary of God." There is an important lesson here. Sometimes we're so ashamed of our doubts and our bitterness that we draw back from God. This is a grave mistake. When we don't know the answers, when we doubt ourselves, or are humiliated by our own feelings, then especially we need to turn our thoughts toward God. We need to enter His temple simply to worship. It is in focusing on the person of the Lord that we are most likely to discover the answer we've been unable to find by searching. Being quiet, looking to God, and listening to Him almost unawares, and the insight may come to us as it came to Asaph. Suddenly, vividly, Asaph gained a new perspective on the wicked whom he had begun to envy: "I understood their final destiny."

Now it all became clear.

Asaph says, "Surely you place them on slippery ground" (73:18). His point is simple and stark. The material success of the wicked has insulated them from a realiza-

tion of their need for God. The fact that their success is rooted in sinful acts makes them even more deaf to the voice of the Deity. If God were real, if God cared, surely He would have slapped them down when they took their first steps down the path of evil. As step followed step, and material prosperity followed, the wicked became even more deaf and blind to God. And, Asaph realizes, they will surely continue down the same path until "You cast them down to ruin. How suddenly they are destroyed, completely swept away by terrors! As a dream when one awakes, so when You arise, O Lord, You will despise them as fantasies" (73:18-20).

The wicked walk in a world of illusion, imagining that the physical universe is all there is. One day God will act in judgment. When that day comes, and the universe as we know it is dissolved, and mankind stands before the judgment throne of God Almighty, then suddenly all will realize what is real, and what is fantasy. But for the wicked, it will be too late.

Thus, the very success of the wicked, their good health, their release from burdens and their privilege and ease, keep them insensible to spiritual realities. Easy is not a blessing but a curse. The wealth of the wicked is not a sign of God's favor, but evidence of judgment to come.

There is a flip side to this insight. The poverty we struggle with, the physical disabilities and emotional pains, make us deeply aware that there is no satisfaction for us in the here and now. Unable to find blessing in this present world, we are pointed beyond it to the spiritual realm, where God beckons us to Him.

Suddenly Asaph sees it all. His envy and his bitterness totally uncalled for. He had had no more insight into God or into blessing than a "brute beast," who is satisfied to gnaw a bone, and never looks beyond the moment. But illuminated by his quick vision of the wicked's end, Asaph is no longer senseless, and no longer ignorant. Everything is back in perspective once again. What a man *is* truly is more important than what a man has. Our possessions will all be left behind at history's end, and all a person will carry with him into eternity is what he personally has become on life's long journey. Those pains that have turned Asaph to God have shaped a person who has "kept his heart pure," and this will prove of far greater value than all the wealth of this passing world could provide.

With you (73:23-28). Asaph concludes his psalm with a catalog of life's true riches, the blessings that he now realizes he has possessed all along.

Asaph is with God. He is no stranger to the Lord, no searcher. Asaph knows God, and God accepts Asaph as His own.

God holds him by his right hand. Asaph is no lonely traveler on life's road. God is with him always, close enough to hold the hand Asaph now lifts up to the Lord.

God guides him with His counsel. Asaph is not lost, but follows a clearly marked trail. The written Word and the Spirit within enable Asaph to discern God's will, and so pick his way safely.

God will take Asaph to glory. Asaph does not stumble into an uncertain future, but walks confidently toward a glory that glows beyond time's horizon.

Finally Asaph has come to the place we must all discover, the realm of contentment. It's not that God has poured out on Asaph the material blessings he once yearned for. It's not that his health has improved, or his situation changed. It is simply that Asaph has realized, as we all must, that "earth has nothing I desire besides You."

Oh, we can *enjoy* the many good things of earth that God gives us so generously. But to desire them? To make the ephemeral our goal, or the transitory the measure of God's blessing? Never! What we need is simply "being with" God. Being with Him, we find ourselves freed from the desire, and thus the dependence on, anything that might be gained here on earth.

And so Asaph sums up what he has at last come to realize. God will destroy the unfaithful. But for us to know good it is enough to make the Sovereign Lord our refuge, and trust ourselves completely to Him.

GROUP RESOURCE GUIDE

Identification: *Share with others*
Mention one thing that people envy others for. List the items suggested on a chalkboard or large sheet of newsprint.

Then compare your list with the things listed by Asaph in 73:2-5. What similarities and differences do you note? How do you explain them?

Exploration: *Probe God's Word*
Together look at 73:6-12 and study Asaph's stark evaluation of the character of the persons he envies. Given that Asaph has specific individuals in mind, does bad character tend to go with great success or ease in this world? If so, why? And, what persons come to mind to illustrate your position, pro or con?

Then break into teams of five to study 73:13-28, and to answer these specific questions:

* Why do the wicked ask, "Does the Most High have knowledge?"
* What is the source of Asaph's envy?
* What "slippery ground" has God placed the wicked on?

* Why does Asaph say he was "a brute beast before You"?
* What characterizes the relationship with God that brings Asaph satisfaction, and frees him from envy?

When your team has answered these questions to its members' satisfaction, come together and share insights.

Reaction: *Respond together to the Word*
In a circle, share what seems to you to be the most important lesson we learn from Asaph and from Psalm 73. Tell why you feel it is important, and how it relates to your own life.

Adoration: *Worship and pray*
Find hymns or choruses that express the conclusion Asaph reaches in this psalm. For instance, "I'd rather have Jesus than anything this world can offer me," says it succinctly. Close your meeting worshiping God in song, expressing your commitment to the insight which this great psalm has shared with us.

THE GREATNESS OF GOD

Overview

The Old Testament begins with the assertion, "In the beginning, God created the heavens and the earth." That simple statement set Old Testament faith apart from all other ancient religions. It introduced a God who was distinct from, and yet the source of the material universe.

The Old Testament often returns to the theme of God as Creator. It reminds us that the Creation is a silent yet universal witness to God's existence, His power, and His personal nature. The New Testament picks up the same themes. Implicit in the fact of creation is a whole web of vital, complex truth about the nature of God and our relationship to Him.

What is so fascinating about the creation theme as it is developed in the psalms is the triumphant note of praise and simple delight that echoes again and again. God as seen in nature is wonderful, amazing, glorious, thoughtful, compassionate, complex—and seeing Him is a pure delight to the believer.

How important it is for us to pause at times, to look away from the problems that sometimes weigh us down, and to look at the big picture. To see in nature, as the psalmist did, the face of a God who is so wonderful and so great that we can unhesitatingly trust our troubles to Him.

Commentary

It's instructive to look at the concepts of origins common in the ancient world. It's even more fascinating to note that none of them can properly be called "creation" stories. For instance, the Mesopotamians believed the universe was formed from the corpse of a slain goddess, Tiamat. Mankind sprang from the blood of murdered god kings, and the spiritual universe was peopled with a host of gods and goddesses who controlled neither it nor the material world. The Greeks believed that the material universe has always existed, and had no explanation at all for the origin of human beings. Again the spiritual world was peopled with many competing gods and goddesses, but again the gods did not really control the universe. Even the gods were subject to Fate, and had no real influence over the shape of the world or the direction of history.

In a way, the dominant modern view is close to these ancient mythologies. The universe is said to have begun in a massive explosion or "big bang," which took place some 15 billion years ago but which cannot be explained. Human beings evolved, not from the spilled blood of some god, but from original single-celled life that was in some unexplained way spontaneously generated by nonliving matter. As for "God," the very concept is unnecessary, for (unexplained!) processes that take place within nature are sufficient to explain everything that exists.

None of these myths, the ancient or the modern "scientific" one, have any notion of the God revealed in Scripture. That God, clearly no invention of human minds which display such a capacity for fantasy, is known only because He has revealed Himself and not because He has been discovered by a spiritually blind mankind.

Yet what is so fascinating is that Scripture consistently insists that God can be known in and through creation, if only man were willing to hear. For instance, Psalm 19 says,

> The heavens declare the glory of God;
> the skies proclaim the work of His hands.
> Day after day they pour fourth speech;
> night after night they display knowledge.
> There is no speech or language

where their voice is not heard.
Their voice goes out into all the earth,
    their words to the ends of the world.
                            Psalm 19:1-4

David's point is most clear. The created universe bears witness to the existence of the Creator. Philosophers speak of an argument from design: the concept that from the existence of order and system a person can discern a mind capable of design, and a power sufficient to impose it. David engages in no philosophical speculation. He simply says that God clearly reveals Himself in His creation, a witness which David recognizes and accepts.

In the New Testament Paul probes this issue more deeply. In Romans 1 Paul notes that "since the creation of the world God's invisible qualities—His eternal power and divine nature—have been clearly seen, being understood from what has been made, so that men are without excuse" (Rom. 1:20). And Paul prefaces this remark with a striking affirmation. Human beings "suppress the truth by their wickedness, since what may be known about God is plain to them, because God has made it plain to [literally, "in"] them" (Rom. 1:18-19). Here Paul relies on no philosophical argument to convince mankind of God's existence intellectually. Instead he simply says that creation makes God "plain to" humanity, for God has "made it plain in them."

Perhaps the best way to understand is to liken creation to a radio station, sending a strong signal throughout the whole world. What Paul says is that man was created by God with a *built-in receiver*. The message creation sends about God is intuitively understood by human beings. But mankind, not willing to receive the message, has "turned down the sound": in Paul's terms, "suppressed the truth" in unrighteousness.

What about the creation myths of the ancient and the evolution myth of moderns? This is simply static, created by human beings who do not like and refuse to acknowledge the real message of the creation. The strident ridicule of creationism, so prevalent in our day, and the angry insistence that mankind must accept the so-called "scientific" view, is little more than noise; noise generated in the vain hope of drowning out testimony of creation to a God the wicked are unwilling to admit could possibly exist.

In this sense the creation stands both as a witness to grace and to judgment. It is grace that moves God to make Himself known to the lost. But man's rejection of the witness of the creation to God is clear evidence that humanity rejects God's self-revelation, and chooses not to know or to love Him.

But creation's message is heard by the believer. For us, listening intently and hearing nature's word about God, the believer finds both peace and delight.

Note, for instance, the response of the psalmist in Psalm 89.

The heavens praise Your wonders,
    O Lord,
Your faithfulness too, in the assembly
    of the holy ones.
For who in the skies above can compare
    with the Lord?
Who is like the Lord among the
    heavenly beings?
In the council of the holy ones God is
    greatly feared;
He is more awesome than all who
    surround Him.
O Lord God Almighty, who is like You?
You are mighty, O Lord, and Your
    faithfulness surrounds You.
You rule over the surging sea;
    when its waves mount up, You still
    them.
You crushed Rahab like one of the slain;
    with Your strong arm You scattered
    Your enemies.
The heavens are Yours, and Yours also
    the earth;
You founded the world and all that is
    in it.
You created the north and the south;
Tabor and Herman sing for joy at Your
    name.
Your arm is endued with power;
    Your hand is strong, Your right hand
    exalted.
                            Psalm 89:4-13

Isaiah also responds to the wonders of creation, but applies them directly to the believer's own experience.

Do you not know?
    Have you not heard?
The Lord is the everlasting God,
    the Creator of the ends of the earth.

He will not grow tired or weary,
  and His understanding no one can
    fathom.
He gives strength to the weary
  and increases the power of the weak.
Even youths grow tired and weary,
  and young men stumble and fall;
but those who hope in the Lord
  will renew their strength.
They will soar on wings like eagles;
  they will run and not grow weary,
  they will walk and not be faint.

                            Isaiah 40:28-31

How wise the psalmist and prophet, and how clear their vision. Even a nature corrupted by sin (Gen. 3:17-18; Rom. 8:20-22) still bears enough of the Creator's stamp so that we can see Him in the things He has made, and can draw comfort from the marvelous messages He has implanted there.

That's why Psalm 104 and the other psalms that celebrate God as Creator can be important to us. They can encourage us to look away from the problems that often demand all our attention, and to sense in nature the patient power of God that is directed to sustaining all that He has made. And to sustaining us as well.

Psalm 104

This psalm has rightly been called "Genesis set to music." It begins by focusing our attention on God as King of creation (104:1-4). The psalmist then reminds us that we live in a stable universe, marked by regular and reliable patterns in the heavens and on earth (104:5-9). What is more, the earth has clearly been designed to function as a home for animal and human life. In guarding the processes that nurture life, God displays personal concern for all in this wonderful world of ours (104:10-23). The infinite variety of God's creation is displayed in the sea, creating a sense of awe in the worshiper (104:24-26). All that lives depends on God, who sustains all creatures great and small (104:27-30). And so, refreshed by his contemplation of nature, the psalmist again praises God for His power, and takes comfort in knowing the Lord (104:31-35).

King of Creation (104:1-4). The psalm begins with a call to praise the Lord (v. 1). Appropriately, the call is directed inward:

"Praise the Lord, O my soul." Corporate worship is important. But corporate worship is rooted in our personal response to God.

Here the psalmist's praise begins with an affirmation: "O Lord my God, You are very great." These four verses use powerful figurative language to express the psalmist's vision of God's greatness. The created universe is likened to clothing and to temporary housing for God as He passes by. Clothing, tents, even chariots, are the stuff from which the ordinary life of ancient peoples was woven. Thus, although vast and awesome in itself, the created universe pales to the ordinary when viewed in relationship to the Lord. Even the most terrifying natural phenomena, wind storms and fire, are subject to Him, as servants to human masters.

While the created universe gives us insight into who God is and what He is like, the universe and God can never be confused. He and it are forever distinct, and He has undisputed primacy.

A stable universe (104:5-9). One of the most important features of the Creation account in Genesis 1 is that it describes the establishment of order and regularity. Darkness and light are separated, and heavenly bodies are placed in such a way as to produce a regular sequence of day and night, and of season succeeding season. Waters and land are separated, and each given a clear role in supporting life. Each kind of animal reproduces after its own kind, with the flexibility required to produce variety, and yet the stability required to maintain each kind, distinct, across the millenniums.

And so the universe God made exhibits that stability and order, that regularity and continuity, which are necessary to provide human beings with a sense of security. The regularity and stability that mark the universe also testify to the character of our God. He is not capricious or unstable. He is consistent and reliable. He is the kind of person with whom we can feel secure, sure that He will act as He has promised, and continue as He has begun. All this is implied in Psalm 104:5-9. God set the earth on foundations. It can never be moved because it is a stable platform for history. Though once Earth was covered by waters, God acted and set boundaries for the seas, which they cannot pass. We live on the land, complex in its networks of hills and valleys and plains, and yet a stable context in which we human beings can live and prosper. That stability of our universe is seen in rock-ribbed mountains and verdant plain, in the waters of the sea that lap against the shore, but never successfully invade the realm God has set aside for man.

Constant concern for the living (104:10-23). But now the psalmist reminds us that for all its magnificence the Creation is in fact a stage, the setting for the living things which are the real focus of God's concern. We can be lost in wonder at the vastness of creation. But at best the mountains and the canyons that stun us with their magnificence, and the planets and the starry hosts whose vastness we can hardly begin to grasp, are cold and overwhelming. It is the living things with which God has filled our world that moves us from wonder to delight, and helps us sense that God is not only great but also good. God is not only far above and beyond His creation, He bends down to become involved in the birth of a fawn, to watch the first stumbling steps of the newborn, and to listen to the voice of the songbird.

And so the psalmist celebrates the springs that give water to the beasts of the field, and nurture the trees in which birds nest. He celebrates the grasses that serve as food for man and beast, and the forests that shelter living creatures. Creation has been shaped to provide a home, and meet the need, of all that live. The creatures of the night, and the men who toil by day, are all provided for in God's creation.

Wonders in the sea (104:24-26). The Hebrews were not a sea-going people. They were not traders or sailors, but farmers. And the unfamiliar oceans aroused a special awe. Yet even these mysterious reaches teemed with life, all of which God formed "to frolic there."

Sustaining life (104:26-30). Every living creature looks to God. He is not only the source of life, but also its sustainer. All living things depend on God for food. To "hide your face" is a figurative expression which means to withhold blessing. Should famine or drought strike the land, living creatures are terrified, for they sense their vulnerability and dependence. Yet even when death comes to the individual, God's Spirit brings the next generation into being. The miracle of reproduction is evidence of spontaneous, continuous acts of creation that replenish and renew life on the face of the earth.

Praises (104:31-36). The psalmist's brief survey of creation's wonders has given him a fresh sense of the glory of God. God might well rejoice in His works! And as for the psalmist, he "will sing to the Lord all my life."

And so the psalm ends as it begins. With an invitation to praise — and with response.

"Praise the Lord, O my soul.

Praise the Lord."

GROUP RESOURCE GUIDE

Identification: *Share with others*
Write on a 3x5 card one "big" problem that troubles you. Hold the card unread.

Then find a nature picture from a stack of magazines that tells you something special about God. Show the picture you selected, and share what it indicates to you.

Exploration: *Probe God's Word*
Divide into teams of five. Each team is to create a poster that sums up the message of Psalm 104 to believers today, using words and/or images from the psalm.

Study the psalm carefully, and attempt to capture its vision of God, and then determine how to express it effectively.

Use large sheets of poster board, crayons or markers, pictures cut from magazines, or any other materials you may wish.

Reaction: *Respond together to the Word*
Show your team's poster and sum up the vision of God you have tried to express.

Adoration: *Worship and pray*
Look now at the "big" problem you described on the 3x5 card at the beginning. In view of God's greatness as revealed in nature, how "big" will your problem be to Him? Praise God for His greatness.

GOD OF OUR HISTORY

Overview

A number of the psalms are historical. That is, they look back and review significant events in Israel's experience with God, and interpret them for the believer. They most often explore human failures, to celebrate both God's judgments and His faithfulness. They draw lessons for the living from the experiences of those who lived in a past which is not dead, but still vividly alive in the Hebrew people's memory.

The historical psalms serve as a pointer for us to a unique dimension in our own experience with God. On the one hand, we are a forgiven people, and our past sins are not only gone, but should be forgotten. On the other hand, if we can look back at our failures without guilt, we often can learn from them.

So historical psalms, like this one, serve not only as a reminder of God's acts in His people's past, but as a pattern of self-examination which you and I may well wish to follow today.

Commentary

Just yesterday I was counseling with a young woman with a past she would just as soon forget. But it was a past that her husband—a man with a past worse than her own—kept throwing up at her. As a young collegian she broke loose from the standards of her home and in her words, "tried everything." She did drugs. She was promiscuous and "slept around." She drank heavily. In particular she was having an affair with the person now her husband while he was married to his own second wife.

And then she was converted. Soundly. The direction of her life was totally reversed. She abandoned her past lifestyle completely, and joined a little Southern Baptist church. She attends church regularly, is faithful at prayer meeting, teaches Sunday School, goes out weekly on visita-tion, and is growing as a truly new person in Christ.

Yesterday she talked quite openly of her past. She knew what she had been. But she also knew what she was now. Today she is a new person in Christ, a forgiven person. She lives as, and she is, a virtuous Christian woman. And her face is marked not with the ravages of sin but with a most attractive innocence.

We Christians have our past. But our past does not have us! We are forgiven, and in forgiveness we have been renewed and given a fresh start. We can look back with total honesty and without shame. Although we are not yet what we will be, we are not, praise God, what we were.

One of the most significant of the verses in Scripture is found first in God's revelation through Jeremiah of His intention to make a "new covenant" with His people (Jer. 31). There, in verses quoted in the New Testament to help explain the significance of Jesus' death, God promises to write His Law in our hearts, and says, "I will forgive their wickedness and will remember their sins no more" (Jer. 31:34).

"Remember" here is *zakar*, a word that not only means the mental act of recall, but also the mental act plus the *behavior appropriate to the act*. Thus for God to "remember His covenant" means to act in accord with His covenant promises. And to "remember their sins no more" means that God will not act against us as our sins deserve. Our sins have been forgiven, and thus, our sins no longer have any impact on our relationship with God. He knows what we did. But He forgets all that. He will behave toward us as if our sins were never committed. We are freed from the dreadful consequences of the mistakes we made in our past.

There is perhaps nothing more important for us to grasp as Christians. What we did in our youth has no bearing on what we will do in our old age. What we did last year can no longer determine what we will do next year. What we did yesterday has no power to corrupt our tomorrow. Because God forgives us, we too are free to "remember our sins no more." We can look back, face what we did, and separate ourselves from past acts. And then we can look ahead, toward a bright and fresh future, as new persons in Christ. We can learn from our failures without being in bondage to them.

That is the secret of the innocence on the face of my young friend. She has looked back, faced the reality of her past, and realizes that in Christ she is not the person she was. Her husband, in a brutal effort to control and dominate her, tries to use her past against her. He can cause her pain. But he cannot crush her. He cannot destroy her innocence. He cannot restore the bondage of the sins that, before they were forgiven and forgotten, dominated her life.

Whether we are reading a psalm like 106, or suddenly recall an incident from our past, or are brutally attacked by a loved one for something we did long ago, we need to understand how to draw value from remembering our flaws. How? First, we recall the details of past failures to alert us to conditions which might make us fall again. Second, we recall the consequences of past failures to assure us that the delights sins promise are a fantasy. Third, we recall them to better grasp the nature of the forgiveness we now enjoy. Fourth, we recall them to stimulate praise for the fact that we are no longer in bondage to our past, and also praise for the grace of a God who forgives us so freely such terrible acts. Finally, we recall them to celebrate our newfound innocence. In remembering what we were, we realize how great a change God has wrought within.

✄ Group Activity: Recovery Group
Step 12 (carry the 12 Step message to others)
Choose a word that sums up how you feel about yourself when you remember sins you have committed in the past. Add your word to a list with those suggested by the others in your group.

Look together at the "new covenant" passage in Jeremiah 31:31-34, and also *at the passages in the N.T. in which it is quoted: Hebrews 8:7-13 and Hebrews 10:11-18. Then choose one of the following statements about the phrase "I will forgive their wickedness and remember their sins no more":*

(1) God will not punish me for forgiven sins.

(2) God will forget my sins so I don't have to remember them anymore.

(3) God will forgive my sins so I can be a new and different person now.

Make an exhaustive list of sins you committed in the past, but which have been forgiven.

Then make another list, this time of ways you are different from the person you were when you committed them.

Share some things from both lists with the rest of the group. When all have shared talk about what the changes you see in your own life mean to you.

Psalm 106

This psalm's review of history focuses attention on the sins of God's people, and is marked by a tone of confession. Yet the psalm also resounds with praise of God's covenant faithfulness, that steadfast love which despite Israel's sins and failures guarantees that God will never let His people go. There is a deep awareness of the nation's flaws, but there is at the same time a thrilling theme of hope.

The psalmist begins with praise of God's grace (106:1-3) and a very personal prayer by the worship leader (106:4-5). This is followed by an extended review of Israel's sins and failures, against which God's many acts of faithful love are seen with stunning clarity (106:6-46). The psalm concludes with a plea to God for salvation (106:47) and with a glad call to praise Him (106:48).

Praise the Lord (106:1-3). The call to praise is an invitation to the public to join in worship. There is a particular focus for the worship to which this psalm calls God's people. Ancient Israel, and we, are invited to praise God because "His love endures forever." That love is expressed in mighty acts God has performed for His people. As we will see, that enduring love is underlined by the fact that God's acts have often been performed for His people despite their unbelief and sins.

God's greatest blessings are reserved for those who maintain justice, who constantly do what is right (106:2). The worship leader calls God's people to remember, that they might turn from the sins that marred the nation's past, for "blessed are they who maintain justice, who constantly do what is right" (106:3). The dark times in our past, the shame, guilt, and disappointment they brought, can help us choose to walk in the light today. They remind us that while God's faithful love is ours at all times, His best gifts are reserved for those who stay close to Him.

Remember me (106:4-5). It is a great joy to be a part of a faith community that stays close to God and experience the full benefits of salvation. Joy that is shared is multiplied, and praise offered by a grateful people is magnified over that offered by one alone. Each individual offering is amplified as we sense the Spirit's flow in one another.

There's another benefit in being a member of a group for an exercise like the recitation of Psalm 106. When we sit alone and look back on our failures it's easy to become discouraged. We feel that we, and we alone, are flawed. Rather than let our failures turn our hearts to God in a fresh appreciation of His grace, we all too often let them push us into the mire of despair. When we are with others who like us have failed, but like us have found forgiveness, we are much more likely to focus on the grace of God and so be lifted up rather than depressed. Just in being with others we realize that what God has for us is prosperity, joy, and the privilege of praise.

Acts of faithful love (106:6-46). It is surely true that God's grace is best seen against the backdrop of human sin and failure. So one impact of recalling our flaws is to sense more clearly the matchless grace and endless love of our God. Now the psalmist leads us to recall a series of historic events which do just this.

The reason is stated in verse 6. "We have sinned, even as our fathers did." The flaws revealed in Israel's history exist in the people of the psalmist's own time. Thus looking back at history provides insight into people of modern times. Whatever we can learn from history, about God, about man, and about the nature of sin, we can apply in our own lives today.

* *rebellion by the Red Sea (106:7-12).*

God brought His people out of Egypt by a series of awesome miracles worked against the oppressors of His people. But when danger threatened they "forgot" His miracles and acted as if relationship with God were of no practical benefit at all. Their rebellion was expressed as a fear so intense they blamed Moses for saving them, and wished they had remained slaves (see Ex. 14).

God overlooked this insult and "saved them from the hand [power] of the foe." And, for a brief moment, their faith was fanned into flame again.

Rebellion on the journey (106:13-23). The psalmist now clusters a series of incidents that illustrate Israel's continuing hardheartedness. Each of these took place after God had provided an even more awesome revelation of Himself at Mount Sinai. Israel complained about the food God provided for them, and demanded meat. God gave them what they demanded, but with it judgment in the form of a terrible disease (Num. 11).

Rebellion was expressed in envy of Moses' and Aaron's relationship with God. This too received immediate and severe judgment (Num. 16).

Perhaps the most terrible rebellion was seen before Sinai itself, when the people made a golden calf and worshiped the idol rather than the living God. The participants in this worship were destroyed, and only Moses' intervention prevented God from destroying them completely (Ex. 32).

Each of these rebellions led to judgment. And yet the judgments were themselves evidence of God's grace. The punishments, like miracles of deliverance, drove home the fact that God was with His people. Only by keeping this reality clearly in view can any of us avoid the traps laid by desire, by envy, and by the wish to create gods for ourselves with whom we are more comfortable than with the Holy God of the Scriptures.

Rebellion at the borders of Canaan (106:24-27). Rebellion was expressed in Israel's refusal to respond to God's Word when He told His people to "go up" into the Promised Land, and in the lack of faith that led to their terror of the inhabitants of the land. And what a lesson this historic incident teaches. Only in obeying God can we find rest. Rebel against Him, doubt His goodness or His love, and an individual or people will surely wander, unsatisfied, through desert places.

Rebellion in the wilderness (106:28-33). Again the psalmist directs the worshipers' attention to incidents that took place during the wilderness wanderings. At Peor rebellion was expressed in the willingness of the Israelites to be sexually seduced into idolatry (Num. 25). The sin of Moabites, the seduction of God's people, led directly to sins by Israelites, and to their judgment.

This spiritual rebellion brings to mind an earlier event, when Moses himself, in a fit of anger, ignored God's command and struck rather than called for water from a rock (Num. 20). Because of this act and his rash words Moses himself was disqualified from entering the Promised Land. In saying trouble came to Moses "because of them" the psalmist does not excuse Moses. But he reminds us again that no sin impacts the individual who commits it alone. The waves caused by any act of sin catch others, and become an occasion for them to join us in rebellion.

Rebellion in the Promised Land (106:34-46). Despite all these sins and failures, God showed His steadfast love by bringing His people into the Promised Land, and establishing them there. But despite this grace, again Israel rebelled. They failed to destroy the pagan peoples of the land, and were corrupted by them. They worshiped their idols, adopted their practices, and so defiled themselves completely.

God is a God of love, but also a God of justice. The sins Israel adopted involved shedding "innocent blood." God could not and would not tolerate such sin, and so He "handed them over to the nations." Israel was invaded by pagan nations who stripped the land of its wealth and resettled its people in pagan lands. This was a culminating punishment, decreed only after a long series of repeated failures. The psalmist says,

Many times He delivered them
  but they were bent on rebellion
  and they wasted away in their sin.
                  Psalm 106:43

Yet the striking thing is that even then God's love was not withdrawn. In an act of total, unmatched grace, and for their sake He remembered His covenant and out of His great love He relented.

                  Psalm 106:45

In His good time He brought a remnant of His people back to the Promised Land, and promised that, in His time, all would return, and all would be blessed.

What a powerful message this review of history brings. On the one hand there is wonder that any people could be so insensitive, forgetful, and corrupt. On the other there is even greater wonder that God could be so patient, so willing to forgive, and so filled with love. Against the background of our past sins, the amazing grace of our God is seen to be more amazing still.

A plea for salvation (106:47). One of the most amazing messages to be found in this sorry rendition of historic sins is that there is hope. The God who has been gracious in the past can be trusted to be gracious in the future. He can save us, not only from the consequences of our sins, but from ourselves. In the day God regathers His people, He will enable them to "give thanks to Your holy name."

No longer will "holy" be a word that strikes terror, as if its only implication were one of judgment. "Holy" will be a word God's people love, for by God's saving acts we will feel an affinity for rather than a fear of the holiness of God. He will renew us, and in renewal we will become something we have never been. Holy, and thus like Him.

That ancient plea for salvation truly has been answered in Christ. We are no longer what we were. Because in Christ God has "gathered us from the nations" and made us His own people, we are now different and new. And our future is isolated from our past.

A call for praise (106:48). Our past tells us what we were, and how far we have come. No wonder the psalmist now invites Israel to praise the Lord. Remembering has reaffirmed the reality of God's great love and grace. And remembering invites us to move into the future renewed, armed with insights from our past, but free from its bondage.

GROUP RESOURCE GUIDE

Identification: *Share with others*
Share your opinion. Is it good or bad for a person to remember past sins and failures? Why?

Exploration: *Probe God's Word*
Listen as someone previously prepared briefly sums up implications of God's promise to "remember your sins no more" (see commentary). Then divide into teams, each of which is to study one or more of the incidents alluded to in Psalm 106. Use the chart on this page to record your insights. Key questions to ask and answer:

What was the nature of the rebellion described?

What was God's response?

What lessons could the Israelites have drawn from this incident?

Regather and complete a master chart that sums up each incident.

Reaction: *Respond together to the Word*
The experiences of the Israelites should stimulate you to remember a number of incidents from your own past. On an 8 1/2 x 11 sheet of paper draw a chart like the one used to analyze Psalm 106. On it briefly describe past sins of your own, note God's response, and list lessons you have learned from the incidents.

If time permits, in groups of three talk about lessons you have learned, and how they affect you now that you have turned your life over to God.

Adoration: *Worship and pray*
Praise God as a person who not only forgives you, but who enables you to put your past behind you and to live a new life in Christ. Ask Him to help you recall your past without guilt or shame, but to learn well the lessons it teaches.

Topical Index

Group Activities Index

	DATE DUE		
11/2/95			
2/14/96			
5/22/96			
11/3/97			